Fodor's

The Complete Guide to Caribbean Cruises

2ND EDITION

**A Cruise Lover's Guide
to Selecting the Right
Trip, with All the Best
Ports of Call**

Fodor's Travel Publications   New York, Toronto, London, Sydney, Auckland
www.fodors.com

FODOR'S THE COMPLETE GUIDE TO CARIBBEAN CRUISES
Editor: Douglas Stallings

Author: Linda Coffman
Editorial Contributors: Carol M. Bareuther, Dianne Barr, John Bigley, Cheryl Blackerby, Marvette Darien, Anita Dunham-Potter, Lynne Helm, Clint Hill, Michele Joyce, Lynda Lohr, Elise Meyer, Paris Permeneter, Vernon O'Reilly Ramesar, Elise Rosen, Ramona Settle, Mark Sullivan, Robin Barr Sussman, Jim and Cythia Tunstall, Jeff Van Fleet, Chelle Koster Walton, CiCi Williamson, Alan Wilson, Pamela Wright, Jane E. Zarem
Editorial Production: Eric B. Wechter
Maps: David Lindroth, *cartographer*; Rebecca Baer and Bob Blake, *map editors*
Design: Fabrizio La Rocca, *creative director*; Guido Caroti, *art director*; Tina Malaney, *designer*; Moon Sun Kim, *cover designer*; Melanie Marin, *senior picture editor*
Production/Manufacturing: Angela L. McLean
Cover Photo: Royal Caribbean International

SPECIAL SALES

This book is available at special discounts for bulk purchases for sales promotions or premiums. Special editions, including personalized covers, excerpts of existing books, and corporate imprints, can be created in large quantities for special needs. For more information, write to Special Markets/Premium Sales, 1745 Broadway, MD 6-2, New York, New York 10019, or e-mail specialmarkets@randomhouse.com.

AN IMPORTANT TIP & AN INVITATION

Although all prices, opening times, and other details in this book are based on information supplied to us at press time, changes occur all the time in the travel world, and Fodor's cannot accept responsibility for facts that become outdated or for inadvertent errors or omissions. So **always confirm information when it matters,** especially if you're making a detour to visit a specific place. Your experiences—positive and negative—matter to us. If we have missed or misstated something, **please write to us.** We follow up on all suggestions. Contact the Caribbean Cruises editor at editors@fodors.com or c/o Fodor's at 1745 Broadway, New York, NY 10019.

PRINTED IN THE UNITED STATES OF AMERICA

10 9 8 7 6 5 4 3 2 1

Be a Fodor's Correspondent

Your opinion matters. It matters to us. It matters to your fellow Fodor's travelers, too. And we'd like to hear it. In fact, we *need* to hear it.

When you share your experiences and opinions, you become an active member of the Fodor's community. That means we'll not only use your feedback to make our books better, but we'll publish your names and comments whenever possible. Throughout our guides, look for "Word of Mouth" excerpts of your unvarnished feedback.

Here's how you can help improve Fodor's for all of us.

Tell us when we're right. We rely on expert writers to give you an insider's perspective. But our writers and staff editors—who are the best in the business—depend on you. Your positive feedback is a vote to renew our recommendations for the next edition.

Tell us when we're wrong. We're proud that we update most of our guides every year. But we're not perfect. Things change. Cruise lines change policies. Shore excursions are added and dropped. Ships lose charm. If our writer didn't quite capture the essence of a ship, tell us how you'd do it differently. If any of our descriptions are inaccurate or inadequate, we'll incorporate your changes in the next edition and will correct factual errors at fodors.com *immediately*.

Tell us what to include. You probably have had fantastic travel experiences that aren't yet in Fodor's. Why not share them with a community of like-minded travelers? Maybe you've taken a shore excursion so special that you don't want to keep it to yourself. Tell us why we should include it. And share your discoveries and experiences with everyone directly at fodors.com. Your input may lead us to add a new listing or highlight a place we cover with a "Highly Recommended" star or with our highest rating, "Fodor's Choice."

Give us your opinion instantly at our feedback center at www.fodors.com/feedback. You may also e-mail editors@fodors.com with the subject line "Caribbean Cruises Editor." Or send your nominations, comments, and complaints by mail to Caribbean Cruises Editor, Fodor's, 1745 Broadway, New York, NY 10019.

You and travelers like you are the heart of the Fodor's community. Make our community richer by sharing your experiences. Be a Fodor's correspondent.

Bon voyage!

Tim Jarrell, Publisher

CONTENTS

CONTENTS

Our Ratings

Sometimes you find terrific travel experiences and sometimes they just find you. But usually the burden is on you to select the right combination of experiences. That's where our ratings come in.

As travelers we've all discovered a place so wonderful that its worthiness is obvious. And sometimes that place is so experiential that superlatives don't do it justice: you just have to be there to know. These sights, properties, and experiences get our highest rating, **Fodor's Choice**.

By default, there's another category: any ship, experience, or establishment we include in this book is by definition worth your time, unless we say otherwise. And we will.

Disagree with any of our choices? Care to nominate a ship or suggest that we rate one more highly? Visit our feedback center at www.fodors.com/feedback.

Budget Well

Hotel and restaurant price categories from ¢ to $$$$ are defined in the opening pages of each chapter. For attractions, we always give standard adult admission fees; reductions are usually available for children, students, and senior citizens.

Want to pay with plastic? **AE, D, DC, MC, V** following restaurant and hotel listings indicate if American Express, Discover, Diners Club, MasterCard, and Visa are accepted.

Restaurants

Unless we state otherwise, restaurants are open for lunch and dinner daily. We mention dress only when there's a specific requirement and reservations only when they're essential or not accepted—it's always best to book ahead.

Hotels

Hotels have private bath, phone, TV, and air-conditioning and operate on the European Plan (a.k.a. EP, meaning without meals), unless we specify that they use the Continental Plan (CP, with a Continental breakfast), Breakfast Plan (BP, with a full breakfast), or Modified American Plan (MAP, with breakfast and dinner) or are all-inclusive (including all meals and most activities). We always list facilities but not whether you'll be charged an extra fee to use them, so when pricing accommodations, find out what's included.

Many Listings

★ Fodor's Choice
★ Highly recommended
⊠ Physical address
✦ Directions
🕮 Mailing address
☎ Telephone
🖷 Fax
⊕ On the Web
✉ E-mail
🎫 Admission fee
🕘 Open/closed times
▶ Start of walk/itinerary
Ⓜ Metro stations
▭ Credit cards

Hotels & Restaurants

🏨 Hotel
🛏 Number of rooms
♨ Facilities
🍽 Meal plans
✕ Restaurant
⌨ Reservations
🏛 Dress code
↘ Smoking
🍸 BYOB
✕🏨 Hotel with restaurant that warrants a visit

Outdoors

⛳ Golf
⛺ Camping

Other

🅲 Family-friendly
🛈 Contact information
⇨ See also
⊠ Branch address
☞ Take note

THE BEST OF CRUISING

Best Suites at Sea

If you want the best accommodations at sea, then look for the plushest suites. The highest-category cabins on today's cruise ships are stocked with extra amenities and services, offering much more room than the typical cruise-ship cabin. While the prices are high, you certainly get what you pay for when you book the best.

- **Cunard Lines'** *Queen Mary 2*. Fit for a queen, or anyone who wants to be treated like one, two Grand Duplex apartments each cover 2,250 square feet. The tastefully decorated main level is connected to the upstairs bedroom and bath by a gently curving staircase. Have the butler serve your guests pre-dinner cocktails as you make a grand entrance.

- **Norwegian Cruise Line's Dawn-class ships.** High atop each ship, two Garden Villas are the ultimate seagoing digs. More apartments than suites, they have bedrooms and bathrooms offering all the comforts of home—if your home is posh—and the private gardens are idyllic retreats.

- **Silversea Cruises'** *Silver Whisper* and *Silver Shadow*. Owner's suites aren't the largest suites on board, but they have an ideal mid-ship location, stylish furnishings, and plenty of room to entertain guests for cocktails or a complete dinner party.

- **Oceania Cruises'** *Regatta*. Aft-facing with huge verandas, Owner's Suites are decorated in an English-country style suitable for a prince or princess. Even the bed is royal, with a draped half-canopy and heavenly Egyptian cotton linens. A butler will serve breakfast there if you choose.

Best Regular Cabins

Cruise-ship accommodations are not created equal; however, you don't have to book the highest-priced cabin to have a comfortable cruise. The following cruise lines offer something a bit above the ordinary for the kind of prices the typical cruiser can afford to pay.

- **Carnival Cruise Line.** Consistently larger than industry standard and with plenty of storage space, Carnival cabins are spacious for two and surprisingly roomy for families. A basket of sample-sized goodies in the bathroom often includes new products, such as cinnamon-flavored toothpaste.

- **Disney Cruise Line.** It's no surprise that cabins are suitable for families of two, three, four, and even five—they were designed especially for them. Whimsical Disney touches in the decor are sure to delight passengers of all ages.

- **Holland America Line.** Comfort is key, and all cabins have the types of conveniences we take for granted at home. DVD and CD players, flat-screen televisions, lighted magnifying make-up mirrors, and baskets of fresh fruit are unexpected bonuses in all categories.

- **Windstar Cruises.** The nautical feel and efficiency of Windstar cabins get our nod. From the view through the portholes to the lockers to stow our gear, these quarters are "ship-y" and ultimately ship-shape.

Best Bathrooms Afloat

Let's face it: cruise-ship bathrooms aren't usually noted for their roominess or luxury. However, there are exceptions. Here's a run-down of our very favorite bathrooms on the high seas.

- **Disney Cruise Line.** A bath-and-a-half configuration makes these bathrooms ideal for families. One bathroom has a sink and toilet, the other a sink and shower or tub/shower combo—perfect for families.

- **Regent Seven Seas Cruises.** Without a doubt, the marble bathrooms with separate shower and full-size tub on *Seven Seas Voyager* and *Seven Seas Navigator* are totally pampering.

- **Seabourn Cruise Line.** Although not the biggest shipboard bathrooms, Seabourn's bath amenities are nonetheless deluxe. Just ask, and your stewardess will draw your bath using deluxe products of your choice from the *Pure Pampering* menu.

- **Silversea Cruises.** Double vanities, marble-clad showers, separate tubs, and fluffy, oversized towels are luxurious appointments, even in standard suites. Top suites add whirlpool jets to the tub for total bathing decadence.

Best Ships for Romantics

There's something about being on the open ocean under a blanket of thousands of stars that gets your heart racing. Whether you're planning your honeymoon or just a quiet getaway for two, these are the ships you should consider above all others.

- **Regent Seven Seas Cruises'** *Seven Seas Mariner* & *Seven Seas Voyager.* Every single suite on these distinctive ships has its own private veranda. The Cordon Bleu restaurants are elegant and the cuisine is sublime—perfect for a quiet dinner for two.

- **SeaDream Yacht Club's** *SeaDream I & II.* Luxurious, intimate settings include snug alcoves for private dining alfresco, a Caviar & Champagne Splash party in the surf, and the feel of being a guest on a private yacht. Suites feature Belgian bed linens, and bathrooms have a to-die-for shower large enough for two with multi-jet massaging shower-heads.

- **Windstar Cruises'** *Wind Surf* & *Wind Spirit.* For sheer enchantment, you can't beat billowing white sails overhead and the thrill of skimming across the sea. Windstar ships are cozy and inviting, with warm, unobtrusive service and coed saunas.

THE BEST OF CRUISING

Best Cruise Lines for Families

A cruise vacation is ideal for families with children. With a safe environment and enough facilities and activities to keep everyone amused, parents can relax, and kids can have fun. Put these cruise lines at the top of your list when you want to bring the kids along.

- **Carnival Cruise Line.** Kid- and teen-friendly spaces packed with toys, games, and activities—combined with nonstop adult action—offer families a casual, laid-back vacation with something for everyone.

- **Disney Cruise Line.** Disney works its legendary magic by creating not only top-notch youth programs, but also activities with adult appeal as well. Add a dash of pixie dust and appearances by Mickey Mouse, and there's a lot of family fun to share.

- **Norwegian Cruise Line.** Facilities for teens and tots on the newest ships, especially *Norwegian Spirit,* have to be seen to be believed. Water parks, playrooms, and discos are elaborate, and even picky kids should find the active programs enticing.

- **Royal Caribbean International.** Well-conceived areas for children and teens, plus sports facilities that invite active family members to play together, are bonuses for parents who want to spend quality family time with the kids.

Best Cruise Lines for Water Sports

When you'd prefer to spend more time under or in the water than onshore, you want a cruise line with a strong water sports program. These lines will keep you both wet and happy.

- **Norwegian Cruise Line.** Underwater program pioneers, NCL's Dive-In instructors offer easy-to-learn snorkel lessons in the shipboard pool or at excursion sites. Even those who aren't certified can get a taste of scuba-diving thrills under direct supervision of instructors.

- **Princess Cruise Line.** The Open Water Diver Program run by accredited professionals is ideal for would-be divers who want to learn to scuba dive and earn a PADI certification in just a week.

- **Star Clippers.** Only *Royal Clipper* has a stern-located water sports marina, but the entire fleet features motorized launches to offer water sports such as banana boating, sunfish sailing, water skiing, and windsurfing. Extensive scuba diving and snorkel programs are available for novice and experienced divers alike.

- **Windstar Cruises & SeaDream Yacht Club.** Water sports marinas are dropped from the stern of each ship for passengers to participate in kayaking, water skiing, windsurfing, and jet skiing to their hearts' content. Weather and sea conditions permitting, of course.

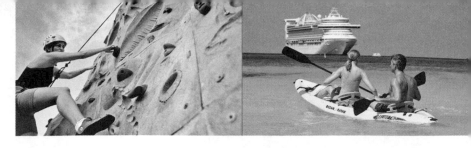

Best Spas Afloat

Some cruisers are more interested in a hot stone massage or a luxurious facial than a midnight buffet. Happily, gone are the days when the most you could expect was a new bouffant hairdo and tips. Today's ships offer better equipped spas with more services than ever.

- **Celebrity Cruise Line Spas.** Attractive, tranquil decor and a full complement of wraps, massages, and deluxe treatments are features of all AquaSpas; however, only Millennium-class ships also feature complimentary bubbly salt-water thalassotherapy pools to melt away tension.

- *Disney Magic & Disney Wonder.* Exclusive to Disney Cruise Line, Spa Villas provide nirvana at sea for couples. Relax on an open-air veranda after a foot exfoliation and some whirlpool time before moving inside to adjacent tables for side-by-side massages. A tea ceremony is a charming finale. (Singles are certainly welcome to indulge in the Spa Villa experience as well!)

- *Norwegian Dawn & Norwegian Jewel.* Massages and facials take a backseat to the elaborate pleasures of long, long indoor lap pools, soothing whirlpools, and indoor relaxation areas worthy of a fine European spa resort.

- *Queen Mary 2.* Utterly decadent, Canyon Ranch operates this plush spa on board Cunard Line's flagship. In addition to offering a wide range of massages and spa treatments, the Aqua Therapy Centre facilities are simply the finest afloat. For a daily fee, you have access to the huge therapy pool, reflexology basins, herbal or Finnish saunas, steam room, and sensory showers.

Best Sports & Fitness Centers

If you'd rather lift more than a mai tai or play something more strenuous than shuffleboard, then consider booking a cruise on a ship with a full-service health club. Gone are the days when a shipboard gym meant a treadmill and some dumbbells in a small room deep in the hull. These days, some shipborne fitness centers are as well-outfitted as your gym at home, and they probably come with much better views. We can especially recommend the following:

- **Carnival Cruise Line's Spirit Class.** Multilevel gyms afford a view of the sea from nearly every stair-stepper, treadmill, and exercise cycle. After your individual workout or aerobics class, a tropical therapy-style pool, saunas, and steam rooms offer relaxation with equally good sea views.

- **Princess Cruises' Grand Class.** Stationary bicycles, treadmills, and step, rowing, and weight machines are positioned for wide-open views of sea and sky during cardiovascular workouts. Laps in the waterfall-generated, swim-against-the-current pool also provide a stimulating workout.

- **Royal Caribbean's Voyager Class & Freedom Class.** Huge and well-equipped gyms and exercise classes almost take a backseat to full-size outdoor basketball courts, rock-climbing walls, and the unique experience of ice-skating at sea. The addition of full-size Everlast boxing rings to Freedom-class gyms gives new meaning to "working up a sweat."

THE BEST OF CRUISING

Best Entertainment at Sea

The quality of cruise-ship entertainment is higher these days than it has ever been. You're likely to find a Las Vegas–quality revue or Broadway–quality show on most cruise ships. Still, some lines stand out with their offerings. These are our favorites.

- **Carnival Cruise Lines.** Flash, dazzle, and special effects worthy of Las Vegas are backdrops for the talented teams of entertainers in Carnival production shows.

- **Disney Cruise Line.** No one knows how to please audience members of all ages like the folks at Disney, and their shipboard showmanship draws standing-room-only crowds and thunderous applause. A magical fireworks display—the only fireworks at sea—is a wondrous and well-loved event.

- **Norwegian Cruise Line.** Professional shows staged by Jean Ann Ryan Productions star highly polished artists, who often include adagio dance pairs and accomplished gymnasts. Performances by Chicago's Second City players are highlights on *Norwegian Dawn* and *Norwegian Jewel*.

- **Royal Caribbean International.** In addition to lavish production shows and guest entertainers fleetwide, only Royal Caribbean's megasized ships feature world-class ice-skating performances.

Best Specialty Restaurants

Virtually every cruise line now offers reservations-only specialty restaurants, which prepare restaurant-quality meals for a special cover charge. Many of these tables are hard to come by, a testament to their quality and imaginative cuisine. Here are the lines that stand apart, offering specialty restaurants that are well worth planning ahead for.

- **Carnival Spirit-class ships.** When Carnival introduced supper clubs, the line took shipboard dining to a new level with a sophisticated ambience and the ingredients for outstanding meals at sea. Anyone familiar with big-city steak houses will recognize the presentation of a tray displaying the evening's entrées.

- **Celebrity Millennium-class ships.** Decorated with authentic ocean-liner artifacts and the actual paneling from the White Star liner *Olympic,* these restaurants feature table-side food preparation, classical music, and food that is described in hushed, reverent tones.

- **Crystal Cruises.** Asian-themed restaurants on Crystal ships receive rave reviews for the beautifully prepared dishes, including ultrafresh sushi. Presentation is as beautiful as the divine food. If you aren't adept with chopsticks, no one will raise an eyebrow if you use a fork.

- **Cunard Line's *Queen Mary 2.*** Cuisine in the Todd English Restaurant, named for the famed chef and restaurateur, is as other-worldly as the exotic Moroccan surroundings in which it is served. The small cover charge for lunch or dinner would hardly be sufficient for a tip at his *Olives* restaurants on land, and you won't have to wait weeks for a reservation at sea.

Best Regular Dining Room Cuisine

With over 2,000 passengers, today's large cruise ships simply can't offer elegant, restaurant-quality food on such a vast scale. However, most cruise lines do manage to provide good food to their passengers. A few do even better, and you may be surprised to find that they aren't always the most luxurious lines.

- **Celebrity Cruises.** Celebrity made its mark with food and service that was decidedly a cut above the average and hasn't wavered over the years. While serving hundreds of diners at set mealtimes, the waiters manage the illusion that yours is the most important meal being presented.

- **Carnival Cruise Line.** Yes, Carnival! The line offers what is possibly the most-improved dining experience at sea. The waiters still take time out to dance and sing, but, with the added touch of chef George Blanc's Signature Selections, the food is tastier, more sensibly portioned, and nicely presented.

- **Regent Seven Seas Cruises.** Creative dishes spiced just so and wines chosen to complement all menus are a hallmark of Regent ships. Service is attentive, but not hovering or intrusive.

- **SeaDream Yacht Club.** A true gourmet meal is hard to come by on land, let alone at sea, but SeaDream chefs accomplish just such a feat. With only 110 passengers on board, every meal is individually prepared.

Best Access for Travelers with Disabilities

The U.S. Supreme Court ruled in 2005 that all cruise lines that call on U.S. ports must make some effort to make their ships more accessible to travelers with disabilities. While it's unlikely that every nook and cranny of every ship will ever be fully accommodating to passengers with mobility problems, some lines have already made great strides in the right direction.

- **Holland America Line.** In the forefront of accessible cruise travel, Holland America offers a variety of services to passengers with mobility, sight, and breathing impairments. Shore tenders are equipped with wheelchair-accessible platforms that simplify transferring wheelchairs and scooters.

- **Princess Cruises.** Not only are accessible staterooms and suites available in a wide range of categories, but Princess takes care to also provide shoreside wheelchair access to appropriate tours on vehicles equipped with lifts.

- **Silversea Cruises.** While suites designed for accessibility are limited, the ships are small and easy to navigate with wide, wide passageways and elevators that reach all decks. Public rooms with broad entryways are clustered together aft, and the distance between them is small.

Best Shops on Board

The need to shop doesn't fade away with the receding coastline, and many cruise lines have now made the experience of onboard shopping a more pleasant one. The best have taken things a step further.

- **Carnival Cruise Line.** You'll find a great selection of popular logo souvenirs, many of them priced under $10, as well as low-priced liquor and sundries and sales on some nifty high-end baubles and trinkets.

- **Crystal Cruises.** Signature apparel, sportswear, formal wear, and luxury cosmetics are all available in thousands of square feet of exclusive boutiques. A favorite is the Crystal Home Collection, featuring The Bistro's Guy Buffet porcelain tableware.

- **Princess Cruise Line.** Should you have the misfortune of lost or delayed luggage, you're in luck. Princess shipboard boutiques are stocked with nearly everything you need to carry on in style.

Best Service

When you go away on a relaxing cruise vacation, you want to be pampered and waited on. While service in all ships is pretty good these days, it's a given that with over 2,000 passengers, large ships just can't give the same kind of personalized service as a smaller ship. So it shouldn't be surprising that the best service at sea is on cruise lines that operate smaller ships.

- **SeaDream Yacht Club.** A Corona with no lime, extra juice in your rum punch: whatever your preference, it will be remembered by all servers on board. They seem to network behind the scenes to ensure perfection.

- **Silversea Cruises.** The mostly-European staff don't seem to understand the word "no." Every attempt is made to satisfy even the most unusual request, even if it means buying a bottle of guava juice in the next port of call.

- **Windstar Cruises.** Graduates of Holland America's training school in Indonesia, Windstar's Filipino and Indonesian stewards and servers go out of their way to provide gracious service with a sincere smile and genuine warmth.

Best Fun & Funky Activities

Being on vacation means having fun. While you may be able to amuse yourself, your fellow passengers sometimes need a little push. The best activities get passengers involved in the fun and give them an opportunity to let loose a bit. We don't claim these are always the most sophisticated activities at sea, but they will make you smile.

- **Carnival contests.** As wacky to watch as they are to participate in, the knobby knees, hairy chest, and men's nightgown contests are something of a throwback, but you have to love the enthusiasm.

- **The Costa toga party.** Do as the Romans did—dress up in a toga (supplies and accessories provided on board) and join in the Bacchanal. Peel a grape for your significant other.

- **Disney "Pirates IN the Caribbean" Deck Party.** Even Captain Hook smiles on a Disney cruise, and nowhere is that more evident than at this fun deck party. Full of high energy and high spirits, we won't spoil the surprise of how Mickey makes his exciting entrance, but the grand finale is the only fireworks show presented from on board a cruise ship while at sea.

Best Shore Excursions

Taking a cruise doesn't mean staying on the ship all the time. The real draw of a cruise is that it gives you the opportunity to visit more places in a single vacation than you might have been able to get to on your own. You can always go snorkeling or take a tour of a rum factory, but the best shore excursions will be remembered long after you've gone back to your regular grind.

- **The America's Club 12-meter Regatta, St. Maarten.** Not only is it a thrill to sail on one of these super-fast yachts, but you can join in to crew the vessel for a real America's Cup–style race. Consistently popular, this one should definitely be booked on board as it will be sold out once you go ashore.

- **Cave Tubing, Belize.** Explore isolated caves where the ancient Maya were said to have conducted religious ceremonies. The current moves your inner tube as you leisurely drift along the waterways connecting jungle caverns.

- **Rain Forest Aerial Tram, Panama Canal.** Whiz through the treetops for the approximately 20-minute ascent through the forest canopy. Guides provide an explanation of the complex ecosystem and point out wildlife along the way.

- **Stingray City, Grand Cayman.** Playful and lively as kittens, the stingrays await visitors on an offshore sandbar reached only by boat. Help your guides feed them while you pet their velvety bodies, and you'll be rewarded with gentle rubbing.

THE BEST OF CRUISING

Best Enrichment Programs

All travel is enlightening, but if you wish to return home with more than souvenir photos and a suntan, you might want to explore the variety of enrichment programs currently offered by cruise lines. Most curricula are available year-round, but the specific courses and lecturers may change. These are the ones we've found most inspirational and entertaining.

- **Crystal Cruises.** Discover your inner artist by learning to play piano in the Crystal Cruises Creative Learning Institute. Expert instruction and lectures can be found in the areas of Arts & Entertainment; Business & Technology; Lifestyle; Wellness; and Wine & Food. Consistently popular is the Computer University@Sea program, which teaches computer basics as well as advanced techniques.

- **Cunard Line.** After a trip through the heavens in the only planetarium at sea, on board *Queen Mary 2,* you can attend lectures presented by Oxford University luminaries and other guest speakers on topics from diplomacy to interior design, or delve into classes ranging from computers to wine appreciation, foreign languages to photography. You can even study acting with graduates of the Royal Academy of Dramatic Art.

- **Holland America Line.** The Explorations Speaker Series features lecturers whose topics may cover the wildlife, history, or culture of world-wide destinations; other subjects of interest might include astronomy, ocean-liner history, wellness, or personal finance. For hands-on cooking classes, gourmet food presentations, and tasting events, each ship has a Culinary Arts Center.

Best Beds

A good night's sleep is important to a feeling of well-being, so why would anyone want to sleep on a lumpy mattress outfitted with pancake-thin pillows and scratchy sheets? No one does. Hotels have been in the process of offering upgraded beds and bedding for years. Cruise lines have now joined the wave, and these are our favorites.

- **Carnival Cruise Lines.** The Carnival Comfort Bed features a thick spring mattress, a down-like non-allergenic pillow, high-quality sheets and pillowcases, and a 100% hypoallergenic down duvet covered by satiny cotton-blend duvet cover.

- **Holland America Line.** The Mariner's Dream bed is an extra-thick Sealy innerspring pillowtop mattress. Hypoallergenic poly or goose down pillows and cuddly down blankets are covered in 300-thread count sheets with a soft, sateen finish.

- **Oceania Cruises.** Inaugurating the bed wars at sea with their "Tranquility Bed," Oceania has outfitted all accommodations with high-quality mattresses, 350-thread count Egyptian cotton linens, silk-cut duvets, and goose down pillows.

- **Royal Caribbean Line.** A thick pillowtop spring mattress is covered by 220-thread count cotton-blend sheets and cushy microfiber pillows. It's all topped with a synthetic duvet with a soft, cotton-blend cover.

Cruising:
The Basics

WORD OF MOUTH

"There is just something about stepping on board a cruise ship that takes me away from everyday living. How fortunate we are to be able to enjoy such luxuries."

—Anne G.

"We have never had a bad cruise; some are just more memorable and enjoyable than others."

—George H.

SHOW ME A WOMAN WHO KNOWS THE IMPORTANCE OF RELAXATION, and I'll bet she's a lot like my ultra-busy mother. When she told me to relax and take a cruise, I listened carefully. Mom said, "Linda, you'll love it. They make your bed, straighten your room, do all the cooking, and wash the dishes. All the things you either hate to do or aren't good at."

A cruise sounded too good to be true. I just had to convince my husband, Mel, whose mantra was "I'll be bored on a ship." He repeated it all the way to Miami, but the complaints mysteriously evaporated upon embarkation. Twenty minutes later, you would have thought the cruise vacation was his idea.

Over lunch at the Lido buffet, I scanned the ship's daily newsletter and found myself in seagoing heaven before I'd even gone out to sea. Not only would I not be cooking or cleaning, but I had my choice of fun and exciting ways to spend the days and evenings on board. Morning walks on the promenade deck led to aerobics before breakfast. After lunch there were lectures and trivia games. Every night was like Saturday night— dressing for dinner, seeing a show, and dancing until the wee hours. Mel's agenda was a bit different. His sea days were spent lounging at the pool. Clearly, he enjoyed relaxing while the captain did the driving.

We found ourselves attended to by an excellent service staff in first-class surroundings and fed multiple-course meals, all for a single, affordable fare. Our only obligation was to enjoy ourselves as the luxurious cruise ship sped from one port of call to the next. Once ashore, we took in the sights, shopped, and discovered a variety of Caribbean cultures. Instead of uncomfortable island-hopping by plane—been there, done that—we visited several destinations while our needs were catered to in high style.

Mel and I enjoy meeting new people, and we made friends for life on our first cruise. Many more years—and cruises—have followed, and we've met more people along the way. We still receive holiday greetings from a newlywed couple who conceived their first child during a rather fateful honeymoon cruise. Over the years, I have met hundreds of other passengers through Internet Web sites I have hosted, and it's always a pleasure to answer their questions and possibly see them on a cruise ship.

Mom's advice forever changed my travel habits. All clichés aside, there is nothing like a cruise.

CARIBBEAN CRUISING MILESTONES

1966	1972	1975
Norwegian Caribbean Line (now Norwegian Cruise Line) begins offering seven-night cruises from the then-obscure Port of Miami.	Carnival Cruise Lines' "Fun Ship" fleet is launched with a single converted ocean liner that runs aground off Miami's Dodge Island during its inaugural voyage.	*The Love Boat* television series, starring Princess Cruises' *Pacific Princess*, introduces the idea of cruise vacations to thousands of weekly fans.

WHAT IS CRUISING?

Ocean travel in the early decades of the 20th century was just another mode of transportation. Much like the airplanes that displaced them, ships were a means of getting to a destination. They were the only practical way of traveling from one continent to another. Even so, venerable ocean liners such as the *Normandie* offered an occasional round-trip pleasure cruise to exotic locales.

Passengers on long-ago cruises didn't have a fun-in-the-sun mindset as they sailed on ocean liners to far-flung corners of the globe. They wanted to broaden their horizons and learn about their ports of call. Perhaps they booked a cruise to Panama to observe the construction of the canal, or like *Normandie*'s passengers, were bound for Brazil and the daring excitement of pre-Lenten Carnaval festivities.

And early cruisers didn't have the comforts of today's cruisers as they steamed toward the unfamiliar. As on *Normandie,* it was common to find air-conditioned comfort only in ships' first-class dining rooms. However, they could at least find relief from Rio's heat in one of that era's few out-door swimming pools at sea. (At that time, if an ocean liner had a per-manent swimming pool at all, it was often indoors and deep in the hull.) They say a ghostly woman in white haunts the *Queen Mary* at the ship's permanent berth in Long Beach harbor. I didn't see her when I toured the floating museum, but I'll bet she's searching for the indoor swim-ming pool.

Carnival Cruise Line executives like to reminisce about the tiny gyms on their early ships, which were converted ocean liners, and then point to how far ship designs have evolved. I remember those ships well. It was even dif-ficult to find the casino on Carnival's first Fun Ship, the *Mardi Gras,* let alone the indoor swimming pool. You won't find claustrophic natatoriums or ill-equipped, windowless gyms on today's modern cruise ships. Designed for contemporary travelers and tastes, these vessels carry passengers amid conveniences unheard of in the heyday of the North Atlantic ocean liner or even on board the earliest ships permanently dedicated to cruising.

There's a lot to like on cruise ships these days. Nearly everything about cruises has changed, from the presence of air-conditioning and roomier

1978	1979	1988
After sailing less than a decade, **Royal Caribbean** "stretches" *Song of Norway*–cutting it in half and inserting a new middle section.	In an unprecedented move, **Norwegian Cruise Line** purchases the SS *France* and rechristens it SS *Norway,* the largest cruise liner to sail from Miami at the time.	**Holland America Line**, one of the most revered names in passenger shipping, is purchased by Carnival Corporation.

cabins to the ever longer list of activities. In the old days, entertainment was staid, and there was no cruise director to lead the merriment. In truth, passengers were usually required to entertain themselves, with after-dinner cigars, brandy, and cards for the gentlemen in a smoking room, and conversation for the ladies in a separate drawing room.

As cruising evolved, swimming pools and pool games became common, and the position of cruise director grew to be the most visible in the hierarchy of shipboard staff. These days, as the average age of cruise passengers drops, more attention is focused on keeping people active. Gyms and spas have grown in size, with today's emphasis on healthy living. Menus now offer lighter fare as well as vegetarian dishes. Poker in the smoking room has been replaced with Las Vegas–style casinos, though poker is once again in vogue.

By night, lavish production shows, cabaret acts, comedy shows, and classical concerts are staged for your enjoyment. Discos and dance clubs rock into the early morning hours. And there's no cover charge or ticket to purchase—all are included in your fare. No one dresses to dine every night anymore, and even traditional formal dinners can be skipped if the casual dining option is more to your liking.

If you ask six couples what they enjoyed most about their Caribbean cruise vacation, you are likely to get a dozen different responses. Although they might not sing anyplace but in the shower at home, they will mention the standing ovation for their karaoke performance in the disco. Nearly everyone raves about the meals, an opportunity to sample unfamiliar dishes with the assurance that if you don't like something, you can get something else simply by asking. The nonstop, attentive service and attention to detail often come as a surprise to first-time cruisers, who may not be used to a server taking their tray at the end of the buffet line and showing them to a table. Women in particular appreciate the ease of unpacking only once and settling into accommodations that visit a variety of destinations.

As you might have guessed, it's the unique social atmosphere that appeals most to me. I rarely encounter the same level of sociability at resorts Mel and I visit, where we typically live out of a suitcase and seldom meet fellow travelers.

Sea cruises also appeal to a range of vacationers who seek a safe and convenient way to travel, particularly if they are going solo. Today's cruise

CARIBBEAN CRUISING MILESTONES

1990	1991	1998
With a refitted vessel from its budget *Fantasy Cruises* line, the Chandris family of Greek shipping prominence launches *Celebrity Cruises*, a premium cruising option.	A boyhood dream for Mikael Krafft becomes a cruise-line reality, when **Star Clippers** sails onto the scene with the tallest clipper ships ever built.	The Magic and Wonder of Walt Disney's beloved resort vacations go to sea with the launch of **Disney Cruise Line**.

ships are lively and luxurious floating resorts that offer something to satisfy the expectations of almost everyone, but each cruise line and cruise ship is different. Most people find that selecting the right cruise is a bit more complicated than booking a land-based resort vacation.

The more you know about cruise travel, the better prepared you will be when it comes time to make your choices. Unfortunately, while cruises have come a long way from the days when ships were viewed as the travel choice of well-heeled newlywed or nearly dead passengers, misconceptions still abound. Most disappointments—and the inevitable complaints—are the result of misunderstandings that stem from unmet expectations. Having the right information debunks the most persistent myths.

My goal is to help you make the right decisions so the cruise you select will be the best fit for you. If you're taking the family, you don't want to sail on a ship without a good children's program. Nor would you be happiest on a ship without a casino if your favorite vacation spot up to now has been Las Vegas. You need the tools to select the proper wardrobe and desirable accommodations. In this book, we'll do our comparison shopping together. I'll give you the dimensions of every cabin category and outline the amenities of every ship plying Caribbean waters so you can pick the cruise ship that fits your needs. Planning to sail away is fun, and I want you to enjoy cruises as much as I do.

Now, let's get started.

WHAT'S ON THE SHIP?

Some people fear they won't know the ropes and will stand out as a first-timer. While some passengers are certain to be repeat cruisers, the majority are in the same boat, so to speak, and will be cruising for the first time. Keep in mind that most of today's larger cruise ships have the same basic arrangement. Once on board, you will encounter a reception area and shore excursion desk, very likely centrally located in a multideck atrium or lobby. Explore a bit further, and you will discover lounges, a main restaurant, buffet restaurant, showroom, Internet–business center, boutiques, photo shop, library, spa, and a gym. Cabins are lined up along quiet passageways. And that is just inside.

Out on open decks there are swimming pools, hot tubs, bars, and a plethora of deck chairs. You're likely to find a deck dedicated to sports with courts

2001	2003	2006
As a testament to their 20-year appeal, the two diminutive Sea Goddess ships are rebuilt in luxurious fashion for the **SeaDream Yacht Club**.	**Carnival Corporation** acquires Princess Cruises, foiling an attempt by Royal Caribbean to become the world's largest cruise company.	**Royal Caribbean** launches the world's largest purpose-built cruise ship, *Freedom of the Seas*. Its sister ships were set to sail in 2007 and 2008.

for volleyball and basketball. Some ships take the facilities up a notch and include waterslides, miniature golf, in-line skating tracks, rock-climbing walls, and even a surf simulator or bowling alley. For joggers there's the outdoor promenade deck or a designated track for running and walking. Children and teens have their own playrooms, swimming pools, video arcades, and, in some cases, lounges and party rooms.

Deck plans and signage point the way to all the features. It may take a couple of hours—or possibly even a couple of days—to get your bearings, but even elevators have helpful signs, or the ubiquitous elevator voice, indicating the public areas found on each deck.

WHAT A CRUISE COSTS

Many would-be cruise passengers are surprised to discover that a cruise won't deplete their bank accounts or max out their credit cards. Cruises are no longer limited to the super-rich. Nearly 12 million people embarked on cruises in 2006, and most of them sailed on ships that were designed and launched in the previous decade. A massive shipbuilding program commenced in the early 1990s and only showed signs of slowing down in 2005; however, a tide has turned, and new ships are once again beginning to appear with regularity. With so many new ships—76 new ships were introduced between 2000 and the end of 2006—cruise lines had a lot of berths to fill and did so by pricing their cruises attractively. Fares in recent years, which could be found as low as $50 per person, per night, are reminiscent of those offered in the 1980s. Even factoring in inflation, you can see that cruises are actually selling for less today than they did 25 years ago, even as the ships and amenities are far superior.

It's no secret that the entire travel industry suffered a downturn after September 11, 2001. Reluctant to fly, many Americans took to the highways on domestic road trips. Cruise lines were in an enviable position compared to resorts, to which travelers might have to fly; if passengers wouldn't fly to traditional embarkation ports, ships could be moved to where passengers were able to reach them by car. Low fares, new ships, and accessible home ports combined to make cruises more popular than ever.

But—and there's always a but—just as passengers nervous about flying were overcoming their fears, along came an unusually active and destructive hurricane season in 2005. Pent-up demand, combined with fewer major new ship introductions in 2005 and 2006, which should have signaled higher fares, were dampened by weather and economic concerns. So, the deals are still out there and cruises on some of the newest, most feature-filled ships are still priced at less than they were in 1990, especially in the Caribbean. As you will see, when you crunch the numbers to compare the total cost of a cruise to that of a traditional resort vacation, a cruise compares favorably.

Imagine you're contemplating a short vacation getaway for two in the tropics and want the best value for your money for a five-day, four-night jaunt. Paradise Island in the Bahamas is a popular destination, so let's compare the costs at a sprawling resort complex there to a short cruise to the Bahamas. Although there are many seasonal price variations to consider, we'll consider the average prices to get an overall estimate for comparison.

Even modest rooms for two can run a whopping $400 per night in the hotel's moderate accommodations. Meals are not included, but an optional dining plan costs $59 per person, per day, plus a mandatory 15% gratuity, and includes a full American breakfast and dinner at your choice of a variety of on-site restaurants. Add in beverages, light lunches, or snacks (not included in the dining plan) and meals can cost about $200 per day for a couple; without a meal plan, you can pay far more to dine at most resorts. So far, just a room and meals add up to $2,400. Not included is round-trip transportation between the airport and the resort or much of anything else once you are on the property—save for use of the swimming pools and beach access. For evening entertainment, if you want to do anything more than walk on the beach, stroll the grounds, or watch television, plan to pay admissions for shows and possibly cover charges for lounges.

A typical cruise isn't an all-inclusive vacation, but it can be a good deal because of what is included—all meals and snacks (including some beverages with meals), games and activities, parties, evening entertainment, and most sports and fitness activities while on board the ship. A contemporary four-night cruise for two to the Bahamas will cost approximately $950 for an outside cabin, including port charges and taxes for your four-night getaway.

That $1,450 difference in the base price goes a long way on a cruise toward extras: shore excursions, alcoholic drinks, spa pampering, souvenirs, and other things that aren't included in the basic fare, such as bingo and a bit of casino action. At the resort, you would still have to pay additional for those, too. You might just decide to take a longer 7-night cruise to maximize the cost of your airfare.

For an even more pleasant surprise, compare the cost of a high-end luxury cruise to suite accommodations at a super-deluxe resort. On a high-end cruise, even more is typically included in the base fares—including complimentary in-suite minibars, wines with lunch and dinner, and other beverages. Guests find it difficult to spend any money beyond their cruise fare, shore excursions, and spa treatments while aboard some luxury cruise ships because they are so all-inclusive. This is rarely the case with an upscale resort, where you can pay dearly for nearly everything.

Add-Ons

Naturally, there are many extras you can spend money on during any vacation, whether you're going on a cruise or staying at a resort. Although low fares have brought cruise vacations within the realm of reality for many people who could only fantasize about them in the past, those same rock-bottom fares can cause consternation to passengers on tight budgets when they factor in the extras that are not included. Increasingly, cruise lines devise creative ways to entice passengers to spend additional money once on board their dream ships. Charge, charge, charge is the mantra; if you heed it, you can see the cost of your cruise vacation rising faster than a helicopter over a Caribbean island volcano.

Although your cruise ticket price includes a lot—accommodations, food, entertainment, taxes, and port charges are covered in the ticket price—there are also many add-ons. Air fare, tips, shore excursions, travel insurance, passports, and even bottled water can increase the bottom line. Holding down the add-on expenses is not easy; after all, the cruise is your vacation, which you deserve, and you want it to be special. However, there are ways to minimize those costs. To get the true picture of what you can expect before your budget floats out of sight, you must consider those extras.

In addition to transportation to your port of embarkation, which is usually not included in the cruise fare these days, there are a few costs that are often overlooked but that add to your overall cruise costs. Before leaving home, consider the cost of passports (now required for all travel to the Caribbean) and travel insurance (an option, but highly recommended).

Adding Up the Cost of the Extras
The majority of on-board extras are strictly discretionary. For instance, whether to purchase alcoholic beverages or cappuccino is your choice, and no one will blink an eye if you shy away from the casino or spa. However, it's unlikely you will be able to avoid all extras. Bottled water seems to be an unavoidable expense these days, and tipping isn't considered an option. Although the extras greatly enhance the overall experience of a cruise, they can quickly add up and exceed your initial budget if you're not careful. Even if you're frugal, you should expect to pay at least $100 (and often much more) beyond the cost of your cruise for tips and incidentals.

Cruise passengers are often caught in something of a catch-22 situation: you must either pay a higher fare up front for a more luxurious cruise or pay for nonincluded items later. Just as you compare the cost of a cruise vacation to a resort vacation, consider the cost of a less-inclusive mainstream cruise versus the cost of a more-inclusive luxury cruise. In addition to the added comfort, you may decide—by determining and budgeting for your personal priorities in advance—that there's not so much difference between the cost of a truly all-inclusive luxury cruise and a less-inclusive mainstream cruise. Of course, it all depends on the cabin category you book and your individual spending habits. Read the fine print in your chosen cruise line's brochure, and you should face no spending bombshells once you are on board.

Cutting Your Bar Tab Down to Size
Bar drinks and wine typically cost about what you would expect to pay at a nice lounge or restaurant in a resort or big city in the United States. Unless you really want a souvenir glass to take home, order umbrella drinks in regular glasses—the keepsake glasses cost extra. Wine by the bottle is a more economical choice at dinner than ordering it by the glass, and any wine you don't finish will be kept for you and served the next night. Gifts of wine or champagne ordered from the cruise line (either by you, a friend, or your travel agent) can be taken to the dining room. Wine from any other source will incur a corkage fee that can run up to $15 per bottle.

1

What Things Cost on Board

HERE'S A LIST of what some of the most popular extras cost on board a ship.

Gratuities: $10–$15 per person, per day

Cocktails: $4–$9

Wine by the glass: $5–$9

Alcoholic coffee drinks: $5–$6

Beer: $4–$6

Bottled water: $2.50–$4

Sodas: $1.25–$2

Specialty ice cream & coffee: $2–$4

Alternative restaurants: $4–$35 per person

Cell phone calls: $2–$5 per minute

Shore excursions: $25–$110

Dry cleaning: $7–$11 per piece (50% of these prices for pressing)

Laundry: $1–$4 per piece

Spa treatments: $100–$175

Salon services: $30–$100

Personal training: $75 per hour

Special exercise classes: $10 per class

Casino gambling: 5¢–$10 for slot machines; $5 and up for table games

Bingo: $5–$10 per card for multiple games in each session

Video Arcade Games: $1–$2 per game

Photographs: $7–$20 each

Internet access: 35¢–$1 per minute

Medical treatment: $75 and up, depending on treatment

Whether or not to BYOB is a hotly debated issue. Many cruise lines look the other way at soft drinks and bottled water toted aboard by arriving passengers, but they are increasingly intolerant of allowing passengers to bring alcoholic beverages on board. Duty-free liquor purchased ashore will be collected when you return to the ship and held until the last night aboard, when it's delivered to your cabin. Similarly, liquor purchases from the ship's own duty-free store will be held until the last night. You will usually be allowed to bring aboard a bottle of wine or champagne for a special occasion in your carry-on when you initially board the ship, but do not even think of carting on a case of beer. If you must BYOB to save money, stick to soft drinks. Or be creative and send yourself a bon voyage gift of your favorite spirits to be delivered to your stateroom, ordered either through the cruise line or from an independent service.

Tap water is always plentiful and free. Why not bring along a powdered drink mix for a flavorful and refreshing change? An insulated cup or mug makes it easy to prepare and keep chilled—cabin stewards fill ice buckets in passenger staterooms at least twice a day. You can also order up a pitcher of fruit juice with your room service breakfast and keep what's left for later; juices are a healthy choice and complimentary with meals (there's usually a charge for juice if you order it at the bar).

In lounges, request the less-expensive bar-brand mixed drinks or the reduced price drink-of-the-day. On some ships discounted beverage cards for unlimited fountain soft drinks are available for approximately $5 a day for children and $6.50 a day for adults. Be sure to attend the Captain's Welcome Aboard Party, where complimentary drinks are served. If you're a repeat passenger, do not miss the repeaters' get together for the same reason. (Anyway, socializing is a big factor in how much you enjoy a cruise; it's not much fun to drink alone in your cabin.)

SHIP SIZES

Although all ships share certain similarities, there's one distinct difference that can be as important as any other single factor in whether you enjoy your cruise: ship size. Choosing the right ship is quite possibly the most important decision you can make when booking your cruise, and your lifestyle and expectations should be major considerations when making this choice. This is one time when size matters and can make or break your vacation.

The size of the ship affects every other aspect of the cruise: entertainment and dining options, the kind of activities you'll be offered, and even the ports of call you can visit. It stands to reason that the larger the ship, the more room there is for features like alternative dining venues, huge show lounges and casinos, elaborate swimming pools, and expansive spa and fitness facilities. This has to be balanced by the fact that there are intriguing ports of call that only smaller ships can visit because of docking or tendering considerations. Keep your priorities in mind while you're examining cruise-line brochures.

Large ships start at approximately 70,000 tons and go up in size from there. These are the ships that have more than 1,800 passengers and often carry as many as 3,600-plus cruisers. They are the megaships that include the bells and whistles modern passengers have come to associate with a cruise. Larger ships offer nonstop activities designed for all interests; they have high-energy Las Vegas or Broadway-style music revues with sophisticated lighting, special effects, and dazzling costumes; there are a variety of restaurants and lounges; dance clubs and discos; well-rounded children's programs; and more. Royal Caribbean's extra-large megaship vessels even include rock-climbing walls, ice-skating rinks, miniature golf courses, and surfing simulators. Carnival's megaships have some of the largest casinos and most lavish spas and exercise facilities afloat.

Mid-size ships range from approximately 25,000 to 70,000 tons and carry between 400 and 1,700 passengers. There's no lack of entertainment and features on these ships, but they tend to not have some of the more extravagant facilities. Alternative dining is generally an option, and in addition to the traditional daytime activities, there will be ample nightlife, a casino, shows, and a spa. By necessity, they are usually on a smaller scale but no less satisfying. Although there are more ships this size in premium and luxury fleets, some older Carnival and Norwegian Cruise Line ships also fall within this range. The most upscale mid-size ships have a higher passenger-space ratio, meaning there's more room per person than on a larger ship. It's usually not difficult to find a deck chair by the pool on a sunny day. Smack in the middle of this range is Regent Seven Seas Cruise's *Seven Seas Voyager,* which has one of the highest pas-

1

RELATIVE SHIP SIZES

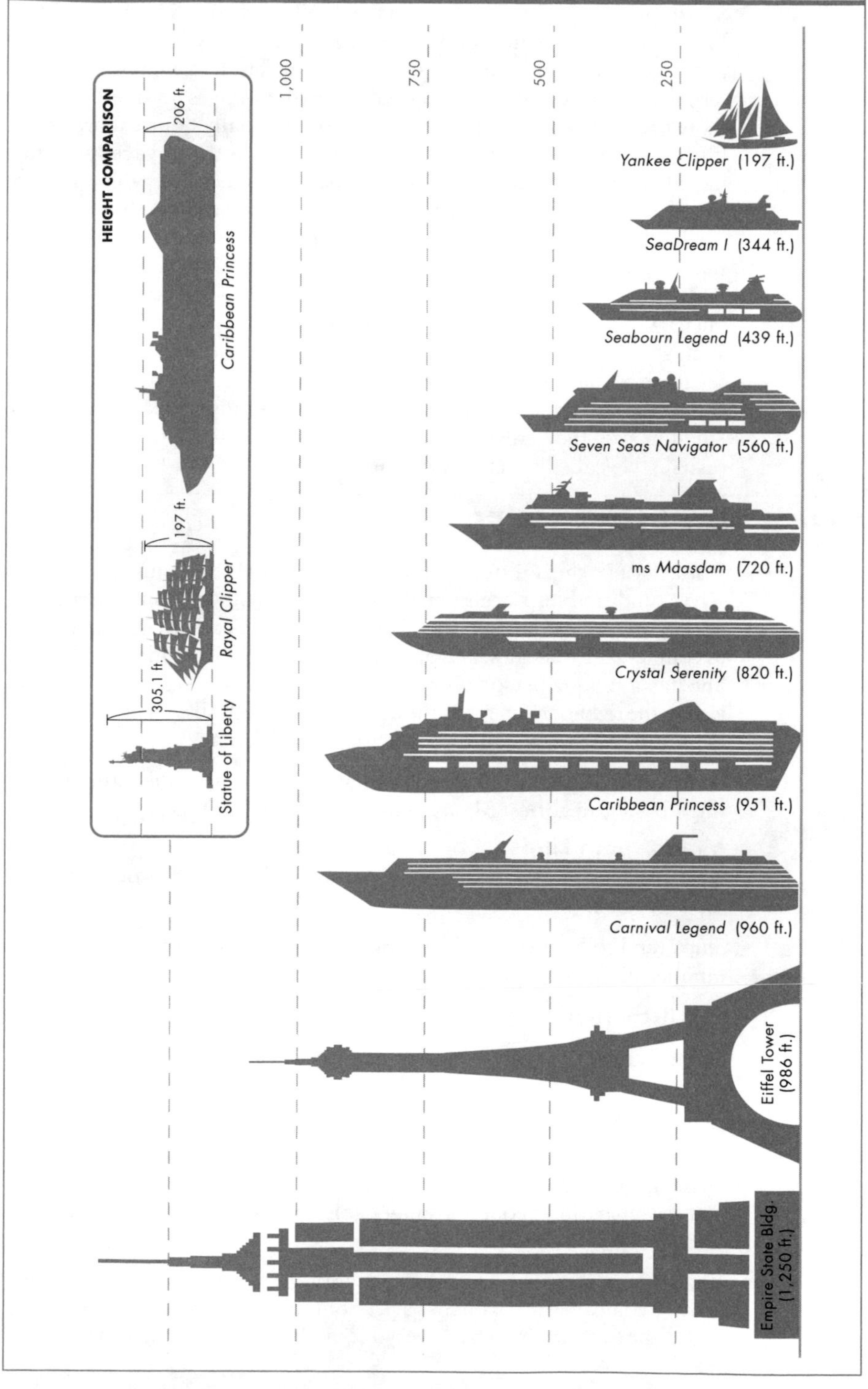

HEIGHT COMPARISON

206 ft.

Caribbean Princess

197 ft.

Royal Clipper

305.1 ft.

Statue of Liberty

1,000

750

500

250

Yankee Clipper (197 ft.)

SeaDream I (344 ft.)

Seabourn Legend (439 ft.)

Seven Seas Navigator (560 ft.)

ms Maasdam (720 ft.)

Crystal Serenity (820 ft.)

Caribbean Princess (951 ft.)

Carnival Legend (960 ft.)

Eiffel Tower (986 ft.)

Empire State Bldg. (1,250 ft.)

senger-space ratios on the seas; if you cruise on this ship, you may wonder where everyone is.

Small ships range from megayachts and sailing vessels of less than 5,000 tons to ships of about 25,000 tons. These ships may have as few as 70 passengers or as many as 350. On smaller vessels, passengers tend to entertain themselves rather than be entertained. Lounges on small ships are more intimate, and the only entertainment is usually done cabaret-style. Intriguing itineraries are more often the focus of the voyage and often include some ports of call such as Mustique or Bequia, which are not suited for larger ships. Restaurants often accommodate all guests in a single open seating. On board luxurious small ships, gracious service and fine dining are paramount, and your table is likely to be set with signature china, European crystal, and heavy silver, and covered by Belgian linens. Good things do come in small packages; a well-kept secret is that Windstar Cruises' superyacht *Wind Surf* has one of the largest spas at sea relative to her size. But not all small ships are luxurious; at the other end of the spectrum is Windjammer Barefoot Cruises' fleet of tall ships. Small in size, they are also laid-back and bare bones, offering an ultra-casual style called barefoot cruising.

TYPES OF CRUISE LINES

Just as cruise ships differ by size and style, so do the cruise lines themselves, and finding a cruise line that matches your personality is as important as finding the right ship. Some cruise lines cater to families, others to couples, active singles, and even food and wine aficionados. Each cruise line has a unique personality that will appeal to different lifestyles. Selecting the right one can mean the difference between struggling with unmet expectations and enjoying the vacation of a lifetime.

Some of the differences are subtle, but today's cruise lines still fall into three basic categories: Mainstream, Premium, and Luxury.

Mainstream Lines

What you'll find. Mainstream cruise lines usually have a little something for everyone:

- Ships tend to be the big, bigger, and biggest at sea, carrying the highest number of passengers per available space.

- Ship decor runs the gamut from glitz and glitter to nautical kitsch.

- Staterooms range from inside cabins for three and four to a variety of outside cabin configurations with or without balconies. Top-notch suites may or may not come with numerous extra amenities.

- Schedules include enough activities to keep even the most hyperactive passenger content. Expect to find deck sports and pool games, team trivia and scavenger-hunt contests, bingo, golf lessons, karaoke, fitness classes, a high-tech gym, and full-service spa.

- Entertainment tends to be high-energy, Las Vegas–style production shows; you can always find a variety of lounges and discos for dancing; and in the liveliest piano bars everyone might be encouraged to sing along.

- Large spas accompany fully equipped gyms; jogging tracks are common, as are multiple swimming pools and hot tubs.

- Dining is generally traditional, with two assigned seatings in the main restaurant for dinner. However, several mainstream cruise lines are experimenting with variations of open-seating dining and alternative restaurant options that allow passengers to dine when and with whom they please. Choice is the keyword on these ships, and you can always find something to eat, either from 24-hour room service or a variety of locations. One thing is typical, though; although generous in quantity, food is often likened to banquet-style fare.

- Service is friendly but not necessarily polished.

- Ideal for families, these cruise lines offer some of the most extensive programs for children and teens.

What won't you find? As a rule, sodas and bottled water aren't complimentary.

Who's on board? First-timers, repeat passengers, young and old alike. Mainstream cruise lines are ideal for singles, families, and groups—anyone who is looking for a fun and exhilarating vacation.

Premium Lines

What You'll Find. Premium lines usually offer a more subdued atmosphere and refined style:

- Ships tend to be newer mid-size to large vessels that carry fewer passengers than mainstream ships and have a more spacious feel.

- Decor is usually more glamorous and subtle, with toned-down colors and extensive original art.

- Staterooms range from inside cabins for three or four to outside cabins with or without balconies to suites with numerous amenities, including butlers on some lines.

- In addition to traditional cruise activities, on-board lectures are common. Port talks often include history and cultural topics in addition to the usual shopping advice.

- Production shows are somewhat more sophisticated, and gentlemen hosts on some sailings keep single ladies dancing the night away.

- An exercise or beauty regimen is a pleasure in the fully outfitted gyms and spas.

- Most ships offer two traditional assigned seatings for dinner. High marks are afforded the quality cuisine and presentation. Many ships have upscale bistros or specialty restaurants, which usually require reservations and command an additional charge. But nowadays, there's also usually a more casual dining option available as well.

- Attentive service is polished and unobtrusive.

- Programs for children and teens are well-run but not as comprehensive as those found on mainstream ships because there aren't usually as many children on board.

CRUISING FAMILY TREE

CARNIVAL CORPORATION

Carnival Cruise Lines: Founded in 1972 by Israeli-born Ted Arison, who got his feet wet at Norwegian Caribbean Line, Carnival's "Fun Ship" fleet of 21 ships is now the largest afloat.

Costa Cruises: Costa's name first appeared in 1854, when Italian founder Giacomo Costa began trading olive oil by sea, and grew to include passenger ships in 1947. Carnival completed a buy-out of the cruise line in 2000.

Cunard Line: Samuel Cunard founded the venerable line in 1839 to carry mail and passengers between Great Britain and North America. After a succession of owners, the company's stability was assured when Carnival bought it in 1998.

Holland America Line: Since 1873, the Dutch company has roamed the globe, carrying passengers and goods worldwide and operating its first vacation cruise in 1895. In 1989 the premium line was purchased by Carnival.

Princess Cruises: Founded by Stanley McDonald in 1965 to carry cruisers from California to Mexico, Princess burst into prominence in 1977 as star of television's The Love Boat. In 2003 Princess joined the list of Carnival-owned cruise lines.

The Yachts of Seabourn: Norwegian industrialist and luxury cruise pioneer Atle Brynestad founded Seabourn in 1987. Partially owned by Carnival since 1991, the line was acquired in full by Carnival in 1999.

DISNEY CORPORATION

Disney Cruise Line: When Disney launched their first ship in 1998, the cruise line had an instant winner with family fun and entertainment for all ages. Even Walt Disney's most beloved character, Mickey Mouse, sails on every cruise.

EASYGROUP

easyCruise: Launched in 2005 by serial entrepreneur Stelios Haji-Ioannou, no-frills easyCruise was designed for the backpacking and hostel set. It fills a niche somewhere between a budget line and flexible passenger ferry.

ROYAL CARIBBEAN CRUISES, LTD.

Celebrity Cruises: Greek shipping tycoon John D. Chandris founded premium Celebrity Cruises in 1989, in essence replacing a previous budget venture, Chandris-Fantasy Cruises. Celebrity was acquired by Royal Caribbean Cruises, Ltd. in 1997. A new deluxe subsidiary, Azamara Cruises, launched in 2007.

Royal Caribbean International: In 1969 a partnership of three Norwegian shipping firms made Wisconsin native Edwin Stephan's dream a reality, and a cruise line composed of modern, purpose-built ships was formed.

STAR CRUISES

Norwegian Cruise Line: Established in 1966 by Norwegian Knut Kloster, the former Norwegian Caribbean Line introduced regularly scheduled Caribbean cruises from Miami. Purchased by Star Cruises in 2000, NCL continues to be an industry innovator.

NIPPON YUSEN KAISHA (NYK)

Crystal Cruises: Founded in 1988 by NYK, one of the world's largest shipping companies, Crystal Cruises strives to offer its passengers the best large, luxury cruise-ship experience in the world.

MEDITERRANEAN SHIPPING COMPANY

MSC Cruises: Established in Naples in 1995, MSC is the family-run cruise division of the world's second-largest container shipping operator. Old hands in the industry, the company began operating the Starlauro line in the 1980s.

CARLSON HOSPITALITY WORLDWIDE

Regent Seven Seas Cruises: RSSC was formed in 1994 when Diamond Cruises merged with Seven Seas Cruises. Previously operating just one ship each, the resulting company has grown to be one of the world's largest luxury cruise lines.

PRIVATELY HELD

Oceania Cruises: Founded by cruise industry veterans Joe Watters and Frank Del Rio in 2003, Oceania's fleet is made up of three mid-size premium vessels. Apollo Management, a private equity fund, made a major investment in 2007.

SeaDream Yacht Club: Seabourn founder Atle Brynestad teamed up with former Seabourn President & CEO Larry Pimentel to establish SeaDream in 2001. The mega-yachts formerly sailed under the Sea Goddess name.

Silversea Cruises: The former owners of Sitmar Cruises, the Lefebvre family of Rome, launched Silversea in 1994 to deliver the most luxurious cruises on the highest-quality ships at sea.

Star Clippers: In 1990, Swedish entrepreneur Mikael Krafft realized his boyhood dream by founding Star Clippers, a modern cruise line that re-creates the golden age of sail with meticulously detailed tall sailing ships.

Windjammer Barefoot Cruises: Over 50 years in the making, the Windjammer line has been inspired by the life of legendary owner Cap'n Mike Burke. The fleet of tall ships is currently operated by Burke's children.

Windstar Cruises: Created in 1984 to offer an alternative to traditional big-ship cruises, Windstar first sailed in 1986. The unique line was sold by Carnival in 2007 to Ambassadors International, Inc., a cruise, marine, travel, and event company.

What won't you find? The cruise staff won't bombard you with noise—announcements are kept to a minimum.

Who's on board? First-timers and experienced passengers who enjoy a more upscale experience in lower-key surroundings. Premium lines attract families, singles, and groups; however, expect the passengers to be older on average, particularly on sailings longer than 7 to 10 days.

Luxury Lines

What you'll find. The air on these deluxe vessels is as rarified as the champagne and caviar:

- Ships range from megayachts for only a hundred or so privileged guests to mid-size vessels, which are considered large for this category. Space is so abundant that you might wonder where the other passengers are hiding.

- Tasteful and elegant surroundings often include such touches as authentic antiques and priceless art collections.

- Spacious staterooms are frequently all suites. On the newest ships, all cabins feature an ocean view or balcony, not to mention a high-tech entertainment center with CD players and TVs with VCRs or DVD. Expect designer bath toiletries, fine linens, and fresh-cut flowers. Some lines include complimentary in-suite bar set-ups for all categories; butlers attend to the needs of guests in exclusive top-category suites.

- Enrichment programs with celebrity and scholarly guest speakers and culinary classes taught by famous chefs augment traditional shipboard activities. Libraries are well-stocked with books, music, and movies to borrow.

- Evening entertainment varies by ship size, from cabaret to stylish production shows to none at all. Luxury-minded passengers tend to entertain themselves.

- Health clubs and spas are fully equipped and staffed with professionals who bring new meaning to indulgence. After jogging or a serious workout, guests can wind down with a swim or savor a relaxing soak in generous hot tubs.

- Open seating is the norm, and guests dine where and with whom they please during dinner hours. Top international chefs are tapped for their culinary expertise in designing menus to please the palate. Meals are prepared to order with the freshest high-quality ingredients and are presented with flair, just like in a top restaurant at home. Complimentary wines accompany meals on most high-end lines.

- At this level, the service staffs anticipate their guests' desires, and it's rare that a special request goes unfulfilled.

- Small, adult-oriented luxury cruise ships are usually inappropriate for children and teens. The lack of organized activities makes these ships undesirable for young families.

What won't you find? No one will be groveling for gratuities. If they're not already included in the fare, they are oh-so-discreetly suggested.

(top) Kayakers from the *SeaDream II*. *(bottom left)* Cocktails on *Crystal Harmony*. *(bottom right)* The sun deck on *Seven Seas Mariner.*

(top left) Norwegian Cruise Line buffet. *(top right)* Jogging on the deck of MSC *Lirica*. *(bottom)* Carnival Victory departing.

(top) Entertainment on Costa. *(bottom left)* Service on Silversea Cruises. *(bottom right)* Deck service on Holland America Line.

(top left) *Star Clipper* under sail. *(top right)* Water slide on a Disney ship. *(bottom)* A luxury suite on *Queen Mary 2.*

(top) MSC *Opera* pool deck. *(bottom left)* The planetarium on *Queen Mary 2*. *(bottom right)* Dinner on Windstar Cruises.

(top) Oceania Cruises' *Regatta*. *(bottom left)* Casino on *Seven Seas Voyager*. *(bottom right)* Compass Rose Bar on Windstar Cruises' *Wind Surf*.

(top left) Captain Max on Windjammer's *Mandalay*. *(top right)* Yoga class on Celebrity Cruises. *(bottom)* An aqua-bike excursion from a Princess ship.

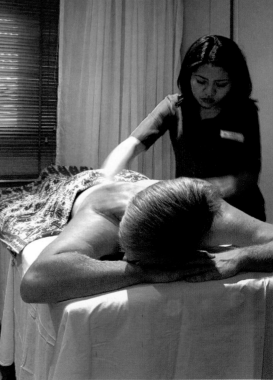

(top) Sky Bar on *Seabourn Legend*. *(bottom left)* Putting practice on Royal Caribbean's *Navigator of the Seas*.
(bottom right) Pampering at SeaDream Spa.

Who's on board? Well-off couples and singles accustomed to the best travel accommodations and service. Small groups and families gravitate to the larger vessels in this category. Traveling in style to collect exotic destinations is highly desirable to luxury-minded passengers.

CABINS

In years gone by, cabins were almost an afterthought. The general attitude of both passengers and the cruise lines used to be that a cabin is a cabin and is used only for changing clothes and sleeping. That's why the cabins on most older cruise ships are skimpy in size and short on amenities.

Until you actually get on board you may not realize that nearly every cabin on your ship is identical. How'd they do that? It's simple, really. Cruise ships are built in sections and, except for some luxury suites, the cabins are prefabricated and dropped into place with everything all ready to hook up, even the plumbing. There are some variations in size, but the main difference between cabins in the myriad price categories is location: on a higher or lower deck, forward or aft, inside or outside.

Cabins high on the ship with a commanding view fetch higher fares. But you should also know that they are also more susceptible to side-to-side movement; in rough seas you could find yourself tossed right out of bed. On lower decks, you'll pay less and find more stability, particularly in the middle of the ship.

Forward cabins have a tendency to be oddly shaped, as they follow the contour of the bow. They are also likely to be noisy; when the ship's anchor drops, you won't need a wake-up call. In rough seas, you can feel the ship's pitch (its upward and downward motion) more in the front.

Should you go for the stern location instead? You're more likely to hear engine and machinery noise there, as well as feel the pitch and possibly some vibration. However, many passengers feel the view of the ship's wake (the ripples it leaves behind as its massive engines move it forward) is worth any noise or vibration they might encounter there.

No location is perfect, but mid-ship on a lower deck is almost always preferable to the extremes—either far forward or aft.

Above all, don't be confused by all the categories listed in cruise line brochures—the categories more accurately reflect price levels based on location than any physical differences in the cabins themselves (keep repeating: prefabricated). Shipboard accommodations fall into four basic configurations: inside cabins, outside cabins, balcony cabins, and suites.

Inside Cabins

An inside cabin is just that: a stateroom that's located inside the ship with no window or porthole. These are always the least expensive cabins and are ideal for passengers who would rather spend their vacation funds on excursions or other incidentals than on upgraded accommodations. Inside cabins are generally just as spacious as outside cabins, and decor and amenities are similar. On the newest vessels, you may even find small refrigerators and a cozy sitting area.

CABIN FEVER: Typical Cabin Features

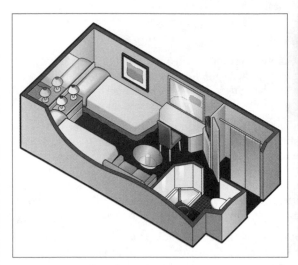

Standard Staterooms

- There are three standard cabin types: Inside, Outside, and Balcony.

- The average size of a standard cabin is 175–180 square feet (including the interior space devoted to bathrooms and closets).

- Strategically placed mirrors as well as clever lighting and furniture placement give the illusion of more space.

- Beds are usually two twins that can be combined to form a single queen (some also have a sofa bed or fold-down upper berths).

- Furnishings typically include bedside tables and reading lamps, a combination desk–vanity table and chair or stool, and possibly a small sitting area with either a chair or love seat and coffee table.

- Hanging closets and drawers and/or shelves are built-in for storage; you may even find unexpected storage beneath the sofa cushions as well as under the beds. Nearly all cabins have a TV and telephone (some with voice mail), an ice bucket and glassware, and many also have a small refrigerator (some are mini-bars).

- Bathrooms feature open or enclosed shelves and a shower. Shampoo, lotion, and soaps or shower gel are usually provided, often in dispensers rather than individual packages.

- A balcony is one of the most popular stateroom amenities and adds an additional dimension to a cruise—personal space with fresh air and sea breezes.

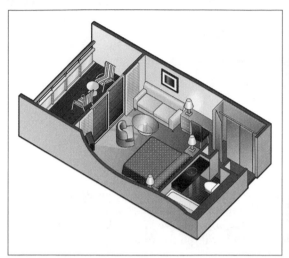

Suites

- A suite is usually at least 300 square feet.

- The sleeping area is separated from the living area, but often by a curtain rather than a wall.

- Some suites have queen- or king-size beds, but often they're two twins that can be combined.

- Furnishings include everything that's in a standard cabin, but some suites have separate dining alcoves and a butler's pantry. There's often a DVD, VCR, or CD player.

- Minibars are usually stocked, but the contents are not always complimentary.

- Storage is generally abundant and many suites have walk-in closets.

- Bathrooms also contain generous storage and usually a bathtub with shower or a separate shower.

- Some bathrooms have twin sinks or jetted tubs.

- A guest powder room is not uncommon in top-of-the-line suites.

- Toiletries may carry designer labels and include a variety of shampoo, conditioner, shower gel, mouthwash, and soaps.

- Bathrobes are almost always furnished for use during the cruise.

- Most suites have balconies; some offer access to a concierge lounge.

To give the illusion of more space, inside cabins may have a mock window (complete with curtain) and rely on the generous use of mirrors for an open feeling. On *Queen Mary 2* and Royal Caribbean's largest vessels, there are even inside cabins with a view of sorts—some are designated atrium staterooms and feature bowed windows overlooking the grand lobby or promenade. Although they don't offer a sea view, these cabins do provide a prime spot for watching Royal Caribbean's nighttime parades on the "street" below.

Many ships locate triple and quad cabins (accommodating three or more passengers) on the inside. Essentially, they look just like a standard double cabin but have bunk beds that either fold down from the wall or disappear into the ceiling. Parents sometimes book an inside cabin for their older children and teens, while their own cabin is an outside across the hall with a window or balcony.

For passengers who want a very dark room for sleeping, an inside cabin is ideal. Use a bit of creativity, and even your inside cabin can have a window on the sea if your ship has a television channel that features a continuous view from the bridge. Tune in that channel before you retire and turn off the sound—it will be dark all night and you will awaken with sunshine and a seascape.

Outside Cabins

A standard outside cabin has either a picture window or porthole. To give the illusion of more space, these cabins might also rely on the generous use of mirrors for an even airier feeling. In addition to the usual amenities, outside staterooms often have a small refrigerator and a sitting area.

Two twin beds can be joined together to create one large bed, the equivalent of a queen- or king-size bed. Going one step further, standard and larger outside staterooms on modern ships are often outfitted with a small sofa or love seat with a cocktail table or small side table. Some of those tables can be raised for dining. The sofas usually contain fold-out beds and can accommodate a third person. Disney Cruise Line's cabins for five even incorporate a clever Murphy bed that drops down from the wall. Floor-to-ceiling curtains that can be drawn from wall to wall to create a private sleeping space are a nice touch in some outside cabins with sitting areas. Cabins that are termed larger may have a combination bathtub-shower instead of just a shower.

Balcony Cabins

A balcony—or veranda—cabin is an outside cabin with floor-to-ceiling glass doors that open onto a private deck. Although the cabin may have large expanses of glass, the balcony is sometimes cut out of the cabin's square footage (depending on the ship). To give the illusion of even more space, a balcony cabin might also rely on the liberal use of mirrors.

> **WORD OF MOUTH**
>
> A cruise is a way for us to kick back and relax and have some time together without any cell phones, pagers, or radios beeping at us. We book ships that offer an elegant experience rather than casual or high-energy atmosphere. Also, for the Caribbean, we tend to book for the ship and stateroom rather than the ports. We spend much of the time in the cabin and on the veranda so for us booking a suite makes sense.   –Sue C.

Back-to-Back Sailings

1

ONE WEEK AT SEA MIGHT NOT BE ENOUGH, so go ahead and book two. Ships with alternating itineraries—Eastern Caribbean one week and Western Caribbean the next—recycle the menus weekly but won't repeat any (or many) ports of call.

Between the time the first cruise ends and the second begins, there are a few things to take into account depending on the cruise line, the port, and customs procedures. Sometimes you're issued a new key-charge card by the purser and invited to relax on board the ship; other times you might have to go into the terminal and check back in. You might even need to get off the ship, go through customs, and then complete the normal boarding process. You'll be informed a day or two before the turnaround, but in every case you do not have to pack up your belongings unless you're changing cabins.

Balconies are usually furnished with two chairs and a table for lounging and casual dining outdoors. However, you should be aware that balconies are not always completely private. Dividers might be opaque and may not extend all the way from ceiling to floor or from the ship's hull to the railing. On some ships, including those with aft-facing balconies, the balconies are stepped like a layer cake; this means that certain balconies are visible from the decks above.

The furnishings and amenities of balcony cabins are otherwise much like those in standard outside cabins. Like outside staterooms, most balcony staterooms have a separate sitting area outfitted with a small sofa or love seat and small table. Some balcony cabins may even have a combination bathtub-shower instead of just a shower.

Suites

Suites are sweet indeed. They are the most lavish accommodations afloat, and although suites are always larger than regular cabins, they do not always have separate rooms for sleeping. Some luxury ships designate all accommodations as suites, and they can range in size from about 250 to 1,500 square feet. The most expansive (and expensive) have large living rooms and separate bedrooms and may also have huge private outdoor sundecks equipped with hot tubs, changing rooms, and dining areas.

Even smaller suites (often termed minisuites) and penthouses are generous in size, and the largest villa suites on Norwegian Cruise Line are more like apartments at sea that measure in at an extraordinary 5,350 square feet.

Suites almost always have amenities that standard cabins do not have. True suites have separate living and sleeping areas, but these areas are still occasionally separated only by a curtain. Depending on the cruise line, you may find a small refrigerator or minibar stocked with complimentary soft drinks, bottled water, and the alcoholic beverages of your choice. A bottle of champagne on ice almost always awaits you upon embarkation. Little extras might include afternoon tea and evening canapés delivered to you and served by a white-gloved butler.

Top-drawer suites on some ships include the luxurious touch of complimentary laundry service, in-cabin Internet connections, and complex entertainment centers with big-screen plasma televisions, VCR/DVD players, and CD stereo systems.

The beds in most suites are two twin-size that can be joined together. Expect roomy closets, abundant storage, and deluxe imported soaps and toiletries in the bathroom. The bathroom may even be outfitted with a jetted tub and separate shower. Butlers' pantries and guest powder rooms are often featured in top-suite categories.

Suite balconies are usually furnished with at least two chairs and a small table for outdoor lounging. Depending on the ship and balcony size, you may also find a table and chairs for alfresco dining and reclining chaise longues for sunbathing. Be aware that the balconies in suites do not always offer 100% privacy. Dividers might be opaque or might not extend all the way from ceiling to floor or from the ship's hull to the railing.

An added bonus to the suite life is the extra level of services many ships offer. At the least you should expect priority boarding and disembarkation, concierge service during the cruise, and top consideration when making restaurant and spa reservations. Even space on sold-out shore excursions may be available to you, or you might be bumped to the top of the waiting list. Some suites come with butler service; the butler can handle tasks from valet services and unpacking your suitcases to daily delivery of tea and hors d'oeuvres. Your butler will make all your reservations for you.

Although minisuites on most contemporary ships have separate sitting areas with a sofa, chair, and a cocktail table, don't let the marketing skill of the cruise lines fool you: so-called minisuites are usually little more than slightly larger versions of standard balcony cabins and don't often include extra services you can get in regular suites. Sometimes you don't even get more elaborate amenities. They're still generally a good value for the price if space matters.

ITINERARIES

It's a common misperception that Caribbean islands and itineraries are pretty much the same. Each island has its own personality and style, some derived from their colonial culture, others from their geography. Most are home to friendly residents and offer pleasant diversions and enough shopping for even the most addicted shopaholic. It's quite possible to take as many as four or five Caribbean cruises and repeat very few islands.

One-week Caribbean cruises come in three distinct flavors: Eastern, Western, and Southern. Longer cruises of 10 and 11 nights are frequently called something like Caribbean Circle or Exotic Caribbean. Short cruises of less than a week generally include ports in the Bahamas and sometimes Key West, Florida.

The Eastern Caribbean is often the choice of first-time cruisers and those veterans who relish more at-sea days. Three, sometimes four, ports of call generally include St. Thomas, St. Maarten, San Juan, and, possibly, a stop at the cruise line's private island for a beach party.

SHIPS BY ITINERARY AND HOME PORT

SHIP	HOMEPORT	DURATION IN NIGHTS	ITINERARY
Carnival Cruise Lines			
Carnival Conquest	Galveston, TX	7	W Caribbean
Carnival Destiny	San Juan, PR or Bridgetown, Barbados	7	S Caribbean
Carnival Ecstasy	Galveston, TX	4 or 5	W Caribbean
Carnival Fantasy	New Orleans, LA	4 or 5	W Caribbean
Carnival Fascination	Miami, FL	3	Bahamas
Carnival Freedom	Miami, FL	7	E or W Caribbean
	Fort Lauderdale, FL	6	W Caribbean
	Fort Lauderdale, FL	8	E or W Caribbean
Carnival Glory	Port Canaveral, FL	7	E or W Caribbean
Carnival Imagination	Miami, FL	4 or 5	W Caribbean
Carnival Inspiration	Tampa, FL	4 or 5	W Caribbean
Carnival Legend	Tampa, FL	7	W Caribbean
Carnival Liberty	Fort Lauderdale, FL	8	E Caribbean
	Miami, FL	7	E or W Caribbean
Carnival Miracle	Fort Lauderdale, FL	8	S or W Caribbean
	New York, NY	8	E Caribbean
Carnival Sensation	Port Canaveral, FL	3 or 4	Bahamas
Carnival Splendor	To Be Announced		
Carnival Triumph	Miami, FL	7	E Caribbean
Carnival Valor	Miami, FL	7	E or Caribbean
Carnival Victory	Miami, FL	7	E or W Caribbean
	Norfolk, VA	6	Bahamas
	Charleston, SC	5	Bahamas
Celebration	Jacksonville, FL	4	Bahamas
	Jacksonville, FL	5	Bahamas & Key West
	Miami, FL	4	W Caribbean
Holiday	Mobile, AL	4 or 5	W Caribbean
Celebrity Cruises			
Celebrity Solstice	To Be Announced		
Azamara Quest	Miami, FL	12 to 14	S Caribbean
Century	Miami, FL	4 or 5	W Caribbean
Constellation	Fort Lauderdale, FL	10 or 11	E or W Caribbean
Galaxy	San Juan, PR	10 or 11	S Caribbean
Millennium	Fort Lauderdale, FL	7	E Caribbean
Summit	San Juan, PR	7	S Caribbean
Costa Cruises			
Costa Fortuna	Fort Lauderdale, FL	7	E or W Caribbean
Costa Mediterranea	Fort Lauderdale, FL	7	E or W Caribbean
Crystal Cruises			
Crystal Serenity	Miami, FL	10 to 14	W Caribbean & Panama Canal
	Miami, FL	14	E Caribbean
Crystal Symphony	Miami, FL	11	W Caribbean & Panama Canal
Cunard Line			
Queen Mary 2	New York, NY	10, 13, or 14	E or W Caribbean
Disney Cruise Line			
Disney Magic	Port Canaveral, FL	7	E or W Caribbean
Disney Wonder	Port Canaveral, FL	3 or 4	Bahamas
easyCruise			
easyCruise One	Phillipsburg, St. Maarten	3, 4 or 7	S Caribbean

Holland America Line

Eurodam	Fort Lauderdale, FL	7	E or S Caribbean
Maasdam	Fort Lauderdale, FL	10	S Caribbean
Noordam	New York, NY	10	E Caribbean
	New York, NY	11	S Caribbean
Statendam	Tampa, FL	7	W Caribbean
	Fort Lauderdale, FL	14	S Caribbean
Veendam	Tampa, FL	7	W Caribbean
	Tampa, FL	14	S Caribbean
Volendam	Fort Lauderdale, FL	10	S Caribbean & Panama Canal
Westerdam	Fort Lauderdale, FL	3	Bahamas
	Fort Lauderdale, FL	7	E, W or S Caribbean
Zuiderdam	Fort Lauderdale, FL	10	S Caribbean & Panama Canal
	Fort Lauderdale, FL	7	E Caribbean

MSC Cruises

MSC Lirica	Fort Lauderdale, FL	11	W or S Caribbean

Norwegian Cruise Line

Norwegian Dawn	Miami, FL	7	E Caribbean
Norwegian Gem	New York, NY	7	Bahamas & Florida
	New York, NY	10 or 11	S Caribbean
Norwegian Jewel	Miami, FL	5	W Caribbean
	Miami, FL	9	S Caribbean
Norwegian Majesty	Charleston, SC	7	W Caribbean
Norwegian Pearl	Miami, FL	5	W Caribbean
	Miami, FL	9	S Caribbean
Norwegian Spirit	New Orleans, LA	7	W Caribbean
Norwegian Sun	Miami, FL	7	W Caribbean

Oceania Cruises

Regatta	Miami, FL	10, 12 or 14	S Caribbean

Princess Cruises

Caribbean Princess	Fort Lauderdale, FL	7	E or W Caribbean
Coral Princess	Fort Lauderdale, FL	10	W Caribbean & Panama Canal
Crown Princess	New York, NY	9	E or W Caribbean
	San Juan, PR	7	S Caribbean
Emerald Princess	Fort Lauderdale, FL	10	E or W Caribbean
Grand Princess	Fort Lauderdale, FL	7	W Caribbean
Ruby Princess	Fort Lauderdale, FL	7	W Caribbean
Sea Princess	Bridgetown, Barbados or Montego Bay, Jamaica	14	S Caribbean

Radisson Seven Seas Cruises

Seven Seas Navigator	Fort Lauderdale, FL	10 or 11	E or W Caribbean
Seven Seas Voyager	Fort Lauderdale, FL	7	E or W Caribbean

Royal Caribbean International

Adventure of the Seas	San Juan, PR	7	S Caribbean
Brilliance of the Seas	Miami, FL	4	Bahamas
	Miami, FL	9	W Caribbean
Empress of the Seas	San Juan, PR	3	E Caribbean
	San Juan, PR	9 or 11	S Caribbean
Enchantment of the Seas	Fort Lauderdale, FL	4, 5 or 7	W Caribbean
Explorer of the Seas	Cape Liberty, NJ	9	E Caribbean
	Cape Liberty, NJ	12	S Caribbean

Freedom of the Seas	Miami, FL	7	E or W Caribbean
Grandeur of the Seas	Tampa, FL	4, 5 or 7	W Caribbean
Independence of the Seas	Fort Lauderdale, FL	6 or 8	W or E Caribbean
Jewel of the Seas	Fort Lauderdale, FL	6	W Caribbean
	Fort Lauderdale, FL	8	E Caribbean
Legend of the Seas	Santo Domingo, DR	7	S Caribbean
Liberty of the Seas	Miami, FL	7	E or W Caribbean
Majesty of the Seas	Miami, FL	3	Bahamas
	Miami, FL	4	Bahamas & Key West
Mariner of the Seas	Port Canaveral, FL	7	E or W Caribbean
Navigator of the Seas	Fort Lauderdale, FL	4 or 5	W Caribbean
Radiance of the Seas	Fort Lauderdale, FL	8	E Caribbean
	Fort Lauderdale, FL	6	W Caribbean
Serenade of the Seas	San Juan, PR	7	S Caribbean
Sovereign of the Seas	Port Canaveral, FL	3 or 4	Bahamas
Voyager of the Seas	Galveston, TX	7	W Caribbean
Seabourn Cruise Line			
Seabourn Legend	St. Thomas, USVI	7	E or S Caribbean
Seabourn Pride	Fort Lauderdale, FL	14	S Caribbean
SeaDream Yacht Club			
SeaDream I	San Juan, PR or	7	S Caribbean
	St. Thomas, USVI		
Sea Dream II	St. John's, Antigua;	7	S Caribbean
	San Juan, PR; or		
	Bridgetown, Barbados		
Silversea Cruise Line			
Silver Cloud	Bridgetown, Barbados	7	S Caribbean
Silver Shadow	Bridgetown, Barbados	9	S Caribbean
	Fort Lauderdale, FL	9 to 14	S or W Caribbean
Silver Wind	San Juan, PR	7 or 8	S or W Caribbean
	Bridgetown, Barbados	7 or 12	S Caribbean
	Fort Lauderdale, FL	12	S Caribbean
Windstar Cruises			
Wind Spirit	St. Thomas, USVI	7	E Caribbean
Wind Surf	Bridgetown, Barbados	7	S Caribbean
Star Clippers			
Royal Clipper	Bridgetown, Barbados	7	S Caribbean
Windjammer			
Barefoot Cruises			
Mandalay	St. Maarten	7	S Caribbean
	Antigua	7	S Caribbean
Polynesia	Road Town, Tortola	7	S Caribbean
	St. Maarten	7	S Caribbean
Yankee Clipper	Grenada	7	S Caribbean

For passengers who consider snorkeling and scuba diving a high priority, the Western Caribbean offers the best options. Typical Western Caribbean ports include Key West, Jamaica, Grand Cayman, Cozumel, Roatan (Honduras), and sometimes a private island.

Southern Caribbean cruises afford the choice of more island destinations—usually as many as five. Often embarking in San Juan, ships on Southern Caribbean itineraries may call on Antigua, Aruba, Barbados, Tortola, Virgin Gorda, Curaçao, Grenada, Martinique, St. Barths, St. Kitts, St. Lucia, and sometimes St. Thomas or St. Maarten. When sailing from a Florida port of embarkation, a Southern Caribbean cruise is generally longer, often 10 to 12 nights.

Abundant sunny days and balmy nights make the Caribbean an ideal vacation destination any time of year. Even brief late afternoon tropical showers simply sweeten the air without overly dampening spirits. However, experienced cruisers know that storms can crop up at the most inopportune times. Passengers numbering in the hundreds of thousands embark on cruises during the official hurricane season, from June 1 through November 30, without a thought about storms on land or at sea. For some, it's the only time of year they can schedule a family vacation. Others don't give it a second thought. After all, the official hurricane season consumes a full six months of the year.

Although it's something to ponder in terms of comfort and convenience, most travelers do not let hurricane season stand in the way of scheduling a cruise during that time frame. Chances are, you'll never encounter a problem, and a ship at sea is not necessarily the worst place to be when a hurricane is looming over the horizon. Modern cruise ships are equipped with sophisticated communications gear and receive regular weather bulletins and storm advisories. Your ship will have the equipment necessary to ensure your safety.

When a hurricane is imminent your major concern should be your embarkation port. When a hurricane barrels down on your embarkation city, flights in and out are certain to be delayed or cancelled by airport closures. Assuming you made it to the ship and have sailed, the itinerary will often be modified as necessary to avoid storms. If a hurricane has a tryst with one of your Caribbean port stops, you will alter course to a different (and possibly more interesting) port. In the extreme, you could end up in the Western Caribbean when your planned itinerary is the Eastern Caribbean. The ship will go where the captain and crew feel it is safest. Your very life depends on their judgment, and they take that responsibility seriously. It's a big ocean out there; happily, there's a lot of room for your ship to maneuver safely.

KEEPING IN TOUCH

Some people just can't get away from it all, but the days when wireless meant something entirely different than a laptop with Wi-Fi capability are a distant memory. No longer do passengers have to depend on the Marconi operator in the radio room to send telegraphed ship-to-shore messages. Technology has gone to sea in a big way, and there's no rea-

What Kids Love About Cruising

As an adult, one of the things I enjoy most in a cruise vacation is having nothing to do. Just lounging away on a deck chair reading a book is pure bliss. For children, however, there is little appeal in these leisurely pleasures. As any parent knows, a child whining "I'm bored!" and "There's nothing to do!" is as welcome as fingernails scraping across a chalkboard.

My daughters, Samantha (age twelve) and Madeleine (age ten) are veteran cruisers, with more than a dozen voyages under each of their belts. Their first cruise was one to remember. In September 1998 we boarded Carnival's *Fascination* in San Juan, Puerto Rico, not knowing that Hurricane Georges planned a stampede through the Eastern Caribbean. Despite the storm and a few missed port calls, the family had a terrific time. If you ask why, you'll get two different answers. Samantha prefers cruises with long days in port so she can get in some quality beach time. Her favorite cruises include day-long calls at a private island in the Bahamas. Madeleine loves hanging out with the Disney characters (especially Mickey Mouse) so our *Disney Magic* voyages are her favorites.

Both Samantha and Madeleine agree that Disney cruises offer the best onboard activities. Highlights include the pool and its water slide and the enormous state-of-the-art activity areas. Even with all the cool onboard offerings, parents should always bring some activities and games for evening wind-down time in the cabin. Crayons, coloring books, clay, and electronic games are vital in helping to keep your children occupied. Do not leave these at home!

When it comes to kids and food on cruises, be prepared for your children to be spoiled beyond their wildest dreams. "I loved all the chocolate donuts on the *Zuiderdam!*" shouts Madeleine. "No, no, the Mickey Mouse ice cream bars on *Disney Magic* were the best!" implores Samantha. "Oh, I forgot, the pizza on *Sun Princess* was awesome," adds Samantha. Madeleine licks her lips and nods in agreement. If your sticky-fingered little darlings are finicky eaters, worry not. There is something aboard for every taste. Cruise staff members really go above and beyond to make a child's wishes come true. Extra chocolates on pillows, a second dessert during the captain's dinner, bottomless Shirley Temples with extra cherries, more pizza—no problem. Believe me, when the kids get back home to meatloaf and no chocolates on pillows at night they'll be screaming to go on their next cruise.

–Anita Dunham-Potter

son for communication junkies to insist on remaining landlocked. Connecting with your family or business from a modern cruise ship is as close as the direct-dial telephone in your cabin. However, since rates vary from a low of $6 to as much as $15 *per minute*, most passengers agree that it's best to reserve their cabin telephone for emergency use only.

The ability to use your own mobile phone from the high seas is a communication alternative that is gaining popularity. It's also cheaper than using a cabin phone if your ship offers the service. Rather ingeniously, some modern cruise ships can act as a cell tower in international waters, so you may be able to use your own cell phone and your own number when roaming at sea. When in port, depending on the agreements your home mobile service provider has established, you may be able to connect to local networks. Rates for using the maritime service, as well as any roaming charges from Caribbean islands, are established by your mobile service carrier and are worth checking into before you leave home. Rates from your ship at sea may range from $2 to $5 per minute, or more. And this is true even if your own mobile phone company provides the roaming service aboard your ship.

E-mail is likely to be the least expensive way to stay in touch, even though charges on board range from 35¢ to $1 per minute to connect to the Internet. There might also be a one-time account activation charge of a few dollars. Cruise-ship computer systems vary widely, and the speed can be maddeningly slow at times. Most ships have a dedicated Internet center where you can go online using the ship's computers; some ships have in-cabin broadband data ports or wireless systems that allow you to use your own laptop or one you can rent on board in public "hot spots." On some vessels wireless access is available ship-wide. As wireless usage becomes more widely available, you may find your ship offers all three options.

You will often save money by purchasing a block of computer time. If the ship's pay-as-you-go rate is 75¢ a minute, you may be able to purchase a plan that allows you to use 250 minutes for $100, which would lower your cost to 40¢ a minute. If you can't send and retrieve e-mail through the Internet by using your own Internet service provider, simply set up a free account with a company like Yahoo or AOL. Using your own e-mail account is usually less expensive than using an e-mail address provided for you by the ship's Internet service, for which you can be charged a fee per e-mail in addition to the per-minute rate.

A few ships still don't have these high-tech communication options, but you won't be cut off totally even then. Some ships offer only a simple e-mail service and charge per e-mail message sent and received. And once on shore, you can find Internet cafés with high-speed connections, often located near the cruise-ship pier; almost any crew member can point the way to them. For business types who must spend extended time online, shoreside cybercafés are usually the cheapest option, and many now offer Wi-Fi as well.

Planning Your Cruise

WORD OF MOUTH

"Before booking a cabin guarantee, you should look at the deck plan and find the worst cabin in that category. Would you be okay with that cabin? If so, then go with the guarantee knowing you'd be okay with the worst cabin just in case you get it."

–pet lover

"I am not so crazy about the big ships, but there is a whole industry out there for a reason. Some people LOVE them! You just have to figure out which type you are."

–Tango

WITH SOMETHING FOR EVERYONE and the option to do nothing at all, cruises are truly the best of all vacation styles for travel companions with different interests. Downtime from everyday stresses is essential for well-being and even if you do nothing more than stare at the sea and horizon, you will find a cruise ship the perfect place to relax. Beyond that, there's a spa where massages and treatments can be an antidote to everyday cares. If you get a natural high from active pursuits, those are at your fingertips both on your cruise ship and in ports of call. There's always a new destination over the horizon to tempt you to explore. You only have to unpack once, and the most important item on your list of things to do is getting back to the ship on time after a day in port.

So you know you want to take a cruise, yet the choices you face seem endless. Whether or not you give it much thought, you probably realize every vacation is about more than money. In addition to spending your hard-earned cash, you're spending your time, and that can be priceless. You could be disappointed if you don't plan wisely. By making informed choices you're less likely to waste your money and precious vacation time.

DOING RESEARCH

Years before the Internet became a savvy traveler's primary information resource, brochures, obtained either from travel agencies or ordered directly from cruise lines, were often the first glimpse of what potential passengers might expect on cruise vacations. In some cases, they still are.

Brochure styles vary from straightforward to as dreamy as a romance novel. Some cruise-line brochures are beautiful enough to qualify as coffee table books. Bear in mind while you are browsing brochures that they are slick marketing devices as well as useful planning tools. Open any cruise brochure, and you're sure to find a dizzying display of information and photographs. What you want are simple facts, organized in an informative manner. What are you likely to find?

First of all, you have to select the right brochure. Although some cruise lines feature their entire fleet and all itineraries in one volume, others publish brochures for specific destinations. Brochures are enticing books, and, fortunately, most contain a table of contents, listing such topics as staterooms, dining options, on-board facilities, activities, entertainment, and children's programs up front.

What more do potential passengers want to know? They want simple facts in language they can follow. Can you bring a bottle of champagne to celebrate a special occasion? Or will one be provided free for the asking? What should you pack to be appropriately dressed? What do the staterooms look like? What is included in the fare (and what is not)? And, most important, what happens if you must cancel in case of an emergency? For answers to those questions and more, begin reading in the *back* of the brochure.

You probably would not start reading a mystery novel on the last page, but if you immediately turn to the last few pages of a cruise brochure you will find the so-called fine print, which everyone needs to know or at least should want to find out. The section may be titled "Things to

Cruise Line Contacts

YOU CAN OBTAIN CRUISE BROCHURES from your travel agent or directly from the cruise line. Here are the phone numbers and Web sites for all the cruise lines covered in this book:

Carnival Cruise Lines (☎ 888/227-6482 ⊕ www.carnival.com)

Celebrity Cruises (☎ 800/437-3111 ⊕ www.celebrity.com)

Costa Cruises (☎ 800/462-6782 ⊕ www.costacruise.com)

Crystal Cruises (☎ 888/799-4625 ⊕ www.crystalcruises.com)

Cunard Line (☎ 800/728-6273 ⊕ www.cunard.com)

Disney Cruise Line (☎ 888/325-2500 ⊕ www.disneycruise.com)

easyCruise (☎ 650/385-0563 [US] or 018/9565-1191 [UK] ⊕ www.easycruise.com)

Holland America Line (☎ 800/577-1728 ⊕ www.hollandamerica.com)

MSC Cruises (☎ 800/666-9333 ⊕ www.msccruises.com)

Norwegian Cruise Line (☎ 800/327-7030 ⊕ www.ncl.com)

Oceania Cruises (☎ 800/531-5658 ⊕ www.oceaniacruises.com)

Princess Cruises (☎ 800/774-6237 ⊕ www.princess.com)

Regent Seven Seas Cruises (☎ 877/505-5370 ⊕ www.rssc.com)

Royal Caribbean International (☎ 800/327-6700 ⊕ www.royalcaribbean.com)

Seabourn Cruise Line (☎ 800/929-9391 ⊕ www.seabourn.com)

SeaDream Yacht Club (☎ 800/707-4911 ⊕ www.seadreamyachtclub.com)

Silversea Cruises (☎ 800/722-9955 ⊕ www.silversea.com)

Star Clippers (☎ 800/442-0551 ⊕ www.starclippers.com)

Windjammer Barefoot Cruises (☎ 800/327-2601 ⊕ www.windjammer.com)

Windstar Cruises (☎ 877/827-7245 ⊕ www.windstarcruises.com)

know before you go," "What you need to know," "Important policies," or even "Terms and conditions." Read it! Read it closely. Also look toward the back of the brochure for details about Air & Sea transportation programs, insurance, and amenity packages to enhance your cruise. Answers to frequently asked questions can be found simply by thumbing through the brochure from back to front.

After absorbing the facts, go back to the front pages of the brochure and take a good look at the illustrations. Would you be happy to share a cruise with the people pictured? Although they are more likely than not models, those people *could* be your shipmates. A brochure that features children in a majority of photos is giving you a solid hint that the cruise line caters to families. Similarly, representations of stylish middle-aged or older couples hint at a particular demographic the line is recruiting.

And here's another thing about those pictures. As a rule, accommodations look exactly like the brochure illustrations and are perfectly adequate for the average passenger; however, most people find their staterooms are somewhat smaller than what they expected. Wide-angle lenses help photographers capture the small space on film, but they also make the cabin appear larger than it is in reality.

CRUISE LINES
AT A GLANCE

Before you narrow your search to a few specific ships, you want the assurance that you aren't looking at the wrong cruise line. To help you decide which cruise line might be most appropriate for you, we have rated several areas important to most passengers on a scale of 5 (most suitable) to 0 (no options) indicated by the ⚓ symbols on the chart at right. A lower number doesn't necessarily indicate an inferior product, however. A cruise line that offers programs for children seasonally will have a lower Family Friendly rating. Although it might have wonderful playrooms with well-planned activities, it will probably be less appealing than a cruise line that caters to families year-round.

Even within a single cruise line's fleet, individual ship facilities can vary widely. The newest vessels often have more dining and entertainment choices and the latest in high-tech gadgetry and gizmos. Look for a general overview here before exploring the details outlined in our Cruise Line Profiles and Cruise Ship Reviews in Chapter 5.

Short cruises are defined as less than seven nights. They are great getaways for busy people as well as a way to sample cruising before committing to a full week, or even longer, at sea.

Although fares are usually quoted per person for an entire cruise, pricing is ultimately based on double occupancy per cabin. For that reason—and also because cruises vary in length—we have simplified our cost ranges to reflect the realistic price of a cabin per night for two passengers. Even fares within a cabin type (inside or outside) vary depending on location, and you may find the category you select is at the high end of a price range even if entry-level fares fall in the lower end.

CRUISE LINE	Cost–Inside Cabin	Cost–Outside Cabin
Carnival Cruise Lines	$	$$
Celebrity Cruises	$$	$$
Costa Cruises	$	$$
Crystal Cruises		$$$$
Cunard Line	$$	$$$
Disney Cruise Line	$$	$$$
easyCruise	$	$
Holland America Line	$$	$$$
Mediterranean Shipping Company	$	$$
Norwegian Cruise Line	$	$$
Oceania Cruises	$$	$$$
Princess Cruises	$	$$
Regent Seven Seas Cruises		$$$$$
Royal Caribbean International	$	$$
Seabourn Cruise Line		$$$$$
SeaDream Yacht Club		$$$$$
Silversea Cruises		$$$$$
Star Clippers	$$$	$$$$
Windjammer Barefoot Cruises		$$$
Windstar Cruises		$$$$

Key to Costs:

$$$$$	over $600
$$$$	$450–$600
$$$	$300–$450
$$	$200–$300
$	$125–$200

Short Cruises	Fine Dining	Service	Lectures/Enrichment Programs	Entertainment/ Shows	Family Friendly	Accessible	Spa	Sports, Facilities
X	▲▲▲▲	▲▲▲		▲▲▲▲▲	▲▲▲▲▲	▲▲▲	▲▲▲▲	▲▲▲▲▲
X	▲▲▲▲	▲▲▲▲	▲▲▲	▲▲▲	▲▲▲	▲▲▲	▲▲▲▲	▲▲▲
	▲▲	▲▲	▲▲	▲▲▲	▲▲	▲▲▲	▲▲▲	▲▲
	▲▲▲▲▲	▲▲▲▲▲	▲▲▲▲▲	▲▲▲	▲▲	▲▲▲▲	▲▲▲▲	▲▲▲
	▲▲▲▲	▲▲▲▲	▲▲▲▲▲	▲▲▲	▲▲▲	▲▲▲▲	▲▲▲▲▲	▲▲▲
X	▲▲▲▲	▲▲▲▲	▲▲▲	▲▲▲▲▲	▲▲▲▲▲	▲▲▲▲	▲▲▲▲▲	▲▲▲▲
	▲	▲						
	▲▲▲▲	▲▲▲▲	▲▲▲▲	▲▲▲	▲▲▲▲	▲▲▲▲	▲▲▲▲	▲▲▲▲
	▲▲	▲▲▲	▲▲▲	▲▲▲	▲▲	▲▲	▲▲▲	▲▲▲
	▲▲▲	▲▲▲		▲▲▲▲▲	▲▲▲▲▲	▲▲▲	▲▲▲▲	▲▲▲▲▲
	▲▲▲▲	▲▲▲▲	▲▲▲	▲▲		▲▲▲	▲▲▲	▲▲
	▲▲▲▲	▲▲▲	▲▲▲▲	▲▲▲	▲▲▲▲	▲▲▲▲▲	▲▲▲▲	▲▲▲▲
X	▲▲▲▲▲	▲▲▲▲▲	▲▲▲▲	▲▲▲		▲▲▲▲	▲▲▲▲▲	▲▲▲
X	▲▲▲	▲▲▲		▲▲▲▲▲	▲▲▲▲▲	▲▲▲▲	▲▲▲▲	▲▲▲▲▲
	▲▲▲▲▲	▲▲▲▲▲	▲▲▲▲▲	▲▲		▲▲	▲▲▲▲	▲▲▲▲
	▲▲▲▲▲	▲▲▲▲▲	▲▲	▲▲		▲	▲▲▲▲	▲▲▲
X	▲▲▲▲▲	▲▲▲▲▲	▲▲▲▲	▲▲▲		▲▲▲	▲▲▲▲	▲▲▲
	▲▲▲▲	▲▲▲▲					▲▲▲	
X	▲	▲▲			▲▲			
	▲▲▲▲	▲▲▲▲▲		▲▲▲			▲▲	▲▲▲

Brochure Speak

SOME ARMCHAIR BROCHURE browsers become enraptured with such descriptions as "crystalline waters" and "historic wonders." These are just some of the buzz words employed to entice you to set sail. But other phrases hint at more practical considerations, and it's helpful to know how to decode the brochure's language:

• A port of embarkation that is close by— or relatively close to home—means you can drive to your cruise or at least find a convenient, and possibly cheap, airline flight. Look for "homeland cruises" and "convenient departure ports" described in the brochures.

• The term "all-inclusive" is a misnomer that is very rarely, if ever, found in a cruise brochure and only found in practice on some luxury lines. Think *nearly* all-inclusive and be sure reread the fine print.

• "Floating resorts" are cruise ships that offer everything from rock-climbing walls and miniature golf courses to facilities and activities that appeal to a wide range of age groups. Think Mall of America afloat. These are usually the biggest and most modern vessels at sea. Other ships may be a bit older, but that does not mean they are less well equipped to offer the expected amenities, activities, and entertainment.

• "Choices" are highly touted, especially when it comes to dining. It's your vacation, and you should be able to choose where to eat and what to wear, within reason. On days when you have been ashore, are tired, or just do not feel like dressing up, it's nice to have the choice of casual dining versus the more prim-and-proper directive to either dress up for a meal in the restaurant or stay in your room.

• "Gourmet dining" is a bit too wishful for what you'll normally get on a mainstream cruise. Unless the cruise is on a smaller, extremely exclusive (and expensive) ship, meals are more likely to resemble very good, high-quality banquet food than the made-to-order meals of shoreside gourmet establishments. There's definitely true gourmet dining at sea, but not on every ship. If you're sailing with more than a few hundred fellow passengers, keep an open mind and do not expect it.

• "Fine dining" is something you can often find on a mainstream cruise. However, it usually comes with an additional price tag. Some alternative restaurants carry cover charges ranging from nominal to hefty.

• "Spacious" is in the eye of the beholder. Only the top-category accommodations on many ships afford the spaciousness of an average hotel room. Look for stateroom diagrams and the square footage of your chosen stateroom category, which may or may not be indicated in the brochure.

• "Elegance" and "luxury" are, again, in the eye of the beholder. A typical Las Vegas resort is not the same as a Miami Beach art deco–era hotel, although each has its own appeal for different tastes. Determine your priorities and make your ship selection carefully. In this case, the pictures in the brochure will often help you see the decor of the ship.

• "Fun" is subjective. No one goes on a vacation not to have fun.

• "Rack rate" fares are never the bottom line. Don't expire from sticker shock—you can expect to pay much less than brochure rate, often as much as half off the published price, depending on when you book your cruise.

Location, location, location. Think of a deck plan as a map of a ship, which, unlike a road map, can give a fairly precise idea of what features the neighborhood will hold, particularly when it's time to select a cabin.

A brief description of ports of call and shore excursions is a practicality covered in most brochures. Ports and itineraries are an important factor in most travelers' cruise selection. The brochures of port-intensive cruise lines tend to offer a tad more insight into the destinations and have more shore-excursion descriptions than their contemporary fun-in-the-sun cousins.

Cruise-line Web sites are also excellent resources for decision-making and planning. Web sites often display even more current information than brochures, which are printed far in advance. In addition, detailed ports of call and shore excursion information is often more extensive online than in brochures.

Use these tools wisely to realize the most satisfying cruise travel experience, but keep an open mind when charting your cruise vacation course. Conditions can change, particularly at sea. Be prepared for modifications in itinerary as well on-board amenities. For the latest information and answers to your questions, a trusted travel agent is a cruise passenger's best tool.

PLANNING FOR YOUR SPECIAL NEEDS

Who takes cruises these days? Some passengers arrive with more in mind than getting a suntan. Couples not only honeymoon on cruises, but they get married on ships or in ports of call. People with disabilities are drawn to the ease of travel by ship, and singles find the atmosphere conducive to making friends. Same-sex couples can blend into the mix just as easily as large groups and multigeneration families. But if you have a special interest or need, you may need to consider some specific things to make your cruise a satisfying experience.

"I'm not the cruise-passenger type." That was another of my husband's arguments against taking the plunge to cruise. You can be sure if you pick the right ship and are breathing, you will find like-minded individuals on board. Cruise ships are small cities at sea; just as the variety of its citizens is the hallmark of a captivating city, a typical ship's passenger manifest can be equally diverse.

Cruisers are quite literally all in the same boat, which tends to drop barriers and lead to more contact than impersonal resort vacations. The ship's social staff strives mightily to foster interaction, and your shipmates are likely to share their experiences and reveal mutual interests when you meet during activities or over cocktails and dinner. Chances are good you will make friends on a cruise, and if you're single, your ship might turn out to be a Love Boat.

Young and old from all walks of life and all points of the compass are discovering the pleasures of the Caribbean by cruise ship. With a bit of forethought, it can be the vacation of a lifetime.

Honeymoons & Anniversaries

With a little careful planning, any cruise can be turned into a special event— a heavenly honeymoon, a renewal of your commitment to each other, or a celebration of a special anniversary.

Cruise lines are certainly aware of the magical effects their vessels have on couples. Nearly all offer options in the way of romance or anniversary packages that can be arranged ahead of time through your travel agent. Packages may include goodies such as a bottle of champagne in your stateroom, logo robes to keep, his-and-hers spa treatments, formal portraits in elegant frames, or breakfast in bed on the morning of your choice. Renewals of vows are sometimes performed privately by the captain upon arrangement or in a festive group setting, followed by a champagne toast to your commitment.

Do-it-yourself romantics might consider these suggestions:

- Enhance your time together by selecting a stateroom with its own private balcony.

- Have champagne breakfast in bed to toast the beginning of a day at sea.

- Request a table for two at late seating and share the memories of your day.

- Dine in the specialty restaurant to celebrate your good taste; after all, you selected each other.

- Dance under the stars to the music only you can hear.

- Pack your favorite scents and sounds to heighten the intimacy of your stateroom. Set the mood for romance with your favorite fragrance lingering in the air while your special song plays on a portable CD player.

- While you're packing, don't forget something whisper soft to lounge in.

Your very own balcony is the ideal setting for spending time alone together; why not also share a room service meal surrounded by sea sounds? Princess Cruises adds a twist to make the occasion even more memorable—Ultimate Balcony Dining. You choose either breakfast ($30 per couple) or dinner ($50 per person), and prepare to be pampered as your own waiter serves it to you on your private balcony.

Weddings

Every couple dreams of a perfect wedding, closely followed by the ideal honeymoon. For many brides and grooms, destination weddings—exchanging vows in an exotic location—are the height of perfection. Tying the knot on a cruise ship offers the best of both worlds: a wedding and honeymoon wrapped into a package that takes the worry out of planning and combines pampering with privacy for newlyweds. Cruise line wedding coordinators take the anxiety out of seemingly insurmountable tasks such as arranging for a marriage license and finding a clergyman—undertakings that assume even more importance in unfamiliar surroundings. Brides-to-be should take note that cruise weddings are increasingly popular. To avoid disappointment, start planning as soon as you've announced your engagement and set a date.

Nearly every cruise line can assist with a ceremony on the ship prior to sailing or while docked in a port of call. Wedding options vary from a simple private ceremony in an intimate ship's chapel to elaborate nuptials and a reception attended by family and friends, who might even sail with the happy couple after sharing their special day. Brides and grooms merely decide what type of wedding they want—aboard ship or ashore

Planning the Perfect Wedding

2

ANDREA AND HER FIANCÉ WERE ON A CARNIVAL CRUISE when she caught a very brief glimpse of a bride and was smitten with the idea of being married on a cruise ship. "Carnival was the first place I called for details," she said. "It was a pleasant surprise to find out they had a whole wedding department. I did no comparison shopping because I knew this was the way I had to do it." Andrea's friends who were also planning weddings spent nearly twice as much on their nuptials as her dream cruise-ship ceremony. First she dealt with the cruise line's wedding department: "Carnival assigns you to a wedding coordinator at a company called A Wedding For You. I worked with two women from there. My travel agent did some planning also."

There were 100 wedding guests on board for Andrea's big day, and 57 of them sailed with the newlyweds. Andrea was thrilled: "What a great time!! It was more like a four-day reception! You are allowed as many sailing guests as you want; however, only 50 people can come aboard to just see the wedding. As soon as the ship was cleared, everyone was allowed to board. We were on the ship by 11:30 and the wedding was at 1. Because the guests boarded so early, we were able to schedule a cocktail hour in the lounge. It worked out nicely. The only drawback was that I wish the actual reception afterward was longer. It was only an hour and a half."

Andrea took advantage of ordering her bouquet and the men's boutonnieres through Carnival and was delighted, but said, "It would have cost a fortune to get bouquets for all seven bridesmaids as well, so we did that on our own. You need to keep in mind that you are not allowed to bring fresh flowers on board the ship—they must be silk. Another snag was the ship only had one videographer, and another wedding on the ship that day booked before we did, so they got his services. Your best bet is book early!"

in a Caribbean port—and what amenities fit their budgets. The cruise line and wedding coordinator take care of the rest.

Services differ between cruise lines, so you should investigate your options before you book your cruise. Packages can include not only the ceremony but also flowers, photographs, a video recording, champagne, wedding cake, and music. Although a number of newer ships—notably those of Carnival, Costa, Norwegian Cruise Line, Princess, and Royal Caribbean—have dedicated wedding chapels, only Princess Cruises can offer the romance of a wedding at sea with the captain officiating on certain ships. Friends and family at home can attend the ceremony virtually by tuning into the Princess Wedding Cam on the Internet.

The Wedding Experience ☎ 877/580-3556 🖷 305/421-1267 ⊕ www. theweddingexperience.com is the exclusive wedding service provider for Royal Caribbean International, Celebrity Cruises, Costa Cruises, Princess Cruises, Carnival Cruise Line, Norwegian Cruise Line, Windstar Cruises, and Holland America Line.

Solo Travel

When you're watching your fellow cruisers walking up the gangway two-by-two, you may think you're cruising on Noah's Ark rather than the Love Boat. But it doesn't take long to find other singles on almost any cruise. They may be sailing on their own or in small groups or with family. However, you need not rely solely on singles get-togethers organized by the ship's social staff to meet your fellow cruisers: head to the gym, the hot tub, or the computer center, where striking up a conversation and forming friendships is less forced. Because families generally opt for the early-dinner seating, request late seating and ask to be assigned to a large table to increase your opportunity to meet others. You are likely to find the maître d' has arranged tables so that passengers who appear to be traveling by themselves are seated together.

Shipboard hours are easily filled with lectures, shows, and activities where singles are urged to join in and where you can find like-minded fellow passengers. Single women may be delighted to discover the cruise line has arranged to have courtly dance hosts on board to make sure they won't be left out of the dancing and other social activities.

By researching the ports of call thoroughly before your cruise, you will not only know which are the must-see sights and where to locate the best shopping opportunities ashore, but you'll also have interesting information to share with fellow passengers. On port days, shore excursions are the most effortless way to see the sights, but don't discount teaming up with newly made friends to explore together independently. If you've been to a port previously, offer to lead a walking tour. Single travelers are eager to share their experiences with one another and an informal group increases everyone's comfort level when in a new environment.

There are distinct advantages to traveling solo on a cruise ship. The desolation of hotel homesickness is unlikely to strike; plus, there's the luxury of having a stateroom with storage and amenities designed for two. There's also a major drawback: cruising single in a couple's world is pricey. Most modern cruise ships do not have single cabins, and nearly all fares are based on double occupancy. Supplements for sailing solo can range from an additional 25% to 100% of the cost of the basic cruise fare, depending on cabin category.

For certain cruises and/or cabin categories, the upscale lines Crystal, Regent Seven Seas, Seabourn, and Silversea charge a relatively low supplement to the solo cruiser's fare for occupying a double cabin. For instance, Seabourn's Run of Ship Single Savings allows guaranteed single occupancy in a Category A or higher suite at 125% or 150% of the double-occupancy fare. If you don't mind relinquishing privacy, some lines, such as Holland America Line and Windjammer Barefoot Cruises, will match you with a roommate. In that case, you pay the lower double-occupancy rate and, if there's no one to pair you up with, you get a cabin to yourself for no additional charge. A singles roommate Match Program is also offered by Princess and Crystal Cruises for occasional hosted singles cruises. Special offers waiving the single supplement are also available from time to time.

The Love Boat image aside, romantic trysts while sailing solo are not necessarily a given. A lot depends on how many other singles are on your ship. With the popularity of cruise travel on the rise among singles, some travel agencies specialize in arranging groups of singles. Windjammer Barefoot Cruises schedules extremely popular annual singles-only cruises without any kind of single supplement.

🛥 **Cruise Mates** ⊕ www.cruisemates.com/articles/single/ is an Internet-only cruise magazine and community with feature articles, a singles group cruise calendar, and message board. **SinglesCruise.com** ☎ 800/393-5000 ⊕ www.singlescruise.com, a member company of Carlson Travel Group, hosts singles group cruises and will match solo cruise passengers with a roommate of the same sex and smoking preference. **Singles Cruise Resource** ☎ 888/724-5123 or 303/690-8937 🖷 303/690-8986 ⊕ www. singlescruiseresource.com, an affiliate agency of Cruises, Inc., the world's largest seller of cruises, caters to the needs of singles by finding affordable cruises and reduced single-supplement fares for solo travelers. **SoloCruiser** ☎ 888/765-6278 🖷 860/236-6177 ⊕ www.solocruiser.com, an affiliate of White Travel, which has been selling cruises since 1972, offers solo travelers escorted group cruises and "Low Single Supplement" cruises on upscale cruise lines.

Families

Cruising can be a great family travel experience. Most parents report that their children have such a great time that they barely see them after boarding. Couples who wish to share adult time on their family cruise vacation no longer find it necessary to engage a nanny or bring along a family member to watch over their little ones. Mom can savor some well-earned beauty rest while Dad heads for a solitary jog on the deck, secure in the knowledge that the children are happy and well-cared for in the youth center.

Youth programs on today's large cruise ships are manned by counselors who have been carefully screened and chosen for their ability to relate to children; most have a background in education or early-childhood development. Their function is to provide a safe environment for age-appropriate play and learning, a day camp at sea. Activities vary by cruise line, but the emphasis is on enjoyable pursuits that can offer an educational bonus. Science and astronomy programs, arts and crafts projects, history and geography of the ports of call, and even training in social graces and dance are only a few of the planned pursuits. The basic complimentary programs usually last all day and, after a late afternoon break, resume in the evening; however, there's usually an hourly charge for late-night babysitting. A notable exception is Cunard Line, which provides complimentary babysitting on their ocean liners.

Take care when researching a family cruise vacation, though, as not all youth programs are equally comprehensive. Most mainstream and premium cruise lines, including Carnival, Costa, Disney, Holland America, Norwegian, Princess, and Royal Caribbean operate their programs all day on sea days, but hours may be limited on port days. Upscale lines that feature seasonal children's programs might close entirely on port days, while others offer little more than babysitting for an additional charge. The best programs schedule escorted educational shore excursions for older children and teens; both Carnival and Disney offer kid-oriented excursions in some ports of call. Disney even has regularly scheduled shoreside activities and excursions for all ages at their own private Bahamian Island, Castaway Cay.

Most children's programs are divided by age group, but infants or toddlers who aren't toilet trained generally will not be accepted. Even on ships with nurseries, counselors will rarely change diapers or assist children with their bathroom needs due to health and legal constraints. The exceptions are Disney Cruise Line and Carnival Cruise Line. On some ships, parents are issued a beeper to summon them in case of a problem.

Baby on Board

NOT EVERY MOM ON BOARD has checked her little one into cruise camp—some of their babies haven't arrived yet. After baby is born, mothers do the pampering thing 24/7, so a cruise is the ideal prestork vacation with lots of time for mothers-to-be to rest up and get pampered.

Expectant moms should be aware of certain time constraints when planning a cruise. Although the stated terms and conditions vary, as a general rule cruise lines will not allow you to sail if you are from 24 to 28 weeks into your pregnancy (or will be before the cruise ends). A statement from your attending physician that establishes your due date might also be required prior to sailing. Also consider, if you're prone to seasickness, combining it with morning sickness might be mistake.

Possibly the pickiest passengers on any ship are those in the 13 to 17 age group. The biggest hurdle to scale with teenagers is usually convincing them that any family vacation can be fun. Teens are . . . like, well, *cool,* and some are not keen to join group activities. However, there are probably an equal number who enjoy checking in at the teen center early in the cruise to meet and hang out with other like-minded teens. Unlike younger children, teens are generally free to come and go as they please in a less-structured environment. Facilities vary, but most ships have at least a video game area and computers. The newest ships have discreetly chaperoned activity centers and discos designed specifically for teens, yet with an adult flavor; vessels without them usually allow teens to dance in the adult disco until about 11 PM.

Most major cruise lines, including Royal Caribbean, Carnival, Disney, Norwegian, Princess, and Holland America, have invested substantially since the late 1990s in their teen programs. Their facilities and programs give teens a place to go to relieve the boredom that used to result in mischievous pranks (think punching elevator buttons to stop on every floor and mixing up the breakfast order tags hung outside stateroom doors late at night). For teens, there can be a lot of freedom on a ship, but there are also rules. During group activities, they are not allowed to smoke, curse, or consume alcoholic beverages. Security will step in if any vandalism or violent behavior is observed. The same is true for younger children enrolled in the ship's youth programs. Children are subject to disciplinary procedures for unacceptable actions. After a warning, a time-out may be issued, and suspension or dismissal from the program is the ultimate punishment for continued unsuitable behavior. Entire families can be put off the ship at the next port for serious infractions.

In case of an emergency, cruise-line counselors are trained to institute YEP, the Youth Evacuation Program. All children under the age of 13 are issued an ID bracelet that must be worn at all times when they register with a shipboard youth program. Upon hearing the ship's emergency signal, parents are instructed to go to their muster stations, stand in the front row, and await the arrival of their children. All children are outfitted with a life jacket, escorted to their assigned muster station, and supervised until they are reunited with their parents.

Family Cruising Do's and Don'ts

IT'S FUN TO TAKE A CRUISE WITH YOUR FAMILY, but there are also some things to keep in mind . . . things you should do and things you shouldn't.

Do's

DO book a cruise early; triple and quad cabins are limited, and ships have a maximum passenger capacity.

DO consider adjoining cabins for parents and older children.

DO find out if the cruise line provides baby supplies (diapers, food, etc.) and bring an adequate supply of other necessities.

DO tell your travel agent if you will need a crib or high chair.

DO bring your own stroller for toddlers.

DO pack a favorite game or stuffed animal.

DO dress up on Formal Night and have a family portrait taken.

DO control your children in public areas, especially around the swimming pool.

DO participate if the children's program invites parents to take part in activities.

DO bring along two-way radios to keep track of family members.

DO plan to spend family time together.

DO invite the grandparents to come along!

Happily, there are few don'ts on a cruise.

Don'ts

DON'T worry. Once you're on board, there's no cooking, no dish washing, no bed making or bathroom clean up to take care of, and, best of all, no small voices in the backseat of the car asking, "Are we there yet?"

DON'T be surprised if the only significant problem you encounter on a cruise is convincing your children they have to leave the ship at the end of the voyage.

The number of children on board any cruise depends a lot on the time of year: peak periods for family cruises are during school holidays and summer vacations. Be sure to attend the youth program orientation with your children and enroll them on the first day of the cruise. Prepaid soft-drink cards that allow children to order an unlimited number of fountain drinks anywhere on the ship cost about $3.50 to $5 a day, plus gratuity, and can be real money-savers.

Families can often save money with special discounted fares for young children occupying the same stateroom as their parents. Although infants sail free on some cruise lines, port charges are usually assessed regardless of your child's age. Holland America Line goes the extra distance for young families, providing not only high chairs, booster chairs, and cribs, but even baby food and diapers with at least 30 days' advance notice. Make sure you or your travel agent requests what you need, and don't forget to reserve a crib for your little one no matter what cruise line you choose.

Disney Cruise Line's staterooms were designed to be particularly family-friendly—nearly all have a split bathroom configuration with one room containing a sink and shower and the other a sink and toilet. Norwegian Cruise Line's newest vessels have many interconnecting cabins, often several in a row—a big advantage for large families who want additional bathrooms as well as space.

Travelers with Disabilities

As recently as the early 1990s, accessibility on a cruise ship meant little more than a few inside staterooms set aside for passengers with mobility impairments. Most public restrooms and nearly all en suite bathrooms had a step-over entryway—even passengers without mobility issues often tripped until they became accustomed to them. Even so, the overall conveniences and relative safety associated with a cruise vacation have always appealed to passengers with disabilities.

Cruise lines have always welcomed passengers with disabilities and, in the wake of the Americans with Disabilities Act (ADA), the cruise industry began demonstrating voluntary ADA compliance by designing new ships from the keel up with expanded accessibility in mind; now that compliance with the ADA has been declared mandatory, you can expect further measures to make cruising easier for passengers with many kinds of disabilities. Nevertheless, physical barriers in both cabins and public rooms remain in many older ships. Facilities planned especially for wheelchair use are more common on newer ships, as are lifts for swimming pools and hot tubs. All ship elevators have raised Braille signage, and even some passageway handrails feature directions in Braille at regular intervals.

All cruise lines offer a limited number of staterooms designed to be wheelchair- and scooter-accessible. Booking a newer vessel will generally assure more choice for passengers with disabilities, including more available cabins in a larger variety of categories, some even with private verandas. Auxiliary aids, such as flashers for the hearing impaired and buzzers for visually impaired passengers, are available on request. Public rooms in these newer ships are more accessible, with ramps and fewer raised thresholds.

When evaluating a cruise, passengers with disabilities (ranging from use of a cane or walker to complete dependence on a wheelchair or reliance on a service animal) should pay particular attention not only to the facilities on board their chosen vessel but also the conditions they are likely to find in ports of call and on shore excursions. More than the usual amount of planning is necessary for smooth sailing. To the extent possible, cruise lines attempt to accommodate guests with a wide range of disabilities. However, they cannot provide personal care and should not be expected to.

Beginning with embarkation, every effort is made to accommodate passengers who require assistance. Even so, certain ship transfer operations may not be fully accessible to wheelchairs or scooters. When a ship is unable to dock, passengers are taken ashore on tenders that are sometimes hard to negotiate even for those without mobility or sensory impairments. Some people with limited mobility may even find it difficult to embark or debark the ship when docked due to the steep angle of gangways caused by high or low tide.

Some health-related problems aren't readily discernible, so if you suffer from a chronic medical condition, inform your travel agent to alert the cruise line and bring along a report from your physician. As a passenger, you must be prepared to care for yourself and your personal needs on a daily basis, and you must be able to participate in the ship's safety practices, particularly the muster drill. If you're unable to function independently, you must travel with a caregiver to provide these services for you; the medical staff aboard a ship won't usually provide any day-to-day care. It's essential that the cruise line be notified of any special medical, physical, or other requirements as early as possible.

Passengers Who Use Service Animals

Cruise lines welcome service animals aboard their fleets, and crew members often go the extra distance to provide for their comfort. However, itineraries may include ports of call that have very specific and strict rules about the importation of animals, and it will be your responsibility to find out what special requirements must be met before your service animal will be allowed off the ship.

The Caribbean islands that are the most open to allowing entry to service animals are Aruba, the Bahamas, the Cayman Islands, Curaçao, St. Maarten, Martinique, Guadeloupe, and Puerto Rico, and the Caribbean coastal areas of Venezuela, Colombia, and Mexico. Island nations that have animal quarantine regulations modeled on the British system include Antigua, Barbados, Grenada, Jamaica, St. Lucia, and Trinidad & Tobago. The entry policy for the Dominican Republic is in flux at this writing. The best places to obtain specific information on required documentation and immunizations are the U.S. State Department (International Travel Information), local customs offices in the specific ports, personal veterinarians, and the Seeing Eye, Inc. If your service animal does not have the proper proof of vaccinations, or if there are local quarantine requirements, it can be denied the right to leave the ship, and you'll be required to stay on board as well.

The Seeing Eye, Inc. ☎ 973/539-4425 ⊕ www.seeingeye.org. **U.S. Department of State, Bureau of Consular Affairs** ☎ 888/407-4747 ⊕ http://travel.state.gov/index.html.

Passengers in Wheelchairs

For persons incapable of walking, a wheelchair is generally their primary mobility aid for getting on and off the ship. In those instances, crew-member squads may offer assistance that involves carrying passengers. Situations sometimes occur when mobility-impaired passengers may not be able to go ashore at the time they prefer. Or, they may be unable to go ashore at all in certain private islands or ports such as Grand Cayman, where there's no pier and all passengers are tendered ashore. For the safety of all concerned, the ship's captain will make the final determination regarding whether it's possible to carry mobility-impaired passengers and their mobility assistance devices ashore (wheelchair, scooter, walker, etc.). The captain will take into account all appropriate conditions, including weather, the ship's location, weight of the guest, and so on. Captains try to realistically accommodate all passenger needs.

However, third-party transfer vehicles and shore excursion facilities may not be fully accessible to those with disabilities. Cruise lines attempt to deal only with companies that comply with legal requirements. How-

Family Radios

THE KIDS ARE IN THE YOUTH CENTER, and you have a beeper in case the counselor feels you're needed. But where's your husband? Don't laugh . . . it happens to me all the time. We're strolling along the Lido deck, and I ask a question. No response. No surprise. My husband has wandered off. Again. Locating him on a ship with 13 passenger decks can mean a lot of walking.

Enter the solution: a simple pair of two-way radios. By and large, they work beautifully on even the largest ships, although interior steel may stop the signal in a few spots. They're worth their weight in gold for keeping track of older children and teens. Some ships have sets for rent, and they are sold in almost any electronics or computer superstore. When shopping for radios, look for:

• **Rugged construction:** You want them to be sturdy and capable of standing up to wear and tear and dropping. Water resistance is pretty important on a ship as well.

• **Subchannels:** These little gems are popular, and the main channels get a lot of use. You want to tune them in to a subchannel to avoid other passengers' chatter.

• **Rechargeable batteries:** It goes without saying, batteries don't last long, even when they're on standby.

Apply common sense when using your radios. There's no need to shout "Can you hear me?" into your handset or tune the volume to an ear splitting decibel.

---

ever, they cannot guarantee that all those companies, particularly those contracted in foreign countries, are able to provide accessible facilities to people with disabilities.

If you need a wheelchair for mobility, bring your own; while most ships carry a limited number of wheelchairs, they generally aren't allowed off the ship and are used only during embarkation, debarkation, and in emergencies. If you need a wheelchair or scooter for mobility but aren't able to travel with it, you can rent one for the duration of your cruise.

Passengers Who Require Oxygen

Passengers who need continuous oxygen for chronic conditions must make their own arrangements prior to travel. Cruise lines do permit oxygen to be brought on board ships for personal use, but passengers are required to provide their own oxygen in these circumstances. There are companies that regularly provide supplemental oxygen and/or oxygen equipment for cruise-ship passengers. Be sure to bring the service company's address and any local contacts in your ports of call.

 Advanced Aeromedical ☎ 800/346-3556 or 757/481-1590 🖷 757/481-2874 ⊕ www. aeromedic.com rents oxygen equipment to cruise-ship passengers. **Care Vacations/ Cruise Ship Assist** ☎ 877/478-7827 or 780/986-6404 🖷 800/648-1116, 780/986-6485, or 780/986-8332 ⊕ www.cruiseshipassist.com is a Canada-based company that rents mobility equipment, including powered and unpowered wheelchairs and scooters, as well as oxygen and oxygen equipment, and provides airport and hotel transfers to passengers with disabilities. The company services most major ports of embarkation in the United States and Canada and also some ports elsewhere in the world. **Scoot Around** ☎ 888/441-7575 or 204/982-0657 🖷 204/478-1172 ⊕ www.scootaround.com rents scooters and powered and regular wheelchairs to cruise-ship passengers. The company will deliver them to your cruise ship in most North American ports of embarkation.

Gay & Lesbian Cruises

Gay cruises have become a big business over the past few years. Several companies now charter entire ships several times a year for all-gay cruises featuring such extras as special entertainment, activities, and parties tailored to their clients' unique tastes. Atlantis Events markets primarily to gay men. RSVP Vacations makes more of an effort to appeal to both gay men and lesbians. Olivia Cruises specializes in all-lesbian trips. R Family Vacations specializes in family trips for gay parents and their kids. Other companies simply book blocks of cabins for gay and lesbian groups and operate as any other affinity group aboard a cruise ship. ⁊ **Atlantis Events** ☎ 310/859-8800, 800/628-5268 reservations ⊕ www.atlantisevents. com. **Olivia Cruises & Resorts** ☎ 800/631-6277 or 415/962-5700 ⊕ www.olivia.com. **R Family Vacations** ☎ 866/732-6822 or 845/348-0397 ⊕ www.rfamilyvacations.com. **RSVP Vacations** ☎ 800/328-7787 ⊕ www.rsvp.net.

Nudist Cruises

Nudist travel has been growing for several years. For reasons that are obvious, all-nude cruises aren't permitted unless a group can charter the entire ship. Bare Necessities Tour & Travel is the only company that offers these cruises, usually several times a year on small- to medium-size ships. For those who are curious: yes, nude passengers must have something to sit on in public areas—a towel or, for the more discerning, an elegant silk scarf. ⁊ **Bare Necessities Tour & Travel** ☎ 800/743-0405 or 512/499-0405 ⊕ www.bare-necessities.com.

Group Travel

Enterprising travel agents have long known that organizing a group is a great way to provide a reduced fare to their clients as well as earn enough free tour-conductor berths for themselves to accompany the group. However, anyone who wants to coordinate a family reunion or simply arrange a carefree vacation for friends to travel together can book a group cruise and receive a discounted rate and free berths. To qualify as a group, your party must usually include a minimum of 16 passengers in at least eight cabins (third and fourth passengers in a cabin do not count), although fewer are required on some upscale cruise lines.

As the number of cabins booked increases, the number of free berths rises proportionally. For large groups, there's also the possibility that the cruise line will kick in a few perks, such as a complimentary cocktail party. Before taking on the responsibilities involved in organizing a group cruise, you should be aware that tour conductor berths are not totally free—port charges and taxes are not included. Be sure group members know the arrangement up front and are in agreement. Some groups feel it's more equitable to split the proceeds from the tour conductor berth in order to reduce everyone's cost.

If family and friends are uninterested and your travel agent has no group cruises planned, there are other ways to reap the benefits of a group cruise fare. College alumni organizations sometimes offer group travel opportunities, as do music and sports clubs, museums, civic and church groups, and even cruise-travel Web sites. Look around for like-minded individuals and you're likely to discover that some of them have cruise plans. **Countryside Travel** ⬧ 544 Brandon Rd., Conroe, TX 77302 ☎ 800/603-5755 ⊕ www.countryside-travel.com specializes in groups and honeymoon cruises. **Cruise Mates** ⬧ 6660 N. 23rd St., Phoenix, AZ 85016 ☎ 602/279-4356 ⊕ www.cruisemates. com/articles/CMcruise/ is an Internet cruise magazine and community that hosts several group cruises a year for online users; bookings are handled by highly qualified independent travel agents. **CruisePlanning.net** ⬧ 900 Grampian Blvd., Williamsport, PA 17701 ☎ 800/561-0802 or 570/323-0112 ⊕ www.cruiseplanning.net is a member of the Cruise Planners network that specializes in group cruises. **Whet Travel Inc.** ⬧ 1881 Washington Avenue, Suite 11E, Miami Beach, FL 33139 ☎ 877/438-9438 ⊕ www.whettravel. com specializes in large affinity groups interested in music and dance. **Skyscraper Tours, Inc.** ⬧ 2954 N. Williamsburg La., Fayetteville, AR 72703 ☎ 888/278-9648 ⊕ www. skyscrapertours.com offers several annual hosted group cruises.

PAYING FOR YOUR TRIP

If you've been thumbing through cruise brochures, you might be reeling from something akin to new car sticker shock, but take heart. No one pays those fares. When shopping for a cruise, don't overlook strategies to save money. Watch the travel section of your Sunday newspaper for cruise-line promotions, and get quotes from several sources, such as local and Internet travel agencies, for comparison.

Take advantage of your buying power as well. Senior citizens often qualify for discounts, as do airline employees who are eligible for low rates from interline agents that serve the airline industry. Residents of certain states (particularly those that have cruise ports) are often able to obtain discounted fares during advertised promotions. Some credit card companies reward their users with travel point programs that can be used for substantial fare reductions or even free cruises. If you're on active military duty, retired from military service, a first responder (police officer, firefighter, paramedic), or educator you may qualify for discounts with some cruise lines. Discounts and promotions have a limited lifetime and might be capacity controlled, but you won't get them if you don't ask. You'll also be required to prove your eligibility.

Many travel agents that specialize in booking cruises belong to consortiums that book blocks of cabins on a number of ships, thus enabling them to pass along group savings to individuals who don't want the hassle of putting together a group of their own, but who want the advantage of the lower group fare. Just because a travel agency is small doesn't mean it can't get you the bargains offered by bigger name-brand agencies. Don't be afraid to ask if there are any such deals available.

Timing and flexibility can also save you money. An affordable one-week cruise in May can cost you hundreds of dollars less per person than the same ship and itinerary in travel-heavy June.

What Impacts Your Fare

YOU THINK AIRLINE FARES ARE CONFUSING? Cruise fares rise and fall like waves during a tropical storm and can seem equally contrary. On a single day it's possible to get as many as a half-dozen different price quotes directly from many cruise lines because fares fluctuate. You and your shipmates paid for the same cruise, but may not have paid the same fare.

One thing never changes—do not ever, under any circumstances, pay brochure rate. You can do better, often as much as half off those inflated fares. These factors can enter the mix when pricing cruises:

• **The date of your cruise:** Fares are seasonal, with the lowest from about the second week of September until the week before Thanksgiving and the highest in summer and during holiday periods.

• **When you book:** Early booking discounts are nearly always offered; last-minute discounts might be available as well.

• **Popularity of the ship:** Some ships are stars and fill quickly, while others are wallflowers and just don't book up as fast.

• **Itinerary:** Certain itineraries hold higher appeal, especially those considered unique or exotic.

• **Age:** No, not the ship's age. Fare discounts may be available for senior citizens, and children sometimes sail free with their parents.

• **Where you live:** Regional discounts may be available, particularly if a cruise line is trying to introduce a ship into a port near where you live.

• **Group pricing:** Even if you're not a member of a group, travel agents may have access to lower group fares.

• **Who your travel agent is:** Top performing agencies can pass along lower fares to their clients.

• **You're a repeat passenger:** Discounts and other goodies are often available to loyal passengers.

• **The accommodations you choose:** Advertisements for low fares inevitably include the word "from . . ." and the figure that follows is going to get you on board in the lowest category; if you want a better cabin, you'll pay more for the space and location you prefer.

When you feel the fare is right, seal the deal. It could be gone in an hour.

Here's one thing that nearly everyone agrees on: it's a great feeling to have the majority of your vacation expenses paid before leaving home. This includes cruises.

The first step in actually booking a cruise is paying a deposit to reserve a cabin. The amount varies by cruise line and the length of the cruise, but it's generally about $250 per person for a one-week sailing. The balance of your fare is usually due from 60 to 75 days prior to the sailing date.

Always pay your cruise fare with a credit card. Though it rarely happens, travel agencies can suffer financial difficulties, or unscrupulous travel sellers can prey on unsuspecting victims and disappear with their money. Credit card companies will support you with a refund in the case of fraud or other unforeseen difficulties. Be sure to check your billing statements to ascertain that the charges are credited to the cruise line and not the travel agent.

Many people balk at the idea of putting such large charges on their credit card. However, by saving a set amount every week until your final cruise payment is due, you can pay the entire balance when your next credit card statement arrives.

In the unfortunate event that you must cancel your trip, most cruise deposits are fully refundable before the final payment date. After that, cancellation fees will apply, and these range from the amount of your deposit to 100% of the entire fare, depending on how long you wait before cancelling your cruise.

WHEN TO BOOK YOUR CRUISE

You will certainly save money if you can book your cruise far in advance. In addition to having a better choice of desirable staterooms, significantly discounted prices are available to those who place a deposit on a cruise anywhere from six months to a year in advance of sailing. Just as department stores schedule first-of-the-year white sales on linens, the cruise industry has its January through March Wave Season, when it books a large number of passengers for the year. Availability is often the best during this period, and some of the year's choice bargains can be booked during the cruise lines' annual sales push.

Most cruise lines guarantee the lowest advertised fare to all passengers who have booked and paid a deposit. Should the price drop before the final payment is due, cruise lines will extend the reduced fare to early bookings. However, if you book early, it will be up to you to discover the fare reduction and request the lesser amount. Acting on your behalf, a good travel agent will monitor fare fluctuations and do that for you.

A wrinkle in cruise pricing is the last-minute discount offered to new bookings after the final payment is due, usually within 60 days of sailing. Cruise lines do not want to sail with empty cabins and will sometimes offer unsold space at deeply reduced fares in specific geographic regions—often through agencies within driving distance of the port of embarkation. Although these discounts can be substantial, your choice of cabins and locations is limited to whatever is left over. Top suites and the lowest-category inside staterooms almost always sell out early. A last-minute reservation could mean your cabin is in a noisy location over the show lounge or under the galley. Although demand for cruises is high, cruise industry insiders advise that you should never assume the date you want is sold out—always check with a travel agent.

If you booked early and cannot take advantage of the last-minute savings, take heart. Ask your travel agent to check into the lower fare for you anyway: some cruise lines will honor it or may give you an upgraded stateroom or, better still, an on-board credit.

CAUTION	

The cruising urban legend that will not die is about someone whose second cousin's mother-in-law packed a bag and arrived at the pier on sailing day. She booked an available cabin on a departing cruise ship and—surprise!—was assigned the owner's suite for mere pennies. If you ever considered just showing up at the pier with your luggage in hopes of booking a last-minute, cut-rate cabin, don't give it another thought. Cruise lines can no longer accept cruise bookings at the dock.

BOOKING YOUR CRUISE

Charting your cruising course doesn't have to be difficult, but it isn't as simple as booking airplane seats or reserving a hotel room. Even after you've settled on a cruise line and cruise ship that's right for you, there will still be many questions to answer and details to get right. First-time cruisers, who may want and need some additional insight and advice, may wish to stick to a traditional travel agent who is close at hand. Of course, if you've taken numerous cruises and are more concerned with the price—and if you're willing to go to bat for yourself if something goes wrong—a Web-based agency might be the way to go.

Using a Travel Agent

Whether it is your first or 50th sailing, your best friend in booking a cruise is a knowledgeable travel agent. The last thing you want when considering a costly cruise vacation is an agent who has never been on a cruise, calls a cruise ship "the boat," or—worse still—quotes brochure rates. The most important steps in cruise travel planning are research, research, and more research; your partner in this process is an experienced travel agent. Booking a cruise is a complex process, and it's seldom wise to try to go it alone, particularly the first time. But how do you find a cruise travel agent you can trust?

First off, look for signs indicating you're dealing with an agency affiliated with Cruise Lines International Association (CLIA). Preferably, your agent should be certified as an Accredited Cruise Counselor (ACC), Master Cruise Counselor (MCC), or Elite Cruise Counselor (ECC) by CLIA. Those agents have completed demanding training programs, including touring or sailing on a specific number of ships. They make it their business to know all they can to serve their clients' needs.

Make sure the travel agency you've chosen belongs to a professional trade organization. In North America, membership in the American Society of Travel Agents (ASTA) indicates an agency has pledged to follow the code of ethics set forth by the world's largest association for travel professionals. In the best of all worlds, your travel agent is affiliated with both ASTA and CLIA. Additionally, many agencies and home-based travel agents belong to such brand-name travel-agent networks as American Express Travel and Uniglobe, which puts the power and support of international corporations in their corner. If you're dealing with a local travel agency, look around the office when you arrive. Racks containing a wide variety of cruise-line brochures and the presence of trade magazines and newspapers are good signs. The agent who makes it a point to read industry publications is an informed agent, one who is likely to keep up with the latest trends and who can provide you with up-to-the-minute data.

Some agencies have preferred-supplier relationships with specific cruise lines and prominently display only their products. If you have done your homework and know what cruise line sounds most appealing to you, be alert if an agent tries to change your mind without very specific reasons.

When you've found a jewel of an agent, then what? Ask many questions. Whether you do that in person, over the phone, or by e-mail is up to

10 Questions to Answer Before Visiting a Travel Agent

IF YOU'VE DECIDED TO USE A TRAVEL AGENT, congratulations. You'll have someone on your side to make your booking and to intercede if something goes wrong. Ask yourself these 10 simple questions, and you'll be better prepared to help the agent do his or her job:

1. Who will be going on the cruise?

2. What can you afford to spend for the entire trip?

3. Where would you like to go?

4. How much vacation time do you have?

5. When can you get away?

6. What are your interests?

7. Do you prefer a casual or structured vacation?

8. What kind of accommodations do you want?

9. What are your dining preferences?

10. How will you get to the embarkation port?

you. However, it's important that you get to know your agent and that your agent gets to know you. Above all else, be honest about your expectations and budget. Seldom can a travel agent who doesn't know you well guess what your interests are and how much you can afford to spend. Don't be shy. If you have champagne taste and a beer budget, say so. Do not hesitate to interview prospective agents and be wary if they do not interview you right back.

Contrary to what conventional wisdom might suggest, cutting out the travel agent and booking directly with a cruise line won't necessarily get you the lowest price. More than 90% of all cruise bookings are handled through travel agents, and many are able to secure group fares or other discounts not offered directly by cruise lines. In fact, cruise-line reservation systems simply are not capable of dealing with tens of thousands of direct calls from potential passengers. They will usually take your reservation and ask if you would like to assign it to a travel agent. Without an agent working on your behalf, you're on your own. A good travel agent is your advocate.

When you use a travel agent to book a cruise, most cruise-line customer service departments are reluctant to respond to your questions over the telephone. Instead, they refer you to your travel agent, who is expected to make queries on your behalf. This is the time a knowledgeable and dedicated travel agent can come in handy. Do not rely on Internet message boards for authoritative responses to your questions—that is a service more accurately provided by your travel agent.

🔁 **Travel Agent Professional Organizations American Society of Travel Agents** (ASTA) ☎ 703/739–2782, 800/965–2782 24-hr hotline 🖶 703/684–8319 ⊕ www.travelsense. org. **Association of British Travel Agents** ☎ 020/7637–2444 🖶 020/7637–0713 ⊕ www. abta.com. **Association of Canadian Travel Agencies** ☎ 866/725–2282 or 613/237–3657 🖶 613/237–7052 ⊕ www.acta.ca. **Australian Federation of Travel Agents** ☎ 02/ 9264–3299 or 1300/363–416 🖶 02/9264–1085 ⊕ www.afta.com.au. **Travel Agents Association of New Zealand** ☎ 04/496–4898 🖶 04/499–0786 ⊕ www.taanz.org.nz.

2

⌘ Cruise Line Organizations Cruise Lines International Association (CLIA) ☎ 754/224-2200 ⊕ www.cruising.org.

⌘ Recommended Travel Agents AAA ☎ 800/222-6953 ⊕ www.csaa.com isn't just for car travel. The company has a searchable database to locate member agencies by zip code.

American Express Travel ☎ 800/297-5627 ⊕ travel.americanexpress.com offers options for online booking or a searchable database of local American Express travel offices.

Countryside Travel ☎ 800/603-5755 ⊕ www.countryside-travel.com specializes in groups and honeymoons.

Cruise Brothers ☎ 800/827-7779 or 401/941-3999 ⊕ www.cruisebrothers.com, in business since the mid-1970s, is one of the largest family-owned, cruises-only agencies in the United States.

Cruise Connections Canada ☎ 800/661-9283 ⊕ www.cruise-connections.com is Canada's leading cruise retailer and one of the largest cruise retailers in North America.

Cruise One ⊕ www.cruiseone.com is affiliated with Boston-based NLG, the world's largest cruise retailer, and offers a satisfaction guarantee. The company has more than 400 member agencies nationwide, and its Web site has a searchable database of member cruise specialists.

Cruise Planners, Inc. ☎ 800/683-0206 ⊕ www.cruiseplanners.com is a network of home-based agent franchises. The Web site offers a searchable database to locate member agencies.

Cruises Inc. ☎ 888/218-4228 or 800/854-0500 ⊕ www.cruisesinc.com is an affiliate of Boston-based NLG, the world's largest cruise retailer, and offers a satisfaction guarantee. The company has more than 450 member agencies nationwide, and its Web site has a searchable database of member cruise specialists.

Cruises Only ☎ 800/278-4737 ⊕ www.cruisesonly.com is affiliated with NLG, the world's largest cruise retailer, and offers a lowest-price guarantee as well as a money-back satisfaction guarantee. Agents are available to assist clients around the clock.

Ensemble Travel ☎ 866/350-7460 ⊕ www.ensembletravel.com is an international network of 1,100 expert travel agencies. Call to be connected to the nearest member agency.

Hartford Holidays ☎ 800/828-4813 or 516/746-6670 ⊕ www.hartfordholidays.com has been family-owned and -operated for 30 years.

Lighthouse Travel ☎ 800/719-9917 or 805/566-3905 ⊕ www.lighthousetravel.com specializes in cruises.

Northstar Cruises ☎ 800/249-9360 or 973/228-5005 ⊕ www.northstarcruises.com is a top producer for most major cruise lines.

Skyscraper Tours, Inc. ☎ 888/278-9648 ⊕ www.skyscrapertours.com offers several annual hosted group cruises.

Uniglobe International ⊕ www.uniglobetravel.com has more than 700 franchise locations worldwide; the Internet Web site has a searchable database of member cruise agencies.

Vacation.com ☎ 800/843-0733 ⊕ www.vacation.com is a network of more than 5,700 travel agency locations across the United States and Canada.

Virtuoso ☎ 866/401-7974 or 817/870-0300 is the world's most exclusive association of upscale travel agencies. Call to locate members specializing in cruises.

Booking Your Cruise Online

In addition to local travel agencies, there are many hard-working, dedicated travel professionals working for Web sites. Both big-name travel sellers and mom-and-pop agencies compete for the attention of cyber-savvy clients, and it never hurts to compare prices from a variety of these sources. Some cruise lines even allow you to book directly with them through their Web sites.

As a rule, Web-based and toll-free brokers will do a decent job for you. They often offer discounted fares, though not always the lowest, so it pays to check around. If you know precisely what you want and how much you should pay to get a real bargain—and you don't mind dealing with an anonymous voice on the phone—by all means make your reservations when the price is right. Just don't expect the personal service you get from an agent you know. Also, be prepared to spend a lot of time and effort on the phone if something goes wrong.

⚡ Online Agencies Cruise.com ⊕ www.cruise.com ☎ 888/333-3116 lays claim to being the largest Web site specializing in discounted cruises on the Internet and offers a lowest-price guarantee.

Cruise Compete ⊕ www.cruisecompete.com ☎ 800/764-4410 allows you to get competing bids from top travel agencies, who respond to your request for bids with their best rates for your trip.

Cruise Direct ⊕ www.cruisedirect.com ☎ 888/407-2784 allows customers to book their own travel arrangements through the Web site and a toll-free number.

Cruise411.com ⊕ www.cruise411.com ☎ 800/553-7090 has a booking engine online that allows you to book directly or temporarily hold most cruise reservations without deposit or payment if you prefer to call in your booking.

Expedia ⊕ www.expedia.com ☎ 800/397-3342 is a full-service online travel seller that books cruises, too.

iCruise.com ⊕ www.icruise.com ☎ 866/389-9219 charges a pretty hefty cancellation fee, so be sure you know what you want before using their booking engine.

jetBlue ⊕ www.jetblue.com ☎ 800/538-2583 now allows you to book cruises on its Web site.

Moment's Notice ⊕ www.moments-notice.com ☎ 888/241-3366 offers a searchable database for last-minute deals; call toll-free for reservations.

Orbitz ⊕ www.orbitz.com ☎ 888/656-4546 is a full-service online travel seller that books cruises.

7 Blue Seas ⊕ www.7blueseas.com ☎ 800/242-1781 offers a comprehensive online cruise information Web site; bookings are made through the toll-free call center.

Travelocity ⊕ www.travelocity.com ☎ 877/815-5446 is a full-service online travel seller with a 24-hour help desk for service issues.

Consumer Protection

Before you actually book your cruise and make your deposit, it's well worth the effort to check with the Better Business Bureau for complaints against the agent you have decided to use. Always pay by credit card, and make sure the correct amount appears on your statement as a charge by the cruise line, not the travel agency. If you've paid by credit card, you can cancel payment or get reimbursed if there's a problem (and you can provide documentation). Check to see what kind of complaints (if any) have been filed against the agency you've chosen to work with and whether they were resolved. Finally, always consider travel insurance that includes default coverage for your travel agency and cruise line.

_▣_ **Canadian Council of Better Business Bureaus** ☎ 416/644-4936 🖷 416/644-4945 ⊕ www.canadiancouncilbbb.ca. **Council of Better Business Bureaus** ☎ 703/276-0100 🖷 703/525-8277 ⊕ www.bbb.org.

Insurance

When you book your cruise, your travel agent should ask you if you want to purchase travel insurance. Travel insurance plans cover trip cancellation and interruption, supplier default, and international medical care—or various combinations of these. If the agent doesn't ask you, you should ask for the information.

Comprehensive travel policies typically cover trip cancellation and interruption, letting you cancel or cut your trip short because of a personal emergency, illness, or, in some cases, acts of terrorism in your destination. Such policies also cover evacuation and medical care. Some also cover you for trip delays because of bad weather or mechanical problems as well as for lost or delayed baggage. Another type of coverage to look for is financial default—that is, when your trip is disrupted because a tour operator, airline, or cruise line goes out of business. Generally you must buy this when you book your trip or shortly thereafter, and it's only available to you if your operator isn't on a list of excluded companies.

If you're going on a cruise (or any trip abroad for that matter), consider buying medical-only coverage at the very least. Neither Medicare nor some private insurers cover medical expenses anywhere outside of the United States besides Mexico and Canada (including time aboard a cruise ship, even if it leaves from a U.S. port). Medical-only policies typically reimburse you for medical care (excluding that related to pre-existing conditions) and hospitalization abroad, and provide for evacuation. You still have to pay the bills and await reimbursement from the insurer, though.

Expect comprehensive travel insurance policies to cost about 4% to 7% of the total price of your trip (it's more like 12% if you're over age 70). A medical-only policy may or may not be cheaper than a comprehensive policy. Always read the fine print of your policy to make sure that you are covered for the risks that are of most concern to you. Compare several policies to make sure you're getting the best price and range of coverage available.

_▣_ **Insurance Comparison Sites InsureMyTrip.com** ⊕ www.insuremytrip.com **Square Mouth.com** ⊕ www.quotetravelinsurance.com.

_▣_ **Comprehensive Travel Insurers Access America** ☎ 800/729-6021 ⊕ www.accessamerica.com **CSA Travel Protection** ☎ 800/873-9855 ⊕ www.csatravelprotection.com **HTH Worldwide** ☎ 610/254-8700 or 888/243-2358 ⊕ www.hthworldwide.com **Travelex Insurance** ☎ 888/457-4602 ⊕ www.travelex-insurance.com **Travel Guard In-**

Self-Insuring

AS THE PUBLISHER OF *CRUISE NEWS DAILY* and a former travel agent with years of experience in cruising, I'm always amazed when people who didn't buy travel insurance—yet need to cancel their cruise—want the cruise line to waive all cancellation penalties because of their special circumstances. No matter how serious or real the problem, the cruise line usually won't waive the penalties. Of course, the cruisers want to make the cruise line the bad guy if they won't even issue a credit on a future cruise for the amount of their penalty. (They "will never sail that cruise line again!")

The insurance industry has a term for people who don't buy insurance. They call them "self-insuring." It makes a lot of sense when you think about it. Instead of paying the insurance company a premium for the small possibility you'll have to cancel your cruise, you're essentially paying it to yourself. Ideally, you should be banking this amount, just as the insurance company does for that inevitable time when you need to collect. Over the course of several trips, your self-insurance fund will very likely cover your cancellation penalties for that one time when you can't make the cruise.

People who are self-insuring need to realize that if they're collecting the premiums themselves instead of giving them to an insurance company, they need to be just as ready to pay out claims when they have to cancel their trip for some unforeseen reason and are assessed a penalty by the cruise line.

—Alan Wilson

ternational ☎ 715/345-0505 or 800/826-4919 ⊕ www.travelguard.com Travel Insured International ☎ 800/243-3174 ⊕ www.travelinsured.com.

Cruise Line Insurance Policies

Nearly all cruise lines offer their own line of insurance. Most policies are underwritten by major insurers and typically include trip cancellation–interruption protection, travel delay protection, emergency medical and/or dental benefits, emergency medical evacuation and transportation to the nearest medical facility, repatriation of remains in case of death, baggage loss or delay protection, and other worldwide emergency assistance. All policies contain coverage limitations and terms and conditions that you should read carefully. Policies purchased through the cruise lines are generally based on the total price of the trip booked with them despite age and are often the most cost-effective coverage for senior citizens. However, they may not cover certain add-on elements such as airfare and the cost of a pre-cruise hotel that you paid for independently. Compare the coverage and rates with similar polices from third-party insurers to determine which is best for you.

Some cruise lines, including Holland America Line, Silversea, and Princess Cruises, offer upgraded levels of cruise insurance that include considerably more liberal cancellation policies. They allow you to cancel up to 24 hours prior to departure for any reason whatsoever and receive either a cash refund or cruise credit of 75% to 100% of your fare. Seabourn goes a step further and covers your cruise payment if you must cancel due to a preexisting condition that is denied by insurance—the cruise line will issue a future travel credit equal to the cancellation penalties imposed.

Keep in mind that insurance purchased from an independent carrier is more likely to include coverage if the cruise line goes out of business before or during your cruise. Although it's a rare and unlikely occurrence, you do want to be insured in the event that it happens.

Medical-Only Plans

It's wise to sign up with a medical-assistance company even if you don't purchase other kinds of general travel insurance. Members get doctor referrals, emergency evacuation or repatriation, hotlines for medical consultation, cash for emergencies, and other assistance. Most general travel insurance policies include medical coverage and evacuation.

🔂 Medical-Only Insurers **International Medical Group** ☎ 800/628-4664 ⊕ www. imglobal.com **International SOS** ☎ 215/942-8000 or 713/521-7611 ⊕ www. internationalsos.com **Wallach & Company** ☎ 800/237-6615 or 504/687-3166 ⊕ www. wallach.com.

MAKING DECISIONS ABOUT YOUR CRUISE

Once you've settled on a specific ship of a particular cruise line, you'll have numerous decisions to make before your travel agent actually completes your booking. You need to settle on your dining arrangements, pick your stateroom, decide how you'll get to the port of embarkation, whether you want to arrive at the port of embarkation early or stay a few days after your cruise, and lay out any special requests or requirements you may have.

Making Dining Arrangements

Your travel agent will ask you to make a number of decisions before he or she books your cruise. When you're sailing on a traditional cruise with assigned dinner seating, your seating selection can set the tone for your entire trip. Which is best? Early dinner seating is generally scheduled between 6 and 6:30 PM, while late seating can begin from 8:15 to 8:45 PM. The best seating depends on you, your lifestyle, and your personal preferences.

You may wish to choose early seating if:

- You have small children accustomed to an early meal and bedtime.
- Your personal routine calls for meals at an earlier hour.
- You retire earlier in the evening and are an early riser.
- You do not want to experience that full feeling at bedtime.
- You want to attend the early shows, enjoy the casino and other activities, and take in the midnight buffet.

Late seating may be better if:

- You're a night owl and do not mind finishing dinner after 10 PM.
- Your itinerary is port-intensive and you don't want to rush to get ready for dinner after a day of touring.
- You like to indulge in a late-afternoon nap.
- You do not care about midnight snacks and like to sleep late in the morning.

- Your personal habit is to dine late.

- You enjoy leisurely dining and linger over coffee at the end of the meal.

  There are also some other factors to consider before you make up your mind:

- Families and groups lean toward early seating, particularly when several generations are traveling together and ages vary widely.

- Older passengers tend to select early seating.

- Americans are more apt to select early seating than European and South American cruisers, who are accustomed to later meal times.

- Early seating diners are encouraged not to linger over dessert and coffee since the dining room has to be readied for late seating.

- Late seating is viewed by some passengers as more romantic and less rushed.

  Cruise lines understand that strict schedules do not satisfy the desires of all modern cruise passengers. Many cruise lines now include alternatives to the set schedules in the dining room, including casual versions of their dinner menus in their Lido buffets, where more flexibility is allowed in dress and meal times. Specialty à la carte restaurants are showing up on more ships, although a surcharge or gratuity is often required.

  Open seating, an amenity primarily associated with more upscale cruise lines, allows passengers the flexibility of dining any time during restaurant hours and being seated with whomever they please.

  Led by Norwegian Cruise Line's Freestyle Cruising concept, more mainstream and premium cruise lines are exploring this adaptation of open seating for more contemporary cruise ships to offer variety and a more personalized experience for their passengers. Princess Cruises offers Personal Choice with full-service dining available around the clock; Carnival Cruise Lines has added a twist with four seating times instead of the usual two, plus casual evening dining in the Lido buffet. Disney Cruise Line has three meal start times in both early and late seatings.

  Some cruise lines will warn you that, while dining preferences may be requested by your travel agent, no requests are guaranteed. And it's true that table assignments are generally not confirmed until embarkation, but the lines do try to satisfy all their guests. If you are unhappy with your dinner seating, see the maître d' during the first day of your cruise for assistance. Changes after the first evening are generally discouraged; there will even be a designated place to meet with dining room staff and iron out seating problems on embarkation day. Check the daily program for the time and location.

Selecting Your Stateroom

Your choice of stateroom or cabin is likely to be a major factor in how you enjoy your cruise. If it truly doesn't matter where you sleep, go ahead and book the least-expensive category guarantee you can find. The cheapest cabin on a ship is typically an inside stateroom on a lower deck. Although ship designers do all they can to make these inside cabins feel less claustrophobic, there's no getting around the fact that you won't have

SPECIALTY RESTAURANTS

CRUISE LINE	SHIP	CUISINE TYPE	CHARGE (PER PERSON)
Carnival	Spirit-class & Conquest-class	Steaks & seafood	$30
Celebrity	Millennium-class & Century	Continental	$30
	Azamara Quest	Mediterranean, steaks & seafood	to be announced
Costa	Costa Fortuna & Mediterranea	Italian/Tuscan Steakhouse	$23 (comp. dinner for two for suite occupants)
Crystal	Crystal Symphony	Italian, Asian	No charge/$6 tip suggested
	Crystal Serenity	Italian, Asian, Sushi	No charge/$6 tip suggested
	All ships	International with wine pairings	$180
Cunard	Queen Mary 2	Mediterranean	$30 dinner, $20 lunch
		International	No charge
Disney	Disney Magic & Wonder	Northern Italian	$10 dinner, $10 Champagne brunch, $5 High Tea
Holland America	All ships	Steaks & seafood	$30 dinner, $15 lunch
Norwegian	Dawn-/Jewel-class	Asian	$13/$10
		Sushi	à la carte or $12.50
		Teppanyaki	à la carte or $20
		Shabu-shabu (Pearl & Gem only)	$12.50
		French Mediterranean	$15/$10
		Steakhouse	$20/$15
		Italian	No charge
	Sun	Steakhouse	$20
		Sushi	$13
		Teppanyaki	à la carte
		French Mediterranean	$15
		Italian	$13
	Majesty	French Mediterranean	$15
		Italian	No charge
Oceania	Regatta	Italian	No charge
		Steakhouse	No charge
Princess	Sun-class	Steakhouse	$15
	Coral-class	Steakhouse	$15
		Italian	$20
	Grand-class	Steakhouse	$15
		Italian	$20 dinner, $20 brunch (sea days only)
	Crown Princess, Emerald Princess	Steaks & seafood	$25
		Italian	$20
Regent Seven Seas	Navigator	Italian	No charge
	Mariner, Voyager	French	No charge
		Asian	No charge
Royal Caribbean	Freedom-, Radiance-class and	Steakhouse	$20
	Mariner & Navigator of the Seas	Italian	$20
	Other Voyager-class and Empress of the Seas	Italian	$20
	Enchantment of the Seas	Steakhouse	$20
	Freedom-class, Voyager-class and Sovereign of the Seas	Johnny Rockets diner	$3.95
Seabourn	Legend & Pride	International & Steakhouse	No charge
Silversea	All ships	International with wine pairings	$150
		Italian	No charge
Windstar	Wind Surf	Steakhouse	No charge

any kind of view to the outside world. There's sometimes a curtain where the porthole or window would typically be in an outside cabin, but it will be covering nothing but blank wall space.

There are a few simple ways you can get a bit more for your money. Fares are determined by the type of accommodation reserved, and guarantee bookings—when you reserve a cabin category instead of a specific stateroom—can save you money. The cruise line will assign you a cabin within the fare category you book, or you may even be upgraded to a higher category. Be aware that you could end up at the very front or back of the ship or—much worse—below the disco. If your plans include dancing until the wee hours, you can snooze until noon and pocket the savings by paying a low fare for one of the Night Owl Staterooms on Carnival Cruise Line's *Carnival Destiny.*

> **WORD OF MOUTH**
>
> We love to cruise and early on found out that we preferred saving money by booking an inside room. This cruise we booked an inside with no assignment. We were told that we would probably get an upgrade and we got a higher deck. It is easy enough to run up or down stairs to see whatever is of interest outside. By running the stairs all day we can also eat all the sumptuous dinners!   –Bev G

On the other hand, if you view your cabin as your sanctuary, you will want a bit more than standard inside for your home-away-from-home. For an inside cabin with a view of the inside action, Royal Caribbean's Voyager-class and Freedom-class ships and Cunard Line's *Queen Mary 2* offer accommodations with windows overlooking interior lobbies. Obstructed-view outside locations offer natural light, but there might be a lifeboat outside your window instead of an ocean view. Moving up a few categories may cost less than you imagine and result in a more comfortable space with a large window or even a balcony. High-end suites should include perks that justify their cost.

Although cruise-ship cabins are not all created equal, they are all designed for comfort, convenience, and practicality. Standard cabins on modern cruise vessels haven't quite achieved parity with land-based resort accommodations in terms of size, but cruise lines recognize that small touches (and more spacious quarters) go a long way toward overall passenger contentment. You're likely to find your cabin equipped with amenities such as a personal safe, robes for use on board, a hair dryer, and bathroom toiletries—the added niceties that hotels have long provided for their guests.

Aside from the little details that vary from cruise line to cruise line, staterooms are furnished for functionality. At the very least, a cabin contains beds (often twin beds that can be combined to form a queen- or king-size bed), a dressing table–writing desk, a chair, drawers or shelf storage, a closet, and a bathroom with shower. There's almost always a television and telephone. Cabins on newer ships often have sitting areas with a sofa or love seat and a coffee table.

The cabin dressing table–writing desk will almost always have two different electric receptacles—one will accept standard U.S.-style plugs (110-volt) and the other is for European-style plugs (220-volt). To plug in more than one gadget at a time, you'll need a power strip, or, for dual voltage appliances, a plug adapter. You'll have to bring along your own adapter—the kind that allows U.S.-style plugs with flat prongs to be inserted into European-style round receptacles. I had always packed a short power strip in order to use more than one appliance until my husband pointed out I could recharge my cell phone while using the computer simply by utilizing the second receptacle with a flat-to-round prong adapter attached. Cabin bathrooms generally feature a dual-voltage plug receptacle suitable for electric shavers only. The hair dryers provided are usually built into the wall or tucked away in a drawer.

If you pay more—sometimes significantly more—you can get more living space and more luxurious amenites, but regardless of your cabin category, careful consideration went into the design and layout of your cabin. Even though shipboard accommodations run the gamut from standard inside cabins to the plushest suites imaginable, you can rest assured that once you enter the ship's public areas, everyone enjoys the same level of ambience and courtesy. No longer divided into classes as they were years ago, cruise ships today are seagoing democracies. Every passenger can expect the same basic choices and services.

Getting to the Cruise Port

For the convenience of one-stop shopping, all cruise lines have a so-called Air & Sea program that will allow you to purchase your airline ticket to the port of embarkation and your cruise ticket at the same time; you'll also get airport transfers. An added bonus is that by bundling all your air, land, and sea transportation together, you can have a cruise vacation that's much more worry-free. On the other hand, forward-thinking cruisers who buy discounted airline tickets in advance can often save a bundle—or at least enough to cover the cost of a pre-cruise overnight hotel. Comparison shopping makes sense if you have the time and inclination to do it.

The main drawback of an Air & Sea program is an obvious one: you can't choose the time you fly. The cruise lines buy the number of seats they need, but the airlines themselves pick the flights. Although all flights are scheduled to give you enough time to make your embarkation, you might find yourself with an inconvenient flight time, and there's not much you can do about that. Even if your preferred air carrier has nonstop service from your gateway airport directly to your port of embarkation, you might be scheduled with an extremely early departure or with multiple stops along the way.

Flights assigned to cruise passengers aren't always the most desirable since cruise lines pay low contracted fares and because independent travelers tend to book the most desirable flights. Basically, that means you're getting what the airlines have open when the time comes to assign flights. If you want to be assured you'll fly on a particular airline at a particular time, request an "air deviation." For a fee—plus any associated airline charges—the cruise line will attempt to book your preference. There's no guarantee you'll get what you want, but they will try.

Your airline tickets are usually issued 30 days before sailing, and the cruise line cannot confirm specific seat assignments. This is where booking

DECIPHER YOUR DECK PLAN

LIDO DECK

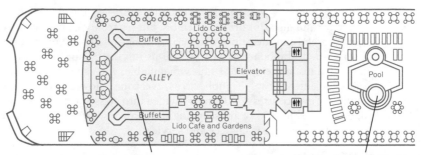

The Lido Deck is a potential source of noise—deck chairs are set out early in the morning and put away late at night; the sound of chairs scraping on the floor of the Lido buffet can be an annoyance.

Music performances by poolside bands can often be heard on upper-deck balconies located immediately below.

UPPER DECK AFT

Take note of where lifeboats are located—views from some outside cabins can be partially, or entirely, obstructed by the boats.

Upper-deck cabins, as well as those far forward and far aft, are usually more susceptible to motion than those in the middle of the ship on a low deck.

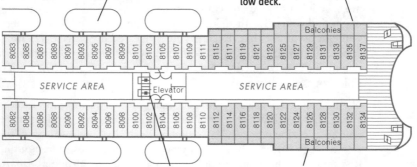

Cabins near elevators or stairs are a double-edged sword. Being close by is a convenience; however, although the elevators aren't necessarily noisy, the traffic they attract can be.

Balcony cabins are indicated by a rectangle split into two sections. The small box is the balcony.

MAIN PUBLIC DECK

Cabins immediately below restaurants and dining rooms can be noisy. Late sleepers might be bothered by early breakfast noise, early sleepers by late diners.

Theaters and dining rooms are often located on middle or lower decks.

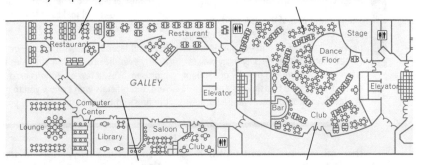

The ship's galley isn't usually labeled on deck plans, but you can figure out where it is by locating a large blank space near the dining room. Cabins beneath it can be very noisy.

Locate the ship's show lounge, disco, children's playroom, and teen center and avoid booking a cabin directly above or below them for obvious reasons.

LOWER DECK AFT

Cabins designated for passengers with disabilities are often situated near elevators.

Interior cabins have no windows and are the least expensive on board.

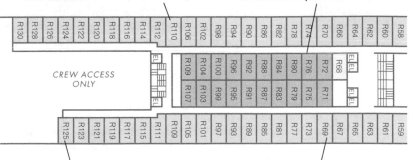

Lower-deck cabins, particularly those far aft, can be plagued by mechanical noises and vibration.

Ocean-view cabins are generally located on lower decks.

Missing the Boat

THE FIRST PORT OF CALL ON YOUR ITINERARY might be Key West, but don't hurry there to board the ship if you missed its initial sailing. By trying to do so you'll violate the Passenger Services Act of 1886 (PSA), which was enacted to protect American passenger shipping interests.

The relevant part of the PSA reads as follows: "No foreign vessel shall transport passengers between ports or places in the United States, either directly or by way of a foreign port, under a penalty of $300 for each passenger so transported and landed." An exception was made for cruise ships: "Foreign-flagged cruise ships may carry passengers from a U.S. port as long as they return them to the same port (a 'cruise to nowhere'). Foreign vessels may also call at intermediate U.S. ports as long as no passenger permanently leaves the vessel at those ports and the vessel makes at least one call at a foreign port."

Even outdated U.S. laws die hard—or hardly ever die—so the PSA still rules the high seas. Yes, a few exceptions exist. And, no, officials won't allow you to pay the fine and board in just any U.S. port.

through a travel agent will help you. Most cruise travel specialists are savvy enough to secure flight numbers 30 days out and nail down seat assignments. Make sure yours does.

There are distinct advantages to using a cruise line's Air & Sea program. When major holidays draw near, an Air & Sea program may be the only way to secure any airline reservation, let alone an affordable one. And when you're taking a one-way cruise you'll have to purchase two one-way tickets, which is often more expensive than a round-trip, unless you purchase the cruise line's budget-friendly air add-on.

These programs have perks other than price. For example, there's comfort in knowing someone is looking out for you and your luggage as well as providing ground transportation to the ship. Uniformed cruise-line agents meet incoming passengers to smooth their way from airport to pier.

Even with Air & Sea flight arrangements, lengthy airline delays can result in literally missing the boat. However, it's a common misconception that when you use a cruise-line's Air & Sea program, the cruise line is responsible for getting you to your ship. On the contrary, the responsibility is with the airline. When cruise lines contract with airlines for tickets, the airline is responsible for getting you to the next port of call if a flight is cancelled; they should even put you on a different airline's flight to ensure that you don't miss the ship if that is possible. However, cruise-line personnel will help you make alternate arrangements. You'll be given an emergency telephone number to call in case your flight is delayed, and the line will help you find alternate flights. They can also assist with hotel arrangements and transfers (often the airline will pay for these if they are at fault).

If you must fly to port the same day your ship sails, it's wise to request the first flight of the day from your departure city. Delays in later flights can snowball, creating air-scheduling havoc and scarce seats as flyers scramble to get on board later flights.

You should also consider your flight home as well. Although your itinerary may state that the ship docks back in its home port at 7 AM, passengers are unlikely to begin leaving the vessel much earlier than 9 AM. Prior to disembarkation, the ship must be cleared by Customs and Immigration and all non–U.S. citizens must be cleared through Immigration on the vessel. In some ports, U.S. citizens pass through Immigration on the ship as well. In other ports, they do so in the terminal before retrieving their luggage and going through customs. In any event, cruise lines normally warn you not to schedule your flight home before noon or even 1 PM, depending on the port location. In New York City, the suggested time is no earlier than mid-afternoon.

Suppose you don't want to fly. After 9/11, cruise lines realized that the traveling public wanted more alternatives, and the solution was surprisingly simple. If passengers couldn't get to the ports easily, bring the ports to them. Although a cruise ship will never dock in Boise, Idaho, there are splendid, underutilized port cities close to major population areas all along the Atlantic and Gulf coasts of the United States that might be closer to where you live, perhaps even within driving distance. There's a lot to discover out there in fly-over country, after all.

In addition to the busiest embarkation ports of Miami, Fort Lauderdale, Port Canaveral, and New York, other cities are also capable of handling passenger ships. Some ships cruise from New Orleans, Tampa, Charleston, or Baltimore. By 2005, relative newcomer Galveston, Texas, ranked as the fifth-busiest cruise port in the United States, thanks largely to a substantial drive-to market. Secure parking is always available, either within the port itself or nearby. Even ports that are better known for moving bananas than people have begun to ride the cruise wave.

Arriving Early at the Embarkation Port

The possibility of flight delays and cancellations is the best reason to pad your vacation with a pre-cruise day of relaxation. Arrive early and unwind—an especially wise move if your home is in the snowbelt and your cruise is in January. The extra expense is well worth the peace of mind.

Pre- and post-cruise packages, which can include hotel accommodations and ground transportation, are offered by most cruise lines. Like airfare, the convenience of a package is sometimes offset by a slightly higher price tag.

With a bit of research, you can make your own independent arrangements at considerable savings. Many hotels near major ports of embarkation have their own packages and offers, which may include transportation to the cruise port. Some hotels offer free parking for the duration of your cruise, a handy addition if you are driving.

> **WORD OF MOUTH**
>
> Definitely take a taxi to and from the Miami airport; it is way cheaper per person and much faster than the cruise-line bus. Plus you don't have the long waits for other passengers, their bags, and the chaos involved in getting on and off the ship.
> –George & Eleanor S.

Getting Ready

3

WORD OF MOUTH

"We're taking a 7-day cruise . . . . There are 2 formal nights. Do we still have to have formal dress if we dine in the alternate restaurants?"

–golfette

"I had read somewhere that U.S. citizens would soon be required to have passports to sail the Caribbean. In the past we've only needed certified copies of birth certificates. Does anyone know the status on this?"

–Holdf

Fodor's Cruise Preparation Timeline

3 Months Before Sailing

• Check with your travel agent or the State Department for the identification required for your cruise. After January 1, 2008, a passport may be required for travel to most cruise destinations in the Caribbean.

• Gather the necessary identification you need. If you need to replace a lost birth certificate, apply for a new passport, or renew one that's about to expire, start the paperwork now. Doing it at the last minute is stressful and often costly.

60 to 75 Days Before Sailing

• Make the final payment on your cruise fare. Though the dates vary, your travel agent should remind you when the payment date draws near. Failure to submit the balance on time can result in the cancellation of your reservation.

• Make a packing list for each person you'll be packing for.

• Begin your wardrobe planning now. Try things on to make sure they fit and are in good repair (it's amazing how stains can magically appear months after something has been dry cleaned). Set things aside in your closet.

• If you need to shop, get started so you have time to find just the right thing (and perhaps to return or exchange just the right thing). You may also need to allow time for alterations. Start early—last-minute shopping for just the right thing can be hazardous to your nerves.

• Make kennel reservations for your pets. (If you're traveling during a holiday period, you may need to do this even earlier.)

• Arrange for a house sitter.

If you're cruising, but your kids are staying home:

• Make child care arrangements.

• Go over children's schedules to make sure they'll have everything they need while you're gone (gift for a birthday party, supplies for a school project, permission slip for a field trip).

• If you have small children, you may want to put together a small bag of treats for them to open while you're gone—make a tape of yourself reading a favorite bedtime story or singing a lullaby (as long as it's you, it will sound fantastic to them).

30 Days Before Sailing

• If you purchased an Air & Sea package, call your travel agent for the details of your airline schedule. Request seat assignments and any special airline meals.

• If your children are sailing with you, check their wardrobes now (do it too early, and the really little kids may actually grow out of garments).

• Make appointments for any personal services you wish to have prior to your cruise. For example, a haircut, manicure, or a pedicure.

• Get out your luggage and check the locks and zippers. Check for anything that might have spilled inside on a previous trip.

• If you need new luggage or want an extra piece to bring home your souvenirs, purchase it now.

2 to 4 Weeks Before Sailing

• Receive your cruise documents through the travel agent.

• Examine the documents for accuracy (correct cabin number, sailing date, and dining arrangements) and make sure names are spelled correctly. If there's something you do not understand, ask your travel agent or the cruise line now.

• Read all the literature in your document package for suggestions specific to your cruise. Most cruise lines include helpful information.

• Pay any routine bills that may be due while you're gone.

• Go over your personalized packing list again. Finish shopping.

1 Week Before Sailing

• Finalize your packing list and continue organizing everything in one area.

• Buy film and check the batteries in your camera.

• Refill prescription medications with an adequate supply (and bring along a copy of the written prescription if this is critical medication).

• Make two photocopies of your passport or ID and credit cards. Leave one copy with a friend, and carry the other copy separately from the originals.

• Get cash and/or traveler's checks at the bank. If you use traveler's checks, keep a separate record of the serial numbers. Get a supply of one-dollar bills for tipping baggage handlers (at the airport, hotel, pier, etc.).

• You may also want to put valuables and jewelry that you won't be taking with you in the safety deposit box while you're at the bank. (See "1 Day Before Sailing"—you may want to put some of the contents of your wallet in the safety deposit box as well.)

• Arrange to have your mail held at the post office or ask a neighbor to pick it up.

• Stop newspaper delivery or ask a neighbor to bring it in for you.

• Arrange for lawn and houseplant care or snow removal during your absence (if necessary).

• Leave your itinerary, the ship's telephone number (plus the name of your ship and your stateroom number), and a house key with a relative or friend. If the ship's telephone number is not included in your documents, your travel agent can get the number for you.

• If traveling with small children, purchase small games or toys to keep them occupied while en route to your embarkation port.

3 Days Before Sailing

• Confirm your airline flights; departure times are sometimes subject to change.

• Put a card with your name, address, telephone number, and itinerary inside each suitcase.

• Fill out the luggage tags that came with your document packet, and follow the instructions regarding when and how to attach them.

• Complete any other paperwork that the cruise line included with your documents (foreign customs and immigration forms, onboard charge application, etc.). Do not wait until you're standing in the pier check-in line to fill them in!

• Do last-minute laundry and tidy up the house.

• Pull out the luggage and begin packing.

The Day Before Sailing

• Take pets to the kennel.

• Water houseplants and lawn (if necessary).

• Dispose of any perishable food in the refrigerator.

• Mail any last-minute bills.

• Set timers for indoor lights.

• Reorganize your wallet. Remove anything you will not need (check-cashing cards, department store or gas credit cards, etc.), put these in an envelope, and leave them in a secure place.

• Finish packing and lock your suitcases.

Departure Day

• Adjust the thermostat and double-check the door locks.

• Turn off the water if there's danger of frozen pipes while you're away.

• Arrange to be at the airport a minimum of two hours before your departure time (follow the airline's instructions).

• Have photo ID and/or passport ready for airport check-in.

• Slip your car keys, parking claim checks, and airline tickets in your carry-on luggage. Never pack these items in checked luggage.

• Breathe a sigh of relief . . . you're on your way.

To expedite your preboarding paperwork, some cruise lines have convenient forms on their Web sites. As long as you have your reservation (or booking) number, you can provide the required immigration information, reserve shore excursions, and even indicate any special requests from the comfort of your home. Be sure to print a copy of the form to present at the pier.

ONCE YOUR IDEAL CRUISE IS BOOKED, it's time to start getting yourself and your family prepared for the trip. Some of the steps you can take are merely for your convenience while others are really important. But it's critical that you prepare in advance for your cruise; don't wait until the last minute, when even a minor oversight could ruin your vacation. As your sailing date approaches, do not hesitate to ask your travel agent if you have any questions.

Many cruise passengers claim that planning is half the fun, and they really throw themselves into the process. That makes sense when you consider you may be out of touch with your home, family, and business when your cruise ship is at sea. Depending on the itinerary, that could be for many hours, even days, at a time.

You'll sleep better if you think ahead. Some of the things you'll need to do before your cruise take time—for instance, obtaining the proper documents; other details may seem relatively simple but can expand in significance if you leave them all for the last minute. By breaking your preparation down into manageable chunks, you'll have plenty of time to get ready and won't be frazzled in the last week before your cruise. The last thing you want is to leave something important undone because you were in a rush. It's easier to leave your worries behind on the dock when you plan with care.

DOCUMENTS

It's every passenger's responsibility to have proper identification. If you arrive at port without the travel documents you need, you will not be allowed to board your cruise ship and the cruise line will not issue you a refund. Most travel agents know the requirements and can guide you to the proper agencies to obtain the documents you need if you don't already have them.

Passports

Cruises to the Bahamas, Mexico, and the Caribbean require proof of citizenship for all passengers. In the past, American citizens could get by with a certified copy of their birth certificate and a government-issued photo identification card, such as driver's license or a military or government employee ID card. However, as of this writing, it is expected that by January 1, 2008, all American citizens will be required to have a passport for all travel by sea to or from the Caribbean, Bermuda, Mexico, Canada, and Central and South America. It's also very important to know that as of January 2007, all passengers were required to have a valid passport for air travel to all destinations in the Caribbean, Canada, and Mexico *except for* Puerto Rico and the U.S. Virgin Islands (for the USVI, you must still show proof of citizenship but are not required to show a passport). So if your cruise leaves from Puerto Rico or St. Thomas, you **do not** need a passport until January 2008 (though you still need that original birth certificate if your cruise leaves from St. Thomas); however, if your cruise leaves from Barbados, the Dominican Republic, or some other island in the Caribbean, you **must** have a valid passport now.

Canadian citizens also need passports now, and resident aliens of the United States need a valid passport from their home country as well as their Alien

Resident Receipt Card (form I-551), which is commonly known as a green card. To embark in a U.S. port, citizens of all other foreign countries—if they aren't permanent residents of the United States—must carry a valid passport and a visa waiver or multiple-entry visa for the United States.

Getting or Renewing a Passport

Since more people will now require passports to travel, you should apply for a passport as far in advance of your cruise as possible if you don't have one or need to renew your current passport. The process usually takes at least six weeks and can take longer during very busy periods. The best time to apply for a passport or to renew is in fall and winter. Before any trip, check your passport's expiration date, and, if necessary, renew it as soon as possible.

You can expedite your passport application if you're traveling within two weeks by paying an additional fee of $60 (in addition to the regular passport fee) and appearing in person at a regional passport office. Also, several passport expediting services will handle your application for you (for a hefty fee, of course) and can get you a passport even sooner. For U.S. citizens, a passport costs $97 if you're 16 or older, $82 if you are under 16. It's valid for 10 years. You can usually renew a passport by mail as long as you can send in your current passport and are over 16 years old. If you're applying for a passport for the first time, you'll have to appear in person to make your application, but most cities and towns large and small have some office that processes passport applications—usually a post office or courthouse; some public libraries or county or state courthouses even process applications.

🔒 **U.S. Passport Information** **National Passport Information Center** ☎ 877/487-2778, 888/874-7793 TDD/TTY ⊕ travel.state.gov.

Permission Letters

But you may need even more documentation than that. Often, single parents or grandparents want to take their children or grandchildren on a cruise; it's also not uncommon for parents to invite their teenager's friend to sail along. An often-overlooked requirement is a notarized letter of permission, which is usually required anytime a child under 18 travels to a foreign country with anyone other than both of his or her parents. The absent or noncustodial parent (or parents) must usually give explicit written permission for their children to travel outside the United States.

Airlines, cruise lines, and immigration agents can—and usually will—deny minor children initial boarding or entry to foreign countries without proper proof of identification and citizenship *and* a permission letter from absent or noncustodial parents. This requirement would apply to any single (divorced, widowed, or simply married-but-solo) parents, grandparents, or family friends taking children on a cruise. Many cruises have been spoiled because groups arrived at the dock or the airport with the kids but without a letter of permission. (Or at the very least, there's been a lot of anxiety waiting for faxed letters to arrive at the last minute.)

There's a good reason for why this letter is now a requirement. According to Department of State Publication 10542: "With the number of international child custody cases on the rise, several countries have instituted

SAMPLE PERMISSION LETTER

Here's the text you might use for a typical letter of permission. You should type this up yourself, putting in all the specific details of your trip in place of the blanks.

CONSENT FOR MINOR CHILDREN TO TRAVEL

Date: _____

I (we): _____

authorize my/our minor child(ren): _____

to travel to: _____ on _____

aboard Airline/Flight Number: _____

and/or Cruise Ship: _____

with _____.

Their expected date of return is: _____.

   In addition, I (we) authorize:_____ to consent to any necessary routine or emergency medical treatment during the aforementioned trip.

Signed: _____(Parent)

Signed: _____(Parent)

Address: _____

_____

_____

Telephone:_____

Sworn to and signed before me, a Notary Public,

this _____ day of _____, 20_____

_____

Notary Public Signature and Seal

passport requirements to help prevent child abductions. For example, Mexico has a law that requires a child traveling alone, or with only one parent, or in someone else's custody, to carry written, notarized consent from the absent parent or parents. No authorization is needed if the child travels alone and is in possession of a U.S. passport. A child traveling alone with a birth certificate requires written, notarized authorization from both parents."

Proof of identity and citizenship is rather straightforward: you need either a certified copy of a birth certificate or a passport for your child. The permission letter is a bit more vexing since most people aren't aware of the necessity to have it, let alone what it should include. An attorney could prepare a formal affidavit, but a simple letter-style document is adequate as long as it's signed before an authorized notary. To be acceptable, it should include specific details about the trip, the custodial adult(s), and the child(ren). Although no one wants to think about medical emergencies while on vacation, it's also wise to include consent for the custodial adult to authorize emergency treatment for the child in case the need should arise.

Some parents, particularly mothers who do not share the same last name as their children, should take no chances and also carry a copy of their divorce decree or, in the case of widows, a death certificate for their spouse.

After going to all the trouble to secure proper documentation, it could turn out that no one even asks for it. Why did you bother? Because if you had not, the possibility existed that your cruise ship may have sailed without you and your very disappointed family. You may even find that it's easier to enter a port of call than to leave it with your own child.

PICKING A CRUISE WARDROBE

So your closet is not full of designer outfits and matching shoes? Not to worry, neither are the closets of most cruise-ship passengers. The reality is that you do not need to overextend a credit card and fill your suitcases with new cruise duds. Despite any fashion anxiety, you probably have almost everything you need.

Cruise wear falls into three categories: casual, informal, and formal. Cruise documents should include information indicating how many evenings fall into each of those categories. You'll know when to wear what by reading your ship's daily newsletter, where each evening's dress code will be prominently announced. Dress codes are primarily directed toward adults, so children's wardrobes can be planned based on what their parents are wearing and the activities they are participating in.

Casual Wear

First and foremost, there's casual wear. This is exactly what it implies: clothing to be comfortable in. Your plans for the day will dictate what you should wear. For warm weather cruises, you'll typically need swimwear, a cover-up, and sandals for pool and beach. Time spent ashore touring and shopping calls

> **WORD OF MOUTH**
>
> Try not to resent the men who wear a navy blue blazer, gray slacks, and the same black shoes for almost every dressy occasion and look just fine. It may be boring, but it's easy to pack!
>
> –Janet N.

for shorts topped with T-shirts or polo-style shirts and comfy walking shoes. Conservative is the rule to live by, and mix-and-match will save room in your suitcase. If you intend to purchase souvenir T-shirts, plan to make them a part of your cruise wardrobe and pack fewer tops.

Evening casual does not mean shorts. For men it's khaki-type slacks and a nice polo or sport shirt. Ladies' evening-casual outfits might consist of sporty dresses, skirts and tops, or pants outfits. By sticking to two colors and a few accessories, you can mix up tops and bottoms for a different look every night.

The first and last nights on board are always casual for obvious reasons—you may not have your luggage before dinner that first night, and you've already packed for home on the last night. Many people consider denim jeans casual wear. Some cruise lines discourage them in the dining room. Use your own judgment, and keep in mind that denim is hot—you might want to wear lighter fabrics in the Caribbean heat.

Informal Wear

Informal dress is a little trickier since it only applies to evening wear and can mean different things depending on the cruise line. Informal for women is a dressier dress or pants outfit; for men it almost always includes a sport coat and often a tie. Check your documents carefully for a specific definition of "informal."

Formal Wear

It has been said that Formal Night is fantasy land for women and torture for men from the sounds of male grumbling, that is. If you like to dress up, this is your night to shine. You'll see women in everything from simple cocktail dresses to elaborate, glittering gowns. Tuxedos (either all black or with a white dinner jacket) or dark suits are required for gentlemen, but a quick review of the dining room will show you that on most mainstream cruises, dark suits prevail. If you have been a mother of the bride lately, chances are your outfit for the wedding is just perfect for formal night. For children, Sunday-best is entirely appropriate.

If a man decides to go all out, then he must decide whether to buy or rent a tuxedo, which is ultimately a point of individual preference. As a rule of thumb, if you're going to wear a tuxedo more than two or three times, it makes economic sense to purchase one. Most cruise lines make it easy to rent the entire outfit, though—and if you do so, it will be waiting for you when you board. Be sure to make these arrangements well before your cruise; your travel agent can get the details from the cruise line.

It has been said that a tuxedo is a rented suit and a dinner jacket is the formal clothing owned by the gentleman wearing it. Whatever the definition or terms of ownership, men look stunning in black tie. If yours is a rental, try it on immediately so alterations can be made if necessary.

Even if you're renting a tuxedo, by all means buy your own studs. You don't have to spend a fortune on them; just get some that look classy. Why? A sure-fire way to spot a rented tuxedo is by the inexpensive studs that come with them. A few words about vests. Many men with a little girth consider them more comfortable than cummerbunds.

Which formal night is most formal? Every woman wants to know the answer to that question because we all have a dress we think is more stylish, or maybe we just feel more beautiful wearing it. Unless you eat like a bird or never gain an ounce, save your roomiest formal outfit for the second formal night.

How glittery can you get without being mistaken for a showgirl? Totally sequined and beaded dresses are not as fashionable as they once were, and you may want to avoid the temptation of borrowing your daughter's frou-frou prom dress as well—neither makes a good fashion statement. When selecting formal outfits, think simple. There's nothing more elegant than a well-cut, simple, black dress. But there's nothing more fun than a flashy or sexy dress that turns heads. It's totally up to you. One of the most practical and useful garments any woman can own is a pair of black, silky cocktail pants. They take up no room at all in the suitcase and don't wrinkle. Best of all, with two dressy tops you have two different formal outfits with a minimum of fuss. Even better, they usually have comfortable elastic waistbands.

If formal is just not a part of your vocabulary or lifestyle, consider booking on one of the cruise lines that have modified it or done away with it altogether. On some cruise lines every night is country-club casual. The ultimate in laid-back can be a cruise on a tall ship where the only clothing suggestion is that you save your clean T-shirt for the captain's dinner.

Other Cruise Wardrobe Tips

For versatility and to stretch your options, coordinate your wardrobe by selecting garments in one or two basic colors to mix and match. No one really notices whether you recycle outfits, so don't be afraid to wear the same things more than once. Create different looks with accessories, either from home or purchased in port. To pack small, take only two pairs of shoes; comfortable all-purpose shoes for day and dressier ones for evening. If you must have your big, clunky athletic shoes, wear them on the plane and pack the others.

An absolute essential for women is a shawl or light sweater. Aggressive air-conditioning can make public rooms uncomfortable, particularly if you're sun burned from a day at the beach.

Expenses for cruise-ship laundry, pressing, and dry-cleaning services can add up fast, especially laundry, as charges are per item and the rates are similar to those charged in hotels. Happily, some ships have a low-cost or free self-serve laundry room (the room usually has an iron and ironing board in addition to washers and dryers). You can make laundry less important when shopping if you look for clothing made of lightweight microfiber. Besides taking up less suitcase space, microfiber sheds wrinkles and dries quickly. In terms of comfort, these fabrics wick moisture away from the body, keeping you cool in the tropics and necessitating fewer clothing changes. Tuck a small bottle of laundry liquid and clothes pins in your suitcase and, in a pinch, you can wash smaller items in your bathroom sink and hang them to dry in the shower. A hair dryer speeds the process along in record time.

After all this obsessing about clothing, consider the unthinkable: what if your luggage is delayed? What if it doesn't show up until the end of the cruise? Unfortunately, this happens. And if it happens to you, do not stress out. Shop here and there and pick up what you need until the next stop—your luggage could appear in the next port. Avoid some of the anxiety lost luggage can cause by carrying on your essentials when you board. Consider using a garment bag or rollaboard containing formal clothing, a bathing suit, and at least one casual outfit just in case.

And here's one last thought about cruise wear: be considerate by adhering to each evening's dress code and do not rush back to your cabin to change into shorts immediately after dinner.

PICKING LUGGAGE

It just so happens that the best luggage for your cruise is also suitable for many other purposes. Airport and pier baggage handlers are notoriously rough with suitcases, so a top consideration is sturdiness. Your suitcase does not have to be top-of-the-line, but it should be built well enough to withstand the rigors of conveyors and sorting machines, not to mention being stacked, dropped, and thrown through the air.

Luggage can be a significant investment, so the right choice in terms of design and durability is important. Brand-name luggage that comes with a good warranty is always desirable, but no-name or private label brands can also stand the test of time.

Hard-sided luggage is usually the longest-wearing of all. In addition to being the most rugged, the built-in locks also make these suitcases the most secure and water-tight. For frequent flyers who want the greatest luggage mileage, it makes sense to look at hard-sided luggage. Improved composition materials have made their shells lighter; however, even when empty they can still be heavy.

If casual observations at airport conveyors are any indication, soft-side suitcases are by far the most popular choice. They're lighter in weight, their zippers can be secured pretty easily, almost all have wheels, and some are expandable for additional packing volume.

What should you look for in a suitcase? Hard-side suitcases should have metal piano hinges and solid hardware. Combination locks are great, but look for those that also have key locks. Unless a clasp is locked, it could snap open. Wheels (preferably in-line skate type) should turn smoothly and be set wide for stability. Retractable handle assemblies should be strong and adjustable for maximum comfort and ease of maneuverability. Padded interiors with pockets and garment tie-downs are fairly standard.

The soft-side suitcases you're considering should be covered in a tightly woven ballistic nylon for the greatest durability since other fabrics can snag, pill, and tear more easily. None of these fabrics is indestructible, but ballistic nylon is usually judged to be the best, especially when it's also Teflon coated. Frame construction is also an important factor in the ultimate stability of the suitcase; it should be strong enough that it does not flex out of shape when the suitcase is fully packed. Corners should be reinforced with rubber bumpers hefty enough to prevent abrasion, which all too often occurs in these vulnerable areas. Wheels and handle assemblies should have the same properties as hard-sided cases; a solid skid plate between the wheels is beneficial to protect the suitcase fabric from damage when inevitable encounters with curbs and escalators occur. Look for self-healing, industrial-grade zippers that move smoothly and have large enough zipper pulls for ease of use. Interiors can include a variety of wet bags, pockets, and other organizers, particularly in the lid-door.

All suitcases should be well balanced with adequate feet so they do not fall over when you're waiting in a check-in line. In addition, many of the newest models include removable garment bags or suiters for wrinkle-free packing.

Even some of the smallest 22-inch suitcases are outfitted with suiters—those fold-up panels that accommodate hanging garments. These are great wrinkle-proof organizers that tuck formal clothing neatly into the suitcase. The handiest are the ones that are removable for times that you don't need them.

Business travelers have long favored garment bags for carry-on ease and quick, wrinkle-free packing. Their bulky favorites are being replaced these days by garment bags on wheels that are virtually rolling closets with multiple pockets and organizers for folded items, shoes, and even toiletries. Look for the same construction qualities as any soft-side suitcase. These bags hold a lot but are not sized as carry-ons.

You know the days of massive steamer trunks are history, but is there a maximum amount of luggage that you can bring on a cruise ship? Yes, there really is a limit of sorts. Although some cruise lines state that each passenger is allowed 200 pounds of personal luggage, you're unlikely to see anyone's bags actually being weighed. However, it's not the cruise-line restrictions that passengers need to worry about. Cruisers arriving at their embarkation port by air should be aware of airline restrictions. Most major airlines enforce suitcase size and weight policies, resulting in a rude (and expensive) surprise to some travelers with large, heavy suitcases.

Unfortunately, many 29-inch to 30-inch suitcases now exceed the maximum size limitation of 62 linear inches (a combination of length, width, depth) for airline checked luggage and are often subject to additional charges. Then there's the matter of suitcase wheel assemblies and whether they're included in the measurements or not. That depends on who you ask, and responses are all over the map. It seems the ultimate arbiter of oversize dimensions is the agent checking in passengers at the airport.

Those 29-inch to 30-inch suitcases are likely to incur excess weight charges, as well. As many travelers discover, they hold so much that they are prone to be overly heavy. Depending on their size, rolling garment bags might also fall into the category of too big to be checked free of charge. These days, you'll usually be charged extra for anything over 50 pounds; on a few airlines the limit is still 70 pounds, but on a few it's even as low as 40 pounds.

Don't even think of expanding a suitcase in the 29-inch to 30-inch size range to accommodate the addition of souvenirs for the trip home—the additional size and weight just will not fly these days without adding a fee as robust as the bag. Take a folding tote bag for purchases, and carry it on the plane home.

Remember that two suitcases in the 24-inch to 26-inch size range will hold as much (or more) than a single larger suitcase and are kinder to your back when you have to lift them. Some airlines allow two free checked bags, some only one. Check with your airline to make sure, and budget for anything you wish to take in excess of the free limit. The charges are quite high for excess baggage; don't be caught by surprise at the airport check-in counter.

Whether you buy new bags or carry your trusty old ones, take the following steps before you leave for the airport:

- Ascertain the exact baggage regulations of the airline(s) you're most likely to fly with and strictly adhere to them.

- For ease of moving through check-in lines, buy luggage pieces that can piggyback on one another.

- Measure suitcases for size and include the wheels just in case.

- Weigh packed suitcases on the bathroom scale.

PACKING

You may find that packing less is more if you follow this experienced travelers' adage: "Pack your suitcases and remove half the contents. Then take twice as much money!" I have a confession. I'm a pack-aholic. I was hopelessly addicted to overburdening my husband with bulging garment bags and suitcases that barely closed. The overflow from my tote bag got stashed in his pockets. Practicality has forced me to change my ways.

I became a confirmed packing list maker following my very first cruise on the SS *Norway*. I overlooked one little grooming essential that I really needed: tweezers. One of my tablemates forgot to pack her hair dryer. And it dawned on us that a cruise is unlike a resort vacation in one important way: there's no local supermarket or drugstore to pop into when you need something. Although many ships stock a variety of sundries, they may not have just what you need and, if they do, the cost can be considerably more than comparable items at home. My tablemate and I were both able to find suitable replacements ashore for our forgotten items, but we spent two days at sea before arriving in our first port of call where we could shop for them.

Aha! A light went on in my brain. If I had checklists, I would be less likely to leave something out of my suitcase. What simplicity. Why hadn't any-one thought of it before? While planning my second cruise, I began by creating basic packing lists for my husband and myself. Over the years I've added and deleted items—for instance, I prefer my own brand of shampoo to the products provided by most hotels and cruise lines. On the other hand, it's seldom necessary to pack a hair dryer these days, al-though some ships' accommodations don't provide them in all cate-

Drugs: What You Can't Pack

IT GOES WITHOUT SAYING that you shouldn't purchase illegal drugs in the islands and try to bring them into the United States at the end of your cruise. In an odd twist, a group of hapless cruisers attempted to actually board a cruise ship in Florida with stashes they planned to consume on board. They were met in the terminal by U.S. Customs, local law enforcement, and a drug-sniffing dog who took the unusual step of examining passengers leaving the United States. It seems the excited group shared their

packing lists with one another on the Internet, and tipped off the authorities. The most common hiding place for their drugs wasn't very original—inside their underwear—and when they realized the search was on it caused quite a melee.

Moral of this story? Other than exercising discretion when sharing your plans openly in a chat room, just say no to buying drugs in foreign ports unless your vacation strategy includes spending time in the brig—or worse, in a Caribbean jail.

gories. I've welcomed suggestions from users of my Web site, CruiseDiva. com, as well. The packing list for babies was compiled entirely from my readers' input.

I begin with personal essentials and a day-by-day schedule of wardrobe requirements, and this has worked fine to rein in my packing excesses. Now, mind you, the following checklists contain just about everything anyone would need on a cruise. As a result, there are many items you can just cross off. How much of each clothing item to pack (such as shirts, shorts, and underwear) is determined by the length of your cruise and your planned activities. A good rule of thumb is to pack one daytime outfit for every two days of travel. However, you may need more shirts and shorts if your plans include adventurous excursions. Clothing tends to get soiled and sweaty under some conditions and you'll want to change more frequently.

Instead of strappy sandals, you may need hiking boots and bug spray, or water shoes and no formal wear. Customize these lists to work for you based on where you're going, what you intend to do, and which cruise line you're traveling with.

Packing for Children & Teens

About the only difference between the wardrobes of parents and younger family members is that children's clothing is smaller and takes up less space in a suitcase. Their requirements will mimic the adult versions of the bathing suits, shorts, T-shirts, shoes, etc., which are outlined in the packing lists. If your plans include dining every night as a family, the children should be suitably attired to conform to the cruise line's dress code, although comfort is more important for their happiness than being overly formal, particularly when it comes to younger children.

Make the planning and packing stage of cruise preparation a family affair by enlisting everyone's help. To make things easy, make stacks of clothing for each child for every day of the cruise, including underwear and socks. Put each day's stack in a zipper top plastic bag and label them Monday, Tuesday, and so on. Once on board the ship, each child can

PACKING LISTS FOR THE FAMILY

Clothing for Women
- gowns or cocktail dresses
- dress shoes and hosiery
- skirts, blouses, or pants outfits
- accessories (scarves, pins, etc.)
- shawl or sweater
- casual shoes
- T-shirts or polo shirts
- shorts or slacks
- bathing suit
- tennis shoes and socks
- undergarments
- sleepwear

Clothing for Men
- tuxedo and accessories (studs, formal shirts, tie, cummerbund, belt); or dark business suit with shirts and ties
- dress shoes and black socks
- sport coat
- slacks and belt
- polo-golf shirts
- khaki pants
- casual shoes
- T-shirts
- shorts
- bathing suit
- tennis shoes and socks
- undergarments
- sleepwear

Packing for Baby
Mothers accustomed to carrying diaper bags chock-full of gear know their babies and toddlers have as many essentials as most infantry divisions in the field. Your own physician should be your guide, but consider these suggestions from a pediatrician and experienced moms when packing for small passengers' general travel needs:

- Benadryl (seasickness or restlessness)
- PediaCare decongestant
- sun block
- adhesive bandages
- Tylenol
- diaper rash ointment
- hat
- disinfectant ointment
- water shoes
- diapers
- bottles
- sipper cups
- diaper wipes
- hand-face wipes
- cotton swabs
- nail clippers
- poolside robe
- bathing suit
- sunglasses
- bottled water
- juice boxes
- favorite blanket or toy
- pacifiers
- thermometer

For flights, the pediatrician suggests giving little ones a sipper cup during airplane take-offs and landings. Also consider bringing an umbrella stroller for walks around the ship and in port with your baby. The stroller is especially handy at airports. Wheel your baby right to the departure gate—the stroller is gate-checked and will be waiting for you at the arrival gate. With limited passenger laundry rooms (and expensive laundry services) on ships, it's handy to bring along a pack of disposable bibs for mealtimes. They keep baby's clothes cleaner and stain-free, avoiding messy garments after meals. The last thing on your mind while cruising is doing laundry!

Essentials for Your Carry-On

Your carry-on is your hedge against lost luggage. In addition to the toiletries, valuables, and medicines you can't do without, you should consider putting a basic change of clothing and fresh undergarments in it as well. In case your luggage is delayed, those items should help you make it through the time it takes for your suitcases to catch up with you.

As of this writing, heightened security measures have restricted the amounts of liquids, gels, and aerosols that can be carried onto airplanes. However, solid cosmetics and personal hygiene items such as lipstick, lip balm, and similar solids are permitted in carry-on bags without restriction. For carry-on liquids and gels, each container must be three ounces or smaller, and all the containers must be placed inside a single, quart-size, zippered, clear plastic bag. One, and only one, plastic bag is allowed per passenger. Exceptions to the size restrictions are made for prescription and over-the-counter medicines, as well as baby formula and breast milk, all of which must be declared before inspection. For the latest regulations on what's allowed and what isn't, check with the Transportation Security Administration (www.tsa.gov).

- makeup remover
- freshener and moisturizer
- cotton balls
- cotton swabs
- toothbrush
- toothpaste
- mouthwash
- dental floss
- perfume
- body and hand lotions
- deodorant
- talcum powder
- sun screen
- eye shadow
- mascara
- powder
- blush
- lipstick
- nail polish and polish remover pads
- shampoo and conditioner (if you want your own brand)
- hair spray
- brushes and combs

- hair dryer (if your cruise ship doesn't provide them)
- curling iron
- shower cap
- feminine hygiene products
- jewelry
- hat or cap
- sunglasses
- shaving kit
- reading glasses
- insulated mug
- travel clock
- short, multiplug extension cord
- notebook and pen
- first-aid supplies (see list below)
- small flashlight
- night light
- duct tape
- cable ties
- lint brush
- liquid laundry soap
- folding tote bag or waist pack
- zip-top bags
- antibacterial hand cleaner
- extra glasses
- contact lens supplies
- camera, film, and extra batteries
- binoculars
- passport, money, documents, and keys

Post-9/11 airline regulations still prohibit sharp objects in carry-on bags, so pack your Swiss Army knife, larger tools (more than 7 inches in length), and razor-type implements (like box cutters, utility knives, and razor blades not in a cartridge) in your checked luggage. Also forbidden in airplanes are cigarette lighters, with the exception of one fueled Zippo lighter, which may be carried in checked luggage if it is encased in a Department of Transportation-approved container. Your safety razor and up to four books of safety (non-strike anywhere) matches may be taken onto the airplane in carry-on baggage. Also prohibited are large containers of liquids, aerosols, and gels—those must be packed in checked luggage. When in doubt about whether an item is allowed in your carry-on, check the current list on the TSA web site. ⊕ www.tsa.gov. Regrettably, the list of prohibited items changes all too often.

3

easily unpack his or her own suitcase and slip the plastic bags into drawers. Every morning they will know what to wear.

Teenagers can be quite independent creatures with very definite ideas about what they prefer to wear. They're likely to insist upon making their own clothing selections. Parents, you might want to keep an eye on what they've chosen to oversee the appropriateness of their wardrobes.

A Travel First-Aid Kit

In addition to clothing, consider packing some indispensable first-aid and emergency items. Not all scrapes happen within close proximity of the ship's medical center, and some minor accidents or illnesses do not require treatment. Be prepared at all times, both on board and ashore, with basic items for first-aid such as a few adhesive bandages and a small bottle of waterless antibacterial hand sanitizer, which can also be used to clean small cuts.

For all-around care, these items should be sufficient:

- adhesive bandages
- first-aid antibacterial cream
- waterless antibacterial hand sanitizer
- aspirin or nonaspirin pain reliever
- anti-nausea medication
- anti-diarrhea medication
- antacid tablets
- antihistamine
- seasickness remedy
- zipper-top plastic bags or ice bag
- dental adhesive
- prescription medications

Even people without dentures may have several capped teeth or fillings. It's rare that a shipboard medical center features a resident dentist, so a small container of dental adhesive or special dental repair kit is handy. A temporary repair can mean the difference between discomfort and relief from sensitivity to hot and cold until a dentist is available in port.

A problem to consider when traveling is edema, the accumulation of excess fluid in body tissues. It's a very common condition, particularly after long airplane flights and while cruising in hot, humid climates. Swollen ankles and feet are regular complaints, but you can take some preventative measures. During pre-cruise flights, drink plenty of water while avoiding caffeine and alcoholic beverages; walk around the plane every hour; and wear special compression stockings. Should swelling still develop, raise your feet and apply an ice-filled zipper-top plastic bag for relief. Sleeping with elevated feet can help as well—try putting a folded blanket or life vest under the mattress.

All medications and first-aid supplies should be in their original containers and should be hand carried—do not pack them in checked luggage.

Tips for Checked Luggage

THE FOLLOWING TIPS APPLY whether you're checking your luggage at the airport or the cruise terminal:

• Arrive at the airport in plenty of time, preferably two hours or more before departure. One of the leading causes of lost luggage is late arrivals—baggage handlers just do not have time to scan your bags and then to get them to the plane.

• Avoid airport curbside check-in. A whopping 87% of lost or stolen luggage originates at those curbside stations.

• One of the most common causes of misrouted bags is gate agent error. Know the three-letter code of your destination airport and verify it on the luggage tag before your bag is put on the conveyor belt.

• Avoid connecting flights whenever possible.

• Make sure the connection times are adequate. Do not accept anything less

than an hour between flights. You might make the plane; however, your luggage may not.

• Secure your bags. Check the locking devices when you arrive at your destination, and report any damage or missing items to the airline or cruise line immediately.

• Label luggage on the inside and outside with your name, phone number, and address (preferably a business address). Include a copy of your itinerary on the inside of your bags so you can be traced more easily.

• Remove any old claim checks from the bags.

• When tagging suitcases for check-in on your ship, use all the tags you receive. Put two tags on each checked bag just in case one is damaged or falls off.

Always have enough prescription medicine on hand for a couple of extra days in case of travel delays when returning home. Contact lens and eyeglasses wearers should consider packing an extra pair.

Packing Strategies

Once your major wardrobe selections are complete and the suitcases are ready, devise a streamlined packing strategy. Here are my suggestions:

• Personalize the packing list and stick with it. Assemble everything on the list before starting to pack, and check items off when they're folded and placed in the suitcase.

• Resist the urge to toss in something "just in case"—that's the item you surely won't need.

• Pack small. Undergarments and knits take only a third of the suitcase space they normally occupy when they're compressed. Simply fill a large zippered storage bag with these articles and force all the air out before zipping it shut. Keep in mind that when you use zippered storage bags to compress clothing, you'll save room and get more in your luggage, but the suitcases could end up heavier because they hold more.

• Plan ahead and shop for sample or small-size containers of favorite toiletries.

• Don't forget that you can only carry onto your flight small containers of liquids and gels (whatever will fit in a single, quart-size zippered storage bag); larger sizes will have to go in your checked bags.

- To help keep garments wrinkle-free, leave them on their hangers, cover them with dry-cleaning bags, and fold over once before placing them in the suitcase. Unpacking is a snap; just open your suitcase and start hanging things in the closet.

- Do not bring along a travel iron to touch up wrinkled garments. Irons are a fire hazard, and their use in passenger cabins is strongly discouraged. Instead, pack a clothing steamer.

- T-shirts can serve as a swimsuit cover up or a nightshirt. Knit sport shirts can do double duty as well; a shirt worn a short time at dinner can easily be donned the next day for touring or lounging on the ship.

- If the ship has self-service laundry facilities you can pack lighter and wash clothes midway through the cruise. Remember, other passengers have the same idea, so you might encounter long lines and surly tempers. Use the ship's laundry service instead. It's pricier, but who wants to spend valuable cruise time washing clothes?

- Use every bit of luggage space. Women's shoes will often fit inside men's. Stuff socks and other small items inside larger space-wasters. A tote bag that folds into its own zippered pocket is handy as a shopping or beach bag and invaluable when it's time to pack the souvenirs that are preventing your suitcase from closing.

- Cross-pack your luggage with your travel companion. Chances are if a suitcase is missing, it'll turn up eventually. In the meantime, you'll both have fresh clothing until it does.

- Valuables should never be packed in your checked luggage. Jewelry, medicine, cameras, travel documents, and a change of underclothes belong in your carry-on. For safety and peace of mind, carry traveler's checks, cash, and copies of your passport and credit cards in a money pouch under your clothing.

- Tuck copies of your packing lists in with your travel documents. If your luggage is waylaid, you'll have a handy record of the contents.

A caveat: Unfortunately, some garments defy the dry-cleaning-bag packing method. Clothing that is slightly creased or wrinkled can often be freshened up by steaming. If you don't have a clothing steamer, just hang those items in the bathroom while taking a hot, steamy shower, and often the wrinkles will fall right out. If all else fails, many ships have ironing stations in their self-service passenger launderettes or, for maximum convenience, send the offending garments to the ship's laundry for pressing.

Frequent travelers have all noticed that luggage often becomes unzipped for one reason or another during baggage handling, either at the airport or cruise terminal. You want to lock your soft-sided luggage, but with current airport security procedures, you may not be able to until after it

Duct Tape—the Essential Travel Tool

SO, YOUR BAGS ARE PACKED and you're ready to cruise? Not quite yet if you skipped the duct tape. You don't want to leave your home port without one of a traveler's handiest necessities. Duct tape no longer belongs only in the garage. Some of its more mundane uses are luggage repair (fix a broken hinge with ease) and security (baggage handlers won't tamper with duct tape; it's too much trouble). Wrapped in duct tape, your luggage is easy to spot in terminals as well. For individuality, duct tape comes in colors, as well as the traditional silver. For even higher suitcase visibility, there are snazzy neon colors. It's water resistant (an important feature for ocean travelers) and can serve as an indestructible luggage tag as well as a strap—just write your name and address on the tape. Best of all, duct tape is easy to tear by hand and you don't need scissors to cut it.

There are literally thousands of uses for duct tape. Every homeowner knows that when something is supposed to stick together and it doesn't, nothing holds like duct tape. What about at sea? Is the bottom ready to fall out of your cabin's vanity drawer? Tape it until the carpenter arrives. You're a late sleeper and the drapes don't quite close? Keep the sun at bay by taping them together. Everyone has had the stitching in a hem unravel at the last minute. Duct tape to the rescue! There are bottle lids to secure, rattles to silence, drawers that won't stay shut when the ship is rolling, and other little things that happen when you least expect them.

One of duct tape's most creative uses is as a replacement for an uplifting foundation garment. Under low-cut or backless dresses—or when a brassiere just won't work with a gown—create your own Wonder Duct Bra. Duct tape sticks well for hours and peels off without pain. Best of all, the variety of colors means more coordinating choices and even less chance of a sliver of silver tape peeping from a black décolleté neckline.

3

---

has been screened. Ask at check-in if you can use cable ties, which can usually be found with electrical supplies in home improvement centers. If your luggage requires hand-screening, a new cable tie should be affixed and you'll find a note inside the suitcase indicating that the contents were examined. If you use a traditional combination or keyed lock, it will be cut off and discarded. Inspectors in foreign countries can't always open the TSA-approved locks.

Once they're attached, cable ties must be removed with scissors or nail clippers. When flying to your embarkation port, never put scissors in your carry-on. Instead, place them in an unlocked outside suitcase pocket or simply pack nail clippers in your carry-on to cut the plastic ties. To keep sticky-fingered baggage handlers from riffling through your things, always secure luggage before checking in at the cruise terminal, and remember to take extra cable ties for the trip home.

Enjoying Your Cruise

WORD OF MOUTH

"We're considering booking a 5-night Caribbean cruise for next summer . . . . There is only one day at sea with 3 port stops. What is there to do during that day when we're at sea?"

—mrg013

"I sail solo often and have always enjoyed myself. I prefer not to hook up with others for excursions as I like to do what I want, whenever I want, and do not feel a need for company. I travel solo and have never felt compromised."

—Kfusto

WITH THE PLANNING, PACKING, AND ANTICIPATION BEHIND THEM, veteran cruisers sometimes view embarkation day as anticlimactic. However, for first-time cruise passengers, embarking on your first ship can be more than exhilarating—it can be downright intimidating.

Take a deep breath. You've come this far, and your ship is within sight. That first glimpse could well be an "oh my gosh" moment if you've booked a megaship. They're huge and dwarf nearly everything in their vicinity. Sit back and savor the moment because soon you'll be busy. There will be a lot happening around you and it will all be new. Procedures may differ slightly from cruise line to cruise line, but don't worry: once you understand the process and know what to expect, you can go with the flow.

Above all, don't stress. There can be advantages to waiting in line when you reach the terminal: your luggage may beat you to your cabin, and you could meet some interesting people. After the check-in and boarding process is behind you, the fun and relaxation begin.

Think of the ship as your first destination, a moveable port of call. Plan to enjoy your time on board as much as you can. Repeat after me: "They won't run out of food."

BOARDING

What exactly can you expect? First of all, keep in mind that your embarkation day cannot officially begin until the ship is clear of departing passengers and their luggage. The disembarkation process can seem as drawn-out as a divorce. While the previous weeks' passengers make their way reluctantly down the gangway, the staff and crew are busy readying the ship for the next sailing. By the time the last straggler departs, trucks are already arriving at the dock with provisions, and a lot of heavy work is going on behind the scenes. Staterooms and public lounges are thoroughly cleaned and readied, and a steady stream of supplies and luggage are brought aboard. There can even be an exchange of crew members, with some leaving and others arriving. The vessel's entire turnaround procedure is as carefully choreographed as the most intricate ballet.

What to Expect

Checking In
Whether you take a bus transfer or taxi from the airport or a hotel, the first people you encounter at the cruise terminal are baggage handlers. They're not cruise-line employees, and they do expect a tip—$2 per suitcase is sufficient. You may be required to show your cruise ticket and picture ID at this point for verification and security purposes. Be sure your ship's luggage tags are securely fastened to your locked suitcases before you hand them over. If you booked a guarantee and haven't received your cabin assignment, your luggage tags may be marked TBA (to be announced), or there may be a blank space where the cabin number should be written in. The baggage handlers will have a copy of the ship's manifest and can give you the proper cabin number.

Cruise-line shoreside staff are milling about to point you in the right direction, and they're easily recognizable in official-looking uniforms with name tags and, often, a clipboard. Once inside the terminal, you might encounter a check-in line. Actual boarding time is often scheduled for noon, but some cruise lines will process early arrivals and then direct them to a holding area. During check-in, you'll be asked to produce your documents and any forms you were sent to complete ahead of time—or a printed copy of those you filled in online—plus proof of citizenship and a credit card (to cover charges on board). You're issued a boarding card that usually also doubles as your stateroom key and shipboard charge card. At some point—either before you enter the check-in area or before you proceed to the ship—you and your hand luggage will pass through a security procedure similar to those at airports.

Everyone is anxious to get on board and begin their vacation, but this is not the time to get cranky if you have to wait. Keep in mind that you cannot board until the ship is ready for you. Once boarding begins, you'll inevitably have your first experience with the ship's photographer and will be asked to pose for an embarkation picture. It only takes a second, so smile. You're under no obligation to purchase any photos taken of you during the cruise, but they're a nice souvenir if you do decide to buy them.

Paying for Things on Board

Let's step back a moment and take a look at what happened when you checked in at the pier. Because a cashless society prevails on cruise ships, an imprint was made of your credit card or you had to place a cash deposit for use against your onboard charges. Then you were issued an onboard charge card that often doubles as your stateroom key. An itemized bill is provided at the end of the voyage listing your purchases. Most onboard expenditures are charged to your shipboard account, with the exception of casino gaming (though some machines now accept your ship charge card as well as coins and paper money).

In order to avoid surprises at the end of your cruise, it's a good idea to set aside your charge slips and request an interim printout of your bill from the purser to ensure accuracy. Should you change your mind about charging onboard purchases, you can always inform the purser and pay in cash or traveler's checks instead. If your cash deposit was more than you spent, you'll receive a refund; if you charge more than the deposit, you'll be asked to put more on your account.

Settling In

Congratulations! Once you cross the gangway, your cruise has begun. The actual boarding procedures can vary; however, you'll have to produce your boarding card for the security officer and, possibly, a picture ID. The security officer may also take your digital image to enter into the ship's security system. When leaving and reboarding the ship in port, your boarding pass is scanned, and your image will appear on a screen for verification.

After you're greeted by the staff members awaiting your arrival, depending on

CAUTION
If your luggage doesn't appear when and where it should (either at the airport or cruise terminal), report the problem immediately before leaving the building and insist on a local phone number so you can follow up.

the cruise line, you'll be directed to your cabin, or a steward will relieve you of your carry-on luggage and accompany you. Stewards on high-end cruise lines such as Seabourn, Regent Seven Seas, SeaDream, and Silversea not only show you the way, but hand you a glass of champagne as a welcome-aboard gesture. Although a tip isn't necessarily expected by the steward who shows you to your cabin, a couple of dollars is usually appreciated by those on mainstream and premium cruise lines. On some luxury lines, gratuities are included in the fare and not expected. Your offer of a tip will be graciously refused.

Some cruise lines restrict access to cabins until a specified time and will direct you to a buffet or restaurant to enjoy lunch while you wait. Once you're in your cabin, make sure that everything is in order. Try the plumbing and set the air-conditioning—your cabin may feel warm while docked, but will cool off quickly when the ship is under way. You should find a copy of the ship's daily schedule in the cabin. Take a few moments to look it over; you'll want to know what time the muster drill takes place (a placard on the back of your cabin door will indicate directions to your emergency station), as well as meal hours and the schedule for various activities and entertainments.

Rented tuxedos are either hanging in the closet or will be delivered sometime during the afternoon, and bon voyage gifts sent by your friends or travel agent usually appear as well. Be patient if you're expecting deliveries, particularly on megaships. Cabin stewards participate in the ship's turnaround and are extremely busy, although yours will no doubt introduce himself at the first available opportunity. It will also be a while before your checked luggage arrives, so, if you haven't had lunch already, your initial order of business is usually the welcome-aboard buffet. Bring along the daily schedule to read more closely while you eat.

While making your way to the Lido buffet, no doubt you'll notice bar waiters offering trays of colorful tropical drinks, often in souvenir glasses that you can keep. Beware: they are not complimentary! If you choose one, you'll be asked to sign for it. Again, as with the photos, you're under no obligation to purchase; however, the glasses are fun souvenirs.

Do your plans for the cruise include booking shore excursions and indulging in spa treatments and salon services? The most popular tours sometimes sell out, spas can be busy during sea days, and salons are particularly busy before formal nights, so your next stops should be the Shore Excursion Desk to book tours and the spa and salon to make appointments.

Dining room seating arrangements are another matter for consideration. Some people like to check the main dining room to determine the location of their table. If it's not to your liking—or if you requested a large table and find yourself assigned to a small one—you'll want to see the headwaiter. He'll be stationed in a lounge with his charts handy to make changes; the daily schedule will indicate where and when to meet with him. If you plan to dine in the ship's specialty restaurants, you'll want to make those reservations as soon as possible.

Do not get in the habit of referring to your cruise ship as a boat. A boat is often carried on a ship, and if you're in a boat, you're either headed for

Common Nautical Terms

BEFORE ACQUAINTING YOURSELF WITH YOUR SHIP, you should add a few nautical terms to your vocabulary:

Berth. Sleeping space on a ship (literally refers to your bed).

Bow. The pointy end of the ship, also known as forward. Yes, it's also the front of the ship.

Bridge. The navigational control center (where the captain drives the ship).

Bulkhead. A wall or upright partition separating a ship's compartments.

Cabin. Your accommodation on a ship (used interchangeably with *stateroom*).

Course. Measured in degrees, the direction in which a ship is headed.

Debark. To leave a ship (also known as disembarkation).

Draft. The depth of water needed to float a ship; the measurement from a ship's waterline to the lowest point of its keel.

Embark. To go on board a ship.

Galley. The ship's kitchen.

Gangway. The stairway or ramp used to access the ship from the dock.

Hatch. An opening or door on a ship, either vertical or horizontal.

Head. A bathroom aboard a ship.

Helm. The apparatus for steering a ship.

Muster. To assemble the passengers and/ or crew on a ship.

Pitch. Plunging in a longitudinal direction; the up-and-down motion of a ship. (A major cause of seasickness.)

Port. The left side of the ship when you're facing forward.

Promenade. Usually outside, a deck that fully or partially encircles the ship, popular for walking and jogging.

Roll. Side-to-side movement of the ship. (Another seasickness culprit.)

Stabilizers. Operated by gyroscopes, these retractable finlike devices below the waterline extend from a ship's hull to reduce roll and provide stability. (Your best friend if you're prone to motion sickness.)

Stern. The rounded end of the ship, also called aft. It's the back end.

Starboard. The right side of the ship when you're facing forward.

Tender. A boat carried on a ship that's used to take passengers ashore when it's not possible to tie up at a dock.

Thrusters. Fanlike propulsion devices under the waterline that move a ship sideways.

Wake. The ripples left on the water's surface by a moving ship.

a day ashore or your ship is sinking! Even more confusing to many passengers are the directional terms "port" and "starboard." An easy way to associate them is by remembering that "port" and "left" each contain four letters.

By late afternoon or early evening, luggage should arrive outside the cabin door, and you can unpack and settle into your cabin to prepare for dinner. Just in case your luggage does not arrive before dinner, as sometimes happens when you're dining at the early seating, it's a good idea to have toiletries and appropriate attire in your carry-on so you can freshen up and change. Dress codes are always casual on the first evening of cruises.

For the rest of the afternoon and into the night you may find other introductory activities scheduled, such as tours of the spa and fitness center, port and shopping talks, and casino gaming lessons. Of course, there will be the compulsory muster drill, either held prior to sailing or within the first 24 hours of every cruise. No matter what terminology is used to describe it—Muster Station, Lifeboat Drill, General Emergency Stations, Compulsory Coast Guard Drill—this exercise is mandatory and required by law.

The Lifeboat Drill

Unpleasant and unlikely as it may seem, emergencies do happen. That's why one of the first things you may notice in your stateroom are the bright orange personal flotation devices (PFD), or life jackets, prominently displayed on the beds. When you're checking your stateroom's features, take a moment to study the emergency card on the back of the door. The cards differ, ship by ship, but usually indicate "you are here"—the location of your cabin—and the direction you should go in case of an emergency. Your muster station will be indicated, usually by number or letter.

Cruise lines take the safety of their guests and vessels very seriously, so shortly before sailing an announcement will be made that the lifeboat drill begins when the alarm bells are sounded. Be prepared with your PFD in hand and proceed to your muster station. Carry the life jacket unless you are instructed to wear it, and be sure the ties don't trail on the floor; it's easy to get tripped up on them as you ascend or descend stairs. Crew members will be stationed at the stairwells on each deck to give directions. Procedures vary—on some cruise lines you'll muster in a public room to receive instructions and then continue to the lifeboat station; on others you'll immediately go to the muster station on an open deck.

In all cases, crew members will be on hand to check your stateroom number off their list and show you how to properly put on your PFD. You'll notice it has two important features: a light that is activated in water and a whistle. An officer assigned to your boat will instruct the group on the procedures to follow if it becomes necessary to actually lower and enter the lifeboats or jump into the water. Should you have the urge to blow the whistle attached to the PFD, restrain yourself—remember, you wouldn't be the first person to do so.

Stewards check the cabins to make sure that everyone attends the muster drill, so don't even think about hiding out and not participating. In an emergency situation, your survival could depend on it. Afterward, stow your life jackets back in the cabin and prepare for sail-away festivities on the pool deck.

The First Evening

A highlight of embarkation day is the first dinner in the main restaurant, where you'll meet your waitstaff and tablemates. Order whatever you like from the menu of appetizers, salads, soups, and entrées, but save room for dessert! Other than iced tea, coffee, hot tea, and tap water, beverages in the dining room are not complimentary on most mainstream and premium ships.

After dinner you'll find the entire ship alive with action. The casino, shops, and lounges will be open to greet guests and the cruise director usually introduces his staff at a Welcome Aboard show in the main theater (shows are scheduled to coordinate with dinner seatings).

Back in your cabin for the night, you'll find that the steward has straightened things up during your absence, filled the ice bucket, provided fresh linens in the bathroom, turned down the bed, left the next day's schedule of activities, and placed a chocolate on your pillow. On mainstream cruise ships you may even find a towel animal—a whimsical creature fashioned from towels—on the bed. Some stewards demonstrate a creative streak, leaving a different one every night.

TIPPING

You don't have to go overboard with extras, but one area not to skimp on is gratuities. Tipping aboard a cruise ship is possibly one of the most delicate—yet frequently debated—topics of conversation among cruise passengers. Whom should you tip? How much should you tip? What is customary and recommended? Should parents tip the full amount for children, or is just half adequate? Why do you have to tip at all?

Like their land-bound contemporaries, cruise-ship service personnel depend on gratuities for a major portion of their compensation. Educate yourself about gratuities by reading your cruise-line brochure, where suggested tipping levels are usually listed in the back with the rest of the fine print. Then read over the small booklet that comes with your cruise documents for up-to-the-minute information.

Before You Board

The whom-to-tip decision is easy. It's up to your discretion to tip anyone who provides a service you would like to recognize. This begins as early as your airport check-in. Porters carrying your bags in airports expect a tip, as do the agents at curbside check-in (even if they charge a fee). Depending on your city, $1 to $2 a bag will do. The same rule applies when you retrieve your suitcases at the baggage claim area at your destination; if you use the services of a porter or skycap, tip him for taking your bags to your bus or taxi. "Wait a minute!" you say, "I'm shelling out all these dollars and I haven't even reached the ship yet." Well, that's true. And one way to avoid tipping is to do everything yourself. It's perfectly acceptable to carry (or roll) your own luggage into and out of airports, but if you accept assistance, you should give a tip.

When transfers to and from your ship are a part of your Air & Sea program, gratuities are generally included for luggage handling. In that case, don't worry about the interim tipping. However, if you take a taxi to the pier and hand over your bags to a stevedore, be sure to tip him. He's the person responsible for getting your suitcases onto a pallet and on their way to the ship, but he's not a cruise-line employee. Stiff this guy, and hours later you may be filing a missing baggage report. Better, treat him with respect and pass along at least $5 with a handshake and big smile.

You're on board. Now what? Relax. With a couple of exceptions, which are addressed below, cash tips won't be expected until the last night of your cruise.

On Board Your Ship

Tipping Procedures

During your last day of cruising there will be a disembarkation talk, which is usually conducted by the cruise director. One member of each family

Recommended Gratuities by Cruise Line

EACH CRUISE LINE has a different tipping policy. Some allow you to add tips to your shipboard account, others expect you to dole out the dollars in cash on the last night of the cruise. Here are the suggested tipping amounts for each line covered in this book. Gratuity recommendations are often higher if you're staying in a suite with extra services, such as a butler. The ship profiles in Chapter 5 give you the details:

Carnival Cruise Line	$10 per person per day
Celebrity Cruises	$10.50 per person per day
Costa Cruises	$8.50 per person per day
Crystal Cruises	$11 per person per day
Cunard Line	$11–$13 per person per day
Disney Cruise Line	$32.50 per person for 3-night cruises, $43.75 per person for 4-night cruises, $76.25 per person for 7-night cruises
easyCruise	Tipping is up to your discretion.
Holland American Line	$10 per person per day
MSC Cruises	$8–$12 per person per day
Norwegian Cruise Line	$10 per person per day
Oceania Cruises	$11.50 per person per day
Princess Cruises	$10 per person per day
Regent Seven Seas Cruises	No tipping expected
Royal Caribbean International	$9.75 per person per day
Seabourn Cruises	No tipping expected
SeaDream Yacht Club	No tipping expected
Silversea Cruises	No tipping expected
Star Clippers	€8 per person per day
Windjammer Cruises	$60 per person per cruise
Windstar Cruises	$11 per person per day

is encouraged to attend and, in addition to customs and immigration procedures, tipping is discussed. (Don't worry if you miss the meeting, it will be replayed on television all day long.)

With the advent of alternative dining venues and options for open seating for dinner on contemporary ships, most cruise lines now either automatically add gratuities to passengers' onboard charge accounts or offer automatic tipping as an option, usually in the amount of $10 per passenger, per day (or, in the case of some lines such as Crystal and Oceania, the amounts may be a few dollars higher; in other cases, a bit lower). If that's your cruise line's policy and the amount suits you, then do nothing. However, you're certainly free to adjust the amounts up or down to more appropriate levels or ask that the charge be removed altogether if you prefer distributing cash gratuities. By the last day of your cruise you'll know whether the cruise line's recommendations are low, high, or right on target for the level of service rendered.

If your ship is one of those on which tips are still given in cash, small white tip envelopes will appear in your stateroom during the last day of the cruise, along with luggage tags and written disembarkation instructions. As a general rule of thumb, you can count on the following amounts falling within the tipping guidelines:

- Room Steward: $3.50 per day
- Dining Room Waiter: $3.50 per day
- Dining Room Asst. Waiter: $2 per day

Give the tip envelopes to your dining room waiter and assistant waiter on the last night of the cruise, at dinner. If you see your room steward in the hall, you can deliver the tip envelope personally, or you may leave it in the cabin when you go to dinner on the last night. When your accommodations include the services of a butler, you should also reward his service in a similar manner. Whatever you do, don't skip out on dinner in the dining room on the final night of your cruise just to avoid tipping. If you prefer to dine elsewhere that evening, by all means do so, but stop by the dining room to recognize the service of the waitstaff.

Those suggestions are per person, per day. For a seven-day cruise , count on gratuities of $63 to $70 per person. In addition, it may be suggested that you tip the headwaiter $5 per person per week. If he's rendered some special service (prepared table-side desserts) or if he's been particularly attentive and kept things moving, by all means give him a tip. If he only shows up that last evening with a smile and his hand out, you needn't feel obliged to tip him.

Some passengers claim that a cash tip offered to their cabin steward at the beginning of a cruise does wonders to produce exceptional service. Although I tried it once, I saw no difference in the level of attention I received.

Of course, some higher-end cruise lines suggest higher gratuity amounts per person, per day, such as Crystal, Cunard, and Oceania. There are also some truly no-tipping-allowed cruise lines, which include SeaDream, Seabourn, Silversea, and Regent Seven Seas Cruises. On these cruises, gratuities are considered prepaid. If you feel the service warrants recognition, ask at the Reception Desk if there's a crew appreciation fund to which you can contribute.

Naturally, it would be gauche to offer a tip to an officer or a member of the cruise line's professional staff. However, if an officer or someone on the cruise staff renders out-of-the-ordinary service or is especially helpful, a letter of praise to the cruise-line's home office can do wonders for that employee's career.

Finally, remember to have some dollar bills on hand when you disembark the ship. There will still be palms to cross in the cruise terminal and at the airport.

Tipping for Your Kids

Parents often argue the need to tip the entire recommended amount for their children, especially little ones. I wonder if the messes their children leave in the bathroom, cabin, and dining room are invisible to these parents. Not to mention that some tykes run their waiters ragged replacing plates of food that they don't like. Simply because children are smaller than adults doesn't mean they are less trouble to clean up after. Parents have already gotten a reduced (third or fourth passenger) fare for their children or, in some cases, free passage. Some cruise lines, such as Celebrity, suggest you tip the cabin steward half the recommended amount for children under 12 when they are the third or fourth person occupying the stateroom.

Automatic Gratuities

On virtually all ships, a 15% gratuity will automatically be added to your bar bills. That would include the fruity welcome drink you signed for when the ship pulled away from the dock as well as cappuccinos and lattes from the specialty coffee bar. If you use salon and spa services, a similar percentage might be added to the bill; if it isn't, then a 15% tip is expected.

The Exceptions

There are exceptions to every rule. These days there are two major exceptions to the no-extra-tipping rule on most cruise ships. The first exception is for room service. Except for bar items and soft drinks, there's no additional charge for what you order from room service; however, it's customary to tip the steward who delivers it and to tip in cash. In most cases, this will not be your regular steward. Depending on what you have ordered and whether it was delivered in a timely manner, $1 to $3 will suffice. If it's just juice and a pot of coffee, the lesser amount will do; a heavy tray with a full dinner would warrant the larger amount.

The second exception is in the à la carte restaurant. More common on modern cruise ships, these dining venues offer a change from the main dining room—often in a private, more intimate atmosphere, with a special menu and personal service. Although there's sometimes no extra charge for the meal, a one-time gratuity may be suggested. Your ship's daily schedule will contain instructions for making reservations and outline tipping protocol. You can usually add a tip to your bill or, if you prefer, offer it discreetly in cash to your main server.

PLACES YOU SHOULD KNOW

Every cruise ship has a distinct personality, whether it's a one-of-a-kind vessel or one of several identical ships built in a class, whose members are virtually indistinguishable from one another (with the possible exception of interior décor). Despite their differences, nearly all ships have certain common elements and other characteristics that set the cruise experience apart from other kinds of travel.

Reception Desk

Sometimes referred to as the Purser's Desk or Information Desk, this is the place to ask questions you might have as well as to take care of any

Past Passengers—an Exclusive Group

YOUR CRUISE IS OVER—pat yourself on the back. Your plans and preparation for an out-of-the-ordinary trip have paid off, and you'll now have lasting memories of a great vacation. Before you even have a chance to fill your scrapbook, the cruise line wants you to consider doing it all over again. And why not? You're a seasoned sailor, so take advantage of your experience. To entice you back on a future cruise, you may find you're automatically a member of an exclusive club—Latitudes (Norwegian Cruise Line), Mariner Society (Holland America Line), Captain's Circle (Princess Cruises), Castaway Club (Disney Cruise Line), Venetian Society (Silversea Cruises)—to name but a few. Members receive the cruise line's magazine for past passengers, exclusive offers, shipboard perks such as a repeaters' party hosted by the captain, and even the opportunity to sail on members-only cruises.

financial matters. The Reception Desk is centrally located in the lobby or atrium and is generally open 24 hours a day for passenger convenience. Should you misplace a personal item, check for it at the Reception Desk, which also functions as the ship's Lost & Found.

Shore Excursion Desk

Manned by a knowledgeable staff, the Shore Excursion Desk can offer not only the sale of ship-sponsored tours but may also be the place to learn more about ports of call and garner information to tour independently. Although staff members—and the focus of their positions—vary widely, the least you can expect are basic information and port maps. Happily, some shore excursion staff members possess a wealth of information and share it without reservation. On some ships the port lecturer may emphasize shopping, and the cruise lines' recommended merchants, with little to impart regarding sightseeing or the history and culture of ports.

Photo Shop

Caribbean cruises are a series of photo opportunities and ship's photographers are on hand to capture boarding, sail-away, port arrivals, and other highlights such as the Captain's Reception. On formal nights there are often several locations where you can have portraits taken in front of your choice of backdrops. Photographers seem to pop up everywhere and take far more pictures than you could ever want; however, they provide a unique remembrance, and there's no obligation to purchase the photos. Prices for the prints, which are put on display, range from $7 to $20, depending on size.

Film, batteries, single-use cameras, and related merchandise may be available in the photo shop. Some ship's photography staffers are capable of processing your film right on board as well as creating a photo CD or prints from digital media.

The Library

Cruise-ship libraries run the gamut from a few shelves of relatively uninspiring titles to huge rooms crammed with volumes of travel guides, classic novels, and the latest best sellers. As a rule, the smaller the ship, the more likely you are to find a well-stocked library. The space allotted to the library falls in proportion to the emphasis on glitzy stage shows, and on small ships the passengers are more likely to lean toward quiet diversions. On ships with sophisticated entertainment centers in staterooms, you may find videocassette or DVD movies as well as books in the library.

Internet Café–Business Center

Just because you're out to sea does not mean you have to be out of touch. Ship-to-shore telephone calls can cost $6 to $15 per *minute,* so it makes economic sense to use e-mail to remain in contact with your home or office. Most ships have at the least basic computer systems while some newer vessels offer more high-tech connectivity—even in-cabin high-speed hookups and wireless connections (Wi-Fi) for either your own laptop computer or one you can rent on board. Expect these services to cost between 35¢ and $1 per minute. However, on many ships you can purchase blocks of time or even unlimited access for the length of your cruise; in these cases, you pay more up front, but you'll save substantially on the per-minute connection charges.

There really is such a thing as a working vacation, and cruise ships are an ideal venue (a substantial portion of this book was written while I was at sea). Meeting rooms with audiovisual equipment are available for corporate functions on many ships. As with any group business function, these facilities should be reserved well in advance of sailing.

DINING ON BOARD

All food, all the time? Not quite, but it's possible to literally eat away the day and most of the night on a cruise. A popular cruise director's joke is "You came on as passengers, and you will be leaving as cargo." While it's meant in fun, it does contain a ring of truth. Food—tasty and plentiful—is available around the clock on most cruise ships, and the dining experience at sea has reached almost mythical proportions. Perhaps it has something to do with legendary midnight buffets, the absence of menu prices, or the vast selection and availability. Whatever the reason, there's a strong emphasis on food aboard cruise ships.

Nearly every cruise passenger can expect numerous opportunities to satisfy hunger pangs: coffee and Danish for early risers, Lido buffet breakfast, sit-down breakfast in the dining room, Lido buffet lunch, sit-down lunch in the dining room, mid-afternoon ice cream and snacks, afternoon tea, casual buffet dinner, formal dining room dinner, and a midnight buffet or canapés offered by waiters passing through public rooms. Whew! You may also find a pizzeria or a specialty coffee bar on your ship—increasingly popular favorites cropping up on ships old and new. Although pizza is complimentary, expect an additional charge for specialty coffees; cappuccino, espresso, and latte usually cost extra at the coffee bar and, possibly, in the dining room. There may also be a charge for fancy pastries and premium ice cream.

Every ship has at least one main restaurant and a Lido, or casual, buffet alternative, and specialty restaurants are an increasingly important option. Meals in the primary and buffet restaurants are included in the cruise fare, as are round-the-clock room service, midday tea and snacks, and late-night buffets. Most cruise lines levy a surcharge for dining in

Joe Farcus

The genius behind Carnival Cruise Line's bold and eclectic ship interiors is marine architect Joe Farcus. History, art, and culture all mingle in Farcus's fertile imagination, and the results are astounding: "entertainment architecture," as he calls it, that carries passengers to another time and place. Farcus views a cruise ship not as a floating hotel but as an experience. As he says, he creates spaces for passengers "to get away from normal life and recharge their batteries." He begins his designs with a central ideal and carries the theme throughout, never losing sight of what people like to do on their vacation. He tries to design spaces to appeal to a broad range of tastes. Do the passengers get it? Do they notice that the carpets draping the ceiling in *Carnival Glory's* Egyptian-themed casino bring to mind a caravan in the desert? While he's sure some people do look beyond the surface, Farcus is more concerned that they have fun in comfortable surroundings. After all, they are spending their valuable time, and his goal is to see them make the most of it.

4

alternative restaurants, and the extra charge may or may not include a gratuity (if not, you should leave one), although there generally is no additional charge on upscale ships.

Cruise lines make every possible attempt to ensure dining satisfaction. If you have special dietary considerations, such as low-salt, kosher, or food allergies, be sure to indicate them well ahead of time, and check to be certain your needs are known by your waiter once on board. In addition to the usual menu items, spa, low-calorie, low-carbohydrate, or low-fat selections and vegetarian as well as children's menus, are usually available. Requests for dishes not featured on the menu can often be granted if you ask in advance.

Legend has it that a nouveau riche passenger's response to an invitation to dine with the captain during a round-the-world cruise was, "I didn't shell out all those bucks to eat with the help!" Although some cruise passengers decline invitations to dine at the captain's table, there are far more who covet such an experience. You'll know you have been included in that exclusive coterie when an embossed invitation arrives in your stateroom on the day of a formal dinner. RSVP as soon as possible; if you're unable to attend, someone else will be invited in your place.

The evening begins with cocktails, either in a reserved area of a public lounge or the captain's quarters, where the ship's social hostess greets you and makes introductions to the captain and other high-ranking officers. After getting acquainted, you're escorted to the captain's table and you take your place according to prearranged seating; place cards show the way. Then you just sit back and enjoy a sumptuous dinner with exquisite service and fine wines. A photographer will likely appear to preserve the memory, and the picture will be delivered to you the next day, perhaps with a copy of the menu or a note of thanks from your host.

Who is invited? Unfortunately, although there are hundreds of passengers on every cruise who would no doubt enjoy dining with him, there's just one captain. However, some factors can work in your favor when guest lists are drawn up. For instance, if you're a frequent repeater of the cruise line, the occupants of an expensive suite, or if you hail from the captain's hometown and speak his native language you may be considered, but you can't count on an invitation. Honeymooning couples are sometimes selected at random, as are couples celebrating a golden wedding anniversary. Attractive unattached female passengers often round out an uneven number of guests. Requests made by travel agents on behalf of their clients sometimes do the trick.

ENTERTAINMENT

It's hard to imagine, but in the early years of cruise travel, shipboard entertainment consisted of little more than poetry readings and recitals that exhibited the talents of fellow passengers. Those bygone days of sedate amusements in an intimate setting have been replaced by lavish showrooms where sequined and feathered showgirls strut their stuff on stage amid special effects unimagined in the past.

Seven-night Caribbean cruises usually include two original production shows—one often a Las Vegas–style extravaganza and the other a best-of-Broadway show featuring old and new favorites from the Great White Way.

Other shows highlight the talents of individual singers, dancers, magicians, comedians, and even acrobats. Don't be surprised if you're plucked from the audience to take the brunt of a comedian's jokes or act as the magician's temporary assistant. Sit in the front row if appearing onstage appeals to you.

Whether it's relegated to a late-afternoon interlude between bingo and dinner, or a featured evening highlight, a passenger talent show is often a don't-miss production. From pure camp to stylishly slick, what passes for talent is sometimes surprising but seldom boring. Stand-up comedy is generally discouraged. Passengers who want their performance skills to be considered should answer the call for auditions and plan to rehearse the show at least once.

Children are often invited to perform skits they learned during cruise camp, either in passenger talent productions or shows presented for parents and other family members. Not to be outdone, the ship's crew might stage a show featuring the music and culture of their homelands.

If you find the show lounge stage a bit intimidating and want to perform in a more intimate venue, look for karaoke. Singing along in a lively piano bar is another shipboard favorite for would-be crooners. Some passengers even take the place of the ship's pianist during breaks to demonstrate their skill.

Other lounges might feature easy-listening music, jazz, or combos for pre- and post-dinner social dancing. Later in the evening, lounges rock with the beat of the 1950s and '60s, and disco reigns into the late-night hours for the truly energetic.

Dance hosts often address the relative disparity between women and men on a cruise by dancing with unaccompanied female passengers on premium-to-upscale ships. In addition to dancing until the wee hours of the morning, hosts are often called upon to greet embarking passengers, give dance lessons, host singles parties and a table in the dining room, and participate in social games, such as bridge, trivia, shuffleboard, and even chess.

Enrichment programs have become a popular pastime at sea. It may come as a surprise that port lecturers on many large contemporary cruise ships offer more information on shore tours and shopping than real insight into the ports of call. If more cerebral presentations are important to you, consider a cruise on a line that features stimulating enrichment programs and seminars at sea. Speakers can include destination-oriented historians, popular authors, business leaders, distinguished government figures, radio or television personalities, and even movie stars.

For a hands-on learning experience, "edutainment" is a relatively new twist in shipboard pursuits. Pottery and needlework classes are a welcome addition to the old standby napkin-folding and scarf-tying demonstrations. If you never seem to find the time at home to master new computer software programs, delve into the fine points of digital photography, or take piano lessons; check for the availability of classes. A small fee is usually charged for courses or supplies, but some demonstrations are free.

CASINOS & GAMBLING

On embarkation day, a sure sign that your ship is in international waters is the opening of the casino. Long gone are the days of brandy, cigars, and shipboard poker in the gentlemen's smoking room. Although you may still find a lounge where brandy and cigars accompany conversation, decorous games of chance have been replaced by lavish casinos pulsating with activity on nearly every cruise ship plying the Caribbean. The most notable exceptions are the family-oriented ships of Disney Cruise Line, which shuns gaming in favor of more wholesome pastimes.

On ships that feature them, the rationale for locating casinos where most passengers must pass either through or alongside them is obvious—the unspoken allure of winning. Who can resist the siren song of coins clanging in slot machines or the urge to try one's luck at roulette? Even nongamblers occasionally succumb to the irresistible urge to give it a try. Although most passengers would not qualify for high-roller status in Las Vegas or Atlantic City, dealers often patiently assist first-time players. Novices can have a rewarding session in the casino by attending one of the gambling demonstrations held early on in the cruise where complimentary drinks are sometimes offered and door-prize drawings held.

In addition to slot machines in a variety of denominations, cruise-ship casinos might feature roulette, craps, and a variety of card games: Caribbean Stud, Let It Ride, Texas Hold 'Em, and blackjack to name a few. Cruise lines strive to provide fair and professional gambling entertainment and supply gaming guides that set out the rules of play and betting limits for each game. Slot machine and poker tournaments are sometimes scheduled as fast-paced diversions on sea days.

Drinking & Gambling Ages

MANY UNDERAGE PASSENGERS HAVE LEARNED to their chagrin that the rules that apply on land are also adhered to at sea. On most mainstream cruise ships you must be 21 to imbibe alcoholic beverages. There are exceptions—for instance, on cruises departing from countries where the legal drinking age is typically lower than 21. By and large, if you haven't achieved the magic age of 21, your shipboard charge card will be coded as booze-free, and bartenders won't risk their jobs to sell you alcohol.

Gambling is a bit looser, and 18-year-olds can try their luck on cruise lines such as Carnival, Celebrity, Holland America, Silversea, Norwegian, and Royal Caribbean; most other cruise lines adhere to the age-21 minimum. Casinos are trickier to patrol than bars, though, and minors who look "old enough" may get away with dropping a few coins in an out-of-the-way slot machine before being spotted on a hidden security camera. If you hit a big jackpot, you may have a lot of explaining to do to your parents.

Casino hours vary based on the itinerary or location of the ship. Most are required to close while in port; others may be able to offer 24-hour slot machines and simply close table games. Every casino has a cashier, and you may be able to charge a cash advance to your shipboard account. If you win big—congratulations!—be prepared to complete a W2G form for the Internal Revenue Service. The U.S. Federal Income Tax Act stipulates that all U.S. citizens and permanent residents are required to pay income tax on gambling winnings, even if they were made overseas.

Only you know if you can afford to lose your seed money. It's important to play responsibly or not at all. If slot machines and casino games are not your thing, you may find the other opportunities to place a bet more appealing. Bingo games and lotteries are amusements that pay off for some participants. Horse racing, with wooden horses that are moved around a track according to the roll of the dice (think board game), is another betting opportunity. Groups generally form a syndicate to buy a horse, name it, and even decorate it in syndicate colors. Betting can be fast, furious, and profitable as long as you choose a winner.

Not as popular as it once was, the ship's pool is a tradition that has nothing to do with swimming; rather, it's a game to estimate how far the ship has traveled in a day. The winner-takes-all pot goes to the player who makes the guess closest to the actual miles. If you think your hand-held GPS gizmo will give you an advantage, think again. Often the winner these days is chosen at random.

SHOPPING ON BOARD

You may consider it your duty to shop. Indeed, duty-free shopping is such a popular cruise-ship pastime that it's possibly second only to eating. Since shopping in many U.S. territories and Caribbean countries is duty-free, you'll find good prices on many goods in your ports of call. But you can shop right on the ship itself.

Shops on board your cruise ships will carry merchandise ranging from funky to fashionable. Expect reasonable prices on souvenirs and logo items as well as imported perfumes, cosmetics, jewelry, electronics, designer items, clothing, and toys. Additionally, liquor and tobacco products can often be purchased at a substantial savings. At the very least you will not have to pay sales tax and may find rare or difficult-to-find imported brands. Art auctions are another shopping opportunity on many cruise ships.

If you're planning to make any sizeable purchase in the Caribbean—whether in duty-free shops or at an art auction—do your homework. Check prices locally and online before you commit a large chunk of money on something that might not live up to its stated value. There's nothing worse than buyer's remorse when a cruise is over and the merchant is hundreds of miles away. Although cruise lines offer a value guarantee when purchases are made from certain recommended stores, going through a refund process can be a headache.

Whatever you do, don't fudge the value of your purchases when completing the U.S. Customs form before disembarkation. If you exceed your personal allowance in the ship's duty-free shop, the customs agents will know. It's a murky little secret that cruise lines notify them of big spenders before docking and, at the very least, agents will bust you for the duty and may even confiscate any items you fail to declare. Your poker face may have paid off in the casino, but do not depend on it to work with U.S. Customs agents. They have seen it all. For more specific information on customs regulations, see Customs & Duties *in* Disembarking, below.

HEALTH & FITNESS

The Spa

With all the usual pampering and service in luxurious surroundings, simply being on a cruise can be a stress-reducing experience. Add to that the menu of spa and salon services at your fingertips, and you have a recipe for total sensory pleasure.

Some spa offerings sound good enough to eat. A Milk & Honey Hydrotherapy Bath, Coconut Rub & Milk Ritual Wrap or Float, and a Javanese Honey Steam Wrap incorporating cinnamon, ginger, coffee, sea salt, and honey are just a few of the tempting items found on spa menus. Other treatments and services that might not sound quite as exotic are nonetheless therapeutic for the body and soul. Steiner Leisure is the largest spa and salon operator at sea (the company operates even Mandara and the Greenhouse spas aboard cruise ships), with facilities on more than 100 cruise ships worldwide.

In addition to facials, manicures, pedicures, massages, and sensual body treatments, other hallmarks of Steiner Leisure are salon services and products for hair and skin. Founded in 1901 by Henry Steiner of London, the single salon prospered when his son joined the business in 1926 and was granted a Royal Warrant as hairdresser to Her Majesty Queen Mary in 1937. A glittering list of royal clients followed, and in 1956 Steiner won its first cruise ship contract to operate the salon on board the *Andes* and ships of the Cunard Line. By the mid-1990s, Steiner Leisure began

Spa Tips

SPAS HAVE GROWN IN POPULARITY. Here are some useful things to keep in mind to help you enjoy your shipboard spa experience:

• Salon appointments for formal nights fill up quickly; book yours as soon as possible.

• Arrive on time or a few minutes early for appointments.

• Prior to your appointment, shower off any sunscreen lotions or oils.

• Towels, robes, and slippers are usually provided for your use, but you may wish to wear your own pool or shower flip-flops.

• Attend the spa orientation—you may win a door prize or be selected for a demonstration (such as a mini-facial).

• Watch for port day specials, packages of discounted spa services.

• Don't feel pressured to purchase any of the products used during your treatment; just say no if they're recommended and you don't want to buy them.

• Check your charge slip before adding a gratuity; most shipboard spas automatically add a tip (however, you may adjust the amount or remove it altogether).

• While spa and salon services are extras that sometimes come with a hefty price tag, you can still indulge yourself in the complimentary or low-cost facilities that are available on most ships. Saunas, steam rooms, therapy pools, and thermal chambers are relaxing alternatives to expensive body wraps and massages. Depending on the ship, some are free.

taking an active role in creating shipboard spas offering a wide variety of wellness therapies and beauty programs for women and men.

Spa services don't usually come cheap, though they are more or less equivalent to what you might pay in any resort spa. Expect to pay $115 for a one-hour Swedish massage ($175 to $210 for a hot stone or specialty massage), $100 to $130 for a facial, and $100 to $110 for an hour of reflexology (therapeutic foot massage). Salon services are also equivalent to what you'd pay in a big-city salon: $30 to $45 for hair styling, $25 to $30 for a manicure, and $40 to $50 for a pedicure. Recently, other kinds of treatments, including teeth whitening and acupuncture, have been on offer aboard some ships. You can brighten your smile for about $200 and manage your aching back for $155 to $175 per session.

The Fitness Center

Cruise vacations can be hazardous to your waistline if you're not careful. Eating "out" for all meals and sampling different cuisines tends to pile on unfamiliar calories. Maintaining a fitness regimen at sea is no problem with a wide assortment of exercise machines such as stationary bikes, treadmills, and stair steppers. As a bonus, shipboard fitness centers with floor-to-ceiling windows have some of the world's most inspiring sea views.

For guests who prefer a more social atmosphere as they burn off sinful chocolate desserts, there are fitness classes for all levels of ability. High-impact energetic aerobics are not for everyone, but any class that raises the heart rate can be toned down and tailored to individual capabilities. In addition, there are stretching classes to warm up for a light jog or brisk walk on deck, and even sit-for-fitness classes for mature passengers or those with delicate joints. Basic aerobics and group exercise classes are usually complimentary, but there's typically a charge of $10 for specialty classes, such as Pilates, Spinning, yoga, and kickboxing. Perhaps you're just starting a fitness program and require individualized attention. Ask about the services of fitness experts or personal trainers to get you off on the right foot. Their fee is usually around $75 per hour.

Watch your ship's daily bulletin for the times classes are scheduled and to determine if your cruise line has a bonus program for participation. Some cruise lines offer prizes—from sun visors and T-shirts to water bottles and tote bags—to passengers who take part in their fitness programs.

You don't have to return from your cruise with extra weight. Even if you don't want to take time out to hit the gym, you can walk on the ship's promenade deck or turn your back on the elevators and use the stairs—they're the ultimate step machines. And you can always control calories by requesting that any sauces be served on the side. Have no fear; it's actually possible to lose weight on a cruise and return home more buff than buffet.

Sports Activities & Programs

Shipboard sports facilities might include a court for basketball, volleyball, or tennis—or all three—a jogging track, or even an in-line skate track. Innovative and unexpected facilities, such as rock-climbing walls, surfing simulators, and bungee trampolines are challenges introduced at sea by Royal Caribbean International. For the less adventurous, more sedate pursuits include table tennis and shuffleboard.

Naturally you'll find at least one swimming pool and, possibly, several. Just be aware that cruise ship pools are usually on the small side, more appropriate for cooling off than doing laps, and that the majority contain filtered salt water. Princess Grand-class ships have challenging swim-against-the-current pools filled with fresh water for swimming enthusiasts.

Golf is a perennial seagoing favorite of players who want to log the Caribbean's most beautiful and challenging courses on their scorecards and take their games to the next level. Shipboard programs can include clinics, use of full-motion golf cages, and even individual instruction from resident pros using state-of-the-art computer analysis. Once ashore, escorted excursions include everything needed for a satisfying round of play, including equipment and tips from the pro, and the ability to schedule tee times at exclusive courses.

STAYING HEALTHY

The Medical Center

Accidents can happen to even the most careful people, and an unexpected illness can strike at any time. That's why almost every ship has a medical center staffed by a physician. Savvy travelers carry a first aid kit that should be adequate for minor scrapes and ailments. For more serious problems, the ship's doctor should be able to treat you as well as any general practitioner or clinic ashore. For really complicated medical conditions, such as a heart attack or appendicitis, the ship's medical team evacuates passengers to the nearest hospital ashore. While at sea, evacuation by helicopter can easily cost thousands of dollars. To cover those expenses, travel insurance is a must.

If you're examined by the ship's doctor, you'll be charged for your office visit. Depending on your illness or injury, fees can run from $75 to several hundred dollars. Any medicines prescribed are extra. Recently, an office visit and medications to treat my simple sinus infection cost me $135. A notable exception is if you're injured in some manner aboard ship or during a shore excursion arranged by the cruise line, in which case your treatment should be free. Unless you carry very comprehensive medical insurance coverage, you probably are not covered for treatment aboard a cruise ship, or in any foreign country for that matter. You'll be expected to pay for any treatment you require at the time you visit the medical center; you'll then file your own claim later. If your medical coverage is through Medicare, you certainly will not be covered outside the United States. It's worth noting once again that all ships of foreign registry are considered to be outside the United States by Medicare; however, this point is not explained clearly in Medicare's manual.

A ship's pharmacy is limited in scope, so it may or may not have what you need if you forget or lose the prescription medications that you regularly take. Just be aware that even if a drug you require is in stock, you should not expect the ship's doctor to dispense medication without examining you.

Common Ailments

Seasickness

Many first-time passengers are anxious about whether they'll be stricken by seasickness, but there's no way to tell until you actually sail. Those who are felled by it claim that only dying will relieve their discomfort. If you have a problem with motion sickness in automobiles and airplanes, you may be more prone to seasickness; however, if you get nauseated in a smallish sailboat, that doesn't necessarily mean you'll get seasick on a large cruise ship. Modern vessels are equipped with stabilizers that eliminate much of the motion responsible for seasickness. Unless your cruise includes the open sea and wind-whipped water, you may not even feel the ship's movement, particularly if your ship is a megaliner. For first-time passengers concerned with seasickness, a megaliner is precisely the ship of choice. They're very stable in the calm waters of the Caribbean.

Seasickness is a balance problem generally attributed to overactive nerve fibers in the inner ear. Your sensory perception gets out of sync as these nerve fibers attempt to compensate for the unfamiliar motion of the ship moving through water. This condition often disappears on its own in a few days, once you get your sea legs, but by that time you've seen far too much of the inside of your bathroom and are ready to bolt the ship at any cost. You need not suffer; there are a number of remedies avail-

CLOSE UP

Nonmedical Seasickness Remedies

NO ONE WANTS TO BE DRUGGED UP and drowsy when they should be enjoying a cruise. There are nearly as many remedies for seasickness as there are sufferers, but they aren't all medicinal. If you want to cure seasickness but avoid additional medication, you may wish to explore a few homeopathic and natural cures.

● **Bitters.** Have the bartender mix up a couple tablespoons of Angostura Bitters in a half glass of water or club soda. Do this right away, and you probably will not need the rest of these remedies.

● **Food.** You may not have an appetite, but you should try to eat something if you become seasick. The nausea associated with seasickness is magnified by an empty stomach. Crackers, bread sticks, or light broth may help. (Any woman who has lived through morning sickness knows the virtues of saltine crackers.) Crackers and apples are recommended for those who cannot keep liquids down—the apples replace vital bodily fluids.

● **Fresh Air.** If nothing else, fresh sea air smells good and is bound to improve your mood. Keeping an eye on the horizon can also help restore your sense of balance.

● **Ginger.** Ginger ale is a widely used home remedy for an upset stomach, and it cannot hurt if you can keep the liquid down. Ginger capsules and crystallized ginger, available in health food stores and supermarkets, are reportedly even more effective.

● **Lying Down.** Spending valuable cruise time in bed is not fun, but a horizontal position may alleviate some of your symptoms.

● **Ice.** A hospital trick to prevent vomiting is an ice bag held against the throat just beneath the chin. It really works.

● **Sea-Bands.** These wristbands work on the principle of acupressure. Each elastic Sea-Band has a round button on the inside; when positioned to press a particular point on the inside of the wrist, the nausea associated with seasickness disappears. Although they look rather tacky with cocktail dresses, they are effective little gems and can be found in many pharmacies, luggage stores, and even at some travel agencies. Many shipboard sundries shops also have them, but if the ship begins to rock and roll, they'll sell out in a heartbeat.

4

---

able to help align your gyros. Seasickness medications are usually available at no charge from the Medical Center or at the Purser's Desk.

Even hardy sailors who never get seasick have been known to avail themselves of medications on occasion. The most common drugs are Dramamine, Dramamine II, and Bonine. All of these are over-the-counter antihistamines that are available at most pharmacies. Antihistamines make most people drowsy, and Dramamine is almost certain to have that effect. Dramamine II and Bonine are nondrowsy formulas, but they still put some people to sleep for a few hours. Considering the alternative, that's not necessarily a bad side-effect. If you want to beat *mal de mer* before it has the chance to sneak up on you, it's better if you take one of these remedies two hours before sailing.

Worn behind the ear, the Transderm Scop patch is a remedy that dispenses a continuous metered dose of medication that's absorbed into the skin and enters the bloodstream. Apply the patch four hours before sailing, and it will continue to be effective for three days. You'll need a prescription from your physician for the patch and, while wearing it, you must be vigilant for possible side-effects that include blurred vision, dry mouth, and drowsiness. Unfortunately, you should neither drink nor drive as long as you are wearing the patch.

If you have a history of motion sickness, do not book an inside cabin. For the terminally seasick, it will begin to resemble a moveable coffin in short order.

Some insensitive people (usually spouses) will tell you seasickness is all in your head. In a way it is—it's that inner ear condition and a very real problem for many unfortunate passengers. There's no better vacation than a week or more at sea, so give these methods a try. If all else fails, the ship's physician can offer an injection that works like a miracle for most passengers.

Contagious Illnesses

When hundreds of cruise passengers report to the infirmary with similar symptoms that have nothing in common with the motion of the ocean, does that necessarily mean their ship has been attacked by a mysterious disease? Hardly, but you'd never know that from news reports about nasty cruise-ship diseases that attack unsuspecting vacationers. Let's face facts—travel by cruise ship often brings together large numbers of people from different regions of North America, as well as other parts of the world. There's no such thing as a cruise-ship disease. In confined quarters, certain respiratory and gastrointestinal diseases can quickly spread through person-to-person contact—just as they do in schools, nursing homes, hospitals, and day-care centers. In addition, when ships dock and passengers go ashore, they might be at risk for diseases prevalent in the ports of call they visit. It's even quite possible that some passengers who become ill during a cruise were infected prior to boarding and were actually sick before their symptoms became apparent.

Because respiratory and gastrointestinal diseases can percolate a few days before their symptoms strike with a vengeance, it's highly likely that some passengers bring their bugs on board with them. Although most people are unaware that they have contracted an illness before embarking, others know they are sick but go aboard anyway, not acknowledging their illness for fear of being denied boarding. They might not seek treatment once on board due to the threat of being confined to their staterooms. These alpha passengers can be the beginning of a shipboard epidemic. Two of the most prevalent diseases that spread through cruise-ship populations are influenza and noroviruses.

INFLUENZA In recent studies, influenza infection among travelers has been found to be quite common and may rank right up there with hepatitis A as one of the most common vaccine-preventable diseases infecting travelers. Seasonal epidemics of influenza generally occur during the winter months on an annual or near-annual basis and can cause disease in all age groups. Although rates of infection are highest among infants, children, and adolescents, rates of serious illness and death are highest among people over 65 years of age and people of any age who have medical conditions that place them at high risk for complications from influenza (e.g., people with chronic cardiopulmonary disease).

When you're traveling, the risk for exposure to influenza depends on the time of year and destination. In the tropics, influenza can occur throughout the year; in the temperate regions of the Southern Hemisphere most activity occurs from April through September. In temperate climates, travelers can also be exposed to influenza in summer, especially when on board a cruise ship with travelers from areas of the world where influenza viruses are circulating. Influenza might be, at best, an inconvenience; however, it can lead to complications, including life-threatening pneumonia, especially among people at increased risk for complications. Annual influenza vaccination is the primary method for preventing influenza and its complications.

NOROVIRUSES Noroviruses are a group of related viruses that cause acute gastroenteritis in humans. Norovirus was recently approved as the official genus name for the group of viruses provisionally described as Norwalk-like viruses or NLV. The incubation period for norovirus-associated gastroenteritis is usually between 24 and 48 hours, but cases can occur within 12 hours of exposure. Symptoms of norovirus infection include vomiting, diarrhea with abdominal cramps, and nausea. Low-grade fever occasionally occurs, and vomiting is more common in children. Dehydration is the most common complication, especially among the young and elderly, and may require medical attention. Symptoms generally last 24 to 60 hours. Recovery is usually complete, and there's no evidence of any serious long-term effect.

Highly contagious noroviruses are transmitted primarily through the fecal-oral route, either by consumption of contaminated food or water or by direct person-to-person spread. During outbreaks of norovirus gastroenteritis, several modes of transmission have been documented. Passengers may be infected initially by contaminated food in a restaurant; they may pass it along to other people directly.

Norovirus is often termed the cruise-ship virus, even though the vast majority—some 60% to 80% of outbreaks—occur on land. According to Princess Cruises, "Statistics have shown that the chance of contracting norovirus on land is 1 in 12; and 1 in 4,000 on a cruise ship." However, the virus is harder to miss on a cruise ship since all the sick passengers and crew members are treated by the same physician, who is required to prepare a special report for the CDC if an outbreak affects 2% or more of the passengers or crew. The CDC may launch an investigation if 3% of passengers or crew members become ill. As of this writing, most ship infirmaries treat passengers who exhibit Norovirus symptoms at no charge.

How to Avoid Illness

Outbreaks of diseases on cruise ships initially led to the creation of the CDC-operated Vessel Sanitation Program (VSP) in the 1970s. Since that time, twice a year, unannounced inspections have been conducted on all cruise ships calling at or sailing from U.S. ports on foreign itineraries. Inspectors use a checklist to score ships on a 100-point system. A score of 86 or higher is satisfactory. Anything below 86 is not satisfactory, or failing. While VSP standards are not mandated by law, the cruise lines voluntarily comply.

In addition to water and food, which are inspected for cleanliness, VSP inspectors scrutinize whirlpool spas, hot tubs, children's facilities, and other areas of cruise ships. Inspection scores are made public and compiled on what VSP calls a green sheet, making it easy to compare all ships. The green sheet for each ship is available on the Internet at the CDC's Web site. Current scores can be faxed, or an inspection report on an individual ship can even be mailed to you if you request it.

No one wants to get sick during a highly anticipated vacation. The best way to avoid illness is to wash your hands thoroughly and often. A waterless, sanitizing hand cleaner is also recommended by the CDC in conjunction with hand washing or when water is unavailable (hand sanitizers are effective and come in travel-size bottles). You'll see dispensers for hand sanitizer on most ships. Some passengers even go so far as to pack a small aerosol can of a germ-killing spray or packaged disinfectant wipes to treat their stateroom furnishings, bedding, and bathrooms before using them.

If all fails and you get sick, seek medical treatment and observe quarantine procedures as long as you are symptomatic so you don't infect other passengers.

🖪 Ship Inspection Reports **Vessel Sanitation Program** ☎ 800/232–4636 ⊕ www.cdc.gov/nceh/vsp.

> **WORD OF MOUTH**
>
> My husband and I discovered we are closet pleasure hounds. He got a massage with warm oils and heated stones and used the Alpha Capsule which involved music, aromatherapy, warmth, and vibration. He said the massage was heavenly, and the Alpha Capsule was pleasant, but over-rated. As for me, I got a deluxe manicure and pedicure, a facial, and a deep conditioning scalp treatment complete with scalp and shoulder massage. I have never felt so relaxed and pampered. It added to an all ready fabulous vacation experience.   –Sherry L.

DAYS AT SEA

All days at sea are not identical, but they do follow a certain rhythm. Most ships schedule activities, port talks, lectures, games, and fitness programs on a nonstop basis. This is the time to personalize your cruise experience—you can participate in any or all scheduled activities or do nothing more strenuous than lift an umbrella drink while reading a book poolside.

No doubt you noticed the shops and casino were closed when you boarded your ship. Local regulations preclude them from opening while in port; however, once at sea, all the ship's facilities are available during set hours.

Let your daily schedule be your guide. You may want to pack a highlighter to mark the events you don't want to miss. If you want to be active, you can take exercise and fitness classes. If you want to revive and beautify yourself, consider spa and salon services (but remember the caveat about booking these in advance, because the spa is busy on sea days). If you like to gamble, there will usually be casino gaming tournaments and bingo games. Lectures might include port or shopping talks, health and

Safety at Sea

SAFETY BEGINS WITH YOU, the passenger. Once settled into your cabin, locate your life vests and review the posted emergency instructions. Make sure the vests are in good condition and learn to secure them properly. Make certain the ship's purser knows if you have a physical infirmity that may hamper a speedy exit from your cabin so that in an emergency he or she can quickly dispatch a crew member to assist you. If you're traveling with children, be sure that child-size life jackets are placed in your cabin.

Within 24 hours of embarkation, you'll be asked to attend a mandatory lifeboat drill. Do so and listen carefully. If you're unsure about how to use your vest, now is the time to ask. Only in the most extreme circumstances will you need to abandon ship—but it has happened. The time you spend learning the procedure may serve you well in a mishap.

In actuality, the greatest danger facing cruise-ship passengers is fire. All cruise lines must meet international standards for fire safety, which require sprinkler systems, smoke detectors, and other safety features. Fires on cruise ships are not common, but they do happen, and these rules have made ships much safer. You can do you part by *not* using an iron in your cabin and taking care to properly extinguish smoking materials. Never throw a lit cigarette overboard—it could be blown back into an opening in the ship and start a fire.

fitness talks, and lifestyle or language classes. Nonstop activities may include bridge lessons and tournaments, pool games, Ping-Pong or shuffleboard, art auctions, dance classes, computer lessons, horse racing (a shipboard classic), or even wine tastings and culinary demonstrations. Most activities are complimentary, but some (wine tasting, for example) may carry a fee. In addition, the library and card room are available for quiet pursuits, as are many of the ship's lounges.

The swimming pool is one of the most popular spots on board during sunny sea days. Towels are provided, but you shouldn't use them to save deck chairs. A lively band usually plays poolside, and the pool bar is a great spot to meet and greet new acquaintances. Even if you're not a sun worshipper, you can enjoy the festivities from a shaded chair.

Breakfast and lunch during sea days are casual and often adhere to open seating in the dining room (meaning you can go at any time during specified hours). Shorts are acceptable in the restaurants but bathing suits are not. If you don't want to change from swimming attire, it's usually not a problem if you slip on shoes and a cover-up before heading for the Lido buffet. Some ships also have a grill near the pool where sunbathers can grab a quick bite without sacrificing any tanning time.

Sea days, particularly if they're the second and next-to-the last days of the cruise, are usually capped by formal evenings. During the first formal night, the captain hosts a reception for all passengers. Upon arrival, you're greeted by the ship's hostess, who introduces you to the master of the vessel (another photo opportunity). Complimentary beverages and hors d'oeuvres are usually served, and the captain takes the stage to introduce his officers and staff.

PORT CALLS

Port calls add an allure to cruise-ship travel that cannot be duplicated by any other type of vacation experience. In a given seven-day cruise, you'll usually have the opportunity to visit at least four unique destinations. Each morning you wake up in a new place, and each afternoon you steam off to the next stop. What you do ashore depends entirely on your interests and comfort level when confronted by a new environment and culture.

> **CAUTION**
>
> The ship's daily program should list the name and telephone number of the port agent. If you have a problem ashore, you can call on the port agent for assistance. Always carry that information with you when going ashore.

After the captain deftly inches your vessel alongside the pier, the gangway appears and everyone is anxious to proceed ashore. If your ship doesn't actually dock, then you'll board tenders for the trip from ship to shore.

But there's always a delay until the announcement that the ship has cleared and you can leave. What's that all about? Simply, before anyone can leave the ship, local immigration officials must approve—or clear—the passengers to go ashore. Procedures vary, depending on the port of call, but generally the identity and nationality of all passengers are verified. This can be accomplished by examining the manifest (often the case in non-U.S. Caribbean ports), or port officials may check individual passports. When ships enter, or reenter, U.S. ports (including Puerto Rico and the U.S. Virgin Islands), all passengers are required to report to Immigration for clearance, even if they do not plan to go ashore.

Shore Excursions

Cruise lines offer shore excursions that appeal to a wide variety of tastes: sightseeing, hiking, biking, sailing, swimming, kayaking, snorkeling, and a host of other activities. These excursions are tried and tested and, as a rule, provide a good experience for the money. If you prefer to do your own touring, you're naturally free to book a private guide or taxi, rent a vehicle, or use public transportation, and delve into whatever interests you. A cautionary rule of thumb is that it's often better to take a ship's tour if you want to explore an area some distance from where the ship is berthed. In case of any delay, your ship will wait for you if you've booked a ship-sponsored excursion. On the other hand, if you're on your own . . . well, you're on your own, and the ship will depart without you if you haven't returned by the announced departure time. Give yourself plenty of time to be back at the ship (not on the dock waiting for a tender) at least a half-hour before it's scheduled to sail.

To make the most of your hours ashore, research your options ahead of time. Guidebooks are an excellent resource, as are Internet sites devoted to travel—particularly the official tourism sites developed by the countries you're visiting. Friends and fellow passengers who have been there and done that can offer valuable insights into your ports of call.

Dressing to Leave

ON THE LAST NIGHT OF YOUR CRUISE, don't shrug off the reminder to set aside clothing to wear ashore before you place your luggage outside your stateroom door. I laughed it off as a corny cruise director's joke. It isn't. On one cruise, a friend accompanying us awoke just in time to report to Immigration that final morning and couldn't find his trousers. Where were they? Oops. Being efficient, he had tucked them into his suitcase the night before! Fortunately, his wife was able to retrieve them, but not before the mandatory 7 AM inspection. Wearing a longish golf shirt and navy blue boxers, he reported as instructed and hoped no one would notice that his shorts weren't a bathing suit. Red-faced, he took a lot of good-natured ribbing during a leisurely breakfast.

4

With the majority of passengers ashore while the vessel is in port, the number of activities on most cruise ships is somewhat curtailed, but programs do not cease entirely. There are still exercise classes, the spa and fitness center remain open, and games and movies are sometimes planned. You can also enjoy the pools in near solitude.

The two activities you won't be able to take part in are gambling and shopping. Customs regulations dictate that both casino and shops close. Also, check your daily schedule for meal times and locations, as they may vary on port days.

DISEMBARKING

All cruises come to an end eventually, and it hardly seems fair that you have to leave when it feels as if your vacation has just begun. The debarkation process actually begins the day before you arrive at your ship's home port. During that day your cabin steward delivers special luggage tags to your stateroom, along with customs forms and instructions.

No matter where you live, keep in mind while packing for home that you need to set aside clothing to wear the next morning when you leave the ship. Many people dress in whatever casual outfits they wear for the final dinner on board, or they change into travel clothes after dinner. Be sure to put your passport or other proof of citizenship, airline tickets, and medications in hand luggage.

After packing, remove all the old tags, except for your personal identification, from your suitcases. Then attach the new debarkation tags (they are color- or number-coded according to post-cruise transportation plans and flight schedules). Follow the instructions provided, and place the luggage outside your stateroom door for pickup during the hours indicated.

A statement itemizing your shipboard charges is delivered before you arise on the morning of debarkation. Plan to get up early enough to check it over for accuracy, finish packing your personal belongings, and vacate your stateroom by the appointed hour. Any discrepancies in your account should be taken care of before leaving the ship, usually at the Purser's Desk.

Room service is not available on most ships on debarkation day; however, breakfast is served in the main restaurant as well as the buffet. After breakfast, there's not much to do but wait comfortably in a lounge or on deck for your tag color or number to be called. Norwegian Cruise Line makes this process more pleasant by allowing passengers to remain in their cabins until it's time to leave the ship. Debarkation procedures can sometimes be drawn out by passengers who are unprepared. This is no time to abandon your patience or sense of humor.

Remember that all passengers must meet with Customs and Immigration officials before debarkation, either on the ship or in the terminal. Procedures vary and are outlined in your instructions. In some ports, passengers must meet with the officials at a specified hour (usually very early) in an onboard lounge; in other ports, customs forms are collected in the terminal and passports and identification papers are examined there as well.

Once in the terminal, you'll find the luggage is sorted by color or number. Locate yours and, if desired, flag down a porter for assistance. Then, either proceed to your prearranged transportation, get in the taxi line, or retrieve your vehicle from the parking lot. Your cruise is complete and you're officially a veteran sailor!

One way to lessen the pain of leaving your ship is to book another cruise while you are on board. Cruise lines make that a seamless process by having cruise counselors on hand who can arrange future sailings for passengers; some even offer incentives to lure you back with lower than usual deposits or onboard credits for your next cruise. The booking can even be transferred to the travel agent of your choosing if that's what you wish.

Customs & Duties

You're always allowed to bring goods of a certain value back home without having to pay any duty or import tax. But there's a limit on the amount of tobacco and liquor you can bring back duty-free, and some countries have separate limits for perfumes; for exact figures, check with your customs department. The values of so-called "duty-free" goods are included in these amounts. When you shop abroad, save all your receipts, as customs inspectors may ask to see them as well as the items you purchased. If the total value of your goods is more than the duty-free limit, you'll have to pay a tax (most often a flat percentage) on the value of everything beyond that limit.

U.S. Customs

ALLOWANCES Individuals entering the United States from the Caribbean are allowed to bring in $800 worth of duty-free goods for your personal use ($1,600 from the U.S. Virgin Islands), including 1 liter of alcohol (2 liters if one was produced in the Caribbean and 5 liters from the USVI), two cartons of cigarettes and 100 non-Cuban cigars. Antiques and original artwork are also duty-free. Remember that any liquids, such as alcohol or perfume, that you buy on your cruise—or anytime before you pass through airport security—will have to be packed into your checked luggage before you board your flight home.

It's Different at Sea

THE POSEIDON ADVENTURE probably wasn't the most comforting movie my husband could have viewed the night before embarking on our first cruise. The film stars an ocean liner that goes bottom-up after being swamped by a monster wave, sending the cast scurrying to reach the keel in an upside-down attempt to be rescued. As we ascended the gangway of SS *Norway* the following morning, my husband grinned wickedly and hummed "There's Got to Be a Morning After."

We encountered no severe weather, no massive wave action, no rocking or swaying that we could even feel. It was almost disappointing to be on a cruise liner and not experience any adventure. Unfortunately, that isn't always the case, as we have subsequently learned. Water is a powerful force, and weather conditions exist that can cause a ship to bob and stagger through thundering waves. The worst are rogue waves that appear out of the depths and smash into ships without warning. Such waves are not uncommon; however, it's rare for a cruise ship to encounter one. Most storms are mildly irritating at best, and their importance only increases in dimension if the weather doesn't clear quickly enough for seasick passengers.

The Cruise Lines International Association (CLIA), whose mission is to promote all measures that foster a safe, secure, and healthy cruise-ship environment, reminds us: "According to the U.S. Coast Guard, cruising is one of the safest modes of transportation. [Since the early 1980s], an estimated 100 million passengers safely enjoyed a cruise vacation. During this period only one passenger death due to a marine incident has been reported on any CLIA member cruise vessel operating from a U.S. port. Cruise ships are built to the highest structural stability standards, as set by the International Maritime Organization (IMO)."

Had *Norwegian Dawn* passengers known how well their ship was constructed, they might have been less anxious when a 70-foot wall of water smacked into the ship in April 2005. The rogue wave reached as high as Deck 10, and windows were broken in two cabins. As frightful as the situation was, only four people received minor injuries, and 62 staterooms were waterlogged (the ship has more than 1,100 cabins). That alone says a lot for the reliability of not only *Norwegian Dawn*, but for all cruise ships at sea that must meet IMO regulations for safety and seaworthiness. CLIA agrees the incident was "an excellent example of the high level of structural integrity found on today's cruise ships."

No one at Norwegian Cruise Line could have foreseen how prophetic one of their past marketing campaigns would become. A 1997 brochure suggested, "Out here, the laws of the land do not apply . . . it's different out here." Passengers should never lose sight of one important difference between a cruise and a resort vacation—a cruise ship is not a hotel. Ships move, and the action of the ocean is as unpredictable as the weather.

SENDING PACKAGES HOME   Although you probably won't want to spend much of your precious shore time looking for a post office, you can send packages home duty-free, with a limit of one parcel per addressee per day (except alcohol or to-bacco products or perfume worth more than $5). You can mail up to $200 worth of goods for personal use; label the package "personal use" and attach a list of the contents and their retail value. If the package contains your used personal belongings, mark it "personal goods returned" to avoid paying duty on your laundry. You may also send up to $100 worth of goods as a gift ($200 from the U.S. Virgin Islands); mark the package "unsolicited gift." Items you mailed do not affect your duty-free allowance on your return.

NONCITIZENS Non-U.S. citizens who are returning home within hours of docking may be exempt from all U.S. Customs duties. Everything you bring into the United States must leave with you when you return home, though. When you reach your own country, you'll have to pay duties there.

🔃 **U.S. Customs and Border Protection** ✉ For inquiries and complaints, 1300 Pennsylvania Ave. NW, Washington, DC 20229 ⊕ www.cbp.gov ☎ 877/227-5511 or 202/354-1000.

PROBLEM SOLVING

There's no such thing as a perfect vacation, so it's probably unrealistic to expect that you'll have a flawless cruise. Various things—small and large—can go wrong. The best piece of advice I can give you is to remember that no one—not your travel agent, not the cruise line, not the crew, and most of all not you—wants problems to occur. Every officer and staff member on your ship has the same goal: to meet passenger expectations and provide a safe and satisfying voyage. The more you know as a passenger, the better you'll be prepared for what happens—and what doesn't—during the cruise.

Some problems are simply matters of miscommunication, some of misguided expectations. Following are a few situations that you may encounter. With expanded knowledge and an understanding of how things work, they do not have to ruin your cruise.

Your Luggage Is Missing

As a rule, the larger the ship, the longer it takes for luggage to be delivered on embarkation day. Being one of the first passengers to board the ship doesn't necessarily mean you'll be the first to get your luggage. Sometimes it will all appear early in the day; however, it may materialize piece by piece during the course of the afternoon or perhaps even later on in the evening. On the largest ships, it's not at all uncommon that you would not receive your checked luggage until after the ship has sailed; this doesn't mean your luggage is not on the ship.

Prompted by a tardy suitcase (and my fretting), my husband once went off on a search-and-recover mission and found it on the opposite side of the ship. You may also find your suitcase delayed by the transposed number scenario. Your cabin number might be 651, but the crew member delivering luggage read the tag as 615 and left it outside the wrong stateroom door. That's an easy mistake to correct, and often the passenger in the other cabin will simply wheel it to your door or inform the steward who will deliver it as soon as possible—remember, they are busy.

If your luggage hasn't arrived by 8 PM and if it appears that all the luggage has been distributed (i.e., you don't see any more in the passageways or being delivered), check with the Reception Desk. Sometimes the room tag affixed to a suitcase has been damaged. In that case, your bag would be set aside until the name on the luggage identification tag could be matched with the manifest. This illustrates why it's very important to have your name on the outside *and* inside of your suitcases.

Cruise Manners

OF COURSE IT'S YOUR VACATION, but do you really want it to be at the expense of others? When it comes to our fellow passengers, it sometimes seems that way. The thing most passengers have in common is the desire to have a satisfying vacation—to explore new places, to relax and revitalize, to spend time with family and friends, or to just have some carefree fun. Unfortunately, it seems that some passengers get a bit carried away with the carefree part and forget to pack one of life's little treasures, the good manners practiced at home in their everyday lives:

• **Adhere to the dress code.** The ship's daily program will indicate the appropriate attire for every evening of the cruise, generally beginning at 6 PM. It's inconsiderate to ignore the guidelines and do as you please. Sitting next to someone wearing sweaty exercise clothing in the show lounge or casino is nothing short of unpleasant.

• **Do not hog the lounge chairs.** Every morning an invisible cadre of passengers pile towels and personal belongings on chaise longues by the pool to save them for later. This is extremely selfish behavior. If you're not using a lounger, it should be available for others.

• **Do not save seats.** Go ahead and set aside a seat for a spouse or traveling companion who is joining you, but do not be thoughtless and try to save entire rows of seats in the show lounge or complete tables in the casual dining area. Again, make room for others.

• **Control your children.** For their safety—and the safety of others—children shouldn't be allowed to roam freely around the ship, run around the swimming pool, splash water on other passengers, cavort in the hot tubs, or play in the elevators. Be mindful of areas indicated for adults only, and do not allow your children to intrude in those spaces. Some parents are in total denial when it comes to the unruly actions of their children (the disruptive kids can't be theirs).

• **Be a considerate smoker.** Those who smoke should only light up their cigarettes, cigars, and pipes in areas clearly approved for that purpose and should never throw lighted cigarettes overboard.

• **Do not jog before daybreak.** It should be obvious that if there are cabins located below the deck where jogging is permitted, then passengers are probably still asleep in them before the sun comes up. Only run on deck during the hours indicated in the daily program.

• **Be mindful of others in the spa and gym.** Wear appropriate work-out attire and wipe down the equipment when you are finished using it. Take your turn in a reasonable amount of time, especially when others are waiting.

• **Turn down the sound.** Portable electronics are wonderful gadgets, but not everyone has the same musical taste as you. In public areas, music players should be used with headphones. When using two-way radios and cell phones, it's seldom necessary to shout.

• **Await your turn.** Events and activities are scheduled in a certain way for a purpose, including the orderly filling of shore tenders and the disembarkation procedure at the end of the cruise. Do not be in such a hurry that you compromise the safety of others.

• **Do not complain while you wait.** No one cares to listen to grumbling and whining. It's a vacation, so lighten up and go with the flow. Instead of complaining, try to strike up a conversation with someone in line.

• **Listen and follow instructions.** This is never more important than during the muster drill! Listening cuts down the need to ask questions and can ensure your safety in case of an emergency.

Don't forget the three Cs at sea—Consideration, Courtesy, and Civility—are your guideposts. And don't forget to bring along a pleasant attitude, your sunniest smile, and good manners.

In the extreme, luggage has been known to be loaded on the wrong ship or accidentally left behind in the cruise terminal. This very rarely happens, but when it does, the purser's staff will do whatever they can to have misdirected suitcases delivered to the ship in the next port of call. In the meantime, they may offer assistance in the form of a shipboard credit so you can purchase clothing and other personal items in the ship's boutiques.

You Need to Switch Staterooms

Congratulations, if you received a last-minute complimentary upgrade or were able to purchase an upgrade to better accommodations at the pier. After you board the ship and inspect your superior digs, tell your steward about the change and request that he take care of getting your luggage to the right stateroom. It's a good idea to be proactive as well, so take the time to stop by your original cabin. You might find your luggage there already, as well as anything that was delivered for you (rented tuxedo, bon voyage gifts, messages, etc.) If the steward is available, tell him your new cabin number. Then, be patient because stewards are very busy on embarkation day.

What if there's something really wrong with your accommodations? Perhaps the air-conditioning doesn't work or there's a major plumbing problem that can't be fixed after repeated attempts. You may be fortunate enough to be moved to a similar cabin, but when ships sail full there often isn't one available. If you're offered a less-expensive category—for instance, your stateroom is outside, but all that is open is an inside— you should expect compensation for the downgrade. The purser may be able to apply a credit for the difference to your shipboard account or advise you that the cruise line will issue a partial refund after the cruise. Permission must be granted by the company's headquarters, so be patient. And get any promise for compensation in writing.

Don't count on moving if you simply don't like your cabin, though. You may notice a small sign on the Reception Desk informing all passengers that the ship is full and change requests cannot be granted. Whether every cabin is occupied or not (the ship may be full to maximum capacity standards), after sailing, the ship's staff is loath to make changes for any reason other than those above.

Your Dining Arrangements Are Unsatisfactory

When you booked your cruise, you requested early seating, but once on board you discover a late dinner-seating assignment (or vice versa). Perhaps you requested a romantic table for two, but find that you're assigned to a table that seats eight. Despite what anyone tells you, cruise lines make no guarantees up front—after all, the dining rooms have only so much space. However, they do want to please all their passengers. They recognize that dining is a highlight of the overall cruise experience, so they make it relatively painless to correct any glitches. The maître d' will be available on embarkation day at a time and place specified in the ship's bulletin to iron out any problems. You may be asked to dine at your assigned table that first night until a more acceptable arrangement can be worked out, at which time you'll be informed of your new table-seating assignment.

Even if you get the seating time and table size you prefer, you could encounter another problem. Sometimes you just don't hit it off with your assigned dining partners, or you meet other people you'd like to spend more time with. Go to the maître d' as soon as possible—no later than the morning of your first full day on board—to make your request for a change. Be patient. He will do his best to accommodate all requests but often changes aren't made on the spot.

You Miss a Port of Call

Sometimes weather conditions or mechanical problems cause a cruise ship to

bypass a particular port of call. If you read the Contract of Carriage on your ticket, you'll see that cruise lines reserve the right to change the itinerary for just cause. They don't make itinerary alterations on a whim. Don't take it personally—they're not trying to ruin your vacation plans. In this case, there's not much you can do.

If you booked a shore excursion on board, your account will automatically be credited for the cancelled tour. Be sure to check your balance for accuracy, though. If you've prebooked your own tour with an independent shore operator and you've paid in advance, the situation may be a bit trickier. Whether you receive a refund depends on the tour company with which you're dealing. Make sure you understand their policy for refunds in the case of a missed port call before finalizing your plans. If you reserved a rental car, the same caveat applies; make sure you understand the car-rental company's cancellation policy.

You Don't Know What's Going On

A problem with communication might more accurately be termed lack of communication. In the event of an unusual situation or emergency, the officers and crew of your vessel are usually more concerned with problem solving than keeping passengers informed. In these situations, it helps to be patient rather than insisting that you are being kept in the dark. The captain and his officers will give you the information you need as soon as they can do so.

A case in point is my experience on the maiden voyage of a brand-new ship. Mel and I noticed while dressing for dinner that our cabin seemed to be getting warm, and it soon became apparent that the entire ship's interior was growing hotter as the evening progressed. Plus, the ship was dead in the water. We were soon informed that an electrical panel had failed and that engineers had shut down the air-conditioning and stopped the ship while making repairs. We appreciated not being left in the dark—a real possibility considering the electrical problem. However, before the captain's announcement over the public address system, the Reception Desk was literally overwhelmed with concerned (and irate) passengers. If you're truly frightened by a situation you don't understand, check with reception.

Effective Complaining

Minor quibbles can be brought to the attention of your waiter (your soup is cold), cabin steward (you need extra pillows), or the Purser's Desk (there's a mysterious charge on your account). For slightly weightier matters, the headwaiter or chief housekeeper should be able to work things out—your dinner partners have atrocious eating habits and you want to switch tables, or your cabin steward isn't cleaning your room satisfactorily. However, for big problems, go to the top. See the hotel director immediately when a situation occurs that you feel needs to be addressed. His assistance will most assuredly be needed if a pipe breaks and floods your accommodations. The most important thing to remember is that you should deal with problems on the ship when they occur; there's not much that can be done after the cruise is over.

If you have a major problem, you'll usually get more satisfaction if you tell the hotel director what you want in terms of compensation, but it's important to be reasonable. If your cabin is flooded, you should expect to be moved and you should expect to have sodden clothing cleaned at no cost to you, and if any of your belongings are ruined, you should expect them to be replaced; you should not expect a refund of your entire fare.

Klaus Lugmaier, long-time Norwegian Cruise Lines hotel director, confides that the most common passenger gripes are bad weather, delays caused by Immigration clearances, and long check-in lines. Possibly his most unusual request was an incident when a passenger wanted to leave the ship during a day at sea and commanded him to order a helicopter. Obviously, there are some requests that cannot be granted under any circumstances.

Keep your travel agent in the loop if something major goes wrong and you need post-cruise assistance. Travel agents have the inside track on solving problems by using channels not available to their clients. Getting better service after your cruise (as well as before it) is just one reason why it's better to use a travel agent.

Comment Cards

Every passenger gets a comment card to complete. Assess your experience honestly, and take the time to make any suggestions you have for improvements. Those comments are taken very seriously. Also, praise crew members by name if you've received particularly good service from them. They could receive a promotion as a result.

Cruise Lines &
Cruise Ships

WORD OF MOUTH

"I like all the noises that precede the sail way. But you have to be in the right places to hear them on large ships. It might take several cruises to hear them all. If you're on an outside deck, you can hear an increase in funnel clatter as the engines at rest are brought back on line, and you can see the exhaust blacken with unburned fuel until the cylinder temperature is right. Soon after that, you hear the boarding doors banging shut or the noise of the gangway being withdrawn. You can hear the squeaks and scrapes of the winches bringing in the lines. Then you hear the horn. If you're directly above the thrusters, you can feel them through your feet or chair as they come to life to dance her away from the pier."

—Steven S.

Seated in an airplane after a week of enjoying an exceptionally nice cruise, I overheard the couple behind me discussing their "dreadful" cruise vacation. What a surprise when they mentioned the ship's name. It was the one I'd just spent a glorious week on. I never missed a meal; they hated the food. My cabin was comfortable and cheery, if not large; their identical accommodations resembled a "cave." In cruising, one size definitely does not fit all. What's appealing to one passenger may be unacceptable to another. Ultimately, most cruise complaints arise from passengers whose expectations were not met. The couple I eavesdropped on were on the wrong ship for them.

Make no mistake about it, cruise ships have distinct personalities. Windstar's sails and lack of formality define their relaxed appeal, while an ethereal sense of peace and tranquillity permeates the more formal Crystal ships. Even those ships belonging to the same class and nearly indistinguishable from one another have certain traits that make them stand out. The most notable examples are vessels in the Carnival fleet, which are built in classes. Although the layouts of the ships in the same class vary little, each has its own, distinctive theme—on Conquest-class ships you might find yourself amid a celebration of color (*Carnival Glory*) or unabashed heroics (*Carnival Valor*).

Cruise ships may appear to be floating resorts, but you can't check out and go someplace else if you don't like your ship. Whichever one you choose will be your home for seven days or more in most cases. The ship will determine the type of accommodations you'll have, what kind of food you'll eat, what style of entertainment you'll see, and even the destinations you'll visit. If you don't enjoy your ship, you probably won't enjoy your cruise.

That is why the most important choice you'll make when booking a cruise is the combined selection of cruise line and cruise ship. Cruise lines set the tone for their fleets, which is why we have classified lines loosely as Mainstream, Premium, and Luxury, plus unique sailing ships. Not all cruise lines in those categories are alike, although they will share many basic similarities. The cruise industry is relatively fluid, meaning that new features introduced on one ship may not be found on all the ships owned by the same cruise line. For instance, you'll find ice-skating rinks only on the biggest Royal Caribbean ships. However, most cruise lines attempt to standardize the overall experience throughout their fleets (for example, there is a rock-climbing wall on *every* Royal Caribbean ship).

Just as trends and fashions evolve over time, cruise lines embrace the ebb and flow of change. To keep up with today's diverse lifestyles, some cruise lines strive to include something that will appeal to everyone on their ships. Others focus on narrower, more traditional elements. Today's passengers have higher expectations, and they sail on ships that are far superior to their predecessors. Happily, they often do so at a much lower comparable fare than in the past.

So, which ship is best? To be honest and direct: only you can determine which ship is best *for you*. You won't find ratings by Fodor's—either quality stars or value scores. Why? Think of those people seated behind me on the airplane. They assuredly would rate their experience differently than I did. Ratings are personal and heavily weighted to the reviewer's opinion. What we've tried to do in these cruise-line and cruise-ship profiles is to give you the telling details that help distinguish one cruise line and cruise ship from another. Rather than inundate you with facts and bury you with opinions, we've tried to be brief and to the point. Travel guides should be empowering, not overwhelming. Use these profiles as a guide, but also ask your friends for their opinions, use a good travel agent who knows the intimate details of the ships he or she sells, and, perhaps most important, trust your own instincts. Your responsibility is to select not only the right cruise line, but the right ship for you, and no one knows your expectations better than you do yourself. It's your precious time and money that are at stake. No matter how knowledgeable your travel agent is, how sincere your friends are, or how clearly any expert lays the cards on the table, you're the only one who really knows what you like. A short wait for a table at dinner might not bother you because you would prefer a casual atmosphere with open seating; however, some people want the security of a set time at an assigned table, where they're served by a waiter who gets to know their preferences. You know what you're willing to trade in order to get what you want most.

RATE YOUR CRUISE SHIP

One way to narrow down your choices is to rate the cruise ships that interest you the most and see which come out on top. Gather cruise-line brochures and take a look at the ship profiles that follow in this chapter. Then rank the ships you wish to compare by making a side-by-side list of each ship's features, assigning each one a ranking, such as:

4 = Gotta have it!

3 = Not essential, but good to have

2 = Can take it or leave it

1 = Don't care; just not important to me

You can create your own list of desired features, which can be as long and specific as you feel it needs to be. It might look something like this:

- Itinerary
- Home port
- Ship size
- Dining options
- Dinner seatings
- Dress code
- Cabin amenities
- Entertainment options
- Activities
- Enrichment programs

- Recreation facilities
- Fitness center
- Spa
- Children's facilities/programs

The cruise-line profiles that follow offer a general idea of what you can expect in terms of the overall experience, quality, and service; individual cruise-ship reviews identify features that apply to particular ships, or classes of ships. You'll want to compare the features of several cruise lines and ships to determine which ones come closest to matching your needs. Then narrow them down further to a few that appeal most to you.

Service is one important characteristic that is difficult to grade. The composition of staff and crew members on any particular ship can change from week to week as employees complete their contracts and are replaced by others returning from their vacations. To get an idea of what level of service you might anticipate, you can use the cruise-industry concept of passenger-to-crew ratio. Basically, it illustrates how many passengers each crew member must serve and, in theory, the lower the number, the higher the service level. Cruise-industry standard is about 2.5 to 1. Luxury lines may have 1 to 1 ratios or better (a few ships have more crew members than passengers). To compute the passenger-to-crew ratios of ships you're considering, simply divide the number of passengers (based on double occupancy) by the number of crew members. You'll find these figures in the ship statistics for each cruise ship.

The overall price you pay for your cruise is always a consideration. Don't think of the bottom line in terms of the fare alone: there are shipboard charges to factor in as well. The ultimate cost isn't computed only in dollars spent; it's in what you get for your money. The real bottom line is value. Many cruise passengers don't mind spending a bit more to get the vacation they really want.

TYPES OF CRUISE LINES

Mainstream Cruise Lines

These are contemporary cruise lines with big, big ships that have all the bells and whistles. More passengers sail on mainstream ships than any others, and mainstream cruises account for the mass appeal of cruise vacations.

The biggest player in the cruise industry is Carnival Cruise Lines. With the most ships and lavish—some would say extraordinary—interiors chockfull of grand public spaces and sports facilities, these ships offer a great deal of choice within the Carnival fleet. Nipping at their heels are Royal Caribbean and Norwegian Cruise Line, whose ships are also big and crammed with features, but neither line is quite as bold as Carnival. Costa Cruises and Disney Cruise Line don't have as many ships in their fleets, but their mainstream appeal lies in different areas. Can't go to Europe? Let Costa deliver a bit of Italy to you. Plan to bring the family? The Disney ships are universally loved by children of all ages.

New for 2008

CARIBBEAN-BOUND SHIPS scheduled for launch in 2008 fall into two categories—some are new vessels that are, essentially, identical to previously introduced ship classes (Royal Caribbean's *Independence of the Seas*, a Freedom-class sister ship) or brand new ship designs (Cunard Line's *Queen Victoria*). Rule of thumb in the cruise industry is "big is better" when building new ships, which explains why Royal Caribbean will eclipse its own biggest vessels with a 220,000-ton behemoth in 2009. However, in a retro move, Princess Cruises and Celebrity's new deluxe cruise line, Azamara Cruises, added a trio of smaller 30,277-ton ships to their fleets in 2007—*Royal Princess*, *Azamara Journey*, and *Azamara Quest*, all relatively new ships that originally sailed for the now-defunct Renaissance Cruises.

Avid cruisers love a brand-new ship, whether it's a unique design or the clone of an earlier one, and cruise lines like to surprise their passengers with innovative features. That explains in part why some of the following new-ship details are still somewhat sketchy.

Carnival Splendor
While *Carnival Splendor* is a larger version of the Conquest-class vessels at 112,000 tons and able to accommodate 3,006 passengers, it will incorporate some unique features for the Carnival line. The most notable is a retractable dome over the mid-ship pool, the first in the fleet. It will also have the largest spa aboard any Carnival vessel, the line's first thalassotherapy pool, and the largest Camp Carnival facilities, above which there will be a water play area featuring "Water Wars," the popular water balloon attraction.

Celebrity Solstice
Celebrity's first post-Panamax vessel—at 118,000 tons—the *Celebrity Solstice* will be a 2,850-passenger vessel measuring 1,033 feet in length and 121 feet in width; it will have larger standard staterooms, 90% of which will be outside, with 85% of those featuring balconies, and an exceptional range of guest-inspired services and amenities. Look for all the trademark elements of the Millennium-class ships—and a few surprises as well. Two sister ships will follow: *Celebrity Equinox* in 2009 and *Celebrity Eclipse* in 2010.

Queen Victoria
The 90,000-ton *Queen Victoria*, entering service late in 2007, promises a dramatic three-tier Grand Lobby with a magnificent staircase and artwork that will offer the first glimpse of her lavish onboard atmosphere to her 2,014 passengers upon embarkation. Elaborate chandeliers adorn the double-height ceiling of the Queens Room and enhance its grandeur; a circular staircase connects the two levels of the mahogany-paneled library; and in the airy and relaxing Winter Garden, a glass roof even opens to admit warm sea breezes. An impressive 86% of staterooms are outside, and 71% will have balconies.

Eurodam
To be delivered in summer 2008, *Eurodam* marks Holland America Line's next class of vessels and, at 86,000 tons, the largest ever constructed for the line. The 2,044-passenger Signature-class ship features 86% outside staterooms, of which 67% have balconies; Signature of Excellence premium amenities will be in all cabins. Additions include the Explorer's Lounge Bar, a new specialty restaurant offering Italian food; a new atrium bar area; an enhanced and reconfigured show lounge with theater-style seating; a pan-Asian restaurant and lounge surrounded by panoramic views; and a new photographic and imaging center. Not to be overlooked are traditional Holland America Line Signature of Excellence features, including the Culinary Arts Center, Explorations Café, and Pinnacle Grill. The line has an option to build a second Signature-class vessel, which would be delivered in spring 2010.

5

Once aboard, you can discover why the mainstream cruise lines are so popular. The furnishings and fittings vary, but all generate their own type of excitement. There's nothing like this in Kansas (or Indiana, Ohio, or Arizona). Glittering and glamorous decor in public areas is the norm. Though it's a bit over-the-top sometimes, the setting is still comfortable and inviting. Accommodations are available in a wide range of sizes and price ranges, from inside cabins with no windows for bargain-basement prices to some of the largest suites at sea that cost a king's ransom.

What you do on a mainstream cruise ship is up to you. Activities are scheduled all day and into the evening. Every evening, the professional entertainment staff goes into high gear, and you can either watch production shows and cabaret or participate in karaoke and passenger games. Try a few hands of blackjack in the casino, even if you're not a gambler (except on Disney ships, which have no casinos).

Lounging in the sun is seemingly the most popular daytime pursuit during Caribbean cruises, but there will be a full-service spa and salon for the pampered set and a fitness center for gym rats. Options ashore are fairly standard—large mainstream ships sail to many of the same Caribbean ports and offer similar, if not exactly the same, excursions.

Food on mainstream ships may be lacking in the gourmet department, but the choices will be vast. You can find something to eat almost 24/7, either in traditional shipboard dining rooms, a casual Lido buffet, or alternative dining restaurants. Norwegian Cruise Line (NCL) and Disney Cruise Line put innovative spins on mainstream ships; NCL offers casual, open-seating dining, while Disney has a unique alternating restaurant concept.

Everyone sets sail to have a good time, and the atmosphere on board is exhilarating, even overwhelming to some people. You're sure to find passengers who share your interests among the couples, singles, and families on these popular ships.

Premium Cruise Lines

Ships in premium fleets have a lot in common with those in mainstream lines. They're just a little more: there's a more refined atmosphere, more gracious surroundings, more attentive service. There are still things like pool games, although not quite the high jinks typical of mainstream ships.

Premium ships are among some of the newest afloat, from medium to very large in size. Holland America Line, Princess Cruises (of *Love Boat* fame), and Celebrity Cruises are among the best-known lines, and they have the largest vessels and fleets. Relative newcomers are Oceania Cruises, Azamara Cruises (the new subsidiary of Celebrity), and MSC Cruises with small, yet growing, fleets. Accommodations usually are a step up in comfort and have refrigerators and other amenities that make them pleasant havens.

Activities tend to be more lifestyle-oriented; computer classes, foreign language lessons, and enrichment programs are more prevalent. Dress codes range from country-club casual at all times to more traditional, usually with two formal nights on a one-week cruise. The overall mix of passengers may be a bit older, but many families sail during summer and peak school vacation periods, so most of the ships have facilities for children, and some premium ships are among the most family-friendly afloat. An exception is Oceania Cruises, which has no children's programs at all.

The social and entertainment staffs on premium vessels are no less busy keeping passengers happy. Although some activities sound similar to those on mainstream ships, including pool games and bingo, everything tends to be a bit more sedate. Afternoon music at the pool might be a jazz quartet instead of a reggae band. Production shows are just as lavish on the larger premium ships; cabaret acts fill in on their off nights and are the norm on smaller ships.

Spas and salons are elaborate, and fitness buffs won't be disappointed by the gym facilities. The itineraries, ports of call, and excursions aren't very different from those on mainstream cruises, but premium cruise lines frequently schedule lengthier cruises to more far-flung destinations.

Premium ships can't boast about true gourmet dining, but they do ramp up the quality and presentation of their food. Celebrity Cruises is highly regarded in this segment for imaginative menus and upscale alternative restaurants. Attentive service shines with more polish and professionalism.

With a few exceptions (notably Princess Cruises' *Caribbean Princess*), ships categorized as premium don't spend the entire year in the Caribbean. From about April or May through October, they reposition to Europe, Alaska, Bermuda, and even Asia. Nevertheless, while in the sunny Caribbean, they aren't your grandparents' cruise lines. Although it may not last as long into the night, the camaraderie that develops naturally at sea is still there.

Luxury Cruise Lines

Step aboard and enter the exclusive realm of foie gras and caviar on ships that run the gamut from megayachts for only a hundred or so guests to one of the largest ships ever built. The deluxe and ultraplush ships that belong to luxury fleets are as good as it gets at sea. You can expect to be welcomed as a valued guest and treated to all the courtesies you would expect at any five-star resort.

At the top end of the top lines, you won't be bothered with signing drink receipts—all beverages (alcoholic or not) are included on the ships of Silversea Cruises, Regent Seven Seas Cruises, Seabourn Cruise Line, and SeaDream Yacht Club. Crystal Cruises serves complimentary soft drinks and bottled water. Cunard Line and Windstar Cruises aren't as inclusive, but have other attributes that nudge them into the luxury category. Most important, all luxury ships provide a level of personal service and courtesy that is unmatched. It's unlikely you'll get more than a few steps from the buffet line before a server relieves you of your plate and shows you to a seat.

With the exception of Cunard, Crystal, and Windstar, luxury ships have all-suite accommodations. Most of these upscale cabins have an ocean view or a private balcony and enough space to throw an intimate predinner cocktail party. These are very social ships, and most are small enough that passengers mix easily. They are also quite formal; guests really like to dress up in their finest. Only Windstar and SeaDream are casual chic.

Dining is the main event of the evening on most luxury ships. Meals are served during a single open seating (exceptions are Cunard and Crystal), and full dinners from the restaurant menu can be served in your stateroom (served course-by-course, of course). On the highest of the high-end ships, wine is poured freely during the meals, and no one is rushed to finish dessert and coffee. Main courses are cooked to order, and the food on some lines approaches the level of that in a fine restaurant in any city.

Classical concerts, lectures on the economy, and scaled-back production shows or cabaret are likely diversions. Passengers tend to entertain themselves and need no more stimulation than interesting conversation to have a pleasant time.

No one will hit you with a volleyball at the pool, but you may have to schedule a tee time to use popular golf simulators. Even on the smallest ships, the libraries are stocked with a wide variety of books, and movies are available to watch in the privacy of your stateroom. A call to room service can bring fresh, hot popcorn to your suite. Luxury ships tend to be adult-oriented; only Cunard and Crystal have dedicated facilities for children.

Elegant and serene, luxury ships are stylish without being stuffy. The well-to-do, sophisticated travelers they attract are collectors of destinations. These ships sail to the Caribbean only part-time, usually during the winter season; otherwise, they are sailing less-charted waters around the world.

Sailing Ships

Sun, sky, sea, and sails. Just add a brisk wind, and you have a perfect combination. The two tall-ship fleets that sail in the Caribbean are truly maritime magic. One of the most magnificent sights at sea is a tall ship under full sail. But the similarity of the two lines stops there.

Star Clippers are super-deluxe sailing vessels that only look as though they've been around for years. In reality, they are modern sailing ships with many of the same comforts and amenities associated with traditional cruise ships.

The Windjammer fleet couldn't be more different. The line's ships date from the early- to mid-20th century and have been reconfigured for cruises that are the most laid-back and casual affairs at sea.

As a rule, passengers who choose tall-ship cruises either love the sea and the activities associated with sailing or envision themselves as pirates exploring the Caribbean in a way that most cruise passengers never experience. What they must have in common is an ability to entertain themselves and a thirst for out-of-the-ordinary experiences. Sailing ships simply don't have room for casinos, elaborate show lounges, or fixed schedules of daily activities. The most exciting event of the day might be a competition to see which group can raise the sail the fastest.

Sailing ships also don't have meals around the clock; room service is limited or nonexistent. Don't look for ice carvings or an elaborate nightly midnight buffet.

Accommodations may be on the plain side, but cabins will be functional and have basic amenities, including a private bath. Luckily, you don't need a lot of closet space on a cruise that requires no formal clothing. On a Windjammer cruise, you don't even need shoes unless you go ashore.

Sailing ships go to very different ports, including the Grenadines, Mustique, the British Virgin Islands, Grenada, and St. Vincent. For the right passengers, they are the only way to see the Caribbean.

ABOUT THESE REVIEWS

For each cruise line described, ships that regularly sail in the Caribbean are grouped by class or similar configuration. Keep in mind that not all ships are deployed in the Caribbean year-round; some head for Alaska and Europe during summer months. Some ships owned by the cruise lines listed do not include regularly scheduled Caribbean cruises on their published itineraries as of this writing. For a complete listing of the ships and the itineraries they are scheduled to follow in the 2008 cruising season, see the chart ⇨ Ships by Itinerary & Home port *in* Chapter 1.

Because cruise ships can float off to far-flung (and not always tropical) regions, many are designed with an eye to less than perfect weather. For that reason, you're likely to find indoor swimming pools featured on their deck plans. Except in rare cases, such as NCL's *Norwegian Dawn,* these are usually dual-purpose pools that can be covered when necessary by a sliding roof or magrodome to create an indoor swimming environment. Our reviews indicate the total number of swimming pools found on each ship, with such permanently and/or temporarily covered pools included in the total and also noted as "# indoors" in parentheses.

When ships belong to the same class—or are basically similar—they're listed together in the subhead under the name of the class; the year each was introduced is also given in the same order in the statistics section. Capacity figures are based on double occupancy, but when maximum capacity numbers are available (the number of passengers a ship holds when all possible berths are filled), those are listed in parentheses. Many larger ships have three- and four-berth cabins that can substantially increase the total number of passengers on board when all berths are booked.

Unlike other cruise guides, we describe not only the features but also list the cabin dimensions for each accommodation category available on the ships reviewed. Dimensions should be considered approximate and used for comparison purposes since they sometimes vary depending on the actual location of the cabin. For instance, while staterooms are largely prefabricated and consistent in size and configuration, those at the front of some ships may be oddly curved to conform to the shape of the bow.

Demand is high, and cruise ships are sailing at full capacity these days, so someone is satisfied by every ship. When you're armed with all the right information, we're sure you'll be able to find one that not only fits your style, but offers you the service and value you expect.

CARNIVAL CRUISE LINES

The world's largest cruise line originated the Fun Ship concept in 1972 with the relaunch of an aging ocean liner, which got stuck on a sandbar during its maiden voyage. In true entrepreneurial spirit, founder Ted Arison shrugged off an inauspicious

Lobby Bar on board *Fantasy*

beginning to introduce superliners only a decade later. Sporting red-white-and-blue flared funnels, which are easily recognized from afar, new ships are continuously added to the fleet and rarely deviate from a successful pattern. If you find something you like on one vessel, you're likely to find something similar on another.

CARNIVAL CRUISE LINES
3655 N.W. 87 Avenue
Miami, FL 33178-2428
305/599–2600 or
800/227–6482
www.carnival.com

Cruise Style: Mainstream

Even the decor is fun; each vessel features themed public rooms, ranging from ancient Egypt to futuristic motifs. More high-energy than cerebral, the entertainment consists of lavish Las Vegas–style revues presented in main show lounges by a company of singers and dancers. Other performers might include comedians, magicians, jugglers, acrobats, and even passengers taking part in the talent show or stepping up to the karaoke microphone. Live bands play a wide range of musical styles for dancing and listening in smaller lounges, and each ship has a disco.

Arrive early to get a seat for bingo and art auctions. Adult activities, particularly the competitive ones, tend to be silly and hilarious and play to full houses. Relaxing poolside can be difficult when Caribbean bands crank up the volume or the cruise director selects volunteers for pool games; fortunately, it's always in fun and mostly entertaining. There's generally a quieter, second pool to retreat to.

Carnival is so sure passengers will be satisfied with their cruise experience that they are the only cruise line to offer a "Vacation Guarantee." Just notify them before arriving at the first port of call if you're unhappy for any reason. Should you choose to disembark at the ship's first non-U.S. port, Carnival will refund the unused portion of your cruise fare and pay for your flight back to your embarkation port. It's a generous offer for which they get very few takers.

Food

Carnival ships have both flexible dining options and casual alternative restaurants. A staggered dining room schedule, which includes a selection of four set meal times on all but the Spirit-class ships (5:45 or 6:15 PM for early dining and 8 or 8:30 PM for late dining), means the ships' galleys serve fewer meals at any one time. The result is better service and higher-quality food preparation. Carnival's less harried restaurant staff deliver a more satisfying dining experience for passengers because they have fewer passengers to cook for and to serve at any given time.

Choices are numerous, and the addition of "George Blanc Signature Selections," created by the French master chef, have elevated Carnival's menus to an unexpected level. While the waiters still sing and dance, the good-to-excellent dining-room food appeals to American tastes and includes second helpings if you want. Upscale supper clubs on certain ships serve cuisine comparable to the best high-end steak houses and seafood restaurants ashore.

Carnival serves the best food of the mainstream cruise lines. In addition to the regular menu, vegetarian, low-calorie, low-carbohydrate, low-salt, and no-sugar selections are available. A children's menu includes such favorites as macaroni and cheese, chicken fingers, and peanut butter-and-jelly sandwiches. If you don't feel like dressing up for dinner, the Lido buffet serves full meals and excellent pizza.

Fitness & Recreation

Manned by staff members trained to keep passengers in ship-shape form, Carnival's trademark spas and fitness centers are some of the largest and best equipped at sea. Spas and salons are operated by Steiner, and treatments include a variety of massages, body wraps, and facials; the latest in hair and nail services are offered in the salons. Tooth-whitening is a recent addition to the roster. State-of-the-art cardiovascular and strength-training equipment, a jogging track, and basic exercise classes are available at no charge in the fitness centers. There's a fee for personal training, body composition analysis, and specialized classes such as yoga and Pilates.

Noteworthy

■ Make yourself at home in one of the most generous standard cabins afloat—185 square feet.

■ Every Carnival passenger enjoys the same service and attention, including nightly turndown service, room service, and 24-hour pizzerias.

■ Watch your weight with healthy selections that are low in calories, cholesterol, salt, and fat from the spa menu.

Top: *Carnival Victory* dining room
Bottom: *Carnival Legend* waterslide

5

CARNIVAL CRUISE LINES

Top: *Carnival Triumph* walking & jogging track
Middle: *Elation* at sea
Bottom: *Carnival Destiny* penthouse suite

Your Shipmates

Carnival's passengers are predominantly active Americans, mostly couples in their mid-30s to mid-50s. Many families enjoy Carnival cruises in the Caribbean year-round. Holidays and school vacation periods are very popular with families, and you'll see a lot of kids in summer.

Dress Code

Two formal nights are standard on seven-night cruises; one formal night is the norm on shorter sailings. Although men are encouraged to wear tuxedos, dark suits or sport coats and ties are more prevalent. All other evenings are casual, although jeans are discouraged in restaurants. All ships request that no shorts be worn in public areas after 6 PM, but that policy is often ignored.

Junior Cruisers

"Camp Carnival" earns high marks for keeping young cruisers busy and content. Run year-round by professionals, dedicated children's areas include great playrooms with separate splash pools. Toddlers from two to five years are treated to puppet shows, sponge painting, face painting, coloring, drawing, and crafts. As long as diapers and supplies are provided, toddlers do not have to be toilet trained to participate. Activities for ages six to eight include arts and crafts, pizza parties, computer time, T-shirt painting, a talent show, and fitness programs. Nine- to eleven-year-olds can play Ping-Pong, take dance lessons, play video games, and participate in swim parties, scavenger hunts, and sports. Teens 12 to 15 particularly appreciate social events, parties, contests, and sports. Every night they have access to the ships' discos from 9:30 until 10:45 PM, followed by late-night movies, karaoke, or pizza.

"Club O2" is geared toward teens from 15 to 17. Program directors play host at the spacious teen clubs, where kicking back is the order of the day between scheduled activities and non-alcoholic parties. The fleetwide "Y-Spa" program for older teens offers a high level of pampering. Staff members also accompany teens on shore excursions designed just for them.

Daytime group babysitting for infants two and under al-

CHOOSE CARNIVAL CRUISE LINES IF:

❶ You want an action-packed casino with a choice of table games and rows upon rows of clanging slot machines.

❷ You don't mind standing in line—these are big ships with a lot of passengers, and lines are not uncommon.

❸ You don't mind hearing announcements over the public-address system reminding you of what's next on the schedule.

lows parents the freedom to explore ports of call without the kids from port arrival until noon. Parents can also pursue leisurely adults-only evenings from 10 PM to 3 AM, when slumber party–style group babysitting is available for children from ages 4 months to 11 years. Babysitting fees are $6 an hour for one child and $4 an hour for each additional child in the same family.

Service

Service on Carnival ships is friendly but not polished. Stateroom attendants are not only recognized for their attention to cleanliness, but also for their expertise in creating towel animals—cute critters fashioned from bath towels that appear during nightly turndown service. They've become so popular that Carnival publishes an instruction book on how to create them yourself.

Tipping

A gratuity of $10 per passenger, per day is automatically added to passenger accounts, and gratuities are distributed to stewards and waitstaff. Passengers may adjust the amount based on the level of service experienced. All beverage tabs at bars get an automatic 15% addition.

Past Passengers

After sailing on one Carnival cruise, you'll receive a complimentary two-year subscription to *Currents*, the company magazine, and access to your past sailing history on the Carnival Web site. You are recognized on subsequent cruises with color-coded key cards—Gold (starting with second cruise) or Platinum (starting with your 10th cruise)—which alert the ship's staff to your status and serve as your entrée to the by-invitation-only repeat passengers' cocktail reception. You're also eligible for exclusive discounts on future cruises, not only on Carnival but on all the cruise lines owned by Carnival Corporation—including Holland America, Princess, Cunard, Costa, Seabourn, and Windstar.

In addition, Platinum members are eligible for "Concierge Club" benefits, including priority embarkation and debarkation, guaranteed dining assignments, supper club and spa reservations, logo items, and complimentary laundry service.

Good to Know

If you've never sailed on a Carnival ship, or haven't sailed on one in recent years, you may not understand how Carnival cruises have evolved. The shipboard atmosphere is still bright, noisy, and fun, but the beer-drinking contests and bawdy, anything-goes image are history. Unfortunately, much like Casual Friday has evolved from no tie in the office to jeans and a polo shirt, it isn't unusual to see Carnival passengers dressed very casually after dinner, even on formal nights. You may be surprised at how quickly some passengers can swap their black ties and gowns for T-shirts and shorts between the dining room and show lounge. The fun of a Carnival cruise can begin before you leave home if you log on to the Carnival Web site at www.carnivalconnections.com, where you will find planning tips, cruise reviews, and a message board.

5

CARNIVAL CRUISE LINES

DON'T CHOOSE CARNIVAL CRUISE LINES IF:

❶ You want an intimate, sedate atmosphere. Carnival's ships are big and bold.

❷ You want elaborate accommodations. Carnival suites are spacious but not as feature-filled as the term "suite" suggests.

❸ You're turned off by men in tank tops. Casual on these ships means casual indeed.

CONQUEST CLASS

Carnival Conquest, Glory,
Valor, Liberty, Freedom

	2002, 2003, 2004, 2005, 2007
	ENTERED SERVICE
	2,974 (3,700 max)
	PASSENGER CAPACITY
	1,160
	CREW MEMBERS
	1,487
	NUMBER OF CABINS
	110,000
	GROSS TONS
	952 feet
	LENGTH
	116 feet
	WIDTH

Public Areas & Facilities

Taking Fun Ships to new lengths and widths, Conquest-class ships are the largest in the Carnival fleet. They're basically larger and more feature-filled versions of earlier Destiny-class vessels. More space translates into additional decks, an upscale Supper Club, and even more bars and lounges; however, well-proportioned public areas belie the ships' massive size. You'll hardly notice that there's slightly less space per passenger after you take a thrilling trip down the spiral waterslide.

Public rooms flow forward and aft from stunning central atriums. Just off each ship's main boulevard is an array of specialty bars, dance lounges, discos, piano bars, and show lounges, plus seating areas along the indoor promenades. The promenade can get crowded between dinner seatings and show lounge performances, but with so many different places to spend time, you're sure to find one with plenty of room and an atmosphere to suit your taste.

WOW Factor

If the atrium doesn't grab your attention immediately, you're in too much of a hurry. Plan to sit down and soak up the details.

Top: *Carnival Glory* at sea
Bottom: Conquest-class balcony cabin

Restaurants

Two formal restaurants serve open-seating breakfast and lunch; dinner is served in four assigned seatings. The casual Lido buffet's food stations offer a variety of choices (including different daily regional cuisines). At night it is the Seaview Bistro for casual dinner. The ship also has a supper club, pizzeria, outdoor grills, a patisserie, a sushi bar, and 24-hour room service.

What Works & What Doesn't

No one got short-changed in the design of these ships. The teen clubs–discos and video arcades are huge and a huge improvement. With appealing spaces dedicated to them, teens tend to get into less mischief. For sybarites, the saunas and steam rooms in the spa have glass walls and ocean views.

A seat at the wine bar should be serene; instead, the volume from adjacent lounges creates the sensation of being surrounded by dueling musicians. Ultracomfortable massage loungers are strategically placed along the indoor promenade; unfortunately, you have to pay to get the effect.

Accommodations

Cabins: As on all Carnival ships, cabins are roomy and generally larger than industry standard. More than 60% have an ocean view and, of those, 60% have balconies. For those suites and ocean-view cabins that have them, private balconies outfitted with chairs and tables add additional living space; extended balconies are 50% larger than standard ones. Every cabin has adequate closet and drawer–shelf storage, as well as bathroom shelves. High thread-count linens and plush pillows and duvets are a luxurious touch in all accommodations. Suites have a whirlpool tub, VCR, and walk-in closet.

Decor: Light-wood cabinetry, pastel colors, mirrored accents, a small refrigerator, a personal safe, a hair dryer in the top vanity–desk drawer, and a sitting area with sofa, chair, and table are typical Conquest-class amenities.

Bathrooms: Shampoo and bath gel are provided in shower-mounted dispensers; you also get an array of sample toiletries, as well as fluffy towels and a wall-mounted magnifying mirror. Bathrobes for use during the cruise are provided for all.

Other Features: A plus for families are a number of connecting staterooms in a variety of ocean-view and interior categories. Balcony dividers can be unlocked to provide connecting access in upper categories. Twenty-five staterooms are designed for wheelchair accessibility.

CABIN TYPE	SIZE (sq. ft.)
Penthouse Suite	345
Suite	230
Ocean View	185
Interior	185

Fast Facts

- 13 passenger decks
- Specialty restaurant, 2 dining rooms, buffet, ice-cream parlor, pizzeria
- Wi-Fi, in-cabin safes, in-cabin refrigerators, some in-cabin VCRs
- 3 pools (1 indoor), children's pool
- Fitness classes, gym, hair salon, 7 hot tubs, sauna, spa, steam room
- 9 bars, casino, dance club, library, showroom, video game room
- Children's programs (ages 2–15)
- Laundry facilities, laundry service
- Computer room

In the Know

The children's playroom has the best view on the ship—looking forward from high over the bow. If your little ones balk at joining Camp Carnival, point out that they're seeing the same thing as the captain; that news seems to captivate kids, even if there's nothing on the horizon.

Carnival Valor: Shooting hoops

Favorites

Best Place to Escape the Crowds: Look for a deck chair in a quiet area of the deck above the aft Lido pool. Most sunbathers there are simply seeking a peaceful and quiet place to read or snooze in the sunshine.

Best Splurge: New York–style supper clubs on these ships are some of the best restaurants—and specialty dining bargains—at sea. Not only is the food outstanding (escargot, Russian caviar, lobster bisque, Alaskan king crab claws, grilled lamp chops, lobster, and several cuts of beef from 9 to 24 ounces), but the presentation is sophisticated and the atmosphere sublime.

Our Favorite Spot for a Nightcap: The grand bar serves up jazz and cigars as well as brandy and cordials and has some comfortable nooks and crannies for privacy. The Internet center is steps away, just in case checking e-mail is important before bedtime.

Best Lunch Choice: Tucked away on the Lido buffet's second floor, an unassuming fish-and-chips counter serves outstanding bouillabaisse.

SPIRIT CLASS
Carnival Spirit, Pride, Legend, Miracle

2001, 2001, 2002, 2004	ENTERED SERVICE
2,124 (2,667 max)	PASSENGER CAPACITY
930	CREW MEMBERS
1,062	NUMBER OF CABINS
88,500	GROSS TONS
960 feet	LENGTH
105.7 feet	WIDTH

Public Areas & Facilities

Spirit-class vessels (the *Carnival Spirit* itself doesn't sail in the Caribbean and isn't listed here) may seem to be a throwback in size, but these sleek ships have the advantage of fitting through the Panama Canal and, with their additional length, include all the trademark characteristics of their larger fleet-mates. They're also racehorses with the speed to reach far-flung destinations.

A rosy red skylight in the front bulkhead of the funnel—which houses the reservations-only upscale Supper Club—caps a soaring, 11-deck atrium. Lovely chapels are available for weddings, either upon embarkation or while in a port of call, and are also used for shipboard religious services.

The upper and lower interior Promenade Decks are unhampered by a mid-ship restaurant or galley, which means that passenger flow throughout the ships is much improved over earlier, and even subsequent, designs.

WOW Factor

True, these are long ships, but not the longest at sea. For some reason, while they aren't actually longer than many others, they seem that way to most passengers.

Top: *Carnival Legend* at sea
Bottom: Spirit-class balcony stateroom

Restaurants

One formal restaurant serves open-seating breakfast and lunch; it also serves dinner in two assigned evening seatings. The casual Lido buffet with stations offers a variety of food choices; at night it becomes the Seaview Bistro for casual dinners. There's also a supper club, pizzeria, outdoor grills, a patisserie, a sushi bar, and 24-hour room service.

What Works & What Doesn't

Carnival's trademark waterslides are situated high atop the ship and far enough away from Lido pools so that they're not a distraction. This class contains numerous quiet nooks and crannies as well as expansive lounges and huge casinos.

These are long ships—really long ships—and you may want to consider any mobility issues when selecting a cabin. Thankfully, there are three banks of well-placed elevators.

Connecting staterooms are relatively scarce throughout the ships; however, balcony dividers can be unlocked between some higher-category cabins.

Accommodations

Cabins: Cabins on Carnival ships are generally more spacious than industry standard, and these are no exception. Nearly 80% have an ocean view and, of those, more than 80% have balconies. Suites and some ocean-view cabins have private balconies outfitted with chairs and tables; extended-balcony cabins have balconies at least 50% larger than average. Every cabin has adequate closet and drawer–shelf storage, as well as bathroom shelves. High thread-count linens and plush pillows and duvets are a luxurious touch in all accommodations. Suites also have a whirlpool tub, VCR, and walk-in closet.

Decor: Light-wood cabinetry, soft pastels, mirrored accents, a small refrigerator, a personal safe, a hair dryer, and a sitting area with sofa, chair, and table are typical for ocean-view cabins and suites. Inside cabins have ample room, but no sitting areas.

Bathrooms: Extras include shampoo and bath gel provided in shower-mounted dispensers and an array of sample toiletries, as well as fluffy towels and a wall-mounted magnifying mirror. Bathrobes for use during the cruise are provided for all.

Other Features: Decks 5, 6, and 7 each have a pair of balcony staterooms that connect to adjoining interior staterooms that are ideal for families because of their close proximity to children and teen areas. Sixteen staterooms are designed for wheelchair accessibility.

CABIN TYPE	SIZE (sq. ft.)
Penthouse Suite	370 (average)
Suite	275
Ocean View	185
Interior	185

Fast Facts

- 12 passenger decks
- Specialty restaurant, dining room, buffet, ice-cream parlor, pizzeria
- Wi-Fi, in-cabin safes, refrigerators, some in-cabin VCRs
- 3 pools (1 indoor), children's pool
- Fitness classes, gym, hair salon, 4 hot tubs, sauna, spa, steam room
- 7 bars, casino, 2 dance clubs, library, showroom, video game room
- Children's programs (ages 2–15)
- Laundry facilities, laundry service
- Computer room

In the Know

Take a walk on the wild side. The gently curving staircase to the Supper Club is clear Plexiglas and definitely a challenge to descend if heights make you dizzy. Try it anyway—it's quite a heady experience. Wimps can use the elevator.

Favorites

Best Place to Escape the Crowds: Delightful enclosed winter garden spaces are located forward on the exterior promenade deck. Air-conditioned and furnished with tables and chairs, they are a quieter choice for reading than the library, which also houses the Internet center.

Best Added Value: The huge gyms and fitness

centers on these ships are great, even for less energetic passengers. A soothing therapy pool sits under a skylight, and his-and-hers saunas and steam rooms have glass walls and sea views.

Best Splurge: Make a reservation for dinner in the Supper Club. The steaks rival Kansas City's finest, and the atmosphere is pure New York.

Our Favorite Place for a Nightcap: Piano bars on Carnival ships are pretty lively early on, but as the evening passes and the sounds grow mellow, these are dimly lighted havens with romantic little alcoves.

Coolest Freebie Serve-yourself ice cream dispensers are located on the Lido deck. Don't forget to add the sprinkles!

Carnival Miracle Gatsby's Garden

DESTINY CLASS
Carnival Destiny, Triumph, Victory

Public Areas & Facilities

The first of the Carnival mega ships weighing in at more than 100,000 tons, everything on the Destiny-class vessels is in keeping with their size—bold interiors highlighted by nine-deck atriums, 200-foot waterslides on their Lido decks, and public areas that often span multiple decks. Though they're all considered "Destiny" ships, the *Carnival Triumph* and *Carnival Victory* have an additional passenger deck and are subsequently bigger and have more cabins and crew than the original *Carnival Destiny*.

The variety of indoor and outdoor spaces range from relatively small lounges with a nightclub atmosphere to huge showrooms. Most public rooms open off wide indoor promenades that branch fore and aft from the spectacular atrium.

Expansive pools and sport decks have plenty of room to spread out for sunning and more active pursuits.

1996, 1999, 2000	Entered Service
2,642 (3,400 max)/2,758 (3,470 max)	Passenger Capacity
1,050/1,100	Crew Members
1,321/1,379	Number of Cabins
101,353/102,000	Gross Tons
893 feet	Length
116 feet	Width

700 ft.
500 ft.
300 ft.

WOW Factor

Try to count all the activities on board. Then add up the things to do ashore. You may feel overwhelmed, not to mention exhausted.

Top: *Carnival Victory* in Miami
Bottom: *Carnival Triumph* atrium

Restaurants

Two restaurants, each spanning two decks, serve open-seating breakfast and lunch; dinner is served in four assigned seatings. Formal dining is supplemented by a casual Lido buffet, which becomes the Seaview Bistro by night. There are also a pizzeria, patisserie, poolside grill, and 24-hour room service.

What Works & What Doesn't

The central Lido pools have tiered sunning decks that offer more areas to lounge with less foot traffic, as well as a good view of the entertainment stage. On *Carnival Destiny*, the gimmicky aft swim-up bar was dropped from subsequent ships.

The galley is situated between dining rooms on deck three, so you won't want to consume too many rum drinks before attempting to find your way to dinner.

Select the location of your balcony cabin on these ships with care. Those on a high deck in the middle of the ship may not be the tranquil havens you expect when the band cranks up the volume on the Lido deck.

Accommodations

Cabins: As on all Carnival ships, cabins are generally larger than cruise-industry standard. More than half have an ocean view and, of those, 60% have balconies. For suites and ocean-view cabins that have them, private balconies are outfitted with chairs and tables, adding additional living space. Every cabin has adequate closet and drawer–shelf storage, as well as bathroom shelves. High thread-count and plump pillows and duvets are a luxurious touch. Suites also have a whirlpool tub, VCR, and walk-in closet.

Decor: Light-wood cabinetry, soft pastels, mirrored accents, a small refrigerator, a personal safe, a hair dryer, and a sitting area with sofa, chair, and table are typical for ocean-view cabins and suites. Inside cabins do not have a sitting area.

Bathrooms: Shampoo and bath gel dispensers are mounted on shower walls; other toiletries are stocked, as well as fluffy towels. Bathrobes for use during the cruise are provided for all.

Other Features: Numerous ocean-view and inside stateroom categories have connecting doors and are suitable for families. In addition, there are slightly larger cabins near the children's playroom and teen center that are designated as family staterooms with floor-to-ceiling windows. Twenty-five staterooms are designed for wheelchair accessibility.

CABIN TYPE	SIZE (sq. ft.)
Penthouse Suite	345
Suite	275
Ocean View	185
Interior	185

Fast Facts

- 12/13 passenger decks (Destiny/Triumph, Victory)
- 2 dining rooms, buffet, ice-cream parlor, pizzeria
- Wi-Fi, in-cabin safes, refrigerators, some in-cabin VCRs
- 3 pools (1 indoor), children's pool
- Fitness classes, gym, hair salon, 7 hot tubs, sauna, spa, steam room
- 7 bars, casino, 3 dance clubs, library, showroom, video game room
- Children's programs (ages 2–15)
- Laundry facilities, laundry service
- Computer room

In the Know

Six balcony cabins (6336, 6344, 6363, 6371, 7316, and 7319 on Destiny; *6424, 6432, 6451, 6459, 7416, and 7419 on* Triumph *and* Victory) *wrap around an aft crew staircase. The configuration—they stretch lengthwise along the hull—creates balconies that are twice as long as the average standard balconies.*

Favorites

Best Place to Escape the Crowds: For some reason, the upper level of the Lido restaurant isn't discovered by many passengers. There are almost always tables readily available to linger over lunch or a casual dinner.

Best Added Value: Thanks to expansion of the "Club O2" Teen Program, teenagers have adult-free spaces

where they can hang out. Among the offerings are video games, chaperoned dance parties, and big-screen TVs that play movies and videos. The dedicated spaces help to keep teens occupied and out of the kind of mischief that inevitably results from boredom.

Best Feature for Younger Kids: Younger passengers haven't been over-

looked, either. These ships are a notable improvement over older fleetmates, with more and better space devoted to children's play areas.

Our Favorite Spot for a Nightcap: When the dinner-and-a-show crowds have cleared, the lobby bar is a surprisingly off-the-beaten-track space with a lot of visual impact.

Carnival Destiny Lido pool deck & waterslide

5

CARNIVAL CRUISE LINES

FANTASY CLASS

Carnival Fantasy, Ecstasy, Sensation, Fascination, Imagination, Inspiration, Elation, Paradise

Public Areas & Facilities

Bathed in fiber-optic light, glitzy Fantasy-class interiors add expansive six-deck atriums and a new dimension to the original Superliner concept. To keep the fun going, these ships offer an almost wearying assortment of places to have a good time. As times and tastes have changed, the ships have evolved as well, with new lobby bars, teen clubs, and Internet centers.

Only one level below the Lido deck, the Indoor Promenade connects major public rooms on a single deck, with only formal dining rooms, shops, and other small spaces one deck below. Large in size and ideal for a short itinerary, these ships have sprawling outdoor pool and sunning areas, but they can feel cramped when sailing at maximum capacity. Cabins provide calm oases from sensory overload, although you'll have to book a suite if you want the solitude of a private balcony.

Generously proportioned fitness centers include huge exercise rooms and miniature golf courses are fun for all ages.

1990, 1991, 1993, 1994, 1995, 1996, 1998, 1998	ENTERED SERVICE
2,052 (2,606 max)	PASSENGER CAPACITY
920	CREW MEMBERS
1,026	NUMBER OF CABINS
70,367	GROSS TONS
855 feet	LENGTH
103 feet	WIDTH

WOW Factor

The indoor promenade fills with music and is where you'll find all the action—from the casino to a variety of show lounges—after the sun goes down.

Restaurants

Two formal restaurants serve open-seating breakfast and lunch; dinner is served in four assigned evening seatings. The Lido restaurant serves buffet breakfast and lunch as well as pizza and serve-yourself ice cream; it's transformed nightly into the Seaview Bistro, a casual dinner alternative. Each ship has a patisserie and sushi bar. Room service is always available.

What Works & What Doesn't

Central atriums are simply stunning when sunlight streams in through skylights—they only take on a flashy air when artificially lighted after dark.

Make no mistake, though, there's a lot of glitz throughout, which can be somewhat overpowering until you become accustomed to it. The children's playrooms are almost hidden, yet recent renovations have increased their size, and the spaces are no longer disappointing. They are chock-full of games and toys, and, an adjacent deck area is available for extra play space; the splash pool is good-size.

Top: *Imagination* at sea
Bottom: *Inspiration* Lido pool deck

Accommodations

Cabins: Fantasy-class ships have a higher percentage of inside cabins than the fleet's newer ships, and only the top two suite categories offer balconies. Every cabin has adequate closet and drawer-shelf storage, as well as bathroom shelves. Light-wood cabinetry and simple decor are the norm for all cabins, while suite embellishments add the convenience of a sitting area and small refrigerator. In addition to the extra space, a whirlpool tub is a deluxe appointment in Penthouse suites. Inside cabins have ample room, and their curtained faux windows mimic those in the more expensive standard ocean-view accommodations. High thread-count linens and plush pillows and duvets add a touch of luxury to all accommodations.

Bathrooms: Extras include shower-mounted shampoo and bath gel dispensers and an array of sample toiletries, as well as fluffy towels. Bathrobes for use during the cruise are provided for all.

Other Features: Oddly, as with earlier Carnival vessels, there are no connecting cabins on Fantasy-class ships. Bring your own hair dryer. Twenty-two staterooms are designed for wheelchair accessibility.

CABIN TYPE	SIZE (sq. ft.)
Penthouse Suite	330
Suite	220
Ocean View	185
Interior	160–185

Fast Facts

- 10 passenger decks
- 2 dining rooms, buffet, ice-cream parlor, pizzeria
- Wi-Fi, in-cabin safes
- 2 pools, children's pool
- Fitness classes, gym, hair salon, 6 hot tubs, sauna, spa, steam room
- 5 bars, casino, dance club, library, showroom, video game room
- Children's programs (ages 2–15)
- Laundry facilities, laundry service
- Computer room

In the Know

Penthouse suites, the most expansive on board, are also in the most desirable area—right in the middle of a lower deck. The lesser suites, however, are high in the sky and all the way forward. To get the best fare, book a suite guarantee; you'll pay less, and the location won't matter that much.

Favorites

Best Place to Escape the Crowds: Head for the libraries, which are ideal retreats for reading or playing board games. There are plenty of games, but you'll want to bring your own reading material. Surprisingly, the library spaces are as large as the piano bar.

Best Added Value: Sushi bars earn high marks for their complimentary creations, although you'll have to pay if you want a glass of sake to drink.

Our Favorite Spot for a Nightcap: These are ships designed for partying, so unless you want to party, it may be difficult to find a late-night hideaway offering peace and quiet. Although it may sound odd, softly lighted seating areas adjacent to the lobby bar can be tranquil retreats.

Best Spot for a Snack: Lido restaurants are spacious and cheery, with banks of windows on three sides. It's worth a walk all the way to the back counter to reach the to-die-for, freshly made pizza and deli-style sandwiches.

Elation Tiffany's lounge

HOLIDAY CLASS
Holiday, Celebration

Public Areas & Facilities

Similar in design and layout, these mid-size ships represent the first wave of superliner construction undertaken by Carnival Cruise Lines. Amazing as it may seem, in some regards they are almost old-fashioned by today's mainstream standards.

Although smaller than their newer fleetmates, and without the visual impact of atriums, many Fun Ship standard features originated with the Holiday class, including spiral waterslides for Lido pool fun and indoor promenades that extend the length of a single side of each ship and from which most public rooms are accessed. These ships introduced the genius of interiors by master designer Joe Farcus, whose themes tie spaces together and add interest and pizzazz to every corner of the ships. The main show lounges span two decks and are suitable venues for high-energy shows and activities that draw a crowd.

Now sailing year-round short itineraries, *Holiday* and *Celebration* offer good value and are ideal for first-time cruisers.

1985, 1987	ENTERED SERVICE
1,452 (1,800)/1,486 (1,896)	PASSENGER CAPACITY
660/670	CREW MEMBERS
726/743	NUMBER OF CABINS
46,052/47,262	GROSS TONS
727/733 feet	LENGTH
92 feet	WIDTH

700 ft.
500 ft.
300 ft.

WOW Factor

These are the cruise ships that ushered in more than two decades of fun at sea, and the party hasn't stopped. The colorful interiors still deliver a lot of punch.

Top: *Celebration* Lido pool deck
Bottom: *Celebration* cabin

Restaurants

Two formal restaurants offer open seating for breakfast and lunch; dinner is served in four assigned seatings. The Lido restaurant serves buffet breakfast and lunch as well as pizza and is transformed nightly into the Seaview Bistro, a casual dinner alternative. Round-the-clock room service is available.

What Works & What Doesn't

Although there's no central atrium and the lobby is a bit blah, the surroundings along the indoor promenade deck are fun and whimsical. From there, it's easy to find your way around to all public spaces. The spa and gym are claustrophobic, and you may find that you have to arise before dawn to secure a deck chair when the ships are fully booked, which occurs nearly every sailing. Least successful of the public rooms, though, are the formal restaurants. Low ceilings and uncomfortable banquettes lend a cramped feeling. Both ships have Carnival's trademark waterslide, and it's a lot of fun to splash directly into the swimming pool.

Accommodations

Cabins: *Holiday* and *Celebration* were among the first ships in Carnival's fleet to have cabins more spacious than industry standard. Though all cabins are roomy, there are a higher percentage of inside cabins than on newer ships, and only a handful of suites have balconies. Every cabin has adequate closet and drawer–shelf storage, as well as bathroom shelves. High thread-count linens and plush pillows and duvets are a luxury touch in all accommodations, but don't forget to pack your own hair dryer.

Decor: Light-wood cabinetry and simple decor are the norm for all cabins, while suites are a bit nicer with the added luxuries of a sitting area, small refrigerator, and whirlpool tub. Inside cabins have ample room, and their curtained faux windows mimic the more expensive standard ocean-view accommodations.

Bathrooms: Shampoo and bath gel are in shower-mounted dispensers, and there's also an array of sample toiletries, as well as fluffy towels. Bathrobes for use during the cruise are provided for all.

Other Features: The lack of interconnecting cabins is made up for by the large number of three- and four-berth accommodations. The larger-than-average size of all standard cabins makes them adequate, if a bit cozy, for close-knit families. Fifteen staterooms on *Holiday* and 14 on *Celebration* are wheelchair-accessible.

CABIN TYPE	SIZE (sq. ft.)
Suite	330 (average)
Ocean View	185
Interior	160–185

Fast Facts

- 9 passenger decks
- 2 dining rooms, buffet, ice-cream parlor, pizzeria
- Wi-Fi, in-cabin safes
- 2 pools, children's pool
- Fitness classes, gym, hair salon, 2 hot tubs, sauna, spa
- 5 bars, casino, 2 dance clubs, library, showroom, video game room
- Children's programs (ages 2–15)
- Laundry facilities, laundry service
- Computer room

5

CARNIVAL CRUISE LINES

In the Know

Board with an open mind. These ships sail from pathfinder embarkation ports for a good reason. They are the oldest vessels in the fleet and were assigned to drive-up markets to test the waters. Although there are no connecting cabins, you'll find wide-open casinos where you won't feel crowded.

Favorites

Best Place to Escape the Crowds: Believe it or not, it's often the lobby! Unlike newer cruise ships, these don't have atriums, so the window-less lobby gets very little through traffic. Nicely furnished with sofas, it's often the quietest spot on board.

Best Added Value: Pizza and ice-cream stations are open around the clock, and sushi is avail-able at no charge before dinner.

Our Favorite Spot for a Nightcap: The casino bar curves around the indoor promenade and serves as a good spot for socializing at the end of an evening.

Best Unexpected Touch of Whimsy: The really cool Trolley (*Celebration*) and Bus Stop (*Holiday*) bars actually integrate a trolley and a bus into their decor; they're also great people-watching spots along their respective ship's wide, interior promenade.

Best Road Trip Ships: Sailing from Mobile, AL (*Holiday*) and Jacksonville, FL (*Celebration*), the Holiday-class ships are within an easy one-day drive from much of the southeastern U.S.

Holiday at sea

CELEBRITY CRUISE LINE

The Chandris Group, owners of budget Fantasy Cruises, founded Celebrity in 1989. Initially utilizing an unlovely, refurbished former ocean liner from the Fantasy fleet, Celebrity gained a reputation for fine food and professional service despite the shabby-chic

Century at anchor

vessel where it was elegantly served. The cruise line eventually built premium, sophisticated cruise ships. Signature amenities followed, including a martini bar, large standard staterooms with generous storage, fully equipped spas, and butler service for top suites. Valuable art collections grace the fleet, which merged with Royal Caribbean International in 1997.

CELEBRITY CRUISES
1050 Caribbean Way
Miami, FL 33132
305/539–6000 or
800/437–3111
www.celebrity.com

Cruise Style: Premium

Even as *Constellation* and *Summit* passengers have been treated to 30-minute performances of "A Taste of Cirque du Soleil," a unique concept at sea, entertainment has never been a primary focus; a lineup of lavish, although somewhat uninspired, revues is presented in the main show lounges by production companies of singers and dancers. In addition to shows featuring comedians, magicians, and jugglers, bands play a wide range of musical styles for dancing and listening in smaller lounges. Cirque du Soleil performers add an interactive element to the custom-built Bar at the Edge of the Earth on *Constellation*.

Two to five guest lecturers participate in the Enrichment Series program on every Celebrity cruise. Presentations may range from financial strategies, astronomy, wine appreciation, photography tips, and politics to the food, history, and culture of ports of call. Culinary demonstrations, bingo, and art auctions are additional diversions throughout the fleet. There are plenty of activities, although you'll have to read the daily program of events to find out about them. There are no public address announcements for bingo or hawking of gold-by-the-inch sales. You can still play and buy, but you won't be reminded repeatedly.

While spacious accommodations in every category are a Celebrity standard, the addition of ConciergeClass, an upscale element on all ships, makes certain premium ocean-view and balcony staterooms almost the equivalent of suites in terms of service. A ConciergeClass stateroom includes numerous extras such as chilled champagne, fresh fruit, and flowers upon arrival, exclusive room-service menus, evening canapés, luxury bedding, pillows, and linens, upgraded balcony furnishings, priority boarding and luggage service, and other VIP perks. At the touch of a single telephone button, a ConciergeClass desk representative is at hand to offer assistance. Suites are still the ultimate, though, and include the services of a butler to assist with unpacking, booking spa services and dining reservations, shining shoes, and even replacing a popped button.

Food

Aside from the sophisticated ambience of its restaurants, the cuisine designed by master chef Michel Roux was always reason enough to cruise on a Celebrity ship. However, in early 2007, Celebrity and Roux ended their affiliation, though his legacy promises to shine into the future. His hands-on involvement—personally creating menus and overseeing all aspects of dining operations—was integral in helping the line achieve the reputation it enjoys today. Happily, every ship in the fleet has a highly experienced team headed by executive chefs and food and beverage managers, who have developed their skills in some of the world's finest restaurants and hotels.

Alternative restaurants on the Millennium-class ships and *Century* offer fine dining and table-side food preparation amid classic ocean liner and Venetian splendor. A less formal evening alternative is offered fleetwide in the Casual Dining Boulevard, where you'll find a sushi bar, pizza and baked pasta, healthy spa items, and an area where you can order from the dining room menu. Reservations are required, but there are no long waits, and reserving a table is usually not a problem. Cova Café serves specialty coffees and pastries in surroundings inspired by the original in Milan; some offerings carry on additional charge. Gourmet Bites, the late-night treats served by white-gloved waiters in public rooms throughout the ships, can include mini–beef Wellingtons and crispy tempura.

To further complement the food, in 2004 Celebrity introduced a proprietary Cellarmaster Selection of wines, which initially included a Russian River Valley chardonnay and a Sonoma County cabernet sauvignon.

Noteworthy

■ Cova Café di Milano on each ship serves genuine coffee and chocolates from Milan.

■ The letter X on the ships' funnels is the Greek letter for C and stands for Chandris, the line's founding family.

■ Fresh-baked pizzas can be delivered to your stateroom in an insulated carrier.

Top: *Millennium* AquaSpa
Bottom: Cinema & conference center Millennium-class

5

CELEBRITY CRUISE LINE

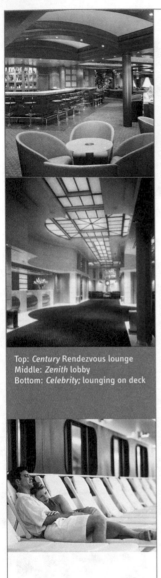

Top: *Century* Rendezvous lounge
Middle: *Zenith* lobby
Bottom: *Celebrity*; lounging on deck

Fitness & Recreation

Celebrity's AquaSpa by Elemis and fitness centers are some of the most tranquil and nicely equipped at sea with thalassotherapy pools on all but *Century* (complimentary on Millennium-class ships; a fee is assessed on Century-class). Spa services are operated by Steiner Leisure, and treatments include a variety of massages, body wraps, and facials. Trendy and traditional hair and nail services are offered in the salons.

State-of-the-art exercise equipment, a jogging track, and basic fitness classes are available at no charge. There's a fee for personal training, body composition analysis, and specialized classes such as yoga and Pilates. Golf pros offer hands-on instruction, and game simulators allow passengers to play world-famous courses. Each ship also has an "Acupuncture at Sea" treatment area staffed by licensed practitioners of Oriental Medicine.

Your Shipmates

Celebrity caters to American cruise passengers, primarily couples from their mid-30s to mid-50s. Many families enjoy cruising on Celebrity's fleet during summer months and holiday periods, particularly in the Caribbean. Lengthier cruises and exotic itineraries attract passengers in the over-60 age group.

Dress Code

Two formal nights are standard on seven-night cruises. Men are encouraged to wear tuxedos, but dark suits or sport coats and ties are more prevalent. Two evenings are designated informal, and other evenings are casual, although jeans are discouraged in restaurants. The line requests that no shorts be worn in public areas after 6 PM, and most people observe the dress code of the evening, unlike on some other cruise lines.

Junior Cruisers

Each Celebrity vessel has a dedicated playroom and offers a four-tier program of age-appropriate games and activities designed for children aged 3 to 6, 7 to 9, 10 to 12, and 13 to 17. Younger children must be toilet-trained to participate in the programs and use the facilities; how-

CHOOSE CELEBRITY CRUISE LINE IF:

❶ You want an upscale atmosphere at a really reasonable fare.

❷ You want piping-hot late-night pizza delivered to your cabin in pizzeria fashion.

❸ You want to dine amid elegant surroundings in some of the best restaurants at sea.

ever, families are welcome to borrow toys for their un-toilet-trained kids. A nominal fee may be assessed for participation in children's dinner parties, the Late-Night Slumber Party, and Afternoon Get-Togethers while parents are ashore in ports of call. Evening in-cabin babysitting can be arranged for a fee. Millennium-class and Century-class ships have teen centers, where teenagers can hang out and attend Coke-tail and pizza parties.

Service
Service on Celebrity ships is unobtrusive and polished. ConciergeClass adds an unexpected level of service and amenities that are usually reserved for luxury ships or passengers in top-category suites on other premium cruise lines.

Tipping
Gratuities (in cash) are personally distributed by passengers on the last night of the cruise. Suggested guidelines are per person, per day: waiter $3.50; assistant waiter $2; maitre d' 75¢; cabin steward $3.50; cabin attendant in ConciergeClass $4; assistant chief housekeeper 75¢; and, for suite occupants only, butler $3.50. Passengers may adjust the amount based on the level of service experienced. For children under 12 who accompany adults as third or fourth occupants of a stateroom, half the suggested amount is recommended. An automatic gratuity of 15% is added to all beverage tabs.

Past Passengers
Once you've sailed with Celebrity, you become a member of the Captain's Club and receive benefits commensurate with the number of cruises you've taken, including free upgrades, the chance to make dining reservations before sailing, and other benefits. Classic members have been on at least one Celebrity cruise. Select members have sailed at least six cruises and get more perks, including an invitation to a senior officer's cocktail party. After 10 cruises, you become an Elite member, and can take advantage of a private departure lounge. Royal Caribbean International, the parent company of Celebrity Cruises, also extends the corresponding levels of their Crown & Anchor program to Celebrity Captain's Club members.

Good to Know

Small refinements add touches of luxury to a Celebrity cruise. White-gloved stewards are present at the gangway upon embarkation to greet weary passengers with the offer of assistance.

In a surprise move, two ships set to join the Celebrity fleet were instead spun off to form a new Celebrity subsidiary, Azamara Cruises. While details were still being unveiled at this writing, the ships *Azamara Journey* and *Azamara Quest* promise to deliver a deluxe cruise experience just short of the luxury category. All passengers will enjoy such upscale amenities as plush bedding and butler service, extensive enrichment programs, a world-class spa, and open-seating in the main restaurant (no formal attire required). Suite guests will receive two nights of complimentary dining in one of the two specialty restaurants—Mediterranean-influenced Aqualina and Prime C for steaks and seafood—while guests in regular rooms will receive one complimentary meal in a specialty restaurant. The suggested daily gratuity rate is $12.25 per person per night.

5

CELEBRITY CRUISE LINE

DON'T CHOOSE CELEBRITY CRUISE LINE IF:

❶ You need to be reminded of when activities are scheduled. Announcements are kept to a minimum.

❷ You look forward to boisterous pool games and wacky contests. These cruises are fairly quiet and adult-centered.

❸ You think funky avant garde art is weird. Abstract modernism abounds in the art collections.

MILLENNIUM CLASS

Millennium, Summit, Infinity, Constellation

Public Areas & Facilities

Millennium-class ships are the largest, newest, and most fea-ture-filled in the Celebrity fleet. Innovations include the Con-servatory, a unique botanical environment; show lounges reminiscent of splendid opera houses; and alternative restau-rants where diners find themselves in the midst of authentic ocean liner decor and memorabilia. The spas simply have to be seen to be believed—they occupy nearly as much space inside as is devoted to the adjacent outdoor Lido deck pool area. Although the spas offer just about any treatment you can think of—and some you probably haven't—they also house a complimentary hydrotherapy pool and spa café. These ships also have the most to offer for families, with the largest children's facilities in the Celebrity fleet.

Rich fabrics in jewel tones mix elegantly with the abundant use of marble and wood accents throughout public areas. The atmosphere is not unlike a luxurious European hotel filled with grand spaces that flow nicely from one to the other with-out any jarring surprises.

2000, 2001,2001, 2002	
ENTERED SERVICE	
1,950 (2,450)	
PASSENGER CAPACITY	
999	
CREW MEMBERS	
975	
NUMBER OF CABINS	
91,000	
GROSS TONS	
965 feet	
LENGTH	
105 feet	
WIDTH	

(vertical scale: 700 ft., 500 ft., 300 ft.)

WOW Factor

In lieu of atriums, Grand Foyers on these ships are stylishly appointed, multideck lobbies, with sweeping staircases crying out for grand entrances.

Top: *Millennium* Cova Café
Bottom: *Millennium* Ocean Grill

Restaurants

The formal two-deck restaurant serves evening meals in two as-signed seatings and is supple-mented by a casual Lido buffet and upscale alternative restau-rant that houses a demonstration kitchen and wine cellar (and also requires reservations and a per-person cover charge). A lunch-eon grill, Cova Café patisserie, and 24-hour room service aug-ment dining choices.

What Works & What Doesn't

There are just too many passengers to expect that your every wish will be granted on ships this size, but crew members try extremely hard to make everyone feel special. Although you'd expect to pay far more for a compa-rable meal ashore, wines suggested to complement alternative restaurant meals are probably a bit too rich for most passen-gers' pocketbooks.

The real gems are the Aquaspa Café, which serves light and healthy cuisine from breakfast until early evening, and the Sushi Café, where masters of the Japanese culinary art prepare the colorful treats.

Accommodations

Cabins: As on all Celebrity ships, cabins are thoughtfully designed with ample closet and drawer–shelf storage, as well as bathroom shelves in all standard inside and outside categories. Some ocean–view cabins and suites have private balconies. Penthouse suites have guest powder rooms.

Amenities: Wood cabinetry, mirrored accents, a small refrigerator, a personal safe, a hair dryer, and a sitting area with sofa, chair, and table are typical standard amenities. Extras include bathroom toiletries (shampoo, soaps, and lotion) and bathrobes for use during the cruise. Suite luxuries vary, but most include a whirlpool tub, VCR, Internet station, and walk–in closet, while all have butler service, personalized stationery, and a logo tote bag. For pure pleasure, Penthouse and Royal suites have outdoor whirlpool tubs on the balconies.

Worth Noting: Most staterooms and suites have convertible sofa beds, and many categories are capable of accommodating third and fourth occupants. Connecting staterooms are available in numerous categories, including the Celebrity suites. Family staterooms feature huge balconies and some have not one, but two sofa beds. Twenty–six staterooms are designed for wheelchair accessibility.

CABIN TYPE	SIZE (sq. ft.)
Penthouse Suite	1,432
Royal Suite/ Celebrity Suite	538/467
Sky Suite/ Family Ocean View	251/271
Concierge Class	191
Ocean View/Interior	170

In the Know

Enhance your personal outdoor space by booking cabins 6035, 6030, or any of the seven cabins forward of those two on deck six. You can't tell from the deck plan, but your balcony will be extra deep, and you won't be looking down into a lifeboat.

Favorites

Best Added Value: There's no charge for use of the thalassotherapy pool in the huge Aqua Spa, a facility that rivals the fanciest ashore.

Best Splurge: There isn't much difference in size between an Ocean-view Stateroom with a balcony and ConciergeClass Stateroom, but if you plan to spend a lot of time in your quarters, the upgrade to ConciergeClass is well worth the extra expense, especially if you're planning your cruise as a honeymoon or other special occasion.

Our Favorite Spot for a Nightcap: Be daring, and alternate between the Martini and Champagne Bar's specialties. With no traffic flowing through the area after the last straggler leaves the dining room, it's a quiet retreat.

Best Way to Curb Your Appetite: The AquaSpa Café serves light and healthy selections for breakfast, lunch, and dinner, as well as fresh fruit smoothies.

Unexpected Freebie: You'll find a logo tote bag in your cabin.

Fast Facts

- 11 passenger decks
- Specialty restaurant, dining room, buffet, ice-cream parlor, pizzeria
- In-cabin broadband (*Constellation*), Wi-Fi, in-cabin safes, in-cabin refrigerators, some in-cabin VCRs, some in-cabin DVDs
- 3 pools (1 indoor), children's pool
- Fitness classes, gym, hair salon, 6 hot tubs, sauna, spa, steam room
- 7 bars, casino, cinema, dance club, library, showroom, video game room
- Children's programs (ages 3–17)
- Dry cleaning, laundry service
- Computer room

Millennium-class conservatory

5

CELEBRITY CRUISE LINE

CENTURY CLASS
Century, Galaxy, Mercury

1995, 1996, 1997	ENTERED SERVICE
1,750 (2,150)/1,870 (2,681)/ 1,886 (2,681)	PASSENGER CAPACITY
858/909/909	CREW MEMBERS
875/935/943	NUMBER OF CABINS
70,606/77,713/77,713	GROSS TONS
815/865/866 feet	LENGTH
105 feet	WIDTH

Public Areas & Facilities

Not quite identical, these sister ships nevertheless have essentially the same layout, though they differ dramatically in décor. *Century* has an eclectic air, while *Galaxy* and *Mercury* are more traditional in design and quietly elegant. All display fine collections of modern and classical art. With an additional 50 feet in length, *Galaxy* and *Mercury* have room for children's pools as well as a third swimming pool with a sliding roof for cover in inclement weather. A 2006 rejuvenation of *Century* added 14 suites and 10 staterooms (both inside and outside), not to mention 314 verandas, the most ever added to an existing cruise ship).

Each vessel has facilities for children and teens, but on *Galaxy* and *Mercury* they seem almost an afterthought. Adults fare better with spectacular spas and sophisticated lounges dedicated to a variety of tastes. The dining rooms are nothing short of gorgeous. Overall, the first impression is that these are fine resort hotels that just happen to float.

WOW Factor

Descend to dine in the tradition of great ocean liners. Both ships have stunning double-height dining rooms with soaring columns and window walls.

Top: *Century;* formal dining
Bottom: *Century* Shipmates
Fun Factory

Restaurants

The formal two-deck restaurant serves evening meals in two assigned seatings and is supplemented by a casual Lido restaurant serving buffet-style breakfast and lunch. (By night, the Lido restaurant is a reservations-only restaurant and Sushi café.) *Century* has both a spa café and an upscale, reservations-only restaurant that has an extra cover charge.

What Works & What Doesn't

The atmosphere throughout is decidedly upscale, despite some over-the-edge art pieces on *Century*. For sheer tranquillity, head for the heavenly AquaSpa. Be forewarned, though, the posh and soothing surroundings translate into dollars; unless you're occupying a suite or have booked a massage or other treatment from the spa menu, plan to pay a fee for relaxing in the huge thalassotherapy saltwater pool on *Galaxy* and *Mercury*. Murano, *Century's* deluxe extra-charge restaurant, has striking Murano-glass chandeliers. Underfoot, jewel-granite resembles the paving of an Italian piazza.

Accommodations

Layout: As on all Celebrity ships, cabins are thoughtfully designed with ample closet and drawer-shelf storage and bathroom shelves. Some ocean-view cabins and suites have balconies with chairs and tables. Penthouse and Royal suites have a whirlpool bathtub and separate shower as well as a walk-in closet; Penthouse suites have a guest powder room. Although Royal and Sky suites are bigger on *Galaxy*, most other cabins are slightly smaller than on *Century*.

Amenities: Light-wood cabinetry, mirrored accents, a refrigerator, a personal safe, a hair dryer, and a sitting area with sofa, chair, and table are typical standard amenities. Extras include bathroom toiletries (shampoo, soaps, and lotion) and bathrobes for use during the cruise. Penthouse and Royal suites have elaborate entertainment

centers with large TVs, while all suites include butler service, personalized stationery, VCR or DVD, and a tote bag.

Worth Noting: On *Galaxy* and *Mercury*, spacious family ocean-view staterooms have a double bed, sofa bed, and upper berth; *Century* has slightly smaller Family Veranda Staterooms.

CABIN TYPE	SIZE (sq. ft.)
Penthouse Suite	1,101
Royal Suite/Sky Suite	522/245
Standard Suite/ Family Ocean View*	220/210
Concierge & Ocean View	175 /172
Interior	174 /171

Cabins sizes are averages.
*Only *Century* has regular suites.

In the Know

While the rest of the industry was rushing to add affordable balconies to a high percentage of staterooms, Celebrity was somewhat slower to get on the bandwagon. When Century *emerged from her dry-dock revitalization in June 2006 with 314 new verandas, the tide had turned.*

Favorites

Best Dessert: Just about any selection from the rolling tea cart on the day Elegant Tea is offered.

Best Splurge: Cova Café di Milano is somewhat loosely styled after its Italian namesake, which opened in 1817 next to Milan's La Scala Opera House. Featuring Cova liqueurs, chocolates, and fresh pastries, it's a delightful sidewalk

café-style spot to order up the best coffee on board while you polish your people-watching skills. There's a charge for the specialty coffee and Cova treats, but complimentary croissants and pastries are available in the morning and late afternoon.

Our Favorite Spot for a Nightcap: The stogie craze has all but died, and the air has cleared in

Michael's Clubs, the lounges formerly devoted to cigar smoking. Now billed as piano bars, they remain quiet spaces for after-dinner cordials.

Unexpected Luxury: Penthouse suites have outdoor whirlpool tubs on their balconies.

Fast Facts

- ■ 10 passenger decks
- ■ Specialty restaurant (*Century* only), dining room, buffet, ice-cream parlor, pizzeria
- ■ Wi-Fi, in-cabin safes, in-cabin refrigerators, some in-cabin VCRs, some in-cabin DVDs
- ■ 2 pools (*Century* only), 3 pools (1 indoor on *Galaxy* & *Mercury*), children's pool (*Galaxy* & *Mercury*)
- ■ Fitness classes, gym, hair salon, 5 hot tubs, sauna, spa, steam room (*Galaxy* & *Mercury*)
- ■ 7 bars (8 on *Galaxy* & *Mercury*), casino, cinema, dance club, library, showroom, video game room
- ■ Children's programs (ages 3–17)
- ■ Dry cleaning, laundry service
- ■ Computer room

Galaxy oasis pool

AZAMARA CLASS
Azamara Journey, Azamara Quest

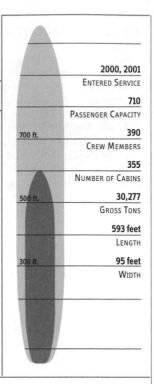

2000, 2001	ENTERED SERVICE
710	PASSENGER CAPACITY
390	CREW MEMBERS
355	NUMBER OF CABINS
30,277	GROSS TONS
593 feet	LENGTH
95 feet	WIDTH

700 ft.

500 ft.

300 ft.

Public Areas and Facilities

At 30,277 tons, *Azamara Quest* and *Azamara Journey* are medium-sized ships are well suited for the itineraries for which they are deployed. (*Azamara Journey* sails remote South American routes.) The ships initially entered service for Renaissance Cruises and served in Spain under the Pullmantur flag until 2007. With their entry into the brand-new Azamara Cruises fleet, a new option will be available to passengers who prefer the boutique-hotel atmosphere of a smaller ship but want the style for which Celebrity is noted.

After separate one-month drydocks, the ships now have a variety of signature Celebrity features, including the Martini Bar, Cova Café, Sushi Café, Michael's Club jazz and piano bar, and AquaSpa. Each ship has two specialty restaurants. The exclusive experience includes butler service and concierge amenities in all 15 categories of accommodations.

WOW Factor

The most photographed spot on board is certainly the dramatic grand staircase, reminiscent of those found on trans-Atlantic liners at the height of the Gilded Age of ocean travel.

Top: Open seating dining
Bottom: Balcony stateroom

Restaurants

Some details were still being developed at this writing, but the formal restaurant serves evening meals in one open seating and is supplemented by a casual Lido buffet and two upscale alternative restaurants (which require reservations and a cover charge). A luncheon grill, Sushi Café, Cova Café patisserie, and 24-hour room service augment dining choices.

What Works and What Doesn't

In the smaller space of mid-size ships, these vessels offer a lot of big-ship features, despite being built to another cruise line's specifications. While most details haven't been unveiled at this writing, Azamara promises everything you'd expect from a traditional premium cruise and more. Expect to have a comfortably sophisticated experience in an intimate environment. One staff member for every two passengers and the attention of a butler for each stateroom ensures unparalleled service at this level.

Accommodations

Layout: Designed for lengthy cruises, all staterooms have ample closet and storage space, and even standard cabins have at least a small sitting area, although bathrooms in lower categories are somewhat tight. Wood cabinetry adds warmth to the décor. In keeping with the trend for more balconies, 73% of all outside cabins and suites have them.

Amenities: Amenities include plush beds and bedding that were installed during the ships' makeovers. Bath toiletries, a hair dryer, TV, personal safe, and robes for use during the cruise are all included, but you must move up to a suite to have a bathtub since lower-category cabins have shower only.

Suites: Full suites are particularly luxurious, with living/dining rooms, entertainment centers, minibars, two TVs, separate bedrooms, whirlpool bathtubs, guest powder rooms, and very large balconies overlooking either the bow or stern. Thirty-two Sky Suites newly incorporated into each ship have a queen size bed, minibar, television, whirlpool, personal safe, and hair dryer.

Worth Noting: Seven staterooms are designated as wheelchair accessible.

CABIN TYPE	SIZE (sq. ft.)
Penthouse/Royal Suites	603/538
Sky Suites/Sunset Veranda	323/215
Oceanview Balcony	215
Oceanview	161
Inside	151

Fast Facts

- 9 passenger decks
- 2 specialty restaurants, dining room, buffet, pizzeria
- Wi-Fi, in-cabin safes, some in-cabin minibars, some in-cabin refrigerators, in-cabin DVDs
- 1 pool
- Fitness classes, gym, hair salon, 2 hot tubs, spa, steam room
- 8 bars, casino, dance club, library, showroom
- Children's programs (ages 3–17)
- Dry cleaning, laundry service
- Computer room

In the Know

Forward-facing Royal Suite balconies offer remarkable views, but depending on the force of the wind when the ship is under way, they can be virtually unusable. Also, it's best to keep the suite balcony doors locked when at sea as they tend to slide open if the ship rolls from side to side.

Favorites

Best Balcony Cabins: Aft-facing Sunset Verandas on decks six and seven are simply standard balcony cabins sandwiched between suites. However, they have much larger balconies than other similar accommodations and terrific views of the ship's wake as well as evening sunsets.

Best Place to Warm Up the Evening: The sophisticated Martini Bar offers 20 variations of this famous cocktail, and the bartenders are willing to follow your instructions to mix your favorite even if it's not on the menu.

Our Favorite Spot for a Nightcap: We like the quiet sounds of a grand piano and deep, welcoming seating that add to the ambience of Michael's Club.

Best Splurge: Sure there's an extra charge, but we just can't pass up the aromatic specialty coffees and divine pastries in Cova Café. The "Best Unexpected Treat" on board is that certain pastries in Cova Café are complimentary throughout the day.

Casual dining

COSTA CRUISES

Europe's number-one cruise line combines a Continental experience, enticing itineraries, and Italy's classical design and style with relaxing days and romantic nights at sea. Genoa-based Costa Crociere, parent company of Costa Cruise Lines, had

Dining alfresco

been in the shipping business for more than 100 years and in the passenger business for almost 50 years when it was bought by Airtours and Carnival Corporation in 1997. In 2000 Carnival completed a buyout of the Costa line and began expanding the fleet with larger and more dynamic ships.

COSTA CRUISES
200 S. Park Road, Suite 200
Hollywood, FL 33021-8541
954/266–5600 or
800/462–6782
www.costacruise.com

Cruise Style: Mainstream

Italian-style cruising is a mixture of Mediterranean flair and American comfort, beginning with a *buon viaggio* celebration and topped off by a signature Roman Bacchanal Parade and zany toga party. The supercharged social staff works overtime to get everyone in the mood and encourages everyone to be a part of the action.

Festive shipboard activities include some of Italy's favorite pastimes, such as playing games of boccie, dancing the tarantella, and tossing pizza dough during the Festa Italiana, an Italian street festival at sea. Other nights are themed as well—a welcome-aboard celebration or Benvenuto A Bordo, hosted by the captain on the first formal night, and Notte Tropical, a tropical deck party with a Mediterranean twist that culminates with the presentation of an alfresco midnight buffet.

There's also a nod to the traditional cruise-ship entertainment expected by North American passengers. Pool games, trivia, bingo, and sophisticated production shows blend nicely with classical concerts in lounges where a wide range of musical styles invite dancing or listening. The enrichment series might include topics such as personal finance as well as the usual health and beauty sessions. Italian language and cooking classes are extremely popular. Every ship has a small chapel suitable for intimate weddings, and Catholic Mass is celebrated most days.

With a nod to American passengers, who make up the majority on board during the Caribbean season, Costa Cruises has eliminated smoking entirely in dining rooms and show lounges. However, smokers are permitted to light up in designated areas in other public rooms, as well as on the pool deck.

A new vessel-building program has brought Costa ships into the 21st century with innovative large-ship designs that reflect their Italian heritage and style without overlooking the amenities expected by modern cruisers.

Food

Costa is noted for themed dinner menus and retractable backdrops that convey the evening's mood. Dining features regional Italian cuisines: a variety of pastas, chicken, beef, and seafood dishes, as well as authentic pizza. European chefs and culinary school graduates, who are members of Chaîne des Rôtisseurs, provide a dining experience that's notable for a delicious, properly prepared pasta course, if not exactly living up to gourmet standards. Vegetarian and healthy diet choices are also offered, as are selections for children. Alternative dining is by reservation only in the upscale supper clubs, which serve choice steaks and seafood from a Tuscan steak-house menu as well as traditional Italian specialties.

While there is normally a per-person charge for the specialty restaurants, suite passengers receive one complimentary dinner for two.

Costa ships also retain the tradition of lavish nightly midnight buffets, a feature that is beginning to disappear on other mainstream lines.

Fitness & Recreation

Taking a cue from the ancient Romans, Costa places continuing emphasis on wellness and sensual pleasures. Spas and salons are operated by Steiner Leisure, and treatments include a variety of massages, body wraps, and facials that can be scheduled à la carte or combined in packages to enjoy during one afternoon or throughout the entire cruise. Hair and nail services are available in the salons.

State-of-the-art exercise equipment in the terraced gym, a jogging track, and basic fitness classes for all levels of ability are available. Costa ships offer a Golf Academy at Sea, with PGA clinics on the ship and golf excursions in most Caribbean ports.

Noteworthy

■ The cuisine of Italian chef Gualtiero Marchesi is served on Versace tableware in Costa's alternative restaurants.

■ Original works of art, including sculptures, paintings, and handcrafted furnishings, are created for all Costa ships.

■ For dessert, Costa chefs tempt you with tiramisu, crème brûlée, cannoli, Sambuca sundaes, and gelato.

Top: Showtime on *Costa*
Bottom: Casino action

Top: *Costa* chefs
Middle: Jogging on deck
Bottom: Las Vegas-style
entertainment

Your Shipmates

Couples in the 35- to 55-year-old range are attracted to Costa Cruises; on Caribbean itineraries approximately 80% of passengers are North Americans, and many of them are of Italian descent. An international air prevails on board and announcements are often made in a variety of languages.

Dress Code

Two formal nights are standard on seven-night cruises. Men are encouraged to wear tuxedos, but dark suits or sport coats and ties are appropriate and more common than black tie. All other evenings are resort casual, although jeans are discouraged in restaurants. It's requested that no shorts be worn in public areas after 6 PM.

Junior Cruisers

Caribbean sailings feature age-specific youth programs that include such daily activities as costume parties, board games, junior aerobics, and even Italian-language lessons for children in four age groups: ages 3 (toilet trained) to 6; ages 7 to 11; junior teens ages 12 to 14; and teens ages 15 to 17. The actual age groupings may be influenced by the number of children on board. Special counselors oversee activities, and specific rooms are designed for children and teens, depending on the ship. Children under three years old can use the playroom facilities if accompanied and supervised by their parents.

Organized sessions for all children between the ages of 3 and 17 are available every day, even when in port, from 9 to 12 and 3 to 6, as well as from 9 to 11:30 in the evening. Parents can enjoy at least a couple of evenings alone by taking advantage of two complimentary Parents Nights Out while their children dine at a supervised buffet or pizza party and take part in evening and night-time activities. Nighttime group babysitting for children ages 3 to 11 is complimentary in the children's area until 1:30 AM. Unfortunately, no late-night babysitting service is offered for children under 3, nor is there in-cabin babysitting.

CHOOSE COSTA CRUISES IF:

❶ You're a satisfied Carnival past passenger and want a similar experience with an Italian flavor.

❷ You want pizza hot out of the oven whenever you get a craving for it.

❸ You're a joiner: there are many opportunities to be in the center of the action.

Service

Service in dining areas can be spotty and rushed but is adequate, if not always overly friendly.

Tipping

A standard gratuity of $8.50 per passenger, per day ($4.25 for children) is automatically added to shipboard accounts and is distributed as follows: $3 to cabin stewards; $3 to waiters; $1.50 to assistant waiters; and $1 to headwaiters. Passengers may adjust the amount based on the level of service experienced. An automatic 15% gratuity is added to all beverage tabs, as well as to checks for spa treatments and salon services.

Past Passengers

The Costa Club has three levels of membership: Aquamarine (2,000 points), Coral (2,001 to 5,000 points) and Pearl (5,001 or more points). Points are assigned for the number of cruising days (100 points per day) and the amount of money spent aboard (40 points for 52 euros).

Membership privileges vary and can include discounts on selected cruises, fruit baskets and bottles of Spumante delivered to your cabin, discounts on boutique merchandise and beauty treatments, or a complimentary dinner in a specialty restaurant.

Good to Know

Mama Mia! Connoisseurs of classical Italian art and design may feel they've died and gone to Caesars Palace. Costa's ships deployed in the Caribbean try to convey what Americans think of as Roman: gilt surfaces, marble columns, and all. Overlook the gaudiness and pay particular attention to the best details: the Murano glass chandeliers and lighting fixtures are simply superb. And when you're packing don't forget to toss something in the suitcase to wear beneath your toga; while sheets and accessories are provided, it's considered bad form to flash fellow passengers during the revelry.

5

COSTA CRUISES

DON'T CHOOSE COSTA CRUISES IF:

❶ You find announcements in a variety of languages annoying.

❷ You want an authentic Italian cruise. The crew has grown more international than Italian as the line has expanded.

❸ You prefer sedate splendor in a formal atmosphere. The Caribbean-based ships are almost Fellini-esque in style.

COSTA FORTUNA, COSTA MAGICA

Public Areas & Facilities

With a bit of interior alteration, *Costa Fortuna* and *Costa Magica* are essentially Euro-clones of parent company Carnival Cruise Line's *Carnival Triumph* and *Carnival Victory*. The mix and size of public rooms was determined to appeal to European as well as North American passengers sailing on itineraries that include the Mediterranean Sea as well as the Caribbean region.

Like Carnival ships designed by Joe Farcus, these Costa beauties have a theme running throughout—the décor is inspired by the grand Italian steamships of the past. Incorporated into the design of these ships, scale models of historic liners grace nearly every public area. A "fleet" of 26 former ships of the Costa fleet boldly "sail" upside down across the ceiling of the atrium. Ceilings in the formal, two-deck dining rooms are also decorated; Michelangelo Restaurant features reproductions of the master's frescoes, while Raffeallo Restaurant displays its namesake's Vatican artwork. Art deco touches add grace to all the public areas.

2003, 2004	ENTERED SERVICE
2,720 (3,470 max)	PASSENGER CAPACITY
1,068	CREW MEMBERS
1,360	NUMBER OF CABINS
105,000	GROSS TONS
890 feet	LENGTH
124 feet	WIDTH

700 ft.

500 ft.

300 ft.

WOW Factor

Art, art, and even more art! Millions of dollars were invested in original paintings, sculptures, wall hangings, and specially designed artisan furnishings.

Top: Romantic dinner
Bottom: *Costa Magica* Grand Suite

Restaurants

Two restaurants, each spanning two decks, serve open-seating breakfast and lunch; dinner is served in two assigned seatings. Club Grand Conte, a reservation-only restaurant and upscale alternative, features a Tuscan steak-house menu of steaks and seafood dishes in addition to Italian specialties. Casual meals and pizza are available in the Lido buffet.

What Works & What Doesn't

Group participation is a major component of a Costa cruise, and Costa Magica's energetic social staff gets the ball rolling by encouraging everyone on board to join in for their signature activities and par-ties. Surprisingly, even the most hesitant often succumb to the coaxing and take part in the antics. Afterward, they may sheepishly reveal they enjoyed wearing a toga. With all this constant activity, though, you may feel that you need a vacation when your cruise is finished. The Internet Café is placed adjacent to the disco, not a spot conducive to peaceful Internet surfing.

Accommodations

Layout: Cabins on *Costa Fortuna* and *Costa Magica* generally follow the outline of their Carnival counterparts, with the notable addition of a Grand Suite category. More than 60% of accommodations have an ocean view and, of those, 60% have balconies. Balconies have chairs and tables, and dividers can be unlocked to connect some cabins. Every cabin has adequate closet and drawer–shelf storage, as well as bathroom shelves. Suites have a generous walk-in closet.

Amenities: Light-wood cabinetry, soft pastel decor, mirrored accents, Murano glass lighting fixtures, a small refrigerator, a personal safe, a hair dryer, and a sitting area with a sofa, chair, and table are typical for ocean-view cabins and suites. Inside cabins have ample room, but sitting areas consist only of a small table and chairs.

Bathrooms: Bathroom extras include shampoo and bath gel in shower-mounted dispensers. Additional features in the suites on *Costa Magica* include a whirlpool tub and double sink. Suite passengers also enjoy an enhanced room-service menu.

Worth Noting: Well-designed lifeboat placement ensures unobstructed sea views from all outside cabin windows. Eight staterooms are designed for wheelchair accessibility.

CABIN TYPE	SIZE (sq. ft.)
Grand Suites	650
Suites	360
Minisuites	300
Ocean View	175
Interior	160

Fast Facts

- 13 passenger decks
- Specialty restaurant, 2 dining rooms, buffet, pizzeria
- In-cabin safes, in-cabin refrigerators
- 3 pools (1 indoor), children's pool
- Fitness classes, gym, hair salon, 6 hot tubs, sauna, spa, steam room
- 7 bars, casino, 2 dance clubs, 2 showrooms, library, video game room
- Children's programs (ages 3–17)
- Laundry service
- Computer room

In the Know

Costa Fortuna and Costa Magica *share many of the same attributes as their Carnival cousins, but make no mistake, these are Costa vessels. In the style that Europeans favor, the casino is much smaller to make room for the huge Conte Di Savoia Grand Bar that houses a suitably large dance floor.*

Favorites

Best Place to Escape the Crowds: The library doesn't have a large collection of books, but it does contain some nifty wraparound cabanalike chairs that envelope the occupants in privacy.

Best Added Value: With floor-to-ceiling glass walls, the saunas and steam rooms for men and women (not coed) are bright and cheery. Better still, they're so huge that they're seldom crowded, and you don't have to book a spa treatment or pay a fee to use them.

Our Favorite Spot for a Nightcap: The Classico Roma Bar is a hideaway with a nautical flavor and a faux fireplace. The clean lines of the mid-century modern style seating belie how comfortable the late-night watering hole is for savoring a cognac or cigar.

Best Splurge: Dinner in the reservations-only Club Grand Conte is well worth the extra charge of $23 per person for the intimate, candlelit atmosphere.

Deck games

COSTA ATLANTICA, COSTA MEDITERRANEA

2000, 2003	ENTERED SERVICE
2,114 (2,682 max)	PASSENGER CAPACITY
920	CREW MEMBERS
1,057	NUMBER OF CABINS
86,000	GROSS TONS
960 feet	LENGTH
106 feet	WIDTH

Public Areas & Facilities

The basic layout of this contemporary ship is nearly identical to parent Carnival Cruise Line's Spirit-class vessels. Interiors were designed by Carnival's ship architect Joe Farcus, whose abundant use of marble reflects Costa's Italian heritage. Artwork commissioned specifically for each ship was created by contemporary artists and includes intricate sculptures in silver and glass. Don't overlook the lighting fixtures, which were created especially for the ship, most of them crafted by the artisans in Venice's Murano glass factories.

The nice flow between public lounges is broken only by piazzas, where you can practice the Italian custom of *passeggiata* (seeing and being seen). And there's plenty to see; these are visually stimulating interiors, with vivid colors and decor elements to arouse a sense of discovery. One of the most elegant spaces on board is the least Italian in appearance—inspired by the Palazzo Roero Di Guarene, the Roero Bar contains cases to display artifacts from four ancient Chinese dynasties.

WOW Factor

As one passenger put it, if earlier Costa ships were Armani (clean, cool, and serene), then this one is Versace (glittering, sexy, and slightly outrageous).

Top: *Costa Mediterranea* at sea
Bottom: European service

Restaurants

A single two-deck-high formal restaurant serves Italian-accented cuisine in two traditional assigned seatings. An upscale, reservations-only alternative restaurant features a Tuscan steak-house menu of steaks and seafood dishes in addition to Italian specialties. The Lido buffet, pizzeria, and 24-hour room service are alternatives to dining room meals.

What Works & What Doesn't

As a nod to the spirit of La Dolce Vita, much socializing takes place during the Italian Bacchanal. However, there's a not-so-subtle current of Americanization underlying the overall experience. Thankfully, that hasn't extended to the lavish midnight buffets and utterly wacky toga party. A quirk, however, is the strange double use of the balcony in the specialty restaurant, which becomes a cigar lounge after regular dinner hours; don't linger over your coffee if you find that offensive. As long as you leave before 10 PM, nothing should distract you from the romantic, candlelit atmosphere.

Accommodations

Layout: *Costa Mediterranea* cabins generally follow the outline of their Carnival counterparts, with the distinctive addition of a Grand Suite category. Nearly 80% of the suites and staterooms have an ocean view, and of those, more than 80% have balconies. Every cabin has adequate closet and drawer–shelf storage, as well as bathroom shelves; suites have a walk-in closet.

Amenities: Light-wood cabinetry, pastel decor, Murano glass lighting fixtures, mirrored accents, a small refrigerator, a personal safe, a hair dryer, and a sitting area with sofa, chair, and table are typical for ocean-view cabins and suites. Inside cabins have somewhat smaller sitting areas for lounging. Suites have VCRs.

Bathroom: Extras include shampoo and bath gel in shower-mounted dispensers. Suites have a whirlpool bathtub.

Worth Noting: Although connecting staterooms are somewhat scarce throughout the ships, balcony dividers can be unlocked to provide connecting access in upper-category staterooms. Eight staterooms are designed for wheelchair accessibility.

CABIN TYPE	SIZE (sq. ft.)
Grand Suites	650
Suites	360
Ocean View*	185
Interior	160

*Extended balcony cabins have balconies at least 50% larger than average.

Fast Facts

- 12 passenger decks
- Specialty restaurant, dining room, buffet, pizzeria
- In-cabin broadband, in-cabin safes, in-cabin refrigerators, some in-cabin VCRs
- 3 pools (1 indoor), children's pool
- Fitness classes, gym, hair salon, 4 hot tubs, sauna, spa, steam room
- 6 bars, casino, cinema, 2 dance clubs, 2 showrooms, video game room
- Children's programs (ages 3–17)
- Laundry service
- Computer room

5

COSTA CRUISES

In the Know

Tucked away far forward is a stunning chapel with an altar, wood pews, stained-glass panels, and religious icons. Unlike other ships' generic wedding chapels, this is a tiny house of worship afloat.

Favorites

Best Place to Escape the Crowds: Forward on the outdoor promenade decks are serene retreats in the form of enclosed terraces, which might have been termed winter gardens on ocean liners.

Best Splurge: Italians consider cappuccino a breakfast beverage, so don't order it in the dining room following dinner—specialty coffees are not available there any-

way. Instead, follow the Roman custom of going out for coffee and head to the Oriental Café, where traditional espresso and cappuccino are served.

Our Favorite Spot for a Nightcap: It may sound unusual, but the lobby bar and the area just aft of the atrium are rather nice places to end the evening. While everyone is busy in the dance

clubs, casino, or show lounges, the lounge-y lobby areas can be almost restful.

Best Retail Therapy: Duty-free boutiques offer enough Italian designer items to satisfy the most addicted shopaholics.

Workout with a sea view

CRYSTAL CRUISES

Winner of accolades and too many hospitality industry awards to count, Crystal Cruises offers a taste of the grandeur of the past along with all the modern touches discerning passengers demand these days. Founded in 1990 and owned by Nippon

Crystal Serenity wraparound promenade

Yusen Kaisha (NYK) in Japan, Crystal ships, unlike other luxury vessels, are large, carrying upward of 900 passengers. What makes them distinctive are superior service, a variety of dining options, spacious accommodations, and some of the highest ratios of space per passenger of any cruise ship.

CRYSTAL CRUISES
2049 Century Park E,
Suite 1400
Los Angeles, CA 90067
888/799-4625 or
310/785-9300
www.crystalcruises.com

Cruise Style: Luxury

Beginning with ship designs based on the principles of feng shui, the Eastern art of arranging your surroundings to attract positive energy, no detail is overlooked to provide passengers with the best imaginable experience. Just mention a preference for a certain food or beverage, and your waiter will have it available whenever you request it.

The complete roster of entertainment and activities includes Broadway-style production shows, and bingo, but where Crystal really shines is in the variety of enrichment and educational programs. Passengers can participate in the hands-on Computer University@Sea, interactive Creative Learning Institute classes, or attend lectures featuring top experts in their fields: keyboard lessons with Yamaha, language classes by Berlitz, wellness lectures with the Cleveland Clinic, and an introduction to Tai Chi with the Tai Chi Cultural Center. Professional ACBL Bridge instructors are on every cruise, and dance instructors offer lessons in contemporary and social dance styles.

An added highlight for women traveling solo is the Ambassador Host Program, which brings cultured gentlemen on each cruise to dine, socialize, and dance with unaccompanied ladies.

Somewhat unique among cruise lines, Crystal Cruises' casinos offer complimentary cocktails to players at the tables and slot machines.

A delightful daily event is afternoon tea in the Palm Court. You're greeted by staff members in 18th-century Viennese brocade and velvet costumes for Mozart Tea; traditional scones and clotted cream are served during English Colonial Tea; and American Tea is a summertime classic created by Crystal culinary artists.

Food

The food alone is a good enough reason to book a Crystal cruise. Dining in the main restaurants is an event starring a Continental-inspired menu of dishes served by European-trained waiters. Off-menu item requests are honored when possible, and special dietary considerations are handled with ease. Full-course vegetarian menus are among the best at sea. Casual poolside dining beneath the stars is offered on some evenings in a relaxed, no-reservations option. A variety of hot-and-cold hors d'oeuvres are served in bars and lounges every evening before dinner and again during the wee hours.

But the specialty restaurants really shine. Jade Garden on *Crystal Symphony* serves traditional Japanese dishes as well as offerings from the menu of Wolfgang Puck's Chinois. Contemporary Asian cuisine is served in *Crystal Serenity*'s Silk Road. The Sushi Bar offers the signature dishes of Nobu Matsuhisa. Both ships have Prego, which serves regional Italian cuisine by Piero Selvaggio, owner of Valentino in Los Angeles and Las Vegas.

Exclusive Wine & Champagne Makers dinners are hosted in the Vintage Room. On select evenings, casual poolside theme dinners are served under the stars.

Crystal has an extensive wine list, including its own proprietary label called C Wines, which are produced in California. Unfortunately, there are no complimentary wines with dinner, as is common on other luxury cruise lines. However, you won't pay extra for bottled water, soft drinks, and specialty coffees; all are included in your basic fare.

Fitness & Recreation

Large spas offer innovative pampering therapies, body wraps, and exotic Asian-inspired treatments by Steiner Leisure. Feng shui principles were scrupulously adhered to in their creation to assure the spas and salons remain havens of tranquility.

Noteworthy

■ Before sailing, each passenger receives a personal e-mail address.

■ Ambassador Hosts on Crystal cruises are cultured, well-traveled gentlemen, who are accomplished dancers and interact with female passengers.

■ Complimentary self-service laundry rooms as well as complete laundry, dry-cleaning, and valet services are available.

Top: *Crystal Serenity* fitness center
Bottom: Crystal casino entrance

5

CRYSTAL CRUISES

Top: Spa treatment
Middle: Keyboard lessons
Bottom: *Crystal Symphony* Crystal penthouse

Fitness centers have a range of exercise and weight-training equipment and workout areas for aerobics classes, plus complimentary yoga and Pilates instruction. In addition, golfers enjoy extensive shipboard facilities, including a driving range practice cage and putting green. Passengers can leave their bags at home and rent top-quality Callaway clubs for use ashore. The line's resident golf pros offer complimentary lessons and group clinics.

Your Shipmates

Affluent, well-traveled couples, from their late-30s and up, are attracted to Crystal's destination-rich itineraries, shipboard enrichment programs, and elegant ambience. The average age of passengers is noticeably higher on longer itineraries.

Dress Code

Formal attire is required on at least two designated evenings, depending on the length of the cruise. Men are encouraged to wear tuxedos, and many do, although dark suits are also acceptable. Other evenings are informal or resort casual; the number of each is based on the number of sea days. The line requests that dress codes be observed in public areas after 6 PM, and few, if any, passengers disregard the suggestion. Most, in fact, dress up just a notch from guidelines.

Junior Cruisers

Although these ships are decidedly adult-oriented, Crystal welcomes children but limits the number of children under age three on any given cruise. Children under six months are not allowed.

Dedicated facilities for children and teens from ages 3 to 17 are staffed by counselors during holiday periods, select summer sailings, and when warranted by the number of children booked. Activities—including games, computer time, scavenger hunts, and arts and crafts—usually have an eye toward the educational. Teenagers can play complimentary video games to their heart's content in Waves, the arcade dedicated for their use. Babysitting can be arranged with staff members for a fee. Baby food, high chairs, and booster seats are available upon request.

❶ You crave peace and quiet. Announcements are kept to a bare minimum, and the ambience is sedate.

❷ You prefer to plan ahead. You can make spa, restaurant, shore excursion, and class reservations when you book your cruise.

❸ You love sushi and other Asian delights; Crystal ships serve some of the best at sea.

Service

Crystal's European-trained staff members provide gracious service in an unobtrusive manner.

Tipping

Tips may be distributed personally by passengers on the last night of the cruise or charged to shipboard accounts. Suggested gratuity guidelines per person, per day are: waiter $4; assistant waiter $2.50; cabin stewardess $4; and, for suite occupants only, butler $4. Passengers may adjust the amount based on the level of service experienced. All beverage tabs include an automatic 15% gratuity, as do spa and salon services. A minimum of $6 per person, per dinner is suggested for the servers in specialty restaurants.

Past Passengers

You're automatically enrolled in the Crystal Society upon completion of your first Crystal cruise and are entitled to special savings and member-only events. Membership benefits increase with each completed Crystal cruise and include such perks as stateroom upgrades, shipboard spending credits, special events, gifts, air upgrades, and even free cruises. Society members also receive Crystal Cruises' complimentary quarterly magazine, which shares up-to-date information on itineraries, destinations, special offers, and Society news.

Good to Know

While two assigned dining room seatings are advertised as an advantage that offers flexibility, the reality is that open-seating is the true mark of choice and the most preferred option at this level of luxury cruising. If you haven't done so in advance, on embarkation day you can reserve a table to dine one night in each specialty restaurant, but don't dawdle until the last minute; if you wait, you may find a line has developed—one of the few lines you'll encounter on board—and all the choice dining times are already booked. You may also be able to reserve additional nights after the cruise is under way, depending on how busy the restaurants are.

5

CRYSTAL CRUISES

DON'T CHOOSE CRYSTAL CRUISES IF:

❶ You don't want to follow the dress code. Everyone does, and you'll stand out—and not in a good way—if you rebel.

❷ You want total freedom. Unlike other luxury cruise lines, Crystal assigns you a seating and a table for dinner.

❸ You want a less structured cruise. With set dining times, Crystal is a bit more regimented than other luxury lines.

CRYSTAL SERENITY

Public Areas & Facilities

Crystal Serenity is Crystal Cruises' long-awaited third ship, the first to be introduced since 1995. Although more than a third larger than Crystal's earlier ships, it's similar in layout and follows the line's successful formula of creating intimate spaces in understated, yet sophisticated surroundings.

Stylish public rooms are uncrowded and uncluttered, yet clubby, in the tradition of elegantly proportioned drawing rooms (even the main show lounge is on a single level). Muted colors and warm woods create a soft atmosphere conducive to socializing in the refined environment. The Palm Court could be mistaken for the kind of British colonial–era lounge you might have seen in Hong Kong or India in the 19th century.

A thoughtful touch is an entirely separate room for scrutinizing the art pieces available for auction. The understatement even continues into the casino, although it contains plenty of slot machines and gaming tables.

700 ft.	**2003** ENTERED SERVICE
	1,080 PASSENGER CAPACITY
	635 CREW MEMBERS
	540 NUMBER OF CABINS
500 ft.	**68,000** GROSS TONS
	820 feet LENGTH
300 ft.	**106 feet** WIDTH

WOW Factor

It's what you don't see that creates a sensation. The Asian restaurants and enrichment programs are unsurpassed afloat and would be difficult to top on land as well.

Restaurants

The formal restaurant serves international cuisine in two assigned evening seatings. There's no additional charge for the intimate Asian and Italian specialty restaurants, but reservations are required, and a gratuity is suggested for the servers. Daytime dining choices include a Lido buffet, poolside grill, a patisserie, and an ice cream bar.

Top: *Crystal Serenity* at sea
Bottom: Sushi bar

What Works & What Doesn't

Crystal Serenity is aptly named. A few anxious moments may pass until dining reservations are secured for the specialty restaurants, but those nerves are nothing compared to what you'd feel trying to get a table at the chef's shoreside counterparts. A West Coast lifestyle prevails, which can be somewhat off-putting to people from fly-over country until they relax and go with the flow. Upscale and tasteful, this ship offers kid-centric spaces, but it isn't a particularly family-friendly cruise experience.

Great for walkers, a wide teak promenade deck encircles the ship.

Accommodations

Layout: As you'd expect on a luxury vessel, *Crystal Serenity* has no inside cabins; however, although suites are generous in size, lesser categories are somewhat smaller than industry standard at this level. All accommodations are designed with ample closet and drawer–shelf storage, as well as bathroom shelves and twin sinks. An impressive 85% of all cabins have private balconies furnished with chairs and tables. Most suites and penthouses have walk-in closets. Crystal Penthouse suites have private workout areas, pantries, and guest powder rooms.

Amenities: Rich wood cabinetry, soft colors, a small refrigerator with complimentary bottled water and soft drinks, a personal safe, a hair dryer, broadband connection for laptop computer, a television with a DVD player, and a sitting area with sofa, chair, and table are typical standard amenities. Most suites and penthouses also have CD players; all have flat-screen TVs, butler service, personalized stationery, and a fully stocked minibar.

Good to Know: Few staterooms have interior interconnecting doors, and accommodations with a third berth are scarce except in penthouse suite categories. Eight staterooms are designed for wheelchair accessibility.

CABIN TYPE	SIZE (sq. ft.)
Crystal Penthouse	1,345
Penthouse Suites	538
Regular Penthouses	403
Deluxe Ocean View (w/balcony)	269
Deluxe Ocean View (regular)	226

All dimensions except for regular Deluxe staterooms (the only category that does not have a veranda) include the balcony square footage.

In the Know

A common occurrence on cruise ships is last-night syndrome (when you return to your cabin after that last dinner to find that certain amenities have vanished). Gone are fruit baskets, minibar beverages, and even unwrapped bars of soap. On Crystal that is not the case; the last night is just like the first.

Favorites

Best Splurge: You don't have to swipe the logo china used in the Bistro to impress your friends back home. It's for sale in one of the boutiques.

Best Added Value: A splendid selection of alternative restaurants is yours to enjoy at no additional cost. You may get the urge to drop at least $20 on the table after dessert—the food and service are that good—but the suggested gratuity is a mere $6.

Our Favorite Spot for a Nightcap: The Avenue Saloon is dark and inviting, just the right spot to duck into following an after-dinner cigar and brandy in the adjacent Connoisseur Club.

Best Bath News: Every bathroom has a full-size tub, Aveda toiletries, plush towels, and bathrobes are provided for use during the cruise. Most suites and penthouses have whirlpool tub and separate shower.

Best Way to Curb Your Aggression: Take a stone sculpting class (part of the Masterpieces of Art program).

Fast Facts

- 9 passenger decks
- 3 specialty restaurants, dining room, buffet, ice-cream parlor
- In-cabin broadband, Wi-Fi, in-cabin safes, some in-cabin minibars, in-cabin refrigerators, in-cabin DVDs
- 2 pools (1 indoor)
- Fitness classes, gym, hair salon, 2 hot tubs, sauna, spa, steam room
- 6 bars, casino, cinema, 2 dance clubs, library, showroom, video game room
- Children's programs (ages 3–17)
- Dry cleaning, laundry facilities, laundry service
- Computer room
- No kids under 6 months

Crystal spa

5

CRYSTAL CRUISES

CRYSTAL SYMPHONY

1995	ENTERED SERVICE
940 (1,010 max)	PASSENGER CAPACITY
545	CREW MEMBERS
470	NUMBER OF CABINS
51,044	GROSS TONS
781 feet	LENGTH
99 feet	WIDTH

Public Areas & Facilities

Crystal Symphony, despite being a relatively large ship with some big-ship features, is noteworthy in the luxury market for creating intimate spaces in understated, yet sophisticated surroundings. Generous per-passenger space ratios have become a Crystal trademark, along with forward-facing observation decks, a Palm Court lounge, and a wide teak promenade encircling the ship. A complete makeover in 2006 refreshed the Bistro Café and shops, reconstructed the casino and Starlite Lounge, and added a new nightclub called Luxe. The extensive refurbishment infused all staterooms and bathrooms with a chic, boutique-style freshness.

Accented by a lovely waterfall, the focal point of the central two-deck atrium is a sculpture of two ballet dancers created especially for the space. Crystal Cove, the lobby lounge, is the spot to meet for cocktails as you make your way to the nearby dining room. Throughout the ship, public rooms shine with low-key contemporary style and flow easily from one to the next with complementary colors and decor.

WOW Factor

The refined and gracious atmosphere without a hint of unnecessary glitter is immediately apparent, but it's the professionalism of the staff that adds sparkle.

Top: Casino gaming
Bottom: Computer University@Sea

Restaurants

The formal restaurant serves international cuisine in two assigned evening seatings. There's no additional charge for the intimate Asian and Italian specialty restaurants, but a gratuity is suggested and reservations required. Daytime dining choices include the Lido buffet, an outdoor grill, ice-cream bar, and the Bistro patisserie.

What Works & What Doesn't

Dedicated areas for children and teens take a backseat to what's offered for adults—the Creative Learning Institute enrichment programs, complimentary Computer University@Sea instruction, and a full roster of distinguished guest speakers barely scratch the surface of what's at hand. Crystal began including complimentary bottled water and soft drinks when *Crystal Serenity* was introduced and also extended the perk to *Crystal Symphony.* Unlike other top-end luxury cruise lines, wine is not included with dinner.

Accommodations

Layout: There are no inside cabins on *Crystal Symphony*. Still, relatively small stateroom sizes are cozy and chic with boutique-hotel style décor; however, all cabins have ample closet and drawer–shelf storage, as well as bathroom shelves. Many have private balconies furnished with chairs and tables. Most suites and penthouses have a walk-in closet. Crystal Penthouse suites have guest powder rooms.

Amenities: Rich wood cabinetry, soft pastel fabrics, a small refrigerator filled with complimentary bottled water and soft drinks, a personal safe, a hair dryer, a television with a DVD player, and a sitting area with sofa, chair, and table are typical standard features in all cabins. Suite and penthouse extras vary, but many have a flat-screen television and CD player. All have butler service, personalized stationery, and

stocked minibars with wine, beer, and choice of liquor.

Bathrooms: Every bathroom has oval glass sinks, granite conters, a full-size tub, Aveda toiletries, plush towels, and bathrobes for use during the cruise. Many suites and penthouses have a whirlpool tub and separate shower.

Good to Know: Seven staterooms are wheelchair-accessible.

CABIN TYPE	SIZE (sq. ft.)
Crystal Penthouse	982
Penthouse Suites	491
Regular Penthouses	367
Deluxe Ocean View (w/balcony)	246
Deluxe Ocean View (regular)	202

All dimensions except for regular Deluxe staterooms (the only category that does not have a veranda) include the balcony square footage.

Fast Facts

- 8 passenger decks
- 2 specialty restaurants, dining room, buffet, ice-cream parlor
- Wi-Fi, in-cabin safes, in-cabin refrigerators, some in-cabin minibars, in-cabin DVDs
- 2 pools (1 indoor)
- Fitness classes, gym, hair salon, 2 hot tubs, sauna, spa, steam room
- 5 bars, casino, cinema, dance club, library, showroom, video game room
- Children's programs (ages 3–17)
- Dry cleaning, laundry facilities, laundry service
- Computer room
- No kids under 6 months

In the Know

Steam rooms and saunas are completely complimentary, and no spa treatments or other purchases are required before using them. Simply go in anytime you please. In addition, bathrobes and disposable slippers are provided for use in the men's and women's locker rooms.

Favorites

Best Added Value: If you feel the need to pack light and do laundry during your cruise or return home with clean clothing in your suitcases, passenger launderettes are complimentary.

Best Way to Take in a Film: The large theater seats almost as many movie buffs as an average multiplex ashore and serves free popcorn.

Screenings alternate between recent releases and classic favorites.

Our Favorite Spot for a Nightcap: Happily, Crystal doesn't mess with a good thing. Just as on *Crystal Serenity*, the Avenue Saloon and its Connoisseur Club annex are winners for a quiet drink before bed.

Best Place to Relax: With no aft-facing passenger

accommodations, *Crystal Symphony*'s stern retains the traditional styling of open decks with plenty of lounge chairs, so you can relax and watch the ship's wake. For a bit more privacy, a canopy-covered sun deck is behind the spa.

Most Difficult Choice: Which one of the proprietary wines will you order with dinner?

Library

CUNARD LINE

One of the world's most distinguished names in ocean travel
since 1840, Cunard Line's history of deluxe transatlantic crossings and worldwide cruising is
legendary for comfortable accommodations, excellent cuisine, and personal service. After

Romantic sunset at sea

a series of owners tried with little success to revive the company's flag-
ging passenger shipping business after the advent of the jet age, Carnival Corporation saved the day in 1998 with an infusion of ready cash
and the know-how to turn the cruise line around. The result is the her-
alded *Queen Mary 2.*

CUNARD LINE
24303 Town Center Drive
Valencia, CA 91355
661/753–1000 or
800/728–6273
www.cunard.com

Cruise Style: Luxury

Entertainment has a decidedly English flavor with nightly
production shows or cabaret-style performances and
even plays starring Great Britain's Royal Academy of Dramatic Arts alumni. An authentic pub gives the liner an
even more British air, while a wide variety of musical styles
can be found for dancing and listening in other bars and
lounges. In the first-ever shipboard planetarium, high-
tech presentations and virtual-reality shows dramatize the
origins of the universe and the history of the galaxies on
a virtual ride through space.

Cunard's fine enrichment programs include lectures by
experts in their fields. Classes vary by cruise and include
a wide assortment of topics taught by top designers,
master chefs, and artists. Even seamanship and navigation courses are offered to novice mariners. Passengers
can plan their activities prior to departure by consulting
the syllabus of courses available online at Cunard Line's
Web site.

Delightful daily events are afternoon tea and the maritime
tradition of sounding the ship's bell at noon. *Queen
Elizabeth 2* continues the tradition of North Atlantic crossings and sails on lengthy worldwide cruises, but she no
longer does regularly scheduled cruises in the Caribbean;

Queen Mary 2 also offers North Atlantic crossings and seasonal shorter cruises, including Caribbean itineraries.

Food
In the tradition of multiclass ocean liners, dining room assignments are made according to the accommodation category booked. You can get as much luxury as you are willing to pay for on *Queen Mary 2,* where passengers in Junior Suites are assigned to the single-seating Princess Grill; the posh Queen's Grill serves passengers booked in duplex apartments and the most lavish suites. All other passengers are assigned to one of two seatings in the dramatic, three-deck-high Britannia Restaurant.

Almost lost in the specialty restaurant hype is acclaimed chef Daniel Boulud, who designed the menus in *Queen Mary 2*'s main restaurants. Although fare in Britannia is reasonably traditional and often outstanding, off-menu requests by Grill passengers are commonly granted—provided the galley has the ingredients. Menus also include vegetarian and low-calorie selections.

Quite possibly the world's most coveted table reservations are those in the restaurant named for Todd English, the celebrity American chef and restaurateur noted for his innovative Mediterranean cuisine and sumptuous desserts. Dinner (for a $35 per person cover charge) was so popular that lunch was added (for $20 per person) so more passengers would have the opportunity to dine in the intimate restaurant.

The Chef's Galley is another small reservations-required restaurant, where diners look on as their food is prepared in an open galley setting; the only charge here is for wine. The King's Court buffet is transformed each evening into three no-charge casual alternative dining spots: the Carvery specializes in carved meats; La Piazza is dedicated to pasta, pizza, and Italian dishes; and Lotus offers Asian regional specialties.

Fitness & Recreation
Swimming pools, golf driving ranges, table tennis, paddle tennis court, shuffleboard, and jogging tracks barely scratch the surface of shipboard facilities dedicated to recreation. Top-quality fitness centers offer high-tech workout equipment, a separate weight room, and classes ranging from aerobics to healthy living workshops.

The Canyon Ranch Spa Club is a one-of-a-kind facility at sea offering salon services for women and men and a menu of more than 60 treatments, including the famous land-based spa's signature 80-minute Canyon Stone Mas-

Noteworthy

■ *Queen Mary 2* uses an Arabic 2 rather than the Roman numeral used by monarchs because it's a sequel to the original ship.

■ The captain steers the *Queen Mary 2* with a single lever or joystick on the bridge.

■ The sound of *Queen Mary 2*'s whistle carries for 10 miles but doesn't disturb passengers on deck.

Top: Cunard White Star service
Bottom: Illuminations planetarium

5

CUNARD LINE

Top: Fine dining
Middle: Royal Court Theater
Bottom: Junior suite

sage. The focal point of the facility is a 30- by 15-foot thalassotherapy pool featuring a deluge waterfall, air tub, massage-jet benches, neck fountains, and air-bed recliner lounges. To further achieve the therapeutic benefits of water and heat, you may want to try the thermal suite with its herbal sauna, Finnish sauna, aromatic steam room, and reflexology basins. Use of these special features is complimentary if you purchase a massage or other body treatment; otherwise, there's a per-day charge.

The daily SpaClub Passport costs $35 and includes use of the fitness center, thermal suite, aqua therapy center, locker rooms, and a choice of fitness classes. Robes, sandals, and complimentary beverages are also available for spa-goers and SpaClub Passport holders in the relaxation lounge.

Your Shipmates

Discerning, well-traveled American and British couples from their late-30s to retirees are drawn to Cunard's traditional style and the notion of a cruise aboard an ocean liner. The availability of spacious accommodations and complimentary self-service laundry facilities make Cunard liners a good option for families, although there may be fewer children on board than you might expect.

Dress Code

Glamorous evenings are typical of Cunard cruises, and specified attire includes formal, informal, and casual. Although resort casual clothing prevails throughout the day, Cunard vessels are ocean liners at heart and, as expected, are dressier than most cruise ships at night. To maintain their high standards, the cruise line requests passengers to dress as they would for dining in fine restaurants.

Junior Cruisers

The kid-friendly Kid Zone has both a dedicated play area and a splash pool for children ages one to six. Separate programs are reserved for older children ages 7 to 12 and teens. Toys and activities range from simple games to more educational computer classes. Children can practice their social graces when they're served their own afternoon teatime goodies. Toddlers are supervised by English nan-

---

CHOOSE CUNARD LINE IF:

❶ You want to boast that you have sailed on the world's largest ocean liner, though larger ships are already on the way.

❷ You enjoy a brisk walk. *Queen Mary 2* is massive, and you'll find yourself walking a great deal.

❸ A posh English pub is your ideal of the perfect place to hang out.

nies. Facilities are only operated until midnight; however, group babysitting is complimentary. Infants under one year are not allowed; children from ages one to two sail free (except for government fees).

Service

Although most crew members are international rather than British, service is formal and sophisticated.

Tipping

Suggested gratuities of $13 per person per day (for Grill Restaurant accommodations) or $11 per person per day (all other accommodations) are automatically charged to shipboard accounts for distribution to stewards and waitstaff. An automatic 15% gratuity is added to beverage tabs for bar service. Passengers can still tip individual crew members directly in cash for any special services.

Past Passengers

After one sailing aboard a Cunard liner, passengers are automatically enrolled as members of Cunard World Club; they are accorded Silver status on their second cruise. Silver-level members receive discounts of up to 50% off Early Booking Savings on all sailings, access to the shipboard World Club Representative and World Club Desk, and a quarterly newsletter, *The Cunarder.*

After completing two Cunard cruises, members are accorded Gold status and are additionally invited to shipboard World Club cocktail receptions and receive a Gold Cunarder pin. Passengers who complete seven sailings, or who have completed a Cunard voyage of 48 consecutive days or more, achieve the Platinum status. Additional benefits to Platinum members include a shipboard World Club cocktail reception, priority check-in and boarding in certain embarkation ports, an invitation to the Senior Officers' party, and a Platinum Cunarder pin.

Good to Know

The idea of a multiple-class ship offends some people's sense of democracy, and Cunard ships are ocean liners that adhere in not-so-subtle fashion to the tradition of class distinctions. This is the 21st century, though, so you won't find steerage class, and even regular folks in the cheaper cabins will enjoy the superior surroundings. However, certain areas of *Queen Mary 2*, including the Queen's Grill Lounge, a private sun terrace, and even a private elevator, are reserved for occupants of privileged accommodations. So luxury on a Cunard ship is a relative experience and certainly more luxurious for some.

5

CUNARD LINE

DON'T CHOOSE CUNARD LINE IF:

❶ You prefer informality, especially in the Caribbean. *Queen Mary 2* is a traditional formal liner.

❷ You want real luxury with no add-on costs.

❸ Your sense of direction is really bad. Nearly everyone gets lost on board at least once.

QUEEN MARY 2

2004	ENTERED SERVICE
2,620 (3,090 max)	PASSENGER CAPACITY
1,253	CREW MEMBERS
1,310	NUMBER OF CABINS
151,400	GROSS TONS
1,132 feet	LENGTH
135 feet	WIDTH

Public Areas & Facilities

With the clever use of design elements, *Queen Mary 2*, one of the largest passenger liners ever built, bears a striking external resemblance to the smaller, older *Queen Elizabeth 2*. The world's grandest and most expensive liner is something of a transitional ship, incorporating classic ocean-liner features—sweeping staircases, soaring public rooms, a 360-degree promenade deck, and a grand ballroom—all comfortably within a hull that also includes a trendy Canyon Ranch Spa and a full-scale planetarium.

Interior spaces blend the traditional style of early-20th-century liners with all the conveniences 21st-century passengers expect. Public rooms are mainly located on two decks low in the ship—remember, this is a liner designed for North Atlantic crossings. Befitting a queen, the grand lobby is palatial with broad, curving staircases and stately columns. Wide passageways lead to a variety of lounges, shops, a casino, showroom, and planetarium. The Queen's room is especially regal, with an arched ceiling and sparkling crystal chandeliers.

WOW Factor

Anyone who claims they aren't impressed just seeing Queen Mary 2 *waiting alongside the dock is probably faking their lack of enthusiasm.*

Top: Intimate lounges
Bottom: Grand duplex

Restaurants

Queen Mary 2 offers different levels of dining assignment that correspond to accommodation category booked. The Britannia Restaurant serves dinner in two seatings to most passengers; those in junior suites and above dine in the single-seating Grill restaurants; those in AA Britannia Club Balcony Cabins dine in the single-seating Britannia Club Dining Room.

What Works & What Doesn't

The full majesty of yesteryear's grand liners is re-created within *Queen Mary 2*'s hull—she appears to be a throwback to the days of opulence and celebrity sightings. Although it's certainly exciting to sail on such an impressive ship, no one harbors the illusion that booking an inside cabin results in the same level of pampering and attention received by occupants of a Penthouse or Royal Suite. So the illusion of total luxury falls short in reality.

On the other hand, proper afternoon tea and great, pub-style fare in the Golden Lion suggest that Britannia still rules the waves.

Accommodations

Layout: Selecting a stateroom or suite on *Queen Mary 2* is a complex endeavor due to the many variations. As expected on the world's most luxurious liner, an impressive 78% of her accommodations are outside cabins and over 86% of these feature spacious private balconies. There are fewer than 300 inside cabins; however, a dozen insides have an atrium view. All accommodations are designed with ample closet, drawer-shelf storage, and bathroom shelves. Private balconies are furnished with chairs, loungers, and tables. Duplex apartment and suite luxuries vary, but most have a whirlpool tub, dressing area, entertainment center, and dining area; all have private balconies. In addition, duplex apartments and most suites feature guest powder rooms and whirlpool tubs; some have his-and-hers dressing rooms.

Amenities: Warm-wood cabinetry, quality fabrics, a small refrigerator, a personal safe, a hair dryer, broadband computer hook-up, interactive television, and a sitting area with sofa or chairs and dual-height table are typical standard amenities. Toiletries, slippers, and bathrobes for use during the cruise are standard.

Good to Know: Thirty cabins are wheelchair-accessible.

CABIN TYPE	SIZE (sq. ft.)
Grand Duplex/Duplex	2,249 /1,194
Royal Suite/Penthouse	796/758
Suite/Jr. Suite	506/381
Deluxe/ Premium Balcony	248/249
Standard Ocean View/Inside	194

In the Know

Yes, you read the deck plan correctly: there's a kennel on Queen Mary 2. But, no, sadly you can't bring Fido or Fluffy along on a Caribbean cruise. Kennel use is restricted to transatlantic crossings, although service animals can avail themselves of the fire hydrant during cruises.

Favorites

Share the Captain's Viewpoint: For a glimpse into all things nautical, visit the bridge observation area. Through glass windows directly behind the main console, you'll have a view of both the long-range and short-range radar. Open on most sea days, access the area by using the "A" stairwell or elevators and stay as long as you like.

Shall We Dance?: The Queen's Room is a true ballroom with the largest ballroom dance floor at sea. Spanning the width of the ship beneath a high, arched ceiling and crystal chandelier, it's a majestic space where you'll want to waltz the night away.

Our Favorite Spot for a Nightcap: So many bars, so little time . . . for the atmosphere of an ocean crossing, the Chart Room wins out. For a nightclub vibe, we prefer the Commodore Club.

Best Splurge: Dine in Todd English, which bears the name of the celebrity chef who designed the menu; his innovative Mediterranean cuisine is the best thing going on the QM2.

Fast Facts

- 14 passenger decks
- 2 specialty restaurants, 3 dining rooms, buffet, ice-cream parlor, pizzeria
- In-cabin broadband, Wi-Fi, in-cabin safes, in-cabin refrigerators, some in-cabin minibars, some in-cabin DVDs
- 5 pools (2 indoor), 2 children's pools
- Fitness classes, gym, hair salon, 7 hot tubs, sauna, spa, steam room
- 11 bars, casino, cinema, 2 dance clubs, library, showroom, video game room
- Children's programs (ages 1–17)
- Dry cleaning, laundry facilities, laundry service
- Computer room
- No kids under age 1

5

CUNARD LINE

Pool deck

DISNEY CRUISE LINE

With the launch of Disney Cruise Line in 1998, families were offered yet another reason to take a cruise. The magic of a Walt Disney resort vacation plus the romance of a sea voyage are a tempting combination, especially for adults who

Disney ships have a classic style.

discovered Disney movies and the Mickey Mouse Club as children. Mixed with traditional shipboard activities, who can resist scheduled opportunities for the young and young-at-heart to interact with their favorite Disney characters?

DISNEY CRUISE LINE
210 Celebration Place, Suite 400
Celebration, FL 34747-4600
407/566-3500 or
888/325-2500
www.disneycruise.com

Cruise Style: Mainstream

A Disney cruise begins even before embarkation if you opt to use bus transfers from the Orlando airport or Walt Disney World. A slick orientation video passes the time and gets everyone revved up for their first view of the ship. Passengers who added a precruise stay at Walt Disney World seamlessly complete their cruise check-in before leaving the resort; check-in for the balance of passengers is handled in the efficient Port Canaveral terminal designed especially for Disney. While waiting to board, capture your children's attention by pointing out the cut-away model of a Disney ship and a map of the Bahamas and Caribbean inlaid in the floor.

Shipboard entertainment leans heavily on popular Disney themes and characters. Parents are actively involved in the audience with their children at production shows, movies, live character meetings, deck parties, and dancing in the family nightclub. Teens have a supervised, no-adults-allowed club space in the forward fake funnel, where they gather for activities and parties. For adults, there are traditional no-kids-allowed bars and lounges with live music, dancing, theme parties, and late-night comedy as well as daytime wine-tasting sessions, game shows, culinary arts and home entertaining demonstrations, and behind-the-scenes lectures on animation and filmmaking.

A giant-size LED screen has been affixed to the forward funnel on *Disney Magic*. Passengers can watch movies and special broadcasts while lounging in the family pool area.

For many *Disney Wonder* passengers, the cruise is a three- or four-night extension of a Walt Disney World vacation, while *Disney Magic* sailings more resemble a traditional seven-night cruise with a Disney twist. All Bahamas and Caribbean cruises call at Castaway Cay, Disney's private Bahamian island with its own pier for convenient dockside debarkation. It's the only cruise line private island with a dock.

Food

Don't expect top chefs and gourmet food. This is Disney, and the fare in Parrot Cay and Animator's Palate, the two casual restaurants, is all-American for the most part. Triton's (*Disney Wonder*) and Lumière's (*Disney Magic*) restaurants are a bit fancier, with French-inspired dishes on the menus. Naturally, all have children's menus with an array of favorite sandwiches and entrées. Vegetarian and healthy selections are also available in all restaurants. A bonus is complimentary soft drinks, lemonade, and iced tea throughout the sailing. A beverage station in the buffet area is always open; however, there is a charge for soft drinks ordered from the bars and room service.

Palo, the adults-only restaurant serving northern Italian cuisine, requires reservations for a romantic evening of fine dining. Although there's a cover charge for dinner, at $10 per person it's a steal and reservations go fast. A champagne brunch on four- and seven-night cruises also commands a $10 surcharge; high tea on seven-night cruises is $5.

Fitness & Recreation

Three swimming pools are designated for different groups: for children (Mickey's Pool, which has a waterslide and requires a parent to be present); for families (Goofy Pool); and adults (Quiet Cove). Young children who aren't potty trained can't swim in the pools but are invited to splash about in the fountain play area near Mickey's Pool. Be sure to bring their swim diapers.

The salon and spa feature a complete menu of hair and nail care services as well as facials and massages. The Tropical Rainforest is a soothing coed thermal suite with heated tile lounges. It's complimentary for the day if you

Noteworthy

■ Disney ships are the first ships since the 1950s to feature two funnels.

■ Many cabins on Disney ships feature faux steamer trunks for storage and efficient split-use bathrooms.

■ There are no casinos on board Disney ships, and smoking areas are strictly limited.

5

DISNEY CRUISE LINE

Top: Dining in Palo, the adults-only restaurant
Bottom: Family fun at Castaway Cay, Disney's private isle in the Bahamas

Top: A day ashore
Middle: Making a splash in
Mickey's pool
Bottom: *Disney Magic* and *Wonder*
at sea

book a spa treatment, or available on a daily or cruise-long basis for a fee. Unique to Disney ships are SpaVillas, three indoor/outdoor treatment suites, each of which has a veranda with a hot tub and an open-air shower. In addition to a nicely equipped fitness center and aerobics studio are a jogging track and basketball court.

Your Shipmates

The young and not so young—singles, couples, and families—all find Disney Cruises appealing. As expected, multigeneration family groups are the core audience for these ships, and the facilities are ideal for family gatherings. What you might not have expected are the numerous newlywed couples celebrating their honeymoons on board.

Dress Code

Three- and four-night *Disney Wonder* cruises are casual; no formal wear is required, and resort casual is the evening dress code for dinner in the Animator's Palate and Parrot Cay dining rooms. A sport coat with tie is appropriate for Triton's (*Disney Wonder*) and Lumière's (*Disney Magic*) restaurants as well as Palo, the adults-only restaurant on both ships; however, you won't be turned away without a tie and could probably get by without the sport coat as well. In addition to the guideline for shorter cruises, one-week cruises on *Disney Magic* schedule a semiformal evening and a formal night, during which men are encouraged to wear tuxedos, but dark suits or sport coats and ties are acceptable.

Junior Cruisers

As expected, Disney ships have extensive programs for children and teens. Parents are issued a pager for peace of mind and to alert them when their offspring need them. Complimentary age-appropriate activities are scheduled from 9 AM to midnight in the Oceaneer Club for ages three (toilet training required) to seven, in Oceaneer Lab for ages 8 to 12. Activities include arts projects, contests, computer games, pool parties, interactive lab stations, and opportunities for individual and group play. Ocean Quest, designed for 10- to 14-year-olds, has video games, plasma-screen TVs, and a ship simulator

CHOOSE DISNEY CRUISE LINE IF:

❶ You want to cruise with the entire family—mom, dad, the kids, and grandparents.

❷ You enjoy having kids around. (There are adults-only areas to retreat to when the fun wears off.)

❸ Your family enjoys Disney's theme parks and can't get enough wholesome entertainment.

where young mariners learn to steer the ship. The emphasis is on fun over education, but subtle educational themes are certainly there.

An hourly fee is charged for child care in Flounder's Reef Nursery, which is open during select hours for infants as young as three months through three years. Supply your own diapers, and nursery attendants will change them. Private, in-cabin babysitting is not available.

The Stack (*Disney Magic*) and Aloft (*Disney Wonder*) are coffeehouse-style clubs with music, a dance floor, large-screen television, and Internet Café. Scheduled activities include challenging games, photography lessons, sporting contests, beach events, and parties, but the Stack is also a great place for teenagers to just hang out with new friends in an adult-free zone.

Service
Friendly service is extended to all passengers with particular importance placed on treating children with the same courtesy extended to adults.

Tipping
Suggested gratuity amounts are calculated on a per person/per cruise rather than per night basis and can be added to onboard accounts or offered in cash on the last night of the cruise. Guidelines include gratuities for your dining room server, assistant server, head server, and stateroom host/hostess for the following amounts: $32.50 for three-night cruises, $43.75 for four-night cruises, and $76.25 for seven-night cruises. Tips for room-service delivery and the dining manager are at each passenger's discretion. An automatic 15% gratuity is added to all bar tabs.

Past Passengers
Castaway Club membership is automatic after completing a Disney cruise. Benefits include a complimentary gift (such as a tote bag or beach towel), communication about special offers, priority check-in, invitations to shipboard cocktail parties during subsequent cruises, and a special toll-free reservation telephone number (800/449–3380) for convenience.

Good to Know

Silhouettes and abstract images of Mickey Mouse are cleverly hidden by Disney's creative designers throughout the ship. See how many Hidden Mickeys you can spot—it's a terrific family game. Another favorite pursuit is autograph collecting; characters and crew members alike are happy to oblige. You can buy autograph books on the ships, but the gift shops won't open until after you sail. Drop in at a Disney store before your cruise and purchase them for your kids; they'll appreciate being prepared from the get-go.

Prior to sailing, go online to reserve shore excursions, a table at the adults-only Palo restaurant, and babysitting in the nursery. Children can also be registered for youth programs, and adults can make spa appointments.

If you didn't do it ahead of time, you can register the kids for their age-appropriate programs in the terminal while you wait to board.

DON'T CHOOSE DISNEY CRUISE LINE IF:

❶ You want to spend a lot of quality time bonding with your kids. Your kids may not want to leave the fun activities.

❷ You want to dine in peace and quiet. The dining rooms and buffet can be boisterous.

❸ You want to gamble. There are no casinos, so you'll have to settle for bingo.

DISNEY MAGIC, DISNEY WONDER

Public Areas & Facilities

Reminiscent of classic ocean liners, Disney vessels have two funnels (the forward one is nonfunctional) and high-tech interiors behind their art deco and art nouveau styling. Whimsical design accents cleverly incorporate the images of Mickey Mouse and his friends without overpowering the warm and elegant decor. Artwork showcases the creativity of Disney artists and animators. The atmosphere is never stuffy.

More than 15,000 square feet—nearly an entire deck—is devoted to children's activity centers, outdoor activity areas, and swimming pools. Theaters cater to family entertainment with large-scale production shows, movies, dances, and lively game shows.

Adults-only hideaways include an avenue of theme bars and lounges tucked into the area just forward of the lobby atrium; the Promenade Lounge, near the aft elevator lobby; and Cove Café, a quiet spot adjacent to the adult pool to relax with coffee or a cocktail, surf the Internet, or read.

1998, 1999	ENTERED SERVICE
1,754 (2,400 max)	PASSENGER CAPACITY
950	CREW MEMBERS
877	NUMBER OF CABINS
83,000	GROSS TONS
964 feet	LENGTH
106 feet	WIDTH

700 ft.

500 ft.

300 ft.

WOW Factor

The ship's horn plays "When You Wish Upon a Star" at sailaway and nearly everyone admits to getting goose bumps.

Restaurants

In a novel approach to dining, passengers (and their waiters) rotate through the three main dining rooms in two assigned seatings. Parrot Cay and Animator's Palate are casual, while Triton's (*Disney Wonder*) and Lumière's (*Disney Magic*) are a bit fancier. Palo is a beautifully appointed northern Italian restaurant for adults only that requires reservations.

What Works & What Doesn't

Top: Friendships are forged on a cruise.
Bottom: Dreams can come true on a Disney cruise.

Even though only potty-trained children can enter the swimming pools, youngsters who wear swim diapers aren't left out entirely; a special filtration system allows them to use the Mickey's Pool play area.

Every parent knows that little details like that can make or break a child's day. Fast-food favorites are alternatives for meals on the go: burgers from Pluto's, pizza from Pinocchio's, and ice cream at Scoops. You

should be aware that, although a Disney cruise isn't all Disney all the time, it can get tiring for passengers who aren't really into it. There's no library, but reading materials are available in the Cove Café.

Accommodations

Layout: Designed for families, Disney ships have some of the roomiest, most functional staterooms at sea. Natural woods, imported tiles, and a nautical flavor add to the decor, which even includes the touch of Disney-inspired artwork on the walls. Most cabins can accommodate at least three people and have a sitting area and unique bath-and-a-half arrangement. Three-quarters of all accommodations are outside cabins, and 44% of those include private balconies with kid-proof door handles and higher-than-usual railings for safety. All cabins have adequate closet and drawer-shelf storage, as well as bathroom shelves.

Amenities: Though not luxurious, Disney cabins are comfortably furnished, and each has a small refrigerator, personal safe, and a hair dryer; bathrobes are provided for use

during the cruise in the top-category staterooms. All suites have concierge service.

Suites: Suites are truly expansive, with master bedrooms separated from the living areas for privacy. All suites have walk-in closets, dining table and chairs, a wet bar, VCR, and large balcony.

Good to Know: Sixteen cabins are wheelchair-accessible.

CABIN TYPE	SIZE (sq. ft.)
Walt & Roy Disney Suites	1,029
2-Bedroom Suite/ 1-Bedroom Suite	945 /614
Deluxe Family Suite	304
Deluxe Balcony/ Ocean View	268 /226
Deluxe Inside/ Standard Inside	214 /184

In the Know

Aesthetically pleasing ship design can result in some quirky interior features. Four Navigator Verandah cabins are semi-obstructed by slanting superstructure (6134, 6634, 7120, 7620); the rest have nautically furnished verandas with views through large portholes cut into the steel.

Favorites

Best Added Value: Soft drinks at meals and beverage stations are included in your cruise fare, so you don't have to max out your onboard account to keep everyone satisfied.

Teen Scene: Disney ship designers recognized that teenagers are at an awkward stage in their lives, so a lot of extra effort went into re-creating the teen territories in

2004. The Stack on *Disney Magic* and Aloft on *Disney Wonder* are more hip dorm lounge than family room–adult-free spaces where teens can have the freedom they crave and where parents are not allowed. However, in Disney style, they are discreetly supervised by counselors.

Our Favorite Spot for a Nightcap: Have no fear—you won't be limited to

milk and cookies. Each ship has a piano bar–jazz club for easy listening and late-night cocktails.

Good for Families: There are plenty of connecting cabins that sleep 3, 4, and 5. Two-bedroom suites sleep up to 7; one-bedroom suites sleep 4 or 5; and deluxe family balcony staterooms sleep up to 5.

5

DISNEY CRUISE LINE

Goofy touches up the paint on *Disney Magic.*

EASYCRUISE

Introduced in Europe with great fanfare in 2005 by Stelios (like many celebrities, he goes by one name), the business model for easyCruise was easily the quirkiest endeavor to hit the cruise industry. Stelios, known as a "serial" entreperneur and the guiding force behind low-fare air carrier easyJet, has designed a cross between a traditional cruise ship and a ferry. Rather than book an entire voyage, independent minded passengers are offered the flexibility to book as few as three nights, embarking and departing in any scheduled port along the way.

easyCruise One

EASYCRUISE (UK) LTD.
The Rotunda,
42/43 Gloucester Crescent,
London, UK NW1 7DL
(30)211/211–6211
www.easycruise.com.

Cruise Style: Mainstream

Aimed at youthful travelers interested in island-hopping and sampling the local nightlife, itineraries are scheduled to arrive in port mid-morning, stay until the partying winds down, and then move on to the next destination. However, a hint that easyCruise may be heading along a more traditional path is that fares are now available in packages consisting of 3, 4, and 7 nights. EasyCruise is still able to offer rock-bottom pricing by eliminating all onboard frills and nearly all necessities. Passengers are encouraged to dine ashore since no meals are included in the cruise fare and on-board meal service is limited. You'll also pay for all cabin services, including cleaning, fresh towels, and bed linens. Fellow passengers on easyCruise don't seem to mind making their own beds.

CHOOSE A CRUISE ON EASYCRUISE IF...

❶ You've never considered a traditional cruise but find the idea of sampling a different destination every day appealing.

❷ You don't mind paying extra for anything and everything on board in exchange for a very low up-front fare.

❸ Your expectations and your budget are low.

Food

The best dining is still found ashore when in port. On board, an upgraded restaurant supplements the diner-quality snacks, sandwiches, and dessert items that have always been available. But the quality of the food is more like Starbucks or Ruby Tuesday. The best offerings are often found at breakfast. You pay for all food on board; there are no meal plans, and, although menus are priced in dollars, the individual items are on the pricey side for what you get. There are few options for passengers with special dietary needs, but numerous choices are suitable for vegetarians.

Fitness & Recreation

A small gym has exercise equipment, but you will be more likely to burn off calories walking in ports and swimming when you head for the beach. There's no pool, but there is a popular hot tub.

Your Shipmates

The plan was to appeal to active adults in their 20s and 30s. In reality, depending on the season and itinerary, passenger ages might lean toward the 40-something and older set. Most passengers hail from Great Britain or North America, with Brits usually in the majority.

Dress Code

This is as informal as cruising can get. The only provision is that you wear clothing.

Service

While it's adequate for food and beverages, you'll have to carry your own bags and make your bed yourself. You can pay for maid service, as well as clean sheets and towels.

Tipping

Tip for dining and drinks as you would at any shoreside bar or restaurant. Other gratuities are completely up to you, but since there is little service, you'll have few opportunities to tip.

Noteworthy

■ An easyCruise is pay-as-you-go cruising. While a low fare gets you on board, virtually nothing else is included.

■ *EasyCruise1* was rebuilt to cram in nearly twice as many passengers as it was designed for. Space and privacy are at a premium.

■ Be prepared to entertain yourself, though there is a nightly DJ and an occasional passenger participation game.

Top: Tropical drinks from the bar
Bottom: Relaxation in the sauna

5

EASYCRUISE

DON'T CHOOSE A CRUISE ON EASYCRUISE IF...

❶ You have a high-maintenance wardrobe and tend to over-pack. Only "suites" have close-to-adequate storage.

❷ Your expectations are for pampering attention and over-the-top services with facilities to match.

❸ You can't take care of yourself and make your own good times without a rigid schedule of activities.

EASYCRUISE ONE

1990	
Entered Service	
170	
Passenger Capacity	
700 ft.	**54**
	Crew Members
	86
	Number of Cabins
500 ft.	**4,077**
	Gross Tons
	290 feet
	Length
300 ft.	**50 feet**
	Width

Public Areas and Facilities

From a small upmarket vessel designed to carry 100 passengers in comfort and luxury, *easyCruiseOne* was transformed by gutting the interiors and replacing them with spartan, modular cabins that sleep nearly twice as many passengers when fully booked. While the bright neon-orange hull emblazoned with "easycruise.com" acted in the past as a beacon to late-night revelers returning from shoreside restaurants and clubs, the garish look has undergone a transformation. A new graphite-gray paint job with discreet orange trim gives the ship a more refined appearance but shouldn't hamper the party spirit of its passengers. Even in its new livery, *easyCruiseOne* is easy to spot late at night—it's likely to be the only ship at the pier.

The ship's public spaces have also been redecorated and now have more of the look of a boutique hotel. While the ship now has a sauna, small spa, and Internet café, the list of what isn't on board is still longer than the list of what is. There's still no swimming pool, casino, library, or even entertainment. This could be called the anti-cruise cruise ship. Easily.

WOW Factor

Budget-conscious cruisers feel the WOW factor in their wallets—even without all the "extras" that are not included, the bottom line on an easyCruise is easy to handle.

Top: New menu options
Bottom: Spa pampering

Restaurants

Meals are served on a come-when-you-want and pay-as-you-go basis. The main restaurant, Fusion on 4, serves all day long. Sun&Moon, the combination bar and café, serves a laundry list of snacks, sandwiches, coffee, and tea. Outdoor seating is available for alfresco dining.

What Works and What Doesn't

For its free-spirited and independent passengers, easyCruise has been a rousing success, particularly in the Caribbean, where the ship not only remains until the party ashore winds down but also arrives early enough so that passengers can enjoy a full day at the beach or sightseeing.

Passengers don't miss the lack of daytime entertainment on the ship because there are no sea days on easyCruise itineraries. With little nighttime entertainment, most cruisers enjoy the easy camaraderie, both on and off the ship.

Accommodations

Layout: Cabin decor has been toned down and is no longer quite so orange. Standard twin cabins for two are tiny, inside cabins tinier; quadruple cabins have two sets of bunk beds. Futon beds set on platforms are standard. Some doubles have windows that resemble square portholes, but all quads are inside. Bathrooms have surprisingly chic, if minimalist, glass basins, but there's no barrier between the shower and the rest of the bathroom, so the floor will likely be soaked. Storage consists of a few hooks and open shelves, so pack light. Toiletries, other than soap in a dispenser, are not provided. With no in-cabin telephones, TVs, or safes, you may wish to leave your valuables at home and pack a travel alarm clock instead. Bring your own hairdryer and beach towels as well. Happily for Americans, electrical outlets deliver 110-volt current with U.S.-style plugs.

Suites: Four suites have small sofas and balconies (as well as more space) but otherwise are similar to regular cabins with the same small bathrooms and plaform futon-style beds. Storage in suites is a bit better but is nothing like what you'd get in even the smallest regular cruise-ship cabin.

Good to Know: New, small windows have been cut through to create an ocean-view for about sixty cabins on Deck 3. Bring earplugs; sound-proofing seems to have been overlooked. One stateroom is designed to be wheelchair accessible.

CABIN TYPE	SIZE (sq. ft.)
Suite	258
Inside/Outside Double	108/129
Quadruple	162

Fast Facts

- 5 passenger decks
- 1 restaurant, 1 café
- gym, 1 hot tub, sauna, spa
- 2 bars
- Computer room, no kids under 14

5

EASYCRUISE

In the Know

Don't look for nightly turn-down service or a chocolate on your pillow. In do-it-yourself fashion, cabin service is not automatic, but is available as an option. You don't have to make your own bed if you are willing to pay the add-on price. Just sign up at the reception desk.

Favorites

Best Place to Wind Down: With happy-hour cocktails in hand, a soak in the hot tub is a relaxing interlude before dressing to head ashore for dinner.

Best Splurge: For more personal space, fares are so low that couples might want to considering booking a quad cabin, but the suites are both much larger and more expensive.

Best Onboard Dining: Breakfast items, available all day in the Fusion on 4 restaurant, are top menu selections among passengers who choose to eat on board.

Best Spot to Get Away From It All: There are a small number of lounge chairs for sunning on Deck 6.

Our Favorite Spot for a Nightcap: With a view over the stern and the stars overhead, we like the new seating area around the hot tub on Deck 5.

Dining al fresco

HOLLAND AMERICA LINE

Holland America Line has enjoyed a distinguished record of traditional cruises, world exploration, and transatlantic crossings since 1873—all facets of its history that are reflected in the fleet's multimillion dollar shipboard art and antiques collec-

Snorkel fun for all ages

tions. Even the ships' names follow a pattern set long ago: all end in the suffix "dam" and are either derived from the names of various dams that cross Holland's rivers, important Dutch landmarks, or points of the compass. The names are even recycled when vessels are retired, and some are in their fifth and sixth generation of use.

HOLLAND AMERICA LINE
300 Elliott Avenue W
Seattle, WA 98119
206/281-3535 or
800/577-1728
www.hollandamerica.com

Cruise Style: Premium Deluxe

Noted for focusing on passenger comfort, Holland America Line cruises are classic in design and style; however, with an infusion of younger adults and families on board, they remain refined without being stuffy or stodgy. Following a basic design theme, returning passengers feel as at home on the newest Holland America vessels as they do on older ones.

Entertainment tends to be more Broadway-stylish than Las Vegas–brash. Colorful revues are presented in main show lounges by the ships' companies of singers and dancers. Other performances might include a range of cabaret acts: comedians, magicians, jugglers, and acrobats. Live bands play a wide range of musical styles for dancing and listening in smaller lounges and piano bars. Movies are shown daily in cinemas that double as the Culinary Arts Centers.

Holland America Line may never be considered cutting edge, but the Signature of Excellence concept introduced in 2003 sets them apart from other premium cruise lines. An interactive Culinary Arts Center offers cooking demonstrations and wine-tasting sessions; Explorations Café (powered by *The New York Times*) is a coffeehouse-style library and Internet center; and the

Explorations Guest Speakers Series is supported by in-cabin televised programming on flat-screen TVs in all cabins; the traditional Crow's Nest observation lounge has a new nightclub-disco layout, video wall, and sound-and-light systems; and facilities for children and teens have been greatly expanded. Signature of Excellence upgrades were completed on the entire Holland America fleet in 2006.

Food

Holland America Line chefs, members of the Confrerie de la Chaîne des Rôtisseurs gourmet society, utilize more than 500 different food items on a typical weeklong cruise to create the modern Continental cuisine and traditional favorites served to their passengers. Vegetarian options as well as healthy Inbalance Spa Cuisine by Jeanne Jones are available, and special dietary requests can be handled with advance notice. Holland America's passengers used to skew older than they do now, so the sometimes bland dishes were no surprise; however, the food quality, taste, and selection have greatly improved in recent years. A case in point is the reservations-required Pinnacle Grill alternative restaurants, where fresh seafood and premium cuts of Sterling Silver beef are used to prepare creative specialty dishes. The $30 per person charge for dinner would be worth it for the Dungeness crab cakes starter and dessert alone. Other delicious traditions are afternoon tea, a Dutch Chocolate Extravaganza, and Holland America Line's signature bread pudding.

Flexible scheduling allows for early (5:45) or late (8:15) seatings in the two-deck, formal restaurants. "As You Wish" open seating from 5 to 9 is being introduced fleet-wide.

Fitness & Recreation

Well-equipped and fully staffed fitness facilities contain state-of-the-art exercise equipment; basic fitness classes are available at no charge. There's a fee for personal training, body composition analysis, and specialized classes such as yoga and Pilates.

Treatments in the Greenhouse Spa include a variety of massages, body wraps, and facials. Hair styling and nail services are offered in the salons. All ships have a jogging track, multiple swimming pools, and sports courts. Some have hydrotherapy pools and soothing thermal suites.

Your Shipmates

No longer just your grandparents' cruise line, today's Holland America Caribbean sailings attract families and dis-

Noteworthy

■ Trays of mints, dried fruits, and candied ginger can be found outside the dining rooms.

■ Passengers are presented with a complimentary cotton canvas carryall bag imprinted with the line's logo.

■ Each ship has a wraparound promenade deck for walking, jogging, or stretching out in the shade on a padded steamer chair.

Top: Casino action
Bottom: Parasailing at Half Moon Cay

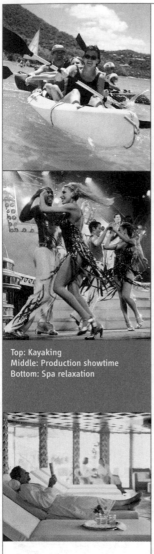

Top: Kayaking
Middle: Production showtime
Bottom: Spa relaxation

cerning couples, mostly from their late-30s on up. Holidays and summer months are peak periods when you'll find more children in the mix. Comfortable retirees are often still in the majority, particularly on longer cruises. Families cruising together who book five or more cabins receive a fountain-soda package for each family member, Club HAL T-shirts for children who participate in the youth program, a family photo for each stateroom, and either dinner for the entire family in the upscale Pinnacle Grill or complimentary water toys at Half Moon Cay (for Caribbean itineraries that call at the private island). If the group is larger,—ten cabins or more—the Head-of-Family is recognized with an upgrade from outside stateroom to a veranda cabin. It's the best family deal at sea, and there's no extra charge.

Dress Code

Evenings on Holland America Line cruises fall into three categories: casual, informal, and formal. Ties are optional, but men are asked to wear a sport coat on one informal night. For the two formal nights standard on seven-night cruises, men are encouraged to wear tuxedos, but dark suits or sport coats and ties are acceptable, and you'll certainly see them. Other nights are casual. It's requested that no T-shirts, jeans, swimsuits, tank tops, or shorts be worn in public areas after 6 PM.

Junior Cruisers

Club HAL is Holland America Line's professionally staffed youth and teen program. Age-appropriate activities planned for children ages three to seven include storytelling, arts and crafts, ice-cream or pizza parties, and games; for children ages 8 to 12 there are arcade games, Sony PlayStations, theme parties, on-deck sports events, and scavenger hunts. Club HAL After Hours offers late-night activities from 10 PM until midnight for an hourly fee. Baby food, diapers, cribs, high chairs, and booster seats may be requested in advance of boarding. Private in-cabin babysitting is sometimes available if a staff member is willing.

Teens aged 13 to 17 have their own lounge with activities including dance contests, arcade games, sports tour-

CHOOSE HOLLAND AMERICA LINE IF:

❶ You crave relaxation. Grab a padded steamer chair on the teak promenade deck and watch the sea pass by.

❷ You like to go to the movies, especially when the popcorn is free.

❸ You want to bring the kids—areas designed exclusively for children and teens are hot new features on all ships.

naments, movies, and an exclusive sun deck on some ships. Select itineraries offer water park–type facilities and kid-friendly shore excursions to Half Moon Cay, Holland America Line's private island in the Bahamas.

Service
Professional, unobtrusive service by the Indonesian and Filipino staff is a fleetwide standard on Holland America Line. It isn't uncommon for a steward or server to remember the names of returning passengers from a cruise taken years before. Crew members are trained in Indonesia at a custom-built facility called the ms *Nieuw Jakarta,* where employees polish their English-language skills and learn housekeeping in mock cabins.

Tipping
$10 per passenger, per day is automatically added to ship-board accounts, and gratuities are distributed to stewards and waitstaff. Passengers may adjust the amount based on the level of service experienced. Room-service tips are usually given in cash (it's the passenger's discretion here). An automatic 15% gratuity is added to bar-service tabs.

Past Passengers
All passengers who sail with Holland America Line are automatically enrolled in the Mariner Society and receive special offers on upcoming cruises as well as insider information concerning new ships and product enhancements. Mariner Society benefits also include preferred pricing on many cruises; Mariner baggage tags, and buttons that identify you as a member during embarkation; an invitation to the Mariner Society champagne reception and awards party hosted by the captain; lapel pins and medallions acknowledging your history of Holland America sailings; a special collectible gift delivered to your cabin; and a subscription to *Mariner,* the full-color magazine featuring news and Mariner Society savings. Once you complete your first cruise, your Mariner identification number will be assigned and available for lookup online.

Good to Know

The sound of delicate chimes still alerts Holland America Line passengers that it's mealtime. Artful flower arrangements never seem to wilt. A bowl of candied ginger is near the dining room entrance if you need a little something to settle your stomach. These simple, but nonetheless meaningful, touches are what make Holland America Line stand out from the crowd.

5

HOLLAND AMERICA LINE

DON'T CHOOSE HOLLAND AMERICA LINE IF:

❶ You want to party hard. Most of the action on these ships ends relatively early.

❷ Dressing for dinner isn't your thing. Passengers tend to ramp up the dress code most evenings.

❸ You have an aversion to extending tips. The line's "tipping not required" policy has been amended.

VISTA CLASS
Zuiderdam, Oosterdam, Westerdam, Noordam

2002, 2003, 2004, 2006	
ENTERED SERVICE	
1,848 (2,272 max)	
PASSENGER CAPACITY	
800	
CREW MEMBERS	
924	
NUMBER OF CABINS	
82,000	
GROSS TONS	
950 feet	
LENGTH	
106 feet	
WIDTH	

Public Areas & Facilities

Ships for the 21st century, Vista-class vessels successfully integrate new youthful and family-friendly elements into Holland America Line's classic fleet. Exquisite Waterford crystal sculptures adorn triple-deck atriums and reflect vivid, almost daring color schemes throughout. Although all the public rooms carry the traditional Holland America names (Ocean Bar, Explorer's Lounge, Crow's Nest) and aren't much different in atmosphere, their louder decor (toned down a bit since the introduction of the *Zuiderdam*) may make them unfamiliar to returning passengers.

Only two decks are termed "promenade," and the exterior teak promenade encircles public rooms, not cabins. As a result, there are numerous outside accommodations with views of the sea restricted by lifeboats on the Upper Promenade Deck. Veterans of cruises on other Holland America class ships will find the layout of public spaces somewhat different; however, everyone's favorite Crow's Nest lounges still offer those commanding views.

WOW Factor

Keep your sunglasses on. The color palette is not only bright and bold, but some of the furniture approaches the edge of funkiness.

Top: *Oosterdam* hydro pool
Bottom: Vista-class ocean-view stateroom

Restaurants

The formal dining room offers two dinner seatings and open seating; alternatives are Pinnacle Grill, which requires reservations and has a cover charge, and the casual Lido café that also serves buffet breakfast and lunch. Terrace Grill serves lunch poolside. The extra-charge Explorations Café offers specialty coffees and pastries. Room service is available 24 hours.

What Works & What Doesn't

Adjacent to the Crow's Nest, outdoor seating areas covered in canvas are wonderful, quiet hideaways during the day as well as at night when the interior is transformed into a dance club—a better choice for dancing than the disco. Missing from the Vista-class ships are self-service laundry rooms, a serious omission for families with youngsters and anyone sailing on back-to-back Caribbean itineraries or cruises of more than a week. The murals in Pinnacle Grill restaurants are strangely chintzy looking, especially considering the priceless art throughout the rest of the ships' interiors.

Accommodations

Layout: Comfortable and roomy, 85% of all Vista-class accommodations have an ocean view, and almost 80% of those also have the luxury of a private balcony furnished with chairs, loungers, and tables. Every cabin has adequate closet and drawer–shelf storage, as well as bathroom shelves. Some suites have a whirlpool tub, powder room, and walk-in closet.

Amenities: All staterooms and suites are appointed with Euro-top mattresses, 250-thread-count cotton bed linens, magnifying halogen-lighted makeup mirrors, hair dryers, a fruit basket, flat-panel TVs, and DVD players. Bathroom extras include Egyptian cotton towels, shampoo, body lotion, and bath gel, plus deluxe bathrobes to use during the cruise.

Suites: Suite luxuries include duvets on beds, a fully stocked minibar; some also have a whirlpool tub, powder room, and walk-in closet. Penthouse Verandah and Deluxe Verandah suites have exclusive use of the private Neptune Lounge, personal concierge service, canapés before dinner, and complimentary laundry, pressing, and dry-cleaning services.

Good to Know: Twenty-eight staterooms are wheelchair-accessible.

CABIN TYPE	SIZE (sq. ft.)
Penthouse Suites	1,000
Deluxe Verandah Suite	380
Superior Verandah Suite	298
Deluxe Ocean View	200
Standard Ocean View/ Inside	194 /185

Fast Facts

- 11 passenger decks
- Specialty restaurant, dining room, buffet, pizzeria
- In-cabin broadband, Wi-Fi, in-cabin safes, in-cabin refrigerators, in-cabin DVDs
- 2 pools (1 indoor)
- Fitness classes, gym, hair salon, 5 hot tubs, sauna, spa, steam room
- 9 bars, casino, cinema, 2 dance clubs, library, showroom, video game room
- Children's programs (ages 3–17)
- Dry cleaning, laundry service
- Computer room

In the Know

If you want complete privacy on your balcony, choose your location carefully. Take a close look at the deck plans for the ones alongside the exterior panoramic elevators. Riders have views of adjacent balconies as well as the seascape.

Favorites

Most Unusual: Tables in the Pinnacle Grill specialty restaurant are set with Frette linens, Riedel stemware, and Bulgari china by Rosenthal, but traditional appointments stop at the table top. The chair design is based on organic forms and resembles delicate, silvery tree branches. Some may require seating assistance, though—in reality, the chairs are cast aluminum and so heavy that they don't budge without a great deal of effort.

Moving with the View: Take a good look at the etched-glass doors of the four outside scenic elevators—they mirror the 1920s motif of the 10 interior elevator doors, which are done in cast aluminum. The design effect may look vaguely familiar because it was modeled after the art deco Chrysler building in New York City.

Our Favorite Spot for a Nightcap: The canvas-covered areas outside the Crow's Nest narrowly edge out second choice—a seat by the faux fireplace in the Oak Room.

Westerdam at sea

ROTTERDAM, AMSTERDAM

Public Areas & Facilities

Amsterdam is a sister ship to *Rotterdam*, which sails on world cruises and extended voyages, and both share Holland America Line flagship status. The most traditional ships in the fleet, their interiors display abundant wood appointments in the public areas on Promenade and Lower Promenade decks and priceless works of art throughout.

The Ocean Bar, Explorer's Lounge, Wajang Theater, and Crow's Nest are familiar lounges to longtime Holland American passengers. Newer additions are a thermal suite in the spa, a culinary-arts demonstration center in the theater, Explorations Café, and expansive areas for children and teens.

Multi-million-dollar collections of art and artifacts are showcased throughout both vessels. In addition to works commissioned specifically for each ship, Holland America Line celebrates its heritage by featuring antiques and artworks that reflect the theme of worldwide Dutch seafaring history.

1997, 2000	ENTERED SERVICE
1,316/1,380 (1,792 max)	PASSENGER CAPACITY
644/647	CREW MEMBERS
658/680	NUMBER OF CABINS
59,652/61,000	GROSS TONS
780 feet	LENGTH
106 feet	WIDTH

WOW Factor

The astrolabe (Amsterdam) *and clock tower* (Rotterdam) *rising above the marble floor of each ship's central atrium are finely detailed sculptures as well as timepieces.*

Restaurants

The formal dining room offers both open and assigned seating. Alternatives are the upscale specialty restaurant Pinnacle Grill, which requires reservations and a cover charge, and the casual Lido café that also serves buffet breakfast and lunch. Terrace Grill serves lunch poolside. The extra-charge Explorations Café offers specialty coffees and pastries. Room service is available 24 hours.

What Works & What Doesn't

The Crow's Nest is the center of late-night activity. Lounges on the Promenade and Upper Promenade decks are lively before and after dinner, but passengers tend to call it a night early after either taking in a movie or one of the production shows. Although outside cabins on the Lower Promenade deck are ideally situated for easy access to fresh air, occupants should heed the warning that the so-called one-way window glass does not offer complete privacy—passersby who get up close can see in, especially after dark, when interior lights are on.

Top: Pinnacle Grill dining
Bottom: Leisurely day at the beach

Accommodations

Layout: Staterooms are spacious and comfortable, although fewer have private balconies than newer fleetmates. Every cabin has adequate closet and drawer–shelf storage, as well as bathroom shelves. Some suites also have a whirlpool tub, powder room, and walk-in closet.

Amenities: All staterooms and suites are appointed with Euro-top mattresses, 250-thread-count cotton bed linens, magnifying halo-lighted mirrors, hair dryers, a fruit basket, flat-panel TVs, and DVD players. Bathrooms have Egyptian cotton towels, shampoo, body lotion, and bath gel, plus deluxe bathrobes to use during the cruise.

Suites: Extras include duvets on beds, a fully stocked minibar, and personalized stationery. Penthouse Verandah and Deluxe Verandah suites have exclusive use of the private Neptune Lounge, personal concierge service, canapés before dinner on request, binoculars and umbrellas for use during the cruise, an invitation to a VIP party with the captain, and complimentary laundry, pressing, and dry-cleaning services.

Good to Know: Connecting cabins are available in a range of categories. Although there are a number of triple cabins to choose from, there are not as many that accommodate four. Twenty-one staterooms are designed for wheelchair accessibility.

CABIN TYPE	SIZE (sq. ft.)
Penthouse Suite	973
Deluxe Verandah Suite	374
Verandah Suite	225
Ocean View	197
Inside	182

Fast Facts

- 9 passenger decks
- Specialty restaurant, dining room, buffet
- Wi-Fi, in-cabin safes, in-cabin refrigerators, some in-cabin minibars, in-cabin DVDs
- 2 pools (1 indoor), 2 children's pools
- Fitness classes, gym, hair salon, 2 hot tubs, sauna, spa, steam room
- 6 bars, casino, cinema, dance club, library, showroom, video game room
- Children's programs (ages 3–17)
- Dry cleaning, laundry facilities, laundry service
- Computer room

In the Know

The creation of the expansive floral stained-glass ceiling that provides a focal point for Amsterdam's *formal dining room required the use of some state-of-the-art technology that was developed especially for the ship. Traditional stained-glass in leaded frames wouldn't have been safe on a moving ship.*

Favorites

Best Place to Escape the Crowds: When there are few children on the ship, adults like to take over the Oasis, which is normally reserved for teenage cruisers.

From Classic to Wacky: On *Amsterdam*, four very special art deco pieces are mounted on the landing just outside the Crow's Nest. The gold-plated *Four Seasons* first graced the *Nieuw*

Amsterdam of 1938, and Holland America Line was able to purchase them from a collector. At the polar opposite of the artistic spectrum, realistic landscapes with surreal touches accent the dining alcoves in the Pinnacle Grill (look closely and you'll notice a Swiss Army knife strutting through a tranquil garden scene).

Our Favorite Spot for a Nightcap: The Ocean Bar is the ideal spot not only for sipping a brandy, but also for a bird's-eye view of the astrolabe. When it's quiet, you can hear the carillon bells play a melody on the hour.

Don't-Miss Munchies: Servers circulate throughout lounges before and after dinner with canapés.

A brisk walk starts the day.

5

HOLLAND AMERICA LINE

VOLENDAM, ZAANDAM

1999, 2000	ENTERED SERVICE
1,440 (1,850 max)	PASSENGER CAPACITY
647	CREW MEMBERS
720	NUMBER OF CABINS
60,906	GROSS TONS
781 feet	LENGTH
106 feet	WIDTH

Public Areas & Facilities

Similar in layout to Statendam-class vessels, these slightly larger sister ships introduced playful art and interior design theme elements to Holland America Line's classic vessels. Triple-deck atriums are distinguished by a fantastic, and fiber-optic lighted, Murano-glass sculpture on *Volendam* and, in an attempt to be hip, an almost scary towering pipe organ on *Zaandam*. Larger than the S-class ships, these ships' atriums open onto three Promenade decks.

The interior decor and much of the artwork found in each vessel has a predominant theme—*Volendam* centers around flowers, and *Zaandam*, music. Look for *Zaandam*'s collection of guitars autographed by famous musicians such as the Rolling Stones and a saxophone signed by former President Bill Clinton. Since the ships are larger than the original Statendam-class ships, the extra space allows for a larger specialty restaurant and a roomier feel throughout.

WOW Factor

Sculptural elements in the atriums are a real departure from the ones in the more sedate lobbies of earlier ships. The pipe organ in particular makes a lasting impression.

Top: Celebrate a special occasion.
Bottom: Deluxe veranda suite

Restaurants

The formal dining room offers both open and assigned seating. Pinnacle Grill, the steak-and-seafood specialty restaurant, requires reservations and a cover charge, and the casual Lido Café also serves buffet breakfast and lunch. Terrace Grill serves lunch poolside. The extra-charge Explorations Café offers specialty coffees and pastries. Room service is available 24 hours.

What Works & What Doesn't

There isn't a bad seat in each vessel's Wajang Theater—something of a curiosity on modern cruise ships. The home of HAL's new Culinary Arts Institute cooking demonstrations, the theaters continue to function as cinemas, and moviegoers still relish the freshly popped popcorn. Newly expanded spa facilities make the gym area somewhat tight and also eliminate the individual men's and women's steam rooms. Passengers now have to pay for use of the thermal suite, which has fancy coed aromatherapy steam rooms.

Accommodations

Layout: Staterooms are spacious and comfortable, with a few more balconies than Statendam-class, but still fewer than newer fleetmates. Every cabin has adequate closet and drawer–shelf storage, as well as bathroom shelves. Some suites have a whirlpool tub, powder room, and walk-in closet.

Amenities: All staterooms and suites are appointed with Euro-top mattresses, 250-thread-count cotton bed linens, magnifying halo-lighted mirrors, hair dryers, a fruit basket, flat-panel TVs, and DVD players. Bathrooms have Egyptian cotton towels, shampoo, body lotion, and bath gel, plus deluxe bathrobes to use during the cruise.

Suites: Suite amenities include duvets on beds, a fully stocked minibar, and personalized stationery. Penthouse Verandah and Deluxe Verandah suites have exclusive use of the private

Neptune Lounge, personal concierge service, canapés before dinner on request, binoculars and umbrellas for use during the cruise, an invitation to a VIP party with the captain, and complimentary laundry, pressing, and dry-cleaning services.

Good to Know: As a nod to families, connecting cabins are featured in a range of categories. However, although the number of triple cabins is generous, there are not many that accommodate four. Twenty-two staterooms are designed for wheelchair accessibility.

CABIN TYPE	SIZE (sq. ft.)
Penthouse Suite	973
Deluxe Verandah Suite	390
Verandah Suite	230
Ocean View	197
Inside	182

Fast Facts

- 10 passenger decks
- Specialty restaurant, dining room, buffet
- Wi-Fi, in-cabin safes, in-cabin refrigerators, some in-cabin minibars, in-cabin DVDs
- 2 pools (1 indoor), 2 children's pools
- Fitness classes, gym, hair salon, 2 hot tubs, sauna, spa
- 6 bars, casino, cinema, dance club, library, showroom, video game room
- Children's programs (ages 3–17)
- Dry cleaning, laundry facilities, laundry service
- Computer room

In the Know

Don't be surprised if you suddenly feel you're in a ticker-tape parade during one of the high-energy production shows. Not only are the show lounges outfitted with revolving stages and hydraulic lifts, but they also feature a moving light system and confetti cannons.

Favorites

Best Place to Escape the Crowds: Grab a book from the library and claim a cozy corner of the Explorer's Lounge while the fun-in-the-sun set is baking on the Lido deck.

Best Value: If you love cooking classes but just can't face anyone during a bad hair day, don't despair. You can watch the culinary-arts demonstration on your cabin television.

Our Favorite Spot for a Nightcap: As on every Holland America ship, the Crow's Nest is the traditional lounge where dancing and late night cocktails go together.

Best Casual Dining: Waiters serve made-to-order entrees in the Lido restaurant at dinner, and an evening poolside barbecue buffet is usually scheduled during each cruise.

Best Pool Game: Use materials supplied by the staff to construct your own model ship. The last one afloat in the treacherous waters of the hot tub is the winner.

Best Afternoon Break: Daily tea time is a delightful mix of not only tea but finger foods, sweets, and socializing with fellow passengers.

Zaandam atrium organ

STATENDAM CLASS
Statendam, Maasdam, Ryndam, Veendam

Public Areas & Facilities

The sister ships included in the S- or Statendam-class retain the most classic and traditional characteristics of Holland America Line vessels. Routinely updated with innovative features, they combine all the advantages of intimate, midsize vessels with high-tech and stylish details.

At the heart of the ships, triple-deck atriums graced by suspended glass sculptures open onto three so-called promenade decks; the lowest contains staterooms encircled by a wide, teak outdoor deck furnished with padded steamer chairs, while interior art-filled passageways flow past lounges and public rooms on the two decks above. It's easy to find just about any area on board, with the possible exception of the main level of the dining room. Either reach the lower dining room floor via the aft elevator, or enter one deck above and make a grand entrance down the sweeping staircase.

1993, 1993, 1994, 1996	ENTERED SERVICE
1,258 (1,627 max)	PASSENGER CAPACITY
602	CREW MEMBERS
55, 451	GROSS TONS
629	NUMBER OF CABINS
720 feet	LENGTH
101 feet	WIDTH

700 ft.

500 ft.

300 ft.

WOW Factor

Carefully chosen antiques and works of art are arranged in passageways, stairwells, and niches all over these ships.

Top: Select from an extensive wine list.
Bottom: Deluxe veranda suite

Restaurants

The formal dining room offers both open and assigned seating. Alternatives are Pinnacle Grill, which requires reservations and a cover charge, and the casual Lido café that also serves buffet breakfast and lunch. Terrace Grill serves lunch poolside. The extra-charge Explorations Café offers specialty coffees and pastries. Room service is available 24 hours.

What Works & What Doesn't

After dark there's a bit more action in public areas; however, you'll find it rather subdued in lounges along the promenade decks. The livelier Crow's Nest is the center of late-night activity. Try to make it to the production shows in time to grab seats on the lower level of the main show lounges—railings on the balcony level obstruct the view from all rows behind the first two or three. Escalators between decks in the lower atrium areas seem out of place; they appear to be more of a curiosity than a real convenience.

Accommodations

Layout: Staterooms are spacious and comfortable, although fewer of them have private balconies than on newer fleetmates. Every cabin has adequate closet and drawer–shelf storage, as well as bathroom shelves. Some suites have a whirlpool tub, powder room, and walk-in closet.

Amenities: Gone are the flowery chintz curtains and bedspreads of yesteryear–all staterooms and suites are now appointed with Euro-top mattresses, 250-thread-count cotton bed linens, magnifying lighted mirrors, hair dryers, a fruit basket, flat-panel TVs, and DVD players. Bathroom extras include Egyptian cotton towels, shampoo, body lotion, and bath gel, plus deluxe bathrobes to use during the cruise.

Suites: Suites have duvets on beds, a fully stocked minibar, and personalized stationery. Penthouse Verandah and Deluxe Verandah suites have exclusive use of the private Neptune Lounge, personal concierge service, canapés before dinner on request, binoculars and umbrellas for use during the cruise, an invitation to a VIP party with the captain, and complimentary laundry, pressing, and dry-cleaning services.

Good to Know: Connecting cabins are featured in a range of categories. Six staterooms are wheelchair-accessible; nine are modified with ramps although doors are standard width.

CABIN TYPE	SIZE (sq. ft.)
Penthouse Suite	946
Deluxe Verandah Suite	385
Verandah Suite	230
Ocean View	196
Inside	186

Fast Facts

- 10 passenger decks
- Specialty restaurant, dining room, buffet
- Wi-Fi, in-cabin safes, in-cabin minibars, in-cabin refrigerators, in-cabin DVDs
- 2 pools (1 indoor), 2 children's pools
- Fitness classes, gym, hair salon, 2 hot tubs, sauna, spa, steam room
- 9 bars, casino, cinema, dance club, library, showroom, video game room
- Children's programs (ages 3–17)
- Dry cleaning, laundry facilities, laundry service
- Computer room

In the Know

Do you recognize the portraits etched into the glass doors to the main show lounges? They are the likenesses of great Dutch artists for whom the spaces are named.

Favorites

Best Place to Escape the Crowds: A padded steamer chair on the teak promenade deck is our favorite cocoon. You'll never want to leave.

Best Dessert: It just might be the best in the world–Holland America Line's signature bread-and-butter pudding with a creamy sauce. Ask for the recipe.

Our Favorite Spot for a Nightcap: Popular with the after-dinner crowd, yet quiet enough for conversation, the Ocean Bar hits just the right balance for late-night socializing.

Best Extra Touches: As you board, you are serenaded by musicians and escorted to your cabin, where you'll find a signature HAL-logo canvas tote bag. Other deluxe touches include complimentary shoeshine service and terry fingertip towels in public restrooms.

Our Choice for Outdoor Dining: Weather permitting, an evening poolside barbecue buffet is usually scheduled during every cruise.

Share a sunset.

MSC CRUISES

With several seasons of Caribbean sailing beneath their hulls, MSC Cruises has sailed past newcomer status in the area. More widely known as one of the world's largest cargo shipping companies, MSC has operated cruises with an eclec-

Pool deck after dark

tic fleet since the late 1980s. Since introducing two graceful, medium-size ships in 2003 and 2004, MSC's expansion plans include operating newer and larger vessels from a larger line-up of home ports in the U.S.

MSC CRUISES
6750 N. Andrews Avenue
Fort Lauderdale, FL 33309
954/662–6262 or
800/666–9333
www.msccruises.com

Cruise Style: Premium

In a shrewd move, MSC transferred 100% of their South Florida commercial shipping operations from Miami to Fort Lauderdale and became the largest tenant at Port Everglades. Literally overnight, even with only two passenger ships deployed there, they earned the status associated with having their own terminal. MSC ships are also distinctive for creative itineraries. Two ports of call on their ship's sailing schedules, La Romana and Cayo Levantado (both in the Dominican Republic), are not often found on typical Caribbean cruise itineraries.

No glitz, no clutter—just elegant simplicity—is the standard of MSC's seaworthy interior decor. Extensive use of marble, brass, and wood reflects the best of Italian styling and design; clean lines and bold colors set their modern sophisticated tone.

While sailing Caribbean itineraries, MSC adopts activities that appeal to American passengers without abandoning those preferred by Europeans (you should be prepared for announcements in Italian as well as English while on board). In addition to the guest lecturers, computer classes, and cooking lessons featured in the enrichment programs, Italian-language classes are a popular option. Nightly shows accentuate the cruise line's

Mediterranean heritage; there might be a flamenco show in the main showroom and live music for listening and dancing in the smaller lounges, while the disco is a happening late-night spot.

The MSC entertainment staff shine off-stage as well as in front of the spotlight. They seek out passengers traveling solo, who might be looking for activity or dance partners, so that they feel fully included in the cruise.

In addition to some of the most reasonable fares in the premium cruise market, MSC doesn't nickel-and-dime passengers during their cruises. Cocktails and wines are sensibly priced. Although it may not last, it's been a long time since Dom Perignon by the bottle has been listed for less than $100 on most other cruise ships.

Food

Dinner on MSC ships is a traditional seven-course event centered around authentic Italian fare. Menus list Mediterranean regional specialties and classic favorites prepared from scratch the old-fashioned way. Some favorites include lamb and mushroom quiche, a Tuscan dish, and veal scaloppine with tomatoes and mozzarella, a recipe from Sorrento in Campania. In its ongoing efforts to appeal to American passengers, MSC purchased a U.S.-based caterer so that most ingredients used during Caribbean cruises are supplied from U.S. sources, although food is still prepared the Italian way. In a nod to American tastes, broiled chicken breast, grilled salmon, and Caesar salad are additions to the dinner menu and are always available. Healthy Choice and vegetarian items are offered as well as tempting sugar-free desserts. A highlight is the bread-of-the-day, freshly baked on board. The nightly midnight buffet is a retro food feast missing from most of today's cruises. Complimentary room service is always available, though the options are somewhat limited.

Fitness & Recreation

Up-to-date exercise equipment, a jogging track, and basic fitness classes for all levels are available in the fitness centers.

Spa treatments include a variety of massages, body wraps, and facials that can be scheduled à la carte or combined in packages to encompass an afternoon or the entire cruise. The hottest hair styling techniques and nail services are offered in the salons. Unlike most cruise lines, MSC Cruises operates its own spas.

Noteworthy

■ Sleek lines and plenty of open deck space are hallmarks of MSC ship design.

■ Traditional midnight buffets are supplemented by late-night snacks offered throughout the lounges by strolling waiters.

■ MSC has adapted their Italian style and menus for North Americans, but not to the extent of becoming fully Americanized.

5

MSC CRUISES

Top: Miniature golf—family fun
Bottom: MSC *Lirica*

Top: Thermal suite
Middle: Expansive pool deck
Bottom: MSC *Lirica* suite with balcony

Your Shipmates

Most passengers are couples in the 35 to 55 year-old range, as well as some family groups who prefer the international atmosphere prevalent on board. Approximately half the passengers on Caribbean itineraries are North Americans.

Dress Code

Two formal nights are standard on seven-night cruises, and three are scheduled on eleven-night cruises. Men are encouraged to wear dark suits, but sport coats and ties are appropriate. All other evenings are casual, although jeans are discouraged in restaurants. It's requested that no shorts be worn in public areas after 6 PM.

Junior Cruisers

Children from ages 3 to 17 are welcome to participate in age-appropriate youth programs. The Mini Club is for ages three to eight, Junior Club for ages 9 to 12, and Teenage Club for youths 13 years and older. Counselors organize daily group activities such as arts and crafts, painting, treasure hunts, games, a mini-Olympics, and shows. Children under age three may use the playroom if accompanied at all times by an adult. Babysitting can be arranged for a fee once you're on board.

Service

Service can be inconsistent, yet it's more than acceptable, even if it's not overly gracious. The mainly Italian staff can seem befuddled by American habits and expectations. Ongoing training and improved English proficiency for staff are top priorities for MSC, and these weaknesses are showing improvement.

Tipping

Passengers may reward staff members with a gratuity for exceptional service should they choose to do so; however, tipping is not obligatory. Customary gratuities are added to your shipboard account. Guidelines are similar to those on other lines (suggested amounts are per person, per day): waiter $3.50–$5; maître d' $1–$2;

CHOOSE MSC CRUISES IF:

❶ You appreciate authentic Italian cooking. This is the real thing, not an Olive Garden clone.

❷ You want your ship to look like a ship. MSC's vessels are very nautical in appearance.

❸ You want the Continental flair of a premium cruise at a fair price.

stateroom attendant \$3.50–\$5. You can always adjust these amounts at the reception desk or even pay in cash, if you prefer. Automatic 15% gratuities are incorporated into all bar purchases.

Past Passengers

At the time of this writing, a past passenger loyalty program was being developed, but details had not been announced.

After sailing on MSC Cruises once, you are eligible to join the MSC Club by completing the registration form found in your cabin or by writing to the club through the line's Web site. Membership benefits include discounts on your cruise fare for the best itineraries, travel cancellation insurance, shore excursions, and even onboard purchases. You will also receive *MSC Club News* magazine.

Good to Know

Mediterranean Shipping Cruises has catered almost exclusively to Europeans since the company's founding, and the changes necessary to conform to the style and habits favored by North Americans seemingly came as a surprise to them when they entered the Caribbean market. For example, Europeans prefer to go out for coffee after dinner; Americans want to be served coffee with their dessert. Unfortunately, this culture clash can cause misunderstandings and some contentiousness. Little things like too-small water glasses and no iced tea can make Americans cranky. To eliminate these issues and broaden their appeal, MSC has enlisted the services of top cruise-industry veterans; most important, though, staff members on board really listen to passengers and take their comments to heart.

5

MSC CRUISES

DON'T CHOOSE MSC CRUISES IF:

❶ Announcements in more than one language get on your nerves.

❷ You aren't able to accept things that are not always done the American way.

❸ Myriad dining choices and casual attire are imperatives. MSC cruises have assigned seating and observe a dress code.

MSC LIRICA, MSC OPERA

Public Areas & Facilities

Though these two sleek, medium-size ships are exactly the same dimensions and differ only slightly in basic layout, *Opera* holds almost 200 more passengers typically and has almost 100 extra cabins. Light and bright by day, intimate and sophisticated by night, the contemporary design may not measure up to the sizzle expected by those North American passengers who don't understand more understated European tastes.

Public rooms are spacious and uniformly elegant with grand touches of marble, brass accents, and lots of wood. The refreshing lack of glitz is more than compensated for by the sparkle of glass and a mixture of primary and neutral colors. With most public areas on the lower two passenger decks, getting acclimated is a breeze. Conveniently located elevator and stairway lobbies make even vertical movement less challenging.

Space around the Lido pools feels particularly lavish, with two swimming pools and hot tubs.

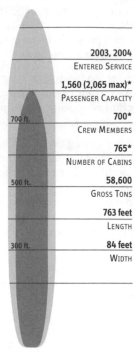

2003, 2004	Entered Service
1,560 (2,065 max)*	Passenger Capacity
700*	Crew Members
765*	Number of Cabins
58,600	Gross Tons
763 feet	Length
84 feet	Width

Opera has 850 cabins and holds 740 crew and 1,700 passengers (2,199 maximum)

WOW Factor

Who knew marble contains so many rich colors? It's everywhere!

Restaurants

Two formal restaurants serve Mediterranean and Italian-accented cuisine in traditional early and late assigned seatings. The Lido buffet, poolside grill, coffee bar, and pizzeria offer casual daytime options. Although there are no true alternative dining restaurants, La Pergola and Il Patio restaurants have outdoor tables protected from the elements by overhead canvas.

What Works & What Doesn't

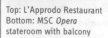

Top: L'Approdo Restaurant
Bottom: MSC *Opera* stateroom with balcony

Oddly, only the forward and aft elevators and stairwells reach all decks; the central ones don't even go as high as the top deck of staterooms. However, this seeming design flaw results in an uninterrupted expanse of wide-open space on the pool deck, so perhaps it wasn't such a bad choice after all.

Encircling the Lido Deck from above is additional sunning space where well-placed glass screens cut the wind.

Lounge chairs are plentiful, and you shouldn't have trouble finding one, even during peak sunning hours.

Accommodations

Layout: There are nearly a dozen state-room price categories; however, they fall into three basic configurations: suite with balcony, ocean view, and inside. The addition of a fourth category on *MSC Opera* (ocean-view cabin with balcony instead of some of the larger suites) increased the number of balconies available, but the size of these new balcony cabins is identical to that of the ocean-view cabins with only windows. Inside cabins were added to nearly an entire deck on MSC Opera as well, which accounts for the higher double-occupancy rate.

Amenities: All cabins are comfortably decorated in primary colors and have a vanity-desk, side chair, television, small minibar refrigerator, personal safe, and a hair dryer. Bathrooms are supplied with MSC Cruises' own brand of shampoo, bath gel, and soaps, plus a handy sewing repair kit. Suites also have a computer connection.

Suites: Suites (which would be more accurately described as minisuites) have a sitting area and a bathroom with bathtub; all but two forward-facing suites on each ship (which are designated family-size suites on *MSC Opera*) have a balcony as well.

Good to Know: Four interior cabins on *MSC Lirica* and five on *MSC Opera* are wheelchair-accessible.

CABIN TYPE	SIZE (sq. ft.)
Suite with Balcony	247
Suite without Balcony	236
Ocean View with Balcony	140
Ocean View without Balcony	140
Inside	140

Fast Facts

- 12 passenger decks
- 2 dining rooms, buffet, pizzeria
- Some in-cabin broadband, Wi-Fi, in-cabin safes, in-cabin minibars
- 2 pools, fitness classes, gym, hair salon, 2 hot tubs, sauna, spa, steam room
- 8 bars, casino, dance club, library, showroom, video game room
- Children's programs (ages 3–17)
- Laundry service
- Computer room

In the Know

Prepare for a treat the first time you use a bath towel. Instead of skimpy standard towels, they are thick bath sheets. The hand towels aren't much smaller than most standard bath towels; they're easily large enough for a woman to wrap her hair in. Beware, though—shower stalls are miniscule.

Favorites

Best Places to Get Away From It All: Head outside behind the disco, where there's an open deck furnished with covered tables and chairs. Because there are no aft-facing cabins, most passenger decks have a small covered area at the stern where you'll find lounge chairs. These are perfect spots for reading or watching the ships' wake disappear behind you, and many people don't discover them.

Best Splurge: Specialty coffees, cocktails, wine, and other alcoholic beverages are some of the most reasonably priced at sea.

Best Added Value: Midnight buffets of the kind rarely seen on cruise ships anymore are an extravaganza worthy of attending even if you aren't hungry. Be sure to bring a camera.

Our Favorite Spot for a Nightcap: High above the stern, cozy seating areas create an intimate atmosphere in the discos, which don't really crank up into high gear (and volume) until quite late. If it's a bit noisy, there's that seating outside.

MSC *Lirica* sauna

NORWEGIAN CRUISE LINE

Norwegian Cruise Line (NCL) set sail in 1966 with an entirely new concept: regularly scheduled Caribbean cruises from the then obscure port of Miami. Good food and friendly service combined with value fares established NCL as a winner for ac-

At anchor in the Caribbean

tive adults and families. With the introduction of the now-retired SS *Norway* in 1979, NCL ushered in the era of cruises on mega-size ships. Innovative and forward-looking, NCL has been a cruise-industry leader for four decades.

NORWEGIAN CRUISE LINE
7665 Corporate Center Drive
Miami, FL 33126
305/436–4000 or
800/327–7030
www.ncl.com

Cruise Style: Mainstream

Noted for top-quality, high-energy entertainment and emphasis on fitness facilities and programs, NCL combines action, activities, and a variety of dining options in a casual, free-flowing atmosphere. Freestyle cruising was born when Asian shipping giant Star Cruises acquired NCL—the new owners were confounded that Americans meekly conformed to rigid dining schedules and dress codes. All that changed with NCL's introduction of a host of flexible dining options that allow passengers to choose open seating in the main dining rooms or dine in any of a number of à la carte and specialty restaurants at any time and with whom they please.

More high jinks than high-brow, entertainment after dark features extravagant Broadway and Las Vegas–style revues presented in main show lounges by lavishly costumed singers and dancers—some of the most talented and professional at sea. Other performers might include comedians, magicians, jugglers, and acrobats. Passengers can get into the act by taking part in talent shows or step up to the karaoke microphone. Live bands play for dancing and listening passengers in smaller lounges, and each ship has a lively disco. Passengers on some ships are treated to performances and improvisation workshops featuring players from Chicago's world famous Second City company, training ground for some of the most gifted comedians in movies and stars of *Saturday Night Live*.

Casinos, bingo sessions, and art auctions are well attended. Adult games, particularly the competitive ones, are fun to participate in and provide laughs for audience members. Goofy pool games are an NCL staple, and the ships' bands crank up the volume during afternoon and evening deck parties. It's lively and enjoyable, even if you just watch the action from a lounge chair.

From a distance, most cruise ships look so similar that it's often difficult to tell them apart, but NCL's largest, modern ships stand out with their distinctive use of hull art. Each new ship is distinguished by murals extending from bow to mid-ship.

When others scoffed at year-round sailings to the Caribbean from New York City, NCL recognized the demand and has sailed with such success that they have increased capacity; *Norwegian Gem* has now joined *Norwegian Dawn* by making New York a home port. To ensure satisfaction, you can take advantage of a Winter Weather Guarantee if foul weather threatens to ruin your vacation plans. Should departure from New York be delayed by more than 12 hours due to weather, you're given the choice of a $100 per person onboard credit or, if you decide to cancel your cruise, you receive a full cruise credit on a future sailing.

Food

Main dining rooms serve what is traditionally deemed Continental fare, although it's about what you would expect at a really good hotel banquet. Health-conscious menu selections are nicely prepared from *Cooking Light* magazine's recipes, and vegetarian choices are always available.

Where NCL really shines is the specialty restaurants, especially the French-Mediterranean Le Bistro (on all ships), the pan-Asian restaurants, and steak houses (on the newer ships). As a rule of thumb, the newer the ship, the wider the variety since new ships were purpose-built with as many as 10 or more places to eat. You may find Spanish tapas, an Italian trattoria, a steak house, and a pan-Asian restaurant complete with a sushi and sashimi bar and teppanyaki room. Some, but not all, carry a cover charge or are priced à la carte and require reservations. An NCL staple, the late-night Chocoholic Buffet continues to be a favorite event.

Noteworthy

■ Numerous connecting staterooms and suites can be combined to create multicabin family accommodations.

■ Freestyle Cruising offers the flexibility of dining with anyone you choose and when you actually wish to eat.

■ The newest ships in the NCL fleet sport hull art— huge murals that make them easily recognizable from afar.

Top: Casual freestyle dining
Bottom: *Norwegian Majesty* suite

Top: Casino play
Middle: Internet café on *Norwegian Dawn*
Bottom: *Norwegian Dream* Superior Ocean View stateroom

Fitness & Recreation

Mandara Spa offers unique and exotic spa treatments fleetwide on NCL, although facilities vary widely. Spa treatments include a long menu of massages, body wraps, and facials and the latest trends in hair and nail services are offered in the salons.

State-of-the-art exercise equipment, jogging tracks, and basic fitness classes are available at no charge. There's a nominal fee for personal training, body composition analysis, and specialized classes such as yoga and Pilates. The Dive-In snorkel and scuba program offers novices the opportunity to participate in shipboard lessons to prepare for underwater exploration in ports of call as well as when visiting NCL's own private island.

Your Shipmates

NCL's mostly American cruise passengers are active couples ranging from their mid-30s to mid-50s. Many families enjoy cruising on NCL ships during holidays and summer months, particularly on Caribbean itineraries. Longer cruises and more exotic itineraries attract passengers in the over-55 age group.

Dress Code

Resort casual attire is appropriate at all times; however, the option of one formal evening is available on all cruises of seven nights and longer. Most passengers actually raise the casual dress code a notch to what could be called casual chic attire.

Junior Cruisers

For children and teens, each NCL vessel offers Kid's Crew program of supervised entertainment for young cruisers ages 2 to 17. Younger children are split into three groups, ages 2 to 5, 6 to 9, and 10 to 12; activities range from storytelling, games, and arts and crafts to dinner with counselors, pajama parties, and treasure hunts.

Evening group "Port Play" is available in the children's area to accommodate parents booked on shore excursions. Babysitting services are available for a fee. Parents whose children are not toilet trained are issued a beeper to alert them when diaper changing is necessary. Children under

CHOOSE NORWEGIAN CRUISE LINE IF:

❶ Doing your own thing is your idea of a real vacation. You could almost remove your watch and just go with the flow.

❷ You want to leave your formal dress-up wardrobe at home.

❸ You're competitive. There's always a pick-up game in progress on the sports courts.

age two cruise free with their parents, and there's no minimum age for infants.

For teens age 13 to 17, options include sports, pool parties, teen disco, movies, and video games. Some ships have their own cool clubs where teens hang out in adult-free zones.

Service

Somewhat inconsistent, service is nonetheless congenial. Although crew members tended to be outgoing Caribbean islanders in the past, they have largely been replaced by Asians who are well-trained, yet are inclined to be more reserved.

Tipping

A fixed service charge of $10 per person, per day is added to shipboard accounts. For children ages 3 to 12, a $5 per person per day charge is added; there's no charge for children under age three. An automatic 15% gratuity is added to bar tabs. Staff members are encouraged to go the extra mile for passengers and are permitted to accept cash gratuities. Passengers in suites who have access to concierge and butler services are asked to offer a cash gratuity at their own discretion.

Past Passengers

Upon completion of your first NCL cruise you're automatically enrolled in Latitudes, the club for repeat passengers. Membership benefits accrue based on the number of cruises completed: Bronze (1–4); Silver (5–8); Gold (9–13); and Platinum (14 or more). Everyone receives "Latitudes," NCL's quarterly magazine, Latitudes pricing, Latitudes check-in at the pier, a ship pin, access to a special customer service desk and liaison on board, a members-only cocktail party hosted by the captain, as well as Polo Club benefits aboard Orient Lines. Higher tiers receive a welcome basket, an invitation to the captain's cocktail party and dinner in Le Bistro, and priority for check-in, tender tickets, and disembarkation.

Good to Know

When considering an NCL cruise, keep in mind that the ships weren't cut from a cookie-cutter mold, and they differ widely in size and detail. Although all are brightly appointed and attempt to offer a comparable experience, the older ships just don't have the panache or the numerous Freestyle dining selections found on the newer, purpose-built ships. Drawbacks for families are the smallish standard cabins that lack adequate storage on the older ships and the absence of self-service laundry facilities on most ships. On the plus side, the newest vessels have many options for families, including large numbers of interconnecting staterooms that make them ideal for even super-size clans. By 2009 NCL will have one of the newest fleets at sea following the introduction of two large, new vessels; older mid-size ships are being transferred to parent Star Cruises in Asia.

5

NORWEGIAN CRUISE LINE

DON'T CHOOSE NORWEGIAN CRUISE LINE IF:

❶ You don't like to pay extra for food on a ship. The best specialty restaurants have extra charges.

❷ You don't want to stand in line. There are lines for nearly everything.

❸ You don't want to hear announcements. They're frequent on these ships— and loud.

DAWN CLASS
Norwegian Star, Norwegian Dawn

Public Areas & Facilities

Purpose-built for NCL's Freestyle Cruising concept, *Norwegian Dawn* and *Norwegian Star*, the latter of which offers only Mexican Riviera and Alaska cruises, each have more than a dozen dining options, a variety of entertainment selections, enormous spas with indoor lap pools, and expansive facilities for children and teens. *Norwegian Dawn* introduced regular cruises year-round to the Caribbean from New York City, and her tropical colors and designs set just the right mood, even in the dead of winter.

These ships unveiled NCL's super-deluxe Garden Villa accommodations, English pubs, and 24-hour dining in the Blue Lagoon Restaurant. Interior spaces are bright and cheerful, especially the atrium area adjacent to the outdoor promenade, which is flooded with sunlight through expansive windows. A second smaller "garden" atrium with a prominent waterfall leads the way to the spa lobby. Located near the children's splash pool is a hot tub for parents' enjoyment.

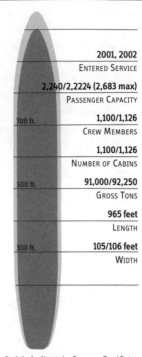

2001, 2002	ENTERED SERVICE
2,240/2,2224 (2,683 max)	PASSENGER CAPACITY
1,100/1,126	CREW MEMBERS
1,100/1,126	NUMBER OF CABINS
91,000/92,250	GROSS TONS
965 feet	LENGTH
105/106 feet	WIDTH

700 ft. / 500 ft. / 300 ft.

Statistics for *Norwegian Dawn* are offered first, followed by those for *Norwegian Star*.

WOW Factor

Reminiscent of European opera houses, the showrooms are grand settings for the lavish production shows and have full proscenium stages.

Top: Cagney's Steakhouse, *Norwegian Dawn*
Bottom: Mini-suite

Restaurants

Continental and specialty dining is offered in a dozen dining rooms and ethnic restaurants with open seating and flexible hours. Main dining rooms are complimentary; specialty restaurants, including NCI's signature Le Bistro, carry a cover charge and require reservations. Casual choices are the Lido Buffet, Blue Lagoon, and poolside grill.

What Works & What Doesn't

In what might be termed a super-size "thermal suite" on other ships, the spa areas feature indoor lap pools surrounded by lounge chairs, large whirlpools, saunas, and steam rooms and—best of all— there's no additional charge to use any of it. Freestyle dining doesn't mean you can get a table in the main dining rooms at precisely the moment you want. However, waiting time can be eliminated by timing your arrival at nonpeak periods. Screens located throughout the ship illustrate the status (full, moderately busy, empty) and waiting time you can expect for each restaurant.

Accommodations

Layout: NCL ships are not noted for large staterooms, but all have a small sitting area with sofa, chair, and table. Most bathrooms are compartmentalized with a sink area, shower, and toilet separated by sliding glass doors. Every cabin has adequate closet and drawer–shelf storage, as well as limited bathroom storage. Suites have walk-in closets.

Amenities: Cherrywood cabinetry, tropical decor, mirrored accents, a small refrigerator, tea/coffeemaker, personal safe, broadband Internet connection, duvets on beds, a wall-mounted hair dryer over the dressing table, and bathrobes for use during the cruise are standard. Bathrooms have a shampoo and bath gel dispenser mounted on the shower wall as well as a magnifying mirror. Suites have whirlpool tubs, entertainment centers with CD/DVD players, and concierge and butler service.

Good to Know: Family-friendly staterooms interconnect in most categories, enabling families of nearly any size to find suitable accommodations. Nearly every stateroom has a third or fourth berth, and some can sleep as many as five and six. Twenty-four staterooms on *Norwegian Dawn* and 20 staterooms on *Norwegian Star* are designed for wheelchair accessibility.

CABIN TYPE	SIZE (sq. ft.)
Garden Villa	5,750/4,390*
Courtyard Villa	574**
Owner's/ Penthouse Suite	750–790/366
Romance/Minisuite	288/229
Ocean View/Inside	158–166/142

* Norwegian Dawn/ Norwegian Jewel
**Norwegian Star only

Fast Facts

- 15 passenger decks
- 4 restaurants, 3 dining rooms, buffet, ice-cream parlor, pizzeria
- In-cabin broadband, Wi-Fi, in-cabin safes, in-cabin refrigerators, some in-cabin DVDs
- 3 pools (1 indoor), children's pool
- Fitness classes, gym, hair salon, 6 hot tubs, sauna, spa, steam room
- 9 bars, casino, cinema, 2 dance clubs, library, showroom, video game room
- Children's programs (ages 2–17)
- Dry cleaning, laundry facilities (*Norwegian Dawn*), laundry service
- Computer room

In the Know

Artwork plays a major role in brightening the interiors of both vessels, but Norwegian Dawn *has a priceless collection of original pop art, featuring original signed works by Andy Warhol, and oil paintings by Impressionists Matisse, Renoir, and Monet.*

Favorites

Second to None: Other ships might have comedy shows, but on these you can look forward to performances by Second City, Chicago's incomparable improvisation artists. Shows are scheduled in the theater as well as in more intimate nightclub settings. Passengers can even get a behind-the-scenes look at the shows during an improv workshop.

Best Place to Escape the Crowds: Try either ship's library. On these ships, it's tucked away inside with no view, but the writing and reading room is a good place to gaze at the sea if your book doesn't hold your attention.

Best Splurge: Three-bedroom Garden Villas are among the largest suites at sea. We love the private whirlpools and outdoor patios for al fresco dining.

Our Favorite Spot for a Nightcap: The sophisticated Star Bar overlooking the pool reminds us of a favorite New York piano lounge with its moody lighting.

Norwegian Dawn at sea

JEWEL CLASS
Norwegian Jewel, Norwegian Jade, Norwegian Pearl, Norwegian Gem

Public Areas and Facilities

Jewel-Class ships are the next step in the continuing evolution of Freestyle ship design: the interior location of some public rooms and restaurants has been tweaked since the introduction of Dawn-Class vessels, and new categories of deluxe accommodations have been added.

These ships have more than a dozen dining options, a variety of entertainment options, enormous spas with thermal suites (for which there is a charge), and expansive areas reserved for children and teens. Pools have water slides and a plethora of lounge chairs, although when your ship is full it can be difficult to find one in a prime location. *Norwegian Pearl* and *Norwegian Gem* introduced the line's first rock-climbing walls as well as Bliss Lounge, which has trendy South Beach decor and the first full-size ten-pin bowling alleys on modern cruise ships.

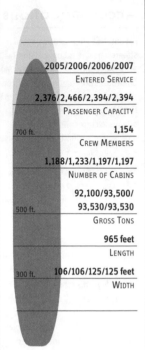

2005/2006/2006/2007	ENTERED SERVICE
2,376/2,466/2,394/2,394	PASSENGER CAPACITY
1,154	CREW MEMBERS
1,188/1,233/1,197/1,197	NUMBER OF CABINS
92,100/93,500/ 93,530/93,530	GROSS TONS
965 feet	LENGTH
106/106/125/125 feet	WIDTH

*Statistics for *Norwegian Jewel* are offered first, followed by those for *Norwegian Jade, Pearl,* and *Gem.*

WOW Factor

From the moment you step aboard, you begin to feel a special tropical ambience. The bright colors and fun surroundings set just the right tone for cruising the Caribbean.

Top: *Norwegian Jewel's* Azura restaurant.
Bottom: Hydro pool in the spa

Restaurants

Continental and specialty dining is offered in a dozen dining rooms and ethnic restaurants with open seating and flexible hours. Main dining rooms are complimentary, but most of the specialty restaurants, including NCL's signature Le Bistro, carry a cover charge and require reservations. The Italian restaurant is still complimentary. Casual choices are the Lido Buffet, Blue Lagoon, and poolside grill.

What Works and What Doesn't

The thermal suites in the spa have large whirlpools, saunas, steam rooms, and a relaxation area with loungers facing the sea. While there is an additional charge to use the facility, you can purchase a cruise-long pass for a discount off the daily charge. Freestyle dining doesn't mean you can get a table in the main dining rooms at precisely the moment you want; however, waiting times can be reduced if you time your arrival at nonpeak periods. Screens located throughout the ship estimate the waiting time you can expect for each restaurant.

Accommodations

Layout: NCL ships are not noted for large staterooms, but all have a small sitting area with sofa, chair, and table. Every cabin has adequate closet and drawer-shelf storage, as well as limited bathroom storage. Suites have walk-in closets.

Amenities: A small refrigerator, tea/coffeemaker, personal safe, ethernet connection, duvets on beds, a wall-mounted hair dryer, and bathrobes are standard. Bathrooms have a shampoo/bath gel dispenser on the shower wall and a magnifying mirror. Suites have whirlpool tubs, entertainment centers with CD/DVD players, and concierge and butler service.

Garden & Courtyard Villas: Garden Villas, with three bedrooms, a living-dining room, and private deck garden with a spa tub, are among the largest suites at sea. Courtyard Villas—

not as large as Garden Villas—nevertheless have an exclusive concierge lounge and a shared private courtyard with pool, hot tub, sundeck, and small gym.

Good to Know: Some staterooms interconnect in most categories, enabling families of nearly any size to find suitable accommodations. Twenty-seven staterooms are wheelchair accessible.

CABIN TYPE	SIZE (sq. ft.)
Garden Villa/ Courtyard Villa	4,390/574
Owner's Suites	823–928*
Penthouse Suite/ Minisuite	575/284
Ocean View with Balcony	205–243
Ocean View/Inside	161/143

*Deluxe Owner's Suites on *Norwegian Pearl* and *Norwegian Gem* only.

Fast Facts

- 15 passenger decks
- 7 restaurants, 2 dining rooms, buffet, ice cream parlor, pizzeria
- In-cabin broadband, Wi-Fi, in-cabin safes, in-cabin refrigerators, some in-cabin DVDs
- 2 pools, children's pool
- Fitness classes, gym, hair salon, 6 hot tubs, spa, steam room
- 9 bars, casino, cinema, dance club, library, showroom, video game room
- Children's programs (ages 2–17)
- Dry cleaning, laundry facilities, laundry service
- Computer room

In the Know

You may feel you've slipped into wonderland when you first encounter some of the fanciful furniture in the lounges aboard each ship and in Bliss Ultra Lounge on Norwegian Pearl *and* Norwegian Gem. *Some are covered in wildly colorful velvets and are designed as thrones and even lounging beds.*

Favorites

Best Place to Escape the Crowds: Try the ship's tranquil library, which is also a good spot to gaze at the sea if your book proves to be less than compelling.

Best Splurge: Courtyard Villas, which are smaller than the pricier Garden Villas, are a good bet for all the privacy and creature comforts you might crave. With access to the courtyard's pool, hot tub,

steam room, exercise area, and private sun deck, it's like a ship within a ship.

Our Favorite Spot for a Nightcap: The dimly lighted Star Bar overlooking the pool reminds us of a favorite piano bar with its comfortable seating and sophisticated atmosphere.

Best Split-Your-Sides Show: Performances by

Second City, Chicago's famous improvisation artists are scheduled in the theater as well as in more intimate nightclub settings. Passengers can even get a behind-the-scenes look at the shows during an improv workshop.

Best Beer Bar: Try Maltings for the most comprehensive beer (and whiskey) menu at sea.

The sports deck

NORWEGIAN SUN

2001	ENTERED SERVICE
1,936 (2,400 max)	PASSENGER CAPACITY
968	CREW MEMBERS
968	NUMBER OF CABINS
77,104	GROSS TONS
853 feet	LENGTH
108 feet	WIDTH

Public Areas & Facilities

Norwegian Cruise Line hadn't introduced many new ships in awhile at the time *Norwegian Sun* was on the drawing board, but it didn't take long before they got the hang of it. With Freestyle Cruising instituted and growing in popularity, the vessel moved into the forefront of the fleet with nine restaurants, an expansive casino, trendy spa, and more family- and kid-friendly facilities.

Rich wood tones and fabric colors prevail throughout. The Observation Lounge is a subdued and tasteful spot for afternoon tea in a light, tropical setting with nothing to distract attention from the expansive views beyond the floor-to-ceiling windows.

An expanded Internet Café with two-dozen computer stations encircles one atrium level, and the Java Café is a welcoming delight on the main atrium floor. Sunshine pours into the atrium through an overhead skylight by day, while at night it's the ship's glamorous hub of activity.

WOW Factor

There isn't a prettier atrium lobby afloat than the one at the heart of Norwegian Sun. *The vaguely art deco brass-and-marble staircases are simply stunning.*

Restaurants

This is a Freestyle ship, so all seating is open; dress is always casual. The two main dining rooms are complimentary; some specialty restaurants carry a cover charge and require reservations. Casual dining choices are the Lido buffet, an ice-cream bar, pizzeria, and a food court.

Top: Las Ramblas Tapas Bar & Restaurant
Bottom: *Norwegian Sun* at sea

What Works & What Doesn't

Dining takes a back seat to nothing else on *Norwegian Sun*, and the food by and large lives up to the stylish decor of all restaurants on board. Side by side, Le Bistro and Las Ramblas restaurants couldn't be more different, yet they share extraordinary sea views. Raised banquette seating along the interior wall of the long, narrow Il Adagio Restaurant ensures all diners a view. Plot your course carefully if you plan to dine in the Seven Seas Restaurant; with the huge galley separating it from the mid-ship Four Seasons Restaurant, you can't get there on a direct route from the atrium.

Accommodations

Layout: Staterooms are a bit more generous in size than on the older vessels in the NCL fleet and contain more than adequate closet and drawer space for a one-week cruise. More than two-thirds have an ocean view, and nearly two-thirds of those have a private balcony. Clever use of primary colors and strategically placed mirrors achieves an open feeling. All have a sitting area with sofa, chair, and table. Suites have walk-in closets.

Amenities: Light-wood cabinetry, mirrored accents, a small refrigerator, tea/coffeemaker, personal safe, broadband Internet connections, duvets on beds, a wall-mounted hair dryer over the dressing table, and bathrobes for use during the cruise are typical standard amenities. Bathrooms have shampoo and bath gel in shower-mounted dispensers as well as limited bathroom storage.

Suites: Suites include such luxuries as whirlpool tubs and entertainment centers. Butlers and a concierge are at the service of suite occupants.

Good to Know: Connecting staterooms are available in several categories, including those with balconies. Oddly sandwiched in between Deck 6 and Deck 7 forward is Deck 6A, which has no direct elevator access. Sixteen cabins are wheelchair-accessible.

CABIN TYPE	SIZE (sq. ft.)
Owner's Suite	828
Penthouse & Romance Suite	504
Minisuite	332
Ocean View Balcony/ Ocean View	221 /145
Deluxe Interior/ Interior	172 /145

Fast Facts

- 11 passenger decks
- 4 specialty restaurants, 2 dining rooms, buffet, ice-cream parlor, pizzeria
- Wi-Fi, in-cabin safes, some in-cabin refrigerators, some in-cabin DVDs
- 3 pools (2 indoor), children's pool
- Fitness classes, gym, hair salon, 4 hot tubs, sauna, spa
- 8 bars, casino, cinema, dance club, library, showroom, video game room
- Children's programs (ages 2–17)
- Dry cleaning, laundry service
- Computer room

In the Know

For newlyweds and couples celebrating a second honeymoon, an elegant honeymoon/anniversary romance suite is a luxurious hideaway for two.

Favorites

Best Dessert: Anything chocolate is well worth the calories; order decadent chocolate treats and linger over coffee and a glass of tawny port to end your meal.

Unique at Sea: Entering uncharted waters for fresh seafood, NCL offers patrons of East Meets West the selection of their own live lobster from the octagonal lobster tank. Have it pre-pared broiled with lemon butter, with hollandaise sauce, or wok-flashed and served atop noodles in a Kaffir lime and lemongrass broth.

Best Added Value: Try all the free food: the tapas in Las Ramblas and healthy selections in Pacific Heights are complimentary.

Our Favorite Spot for a Nightcap: The pianist in the Windjammer Bar will be happy to play requests. To accompany a late-night cognac, an adjacent nook set aside for cigar smokers has oversize leather chairs and a clubby atmosphere.

Best Late-Night Munchies: Head for the Sports Bar for live broadcasts of sporting events and snacks.

Stateroom with balcony

NORWEGIAN SPIRIT

Public Areas & Facilities

In a curious East-goes-West journey, *Norwegian Spirit* was originally built for the Freestyle Cruising concept and launched as *SuperStar Leo* for Norwegian Cruise Line's Asian parent, Star Cruises. In winter 2004, NCL's Hawaiian venture nearly sank when a freakish storm filled its almost-completed flagship with water while it was nearing completion in Germany. With a month's worth of bookings and no new ship, arrangements were made to deploy a substitute in Hawaii and transfer *SuperStar Leo* to fill the gap it left in its wake.

Rechristened in spring 2004 and updated to better suit American tastes, *Norwegian Spirit* still retains fine examples of Asian artwork as well as a few elements that may seem a bit out of place. In addition to the usual array of shipboard bars and lounges, passengers may be puzzled to find a mahjongg room and a huge amphitheater area overlooking the children's outdoor pool. As is customary in Asia, facilities for children and teens are particularly extensive, only rivaled by the Disney Cruise Line ships.

1999	Entered Service
1,966 (2,475 max)	Passenger Capacity
965	Crew Members
983	Number of Cabins
77,000	Gross Tons
880 feet	Length
106 feet	Width

700 ft.
500 ft.
300 ft.

WOW Factor

Elegantly appointed, Windows Restaurant is striking in its simplicity. Breathtaking vistas through the aft-facing floor-to-ceiling Palladian windows are attention-stealers.

Top: Shogun Asian Restaurant
Bottom: *Norwegian Spirit* at sea

Restaurants

All restaurants and dining rooms have open seating and flexible hours. The two main dining rooms are complimentary; most specialty restaurants carry a cover charge and require reservations. The Italian La Trattoria is an additional evenings-only option in the Lido. Casual daytime choices are the Lido buffet, an ice-cream bar, pizzeria, and a food court–style eatery.

What Works & What Doesn't

Security measures preclude a tour of the ship's bridge, but passengers can still watch the action from the bridge viewing gallery reached via staircase from the Galaxy of the Stars observatory lounge. Although the children's water park area is fantastic, the main swimming pool feels cramped and on the small side. There are many things to like about the champagne bar, but the neon lights in the ceiling are not among them; they are a tacky surprise in the otherwise serene atmosphere.

Accommodations

Layout: Over two-thirds of Norwegian Spirit's cabins are outside with ocean views, and more than two-thirds of those have private balconies. Cabins have adequate space, including a sitting area with sofa, chair, and table. Every cabin has adequate closet and drawer–shelf storage, as well as limited bathroom storage. Most bathrooms are compartmentalized with sink area, shower, and toilet separated by sliding glass doors. Suites have walk-in closets.

Amenities: Light-wood cabinetry, mirrored accents, a small refrigerator, tea/coffeemaker, personal safe, Internet connection, duvets on beds, a wall-mounted hair dryer over the dressing table, bathrobes for use during the cruise. Electrical outlets are designed for Asian-style 220 volts and, although there's a 110-volt receptacle, it should be reserved for low-wattage appliances.

Plug in a megawatt hair dryer, and you'll likely get to meet a ship's engineer because you blew out the power. Bathrooms have shampoo and bath gel in a shower-mounted dispenser.

Suites: Suites include such luxuries as whirlpool tubs and entertainment centers with DVD players.

Good to Know: Only four staterooms are designed for wheelchair accessibility and they are all interior.

CABIN TYPE	SIZE (sq. ft.)
Owners Suite	605
Deluxe Penthouse	555
Penthouse	436
Ocean View Balcony/ Ocean View	201 /157
Interior	149

Fast Facts

- 10 passenger decks
- 4 specialty restaurants, 2 dining rooms, buffet, ice-cream parlor, pizzeria
- Wi-Fi, in-cabin safes, some in-cabin refrigerators, some in-cabin DVDs
- 3 pools (2 indoor), children's pool
- Fitness classes, gym, hair salon, 4 hot tubs, sauna, spa
- 8 bars, casino, cinema, dance club, library, showroom, video game room
- Children's programs (ages 2–17)
- Dry cleaning, laundry service
- Computer room

In the Know

More than just the splash pool typically found on cruise ships, Buccaneer's Wet & Wild is an astonishing water park at sea with slides, fountains, caves, and enough pretend pirate-theme details to spark any child's imagination for hours.

Stateroom with balcony

Favorites

Best Place to Escape the Crowds: If you aren't a card player or would prefer to do your singing in the shower rather than a karaoke room (private or not), then you may find solitude in the library or writing room.

Best Spot for a Snack: The Bier Garten overlooking the central Lido pool serves burgers, hot dogs, salads, and German bratwurst and sauerkraut

all day long. Surrounded by picnic tables, it offers a bird's-eye view of the swimming pool and all the action.

Our Favorite Spot for a Nightcap: Henry's Pub is an inviting bar with a homey feel and abundance of wood. Even the floors are hardwood.

Best Place to Engage Children: If the kids get bored, take them to the

bridge viewing gallery, where they can catch a glimpse of the captain and his officers at work.

Best Place to Celebrate: Order flutes of bubbly to toast each other over foie gras and caviar. Who needs a special occasion to indulge in the Champagne Bar?

5

NORWEGIAN CRUISE LINE

NORWEGIAN MAJESTY

Public Areas & Facilities

Built in 1992, *Norwegian Majesty* was stretched in 1999, when a 112-foot midsection was added to increase her size. Although that meant more space, unfortunately there were some features that couldn't be added, including balconies: none of the staterooms have them.

Nevertheless, she's a lovely ship, and her public rooms reflect a quiet glamour in jewel-tone colors and an art deco flavor reminiscent of Miami Beach. The ship's size makes her easily navigable, and what she lacks in quantity, she more than makes up for in quality, including wood finishes and polished brass accents. The wraparound promenade deck gives her the feel of an ocean liner and more than makes up for somewhat low ceilings inside.

1992	ENTERED SERVICE
1,462 (1,790 max)	PASSENGER CAPACITY
620	CREW MEMBERS
731	NUMBER OF CABINS
40,876	GROSS TONS
680 feet	LENGTH
91 feet	WIDTH

700 ft.

500 ft.

300 ft.

WOW Factor

Nothing beats views overlooking the bow of any ship, and Norwegian Majesty *has both indoor and outdoor spaces where you can see where you are going.*

Top: Monte Carlo casino
Bottom: *Norwegian Majesty* at sea

Restaurants

Two main dining rooms serve Continental cuisine, with open dinner seating. NCL's signature Le Bistro carries a cover charge and requires reservations. Italian fare is served nightly in the Royal Observatory by reservation. Casual daytime choices are the Lido buffet, adjacent outdoor grill, pizzeria, and ice-cream bar. Room service is available around the clock.

What Works & What Doesn't

Norwegian Majesty doesn't dazzle; instead, public areas have classic deco-inspired interiors for cruising in comfortable style. At the ship's heart, the Crossroads lobby on Atlantic Deck anchors several lounges, the Internet Café, library, card room, video arcade, main dining rooms, Le Bistro, and duty-free shops. Presented in the low-ceiling Palace Theater, production shows are appealing with an intimate, almost cabaret-style flavor.

Accommodations

Layout: Although there are numerous cabin categories from which to choose, all staterooms are configured in six basic layouts, and fares are determined mostly by size and location. Take care when selecting a location: even some accommodations in the top categories have obstructed or partially obstructed views. Take time to examine the deck plans carefully because many cabins have two lower beds that cannot be pushed together or a double bed that cannot be split apart. If you plan to share a cabin with the kids, you might want to consider a superior category or even a suite—standard cabins are really miniuscule.

Amenities: Wood cabinetry adds warmth to what are basic furnishings in all superior and standard ocean-view and inside cabins. Built during an era when cabins were designed for dressing and sleeping, they contain a desk-vanity and chair and hair dryers; only the superior ocean-view category has a small refrigerator. Bathroom amenities include shampoo, lotion, soap, and bathrobes for use during the cruise.

Suites: Suites have floor-to-ceiling bay windows, stereo with CD library, VCR, a personal safe, hair dryer, and small refrigerator.

Good to Know: Seven staterooms are wheelchair-accessible.

CABIN TYPE	SIZE (sq. ft.)
Owner's Suite	374
Suite	235
Superior Ocean View	145
Superior Inside	145
Standard Ocean View/Inside	108

Fast Facts

- 9 passenger decks
- 2 specialty restaurants, 2 dining rooms, buffet, ice-cream parlor, pizzeria
- Wi-Fi, in-cabin safes, some in-cabin refrigerators, some in-cabin VCRs
- 2 pools, children's pool
- Fitness classes, gym, hair salon, 2 hot tubs, sauna, spa
- 8 bars, casino, dance club, library, showroom, video game room
- Children's programs (ages 2–17)
- Dry cleaning, laundry service
- Computer room

In the Know

When the sun goes down, the Royal Observatory is transformed into an Italian trattoria, where meals include individually prepared pasta dishes. Crisp linens cover cozy tables for two or four, and it's dining with a magnificent view and no cover charge. Grab a reservation before the word gets around.

Seven Seas Restaurant

Favorites

Best Snacking Spots: For late-night attacks of the munchies, head for the Rendezvous Lounge or the casino, where snacks are served from 11:30 PM until 12:30 AM and midnight to 1 AM, respectively.

Best Place for Sea Air: Walkers, joggers, and even moonlight strollers will be pleased to find a 360-degree wraparound teak promenade deck, a traditional feature missing from most new cruise ships. It's also a fine place to escape the crowds and enjoy a bit of solitude at the ship's rail.

Our Favorite Spot for a Nightcap: Snuggled between the Royal Fireworks dance club and Rendezvous piano bar, the House of Lords Lounge is a quiet retreat. Music from nearby lounges is audible but doesn't hinder conversation.

Best Retro Design Element: The art deco-style faux skylight that crowns the lobby could easily adorn any Miami Beach interior.

OCEANIA CRUISES

This distinctive cruise line was founded by Frank Del Rio and Joe Watters, cruise-industry veterans with the know-how to satisfy the wants of inquisitive passengers. By offering itineraries to interesting ports of call and upscale touches—all for

Oceania's *Regatta*

fares much lower than you would expect—they are succeeding quite nicely. Oceania Cruises set sail in 2003 to carve a unique, almost boutique niche in the cruise industry by obtaining mid-size R-class ships that formerly made up the popular Renaissance Cruises fleet.

OCEANIA CRUISES
8120 N.W. 53rd Street,
Suite 100
Miami, FL 33166
305/514–2300 or
800/531–5658
www.oceaniacruises.com

Cruise Style: Premium

Intimate and cozy public spaces reflect the importance of socializing on Oceania ships. Indoor lounges feature numerous conversation areas, and even the pool deck is a social center. The Patio is a shaded slice of deck adjacent to the pool and hot tubs. Defined by billowing drapes and carpeting underfoot, it is furnished with plush sofas and chairs ideal for relaxation. Evening entertainment leans toward light cabaret, solo artists, music for dancing, and conversation with fellow passengers; however, you'll find lively karaoke sessions on the schedule as well. The sophisticated, adult atmosphere on days at sea is enhanced by a combo performing jazz or easy-listening melodies poolside.

While thickly padded single and double loungers are arranged around the pool, if more privacy appeals to you, eight private cabanas are available for rent on Deck 11. Each one has a double chaise longue with a view of the sea; overhead drapery can be drawn back for sunbathing, and the side panels can be left open or closed. Waiters are on standby to offer chilled towels or serve occupants with beverages or snacks. In port, this luxury will set you back $50, but at sea it is $100 per day. In addition, you can request a spa service in your cabana.

Varied, destination-rich itineraries are an important characteristic of Oceania Cruises, and most Caribbean sailings are in the 10- to 12-night range. Before arrival in ports of call, lectures are presented on the historical background, culture, and traditions of the islands.

Culinary demonstrations by guest presenters and Oceania's own executive chefs are extremely popular. Lectures on varied topics, computer courses, hands-on arts and crafts classes, and wine or champagne seminars round out the popular enrichment series on board.

Food

Several top cruise-industry chefs were lured away from other cruise lines to ensure that the artistry of world-renowned master chef Jacques Pépin, who crafted five-star menus for Oceania, is properly carried out. The results are sure to please the most discriminating palate. Oceania simply serves some of the best food at sea, particularly impressive for a cruise line that charges far less than luxury rates. The main restaurant offers trendy, French-Continental cuisine with an always-on-the-menu steak, seafood, or poultry choice and vegetarian option.

Intimate specialty restaurants require reservations, but there's no additional charge for Toscana, the Italian restaurant, or Polo Grill, the steak house. A fourth dinner option is Tapas on the Terrace, alfresco dining at the Terrace Café (the daytime Lido deck buffet). Although service is from the buffet, outdoor seating on the aft deck is transformed into a charming Spanish courtyard with Catalonian-style candleholders and starched linens.

The Terrace Café also serves breakfast and lunch buffet-style and has a small pizzeria window that operates during the day. At an outdoor poolside grill you can order up burgers, hot dogs, and sandwiches for lunch and then take a seat; waiters are at hand to serve you either at a nearby table or your lounge chair by the pool. Afternoon tea is a decadent spread of finger foods and includes a rolling dessert cart, which has to be seen to be believed.

Fitness & Recreation

Although small, the spa, salon, and well-equipped fitness center are adequate for the number of passengers on board. In addition to individual body-toning machines and complimentary exercise classes, there's a walking-jogging track circling the top of the ship. A personal trainer is available for individual instruction for an additional charge.

The spa menu lists massages, body wraps, and facials, while a full range of hair and beauty services are avail-

Noteworthy

■ The Oceania signature Tranquility Bed has a firm mattress, 350-thread count linens, goose-down pillows, and a silk-cut duvet.

■ Instead of on easels cluttering passageways, artworks for auction are displayed on stairwell landings and in lounges.

■ Pool decks are outfitted with attractive wood tables and chairs, market umbrellas, and couples lounge chairs with cushy pads and colorful bolsters.

Top: Penthouse suite
Bottom: Toscana Restaurant

Top: Cocktails before dinner
Middle: Veranda stateroom
Bottom: Martini's Lounge

able for women and men in the salon. Just forward of the locker rooms you can find a large therapy pool and quiet deck for relaxation and sunning on padded wooden steamer chaises. Locker rooms contain good-size steam rooms and rain showers, but no saunas.

Your Shipmates

Oceania Cruises appeal to singles and couples from their late-30s to well-traveled retirees, who have the time for and prefer longer cruises. Most are American couples attracted to the casually sophisticated atmosphere, creative cuisine, and high level of service. Many are past passengers of the now-defunct Renaissance Cruises who are loyal to their favorite ships, which now offer a variety of destination-rich itineraries.

Dress Code

Leave the formal wear at home—attire on Oceania ships is country-club casual every evening, although some guests can't help dressing up to dine in the beautifully appointed restaurants. A jacket and tie are never required for dinner, but many men wear sport jackets, as they would to dine in an upscale restaurant ashore. Jeans, shorts, T-shirts, and tennis shoes are discouraged after 6 PM in public rooms.

Junior Cruisers

Oceania Cruises are adult-oriented and not a good choice for families, particularly those traveling with infants and toddlers. No dedicated children's facilities are available, and parents are completely responsible for the behavior and entertainment. Teenagers with sophisticated tastes (and who don't mind the absence of a video arcade) might enjoy the intriguing ports of call.

Service

Highly personalized service by a mostly European staff is crisp and efficient without being intrusive. Butlers are on hand to fulfill the requests of suite guests and will even assist with packing and unpacking when asked.

CHOOSE OCEANIA CRUISES IF:

❶ Socializing plays a more important role in your lifestyle than boogying the night away.

❷ You love to read. These ships have extensive libraries that are ideal for curling up with a good book.

❸ You have a bad back. You're sure to love the Tranquility Beds.

Tipping

Gratuities of $11.50 per person, per day are added to ship-board accounts for distribution to stewards and waitstaff; an additional $3.50 per person, per day is added for oc-cupants of suites with butler service. Passengers may ad-just the amount based on the level of service experienced. An automatic 18% gratuity is added to all bar tabs for bartenders and drink servers.

Past Passengers

After you take one Oceania cruise, you'll receive several benefits along with a free subscription to *The Oceania Club Journal*. Shipboard Club parties hosted by the cap-tain and senior officers, complimentary amenities or ex-clusive privileges on select sailings, an Oceania Club membership recognition pin after 5, 10, 15, and 20 cruises, and special pricing and mailings about upcom-ing promotions are some of the benefits. Members fur-ther qualify for elite-level status based on the number of sailings aboard Oceania Cruises. Starting with your fifth cruise, you begin to accrue more valuable benefits on every cruise you take, beginning with a $200 shipboard credit per stateroom on cruises five through nine. On your tenth cruise, you will receive a $400 shipboard credit per stateroom plus complimentary gratuities on cruises 10 through 14. Once you take your 20th cruise, you get a free cruise as well as complimentary spa treatments, shore excursions, and gratuities on all future cruises.

Good to Know

When these ships were oper-ated by Renaissance, they were entirely smoke-free, and many people booked cruises because of that. Now, two very small areas are set aside for smokers, one near the pool bar and the other set in a portside corner of the Horizons Lounge. Staterooms and balconies continue to be no-smoking zones, and if you light up in either spot, you could find yourself put ashore in the next port.

5

OCEANIA CRUISES

DON'T CHOOSE OCEANIA CRUISES IF:

❶ You like the action in a huge casino. Oceania casinos are small, and seats at a poker table can be difficult to get.

❷ You won't take a cruise without your children. Most passengers book with Oceania anticipating a kid-free atmosphere.

❸ Glitzy production shows are your thing. Oceania's showrooms are decidedly low-key.

REGATTA, INSIGNIA, NAUTICA

1998, 1998, 2000	ENTERED SERVICE
684 (824 max)	PASSENGER CAPACITY
400	CREW MEMBERS
342	NUMBER OF CABINS
30,200	GROSS TONS
594 feet	LENGTH
84 feet	WIDTH

Public Areas & Facilities

Carefully furnished to impart the atmosphere of a private English country manor, this mid-size ship is casual yet elegant, with a sweeping central staircase and abundant flower arrangements. Brocade and toile fabrics cover the windows, overstuffed sofas, and wing chairs to create a feeling throughout that is warm and intimate. The entire effect is that of a weekend retreat in the English countryside.

Authentic-looking faux fireplaces are inviting elements adjacent to a cozy seating area in the Grand Bar, near the Martini Bar's grand piano, and in the beautiful library—one of the best at sea with an enormous selection of best sellers, nonfiction, and travel books. The casino is quite small and can feel cramped, nor does it allow smoking. There might be a wait for a seat at a poker table; however, there are enough slot machines to go around.

Other than decorative trompe l'oeil paintings in several public areas, the artwork is ordinary.

WOW Factor

Everyone has to have a photograph taken on the lobby staircase—it's practically a twin of the one in the movie Titanic.

Top: Teatime in Horizons
Bottom: Breakfast in bed

Restaurants

Oceania passengers enjoy the flexibility of four open-seating restaurants: the Grand Dining Room; Toscana and Polo Grill, the reservations-required alternative restaurants; and Terraces, the buffet restaurant, which transforms into Tapas after dark for a relaxed atmosphere and alfresco dining. All dining venues have nearby bars, and there's no additional cover charge.

What Works & What Doesn't

A relaxed, social atmosphere pervades all areas on board, particularly during sea days. Passengers mix easily and create their own entertainment, depending very little on organized activities. Shipboard charges can add up fast since drink prices and even Internet services are above the average charged by most cruise lines. The one miniuscule self-serve laundry room can get steamy, particularly when there's a wait for the machines. The absence of a sauna in the spa is an unfortunate oversight, although you'll be happy to find a rain shower and nifty tiled steam room in the changing areas.

Accommodations

Layout: Private balconies outfitted with chairs and tables add additional living space to nearly 75% of all outside accommodations. All cabins have a vanity–desk and a sitting area with sofa, chair, and table. Every cabin has generous closet and drawer–shelf storage and bathroom shelves. Owner's and Vista suites have a separate living–dining room as well as a separate powder room.

Amenities: Dark-wood cabinetry, soothing blue decor, mirrored accents, personal safe, Tranquility Beds, 350-thread-count linens, goose-down pillows, silk-cut duvets are typical stateroom features. Bathrooms have a hair dryer, shampoo, lotion, and bath gel, plus robes.

Suites: Owner's and Vista Suites have an entertainment center with a DVD and CD player, a small refrigerator, and a second TV in the bedroom; the main bathroom has a combination shower–whirlpool tub. Penthouse suites also have refrigerators and bathtubs. Butlers are on hand to coordinate reservations and serve evening canapés and dinner ordered from any of the ship's restaurants.

Good to Know: Several cabins accommodate third and fourth passengers, but few have connecting doors. Three staterooms are designed for wheelchair accessibility.

CABIN TYPE	SIZE (sq. ft.)
Owner's/Vista Suite	962 /786
Penthouse Suite	322
Concierge Ocean View	216
Deluxe/Standard Ocean View	165 /150–165
Inside	160

Fast Facts

- 9 passenger decks
- 2 specialty restaurants, dining room, buffet, pizzeria
- In-cabin broadband, Wi-Fi, in-cabin safes, some in-cabin refrigerators, some in-cabin DVDs
- Pool
- Fitness classes, gym, hair salon, 3 hot tubs, spa, steam room
- 4 bars, casino, dance club, library, showroom
- Dry cleaning, laundry facilities, laundry service
- Computer room
- No-smoking cabins

5

OCEANIA CRUISES

In the Know

Don't plot to take the divine linens home with you—it's been tried with embarrassing consequences. Take heart, though. You can purchase the luxurious sheets, pillow slips, and duvet covers on the cruise line's Web site, and the prices are reasonable.

Favorites

Best Place to Get Away From It All: Passengers don't always discover the teak deck just forward of the spa and fitness center. Padded wood steamer chairs surrounding a large saltwater therapy pool are the ideal spot to sunbathe and watch the ship's bow slice through the water.

Best Dessert: Choose anything chocolate from the dessert cart at teatime.

Our Favorite Spot for a Nightcap: Despite its location adjacent to the casino, Martini's feels more like a living room with its cushy seating and fireplace. With a pianist playing softly in the background, you'll be disturbed only if some lucky player hits a jackpot.

Best Splurge: Certain staterooms on decks 7 and 8 receive an extra level of service and amenities, including chilled champagne on embarkation, an in-cabin refrigerator, 20-inch TV, DVD player, cashmere throw, plush robes and slippers, a complimentary tote bag, and updated bathroom amenities, plus complimentary shoe shine service; these guests also receive priority embarkation, luggage delivery, and priority restaurant reservations.

Regatta at sea

PRINCESS CRUISES

Princess Cruises may be best known for introducing cruise travel to millions of viewers, when its flagship became the setting for *The Love Boat* television series in 1977. Since that heady time of small-screen stardom, the Princess fleet has grown both in the num-

Kayaking at Princess Cays

ber and size of ships plying Caribbean waters. Although most are large in scale, Princess vessels manage to create the illusion of intimacy through the use of color and decor in understated yet lovely public rooms graced by multimillion-dollar art collections.

PRINCESS CRUISES
24305 Town Center Drive
Santa Clarita, CA 91355-4999
661/753-0000 or
800/774-6237
www.princess.com

Cruise Style: Premium

Princess has also become more flexible lately; Personal Choice Cruising offers alternatives for open-seating dining (when you wish and with whom you please) and entertainment options as diverse as those found in resorts ashore.

Welcome additions to Princess's roster of adult activities, which still include standbys like bingo and art auctions, are ScholarShip@Sea Enrichment programs featuring guest lecturers, cooking classes, wine-tasting seminars, pottery workships, and computer and digital photography classes. Nighttime production shows tend toward Broadway-style revues presented in the main show lounge, and performers might include comedians, magicians, jugglers, and acrobats. Live bands play a wide range of musical styles for dancing and listening in smaller lounges throughout the ships and each ship has a disco.

A spirited Island Night deck party is held during every Caribbean cruise; on Pub Night the cruise director's staff leads a rollicking evening of fun with passenger participation. At the conclusion of the second formal night, champagne trickles down over a champagne waterfall, painstakingly created by the arrangement of champagne glasses in a pyramid shape. It's a great photo-op when several women are invited to join the maître d' atop the platform to assist in the pouring.

Lovely chapels or the wide-open decks are equally romantic settings for weddings at sea. Princess Cruises explode the myth that just any captain of any ship can marry starry-eyed couples. Legally, ceremonies with the captain officiating can only be performed on certain Grand-class Princess vessels. It's an option not offered by any other cruise line in the Caribbean.

Food

Personal choices regarding where and what to eat abound, but there's no getting around the fact that Princess ships are large and carry a great many passengers. Unless you opt for traditional assigned seating, you could experience a brief wait for a table in one of the open-seating dining rooms.

Menus are varied and extensive in the main dining rooms, and the results are good to excellent considering how much work is going on in the galleys. Vegetarian and healthy lifestyle options are always on the menu, as well as steak, fish, or chicken. A special menu is designed especially for children.

Alternative restaurants are a staple throughout the fleet, but vary by ship class. Grand-class ships have upscale steak houses and Sabatini's for Italian food; both require reservations and carry an extra cover charge. Sun-class ships offer complimentary sit-down dining in the pizzeria and a similar steak house option, although it's in a sectioned-off area of the buffet restaurant. On *Caribbean, Crown,* and *Emerald Princess,* a casual evening alternative to the dining rooms and usual buffet is Café Caribe—adjacent to the Lido buffet restaurant, it serves cuisine with a Caribbean flair. With a few breaks in service, Lido buffets on all ships are almost always open, and a pizzeria and grill offer casual daytime snack choices. The fleet's patisseries and ice-cream bars charge for specialty coffee, some pastries, and premium ice cream.

An utterly posh dining opportunity for passengers who have balconies and want to celebrate a special occasion is Ultimate Balcony Dining. Breakfast is $30 per couple, dinner $50 per person. A server is on duty throughout the four-course dinner, and a photographer also stops by to capture the romantic evening.

Fitness & Recreation

Spa rituals include a variety of massages, body wraps, and facials; numerous hair and nail services are offered

Noteworthy

■ The traditional gala champagne waterfall on formal night is a not-to-be-missed event.

■ Bathrobes are provided for use during your cruise—all you have to do is ask the room steward to deliver them.

■ Wheelchair-accessible staterooms with 33-inch wide entry and bathroom doorways, plus bathrooms fitted to ADA standards, are available in an array of categories.

Top: Place a bet in the casino
Bottom: Disco into the night

5

PRINCESS CRUISES

Top: Sunset at sea
Middle: Morning stretch
Bottom: Freshwater Jacuzzis

in the salons. Both the salon and spa are operated by Steiner Leisure, and the menu of spa services includes special pampering treatments designed specifically for men and teens as well as couples.

Modern exercise equipment, a jogging track, and basic fitness classes are available at no charge. There's a nominal fee for personal training, body composition analysis, and specialized classes such as yoga and Pilates. Grand-class ships have a resistance pool so you can get your laps in effortlessly. You can even earn PADI scuba-diving certification in just one week by participating in the Open Water Diver program—be sure to check for program availability on your selected cruise date.

Your Shipmates

Princess Cruises attract mostly American passengers, ranging from their mid-30s to mid-50s. Families enjoy cruising together on the Princess Caribbean fleet, particularly during holiday seasons and summer months, when many children are on board. Longer cruises appeal to well-traveled retirees and couples who have the time.

Dress Code

Two formal nights are standard on seven-night cruises; an additional formal night may be scheduled on longer sailings. Men are encouraged to wear tuxedos, but dark suits are appropriate. All other evenings are casual, although jeans are discouraged in restaurants, and it's requested that no shorts be worn in public areas after 6 PM.

Junior Cruisers

For young passengers aged 3 to 17, each Princess vessel has a playroom, teen center, and programs of supervised activities designed for different age groups: ages 3 to 7, 8 to 12, and 13 to 17. Activities to engage youngsters include arts and crafts, pool games, scavenger hunts, deck parties, backstage and galley tours, games, and videos. Events such as dance parties in their own disco, theme parties, athletic contests, karaoke, pizza parties, and movie fests occupy teenage passengers. With a nod toward science and educational entertainment, children also participate in learning programs focused on the environment and wildlife in areas where the ships sail. The

CHOOSE PRINCESS CRUISES IF:

❶ You're a traveler with a disability. Princess ships are some of the most accessible at sea.

❷ You'd like to gamble but hate a smoke-filled casino. Princess casinos are well-ventilated and spacious.

❸ You want a balcony. Princess ships feature them in abundance at affordable rates.

Adventures Ashore program features appealing tours for children and teens while in port.

To afford parents independent time ashore, youth centers operate as usual during port days, including lunch with counselors. For a nominal charge, group babysitting is available nightly from 10 PM until 1 AM. Family-friendly conveniences include self-service laundry facilities and two-way family radios that are available for rent at the Purser's Desk. Infants under six months are not permitted; private in-cabin babysitting is not available on any Princess vessel. Children under age three are welcome in the playrooms if supervised by a parent.

Service
Professional service by an international staff is efficient and friendly. It's not uncommon to be greeted in passageways by smiling stewards who know your name.

Tipping
A gratuity of $10 per person, per day is added to shipboard accounts for distribution to stewards and waitstaff. Passengers may adjust the amount based on the level of service experienced. An automatic 15% is added to all bar tabs for bartenders and drink servers; gratuities to other staff members may be extended at passengers' discretion.

Past Passengers
Membership in the Captain's Circle is automatic following your first Princess cruise. All members receive a free subscription to *Captain's Circle News,* a quarterly newsletter, as well as discounts on selected cruises.

Perks are determined by the number of cruises completed: Gold (2 through 5), Platinum (6 through 15), and Elite (16 and above). While Gold members only receive the magazine, an invitation to an onboard event, and the services of the Circle Host on the ship, benefits really begin to accrue once you've completed five cruises. Platinum members receive upgraded insurance (when purchasing the standard policy), expedited check-in, a debarkation lounge to wait in on the ship, and, best of all, free Internet access during the cruise. Elite benefits are even more lavish, with many complimentary services.

Good to Know

Some people like the time-honored tradition of assigned seating for dinner, so they can get to know their table companions and their servers; others prefer to choose with whom they dine as well as when. Princess lets you have things your way or both ways. If you're unsure whether Personal Choice is for you, select Traditional dining when you reserve your cruise. You can easily make the switch to anytime dining once on board; however, it can be impossible to change from Personal Choice to Traditional.

5

PRINCESS CRUISES

DON'T CHOOSE PRINCESS CRUISES IF:

❶ You have a poor sense of direction. The ships, especially the Grand-class ships, are very large.

❷ You want to meet *The Love Boat* cast. That was just a TV show, and it was more than three decades ago.

❸ You're too impatient to stand in line or wait. Debarkation from these large ships can be a nightmare.

CARIBBEAN, CROWN, EMERALD, RUBY PRINCESS

2004, 2006, 2007, 2008	ENTERED SERVICE
3,100	PASSENGER CAPACITY
1,200	CREW MEMBERS
1,550	NUMBER OF CABINS
113,000	GROSS TONS
951 feet	LENGTH
206 feet	WIDTH

Public Areas & Facilities

With dramatic atriums and Skywalker's Disco (the spoiler hovering 150 feet above the stern), *Caribbean Princess* is a super-size version of the older Grand-class vessels with an extra deck of passenger accommodations.

Not quite identical to *Caribbean Princess, Crown, Emerald,* and *Ruby Princess* have introduced more dining options. Several signature public spaces have been redesigned or relocated on both ships as well—the atrium on *Crown, Emerald,* and *Ruby Princess* resembles an open piazza and sidewalk café; Sabatini's Italian Trattoria is found on a top deck with views on three sides and adjacent space for alfresco dining; and Skywalker's Disco is forward near the funnel (where it's topped with a sports court).

Inside spaces on all three vessels are quietly neutral, with touches of glamour in the sweeping staircases and marble-floor atriums. Surprising intimacy is achieved by the number of public rooms and restaurants that swallow up passengers.

WOW Factor

Visible from afar, the huge screen for Movies Under the Stars proved to be such a WOW that other cruise lines have installed them.

Top: *Caribbean Princess* at sea
Bottom: Broadway-style revues

Restaurants

Passengers have the choice between two traditional dinner seating times in an assigned dining room or open seating in the ships' other two formal dining rooms. Alternative dinner options include reservations-only Sabatini's and Sterling Steakhouse (with a supplement), as well as Café Caribe, a Caribbean buffet with linen-dressed tables and limited waiter service.

What Works & What Doesn't

Movies Under the Stars on the huge poolside screen may have seemed like a gimmick, but the clever programming and interactive party atmosphere have proven to be a big hit. Popcorn is free, but other movie snacks aren't. Passengers who opt for Personal Choice dining may encounter a short wait for a table unless they're willing to join other diners. Personal Choice is all about flexibility, and it's no big deal to just go to a different dining room that might not be as busy. *Crown Princess* introduces pub snacks to the trademark Wheelhouse Bar.

Accommodations

Layout: On these ships 80% of the outside staterooms have balconies. The typical stateroom has a sitting area with a chair and table; even the cheapest categories have ample storage. Minisuites have a separate sitting area, walk-in closet, combination shower–tub, and a balcony, as well as two TVs. Grand Suites have a separate sitting room and dining room, as well as a walk-in closet. Owner's, Penthouse, Premium, and Vista suites have a separate sitting room with a sofa bed and desk, as well as a walk-in closet.

Amenities: Decorated in attractive pastel hues, all cabins have refrigerators, hair dryers, a personal safe, and bathrobes to use during the cruise. Bathrooms have shampoo, lotion, and bath gel.

Good to Know: Two family suites are interconnecting staterooms with a bal-cony that each sleep up to eight people (D105/D101 and D106/D102). Staterooms in a variety of categories will accommodate three and four people, and some adjacent cabins can be interconnected through interior doors or by unlocking doors in the balcony dividers. Twenty-five staterooms are designed for wheelchair accessibility and range in size from 234 to 396 square feet, depending upon the category.

CABIN TYPE	SIZE (sq. ft.)
Grand Suite	1,279
Other Suites	461–689
Family Suite/Minisuite	607/324
Ocean view Balcony/Standard Balcony	233–285/158–182
Inside	163

All dimensions include the square footage for balconies.

Fast Facts

- 15 passenger decks
- 2 specialty restaurants, 3 dining rooms, buffet, ice-cream parlor, pizzeria
- Wi-Fi, in-cabin safes, in-cabin refrigerators
- 4 pools (1 indoor), children's pool
- Fitness classes, gym, hair salon, 7 hot tubs, sauna, spa, steam room
- 9 bars, casino, cinema, 2 dance clubs, library, 2 showrooms, video game room
- Children's programs (ages 3–17)
- Dry cleaning, laundry facilities, laundry service
- Computer room
- No kids under 6 months

In the Know

These ships are marginally larger than Grand-class with the addition of the extra passenger deck, but do they seem crowded with the extra passengers on board? Not necessarily, although when booked to maximum capacity, lines can form with more frequency than on their smaller fleetmates.

Favorites

Best Place to Escape the Crowds: The terrace overlooking the aft swimming pool is a little-used spot after dark, but bring your own refreshments if you plan to stay a while because the adjacent bar may close early.

Best Dessert: Any soufflé is scrumptious, and a scoop of ice cream on the side is a special treat. Try them all!

Our Favorite Spot for a Nightcap: The dimly lighted Wheelhouse Bar has oversized comfy chairs and a clubby feel.

Best Splurge: Book a suite to get two TVs, a wet bar, and a separate shower and tub (whirlpool tub in Grand Suites). An extended room-service menu is also available for suite passengers, as are priority dining reservations and all the amenities extended to Elite Captain's Circle members.

Best Place to De-Stress: Only on *Crown* and *Emerald Princess*, it's the adults-only Sanctuary, a private, partially shaded deck with posh loungers, waiter service for snacks and drinks, and a small fee to keep capacity down.

Movies Under the Stars

CORAL CLASS
Coral Princess, Island Princess

2003, 2003	ENTERED SERVICE
1,970	PASSENGER CAPACITY
900	CREW MEMBERS
985	NUMBER OF CABINS
92,000	GROSS TONS
964 feet	LENGTH
106 feet	WIDTH

Public Areas & Facilities

Princess includes *Coral Princess* (as well as *Island Princess*, which cruises the Pacific coast) in the Sun-class category; however, she's a larger ship with a similar capacity, which means much more space per passenger. All the Personal Choice features attributed to the larger Grand-class ships were incorporated into this new design as well as a few unique additions, such as a demonstration kitchen and ceramics lab complete with kiln where ScholarShip@Sea programs are presented. The four-story atrium is similar to that on Sun-class ships, but public rooms are mainly spread fore and aft on two lower decks.

While signature rooms such as the Wheelhouse Bar are more traditional, the casino has a subtle London-like atmosphere with themed slot machines; Crooner's Bar is a retro 1960s Vegas-style martini and piano bar. In addition to the stately Princess Theater showroom, the Universe Lounge has three stages for shows and flexible seating on two levels, making it a multipurpose space.

WOW Factor

Engine pods on the funnel give Coral Princess *a space-age appearance of jet speed but function mainly as decoration. The ship can easily make 24 knots, but doesn't fly.*

Top: Fast-paced shows
Bottom: Aqua biking

Restaurants

One dining room has two traditional assigned dinner seatings; a second dining room is for open-seating Personal Choice cruisers. Alternative dining options are the two specialty restaurants, Sabatini's and Bayou Café Steakhouse, both of which have a surcharge and require reservations. A pizzeria, grill, patisserie, and ice-cream bar offer casual dining options and snacks.

What Works & What Doesn't

As many as 20 courses in the ScholarShip@Sea Program are offered on each cruise, and you can select from ceramics, cooking fundamentals, computer, and photography classes or attend lectures on a wide range of topics. No one should have trouble finding their way around or feel crowded on *Coral Princess*. Oddly, the library and card room are situated so they are often used as passageways, which results in a bit more noise than usual in areas that should be quiet.

Accommodations

Layout: Stepped out in wedding-cake fashion, over 83% of ocean-view staterooms include Princess Cruises' trademark private balconies. Even the least expensive inside categories have plentiful storage and a small sitting area with chair and table. Suites have two televisions, a sitting area, wet bar, large walk-in closet, and separate bathtub and shower. Minisuites have a separate sitting area, two televisions, walk-in closet, and a combination bathtub/shower.

Amenities: Decorated in attractive pastels and light-wood tones, typical staterooms have a personal safe, hair dryer, refrigerator, and bathrobes for use during the cruise. Bathrooms have shampoo, lotion, and bath gel.

Suites: Occupants of sixteen suites receive complimentary Internet access, dry cleaning, and shoe polishing, after-noon tea and evening canapés delivered to their suites, and priority embarkation, disembarkation, and tendering privileges. An extended room service menu is also available for them, as are priority reservations for dining and shore excursions.

Good to Know: Twenty staterooms are designed for wheelchair accessibility and range in size from 217 to 374 square feet, depending upon category.

CABIN TYPE	SIZE (sq. ft.)
Suite	470
Minisuite	285–302
Oceanview Balcony	217–232
Ocean view Stand./ Deluxe	162/212
Inside	156

All dimensions include the square footage for balconies.

Fast Facts

- 11 passenger decks
- 2 specialty restaurants, 2 dining rooms, buffet, ice-cream parlor, pizzeria
- Wi-Fi, in-cabin safes, in-cabin refrigerators
- 3 pools (1 indoor), children's pool
- Fitness classes, gym, hair salon, 5 hot tubs, sauna, spa, steam room
- 7 bars, casino, 2 dance clubs, library, 2 showrooms, video game room
- Children's programs (ages 3–17)
- Dry cleaning, laundry facilities, laundry service
- Computer room
- No kids under 6 months

In the Know

Most mid-ship ocean-view cabins on Emerald Deck are designated as obstructed view, and even some balcony staterooms on Emerald and Dolphin Decks are considered partially obstructed. And when balconies are arranged in a stepped-out design, the lower ones aren't totally private.

Lavish buffets in Horizon Court

Favorites

Best Splurge: Surprise your sweetie with flowers or chocolates delivered to your cabin from the shipboard floral shop. Orders are taken at the Passenger Services Desk.

Best Place to Escape the Crowds: Claim a padded steamer chair on the wrap-around promenade deck for a quiet spot to read or nap.

Most Appreciated Addition: The Fine Art Gallery is a dedicated spot for art-auction stock, meaning that displays don't clutter the passageways and distract from the art pieces selected to complement the décor.

Our Favorite Spot for a Nightcap: With seating for only 15, the clubby Churchill's has a custom humidor and call-button for bar service that summons a server from the nearby Crooner's Bar.

Best for Families: Cabins that sleep third and fourth passengers are numerous, and the best bet for families are interconnecting balcony staterooms on Aloha Deck (A624–A631 and A704–A722), which are adjacent to facilities dedicated to children and teens.

5

PRINCESS CRUISES

GRAND CLASS
*Grand Princess, Golden Princess,
Star Princess*

Public Areas & Facilities

When *Grand Princess* was introduced as the world's largest cruise ship in 1998, she also boasted one of the most distinctive profiles. Not only did the Skywalker's Disco appear futuristic, hovering approximately 150 feet above the water line, but Grand-class vessels also advanced the idea of floating resort to an entirely new level with more than 700 staterooms that included private balconies.

Like their predecessors, the interiors of Grand-class ships feature soothing pastel tones with splashy glamour in the sweeping staircases and marble-floor atriums. Surprisingly intimate for such large ships, human scale in public lounges is achieved by judicious placement of furniture as unobtrusive room dividers.

The 300-square-foot Times Square–style LED screen that hovers over *Grand Princess*'s Terrace Pool shows up to seven movies or events daily.

700 ft.	**1998, 2001, 2002**
	ENTERED SERVICE
	2,600
	PASSENGER CAPACITY
	1,100/1,100/1,200
	CREW MEMBERS
	1,300
	NUMBER OF CABINS
500 ft.	**109,000**
	GROSS TONS
	951 feet
	LENGTH
300 ft.	**201 feet**
	WIDTH

WOW Factor

When Grand Princess *was introduced in Europe, she was affectionately dubbed the* Shopping Cart *because her stern spoiler reminded Europeans of a grocery cart.*

Top: *Star Princess* at sea
Bottom: Grand-class
balcony stateroom

Restaurants

Passengers choose between two traditional dinner seatings in an assigned dining room or open-seating in the ships' other two formal dining rooms. Alternative evening dining options include reservations-only Sabatini's Italian Trattoria and Sterling Steakhouse specialty restaurants (both with a cover charge). The Horizon Court buffet is a casual option.

What Works & What Doesn't

Four pools, each with a distinctive personality, ensure it's nearly always possible to find a sun lounger—either in the midst of the action or a quiet corner. Sports bars get jam-packed and lively when important games are televised; however, they're also the only indoor bars where cigar smoking is allowed and can become stuffy and close. The Wheelhouse Bar has a combo for pre-dinner dancing and easy listening during the cocktail hour.

Accommodations

Layout: On these ships, 80% of the outside staterooms have balconies. The typical stateroom has a sitting area with a chair and table; even the cheapest categories have ample storage. Minisuites have a separate sitting area, walk-in closet, combination shower–tub, and a balcony, as well as two TVs. Grand Suites have a separate sitting room and dining room, as well as a walk-in closet. Owner's, Penthouse, Premium, and Vista suites have a separate sitting room with a sofa bed and desk, as well as a walk-in closet.

Amenities: Decorated in attractive pastel hues, all cabins have refrigerators, hair dryers, a personal safe, and bathrobes to use during the cruise. Bathrooms have shampoo, lotion, and bath gel.

Good to Know: Two family suites are interconnecting staterooms with a balcony that each sleep up to eight people (D105/D101 and D106/D102). Staterooms in a variety of categories will accommodate three and four people, and some adjacent cabins can be interconnected through interior doors or by unlocking doors in the balcony dividers. Twenty-eight staterooms are wheelchair-accessible.

CABIN TYPE	SIZE (sq. ft.)
Grand Suite	730/1,314*
Other Suites	468–591
Family Suite/Minisuite	607/323
Ocean View Balcony/ Standard	232–274/168
Inside	160

All dimensions include the square footage for balconies. *Grand Princess* dimensions followed by *Golden* and *Star Princess*

In the Know

Port and starboard balconies are stepped out from the ships' hulls in wedding-cake fashion. That means, depending on location, yours will likely be exposed a bit—or a lot—to passengers on higher decks. Exceptions are balconies on Emerald deck, which are covered.

Favorites

Best Place to Escape the Crowds: Skywalker's Disco has comfy semiprivate alcoves facing port and starboard and is virtually deserted during the day. It's the ideal spot to read or just watch the sea. The bar isn't open, though, so bring your own refreshments if you plan to stay awhile.

Best Added Value: For a few dollars you can wash and dry a load of dirty clothing in the convenient self-service passenger laundry rooms. You'll also find irons there to touch up garments wrinkled from packing.

Our Favorite Spot for a Nightcap: The Wheelhouse Bar, with soft lighting, comfortable leather chairs, shining brass accents, ship paintings, and nautical memorabilia, has become a Princess tradition.

Best Balcony Cabins: Nearly famous for the huge size of their balconies are minisuites E728 and E729. Both spaces are great for relaxing and entertaining, but you'll probably hear the band during shows in the Vista Lounge below E728 and a strange mechanical-sounding noise in E729.

Fast Facts

- 14 passenger decks
- 2 specialty restaurants, 3 dining rooms, buffet, ice-cream parlor, pizzeria
- Wi-Fi, in-cabin safes, in-cabin refrigerators
- 4 pools (1 indoor), children's pool
- Fitness classes, gym, hair salon, 9 hot tubs, sauna, spa, steam room
- 9 bars, casino, outdoor cinema, 2 dance clubs, library, 2 showrooms, video game room
- Children's programs (ages 3–17)
- Dry cleaning, laundry facilities, laundry service
- Computer room
- No kids under 6 months

Golden Princess grand plaza atrium

5

PRINCESS CRUISES

SUN CLASS

Sun Princess, Dawn Princess, Sea Princess

Public Areas & Facilities

Refined and graceful, Sun-class ships offer the choices attributed to larger Grand-class ships without sacrificing the smaller-ship atmosphere for which they're noted. The four-story atrium with a circular marble floor, stained-glass dome, and magnificent floating staircase are ideal settings for relaxation, people-watching, and making a grand entrance.

Onboard decor is a combination of neutrals and pastels, which is easy on the eyes after a sunny day ashore. The main public rooms are situated in a vertical arrangement on four lower decks and, with the exception of Promenade Deck, cabins are located forward and aft. In a nice design twist, the casino is somewhat isolated, and passengers aren't forced to use it as a passageway to reach dining rooms or the art deco main show lounge.

Sea Princess also has an outdoor Movies Under the Stars LED screen.

1995, 1997, 1998	ENTERED SERVICE
1,950	PASSENGER CAPACITY
900	CREW MEMBERS
975	NUMBER OF CABINS
77,000	GROSS TONS
856 feet	LENGTH
106 feet	WIDTH

700 ft.
500 ft.
300 ft.

WOW Factor

From the marble floor at its base to the stained-glass dome atop the atrium, a delicate circular staircase seems to float higher and higher between decks.

Top: *Sea Princess* at sea
Bottom: Sun-class ocean-view stateroom

Restaurants

Sun-class ships have one dining room with two traditional assigned dinner seatings and one open-seating dining room for Personal Choice cruisers. Alternatives are the reservations-only Sterling Steakhouse specialty restaurant (a section of the buffet that's dressed up for the evening and for which there's a charge) and the complimentary pizzeria.

What Works & What Doesn't

Horizon Court Lido buffet restaurants occupy one of the most prestigious spots on these ships—far forward, with a true view of the horizon. There's nothing about the interior decor that'll knock your socks off—some areas still have echoes of *The Love Boat* television series sets—but the cool palette enhanced by marble accents showcases impressive original artwork and murals. These are large ships, but not large enough to overcome the invasive nature of regularly scheduled art auctions. Why, oh why, do the auction displays have to intrude on the carefully selected artworks that are chosen to enhance the decor?

Accommodations

Layout: Princess Cruises' trademark is an abundance of staterooms with private balconies, yet even the least expensive inside categories have ample storage and a small sitting area with a chair and table. Suites have two TVs, a separate sitting area, dining-height table with chairs, walk-in closets, double-sink vanities, and a separate shower and whirlpool tub. Minisuites have a separate sitting area, two TVs, walk-in closet, and separate shower and whirlpool tub.

Amenities: Decorated in pastel colors, staterooms typically have mirrored accents, a personal safe, a refrigerator, a hair dryer, and bathrobes for use during the cruise. Bathrooms have shampoo, lotion, and bath gel.

Good to Know: Cabins that sleep third and fourth passengers aren't as numerous as on other Princess ships, and no

staterooms have interconnecting interior doors. Adjacent cabins with balconies can be interconnected by unlocking doors in the balcony dividers. Nineteen staterooms are designed for wheelchair accessibility and range in size from 213 to 305 square feet, depending upon category.

CABIN TYPE	SIZE (sq. ft.)
Suite	538–695
Minisuite	370–536
Ocean View Balcony/Deluxe	179 /173
Ocean View Standard	135–155
Interior	135–148

All dimensions include the square footage for balconies.

Fast Facts

- 10 passenger decks
- 2 dining rooms, buffet, ice-cream parlor, pizzeria
- Wi-Fi, in-cabin safes, in-cabin refrigerators
- 3 pools (1 indoor), children's pool
- Fitness classes, gym, hair salon, 5 hot tubs, sauna, spa, steam room
- 7 bars, casino, 2 dance clubs, library, 2 showrooms, video game room
- Children's programs (ages 3–17)
- Dry cleaning, laundry facilities, laundry service
- Computer room
- No kids under 6 months

In the Know

Check and double-check your bed configurations when booking an outside quad cabin for your family. There are balcony cabins with three and four berths, but some have two lower twin-size beds that cannot be pushed together to form a queen.

Favorites

Best Place to Escape the Crowds: You can always escape to the cozy, wood-panel reading room, where each oversize chair faces its own bay window.

Best Dessert: As on other Princess ships, the soufflés can't be beat. It doesn't matter what flavor is on the menu; they're all divine, but chocolate with a warm berry sauce is truly to die for.

Best Splurge: Treat yourself by day to specialty coffees and fresh pastries at the patisserie. In the evening, a flute of bubbly champagne and a caviar snack are indulgent pleasures at the wine and caviar bar.

Our Favorite Spot for a Nightcap: For after-dinner drinks and a late-night rendezvous, the elegant Rendez-Vous Lounge gets our nod.

Best Value: There's no charge to dine at night in the pizzeria, which offers traditional Italian dishes in a trattoria-style setting.

Riviera pool

REGENT SEVEN SEAS CRUISES

The December 1994 merger of Radisson Diamond Cruises and Seven Seas Cruise Line launched Radisson Seven Seas Cruises with an eclectic fleet of vessels that offered a nearly all-inclusive cruise experience in sumptuous, contemporary surroundings. Wholly

The end of a perfect day

owned by Carlson Hospitality Worldwide, the line was re-branded as Regent Seven Seas Cruises in 2006. Even more inclusive than in the past, the line has maintained its traditional tried-and-true formula—delightful ships offering exquisite service, generous staterooms with abundant amenities, a variety of dining options, and superior lecture and enrichment programs.

REGENT SEVEN SEAS CRUISES
1000 Corporate Drive, Suite 500
Fort Lauderdale, FL 33334
954/776-6123 or
877/505-5370
www.rssc.com

Cruise Style: Luxury

Guests are greeted with champagne upon boarding and find an all-inclusive beverage policy that offers not only soft drinks and bottled water, but also cocktails and select wines at all bars and restaurants throughout the ships.

The cruises are destination-focused, and most sailings host guest lecturers—historians, anthropologists, naturalists, and diplomats. Spotlight cruises center around popular pastimes and themes, such as food and wine, photography, history, archaeology, literature, performing arts, design and cultures, active exploration and wellness, antiques, jewelry and shopping, the environment, and marine life. Passengers need no urging to participate in discussions and workshops led by celebrated experts. All passengers have access to these unique experiences on board and on shore.

Activities and entertainment are tailored for each of the line's distinctive ships with the tastes of sophisticated passengers in mind. Don't expect napkin-folding demonstrations or nonstop action. Production revues, cabaret acts, concert-style piano performances, solo performers, and comedians may be featured in show lounges, with combos playing for listening and dancing in lounges and bars throughout the ships. Casinos are more akin to Monaco than Las Vegas. All ships display tasteful and varied art collections, including pieces that are for sale.

Food

Menus may appear to include the usual beef Wellington and Maine lobster, but in the hands of Regent Seven Seas chefs, the results are some of the most outstanding meals at sea. Specialty dining varies within the fleet, but the newest ships, *Seven Seas Voyager* and *Seven Seas Mariner,* have the edge with the sophisticated Signatures, which features the cuisine of Le Cordon Bleu of Paris, and Latitudes, offering a set "tasting" menu inspired by Indochine cooking. The authentic fare is prepared using French cooking techniques and served in traditional family style by Asian waiters. In addition, Mediterranean-influenced bistro dinners that need no reservations are served in La Veranda, the venue that is the daytime casual Lido buffet restaurant.

Evening alternative dining in *Seven Seas Navigator*'s Portofino is a lively affair that focuses on food and wines from four major regions of Italy and requires reservations.

Held in a tranquil setting, Wine Connoisseurs Dinners bring together people with an interest in wine and food. Each of five courses on the degustation menu is complemented by a fine wine pairing. Participation begins at $120 per person, and the dinners can be scheduled as many times as demand warrants.

Room service menus are fairly extensive, and you can also order directly from the restaurant menus during regular serving hours.

Although special dietary requirements should be relayed to the cruise line before sailing, general considerations such as vegetarian, low-salt, or low-cholesterol food requests can be satisfied on board the ships simply by speaking with the dining room staff. Wines chosen to complement dinner menus are freely poured each evening.

Fitness & Recreation

Although gyms and exercise areas are well-equipped, these are not large ships, so the facilities tend to be on the small size. Each ship has a jogging track, and the larger ones feature a variety of sports courts.

Exclusive to Regent Seven Seas, the spa and salon are operated by high-end Carita of Paris. The extensive range of beauty treatments offered follow the Carita approach of tailoring services to the unique needs of the individual

Noteworthy

■ Passengers enjoy open-seating dining with complimentary wines of the world in the elegant restaurants.

■ Italian fare with flair is an alternate dinner option on each Regent ship.

■ Regent's ship photographers are most unobtrusive. You may have to ask for your picture to be taken—a far cry from most cruise ships.

Top: Sunrise jog
Bottom: *Seven Seas Navigator*

Top: Fitness center
Middle: Pool decks are never crowded
Bottom: Pampering in the Carita of Paris spa

for maximum results. Facials are on the pricey side, but massage treatments are quite reasonable when compared to those in other cruise-ship spas.

Your Shipmates

Regent Seven Seas Cruises are inviting to active, affluent, well-traveled couples ranging from their late-30s to retirees who enjoy the ships' chic ambience and destination-rich itineraries. Longer cruises attract veteran passengers in the over-60 age group.

Dress Code

Formal attire is required on designated evenings. Men are encouraged to wear tuxedos, and many do so, although dark suits are acceptable. Cruises of 7 to 10 nights usually have one or two formal nights; longer cruises may have three. Other evenings are informal or resort casual; the number of each is based on the number of sea days. It's requested that dress codes be observed in public areas after 6 PM.

Junior Cruisers

Regent Seven Seas' vessels are adult-oriented and do not have dedicated children's facilities. However, a Club Mariner youth program for children from ages 6 to 11 and 12 to 17 is offered on selected sailings, both during summer months and during school holiday periods. Supervised by counselors, the organized, educational activities focus on nature and the heritage of destinations the ship will visit. Activities, including games, craft projects, movies, and food fun, are organized to ensure that every child has a memorable experience. Teens are encouraged to help counselors select the activities they prefer.

Service

The efforts of a polished European staff go almost unnoticed, yet special requests are handled with ease. Butlers provide an additional layer of personal service to guests in the top-category suites.

CHOOSE REGENT SEVEN SEAS CRUISES IF:

❶ You want to learn the secrets of cooking like a Cordon Bleu chef (for a charge, of course).

❷ You want to stay connected. Internet packages are reasonably priced by the hour.

❸ A really high-end spa experience is on your agenda.

Tipping

Gratuities are included in the fare, and none are expected. To show their appreciation, passengers may elect to make a contribution to a crew welfare fund that benefits the ship's staff.

Past Passengers

Membership in the Seven Seas Society is automatic upon completion of a Regent Seven Seas cruise. Members receive 5%–10% cruise fare savings on select sailings; exclusive shipboard and shoreside special events on select sailings; a Seven Seas Society recognition cocktail party on every sailing; and *Inspirations* newsletter highlighting special events, sailings, and destination- and travel-related information. The tiered program offers rewards based on the number of nights you have sailed with RSSC. The more you sail, the more you accrue. Basic benefits are offered to members with less than 20 nights; from 21 through 74 nights, Silver members also receive complimentary Internet access on board, free pressing, and an hour of free phone time; from 75 through 199 nights, Gold members are awarded priority disembarkation at some ports, another hour of complimentary phone time, more complimentary pressing, an exclusive Gold & Platinum activity aboard or ashore on every sailing, and priority reservations at restaurants and spas; from 200 through 399, Platinum members can add complimentary air deviation services (one time per sailing), six hours of complimentary phone use , and unlimited free pressing and laundry services; Titanium members who have sailed 400 or more nights get free dry cleaning and free transfers.

Good to Know

So why did Carlson Hospitality change the name from Radisson to Regent Seven Seas? It probably seemed logical in the beginning to give their new cruise line a recognizable name—Radisson. However, the name wasn't recognizable for the right reasons. Radisson Seven Seas Cruises aspired to be recognized as upscale (which it was), while the Radisson hotel chain is a decidedly middle-of-the-road. The hotel name turned off some potential passengers who didn't perceive the cruise line as being luxurious or exclusive. It just so happened that Carlson Hospitality's small, but growing, Regent chain of hotels is more in tune with today's definition of luxury and a better fit to co-brand with a top-of-the-line cruising experience. Voila! Early in 2006, a "fleet christening" accomplished the renaming and, best of all, the cruise line's initials didn't change and neither did its Web site address.

DON'T CHOOSE REGENT SEVEN SEAS CRUISES IF:

❶ Connecting cabins are a must. Very few are available, and only the priciest cabins connect.

❷ You can't imagine a Caribbean cruise without the hoopla of pool games and steel bands.

❸ You think dressing up for dinner is too much trouble. Most passengers look forward to the ritual.

SEVEN SEAS VOYAGER

2003	ENTERED SERVICE
700	PASSENGER CAPACITY
447	CREW MEMBERS
350	NUMBER OF CABINS
46,000	GROSS TONS
670 feet	LENGTH
95 feet	WIDTH

700 ft.
500 ft.
300 ft.

Public Areas & Facilities

The world's second all-balcony, all-suite ship continues the Regent Seven Seas tradition of offering posh accommodations on a vessel with generous space for every passenger.

Lounges are predominantly decorated in soothing neutrals and cool marine blues with splashes of color, soft leather, and glass-and-marble accents. Even areas that can accommodate all (or nearly all) passengers at once, including the formal dining room and show lounge, appear intimate; good design elements don't hint at their size and indoor spaces seem smaller than they actually are. With so much room, public areas are seldom crowded, and you won't have to hunt for a deck chair by the swimming pool.

The two-tiered Constellation Theater is a state-of-the-art show room with a full-size proscenium stage, where Broadway-inspired shows created by renowned producer Peter Grey Terhune are staged.

WOW Factor

After an effortless check-in and warm greeting, can it get any better? Yes, when you're offered a chilled flute of champagne to sustain you as you are escorted to your suite.

Restaurants

Four restaurants function on an open-seating basis. In addition to Compass Rose, the main dining room, choices include Signatures, Le Cordon Bleu restaurant, and Latitudes, which features Indo-chine cuisine prepared in an open galley (reservations required); and La Veranda, the daytime buffet, which is a Mediterranean bistro by night.

What Works & What Doesn't

Top: Afternoon tea in Horizon Lounge
Bottom: *Seven Seas Voyager*

In a successful, if somewhat unorthodox, blending of indoor and outdoor spaces, Horizon Lounge treats passengers to a variety of diversions, from afternoon tea to a piano duet at night followed by dancing, either inside or just outside under the stars. With private balconies for all and a 360-degree jogging track encircling the deck above the pool, there's no real necessity for a lengthy promenade deck, and most passengers probably won't miss it.

Accommodations

Layout: Rich-textured fabrics and warm-wood finishes add a touch of coziness to the larger-than-usual suite accommodations in all categories. Every suite has a vanity-desk, walk-in closet, and sitting area with sofa, chairs, and table. Marble bathrooms have a separate tub and shower. Most balconies are approximately 50 square feet in size.

Amenities: All suites have an entertainment center with CD/DVD player, stocked refrigerator, stocked bar, personal safe, hair dryer, and fine linens and duvets on the bed. Bathrooms have robes for use during the cruise and toiletries including shampoo, lotion, and bath gel.

Top-Category Suites: The top three suite categories feature Bose Wave Music Systems. Butler service is available for passengers in Master, Grand, Navigator, and Penthouse Suites. The top-category Master Suites have a separate sitting–dining room, two bedrooms (each has its own TV), a powder room as well as two full bathrooms (the master bath has dual vanities, a bidet, separate shower, and whirlpool tub). Some of the other high-end suites do not have the powder room or whirlpool tubs.

Good to Know: Four suites are designed for wheelchair accessibility and are equipped with showers only.

CABIN TYPE	SIZE (sq. ft.)
Master Suite	1,152–1,216
Grand Suite	753
Seven Seas Suite	441–495
Penthouse Suite	320
Deluxe Suite	306

Fast Facts

- 9 passenger decks
- 2 specialty restaurants, dining room, buffet
- Wi-Fi, in-cabin safes, in-cabin refrigerators, in-cabin DVDs
- Pool
- Fitness classes, gym, hair salon, 2 hot tubs, sauna, spa, steam room
- 5 bars, casino, dance club, library, showroom
- Children's programs (ages 6–17)
- Dry cleaning, laundry facilities, laundry service
- Computer room

5

REGENT SEVEN SEAS CRUISES

In the Know

Regent combined the best features from their other ships when planning the Seven Seas Voyager, *and the result is an elegant vessel with a lot of room per passenger, more easily navigable layout of public rooms, and arguably some of the best bathrooms at sea, even in entry-level suites.*

Favorites

Best Splurge: Shopping in the well-stocked boutiques is always a pleasure.

Best Added Value: The self-service passenger launderettes with ironing stations on every accommodations deck are complimentary. Plan carefully, or you may have a slight wait because they get a lot of use.

Our Favorite Spot for a Nightcap: Every suite has a balcony, and there's no better spot for sharing quiet conversation and a libation before retiring.

Best Suite Locations: The dimensions of the upper-category suites can vary depending on where they are on the ship. Seven Seas Suites located aft are larger than those located mid-

ship and have enormous balconies that measure 215 square feet. Also facing aft, Horizon View suites are simply standard Deluxe Suites, but with balconies that range in size from 105 to 180 square feet, depending on deck location.

Attentive butler service

SEVEN SEAS MARINER

Public Areas & Facilities

The world's first all-balcony, all-suite ship introduced the innovative Regent Seven Seas concept of luxury while retaining the tradition of stylish accommodations on a vessel with exceptionally generous space per passenger throughout.

Modern by design, traditional lounges feature comfortable furnishings with large expanses of glass to bring the sea views inside and fill interiors with sunlight. Mariner Lounge serves as a piano bar and a delightful spot to meet for predinner cocktails and conversation. Paneled walls separating the bar from the groupings of deep navy chairs and love seats contain niches with classical bronze sculptures.

A spiral staircase provides a grand entrance from the casino to Stars Nightclub, a late-night dance club, where wood paneling, granite-color wall coverings, and contrasting blue tub chairs and square high-back chairs in paler shades create an interesting and eclectic mix of styles. The room's centerpiece is the unusual staircase.

2001	ENTERED SERVICE
700	PASSENGER CAPACITY
445	CREW MEMBERS
350	NUMBER OF CABINS
50,000	GROSS TONS
709 feet	LENGTH
93 feet	WIDTH

WOW Factor

From the atrium, three glass elevators climb skyward past remarkable human shadow sculptures mounted on the opposite wall.

Top: Atrium
Bottom: *Seven Seas Mariner*

Restaurants

Four restaurants function on an open-seating basis with no dining assignments. In addition to Compass Rose, the main dining room, choices include Signatures, Le Cordon Bleu restaurant (reservations required); Latitudes, which serves Indochine cuisine (reservations required); and La Veranda, the daytime buffet that's converted to an evening bistro serving Mediterranean cuisine.

What Works & What Doesn't

There's no getting around the appeal of balconies for all suites and the abundance of space per passenger, but those appealing features have a small downside as well. The beautifully appointed lounges appear almost deserted at times, and you may wonder where everyone is. Dedicated to after-dinner brandy and cigars, Connoisseur Club is the one lounge that is disappointing; although the very masculine setting has oversize buttery soft leather chairs, huge cigar proportioned ashtrays, and even a faux fireplace, it looks sterile and isn't very inviting.

Accommodations

Layout: Rich, textured fabrics and warm-wood finishes add a touch of coziness to the larger-than-usual suite accommodations in all categories. Every suite has a vanity-desk, walk-in closet, and sitting area with sofa, chairs, and table. Marble bathrooms have a combination tub–shower. Master suites have two bedrooms (each with a TV) and a separate sitting–dining room, as well as a guest powder room and two full baths (with dual vanities, bidet, separate shower, and whirlpool tub in the master bedroom), not to mention two balconies (one for each bedroom). Other suites have but a single bedroom; forward Penthouse, Horizon, and Seven Seas suites do not have the guest powder room or whirlpool tub.

Amenities: Every suite has an entertainment center with CD/DVD player, stocked refrigerator, stocked bar, personal safe, hair dryer, and beds dressed with fine linens and duvets. Bathrooms have robes for use during the cruise; toiletries include shampoo, lotion, and bath gel.

Top-Category Suites: The top three suite categories have Bose Wave Music Systems; butler service is available for passengers in Master, Grand, Navigator, Penthouse, and Horizon suites.

Good to Know: Six suites are wheelchair-accessible and are equipped with showers only.

CABIN TYPE	SIZE (sq. ft.)
Master Suite	1,204
Grand/Mariner Suite	903/650
Seven Seas Suite	505–561
Horizon/Penthouse Suite	359/376
Deluxe Suite	252

Fast Facts

- 8 passenger decks
- 2 specialty restaurants, dining room, buffet
- Wi-Fi, in-cabin safes, in-cabin refrigerators, in-cabin DVDs
- Pool
- Fitness classes, gym, hair salon, 2 hot tubs, sauna, spa, steam room
- 5 bars, casino, dance club, library, showroom
- Children's programs (ages 6–17)
- Dry cleaning, laundry facilities, laundry service
- Computer room

In the Know

You might find the standard combination bathtub–shower a tight fit if you're over 6 feet tall. The ceiling isn't too low—it's the bathtub height that can cause a problem. The solution is booking a minimum of a Mariner Suite for a separate shower stall.

Favorites

Best Splurge: Individually tailored services in the upscale Carita of Paris spa are a divine indulgence. Don't be concerned about a hard sell since the staff focuses on pampering, not pressure.

Best Added Value: The specialty restaurants, with superb food and service, are fine dining at its finest—and at no additional cost.

Best Seat in the House: It doesn't matter where you sit—the view is unobstructed from every seat in the show lounge.

Our Favorite Spot for a Nightcap: Chairs and tables provide a peaceful aft-facing retreat for stargazing just outside the Horizon Lounge.

Best Bathroom News: In a rather nifty move, bathrooms in 47 suites were rebuilt in 2005 to include rain showers with tiled seats. Accommodations that have them are scattered throughout categories ranging from Deluxe Suites to Horizon Suites.

Perfect your swing

5

REGENT SEVEN SEAS CRUISES

SEVEN SEAS NAVIGATOR

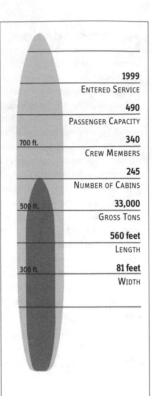

1999	ENTERED SERVICE
490	PASSENGER CAPACITY
340	CREW MEMBERS
245	NUMBER OF CABINS
33,000	GROSS TONS
560 feet	LENGTH
81 feet	WIDTH

Public Areas & Facilities

The first ship outfitted uniquely to Regent Seven Seas' specifications, the *Seven Seas Navigator* is a particular favorite of
returning passengers for its small-ship intimacy, big-ship features, and comfortable, well-designed cabins.

The generous use of wood and the addition of deep-tone accents to the predominantly blue color palette give even the
larger lounges an inviting feel. Artwork and elaborate flower
arrangements add a bit of sparkle and interest to the somewhat angular modern decor.

Due to the aft location of the two-deck-high main showroom,
the only lounges that afford sweeping seascapes are
Galileo's—typically the most popular public space, with
nightly entertainment—and the Vista Lounge. Although views
from the Vista Lounge are spectacular, there's no permanent
bar, and it's primarily a quiet spot for reading when there
are no lectures or activities scheduled there.

WOW Factor

*There are no massive atriums on ships this size, but with staircases that seem to float
in mid-air,* Seven Seas Navigator's *modest atrium is nonetheless impressive.*

Top: Casino
Bottom: Navigator suite

Restaurants

Two restaurants, including Compass Rose, the main dining room,
function on an open-seating
basis, so there are no set dining
assignments. For alternative dining, Portofino Grill, the daytime
buffet, is converted to a reservations-only evening trattoria serving Mediterranean cuisine
accompanied by spirited Italian-
style entertainment. A poolside
grill serves casual daytime meals.

What Works & What Doesn't

Navigating the *Navigator*
is a relatively simple
matter with most public
rooms and the formal
Compass Rose
Restaurant clustered aft
on three decks adjacent
to the atrium. Aft-facing
outdoor tables adjoining
Portofino Grill are
extremely popular for
alfresco dining on sunny
days; unfortunately,
seating is somewhat lim-
ited. Internet use can be
heavy on sea days, and
the lines that form in the
computer area can add a
bit of congestion—and
inevitable noise—to the
adjacent library, a space
that should be a quiet
haven.

Accommodations

Layout: Attractive textured fabrics and honeyed wood finishes add a touch of coziness to the larger-than-usual suites in all categories, 90% of which have balconies. All have a vanity-desk, walk-in closet, and sitting area with a sofa, chairs, and table. Marble bathrooms have a separate tub and shower. Master Suites have a separate sitting-dining room, a separate bedroom, and a powder room; only Grand Suites also have a powder room.

Amenities: Every suite has an entertainment center with CD/DVD player, stocked refrigerator, stocked bar, personal safe, hair dryer, and beds dressed with fine linens and duvets. Bath toiletries include shampoo, lotion, and bath gel.

Suites: Master Suites have a second TV in the bedroom, butler service, and whirlpool tub in the master bathroom.

Grand and Navigator Suites are similarly outfitted. The top three suite categories feature Bose Wave Music Systems. Penthouse suites, which include butler service, are only distinguished from Deluxe suites by location and do not have a whirlpool bathtub.

Good to Know: Very few suites have the capacity to accommodate three people, and only 10 far-forward suites adjoin with those adjacent to them. Four suites are wheelchair-accessible.

CABIN TYPE	SIZE (sq. ft.)
Master Suite	1,067
Grand Suite	539
Navigator Suite	448
Penthouse/ Balcony Suite	301
Window Suite	301*

*except for Suite 600, which measures 516

Fast Facts

- 8 passenger decks
- Specialty restaurant, dining room, buffet
- Wi-Fi, in-cabin safes, in-cabin refrigerators, in-cabin DVDs
- Pool
- Fitness classes, gym, hair salon, hot tub, sauna, spa, steam room
- 4 bars, casino, dance club, showroom
- Children's programs (ages 6–17)
- Dry cleaning, laundry facilities, laundry service
- Computer room

5

REGENT SEVEN SEAS CRUISES

In the Know

From Russia, With Love: Regent Seven Seas took over an unfinished hull that was originally destined to be a Soviet spy ship and redesigned it to create the Seven Seas Navigator. They did such a good job completing the interiors that even James Bond would feel right at home.

Favorites

Best Added Value: The library contains hundreds of novels, bestsellers, and travel books, as well as newspapers, movies for in-suite viewing, and even a selection of board games.

Best Dance Floor: Galileo's smallish dance floor may seem somewhat cramped, but when the doors are opened to the adjacent stern-facing deck, it becomes a magi-

cal spot to dance beneath the stars.

Our Favorite Spot for a Nightcap: The Navigator Lounge is just about as cozy a space as anyone could want for a late-night chat before retiring.

Best Balconies: Grand Suites on deck 8 have considerably larger wraparound balconies than those with only

side-facing balconies on deck 7.

Most Fun With Food: Loyal passengers mourned the sale of the *Radisson Diamond* and the loss of its lively Italian trattoria experience known as Don Vito's. Happily, the singing waiters and festivities have reappeared aboard *Navigator*.

Casual poolside dining

ROYAL CARIBBEAN INTERNATIONAL

Big, bigger, biggest! More than a decade ago, Royal Caribbean launched *Sovereign of the Seas*, the first of the modern megacruise liners, which continues to be an all-around favorite of passengers who enjoy traditional cruising ambience

Jet skiing in Labadee

with a touch of daring and whimsy tossed in. Plunging into the 21st century, each ship in the current fleet carries more passengers than the entire Royal Caribbean fleet of the 1970s and has features—such as new surfing pools—that were unheard of in the past.

**ROYAL CARIBBEAN
INTERNATIONAL**
1050 Royal Caribbean Way
Miami, FL 33132–2096
305/539–6000 or
800/327–6700
www.royalcaribbean.com

Cruise Style: Mainstream

All Royal Caribbean ships are topped by the company's distinctive signature Viking Crown Lounge. These lofty perches allow passengers to contemplate the passing seascape by day and dance away the night in a heavenly space high above the water. Expansive multideck atriums and the generous use of brass and floor-to-ceiling glass windows give each vessel a sense of spaciousness and style.

A variety of lounges and high-energy stage shows draw passengers of all ages out to mingle and dance the night away. Production extravaganzas showcase singers and dancers in lavish costumes. Comedians, acrobats, magicians, jugglers, and solo entertainers fill show lounges on nights when the ships' companies aren't performing. Professional ice shows are a highlight of cruises on Voyager- and Ultra Voyager-class ships—the only ships at sea with ice-skating rinks.

The action is nonstop in casinos and dance clubs after dark, while daytime hours are filled with poolside games and traditional cruise activities. Port talks tend to lean heavily on shopping recommendations and the sale of shore excursions.

Food

Dining is an international experience with nightly changing themes and cuisines from around the world. Passenger preference for casual attire and a resortlike atmosphere has prompted the cruise line to add laid-back alternatives to the formal dining rooms in the Windjammer Café and, on certain ships, the fun and retro Johnny Rockets Diner; Seaview Café evokes the ambience of an island beachside stand.

Room service is available 24 hours, but choices are limited. Only certain dishes that travel well can be ordered from the restaurant menu during dinner hours.

Royal Caribbean doesn't place emphasis on celebrity chefs or specialty alternative restaurants, although they have introduced a more upscale and intimate dinner experience in the form of Portofino, an Italian-specialty restaurant, and/or Chops Grille, a steak house, on Radiance- and Voyager-class ships, as well as *Enchantment of the Seas* and *Empress of the Seas* and the Freedom-class ships.

Fitness & Recreation

Royal Caribbean has pioneered such new and unheard of features as rock-climbing walls, ice-skating rinks, bungee trampolines, and even the first self-leveling pool tables on a cruise ship. Interactive parks, boxing rings, surfing simulators, and cantilevered whirlpools suspended 112 feet above the ocean made their debuts on the Freedom-class ships.

Facilities vary by ship class, but all Royal Caribbean ships have state-of-the-art exercise equipment, jogging tracks, and rock-climbing walls; passengers can work out independently or in classes guaranteed to sweat off extra calories. Most exercise classes are included in the fare, but there's a fee for specialized spinning, yoga, and Pilates classes, as well as the services of a personal trainer. Spas and salons are top-notch, with full menus of day spa–style treatments and services for pampering and relaxation for adults and teens.

Your Shipmates

Royal Caribbean cruises have a broad appeal for active couples and singles, mostly in their 30s to 50s. Families are partial to the newer vessels that have larger staterooms, huge facilities for children and teens, and seemingly endless choices of activities and dining options.

Noteworthy

■ Each ship's Schooner Bar features nautically-inspired decor, right down to a unique scent.

■ The signature Viking Crown Lounge found on every RCI ship was originally inspired by the Seattle World's Fair Space Needle.

■ Hot tubs and certain swimming pools are designated for adults only on Royal Caribbean ships.

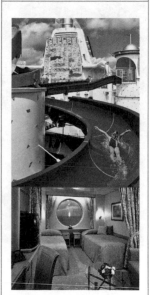

Top: Adventure Beach for kids
Bottom: Voyager-class Interior Stateroom

Top: Miniature golf
Middle: *Adventure of the Seas*
Bottom: *Serenade of the Seas* rock climbing wall

Dress Code

Two formal nights are standard on seven-night cruises; one formal night is the norm on shorter sailings. Men are encouraged to wear tuxedos, but dark suits or sport coats and ties are more prevalent. All other evenings are casual, although jeans are discouraged in restaurants. It's requested that no shorts be worn in public areas after 6 PM, although there are passengers who can't wait to change into them after dinner.

Junior Cruisers

Supervised age-appropriate activities are designed for children ages 3 through 17; babysitting services are available as well (either group sitting or in-stateroom babysitting, but sitters will not change diapers). Children are assigned to the Adventure Ocean youth program by age. They must be at least three years old and toilet trained to participate (children who are in diapers and pull-ups or who are not toilet trained are also not allowed in swimming pools or whirlpools). Youngsters who wish to join a different age group must participate in one daytime and one night activity session with their proper age group first; the manager will then make the decision based on their maturity level. All participants earn credits for activities which they can trade for prizes at the end of the cruise.

In partnership with toy maker Fisher-Price, Royal Caribbean offers interactive 45-minute Aqua Babies and Aqua Tots play sessions for children from 6 months to 36 months of age. The playgroup classes, which are hosted by youth staff members, were designed by early childhood development experts for parents and their babies and toddlers, and teach life skills through playtime activities.

A teen center with a disco is an adult-free gathering spot that will satisfy even the pickiest teenagers. A flat-rate soda card program is a bonus for family budgets—children can have all the fountain soft drinks they desire for a single charge. Pluses are family-size staterooms on certain ships; drawbacks are the small standard cabins in the older vessels and the lack of self-service laundry facilities.

CHOOSE ROYAL CARIBBEAN INTERNATIONAL IF:

❶ You want to see the sea from atop a rock wall—it's one of the few activities on these ships that's free.

❷ You're active and adventurous. Even if your traveling companion isn't, there's an energetic staff on board to cheer you on.

❸ You want your space. There's plenty of room to roam; quiet nooks and crannies are there if you look.

Service

Service on Royal Caribbean ships is friendly, but not consistent. Assigned meal seatings assure that most passengers get to know the waiters and their assistants, who in turn get to know the passengers' likes and dislikes; however, that can lead to a level of familiarity that is uncomfortable to some people. Some ships have a concierge lounge for the use of suite occupants and top-level past passengers.

Tipping

Tips can be prepaid when the cruise is booked, added on to shipboard accounts, or given in cash on the last night of the cruise. Suggested gratuities per passenger, per day are: $3.50 for the cabin steward; $3.50 for the waiter; $2 for the assistant waiter; and $0.75 for the headwaiter. Passengers may adjust the amounts based on the level of service experienced. An automatic 15% gratuity is automatically added to all bar tabs.

Past Passengers

After one cruise, you can enroll in the Crown & Anchor Society. All members receive the *Crown & Anchor* magazine and have access to the member section on the Royal Caribbean Web site. All members receive an Ultimate Value Booklet, an invitation to a complimentary wine tasting, a welcome back party, and commemorative gift. Platinum members (after five cruises) also have the use of a private departure lounge and receive priority check-in (where available), the onboard use of robes during the cruise, an invitation to an exclusive onboard event, and complimentary custom air arrangements.

Diamond members (after 10 cruises) also receive consideration on a priority wait list for sold-out shore excursions and spa services, concierge service on select ships, priority departure from the ship, complimentary custom air fee, special rates on balcony and suite accommodations, and a priority wait list for dining room seating. When you achieve Diamond Plus status (after 24 cruises), you're offered behind-the-scenes tours and preferred seating in main dining rooms. Comparable Crown & Anchor membership status is also extended to members who sail on Royal Caribbean's sister cruise line, Celebrity Cruises.

Good to Know

Royal Caribbean ships are truly resorts afloat with an emphasis on recreation and family enjoyment. You could spend a week on board the huge Voyager-class and Freedom-class ships and never leave. You would also be hard-pressed to try to do everything at hand, so it's important to pace yourself by setting priorities and budgeting your time. A good idea is to try new things that you may not be able to do at home—climb a rock wall and learn to snorkel, for example.

5

ROYAL CARIBBEAN INTERNATIONAL

DON'T CHOOSE ROYAL CARIBBEAN INTERNATIONAL IF:

❶ Patience is not one of your virtues. Lines are not uncommon.

❷ You want to do your own laundry. There are no self-service facilities on any Royal Caribbean ships.

❸ You don't want to hear announcements, especially in your cabin. There are a lot on these cruises.

FREEDOM CLASS

Freedom, Liberty, Independence of the Seas

2006, 2007, 2008	ENTERED SERVICE
3,634	PASSENGER CAPACITY
1,360	CREW MEMBERS
1,815	NUMBER OF CABINS
160,000	GROSS TONS
1,112 feet	LENGTH
185 feet	WIDTH

Public Areas and Facilities

The world's largest cruise ships (for now) live up to Royal Caribbean's reputation for imaginative thinking that results in features to stir the imagination and provide a resort-like atmosphere at sea. Whether you are hanging ten in the surf simulator, going a few rounds in the boxing ring, or strolling the Royal Promenade entertainment boulevard, there's almost no reason to go ashore.

The layout is more intuitive than you might expect on such a gigantic ship. Freedom-class vessels have a familiar mall-like Promenade lined with shops and bistros, an ice skating rink/theater, numerous lounges, and dining options but are not simply enlarged Voyager-class ships. With plenty of room, even the most intimate spaces do not feel crowded. A good fit for extended families, these ships have expansive areas devoted to children and teens and enough adults-only spaces to satisfy everyone.

WOW Factor

The FlowRider surfing simulator is such an exciting attraction that bleacher seating on threes sides of the deck is often full of spectators—everyone enjoys being a part of the action.

Restaurants

Triple-deck-high formal dining rooms serve meals in two evening seatings and are supplemented by two specialty restaurants, Portofino and Chops Grille, which charge a supplement and are open by reservation only. The casual Lido buffet offers service nearly around the clock, and Johnny Rockets is a popular option, though it too has a separate charge, albeit a modest one.

What Works and What Doesn't

Top: Dining is fun in Johnny Rockets
Bottom: Hang ten on the surf simulator

"Of the Seas" takes on new meaning with a combination of pools that encompass 43% more space than Voyager-class ships. The H2O Zone waterpark with interactive fountains is the ideal play area for kids; a sports pool accommodates water volleyball, basketball, and golf; and a Solarium contains a tranquil pool for adults, as well as hammocks for relaxation and two huge hot tubs cantilevered twelve feet from the sides of the ship. The self-serve frozen yogurt bar is a cool treat, but its location near the kids' pool means that it often ends up messy.

Accommodations

Layout: As on other Royal Caribbean ships, cabins are bright and cheerful. Although 60% are outside cabins—and a whopping 78% of those have private balconies—bargain inside cabins, including some that are uniquely configured with a bowed window for a view overlooking the action-packed promenade, are plentiful. Cabins in every category have adequate closet and drawer–shelf storage, as well as bathroom shelves. Family ocean-view cabins with a window sleep up to six people with two twin beds (convertible to queen-size), bunk beds in a separate area, a sitting room with a sofa bed, a vanity area, and a shower-only bathroom. At 1,215 square feet, the Presidential Suite sleeps 14 people and has an 810-square-foot verandah with a hot tub and bar.

Amenities: Wood cabinetry, a small refrigerator/minibar, ethernet connec-tion, vanity-desk, flat-panel TV, personal safe, a hair dryer, and a sitting area with sofa, chair, and table are typical features in all categories. Bathrooms have shampoo and bath gel. Premium beds and bedding complete the comfortable package.

Good to Know: Thirty-two staterooms are wheelchair accessible.

CABIN TYPE	SIZE (sq. ft.)
Royal/Presidential Suite	1,406/1,215
Owner's/Grand Suite	614/387
Junior Suite/Family Stateroom	287/293
Balcony Stateroom	177–189
Oceanview/Inside	161–214/149–152

Fast Facts

- 15 passenger decks
- 2 specialty restaurants, dining room, buffet, ice cream parlor, pizzeria
- In-cabin broadband, Wi-Fi, in-cabin safes, some in-cabin minibars, in-cabin refrigerators, some in-cabin DVDs
- 3 pools, children's pool
- Fitness classes, gym, hair salon, 7 hot tubs, sauna, spa, steam room
- 14 bars, casino, cinema, 2 dance clubs, library, 3 showrooms, video game room
- Children's programs (ages 3–17)
- Dry cleaning, laundry service
- Computer room

In the Know

Shipboard personnel expressed concern upon realizing the posteriors of the cows atop Ben & Jerry's marquee were aimed at the bay window of atrium-view stateroom 6305. They suggested the occupants be offered free ice cream during their cruise, so the ships now have a Ben & Jerry's "Sweet"—the only stateroom like it at sea.

Favorites

Best Splurge: Burgers, onion rings, and all the trimmings in Johnny Rockets diner are a deal at only $3.95 (the malts are extra).

Our Favorite Spot for a Nightcap: Soft lights, hot music, and drinks with the best view on board— the jazz club in the Viking Crown Lounge has it all.

Grown-up Stuff: Kids, don't even think of trying to crash Twenty Nightclub, a late-night adult dance party that takes place in the open-air Solarium. You won't get past the doorman who guards the entry.

Float With the Flow: Full of bright and whimsical "family" figures— including a puppy—the H2O Zone is a fun place to beat the heat beneath a waterfall, fountain sprays, and in a lazy river (where the fountain sculptures mist everyone who floats by). Parents can join in or watch the kids from adjacent shaded hot tubs or convenient deck chairs.

Best Photo Op: Pose seated inside the Morgan car on *Freedom of the Sea's* Royal Promenade.

Climb the wall.

5

VOYAGER CLASS

Voyager, Explorer, Adventure, Navigator, Mariner of the Seas

1999, 2000, 2001, 2002, 2003	
ENTERED SERVICE	
3,114 (3,835 max)	
PASSENGER CAPACITY	
1,185	
CREW MEMBERS	
1,557	
NUMBER OF CABINS	
142,000	
GROSS TONS	
1,020 feet	
LENGTH	
158 feet	
WIDTH	

700 ft.

500 ft.

300 ft.

Public Areas & Facilities

A truly massive building program introduced one of these gigantic Voyager-class ships per year over a five-year period. With their rock-climbing walls, ice-skating rinks, in-line skating tracks, miniature golf, and multiple dining venues, they are destinations in their own right. Sports enthusiasts will be thrilled with nonstop daytime action.

Only the unique horizontal, multiple-deck promenade–atriums on Voyager-class vessels can stage some of the pageantry for which Royal Caribbean is noted. Fringed with boutiques, bars, and even coffee shops, the mall-like expanses set the stage for evening parades and events, as well as simply spots to kick back for some people-watching.

Other public rooms are equally dramatic. Though it's considered to be three separate dining rooms, the triple-deck height of the single space is stunning. These ships not only carry a lot of people, but carry them well. Space is abundant, and crowding is seldom an issue.

WOW Factor

A lot of things on these ships is impressive, but the Royal Promenade, particularly when a parade or other event is center stage, may elicit the biggest "Wow!"

Top: Rock-climbing wall
Bottom: Fitness class

Restaurants

Triple-decker formal dining rooms serve meals in two evening seatings and are supplemented by Portofino, a reservations-only Italian restaurant that charges a supplement. Additionally, *Mariner of* *the Seas* and *Navigator of the Seas* also feature Chops Grille. The casual Lido buffet offers an Island Grill for casual dinners and does not require reservations.

What Works & What Doesn't

Active families will surely find something to keep everyone busy—rock climbing, ice-skating, full-size basketball courts, in-line skating, miniature golf. The good news is that equipment to participate in all those sports activities is provided at no additional charge. The bad news is that, with the exception of the gym and some fitness classes, nearly everything else on board—including soft drinks, specialty coffees, meals in the alternative dining venues, spa services, bingo, and alcoholic beverages—carries a price tag. More good news is that snacks and pizza in Café Promenade are free.

Accommodations

Layout: As on other Royal Caribbean ships, cabins are bright and cheerful. Although more than 60% are outside—and a hefty 75% of those have private verandas—there are still plenty of bargain inside cabins, some with a bowed window for a view overlooking the action-packed promenade. Cabins in every category have adequate closet and drawer–shelf storage and bathroom shelves. Junior Suites have a sitting area, vanity area, and bathroom with bathtub. Family ocean-view cabins with a window sleep up to six people and can accommodate a roll-away bed and/or crib, have two twin beds (convertible to a queen), and additional bunk beds in a separate area, a separate sitting area with a sofa bed, vanity area, and a private bathroom with shower.

Amenities: Wood cabinetry, a small refrigerator–minibar, computer connection, vanity-desk, TV, personal safe, a hair dryer, and a sitting area with sofa, chair, and table are typical Voyager-class features in all categories. Bathrooms have shampoo and bath gel.

Good to Know: Twenty-six staterooms are designed for wheelchair accessibility.

CABIN TYPE	SIZE (sq. ft.)
Royal Suite	1,188–1,325
Other Suites*	277–610
Superior/Deluxe/ Family Ocean View**	173–328
Large/Standard Ocean View	211 /161–180
Interior	153–167

*Owner's (506–618 sq. ft.), Grand (381–390 sq. ft.), Royal Family (512–610 sq. ft.), Jr. (277–299 sq. ft).
**Superior (202–206 sq. ft.), Deluxe (173–184 sq. ft.), Family (265–328 sq. ft.).

Fast Facts

- 14 passenger decks
- Specialty restaurant (2 on *Mariner* and *Voyager*), dining room, buffet, ice-cream parlor, pizzeria
- In-cabin broadband, Wi-Fi, in-cabin safes, in-cabin refrigerators, some in-cabin VCRs, some in-cabin DVDs
- 3 pools, children's pool (only *Voyager, Explorer,* and *Adventure*)
- Fitness classes, gym, hair salon, 7 hot tubs, sauna, spa, steam room
- 12 bars, casino, cinema, 2 dance clubs, library, 3 showrooms, video game room
- Children's programs (ages 3–17)
- Dry cleaning, laundry service
- Computer room

In the Know

Long queues can form at security and check-in counters before the boarding process begins because many passengers arrive early and clog the terminal before the scheduled boarding time. Avoid the hassle by arriving a bit later to breeze through and start your cruise relaxed.

Favorites

Best Place to Escape the Crowds: The clubby and quiet cigar bars are comfortable retreats day and night. Even nonsmokers can't fail to be impressed with a ventilation system that eliminates any lingering scent.

Fun & Funky: In the sports bars, at the ships' rail, and around the pools, colorful sculptures add a touch of whimsy.

Best Added Value: Although you could spend extra for specialty coffee and ice cream, it's possible to grab a complimentary snack instead in the Café Promenade.

Our Favorite Spot for a Nightcap: Music and drinks with a view gets our vote—the jazz clubs in the Viking Crown Lounge have it all.

Suite Stuff: Full suites and family suites have concierge service, balconies, and sitting areas. All suites are furnished with a DVD/VCR player and stereo; bathrooms with a tub and double sinks; and (in many) walk-in closets. Top-category suites have flat-screen TVs, whirlpool tubs, dining rooms, multiple bedrooms, and even hot tubs on balconies.

Relax poolside.

RADIANCE CLASS

Radiance of the Seas, Brilliance of the Seas,
Serenade of the Seas, Jewel of the Seas

2001, 2002, 2003, 2004	Entered Service
2,112 (2,501 max)	Passenger Capacity
857	Crew Members
1,056	Number of Cabins
90,090	Gross Tons
962 feet	Length
106 feet	Width

Public Areas & Facilities

Considered by many people to be the most beautiful vessels in the Royal Caribbean fleet, Radiance-class ships are large but sleek and swift, with sun-filled interiors and panoramic elevators that span 10 decks along the ships' exteriors.

High-energy and glamorous spaces are abundant throughout these sister ships. From the rock-climbing wall, children's pool with waterslide, and golf area to the columned dining room, sweeping staircases, and the tropical garden of the solarium, these ships hold appeal for a wide cross section of interests and tastes.

The ships are packed with multiple dining venues, including the casual Windjammer, which has both indoor and outdoor seating, and the Latte-Tudes patisserie, which sells specialty coffees, pastries, and ice cream treats.

WOW Factor

Vast expanses of glass bring the outdoors inside, so there's no excuse to miss a sunset, even if you're on an elevator.

Top: Pool deck
Bottom: Sports courts

Restaurants

The double-deck formal dining room serves meals in two evening seatings and is supplemented by Portofino Italian restaurant and Chops Grill steak house, each of which requires reservations. The casual Lido buffet serves three meals a day, and the Seaview Café is open for quick lunches and dinners. A pizzeria serves pizza by the slice.

What Works & What Doesn't

Radiance-class ships take the concept of expanses of glass in a new direction, with panoramic elevators allowing sea views while you move vertically through the ship. Aft on deck six, four distinct lounges and the billiard room form a clubby adult entertainment center furnished in rich colors and accented by warm woods. With the traditional and nautical-leaning decor on these otherwise classy ships, the weird free-form atrium sculptures are a jarring throwback to earlier design elements.

Accommodations

Layout: With the line's highest percentage of outside cabins, standard staterooms are bright and cheery as well as roomy. Nearly three-quarters of the outside cabins have private balconies. Every cabin has adequate closet and drawer–shelf storage, as well as bathroom shelves.

Amenities: Light-wood cabinetry, small refrigerator–minibar, computer connection, vanity–desk, TV, personal safe, hair dryer, and a sitting area with sofa, chair, and table are typical Radiance-class features in all categories. Bathroom extras include shampoo and bath gel.

Suites: All full suites and family suites have private balconies and include concierge service. Top-category suites have wet bars, separate living/dining areas, multiple bathrooms, entertainment centers with flat-screen TVs, VCRs, and stereos. Some bathrooms have twin sinks, steam showers, and whirlpool tubs. Junior suites have a sitting area, vanity area, and bathroom with a tub.

Good to Know: Nineteen staterooms are wheelchair-accessible.

CABIN TYPE	SIZE (sq. ft.)
Royal/Owner's Suite	1,001/512
Other Suites*	277–610
Superior/Deluxe Ocean View	204/179
Large/Family Ocean View	170/319
Interior	165

*Grand (358–384 sq. ft.), Royal Family (533–586 sq. ft.), Jr. (293 sq. ft.).

Fast Facts

- 12 passenger decks
- 2 specialty restaurants, dining room, buffet, pizzeria
- In-cabin broadband, Wi-Fi, in-cabin data ports, in-cabin safes, in-cabin refrigerators, some in-cabin VCRs
- 2 pools (1 indoor), children's pool
- Fitness classes, gym, hair salon, 3 hot tubs, sauna, spa, steam room
- 11 bars, casino, cinema, dance club, library, showroom, video game room
- Children's programs (ages 3–17)
- Dry cleaning, laundry service
- Computer room

In the Know

Other cruise ships may have rollicking sports bars (and these do as well), but only on the Radiance-class Royal Caribbean vessels will you find self-leveling pool tables.

Favorites

Best Place to Escape the Crowds: Not everyone discovers the out-of-the way Seaview Cafés, making them a favored casual dining spot for those passengers who take the time to locate them.

Our Favorite Spot for a Nightcap: In a setting overlooking the atriums, yet with intimate seating arrangements, the Champagne Bars offer privacy at the heart of the action.

Best Family Quarters: Particularly spacious, family ocean-view cabins, which sleep up to six people and can accommodate a roll-away bed and/or a crib, have two twin beds (convertible into one queen-size), additional bunk beds in a separate area, a separate sitting area with a sofa bed, a vanity area, and a bathroom with a shower.

Shared moments on your personal balcony

5

ROYAL CARIBBEAN INTERNATIONAL

ENCHANTMENT OF THE SEAS

Public Areas & Facilities

In 2005 *Enchantment of the Seas* was the third Royal Caribbean ship to be lengthened to increase her capacity and facilities. After she was cut in half, a new, 73-foot middle section containing 151 staterooms and suspension bridges that span the pool area and overhang the sea were added. Not only was the pool area expanded by almost 50%, but four bungee trampolines were installed—a first at sea. For real thrills you can soar high above the bow while safely tethered to the trampoline.

For a buzz of a different sort, a new pool bar juts out over the water where peek-a-boo windows set into the deck afford views of the sea below. Nearby floor-mounted water jets create a splash deck for children that transforms into a lighted fountain after dark. Recreational facilities and the spa were also expanded during the renovation. Not to be overlooked, interiors now include the South Beach–style Bolero's lounge as well as Latte-Tudes coffee and ice-cream bar, a specialty steak-house restaurant, and an enlarged Windjammer Café.

1997	Entered Service
2,252 (2,730 max)	Passenger Capacity
840	Crew Members
1,126	Number of Cabins
81,500	Gross Tons
989 feet	Length
106 feet	Width

700 ft.

500 ft.

300 ft.

WOW Factor

Dramatic arches on both sides of the ship's Lido Deck support futuristic-looking 75-foot suspension bridges.

Top: Formal dining
Bottom: Ocean view stateroom

Restaurants

The double-deck formal dining room serves meals in two assigned evening seatings. Chops Grill steak house requires reservations and carries a supplement. The casual Windjammer buffet serves three meals a day, including a laid-back dinner. A counter in the Solarium serves pizza by the slice and Latte-Tudes sells specialty coffees and pastries. Room service is 24 hours a day.

What Works & What Doesn't

When increasing the number of cabins—and thereby accommodating more passengers—other areas of a ship can suffer overload, particularly the dining rooms, lounges, pool area. In the case of *Enchantment of the Seas,* those potential problems received careful consideration. The transformation of an underutilized lounge into Chops Grille and the addition of both a concierge lounge and Bolero's Latin nightclub were brilliant moves.

Two new family cabins that sleep six to eight were also added during the stretch.

Accommodations

Layout: Cabins are light and comfortable, although the smallest can be a tight squeeze for more than two adults. Every cabin has adequate closet and drawer–shelf storage, as well as bathroom shelves.

Amenities: Light woods, pastel colors, a vanity–desk, TV, personal safe, a hair dryer, and a sitting area with sofa, chair, and table are typical features in all categories. Bathrooms have shampoo and bath gel.

Suites: All full suites and family suites have private balconies, a small refrigerator–minibar; full suites include concierge service. Royal Suites have a living room, wet bar, separate dining area, TV, stereo, and VCR, separate bedroom, bathroom (with twin sinks, a whirlpool tub, steam shower, and bidet), and separate powder room. Owner's Suites have separate living area, minibar, TV, stereo, and VCR, dinette area, and bathroom with twin sinks, bathtub, separate shower, and bidet. Grand Suites have a sitting area, stereo and VCR, bathroom with combination bathtub–shower, and double sink.

Good to Know: Fourteen staterooms are designed for wheelchair accessibility.

CABIN TYPE	SIZE (sq. ft.)
Royal/Owner's Suite	1,119/511
Other Suites*	277–610
Superior/Large Ocean View	190/154
Family Ocean View/ Interior	449/230
Large/Standard Interior	146/140

*Grand (349 sq. ft.), Royal Family (532 sq. ft.), Jr. (245 sq. ft).

Fast Facts

- 11 passenger decks
- Specialty restaurant, dining room, buffet, ice-cream parlor, pizzeria
- Wi-Fi, in-cabin safes, some in-cabin refrigerators, some in-cabin VCRs
- 3 pools (1 indoor), children's pool
- Fitness classes, gym, hair salon, 6 hot tubs, sauna, spa
- 6 bars, casino, dance club, library, showroom, video game room
- Children's programs (ages 3–17)
- Dry cleaning, laundry service
- Computer room

In the Know

From a seat in Viking Crown Lounge, you could look the Statue of Liberty in the eye. With practice, you might be able to jump that high on a bungee trampoline.

Favorites

Family-Friendly Splurge: Lunch with the kids at Johnny Rockets is worth the extra charge. The popular diner that was added to *Enchantment of the Seas* during her stretch has a flat charge for food (though the malts are extra), but is a lot cheaper than its shoreside counterparts.

Best Added Value: With a nod to variety, the jogging track contains a vitality course. Between laps, fitness stops offer runners the opportunity to jump rope, use sit-up/press-up bars and a step-up station, as well as cool down by performing suggested stretching moves.

Our Favorite Spot for a Nightcap: The poolside Island Bar is only steps away from the splash deck, which is transformed at night into a decorative fountain with fiber-optic lights playing off the water.

Best Place to Escape the Crowds: The tranquil solitude of the library, with oversized leather chairs, can be welcoming; however it has an under-abundance of books, so bring your own reading material.

Enchantment of the Seas at sea

VISION CLASS

*Legend, Splendour, Grandeur,
Rhapsody, Vision of the Seas*

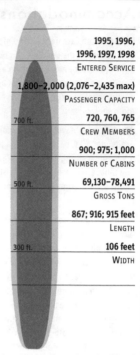

1995, 1996, 1996, 1997, 1998	ENTERED SERVICE
1,800–2,000 (2,076–2,435 max)	PASSENGER CAPACITY
720, 760, 765	CREW MEMBERS
900; 975; 1,000	NUMBER OF CABINS
69,130–78,491	GROSS TONS
867; 916; 915 feet	LENGTH
106 feet	WIDTH

Legend and *Splendour* are the smallest, followed by *Grandeur*, then *Rhapsody* and *Vision*.

Public Areas & Facilities

The first Royal Caribbean ships to offer private balconies in a number of categories, these Vision-class vessels, named for sister ship *Vision of the Seas* (which does not sail in the Caribbean and is not profiled here), have acres of glass skylights that allow sunlight to flood in and windows that offer wide sea vistas. The soaring central atrium at the heart of each ship is anchored by champagne bars and fills with music after dark.

Built in pairs, the ships follow the same general layout but are different in overall size and the total number of passengers on board. Cabin sizes also vary somewhat; as the total size of the ships increased from *Legend* and *Splendour* at 69,130 tons (1,800 passengers) to *Grandeur* at 74,140 tons (1,950 passengers), and finally, *Rhapsody* and *Vision* at 78,491 tons (2,000 passengers), so did the size of the accommodations. In some categories, it's only a matter of a few feet, so don't look for huge—or even noticeable—differences.

WOW Factor

Lots and lots of wide-open space everywhere and a bit more glitter than other Royal Caribbean ships give the Vision-class vessels a distinctive look and feel.

Restaurants

The double-deck-high formal dining room serves meals in two assigned evening seatings. Windjammer, the casual Lido buffet, serves three meals a day, including a laid-back dinner. Room service is available 24 hours a day, and a poolside grill serves burgers in the solarium.

Top: Viking Crown Lounge overlooks the pool deck
Bottom: *Splendour of the Seas*

What Works & What Doesn't

Open, light-filled public areas offer sea views from almost every angle on these ships. Each vessel features double-deck-height dining rooms with sweeping staircases that are a huge improvement over previous ship designs. Some lounges, particularly the popular Schooner Bars, serve as a thoroughfare and suffer from continuous traffic flow before and after performances in the ships' main show lounges. These ships were the first in the fleet to include indoor/outdoor solarium pools with expansive adjacent fitness centers and spas.

Accommodations

Layout: Cabins are airy and comfortable, but the smaller categories are a tight squeeze for more than two adults. Every cabin has adequate closet and drawer–shelf storage.

Amenities: Light woods, pastel colors, vanity–desk, TV, personal safe, a hair dryer, and a sitting area with sofa, chair, and table are typical Vision-class features in all categories. Bathrooms have shampoo and bath gel.

Suites: All full suites and family suites have private balconies and a small minibar; full suites also include concierge service. Royal Suites have a living room, wet bar, separate dining area, entertainment center with TV, stereo, and VCR, separate bedroom, and a bathroom (twin sinks, whirlpool tub, separate steam shower, bidet) and separate powder room. Owner's Suites have a separate living area, minibar,

entertainment center with TV, stereo, and VCR, dinette area, and one bathroom (twin sinks, bathtub, separate shower, bidet). Grand Suites have similar amenities on a smaller scale.

Good to Know: On *Legend* and *Splendour*, 17 cabins are wheelchair-accessible; on *Grandeur*, *Vision*, and *Rhapsody*, 14 cabins are wheelchair-accessible.

CABIN TYPE	SIZE (sq. ft.)
Royal Suite	1,074
Owner's/Grand Suite	523/355
Royal Family/Jr. Suite	512/240
Superior/Large Ocean View*	193/154
Interior	135–174

All cabin sizes are averages of the 5 ships since cabins vary somewhat in size among the Vision-class ships (all *Legend* and *Splendour* cabins are the same size). *Rhapsody has Family Ocean View cabins at 237 sq. ft.

In the Know

All suites on Vision-class ships are not created equal. A Royal Family Suite is a roomy choice for parents with younger children, but goodies that other suites receive—including bathrobes to use on board, welcome-aboard champagne, evening canapés, and concierge service—aren't included.

Favorites

Best Added Value: With no real specialty restaurants, it's an advantage to be able to order some items from the dining room menu through room service. Only those dishes that travel well are offered, but there are plenty from which to choose for a private dinner or balcony picnic.

Best Dance Spot: The Viking Crown Lounge is a rocking late-night dance club where the DJ spins pop tunes until well into the early hours of the morning. You can probably count on hearing *YMCA* at least once.

Our Favorite Spot for a Nightcap: Tucked into an atrium nook, the Champagne Bar on each ship is not only an elegant spot for predinner drinks and dancing, but also for quiet after-dinner or after-the-show drinks and conversation.

Fast Facts

- 11 passenger decks
- Dining room, buffet, ice-cream parlor, pizzeria
- Wi-Fi, in-cabin safes, some in-cabin refrigerators, some in-cabin VCRs
- 2 pools (1 indoor)
- Fitness classes, gym, hair salon, 6 hot tubs, sauna, spa
- 6 bars, casino, dance club, library, showroom, video game room
- Children's programs (ages 3–17)
- Dry cleaning, laundry service
- Computer room

Vision-class Owner's Suite

SOVEREIGN CLASS
Sovereign, Monarch, Majesty of the Seas

Public Areas & Facilities

Precursor of vessels to come, *Sovereign of the Seas* was the largest cruise ship afloat when it was introduced in 1988. Two sister ships followed and, although they all share the same layout, subtle differences exist in size and the number of passengers they carry. *Sovereign* and *Monarch* have received major refurbishments, with the addition of a new Miami Beach–style Latin club, and a Johnny Rockets diner. Other improvements include an expanded spa and enlarged areas for children and teens. Balconies were also added to 62 junior suites. *Majesty* had a similar rejuvenation in 2007.

The futuristic atrium, combined with the abundant use of marble and gleaming metal, virtually assured the Sovereign-class ships design longevity. The addition of rock-climbing walls and other features found on subsequent Royal Caribbean vessels, plus sparkling new interior colors, belie the age of these ships.

1988, 1991, 1992	ENTERED SERVICE
2,292 (2,773 max)/2,350 (2,744 max)	PASSENGER CAPACITY
840/822	CREW MEMBERS
1,146/1,175	NUMBER OF CABINS
73,192/73,941	GROSS TONS
880 feet	LENGTH
106 feet	WIDTH

700 ft.
500 ft.
300 ft.

WOW Factor

Even at their age, the multideck atriums—cruise ship firsts—are still stunning.

Top: Formal dining room
Bottom: *Sovereign of the Seas* Owner's Suite

Restaurants

Two formal dining rooms serve breakfast and lunch in open seatings and dinner in two assigned seatings. The Windjammer casual Lido buffet serves three meals a day, including a casual dinner option. In addition, *Sovereign* has Sorrento's Pizza and Johnny Rockets in the Windjammer, as well as Latte-Tudes, a patisserie serving specialty coffees and Ben & Jerry's ice cream.

What Works & What Doesn't

The hottest clubs at sea are Latin-flavored, and Sovereign-class ships got them during rejuvenations that also saw the addition of the Johnny Rockets diner. Unfortunately, some remnants of late-1980s design are difficult to overcome, including few balconies and low ceilings in the dining rooms. The rock-climbing walls are certainly impressive enough, but they really look like an afterthought, and their awkward position spoils the view overlooking the stern from the Viking Crown Lounge.

Accommodations

Layout: Cabins are comfortable, but standard ocean-view and inside categories are a tight squeeze for more than two occupants. When these ships were conceived, staterooms were viewed as primarily for sleeping and changing clothes, so even the suites are on the small size by current standards. Every cabin has adequate closet and drawer-shelf storage. The added personal space provided by the balconies in suites and junior suites on both Sovereign and Majesty is a real plus.

Amenities: Light woods, mirrored accents, a vanity-desk, TV, personal safe, and a hair dryer are typical Sovereign-class features in all categories. Bathrooms have shampoo and bath gel.

Suites: All suites and junior suites have a minibar, balcony, and bathtub. Royal Family Suites (on *Majesty of the Seas*

only) have a sitting area, dining area, two bedrooms (one with two twin beds and an upper bunk, one with queen-size bed), and two bathrooms.

Good to Know: Third and fourth Pullman beds are found in a variety of stateroom categories, as are connecting staterooms—a plus for families that require more room to spread out. Six staterooms are designed for wheelchair accessibility.

CABIN TYPE	SIZE (sq. ft.)
Royal Suite	670
Owner's/Grand Suite	446/382
Royal Family*/Jr. Suite	371/264
Superior/Standard Ocean View	157/122
Interior	119

*Only on *Majesty of the Seas*

Fast Facts

- 11 passenger decks
- 2 dining rooms, buffet, pizzeria
- Wi-Fi, some in-cabin safes, some in-cabin refrigerators, some in-cabin VCRs
- 2 pools
- Fitness classes, gym, hair salon, 2 hot tubs, sauna (*Majesty* only), spa
- 7 bars, casino, 2 dance clubs, library, showroom, video game room
- Children's programs (ages 3–17)
- Dry cleaning, laundry service
- Computer room

In the Know

These ships are ideally suited for short cruises, especially since the addition of more expansive facilities for younger children and teens and a redesigned fitness center and spa.

Favorites

Teen-Friendly: *Sovereign* has a bit of an advantage since her 2004 makeover with a teen disco, computer room, private outdoor deck space, and no-adults-allowed lounge, but *Majesty* also has a disco where parties and events are held just for teenagers.

Best Nautical Spaces: Each ship has a Schooner Bar, Royal Caribbean's signature piano bar with seagoing flair (models of sailing ships and even a smoky tar scent set the tone).

Our Favorite Spot for a Nightcap: The Viking Crown Lounge is not only our favorite place for catching the sunset; we also like the space for the last drink of the day.

Best Way to Stay Connected: In addition to an Internet center, Wi-Fi hot spots are conveniently located in public rooms, and cell phone access at sea is a hot new feature.

Majesty of the Seas: The Centrum

EMPRESS OF THE SEAS

Public Areas & Facilities

Unique for her smaller size in a fleet of large and megalarge ships, *Empress of the Seas* was brought up-to-the-minute in 2004 with such features as a rock-climbing wall and alternative dining options.

The central atrium is something of a surprise on a ship this size; piercing six decks, it's a lovely space with its skylight, fountain, and abundant brass accents. Small can still be spacious, and *Empress of the Seas* has lounges and bars that are roomy enough, yet feel cozy and warm.

A wooden promenade completely encircles the ship and is an ideal spot for a quiet moonlight stroll, particularly after dinner, when interior passageways tend to get somewhat congested.

Royal Caribbean plans to transfer *Empress* to Pullmantur, the Madrid-based cruise line that Royal Caribbean Cruises Ltd. purchased in 2006. The last voyage of *Empress* as a Royal Caribbean ship will be March 7, 2008.

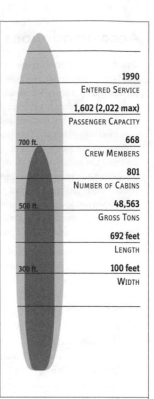

1990	Entered Service
1,602 (2,022 max)	Passenger Capacity
668	Crew Members
801	Number of Cabins
48,563	Gross Tons
692 feet	Length
100 feet	Width

700 ft.

500 ft.

300 ft.

WOW Factor

Working out in a fitness center located at the highest point of the ship offers quite a rush and unique point of view.

Restaurants

The two-level formal dining room serves open seating breakfast and lunch during posted hours and dinner in two assigned seatings. As an alternative, Portofino is an intimate, Italian restaurant (reservations required) with a supplemental charge. The casual Windjammer buffet serves three meals a day and Latte-Tudes is the spot for specialty coffees and ice cream.

Top: Bolero's Lounge
Bottom: Royal Suite

What Works & What Doesn't

In a fleet of large vessels, *Empress of the Seas* is the little ship that could. Her appeal for many lies in her small size. From the serene sounds of the fountain at the base of her atrium to the excitement of Bolero's, the Latin-theme bar, she has some big-ship innovations in an appealing small package. Although upgraded, there's no getting around the size of the cabins, nearly half of which are inside. Lounge chairs are lined up side-by-side around the pool with barely inches (or no inches) between them. At best, it feels claustrophobic.

Accommodations

Layout: Cabins are comfortable but small and all categories will be a bit cozy for more than two occupants; the standard bathrooms are spartan. The added personal space provided by balconies in suites and junior suites is a huge bonus with such small cabins; the largest balconies are those overlooking the bow and stern. Every cabin has adequate closet and drawer-shelf storage.

Amenities: Light-wood tones, mirrored accents, a vanity-desk, TV, computer connection, personal safe, and a hair dryer are typical features in all categories. Bathrooms provide shampoo and bath gel.

Suites: Royal Suites have a living room, wet bar, separate dining area, entertainment center with a TV, separate bedroom, walk-in closet, and bathroom with whirlpool bathtub and separate shower. Owner's Suites have separate living area, minibar, and bathroom with shower. Junior Suites have a sitting area, small refrigerator, walk-in closet, and bathroom with combination tub-shower.

Good to Know: Numerous cabins are configured for third- and fourth-passenger occupancy; however, the availability of connecting accommodations is meager, so book early if you need more space. Four staterooms are wheelchair-accessible.

CABIN TYPE	SIZE (sq. ft.)
Royal Suite	596
Owner's	303
Jr. Suite	194
Superior/Standard Ocean View	157/139
Small Ocean View/ Interior	108/117

Fast Facts

- 9 passenger decks
- Specialty restaurant, dining room, buffet, ice-cream parlor
- In-cabin broadband, Wi-Fi, some in-cabin safes, some in-cabin refrigerators
- 2 pools
- Fitness classes, gym, hair salon, 4 hot tubs, sauna, spa
- 5 bars, casino, dance club, showroom, video game room
- Children's programs (ages 3–17)
- Dry cleaning, laundry service
- Computer room

In the Know

Don't discount Empress of the Seas *as too old and too small for a family cruise—she has expanded facilities for children and teens, a good-size spa with sauna, as well as a nice, if oddly placed, fitness center perched high atop the Viking Crown Lounge.*

Favorites

Best Bet After Dark: When the sun goes down, the Sun Deck morphs into a moonlit poolside dance spot featuring fountains and intimate alfresco seating areas.

Our Favorite Spot for a Nightcap: Bolero's is the place to go if your taste runs to mojitos, caipirinhas, and specialty tequilas. Just steps away is the promenade deck, a peaceful retreat in the wee hours.

Best Splurges: Dinner in Portofino and coffee, pastries, or ice cream from Latte-Tudes are worth the extra price.

Best Way to Work Off Those Calories: You don't have to live at the gym to make room in your diet for all the extra food. Simply walk around and around the ship on the 360-degree promenade deck and then bypass the elevators in favor of the stairs.

The Centrum

SEABOURN CRUISE LINE

Seabourn was founded on the principle that dedication to personal service in elegant surroundings would appeal to sophisticated, independent-minded passengers whose lifestyles demand the best. Lovingly maintained since their introduction in 1987—and routinely updated with new features—the megayachts of Seabourn have proved to be a smashing success over the years. They remain favorites with people who can take care of themselves but would rather do so aboard a ship that caters to their individual preferences.

Make memories to last a lifetime.

SEABOURN CRUISE LINE
6100 Blue Lagoon Drive,
Suite 400
Miami, FL 33126
305/463–3000 or
800/929–9391
www.seabourn.com

Cruise Style: Luxury

Recognized as a leader in small-ship, luxury cruising, Seabourn delivers all the expected extras—complimentary wines and spirits, a stocked minibar in all suites, and elegant amenities. Expect the unexpected as well—from travel document portfolios and luggage tags by Tumi to the pleasure of a complimentary minimassage while lounging at the pool. If you don't want to lift a finger, Seabourn will even arrange to have your luggage picked up at home and delivered directly to your suite—for a price.

Dining and evening socializing are generally more stimulating to Seabourn passengers than splashy song-and-dance revues; however, proportionately scaled production shows and cabarets are presented in the main showroom and smaller lounge. Movies Under the Stars are shown on the wind-protected sun deck at least one evening on virtually all cruises as long as the weather permits. The library stocks not only books, but also movies for those who prefer to watch them in the privacy of their suites—popcorn will naturally be delivered with a call to room service.

The Dress Circle Series enrichment program features guest appearances by luminaries in the arts and world affairs. Due to the size of Seabourn ships, passengers have the opportunity to mingle with presenters and interact one-on-one.

Peace and tranquillity reign on these ships, so the daily roster of events is somewhat thin. Wine-tastings, lectures, and other quiet pursuits might be scheduled, but most passengers are pleased to simply do what pleases them.

One don't-miss activity is the daily team trivia contest. Prizes are unimportant: it's the bragging rights that most guests seek.

Food
Exceptional cuisine created by celebrity chef Charlie Palmer is prepared *à la minute* and served in open-seating dining rooms. Upscale menu offerings include foie gras, quail, fresh seafood, and jasmine crème brûlée. Dishes low in cholesterol, salt, and fat, as well as vegetarian selections, are prepared with the same attention to detail and artful presentation. Wines are chosen to complement each day's luncheon and dinner menus, and caviar is always available. A background of classical music sets the tone for afternoon tea. The weekly Gala Tea features crèpes Suzette.

A casual dinner alternative is "Tastings @ 2," serving innovative cuisine in multiple courses nightly in the Veranda Café, where outdoor tables enhance the romantic atmosphere. Evening attire in the Veranda Café is specified as casual or elegant casual—when men are asked to wear a jacket but no tie. A second, and even more laid back, dinner alternative is offered on select occasions in the open-air Sky Bar, where grilled seafood and steaks are served. "Sky Grill" dinners are scheduled on a couple of nights during each cruise, weather permitting. Both Tastings @ 2 and Sky Grill require reservations, but happily there is no additional charge for either.

Room service is always available. Dinner can even be served course by course in your suite during restaurant hours.

Fitness & Recreation
A full array of exercise equipment, free weights, and basic fitness classes are available in the small gym, while some specialized fitness sessions are offered for a fee.

Many passengers are drawn to the pampering spa treatments, including a variety of massages, body wraps, and facials. Hair and nail services are offered in the salon. Both spa and salon are operated by Steiner Leisure.

Noteworthy

■ Dinner can always be served in your suite, served course by course from the regular menu.

■ Nearly half the suites on Seabourn ships have mini-balconies with doors that open to admit fresh sea breezes.

■ Complimentary shore experiences can range from a beach barbecue to a private cocktail reception at the Puerto Rican Museum of Art.

Top: A good book and breakfast in bed
Bottom: The Club

Top: French balcony
Middle: Dining by candlelight in
The Restaurant
Bottom: Relax on deck.

The water sports marina at the stern is popular with active passengers who want to Jet Ski, windsurf, kayak, or swim in the integrated salt-water pool while anchored in calm waters.

Your Shipmates

Seabourn's yachtlike vessels appeal to well-traveled, affluent couples of all ages who enjoy destination-intense itineraries, a subdued atmosphere, and exclusive service. Passengers tend to be 50-plus and retired couples who are accustomed to evening formality.

Dress Code

Two formal nights are standard on seven-night cruises and three to four nights, depending on the itinerary, on two-week cruises. Men are required to wear tuxedos or dark suits after 6 PM, and the majority prefer black tie. All other evenings are elegant casual, and slacks with a jacket over a sweater or shirt for men and sundresses, skirts, or pants with a sweater or blouse for women are suggested.

Junior Cruisers

Seabourn Cruise Line is adult-oriented and unable to accommodate children under one year. A limited number of suites are available for triple-occupancy; anyone two years of age and older traveling as the third passenger in a suite pays 50% of the Category A brochure fare. No dedicated children's facilities are present on these ships, so parents are responsible for the behavior and entertainment of their children.

Service

Personal service and attention by the professional staff are the orders of the day. Your preferences are noted and fulfilled without the necessity of reminders. It's a mystery how nearly every staff member knows your name within hours, if not minutes, after you board.

CHOOSE SEABOURN CRUISE LINE IF:

❶ You consider fine dining the highlight of your vacation.

❷ You own your own tuxedo. These ships are dressy, and most men wear them on formal evenings.

❸ You feel it's annoying to sign drink tabs; everything is included on these ships.

Tipping

Tipping is neither required nor expected.

Past Passengers

Once you have completed your first Seabourn cruise, you are automatically enrolled in the Seabourn Club for past guests. Benefits include up to a 50% discount on selected cruises (not combinable with Early Booking Savings); the Seabourn Club newsletters and periodic mailings featuring destinations, special programs, and exclusive savings; and an exclusive online e-mail contact point to the Club Desk through the membership page on the Seabourn Web site.

On the ships, Club members receive a 5% discount on future bookings; special recognition for frequent cruisers; and a Club party hosted by the captain. Passengers who sail 140 days aboard Seabourn are awarded a complimentary cruise of up to 14 days.

Good to Know

Shore excursions often include privileged access to historic and cultural sites when they are not open to the general public. A highlight of Seabourn's Caribbean cruises is the picnic on a private beach when the uniformed captain and crew members wade into the surf to serve champagne and caviar to guests enjoying a refreshing dip in the sea.

5

SEABOURN CRUISE LINE

DON'T CHOOSE SEABOURN CRUISE LINE IF:

❶ Dressing down is on your agenda.

❷ You absolutely must have a spacious private balcony; they are limited in number and book fast.

❸ You need to be stimulated by constant activity.

SEABOURN LEGEND, PRIDE, SPIRIT

Public Areas & Facilities

The height of absolute luxury, *Seabourn Legend* and *Seabourn Pride* surround passengers in comfort and understated style punctuated by polished brass accents and etched-glass panels. Public rooms are intimate, but that isn't to say cramped, although predinner cocktail gatherings tend to strain the room available in the popular Club bar.

The relative amount of ship-wide space devoted to passengers is among the highest in the cruise industry, and the public areas and deck spaces were designed so that no one aboard feels crowded. Fresh flower arrangements add a gracious touch to the classic decor of every public room.

After an ambitious program of extensive refurbishment, which was completed in 2006, each of Seabourn's yacht-like vessels emerged from drydock in ship-shape.

1992, 1988, 1989	ENTERED SERVICE
208	PASSENGER CAPACITY
160	CREW MEMBERS
104	NUMBER OF CABINS
10,000	GROSS TONS
439 feet	LENGTH
63 feet	WIDTH

700 ft.

500 ft.

300 ft.

WOW Factor

As the high crew member-to-guest ratio suggests, service is nonstop. If you're the slightest bit indecisive, the staff seems to anticipate your wishes.

Top: Sky Bar
Bottom: Balcony Suite

Restaurants

The formal restaurant offers open seating during scheduled hours. For a more laid-back setting, the Veranda Café has indoor and outdoor seating for breakfast and lunch, plus reservations-required tasting dinners in a smart-casual atmosphere every evening, including formal nights. The grill serves outdoors when weather permits.

What Works & What Doesn't

Everything on board is in keeping with the ship's small scale, including entertainment, which leans toward pianists or singers accompanied by a small combo for dancing. Repeat passengers can't keep the secret whirlpool on the ship's bow from being discovered—it's a preferred spot for watching the sun set. A single outdoor swimming pool is deep, but not long enough for serious laps. Art, or the absence of it, is noteworthy on a ship of this style. Some well-chosen, colorful pieces would add vibrancy to the otherwise predominantly blue and neutral color schemes.

Accommodations

Layout: All suites are on three mid-level decks and none are aft, which can be noisy on a ship with a water-sports marina. The roomy accommodations are truly of suite proportion: large walk-in closets, a spacious sitting area with coffee table that converts to a dining table for meals, a vanity–desk, and a marble bathroom with a separate shower and tub (in most suites). Owner's, Classic, and Double suites actually have a dining table and chairs; Owner's suites have a guest bathroom. Both Owner's and Classic suites have fully furnished balconies.

Amenities: Amenities are also befitting a true luxury suite: flat-screen TV with DVD player, Bose Wave CD stereo, a personal safe, and hair dryer. Other amenities include a stocked minibar, fresh fruit and flowers, a world atlas, personalized stationery, shampoo, con-

ditioner, designer soap and lotion, Egyptian cotton towels and robes, slippers, umbrellas, and beds dressed with silky, high thread-count linens. The only apparent difference between the sister ships is that *Seabourn Pride* has twin sinks in the bathrooms, while *Seabourn Legend* bathrooms have but one.

Good to Know: Four suites are designed for wheelchair accessibility.

CABIN TYPE	SIZE (sq. ft.)
Owner's Suite	530–575
Classic Suite	400
Double Suite	554
Balcony Suite*	277
Ocean View Suite	277

*The balcony isn't functional.

5

SEABOURN CRUISE LINE

In the Know

Brush up on obscure facts before boarding if you plan to participate in Team Trivia: the hotly contested competition can be brutal. Bridge is another serious pastime on Seabourn cruises, and you're sure to find a foursome. Decks and score pads are provided on board, so leave your cards at home.

Favorites

Floating Pleasure: For pure indulgence, make a selection from the aromatherapy bath menu before a soak in the tub. Your cabin attendant will even draw it for you, although you'll have to wash your own back and dry yourself off afterward.

Best Added Value: Complimentary Massage Moments on deck are soothing tension tamers

and an antidote to travel weariness.

Our Favorite Spot for a Nightcap: The deck surrounding the whirlpool on Deck 5 is usually deserted after dark and terribly romantic on a starry night.

Make It a Double: Double suites consist of two standard suites combined, with one half furnished as a living-dining

room and two full bathrooms. They're the ultimate indulgence if you have the money.

Suite-est Indulgence: A limited number of mini-balconies are available in standard suites; however, they're simply for fresh air, as there's no room to stand outside on them. Go this route if you want a taste of the sea air but can't upgrade to a full balcony.

Water-sports marina

SEADREAM YACHT CLUB

SeaDream yachts began sailing in 1984 beneath the Sea Goddess banner and, after a couple of changes of ownership and total renovation in 2002, they have evolved into the ultimate boutique ships. A voyage on one of these sleek

Take to the sea on a Jet Ski when your ship is at anchor.

megayachts is all about personal choice. Passengers enjoy an unstructured holiday at sea doing what they please, making it easy to imagine the diminutive vessel really is a private yacht. The ambience is refined and elegantly casual.

SEADREAM YACHT CLUB
2601 S. Bayshore Drive,
Penthouse 1B
Coconut Grove, FL 33133
305/856-5622 or
800/707-4911
www.seadreamyachtclub.
com

Cruise Style: Luxury

Fine dining and socializing with fellow passengers and the ships' captains and officers are preferred yachting pastimes. Other than a pianist in the tiny piano bar, a small casino, and movies in the main lounge, there's no roster of activities. The late-night place to be is the Top of the Yacht Bar, where passengers gather to share the day's experiences and kick their shoes off to dance on the teak deck. The captain hosts welcome aboard and farewell cocktail receptions in the Main Salon each week. Otherwise, you're on your own to do as you please.

A well-stocked library has books and movies for those who prefer quiet pursuits in the privacy of their staterooms. In addition, MP3 jukeboxes stocked with all types of music—enough to play for a complete sailing without repeating a selection—are available for personal use at no charge.

The weekly picnic on a private beach is considered by many passengers as their most memorable experience ashore during a SeaDream cruise. It begins with tropical drinks served during a wet landing from Zodiacs and is followed by SeaDream's signature champagne and caviar splash served to passengers from a surfboard bar in the crystal-clear water.

SeaDream yachts are often chartered by families, corporations, and other affinity groups, but the company does not charter both ships at the same time. If your chosen sailing is closed to you because of a charter, the other yacht will be available.

Food
Every meal is prepared-to-order using the freshest seafood and U.S. Prime cuts of beef. Menus include vegetarian alternatives and Asian wellness cuisine for the health-conscious. Cheeses, petits fours, and chocolate truffles are offered after dinner with coffee, and the Grand Marnier soufflé is to die for. A weekly dining event, the Chef's Menu Gustation, features an interesting medley of dishes planned by the executive chef for their variety and flavor; portions are sensibly sized, enabling diners to enjoy each course.

Weather permitting, daily breakfast, lunch, and special dinners are served alfresco in the canopied Topsider Restaurant. Wines are chosen to complement each luncheon and dinner menu from shipboard cellars that stock 3,500 bottles on each ship. Sommeliers are more than happy to discuss the attributes of each vintage and steam off the labels if you want to search for them at home. Snacks, from caviar to popcorn, are always available and delivered wherever you might be when hunger strikes, although there is a charge for caviar.

Room service is always available, but not just in your suite; you can dine anywhere you wish on deck.

Fitness & Recreation
Small gyms on each ship are equipped with treadmills, elliptical machines, recumbent bikes, and free weights. A personal trainer is available for consultation, and tai chi, yoga and aerobics classes are offered on deck as requested by passengers.

The yachts' unique SeaDream Spa facilities are also on the small side, yet offer a full menu of individualized, gentle Asian pampering treatments including massages, facials, and body wraps utilizing Eastern techniques. Hair and nail services are offered in the salon. SeaDream Spa is a member of the Thai Spa Association; products utilized for spa and salon services are among the best available from around the world. Massages are also available in cabanas ashore during the private beach party. It's recommended that passengers schedule time for use of the sauna, as its size limits the number of people who can comfortably use it at once.

Noteworthy

■ You may use an MP3 jukebox stocked with all types of music at no charge during your cruise.

■ The bar is always open with a wide selection, but an additional fee applies to certain wines and premium liquor brands.

■ Activities directors conduct informal talks prior to each port of call to help you orient yourself ashore.

Top: Relax on a Balinese dream bed.
Bottom: Fitness class

5

SEADREAM YACHT CLUB

Top: Dining at Topside Restaurant
Middle: SeaDream Spa
Bottom: Kayak from the ship's own marina.

The water-sports marina is popular with active passengers who want to water-ski, kayak, windsurf, or take a Jet Ski for a whirl while anchored in calm waters. Mountain bikes are available for use ashore, and a Segway people-mover can be rented for a unique spin around the pier. On board, the state-of-the-art golf simulator offers play on 30 worldwide championship golf courses.

Your Shipmates

SeaDream yachts attract energetic, affluent travelers of all ages, as well as groups. Passengers tend to be couples in their mid-40s up to retirees who enjoy the unstructured informality, subdued ambience, and utterly exclusive service.

These ships are not recommended for passengers who use wheelchairs. Although there's one stateroom considered accessible, public facilities have thresholds and the elevator doesn't reach the uppermost deck. Tide conditions can cause the gangway to be steep when docked, and negotiating shore tenders would be impossible.

Dress Code

Leave the formal duds at home—every night is yacht casual on SeaDream. Men wear open-collar shirts and slacks; sport coats are preferred but not required. A tie is never necessary. For women, sundresses, dressy casual skirts and sweaters, or pants and tops are the norm.

Junior Cruisers

SeaDream yachts are adult-oriented. High chairs and booster seats are available for the youngsters occasionally on board, but no children's facilities or organized activities are available. Parents are responsible for the behavior and entertainment of their children. Addtionally, children under the age of one are not allowed.

Service

Personal service and attention to detail are amazing; everyone will greet you by name within minutes of boarding. Passenger preferences are shared among staff members, who all work hard to assist one another. You seldom, if ever, have to repeat a request. Waiting in line for anything is unthinkable.

CHOOSE SEADREAM YACHT CLUB IF:

❶ You enjoy dining as an event, as courses are presented with a flourish and wines flow freely.

❷ You don't like to hear the word "no."

❸ You have good sea legs. In rough seas, the SeaDream yachts tend to bob up and down.

Tipping
Tipping is neither required nor expected.

Past Passengers
The SeaDream Club was designed to extend appreciation to past passengers, who are automatically enrolled
in the club upon completion of one sailing. Members receive the *SeaDreamer* newsletter, which is published
three times a year and features news and photos from
the SeaDream yachts, profiles of the yachts' captains
and other onboard personalities, profiles of various ports
of call, news of special sailings, and other information
of interest.

Other SeaDream Club benefits include advance notice of
new itineraries, an annual club-members cruise, perks for
introducing new passengers to SeaDream, a priority wait
list on sold-out cruises, the ability to reserve spa appointments and shore excursions online, 5% savings
when booking a future cruise while on board, an onboard
club member cocktail party, and special savings in the
ships' Boutique and Asian Spa.

Good to Know

Don't miss cocktails before
dinner, when the activities
director gives a brief
overview of the next day's
port of call and other hap-
penings. There's a daily
schedule, but you'll miss a
lot of fun and camaraderie if
you skip the cocktail hour.
You may also miss a last-
minute decision by the captain to extend a port call or
even change the order of
ports if there's something interesting going on ashore.

5

SEADREAM YACHT CLUB

DON'T CHOOSE SEADREAM YACHT CLUB IF:

❶ You like to dress up. A sport
coat is okay, but no one
ever wears a tie on these
ships.

❷ You must have a balcony:
there are none.

❸ You need structured activities: you'll have to plan
your own.

SEADREAM I, SEADREAM II

Public Areas & Facilities

Although these vessels are not huge, the public rooms are quite spacious; the Main Salon and Dining Salon are large enough to comfortably seat all passengers at once. Decor is elegant in its simplicity and surprisingly non-nautical. Instead, it's modern and sleek, utilizing the hues of the sea, sky, and sandy beaches. Oriental rugs cover polished teak floors in the reception area, and in the large, sun-splashed library, where you'll find over 1,000 books from which to select as well as computers to access the Internet. The library also lends movies to watch on the flat-screen TV/DVD player in your suite.

Balinese dream beds are the ideal spot to relax by day, either for sunbathing or reading beneath an umbrella. A telescope mounted at each ship's stern is handy for spotting land and other vessels at sea.

1984, 1985	ENTERED SERVICE
110	PASSENGER CAPACITY
90	CREW MEMBERS
55	NUMBER OF CABINS
4,300	GROSS TONS
344 feet	LENGTH
47 feet	WIDTH

700 ft.

500 ft.

300 ft.

WOW Factor

Every passenger is treated like the most important guest on board. Crew members take all requests very seriously.

Top: The Top of the Yacht Bar
Bottom: SeaDream yacht at sea

Restaurants

The formal restaurant offers open-seating dining during scheduled hours. For a more casual setting, the Topside restaurant has outdoor seating for breakfast and lunch—either with table service or from a small buffet—plus scheduled dinners alfresco (the indoor restaurant is also open for those who do not wish to dine outside).

What Works & What Doesn't

Exceptional food and service in a comfortable, yet sophisticated yachting atmosphere are the allure of these diminutive ships. No smoking is allowed indoors, which is either refreshing or an annoyance, depending on your point of view (and habits).

Cocktail glasses (and even a corkscrew) are provided in suite cabinets; however, there's a charge for wines and spirits ordered for your suite. This is somewhat odd considering the open-bar policy throughout the ships and the complimentary soft drinks, bottled water, and beer that are provided in passengers' mini-refrigerators.

Accommodations

Layout: Every stateroom is outside with an ocean view; every cabin has a sitting area, and there's plenty of drawer space for storage. A curtain can be drawn between the bed and sitting area for privacy. Bathrooms are marble-clad and have large, glass-enclosed showers with twin shower heads that make up for the tiny overall size of the bathrooms.

Amenities: All cabins contain an entertainment center with a large, flat-screen TV, CD, and DVD system, broadband Internet connection, personalized stationery, and a wet bar stocked with complimentary beer, soft drinks, and bottled water. A lighted, magnifying mirror and hair dryer are at a vanity table. Beds are dressed with Belgian linens and your choice of synthetic or down pillows and a duvet or woolen blankets. Bathrooms are stocked with deluxe Bulgari shampoo, shower gel, soap, and lotion. Turkish cotton bathrobes and slippers are provided for use during the cruise.

Good to Know: The single Owner's suite has a living room, dining area, separate bedroom, a bathroom with a sea view (as well as a separate tub and shower), and a guest bathroom. Commodore Club staterooms are basically double staterooms with one side configured as a sitting–dining area room; they feature two identical bathrooms with showers. One stateroom is designed for wheelchair accessibility.

CABIN TYPE	SIZE (sq. ft.)
Owner's Suite	450
Commodore Club	390
Yacht Club*	195

*16 of the Yacht Club staterooms are convertible to 8 Commodore staterooms, giving a variable passenger capacity.

Fast Facts

- 5 passenger decks
- Dining room, buffet
- In-cabin safes, in-cabin refrigerators, in-cabin broadband, in-cabin DVDs
- Pool
- Fitness classes, gym, hair salon, hot tub, sauna, spa
- 3 bars, casino, library, showroom
- Dry cleaning, laundry service
- Computer room
- No-smoking cabins

In the Know

The Balinese sun beds adjacent to the Top of the Yacht Bar have such thick, comfortable pads that passengers occasionally choose to spend the night there after everyone else has gone below deck to their quarters.

Favorites

How'd They Do That?: The weekly barbeque held on a deserted stretch of beach would be a highlight even if it didn't include champagne and caviar. Servers are somehow able to do forward flips in the surf while gripping champagne bottles and never spill a drop.

It's Your Yacht: There's a good selection of music CDs at the Top of the Yacht Bar, but feel free to bring some from home if you have favorites for listening and dancing.

Best Added Value: The single stateroom (215) that is designed for accessibility has a huge bathroom and can be booked by anyone unless it's required by a person with mobility challenges.

Our Favorite Spot for a Nightcap: The Top of the Yacht Bar is the sociable choice; however, for a bit of privacy, take your brandy to one of the secluded alcoves on either side of the open-air Topsiders Restaurant.

Best Eye Opener: Coffee and pastries are set out at Top of the Yacht Bar for early risers.

Pool deck

SILVERSEA CRUISES

Silversea Cruises was launched in 1994 by the former owners of Sitmar Cruises, the Lefebvre family of Rome, whose concept for the new cruise line was to build and sail the highest-quality luxury ships at sea. Intimate ships, paired with exclusive

The most captivating view on board

amenities and unparalleled hospitality are the hallmarks of Silversea cruises. All-inclusive air-and-sea fares can be customized to include not just round-trip airfare, but all transfers, porterage, and deluxe precruise accommodations as well.

SILVERSEA CRUISES
110 E. Broward Boulevard
Fort Lauderdale, FL 33301
954/522–4477 or
800/722–9955
www.silversea.com

Cruise Style: Luxury

Personalization is a Silversea maxim. Although their ships offer more activities than other comparably sized luxury vessels, you can either take part in those that interest you or opt instead for a good book and any number of quiet spots to read or snooze in the shade.

Guest lecturers are featured on nearly every cruise; language, dance, and culinary lessons and excellent wine appreciation sessions are always on the schedule of events. Silversea also schedules culinary arts cruises and a series of wine-focused voyages that feature award-winning authors, international wine experts, winemakers, and acclaimed chefs from the world's top restauratns. During afternoon tea, ladies gather for conversation over needlepoint, and the ranks of highly competitive trivia teams increase every successive afternoon.

After dark, the Bar is a predinner gathering spot and the late-night place for dancing to a live band. A multitiered show lounge is the setting for spirited production shows, classical concerts, magic shows, big-screen movies, and folkloric entertainers from ashore. A small casino offers slot machines and gaming tables.

Food

Dishes from the galleys of Silversea's Master Chefs are complemented by those of La Collection du Monde, created by Silversea's culinary partner, the world-class chefs of Relais & Châteaux. Menus include hot-and-cold appetizers, at least four entrée selections, a vegetarian alternative, and Cruiselite cuisine (low in cholesterol, sodium, and fat). Special off-menu orders are prepared whenever possible, provided that the ingredients are available on board. In the event that they aren't, you may find after a day in port that a trip to the market was made in order to fulfill your request.

Chef Marco Betti, the owner of Antica Pasta restaurants in Florence, Italy, and Atlanta, Georgia, has designed a new menu for La Terrazza that focuses on one of the most luxurious food trends, the "slow food" movement. The goal of the movement is to preserve the gastronomic traditions of Italy through the use of fresh, traditional foods, and it's spread throughout the world. At La Terrazza (by day the Terrace Café, a casual buffet) the menu showcases the finest in Italian cooking, from classic favorites to Tuscan fare. The restaurant carries no surcharge; however, seating is limited, so reservations are a must to ensure a table. It's one reservation you'll be glad you took the time to book.

An intimate dining experience aboard each vessel is the Wine Restaurant by Relais & Châteaux—Le Champagne (*Silver Shadow, Silver Whisper*) or La Saletta (*Silver Wind, Silver Wind, Silver Cloud*). Adding a dimension to dining, the exquisite cuisine is designed to celebrate the wines served—a different celebrated vintage is served with each course. Menus and wines are chosen by Relais & Chateaux sommeliers to reflect regions of the world noted for their rich wine heritage.

An evening poolside barbeque is a weekly dinner event, weather permitting. A highlight of every cruise is the Galley Brunch, when passengers are invited into the galley to select from a feast decorated with imaginative ice and vegetable sculptures. Even when meals are served buffet-style in the Terrace Café, you will seldom have to carry your own plate as waiters are at hand to assist you to your table. Wines are chosen to complement each day's luncheon and dinner menus.

Grilled foods, sandwiches, and an array of fruits and salads are served daily for lunch at the poolside Grill. Always available are extensive selections from the room-service menu. The full restaurant menu may also

Noteworthy

■ Prior to departure, Silversea provides a list of port addresses, to which your mail can be forwarded throughout your voyage.

■ Gentlemen are no longer required to wear a tie with their jackets on informal evenings.

■ Silversea does not utilize the services of photographers aboard their ships.

Top: Stylish entertainment
Bottom: Terrace Café alfresco dining

Top: Table tennis
Middle: Caring, personal service
Bottom: Veranda Suite

be used for room service orders, which can be served course by course in your suite during regular dining hours.

Fitness & Recreation

The rather small gym is equipped with cardiovascular and weight-training equipment, and fitness classes are held in the mirror-lined, but somewhat confining, exercise room.

South Pacific–inspired Mandara Spa offers numerous treatments including exotic sounding massages, facials, and body wraps. Hair and nail services are available in the busy salon. A plus is that appointments for spa and beauty salon treatments can be made online from 60 days until 48 hours prior to sailing.

Golfers can sign up with the pro on board for individual lessons utilizing a high-tech swing analyzer and attend complimentary golf clinics or participate in a putting contest.

Your Shipmates

Silversea Cruises appeal to sophisticated, affluent couples who enjoy the country-clublike atmosphere, exquisite cuisine, and polished service on board, not to mention the exotic ports and unique experiences ashore.

Dress Code

Two formal nights are standard on seven-night cruises and three to four nights, depending on the itinerary, on longer sailings. Men are required to wear tuxedos or dark suits after 6 PM. All other evenings are either informal, when a jacket is called for (a tie is optional, but most men wear them), or casual, when slacks with a jacket over an open-collar shirt for men and sporty dresses or skirts or pants with a sweater or blouse for women are suggested.

Junior Cruisers

Silversea Cruises is adult-oriented and unable to accommodate children less than one year of age, and the cruise line limits the number of children under the age of three on board. No dedicated children's facilities are available, so parents are responsible for the behavior and entertainment of their children.

CHOOSE SILVERSEA CRUISES IF:

❶ Your taste leans toward learning and exploration.

❷ You enjoy socializing as well as the option of live entertainment, just not too much of it.

❸ You like to plan ahead. You can reserve shore tours, salon services, and spa treatments online.

Service

Personalized service is exacting and hospitable, yet discreet; the staff strive for perfection and often achieve it. The attitude is decidedly European and begins with a welcome-aboard flute of champagne, then continues throughout as personal preferences are remembered and satisfied. The word "no" doesn't seem to be in the staff vocabulary in any language. Guests in top-category suites are pampered by butlers who are certified by the Guild of Professional Butlers.

Tipping

Tipping is neither required nor expected.

Past Passengers

Membership in the Venetian Society is automatic upon completion of one Silversea cruise. Members begin accruing Venetian Society cruise days and are eligible for discounts on select voyages; onboard recognition and private parties; milestone rewards; exclusive gifts; the *Venetian Society Newsletter*; ship visitation privileges; complimentary early embarkation or late debarkation at certain milestones; members-only benefits at select Leading Hotels of the World and Relais & Châteaux hotels and resorts; and select offers through Silversea's preferred partners.

Through the Friends of Society programs, members can double their accumulated cruise days and receive a shipboard spending credit by inviting friends or family members to sail on select Venetian Society sailings. Friends or family will enjoy the same Venetian Society savings as members for those cruises, a really nice perk.

Good to Know

You might expect a bit of stodginess to creep in at this level of ultraluxury, but you wouldn't necessarily be correct. Socializing isn't quite as easy-going as on smaller ships, and some passengers can come off as a bit stand-offish. However, you will encounter like-minded fellow passengers if you make the effort to participate in group activities, particularly the highly competitive afternoon-trivia sessions. With an increasingly younger crowd on board, you are more likely to encounter partyers at late-night disco sessions than couples waltzing between courses during dinner.

5

SILVERSEA CRUISES

DON'T CHOOSE SILVERSEA CRUISES IF:

❶ You want to dress informally at all times on your cruise.

❷ You need highly structured activities and have to be reminded of them.

❸ You prefer the glitter and stimulation of Las Vegas to the understated glamour of Monaco.

SILVER CLOUD, SILVER WIND

Public Areas and Facilities

These two yacht-like gems are all about style, understatement, and personal choice, so if you want to snuggle into a book in the well-stocked library, no one will lift an eyebrow. While there simply isn't room on these ships for huge rooms, the public spaces are more than adequate and designed to function well. These ships served as the models for their larger sisters, *Silver Shadow* and *Silver Whisper,* which expanded on the smaller ships' concept of locating all passenger accommodations forward and public rooms aft.

The Restaurant is one of the loveliest dining rooms at sea with a domed ceiling and musicians to provide dance music between courses. Either The Bar or Panorama Lounge are comfortable spots to socialize, dance, or enjoy cocktails before or after the evening entertainment, which might include a classical concert or smallish production show in the showroom or Moonlight Movies, feature films shown outside on the Pool Deck.

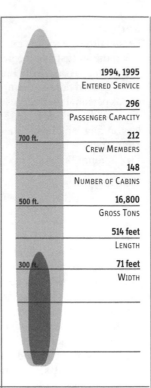

700 ft.	**1994, 1995** ENTERED SERVICE
	296 PASSENGER CAPACITY
	212 CREW MEMBERS
	148 NUMBER OF CABINS
500 ft.	**16,800** GROSS TONS
	514 feet LENGTH
300 ft.	**71 feet** WIDTH

WOW Factor

Cold towels and chilled fruit poolside and a fridge stocked with chilled water in the fitness area don't go unnoticed by appreciative passengers.

Top: The bar
Bottom: Royal Suite

Restaurants

The Restaurant has open seating for all meals. Saletta has a special tasting menu with wine pairings for an extra charge. La Terrazza is the indoor-outdoor buffet; on most evenings it serves as an alternative restaurant. The Pool Grill offers casual fare. Room service is available 24 hours a day, and items from The Restaurant menu can be served course-by-course.

What Works and What Doesn't

Silversea is one of the most all-inclusive cruise lines, and the ambiance onboard is comfortably upscale, heightened by never having to sign a bar ticket. Wine is poured freely at lunch and dinner, and no one has to cringe when ordering a round of drinks for new friends, which reinforces camaraderie between passengers. While the minimalist modern décor is accented by beautiful flower arrangements throughout the ship, the artwork is somewhat uninspired. However, whatever might be lacking in terms of decorative art is more than made up for by the excellent enrichment programs. Afternoon trivia contests during tea are particularly spirited.

Accommodations

Layout: All accommodations are considered suites; all are outside and have at least an ocean view; an outstanding 80% also have private balconies. Suite interiors are enhanced with appealing artwork, flowers, sitting areas, and bedding topped with plush duvets and choice of pillow style. A writing desk, refrigerator, TV with DVD player, dressing table with lighted mirror and hair dryer, walk-in closet, and personal safe are all standard. The marbled bathrooms have full-sized bathtubs.

Amenities: Champagne on ice awaits the arrival of all passengers, and it is replenished as desired; the beverage cabinet is stocked daily on request with individual selections of wines, spirits, and beverages. A fruit basket is replenished daily. Bathrooms are stocked with European toiletries, and slippers and bathrobes are provided for use during the cruise.

Good to Know: Teak-floored balconies have patio furniture and floor-to-ceiling glass doors. Two suites are wheelchair-accessible.

CABIN TYPE	SIZE (sq. ft.)
Grand and Rossellini Suite	1,314
Royal Suite 1,031	
Owner's Suite	827
Silver Suite 541	
Veranda Suite/Vista Suite	295/240

**Cabin sizes include the square footage of any balcony.

Fast Facts

- 6 passenger decks
- 2 specialty restaurants, dining room, buffet
- WiFi, in-cabin safes, some in-cabin minibars, some in-cabin refrigerators, in-cabin DVDs
- 1 pool
- Fitness classes, gym, hair salon, 1 hot tub, sauna, spa, steam room
- 3 bars, casino, dance club, library, showroom
- Dry cleaning, laundry facilities, laundry service
- Computer room

5

SILVERSEA CRUISES

In the Know

Silversea's spokesperson Isabella Rossellini is the personification of the line's standard of glamour and sophistication. Rossellini makes her home away from home aboard each Silversea ship in a suite she has personally selected, customized, and renamed. You can book the "Rossellini Suite" on any Silversea ship.

Favorites

Our Favorite Spot for a Nightcap: Le Champagne, the wine and cigar room on Deck Eight, is a cozy retreat with sumptuous leather chairs. It's just naturally a haven for a rare port after dinner or a nightcap accompanied by a fine cigar.

Best Place to Get Away: Practice yoga, train with the latest Pilates program, or work out utiliz-ing state-of-the-art fitness equipment while drawing inspiration from the breathtaking, panoramic views of the ocean from the Fitness Center.

Best Way to Expand Your Mind: Every cruise features regionally specific lectures by noted historians, ambassadors, state leaders, authors and geographers—all experts and each sharing special insights into areas of the world they know intimately. Guest chefs and wine experts also join special Culinary Arts and Wine Series Voyages.

Best Added Value: Silversea is so all-inclusive that you seldom need to reach for your charge card, but what we appreciate most is feeling like a valued guest in a gracious vacation retreat. We consider that priceless.

The pool deck.

SILVER SHADOW, SILVER WHISPER

Public Areas & Facilities

The logical layout of these sister ships, with suites located in the forward two-thirds of the ship and public rooms aft, makes orientation simple. The clean, modern decor that defines public areas and lounges might almost seem stark, but it places the main emphasis on large expanses of glass for sunshine and sea views as well as passenger comfort.

Silversea ships boast unbeatable libraries stocked with best-sellers, travel books, classics, and movies for in-suite viewing. Extremely wide passageways in public areas are lined with glass-front display cabinets full of interesting and unusual artifacts from the places the ships visit.

The Humidor by Davidoff is a clubby cigar smoking room with overstuffed leather seating and a ventilation system that even nonsmokers can appreciate.

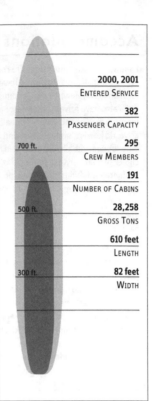

700 ft.	**2000, 2001**
	ENTERED SERVICE
	382
	PASSENGER CAPACITY
	295
	CREW MEMBERS
	191
500 ft.	NUMBER OF CABINS
	28,258
	GROSS TONS
	610 feet
	LENGTH
300 ft.	**82 feet**
	WIDTH

WOW Factor

Pommery champagne on ice welcomes you to your suite. And the champagne flows freely throughout your cruise.

Top: The casino
Bottom: *Silver Whisper* at sea

Restaurants

The formal restaurant offers open-seating during scheduled hours. Specialty dining is offered by reservation in Le Champagne (extra charge) and La Terrazza. For a more casual meal, the Ter- race Café has indoor and outdoor seating for buffet-style breakfast and lunch. The poolside Grill offers an ultracasual lunch option.

What Works & What Doesn't

Sailing on a Silversea ship is like spending time as a pampered guest at a home in the Hamptons. Everything is at your fingertips, and if it isn't, all you have to do is ask. Silversea is so all-inclusive that you'll find your room key–charge card is seldom used for anything but opening your suite door. Room service is prompt, and orders arrive with crystal, china, and even a linen tablecloth for a complete dining room–style setup in your suite. In an odd contrast to the contents of display cases and lovely flower arrangements, artwork on the walls is fairly ho-hum and not at all memorable.

Accommodations

Layout: Every suite is outside with an ocean view, and more than 80% have a private teak-floor balcony. Standard suites have a sitting area that can be curtained off from the bed for more privacy. Marble bathrooms have double sinks and a separate, glass-enclosed shower as well as a tub. All suites have generous walk-in closets.

Amenities: Standard suites have an entertainment center with a TV and DVD or VCR, personalized stationery, a cocktail cabinet, personal safe, and a refrigerator stocked with complimentary beer, soft drinks, and bottled water. A hair dryer is provided at a vanity table, and you can request a magnifying mirror. Beds are dressed with high-quality linens, duvets, or blankets, and your choice of synthetic or down pillows. Bathrooms have huge towels and terry bathrobes for use during the cruise as

well as designer shampoo, soaps, and lotion.

Top Suites: In addition to much more space, top-category suites have all the standard amenities plus dining areas, separate bedrooms, and CD players. Silver suites and above have whirlpool tubs. The top three categories have separate powder rooms.

Good to Know: Two suites are designed for wheelchair accessibility.

CABIN TYPE	SIZE (sq. ft.)
Grand Suite	1,286–1,435
Royal Suite	1,312–1,352
Owner's Suite	1,208
Silver/Medallion Suite	701/521
Verandah/Vista Suite	345/287

Fast Facts

- 7 passenger decks
- 2 specialty restaurants, dining room, buffet
- Wi-Fi, in-cabin safes, in-cabin refrigerators, some in-cabin DVDs, some in-cabin VCRs
- Pool
- Fitness classes, gym, hair salon, 2 hot tubs, sauna, spa, steam room
- 3 bars, casino, dance club, library, showroom
- Dry cleaning, laundry facilities, laundry service
- Computer room

5

SILVERSEA CRUISES

In the Know

Nine Vista suites on deck five have doors to the outside that access a common, semiprivate veranda area. Even though the area is not furnished, it's like having a balcony without paying a higher fare.

Favorites

Best Added Value: The spas' complimentary saunas and steam rooms are tiny treasures. Although small, they are adequate and seldom occupied.

Most Appreciated Freebie: Also on the small side are the totally free laundry rooms (even the soap is included). Perfectly adequate for ships this size, they are frequently in use. Just

about the only line you're likely to encounter on a Silversea ship is the one to use a washing machine.

Best Nightly Treat: Other cruise lines leave a chocolate on your pillow to wish you sweet dreams. Silversea's little gold boxes of Godiva chocolates are distinctively a cut above the usual.

Our Favorite Spot for a Nightcap: We love to sink into a cushy leather seat in the candlelighted cigar lounge to end a full evening of dinner and dancing.

The Poolside Grille: lunch and light snacks

STAR CLIPPERS

In 1991 Star Clippers unveiled a new tall-ship alternative to sophisticated travelers, whose desires included having an adventure at sea but not on board a conventional cruise ship. Star Clippers vessels are four- and five-masted sailing beau-

Sun yourself on the bow netting.

ties—the world's largest barquentine and full-rigged sailing ships. Filled with modern, high-tech equipment as well as the amenities of private yachts, the ships rely on sail power while at sea unless conditions require the assistance of the engines. Minimal heeling, usually less than 6%, is achieved through judicious control of the sails.

STAR CLIPPERS
7200 N.W. 19th Street,
Suite 206
Miami, FL 33126
305/442–0550 or
800/442–0551
www.starclippers.com

Cruise Style: Sailing Ship

A boyhood dream became a cruise-line reality when Swedish entrepreneur Mikael Krafft launched his fleet of authentic re-creations of classic 19th-century clipper ships. The day officially begins when the captain holds an informative daily briefing on deck with a bit of storytelling tossed in. Star Clippers are not cruise ships in the ordinary sense with strict agendas and pages of activities. You're free to do what you please day and night, but many passengers join the crew members topside when the sails or raised or for some of the lighthearted events like crab-racing contests, scavenger hunts, and a talent night. The informality of singing around the piano bar typifies an evening on one of these ships, although in certain ports local performers come on board to spice up the action with an authentic taste of the local music and arts.

The lack of rigid scheduling is one of Star Clippers' most appealing attractions. The bridge is always open, and passengers are welcome to peer over the captain's shoulder as he plots the ship's course. Crew members are happy to demonstrate how to splice a line, reef a sail, or tie a proper knot.

As attractive as the ships' interiors are, the focal point of Star Clippers cruises is the outdoors. Plan to spend a lot of time on deck soaking in the sun, sea, and sky. It doesn't get any better than that. Consider also that each ship has at least two swimming pools. Granted, they are tiny, but they are a refreshing feature uncommon on true sailing ships and all but the most lavish yachts.

Although the Star Clippers ships are motorized, their engines are shut down whenever crews unfurl the sails (36,000 square feet on *Star Clipper* and 56,000 square feet on *Royal Clipper*) to capture the wind. On a typical cruise, the ships rely exclusively on sail power anytime favorable conditions prevail.

As the haunting strains of Vangelis's symphony "1492: Conquest of Paradise" are piped over the PA system and the first of the sails are unfurled, the only thing you'll hear on deck is the sound of the music and the calls of the line handlers until every sail is in place. While the feeling of the wind powering large ships through the water is spine-tingling, you will miss the wondrous sight of your ship under sail unless the captain can schedule a photo opportunity utilizing one of the tenders. It's one of the most memorable sights you'll see if this opportunity avails itself. However, when necessary, the ships will cruise under motor power to meet the requirements of their itineraries.

Food
Not noted for gourmet fare, the international cuisine is what you would expect from a trendy shoreside bistro, albeit an elegant one. All meals are open-seating in the formal dining room during scheduled hours; breakfast and lunch—an impressive spread of seafood, salads and grilled items—are served buffet-style, while dinners are leisurely affairs served in the European manner. Hint: If you want your salad *before* your main course, just ask; the French style is to serve it after the main course. Menus, created in consultation with chef Jean Marie Meulien (who has been awarded Michelin stars throughout his career), include appetizers, soups, pasta, a sorbet course, at least three choices of entrees, salad, cheese, and, of course, dessert. Caribbean-inspired entrees, vegetarian, and light dishes are featured. A maître d' is present at the more formal evening meals to seat passengers, but it isn't uncommon on these small ships for them to arrange their own groups of dinner company.

Early risers on each ship find a Continental breakfast offered at the Tropical Bar, and coffee and fresh fruit are always available in the Piano Bar. Should you want to

Noteworthy

■ Don't ask for connecting staterooms on Star Clippers ships—there are none.

■ Look for secret hide-aways on one of the hidden balconies on either side of *Royal Clipper*'s bow.

■ You are free to dine when and with whomever you wish on Star Clippers ships, including with the officers, who join passengers in the dining room most nights.

5

STAR CLIPPERS

Top: Cooling off in one of the pools
Bottom: *Royal Clipper* Deluxe Suite

Top: View from the bow
Middle: *Royal Clipper* Piano bar
Bottom: *Royal Clipper* Spa

remain in your swimsuit, casual buffets are set up adjacent to the Tropical Bar at noon (the "Deck Snack Buffet") and at 5 PM (the "Afternoon Snack"). Some of the "snacks" are themed and quite popular—a Neptune seafood luncheon, snacks with waffles or crepes, and a taco bar. On select itineraries, an outdoor barbecue is served on shore.

With the exception of occupants of Owner's Suites and Deluxe Suites on *Royal Clipper,* there is no room service available unless you are sick and can't make it to the dining room for meals.

Fitness & Recreation

Formal exercise sessions take a backseat to water sports, although aerobics classes and swimming are featured on all ships. Only *Royal Clipper* has a marina platform that can be lowered in calm waters to access water sports and diving; however, the smaller ships replicate the experience by using motorized launches to reach reefs for snorkeling. A gym-spa with an array of exercise equipment, free weights, spa treatments and unisex hair services are also found only on *Royal Clipper.* Despite the lack of a formal fitness center on *Star Clipper,* morning aerobics or yoga classes are usually held on deck for active passengers. Massages, manicures, and pedicures can be arranged as well.

Your Shipmates

Star Clippers cruises draw active, upscale American and European couples from their 30s on up, who enjoy sailing but in a casually sophisticated atmosphere with modern conveniences. Many sailings are equally divided between North Americans and Europeans, so announcements are made in several languages accordingly.

This is not a cruise line for the physically challenged; there are no elevators or ramps, nor are staterooms or bathrooms wheelchair-accessibile. Gangways and shore launches can also be difficult to negotiate.

Dress Code

All evenings are elegant casual, so slacks with an open-collar shirt are fine for men, and sundresses, skirts, or

CHOOSE STAR CLIPPERS IF:

❶ You wouldn't consider a vacation on a traditional cruise ship but are a sailing enthusiast.

❷ You love water sports, particularly snorkeling and scuba diving.

❸ You want to anchor in secluded coves and visit islands that are off the beaten path.

pants with a sweater or blouse suggested for women. Coats and ties are never required. Shorts and T-shirts are not allowed in the dining room at dinner.

Junior Cruisers

Star Clippers ships are adult-oriented. Although children are welcome and may participate in shipboard activities suited to their ability, there are no dedicated youth facilities. Parents are responsible for the behavior and entertainment of their children. Mature teens who can live without video games and a lot of other teens are the best young sailors.

Service

Service is friendly and gracious, similar to what you would find in a boutique hotel or restaurant. You may find that you have to flag down a waiter for a second cup of coffee, though.

Tipping

Gratuities are not included in the cruise fare and are extended at the sole discretion of passengers. The recommended amount is 8 euros per person per day. Tips are pooled and shared; individual tipping is discouraged. You can either put cash in the tip envelope that will be provided to you and drop it at the purser's office or charge gratuities to your shipboard account. An automatic 15% gratuity is added to each passenger's bar bill.

Past Passengers

Top Gallant is the loyalty club for past passengers. No specific fare discount is offered to members; however, they receive a newsletter and special offers on fare reductions from time to time. Nearly 60% of all passengers choose to make a repeat voyage on Star Clippers ships.

Funds

Note that while fares are quoted in U.S. dollars, all shipboard charges are in euros. Accounts can be settled with cash, traveler's checks, or credit cards on the final day of your cruise.

Good to Know

Fresh air is prevalent inside as well as on deck. Smoking is restricted to limited public rooms and not permitted in cabins. For the ultimate in fresh air, an unparalleled treat is the climb to a lookout station at the first yardarm on each of *Royal Clipper*'s masts where you can relax on a teak settee and take in the view.

5

STAR CLIPPERS

DON'T CHOOSE STAR CLIPPERS IF:

❶ You have a preexisting or potentially serious medical condition. There's no physician on board.

❷ You must have a private balcony—there are a few, but only in top accommodation categories.

❸ You can't live without room service. Only *Royal Clipper* has it, and only in a few high-end suites.

ROYAL CLIPPER

Public Areas & Facilities

Royal Clipper is the first five-masted, full-rigged sailing ship built since 1902. As the largest true sailing clipper ship in the world today, she carries 42 sails with a total area of 56,000 square feet.

Unusual for a sailing ship, a three-deck atrium graces the heart of the vessel.

Her interior is decorated in Edwardian-era style with abundant gleaming woods, brass fixtures, and nautical touches. Light filters into the piano bar, three-deck high atrium, and the dining room through the glass bottom and portholes of the main swimming pool located overhead.

The rarely used Observation Lounge is located forward of the deluxe suites and affords great sea views. It is also the location of the computer station for all Internet access.

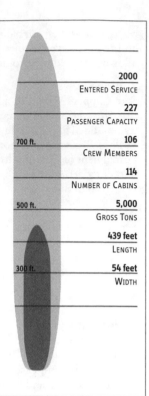

700 ft.	2000
	ENTERED SERVICE
	227
	PASSENGER CAPACITY
	106
	CREW MEMBERS
	114
	NUMBER OF CABINS
500 ft.	5,000
	GROSS TONS
	439 feet
	LENGTH
300 ft.	54 feet
	WIDTH

WOW Factor

Expanses of teak, neatly coiled rope, and honest-to-goodness speed under sail: Royal Clipper *can crank out 20 knots without the engines.*

Top: *Clipper* dining room
Bottom: Preparing to dive

Restaurants

The multilevel dining room serves a single, open-seating breakfast, lunch, and dinner. For early-risers, a Continental breakfast is set up in the piano bar, and a buffet lunch is sometimes offered in the Tropical Bar, as are late-afternoon snacks and predinner canapés. Room service is only available to occupants of the Owner's Suites and Deluxe Suites.

What Works & What Doesn't

The feeling of the wind powering this large vessel through the water is spine-tingling. Unfortunately, you will miss the glorious sight of her under way unless the captain can schedule a photo-op via one of the tenders. Always lively and the center of most of the action day and night, the Tropical Bar on the main deck is where the evening entertainment happens. Outdoors, on the teak deck, is the place to be. The library, with its cushy seating and faux fireplace, is a cozy place to read or play board games; it also offers a surprisingly good selection of books.

Accommodations

Layout–Amenities: Think yacht, and the cabin sizes make sense. Although efficiently laid out with tasteful, sea-going appointments and prints of clipper ships and sailing yachts on the walls, cabins are small by comparison to most cruise ships. All have a TV, personal safe, desk–vanity, small settee, hair dryer, and marble bathroom with standard toiletries. Closet space is compact, and bureau drawers are narrow, but an under-the-bed drawer is a useful nautical touch for extra storage.

Suites: Owner's Suites, Deluxe Suites, and Category 1 cabins have a sitting area, minibar, whirlpool tub–shower combinations, and bathrobes to use during the cruise. Deluxe Suites also feature a private veranda. Category 1 cabins have doors that open onto a semiprivate area on the outside deck.

Only the two Owner's Suites have connecting doors.

Good to Know: Cabins are equipped with 220-volt electrical outlets and a 110-volt outlet suitable only for electric shavers. For 110-volt appliances, you'll need to bring a transformer; for dual-voltage appliances, pack a plug converter. None of the staterooms is designed for wheelchair accessibility, nor are there any elevators. Only the two Owner's Suites have interconnecting doors.

CABIN TYPE	SIZE (sq. ft.)
Owner's Suite	355
Deluxe Suite & Cat. 1 Ocean View	204
Standard Ocean View	150
Cat. 5 Ocean View	118
Inside	107

Fast Facts

- 5 passenger decks
- Dining room
- In-cabin safes, some in-cabin refrigerators, some in-cabin DVDs
- 3 pools
- Fitness classes, gym, hair salon, spa, steam room
- 3 bars, library
- Dry cleaning, laundry service
- Computer room
- No-smoking cabins

5

STAR CLIPPERS

In the Know

Most cabin showers have only a 1-inch marble lip, so water tends to spread across the bathroom floor in bumpy seas. While there's a second drain outside the shower, anything left on the floor will get soaked. A rolled-up beach towel outside the shower will help contain the flood.

Favorites

Heads Up: In Category 3 cabins forward, you'll notice a definite slant to the floor, due to the location near the bow. You may also feel a bit more motion forward than aft and should also remember that creaking sounds are common on sailing ships.

Best Splurge: Massages in the spa are no-nonsense and reasonably priced.

Best Place to Escape the Crowds: Lookout stations at the first yardarm on each mast are the most private spaces on board and afford the best views–provided that you aren't bothered by heights.

Our Favorite Spot for a Nightcap: Almost anywhere outside at the rail is about perfect on a moonlit night.

Best Snack Spot: Coffee and fresh fruit are always available in the Piano Bar.

Best Underwater View: Peek-a-boo submarine portholes are adjacent to the gym and spa in the Captain Nemo Lounge, where underwater marine life can be spotted when the ship is at anchor.

Royal Clipper under sail

STAR CLIPPER

Public Areas & Facilities

With its bright, brass fixtures, teak-and-mahogany paneling and rails, and antique prints and paintings of famous sailing vessels, *Star Clipper*'s interior decor reflects the heritage of grand sailing ships.

Lighted from overhead by porthole-shape skylights, an atrium-like effect is created by the central opening in the piano bar, which leads to a graceful staircase and the dining room one deck below. The centerpiece of the vaguely Edwardian-style library is a belle époque–period fireplace.

The Piano Bar is noted for being intimate and cozy. The Tropical Bar, one of the most popular areas on board, is the center of social activity, for predinner cocktails and late-night socializing and dancing. It's the covered outdoor lounge adjacent to the open deck space, where local entertainers often perform.

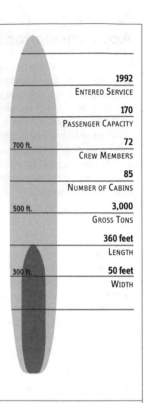

1992	ENTERED SERVICE
170	PASSENGER CAPACITY
72	CREW MEMBERS
85	NUMBER OF CABINS
3,000	GROSS TONS
360 feet	LENGTH
50 feet	WIDTH

WOW Factor

You can't help but appreciate the silence and harmony with the sea when the engines are turned off and the ship is under sail.

Top: Dining on *Star Clipper*
Bottom: Friendly, efficient service

Restaurants

The mahogany-paneled dining room serves a single open-seating breakfast, lunch, and dinner. For early-risers, a Continental breakfast is set up in the piano bar, and a buffet lunch is sometimes served on deck. Late-night canapés are offered in the piano bar. There's no room service unless you're sick and can't make it out to meals.

What Works & What Doesn't

If the sheer beauty of real sailing isn't enough to satisfy your inner pirate, creature comforts are only as far away as your fingertips. However, the bathroom taps can be frustrating until you are accustomed to the regulated water flow. To conserve water, the flow shuts off with annoying regularity, and you have to press a button to restart it. The beds in four Category 5 cabins aft are raised several feet off the floor, and most passengers require the ladder to climb into them. That could be a problem after a long day and a bit too much rum punch.

Accommodations

Layout–Amenities: Traditional, yacht-y, and efficiently designed, *Star Clipper*'s cabins are adequate but far from spacious by modern standards. All cabins have a personal safe, desk–vanity, small settee, hair dryer, TV (except Category 6 inside), and marble bathroom with standard toiletries.

As would normally be expected on a sailing vessel, staterooms forward and aft are more susceptible to motion than those amidship. There is also a noticeable slant to the floor in cabins near the bow. Unless you are particularly agile, you will want to avoid the inside cabins on Commodore Deck, where beds are strictly upper and lower berths. Some cabins are outfitted with a third, pull-down berth, but most passengers will find the space too cramped for three occupants.

Top-Category Cabins: The Owner's Cabin and Category 1 cabins have a minibar, whirlpool tub–shower combination, and the use of bathrobes during the cruise. Category 1 cabin doors open onto the outside deck, and the Owner's Cabin has a sitting room.

Good to Know: All cabins are equipped with 110-volt electrical outlets and a 110-volt outlet in the bathroom that is suitable only for electric shavers. None of the staterooms are designed for wheelchair accessibility, nor do any staterooms have connecting doors.

CABIN TYPE	SIZE (sq. ft.)
Owner's Suite	266
Cat. 1 Ocean View	150
Cat. 2 Ocean View	129
Standard Ocean View	118
Inside	97

Fast Facts

- 4 passenger decks
- Dining room
- In-cabin safes
- 2 pools
- Fitness classes
- 2 bars, library, laundry service
- Computer room
- No-smoking cabins

In the Know

For tranquillity and ample sunbathing space, head to the stern or the bowsprit net. The sails block less sunlight on the deck around the aft pool, and it tends to be quieter, but crawling onto the netting at the bowsprit is even better.

Favorites

Best Place to Escape the Crowds: On a ship this size there aren't too many spots to get away from fellow passengers. Fortunately, there aren't that many passengers, and there's seldom what anyone would consider a crowd.

Our Favorite Spot for a Nightcap: The banquettes that line the piano bar provide a suitably cozy spot to end your evening.

Best Meet-and-Mingle Spot: It's the dining room. Booths and tables that seat six to eight are designed to maximize socializing. There are no tables for two, and few passengers seem to mind.

Best Place to Get Caffeinated: Stop by the Piano Bar anytime for a jolt of java. Complimentary coffee and tea are available there around the clock. Specialty coffee beverages (for which there is a charge) are served only during bar hours.

Star Clipper under sail

5

STAR CLIPPERS

WINDJAMMER BAREFOOT CRUISES

The world's largest fleet of tall ships evolved from a modest beginning—a single 19-foot sloop, *The Hangover,* on which legendary company founder Mike Burke sailed his friends from South Florida to the Bahamas. Each Windjammer ship

Quiet time on deck

is unique and has a distinctive pedigree. Rescued from the scrappers when no one else recognized their potential, each vessel has been carefully renovated to sail the far reaches of the Caribbean and anchor in pristine waters where traditional cruise ships can't go.

**WINDJAMMER BAREFOOT
CRUISES**
Box 190120,
Miami, FL 33119-0120
305/672-6453 or
800/327-2601
www.windjammer.com

Cruise Style: Sailing Ship

Windjammer offers as much a state of mind as a cruise. Jammers, as passengers are called, view themselves as cut from the same cloth as the infamous Cap'n Mike Burke—adventurous and irreverent. As soon as you are on board, you are a Jammer. You may find your heart swelling with the buccaneer spirit in the time it takes the wind to fill the sails of your tall ship.

Not quite as wild and crazy as in years past, Windjammer cruises are still about as unconventional as you can get and still be cruising. Instead of a cruise director and social staff, an activities mate is on hand to assist you with things to do ashore and to lead the merriment on board. Even the ships' captains wear shorts and go barefoot. You might also find that your itinerary is relatively flexible, depending on the wind and weather.

Barefoot cruising days officially begin with Bloody Marys on deck during story time, when the captain holds a briefing to share island information, lore, and tall tales laced with good-natured humor. From that point on, you're on your own and free to do what you please at any time (and within reason), both on board and ashore.

Many passengers join the crew to work the sails and for some laid-back nautical games like crab-racing contests and masquerading as pirates. Swizzle time comes late every afternoon when passengers need no encouragement to show up for their daily complimentary ration of grog and finger food. Don't be surprised if that pretty woman at the costume party turns out to be your ship's captain in drag.

Local bands come on board in some ports for dancing to island music. Unfortunately, they often have to pack up early when the ships are ready to sail. If your ship happens to stay late or overnight in port, you're free to dine ashore or join crew members in one of their favorite watering holes.

SV *Legacy* is the only ship in the fleet that has passed the stringent United States Coast Guard inspection and, as a result, is the only Windjammer ship that schedules cruises from the U.S. mainland. All ships comply with international safety standards; only SV *Legacy* also complies with 1966 fire-safety standards.

Food
Plentiful and filling, food is acceptable and sometimes excellent, but the easy camaraderie is the focus of meal times. Pastries and coffee are available on deck at sunrise before breakfast is served in the dining salon. Buffet lunches are set up on deck, weather permitting, and sit-down dinners consist of salads, a choice between two entrées, side dishes, desserts, and free-flowing white and red table wines at no charge. Vegetarian and health-conscious meals are available upon request. When the weather cooperates, there's usually one dinner barbeque on deck, and afternoon beach picnics are held on certain islands.

There is no room service on any of the ships, but if you are feeling under the weather, the cook might take pity on you and send a bowl of soup to your cabin.

Fitness & Recreation
These are not frou-frou ships (translation: big, white, conventional cruise liners) and have no gyms, spas, or salons. Serious exercise is stair-climbing (translation: don't expect elevators, either) and swimming, either at the beaches or sometimes right from the ship (translation: no swimming pools or hot tubs). For more vigorous workouts, soft-adventure shore excursions feature activities such as biking, hiking, kayaking, and snorkeling. Leave your own gear at home—a mask, snorkel, and fins can be rented for $25 a week.

Noteworthy

■ Bring your blanket and pillow up on deck if you want to sleep under the stars.

■ Barefoot is preferred, but if you must wear shoes, make sure the soles are appropriate. Topsider-style boat shoes are best.

■ You can swap books with other passengers, but there's not much in the way of reading materials on board.

Top: Everyone can take a turn at the ship's wheel.
Bottom: Sunning and simple diversions

5

WINDJAMMER BAREFOOT CRUISES

Top: Coral reefs
Middle: Casual dining
Bottom: Masquerade as a pirate

Your Shipmates

Active, unpretentious, adventurous singles, couples, and families of all ages are likely to be your mates on a Windjammer tall ship. Singles-only theme cruises guarantee a balance between the sexes, but you have to arrange your own romance.

These are not ships for physically challenged travelers; there are no elevators, ramps, cabins, or bathrooms with wheelchair accessibility. Shore launches can be difficult to navigate.

Dress Code

Dress is always casual, all the time. Shorts and T-shirts are the order of the day and night. Barefooting is taken seriously, and anyone dressing to impress just might be forced to walk the plank. According to Windjammer regulars, "If you have to check a bag at the airport, you've packed too much." You may want to get a pedicure before leaving home, but leave your flip-flops behind. Bare feet are preferred on board for safety reasons. Plan appropriately for activities such as hiking, when you will need sturdy shoes, or dinner ashore when men should respectfully wear long pants and women usually wear sundresses or slacks and top. Save your clean T-shirt for the captain's party. That's as close as you'll get to a formal night on board a Windjammer ship.

Junior Cruisers

In summer months there are water-sports programs for children and teens sailing on *Legacy* and *Polynesia* (a maximum of 20 children per ship). Counselors keep an eye on kids from ages 6 through 12 in the Junior Jammers program as they learn to snorkel (providing they can swim) and participate in games, skits, scavenger hunts, and even take a turn at the ship's helm.

In the Cadet Sailing program for teens 13 through 17, activities include snorkeling, diving, kayaking, and hiking, as well as Caribbean cultural experiences and tall ship sailing instructions.

CHOOSE WINDJAMMER BAREFOOT CRUISES IF:

❶ You wouldn't be caught dead on a frou-frou cruise ship.

❷ You enjoy active water sports, especially snorkeling and diving.

❸ You have always dreamed of being a pirate.

Service

Service is easy-going, friendly, and carried out in the warm "no problem, mon" air of the Caribbean islands that most crew members call home. You'll likely feel as if you are a member of the extended family by the end of the cruise.

Tipping

Gratuities are optional, but you may extend them the last day of the cruise, either in cash, which should be placed in an envelope and deposited in a designated box, or by charging them to your account. The recommended amount is $75 per passenger, per week. All tips are pooled and shared by the entire crew, with the exception of officers.

Past Passengers

For a $25 membership fee, past passengers receive the Windjammer Barefoot Cruises newsletter, notice of special discounts, and a $25 discount for booking two sailings back-to-back.

Good to Know

Fares for Windjammer cruises look pretty reasonable, and they are. But here's the scoop: count the length of the days and nights because they aren't all technically one-week sailings. However, the Stow-Away option offered for the night before official sailing day was a good deal, allowing you to board the evening before you sail, have dinner, and spend the night for $55 per person. Unfortunately, it's now going away—in a sense. With costs rising, Windjammer announced price increases with a twist. To offset higher fares, the line no longer charges for port fees or the Stow-Away night, which is more often than not unavailable.

5

WINDJAMMER BAREFOOT CRUISES

DON'T CHOOSE WINDJAMMER BAREFOOT CRUISES IF:

❶ Decorum is paramount to you. If someone suggests it, fellow passengers might even moon a big cruise ship.

❷ You have a preexisting or potentially serious medical condition. There's no well-equipped infirmary on board.

❸ You can't entertain yourself.

SV LEGACY

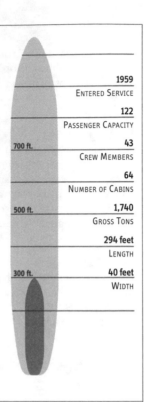

1959	ENTERED SERVICE
122	PASSENGER CAPACITY
43	CREW MEMBERS
64	NUMBER OF CABINS
1,740	GROSS TONS
294 feet	LENGTH
40 feet	WIDTH

History

Flagship of the Windjammer Barefoot Cruises fleet, the four-masted barquentine *Legacy* began sailing in 1959 as *France II*, a meteorological research vessel for the French government. After Windjammer acquired her in 1989, she was renovated with custom interiors, roomy accommodations, and up-to-date navigational systems.

Legacy blends polished wood-and-brass work below and teak decks above with relative creature comforts.

Restaurants

The air-conditioned dining room serves breakfast and dinner in a family-style setting. For early-risers, a Continental breakfast with Bloody Marys is set up on deck, and lunch is offered buffet-style on deck when weather permits. Snacks and predinner appetizers are served on deck with complimentary Rum Swizzles. Inexpensive red and white wines are included at dinner.

Accommodations

You won't find many of the amenities associated with traditional cruise ships on SV *Legacy*, although it's the roomiest and most comfortable vessel in the Windjammer fleet. There are 11 cabin categories, but with the exception of Burke's Berth, the nicely appointed Owner's cabin, and a few wood touches to warm the appearance of all others, they're still spartan. Burke's Berth has a double bed, small settee, vanity, entertainment center, bar, refrigerator, picture windows, and private bathroom. All other cabins are a mix of double beds and upper and lower berths and accommodate from one to four passengers. Some have windows, others portholes. All have private bathrooms with showers, and storage is adequate for the minimal wardrobe most passengers pack.

Cabin Size: As on any true sailing vessel of this vintage, the size and layout varies widely from cabin to cabin.

Top: Burke's Berth, the Owner's Quarters
Bottom: *Legacy*

In the Know

Legacy is a good choice for first-time Windjammers. Although it's a bit cushier in terms of facilities, none of the bold 'jamming attitude is missing. For reassurance, just take a good look at the carved figurehead: that's no mermaid—it's Cap'n Mike Burke himself with a beer in hand.

Fast Facts

- 4 masts
- Dining room
- Some refrigerators
- Bar
- Some children's programs (ages 6–17)
- No-smoking cabins

SV MANDALAY

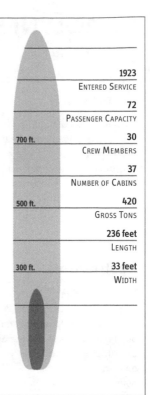

1923	ENTERED SERVICE
72	PASSENGER CAPACITY
30	CREW MEMBERS
37	NUMBER OF CABINS
420	GROSS TONS
236 feet	LENGTH
33 feet	WIDTH

700 ft.
500 ft.
300 ft.

History

Built in 1923 for financier E. F. Hutton and christened *Hussar* (the fourth of Hutton's yachts to bear that name), she was legendary for her first-rate appointments. Sold in the 1930s to a private owner, the barquentine was eventually acquired by Columbia University. While accumulating over 1¼ million mi beneath her sails during research expeditions to far-flung worldwide destinations, crews gathered evidence to confirm the theory of the continental drift. Windjammer acquired her in 1982.

Restaurants

The open-air dining room serves breakfast and dinner in a convivial family-style setting. Continental breakfast with Bloody Marys is set up on deck at sunrise, and lunch is offered buffet-style on deck when weather permits. Snacks and predinner appetizers are served on deck with complimentary Rum Swizzles. Inexpensive red and white wines are included at dinner.

Accommodations

You won't find many of the amenities associated with traditional cruise ships on SV *Mandalay*. There are four cabin categories with differing features; however, the most distinctive include traditional wood paneling. Admiral Suites, the Captain's Cabin, and Deck Cabins are on the main deck with doors that open to the outside; some have small refrigerators. Two Deck Cabins share a bath with shower, but have skylights as a sort of bonus. All other cabins are considered Standard, with upper and lower berths and private bathrooms with showers. Storage is adequate for the minimal wardrobe most passengers pack.

Cabin Size: As on any true sailing vessel of this vintage, size and layout vary widely from cabin to cabin. Selection strategy is necessary to determine the type of bed or berths that will satisfy your requirements and to find the roomiest or best location in that category.

In the Know

Bring your own beach towel. They're not provided, and borrowing ship's towels for use ashore is strongly discouraged, although there are no towel police.

No longer a rich man's yacht, *Mandalay* retains some polished woods but few traces of her former glory.

Fast Facts

- 3 masts
- Dining room
- Some in-cabin refrigerators
- Bar
- No-smoking cabins

Top: Deck cabin
Bottom: *Mandalay*

SV POLYNESIA

History

Built in 1938, and launched as *Argus,* this was one of the last vessels of the Portuguese Grand Banks fishing fleet. Never posh by any stretch of the imagination, the schooner was acquired by Windjammer in 1975 and christened *Polynesia.* She hosts Windjammer's popular singles cruises as well as the seasonal children's program.

Restaurants

The air-conditioned dining room serves breakfast and dinner in a family-style setting, but there's always Continental breakfast with Bloody Marys on deck; lunch is offered buffet-style on deck when weather permits. Snacks and predinner appetizers are served on deck with complimentary Rum Swizzles. Inexpensive red and white wines are included in the fare and poured freely at dinner.

700 ft.	**1938**
	ENTERED SERVICE
	112
	PASSENGER CAPACITY
	45
	CREW MEMBERS
	53
	NUMBER OF CABINS
500 ft.	**430**
	GROSS TONS
	248 feet
	LENGTH
300 ft.	**36 feet**
	WIDTH

Accommodations

The usual amenities associated with traditional cruise ships are absent on SV *Polynesia* unless you provide them yourself. In fact, with so many cabins below decks, she feels more cramped than the fleet's other vessels when full. There are four cabin categories with differing features; however, the nicest are those on the main deck—the Admiral Suites and Commodore Deluxe cabins, which have doors that open to the outside, private bathrooms with shower, and small refrigerators (in the suites only). Standard cabins have upper and lower berths and private bathrooms with showers. Three Ensign cabins are quads with two sets of upper and lower berths. Storage is adequate for the minimal wardrobe most passengers pack.

Cabin Size: As on any true sailing vessel of this vintage, size and layout vary widely from cabin to cabin. Selection strategy is necessary to determine the type of cabin to satisfy your requirements and to find the roomiest or best location in that category.

Top: Admiral Suite
Bottom: *Polynesia*

In the Know

Heads on board are the real deal in terms of nautical plumbing. Your sink and shower are controlled by a single water-conserving faucet that must be held to keep the water flowing. It may take some practice, but you'll get the hang of it quickly.

Fast Facts

- 4 masts
- Dining room
- Some refrigerators
- Bar
- Some children's programs (ages 6–17)
- No-smoking cabins

SV YANKEE CLIPPER

History

Christened the *Cressida* in 1927, the graceful German schooner was the only armor-plated private yacht in the world during her heyday. After the U.S. government commandeered the yacht as booty following World War II, George Vanderbilt purchased her for racing off the California coast, renaming her *Pioneer*. Once hailed as one of the fastest tall ships on the West Coast, she was rescued from the scrappers in 1965 by Windjammer and given a new lease on life as *Yankee Clipper*.

700 ft.	**1927** ENTERED SERVICE
	64 PASSENGER CAPACITY
	30 CREW MEMBERS
	31 NUMBER OF CABINS
500 ft.	**327** GROSS TONS
	197 feet LENGTH
300 ft.	**30 feet** WIDTH

Restaurants

The air-conditioned dining room serves breakfast and dinner in a family-style setting. Continental breakfast with Bloody Marys is set up on deck for early risers, and lunch is offered buffet-style on deck when weather permits. Snacks and predinner appetizers are served on deck with complimentary Rum Swizzles. Inexpensive red and white wines are included at dinner.

Accommodations

Like other Windjammer ships, SV *Yankee Clipper* doesn't boast the characteristics associated with traditional cruise ships. Four cabin categories offer differing features; however, the nicest are those on the main deck—the Admiral Suites, Captain's Cabins, and Deck Cabins, which have doors that open to the outside, either windows or portholes, and private bathrooms with shower. Small refrigerators are a bonus in the Admiral Suites and Captain's Cabins only. Standard cabins have upper and lower berths, portholes, and private bathrooms with showers. Storage is adequate for the minimal wardrobe most passengers pack.

Cabin Size: As on any true sailing vessel of this vintage, size and layout vary widely from cabin to cabin. Selection strategy is necessary to determine the type of bed or berths that will satisfy your requirements and to find the roomiest or best location in that category.

In the Know

Prepare to dry your hair outside using wind power. Although the hair dryer you bring from home will probably work, most people are so laid-back by the second day on board that they prefer going natural. A curling iron is fashion overkill.

Fast Facts

- 3 masts
- Dining room
- Some in-cabin refrigerators
- Bar
- No-smoking cabins

Top: Standard cabin
Bottom: *Yankee Clipper*

WINDSTAR CRUISES

Are they cruise ships with sails or sailing ships designed for cruises? Since 1986, these masted sailing yachts have filled an upscale niche. They often visit ports of call inaccessible to huge, traditional cruise ships and offer a unique perspective of the Caribbean.

Your Windstar ship at anchor

However, Windstar ships seldom depend on wind alone to sail. Nevertheless, if you're fortunate and conditions are perfect, as they sometimes are, the complete silence of pure sailing is heavenly. Stabilizers and computer-controlled ballast systems ensure no more than a mere few degrees of lean, making the ships reliably stable in heavy sea conditions.

WINDSTAR CRUISES
2101 Fourth Avenue
Suite 1150
Seattle, WA 98119
206/292-9606 or
877/827-7245
www.windstarcruises.com

Cruise Style: Luxury

When you can tear yourself away from the sight of thousands of yards of Dacron sail overhead, it doesn't take long to read the daily schedule of activities on a typical Windstar cruise. Simply put, there are very few scheduled activities. Diversions are for the most part social, laid-back, and impromptu. You can choose to take part in the short list of daily activities, borrow a book, game, or DVD from the library or do nothing at all. There's never pressure to join in or participate if you simply prefer relaxing with a fully-loaded iPod, which you can check out on board.

Evening entertainment is informal, with a small dance combo playing in the main lounges. Compact casinos offer games of chance and slot machines, but don't look for bingo or other organized contests. A weekly show by the crew is delightful; attired in the traditional costumes of their homelands, they present music and dance highlighting their cultures. You may also find occasional movies in the main lounges, which are outfitted with state-of-the-art video and sound equipment. Most passengers prefer socializing, either in the main lounge or an outdoor bar where Cigars Under the Stars attracts not only cigar aficionados, but stargazers as well.

Welcome aboard and farewell parties are hosted by the captain, and most passengers attend those as well as the nightly informational sessions regarding ports of call and activities that are presented by the activities staff during predinner cocktails.

A multi-million-dollar "Degrees of Difference" initiative enhanced each ship from stern to stern in 2006–07. The Yacht Club, which replaces the library on *Wind Surf*, is envisioned to be the social hub of the ship, with computer stations, a coffee bar, and a more expansive feel than the room it replaced. You will be able to join other passengers in comfortable seating around a large flat-screen TV to cheer on your favorite team during sporting events. In addition, all accommodations and bathrooms have been remodeled with updated materials; new weights and televisions were added to the gym; a couples massage room enhances the *Wind Surf* spa; the casual Veranda was expanded; the decks now have Balinese sun beds, and cooling mist sprayers are near the pools. Updates to *Wind Spirit* were not completed at this writing but are expected to be similiar to those on other ships.

Food

Since 1994, Windstar menus have featured Signature Cuisine, a collection of dishes originated by trendy West Coast chef and restaurateur Joachim Splichal and his Patina Group of bistro-style restaurants. Splichal integrates new recipes into the menus regularly in Windstar Cruises' main restaurants and also at Degrees, the alternative restaurant on *Wind Surf*. Splichal and his culinary team spend time aboard each ship with Windstar's executive chefs perfecting the menus and recipes.

In a nod to healthy dining, low-calorie and low-fat Sail Lite spa cuisine alternatives created by chef and cookbook author Jeanne Jones are prepared to American Heart Association guidelines. Additional choices are offered from the vegetarian menu.

Alcoholic beverages and soft drinks are not included in your cruise fare. Neither are the contents of the stocked minibar in your cabin.

A mid-cruise deck barbeque featuring grilled seafood and other favorites is fine dining in an elegantly casual alfresco setting. Desserts are uniformly delightful, and you'll want to try the bread pudding, a Windstar tradition available at the luncheon buffet. With daily tea and hot-and-cold hors d'oeuvres served several times during the afternoon and evening, no one goes hungry. Room service is always available, and you can place your order

Noteworthy

■ The shipboard computers that monitor wind velocity and direction also control heeling of the ships to less than six degrees.

■ Evening entertainment on Windstar usually includes a trio for dancing, a small casino, and stargazing.

■ Windstar ships have hot tubs and saltwater swimming pools in addition to retractable stern-mounted water-sports marinas.

Top: Cuisine by Chef Charlie Palmer
Bottom: Compass Rose Bar on
Wind Surf

Top: Backgammon on deck
Middle: Scuba with the dive masters
Bottom: *Wind Surf* stateroom

for dinner from the restaurant's menu during scheduled dining hours.

Fitness & Recreation

Most of the line's massage and exercise facilities are quite small, as would be expected on a ship that carries fewer than 150 passengers; however, *Wind Surf*'s WindSpa and fitness areas are unexpectedly huge. An array of exercise equipment, free weights, and basic fitness classes are available in the gym and Nautilus room. There is an extra charge for Pilates and yoga classes. A wide variety of massages, body wraps, and facial treatments are offered in the spa, while hair and nail services are available for women and men in the salon. Both spa and salon are operated by Steiner Leisure.

Stern-mounted water-sports marinas are popular with active passengers who want to kayak, windsurf, and water ski. Watery activities are free, including the use of snorkel gear that can be checked out for the entire cruise. The only charge is for diving; PADI-certified instructors offer a two-hour course for noncertified divers who want to try scuba and are also available to lead experienced certified divers on underwater expeditions. The dive teams take care of everything, even prepping and washing down the gear. If you prefer exploring on solid ground, sports coordinators are often at hand to lead an early-morning guided walk in port.

Your Shipmates

Windstar Cruises appeal to upscale professional couples in their late-30s to 60s and on up to retirees, who enjoy the unpretentious, yet casually sophisticated atmosphere, creative cuisine, and refined service.

Windstar's ships were not designed for accessibility, and are not a good choice for the physically challenged. Although every attempt is made to accommodate passengers with disabilities, *Wind Surf* has only two elevators, and the smaller ships have none. There are no staterooms or bathrooms with wheelchair accessibility, and gangways can be difficult to navigate, depending on the tide and angle of ascent. Service animals are permitted to sail if arrangements were made at the time of booking.

CHOOSE WINDSTAR CRUISES IF:

❶ You want a high-end experience, yet prefer to dress casually every night on your vacation.

❷ You love water sports, particularly scuba diving.

❸ You're a romantic: tables for two are plentiful in the dining rooms.

Dress Code

All evenings are country-club casual, and slacks with a jacket over a sweater or shirt for men and sundresses, skirts or pants with a sweater or blouse for women are suggested. Coats and ties for men are not necessary, but some male passengers prefer to wear a jacket with open-collar shirt to dinner.

Junior Cruisers

Windstar Cruises' unregimented atmosphere is adult-oriented, and children are not encouraged. Children less than two years of age are not allowed at all; older children traveling as the third passenger in a stateroom with their parents incur the applicable third person fare. No dedicated children's facilities are available, so parents are responsible for the behavior and entertainment of their children.

Service

Personal service and attention by the professional staff is the order of the day. Your preferences are noted and fulfilled without the necessity of reminders. Expect to be addressed by name within a short time of embarking.

Tipping

For many years, Windstar sailed under a "tipping not required" policy. Windstar has now changed that policy. A service charge of $11 per guest, per day (including children) is now added to each shipboard account. A 15% service charge is now added to all bar bills. All these proceeds are paid directly to the crew.

Past Passengers

Windstar guests who cruise once with the line are automatically enrolled in the complimentary Foremast Club. Member benefits include savings on many sailings in addition to the Advance Savings Advantage Program discounts, Internet specials, and a free subscription to the Foremast Club magazine.

Good to Know

Don't offer to help hoist the sails. They're operated by computer from the bridge and unfurl at the touch of a button in only two minutes. If you're interested in how everything works, take advantage of the open bridge policy and drop in for a chat with the captain.

5

WINDSTAR CRUISES

DON'T CHOOSE WINDSTAR CRUISES IF:

❶ You must have a spacious private balcony; there are none.

❷ You're bored unless surrounded by constant stimulation; activities are purposely low-key.

❸ You have mobility problems.

WIND SURF

Public Areas & Facilities

To make finding your way around simple, remember that all dining and entertainment areas are located on the top three decks, with restaurants located forward and indoor–outdoor bars facing aft. The main lounge and casino are mid-ship on Main Deck, as is the library. The fitness center is one deck higher. Most public areas have expansive sea views, although an exception is the WindSpa, which is tucked away aft on Deck 2 just forward of the water-sports platform and large sauna. Stairways are rather steep, but forward and aft elevators assure that moving about is relatively easy.

Don't expect nautical kitsch to predominate *Wind Surf*'s decor. Although the main lounge has an understated sailing-flag motif, all other public areas are simply designed for comfort, with deep seats and an abundance of polished teak. Fresh flower arrangements and sailing-related artwork are lovely touches shipwide.

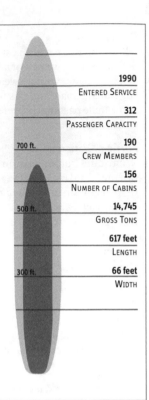

1990	ENTERED SERVICE
312	PASSENGER CAPACITY
190	CREW MEMBERS
156	NUMBER OF CABINS
14,745	GROSS TONS
617 feet	LENGTH
66 feet	WIDTH

700 ft.
500 ft.
300 ft.

WOW Factor

The sight of crisp white sails being raised against a clear, blue Caribbean sky is positively breathtaking.

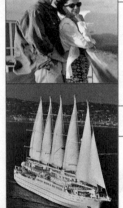

Restaurants

The formal restaurant has open-seating dining and is large enough to serve all passengers at once. For a more casual setting, the Veranda Café has indoor and outdoor seating for breakfast and lunch. An adjacent grill whips up cooked-to-order breakfast items and serves barbeque selections outdoors when weather permits. Degrees is a reservations-only, casual alternative.

What Works & What Doesn't

Superb service is delivered with a smile by waiters and stewards who greet you by name from almost the moment you board. Utter contentment is assured with such a high ratio of staff members to pamper passengers. The open bridge policy means you can stop by when you wish for a chat with the captain or his navigation staff; however, don't count on a warm reception at all times. They may be busier than they appear to be. Keep in mind that tightened security measures also might prevent you from stopping in for a visit.

Top: Sea views at the rail
Bottom: *Wind Surf* at sea

Accommodations

Layout–Amenities: *Wind Surf*'s ocean-view staterooms are a study in efficiency and clever design. Hanging lockers ("closets" to nonsailors) are generous. A small enclosed cabinet conceals a personal safe and an entertainment center features a flat-screen TV and DVD and CD players. The combination vanity–desk and bedside table have drawers for ample storage. A few standard cabins have upper fold-down Pullman berths for a third passenger.

Suites: Double the size of standard staterooms, suites were created by reconfiguring two standard cabins to create accommodations with twice as much storage, two bathrooms, and a generous sitting area with a sofa bed to offer a berth for a third passenger. The bedroom and sitting room can be separated by drawing a curtain for privacy. Two super-size bridge suites have living

and dining areas, a separate bedroom, walk-in closet, and bathroom with a whirlpool tub and separate shower.

Good to Know: Special touches in each stateroom and suite are fresh flowers, terry robes for use during the voyage, and bath toiletries. Teak-floor bathrooms are sensibly laid out and spacious enough for two people to actually share the space. All staterooms and suites are equipped with barware, a minibar, and hair dryer. Voltage is 220, so converters are needed for most small appliances. There are no cabins configured for wheelchair accessibility.

CABIN TYPE	SIZE (sq. ft.)
Suite	376
Ocean View	188
Bridge Suite	500

Fast Facts

- 6 passenger decks
- Specialty restaurant, dining room, buffet
- Wi-Fi, in-cabin safes, in-cabin refrigerators, in-cabin DVDs
- 2 pools
- Fitness classes, gym, hair salon, 2 hot tubs, sauna, spa
- 3 bars, casino, dance club, library
- Laundry service
- Computer room

5

WINDSTAR CRUISES

In the Know

Don't be alarmed if you go below deck and find the passageways blocked. Those watertight doors are normally tucked out of sight but must be closed when Wind Surf *is departing from (or arriving in) port.*

Favorites

Don't Miss: Teatime at the Compass Rose, where sweets are served in addition to the finger foods and a duo performs easy-listening tunes, is a highlight every afternoon.

Best Added Value: All cabins are outside and none have obstructed views.

Best Dessert: Hands-down, the best dessert is the signature bread pudding. Look for it daily at the lunch buffet.

Our Favorite Spot for a Nightcap: The deck behind the Compass Rose Bar is close enough to enjoy good service and music and yet far enough away for privacy.

Closest Thing to a Sports Bar: Smoke your cigars under the stars outside the Terrace Bar, which has a high-tech humidor and a flat-screen TV.

Most Cuddle-Worthy Hangouts: A hammock for two or a Balinese sun bed offer opportunities for relaxing with your loved one.

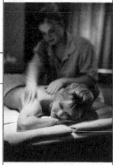

Unwind with a soothing massage.

WIND SPIRIT

Public Areas & Facilities

Comfort is the key element that ties *Wind Spirit*'s interiors together. Blue and cream, echoing hues of the sea and sandy beaches, predominate in the formal restaurant and cozy main lounge, where you'll find a tiny casino tucked into a corner. With its large windows and a skylight, the lounge is flooded with natural light during daytime hours.

Public spaces are proportionately small on such a diminutive vessel and feature yachtlike touches of polished wood, columns wrapped in rope, and nautical artwork shipwide as well as abundant fresh flower arrangements. The library contains books, movies to play in your cabin, and a computer for sending or receiving e-mail (although there's no Internet access at this writing).

Passenger accommodations and public areas are all found in the aft two-thirds of the ship, with dining and entertainment located on the top two decks.

1988	ENTERED SERVICE
148	PASSENGER CAPACITY
90	CREW MEMBERS
74	NUMBER OF CABINS
5,350	GROSS TONS
440 feet	LENGTH
52 feet	WIDTH

700 ft.

500 ft.

300 ft.

WOW Factor

No question, it's the sails that take your breath away—their first appearance is beguiling.

Top: Elegant dining in a casual atmosphere
Bottom: A sunny day at the pool

Restaurants

The formal restaurant offers open seating during scheduled hours and is large enough to serve all passengers at once. For a more casual setting, the Veranda Café has indoor and outdoor seating for breakfast and lunch. A grill whips up cooked-to-order breakfast items, and an outdoor barbeque when weather permits.

What Works & What Doesn't

Water babies, no matter what their age, naturally gravitate to the watersports platform when the ship is at anchor in calm water. Water toys and activities, including sail boats, sailboards, and kayaks—as well as water skiing and banana boat rides—are plentiful, and there's seldom a wait. In contrast, with so much time spent outside, the aft pool and hot tub are popular relaxation spots and apt to feel crowded. The pool bar has a permanent food station for Continental breakfast, afternoon tea, desserts, and evening canapés.

Accommodations

Layout–Amenities: *Wind Spirit*'s ocean-view staterooms are ingeniously designed for efficiency. Hanging lockers (closets) are generous and contain shoe racks and shelves for gear. A small enclosed cabinet conceals a personal safe, and an entertainment center includes a flat-screen TV and DVD and CD players. The combination vanity–desk and bedside table have drawers for ample storage.

Suites: A single Owner's Suite, the only premium accommodation on board, has a sitting area with a sofa bed to offer a berth for a third passenger.

Good to Know: Special touches in each stateroom are fresh flowers, terry robes for use during the voyage, and bath toiletries. The teak-floor bathrooms are big enough for two. All staterooms and suites are equipped with barware, a minibar, and hair dryer (voltage is standard 110 AC); portholes have deadheads, which can be closed in high seas. Ten staterooms have adjoining doors, and a limited number of standard cabins have upper fold-down Pullman berths for a third passenger. There are no cabins configured for wheelchair accessibility.

CABIN TYPE	SIZE (sq. ft.)
Suite	220
Ocean View	188

Fast Facts

- 5 passenger decks
- Dining room, buffet
- Wi-Fi, in-cabin safes, in-cabin refrigerators, in-cabin DVDs
- Pool
- Fitness classes, gym, hair salon, hot tub, sauna
- 2 bars, casino, dance club, library
- Laundry service
- Computer room

5

WINDSTAR CRUISES

In the Know

Slide out the ingenious hidden table in your stateroom cabinetry, and pull up a chair for relaxed room-service dining.

Favorites

Best Splurge: A scuba-diving adventure—the dive team rigs and maintains the gear so just sign up and be ready—allows even novices to participate after they complete a two-hour course.

Best Added Value: Each evening before dinner, most passengers gather in the lounge for really informative port talks while hot-and-cold appetizers are served by roaming waiters.

Our Favorite Spot for a Nightcap: Deck chairs by the pool, especially on a starry night when the sails are raised, are the best place to sit for a quiet drink.

Best Thoughtful Touch: Select a movie from the extensive DVD collection to watch in the privacy of your stateroom, and don't forget the popcorn. Just call room service.

Best Way to Beat the Heat: Mist sprayers near the pool offer a refreshing way to keep cool.

Wind Spirit at sea

Ports of Embarkation

WORD OF MOUTH

"I want to go on a birthday cruise in Jan. with a friend and another couple. Charleston, S.C. is the best departure port for all of us. Any cruise lines leave from there?"   —Minette

"Any ideas for a few hours in the port area—restaurants/walks/shopping? We'll be in [New Orleans] for a few days pre-cruise also, so this will be our last chance to enjoy and say good-bye to the city."   —CaliNurse

"We are taking a cruise out of Miami and wanted to stay in Miami for a day or 2 before the cruise. How far is Miami (by the beach) from the Port? Does anybody have any recommendations for hotels? "   —AimeeNC

MIAMI IS THE WORLD'S CRUISE CAPITAL, and more cruise ships are based here year-round than anywhere else. Caribbean cruises depart for their itineraries from several ports on either of Florida's coasts, as well as cities on the Gulf Coast and East Coast of the United States. Generally, if your cruise is on an Eastern Caribbean itinerary, you'll likely depart from Miami, Fort Lauderdale, Jacksonville, or Port Canaveral; short 3- and 4-day cruises to the Bahamas also depart from these ports. Most cruises on Western Caribbean itineraries depart from Tampa, Mobile, New Orleans, Galveston, or Houston, though some depart from Miami as well. Cruises from ports farther up the East Coast of the United States, including such ports as Baltimore, Maryland, Charleston, South Carolina, and even New York City, usually go to the Bahamas or Key West and often include a private-island stop or a stop elsewhere in Florida. Cruises to the Southern Caribbean might depart from Miami if they are 10 days or longer, but more likely they will depart from San Juan, Puerto Rico, or some other port deeper in the Caribbean.

Regardless of which port you depart from, air connections may prevent you from leaving home on the morning of your cruise or going home the day you return to port. Or you may wish to arrive early simply to give yourself a bit more peace of mind, or you may just want to spend more time in one of these interesting port cities. Many people choose to depart from New Orleans just to have an excuse to spend a couple of days in the city before or after their cruise.

PORT ESSENTIALS

Car Rental

🖪 Major Agencies **Alamo** ☎ 800/462-5266 ⊕ www.alamo.com. **Avis** ☎ 800/230-4898 ⊕ www.avis.com. **Budget** ☎ 800/527-0700 ⊕ www.budget.com. **Hertz** ☎ 800/654-3131 ⊕ www.hertz.com. **National Car Rental** ☎ 800/227-7368 ⊕ www.nationalcar.com.

SURCHARGES To avoid a hefty refueling fee, fill the tank just before you turn in the car, but be aware that gas stations near the rental outlet may charge more than those farther away. It's almost never a deal to buy the tank of gas that's in the car when you rent it; the understanding is that you'll return it empty, but some fuel usually remains. Surcharges may apply if you are under 25 or over 75 years old, if you want to add an additional driver to the contract, or if you want to drive over state borders or out of a specific radius from your point of rental. You'll pay extra for child seats (about $6 a day), which are compulsory for children under five, and usually for additional drivers (about $10 per day).

Dining

Unless otherwise noted, all prices are given in U.S. dollars. The following price categories are used in this book.

WHAT IT COSTS In US$				
$$$$	**$$$**	**$$**	**$**	**¢**
AT DINNER over $30	$20–$30	$12–$20	$8–$12	under $8

Prices are per person for a main course at dinner and do not include any service charges or taxes.

Lodging

Whether you are driving or flying into your port of embarkation, it is often more convenient to arrive the day before or to stay for a day after your cruise. Thus, we offer lodging suggestions for each port of embarkation.

The lodgings we list are convenient to the cruise port and the cream of the crop in each price category. We always list the facilities that are available, but we don't specify whether they cost extra; when pricing accommodations, always ask what's included. Properties are assigned price categories based on the range between their least expensive standard double room at high season (excluding holidays) and the most expensive. But if you find everything sold out or wish to find a more predictable place to stay, there are chain hotels at almost all ports of embarkation.

Assume that hotels operate on the **European Plan** (EP, with no meals) unless we specify that they use either the **Continental Plan** (CP, with a Continental breakfast), **Breakfast Plan** (BP, with a full breakfast), or the **Modified American Plan** (MAP, with breakfast and dinner). The following price categories are used in this book.

WHAT IT COSTS In US$				
$$$$	**$$$**	**$$**	**$**	**¢**
FOR 2 PEOPLE over $250	$175–$250	$120–$175	$70–$120	under $70

Prices are for a double room, excluding service and taxes.

CHARLESTON, SOUTH CAROLINA

Eileen Robinson Smith

Charleston looks like a movie set or an 18th-century etching brought to life. The spires and steeples of more than 180 churches punctuate her low skyline, and tourists ride in horse-pulled carriages that pass grandiose, centuries-old mansions and antique gardens brimming with heirloom plants. Preserved through the poverty following the Civil War, and natural disasters like fires, earthquakes, and hurricanes, much of Charleston's earliest public and private architecture still stands. And thanks to a rigorous preservation movement and strict Board of Architectural Review, the city's new structures blend with the old ones. If you're embarking your cruise ship here, it's worth coming a few days early to explore the historic downtown and to eat in one of the many superb restaurants. In late spring, plan in advance for the Spoleto U.S.A. Festival. For 30 memorable years, arts patrons have gathered to enjoy both international and regional concerts, dance performances, operas, improv shows, and plays at creative venues citywide.

Essentials

HOURS Most shops are open from 9 or 10 AM to at least 6 PM, but some are open later. A new city ordinance requires bars to close by 2 AM.

INTERNET While almost all hotels (and even B&Bs) offer some kind of Internet service, Internet cafés are rare in the Charleston historic district; however, many coffee shops, including all the local Starbucks, offer Wi-Fi for a fee.

VISITOR INFORMATION The **Charleston Visitor Center** (✉ 375 Meeting St., Upper King ⌖ 423 King St., 29403 ☎ 843/853–8000 or 800/868–8118 ⊕ www.charlestoncvb.

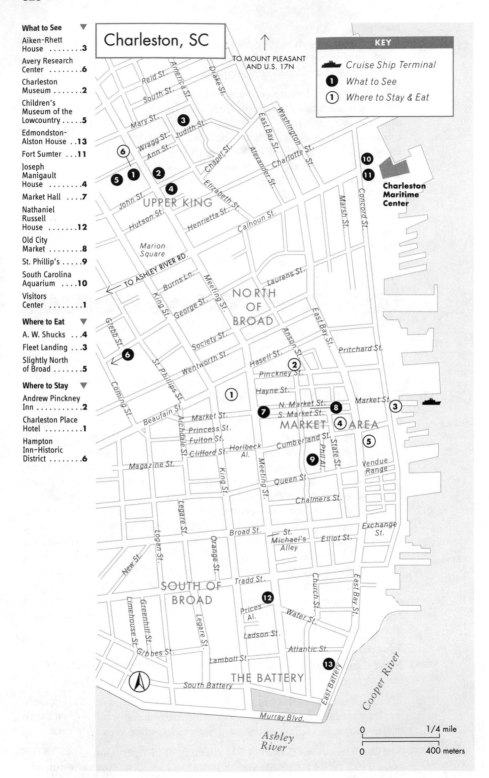

Charleston, SC

↑
TO MOUNT PLEASANT
AND U.S. 17N

KEY

Cruise Ship Terminal

❶ What to See

① Where to Stay & Eat

Charleston
Maritime
Center

UPPER KING

Marion
Square

TO ASHLEY RIVER RD.

NORTH
OF
BROAD

MARKET AREA

Vendue
Range

SOUTH OF
BROAD

THE BATTERY

Cooper River

Ashley
River

0   1/4 mile

0   400 meters

com), which is one of the most handsome in the country, is housed in a marvelous restoration of a 19th-century railroad warehouse with local artwork and multi-media displays of Charleston. It has information on Kiawah Island, Seabrook Island, Mount Pleasant, North Charleston, Edisto Island, Summerville, and the Isle of Palms, too.

The Cruise Port

Cruise ships embarking in Charleston leave from the Union Pier Terminal, which is in Charleston's historic district. If you are driving, however, and need to leave your car parked, take the East Bay Street exit off the new, majestic Arthur Ravenel, Jr. Bridge on I–17 and follow the signs to the Charleston Aquarium.

🚢 **Port of Charleston** ⊠ 196 Concord St., Market area, at foot of Market St. ☎ 843/ 577–8776 for Union Pier ⊕ www.port-of-charleston.com.

AIRPORT TRANSFERS
Several cab companies service the airport, including the new Charleston Black Cab Company, which operates a fleet of genuine London cabs with uniformed drivers and costs no more than calling a regular cab—about $24.50 to downtown. Airport Ground Transportation arranges shuttles, which cost $14 per person to the downtown area, $25 round-trip. CARTA's bus #11, a public bus, now goes to the airport for a mere $1.25; it leaves downtown from the Meeting/Mary St. parking garage every 50 minutes, starting at 5:45 AM until 11:09 PM.

PARKING
An outdoor parking lot is near the pier and patrolled 24 hours a day. Parking costs $15 per day ($105 per week) for regular vehicles, $25 per day ($150 per week) for RVs or other vehicles more than 20 feet in length. You pay in advance, but credit cards are not accepted. A free shuttle bus takes you to the cruise-passenger terminal. Be sure to drop your large luggage off at Union Pier before you park your car; only carry-on size luggage is allowed on the shuttle bus. If you have any bags larger than 22 inches by 14 inches, they will have to be checked before you park. You'll need your cruise tickets to board the shuttle bus.

CHARLESTON BEST BETS

- **Viewing Art.** The city is home to more than 133 galleries, so you'll never run out of places to see world-class art. The Charleston Museum and dozens of others add to the mix.

- **The Battery.** The views from the point—both natural and man-made—are the loveliest in the city. Look west to see the harbor; to the east you'll find elegant Charleston mansions.

- **Historic Homes.** Charleston's preserved 19th-century houses, including the Nathaniel Russell House, are highlights.

Exploring Charleston

Numbers in the margin correspond to points of interest on the Charleston map.

The heart of the city is on a peninsula, sometimes just called "downtown" by the nearly 60,000 residents who populate the area. Walking Charleston's peninsula is the best way to get to know the city. If you don't wish to walk, there are bikes, pedicabs, and trolleys. Street parking is irksome, as meter readers are among the city's most efficient public servants.

Parking garages, both privately and publicly owned, charge around $1.50 an hour.

❸ Aiken-Rhett House. This stately 1818 mansion still has its original wallpaper, paint colors, and some of its furnishings. The kitchen, slave quarters, and work yard are much as they were when the original occupants lived here, making this one of the most complete examples of urban slave life of the period. Confederate general P. G. T. Beauregard made his headquarters here during his 1864 Civil War defense of Charleston. ⊠ *48 Elizabeth St., Upper King* ☎ *843/723–1159* ⊕ *www. historiccharleston.org* 🎟 *$10, $16 with admission to Nathaniel Russell House* ⊗ *Mon.–Sat. 10–5, Sun. 2–5.*

❻ Avery Research Center for African-American History and Culture. This center, part museum and part archives, was once a school for freed slaves. Collections include slavery artifacts (manacles, bills of sale, slave badges), old manuscripts, and African artifacts with ties to Lowcountry slaves. A riveting mural chronicles the Middle Passage—the journey slaves made from Africa to Charleston's shores. The free tour includes a brief film. Although it's a short five-block walk from the Cistern quad, Avery Research Center is affiliated with the College of Charleston. ⊠ *125 Bull St., College of Charleston Campus* ☎ *843/953–7609* ⊕ *www.cofc.edu* 🎟 *Free* ⊗ *Weekdays noon–5, mornings by appointment.*

★ ☾ ❷ Charleston Museum. Founded in 1773, the country's oldest museum is now housed in a contemporary complex. The museum's decorative arts holdings and its permanent Civil War exhibit are extraordinary. There are more than 500,000 items in the collection. In addition to displaying Charleston silver, fashions, toys, snuffboxes, and the like, there are exhibits relating to natural history, archaeology, and ornithology. The 1803, Federal-style **Joseph Manigault House,** owned by the Charleston Museum, is across the street. George Washington once slept at the 1772 **Heyward-Washington House,** which is seven blocks southeast of its parent, the Charleston Museum. ⊠ *360 Meeting St., Upper King* ☎ *843/722–2996* ⊕ *www. charlestonmuseum.org* 🎟 *$10* ⊗ *Mon.–Sat. 9–5, Sun. 1–5.*

★ ☾ ❺ Children's Museum of the Lowcountry. Daily art projects and other exhibits promote hands-on science, culture, and creativity for toddlers up to 12-year-olds. Kids can climb on a replica of a local shrimp boat, play in exhibits that show how water evaporates from and returns to the Lowcountry, wander the inner workings of a medieval castle, and more. This kids' museum is both exceptional and fun. ⊠ *25 Ann St., Upper King* ☎ *843/ 853–8962* ⊕ *www.explorecml.org* 🎟 *$7* ⊗ *Tues.–Sat. 10–5, Sun. 1–5.*

⓭ Edmonston-Alston House. First built in 1825 in late-Federal style, the Edmondston-Alston House was transformed into the imposing Greek Revival structure you see today during the 1840s. Tours of the home—furnished with antiques, portraits, Piranesi prints, silver, and fine china—are informative and in-depth. The home commands an excellent view of Charleston Harbor. ⊠ *21 E. Battery, South of Broad* ☎ *843/ 722–7171* ⊕ *www.middletonplace.org* 🎟 *$10* ⊗ *Tues.–Sat. 10–4:30, Mon. 1:30–4:30.*

★ ☙ ⑪ **Ft. Sumter National Monument.** On a man-made island in Charleston Harbor, Confederate forces fired the first shot of the Civil War on April 12, 1861. After a 34-hour bombardment, Union forces surrendered and Confederate troops occupied Sumter, which became a symbol of Southern resistance. The Confederacy held the fort, despite almost continual bombardment, from August 1863 to February 1865; when it was finally evacuated, the place was a heap of rubble. Today, the National Park Service oversees the Ft. Sumter National Monument complex. The **Ft. Sumter Liberty Square Visitor Center,** next to the South Carolina Aquarium, contains exhibits on the Civil War. You reach the island by ferry; there are six ferry crossings daily from mid-March through mid-August, some leaving from Liberty Square, others from Patriots Point. The schedule is abbreviated from mid-August to mid-March. Check the Spirit Line Cruises web site for details. ⊠ *340 Concord St., Upper King* ☎ *843/577–0242 for Liberty Square Visitor Center* ⊕ *www.nps.gov/fosu or www.spiritlinecruises.com* 🎟 *Fort free; ferry $14* ⊙ *Apr.–early Sept., daily 10–5:30; early Sept.–Mar., daily 10-4.*

❹ **Joseph Manigault House.** A National Historic Landmark and an outstanding example of Federal architecture, this home was designed by Charleston architect Gabriel Manigault in 1803 and is noted for its carved-wood mantels, elaborate plasterwork, and garden "folly." Furnishings are antiques from France, England, and Charleston; the pieces of rare tricolor Wedgwood are noteworthy. ⊠ *350 Meeting St., Upper King* ☎ *843/722–2996* ⊕ *www.charlestonmuseum.org* 🎟 *$10* ⊙ *Mon.–Sat. 10–5, Sun. 1–5.*

❼ **Market Hall.** Built in 1841, this imposing landmark was modeled after the Temple of Nike in Athens. The hall contains the **Confederate Museum,** in which the United Daughters of the Confederacy preserve and display flags, uniforms, swords, and other Civil War memorabilia. ⊠ *188 Meeting St., Market area* ☎ *843/723–1541* 🎟 *$5* ⊙ *Tues.–Sat. 11–3:30.*

⑫ **Nathaniel Russell House.** One of the nation's finest examples of Adam-style architecture, the Nathaniel Russell House was built in 1808. The interior is distinguished by its ornate detailing, its lavish period furnishings, and the "free-flying" circular staircase that spirals three stories with no visible support. The garden is well worth a stroll. ⊠ *51 Meeting St., South of Broad* ☎ *843/724–8481* ⊕ *www.historiccharleston.org* 🎟 *$7, garden free, combination ticket with Aiken-Rhett House $14* ⊙ *Mon.–Sat. 10–5, Sun. 2–5.*

☙ ❽ **Old City Market.** Although often called the Slave Market, slaves were not sold here. Instead, it's where household slaves once shopped for produce and fish. Today, stalls are lined with restaurants and shops selling children's toys, Charleston souvenirs, crafts, praline candies, and more. Local "basket ladies" weave and sell sweetgrass, pine-straw, and palmetto-leaf baskets—a craft passed down through generations from their West African ancestors. ⊠ *N. and S. Market Sts. between Meeting and E. Bay Sts., Market area* ⊙ *Daily 9–dusk.*

❾ **St. Philip's (Episcopal) Church.** The namesake of Church Street, this graceful late-Georgian building is the second on its site: the congregation's first building burned down in 1835 and was rebuilt in 1838. During the Civil

War, the steeple was a target for shelling; one Sunday a shell exploded in the churchyard—the minister continued his sermon. Afterward, the congregation gathered elsewhere for the duration of the war. Notable Charlestonians (like John C. Calhoun) can be found in the graveyard, which flanks the church. ⊠ *146 Church St., Market area* ☎ *843/722–7734* ⊕ *www.stphilipschurchsc.org* ⊙ *Church: weekdays 9–11 and 1–4; cemetery: daily 9–4.*

★ ⊙ ⑩ **South Carolina Aquarium.** The 380,000-gallon Great Ocean Tank has the tallest aquarium window in North America. Exhibits display more than 10,000 living organisms. You travel through the five major regions of the Southeast Appalachian Watershed as found in South Carolina, from the mountains to the ocean. Little ones can pet stingrays at one touch tank and horseshoe crabs and conch at another. The adjacent Fountain Walk has fun shops and restaurants, including the Toucan Reef. The views here of the new Arthur Ravenel Bridge (North America's longest cable-stayed bridge) and the harbor's fascinating marine activity, are ideal photo ops. ⊠ *100 Aquarium Wharf, Upper King* ☎ *843/720–1990 or 800/722–6455* ⊕ *www.scaquarium.org* ⊠ *$16* ⊙ *Mid-Apr.–mid-Aug., Mon.–Sat. 9–5, Sun. noon–5; mid-Aug.–mid-Apr., Mon.–Sat. 9–4, Sun. noon–4.*

❶ **Charleston Visitors Center.** The center's 20-minute film is a fine introduction to the city. The first 30 minutes are free at the parking lot; after that it is $1.50 per hour. Garage parking here is $1.50 per hour, $10 a day. ⊠ *375 Meeting St., Upper King* ☎ *843/853–8000 or 800/868–8118* ⊕ *www.charlestoncvb.com* ⊠ *Free* ⊙ *Apr.–Aug., daily 8:30–5:30; Sept.–Mar., Mon.–Sat. daily 8:30–5.*

Shopping

King Street is the major shopping street in town. Lower King (from Broad to Market streets) is lined with high-end antiques dealers. Middle King (from Market to Calhoun streets) is a mix of national chains like Banana Republic and Pottery Barn. Upper King (from Calhoun Street to Cannon street) is the up-and-coming area where fashionistas like the alternative shops like Putumayo. **Shops at Charleston Place** (⊠ 130 Market St., Market Area) is home to Gucci, Caché, St. John, Godiva, The Limited, Express, Brookstone, and more. The Market area is a cluster of shops and restaurants centered around the **Farmers' Market** (⊠ E. Bay and Market Sts., Market area). Sweetgrass basket weavers work here, and you can buy the resulting wares.

Where to Eat

$–$$ ✕ **A.W. Shucks.** The State Street door opens to a typical Lowcountry oyster bar, as earthy as pluff-mud, with the freshest shellfish outside of water. The South Market Street exit drops down to the deck, a perfect location to people-watch the market activity. A centuries-old warehouse, this family restaurant is where you can still get a root beer float, and local specialties like shrimp and grits, and a steam pot—a bountiful cauldron of shellfish, crab legs, smoked sausage, potatoes, and corn on the cob. T-shirts that read "Big Mussels, Great Legs & Fantastic Tails" could be your funky souvenir gift. ⊠ *70 State St.* 843/723–1151 ⊟ AE.

★ ✕ **Slightly North of Broad.** This former
$$$–$$$$ warehouse with brick-and-stucco walls
has a chef's table that looks directly
into the open kitchen. It's a great place
to perch, as Chef Frank Lee, who wears
a baseball cap instead of a toque, is one
of the city's culinary characters. Known
for his talent in preparing game, his
venison is exceptional. Many of the
items come as small plates, which make them perfect for sharing. The
braised lamb shank with a ragout of white beans, arugula and a red demi-
glace is divine and is an example of a "main" on the $9.95 Express Lunch,
a phenomenal value. ✉ *192 East Bay St.* ☎ *843/723–3424* ▭ *AE, D,
MC, V* ☺ *No lunch Sat., Sun.*

WAITER KNOWS BEST

If your waiter frowns when you
make a menu selection, follow his
lead. He knows what's good on
the dining room menu and what
isn't.

¢–$ ✕ **Fleet Landing.** This is one fun place, smack in the marsh within sight of
the cruise-ship dock, so there's little danger of being left behind. A youth-
ful redo of a former Navy depot, there are B&W pics from the 1940s and
orange life preservers as art. You can sit out on the deck and—to the envy
of the circling seagulls—ingest the freshest of bivalves. On Saturdays, buck-
ets of steamed oysters are $8.95; a guitarist sings southern rock at Sun-
day brunch. The menu includes classic Charleston dishes like blue crab
cakes, fried platters, and *moderne* salads like fried oysters atop warm spinach
with a bacon vinaigrette; there's always pecan pie. ✉ *186 Concord St.*
☎ *843/722–8100* ▭ *AE, D, MC, V.*

Where to Stay

While the city's best hotels and B&Bs are in the historic district, most of
them do not have free parking. If you stay outside of downtown in a chain
hotel, you will give up much in charm and convenience but pay signifi-
cantly less. High-season rates are traditionally March through May and
September through November.

★ **$$$$** 🏨 **Charleston Place Hotel.** Even casual passersby enjoy gazing up at the hand-
blown Moreno glass chandelier in the hotel's open lobby, clicking across
the Italian marble floors, and admiring the antiques from Sotheby's. A
gallery of upscale shops complete the ground floor offerings. Rooms are
furnished with period reproductions. The impeccable service is what you
would expect from an Orient-Express property, particularly on the Club
Level. A truly deluxe day spa, with an adjacent fitness room, has an invit-
ing indoor pool illuminated by skylights. ✉ *205 Meeting St., Lower King,
29401* ☎ *843/722–4900 or 800/611–5545* 🖶 *843/722–0728* ⊕ *www.
charlestonplacehotel.com* ➷ *400 rooms, 42 suites* ⚙ *In room: safe,
dial-up. In hotel: 2 restaurants, room service, bar, gym, spa, concierge
floor, public Internet, parking (fee), no-smoking rooms* ▭ *AE, D, DC,
MC, V* ⦿ *EP.*

$$$ 🏨 **Hampton Inn–Historic District.** Hardwood floors and a fireplace in the lobby
of what was once an 1800s warehouse help elevate this chain hotel a bit
above the rest. Spindle posts on the headboards give guest rooms a little personality. Rooms are not large but have little perks like coffeemak-
ers. The location is perfect for exploring downtown. ✉ *373 Meeting St.,
Upper King 29403* ☎ *843/723–4000 or 800/426–7866* 🖶 *843/722–3725*

⊕ *www.hamptoninn.com* ⤳ *166 rooms, 5 suites* ↺ *In room: refriger-ator (some), dial-up. In hotel: pool, laundry facilities, laundry service, public Internet, parking (fee), no-smoking rooms* ⊟ *AE, D, DC, MC, V* ⊠|◯| *BP.*

$$–$$$ ⊡ **Andrew Pinckney Inn.** The lobby of this boutique inn has a homey am-bience that blends South Carolina and the West Indies. The two-story town-house suites, which sleep four, are ideal for longer stays. A heavenly breakfast with fresh-baked pastries and biscuits with sausage gravy is taken on its rooftop, which overlooks the church spires. It's in the bustling mar-ket area, so ask for an interior room. ⊠ *40 Pinckney St., 29401* ☏ *843/937–8800 or 800/505–8983* ⊟ *843/937–8810* ⊕ *www.andrewpinckneyinn. com* ⤳ *41 rooms, 3 town houses, 1 suite* ↺ *In hotel: refrigerator (some), dial-up, Wi-Fi. In hotel: public Internet, parking (fee), no-smoking* ⊟ *AE, MC, V* ⊠|◯| *BP.*

FORT LAUDERDALE, FLORIDA

Lynne Helm

In the 1960s, Fort Lauderdale's beachfront was lined with T-shirt shops interspersed with quickie-food outlets, and downtown consisted of a lone office tower, some dilapidated government buildings, and motley other structures waiting to be razed. Today the beach is home to upscale shops and restaurants, while downtown has exploded with new office and lux-ury residential development. The entertainment and shopping areas—Las Olas Boulevard, Las Olas Riverfront, and Himmarshee Village—are thriving. And Port Everglades is giving Miami a run for its money in pas-senger cruising, with a dozen cruise-ship terminals hosting more than 20 cruise ships with some 3,000 departures annually. A captivating shore-line with wide ribbons of sand for beachcombing and sunbathing makes Fort Lauderdale and Broward County a major draw for visitors and often tempts cruise-ship passengers to spend an extra day or two in the sun. Fort Lauderdale's 2-mi (3-km) stretch of unobstructed beachfront has been further enhanced with a sparkling promenade designed more for the pleasure of pedestrians than vehicles.

Essentials

HOURS Many museums close on Monday.

INTERNET If you have your own laptop, Broward County has created a fairly extensive wireless broadband network with nu-merous Wi-Fi hot spots in downtown Fort Lauderdale, providing free Internet access to anyone using suitably equipped laptops. There's also free Wi-Fi in the airport.

BOAT TOURS **Water Bus** (☏ 954/467–6677 ⊕ www. watertaxi.com), also known as Water Bus, provides service along the Intra-coastal Waterway in Fort Lauderdale between the 17th Street Causeway and Oakland Park Boulevard daily from 10:30 AM until midnight.

FORT LAUDERDALE BEST BETS

■ **The Beach.** With more than 20 mi of ocean shoreline, don't miss soaking up the scene at Greater Fort Lauderdale's best beaches including those along Lauderdale-by-the-Sea and Fort Lauderdale.

■ **The Everglades.** Take in the wild reaches in or near the Ever-glades with an airboat ride. Mosquitos are friendly, so arm yourself accordingly.

■ **The Riverwalk.** This is a great place to stroll before and after performances, dinner, libations, and other entertainment.

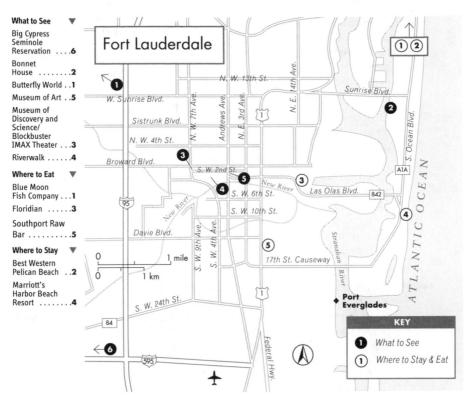

VISITOR **Chamber of Commerce of Greater Fort Lauderdale** (✉ 512 N.E. 3rd Ave., Fort
INFORMATION Lauderdale 33301 ☎ 954/462–6000 ⊕ www.ftlchamber.com). **Greater
Fort Lauderdale Convention & Visitors Bureau** (✉ 100 E. Broward Blvd., Suite
200, Fort Lauderdale 33301 ☎ 954/765–4466 ⊕ www.sunny.org). **Hollywood Chamber of Commerce** (✉ 330 N. Federal Hwy., Hollywood 33020
☎ 954/923–4000 ⊕ www.hollywoodchamber.org).

The Cruise Port

Port Everglades, Fort Lauderdale's cruise port (nowhere near the Everglades, but happily near the beach and less than 2 mi (3 km) from the
airport), is among the world's largest, busiest ports. It's also the straight-
est, deepest port in the southeastern United States, meaning you'll be out
to sea in no time flat once your ship sets sail. A few words of caution:
Schedule plenty of time to navigate the port from the airport, your hotel,
or wherever else you might be staying, especially if you like to be among
the first to embark for your sailing. Increased security combined with
increased traffic, larger parking facilities, construction projects, roadway
improvements, and other obstacles mean the old days of popping over
to Port Everglades and running up a gangplank in the blink of an eye
are history.

If you are driving, there are two entrances to the port. One is from 17th
Street, west of the17th Street Causeway Bridge, turning south at the traffic light onto Eisenhower Boulevard. Or to get to the main entrance, take
either State Road 84, running east–west, to the intersection of Federal

Highway and cross into the port, or take I–595 East straight into the Port (I–595 becomes Eller Drive once inside the Port).

🚢 **Port Everglades** ✉1850 Eller Dr. ☎954/523–3404 ⊕ www.porteverglades.org.

AIRPORT TRANSFERS
Fort Lauderdale–Hollywood International Airport is 4 mi (6 km) south of downtown and 2 mi (3 km) (about 5 to 10 minutes) from the docks. If you haven't arranged an airport transfer with your cruise line, you can take a taxi to the cruise-ship terminals. The ride in a metered taxi costs about $12 to $15, depending on your departure terminal. Taxi fares are $4.50 for the first mile and $2.40 for each additional mile, and 40¢ per minute for waiting time. If you are staying over, Airport Express provides limousine service to all parts of Broward County; fares to most Fort Lauderdale beach hotels are in the $25 range

> **IT'S A GIRL**
>
> Even as far back as ancient times, mariners have traditionally referred to their ships as "she." To a seaman, a ship is as beautiful and comforting as his mother or sweetheart. You could say a good ship holds a special place in his heart.

PARKING
Two covered parking facilities close to the terminals are Northport (with 2,500 spaces, expanding to 4,250) and Midport (for 2,000 cars). Use the Northport garage if your cruise leaves from Piers 1, 2, or 4; use Midport if your cruise leaves from Piers 18, 19, 21, 22/24, 25, 26, 27, or 29. The cost is $2 for the first hour, $5 for one to five hours, or $12 per day for either garage ($15 for oversized vehicles up to 40 feet). To save a few bucks on your parking tab, Park 'N Fly provides remote parking just outside Port Everglades, at the exit off I–595, with shuttle service assistance to all cruise terminals. Rates are $10 per day, $70 per week.

🚢 **Park 'N Fly** ✉ 2200 N.E. 7th Ave., at the Port Everglades exit off I–595 ☎ 954/779-1776 ⊕ www.pnf.com.

Exploring Fort Lauderdale

In a state where gaudy tourist zones often stand aloof from workaday downtowns, Fort Lauderdale is unusual in that the city exhibits consistency at both ends of the 2-mi (3-km) Las Olas corridor. The sparkling look results from efforts to thoroughly improve both beachfront and downtown.

Numbers in the margin refer to points of interest on the Fort Lauderdale map.

7 **Big Cypress Seminole Reservation.** Some distance from Fort Lauderdale's tranquil beaches, but worth the hour-plus drive, the reservation has two very different attractions. At the **Billie Swamp Safari,** experience the majesty of the Everglades firsthand. Daily tours of the wetlands and hammocks, where wildlife abounds, yield sightings of deer, water buffalo, bison, wild hogs, hawks, eagles, alligators, and occasionally the rare Florida panther. Animal and reptile shows are also offered. Eco-heritage tours are provided aboard motorized swamp buggies, and airboat rides are available, too. On the property is Swamp Water Café, which serves Seminole foods. ✉ *19 mi north of I–75 Exit 49* ☎ *863/983–6101 or 800/949–6101* ⊕ *www.seminoletribe.com* 🎫 *Free to visit the reservation's Seminole village; swamp buggy tour $25; combined ecotour, show, airboat ride $43* ☉ *Daily 8:30–5.*

Not far from the Billie Swamp Safari is the **Ah-Tha-Thi-Ki Museum,** whose name means "a place to learn, a place to remember." It is just that. The museum documents and honors the culture and tradition of the Seminole Tribe of Florida through artifacts, exhibits, and reenactments of rituals and ceremonies. The site includes a living-history Seminole village, nature trails, and a boardwalk through a cypress swamp. ⊠ *17 mi north of I–75 Exit 49* ☎ *863/902–1113* ⊕ *www.seminoletribe.com* ✉ *$6* ⊘ *Daily 9–5.*

② **Bonnet House.** A 35-acre oasis in the heart of the beach area, this subtropical estate, having survived a big hit from 2005's Hurricane Wilma, remains as a tribute to the history of Old South Florida. The charming home was the winter residence of the late Frederic and Evelyn Bartlett, artists whose personal touches and small surprises are evident throughout. Whether you're interested in architecture, artwork, or the natural environment, this is a special place. Be on the lookout for playful monkeys swinging from trees, a source of amusement at even some of the most solemn outdoor weddings on the grounds. Hours can vary, so call first. ⊠ *900 N. Birch Rd.* ☎ *954/563–5393* ⊕ *www.bonnethouse.org* ✉ *House tours $15, grounds only $9* ⊘ *Wed.–Fri. 10–3, weekends noon–4.*

6

☝ ① **Butterfly World.** As many as 80 butterfly species from South and Central America, the Philippines, Malaysia, Taiwan, and other Asian nations are typically found within this 3-acre site inside Tradewinds Park. A screened aviary called North American Butterflies is reserved for native species. The Tropical Rain Forest Aviary is a 30-foot-high construction, with observation decks, waterfalls, ponds, and tunnels where thousands of colorful butterflies flutter about. There's also a bug zoo. ⊠ *3600 W. Sample Rd., Coconut Creek* ☎ *954/977–4400* ⊕ *www.butterflyworld.com* ✉ *$18.95* ⊘ *Mon.–Sat. 9–5, Sun. 1–5.*

⑤ **Museum of Art.** In an Edward Larrabee Barnes–designed building that's considered an architectural masterpiece, this museum's impressive permanent collection has 20th-century European and American art, including works by Picasso, Calder, Dalí, Mapplethorpe, Warhol, and Stella, as well as a notable collection of works by celebrated Ashcan School artist William Glackens. When its building opened in 1986, the museum helped launch revitalization of the downtown district and nearby Riverwalk area, and it since has become a magnet for special traveling exhibits (with higher admission fees). ⊠ *1 E. Las Olas Blvd.* ☎ *954/763–6464* ⊕ *www. moafl.org* ✉ *$7 and up, depending on exhibit* ⊘ *Feb–mid-Dec., Fri.–Wed. 11–7, Thurs. 11–9; mid-Dec.–Jan., Fri.–Mon. and Wed. 11–7, Thurs. 11–9.*

☝ ③ **Museum of Discovery and Science/Blockbuster IMAX Theater.** The aim here is to show children—*and* adults—the wonders of science in an entertaining fashion. The 52-foot-tall Great Gravity Clock in the courtyard entrance lets arrivals know a cool experience awaits. Inside, exhibits include Living in the Everglades, a hands-on exhibit and nature trail telling about Florida's Everglades restoration; Kidscience, encouraging youngsters to explore the world around them; and Gizmo City, a look at how gadgets work. Florida Ecoscapes has a living coral reef as well as live bees, bats, frogs, turtles, and alligators. An IMAX theater, part of the complex, shows films (some 3-D) on a five-story-high screen. ⊠ *401 S.W.*

2nd St. ☎ *954/467–6637 museum, 954/463–4629 IMAX* ⊕ *www.mods. org* ✉ *Exhibits $9, IMAX Show $9, combo ticket $14* ۞ *Mon.–Sat. 10–5, Sun. noon–6.*

④ Riverwalk. Fantastic views and entertainment prevail on this lovely paved promenade on the New River's north bank, with more strolling area on the south bank winding past the courthouse. On the first Sunday of every month a jazz brunch attracts visitors. The walk has been extended 2 mi (3 km) on both sides of the beautiful urban stream, connecting the fa-cilities of the Arts and Science District.

Beaches

Fort Lauderdale's **beachfront** offers the best of all possible worlds, with easy access not only to a wide band of beige sand but also to restaurants and shops. For 2 mi (3 km) heading north, beginning at the Bahia Mar yacht basin, along Route A1A you'll have clear views, typically across rows of colorful beach umbrellas, to the sea and ships passing into and out of nearby Port Everglades. If you're on the beach, gaze back on an exceptionally graceful promenade.

Pedestrians rank above cars in Fort Lauderdale. Broad walkways line both sides of the beach road, and traffic has been trimmed to two gen-tly curving northbound lanes, where in-line skaters skim past slow-mov-ing cars. On the beach side, a low masonry wall doubles as an extended bench, separating sand from the promenade. At night the wall is ac-cented with ribbons of fiber-optic color, quite pretty when working, although outages are frequent. The most crowded portion of beach is between Las Olas and Sunrise boulevards. Tackier aspects of this one-time strip—famous for the springtime madness spawned by the film *Where the Boys Are*—are now but a fading memory, with the possible exception of the icon Elbo Room, an ever-popular bar at the corner of Las Olas and A1A.

North of the redesigned beachfront are another 2 mi (3 km) of open and natural coastal landscape. Much of the way parallels the Hugh Taylor Birch State Recreation Area, preserving a patch of primeval Florida.

Shopping

Las Olas Boulevard holds the city's best boutiques, plus top restaurants and art galleries, all along a beautifully landscaped street. When you're downtown, check out the Las Olas Riverfront, a shopping, dining, and entertainment complex.

Where to Eat

For price categories, *see* Dining at the beginning of this chapter.

★ ✕ **Blue Moon Fish Company.** Most tables have stellar views of the Intracoastal
$$$–$$$$ Waterway, but Blue Moon's true—if pricey—magic comes from the kitchen, where chefs Baron Skorish and Bryce Statham create moon-and-stars-worthy seafood dishes. Start with the raw bar, a sushi sampler, or the pan-seared fresh shucked oysters. Salads include a hydroponic bibb with hearts of palm, and entrée favorites include shiitake-mushroom-crusted halibut, big-eye tuna, or (for carnivores) veal tenderloin. Always book ahead for the Sunday champagne brunch. ✉ *4405 W. Tradewinds Ave.* ☎ *954/267–9888* ⊟ *AE, D, DC, MC, V.*

$–$$ ✕ **Floridian.** This Las Olas landmark with photos of Marilyn Monroe, Richard Nixon, and local notables past and present dishes up some of the best breakfasts around, with oversize omelets that come with biscuits, toast, or English muffins, plus a choice of grits or tomatoes to go with friendly, efficient service. With sausage or bacon on the side, the feast will make you forget about eating again soon. Count on savory sandwiches and hot platters for lunch and dinner. It's open 24 hours every day—even during hurricanes, as long as the power holds out. Feeling flush? Try the Fat Cat Breakfast (New York strip steak, hash browns or grits, toast, and a worthy champagne) or the Not-So-Fat-Cat, with the same grub and a lesser-quality vintage. ⊠ *1410 E. Las Olas Blvd.* ☎ *954/463–4041* ▭ *No credit cards.*

$–$$ ✕ **Southport Raw Bar.** If you're lodging near the port and prefer to stick within the area for meals, you can't go wrong at this unpretentious spot where the motto, seen on bumper stickers for miles around, proclaims "Eat fish, live longer, eat oysters, love longer, eat clams, last longer." Raw or steamed clams, raw oysters, and combos, along with peel-and-eat shrimp, are market-priced. Hoagies, subs, and burgers are the ticket for under $10. Sides range from Bimini bread to key lime pie, with conch fritters and beer-battered onion rings in between. Order wine by the bottle or glass and beer by the pitcher, bottle, or can. Eat outside overlooking a canal, or inside at booths, tables, or the bars, in front and back. Limited parking is free, and a shopping center lot is across the street. ⊠ *1536 Cordove Rd.* ☎ *954/525–2526* ▭ *MC, V.*

Where to Stay

Fort Lauderdale has a growing and varied roster of lodging options, from beachfront luxury suites to intimate B&Bs to chain hotels along the Intracoastal Waterway. If you want to be on the beach, be sure to mention this when booking your room, since many hotels advertise "waterfront" accommodations that are actually on inland waterways, not the beach.

For price categories, *see* Lodging at the beginning of this chapter.

$$–$$$$ ▥ **Marriott's Harbor Beach Resort.** Look down from the upper stories (14 in **Fodor'sChoice** all) at night, and this 16-acre property, on the secluded south end of Fort ★ Lauderdale Beach, shimmers like a jewel. Spacious guest rooms have rich tropical colors, lively floral art prints, and warm woods. Part of the hotel's big-budget renovation is the addition of a European spa. No other hotel on the beach gives you so many activity options. ⊠ *3030 Holiday Dr., 33316* ☎ *954/525–4000 or 800/222–6543* 🖷 *954/766–6152* ⊕ *www. marriottharborbeach.com* ⮑ *602 rooms, 35 suites* ⚴ *In-room: dial-up. In-hotel: 3 restaurants, bars, tennis courts, pools, gym, spa, beachfront, water sports, children's programs (ages 5–12)* ▭ *AE, D, DC, MC, V.*

𝒞 $$–$$$ ▥ **Best Western Pelican Beach.** On the north end of Fort Lauderdale beach **Fodor'sChoice** and under new ownership, this already lovely property has been entirely ★ transformed into a nonsmoking resort with a restaurant and lounge, an old-fashioned ice-cream parlor, and Fort Lauderdale's only Lazy River pool, allowing guests to float around a moatlike "river" via circulating current. For small fry, there's also a Funky Fish program. Of 156 rooms and one-bedroom suites in the new building, 117 are oceanfront. With the new building all aglow, the original Sun Tower is getting a makeover. ✉ *2000 N. Atlantic Blvd., 33305* ☎ *954/568–9431 or 800/525–6232* 🖷 *954/565–2622* ⊕ *www.pelicanbeach.com* ⮐ *180 rooms* ♿ *In-hotel: restaurant, bar, pools* ▭ *AE, DC, MC, V.*

GALVESTON, TEXAS

Robin Barr
Sussman

A thin strip of island in the Gulf of Mexico, Galveston is big sister Houston's beach playground—a year-round coastal destination just 50 mi away. Many of the first public buildings in Texas, including a post office, bank, and hotel, were built here, but most were destroyed in the Great Storm of 1900. Those that endured have been well preserved, and the Victorian character of the Strand shopping district and the neighborhood surrounding Broadway is still evident. On the Galveston Bay side of the island (northeast), quaint shops and cafés in old buildings are near the Seaport Museum, harbor-front eateries, and the cruise-ship terminal. On the Gulf of Mexico side (southwest), resorts and restaurants line coastal Seawall Boulevard. The 17-foot-high seawall abuts a long ribbon of sand and provides a place for rollerblading, bicycling, and going on the occasional surrey ride.

Galveston is a port of embarkation for cruises on Western Caribbean itineraries; some Panama Canal cruises leave from here as well. It's an especially popular port of embarkation for people living in the southeastern states who don't wish to fly to their cruise. Carnival, Royal Caribbean, and Princess have made Galveston the home port for their ships.

Essentials

HOURS Shops in the historic district are usually open until at least 7, but some stay open later. This is also the city's nightlife district, and that is hopping until late.

INTERNET The best place to check your e-mail is at your hotel. Most of the hotels in Galveston offer some kind of Internet service, though usually for a fee. If you have a laptop, the city has a relatively extensive network of free Wi-Fi zones, including several spots on The Strand.

VISITOR INFORMATION **Strand Visitors Center** (✉ 2215 Strand ⊕ www.galveston.com) has free brochures and maps and is open daily.

The Galveston Cruise Port

The relatively sheltered waters of Galveston Bay are home to the Texas Cruise Ship Terminal. It's only 30 minutes to open water from here. Driving south from Houston on I–45, you cross a long causeway before reaching the island. Take the first exit, Harborside Drive, left after you've crossed the causeway onto Galveston Island. Follow that for a few miles to the port. Turn left on 22nd Street (also called Kemper Street); there is a security checkpoint before you continue down a driveway. The drop-off point is set up much like an airport terminal, with pull-through lanes and curbside check-in.

🚩 **Port of Galveston** ✉ Harborside Dr. and 22nd St. ☎ 409/765–9321 ⊕ www.portofgalveston.com.

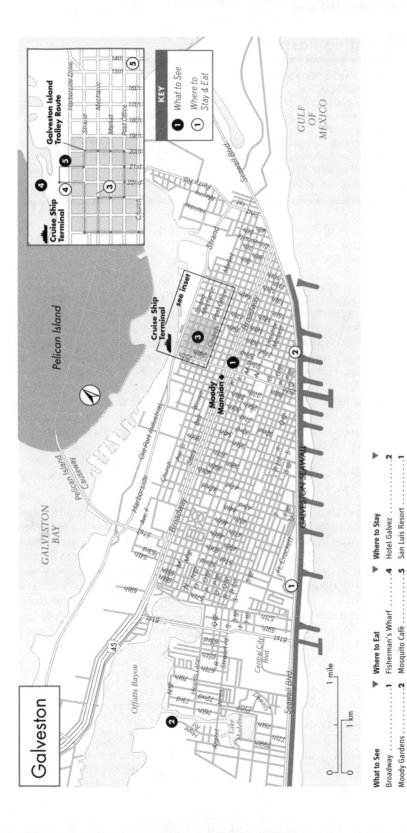

Galveston

GULF OF MEXICO

GALVESTON SEAWALL

Pelican Island

GALVESTON BAY

Pelican Island Causeway

Offatts Bayou

Moody Mansion ◆

Cruise Ship Terminal

see inset

Cruise Ship Terminal

Galveston Island Trolley Route

KEY

1 What to See

1 Where to Stay & Eat

0 — 1 km

0 — 1 mile

What to See ▼

Broadway **1**
Moody Gardens **2**
Pier 21 Theater **5**
The Strand **3**
Texas Seaport Museum **4**

Where to Eat ▼

Fisherman's Wharf **4**
Mosquito Café **5**

Where to Stay ▼

Hotel Galvez **2**
San Luis Resort **1**
Tremont House **3**

Boarding Passes

SIMPLE PAPER BOARDING passes seem almost as antiquated as the custom of tossing streamers at the sailaway. Environmental awareness nixed the streamers in the 1980s, while modern ID cards and scanning equipment record passenger comings and goings on the majority of cruise ships these days. With a swipe through a machine (it looks much like a credit card swipe at the supermarket), security personnel know who is on board the vessel at all times. On most large ships, passengers' images are recorded digitally at check-in so that when they leave for shore or reboard the ship, security screens display their likeness when their boarding passes are inserted into the scanning machines.

AIRPORT TRANSFERS
The closest airports are in Houston, 50 mi from Galveston. Houston has two major airports: Hobby Airport, 9 mi (15 km) southeast of downtown, and George Bush Intercontinental, 15 mi (24 km) northeast of the city.

Unless you have arranged airport transfers through your cruise line, you'll have to make arrangements to navigate the miles between the Houston airport at which you land and the cruise-ship terminal in Galveston. Galveston Limousine Service provides scheduled transportation (return reservations required) between either airport and Galveston hotels or the cruise-ship terminal. Hobby is a shorter ride (1 hour, $35 one-way, $60 round-trip), but Intercontinental (2 hours, $40 one-way, $70 round-trip) is served by more airlines, including international carriers. Taking a taxi allows you to set your own schedule but can cost twice as much (it's also important to note that there aren't always enough taxis to handle the demands of disembarking passengers, so you might have to wait after you leave your ship). Negotiate the price before you get in.
🛈 **Galveston Limousine Service** ☎ 800/640-4826 ⊕ www.galvestonlimousineservice. com.

PARKING
Parking is coordinated by the Port Authority. After you drop off your checked luggage and passengers at the terminal, you receive a color-coded parking pass from the attendant, with directions to a parking lot for your cruise departure. The lots are approximately ½ mi (1 km) from the terminal. Check-in, parking, and boarding are generally allowed four hours prior to departure. A shuttle bus (carry-on luggage only) runs back and forth between the lots and the terminal every 7 to 12 minutes on cruise arrival and departure days (be sure to drop off your luggage *before* you park the car). The lot is closed other days. Port Authority security checks the well-lighted, fenced-in lots every two hours; there is also a limited amount of covered parking. Parking for a 5-day cruise is $50 ($60 covered), 7-day is $70 ($80 covered), and 11-day is $85 ($100 covered). Cash, traveler's checks, and credit cards (Visa and MasterCard only) are accepted for payment, which must be made in advance.

Exploring Galveston

❶ **Broadway.** The late 1800s were the heyday of Galveston's port (before Houston's was dug out). Victorian splendor is evident in the meticulously restored homes of this historic district, some of which are now museums. If you're in town the first two weekends of May, don't miss the **Galveston Historic Homes Tour.** In addition to visiting the neighborhood's museums, you can walk through privately owned homes dating from the 1800s. For more information about area house museums or the tour, contact the Heritage Visitors Center. **Moody Mansion** (✉ 2618 Broadway ☎ 409/762–7668), the residence of generations of one of Texas's most powerful families, was completed in 1895. Tour its interiors of exotic woods and gilded trim filled with family heirlooms and personal effects. **Ashton Villa** (✉ 2328 Broadway ☎ 409/762–3933), a formal Italianate villa, was built in 1859 of brick. Look for the curtains that shielded the more modest Victorian guests from the naked Cupids painted on one wall. ✉ *2328 Broadway* ☎ *409/765–7834* ⊕ *www.galvestonhistory.org* 🎫 *Visitor center free, museums $6 each, tour $20* ⊙ *Mon.–Sat. 10–4, Sun. noon–4.*

☝ **②** **Moody Gardens** is a multifaceted entertainment and educational complex inside pastel-colored glass pyramid buildings. Attractions include the 13-story **Aquarium Pyramid,** showcasing marine life from four oceans in tanks and touch pools; **Rainforest Pyramid,** a 40,000-square-foot tropical habitat for exotic flora and fauna; **Discovery Pyramid,** a joint venture with NASA featuring more than 40 interactive exhibits; and two **IMAX theaters,** one of which has a space adventure ride. Outside, **Palm Beach** has white-sand beach, landscaped grounds, man-made lagoons, a kid-size waterslide and games, and beach chairs. ✉ *1 Hope Blvd.* ☎ *409/741–8484 or 800/582–4673* ⊕ *www.moodygardens.com* 🎫 *$8.95–$15.95 per venue, $44.95 day pass* ⊙ *Memorial Day–Labor Day, daily 10–9; Labor Day–Memorial Day, weekdays 10–6, weekends 10–8.*

⑤ **Pier 21 Theater.** At this theater on the Strand, watch the Great Storm of 1900 come back to life in a multimedia presentation that includes video clips of archival drawings, still photos, and narrated accounts from survivors' diaries. Also playing is a film about the exploits of pirate Jean Lafitte, who used the island as a base. ✉ *Pier 21, Harborside Dr. and 21st St.* ☎ *409/ 763–8808* ⊕ *www.galvestonhistory.org/plc-pier21.htm* 🎫 *Great Storm $5, Pirate Island $4* ⊙ *Sun.–Thurs. 11–6, Fri. and Sat. 11–8.*

③ **The Strand.** This shopping area is defined by the architecture of its 19th- and early-20th-century buildings, many of which survived the storm of 1900 and are on the National Register of Historic Places. When Galveston was still a powerful port city—before the Houston Ship Channel was dug, diverting most boat traffic inland—this stretch, formerly the site of stores, offices, and warehouses, was known as the Wall Street of the South. As you stroll up the Strand, you pass dozens of shops and cafés. ✉ *Between Strand and Postoffice St., 25th and 19th sts.*

GALVESTON BEST BETS

- **Historic Homes.** The island has some lovely historic homes to explore, particularly during early May, when the Historic Homes Tour lets you into many that aren't usually open to the public.

- **Moody Gardens.** There are enough activities at this park to keep any kid happy.

- **The Strand.** Galveston's historic district is a great place to stroll, shop, and eat.

4 **Texas Seaport Museum.** Aboard the restored 1877 tall ship *Elissa,* detailed interpretive signs provide information about the shipping trade in the 1800s, including the routes and cargoes this ship carried into Galveston. Inside the museum building is a replica of the historic wharf and information about the ethnic groups that immigrated through this U.S. point of entry after 1837. The tall ship *Elissa* was refurbished in 2005. ✉ *Pier 21* ☎ *409/763–1877* ⊕ *www.tsm-elissa.org* ✍ *$8* ⊙ *Daily 10–5.*

Beaches

The **Seawall** (✉ Seawall Blvd. from 61st St. to 25th St.) on the gulf-side waterfront attracts runners, cyclists, and rollerbladers. Just below it is a long, free beach near many big hotels and resorts. **Stewart Beach Park** (✉ 6th St. and Seawall Blvd. ☎ 409/765–5023) has a bathhouse, amusement park, bumper boats, miniature-golf course, and a water coaster in addition to salt water and sand. It's open weekdays 9 to 5, weekends 8 to 6 from March through May; weekdays 8 to 6 and weekends 8 to 7 from June through September; and weekends 9 to 5 during the first two weekends of October. Admission is $5 per vehicle. **Galveston Island State Park** (✉ 3 Mile Rd., 10 mi (16 km) southwest on Seawall Blvd. ☎ 409/737–1222), on the western, unpopulated end of the island, is a 2,000-acre natural beach habitat ideal for birding, walking, and renewing your spirit. It's open daily from 8 AM to 10 PM; admission is $3.

Shopping

The **Strand** is the best place to shop in Galveston. Old storefronts are filled with gift shops, antiques stores, and one-of-a-kind boutiques. The area is bounded by Strand and Postoffice Street (running east–west) and 25th and 19th streets (running north–south). More than 50 antiques dealers are represented at **The Emporium at Eibands** (✉ 2201 Postoffice St. ☎ 409/763–5495), an upscale showroom filled with furniture, books, art, and jewelry.

Where to Eat

For price categories, *see* Dining at the beginning of this chapter.

$$–$$$ ✕ **Fisherman's Wharf.** Even though Landry's has taken over this harborside institution along with just about everything else on the Kemah Boardwalk, locals keep coming here for the reliably fresh seafood and reasonable prices. Dine indoors or watch the boat traffic (and waiting cruise ships) from the patio. Start with a cold combo, like boiled shrimp and grilled rare tuna. The fried fish, shrimp, and oysters are hard to beat as an entrée. ✉ *Pier 22, Harborside Dr. and 22nd St.* ☎ *409/765–5708* ⊟ *AE, D, DC, MC, V.*

$$–$$$ ✕ **Mosquito Café.** This chichi eatery in Galveston's historic East End serves fresh, contemporary food—some vegetarian—in a hip, high-ceilinged dining room and on an outdoor patio. Wake up to a fluffy egg frittata or a homemade scone topped with whipped cream, or try a large gourmet salad later on. The grilled snapper with Parmesan grits is a hit in the evening. ✉ *628 14th St.* ☎ *409/763–1010* ⊟ *AE, D, DC, MC, V* ⊙ *No dinner Sun.–Wed.*

CAUTION	

Do not forget to pack and use your sunscreen. Why take the chance of a nasty sunburn ruining a great cruise vacation? Protect your skin from injury and aging.

Where to Stay
For price categories, *see* Lodging at the beginning of this chapter.

$$–$$$$ ⬚ **San Luis Resort.** A long marble staircase alongside a slender fountain with sculpted dolphins welcomes you to the waterfront elegance of this resort. The upper-floor facade isn't much to look at, but don't let that fool you; inside, the colors of the cool, cream marble and taupe stone in the lobby are echoed in the guest rooms. The sculptural lines of pink granite on the headboards and armchairs say Italian villa. All rooms have balconies facing the gulf, and prices rise with the floor height. Back on ground level, step into the meandering (and heated) grotto pool with a rock waterfall set amid coconut palms and bougainvillea; then have a Balinese massage (or a wildflower compress) at the Spa San Luis. The resort offers free parking for the duration of a cruise as well as transportation to the cruise terminal. ⊠ *5222 Seawall Blvd., 77551* ☎ *409/744–1500 or 800/445–0090* 🖨 *409/744–8452* ⊕ *www.sanluisresort.com* ⇆ *246 rooms* ⬚ *In room: dial-up. In hotel: Restaurant, room service, bars, tennis courts, pools, gym, spa, children's programs (ages 4–12), laundry service, executive floor, public Internet, parking (free), no-smoking rooms* ▤ *AE, D, DC, MC, V.*

$$–$$$ ⬚ **Hotel Galvez.** This renovated six-story Spanish colonial hotel, built in 1911, was once called "Queen of the Gulf." Teddy Roosevelt and Howard Hughes are just two of the many well-known guests who have stayed here. Traditional dark wood and plush upholstery pieces furnish both the public and private areas. A pool, swim-up bar, and outdoor grill have been added to the tropical garden facing the sea. ⊠ *2024 Seawall Blvd., 77550* ☎ *409/765–7721* 🖨 *409/765–5780* ⊕ *www.wyndham.com* ⇆ *231 rooms* ⬚ *In room: dial-up, Ethernet. In hotel: restaurant, pool, gym, laundry service, public Internet, no-smoking rooms* ▤ *AE, DC, MC, V.*

$–$$ ⬚ **Tremont House.** A four-story atrium lobby, with ironwork balconies and full-size palm trees, showcases an 1872 hand-carved rosewood bar in what was once a busy dry-goods warehouse. It is actually a historic place: Republic of Texas president Sam Houston presented his last speech at this hotel, both Confederate and Union soldiers bunked here, and Great Storm victims took refuge under this roof. Rooms have high ceilings and 11-foot windows. Period reproduction furniture and Victorian-pattern wallpapers add to the authenticity. It's the closest full-service lodging to the port, just a short walk from shopping on the Strand. ⊠ *2300 Ship's Mechanic Row, 77550* ☎ *409/763–0300* 🖨 *409/763–1539* ⊕ *www.wyndham.com* ⇆ *119 rooms* ⬚ *In room: dial-up, Ethernet. In hotel: restaurant, room service, bar, laundry service, public Internet, parking (fee), no-smoking rooms* ▤ *AE, D, DC, MC, V.*

HOUSTON, TEXAS

Robin Barr Sussman

Unbridled energy has always been Houston's trademark. Once a swamp near the junction of the Buffalo and White Oak bayous, Houston is now the nation's fourth-largest city and the energy capital of the United States. Excellent museums, galleries, and performance halls affirm the city's commitment to the arts, and its many ethnic restaurants add to the cosmopolitan flavor. Just a few hours' sailing time from the Gulf of Mex-

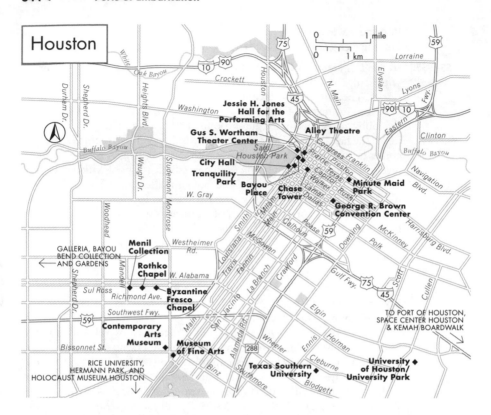

ico, the Port of Houston—a vibrant component to the regional economy—comprises the port authority and the 150-plus private industrial companies along the Houston Ship Channel. At this writing, Norwegian Cruise Line bases two ships at Houston's single cruise terminal, operating week-long voyages to the Western Caribbean, including such ports as Roatan Island, Honduras; Belize City; and Cozumel, Mexico. This cruise terminal is convenient for Houstonians and residents of the smaller cities in the bay area.

Essentials

HOURS Some museums are closed on Monday. Stores in malls tend to be open later, often until 9 PM.

INTERNET Since Houston is so spread out, it's best if you check your email at your hotel rather than go searching for a far-flung Internet café.

VISITOR INFORMATION **Greater Houston Convention & Visitors Bureau** (🏠 901 Bagby St. 🕿 713/437–5200 ⊕ www.visithoustontexas.com).

The Port of Houston

The Port of Houston is a 25-mi-long complex of diversified public and private industrial terminal facilities designed to handle general cargo. The facilities of this massive port cover several municipal jurisdictions, including the cities of Houston, Pasadena, Galena Park, LaPorte, Baytown, Deer Park, and Morgan's Point. Within the public terminal facilities is the Barbours

Cut Cruise Terminal, which is located in Morgan's Point, near LaPorte, Texas. Norwegian Cruise Line vessels call on the terminal Saturdays and Sundays. To reach the port by car, from downtown Houston, take I–45 south to 610 N, then continue to 225 E. Turn on 146 S to Barbours Cut Boulevard and turn left. Drive 3 mi (5 km) to reach the cruise terminal. The new Bayport Cruise Terminal opened in 2007.

⚓ **Port of Houston** ✉ Barbours Cut Terminal, 820 North L St., Pier C-7, Morgan's Point ✉ 111 E. Loop N, Houston ☎ 713/670-2400 ⊕ www.portofhouston.com

> ## HOUSTON BEST BETS
>
> - **Kemah Boardwalk.** This bayside entertainment and dining center is a good family destination.
> - **Menil Collection.** Art lovers will appreciate this eclectic collection—and it's all free.
> - **NASA Space Center.** Though not as extensive in its visitor facilities (or as expensive) as the Kennedy Space Center in Florida, this is still worth a trip.

AIRPORT TRANSFERS
There are two major airports in Houston. Bush Intercontinental Airport, 15 mi (24 km) northeast of downtown Houston, is 40 mi (64 km) and approximately 45 minutes from the Port of Houston. William P. Hobby Airport, southeast of downtown, is closer, at 20 mi (32 km) and approximately 25 minutes. You may purchase a transfer option from the cruise line when you book your cruise, or you can arrange your own transfers. A private car transfer from Airport Taxi & Town Car will cost $65–$70 from Houston Hobby and $85 to $90 from Bush Intercontinental; Yellow Cab Houston charges by distance traveled, and their rates will usually be much cheaper than those of a private car service from Hobby and slightly cheaper from Bush Intercontinental (you can estimate your fare on the company's Web site). Visit Houston's official visitor's Web site to research hiring a taxi and current rates.

⚓ **Airport Taxi & Town Car** ☎ 281/630-1137 ⊕ www.24hrairporttaxi.com. **Yellow Cab Houston** ☎ 713/236-1111 ⊕ www.yellowcabhouston.com.

PARKING
Outdoor parking facilities operated by the Port of Houston Authority are available at the cruise-ship pier. Twenty-four hour security is provided, and the facility is secured for the duration of the cruise. Rates are $7 per day. Note that parking fees must be paid with cash or traveler's checks; you can't use credit cards. The parking lot is very close to the terminal. Drive to the front of the terminal, and drop your baggage with the porters; then drive to the parking booth and pay; you'll be able to walk to the terminal.

Exploring Houston

Houston can be divided neatly into three major areas. One is its very modern downtown (including the theater district), which spurred one architecture critic to declare the city "America's future." Another is the area a couple of miles south of downtown, the museum district, where some of the Southwest's leading museums are found along with Rice University and the internationally renowned Texas Medical Center. There is the thriving shopping and business center west of downtown, known as both the Galleria and Uptown. Finally, there are neighborhoods south of downtown Houston that are convenient to the cruise port ripe for exploring.

DOWNTOWN Texas Avenue, downtown's main street, is 100 feet wide, precisely the width needed to accommodate 14 Texas longhorns tip to tip in the days when cattle were driven to market along this route. One good way to start any trip to downtown Houston is to take in the entire urban panorama from the observation deck (weekdays only) of I. M. Pei's 75-story **Chase Tower** (✉ 600 Travis St.), built in 1981. **Tranquility Park** (✉ between Walker and Rusk Sts. east of Smith St.), a cool oasis of fountains and walkways, was built to commemorate the first landing on the moon by the *Apollo 11* mission.

Minute Maid Park is a state-of-the-art baseball stadium with a retractable roof to defy Houston's frequently changing weather. The stadium incorporates the 1911 Union Station (designed by Warren and Wetmore of New York's Grand Central Station fame), which houses the ball club offices, retail stores, and eateries.

THE MUSEUM Most museums are clustered within an area bordering the verdant cam-
DISTRICT pus of Rice University, one of Texas's finest educational institutions, and Hermann Park, the city's playground. Walking from one institution to the other is possible, but the expanse can be taxing; it's best to segment your visit.

The **Museum of Fine Arts** is remarkable for the completeness of its enormous collection, housed in a complicated series of wings and galleries, many designed by Ludwig Mies van der Rohe. The Audrey Jones Beck Building, the work of famed Spanish architect Rafael Maneo, opened in 2000, doubling the museum's size. Renaissance and 18th-century art is particularly well represented, and there's a nice selection of Impressionist and Post-Impressionist works and a museum store. The **Lillie and Hugh Roy Cullen Sculpture Garden** (✉ 1001 Bissonnet St., at Montrose Ave.), across the street from the Museum of Fine Arts, displays 19th- and 20th-century sculptures by Rodin, Matisse, Giacometti, and Stella in an outdoor space designed by Isamu Noguchi. It's open daily from 9 AM–10 PM. ✉ *1001 Bissonnet St., north of Rice University, between Montrose Blvd. and Main St., Museum District* ☎ *713/639–7300* ⊕ *www.mfah. org* 🖼 *Museum $7, free Thurs.; garden free* ☉ *Tues. and Wed. 10–5; Thurs. 10–9, Fri. and Sat. 10–8; Sun. 12:15–7.*

The **Contemporary Arts Museum**, housed in an aluminum-sheathed trapezoid, is the home of avant-garde art in Houston, with many traveling exhibitions and a whimsical gift shop. ✉ *5216 Montrose Blvd.* ☎ *713/ 284–8250* ⊕ *www.camh.org* 🖼 *Free* ☉ *Tues. and Wed. 10–5; Thurs. 10–9, Fri. and Sat. 10–5; Sun. 12–5.*

The **Menil Collection** is one of the city's premier cultural treasures. Italian architect Renzo Piano designed the spacious building with airy galleries. John and Dominique de Menil collected the eclectic art, which ranges from tribal African sculptures to Andy Warhol's paintings of Campbell's soup cans. A separate gallery across the street houses the paint-

CAUTION	
An endlessly ringing telephone is a hint that you are not home. Before leaving the house, either turn off the telephone ringers or set the answering machine to pick up after two rings.	

ings of American artist Cy Twombly. ⊠ *1515 Sul Ross St.* ☎ *713/525–9400* ⊕ *www.menil.org* ✉ *Free* ⊙ *Wed.–Sun. 11–7.*

OTHER NEIGHBORHOODS

Kids and adults can learn about space exploration at **Space Center Houston.** Life on the deck of a space shuttle is simulated in the **Space Center Plaza.** In the **Kids Space Place,** children can ride on the lunar rover and try out tasks in the *Apollo* command module. The adjacent **Johnson Space Center** tour includes a visit to Mission Control and laboratories that simulate weightlessness and other space-related concepts. Allow several hours for your visit. ⊠ *1601 NASA Rd. 1, off I–45, 25 mi south of Downtown* ☎ *281/244–2100* ⊕ *www.spacecenter.org* ✉ *$18.95* ⊙ *Weekdays 10–5, weekends 10–6.*

Take a detour off I–45 between Houston and Galveston to the **Kemah Boardwalk,** a cluster of restaurants, amusement rides, game arcades, and inns on the bustling ship channel. It's a family-oriented destination where you can catch a Gulf breeze, eat seafood, shop, and watch personal and commercial marine craft motor by. ⊠ *Bradford and 2nd St., Kemah* ☎ *877/285–3624* ⊕ *www.kemahboardwalk.com.*

Shopping
You can shop for just about anything in Houston. Shopping centers sprawl across the metropolis from the suburbs at points north (The Woodlands) and south (SugarLand), but the best concentration of fine and specialty stores is inside and just immediately outside Loop–610, commonly referred to as center of the city.

The city's premier shopping area is the **Galleria,** or **Uptown,** area; the business, office towers, and shopping complexes in the area have made it one of the most important business districts in the city. Many of Houston's best restaurants are here, and the River Oaks neighborhood, with its multi-million-dollar mansions and garden parkways, is nearby. The **Galleria Mall** (⊠ Westheimer Rd. at Post Oak Blvd.), the region's anchor shopping complex, is famous for high-quality stores like Neiman Marcus, Saks Fifth Avenue, and Tiffany & Co. **Uptown Park** (⊠ Uptown Park Blvd. at Post Oak Blvd.) is a charming European-style outdoor shopping center with cafés, upscale restaurants, designer-clothing boutiques, and fine jewelry shops north of the Galleria Mall off Post Oak Boulevard.

For antiques, vintage clothing, and folk art, try the stores in the **Heights,** a re-gentrified neighborhood north of I–10 (19th Street between Heights Boulevard and Yale Street). The **Museum District** is known for art galleries.

Nightlife
There are other hot spots around Houston, but downtown is the main magnet for after-hours activity, with new clubs and restaurants springing up all the time in renovated storefronts and warehouses. **Bayou Place** (⊠ 500 Texas Ave.), Houston's largest entertainment complex, is a 130,000-square-foot, two-story center of evening activity, with restaurants, clubs, a theater, and the Angelika Film Center, a spinoff of the New York City cinema showing independent and foreign films.

Where to Eat
From Vietnamese to Latin American, contemporary American or Indian, the Bayou City is among the more diverse places in Texas. Houston's

food culture also mandates barbecue and Tex-Mex, high-end steak houses, and contemporary Italian restaurants as staples. It's a cosmopolitan scene with booming downtown eateries; increasingly, excellent hotel restaurants have become major dining destinations. About 20 mi (32 km) south of downtown Houston, you can experience the Kemah Boardwalk, a waterfront dining park and shopping center that is located near Clear Lake, just south of the port of Houston cruise terminal.

$$–$$$ ✕ **Aquarium Restaurant.** This one-of-a-kind restaurant on the Kemah Boardwalk serves quality seafood and has a sea-themed decor with floor-to-ceiling aquarium tanks. The whole family will be in awe of the myriad sea creatures, fish, sharks, and colorful coral on display. It's a wide-ranging menu that moves easily between fancy seafood entrées and casual, kid-friendly meals. ⊠ *11 Kemah Waterfront, Kemah* ☎ *281/334–9010* ▤ *AE, D, DC, MC, V.*

$–$$$ ✕ **Ibiza.** Gutsy, sometimes playful, cuisine prepared by Chef Charles Clark is served in a bustling dining room as seductive as its namesake island off the coast of Spain. Generous portions of seasonal dishes intermingle with delectable Spanish tapas and hearty entrées such as "six-hour" braised lamb shank with Spanish mint oil. Oenophiles will appreciate Ibiza's ever-changing wine list of rare tastes at fair prices. Don't miss the outdoor patio on pretty days, the Sunday paella, or the homemade sangria chock-full of fresh fruit. ⊠ *2450 Louisiana St., suite 300* ☎ *713/524–0004* ⌖ *Reservations essential* ▤ *AE, D, DC, MC, V* ◷ *Closed Mon.*

¢–$ ✕ **Goode Company.** Down-home Texas barbecue is prepared ranch-style—mesquite-smoked and served with tasty red sauce. Patrons line up on the sidewalk to eat at picnic tables on the covered patio. A standard order is the chopped-beef brisket sandwich on jalapeño-cheese bread. Don't skip the celebrated pecan pie for dessert. For hamburgers, tacos, and great weekend breakfasts, visit Goode Company Hamburgers and Taqueria right across the street on Kirby Drive. ⊠ *5109 Kirby Dr.* ☎ *713/522–2530* ▤ *AE, D, DC, MC, V.*

Where to Stay

Sprawling Houston has a seemingly endless variety of respectable hotels that are convenient to the port of Houston cruise terminal. However, the revitalized downtown offers both a central location and quick access to I–45 S and the port. Downtown Houston offers world-class hotels, a vibrant nightlife, and varied, if trendy, restaurants. Moderate hotels are even closer to the port of Houston in LaPorte, which is a mostly industrial area, so do not expect the same urban scene. Although rack rates for many Houston hotels seem high, they drop dramatically on weekends or if you make your reservation online or in advance.

$$$ ⊡ **Alden Houston.** Formerly named The Sam Houston Hotel, this small luxury boutique hotel is decidedly modern and well located near bustling Main Street and the ballpark. The guest rooms are stylish, with fine linens, granite bathrooms, high-tech work stations, and suites with plasma TVs. The hotel's award-winning restaurant, 17, is just as modern and attracts a hip international crowd of epicures hungry for contemporary American food. Don't miss it. ⊠ *1117 Prairie St., 77002* ☎ *832/200–8800 or*

877/348–8800 🖷 832/200–8822 ⊕ *www.aldenhotels.com* 🛏 *97 rooms* ♨ *In room: DVD, refrigerator, Wi-Fi. In hotel: Restaurant, room service, bar, gym, concierge, laundry service, public Wi-Fi, some pets allowed* 🖃 *AE, D, DC, MC, V* ⑩ *EP.*

$–$$$ 🖼 **Hilton Houston NASA Clear Lake** On the shores of Clear Lake, this Hilton offers a number of water sports and easy access to NASA, which is across the street. ⊠ *3000 NASA Rd. 1, 77058* ☏ *281/333–9300* 🖷 *281/333–3750* ⊕ *www.hilton.com* 🛏 *243 rooms* ♨ *In hotel: Restaurant, room service, bar, pool, gym, public Internet* 🖃 *AE, D, DC, MC, V* ⑩ *EP.*

JACKSONVILLE, FLORIDA

Kerry
Speckman

One of Florida's oldest cities and at 730 square mi (1,891 square km) the largest city in the continental United States, Jacksonville makes for an underrated vacation spot; it's a worthwhile vacation spot for an extra day or two before or after your cruise. It offers appealing downtown riverside areas, handsome residential neighborhoods, the region's only skyscrapers, a thriving arts scene, and, for football fans, the NFL Jaguars and the NCAA Gator Bowl. Remnants of the Old South flavor the city, especially in the Riverside/Avondale historic district, where moss-draped oak trees frame prairie-style bungalows and Tudor Revival mansions; and palm trees, Spanish bayonet, and azaleas populate Jacksonville's landscape.

Essentials

HOURS Many museums close on Monday.

INTERNET Most people access the Internet in their hotel. If you are in town for just the day (or if your hotel has expensive or inadequate Internet access options), there are Internet cafés. **Docking Station** (⊠ 1301-11 Monument Rd. ☏ 904/722–3625 ⊕ dstationtech.com).

VISITOR
INFORMATION
Jacksonville & The Beaches Convention & Visitors Bureau (⊠ 550 Water St., Suite 1000, Jacksonville 32202 ☏ 904/798–9111 or 800/733–2668 ⊕ www.jaxcvb.com).

The Cruise Port

Limited in the sizes of ships it can berth, JAXPORT currently serves as home port to the Carnival *Celebration,* which departs weekly on 4- and 5-night cruises to Key West and the Bahamas. Plans are in the works to move the port to a more accessible location within the next several years, but in the meantime, cruises depart from a temporary cruise facility. The facility is fairly sparse, consisting basically of some vending machines and restrooms, but the embarkation staff receives high marks, having won a good-service award from Carnival Cruise Line in 2004 and 2005.

JAXPORT is about 15 minutes from the Jacksonville International Airport. Take I–95 S to S.R. 9-A E. Follow 9-A to Heckscher Drive (S.R. 105) west until you reach August Drive. Head south on August Drive, and follow the signs to the cruise terminal.

🗗 **Jacksonville Port Authority** ⊠ 9810 August Dr., Jacksonville, FL ☏ 904/630–3006 ⊕ www.jaxport.com.

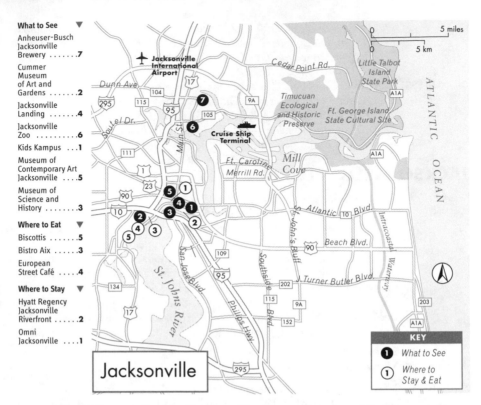

Jacksonville

AIRPORT TRANSFERS The transfer from Jacksonville airport takes about 15 minutes and costs $20 to $25 for up to four passengers by taxi. Express Shuttle costs $10 per person and departs the airport every 15 minutes.

🛈 **Express Shuttle USA** ☎ 904/353-8880. **Gator City Taxi & Shuttle** ☎ 904/355-8294. **Yellow Cab** ☎ 904/260-1111.

PARKING There is a fenced and guarded parking lot next to the cruise terminal, within walking distance. Parking costs $12 per day for regular vehicles, $20 for RVs. You must pay in advance by cash or major credit card.

Exploring Jacksonville

Because Jacksonville was settled along both sides of the twisting St. Johns River, a number of attractions are on or near a riverbank. Both sides of the river, which is spanned by myriad bridges, have downtown areas and waterfront complexes of shops, restaurants, parks, and museums; some attractions can be reached by water taxi or the Skyway Express monorail system—scenic alternatives to driving back and forth across the bridges—but a car is generally necessary.

❼ Anheuser-Busch Jacksonville Brewery. Beer lovers will appreciate this behind-the-scenes look at how barley malt, rice, hops, and water form the "King of Beers." Guided tours take guests through the entire brewing and bottling process. Or you can high-tail it through the self-guided tour and head straight to the free beer tastings, which is all that true beer lovers really care about anyway. Leave the kids at home, though, since guests must be at least 18 to visit the brewery or shops. ✉ *111 Busch Dr.* ☎ *904/*

696–8373 ⊕ *www.budweisertours.com* ✉ *Free* ⏱ *Mon.–Sat. 10–4; guided tours Mon.–Sat. 10–3 on the half hr.*

② Cummer Museum of Art and Gardens. The world-famous Wark Collection of early-18th-century Meissen porcelain is just one reason to visit this former riverfront estate; it also includes 13 permanent galleries with more than 5,000 items spanning 8,000 years and 3 acres of riverfront gardens reflecting Northeast Florida's blooming seasons and indigenous varieties. For the kids, Art Connections allows them to experience art through hands-on, interactive exhibits. The latest museum's addition, the Thomas H. Jacobsen Gallery of American Art, focuses on works by American artists including Max Weber, N. C. Wyeth, and Paul Manship. ✉ *829 Riverside Ave.* ☎ *904/356–6857* ⊕ *www.cummer.org* ✉ *$8* ⏱ *Tues. and Thurs. 10–9, Wed., Fri., and Sat. 10–5, Sun. noon–5.*

JACKSONVILLE BEST BETS

■ **Jacksonville Zoo.** One of the best mid-sized zoos you'll visit.

■ **Kids Kampus.** If you are traveling with your family, this park may become your favorite place in the city.

■ **Museum of Contemporary Art Jacksonville.** Though small, this is excellent museum is an unexpected treat in Northeast Florida.

④ Jacksonville Landing. During the week, this riverfront festival marketplace caters to locals and tourists alike, with more than 40 specialty shops with home furnishings, apparel, and toys, nine full-service restaurants—including a brew pub, Italian bistro, and steak house—and an internationally-flavored food court (though the view is probably the best thing on any of their menus). On the weekends, the Landing hosts more than 250 events each year, ranging from the good clean fun of the American Cancer Society Duck Race to the just plain obnoxious Florida–Georgia game after-party, as well as live music (usually of the local cover band variety) in the courtyard. ✉ *2 Independent Dr.* ☎ *904/353–1188* ⊕ *www.jacksonvillelanding.com* ✉ *Free* ⏱ *Mon.–Thurs. 10–8, Fri. and Sat. 10–9, Sun. noon–5:30; some restaurants open earlier and close later.*

⑥ Jacksonville Zoo & Gardens. Encompassing more than 120 acres on Jacksonville's Northside, this mid-size zoo is home to thousands of amphibians, birds, invertebrates, mammals, and reptiles from barking tree frogs and Madagascar hissing cockroaches to dusky pygmy rattlesnakes and giant anteaters. Among the zoo's outstanding exhibits is its collection of rare waterfowl and the Serona Overlook, which showcases some of the world's most venomous snakes. The Florida Wetlands is a 2½-acre area with black bears, bald eagles, white-tailed deer, and other animals native to Florida. The African Veldt has alligators, elephants, and white rhinos, among other species of African birds and mammals. The zoo's newest exhibit, the Range of the Jaguar, includes 4 acres of exotic big cats as well as 20 other species of animals. A new $6.7-million Kids' Zone complete with a splash park, forest play area, maze, and discovery building is expected to be completed by the end of 2006. ✉ *370 Zoo Pkwy., off Heckscher Dr. E* ☎ *904/757–4463* ⊕ *www.jaxzoo.org* ✉ *$11* ⏱ *Daily 9–5.*

FodorśChoice ★

Kids Kampus. Directly on the St. Johns River adjacent to Metropolitan Park, this 10-acre recreational facility, developed by local educators, encourages children's natural curiosity with climbing and sliding apparati, engaging playscapes, mini-representations of Jacksonville landmarks, like Bay Street, Kings Road, and the main post office, and a

> **BRING GEORGE**
>
> Whenever you leave for a cruise, carry a supply of one-dollar bills. They'll come in handy for tipping airport skycaps and porters at the pier.

splash park. It's not exactly Disney World, but parents looking for a way to entertain the kids for a couple of hours, especially in the sweltering Florida heat, report it just might be the happiest place on earth. The "kampus" also has a picnic pavilion and jogging trail. ⊠ *1410 Gator Bowl Blvd.* ☏ *904/630–5437* ⊠ *Free* ☉ *Mar.–Oct., Mon.–Sat. 8–8, Sun. 10–8; Nov.–Feb., Mon.–Sat. 8–6, Sun. 10–6.*

Museum of Contemporary Art Jacksonville In this loftlike downtown build-
FodorśChoice ing, the former headquarters of the Western Union Telegraph Company, ★ a permanent collection of 20th-century art shares space with traveling exhibitions. The museum encompasses five galleries and ArtExplorium, a highly interactive educational exhibit for kids. MOCA Jacksonville (previously known as the Jacksonville Museum of Modern Art) also hosts film series, lectures, and workshops throughout the year. ⊠ *Hemming Plaza, 333 N. Laura St.* ☏ *904/366–6911* ⊕ *www.jmoma.org* ⊠ *$6, free Wed. 5–9 and Sun.* ☉ *Tues. and Fri. 11–5, Wed. and Thurs. 11–9, Sat. 11–4, Sun. noon–4.*

Museum of Science and History. You won't find any mad scientists here, but you'll probably find lots of giggling ones. Targeted at the elementary and middle school set, MOSH aims to educate and entertain kids about science and history through a variety of interactive exhibits like the JEA Science Theatre, where they'll participate in live experiments related to electricity and electrical safety; the Florida Naturalist's Center, where they can explore Northeast Florida wildlife (like American alligators, gopher turtles, and various native snakes and birds); and the Universe of Science, where they'll learn about properties of physical science through hands-on demonstrations. Other permanent exhibits include Atlantic Tails, a hands-on exploration of whales, dolphins, and manatees; Currents of Time, chronicling 12,000 years of Northeast Florida history; and Prehistoric Park, featuring a life-size Allosaurus skeleton. The Alexander Brest Planetarium hosts daily shows on astronomy (request your seating pass from the front desk 30 minutes prior to any showing) and, on weekends, Cosmic Concerts, 3-D laser shows set to pop music. ⊠ *1025 Museum Circle* ☏ *904/396–6674* ⊕ *www.themosh.org* ⊠ *$8, Cosmic Concerts $3–$6* ☉ *Weekdays 10–5, Sat. 10–6, Sun. 1–6.*

Shopping

At **Five Points** (⊠ Intersection of Park, Margaret, and Lomax Sts.) you'll find a small but funky shopping district of new and vintage clothing boutiques, shoe stores, and antiques shops, as well as a handful of eateries and bars, not to mention some of the most colorful characters in the city. **San Marco Square** (⊠ San Marco and Atlantic Blvds.) has dozens of interesting apparel, home, and jewelry stores and restaurants in 1920s Mediterranean Revival-style buildings. **The Shoppes of Avondale** (⊠ St. Johns Ave., between Talbot Ave. and Dancy St.) consist mostly of upscale clothing and accessories boutiques, art galleries, home-furnishing shops, a chocolatier, and trendy restaurants.

Where to Eat

JAXPORT's location on Jacksonville's Westside means there aren't too many nearby restaurants. But by taking a 10- to 15-minute drive south, you'll find a wealth of restaurants for all tastes and price categories.

For price categories, *see* Dining at the beginning of this chapter.

★ **$$–$$$** ✕ **Bistro Aix.** When a Jacksonville restaurant can make Los Angelesians feel like they haven't left home, that's saying a lot. With its slick black leather booths, 1940s brickwork, velvet drapes, and intricate marbled globes, Bistro Aix (pronounced "X") is just that place. Regulars can't get enough of the creamy onion soup, crispy calimari, and house-made potato chips with warm blue cheese appetizers or entrées like oak-fired fish "Aixoise," grilled salmon, and filet mignon; while Aix's on-site pastry chef ensures no sweet tooth leaves unsatisfied. For the most part, wait staff are knowledgeable and pleasant, though some patrons find their demeanor snooty, except, of course, those patrons from L.A. Call ahead for preferred seating. ⊠ *1440 San Marco Blvd.* ☎ *904/398–1949* ⌖ *Reservations not accepted* ▤ *AE, D, DC, MC, V* ⊗ *No lunch weekends.*

$–$$ ✕ **Biscottis.** The local artwork on the redbrick walls is a mild distraction from the jovial crowds (from yuppies to soccer moms to metrosexuals) jockeying for tables in this midsize restaurant. Elbows almost touch, but no one seems to mind. The menu offers the unexpected: wild-mushroom ravioli with a broth of corn, leek, and dried apricot; or curry grilled swordfish with cucumber fig bordelaise. And if you ever have trouble finding the place, just follow the trail of drool down St. Johns Avenue, which leads directly to Biscottis decadent dessert case (we hear the peanut butter ganache is illegal in three states). ⊠ *3556 St. Johns Ave.* ☎ *904/387–2060* ⌖ *Reservations not accepted* ▤ *AE, MC, V.*

¢ ✕ **European Street Cafe.** Wicker baskets and lofty shelves brimming with European confections and groceries like Toblerone and Nutella fill practically every inch of space not occupied by café tables. The menu can be similarly overwhelming, with nearly 100 deli sandwiches and salads. This spot is favored by area professionals looking for a quick lunch, as well as the under-forty set doing 23-ounce curls with one of the restaurant's 20-plus beers on tap (plus more than 100 in bottles). ⌖ *Reservations not accepted* ▤ *AE, D, MC, V.*

Where to Stay

Hotels near the cruise terminals are few and far between, so most cruisers needing a room make the drive to Downtown (15 minutes) or to the Southbank or Riverside (20 minutes).

For price categories, *see* Lodging at the beginning of this chapter.

$$–$$$ ▦ **Hyatt Regency Jacksonville Riverfront.** In Jacksonville, it doesn't get much more convenient than this downtown, waterfront hotel. Perched on the north bank of the St. Johns River, the nine-story property is within walking distance of the Jacksonville Landing, Florida Theatre, and T-U Center, as well as corporate office towers and the county courthouse. The former Adam's Mark Hotel has undergone some significant changes, most notably in its dining options with the addition of the Plaza III Steakhouse, and its guest rooms with a splashier Florida-style decor, triple-sheeted beds, and (gasp!) hotel windows that actually open, while retaining some of its best features, namely the roof-top swimming pool and club level rooms, where guests enjoy complimentary breakfast every morning and hors d'oeuvres every night. Unfortunately, the heavily-mirrored, over-chandeliered, and excessively-sconced lobby remains largely intact. ⊠ *225 E. Coastline Dr., 32202* ☎ *904/633–9095 or 800/444–2326* 🖷 *904/633–9988* ⊕ *www.jacksonville.hyatt.com* ⤴ *966 rooms, 21 suites* ⚘ *In-room: refrigerator (some), Ethernet,. In-hotel: 3 restaurants, room service, bar, pool, gym, concierge, laundry facilities, laundry service, concierge, executive floor, public Wi-Fi, parking (fee), no-smoking rooms* ⊟ *AE, D, DC, MC, V.*

★ **$–$$$** 🏨 **Omni Jacksonville Hotel.** Further cementing its reputation as Jacksonville's most luxurious hotel, the 16-story Omni underwent a multi-million-dollar renovation enhancing practically every area of the property. Guest rooms are done in a "downtown urban style" with neutral colors (creams and grays), dark wood, stainless steel, and flat-screen TVs and feature complimentary Wi-Fi. The splashy marble-floor lobby leads to the reception area, an upscale lounge—J Bar—and Juliette's Bistro with cozy banquettes and tables that look up to a soaring atrium. It also scores high marks for its family-oriented atmosphere, including Nintendo in every room, no adult films, and the Omni Kids Rule program. Bell service is also exemplary: with most porters having 10-plus years on the job, they can, and will, help you find just about anything. Parking, however, can be a bear when there's a show at the Times-Union Center for the Performing Arts across the street. ⊠ *245 Water St., 32202* ☎ *904/355–6664 or 800/843–6664* 🖷 *904/791–4812* ⊕ *www.omnijacksonville.com* ⤴ *354 rooms, 4 suites* ⚘ *In-room: kitchen (some), Wi-Fi. In-hotel: restaurant, room service, bar, pool, gym, children's programs (ages 3–10), laundry service, concierge, public Wi-Fi, parking (fee), some pets allowed, no-smoking rooms* ⊟ *AE, D, DC, MC, V.*

MIAMI, FLORIDA

Miami is the busiest of Florida's very busy cruise ports. Because there's so much going on here, you might want to schedule an extra day or two before and/or after your cruise to explore North America's most Latin city. Downtown is a convenient place to stay if you are meeting up with a cruise ship, but at night, except for Bayside Marketplace, the AmericanAirlines Arena, and a few ever-changing clubs in warehouses, the area is deserted. Travelers spend little time here, since most tourist attractions are in other neighborhoods. Miami Beach, particularly the 1-square-mi Art Deco District in South Beach—the section south of 24th to 28th streets—is the heart of Miami's vibrant nightlife and

CAUTION	
Airline carry-on restrictions are being updated continuously. Check with your airline before packing, and be aware that large purses will sometimes be counted as a carry-on item!	

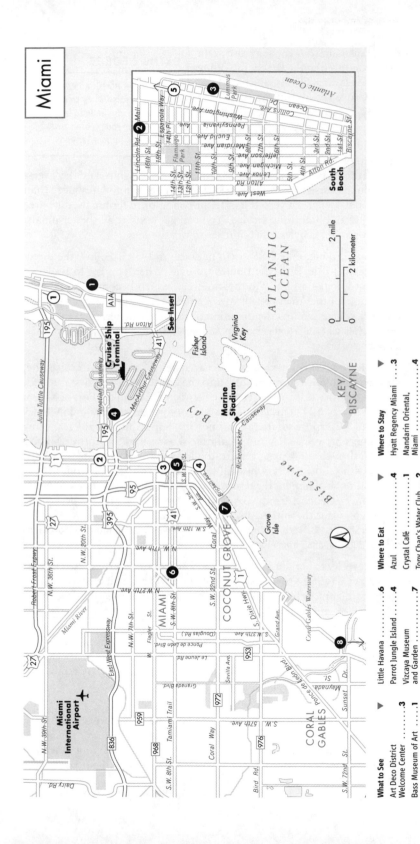

Miami

South Beach

Atlantic Ocean

Lummus Park

Lincoln Rd.
16th St.
Española Way
74th Pl.
Mall
Ave.
Pennsylvania
Washington Ave.
Collins Ave.
Ocean Dr.
15th St.
Euclid Ave.
14th St.
Meridian Ave.
Michigan Ave.
Jefferson Ave.
Flamingo Park
13th St.
12th St.
Lenox Ave.
West Ave.
Alton Rd.
11th St.
10th St.
9th St.
5th St.
1st St.
2nd St.
3rd St.
4th St.
Biscayne St.

Miami International Airport

Julia Tuttle Causeway

Robert Frost Expwy.

N.W. 39th St.

N.W. 36th St.

N.W. 20th St.

N.W. 17th Ave.

N.W. 27th Ave.

N.W. 7th St.

N.W. 8th St.

Miami River

East-West Expressway

Le Jeune Rd.

Ponce de Leon Blvd.

Flagler St.

MIAMI

S.W. 8th St.

S.W. 1st Ave.

S.W. 12th Ave.

S.W. 17th Ave.

Coral Way

Biscayne Blvd.

See Inset

A1A

Alton Rd.

Cruise Ship Terminal

Venetian Causeway

MacArthur Causeway

41

Fisher Island

Virginia Key

Marine Stadium

Rickenbacker Causeway

KEY BISCAYNE

Biscayne Bay

Grove Isle

COCONUT GROVE

Coral Gables Waterway

S.W. 32nd Ave.

S.W. 37th Ave. (Douglas Rd.)

Grand Ave.

S. Dixie Hwy.

S. Bayshore Dr.

CORAL GABLES

Sunset Dr.

Bird Rd.

Coral Way

S.W. 57th Ave.

S.W. 72nd St.

S.W. 8th St.

Tamiami Trail

Sevilla Ave.

Granada Blvd.

Maynada St.

Dairy Rd.

Coral Way

ATLANTIC OCEAN

0   2 mile
0   2 kilometer

What to See

Art Deco District Welcome Center **3**

Bass Museum of Art **1**

Brickell Village **5**

Fairchild Tropical Garden **8**

Lincoln Road Mall **2**

Little Havana **6**

Parrot Jungle Island **4**

Vizcaya Museum and Garden **7**

Where to Eat

Azul **4**

Crystal Café **1**

Tony Chan's Water Club ..**2**

Where to Stay

Hyatt Regency Miami **3**

Mandarin Oriental, Miami **4**

Townhouse **5**

restaurant scene. But you may also want to explore beyond the beach, including the Little Havana, Coral Gables, and Coconut Grove sections of the city.

The Cruise Port

The Port of Miami, in downtown Miami near Bayside Marketplace and the MacArthur Causeway, justifiably bills

> **BRING GEORGE**
>
> Pack a pad of Post-It notes when you take a cruise. They come in handy when you need to leave messages for your cabin steward, family, and shipboard friends.

itself as the Cruise Capital of the World. Home to 18 ships and the largest year-round cruise fleet in the world, the port accommodates more than 3 million passengers a year. It has 12 air-conditioned terminals, duty-free shopping, and limousine service. You can get taxis at all the terminals, and car-rental agencies offer shuttles to off-site lots.

If you are driving, take I–95 north or south to I–395. Follow the directional signs to the Biscayne Boulevard exit. When you get to Biscayne Boulevard, make a right. Go to 5th Street, which becomes Port Boulevard (look for the AmericanAirlines Arena); then make a left and go over the Port Bridge. Follow the directional signs to your terminal.
🚢 **Port of Miami** ✉ 1015 North American Way ☎ 305/371-7678 ⊕ www.co.miami-dade.fl.us/portofmiami.

AIRPORT TRANSFERS If you have not arranged an airport transfer through your cruise line, you have a couple of options to get to the cruise port. The first is a taxi, and the fares are reasonable. The fare between MIA and the Port of Miami is a flat fare of $24. This fare is per trip, not per passenger, and includes tolls and $1 airport surcharge but not tip. SuperShuttle vans transport passengers between MIA and local hotels, as well as the Port of Miami. At MIA the vans pick up at the ground level of each concourse (look for clerks with yellow shirts, who will flag one down). Service from MIA is available on demand; for the return it's best to make reservations 24 hours in advance. The cost from MIA to the cruise port is $15 per person, or $55 if you want the entire van to yourselves.
🚢 **SuperShuttle** ☎ 305/871-2000 from MIA, 954/764-1700 from Broward [Fort Lauderdale], 800/874-8885 from elsewhere.

PARKING Street-level lots are right in front of each of the cruise terminals. The cost is $12 per day ($24 for RVs), payable in advance. You can pay with a credit card at most terminals (except for numbers 2 and 10), though it's MasterCard and Visa only.

VISITOR INFORMATION 🚢 **Greater Miami Convention & Visitors Bureau** ✉ 701 Brickell Ave., Suite 2700, Downtown, 33131 ☎ 305/539-3000 or 800/933-8448 ⊕ www.gmcvb.com ✉ Bayside Marketplace tourist information center, 401 Biscayne Blvd., Bayside Marketplace, 33132 ☎ 305/539-2980.

Where to Stay

Staying in downtown Miami will put you close to the cruise terminals, but there is little to do at night. South Beach is the center of the action in Miami Beach, but it's fairly distant from the port. Staying in Miami Beach, but north of South Beach's Art Deco District, will put you on the beach but nominally closer to the port.

For price categories, *see* Lodging at the beginning of this chapter.

$$$$
Fodor'sChoice
★
Mandarin Oriental, Miami. If you can afford to stay here, do. The location, at the tip of Brickell Key in Biscayne Bay, is superb. Rooms facing west overlook the downtown skyline; to the east are Miami Beach and the blue Atlantic. There's also beauty in the details: sliding screens that close off the baths, dark wood, crisp linens, and room numbers hand-painted on rice paper at check-in. The Azul restaurant, with an eye-catching waterfall and private dining area at the end of a catwalk, serves a mix of Asian, Latin, Caribbean, and French cuisine. The hotel has a 20,000-square-foot private beach and an on-site spa. ⊠ *500 Brickell Key Dr., Brickell Key, 33131* ☎ *305/913–8288 or 866/888–6780* 🖷 *305/913–8300* ⊕ *www.mandarinoriental.com* 🛏 *327 rooms, 31 suites* ⚫ *In-room: safe, dial-up. In-hotel: 2 restaurants, bars, pool, spa, concierge, laundry service, parking (fee)* ⏐⊙⏐ *EP* ⊟ *AE, D, DC, MC, V.*

$$$
Hyatt Regency Miami. If your vacation is based on boats, basketball, business, or bargains, you can't do much better than the Hyatt Regency, thanks to its adjacent convention facilities and prime location near the Brickell Avenue business district, Bayside Marketplace, AmericanAirlines Arena, the Port of Miami, and downtown shopping. Distinctive public spaces are more colorful than businesslike, and guest rooms are a blend of avocado, beige, and blond. The James L. Knight International Center is accessible without stepping outside, as is the downtown Metromover and its Metrorail connection. The hotel is situated at the mouth of the Miami River. ⊠ *400 S.E. 2nd Ave., Downtown, 33131* ☎ *305/358–1234 or 800/233–1234* 🖷 *305/358–0529* ⊕ *www.miamiregency.hyatt.com* 🛏 *561 rooms, 51 suites* ⚫ *In-room: safe, refrigerator, Wi-Fi. In-hotel: restaurant, room service, bar, pool, gym, concierge, public Wi-Fi, parking (fee)* ⏐⊙⏐ *EP* ⊟ *AE, D, DC, MC, V.*

$$–$$$
Fodor'sChoice
★
Townhouse. The Townhouse looks like a big adult playhouse and fits the bill as the most lighthearted hotel on South Beach. A red plastic beach ball welcomes you to spotless rooms bleached white. The rooftop terrace has red waterbeds and a signature water tower. It's no wonder you find loud parties here on weekend nights. The hotel was designed by India Madhavi; thank him for the bright, inviting lobby with two, big, red (of course) bikes, kickstands down, for rent. Off to one side, a delightful sun room is a great place to read the paper over a generous Continental breakfast. Just outside, a porch deck has swings and comfortable chairs. A hip sushi restaurant, Bond St. Lounge, is downstairs. ⊠ *150 20th St., South Beach, 33139* ☎ *305/534–3800 or 877/534–3800* 🖷 *305/534–3811* ⊕ *www.townhousehotel.com* 🛏 *69 rooms, 3 suites* ⚫ *In-room: safe, Ethernet, Wi-Fi. In-hotel: restaurant, room service, bar, bicycles, laundry facilities, laundry service, public Wi-Fi, parking (fee), no-smoking rooms.* ⊟ *AE, D, MC, V.*

Where to Eat

At many of the hottest spots, you'll need a reservation to avoid a long wait for a table. And when you get your check, note whether a gratuity is included; most restaurants add 15% (ostensibly for the convenience of—and protection from—Latin-American and European tourists who are used to this practice in their homelands and would not normally tip), but you can reduce or supplement it depending on your opinion of the service.

For price categories, *see* Dining at the beginning of this chapter.

$$–$$$$ ✕ **Azul.** This sumptuous eatery has truly conquered the devil in the details. In addition to chef Clay Conley's exquisite French–Caribbean cuisine, the thoughtful touches in service graciously anticipate your needs. Does your sleeveless top mean your shoulders are too cold to properly appreciate the Swiss chard–stuffed pompano with caramelized pears? Ask for one of the house pashminas. Need somewhere to properly place your Birken bag? Ask for a purse stand. Forgot your reading glasses and can't decipher the hanger steak with foie gras sauce? Request a pair from the host. Want to see how the other half lives? Descend the staircase to Café Sambal, the all-day casual restaurant overlooking the shimmering waters and luxurious high-rise buildings of Biscayne Bay. ⊠ *Mandarin Oriental Hotel, 500 Brickell Key Dr., Brickell Key* ☎ *305/913–8288* ⚕ *Reservations essential* ☱ *AE, MC, V* ⊘ *No lunch weekends.*

$–$$$$ ✕ **Tony Chan's Water Club.** Off the lobby of the Doubletree Grand Hotel, this spot overlooks a bayside marina. On the menu of more than 200 appetizers and entrées are minced quail tossed with bamboo shoots and mushrooms wrapped in lettuce leaves. Indulge in a seafood spectacular of shrimp, conch, scallops, fish cakes, and crabmeat tossed with broccoli in a bird's nest, or go for pork chops sprinkled with green pepper in a black bean–garlic sauce. A lighter favorite is steamed sea bass with ginger and garlic. ⊠ *1717 N. Bayshore Dr., Downtown* ☎ *305/374–8888* ☱ *AE, D, DC, MC, V* ⊘ *No lunch weekends.*

$$–$$$ ✕ **Crystal Café.** Classic dishes like beef Stroganoff and chicken *paprikash* are updated and lightened up here; osso buco falls off the bone (there's also a seafood version with salmon). More contemporary items include chicken Kiev, stuffed with goat cheese and topped with a tricolor salad, and pan-seared duck breast with raspberry sauce. Multiple Golden Spoon award–winning Macedonian chef-proprietor Klime Kovaceski takes pride in serving more food than you can possibly manage, including home-baked rhubarb pie. ⊠ *726 41st St., Miami Beach* ☎ *305/673–8266* ☱ *AE, D, DC, MC, V* ⊘ *Closed Mon. No lunch.*

Beaches

The **beach on Ocean Drive from 1st to 22nd Street**—primarily the 10-block stretch from 5th to 15th Street—is one of the most talked-about beachfronts in America. The beach is wide, white, and bathed by warm aquamarine waves. Separating the sand from the traffic of Ocean Drive is palm-fringed Lummus Park, with its volleyball nets and chickee huts for shade. The beach also has some of the funkiest lifeguard stands you'll ever see, pop stars shooting music videos, and visitors from all over the world. Popular with gays is the beach at **12th Street.** Because much of South Beach has an adult flavor—women are often casually topless—many families prefer the beach's quieter southern reaches, especially **3rd Street Beach** (⊠ Ocean Dr. and 3rd St., South Beach). Unless you're parking south of 3rd Street, metered spaces near the waterfront are rarely empty. Instead, opt for a public garage and walk; you'll have lots of fun people-watching, too. ☎ *305/673–7714.*

Shopping

In Greater Miami you're never more than 15 minutes from a major commercial area that serves as both a shopping and entertainment venue for tourists and locals. The shopping is great on a two-block stretch of **Collins Avenue** between 6th and 8th streets. The busy **Lincoln Road Mall** is just a few blocks from the beach and convention center, making it popular with locals and tourists. There's an energy to shopping here, especially on weekends, when the pedestrian mall is filled with locals. Creative merchandise, galleries, and a Sunday-morning antiques market can be found among the art galleries and cool cafés. An 18-screen movie theater anchors the west end of the street. **Bayside Marketplace** (⊠ 401 Biscayne Blvd., Downtown), the 16-acre shopping complex on Biscayne Bay, has more than 100 specialty shops, live entertainment, tour-boat docks, and a food court. It's open late (until 10 during the week, 11 on Friday and Saturday), but its restaurants stay open even later. Browse, buy, or simply relax by the bay with a tropical drink.

Nightlife

Most of the city's nightlife scene is concentrated in South Beach. The best, most complete source is the *New Times,* a free weekly distributed throughout Miami–Dade County each Thursday. Greater Miami's English-language daily newspaper, the *Miami Herald,* publishes reliable reviews and comprehensive listings in its "Weekend" section on Friday and in the "IN South Florida" section on Sunday. Various tabloids reporting on South Beach entertainment and the Miami social scene come and go but *Ocean Drive Magazine* remains the most reliable glossy monthly publication for what's new and hot in the city's fashion, nightlife, and dining scenes. Buy it on the newsstands at Publix or Books & Books, or pick it up for free in South Beach's high-end hotels, salons, and boutiques. *Wire* covers the gay scene.

Exploring Miami

In the 1950s, Miami was best known for alligator wrestlers and you-pick strawberry fields or citrus groves. Well, things have changed. Miami on the mainland is South Florida's commercial hub, while its sultry sister, Miami Beach (America's Riviera), encompasses 17 islands in Biscayne Bay. Seducing winter refugees with its sunshine, beaches, palms, and nightlife, this is what most people envision when planning a trip to what they think of as Miami. If you want to do any exploring, you'll have to drive.

❸ Art Deco District Welcome Center. Run by the Miami Design Preservation League, the center provides information about the buildings in the district. A gift shop sells 1930s–1950s art deco memorabilia, posters, and books on Miami's history. Several tours—covering Lincoln Road, Espanola Way, North Beach, the entire Art Deco District, among others—start here. You can rent audiotapes for a self-guided tour, join one of the regular morning (Wed. & Fri.-Sun.) or Thursday-evening walking tours, or take a bicycle tour. ⊠ *1001 Ocean Dr., at Barbara Capitman Way (10th St.), South Beach* ☎ *305/531–3484 or 305/672–2014* ☞ *Tours $20* ☉ *Sun.-Thurs. 10–7, Fri.-Sat. 10–6.*

❶ Bass Museum of Art. European art is the focus of this impressive museum in historic Collins Park, a short drive north of SoBe's key sights. Works on display include *The Holy Family,* a painting by Peter Paul Rubens; *The Tournament,* one of several 16th-century Flemish tapestries; and works by Albrecht Dürer and Henri de Toulouse-Lautrec. An $8 million, three-phase expansion by architect Arata Isozaki added another wing, cafeteria, and theater, doubling the museum's size to nearly 40,000 square feet. ⊠ *2121 Park Ave., South Beach* ☎ *305/673–7530* ⊕ *www.bassmuseum. org* ⊠ *$8* ⊘ *Tues.–Sat. 10–5, Thurs. 10–9, Sun. 11–5.*

⑤ Brickell Village. Brickell (rhymes with "fickle") is an up-and-coming downtown area with new low- and high-rise condos, a shopping area, Brickell Park, and plenty of popular restaurants. **Perricone's Marketplace and Café** (⊠ 15 S.E. 10th St., Brickell Village) is the biggest and most popular of the area's many Italian restaurants, in a 120-year-old Vermont barn. The cooking is simple and good. Buy your wine from the on-premises deli and bring it to your table for a small corking fee. ⊠ *Between Miami River and S.W. 15th St., Brickell Village.*

⑧ Fairchild Tropical Garden. Comprising 83 acres, this is the largest tropical
FodorsChoice   botanical garden in the continental United States. Eleven lakes, a rain
★   forest, and lots of palm trees, cycads, and flowers, including orchids, mountain roses, bellflowers, coral trees, and bougainvillea make it a garden for the senses—and there's special assistance for the hearing impaired. Take the free guided tram tour, which leaves on the hour. Spicing up the social calendar are garden sales (don't miss the Ramble in November or the International Mango Festival in July), moonlight strolls, and symphony concerts. A gift shop in the visitor center is a popular source for books on gardening and horticulture, ordered by botanists the world over. ⊠ *10901 Old Cutler Rd., Coral Gables* ☎ *305/667–1651* ⊕ *www. fairchildgarden.org* ⊠ *$20* ⊘ *Daily 9:30–4:30.*

② Lincoln Road Mall. The Morris Lapidus–renovated Lincoln Road, just a few
FodorsChoice   blocks from the beach and convention center, is fun, lively, and friendly
★   for people old, young, gay, and straight—and their dogs. Folks skate, scoot, bike, or jog here past the electronics stores at the Collins Avenue end toward the chichi boutiques and outdoor cafés heading west. An 18-screen movie theater anchors the west end of the street. The best times to hit the road are during Sunday-morning farmers' markets and on weekend evenings when cafés are bustling; art galleries, like Romero Britto's Britto Central, schedule openings; street performers take the stage; and bookstores, import shops, and clothing stores are open late. ⊠ *Lincoln Rd. between Collins Ave. and Alton Rd., South Beach.*

⑥ Little Havana. More than 40 years ago the tidal wave of Cubans fleeing the Castro regime flooded into an older neighborhood west of downtown Miami. Don't expect a sparkling and lively reflection of 1950s Havana, however. What you will find are ramshackle motels and cluttered storefronts. With a million Cubans and other Latinos—who make up more than half the metropolitan population—dispersed throughout Greater Miami, Little Havana and neighboring East Little Havana remain magnets for Hispanics and Anglos alike, who come to experience the flavor of traditional Cuban culture. That culture, of course, functions in Spanish. Many Little Havana residents and shopkeepers speak little or no English. In Little Havana's commercial heart, **Calle Ocho** (⊠ S.

W. 8th St., Little Havana), experience such Cuban favorites as hand-rolled cigars or sandwiches piled with meats and cheeses. Although the entire area deserves exploring, if time is limited, try the stretch from Southwest 14th to 11th avenues. In **Plaza de la Cubanidad** (⊠ W. Flagler St. and S.W. 17th Ave., Little Havana) redbrick sidewalks surround a fountain and monument with the words of José Martí, a leader in Cuba's struggle for independence from Spain and a hero to Cuban refugees and immigrants in Miami. The quotation, LAS PALMAS SON NOVIAS QUE ESPERAN (The palm trees are waiting brides), counsels hope and fortitude to the Cubans.

❹ **Parrot Jungle Island.** One of South Florida's original tourist attractions, Parrot Jungle opened in 1936 and has relocated to Watson Island, linked by the MacArthur Causeway (I–395) to Miami and Miami Beach. In addition to a thousand exotic birds, the attraction includes a 17-foot Asian crocodile, a 9-foot albino alligator, a serpentarium filled with venomous snakes, a petting zoo, and a two-story-high aviary with more than 100 free-flying macaws. A restaurant with indoor and outdoor seating overlooks a lake where 60 postcard-perfect Caribbean flamingos hang out. Orchids and ferns and even trees from the original site were transplanted along a Disneyesque jungle river that meanders through the park. ⊠ *980 MacArthur Causeway, Watson Island* ☎ *305/258–6453* ⊕ *www. parrotjungle.com* ⊠ *$27.95 plus $7 parking* ⊙ *Daily 10–6; last admission 4:30.*

❼ **Vizcaya Museum & Gardens.** Of the 10,000 people living in Miami between 1912 and 1916, about 1,000 of them were gainfully employed by Chicago industrialist James Deering to build the $20-million Italian Renaissance–style winter residence. Once comprising 180 acres, the grounds now cover a still-substantial 30-acre tract, including a native hammock and more than 10 acres of formal gardens and fountains overlooking Biscayne Bay. The house, open to the public, contains 70 rooms, 34 of which are filled with paintings, sculpture, antique furniture, and other decorative arts dating from the 15th through the 19th century and representing the Renaissance, baroque, rococo, and neoclassical styles. ⊠ *3251 S. Miami Ave., Coconut Grove* ☎ *305/250–9133* ⊕ *www. vizcayamuseum.com* ⊠ *$12* ⊙ *House daily 9:30–4:30, garden daily 9:30–5:30.*

Fodor'sChoice
★

MOBILE, ALABAMA

Clint Hill

Fort Condé was the name given by the French in 1711 to the site known today as Mobile; around it blossomed the first white settlement in what is now Alabama. For eight years it was the capital of the French colonial empire, and it remained under French control until 1763, long after the capital had moved to New Orleans. Mobile, known as the "Port City"— not to mention the birthplace of Mardi Gras—is noted for its tree-lined boulevards fanning westward from the riverfront. In the heart of busy downtown is Bienville Square, a park with an ornate cast-iron fountain and shaded by centuries-old live oaks. One of the city's main thoroughfares, Dauphin Street, has many thriving restaurants, bars, and shops.

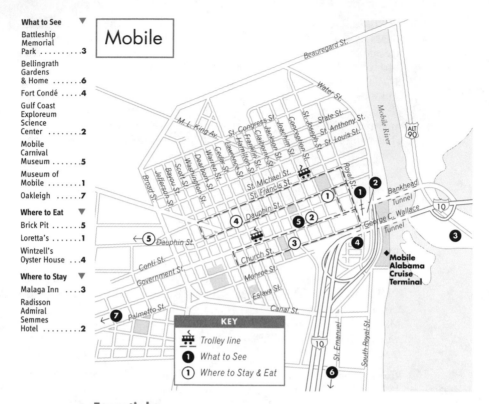

Essentials

HOURS Most stores are open from 10 or 11 until 7 or 8.

INTERNET Your best bet for Internet service in Mobile is your hotel since Internet cafés are few and far between. You can get online at the **Mobile Public Library** (⊠ 704 Government St. ☎ 251-208-7076); at this writing, it was operating from a temporary branch, but the main library just across the street was expected to reopen in 2007.

VISITOR **Mobile Bay Convention & Visitor's Bureau** (⊠ 1 S. Water St., Mobile,
INFORMATION AL ☎ 251/208–2000 or 800/566–2453 ⊕ www.mobilebay.org).

The Cruise Port

Only one ship is based in Mobile at this writing, and it does shorter (four- and five-day) Western Caribbean itineraries. The cruise terminal is near the downtown area. Free shuttles from Mobile's public transit system, Moda, are provided to the cruise terminal from throughout downtown Mobile on days when ships are in port. It's a good home port to consider if you want to drive to your cruise embarkation point, but it's less convenient by air, with just a few airlines flying to the Mobile Regional Airport; however, the Biloxi and Pensacola airports are a relatively short drive away.

🛈 **Mobile Alabama Cruise Terminal** ⊠ 201 S. Water St., Mobile, AL ☎ 251/338–7447 ⊕ www.shipmobile.com.

AIRPORT
TRANSFERS
Taxis are available to the cruise terminal, or you can call the Mobile Regional
Airport Shuttle, which will transport
you for $20 ($30 round-trip). Mobile
Bay Transportation Company also operates airport transfers for $13 one-way
and $25 round-trip.

🖪 Mobile Bay Transportation Company ☎ 251/
633-5693 or 800/272-6234 ⊕ www.
mobilebaytransportation.com.

Mobile Regional Airport Shuttle ☎ 251/633-
0313 or 800/357-5373 ⊕ www.mobairport.com.

> ### MOBILE BEST BETS
>
> ■ **Bellingrath Gardens.** One of the finest gardens in the South is just outside Mobile.
>
> ■ **Battleship Memorial Park.** Many people come to Mobile just to tour the USS *Alabama*.
>
> ■ **Oakleigh.** This well-preserved antebellum home is furnished with period antiques; it's a great experience if you like history.

PARKING
Parking is available in a garage next to
the cruise terminal. It costs $50 to park for a 4-day cruise, $60 for a 5-
day cruise; RVs cost double. You can pay by cash or credit card.

Exploring Mobile

Bullets in the margins refer to points of interest on the Mobile map.

③ Battleship Memorial Park. On Mobile Bay, east of downtown, is the site of
the 155-acre park where the battleship USS *Alabama* is anchored. A self-
guided tour gives a fascinating glimpse into the World War II vessel, which
had a crew of 2,500. Dry-docked next to it is the USS *Drum,* a World
War II submarine. Other exhibits include the B-52 bomber *Calamity Jane.*
⊠ *2703 Battleship Pkwy., Mobile* ☎ *251/433–2703 or 800/426–4929*
⊕ *www.ussalabama.com* 🖾 *$12* ☺ *Apr.–Sept., daily 8–6; Oct.–Mar.,
daily 8–4.*

⑥ Bellingrath Gardens & Home. One of the most popular gardens in the South
FodorsChoice is Bellingrath, famous for its magnificent azaleas, which are part of 65
★ acres of gardens set amid a 905-acre semitropical landscape. Showtime
for the azaleas is mid- to late-March, when some 250,000 plantings of
200 different species are ablaze with color. But Bellingrath is a year-round
wonder, with more than 75 varieties of roses blooming in summer,
60,000 chrysanthemum plants cascading in fall, and red fields of poin-
settias brightening winter. Countless species and flowering plants spring
up along the Fowl River, surround streams, and a lake populated by ducks
and swans. A free map lets you plan your own strolls along flagstone
paths across charming bridges. In April and October, large numbers of
migratory birds drop by. You can also visit the home of Coca-Cola bottling pioneer Walter D. Bellingrath. Forty-five-minute boat cruises on the
Fowl River aboard the *Southern Belle* leave from the dock next to the
home daily at 10, noon, and 2 from mid-February through Thanksgiving. Take I–10 West to Exit 15, then follow CR 59 South to Theodore.
⊠ *12401 Bellingrath Gardens Rd., Theodore* ☎ *251/973–2217, 800/
247–8420, 251/973–1244 for boat cruises* ⊕ *www.bellingrath.org*
🖾 *Gardens $10; gardens and home $18; gardens, home, and cruise $26*
☺ *Gardens daily 8–5, home daily 9–4.*

④ Ft. Condé. In 1711, France built this fort that would one day expand and
become Mobile. The city's French origins endure in its creole cuisine. Now,

6

150 years after the fort was destroyed, its remains were discovered during construction of the I–10 interchange. A reconstructed portion houses the city's **visitor center,** as well as a museum. Costumed guides conduct tours. ⊠ *150 S. Royal St., Mobile* ☎ *251/208–7304* ⊠ *Free* ⊙ *Daily 8–5.*

Gulf Coast Exploreum Science Center. Near Ft. Condé, Mobile's science museum for children hosts traveling exhibits and an IMAX dome theater. ⊠ *65 Government St., Mobile* ☎ *251/208–6883 or 877/625–4386* ⊕ *www.exploreum. net* ⊠ *$18.25* ⊙ *Weekdays 9–5, Sat. 10–5, Sun. noon–5.*

Mobile Carnival Museum. Mobile celebrates its heritage in this converted 1870 townhouse dedicated to all things Mardi Gras. The pre-Lenten festival was first celebrated in the New World here in Mobile in 1703, and the museum allows the party to continue 365 days a year. Displays include regal costumes of past kings and queens, traditional Mardi Gras "throws" (items that are thrown from the floats during parades), and even full-sized floats. ⊠ *355 Government St.* ☎ *251/432–3324* ⊕ *www. carnivalmuseum.com* ⊠ *$5* ⊙ *Mon., Wed., Fri., Sat. 9–5.*

Museum of Mobile. The museum opened in 2001 in the renovated circa-1857 Southern Market/Old City Hall building next to the Exploreum. Interactive exhibits and special collections of antique silver, weapons, and more tell the 300-year history of Mobile. ⊠ *111 S. Royal St., Mobile* ☎ *251/208–7569* ⊕ *www.museumofmobile.com* ⊠ *$5* ⊙ *Mon.–Sat. 9–5, Sun. 1–5.*

★ **Oakleigh.** About 1½ mi (2 ½ km) from Ft. Condé, in the heart of the historic Oakleigh Garden District, is an antebellum Greek Revival–style mansion, built between 1833 and 1838. Costumed guides give tours of the home, which has fine period furniture, portraits, silver, jewelry, kitchen implements, toys, and more. Tickets include a tour of neighboring **Cox-Deasy House,** an 1850s cottage furnished with simple 19th-century pieces. ⊠ *350 Oakleigh Pl., Mobile* ☎ *251/432–1281* ⊕ *www. historicmobile.org* ⊠ *$7* ⊙ *Oakleigh: Tues.–Sat. 9–3.*

Shopping

Most shopping in Mobile is in malls and shopping centers in the suburbs. Stores are generally open Monday to Saturday 10–9, Sunday 12–6. Antiques buffs may be interested in Mobile's many antiques stores that are in the Loop area of midtown (where Government Street, Airport Boulevard, and Dauphin Island Parkway converge); several shops are within walking distance of each other.

Nightlife

Most of Mobile's nightlife centers around the downtown's former commercial district, Dauphin Street, which today has a number of restaurants and nightspots spread out over several blocks. Mobilians have taken to calling the area LoDa, short for Lower Dauphin.

Where to Eat

For price categories, *see* Dining at the beginning of this chapter.

> **CAUTION**
>
> Notify the cruise line of any special dietary restrictions when booking your cruise and follow up on the arrangements a couple of months before embarking.

$–$$$ ✕ **Loretta's.** At a colorful corner a block off Dauphin Street, this place has its own dramatic flair. It's hidden behind a wall of glass covered in creeping fig, with a unique style—gleaming silver palm trees and whimsical, mismatched salt and pepper shakers. In the kitchen, owner-chef Christopher Hunter adds creative nuances to Southern favorites, such as sausage-stuffed pork loin and pan-seared sashimi tuna steak. ⊠ *19 S. Conception St.* ☎ *251/432–2200* ▤ *AE, D, DC, MC, V* ⊗ *Closed Sun. and Mon. No lunch Sat. No dinner Tues.*

> ### FRESH, WRINKLE-FREE
>
> You can tuck fabric softener sheets between garments as you pack to keep your clothing smelling fresh during travels. Dry cleaning bags are good to keep out wrinkles.

$–$$$ ✕ **Wintzell's Oyster House.** "Oysters—fried, steamed, or nude" is the motto for this downtown Mobile institution. Founded in 1938 by Oliver Wintzell, the restaurant is in the same location and with few cosmetic changes since it was founded, the walls still covered by Oliver's home-spun sayings. You can get your oysters by the dozen or half-dozen, but won't go wrong sampling any of the seafood on the menu or simply enjoying a cup of homemade gumbo. ⊠ *605 Dauphin St.* ☎ *251/432–4605* ▤ *AE, D, DC, MC, V.*

¢–$ ✕ **Brick Pit.** It's "the best damn barbecue in the state of Alabama," owner Bill Armbrecht insists. Chicken, ribs, and pork are smoked for hours over a blend of hickory and pecan to achieve a distinct flavor. Barbecue sauce comes spicy or sweet, with soft white bread for dipping. Be sure to add your name to the graffiti scrawled in red marker all over the walls and ceiling. Try the smoked pulled-pork plate. ⊠ *5456 Old Shell Rd.* ☎ *251/ 343–0001* ▤ *AE, DC, MC, V* ⊗ *Closed Sun. and Mon.*

Where to Stay

Several local hotels offer cruise packages that include lodging, parking for the duration of your cruise, and a shuttle to the cruise terminal.

For price categories, *see* Lodging at the beginning of this chapter.

$$ ▦ **Radisson Admiral Semmes Hotel.** This restored 1940 hotel in the historic district is a favorite with local politicians. It's also popular with partygoers, particularly during Mardi Gras, because of its excellent location directly on the parade route. The spacious, high-ceiling rooms have a burgundy-and-green color scheme and are furnished in Queen Anne and Chippendale styles. ⊠ *251 Government St., 36602* ☎ *251/432–8000 or 800/333–3333* ☐ *251/405–5942* ⊕ *www.radisson.com* ⟿ *148 rooms, 22 suites* ⚭ *In room: Ethernet. In hotel: Restaurant, room service, bar, pool, laundry service, public Wi-Fi, no-smoking rooms* ▤ *AE, D, DC, MC, V.*

$–$$ ▦ **Malaga Inn.** A delightful, romantic getaway, this place comprises two townhouses built by a wealthy landowner in 1862. The lobby is furnished with 19th-century antiques and opens onto a landscaped central courtyard with a fountain. The rooms are large, airy, and furnished with antiques. The Malaga is on a quiet street downtown, within walking distance of the Museum of Mobile and the Gulf Coast Exploreum, and offers a cruise package. ⊠ *359 Church St., 36602* ☎ *251/438–4701 or 800/235–1586* ☐ *251/438–4701 Ext. 123* ⊕ *www.malagainn.com* ⟿ *35 rooms, 3 suites* ⚭ *In room: Wi-Fi. In hotel: pool, public Wi-Fi* ▤ *AE, D, MC, V.*

6

NEW ORLEANS, LOUISIANA

Tucked between the Mississippi River and Lake Ponchartrain, New Orleans is mostly below sea level, and when Hurricane Katrina struck in August 2005, the city's levees strained under the force of the strong storm's wind and rain, finally breaking. The resulting floods covered 80% of New Orleans. Fortunately, much of the Big Easy that is well known to tourists was relatively untouched by the floods, including most of the French Quarter, the River Walk, the Garden District, and most of Uptown. Within months, these areas rebounded. Although the city is still recovering, all the aforementioned areas are up and running and eager to welcome visitors.

> ## NEW ORLEANS BEST BETS
>
> ■ **Aquarium of the Americas.** Especially good for families is this fantastic aquarium near the city's convention center.
>
> ■ **Eating Well.** A highlight in New Orleans is dining. If you ever wanted to splurge on a great restaurant meal, this is the place to do it. At the very least, have a beignet at Café du Monde.
>
> ■ **Hermann-Grima House.** This is one of the best-preserved historic homes in the French Quarter.

Essentials

HOURS Shops in the French Quarter tend to be open late, but stores in most of the malls close by 9. Restaurants tend to be open late as well.

INTERNET **French Quarter Postal Emporium** (✉ 1000 Bourbon St. ☎ 504/525–6651 ⊕ www.frenchquarterpostal.com) offers Internet service and is also a mailing center.

VISITOR INFORMATION You can get information about visiting New Orleans from the Louisiana Office of Tourism and the New Orleans Convention & Visitors Bureau.

Louisiana Office of Tourism ✉ Box 94291, Baton Rouge, LA 70804-9291 ☎ 800/633-6970 ⊟ 225/342-8390 ⊕ www.louisianatravel.com. **New Orleans Convention & Visitors Bureau** ✉ 2020 St. Charles Ave., 70130 ☎ 800/672-6124 or 504/566-5011 ⊟ 504/566-5021 ⊕ www.neworleanscvb.com ✉ in the U.K.: ✉ 33 Market Pl., Hitchin, Nertfordshire SG5 1DY ☎ 01462-455323 ⊟ 01462-455391.

The Cruise Port

The Julia Street Cruise Terminal is at the end of Julia Street on the Mississippi River; the Erato Street Terminal is just to the north. Both terminals are behind the Ernest M. Morial Convention Center. You can walk to the French Quarter from here in about 10 minutes; it's a short taxi ride to the Quarter or nearby hotels. Carnival and Norwegian base ships here at least part of the year, and the *Delta Queen, Mississippi Queen,* and *American Queen* river steamboats leave from the Robin Street Wharf, just south of the Julia Street terminals.

If you are driving, you'll probably approach New Orleans on I–10. Take the Business 90 West/Westbank exit, locally known as Pontchartrain Expressway, and proceed to the Tchoupitoulas Street/South Peters Street exit. Continue to Convention Center Boulevard, where you will take a

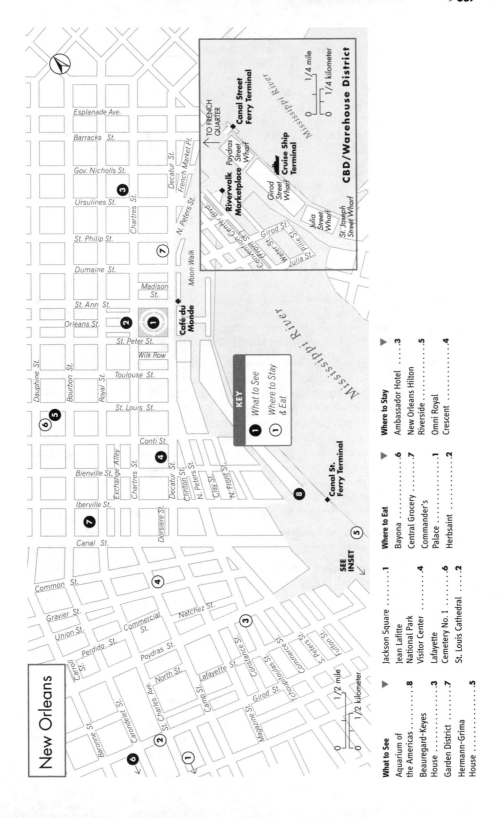

New Orleans

What to See ▸

Aquarium of
the Americas **8**
Beauregard-Keyes
House **3**
Garden District **7**
Hermann-Grima
House **5**
Jackson Square **1**
Jean Lafitte
National Park
Visitor Center **4**
Lafayette
Cemetery No. 1 ....**6**
St. Louis Cathedral **2**

Where to Eat ▸

Bayona **6**
Central Grocery **7**
Commander's
Palace **1**
Herbsaint **2**

Where to Stay ▸

Ambassador Hotel **3**
New Orleans Hilton
Riverside **5**
Omni Royal
Crescent **4**

KEY

① What to See
① Where to Stay
   & Eat

CBD/Warehouse District

Canal Street
Ferry Terminal

Cruise Ship
Terminal

Riverwalk
Marketplace

Poydras
Street
Wharf

Girod
Street
Wharf

Julia
Street
Wharf

St. Joseph
Street Wharf

Mississippi River

TO FRENCH
QUARTER

0   1/4 mile
0   1/4 kilometer

368 < **Ports of Embarkation**

right turn. Continue to Henderson Street, where you will turn left, and then continue to Port of New Orleans Place. Take a left on Port of New Orleans Place to Julia Street Terminals and to the Erato Street Cruise Terminal 1. 🚢 **Port of New Orleans** ✉ Port of New Orleans Pl. at foot of Julia St. ☎ 504/522-2551 ⊕ www.portno.com.

AIRPORT **TRANSFERS** Shuttle-bus service to and from the airport and the cruise port is available through Airport Shuttle New Orleans. Buses leave regularly from the ground level near the baggage claim. Return

YOUR CARD, PLEASE

Print cards with your name, address, phone number, and email address to share with new friends. Stiff, business card–style paper can be purchased at nearly any office supply store, and you can make the cards on your computer at home. Having your cards handy sure beats hunting for pens and scribbling on scraps of paper to swap addresses.

trips to the airport need to be booked in advance. The cost one-way is $13 per person, and the trip takes about 45 minutes.

A cab ride to or from the airport from uptown or downtown New Orleans costs $28 for the first two passengers and $12 for each additional passenger. At the airport, pickup is on the lower level, outside the baggage claim area. There may be an additional charge for extra baggage. 🚢 **New Orleans Tours Airport Shuttle** ☎ 504/522-3500 or 866/596-2699.

PARKING If you are spending some time in the city before or after your cruise, finding a parking space is fairly easy in most of the city, except for the French Quarter, where meter maids are plentiful and tow trucks eager. If in doubt about a space, pass it up and pay to use a parking lot. Avoid parking spaces at corners and curbs: less than 15 feet between your car and the corner will result in a ticket. Watch for temporary NO PARKING signs, which pop up along parade routes and film shoots. Long-term and overnight parking are extremely expensive at hotels and garages. Parking for the duration of your cruise is available for $14 per night and is on Erato Street; if you want, SeaCaps will take your bags directly to the ship so you just have to deal with your hand luggage.

Exploring New Orleans
Bullets in the margins refer to points of interest on the New Orleans map.

The **French Quarter,** the oldest part of the city, lives up to all you've heard: it's alive with the sights, sounds, odors, and experiences of a major entertainment hub. At some point, ignore your better judgment and take a stroll down **Bourbon Street,** past the bars, restaurants, music clubs, and novelty shops that have given this strip its reputation as the playground of the South. Be sure to find time to stop at Café du Monde for chicory-laced coffee and beignets. With its beautifully landscaped gardens surrounding elegant antebellum homes, the **Garden District** is mostly residential, but most home owners do not mind your enjoying the sights from outside the cast-iron fences surrounding their magnificent properties.

🐊 **⑧** **Aquarium of the Americas.** Each of the four major exhibit areas—the Amazon Rain Forest, the Caribbean Reef, the Mississippi River, and the Gulf Coast—has fish and animals native to that environment. A fun exhibit

Fodor's Choice ★

called Beyond Green houses more than 25 frog species and includes informative displays. The aquarium's spectacular design allows you to feel part of the watery worlds by providing close-up encounters with the inhabitants. A gift shop and café are on the premises. You can get a combined ticket for the aquarium and the Audubon Zoo, including a round-trip cruise down the river. ⊠ *1 Canal St., French Quarter* ☎ *504/ 581–4629 or 800/774–7394* ⊕ *www.auduboninstitute.org* ✉ *Aquarium $17; combination ticket for aquarium, zoo, and IMAX theater $28* ⊙ *Aquarium Sun.–Thurs. 9:30–6 (last ticket sold at 5), Fri. and Sat. 9:30–7 (last ticket sold at 6).*

❸ Beauregard-Keyes House. This stately 19th-century mansion with period furnishings was the temporary home of Confederate general P. G. T. Beauregard. The house and grounds had severely deteriorated by the 1940s, when the well-known novelist Frances Parkinson Keyes moved in and helped restore it. Her studio at the back of the large courtyard remains intact, complete with family photos, original manuscripts, and her doll and teapot collections. If you do not have time to tour the house, take a peek through the gates at the beautiful walled garden at the corner of Chartres and Ursulines streets. Landscaped in the same sun pattern as Jackson Square, the garden is in bloom throughout the year. ⊠ *1113 Chartres St., French Quarter* ☎ *504/523-7257* ✉ *$5* ⊙ *Mon.–Sat. 10-3, tours on the hr.*

❼ Garden District. The Garden District is divided into two sections by Jackson Avenue. Upriver from Jackson is the wealthy **Upper Garden District,** where the homes are meticulously kept. Below Jackson, the **Lower Garden District** is considerably rougher. Though the homes here are often just as structurally beautiful, most of them lack the recent restorations of those of the Upper Garden District. The streets are also less well patrolled; wander cautiously. **Magazine Street,** lined with antiques shops and coffeehouses (ritzier along the Upper Garden District, hipper along the Lower Garden District), serves as a southern border to the Garden District, and St. Charles Avenue forms the northern border.

❺ Hermann-Grima House. One of the largest and best-preserved examples of American architecture in the Quarter, this Georgian-style house has the only restored private stable and the only working 1830s Creole kitchen in the Quarter. American architect William Brand built the house in 1831. You'll want to check the gift shop, which has many local crafts and books. ⊠ *820 St. Louis St., French Quarter* ☎ *504/525-5661* ✉ *$6, combination ticket with the Gallier House $10* ⊙ *Tours weekdays 10, 11, noon, 2, 3.*

FodorśChoice
★

❶ Jackson Square. Surrounded by historic buildings and filled with plenty of the city's atmospheric street life, the heart of the French Quarter is today a beautifully landscaped park. Originally called the Place d'Armes, the square was founded in 1718 as a military parade ground. It was also the site of public executions carried out in various styles, including burning at the stake, beheading, breaking on the wheel, and hanging. A **statue of Andrew Jackson,** victorious leader of the Battle of New Orleans in the War of 1812, commands the center of the square; the park was renamed for him in the 1850s. Among the notable buildings around the square are **St. Louis Cathedral** and **Faulkner House.** Two Spanish colonial–style buildings, the **Cabildo** and the **Presbytère,** flank the cathedral. The handsome rows of brick apartments on each side of the square are the **Pontalba Buildings.** The park is landscaped in a sun pattern, with walkways set like rays streaming out from the center, a popular garden design in the royal court of King Louis XIV, the Sun King. ⊠ *French Quarter ⊙ Park daily 8–dusk; flagstone paths on park's periphery open 24 hrs.*

★ ❹ **Jean Lafitte National Park Visitor Center.** This center has free visual and sound exhibits on the customs of various communities throughout the state, as well as information-rich daily history tours of the French Quarter. The one-hour daily tour leaves at 9:30 AM; tickets are handed out one per person (you must be present to get a ticket), beginning at 9 AM, for that day's tours only. Arrive at least 15 minutes before tour time to be sure of a spot. The office also supervises and provides information on Jean Lafitte National Park Barataria Unit across the river from New Orleans, and the Chalmette Battlefield, where the Battle of New Orleans was fought in the War of 1812. ⊠ *419 Decatur St., French Quarter* ☏ *504/589–2636 ⊙ Daily 9–5.*

★ ❻ **Lafayette Cemetery No. 1.** Begun around 1833, this was the first planned cemetery in the city, with symmetrical rows, roadways for funeral vehicles, and lavish aboveground vaults and tombs for the wealthy families who built the surrounding mansions. In 1852, 2,000 yellow fever victims were buried here. The cemetery and environs figure in Anne Rice's popular series *The Vampire Chronicles,* and movies such as *Interview with the Vampire* have used this walled cemetery for its eerie beauty. The cemetery remained intact following Hurricane Katrina, and you can wander the grounds on your own or take an organized tour. One guided tour is arranged by **Save Our Cemeteries** (☏ 504/525–3377). ⊠ *1400 block of Washington Ave., Garden District* ⊠ *Cemetery free, tour $6 ⊙ Weekdays 7–2:30, Sat. 7–noon; tours Mon., Wed., Fri., and Sat. at 10:30.*

❷ **St. Louis Cathedral.** The oldest active cathedral in the United States, this church at the heart of the Old City is named for the 13th-century French king who led two crusades. The current building, which replaced two structures destroyed by fire, dates from 1794, although it was remodeled and enlarged in 1851. The austere interior is brightened by murals covering the ceiling and stained-glass windows along the first floor. While staff shortages post-Katrina have suspended the tour schedule, new tour guides are currently being trained, and tours of the cathedral should resume in 2006. The statue of the Sacred Heart of Jesus dominates **St. Anthony's Garden,** which extends behind the rectory to Royal Street. This statue was damaged during the storm, losing the thumb and forefinger of one hand. The pieces have been recovered, but the statue's injuries have yet to be repaired. ⊠ *615 Père Antoine Alley, French Quarter* ☏ *504/525–9585* ⊠ *Free ⊙ Tours Mon.–Sat. 9–4:30, Sun. 1–4:30.*

Shopping

The fun of shopping in New Orleans is in the regional items available throughout the city, in the smallest shops or the biggest department stores. You can take home some of the flavor of the city: its pralines (pecan candies), seafood (packaged to go), Louisiana red beans and rice, coffee (pure or with chicory), and creole and Cajun spices (cayenne pepper, chili, and garlic). The French Quarter is well known for its fine antiques shops, located mainly on Royal and Chartres streets. The main shopping areas in the city are the French Quarter, with narrow, picturesque streets lined with specialty, gift, fashion, and antique shops and art galleries; the Central Business District (CBD), populated mostly with jewelry, specialty and department stores; and the Warehouse District, best known for contemporary arts galleries and cultural museums. **Jax Brewery** (✉ 600 Decatur St., French Quarter ☎ 504/566–7245 ⊕ www.jacksonbrewery.com), a historic building that once was a factory for Jax beer, now holds a Jax Beer museum and an upscale mall filled with both local shops and national chains. **Riverwalk Marketplace** (✉ 1 Poydras St. ☎ 504/522–1555 ⊕ www.riverwalkmarketplace.com), along the riverfront, has a ½-mi-long (1-km-long) marketplace with 180 local and nationally known shops and restaurants, including Café du Monde.

Nightlife

No American city places such a premium on pleasure as New Orleans. From swank hotel lounges to sweaty dance clubs, refined jazz clubs and raucous Bourbon Street bars, this city is serious about frivolity. And famous for it. Partying is more than an occasional indulgence in this city—it's a lifestyle. Bars tend to open in the early afternoon and stay open into the morning hours; live music, though, follows a more restrained schedule. Some jazz spots and clubs in the French Quarter stage evening sets around 6 PM or 9 PM; at a few clubs, such as the Palm Court, the bands actually finish by 11 PM. But this is the exception: for the most part, gigs begin between 10 and 11 PM, and locals rarely emerge for an evening out before 10. Keep in mind that the lack of legal closing time means that shows advertised for 11 may not start until after midnight.

★ **Preservation Hall** (✉ 726 St. Peter St., French Quarter ☎ 504/522–2841 or 504/523–8939), the jazz tradition that flowered in the 1920s, is enshrined in this cultural landmark. A bust of legendary New Orleans pi-
★ anist Professor Longhair, or "Fess," greets visitors at the door of **Tipitina's** (✉ 501 Napoleon Ave., Uptown ☎ 504/895–8477), which takes its name from one of his most popular songs. As the concert posters pinned to the walls attest, Tip's hosts a wide variety of touring bands and local acts. The long-running Sunday afternoon Cajun dance still packs the floor. The Tipitina's Foundation has an office and workshop upstairs, where local musicians affected by Hurricane Katrina can network, gain access to resources, and search for gigs.

Sightseeing Tours

Several local tour companies give two- to four-hour city tours by bus that include the French Quarter, the Garden District, uptown New Orleans, and the lakefront. Prices range from $25 to $125 per person, depending on the kind of experience. Both Gray Line and New Orleans Tours offer a longer tour that combines a two-hour city tour by bus with a two-hour steamboat ride on the Mississippi River. Gray Line and Tours by Isabelle both offer tours of Hurricane Katrina devastation as well. **Gray Line** ☎ 800/535–7786 or 504/569–1401 ⊕ www.graylineneworleans.com. **New Orleans Tours** ☎ 888/486–8687 or 504/529–4567 ⊕ www.notours.com. **Tours by Isabelle** ☎ 877/665–8687 or 504/391–3544 ⊕ www.toursbyisabelle.com.

Where to Eat

For price categories, *see* Dining at the beginning of this chapter. Don't miss beignets and rich, chicory-laced coffee at **Café du Monde** (⊠ 800 Decatur St.), in the French Quarter, though there's also an outlet in the Riverwalk.

$$$–$$$$ ✕ **Commander's Palace.** No restaurant captures New Orleans's gastro-
Fodor'sChoice nomic heritage and celebratory spirit as well as this one, long consid-
★ ered the Grande Dame of New Orleans fine dining. The post-Katrina renovation has added new life, especially upstairs, where the Garden Room's glass walls have marvelous views of the giant oak trees on the patio below; other rooms promote conviviality with their bright pastels. The menu's classics include foie-gras-and-rabbit pie; a spicy and meaty turtle soup; terrific grilled veal chops with grits; and a wonderful sautéed Gulf fish coated with crunchy pecans. Among the addictive desserts is the bread-pudding soufflé. ⊠ *1403 Washington Ave., Garden District* ☎ *504/899–8221* ⌀ *Reservations essential* 🖃 *AE, D, DC, MC, V.*

$–$$ ✕ **Herbsaint.** Upscale food and moderate prices are among Herbsaint's as-
Fodor'sChoice sets. Chef Donald Link turns out food that sparkles with robust flavors
★ and top-grade ingredients. "Small plates" and side dishes such as charcu-terie, a knock-'em-dead shrimp bisque, house-made pasta, and cheese- or nut-studded salads are mainstays. Don't overlook the rich and flavorful shrimp and green chile grits cakes with tasso cream sauce. More substan-tial appetites are courted with duck and dirty rice, and chili-glazed pork belly. For dessert, the warm chocolate beignets filled with molten choco-late are deserving of love poems. The plates provide most of the color in the lighthearted, often noisy, rooms. The wine list is expertly compiled and reasonably priced. ⊠ *701 St. Charles Ave., CBD* ☎ *504/524–4114* ⌀ *Reser-vations essential* 🖃 *AE, D, DC, MC, V* ☉ *Closed Sun. No lunch Sat.*

$–$$$ ✕ **Bayona.** "New World" is the label Louisiana native Susan Spicer ap-
Fodor'sChoice plies to her cooking style, which results in such signature dishes as the
★ goat cheese crouton with mushrooms in Madeira cream, and crispy-fried smoked quail on a salad with bourbon-molasses vinaigrette. Vegetarian options include a farmers' market medley with cheddar spoon bread. These and other imaginative dishes are served in an early-19th-century Creole cottage that fairly glows with flower arrangements, elegant photographs, and trompe l'oeil murals suggesting Mediterranean landscapes. Don't skimp on pastry chef Megan Roen's sweets, such as churros with choco-late mousse, and mint julep ice cream.
⊠ *430 Dauphine St., French Quarter* ☎ *504/525–4455* ⌀ *Reservations essen-tial* 🖃 *AE, DC, MC, V* ☉ *Closed Sun. No lunch Sat.*

¢–$$ ✕ **Central Grocery.** This old-fashioned
Fodor'sChoice Italian grocery store produces authen-
★ tic muffulettas, one of the gastronomic gifts of the city's Italian immigrants. Good enough to challenge the po'boy as the local sandwich champs, they're made by filling round loaves of seeded bread with ham, salami, mozzarella,

---

GET MUGGED

Take along an insulated mug with a lid that you can fill at the bever-age station in the buffet area. Your drinks will stay hot or cold, and you won't have to worry about spills. Most bartenders will fill the mug with ice and water or a soft drink. With a straw, your ice will not melt instantly while you lounge at the pool.

and a salad of marinated green olives. Each sandwich, about 10 inches in diameter, is sold in wholes and halves. You can eat your muffuletta at a counter, but some prefer to take theirs out to a bench on Jackson Square or the Moon Walk along the Mississippi riverfront. The Grocery closes at 5:30 PM. ⊠ *923 Decatur St., French Quarter* ☎ *504/523–1620* ▤ *D, MC, V.*

> **CAUTION**
>
> Items confiscated by airport security will not be returned to you. If you are uncertain whether something will pass the security test, pack it in your checked luggage.

Where to Stay

You can stay in a large hotel near the cruise-ship terminal, in the Warehouse District, or in the French Quarter. Hotel rates in New Orleans tend to be on the high end, though deals abound.

For price categories, *see* Lodging at the beginning of this chapter.

$$$$ 🏨 **New Orleans Hilton Riverside.** This sprawling multilevel complex is smack on the Mississippi with superb river views. Guest rooms have French-provincial furnishings; the 180 rooms that share a concierge have fax machines. On Sunday the hotel's Kabby's Restaurant hosts a jazz brunch. The Riverfront streetcar stops out front. Adjacent to Riverwalk Shopping Center and directly across the street from Harrah's New Orleans casino, the hotel has a resident golf pro and a four-hole putting green. The health club is among the best in town. ⊠ *Poydras St. at the Mississippi River, CBD, 70140* ☎ *504/561–0500 or 800/445–8667* 🖷 *504/ 568–1721* ⊕ *www.hilton.com* 🛏 *1,600 rooms, 67 suites* ⌂ *In-room: Wi-Fi. In-hotel: 3 restaurants, tennis courts, pools, gym, parking (fee), no-smoking rooms* ▤ *AE, D, DC, MC, V.*

$$–$$$$ 🏨 **Omni Royal Crescent.** This elegant white-marble hotel built in 1960 is a
FodorsChoice replica of the grand St. Louis Hotel of the 1800s. Sconce-enhanced
★ columns, gilt mirrors, fan windows, and three magnificent chandeliers re-create the atmosphere of old New Orleans. Some rooms have marble baths and marble-top dressers and tables; others have balconies. The recently renovated Rib Room, on the lobby level, has been one of the city's culinary showpieces for more than 40 years. The rooftop pool has the city's best overhead view of the French Quarter. ⊠ *621 St. Louis St., French Quarter, 70140* ☎ *504/529–5333 or 800/843–6664* 🖷 *504/529–7089* ⊕ *www.omnihotels.com* 🛏 *346 rooms, 16 suites* ⌂ *In-room: Wi-Fi. In-hotel: restaurant, pool, gym, parking (fee)* ▤ *AE, D, DC, MC, V.*

$$–$$$ 🏨 **Ambassador Hotel.** Guest rooms at this hotel conveniently bordering the CBD and Warehouse District have real character. Four-poster iron beds, armoires, and local jazz prints are among the furnishings. Exposed brick walls, ceiling fans, and wood floors add to the ambience of the pre–Civil War building. This is a good alternative to huge convention hotels, but it's still just steps from all the major downtown attractions and the Convention Center. The hotel is a five-minute walk from Harrah's New Orleans Casino. ⊠ *535 Tchoupitoulas St., CBD, 70130* ☎ *504/527–5271 or 800/ 455–3417* 🖷 *504/599–2107* ⊕ *www.ahno.com* 🛏 *165 rooms* ⌂ *In-room: Wi-Fi; In-hotel: restaurant, bar, parking (fee)* ▤ *AE, D, DC, MC, V.*

6

NEW YORK, NEW YORK

A few cruise lines now base Caribbean-bound ships in New York City year-round, though most of the market is made up of ships doing seasonal cruises to New England and Bermuda. If you're coming to the city from the immediate area, you can easily arrive the day before and do a bit of sightseeing and perhaps take in a Broadway show. The cruise port in Manhattan is fairly close to Times Square and Midtown hotels and theaters. But the New York City region now has three major cruise ports. You can also leave from Cape Liberty Terminal in Bayonne, New Jersey, on both Celebrity and Royal Caribbean ships. In 2006, a new cruise-ship terminal opened in Red Hook, Brooklyn, and this terminal serves Carnival and Princess ships as well as Cunard's *Queen Mary 2*.

> ## NEW YORK CITY BEST BETS
>
> ■ **An Art Museum.** Take your pick: the Met, MOMA, or the Frick, but this is a true highlight of New York.
>
> ■ **A Broadway Show.** The theater experience in New York is better than almost anywhere else in the world.
>
> ■ **Statue of Liberty.** Just the sight of Lady Liberty will melt the coldest heart, though the highlight of the trip is actually the Ellis Island museum, not the statue itself.

Essentials

HOURS They say that New York never sleeps, and that's particularly true around Times Square, where some stores are open until 11 PM or later even during the week. But most stores outside of the immediate Times Square area are open from 9 or 10 until 6 or 7. Many museums close on Monday.

INTERNET Internet service is offered by most New York hotels, and there are independent Internet cafés all over town. You might even see cheap Internet service in pizzerias and delis. Starbucks offers wireless service for a fee, but if you have your own laptop, you can use the free outdoor Wi-Fi network in Bryant Park (6th Ave., between 42nd and 41st streets).

VISITOR INFORMATION **NYC & Company Convention & Visitors Center** (✉ 810 7th Ave., between W. 52nd and W. 53rd Sts., 3rd fl., Midtown West ☎ 212/484–1222 ⊕ www.nycvisit.com). **Times Square Information Center** (✉ 1560 Broadway, between 46th and 47th Sts., Midtown West ☎ 212/768–1560 ⊕ www.timessquarenyc.org).

The Cruise Port

The **New York Passenger Ship Terminal** is on the far west side of Manhattan, five very long blocks from the Times Square area, between 48th and 52nd streets; the vehicle entrance is at 55th Street. Traffic can be backed up in the area on days that cruise ships arrive and depart, so allow yourself enough time to check in and go through security. There are no nearby subway stops, though city buses do cross midtown at 50th and 42nd streets. If you don't have too much luggage, it is usually faster and more convenient to have a taxi drop you off at the intersection across the street from the entrance to the lower-level of the terminal area be-

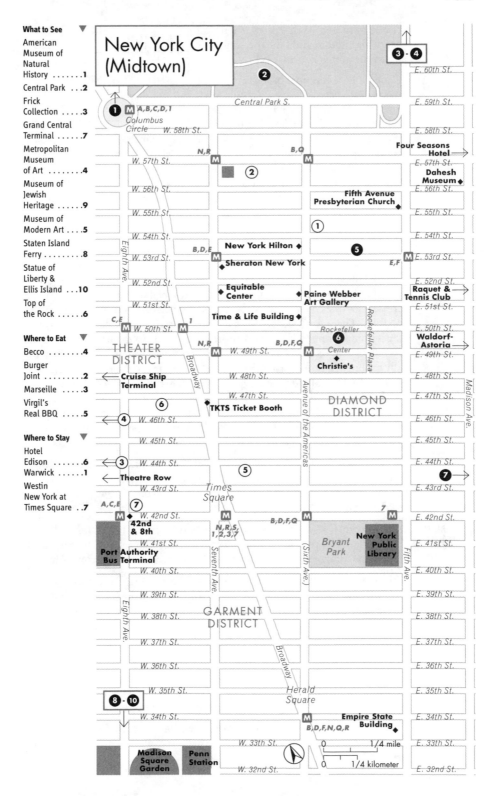

What to See ▼

American Museum of Natural History **1**

Central Park ...**2**

Frick Collection **3**

Grand Central Terminal **7**

Metropolitan Museum of Art **4**

Museum of Jewish Heritage **9**

Museum of Modern Art **5**

Staten Island Ferry **8**

Statue of Liberty & Ellis Island ...**10**

Top of the Rock **6**

Where to Eat ▼

Becco **4**

Burger Joint **2**

Marseille **3**

Virgil's Real BBQ **5**

Where to Stay ▼

Hotel Edison **6**

Warwick **1**

Westin New York at Times Square ..**7**

New York City (Midtown)

Central Park S.

E. 60th St.

E. 59th St.

Columbus Circle   W. 58th St.   E. 58th St.

E. 57th St.

W. 57th St.   **Four Seasons Hotel**

Dahesh Museum

W. 56th St.   E. 56th St.

Fifth Avenue Presbyterian Church

W. 55th St.   E. 55th St.

W. 54th St.   E. 54th St.

New York Hilton

W. 53rd St.   **Sheraton New York**   E. 53rd St.

W. 52nd St.   E. 52nd St.

Equitable Center   **Paine Webber Art Gallery**   **Raquet & Tennis Club**

W. 51st St.   E. 51st St.

Time & Life Building   E. 50th St.

W. 50th St.   Rockefeller   **Waldorf-Astoria**

W. 49th St.   Center   E. 49th St.

W. 48th St.   **Christie's**   E. 48th St.

Cruise Ship Terminal

W. 47th St.   E. 47th St.

DIAMOND DISTRICT

TKTS Ticket Booth

W. 46th St.   E. 46th St.

W. 45th St.   E. 45th St.

W. 44th St.   E. 44th St.

Theatre Row

W. 43rd St.   E. 43rd St.

Times Square

W. 42nd St.   E. 42nd St.

42nd & 8th

W. 41st St.   **Bryant Park**   **New York Public Library**   E. 41st St.

Port Authority Bus Terminal

W. 40th St.   E. 40th St.

W. 39th St.   E. 39th St.

GARMENT DISTRICT

W. 38th St.   E. 38th St.

W. 37th St.   E. 37th St.

W. 36th St.   E. 36th St.

W. 35th St.   E. 35th St.

Herald Square

W. 34th St.   **Empire State Building**   E. 34th St.

W. 33rd St.   E. 33rd St.

Madison Square Garden   **Penn Station**

0   1/4 mile

0   1/4 kilometer

W. 32nd St.   E. 32nd St.

THEATER DISTRICT

Eighth Ave.

Broadway

Seventh Ave.

Avenue of the Americas

(Sixth Ave.)

Rockefeller Plaza

Fifth Ave.

Madison Ave.

A,B,C,D,1

N,R   B,Q

B,D,E

C,E

N,R   B,D,F,Q

A,C,E

N,R,S, 1,2,3,7   B,D,F,Q   7

B,D,F,N,Q,R

E,F

tween 48th and 49th streets; then you can walk right in and take the elevators up to the embarkation level.

Cape Liberty Terminal in Bayonne is off Route 440. From the New Jersey Turnpike, take Exit 14A, then follow the signs for 440 South, and make a left turn into

> **CAUTION**
>
> Do not pack photo film in checked luggage since the newest airport screening equipment will ruin it. Put it in your carry-on instead.

the Cape Liberty Terminal area (on Port Terminal Boulevard). If you are coming from Long Island, you cross Staten Island, and after crossing the Bayonne Bridge take 440 North, making a right into the terminal area. If you are coming from Manhattan, you can also reach the terminal by public transit. Take the New Jersey Transit light-rail line that connects to the PATH trains in Hoboken; get off at the Bayonne stop, and from there you can take a taxi to the terminal (about 2 mi away); sometimes there is a free shuttle bus on cruise sailing dates, but confirm that with your cruise line.

The new **Brooklyn Cruise Terminal** at Pier 12 in Red Hook, which opened in April 2006, is not convenient to public transportation, so you should plan to take a taxi, drive, or take the bus transfers offered by the cruise lines (the cost for this is about $40 per person from either LaGuardia or JFK). There is a secure, 500-car outdoor parking lot on site. To reach the terminal from La Guardia Airport, take I–278 W (the Brooklyn-Queens Expressway), Exit 26 - Hamilton Avenue; the terminal entrance is actually off Browne Street. From JFK, take I–278 E (again, the Brooklyn-Queens Expressway), and then the same exit. If you arrive early, there's not much in the neighborhood, but there are a few neighborhood delis and restaurants with in a 10- to 15-minute walk; the area is a safe place to walk around during daylight hours. Red Hook is the home of ships from the Carnival, Princess, and Cunard cruise lines.

🚢 **Cape Liberty Terminal** ✉ 14 Port Terminal Blvd., Bayonne, NJ ☎ 201/823–3737 ⊕ www. cruiseliberty.com. **New York Passenger Ship Terminal** ✉ 711 12th Ave., Midtown West, New York, NY ☎ 212/246–5450 ⊕ www.nycruiseterminal.com ✉ Pier 12, Building 112, Red Hook Brooklyn, NY ☎ 718/858–3450.

AIRPORT TRANSFERS A cab from JFK to the passenger-ship terminal in **Manhattan** will cost $45 (a flat fare) plus toll and tip; expect to pay at least $35 on the meter if you are coming from LaGuardia and at least $45 or $50 from Newark.

From Newark Airport, it's approximately $30 to **Cape Liberty,** $75 from JFK (plus toll and tip), and $80 from La Guardia (plus toll and tip). Royal Caribbean offers bus service from several Mid-Atlantic and Northeast cities on sailing dates, but confirm that with the cruise line.

If your cruise is leaving from **Red Hook,** the taxi fare will be much cheaper if you fly into either La Guardia (about $30) or JFK (about $40); you'll pay at least $60 from Newark Airport. Cruise lines provide bus transfers from all three of the area's airports, but it may be cheaper to take a taxi if you are traveling with more than one other person.

PARKING You can park at the New York Passenger Ship Terminal for $24 a day; the fee is payable in advance in cash or traveler's checks (no credit cards).

Parking at Cape Liberty Terminal in Bayonne is $15 per day, payable only in cash, traveler's checks, and major credit cards.

Parking at Red Hook, Brooklyn, costs $18 per day.

Top Attractions

There's no way to do justice to even the most popular tourist stops in New York. If you have only a day in the city, choose one or two attractions and buy a daily unlimited subway pass to get around. There's a moving series of panels about the World Trade Center at the so-called "Ground Zero" site across from the Millennium Hotel (take the 1 train to Cortlandt Street or the E to World Trade Center); there's another series of memorial panels underneath at the World Trade Center PATH station, which is accessible from the main, streetside memorial area.

Bullets in the margins refer to points of interest on the Midtown Manhattan map.

❶ **American Museum of Natural History.** With 45 exhibition halls and more than 32 million artifacts and specimens, the world's largest and most important museum of natural history can easily occupy you for half a day. The dioramas might seem dated but are fun. The dinosaur exhibits are probably the highlight. Attached to the museum is the **Rose Center for Earth and Space** with various exhibits and housing the **Hayden Planetarium** and an **IMAX Theater.** ⊠ *Central Park W at W. 79th St., Upper West Side* ☎ *212/769–5200* ⊕ *www.amnh.org* ⊠ *$14 suggested donation, includes admission to Rose Center; museum and planetarium show combination ticket $30. Prices may vary for special exhibitions* ⊗ *Daily 10–5:45* Ⓜ *Subway: B, C to 81st St.*

❷ **Central Park.** Without the Central Park's 843 acres of meandering paths, tranquil lakes, ponds, and open meadows, New Yorkers might be a lot less sane. You can drop by the zoo (near 64th Street, on the east side) or the famous Bethesda Fountain (mid-park, at around 72nd Street), but the main draw is just to wander the lanes. Central Park has one of the lowest crime rates in the city. Still, use common sense and stay within sight of other park visitors, and don't go into the park after dark. Directions, park maps, and event calendars can be obtained from volunteers at two 5th Avenue **information booths,** at East 60th Street and East 72nd Street. ☎ *212/408–0266 for schedule of park events, 212/360–2727 for schedule of walking tours* ⊕ *www.nycgovparks.org* Ⓜ *Subway: A, C, or 1 to Columbus Circle.*

❸ **Frick Collection.** Coke-and-steel baron Henry Clay Frick (1849–1919) amassed this superb art collection far from the soot and smoke of Pittsburgh, where he made his fortune. The mansion was designed by Thomas Hastings and built in 1913–14. It opened in 1935, but still resembles a gracious private home, albeit one with bona fide masterpieces in almost every room. This is the best small museum in town by a mile. ⊠ *1 E. 70th St., at 5th Ave., Upper East Side* ☎ *212/288–0700* ⊕ *www.frick. org* ⊠ *$15* ☞ *Children under 10 not admitted; those under 16 must be accompanied by an adult* ⊗ *Tues.–Sat. 10–6, Sun. 11–5* Ⓜ *Subway: 6 to 68th St./Hunter College.*

6

❼ Grand Central Terminal. Grand Central is not only the world's largest railway station (76 acres) and the nation's busiest (500,000 commuters and subway riders use it daily), but also one of the world's greatest public spaces, "justly famous," as critic Tony Hiss has said, "as a crossroads, a noble building . . . and an ingenious piece of engineering." A massive four-year renovation completed in October 1998 restored the 1913 landmark to its original splendor—and then some. *Main entrance* ⊠ *E. 42nd St. at Park Ave., Midtown East* ☎ *212/935–3960* ⊕ *www.grandcentralterminal. com* Ⓜ *Subway: 4, 5, 6, 7, S to 42nd St./Grand Central.*

❹ Metropolitan Museum of Art. One of the world's greatest museums, the Met is also the largest art museum in the Western Hemisphere—spanning four blocks and encompassing 2 million square feet. Its permanent collection of nearly 3 million works of art from all over the world includes objects from the Paleolithic era to modern times. There's something for everyone here, but it's a bit overwhelming, so don't even try to see it all. ⊠ *5th Ave. at 82nd St., Upper East Side* ☎ *212/535–7710* ⊕ *www.metmuseum. org* ⊠ *$20 suggested donation* ⊗ *Tues.–Thurs. and Sun. 9:30–5:30, Fri. and Sat. 9:30–9* Ⓜ *Subway: 4, 5, 6 to 86th St.*

❾ Museum of Jewish Heritage—A Living Memorial to the Holocaust. In a granite hexagon rising 85 feet above Robert F. Wagner Jr. Park at the southern end of Battery Park City, this museum pays tribute to the 6 million Jews who perished in the Holocaust. It's one of the best such museums in the country. ⊠ *36 Battery Pl., Battery Park City, Lower Manhattan* ☎ *646/ 437–4200* ⊕ *www.mjhnyc.org* ⊠ *$10* ⊗ *Thurs. and Sun.–Tues. 10–5:45; Wed. 10–8; Fri. and eve. of Jewish holidays 10–3 (until 5 during Daylight Saving Time)* Ⓜ *Subway: 4, 5 to Bowling Green.*

❺ Museum of Modern Art (MoMA). The masterpieces—Monet's *Water Lilies,* Picasso's *Les Demoiselles d'Avignon,* Van Gogh's *Starry Night*—are still here, but for now the main draw at MoMA is, well, MoMA. A "modernist dream world" is how critics described the museum after its $425 million face-lift. Unfortunately, the museum was an instant success, which means lines are sometimes down the block. For the shortest wait, get here before the museum opens; you can avoid some of the crowding by entering through the 54th Street side. Be prepared for sticker shock when you buy your ticket. ⊠ *11 W. 53rd St., between 5th and 6th Aves., Midtown East* ☎ *212/708–9400* ⊕ *www.moma.org* ⊠ *$20* ⊗ *Sat.–Mon., Wed., and Thurs. 10:30–5:30; Fri. 10:30–8* Ⓜ *Subway: E, V to 5th Ave./53rd St.; B, D, E to 7th Ave.; B, D, F, V to 47th–50th Sts./Rockefeller Center.*

❽ Staten Island Ferry. The best transit deal in town is the Staten Island Ferry, a free 20- to 30-minute ride across New York Harbor providing great views of the Manhattan skyline, the Statue of Liberty, the Verrazano-Narrows Bridge, and the New Jersey coast. Ferries embark on various schedules: every 15 minutes during rush hours, every 20–30 minutes most other times, and every hour on weekend nights and mornings. If you can manage it, catch one of the older blue-and-orange ferries, which have outside decks. ⊠ *State and South Sts., Lower Manhattan* ☎ *718/390–5253* Ⓜ *Subway: 4, 5 to Bowling Green; 1, 9 to South Ferry.*

⑩ **Statue of Liberty & Ellis Island.** Though you must endure a long wait and oner- ous security, it's worth the trouble to see one of the iconic images of New York. But the truth is there's not much to see in the statue itself. You can no longer climb up to the crown, just view the inside from the base. There's a small museum on-site. Much more interesting—and well worth exploring—is the Ellis Island museum, which traces the story of immigra- tion in New York City with moving exhibits throughout the restored pro- cessing building. Other parts of the island are still ruins. Make reservations and go early if you want to see everything. The ferry stops first at the statue and then continues to Ellis Island. ⊠ *Castle Clinton, Battery Park, Lower Manhattan* ☎ *212/363–3200 for park service, 212/269–5755 for ferry in- formation, 866/782–8834 for ticket reservations, 212/363–3200 for Ellis Island, 212/883–1986 for Wall of Honor information* ⊕ *www.nps.gov/ stli/, www.statuereservations.com for reservations* ⌧ *Statue and museums free, ferry $11.50 round-trip* ☉ *Daily 9:30–5; extended hrs in summer* Ⓜ *Sub- way: 5 to Bowling Green; 1, 9 to South Ferry; or W to Whitehall.*

★ ⑥ **Top of the Rock.** Rockefeller Center's multifloor observation deck, first opened in 1933, and closed in the early 1980s, reopened in 2005. The experi- ence is infinitely better than that at the Empire State Building, where in- terminable lines spoil most of the fun. Arrive just before sunset for the best views (which include the Empire State Building). ⊠ *Entrance on 50th St., between 5th and 6th Aves., Midtown West* ☎ *877/692–7625 or 212/ 698–2000* ⊕ *www.topoftherocknyc.com* ⌧ *$17.50* ☉ *Daily 8–mid- night; last elevator at 11:30* PM.

Shopping

You can find almost any major store from virtually any designer or chain in Manhattan. High-end designers tend to be along **Madison Avenue,** between 55th and 86th streets. Some are along **57th Street,** between Madi- son and 7th avenues. **Fifth Avenue,** starting at Saks Fifth Avenue (at 50th Street) and going up to 59th Street, is a hodgepodge of high-end stores and more accessible options, including the high-end department store Bergdorf-Goodman, at 58th Street. More interesting and individual stores can be found in **SoHo** (between Houston and Canal, West Broad- way and Lafayette), and the **East Village** (between 14th Street and Hous- ton, Broadway and Avenue A). **Chinatown** is chock-full of designer knockoffs, crowded streets, and dim sum palaces; though frenetic dur- ing the day, it's a fun stop. The newest group of stores in Manhattan is at the **Time-Warner Center,** at Columbus Circle (at 8th Avenue and 59th Street); the high-rise mall has upscale stores and some of the city's best- reviewed and most expensive new restaurants.

Broadway Shows

Scoring tickets to Broadway shows is fairly easy except for the very top draws. For the most part, the top ticket price for Broadway musicals is about $110; the best seats for Broadway plays can run as high as $90. **Telecharge** (☎ 212/ 239–6200 ⊕ www.telecharge.com) sells

CAUTION	

Store any irreplaceable valuables in the ship purser's safe rather than the one in your cabin. Some insurance policies will not cover the loss of items left in your cabin.

6

tickets to most Broadway shows. **Ticketmaster** (☎ 212/307–4100 ⊕ www.
ticketmaster.com) sells a lot of Broadway tickets, but probably runs second to Telecharge.

For tickets at 25% to 50% off the usual price, head to **TKTS** (✉ Duffy
Sq., W. 47th St. and Broadway, Midtown West Ⓜ Subway: N, R, W to
49th St.; 1, 9 to 50th St. ✉ South St. Seaport at Front and John Sts.,
Lower Manhattan Ⓜ Subway: 2, 3 to Fulton St.). The kiosks accept cash
and traveler's checks—no credit cards.

Where to Eat

The restaurants we recommend below are all in Midtown West, near Broadway theaters and hotels. Make reservations at all but the most casual
places or face a numbing wait.

For price categories, *see* Dining at the beginning of this chapter.

$$ ✕ **Marseille.** With great food and a convenient location near several
Broadway theaters, Marseille is perpetually packed. Chef Andy d'Am-
ico's Mediterranean creations are continually impressive. Grilled sardines
are served with shards of black pepper brittle and tiny cubes of lemon
gelée. The daube is classic: a hunk of beef is slowly braised into submis-
sion in red wine, then plated on a crispy square of fried polenta with diced
sautéed root vegetables. Leave room for the spongy beignets with choco-
late and raspberry dipping sauces. ✉ *630 9th Ave., at W. 44th St., Mid-
town West* ☎ *212/333–3410* ⚹ *Reservations essential* ⊟ *AE, DC, MC,
V* Ⓜ *Subway: 6 to 51st St./Lexington Ave.*

$$ ✕ **Becco.** An ingenious concept makes Becco a prime Restaurant Row choice
for time-constrained theatergoers. There are two pricing scenarios: one
includes an all-you-can-eat selection of antipasti and three pastas served
hot out of pans that waiters circulate around the dining room; the other
adds a generous entrée to the mix. The pasta selection changes daily but
often includes gnocchi, fresh ravioli, and something in a cream sauce.
The entrées include braised veal shank, grilled double-cut pork chop, and
rack of lamb, among other selections. ✉ *355 W. 46th St., between 8th
and 9th Aves., Midtown West* ☎ *212/397–7597* ⚹ *Reservations essential* ⊟ *AE, DC, MC, V* Ⓜ *Subway: A, C, E to 42nd St.*

Ⓒ **$$** ✕ **Virgil's Real BBQ.** Neon, wood, and Formica set the scene at this mas-
sive roadhouse in the theater district. Start with stuffed jalapeños or—
especially—unbelievably succulent barbecued chicken wings. Then, what
the hell: go for the "Pig Out"—a rack of pork ribs, Texas hot links, pulled
pork, rack of lamb, chicken, and, of course, more. It's that kind of place.
There are also five domestic microbrews on tap and a good list of top
beers from around the world. The place is absolutely mobbed prethe-
ater, so if that's when you're going, arrive by 6 PM or you'll miss your
curtain. ✉ *152 W. 44th St., between 6th Ave. and Broadway, Midtown
West* ☎ *212/921–9494* ⚹ *Reservations essential* ⊟ *AE, MC, V* Ⓜ *Sub-
way: N, Q, R, S, W, 1, 2, 3, 7 to 42nd St./Times Sq.*

¢ ✕ **Burger Joint.** What's a college burger bar, done up in particleboard and
rec room decor, doing hidden inside of a five-star Midtown hotel? This
tongue-in-cheek lunch spot buried in the Parker Meridien does such bois-
terous midweek business that lines often snake through the lobby. Step-
ping behind the beige curtain you can find baseball cap–wearing

grease-spattered cooks dispensing paper-wrapped cheeseburgers and crisp thin fries. The burgers—featuring no Kobe beef or foie gras—are straightforward, cheap, and delicious. ⊠ *118 W. 57th St, between 6th and 7th Aves., Midtown West* ☎ *212/245–5000* ▤ *No credit cards* Ⓜ *Subway: F to 57th St.*

Where to Stay

There are no real bargains in the Manhattan hotel world, and you'll find it difficult to get a decent room for under $250. However, occasional weekend deals can be found. All the hotels we recommend for cruise passengers are in Midtown, on the west side, due to the area's relatively easy proximity to the cruise ship terminal.

For price categories, *see* Lodging at the beginning of this chapter.

$–$$$$ ⌂ **Warwick.** Astonishingly, this palatial hotel was built by William Randolph Hearst in 1927 as a private hotel for his friends and family. The Midtown favorite is well placed for the theater district. The marble-floor lobby buzzes with activity; the Randolph Bar is on one side and Murals on 54, a Continental restaurant, is on the other. Handsome, Regency-style rooms have soft pastel color schemes, mahogany armoires, and marble bathrooms. The Cary Grant suite was the actor's New York residence for 12 years, and encapsulates a more refined moment in New York glamour. ⊠ *65 W. 54th St., at 6th Ave., Midtown West 10019* ☎ *212/247–2700 or 800/223–4099* 🖶 *212/713–1751* ⊕ *www.warwickhotels.com* ⇨ *359 rooms, 66 suites* ◊ *In-room: safe, refrigerator, dial-up, Wi-Fi. In-hotel: 2 restaurants, room service, bar, gym, laundry service, concierge, parking (fee), no-smoking rooms* ▤ *AE, DC, MC, V* Ⓜ *Subway: E, V to57th Street.; N, Q, R, W to 57th St.*

$ ⌂ **Hotel Edison.** This offbeat old hotel is a popular budget stop for tour groups from both the United States and abroad. The simple, serviceable guest rooms are clean and fresh. The loan-shark murder scene in *The Godfather* was shot in what is now Sofia's restaurant, and the pink-and-blue plaster Edison Café, known half jokingly as the Polish Tea Room, is a theater-crowd landmark consistently recognized as New York City's best coffee shop. ⊠ *228 W. 47th St., between Broadway and 8th Ave., Midtown West 10036* ☎ *212/840–5000 or 800/637–7070* 🖶 *212/596–6850* ⊕ *www.edisonhotelnyc.com* ⇨ *770 rooms, 30 suites* ◊ *In-room: Wi-Fi. In-hotel: restaurant, bars, gym, laundry service, airport shuttle, parking (fee), no-smoking rooms* ▤ *AE, D, DC, MC, V* Ⓜ *Subway: C, E to 50th St., R to 49th St.*

$ ⌂ **The Westin New York at Times Square.** The Westin changed the skyline of Midtown with this soaring skyscraper that subtly mimics the flow of the city—look for subway patterns in the carpets and the city reflected on the building's exterior. A thoughtful staff helps make the cavernous lobby and throngs of guests tolerable. Exceptionally large rooms are blissfully quiet and built to give you optimal views—especially the light-filled corner rooms. The much-noted Heavenly Bed and double showerheads are indeed praiseworthy, but for even more comfort, spa-floor rooms come with massage chairs, aromatherapy candles, and other pampering pleasures. ⊠ *270 W. 43rd St., at 8th Ave., Midtown West 10036* ☎ *212/201–2700 or 866/837–4183* 🖶 *212/201–2701* ⊕ *www.westinny.com* ⇨ *737 rooms, 126 suites* ◊ *In-room: safe, refrigerator, dial-up, Wi-Fi. In-hotel:*

restaurant, room service, bars, gym, spa, laundry service, concierge, parking (fee), some pets allowed, no-smoking rooms ▭ *AE, D, DC, MC, V* Ⓜ *Subway: A, C, E to 42nd St./Times Sq.*

NORFOLK, VIRGINIA

CiCi
Williamson

Founded in 1680, Norfolk is no newcomer to the cruise business. One famous passenger, Thomas Jefferson, arrived here in November 1789 after a two-month crossing of the Atlantic. Over 200 years later, this historic seaport welcomes more than 300,000 cruise passengers annually. Situated at the heart of nautical Hampton Roads, Norfolk is home to the largest Naval Base in the world and is also a major commercial port.

Essentials

HOURS Most stores are open Monday through Friday from 10 to 9. Some museums close on Monday and/or Tuesday.

INTERNET Most of the hotels offer free Wi-Fi service if you have your own laptop. If not, you may be able to find an Internet café, but the local Norfolk Public Library has free Internet access, so why pay? **Norfolk Public Library** (✉ 301 E. City Hall Ave. ☎ 757/664–7337 ⊕ www.npl.lib.va.us).

VISITOR   **Hampton Roads Transit kiosk** (✉ Waterfront, 333 Waterside Dr. ☎ 757/
INFORMATION 623–3222 ⊕ www.watersidemarketplace.com) is the launching point for tours of the city. **Norfolk Convention & Visitors Bureau** (✉ End of 4th View St. ☎ 757/441–1852 or 800/368–3097 ⊕ www.norfolkcvb.com).

Norfolk Cruise Terminal

The new, state-of-the-art Half Moone Cruise Terminal opened in April 2007. Attached to Celebration Center, a large meeting and event space, it's within walking distance to several attractions and amenities in the downtown area.

Parking is off-site at the Ceder Grove parking lot, which is about 14 blocks from the waterfront and the cruise terminal. From I–264, take the City Hall exit (Exit 10). At the light, turn right on St. Paul's Boulevard, and follow the signs to the Cedar Grove parking lot.

🛈 **Half Moone Cruise Terminal & Celebration Center** ✉ 1 Waterside Dr. ☎ 757/664–1000 for cruise hotline ⊕ www.cruisenorfolk.org.

AIRPORT   Norfolk International Airport (ORF) is
TRANSFERS 9 mi (15 km) and 20 minutes away from the cruise terminal. One-way, shared shuttle costs range from $6.25 to $20 per person, and a taxi costs about $18 to $25.
🛈 **Norfolk Airport Express** ☎ 800/643–2197 ⊕ www.norfolkairportexpress.com. **Norfolk International Airport (ORF)** ✉ 200 Norview Ave. ☎ 757/857–3200 ⊕ www.norfolkairport.com.

PARKING Before parking, drop your luggage at Nauticus, where you'll also find the

---

NORFOLK BEST BETS

- **Chrysler Museum of Art.** Though far from New York, Chicago, or Los Angeles, this is one of the major art museums in the U.S.

- **Nauticus.** The National Maritime Center is one of the region's most popular attractions and especially good for families.

- **Norfolk Naval Station.** This giant naval station, the home of the Atlantic Fleet, is an impressive site in itself.

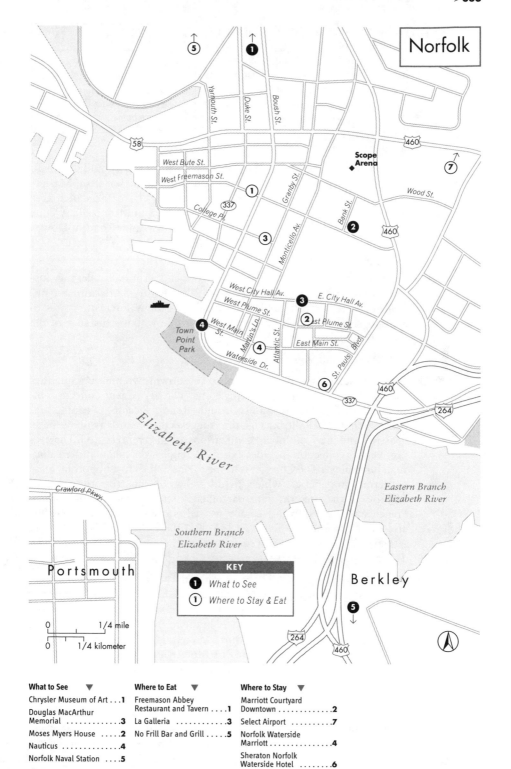

Norfolk

Scope Arena

Town Point Park

Elizabeth River

Crawford Pkwy.

Eastern Branch Elizabeth River

Southern Branch Elizabeth River

P o r t s m o u t h

B e r k l e y

KEY

❶ *What to See*

① *Where to Stay & Eat*

0 _____ 1/4 mile
0 _____ 1/4 kilometer

What to See ▼

Chrysler Museum of Art . . . **1**

Douglas MacArthur
Memorial **3**

Moses Myers House **2**

Nauticus **4**

Norfolk Naval Station **5**

Where to Eat ▼

Freemason Abbey
Restaurant and Tavern **1**

La Galleria **3**

No Frill Bar and Grill **5**

Where to Stay ▼

Marriott Courtyard
Downtown **2**

Select Airport **7**

Norfolk Waterside
Marriott **4**

Sheraton Norfolk
Waterside Hotel **6**

cruise terminal. Depending upon the cruise line you're sailing, park your car in one of two lots, both patrolled by roving security officers. The West Plume Street Garage serves Radisson and accepts cash and traveler's checks only ($10 daily), to be paid when entering. The garage is located directly across the street from Nauticus.

BEACH AND BUY

A nylon tote bag that folds compactly into its own pocket can be used as a beach bag during your cruise and as an extra carry-on for your return home.

Cedar Grove Parking serves Holland America, Celebrity, and Carnival. The parking fee ($10 daily) is paid upon entering the lot; Visa, Master-Card, American Express, cash, and traveler's checks are accepted. Less than 1 mi (1 ½ km) from I–264, this lot is located on Monticello Avenue between Virginia Beach Boulevard and Princess Anne Road in Downtown Norfolk. Complimentary shuttles run regularly to Nauticus.

Exploring Norfolk

History meets high-tech in this waterfront city. From 18th-century historic homes and a major art museum to 20th-century battleships and nuclear-powered aircraft carriers, Norfolk has many interesting sites to explore, several of them free and most within walking distance of the cruise terminal.

Bullets in the margins refer to points of interest on the Norfolk map.

★ ❶ **Chrysler Museum of Art.** By any standard this downtown museum qualifies as one of America's major art museums. The permanent collection includes works by Rubens, Gainsborough, Renoir, Picasso, Cézanne, Matisse, Warhol, and Pollock, a list that suggests the breadth available here. Classical and pre-Columbian civilizations are also represented. The decorative-arts collection includes exquisite English porcelain and art nouveau furnishings. The Chrysler is home to one of the most important glass collections in America, which includes glass objects from the 6th century BC to the present, with particularly strong holdings in Tiffany, French art glass, and English cameo, as well as artifacts from ancient Rome and the Near and Far East. ✉ *245 W. Olney Rd.* ☎ *757/664–6200* ⊕ *www.chrysler.org* ✑ *$7; Wed. by voluntary contribution* ☉ *Wed. 10–9, Thurs.–Sat. 10–5, Sun. 1–5.*

❸ **Douglas MacArthur Memorial.** The memorial is the burial place of one of America's most distinguished military officers. General Douglas MacArthur (1880–1964) agreed to this Navy town as the site for his monument because it was his mother's birthplace. In the rotunda of the old City Hall, converted according to MacArthur's design, is the mausoleum; 11 adjoining galleries house mementos of MacArthur's career, including his signature corncob pipe and the Japanese instruments of surrender that concluded World War II. However, this is a monument not only to General MacArthur but to all those who served in wars from the Civil to the Korean War. Its Historical Center holds 2 ½ million documents and more than 100,000 photographs, and assists scholars, students, and researchers from around the world. The general's staff car is on display in the gift shop, where a 24-minute biography is shown. ✉ *Bank St. and City Hall Ave.* ☎ *757/441–2965* ⊕ *www.macarthurmemorial.org* ✉ *By donation* ◷ *Mon.–Sat. 10–5, Sun. 11–5.*

2 **Moses Myers House.** The federal-style redbrick home built by its namesake in 1792 is exceptional, and not just for its elegance. In the long dining room, a wood writing desk holds a collection of fine china—and a set of silver kiddush cups (Moses Myers was Norfolk's first permanent Jewish resident). A transplanted New Yorker, Myers made his fortune in Norfolk in shipping, then served as a diplomat and a customhouse officer. His grandson married James Madison's grandniece, his great-grandson served as mayor, and the family kept the house for five generations. The furnishings, 70% of them original, include family portraits by Gilbert Stuart and Thomas Sully. ✉ *331 Bank St.* ☎ *757/333–1085* ⊕ *www. chrysler.org/houses.asp* ✉ *Free* ◷ *Wed.–Sat. 10–4, Sun. 1–4.*

★ ⟳ **4** **Nauticus.** A popular attraction on Norfolk's redeveloped waterfront is the National Maritime Center. With more than 70 high-tech exhibits on three "decks," the site places ancient shipbuilding exhibits next to interactive displays depicting the modern naval world. Weather satellites, underwater archaeology, and the Loch Ness Monster all come together here. The battleship USS *Wisconsin,* still maintained in a state of reduced readiness to allow reactivation, has found a home here. Most of its interior is off-limits, but its enormous gun turrets and conning tower are impressive up close. The *Wisconsin,* tied up just outside the museum, and the Hampton Roads Naval Museum, within Nauticus, are both operated by the U.S. Navy and can be toured without paying Nauticus's admission price. There are additional fees for the AEGIS Theater and Virtual Adventures. ✉ *1 Waterside Dr.* ☎ *757/664–1000* ⊕ *www.nauticus.org, www.thenmc.org, www.hrnm.navy.mil* ✉ *$10* ◷ *Memorial Day–Labor Day, daily 9–5; Labor Day–Memorial Day, Tues.–Sat. 10–5, Sun. noon–5.*

⟳ **5** **Norfolk Naval Station.** On the northern edge of the city, this naval base Fodor'sChoice is an impressive sight, home to more than 100 ships of the Atlantic Fleet. ★ The base was built on the site of the Jamestown Exposition of 1907: many of the original buildings survive and are still in use. Several large aircraft carriers, built at nearby Newport News, call Norfolk home port and can be seen from miles away, especially at the bridge-tunnel end of the base. You may see four or even more, each with a crew of up to 6,300, beside slightly smaller amphibious carriers that discharge marines in both helicopters and amphibious assault craft. The submarine piers, floating drydocks, supply center, and air station are all worth seeing. *The Victory Rover* and *Carrie B.* provide boat tours from downtown Norfolk to the naval station, and Hampton Roads Transit operates tour trolleys most of the year, departing from the naval-base tour office. Visitor access is by tour only, and photo ID is required to enter the base. ✉ *9079 Hampton Blvd.* ☎ *757/444–7955* ⊕ *www.navstanorva.navy. mil/tour* ✉ *Tour $7.50* ◷ *Tours Oct. 29–Mar. 18, Tues.–Sun. 1:30; Mar. 19–May 20, Tues.–Sun. 11–2 on the hr; May 21–Sept. 2, Tues.–Sun. 10–2 every ½ hr.*

Shopping

If you forget to pack an item for your cruise, you'll find stores galore within walking distance of the cruise terminal at the handsome MacArthur Center Mall. A car is helpful if you want to visit **Ghent**, where you'll find an eclectic mix of shops, including antiques stores and restaurants. It's a turn-of-the-20th-century neighborhood that runs from the Elizabeth River to York Street, to West Olney Road and Llewellyn Avenue. Colley Avenue and 21st Street is the hub.

The center of Norfolk's downtown, the **MacArthur Center** (⊠ 300 Monticello Ave. ☎ 757/627–6000) has more than 100 stores, including anchors Nordstrom and Dillard's. There are restaurants downstairs and numerous fast-food outlets upstairs offering a variety of reasonably tolerable food.

Where to Stay

Within walking distance of the cruise terminal are three handsome hotels, two modern and one century-old boutique hostelry. You can also take the water taxi from Waterside ($1 per person, leaving half-hourly) across the Elizabeth River to Portsmouth to a lower-priced hotel. If you have a car, there are numerous chain motels on the outskirts of town.

$$–$$$$ 🏨 **Norfolk Waterside Marriott.** This hotel in the redeveloped downtown area is connected to the Waterside Festival Marketplace shopping area by a ramp and is close to Town Point Park, site of many festivals. The handsome lobby, with wood paneling, a central staircase, silk tapestries, and Federal-style furniture, sets a high standard that continues throughout the hotel. Rooms are somewhat small, but each has most everything the business traveler could ask for—including two telephones, voice mail, and Internet access. ⊠ *235 E. Main St., 23510* ☎ *757/627–4200 or 800/228–9290* 🖷 *757/628–6452* ⊕ *www.marriott.com* ⤳ *396 rooms, 8 suites* ⟡ *In room: dial-up. In hotel: 2 restaurants, bar, pool* ▤ *AE, D, DC, MC, V* ⫶⊙⫶ *EP.*

$–$$$ 🏨 **Sheraton Norfolk Waterside Hotel.** Modern is the word for this hotel's furnishings, from the bright, spacious lobby to the ample rooms and large suites. A ground-floor bar with dramatic 30-foot windows overlooks the Elizabeth—many rooms also have a beautiful view over the water. This property is convenient to the Waterside Festival Marketplace shopping area. ⊠ *777 Waterside Dr., 23510* ☎ *757/622–6664* 🖷 *757/625–8271* ⊕ *www.sheraton.com* ⤳ *426 rooms, 20 suites* ⟡ *In hotel: Restaurant, bar, pool* ▤ *AE, D, DC, MC, V* ⫶⊙⫶ *EP.*

$$ 🏨 **Marriott Courtyard Downtown.** Built in 2005, this eight-story hotel is near everything visitors want to see and where business travelers need to be. It's next door to the MacArthur Memorial and near the MacArthur Center and Nauticus. A handsome, inviting lobby has a tailored look; the modern guest rooms have a large desk, comforters, hair dryers, coffeemakers, irons, ironing boards, and a free daily newspaper. ⊠ *520 Plume St., 23510* ☎ *757/963–6000 or 800/321–2211* 🖷 *757/963–6001* ⊕ *www. marriott.com* ⤳ *137 rooms, 3 suites* ⟡ *Restaurant, room service, in-room data ports, refrigerators, cable TV with movies, in-room broadband, indoor pool, wading pool, exercise equipment, shop, dry cleaning, laundry facilities, laundry service, business services, meeting rooms, parking (fee), no-smoking rooms* ▤ *AE, D, DC, MC, V.*

$–$$ ⊞ **Holiday Inn Select Airport.** Surprisingly plush for a Holiday Inn property, this airport location welcomes business travelers with an elegant lobby bar and fireplace. Rooms are outfitted with two phone lines, high-speed DSL Internet access, and voice mail; the lobby has free Wi-Fi. Behind the hotel is Lake Wright where guests may stroll or relax. ⊠ *Lake Wright Executive Center, 1570 N. Military Hwy., 23502* ☎ *757/213–2231* 🖷 *757/213–2232* ⊕ *www.hiselect.com/norfolkva* ⤳ *147 rooms* 🔥 *Restaurant, microwaves, refrigerators, indoor pool, gym, hot tub, lobby lounge, laundry facilities, business services, meeting rooms, airport shuttle* ⊟ *AE, D, DC, MC, V.*

Where to Eat

In addition to hotel restaurants, downtown Norfolk has many fine-dining restaurants and casual eateries in Waterside Festival Marketplace, which offers a versatile food court. In the MacArthur Center Mall, you'll find Johnny Rockets and Castaldi's—promising good value.

★ **$$–$$$$** ✕ **La Galleria.** This restaurant has a favorable reputation in Norfolk. The interior is classic Mediterannean and includes Ionic columns and large urns imported from Italy. There's entertainment Friday and Saturday nights. Among the menu choices are *vongole al forno* (baked clams sprinkled with herbs, garlic, and bread crumbs) as an appetizer, and many excellent pastas and main courses, such as veal, chicken, steaks, and fish (for example, salmon sautéed in herbs, garlic, and white wine). ⊠ *120 College Pl.* ☎ *757/623–3939* ⊟ *AE, DC, MC, V.*

$–$$$ ✕ **Freemason Abbey Restaurant and Tavern.** This former church near the historic business district has been drawing customers for a long time, and not without reason. It has 40-foot-high cathedral ceilings and large windows, making for an airy, and dramatic, dining experience. You can sit upstairs, in the large choir loft, or in the main part of the church downstairs. Beside the bar just inside the entrance is an informal sort of "diner" area, but with the whole menu to choose from. Regular appetizers include artichoke dip and Santa Fe shrimp. There's a dinner special every weeknight, such as lobster, prime rib, and wild game (wild boar or alligator, for example). ⊠ *209 W. Freemason St.* ☎ *757/622–3966* ⊟ *AE, D, DC, MC, V.*

★ **¢–$$** ✕ **No Frill Bar and Grill.** This expansive café is in an antique building in the heart of Ghent. Beneath a tin ceiling and exposed ductwork, a central bar is surrounded by several dining spaces with cream-and-mustard walls and wooden tables. Signature items include its ribs; the Funky Chicken Sandwich, a grilled chicken breast with bacon, tomato, melted Swiss cheese, and Parmesan pepper dressing on rye; and the Spotswood Salad of baby spinach, Granny Smith apples, and blue cheese. ⊠ *806 Spotswood Ave., at Colley Ave.* ☎ *757/627–4262* ⊟ *AE, MC, V.*

PORT CANAVERAL, FLORIDA

Kerry
Speckman

This once-bustling commercial fishing area is still home to a small shrimping fleet, charter boats, and party fishing boats, but its main business these days is as a cruise-ship port. Cocoa Beach itself isn't the spiffiest place around, but what is becoming quite clean and neat is the north end of the port where the Carnival, Disney, and Royal Caribbean cruise

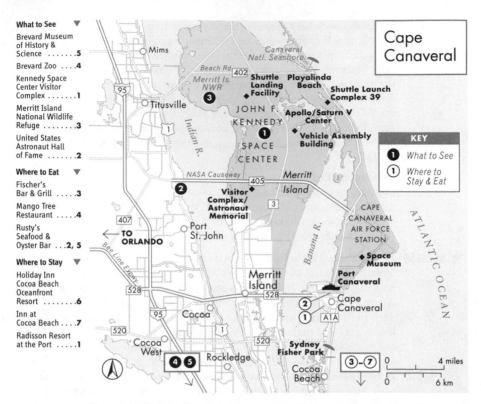

lines set sail, as well as Sun Cruz and Sterling casino boats. Port Canaveral
is now Florida's second-busiest cruise port. Because of Port Canaveral's
proximity to Orlando theme parks (about an hour away), many cruisers combine a short cruise with a stay in the area. The port is also convenient to popular Space Coast attractions such as the Kennedy Space
Center and United States Astronaut Hall of Fame in Titusville.

Essentials

HOURS   Most of the area's attractions are open every day.

INTERNET   Most people choose to go online at their hotel.

VISITOR   **Cocoa Beach Area Chamber of Commerce** (✉ 400 Fortenberry Rd., Mer-
INFORMATION   ritt Island 32952 ☎ 321/459–2200 ⊕ www.visitcocoabeach.com).

The Cruise Port

Port Canaveral is the second-busiest cruise port in the world, with more
than 4.6 million passengers passing through its terminals annually. The port
has six cruise terminals and is home to Carnival Cruise Lines, Disney Cruise
Line, and Royal Caribbean International. Other cruise lines, such as Holland America and Norwegian Cruise Line, operate seasonally. The port
serves as the embarkation point for three-, four-, and seven-day cruises to
the Bahamas, Key West, Mexico, Jamaica, and the Virgin Islands.

In Brevard County, Port Canaveral is on State Road (S.R.) 528, also known
as the Beeline Expressway, which runs straight to Orlando, which has
the nearest airport. To drive to Port Canaveral from there, take the

north exit out of the airport, staying to the right, to S.R. 528 (Beeline Expressway) East. Take S.R. 528 directly to Port Canaveral; it's about a 45-minute drive.

🚩 **Canaveral Port Authority** ⊠ 9150 Christopher Columbus Dr., Cape Canaveral ☎ 321/783-7831 or 888/767-8226 ⊕ www.portcanaveral. org.

AIRPORT TRANSFERS If you are flying into the area, most visitors choose to fly into Orlando; the Orlando airport is 45 minutes away from the docks. If you have not arranged airport transfers with your cruise line, then you will need to make your own arrangements. Taxis are expensive, but many companies offer minivan and bus shuttles to Port Canaveral. They are all listed on the Canaveral Port Authority Web site. Some shuttles charge for the entire van, which is a good deal for groups but not for individuals or couples; some will charge a per-person rate. Expect to pay at least $25 per person each way. But you will need to make a reservation in advance regardless of which service you use. Some cruisers who want to do some exploring before the cruise rent a car at the airport and drop it off at the port, which houses several major rental-car agencies.

🚩 **AAA Cruise Line Connection** ☎ 407/908-5566 ⊕ www.aaasuperride.com. **Art's Shuttle** ☎ 371/783-2112 or 800/567-5099 ⊕ www.artsshuttle.com. **Busy Traveler Transport Service** ☎ 321/453-5278 or 800/496-7433 ⊕ www.abusytraveler.com.

PARKING Outdoor, gated lots and a six-story parking garage are near the terminals and cost $12 per day for vehicles up to 20 feet in length and $24 per day for vehicles over 20 feet, which must be paid in advance, either in cash, traveler's checks, or by major credit card (MasterCard and Visa only).

Exploring the Cape Canaveral Area

With the Kennedy Space Center just 20 minutes away, there is plenty to do in and around Cape Canaveral, though many folks opt to travel the extra hour into Orlando to visit the popular theme parks.

🌀 ❺ **Brevard Museum of History & Science.** To see what the local lay of the land looked like in other eras, check out this local science museum. Hands-on activities for children are the draw here. Not to be missed is the Windover Archaeological Exhibit of 7,000-year-old artifacts indigenous to the region. The museum's nature center has 22 acres of trails encompassing three distinct ecosystems—sand pine hills, lake lands, and marshlands. ⊠ *2201 Michigan Ave., Cocoa* ☎ *321/632–1830* ⊕ *www.brevardmuseum. com* ⊠ *$6* ⊗ *Mon.–Sat. 10–4, Sun. noon–4.*

🌀 ❹ **Brevard Zoo.** It took 20,000 volunteers two weeks to turn 56 acres of forest and wetlands into the only American Zoo and Aquarium Association–accredited zoo built by a community. Stroll along the shaded boardwalks and get a close-up look at alligators, crocodiles, giant

Fodor'sChoice ★

■ **Kennedy Space Center.** Kennedy Space Center in Titusville is the region's biggest attraction.

■ **Merritt Island.** If you want to get out and commune with nature, this is the place, especially for bird-watchers.

■ **Orlando Theme Parks.** With Orlando just an hour away, many cruisers combine a theme-park visit with their cruise.

6

anteaters, marmosets, jaguars, eagles, river otters, kangaroos, exotic birds, and kookaburras. Alligator, crocodile, and river otter feedings are held on alternate afternoons—although the alligators do not dine on the otters. You can also paddle kayaks and keep an eye open for the 4,000 species of wildlife that live in 22 acres waters and woods. ⊠ *8225 N. Wickham Rd., Melbourne* ☎ *321/254–9453* ⊕ *www.brevardzoo.org* ⊡ *$10.50; train ride $3* ⊙ *Daily 9:30–5.*

① Kennedy Space Center Visitor Complex. This "must-see" sight is just southeast of Titusville. Following the lead of the theme parks, they've switched to a one-price-covers-all admission. To get the most out of your visit to the space center, take the basic bus tour (included with admission), which makes stops at several facilities. Buses depart every 15 minutes, and you can get on and off any bus whenever you like. If you want a more special experience, you can pay for many different add-ons. As you approach the Kennedy Space Center grounds, tune your car radio to AM1320 for attraction information. New for 2007, the $60-million Shuttle Launch Experience uses a sophisticated motion-based platform, special effects seats, and high-fidelity visual and audio components to simulate the sensations experienced in an actual Space Shuttle launch. It's included in the basic admission price, which also includes whatever film is showing in the IMAX theater. ⊠ *Rte. 405, Kennedy Space Center, Titusville* ☎ *321/449–4444* ⊕ *www.kennedyspacecenter.com* ⊡ *General admission (includes bus tour, IMAX movies, Visitor Complex shows and exhibits, and the Astronaut Hall of Fame) $38* ⊙ *Space Center daily 9 AM–5:30, last regular tour 3 hrs before closing; closed certain launch dates; IMAX I and II Theaters daily 10–5:40.*

③ Merritt Island National Wildlife Refuge. If you prefer wading birds over waiting in line, don't miss the 140,000-acre wildlife refuge that adjoins the Canaveral National Seashore. It's an immense area dotted by brackish estuaries and marshes and patches of land consisting of coastal dunes, scrub oaks, pine forests and flat woods, and palm and oak hammocks. You can borrow field guides and binoculars at the visitor center to track down various types of falcons, osprey, eagles, turkeys, doves, cuckoos, loons, geese, skimmers, terns, warblers, wrens, thrushes, sparrows, owls, and woodpeckers. A 20-minute video about refuge wildlife and accessibility—only 10,000 acres are developed—can help orient you. Several well-marked trails help you explore. ⊠ *Rte. 402 across Titusville Causeway, Titusville* ☎ *321/861–0667* ⊕ *merrittisland.fws.gov* ⊡ *Free* ⊙ *Daily sunrise–sunset; visitor center open weekdays 8–4:30, Sat. 9–5.*

② United States Astronaut Hall of Fame. The original *Mercury* 7 team and the later Gemini, Apollo, Skylab, and shuttle astronauts contributed to make this the world's premium archive of astronauts' personal stories. Authentic memorabilia and equipment from their collections tell the story of human space exploration. You'll watch videotapes of historic moments in the space program and see one-of-a-kind items like Wally Schirra's relatively archaic Sigma 7 Mercury space capsule, Gus Grissom's spacesuit (colored silver only because NASA thought silver looked more "spacey"), and a flag that made it to the moon. Definitely don't miss the **Astronaut Adventure**, a hands-on discovery center with interactive ex-

FodorsChoice ★

FodorsChoice ★

hibits that help you learn about space travel. ⊠ *Rte. 405, Kennedy Space Center, Titusville, before the Causeway* ☎ *321/449–4444* ⊕ *www. kennedyspacecenter.com* ⊠ *$17 (included in Kennedy Space Center admission price)* ⊙ *Daily 10–6:30.*

Beaches

After crossing a long and high bridge just east of Cocoa Village, you'll be dropped down upon a barrier island. A few miles farther and you'll reach the Atlantic Ocean and picture-perfect **Cocoa Beach** at Route A1A. This is one of the Space Coast's nicest beaches, with many wide stretches that are excellent for biking, jogging, power walking, or strolling. In some places there are dressing rooms, showers, playgrounds, picnic areas with grills, snack shops, and surf-side parking lots. Beach vendors offer necessities, and guards are on duty in summer. Cocoa Beach is considered the capital of Florida's surfing community. North of Cocoa, **Playalinda Beach** (⊠ Rte. 402, Titusville ☎ 321/267–1110), part of the **Canaveral National Seashore,** is the longest undeveloped stretch on Florida's Atlantic coast—hundreds of giant sea turtles come ashore here between May and August to lay their eggs. The park's extreme northern area is favored by nude sunbathers. There are no lifeguards, but park rangers patrol. Take Exit 80 from I–95 and follow Route 406 east across the Indian River, then Route 402 east for another 12 mi (19 km). It's open daily from 6 to 8 (Apr.–Oct.) and 8 to 6 (Nov.–Mar.), and admission is $5 per vehicle. **Sidney Fischer Park** (⊠ 2100 block of Rte. A1A, Cocoa Beach ☎ 321/868–3252) has showers, playgrounds, changing areas, picnic areas with grills, snack shops, and plenty of well-maintained, inexpensive, surf-side parking lots. Beach vendors carry necessities for sunning and swimming. The parking fee is $5 for cars and RVs.

Shopping

In downtown Cocoa, cobblestone walkways wend through **Cocoa Village,** along Brevard Avenue and Harrison Street, a cluster of restored turn-of-the-20th-century buildings now occupied by restaurants and specialty shops purveying crafts, fine art, and clothing. It's impossible to miss the **Ron Jon Surf Shop** (⊠ 4151 N. Atlantic Ave., Rte. A1A ☎ 321/799–8888 ⊕ www.ronjons.com). With a giant surfboard and an aqua, teal, and pink art-deco facade, Ron Jon takes up nearly two blocks along Route A1A.

Fodor'sChoice
★

Where to Eat

For price categories, *see* Dining at the beginning of this chapter.

★ $$–$$$$ ✕ **Mango Tree Restaurant.** Adult sufferers of attention deficit disorder may want to steer clear of this overstimulating restaurant that resembles an exotic garage sale. Hanging orchids, live swans, climbing vines, ornate planters, palmetto bushes, tropical birds, and a koi pond are just a few of the colorful distractions you'll encounter—and that's just on the way in. Once inside the restaurant, the blur of colors, sounds, and smells only intensifies. The *lobsterocki* appetizer (Maine lobster

> **WRITE EASY**
>
> Address a page of stick-on labels before you leave home; use them for postcards to the folks back home and you will not have to carry along a bulky address book.

wrapped in bacon with teriyaki cream sauce) is a favorite with regulars, as are the Indian River crab cakes, coq au vin, or veal Française (scaloppine with mushroom sauce), none of which, unfortunately, comes with a side of Ritalin. ⊠ *118 N. Atlantic Ave., Cocoa Beach* ☎ *321/799–0513* ▤ *AE, MC, V* ⊗ *Closed Mon. No lunch.*

> **BATTERY ALERT**
>
> Even if you don't think you'll need them, bring along extra camera batteries and change them before you think the old ones are "dead."

¢–$$$ ✕ **Rusty's Seafood & Oyster Bar.** Oysters, prepared raw, steamed, or casino style, are just one of the draws at this casual eatery. Waitresses sporting nylon short-shorts and daily happy hour specials (dollar drafts and 2-for-1 cocktails) are undoubtedly the others. Rusty's quick service and proximity to the cruise ships make it a favorite for those about to hit the high seas. Other menu items include seafood gumbo, spicy wings, steamed crab legs, burgers, and baskets of fish-and-chips, clam strips, or fried calamari. ⊠ *2 S. Atlantic Ave.* ☎ *321/783–2401* ⊠ *628 Glen Cheek Dr., Port Canaveral* ☎ *321/783–2033* ▤ *AE, D, MC, V.*

¢–$$ ✕ **Fischer's Bar & Grill.** This casual eatery, owned by the same family that runs the more upscale Bernard's Surf, is a perfect spot for winding down after a tough day at the beach. Although complete dinners are available, people tend to come for the salads, pasta, burgers, and platters of tasty fried shrimp. The family's fleet of fishing boats brings in fresh seafood daily. Happy hour is from 4 to 7. ⊠ *2 S. Atlantic Ave., Cocoa Beach* ☎ *321/783–2401* ▤ *AE, D, MC, V.*

Where to Stay

Many local hotels offer cruise packages that include one night's lodging, parking for the duration of your cruise, and transportation to the cruise port.

For price categories, *see* Lodging at the beginning of this chapter.

$$–$$$ ▦ **Holiday Inn Cocoa Beach Oceanfront Resort.** When two adjacent beach hotels were redesigned and a promenade park landscaped between them, the Holiday Inn Cocoa Beach Resort was born. Hit hard by the 2004 hurricanes, the oceanfront property underwent a multi-million-dollar renovation with a complete exterior makeover and updates to guest rooms and meeting rooms.Standard rooms are plush, modern, and designed in bright tropical colors; suites and villas have a Key West feel with louvered doors and rattan ceiling fans. Lodging options include standard and king rooms; oceanfront suites, which have a living room with sleeper sofa; villas; or bi-level lofts. Kids are given the royal treatment with specially-designed KidsSuites that feature bunkbeds and video games and a pirate ship pool with water-blasting cannons. ⊠ *1300 N. Atlantic Ave., Cocoa Beach, 32931* ☎ *321/783–2271 or 800/206–2747* ☐ *321/784–8878* ⊕ *www.hicentralflorida.com/cocoa.html* ⤳ *500 rooms, 119 suites* ♨ *In-room: safe, kitchen (some), refrigerator (some), Wi-Fi. In-hotel: restaurant, bars, tennis courts, pool, gym, beachfront, laundry facilities, laundry service, executive floor, parking (no fee)* ▤ *AE, DC, MC, V.*

$$–$$$ ▦ **Radisson Resort at the Port.** For cruise-ship passengers who can't wait to get underway, this splashy resort, done up in pink and turquoise, already

feels like the Caribbean. Guest rooms have wicker furniture, hand-painted wallpaper, tropical-themed decor, and ceiling fans. The pool is lushly landscaped and features a cascading 95-foot mountain waterfall. This resort, directly across the bay from Port Canaveral, is not on the ocean, but it does provide complimentary transportation to the beach, Ron Jon Surf Shop, and the cruise-ship terminals at Port Canaveral. ✉ *8701 Astronaut Blvd., Cape Canaveral, 32920* ☎ *321/784–0000* 📠 *321/784–3737* 🌐 *www.radisson.com/capecanaveralfl* *284 rooms, 72 suites* *In-room: refrigerator (some), kitchen (some), Ethernet. In-hotel: restaurant, bar, tennis court, pool, gym, laundry facilities, laundry service* 💳 *AE, DC, MC, V.*

★ $$ **Inn at Cocoa Beach.** One of the area's best, this charming oceanfront inn has spacious, individually decorated rooms with four-poster beds, upholstered chairs, and balconies or patios; most have ocean views. Deluxe rooms are much larger, with a king-size bed, sofa, and sitting area; most also have a dining table. Jacuzzi rooms are different sizes; several have fireplaces, and all have beautiful ocean views. Included in the rate are afternoon socials in the breezeway, evening wine and cheese, and a sumptuous Continental breakfast. ✉ *4300 Ocean Beach Blvd., Cocoa Beach, 32931* ☎ *321/799–3460, 800/343–5307 outside Florida* 📠 *321/784–8632* 🌐 *www.theinnatcocoabeach.com* *50 rooms* *In-room: safe, VCR (some) Wi-Fi. In-hotel: pool, beachfront, public Wi-Fi, parking (no fee), no smoking rooms* 💳 *AE, D, MC, V* *BP.*

6

SAN JUAN, PUERTO RICO

Mark Sullivan

In addition to being a major port of call, San Juan is also a common port of embarkation for cruises on Southern Caribbean itineraries. For information on dining, shopping, nightlife, and sightseeing *see* San Juan, Puerto Rico *in* Chapter 7.

The Cruise Port

Cruise ships dock within a couple of blocks of Old San Juan. The Paseo de la Princesa, a tree-lined promenade beneath the city wall, is a nice place for a stroll—you can admire the local crafts and stop at the refreshment kiosks. A tourist information booth is in the cruise terminal area. Major sights in the Old San Juan area are mere blocks from the piers, but be aware that the streets are narrow and steeply inclined in places. Even if you have only a few hours before your cruise, you'll have time to do a little sightseeing.

AIRPORT TRANSFERS

The ride from the Luis Muñoz Marín International Airport, east of downtown San Juan, to the docks in Old San Juan takes about 20 minutes. The white "taxi turistico" cabs, marked by a logo on the door, have a fixed rate of $19 to the cruise ship piers; there is a 50¢ charge for luggage. Other taxi companies charge by the mile, which can cost a little more. Be sure the driver starts the meter, or agree on a fare beforehand.

VISITOR INFORMATION

Puerto Rico Tourism Company 🌐 www.gotopuertorico.com ☎ 787/721–2400 or 800/866–7827.

Where to Stay

If you are planning to spend one night in San Juan before your cruise departs, you'll probably find it easier to stay in Old San Juan, where the cruise ship terminals are. But if you want to spend a few extra days in the city, there are other possibilities near good beaches a bit farther out. We make some nightlife suggestions in the San Juan port of call section (see ⇨ San Juan *in* Chapter 7).

For price categories, *see* Lodging at the beginning of this chapter.

$$ ▦ **Sheraton Old San Juan.** This hotel's triangular shape subtly echoes the cruise ships docked nearby. Rooms facing the water have dazzling views of these behemoths as they sail in and out of the harbor. Others have views over the rooftops of Old San Juan. The rooms have been plushly renovated and have nice touches like custom-designed beds. On the top floor you'll find a sunny patio with a pool and whirlpool bath, as well as a spacious gym with the latest equipment; the concierge level provides hassle-free check-ins, Continental breakfasts, and evening hors d'oeuvres. ⊠ *100 Calle Brumbaugh, Old San Juan 00901* ☎ *787/721–5100 or 866/376–7577* 🖷 *787/289–1910* ⊕ *www.sheratonoldsanjuan.com* 📁 *200 rooms, 40 suites* ⚬ *In-room: safe, Ethernet. In-hotel: restaurant, room service, bar, pool, gym, laundry service, executive floor, public Internet, public Wi-Fi, parking (fee), no-smoking rooms* ▤ *AE, D, DC, MC, V* ⦙◯⦙ *EP.*

$$$–$$$$ ▦ **Normandie Hotel.** One of the Caribbean's finest examples of art-deco
Fodor'sChoice architecture, this ship-shaped hotel hosted high-society types back in the
★ 1940s. After a stem-to-stern renovation, it's ready to sail again. Egyptian motifs in the grand ballroom and other period details have been meticulously restored. Guest rooms, many of them as big as suites, are decorated in sensuous shades of cream and oatmeal. Business travelers will appreciate the huge desks outfitted with broadband access. Relaxation-seekers need look no further than the sparkling pool or the compact spa with its massage area overlooking the ocean. N Bar, on the second floor, has quickly become a see-and-be-seen place for the city's trendy crowd. ⊠ *499 Av. Muñoz Rivera, Puerta de Tierra 00901* ☎ *787/729–2929* 🖷 *787/729–3083* ⊕ *www.normandiepr.com* 📁 *58 rooms, 117 suites* ⚬ *In-room: safe, refrigerator, Wi-Fi. In-hotel: Restaurant, room service, bars, pool, gym, spa, beachfront, laundry service, public Internet, parking (fee), no-smoking rooms* ▤ *AE, MC, V* ⦙◯⦙ *EP.*

$–$$ ▦ **Numero Uno.** The name refers to the address, but Numero Uno is also how this small hotel rates with its guests. It's not unusual to hear people trading stories about how many times they've returned to this relaxing retreat. Behind a whitewashed wall is a patio where you can catch some rays beside the pool, dine in the restaurant, or enjoy a cocktail at the bar. A few steps away, a sandy beach beckons; guests are provided with beach chairs and umbrellas. Rooms are decorated in sophisticated shades of cream and taupe; several have ocean views. ⊠ *1 Calle Santa Ana, Ocean Park 00911* ☎ *787/726–5010* 🖷 *787/727–5482* ⊕ *www.numero1guesthouse.com* 📁 *11 rooms, 2 apartments* ⚬ *In-room: kitchen (some), refrigerator, Ethernet. In-hotel: restaurant, bar, pool, beachfront, no elevator* ▤ *AE, MC, V* ⦙◯⦙ *CP.*

TAMPA, FLORIDA

Jim and
Cynthia
Tunstall

Although glitzy Miami seems to hold the trendiness trump card and Orlando is the place your kids want to visit annually until they hit middle school, the Tampa Bay area has that elusive quality that many attribute to the "real Florida." The state's second-largest metro area is less fast-lane than its biggest (Miami), or even Orlando, but its strengths are just as varied, from broad cultural diversity to a sun-worshipping beach culture. Florida's third-busiest airport, a vibrant business community, world-class beaches, and superior hotels and resorts—many of them historic—make this an excellent place to spend a week or a lifetime. Car-

TAMPA BEST BETS

- **Busch Gardens.** The area's best theme park is a good family destination.
- **Florida Aquarium.** The aquarium is next to the cruise-port, so you can just walk, making it a good option even if you have a couple of hours to kill before boarding (they'll even store your luggage if you want to visit after disembarking).
- **Ybor City.** For nightlife and restaurants, this historic district is Tampa's hot spot.

nival and Royal Caribbean base several ships in Tampa for cruises to the Western Caribbean, Holland America bases one ship, and several other lines base ships here seasonally.

Essentials

HOURS Some museums are closed on Mondays.

INTERNET Most people choose to access the Internet through their hotels. Most Starbucks outlets offer Internet service for a fee if you have your own laptop.

VISITOR
INFORMATION St. Petersburg/Clearwater Area Convention & Visitors Bureau (✉ 13850 58th St. N, Suite 2200, Clearwater 33760 ☎ 727/464–7200 or 877/352–3224 ⊕ www.floridasbeach.com). Tampa Bay Convention and Visitors Bureau (✉ 400 N. Tampa St., Suite 2800, Tampa 33602 ☎ 813/223–1111 or 800/368–2672 ⊕ www.visittampabay.com).

The Cruise Port

Tampa is the largest shipping port in the state of Florida, and it's becoming ever more important to the cruise industry, now with three passenger terminals. In Tampa's downtown area, the port is linked to nearby Ybor City and the rest of the Tampa Bay Area by the TECO streetcar line.

To reach the port by car, take I–4 West to Exit 1 (Ybor City), and go south on 21st Street. To get to Terminals 2 and 6, turn right on Adamo Drive (Highway 60), then left on Channelside Drive.
🚢 Tampa Port Authority ✉ 1101 Channelside Dr. ☎ 813/905–7678, 813/905–5045, or 800/741–2297 ⊕ www.tampaport.com.

AIRPORT
TRANSFERS Bay Shuttle provides van-shuttle service from Tampa International Airport to the cruise-ship terminals for a fee of $11 for each passenger. Make a reservation when you arrive at the airport at their booth in ground transportation. Super Shuttle will take passengers from the Tampa airport to the cruise terminal for $19 for the first passenger and $10 for each additional passenger.

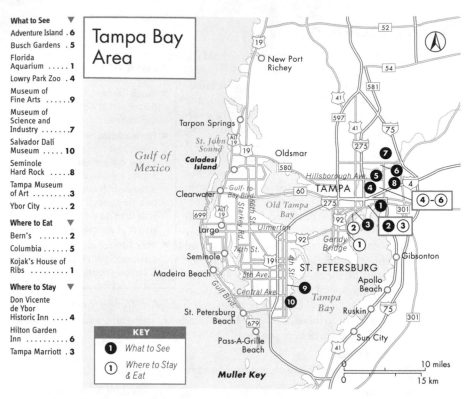

Bay Shuttle ☎ 813/259–9998 ⊕ www.tampabayshuttle.com. **Super Shuttle** ☎ 800/258–3826 ⊕ www.supershuttle.com.

PARKING Parking is available at the port directly across from the terminals. For Terminals 2 and 3 (Carnival and Royal Caribbean), parking is in a garage across the street. For Terminal 6 (Holland America), parking is outdoors in a guarded, enclosed lot. The cost is $12 a day, payable by credit card (MasterCard or Visa) or in cash.

Exploring the Tampa Bay Area

Florida's west coast crown jewel as well as its business and commercial hub, Tampa has high-rises and heavy traffic. Amid the bustle is the region's greatest concentration of restaurants, nightlife, stores, and cultural events.

Numbers in the margin refer to points of interest on the Tampa Bay Area map.

☞ ⑥ **Adventure Island.** Waterslides, pools, and artificial-wave pools create a 30-acre wonderland at this water park, a corporate cousin of Busch Gardens. The park's newest thrill ride, Riptide, is a competitive adventure for racing three other riders through twisting tubes and hairpin turns. Rides such as the Key West Rapids and Tampa Typhoon are creative, if geographically incorrect. (There are no rapids in Key West and *typhoon* is a term used only in Pacific regions—Tampa Hurricane just wouldn't have had the same alliterative allure.) The park's planners took the younger kids into account, with offerings such as Fabian's Funport, which has a scaled-down wave pool and interactive water gym. Along with a championship volleyball complex and a surf pool, you'll find cafés, snack bars, picnic and sunbathing areas, and changing rooms. ⊠ *1001 Malcolm McKinley Dr., less than 1 mi (1½ km) north of Busch Gardens, Tampa* 🕾 *813/987–5660 or 888/800–5447* ⊕ *www.adventureisland.com* 🎫 *$34.95* ☉ *Mid-Mar.–late Oct., daily 10–5.*

Busch Gardens. More than 2,000 animals and dazzling live entertainment are just part of the attractions at this sprawling, carefully manicured theme park. The 335-acre adventure park's habitats offer views of some of the world's most endangered and exotic animals.

SheiKra, North America's first dive coaster, opened in mid-2005. On the wings of an African hawk, riders fly through a three-minute journey 200 feet up, then 90 degrees straight down at 70 mi per hour. The park's coaster lineup also includes steel giants **Kumba** and **Montu,** a double wooden roller coaster called **Gwazi,** and **Cheetah Chase**—a five-story family coaster full of hairpin turns and breathtaking dips. The off-road safari **Rhino Rally** brings you face to face with elephants, white rhinos, and Nile crocodiles. **Land of the Dragons** is a 4-acre playland for children that has rides, special shows, play areas, and a three-story tree house with towers and stairways. You can also take a beer-tasting class—after all, Anheuser-Busch owns the park. ⊠ *3000 E. Busch Blvd., 8 mi (13 km) northeast of downtown Tampa and 2 mi (3 km) east of I–275 Exit 50, Tampa* 🕾 *813/987–5082 or 888/800–5447* ⊕ *www.buschgardens.com* 🎫 *$61.95* ☉ *Daily 9–6; later in summer during special events.*

Florida Aquarium. The $84-million aquarium is no overpriced fishbowl; it's a dazzling architectural landmark with an 83-foot-high multitiered glass dome and 200,000 square feet of air-conditioned exhibit space. It has more than 10,000 aquatic plants and animals representing species native to Florida and the rest of the world. The aquarium's most impressive single exhibit is the Coral Reef, in a 500,000-gallon tank ringed with viewing windows, including an awesome 43-foot-wide panoramic opening. Part of the tank is a walkable tunnel, almost giving the illusion of venturing into underwater depths. The outdoor Explore-a-Shore exhibit, which packs appeal for younger kids, is an aquatic playground with a water slide, water jet sprays, and a climbable replica pirate ship. ⊠ *701 Channelside Dr., Tampa* 🕾 *813/273–4000* ⊕ *www.flaquarium.org* 🎫 *Aquarium $17.95; Bay Spirit, Wild Dolphin Ecotour $19.95* ☉ *Daily 9:30–5.*

Lowry Park Zoo. In Tampa's 56-acre zoo, exotic creatures live in their lush, natural habitats. Visit the zoo's newest exhibit area, Safari Africa, with a baby African elephant (born in October 2005) and four adult elephants. Feed a giraffe, ride a camel, see the zebra play, and experience a "white rhino encounter." Check out the Asian Domain, with tigers and Indian rhinos, and Primate World, including chimpanzees and colobus monkeys. Spot some fancy flying in the free-flight bird aviary, and come face to face with alligators, panthers, bears, and red wolves at the Florida Wildlife Center. Gentle goats and kangaroos populate the Wallaroo Station children's zoo, and gentle creatures of another kind headline at the Manatee Amphitheater and Aquatic Center. ⊠ *1101 W. Sligh Ave., Tampa* 🕾 *813/ 935–8552* ⊕ *www.lowryparkzoo.com* 🎫 *$14.95* ☉ *Daily 9:30–5.*

⑨ Museum of Fine Arts. Outstanding examples of European, American, pre-Columbian, and Far Eastern art are at St. Petersburg's major art museum. There are also photographic exhibits. Staff members give narrated gallery tours two to five times a day. ⊠ *255 Beach Dr. NE, St. Petersburg* ☎ *727/896–2667* ⊕ *www.fine-arts.org* ⊠ *$8* ⊙ *Tues.–Sat. 10–5, Sun. 1–5.*

⑦ Museum of Science & Industry (MOSI). This fun and stimulating scientific playground is a place where you learn about Florida weather, anatomy, flight, and space by seeing *and* by doing. At the Gulf Coast Hurricane Exhibit you can experience what a hurricane and its 74-mph winds feel like (and live to write home about it). The Bank of America BioWorks Butterfly Garden is a 6,400-square-foot engineered ecosystem project that not only serves as a home for free-flying butterflies but also demonstrates how wetlands can clean water. The 100-seat Saunders Planetarium—Tampa Bay's only planetarium—has afternoon and evening shows, one of them a trek through the universe. There's also an IMAX theater, where films are projected onto a hemispherical 82-foot dome. Kids in Charge, a 40,000-square-foot science center with interactive exhibits aimed at the 12-and-under set, opened in 2005, complete with a flight simulator. ⊠ *4801 E. Fowler Ave., 1 mi 1½ km) north of Busch Gardens, Tampa* ☎ *813/987–6300 or 800/995–6674* ⊕ *www.mosi.org* ⊠ *$19.95* ⊙ *Weekdays 9–5, weekends 9–7.*

⑩ Salvador Dalí Museum. The world's most extensive collection of originals by the Spanish surrealist Salvador Dalí is found here. The collection includes 95 oils, more than 100 watercolors and drawings, and 1,300 graphics, sculptures, photographs, and objets d'art, including floor-to-ceiling murals. Frequent tours are led by well-informed docents. How did the collection end up here? A rich northern industrialist and friend of Dalí, Ohio magnate A. Reynolds Morse, was looking for a museum site after his huge personal Dalí collection began to overflow his mansion. The people of St. Petersburg vied admirably for the collection, and the museum was established here as a result. ⊠ *1000 3rd St. S, St. Petersburg* ☎ *727/823–3767 or 800/442–3254* ⊕ *www.salvadordalimuseum.org* ⊠ *$15* ⊙ *Mon.–Wed., Fri., and Sat. 9:30–5:30; Thurs. 9:30–8; Sun. noon–5:30.*

⑧ Seminole Hard Rock Hotel & Casino. If you've brought your body to Tampa but your heart's in Vegas, you can satisfy that urge to hang around a poker table at 4 AM here. The casino has poker tables and gaming machines, and Las Vegas–style level-three slot machines are slated to open in mid-2006. The casino lounge serves drinks 24 hours a day. Floyd's restaurant has dinner and nightlife. ⊠ *5223 N. Orient Rd., off I–4 at N. Orient Rd. Exit* ☎ *813/627–7625 or 866/762–5463* ⊕ *www.seminolehardrock.com* ⊠ *Free* ⊙ *Daily 24 hrs.*

③ Tampa Museum of Art. The 35,000-square-foot museum has an impressive permanent collection of Greek and Roman antiquities and 20th–21st-century sculpture, along with five galleries that host traveling exhibits, which range from contemporary to classical. ⊠ *600 N. Ashley Dr., Downtown* ☎ *813/274–8130* ⊕ *www.tampamuseum.com* ⊠ *$8* ⊙ *Tues.–Sat. 10–5, Sun. 11–5; 3rd Thurs. of month open until midnight.*

Fodor$Choice
★

② **Ybor City.** One of only three National Historic Landmark districts in
Fodor'sChoice Florida, Tampa's lively Cuban enclave has brick streets and wrought-iron
★ balconies. Cubans brought their cigar-making industry to Ybor (pronounced *ee*-bore) City in 1866, and the smell of cigars—hand-rolled by
Cuban immigrants—still wafts through the heart of this east Tampa area,
along with the strong aroma of roasting coffee. These days the neighborhood is emerging as Tampa's hot spot as empty cigar factories and
social clubs are transformed into boutiques, galleries, restaurants, and
nightclubs that rival those in Miami's sizzling South Beach. Take a stroll
past the ornately tiled **Columbia** restaurant and the stores lining 7th Avenue. Guided walking tours of the area ($5) enable you to see artisans
hand-roll cigars following time-honored methods. Step back into the past
at **Centennial Park** (⊠ 8th Ave. and 18th St.), which re-creates a period
streetscape and hosts the Fresh Market every Saturday. ☾ Ybor City's
destination within a destination is the dining and entertainment palace
Centro Ybor (⊠ 1600 E. 7th Ave.). It has shops, trendy bars and restaurants, a 20-screen movie theater, and GameWorks, an interactive playground developed by Steven Spielberg. The **Ybor City Museum State Park**
provides a look at the history of the cigar industry. Admission includes
a tour of La Casita, one of the shotgun houses occupied by cigar workers and their families in the late 1890s. ⊠ *1818 E. 9th Ave., between
Nuccio Pkwy. and 22nd St., from 7th to 9th Aves.* ☎ *813/247–6323*
⊕ *www.ybormuseum.org* ☜ *$3* ☉ *Daily 9–5; walking tours Sat. 10:30.*

Beaches

Spread over six small islands, or keys, 900-acre **Fort De Soto Park** (⊠ 3500
Pinellas Bayway S, Tierra Verde ☎ 727/582–2267) lies at the mouth of
Tampa Bay. It has 7 mi (11 km) of beaches, two fishing piers, picnic and
camping grounds, and a historic fort. The fort was built on the southern
end of Mullet Key to protect sea lanes in the gulf during the Spanish-Amer-
ican War. Roam the fort or wander the beaches and the islands. **Pass-A-Grille
Beach** (⊠ Off Gulf Blvd. [Rte. 699], St. Pete Beach), at the southern end of
St. Pete Beach, has parking meters, a snack bar, restrooms, and showers.
St. Pete Beach (⊠ 11260 Gulf Blvd., St. Pete Beach) is a free beach on Treasure Island. There are dressing rooms, metered parking, and a snack bar.

Shopping

The **Channelside shopping and entertainment complex** (⊠ 615 Channelside Dr.,
Downtown) offers movie theaters, shops, restaurants, and clubs; the official Tampa Bay visitors center is also here. **Old Hyde Park Village** (⊠ Swan
Ave. near Bayshore Blvd., Hyde Park) is a gentrified shopping district
like the ones you find in every major American city. Williams-Sonoma
and Brooks Brothers are mixed in with bistros and sidewalk cafés. If you
are shopping for hand-rolled cigars, head for 7th Avenue in **Ybor City**, where
a few hand-rollers practice their craft in small shops.

Nightlife

The biggest concentration of nightclubs, as well as the widest variety, is
found along 7th Avenue in Ybor City. It becomes a little like Bourbon
Street in New Orleans after the sun goes down.

Where to Eat in the Tampa Bay Area

For price categories, *see* Dining at the beginning of this chapter.

$$$–$$$$ ✕ **Bern's Steak House.** Fine mahogany paneling and ornate chandeliers de-
FodorsChoice fine the elegance at legendary Bern's, which many feel is Tampa's best
★ restaurant. Owner David Laxer ages his own beef, grows his own or-
ganic vegetables, roasts his own coffee, and maintains his own saltwa-
ter fish tanks. Cuts of topmost beef are sold by weight and thickness.
The wine list includes some 6,500 selections (with 1,800 dessert wines).
After dinner, tour the kitchen and wine cellar before having dessert up-
stairs in a cozy booth. ✉ *1208 S. Howard Ave., Hyde Park, Tampa* ☎ *813/
251–2421, 800/282–1547 in Florida* ⩜ *Reservations essential* ▤ *AE,
D, MC, V* ☻ *No lunch.*

$$–$$$ ✕ **Columbia.** A fixture since 1905, this magnificent structure with spacious
dining rooms and a sunny courtyard takes up an entire city block. The
paella is possibly the best in Florida, and the 1905 salad—with ham, olives,
cheese, and garlic—is legendary. The menu has Cuban classics such as
ropa vieja (shredded beef with onions, peppers, and tomatoes) and *arroz
con pollo* (chicken with yellow rice). There's flamenco dancing most nights.
Buy hand-rolled cigars in the bar. ✉ *2117 E. 7th Ave., Ybor City, Tampa*
☎ *813/248–4961* ▤ *AE, D, DC, MC, V.*

¢–$ ✕ **Kojak's House of Ribs.** Family-run since its doors opened in 1978, this ca-
sual eatery has been voted a Tampa favorite year after year in local polls.
Day and night the three indoor dining rooms and outdoor dining terrace
are crowded with hungry patrons digging into tender barbecued ribs. There's
chicken on the menu, too, and heaping sides of coleslaw, potato salad,
parsley potatoes, and corn on the cob. ✉ *2808 Gandy Blvd., South
Tampa, Tampa* ☎ *813/837–3774* ▤ *AE, D, DC, MC, V* ☻ *Closed Mon.*

Where to Stay in the Tampa Bay Area

If you want to be close to the cruise-ship terminal, then you'll have to
stay in Tampa, but if you want to spend more time in the area and per-
haps stay on the beach, St. Petersburg and the beaches are close by.

For price categories, *see* Lodging at the beginning of this chapter.

$$$$ ▥ **Tampa Marriott Waterside.** Across from the Tampa Convention Center,
this downtown hotel was built for conventioneers but is also convenient
to popular tourist spots such as the Florida Aquarium, the St. Pete Times
Forum hockey arena, and shopping and entertainment districts Chan-
nelside, Hyde Park, and Ybor City. At least half of the rooms and most
of the suites overlook the channel to Tampa Bay; the bay itself is visible
from the higher floors of the 27-story hotel. The lobby coffee bar over-
looks the water. Il Terrazzo is the hotel's formal, Italian dining room.
✉ *700 S. Florida Ave., Downtown, 33602* ☎ *813/221–4900* 🖶 *813/
221–0923* ⊕ *www.tampawaterside.com* ⤢ *681 rooms, 36 suites* ⟐ *In-
room: safe, kitchen (some), high-speed Internet, Wi-Fi in lobby. In-hotel:
3 restaurants, room service, bars, pool, gym, spa, concierge, laundry fa-
cilities, laundry service, executive floor, parking (fee), no-smoking rooms*
▤ *AE, D, DC, MC, V.*

★ **$$–$$$** ▥ **Don Vicente de Ybor Historic Inn.** This boutique hotel is in a restored build-
ing constructed in 1895 by Vicente Martinez Ybor, the founder of Ybor
City. From the beige stucco exterior to the white marble staircase in the
main lobby, the hotel is an architectural tour de force. Rooms have an-
tique furnishings, Persian rugs, and four-poster canopied beds. Most rooms

have wrought-iron balconies. The clubs and shops of Ybor City are within a short walk. ✉ *1915 Republica de Cuba, Ybor City, 33605* ☎ *813/ 241–4545* 🖷 *813/241–6104* ⊕ *www.donvicenteinn.com* ⤺ *13 rooms, 3 suites* ♿ *In-room: Ethernet. In-hotel: restaurant, bar, laundry service, Wi-Fi* ▭ *AE, D, DC, MC, V* ⎟◎⎟ *BP.*

$$–$$$ 🖼 **Hilton Garden Inn Tampa Ybor Historic District.** Architecturally, this property pales when compared to the century-old classic structures around it in Ybor City. But it is convenient: it's across the street from the Centro Ybor complex, 3 mi (5 km) from downtown Tampa, and 7 mi (11 km) from Tampa International Airport. The hotel restaurant has a full breakfast buffet and doesn't try to compete with the culinary heavyweights in a six-block radius. Rooms are business traveler–friendly, with high-speed Internet access, dual phone lines, large desks, and ergonomic chairs. ✉ *1700 E. 9th Ave., Ybor City, 33605* ☎ *813/769–9267* 🖷 *813/ 769–3299* ⊕ *www.tampayborhistoricdistrict.gardeninn.com* ⤺ *84 rooms, 11 suites* ♿ *In-room: refrigerator, Ethernet. In-hotel: restaurant, pool, laundry facilities, laundry service, Wi-Fi* ▭ *AE, D, DC, MC, V* ⎟◎⎟ *EP.*

6

Ports of Call

WORD OF MOUTH

"I love planning a trip and seeing the island on my own terms . . . and not with hordes of other people . . .. It takes a little more work to research and make arrangements, but it is always worth it to me."
—Cathy

"[T]hese excursion companies depend on the cruise industry for their living, and they are all very much aware of the sailing times. Don't be scared off from arranging your own tours because of the threat of [the ship] leaving without you."   —PumpkinEater

"There are times when it is a good idea to book with the ship. Last year we did a tour that let us swim with the dolphins then it took us to the ship's private beach."   —toontown

NOWHERE IN THE WORLD are conditions better suited to cruising than in the Caribbean Sea. Tiny island nations, within easy sailing distance of one another, form a chain of tropical enchantment that curves from Cuba in the north all the way down to the coast of Venezuela. There's far more to life here than sand and coconuts, however. The islands are vastly different, with a variety of cultures, topographies, and languages represented. Colonialism has left its mark, and the presence of the Spanish, French, Dutch, Danish, and British is still felt. Slavery, too, has left its cultural legacy, blending African overtones into the colonial/Indian amalgam. The one constant, however, is the weather. Despite the islands' southerly latitude, the climate is surprisingly gentle, due in large part to the cooling influence of the trade winds.

The Caribbean is made up of the Greater Antilles and the Lesser Antilles. The former consist of those islands closest to the United States: Cuba, Jamaica, Hispaniola (Haiti and the Dominican Republic), and Puerto Rico. (The Cayman Islands lie south of Cuba.) The Lesser Antilles, including the Virgin, Windward, and Leeward islands and others, are greater in number but smaller in size, and constitute the southern half of the Caribbean chain.

GOING ASHORE

Traveling by cruise ship presents an opportunity to visit many places in a short time. The flip side is that your stay in each port of call will be brief. For this reason cruise lines offer shore excursions, which maximize passengers' time. There are a number of advantages to shore excursions arranged by your ship: in some destinations, transportation may be unreliable, and a ship-packaged tour is the best way to see distant sights. Also, you don't have to worry about missing the ship. The disadvantage of a shore excursion is the cost—you usually pay more for the convenience of having the ship do the legwork for you, but it's not always a lot more. Of course, you can always book a tour independently, hire a taxi, or use foot power to explore on your own. For each port of call included in this guide, we've provided some suggestions for the best ship-sponsored excursions—in terms of both quality of experience and price—as well as some suggestions for what to do if you want to explore on your own.

Arriving in Port

When your ship arrives in a port, it will tie up alongside a dock or anchor out in a harbor. If the ship is docked, passengers walk down the gangway to go ashore. Docking makes it easy to move between the shore and the ship.

Tendering

If your ship anchors in the harbor, you will have to take a small boat—called a launch or tender—to get ashore. Tendering is a nuisance. Passengers wishing to disembark may be required to gather in a public room, get sequenced boarding passes, and wait until their numbers are called. The ride to shore may take as long as 20 minutes. If you don't like waiting, plan to go ashore an hour or so after the ship drops its anchor. On a very large ship, the wait for a tender can be quite long and frustrating.

Because tenders can be difficult to board, passengers with mobility problems may not be able to visit certain ports. The larger ships are more likely to use tenders. It is usually possible to learn before booking a cruise whether the ship will dock or anchor at its ports of call.

Before anyone is allowed to walk down the gangway or board a tender, the ship must be cleared for landing. Immigration and customs officials board the vessel to examine passports and sort through red tape. It may be more than an hour before you're allowed ashore. You will be issued a boarding pass, which you'll need to get back on board.

Returning to the Ship

Cruise lines are strict about sailing times, which are posted at the gangway and elsewhere and announced in the daily schedule of activities. Be sure to be back on board (not on the dock waiting to get a tender back to the ship) at least a half-hour before the announced sailing time or you may be stranded. If you are on a shore excursion that was sold by the cruise line, however, the captain will wait for your group before casting off. That is one reason many passengers prefer ship-packaged tours.

If you're not on one of the ship's tours and the ship sails without you, immediately contact the cruise line's port representative, whose phone number is often listed on the daily schedule of activities. You may be able to hitch a ride on a pilot boat, although that is unlikely. Passengers who miss the boat must pay their own way to the next port.

CARIBBEAN ESSENTIALS

Currency
The U.S. dollar is the official currency on Puerto Rico, the U.S. Virgin Islands, and the British Virgin Islands. On Grand Cayman you will usually have a choice of Cayman or U.S. dollars when you take money out of an ATM, and you may even be able to get change in U.S. dollars. In most other Caribbean ports, U.S. paper currency (not coins) is accepted readily, but you may need to change a few dollars into local currency for phone calls, tips, and taxis. When you pay in dollars you'll almost always get change in local currency, so it's best to carry bills in small denominations. If you need local currency (say, for a trip to one of the French islands that uses the euro), change money at a local bank or use an ATM for the best rate. Most major credit cards are accepted all over the Caribbean, except at local market stalls and small establishments.

Keeping in Touch
Internet cafés are now fairly common on most islands, and you'll sometimes find Internet cafés in the cruise-ship terminal itself—or perhaps in an attached or nearby shopping center. If you want to call home, most cruise-ship facilities have phones that accept credit cards or local phone cards (local phone cards are almost always the cheapest option). And

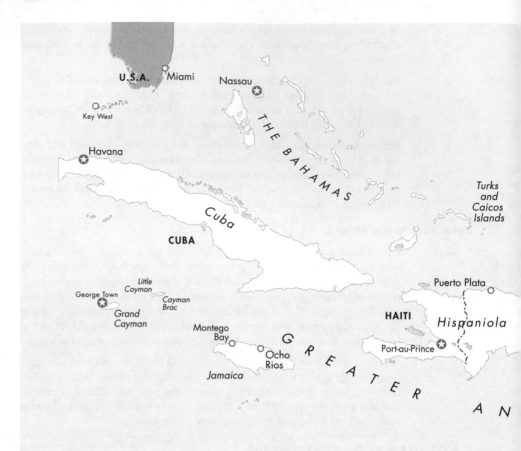

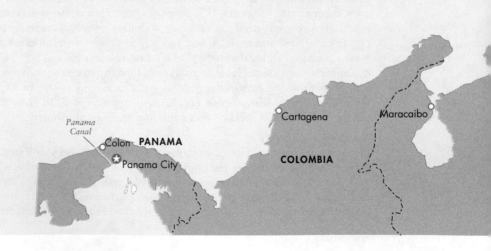

Caribbean

ATLANTIC OCEAN

LEEWARD ISLANDS

DOMINICAN
REPUBLIC

Santo
Domingo

San Juan

St. John
St. Thomas
Tortola
Virgin Gorda
Anguilla
St. Barthélemy

Puerto
Rico

St.
Croix

St. Maarten/
St. Martin
St. Eustatius
St. Kitts
Nevis
Montserrat
Guadeloupe

Saba
Barbuda

Antigua

Marie
Galante

TILLES

Sea

WINDWARD

Dominica

Martinique
Fort-de-France

St. Lucia

Barbados

Bridgetown

St. Vincent
Bequia
The
Grenadines
Carriacou
St. George's
Grenada

Tobago

LESSER ANTILLES

Aruba
Willemstad
Bonaire
Islas Los
Roques
Curaçao

Port of Spain
Trinidad

La Guaira

Caracas

VENEZUELA

0		200 miles
0		300 km

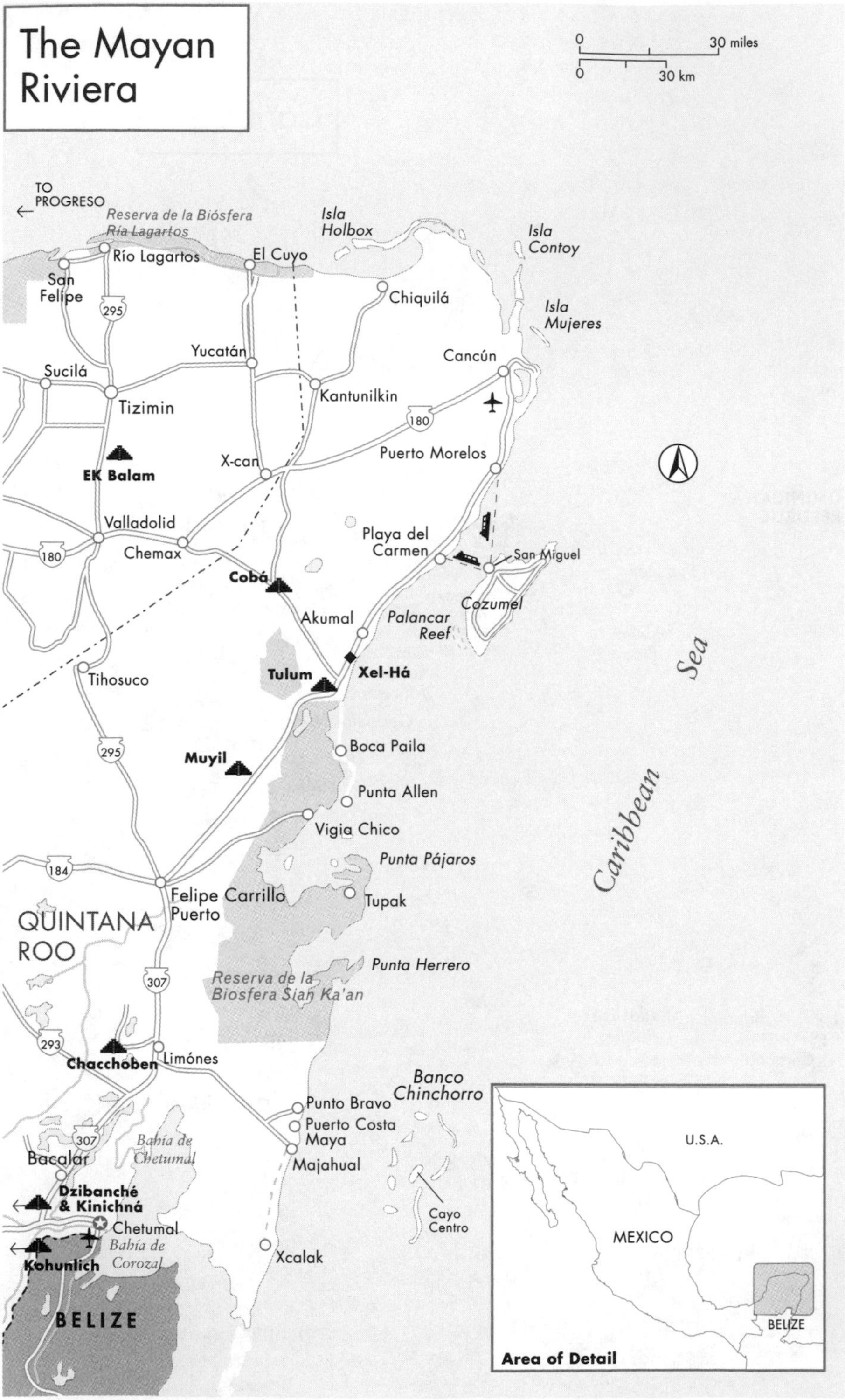

The Mayan Riviera

0   30 miles

0   30 km

TO PROGRESO

Reserva de la Biósfera
Ría Lagartos

Isla Holbox

Isla Contoy

Río Lagartos

El Cuyo

Chiquilá

San Felípe

Isla Mujeres

295

Yucatán

Cancún

Sucilá

Kantunilkin

Tizimin

180

EK Balam

X-can

Puerto Morelos

Valladolid

Playa del Carmen

180

Chemax

San Miguel

Cobá

Cozumel

Akumal

Palancar Reef

Tihosuco

Tulum

Xel-Há

Muyil

Boca Paila

295

Punta Allen

Vigia Chico

Punta Pájaros

184

Felipe Carrillo Puerto

Tupak

QUINTANA ROO

Punta Herrero

307

Reserva de la
Biosfera Sian Ka'an

Chacchoben

Limónes

293

Caribbean Sea

Banco Chinchorro

307

Bahía de Chetumal

Punto Bravo

Puerto Costa Maya

Bacalar

Majahual

Dzibanché & Kinichná

Cayo Centro

Chetumal

Kohunlich

Bahía de Corozal

Xcalak

BELIZE

Area of Detail

U.S.A.

MEXICO

BELIZE

on most islands, GSM multi-band mobile phones will work, though roaming charges may be steep (some plans include Puerto Rico and the U.S. Virgin Islands in their nationwide calling regions).

Where to Eat

Cuisine on the Caribbean's islands is as varied as the islands themselves. The region's history as a colonial battleground and ethnic melting pot creates plenty of variety and adds lots of unusual tropical fruit and spices. In fact, the one quality that defines most Caribbean cooking is its spiciness, acquired from nutmeg, mace, allspice, peppers, saffron, and many other seasonings grown in the islands. Dress is generally casual, although throughout the islands, beachwear is inappropriate most anywhere except on the beach. Unless otherwise noted, prices are given in U.S. dollars. The following price categories are used in this book.

> **BUYING LIQUOR & PERFUME**
>
> If you buy duty-free liquor or perfume while in a Caribbean port, don't forget that you may not bring it aboard your flight home. You will have to put it in your checked bags. Many liquor stores will pack your bottles in bubble wrap and pack them in a good cardboard box. Take advantage of this service.

	WHAT IT COSTS In US$				
	$$$$	**$$$**	**$$**	**$**	**¢**
AT DINNER	over $30	$20–$30	$12–$20	$8–$12	under $8

Prices are per person for a main course at dinner and do not include any service charges.

Shore Excursions

Typical excursions include an island or town bus tour, a visit to a beach or rum factory, a boat trip, a snorkeling or diving trip, and charter fishing. In recent years, however, shore excursions have gotten more adventurous with mild river rafting, parasailing, jet skiing, hiking, and biking added to the mix. It's often easier to take a ship-arranged excursion, but it's almost never the cheapest option.

If you prefer to break away from the pack, find a knowledgeable taxi driver or tour operator—they're usually within a stone's throw of the pier—or wander around on your own. A group of four to six people will usually find this option more economical and practical than will a single person or a couple.

Renting a car is also a good option on many islands—again, the more people, the better the deal. But get a good island map before you set off, and be sure to find out how long it will take you to get around.

Conditions are ideal for water sports of all kinds—scuba diving, snorkeling, windsurfing, sailing, waterskiing, and fishing excursions abound. Your shore-excursion director can usually arrange these activities for you if the ship offers no formal excursion.

PRIVATE ISLANDS

Linda Coffman When evaluating the "best" Caribbean ports of call, many repeat cruise passengers often add the cruise lines' own private island to their lists of preferred destinations.

The cruise lines established "private" islands to provide a beach break on an island (or part of one) reserved for their exclusive use. While most passengers don't select an itinerary based solely upon calling at a private island, they usually consider them a highlight of their cruise vacation. The very least you can expect of your private island is lush foliage and a wide swath of beach surrounded by azure water. Facilities vary, but a beach barbeque, water-sports equipment rental, lounge chairs, hammocks, and restrooms are standard. Youth counselors come ashore to conduct sand castle building competitions and lead junior pirates on swashbuckling island treasure hunts.

The use of strollers and wheelchairs equipped with all-terrain wheels may be offered on a complimentary first-come, first-served basis. However, with the exception of some participation sports on the beach, plan to pay for most water toys and activities. Costs associated with private island fun and recreation can range from $6 for use of a snorkel vest (you may use your own snorkel equipment; however, in the event a floatation vest is required for safety, you must rent one) to $30 for rental of an entire snorkeling outfit for the day (mask, fins, snorkel vest, a mesh bag, fish identification card, and fish food). You can often take a banana boat ride for $16 to $19 (15-minute ride), sail a small boat or catamaran for $30 to $50 (one hour), paddle a kayak for $18 to $30 (half-hour), ride a jet ski for $59 to $95 (45 minutes to one hour), or parasail for a hefty $69 to $79 (10 minutes or less). Floating mats are a relative bargain at $10 for all day lounging in the water. You might also find open-air massage cabanas with pricing comparable to the spa charges on board.

There is generally no charge for food or basic beverages, such as those served on board ship. While soft drinks and tropical cocktails can be charged to your shipboard account, you might want to bring a small amount of cash ashore for souvenir shopping, which is usually possible from vendors set up on or near the beach. You will also want to bring beach towels ashore and return them to the ship at the end of the day because, as Princess Cruises reminds passengers, "Although the locals may offer to do this for you, unfortunately we seldom see the towels again!"

Even if you do nothing more than lie in a shaded hammock and sip fruity tropical concoctions, the day can be one of the most fun and relaxing of your entire cruise.

Islands by Cruise Line

Carnival Cruise Lines is currently the only major cruise line without an extensive private island experience available to the entire fleet. However, select Carnival itineraries include calls at Half Moon Cay, Holland America Line's private paradise. Similarly, certain Regent Seven Seas cruises include beach party days at Princess Cays and Cayo Leventado.

Not a "private island" destination in the strictest sense, the yachts of Seabourn and SeaDream offer passengers a day ashore on secluded private beaches where they can enjoy lavish barbeques and take a break from swimming and snorkeling to indulge in champagne and caviar served in the surf.

COSTA CRUISES   An unspoiled island paradise, Costa's **Catalina Island** is located just off the coast of the Dominican Republic. Passengers can participate in Costa's "Beach Olympics," schedule a seaside massage, or just kick back on a chaise lounge or a complimentary water float. Water toy rentals, banana boat rides, and sailing tours are available from independent concessionaires. Local vendors set up souvenir shops offering crafts and T-shirts. The ship provides the food for a lunch barbeque and tropical beverages at the beach bar.

Activities: Snorkeling, sailing, jet skiing, waterskiing, hiking, volleyball, organized games, massages, shopping.

DISNEY   Unique among private islands, Disney's **Castaway Cay** has a dock, so pas-
CRUISE LINE   sengers simply step ashore (rather than tendering, as is required to reach all other private islands). Like everything associated with Disney, the line's private island is almost too good to be true. Located in the Abacos, a chain in the Bahamas, only 10% of Castaway Cay is developed, leaving plenty of unspoiled area to explore in Robinson Crusoe fashion. Trams are provided to reach separate beaches designated for children, teens, families, and adults, and Disney is the only line to offer age-specific activities and extensive, well-planned children's activities. Biking and hiking are so popular that a second nature trail, complete with an observation tower, has been added. Excursions range from as passive as a glass-bottom boat tour to the soaring excitement of parasailing. An interactive experience with stingrays is educational and safe—the gentle creatures' barbs are blunted for safety. In addition to barbeque fare and several beverage stations, beach games, island-style music, and a shaded game pavilion, there are shops, massage cabanas by the sea, and even a post office.

Activities: Snorkeling, kayaking, parasailing, sailing, jet skiing, paddleboats, water cycles, fishing, bicycles, basketball, billiards, hiking, Ping-Pong, shuffleboard, soccer, volleyball, organized games, massages, shopping.

HOLLAND   Little San Salvador, one of the Bahamian out-islands, was renamed **Half**
AMERICA LINE   **Moon Cay** by Holland America Line to honor Henry Hudson's ship (depicted on the cruise line's logo) as well as to reflect the beach's crescent shape. Even after development, the island is still so unspoiled that it has been named a Wild Bird Preserve by the Bahamian National Trust. Passengers, who are welcomed ashore at a West Indies Village complete with shops and straw market, find Half Moon Cay easily accessible—all facilities are connected by hard-surfaced and packed-sand pathways and meet and exceed ADA requirements. An accessible tram also connects the welcome center with the food pavilion; wheelchairs with balloon tires are available. In addition to the beach area for lazing in the sun or shade, the island has a post office, Bahamian-style chapel, a lagoon where you can interact with stingrays, and, for family fun, you'll find a beachfront water park with water slides and fanciful sea creatures tethered to the sandy bottom of the shallow water. Massage services are available as are fitness activities. Air-conditioned cabanas can be rented for the day, with or without the services of your own butler.

Activities: Scuba diving, snorkeling, windsurfing, kayaking, parasailing, sailing, jet skiing, Aqua Bikes, fishing, bicycles, basketball, hiking, horseback riding, shuffleboard, volleyball, massages, shopping.

MSC CRUISES **Cayo Leventado,** roughly translated as "Floating Island," is located off the Samaná Peninsula on the northeast coast of the Dominican Republic. The unspoiled cay is leased by Bahia Cruises, a development company that has installed beach chairs, umbrellas, bars, a dining facility, and acres of walking paths through the topical rain forest. Not owned outright by MSC Cruises, the private island is available to other cruise lines. In addition to lazing in the sun, swimming in the warm surf, and participating in spirited beach games, you can choose from several tours. Tours offered are a Jeep safari, hiking to a mountain waterfall with horseback riding, a speedboat excursion to a bird sanctuary, a sail-and-snorkel adventure, and even seasonal whale-watching boat trips.

Activities: Snorkeling, sailing, hiking, volleyball, organized games.

Many ships now tender passengers ashore in the town of Samaná; for more information on this port, see ⇨ Samaná, Dominican Republic, *below.*

NORWEGIAN CRUISE LINE Only 120 miles east of Fort Lauderdale in the Berry Island chain of the Bahamas, much of **Great Stirrup Cay** looks as it did when it was acquired by Norwegian Cruise Line in 1977. The first uninhabited island purchased to offer cruise-ship passengers a private beach day, Great Stirrup Cay's white sand beaches are fringed by coral and ideal for snorkeling. Permanent facilities have been added to and improved in the intervening years, but bougainvillea, sea grape, and coconut palms are still as abundant as the colorful tropical fish that inhabit the reef. To reduce beach erosion and preserve the environment, a seawall was erected. A straw market, water sports centers, bars, volleyball courts, beachside massage stations, and food pavilion round out the facilities.

Activities: Snorkeling, kayaking, parasailing, sailing, paddleboats, Ping-Pong, hiking, volleyball, organized games, massages, shopping.

PRINCESS CRUISES **Princess Cays** is a 40-acre haven on the southern tip of Eleuthera Island in the Bahamas. Not quite an uninhabited island, it nevertheless offers a wide ribbon of beach, long enough for passengers to splash in the surf, relax in a hammock, or limbo to the beat of local music and never feel crowded. In a similar fashion to booking shore excursions, water-sports equipment can be reserved ahead of time, either on board the ship or through the Princess Web site. Nestled in a picturesque palm grove, private bungalows with air-conditioning and ceiling fans and a deck for lounging can be rented for parties of up to six. In addition to three tropical bars and the area where a Bahamian barbeque is served, permanent facilities include small shops that sell island crafts and trinkets, but if you head around the back and through the fence, independent vendors sell similar goods for lower prices.

Activities: Snorkeling, kayaking, parasailing, sailing, paddleboats, Aqua Bikes, hiking, organized games, shopping.

Royal Caribbean and Celebrity Cruises passengers have twice as many opportunities to visit a private island. The lines share two, and many Caribbean itineraries include one or the other.

Coco Cay is a 140-acre island in the Berry Island chain between Nassau and Freeport. Originally known as Little Stirrup Cay, it's within view of Great Stirrup Cay (NCL's private island) and the snorkeling is just as good, especially around a sunken airplane and a replica of Blackbeard's flagship, *Queen Anne's Revenge.* In addition to activities and games ashore, Coco Cay boasts the largest Aqua Park in the Caribbean, where children and adults alike can jump on an in-water trampoline or climb a floating sand castle before they dig into a beach barbeque or explore a nature trail. The newest attractions include an inflatable 40-foot water slide (fun for adults and kids alike) and a Power Wheels track where youngsters age 3 to 8 can take a miniature car for a spin at a sedate 3 mph.

Activities: Scuba diving, snorkeling, jet skiing, kayaking, parasailing, hiking, volleyball, organized games, shopping.

Labadee is a 260-acre peninsula approximately 6 mi (10 km) from Cap Haitien on the secluded north coast of Haiti (the port of call will often be called "Hispaniola"). In addition to swimming, water sports, an Aqua Park with floating trampolines and water slides, and nature trails to explore, bonuses on Labadee are an authentic folkloric show presented by island performers and a market featuring work of local artists and crafters, where you might find an interesting painting or unique wood carving. Due to the proximity of Labadee to mainland Haiti, it is sometimes necessary to cancel calls there due to political unrest. In that event, an alternate port is usually scheduled.

Activities: Snorkeling, jet skiing, kayaking, parasailing, hiking, volleyball, organized games, shopping.

ANTIGUA

Jordan Simon   Some say Antigua has so many beaches that you could visit a different one every day for a year. Most have snow-white sand, and many are backed by lavish resorts that offer sailing, diving, windsurfing, and snorkeling. The largest of the British Leeward islands, Antigua was the headquarters from which Lord Horatio Nelson (then a mere captain) made his forays against the French and pirates in the late 18th century. You may wish to explore English Harbour and its carefully restored Nelson's Dockyard, as well as tour old forts, historic churches, and tiny villages. Appealing aspects of the island's interior include a small tropical rain forest ideal for hiking, ancient Native American archaeological digs, and restored sugar mills. Due to time constraints, it's best to make trips this far from port with an experienced tour operator. But you can easily take a taxi to any number of fine beaches on your own and escape from the hordes descending from the ship.

Essentials

CURRENCY   Eastern Caribbean (E.C.) dollar (EC$2.70 to US$1). U.S. dollars are generally accepted, but change is given in E.C. dollars.

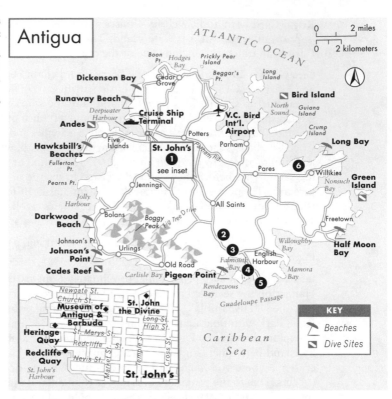

Antigua

ATLANTIC OCEAN

0   2 miles
0   2 kilometers

KEY

Beaches
Dive Sites

HOURS Banks are generally open weekdays from 8 to 1 and 3 to 5. Although some stores still close for lunch, most are open Monday through Saturday from 9 to 5; if a cruise ship is in port, shops in Heritage and Redcliffe Quays are likely to open Sunday.

INTERNET There are some small Internet cafés in St. John's and English Harbour; ask at the tourist information booth at the cruise-ship pier.

TELEPHONES A GSM tri-band mobile phone will usually work in Antigua. You can use the Caribbean Phone Card (available in $5, $10, and $20 denominations in most hotels and post offices) for local and long-distance calls. To call the United States and Canada, dial 1 + the area code + the seven-digit number, or use the phone card or one of the "CALL USA" phones, which are available at several locations, including the cruise terminal at St. John's and the English Harbour Marina.

Coming Ashore

Though some ships dock at the deep-water harbor in downtown St. John's, most use Heritage Quay, a multimillion-dollar complex with shops, condominiums, a casino, and a food court. Most St. John's attractions are an easy walk from Heritage Quay; the older part of the city is eight blocks away. A tourist information booth is in the main docking building.

If you intend to explore beyond St. John's, consider hiring a taxi driver-guide. Taxis meet every cruise ship. They're unmetered; fares are fixed, and drivers are required to carry a rate card. Agree on the fare before setting off, and plan to tip drivers 10%. Some cabbies may take you from St. John's to English Harbour and wait for a "reasonable" amount of time (about a half-hour) while you look around, for about $50; you can usually arrange an island tour for around $25 per hour. Renting your own car isn't usually practical, since you must purchase a $20 temporary driving permit in addition to the car-rental fee, which is usually about $50 per day in the high season.

Shore Excursions

We consider these to be among the better shore excursions for Antigua. They may not be offered by all lines, and tour names may differ as well. Times and prices are approximate.

Highlights Tour. Most highlights tours stop at Nelson's Dockyard and Shirley Heights. Longer versions usually include a beach stop, often at Pigeon Point Beach. Tours usually include a break for refreshments. ⊙ 3–4½ hrs 🎟 $48.

4x4 Off-Road Historical Adventure. By taking a four-wheel-drive vehicle, you'll get to explore some of the quieter, off-the-beaten-track areas of the island, including Betty's Hope. Most of these tours include at least a short beach stop and refreshments. ⊙ 3 hrs 🎟 $59–$66.

Helicopter to Montserrat. If you'd like an upclose look at the island's smoldering active volcano, book this expensive but worthwhile aerial tour. ⊙ 2 hrs 🎟 $250.

Kayak & Snorkel Tour. These guided snorkeling tours usually visit one of the uninhabited islands off Antigua's east coast. After the kayaking trip, there's always time to relax on the beach. ⊙ 4½ hrs 🎟 $69.

Zip Line Tour. Antigua's first zip-line tour opened in 2006. It's sometimes hard to get a spot if you don't book through the ship. ⊙ 4½ hrs 🎟 $69.

Exploring Antigua

Numbers in the margin correspond to points of interest on the Antigua map.

❸ **Falmouth.** This town sits on a lovely bay backed by former sugar plantations and sugar mills. The most important historic site here is St. Paul's Church, which was rebuilt on the site of a church once used by troops during the Nelson period.

❷ **Fort George.** East of Liberta—one of the first settlements founded by freed slaves—on Monk's Hill, this fort was built from 1689 to 1720. Among the ruins are the sites for 32 cannons, water cisterns, the base of the old flagstaff, and some of the original buildings.

ANTIGUA BEST BETS

■ **Dickenson Bay Beach.** One of Antigua's best beaches is just north of St. John's, and it has myriad water-sports outfitters and many beach bars where you can rent chairs and get refreshments.

■ **Nelson's Dockyard.** This is one of the Caribbean's best historic sights, and if you tire of history, it has abundant stores, restaurants, and bars.

■ **Eco-Tourism.** Some of the most interesting tours on Antigua explore the island's forested interior on foot or surrounding coves by kayak. Since some areas are far from St. John's, it's usually best to book these tours with your ship.

7

4 Nelson's Dockyard. Antigua's most famous attraction is the world's only Georgian-era dockyard still in use, a treasure trove for history buffs and nautical nuts alike. In 1671 the governor of the Leeward Islands wrote to the Council for Foreign Plantations in London, pointing out the advantages of this landlocked harbor. By 1704 English Harbour was in regular use as a garrisoned station.

> **CAUTION** ⚠
>
> Do not bother packing beach towels; they will be provided for your use on board the cruise ship and will be given out when you go ashore.

In 1784 26-year-old Horatio Nelson sailed in on the HMS *Boreas* to serve as captain and second-in-command of the Leeward Island Station. Under him was the captain of the HMS *Pegasus,* Prince William Henry, duke of Clarence, who was later crowned King William IV. The prince acted as best man when Nelson married Fannie Nisbet on Nevis in 1787.

When the Royal Navy abandoned the station at English Harbour in 1889, it fell into a state of decay, though adventuresome yachties still lived there in near-primitive conditions. The Society of the Friends of English Harbour began restoring it in 1951; it reopened with great fanfare in 1961. Within the compound are crafts shops, restaurants, and two splendidly restored 18th-century hotels, the Admiral's Inn and the Copper & Lumber Store Hotel, which are worth peeking into. (The latter, occupying a supply store for Nelson's Caribbean fleet, is a particularly fine example of Georgian architecture and has an interior courtyard evoking Old England.) The Dockyard National Park also includes serene nature trails accessing beaches, rock pools, and crumbling plantation ruins and hilltop forts.

The **Dockyard Museum,** in the original Naval Officer's House, presents ship models, mock-ups of English Harbour, displays on the people who worked there and typical ships that docked, silver regatta trophies, maps, prints, antique navigational instruments, and Nelson's very own telescope and tea caddy. ⊠ *English Harbour* ☎ *268/481–5022, 268/463–1060, 268/481–5028 for the National Parks Department* ⊕ *www.antiguamuseums.org* ✉ *$2 suggested donation* ⊙ *Daily 8–5.*

1 St. John's. Antigua's capital, with some 45,000 inhabitants (approximately half the island's population), lies at sea level at the inland end of a sheltered northwestern bay. Although it has seen better days, a couple of notable historic sights and some good waterfront shopping areas and restaurants make it worth a visit. Signs at the **Museum of Antigua & Barbuda** say PLEASE TOUCH, encouraging you to explore Antigua's past. Try your hand at the educational video games or squeeze a cassava through a *matapi* (grass sieve). Exhibits interpret the nation's history, from its geological birth to its political independence in 1981. The museum occupies the former courthouse, which dates from 1750. The superlative gift shop carries such unusual items as calabash purses, seed earrings, and lignum vitae pipes, as well as historic maps and local books. ⊠ *Church and Market Sts.* ☎ *268/462–1469* ⊕ *www.antiguamuseums.org* ✉ *$2 suggested donation* ⊙ *Sun.–Thurs. 8:30–4, Fri. 8:30–3, Sat. 10–2.*

At the south gate of the **Anglican Cathedral of St. John the Divine** are figures of St. John the Baptist and St. John the Divine said to have been taken from one of Napoléon's ships and brought to Antigua. The original church was built in 1681, replaced by a stone building in 1745, and destroyed by an earthquake in 1843. The present neo-baroque building dates from 1845; the parishioners had the interior completely encased in pitch pine, hoping to forestall future earthquake damage. The church attained cathedral status in 1848. Tombstones bear eerily eloquent testament to the colonial days. ⊠ *Between Long and Newgate Sts.* ☎ *268/461–0082.*

Redcliffe Quay, at the water's edge just south of Heritage Quay, is the most appealing part of St. John's. Attractively restored (and superbly re-created) buildings in a riot of cotton-candy colors house shops, restaurants, and boutiques and are linked by courtyards and landscaped walkways.

❺ Shirley Heights. This bluff affords a spectacular view of English Harbour. The heights are named for Sir Thomas Shirley, the governor who fortified the harbor in 1787. At the top is Shirley Heights Lookout, a restaurant built into the remnants of the 18th-century fortifications. Most notable for its boisterous Sunday barbecues that continue into the night with live music and dancing, it serves dependable burgers, pumpkin soup, grilled meats, and rum punches. Not far from Shirley Heights is the **Dows Hill Interpretation Centre,** where observation platforms provide still more sensational vistas of the English Harbour area. A multimedia sound-and-light presentation on island history and culture, spotlighting lifelike figures and colorful tableaux accompanied by running commentary and music, results in a cheery, if bland, portrait of Antiguan life from Amerindian times to the present. ☎ *268/460–2777 for National Parks Authority* ⊡ *EC$15* ☉ *Daily 9–5.*

☾ ❻ Stingray City Antigua. A carefully reproduced "natural" environment has been nicknamed by staffers the "retirement home," though the 30-plus stingrays, ranging from infants to seniors, are frisky. You can stroke, feed, even hold the striking gliders, as well as snorkel in deeper, protected waters. The tour guides do a marvelous job of explaining the animals' habits—from feeding to breeding—and their predators (including man). ⊠ *Seaton's Village* ☎ *268/562–7297 or 268/463–1944.*

Shopping

Redcliffe Quay, on the waterfront at the south edge of St. John's, is by far the most appealing shopping area. Several restaurants and more than 30 boutiques, many with one-of-a-kind wares, are set around landscaped courtyards shaded by colorful trees. **Heritage Quay,** in St. John's, has 35 shops—including many that are duty-free. There are also shops along **St. John's, St. Mary's, High,** and **Long streets.** The tangerine-and-lilac-hue four-story **Vendor's Mall** at the intersection of Redcliffe and Thames streets gathers the pushy, pesky vendors that once clogged the narrow streets. It's jammed with stalls; air-conditioned indoor shops sell some higher-price, if not higher-quality, merchandise.

★ The **Goldsmitty** (⊠ Redcliffe Quay, St. John's ☎ 268/462–4601) is Hans Smit, an expert goldsmith who turns gold, black coral, and precious and semiprecious stones into one-of-a-kind works of art.

Isis (✉ Redcliffe Quay, St. John's ☎ 268/462–4602) sells island and international bric-a-brac, such as antique jewelry, hand-carved walking sticks, and glazed pottery. **Jacaranda** (✉ Redcliffe Quay, St. John's ☎ 268/462–1888) sells batik, sarongs, and swimwear as well as Caribbean food, perfumes, soaps, and artwork. **Map Shop** (✉ St. Mary's St., St. John's ☎ 268/462–3993) offers a fine assortment of books on Caribbean cuisine, flora, fauna, and history, as well as maps. **Noreen Phillips** (✉ Redcliffe Quay, St. John's ☎ 268/462–3127) creates glitzy appliquéd and beaded evening wear—inspired by the colors of the sea and sunset—in sensuous fabrics ranging from chiffon and silk to Italian lace and Indian brocade.

★   At **Galley Boutique** (✉ Nelson's Dockyard, English Harbour ☎ 268/460–1525), Janey Easton personally seeks out exclusive creations from both international (Calvin Klein, Adrienne Vittadini) and local Caribbean designers, ranging from swimwear to evening garb. She also sells handicrafts and lovely hammocks.

Activities

Adventure Tours
Adventure Antigua (☎ 268/727–3261 ⊕ www.adventureantigua.com) is run by enthusiastic Eli Fuller, who is knowledgeable not only about the ecosystem and geography of Antigua but also about its history and politics. The company offers an exceptional day-long boat tour of the island. An "Xtreme Tour" takes you on a circumnavigation of the island on a racing speedboat. **"Paddles" Kayak Eco Adventure** (✉ Seaton's Village ☎ 268/463–1944 or 268/560–3782 ⊕ www.antiguapaddles.com) takes you on a 3½-hour tour of serene mangroves and inlets with informative narrative about the fragile ecosystem of the swamp and reefs and the rich diversity of flora and fauna. The tour ends with a hike to sunken caves and snorkeling in the North Sound Marine Park. Experienced guides double as kayaking and snorkeling instructors, making this an excellent opportunity for novices.

DIVING   With all the wrecks and reefs, there are lots of undersea sights to explore, from coral canyons to sea caves. The most accessible wreck is the schooner *Andes,* not far out in Deep Bay, off the Five Islands Peninsula. Among the favorite sites are **Green Island, Cades Reef,** and **Bird Island** (a national park). **Dockyard Divers** (✉ Nelson's Dockyard, English Harbour ☎ 268/460–1178), owned by British ex-merchant seaman Captain A. G. "Tony" Fincham, is one of the island's most established outfits and offers diving and snorkeling trips, PADI courses, and dive packages with accommodations. They're geared to seasoned divers, but work patiently with novices.

Beaches
Antigua's beaches are public, and many are dotted with resorts that have water-sports outfitters and beach bars. Most hotels have taxi stands, so getting back to the ship isn't usually a problem. Sunbathing topless or in the buff is strictly illegal except on one of the small beaches at Hawksbill Beach Hotel on the Five Islands Peninsula. Most cruise-ship beach excursions go to the beaches on the west coast.

Dickenson Bay, the closest accessible beach to St. John's, is a lengthy stretch of powder-soft white sand and exceptionally calm water, where you'll find small and large hotels, water sports, concessions, and beachfront restaurants. **Half Moon Bay,** a ¾-mi (1-km) crescent, is a prime snorkeling and windsurfing area. On the Atlantic side of the island the water can be quite rough (the eastern end is calmer). **Johnson's Point/Crab Hill** is a series of connected, deliciously deserted beaches of bleached white sand on the southwest coast overlooking Montserrat. You can explore a ruined fort at one end; notable beach bars are OJ's (try the snapper) and Turner's. **Pigeon Point,** near Falmouth Harbour, has two fine white-sand beaches; the leeward side is calmer, while the windward side is rockier, with sensational views and snorkeling around the point. Several restaurants and bars are nearby, though Billy's satisfies most on-site needs. **Runaway Beach,** a stretch of glittering sand, is still rebuilding after years of hurricane erosion. Both the water and the scene are relatively calm, and beach bars such as the raucous Bikini's offer cool shade and cold beer.

Where to Eat

In restaurants, a 10% service charge and 7% tax are usually added to the bill.

★ **$$–$$$$** ✕ **Coconut Grove.** Coconut palms grow through the roof of this open-air thatched restaurant, waves lap the white sand, and the warm waitstaff provides just the right level of service. Jean-François Bellanger's superbly presented dishes fuse French culinary preparations with island ingredients. Top choices include pan-seared snapper medallions served with roasted sweet potato in a saffron white-wine curry; tuna tartare accented by tapenade with molasses drizzle and guacamole; and chicken stuffed with creole vegetables in mango-kiwi sauce. The kitchen can be uneven, and the wine list is merely serviceable. Nonetheless, Coconut Grove straddles the line between casual beachfront boîte and elegant eatery with aplomb. ⊠ *Siboney Beach Club, Dickenson Bay* ☎ *268/462–1538* ▭ *AE, D, MC, V.*

$$–$$$$ ✕ **george.** This downtown eatery is a loving evocation of the building owner's original Georgian family home. The contemporary colonial design is stunning: beamed ceilings, teal-and-aqua walls, high-back hardwood chairs, and jalousie shutters that close off to form a second-floor gallery overlooking the busy street scene. The menu updates West Indian classics, from jerk burgers to slow-roasted spare ribs with a caramelized passion fruit–pineapple glaze to pepper-seared tuna marinated in sesame-ginger oil. The congenial new British managers plan to add children's and vegetarian menus. Indulge in the bartenders' extensive "Naughty List" of cocktails. ⊠ *Market and Redcliffe Sts., St. John's* ☎ *268/562–4866* ▭ *AE, D, MC, V.*

ARUBA

Vernon
O'Reilly
Ramesar

Few islands can boast the overt dedication to tourism and the quality of service that Aruba offers. The arid lansdcsape is full of attractions to keep visitors occupied, and the island offers some of the most dazzling beaches in the Caribbean. Casinos and novelty nightclubs abound in Oranjestad, giving the capital an almost Las Vegas appeal. To keep tourists coming back year after year, the island boasts a tremendous variety of restaurants ranging from upscale French eateries to toes-in-the-sand casual dining. Aruba may not be an un-explored paradise, but hundreds of thousands of tourists make it a point to beat a path here every year. Because it's not a very large island, cruise-ship visitors can expect to see a large part of the island on their day ashore. Or they can simply see a lot of the beautiful beaches. Whether you're planning to be active or to simply relax, this is an ideal cruise port.

Essentials

CURRENCY The Aruban florin (AFl1.79 to US$1). Arubans accept U.S. dollars readily, so you need only acquire local currency for pocket change. Note that the Netherlands Antilles florin used on Bonaire and Curaçao is not accepted on Aruba.

ARUBA BEST BETS

■ **Beaches.** With few interesting historical sights and not-so-great desert scenery, Aruba's real pleasures are on its dazzling west coast. Palm Beach is as beautiful a stretch of sand as you are likely to find anywhere. You might even learn to windsurf.

■ **Nightlife.** If your ship stays in port late (and in Aruba, many do), take advantage of the island's great bar scene and also its many casinos.

■ **Snorkeling.** Though you can't dive here, you can snorkel to get a glimpse of what's under the sea.

HOURS Stores are open Monday through Saturday from 8:30 or 9 to 6. Some stores stay open through the lunch hour (noon to 2), and many open when cruise ships are in port on Sunday and holidays. Most of the larger supermarkets are open on Sunday from 8 to noon.

INTERNET **Café Internet** (⊠ 8 Royal Plaza Mall, Oranjestad ☎ 297/582–4609).

TELEPHONES When making calls to anywhere in Aruba, simply dial the seven-digit number. AT&T customers can dial 800–8000 from special phones at the cruise dock and in the airport's arrival and departure halls. Otherwise dial 121 to contact the international operator to place an international call.

Coming Ashore

The Port of Oranjestad is a busy place and is generally full of eager tourists looking for souvenirs or a bite to eat. The port can accommodate up to five ships at a time (and frequently does). The Renaissance Mall is located right on the port, as are a number of souvenir shops and some decent and inexpensive eating places. The main shopping areas of Oranjestad are all within 10 minutes walk from the port.

Taxis can be flagged down on the street that runs alongside the port (look for license plates with a "TX" tag). Rates are fixed (i.e., there are no meters; the rates are set by the government and displayed on a chart), though you and the driver should agree on the fare before your ride begins. Rides to Eagle Beach run about $5; to Palm Beach, about $8. If you want to rent a car, you can do that for a reasonable price; driving is on the left, just as in the U.S., and it's pretty easy to get around, though a 4-wheel drive vehicle does help in reaching some of the more out-of-the-way places.

Shore Excursions

We consider these to be among the better shore excursions for Aruba. They may not be offered by all lines, and tour names may differ as well. Times and prices are approximate.

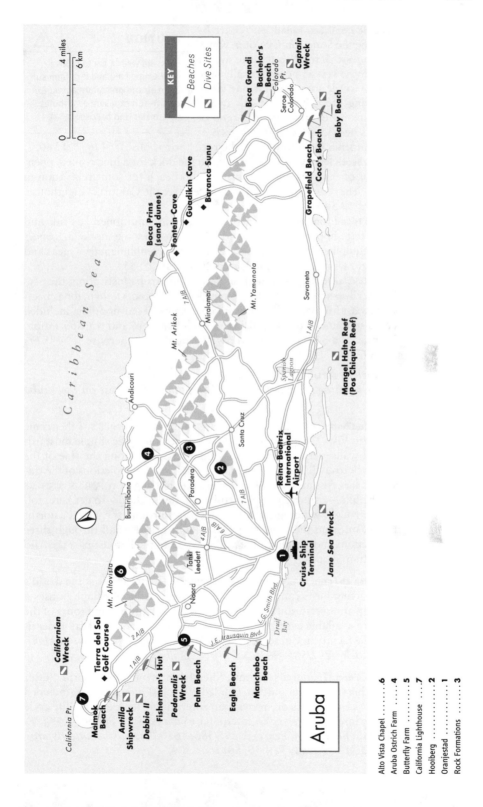

Aruba

KEY

⊿ Beaches

◩ Dive Sites

Caribbean Sea

California Pt.

- Californian Wreck
- Malmok Beach
- Antilla Shipwreck
- Debbie II
- Tierra del Sol Golf Course
- Fisherman's Hut
- Pedernalis Wreck
- Palm Beach
- Eagle Beach
- Manchebo Beach
- Mt. Altovista

Bushiribana
Andicouri
Noord
Tanki Leendert
Paradera
Santa Cruz
Mt. Arikok
Miralamar
Mt. Yamanota
Savaneta

Boca Prins (sand dunes)
- Fontein Cave
- Guadikin Cave
- Baranca Sunu

Boca Grandi
Bachelor's Beach
Captain Wreck
Seroe Colorado
Colorado Pt.
Baby Beach
Coco's Beach
Grapefield Beach

Mangel Halto Reef (Pos Chiquito Reef)

Spanish Lagoon

Reina Beatrix International Airport

Cruise Ship Terminal

Jane Sea Wreck

L.G. Smith Blvd.
J.E. Irausquin Blvd.
Druif Bay

7 A/B
6 A/B
4 A/B
2 A/B
1 A/B

4 miles
6 km

Aruba Sea and See Island Tour. Start by boarding the *Seaworld Explorer,* which lets you sit 5 feet under the water (though the vesssel never actually submerges) to see some spectacular views of marine life. Then it's back to the shore for an exploration of some of Aruba's best-loved attractions such as the California Lighthouse and the rock formations. ⊘ *4 hrs* ▱ *$60.*

> **CAUTION**
>
> Pack and wear a hat to protect your scalp, ears, and face from sun damage and premature aging. Excessive sun exposure contributes to wrinkles and dark spots.

Cruise & Beach Tour. Board a catamaran at the dock for a music-filled, open-bar tour of the coast with a stop at Palm Beach for some relaxation in the sun. The return trip offers the chance to see the California Lighthouse. ⊘ *3 hrs* ▱ *$45.*

De Palm Island Snorkeling Adventure. After an air-conditioned bus ride and a short ferry hop to De Palm Island, it's time to do some snorkeling. Snorkeling equipment is provided as are unlimited complimentary snacks and beverages while on De Palm Island ⊘ *3 ½ hrs* ⊘ *$55.*

Kukoo Kunuku Bar Hop & Dinner Tour. Board this Aruba institution, the psychedelically painted 1957 Chevy bus called the *Kukoo Kunuku,* for a champagne toast followed by dinner and an evening of bar-hopping. Included is a so-so dinner, your first drink at each bar stop, and transportation. The price is a $15 premium over what you'd pay otherwise. ⊘ *4–5 hrs* ▱ *$69.*

Exploring Aruba

Numbers in the margin correspond to points of interest on the Aruba map.

⑥ Alto Vista Chapel. Alone near the island's northwest corner sits the scenic little Alto Vista Chapel. The wind whistles through the simple mustard-colored walls, eerie boulders, and looming cacti. Along the side of the road back to civilization are miniature crosses with depictions of the stations of the cross and hand-lettered signs exhorting PRAY FOR US, SINNERS and the like—a simple yet powerful evocation of faith. To get here, follow the rough, winding dirt road that loops around the island's northern tip, or, from the hotel strip, take Palm Beach Road through three intersections and watch for the asphalt road to the left just past the Alto Vista Rum Shop.

★ ④ Aruba Ostrich Farm. Everything you ever wanted to know about the world's largest living birds can be found at this farm. A large palapa houses a gift shop and restaurant (popular with large bus tours), and tours of the farm are available every half hour. This is operation is virtually identical to the facility in Curaçao; it's owned by the same company. ⊠ *Makividiri Rd.* ☎ *297/585–9630* ▱ *$10* ⊘ *Daily 9–5.*

⑤ Butterfly Farm. Hundreds of butterflies from around the world flutter about this spectacular garden. Guided 20- to 30-minute tours (included in the price of admission) provide an entertaining look into the life cycle of these insects, from egg to caterpillar to chrysalis to butterfly. ⊠ *J. E. Irausquin Blvd., Palm Beach* ☎ *297/586–3656* ⊕ *www.thebutterflyfarm. com* ▱ *$12* ⊘ *Daily 9–4:30; last tour at 4.*

❼ **California Lighthouse.** The lighthouse, built by a French architect in 1910, stands at the island's far northern end. Although you can't go inside, you can ascend the hill to the lighthouse base for some great views. In this stark landscape, you might feel as though you've just landed on the moon. The lighthouse is surrounded by huge boulders that look like extraterrestrial monsters and sand dunes embroidered with scrub that resemble undulating sea serpents.

❷ **Hooiberg.** Named for its shape (*hooiberg* means "haystack" in Dutch), this 541-foot peak lies inland just past the airport. If you have the energy, climb the 562 steps to the top for an impressive view of Oranjestad.

❶ **Oranjestad.** Aruba's charming capital is best explored on foot. The palm-lined thoroughfare in the center of town runs between pastel-painted buildings, old and new, of typical Dutch design. You'll find many malls with boutiques and shops here.

The **Archaeological Museum of Aruba** has two rooms chock-full of fascinating artifacts from the indigenous Arawak people, including farm and domestic utensils dating back hundreds of years. ⊠ *J. E. Irausquin Blvd. 2A, Oranjestad* ☎ *297/582–8979* ⊑ *Free* ☉ *Weekdays 8–noon and 1–4.*

🖰 The **Experience Aruba Panorama** brings the island's history and culture to life in a 22-minute cinematic extravaganza that fills five massive screens measuring a total of 13 feet high and 66 feet wide. The breathtaking shows begin in the Crystal Theater at the Renaissance Aruba Beach Resort every hour from 11 to 5. ⊠ *L. G. Smith Blvd. 82, Oranjestad* ☎ *297/583–6000* ⊑ *$12* ☉ *Mon.–Sat. 11–5.*

One of the island's oldest edifices, **Fort Zoutman** was built in 1796 and played an important role in skirmishes between British and Curaçao troops in 1803. The Willem III Tower, named for the Dutch monarch of that time, was added in 1868 to serve as a lighthouse. Over time, the fort has been a government office building, a police station, and a prison; now its historical museum displays Aruban artifacts in an 18th-century house. ⊠ *Zoutmanstraat* ☎ *297/582–6099* ⊑ *Free* ☉ *Weekdays 8–noon and 1–4.*

★ The **Numismatic Museum** displays more than 40,000 historic coins and paper money from around the world. A few pieces were salvaged from shipwrecks in the region. Some of the coins circulated during the Roman Empire, the Byzantine Empire, and the ancient Chinese dynasties; the oldest dates to the 3rd century BC. The museum—which is next to the central bus station—had its start as the private collection of an Aruban who dug up some old coins in his garden. It's now run by his granddaughter. ⊠ *Westraat* ☎ *297/582–8831* ⊑ *$5* ☉ *Mon.–Thurs. 9–4, Fri. 9–1, Sat. 9–noon.*

❸ **Rock Formations.** The massive boulders at Ayo and Casibari are a mystery, as they don't match the island's geological makeup. You can climb to the top for fine views of the arid countryside. On the way you'll doubtless pass Aruba whip-tail lizards—the males are cobalt blue, the females blue with dots. The main path to Casibari has steps and handrails (except on one side), and you must move through tunnels and along narrow steps and ledges to reach the top. At Ayo you can find ancient pictographs in a small cave (the entrance has iron bars to protect the drawings from vandalism). You may also encounter a boulder climber, one of many who are increasingly drawn to Ayo's smooth surfaces. Access to Casibari is via Tanki Highway 4A to Ayo via Route 6A; watch carefully for the turnoff signs near the center of the island on the way to the windward side.

Shopping

Caya G. F. Betico Croes in Oranjestad is Aruba's chief shopping street. Several malls—gabled, pastel-hued re-creations of traditional Dutch colonial architecture—house branches of such top names as Tommy Hilfiger, Little Switzerland, Nautica, and Benetton; the ritziest are the **Royal Plaza** and **Renaissance Mall,** both right near the cruise-ship pier. There are excellent deals to be found on jewelry, watches, liquor, and clothing.

★ If you're in the mood to splurge, **Agatha Boutique** (⊠ Renaissance Mall, L. G. Smith Blvd. 82, Oranjestad ☎ 297/583–7965) has high-style clothing and accessories by Aruba-based New York fashion designer Agatha
★ Brown. **Art & Tradition Handicrafts** (⊠ Caya G. F. Betico Croes 30, Oranjestad ☎ 297/583–6534 ⊠ Royal Plaza Mall, L. G. Smith Blvd. 94, Oranjestad ☎ 297/582–7862) sells intriguing souvenirs, most locally made. Filling 6,000 square feet of space, **Boolchand's** (⊠ Renaissance Mall, L. G. Smith Blvd. 82, Oranjestad ☎ 297/583–0147) sells jewelry and watches. It also stocks leather goods, cameras, and electronics. **Confetti** (⊠ Renaissance Mall, L. G. Smith Blvd. 82, Oranjestad ☎ 297/583–8614) has the hottest European and American swimsuits, cover-ups, and beach essentials. A venerated name in Aruba, **J. L. Penha & Sons** (⊠ Caya G. F. Betico Croes 11/13, Oranjestad ☎ 297/582–4160 or 297/582–4161) sells high-end perfumes and cosmetics. It stocks such brands as Boucheron, Cartier, Dior, and Givenchy.

Activities

BIKING Pedal pushing is a great way to get around the island; the climate is perfect, and the trade winds help to keep you cool. **Melchor Cycle Rental** (⊠ Bubali 106B, Noord ☎ 297/587–1787) rents ATVs and bikes. **Rancho Notorious** (⊠ Boroncana, Noord ☎ 297/586–0508 ⊕ www.ranchonotorious.com) organizes mountain-biking tours.

DIVING & With visibility of up to 90 feet, the waters around Aruba are excellent
SNORKELING for snorkeling and diving. Both advanced and novice divers will find plenty to occupy their time, as many of the most popular sites, including some interesting shipwrecks, are found in shallow waters ranging from 30 feet
★ to 60 feet. **De Palm Watersports** (⊠ L. G. Smith Blvd. 142, Oranjestad ☎ 297/582–4400 or 800/766–6016 ⊕ www.depalm.com) is one of the best choices for your undersea experience, and the options go beyond basic diving. You can don a helmet and walk along the ocean floor near De Palm Island, home of huge blue parrot fish. You can even do Snuba— which is like scuba diving but without the heavy air tanks—from either a boat or from an island; it costs $56.

GOLF The **Links at Divi Aruba** (⊠ J. E. Irausquin Blvd. 93, Oranjestad ☎ 297/ 581–4653) is a 9-hole course designed by Karl Litten and Lorie Viola. The par-36 paspalum grass course (best for seaside courses) takes you past beautiful lagoons. Amenities include a golf school with professional instruction, a swing analysis station, a driving range, and a two-story golf clubhouse with a pro shop. Two restaurants are available: Windows on Aruba for fine dining and Mulligan's for a casual and quick lunch. Greens fees are $75 for 9 holes, $110 for 18 (high season); guests of the Divi Village Golf & Beach Resort pay a reduced rate.

KAYAKING   Kayaking is a popular sport on Aruba, especially along the south coast, where the waters are calm. It's a great way to explore the coastline. **Aruba Kayak Adventure** (⊠ Ponton 90, Oranjestad ☎ 297/587–7722 ⊕ www.arubakayak.com) has excellent half-day kayak trips, which start with a quick lesson before you paddle through caves and mangroves and along the scenic coast. The tour makes a lunch stop at De Palm Island, where snorkeling is included as part of the $77 package.

Beaches

Beaches in Aruba are beautiful and clean and easily reachable from the cruise-ship terminal in Oranjestad. On the north side of the island the water is too choppy for swimming, but the views are great. **Eagle Beach** (⊠ J. E. Irausquin Blvd., north of Manchebo Beach), on the southwestern coast, across the highway from what is quickly becoming known as Time-Share Lane, is one of the Caribbean's—if not the world's—best beaches. **Fisherman's Huts** (⊠ 1 A/B, at the Holiday Inn SunSpree Aruba) is a windsurfer's haven with good swimming conditions. Take a picnic lunch (tables are available) and watch the elegant purple, aqua, and orange sails struggle in the wind. **Manchebo Beach** (⊠ J. E. Irausquin Blvd., at the Manchebo Beach Resort) is impressively wide, and this is the spot where officials turn a blind eye to the occasional topless sunbather. This beach merges with Druif Beach, and most locals use the name Manchebo to refer to both. **Palm Beach** (⊠ J. E. Irausquin Blvd., between the Westin Aruba Beach Resort and the Marriott Aruba Ocean Club) is the center of Aruban tourism, offering good opportunities for swimming, sailing, and other water sports. In some spots you might find a variety of shells that are great to collect, but not as much fun to step on barefoot—bring sandals just in case.

FodorsChoice ★ (next to Eagle Beach)

Where to Eat

Restaurants usually add a 10% to 15% service charge.

$$–$$$ ✕ **Qué Pasa?** This funky eatery recently moved into new digs down the street from its former address; it now serves as something of an art gallery–restaurant. The colors of both the interior and exterior make quite an artistic statement themselves. Despite the name, there isn't a Mexican dish on the menu, which includes everything from sashimi to ribs, but everything is done with Aruban flair and is served by a helpful and friendly staff; the fish dishes are especially good. The bar area is lively and friendly. ⊠ *Wilheminastraat 18, Oranjestad* ☎ *297/583–4888* 🖃 *MC, V.*

$–$$$ ✕ **Rumba Bar & Grill.** In the heart of Oranjestad, this lively bistro has an open kitchen where you can watch the chef prepare tasty international fare over a charcoal grill (mostly grilled seafood and beef). The presentations are fanciful, with entrées forming towering shapes over beds of colorful vegetables and sauces. You can dine on the terrace and soak up the local color, or inside amidst wicker and warm pink hues; the crowd is always worth watching. It's an AGA Dine-Around member. ✉ *Haven-straat 4, Oranjestad* ☎ *297/588–7900* ▭ *AE, D, MC, V.*

BARBADOS

Jane Zarem

Barbadians (Bajans) are a warm, friendly, and hospitable people, who are genuinely proud of their country and culture. Although tourism is the island's number one industry, the island has a sophisticated business community and stable government, so life here doesn't skip a beat after passengers return to the ship. Barbados is the most "British" island in the Caribbean. Afternoon tea is a ritual, and cricket is the national sport. The atmosphere, though, is hardly stuffy. This is still the Caribbean, after all. Beaches along the island's south and west coasts are picture-perfect, and all are available to cruise passengers. On the rugged east coast, the Atlantic Ocean attracts world-class surfers. The northeast is dominated by rolling hills and valleys; the interior of the island is covered by acres of sugarcane and dotted with small villages. Historic plantations, a sta-lactite-studded cave, a wildlife preserve, rum distilleries, and tropical gardens are among the island's attractions. Bridgetown, the capital, is a bustling city with more traffic than charm.

Essentials

CURRENCY Barbados dollar (BDS$), with BDS$1.99 to US$1 at this writing. U.S. dollars are generally accepted, but change is given in Barbados dollars.

HOURS Banks are open Monday through Thursday from 8 to 3, Friday from 8 to 5 (some branches in supermarkets are open Saturday morning from 9 to noon). The General Post Office in Cheapside, Bridgetown, is open weekdays from 7:30 to 5, and branches in each parish are open weekdays from 8 to 3:15. Most stores in Bridgetown are open weekdays from 8:30 or 9 to 4:30 or 5, Saturday from 8:30 to 1 or 2. Stores in shopping malls outside of Bridgetown may stay open later.

INTERNET You'll find Internet cafés in and around Bridgetown and at St. Lawrence Gap on the south coast. Rates range from $2 for 15 minutes to $8 or $9 per hour. **Bean-n-Bagel Internet Cafe** (✉ St. Lawrence Gap, Dover). **Connect Internet Cafe** (✉ Shop #9, 27 Broad St., Bridgetown).

TELEPHONES A multi-band GSM phone will usually work in Barbados. You can purchase phone cards at the cruise-ship terminal. Direct-dialing to the United States, Canada, and other countries is efficient and reasonable. Some toll-free numbers cannot be accessed in Barbados. To charge your overseas call on a major credit card without incurring a surcharge, dial 800/744–2000 from any phone.

Coming Ashore

Up to eight ships at a time can dock at Bridgetown's Deep Water Harbour, on the northwest side of Carlisle Bay. The cruise-ship terminal has duty-free shops, handicraft vendors, a post office, a telephone station, a tourist information desk, and a taxi stand. To get downtown, follow the shoreline to the Careenage. It's a 15-minute walk or a $3 to $5 cab ride.

Taxis await ships at the pier. Drivers accept U.S. dollars and expect a 10% tip. Taxis are unmetered and operate at a fixed hourly rate of $25 per carload (up to three passengers). Most drivers will cheerfully narrate an island tour. You can rent a car with a valid driver's license, but rates are steep—during the high season, up to $85 per day.

Shore Excursions

We consider these to be among the better shore excursions for Barbados. They may not be offered by all lines, and tour names may differ as well. Times and prices are approximate.

Barbados Highlights Tour. This affordable tour takes in the historical highlights of the island, including Gun Hill Signal Station and Sunbury Plantation. ☉ *4 hrs* ✆ *$38.*

> **BARBADOS BEST BETS**
>
> - **The East Coast.** The island's windward coast, with its crashing surf, is one of the Caribbean's most beautiful sights. It may remind you of California's Big Sur.
> - **Harrison's Cave.** The island's most popular attraction is an extensive cave system in the limestone deep beneath Barbados.
> - **St. Nicholas Abbey.** Not an abbey at all, this is the island's oldest great house; it's one of the oldest Jacobean-era houses still standing in the Western Hemisphere.

Barbados Rainforest Hike & Cave Adventure. This excursion combines a trip to a small slice of remaining rain forest as well as the island's top attraction, Harrison's Cave. ☉ *4 hrs* ✆ *$74.*

Kayak and Turtle Encounter. This trip involves 45 minutes of kayaking followed by snorkeling in an area frequented by turtles; the guides feed the turtles while guests snorkel among them; snorkeling equipment is provided. You'll get drinks on the boat ride back. ☉ *3½ hrs* ✆ *$76.*

Mount Gay Rum Distillery/Banks Beer Tour. Exactly what the title describes, a rum distillery and brewery tour. Beer and rum lovers will enjoy this tour best; samples are provided. ☉ *4 hrs* ✆ *$39.*

Exploring Barbados

Numbers in the margin correspond to points of interest on the Barbados map.

BRIDGETOWN This bustling capital city is a major duty-free port with a compact shopping area. The principal thoroughfare is Broad Street, which leads west from National Heroes Square.

➋ **Jewish Synagogue.** Providing for the spiritual needs of one of the oldest Jewish congregations in the Western Hemisphere, this synagogue was formed by Jews who left Brazil in the 1620s and introduced sugarcane to Barbados. The adjoining cemetery has tombstones dating from the 1630s. The original house of worship, built in 1654, was destroyed in an 1831 hurricane, rebuilt in 1833, and restored by the Barbados National Trust in 1992. The building is open to the public year-round. ✉ *Synagogue La., St. Michael* ☎ *246/426–5792* ✆ *Donation requested* ☉ *Weekdays 9–4.*

➊ **Parliament Buildings.** Overlooking National Heroes Square in the center of town, these Victorian buildings were built around 1870 to house the British Commonwealth's third-oldest parliament. A series of stained-

Barbados

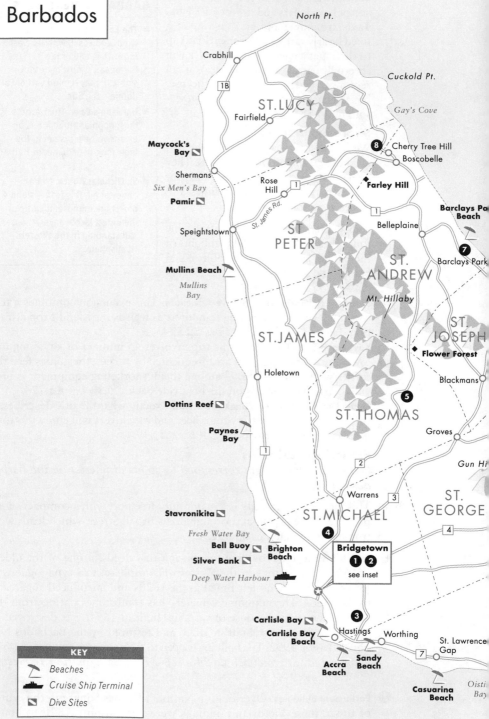

North Pt.

Crabhill

Cuckold Pt.

1B

ST. LUCY
Gay's Cove

Fairfield

Maycock's
Bay

Cherry Tree Hill
8
Boscobelle

Shermans

Six Men's Bay

Rose
Hill

1

Farley Hill

Pamir

St. James Rd.

Belleplaine

Barclays Pa
Beach

Speightstown

ST.
PETER

ST.
ANDREW

7

Mullins Beach

Barclays Park

Mullins
Bay

Mt. Hillaby

ST.
JOSEPH

ST. JAMES

Flower Forest

Holetown

Blackmans

Dottins Reef

5

Paynes
Bay

ST. THOMAS

Groves

1

Gun Hi

2

Stavronikita

Warrens

3

ST.
GEORGE

ST. MICHAEL

Fresh Water Bay

Bell Buoy

Brighton
Beach

4

4

Silver Bank

Bridgetown

Deep Water Harbour

1 2

see inset

Carlisle Bay

3

Carlisle Bay
Beach

Hastings

Worthing

St. Lawrence
Gap

Accra
Beach

Sandy
Beach

7

Casuarina
Beach

Oisti
Bay

KEY

- Beaches
- Cruise Ship Terminal
- Dive Sites

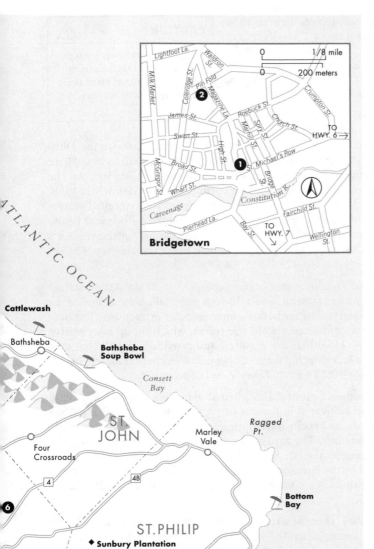

glass windows depicts British monarchs from James I to Victoria. ⊠ *Broad St., St. Michael* ☎ *246/427–2019* ✆ *Donations welcome* ⊙ *Tours weekdays at 11 and 2, when parliament isn't in session.*

> **CAUTION** ⚠
>
> If you don't want to rely on shipboard wake-up calls, be sure to bring your own travel alarm clock; most staterooms do not have them.

CENTRAL & WEST

👆 **6** **Gun Hill Signal Station.** The 360-degree view from Gun Hill, 700 feet above sea level, was what made this location of strategic importance to the 18th-century British army. Using lanterns and semaphore, soldiers based here could communicate with their counterparts at The Garrison, on the south coast, and at Grenade Hill in the north. Time moved slowly in 1868, and Captain Henry Wilkinson whiled away his off-duty hours by carving a huge lion from a single rock—which is on the hillside just below the tower. Come for a short history lesson but mainly for the view; it's so gorgeous, military invalids were once sent here to convalesce. ⊠ *Gun Hill, St. George* ☎ *246/429–1358* ✆ *$4.60* ⊙ *Weekdays 9–5.*

👆 **5** **Harrison's Cave.** This limestone cavern, complete with stalactites, stalagmites, subterranean streams, and a 40-foot waterfall, is a rare find in the Caribbean—and one of Barbados's most popular attractions. The one-hour tours are conducted via electric trams, which fill up fast; reserve ahead of time. Hard hats are required and provided, but all that may fall on you is a little dripping water. ⊠ *Hwy. 2, Welchman Hall, St. Thomas* ☎ *246/438–6640* ✆ *$13* ⊙ *Daily 9–6; last tour at 4.*

Fodor'sChoice
★

NORTH & EAST

7 **Andromeda Gardens.** Beautiful and unusual plant specimens from around the world are cultivated in 6 acres of gardens that are nestled among streams, ponds, and rocky outcroppings overlooking the sea above the Bathsheba coastline. The gardens were created in 1954 with flowering plants collected by the late horticulturist Iris Bannochie. They're now administered by the Barbados National Trust. The Hibiscus Café serves snacks and drinks. ⊠ *Bathsheba, St. Joseph* ☎ *246/433–9261* ✆ *$6* ⊙ *Daily 9–5.*

8 **St. Nicholas Abbey.** There's no religious connection here at all. The island's oldest great house (circa 1650) was named after the British owner's hometown, St. Nicholas parish near Bristol, and Bath Abbey nearby. Its stone-and-wood architecture makes it one of only three original Jacobean-style houses still standing in the Western Hemisphere. It has Dutch gables, finials of coral stone, and beautiful grounds. The first floor, fully furnished with period furniture and portraits of family members, is open to the public. Fascinating home movies, shot by the last owner's father, record Bajan life in the 1930s. The Calabash Café, in the rear, serves snacks, lunch, and afternoon tea. ⊠ *Cherry Tree Hill, St. Peter* ☎ *246/422–5357* ✆ *$12.50* ⊙ *Weekdays 10–3:30.*

SOUTH

👆 **3** **Barbados Museum.** This intriguing museum, in the former British Military Prison (1815) in the historic Garrison area, has artifacts from Arawak days (around 400 BC) and galleries that depict 19th-century military history and everyday life. You can see cane-harvesting tools, wedding dresses, ancient (and frightening) dentistry instruments, and slave sale accounts kept in a spidery copperplate handwriting. The museum's Harewood Gallery showcases the island's flora and fauna; its Cunard Gallery has a permanent collection of 20th-century Barbadian and Caribbean paintings and engravings; and its Connell Gallery features European decorative arts. Additional galleries include one for children; the museum also has a gift shop and a café. ⊠ *Hwy. 7, Garrison Savannah, St. Michael* ☎ *246/427–0201 or 246/436–1956* ⊕ *www.barbmuse.org. bb* ☞ *$4* ☉ *Mon.–Sat. 9–5, Sun. 2–6.*

🐚 **❹ Tyrol Cot Heritage Village.** This interesting coral-stone cottage just south of Bridgetown was constructed in 1854 and has been preserved as an example of period architecture. In 1929 it became the home of Sir Grantley Adams, the first premier of Barbados and the namesake of its international airport. Part of the Barbados National Trust, the cottage is now filled with antiques and memorabilia of the late Sir Grantley and Lady Adams. It's also the centerpiece of an outdoor "living museum," where artisans and craftsmen have their workshops in a cluster of traditional chattel houses. The crafts are for sale, and refreshments are available at the "rum shop." ⊠ *Rte. 2, Codrington Hill, St. Michael* ☎ *246/ 424–2074 or 246/436–9033* ☞ *$6* ☉ *Weekdays 9–5.*

Shopping

Duty-free shopping is found in Bridgetown's Broad Street department stores and their branches in Holetown and at the cruise-ship terminal. (Note that to purchase items duty-free, you must show your passport and cabin key card). Stores are generally open weekdays 8:30–4:30 and Saturdays 8:30–1. **Best of Barbados** (⊠ Worthing, Christ Church ☎ 246/ 421–6900), which has a total of seven locations, offers high-quality artwork and crafts in both "native" style and modern designs; everything is made or designed on Barbados. **Earthworks Pottery** (⊠ No. 2, Edgehill Heights, St. Thomas ☎ 246/425–0223) is a family-owned and -operated pottery where you can purchase anything from a dish or knickknack to a complete dinner service or one-of-a-kind art piece. You can find the characteristically blue or green pottery for sale in gift shops throughout the island, but the biggest selection (including some "seconds") is at the pottery, where you also can watch the potters work. **Pelican Craft Centre** (⊠ Princess Alice Hwy., Bridgetown, St. Michael ☎ 246/427–5350) is a cluster of workshops halfway between the cruise-ship terminal and downtown Bridgetown, where craftspeople create and sell locally made leather goods, batik, basketry, carvings, jewelry, glass art, paintings, pottery, and other items. It's open weekdays 9 to 5 and Saturday 9 to 2, with extended hours during holidays or to accommodate cruise-ship arrivals.

Sports & Activities

FISHING **Billfisher II** (☎ 246/431–0741), a 40-foot Pacemaker, accommodates up to six passengers with three fishing chairs and five rods. Captain Winston ("The Colonel") White has been fishing these waters since 1975. His full-day charters include a full lunch and guaranteed fish (or a 25% refund); all trips include drinks and transportation to and from the boat. **Blue Jay** (☎ 246/429–2326 ⊕ www.bluemarlinbarbados.com) is a spacious, fully equipped, 45-foot Sport Fisherman with a crew that knows the denizens of blue marlin, sailfish, barracuda, and kingfish. Four to six people can be accommodated—it's the only charter boat on the island with four chairs. Most fishing is done by trolling. Drinks, snacks, bait, tackle, and transfers are provided.

GOLF   **Barbados Golf Club** (✉ Hwy. 7, Durants, Christ Church ☎ 246/428–8463 ⊕ www.barbadosgolfclub.com), the first public golf course on Barbados, is an 18-hole championship course (6,805 yards, par 72) redesigned in 2000 by golf course architect Ron Kirby. Greens fees are $119 for 18 holes, plus a $13 per person cart fee. Unlimited three-day and seven-day golf passes are available. Several hotels offer preferential tee-time reservations and reduced rates. Club and shoe rentals are available. At the prestigious **Country Club at Sandy Lane** (✉ Hwy. 1, Paynes Bay, St. James ☎ 246/432–2829 ⊕ www.sandylane.com/golf), golfers can play on the Old Nine or on either of two 18-hole championship courses: the Tom Fazio–designed Country Club Course or the spectacular Green Monkey Course, which opened in October 2004 and is reserved for hotel guests and club members only. Greens fees in high season are $85 for 9 holes or $200 for 18 holes. Golf carts are equipped with GPS, which alerts you to upcoming traps and hazards, provides tips on how to play the hole, and allows you to order refreshments!

Beaches

All beaches in Barbados are open to cruise-ship passengers. The west coast has the stunning coves and white-sand beaches dear to the hearts of postcard publishers, plus calm, clear water for snorkeling, scuba diving, and swimming. Waterskiing, snorkeling, and parasailing are available on most beaches along the west and south coasts. Windsurfing is best on the south coast. Popular **Accra Beach,** in Rockley, has gentle surf and a lifeguard. There are plenty of places to eat and drink and to rent watersports equipment. Calm as a lake and just north of Bridgetown, **Brighton Beach** is also the home to the Malibu Beach Club. At **Carlisle Bay,** at Needham's Point, just south of Bridgetown, a broad half-circle of white sand is one of the island's best beaches. At the Boatyard, on Bay Street, you can rent umbrellas and beach chairs and buy refreshments. Picturesque **Mullins Beach,** just south of Speightstown, is a perfect place to spend the day. The water is safe for swimming and snorkeling and Suga Suga Restaurant serves snacks, meals, and drinks—and rents chairs and umbrellas. South of Holetown, **Paynes Bay** is lined with luxury hotels. It's a very pretty area, with plenty of beach to go around and good snorkeling. Public access is available opposite the Coach House. You can grab a bite to eat or a cold drink at Bomba's Beach Bar.

Where to Eat

A 15% V.A.T. (value-added tax) is in effect in Barbados. Most restaurant prices are V.A.T.-inclusive. A 10% service charge is added to most restaurant bills; if no service charge is added, tip waiters 10% to 15%.

$$–$$$ ✕ **Atlantis Hotel Restaurant.** People have been stopping by for lunch with a view here since 1945, when Mrs. Enid Maxwell bought this property, a quaint, 19th-century seaside hotel. New owners have kept up Mrs. Maxwell's tradition—all Bajan cuisine that complements the natural environment. Each Wednesday and Sunday the enormous buffet includes pumpkin fritters, rice and peas, breadfruit casserole, steamed fish creole, oven-barbecued chicken, pepper pot, macaroni pie, ratatouille, and more.

Homemade coconut pie tops the dessert list. The Atlantis is a lunch stop for organized day tours, so it sometimes get crowded. ⊠ *Atlantis Hotel, Tent Bay, Bathsheba, St. Joseph* ☎ *246/433–9445* ⊟ *AE, MC, V.*

$$ ✕ **Waterfront Cafe.** This friendly bistro alongside the Careenage is the perfect place to enjoy a drink, snack, or meal—and to people-watch. Locals and tourists alike gather for all-day alfresco dining on sandwiches, salads, fish, pasta, pepper pot stew, and tasty Bajan snacks such as buljol, fish cakes, or plantation pork (plantains stuffed with spicy minced pork). The panfried flying fish sandwich is especially popular. In the evening you can gaze through the arched windows while savoring nouvelle Caribbean cuisine, enjoying cool trade winds, and listening to live jazz. There's a special Caribbean buffet and steel-pan music on Tuesday night from 7 to 9. ⊠ *The Careenage, Bridgetown, St. Michael* ☎ *246/427–0093* ⊟ *AE, DC, MC, V* ☺ *Closed Sun.*

BELIZE

Lan Sluder

Belize probably has the greatest variety of flora and fauna of any country of its size in the world. Here, you'll often find more iguanas or howler monkeys than humans. A few miles off the mainland is the Belize Barrier Reef, a great wall of coral stretching the entire 333 km (200 mi) length of the coast. Over 200 cayes (pronounced keys) dot the reef like punctuation marks, and three coral atolls lie farther out to sea. All are superb for diving and snorkeling. Many, like Ambergris Caye (pronounced Am-bur-griss Key) and Caye Caulker, are jolly resort islands with ample supplies of bars and restaurants, easily reachable on day trips from Belize City. The main choice you'll have to make is whether to stay in Belize City for a little shopping, a little walking, and perhaps lunch or a dram at one of the Fort George hotels or restaurants, or alternatively to head out by boat, rental car, taxi, or tour on a more active adventure.

Essentials

CURRENCY The Belize dollar (BD$2 to US$1). Since the U.S. dollar is universally accepted, there's no need to acquire Belize currency.

FLIGHTS Especially if you are going to Ambergris Caye, you may prefer to fly, or you can water taxi over and fly back. There are hourly flights on two airlines. The flight to Caulker takes about 15 minutes and that to San Pedro about 25 minutes. The cost is BZ$115 round-trip to either island. Be sure you fly out of Belize City's Municipal, not out of the international airport north of the city. **Maya Island Airways** (☎ 501/223–1140, 800/225–6732 in the U.S. ⊕ www.mayaairways.com) has hourly flights, and you can make a reservation on the company Web site. **Tropic Air** (☎ 501/226–2012 or 800/422–3435 in the U.S. ⊕ www.tropicair.com) also has frequent flights.

HOURS Banks are open Monday through Thursday from 8 to 1, and Friday from 8 to 1 and 3 to 6. Shops are open from 8 to 12 and from 2 to 8 (although some shops in Belize City do not close for lunch). Few shops are open on Sunday. Most sights and museums close by 4 or 4:30 and have abbreviated hours on weekends.

INTERNET Click & Sip Internet Café (⊠ Fort St. in Tourist Village, Belize City ☎ 223/1305). **M-Business Solutions** (⊠ 13 Cork St., in Great House, Belize City ☎ 223/6766 ⊕ www.officeservices.bz).

TELEPHONES Calling locally or internationally is easy, but rates are high; around 75¢ a minute for calls to the U.S. To call the United States, dial 001 or 10–10–199 plus the area code and number. Pay phones, which are located in the Tourist Village where you are tendered, and elsewhere downtown, accept only pre-paid Belize Telecommunications Ltd. phone cards, available in shops in denominations from $2.50 to $25. Special "USA Connect" pre-paid cards, for sale at some stores in Belize City, in denominations of $2.50 to $10, claim discounts of as much as 57% for calls to the U.S. only. Your U.S.-based GSM phone will probably work on Belize's GSM 1900 system. Foreign calling cards are blocked in Belize. Call 113 for local directory assistance, and 115 for an operator.

Coming Ashore

Because Belize City's harbor is shallow, passengers are tendered in. If you're going the independent route, try to get in line early for the tenders, as it sometimes takes 90 minutes or more for all the passengers to be brought ashore. You arrive at the Fort Pointe Tourist Village, which opened in 2002. It has an antiseptic collection of gift shops, restaurants, and tour operators nicely situated along the harbor. Bathrooms are spic-n-span, too. At this writing, Carnival Cruise Lines still plans to build a much-delayed $50-million cruise terminal in another part of the city, but it is unlikely to come online until at least 2008.

Taxis, tour guides, and car rental desks are readily available. Taxi trips—official taxis have green license plates—within Belize City's small downtown area are supposed to be set at $3.50 plus 50¢ for each additional passenger, although some drivers meeting the cruise ships try to charge whatever the traffic will bear. Taxis don't have meters, so settle on the fare in advance; you shouldn't have to pay more than $6 or $7 to go anywhere in the city. Hourly rates are negotiable, but expect to pay around $25 or $30, or $150 for the day. There's no need to tip cab drivers. Horse and buggy tours of Belize City are available at the Tourist Village. You'll pay around $20 per person for a one-hour city tour. You can also rent a car. Crystal, a local company, has a branch at the Tourist Village, and Hertz and Budget will also arrange cars for cruise passengers, but rates can be high (at least $75 per day), and gas is about $5 per gallon. Green directional signs point you to nearby destinations such as the Belize Zoo.

SHORE EXCURSIONS If you don't want to rent a car or arrange your own private tours, then do a ship-sponsored excursion. We consider these to be among the bet-

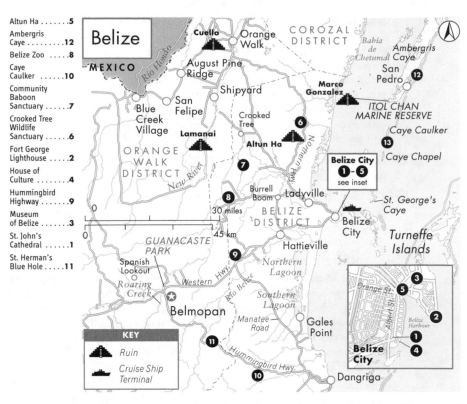

ter shore excursions for Belize. They may not be offered by all lines, and tour names may differ as well. Times and prices are approximate.

Altun Ha. If you have never seen Mayan ruins before, then consider this tour. ⊙ *4 hrs* 🎫 *$59.*

Belize Zoo & Belize City. After a trip to the Belize Zoo, you get a short city tour. ⊙ *4 hrs* 🎫 *$49.*

Cave Tubing and Jungle Walk. This popular cave-tubing excursion requires a 45-minute walk through the jungle to the cave entrance after a one-hour ride. The tubing itself takes about an hour, then you have lunch and can either rest or explore further. ⊙ *7 hrs* 🎫 *$79.*

Shark Ray Alley & San Pedro. This excursion takes you to Hol Chan Marine Reserve, where you swim among stingrays and baby nurse sharks and then on to a good snorkeling spot at Horseshoe Reef. Then it's lunch in San Pedro. 🎦 *7 hrs* 🎫 *$79.*

Exploring Belize

Numbers in the margins correspond to points of interest on the Belize map.

Belize City. Many Belize hands will tell you the best way to see Belize City is through a rear-view window. But, with an open mind to its peculiarities, and with a little caution (the city has a crime problem, but the tourist police keep a close watch on cruise-ship passengers), you may decide Belize City has a raffish, atmospheric charm rarely found in other Caribbean ports of call. You might even see the ghost of Graham Greene at a hotel bar. A 5- to 10-minute stroll from the perky Tourist Village brings you into the other worlds of Belize City. On the north side of Haulover Creek is the colonial-style world of the Fort George section, where large old homes, stately but sometimes down at the heels, take the breezes off the sea and share their space with hotels and restaurants. On the south side is the bustling world of Albert Street, the main commercial thoroughfare. But don't stroll too far. Parts of Belize City are unsafe by night or day. During the daylight hours, as long as you stay within the main commercial district and the Fort George area—and ignore the street hustlers—you should have no problem.

② **Fort George Lighthouse** towers over the entrance to Belize Harbor at the tip of Fort George Point. ⊠ *Marine Parade.*

④ The city's finest colonial structure, the **House of Culture** is said to have been designed by the illustrious British architect Sir Christopher Wren. Built in 1814 it was once the residence of the governor general, the queen's representative in Belize. Queen ⊠ *Regent St. at Southern Foreshore* ☎ *227/3050* ⌦ *BZ$10* ☉ *Weekdays 9–4.*

⑤ From the **Marine Terminal** you can catch a boat to Ambergris Caye, Caye Caulker, St. George's Caye, and Caye Chapel, from this white clapboard building, which was a firehouse in the 1920s. The **Coastal Zone Museum** is on the main floor and has information about the reef and the creatures that live there. On the second floor is the **Marine Museum,** where you can wander among models of boats that have sailed these waters and tools used by shipwrights. One ticket gets you into both museums. ⊠ *10 N. Front St., at Queen St.* ☎ *223/1969* ⌦ *BZ$8* ☉ *Mon.–Sat.*

③ *8–5:30.*Debuting in 2002, the **Museum of Belize.** located in the Central Bank of Belize building complex, has displays on Belize history and culture ranging from ancient Maya artifacts to a cell from the old jail built in 1853. ⊠ *Gabourel La.* ☎ *223/4524* ⌦ *BZ$10* ☉ *Weekdays 9–5.*

① **St. John's Cathedral,** at the south end of Albert Street, is the oldest Anglican church in Central America and the only one outside England where kings were crowned. From 1815 to 1845 four kings of the Mosquito Coast (a British protectorate along the coast of Honduras and Nicaragua) were crowned here. ⊠ *Albert St.* ☎ *227/2137.*

⑥ **Altun Ha.** If you've never visited an ancient Maya site, make a trip to Altun Ha, 45 km (28 mi) north of Belize City. ✛ *From Belize City, take the Northern Hwy. north to Mile 18.9. Turn right (east) on the Old Northern Hwy., which is only partly paved, and go 10½ mi (17 km) to the signed entrance road to Altun Ha on the left. Follow this paved road 2 mi (3 km) to the visitor center* ☎ *609/3540* ⌦ *BZ$10* ☉ *Daily 9–5.*

⑧ **Belize Zoo.** One of the smallest, but arguably one of the best, zoos in the world, this park houses only animals native to Belize. Highlights include spotted and rare black jaguars, the puma, margay, ocelot, jaguarondi, and the Bairdís tapir, the national animal of Belize. ⊠ *Western Hwy., 30 mi (49 km) west of Belize City* ☎ *220/8004* ⊕ *www.belizezoo.org* ⌦ *BZ$15* ☉ *Daily 9–5.*

⑦ **Community Baboon Sanctuary.** This interesting wildlife conservation project is a haven for nearly 1,000 black howler monkeys and numerous other species of birds and mammals. ⊠ *Community Baboon Sanctuary, 31 mi (50 km) northwest of Belize City* ☎ *220/2181* ✉ *BZ$10* ☉ *Daily 8–5.*

7 **Crooked Tree Wildlife Sanctuary.** This interesting wildlife conservation project is a haven for nearly 1,000 black howler monkeys and numerous other species of birds and mammals. ⊠ *Turn west off Northern Hwy. at Mile 30.8, then drive 2 mi (3 km)* ☎ *223/4987 for Belize Audubon Society* ⊕ *www.belizeaudubon.org/html/parks/ctws.htm* ✉ *BZ$8.*

10 **Hummingbird Highway.** This 78-km (49-mi) pavedtwo-lane, which turns south off the Western Highway, is the country's most scenic route. As you go south toward Dangriga Town, on your right rise the jungle-covered Maya Mountains.Less than half an hour south of Belmopan on the

11 Hummingbird is the **St. Herman's Blue Hole Natural Park,** a natural turquoise pool surrounded by mosses and lush vegetation, excellent for a cool dip. ☉ *Daily 8–4:30* ⊠ *Mile 42.5, Hummingbird Hwy.* ✉ *BZ$8.*

12 **Ambergris Caye.** Ambergris is the queen of the cayes. With a population around 5,000, the island's only town, San Pedro, remains a small, friendly, and prosperous village. It has one of the highest literacy rates in the country and an admirable level of awareness about the fragility of the reef. The large number of substantial private houses being built on the edges of town is proof of how much tourism has enriched San Pedro. A water taxi from the Marine Terminal takes about 75 minutes and costs $27.50 round-trip. You can also fly.

Hol Chan Marine Reserve (Maya for "little channel"), Maya for little channel, is 6 km (4 mi) from San Pedro at the southern tip of Ambergris. Because fishing is forbidden here, snorkelers and divers can see teeming marine life. You can also snorkel with nurse sharks and rays (which gather here to be fed) at Shark-Ray Alley, a sandbar that is part of the reserve. You need above-average swimming skills, as the current is often strong. ⊠ *Southern tip, Ambergris Caye* ✉ *BZ$20 plus cost of snorkel tour.*

13 **Caye Caulker.** On Caye Caulker, where the one village is home to around 800 people, brightly painted houses on stilts line the coral sand streets. Although the island is being developed more each year, flowers still outnumber cars 10 to 1 (golf carts, bicycles, and bare feet are the preferred means of transportation). The living is easy, as you might guess from all the NO SHIRT, NO SHOES, NO PROBLEM signs at the bars. This is the kind of place where most of the listings in the telephone directory give addresses like "near football field." A water taxi from the Marine Terminal costs about $10 each way and takes about 45 minutes.

Shopping

Belize does not have the crafts tradition of its neighbors Guatemala and Mexico, and imported goods are expensive due to high duties, but hand-carved items of Zircote or other local woods make good souvenirs. Near the Swing Bridge at Market Square is the **Commercial Center,** which has some food and craft vendors on the first floor, and a restaurant and shops on the second. The **Fort Pointe Tourist Village,** where the ship tenders come in, is a collection of bright and clean gift shops selling T-shirts and Belizean and Guatemalan crafts. Beside the Tourist Village is an informal

Street Vendor Market, with funkier goods and performances by a "Bruk-down" band or a group of Garifuna drummers.

Opened in 2004, **Fine Arts Gallery** (⊠ 1 Fort St., next to the Tourist Village ☎ 501/223–7773) quickly became one of Belize's top spots to shop for art. It has original paintings by many of Belize's best-known artists, including Pen Cayetano, Walter Castillo, and Patrick Chevailler, along with prints by Carolyn Carr and other artists. The **Image Factory** (⊠ 91 N. Front St. ☎ 501/223–4151) is run by a nonprofit foundation. Its exhibitions change monthly and its store sells works by more than 20 Belizean artists. **National Handicraft Center** (⊠ 2 S. Park St. ☎ 501/223–3636) has Belizean souvenir items, including hand-carved figurines, hand-made furniture, pottery, and woven baskets.

Activities

CANOPY TOURS You may feel a little like Tarzan as you dangle 80 feet above the jungle floor, suspended by a harness, moving from one suspended platform to another. **Jaguar Paw Lodge** (⊠ Off Mile 37 of the Western Hwy. ☎ 501/820–2023) opened the first zip-line aerial canopy tour in Belize in 2004. It has eight platforms set 100 to 250 feet apart. At the last platform you have to rappel to the ground. The cost is around $60 to $80. There is a 240-pound weight limit.

CAVE TUBING Very popular with cruise passengers are river-tubing trips that go through a cave, where you'll turn off your headlamp for a minute of absolute darkeness, but these are not for the claustrophic or those afraid of the dark. **Cave-Tubing in Belize** (☎ 605/1573 ⊕ www.cave-tubing.com) specializes in cave tubing trips. Tour guide Reginald Tripp, of **Reggie's Tours** (⊠ 29 Clinic Rd., Ladyville ☎ 501/225–2195 ⊕ www.regtour.com), has carved out a profitable niche running independent cave tubing trips for cruise passengers ($45), to Altun Ha ($45), and other tours.

DIVING & SNORKELING Most companies on Ambergris Caye offer morning and afternoon single-tank dives; snorkel trips begin mid-morning or early afternoon. Dive and snorkeling trips that originate in Caye Caulker are a bit cheaper. **Amigos del Mar** (⊠ Off Barrier Reef Dr., near Mayan Princess Hotel, Ambergris Caye ☎ 501/226–2706 ⊕ amigosdive.com) is probably the most consistently recommended dive operation on the island. It offers a range of local dives and snorkel trips. For trips to the Blue Hole and local dives, **Paradise Down** (⊠ Front St. north of the public pier, Caye Caulker ☎ 501/226–0437) has three well-equipped dive boats.

GOLF **Caye Chapel Island Resort** (⊠ Caye Chapel, 16 mi (25 km) northeast of Belize City ☎ 501/226–8250) has a beautiful 18-hole seaside course occupying much of Caye Chapel. Water taxis to Caye Caulker will drop you here ($10), or you can fly the 12 minutes to the island's private airstrip, by prior arrangement with the resort, for $100 round-trip. Unlimited golf, with clubs and cart rental and a poolside lunch, costs $200. Reservations are required.

INDEPENDENT TOURS Several Belize City–based tour guides and operators offer custom trips for ship passengers; companies will usually meet you at the Tourist Village. Katie Valk of **Belize Trips** (☎ 223/0376 ⊕ www.belize-trips.com), a New Yorker with attitude (softened by some 15 years' residency in Belize), can organize a custom trip to just about anywhere in the country. **Coral Breeze Ltd.** (⊕ www.coralbreezelimited.com) has a variety of trips for cruise-ship passengers, including cave tubing ($59, with lunch), scuba diving ($139 for two-tank dive), Altun Ha and Belize City tour ($39), and a snorkel tour with lunch ($69).

Beaches

Although the barrier reef just offshore limits the wave action, which, over eons, builds classic wide sandy beaches, and there is a good deal of seagrass on the shore bottom, Ambergris Caye's beaches are among the best in Belize. All beaches in Belize are public. **Mar de Tumbo,** 1½ mi (3 km) south of town near Tropica Hotel, is the best beach on the south end of the island. **North Ambergris,** accessible by water taxi from San Pedro or by golf cart over the new bridge to the north, has miles of narrow beaches and fewer people. **Ramon's Village's beach,** right across from the airstrip, is the best in the town area. The beaches on Caulker are not as good as those on Ambergris. Along the front side of the island is a narrow strip of sand, but the water is shallow and swimming conditions are poor. **The Split,** on the north end of the village (turn to your right from the main public pier), is the best place on Caye Caulker for swimming.

Where to Eat

★ ✕ **Harbour View.** For the most romantic setting in the city, ask for a table
$$$–$$$$ on the wraparound balcony overlooking the harbor. The friendly staff and consistently excellent food also make the Harbour View a favorite of Belize's power brokers. The seafood is especially good; try the snapper with mango chutney, cooked in a banana leaf. Pork dishes, especially Pork Picasso with a hot pepper relish, also are delicious. ⊠ *Fort St. near Tourist Village* ☎ *223/6420* ▤ *AE, D, MC, V.*

$–$$ ✕ **Wet Lizard.** Right next to the Tourist Village, overlooking cruise ship terminals 3 and 4, there's no question of the target market of the Wet Lizard. Even so, it's become a popular bar and a place to grab a sandwich or hamburger, even for those not on a cruise ship. An expansion added a gift shop and upper deck with bright green roof trim. ⊠ *1 Fort St.* ☎ *223/2664* ▤ *MC, V.*

BEQUIA, ST. VINCENT & THE GRENADINES

Jane Zarem

Bequia (pronounced *beck*-way) is the Carib word for "island of the cloud." Part of St. Vincent and the Grenadines, hilly and green Bequia is 9 mi (14½ km) south of St. Vincent's southwestern shore and the largest and most populous of the 32 islands and cays that make up the Grenadines. The capital is Port Elizabeth, a tiny town with waterfront bars, restaurants, and shops where you can buy handmade souvenirs, including the exquisitely detailed model sailboats for which Bequia is famous. Although boatbuilding, whaling, and fishing have been the predominant industries here for generations, sailing and Bequia have now become almost synonymous. Bequia's picturesque Admiralty Bay is one of the prettiest anchorages in the Caribbean and a favored anchorage for private and chartered yachts. With superb views, snorkeling, hiking, and swimming at several gold-sand beaches, the island has much to offer the international mix of visitors who frequent its shores.

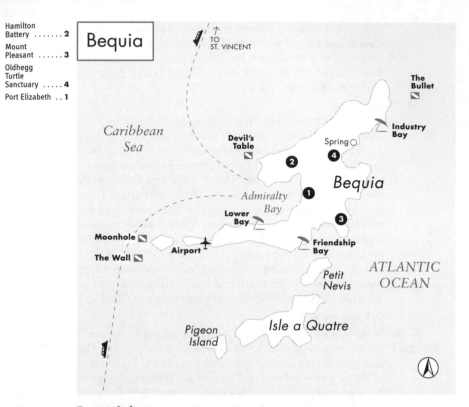

Essentials

CURRENCY Eastern Caribbean (E.C.) dollar (EC$2.70 to US$1). U.S. dollars are generally accepted, but change is given in E.C. dollars.

HOURS Shops are open weekdays from 8 to 5, Saturday 8 to noon. Most are closed Sunday. Banks on Bequia are open Monday through Thursday from 8 to 1 and Friday 8 to 5.

INTERNET You'll find several Internet cafés in Port Elizabeth, including the following. **Lenroc Internet Cafe** (✉ Back St., Port Elizabeth, Bequia). **Sunset Internet Cafe** (✉ Front St., Port Elizabeth, Bequia). **Surf 'n' Send Internet Cafe** (✉ Belmont Walkway, Port Elizabeth, Bequia).

TELEPHONES Public telephones are located on the jetty and at the Bayshore Mall in Port Elizabeth. Prepaid phone cards, which can be used throughout St. Vincent and many other Caribbean islands, are sold at shops in Port Elizabeth. The phone cards can be used for local or international calls.

Coming Ashore

Cruise ships that call on Bequia anchor offshore in Admiralty Bay and tender passengers to the jetty in Port Elizabeth or to nearby beaches. Although it's the capital of Bequia, Port Elizabeth is a tiny waterfront town that is only a few blocks long and one block deep. A tourist information booth is located on the jetty, shops and restaurants face the bay, and taxis are always lined up under the almond trees to meet cruise-ship passengers and the St. Vincent-Bequia ferry, which docks alongside the jetty. Water taxis are available for transportation between the jetty and nearby beaches for a couple of dollars per person each way, but keep in mind that most of these operators are not insured: ride at your own risk.

To see the views, villages, beaches, and other places of interest in Bequia, the best bet is to hire a taxi. Most taxis are pickup trucks, with a covered bed that is fitted with seating for four or six people. The driver will show you the sights in a couple of hours, point out a place for lunch, and drop you (if you wish) at a beach for swimming and snorkeling and pick you up later on. Negotiate the fare in advance, but expect to pay about $17 per person per hour for the tour. A rental car will cost about $55 per day and, unless you already have an international driver's license, requires a temporary local permit—available for EC$50 (US$20) at the Revenue Office in Port Elizabeth.

> ## BEQUIA BEST BETS
>
> ■ **Island Tour.** Taxi drivers are always available at the jetty in Port Elizabeth (2 hours, about $40). If you wish, the driver will stop for lunch or for a swim at the beach and pick you up after.
>
> ■ **Ferry to St. Vincent.** Ferries (EC$25 round-trip) make the 60-minute trip to St. Vincent several times each day. Once in St. Vincent, you can easily explore Kingstown and visit Fort Charlotte and the Botanical Garden before heading back to Bequia. Ferries dock at the jetty in Port Elizabeth.

Shore Excursions

We consider these to be among the better shore excursions for Bequia. They may not be offered by all lines, and tour names may differ as well. Times and prices are approximate.

Island Tour. Island tours by safari van will show you most of the highlights, including some of the beautiful views; almost all tours include a stop at the Oldhegg Turtle Sanctuary. ⊙ *2½ hrs* ⬜ *$28–$35.*

Mustique. You sail to Mustique and have a short island tour, then there is time to relax on the beautiful beaches or go to Basil's Bar. Tours by speedboat tend to be cheaper (almost half as much) but also less relaxing. ⊙ *6–7 hrs* ⬜ *$85–$170.*

Snorkeling Trip. You can get a glimpse of the sea life in the Grenadines on a snorkeling excursion. ⊙ *2½ hrs* ⬜ *$40.*

Exploring Bequia

Numbers in the margin correspond to points of interest on the Bequia map.

❷ Hamilton Battery. Just north of Port Elizabeth, high above Admiralty Bay, the 18th-century battery was built to protect the harbor from marauders. Today it's a place to enjoy a magnificent view.

❸ Mt. Pleasant. Bequia's highest point (an elevation of 881 feet) is a reasonable goal for a hiking trek. Alternatively, it's a pleasant drive. The reward is a stunning view of the island and surrounding Grenadines.

★ ☾ **❹ Oldhegg Turtle Sanctuary.** In the far northeast of the island, Orton "Brother" King, a retired skin-diving fisherman, tends to endangered hawksbill turtles. He'll be glad to show you around and tell you how his project is increasing the turtle population in Bequia. ⊠ *Park Beach, Industry* ☎ *784/458–3245* ✉ *$5 donation requested* ☉ *By appointment only.*

★ ❶ **Port Elizabeth.** Bequia's capital is on the northeast side of Admiralty Bay. The ferry from St. Vincent docks at the jetty, in the center of the tiny town, which is only a few blocks long and a couple of blocks deep. Walk north along Front Street, which faces the water, to the open-air market, where you can buy local fruits and vegetables and some handicrafts; farther along, you can find the model-boat builders' workshops for which Bequia is renowned. Walk south along Belmont Walkway, which meanders along the bay front past shops, cafés, restaurants, bars, and hotels.

Shopping
Long renowned for their boatbuilding skills, Bequians have translated that craftsmanship to model-boat building. In their workshops in Port Elizabeth you can watch as hair-thin lines are attached to delicate sails or individual strips of wood are glued together for decking. Other Bequian artisans create scrimshaw, carve wood, crochet, or work with fabric—designing or hand-painting it first, then creating clothing and gift items for sale.

Most of Bequia's shops are located just steps from the jetty in Port Elizabeth, along Front Street and Belmont Walkway. North of the jetty there's an open-air market, and farther along the road are the model-boat builders' shops. Opposite the jetty, at Bayshore Mall, shops sell ice cream, baked goods, stationery, gifts, and clothing; there's also a grocery, liquor store, pharmacy, travel agent, and bank. On Belmont Walkway, south of the jetty, shops and studios showcase gifts and handmade articles.

Bequia Bookshop (⊠ Belmont Walkway, Port Elizabeth ☎ 784/458–3905) has Caribbean literature, plus cruising guides and charts, Caribbean flags, beach novels, souvenir maps, and exquisite scrimshaw and whalebone pen knives hand-carved by Bequian scrimshander Sam McDowell.

Local Color (⊠ Belmont Walkway, Port Elizabeth ☎ 784/458–3202), above the Porthole restaurant—near the jetty—has an excellent and unusual selection of handmade jewelry, wood carvings, scrimshaw, and resort clothing.

★ **Mauvin's Model Boat Shop** (⊠ Front St., Port Elizabeth ☎ 784/458–3344) is where you can purchase the handmade model boats for which Bequia is known. You can even special-order a replica of your own yacht. They're incredibly detailed and quite expensive—from a few hundred to several thousand dollars. The simplest models take about a week to make.

★ **Sargeant Brothers Model Boat Shop** (⊠ Front St., Port Elizabeth ☎ 758/458–3344) sells handmade model boats and will build special requests on commission.

Housed in the ruins of an old sugar mill, **Spring Pottery & Studios** (⊠ Spring ☎ 784/457–3757) is the working pottery of Mike Goddard and Maggie Overal, with gallery exhibits of ceramics, paintings, and crafts—their own and those of other local artists. All works are for sale.

Activities

BOATING & SAILING ★

With regular trade winds, visibility for 30 mi (48 km), and generally calm seas, Bequia is a center for some of the best blue-water sailing you can find anywhere in the world, with all kinds of options: day sails or weekly charters, bareboat or fully crewed, monohulls or catamarans—whatever your pleasure. Prices for day trips run $50 to $75 per person, depending on the destination.

Friendship Rose (⊠ Port Elizabeth ☎☎ 784/458–3373), an 80-foot schooner that spent its first 25 years as a mail boat, was subsequently refitted to take passengers on day trips from Bequia to Mustique and the Tobago Cays. The 65-foot catamaran *Passion* (⊠ Belmont ☎ 784/458–3884), custom-built for day sailing, offers all-inclusive daylong snorkeling and/or sportfishing trips from Bequia to Mustique, the Tobago Cays, and St. Vincent's Falls of Baleine. It's also available for private charter. The Frangipani Hotel owns the *S. Y. Pelangi* (⊠ Port Elizabeth ☎ 784/458–3255 ⊕ www.frangipanibequia.com), a 44-foot CSY cutter, for day sails or longer charters; four people can be accommodated comfortably, and the cost is $200 per day.

DIVING & SNORKELING

About 35 dive sites around Bequia and nearby islands are accessible within 15 minutes by boat. The leeward side of the 7-mi (11-km) reef that fringes Bequia has been designated a marine park. The **Bullet,** off Bequia's northeast point, has limited access because of rough seas but is a good spot for spotting rays, barracuda, and the occasional nurse shark. **Devil's Table** is a shallow dive at the northern end of Admiralty Bay that's rich in fish and coral and has a sailboat wreck nearby at 90 feet. **Moonhole** is shallow enough in places for snorkelers to enjoy. The **Wall** is a 90-foot drop, off West Cay. Expect to pay dive operators $50 for a one-tank and $85 for a two-tank dive, including equipment. Dive boats welcome snorkelers for about $10 per person, but for the best snorkeling in Bequia, take a water taxi to the bay at Moonhole and arrange a pickup time.

Bequia Dive Adventures (⊠ Belmont Walkway, Admiralty Bay, Port Elizabeth ☎ 784/458–3826 ⊕ www.bequiadiveadventures.com) offers PADI instruction courses and takes small groups on three dives daily; harbor pickup and return is included for customers staying on yachts. **Dive Bequia** (⊠ Belmont Walkway, Admiralty Bay, Port Elizabeth ☎ 784/458–3504 ⊕ www.dive-bequia.com), at the Gingerbread Hotel, offers dive and snorkel tours, night dives, and full equipment rental. Resort and certification courses are available.

Beaches

Bequia has clean, uncrowded white-sand beaches. Some are a healthy trek or water taxi ride from the jetty at Port Elizabeth; others require land transportation.

Friendship Bay. This horseshoe-shape, protected beach on Bequia's mid-south coast can be reached by land taxi. It's a great beach for swimming, snorkeling, and windsurfing; you can rent any equipment you need at Friendship Bay Resort and also grab a bite to eat or a cool drink at the hotel's Moskito Bar & Restaurant.

Hope Bay. Getting to this beach facing Bequia's Atlantic side involves a long taxi ride (about $7.50) and a mile-long (1½-km-long) walk downhill on a semi-paved path. Your reward is a magnificent crescent of white sand, total seclusion, and—if you prefer—nude bathing. Be sure to ask your taxi driver to return at a prearranged time. Bring your own lunch and drinks; there are no facilities. Even though the surf is fairly shallow, swimming may be dangerous because of the undertow.

Industry Bay. This nearly secluded beach is fringed with towering palms on the northeast (windward) side of the island; getting here requires transportation from Port Elizabeth. This is a good beach for snorkelers, but there could be a strong undertow. Bring a picnic; the nearest facilities are at Spring on Bequia resort, a 10- to 15-minute walk from the beach.

★ **Lower Bay.** This broad, palm-fringed beach south of Port Elizabeth and Princess Margaret Beach is reachable by land or water taxi or a healthy hike. It's an excellent beach for swimming and snorkeling. There are restaurants here, as well as facilities to rent water-sports equipment.

Princess Margaret Beach. Quiet and wide, with a natural stone arch at one end, the beach is a half-hour hike over rocky bluffs from Port Elizabeth's Belmont Walkway—or you can take a water or land taxi. Though it has no facilities, it's a popular spot for swimming, snorkeling, or snoozing under the palm and sea grape trees.

Where to Eat

$$–$$$ ✕ **Gingerbread.** The airy dining-room veranda at the Gingerbread Hotel offers a panoramic view of Admiralty Bay and the waterfront activity. The lunch crowd can enjoy barbecued beef kebabs or chicken with fried potatoes or onions, grilled fish, homemade soups, salads, and sandwiches. In the evening, steaks, seafood, and curries are specialties of the house. Save room for warm, fresh gingerbread—served here with lemon sauce. In season, dinner is often accompanied by live music. ⊠ *Gingerbread Hotel, Belmont Walkway, Admiralty Bay, Port Elizabeth* ☎ *784/ 458–3800* ⚑ *Reservations essential* ▭ *AE, D, MC, V.*

$–$$ ✕ **Mac's Pizzeria.** Overheard at the dock in Mustique: "We're sailing over to Bequia for pizza." The two-hour sunset sail to Admiralty Bay is worth the trip to Mac's, which has been serving pizza in Bequia since 1980. Choose from 17 mouthwatering toppings (including lobster), or select homemade quiche, conch fritters, pita sandwiches, lasagna, or soups and salads. Mac's home-baked cookies, muffins, and banana bread (by the slice or the loaf) are great for dessert or a snack. Or top off your meal with a scoop or two of Maranne's homemade ice cream in tropical flavors. The outdoor terrace offers fuchsia bougainvillea and water views. ⊠ *Belmont Walkway, Admiralty Bay, Port Elizabeth* ☎ *784/458–3474* ⚑ *Reservations essential* ▭ *AE, D, MC, V.*

BERMUDA

Basking in the Atlantic, 508 mi (817 km) due east of Cape Hatteras, North Carolina, restrained, polite Bermuda is a departure from other sunny, beach-strewn isles. You won't find laid-back locals wandering around barefoot proffering piña coladas. Bermuda is somewhat formal, and despite the gorgeous weather, residents wearing stockings and heels or jackets, ties, Bermuda shorts, and knee socks are a common sight, whether on the street by day or restaurants at night. On Bermuda's 22 square miles (57 square km) you will discover that pastel cottages, quaint shops, and manicured gardens betray a more staid, suburban way of life. A self-governing British colony since 1968, Bermuda has maintained some of its English character even as it is increasingly influenced by American culture. Most cruise ships make seven-night loops from U.S. embarkation ports, with four nights at sea and three tied up in port. Increasingly popular are round-trip itineraries originating in northeastern embarkation ports that include a single day or overnight port call in Bermuda before continuing south to the Bahamas or Caribbean.

BERMUDA BEST BETS

- **Gibb's Lighthouse.** Make the climb to the top, where the reward is an expansive view of the inlets and harbors.
- **Bermuda Maritime Museum.** Absorb Bermuda's nautical and military history in this Royal Navy Dockyard museum.
- **St. George's.** Attend the pierside show hosted by the town crier, where gossips and nagging wives are drenched in a dunking stool.

Essentials

CURRENCY The Bermuda dollar (B$) is on par with the U.S. dollar. You can use American money anywhere, but change is often given in Bermudian currency. ATMs are common.

HOURS Banks are usually open on weekdays from 9 or 9:30 to 3:30 or 4:30. Shops are generally open Monday through Saturday from 9 to 5 and closed on Sunday. Some sights close on Sunday.

INTERNET Expect to pay as much as $12 per hour to check the Internet on Bermuda. **Internet Lane** (✉ The Walkway, 22 Reid St., Hamilton ☎ 441/296–9972).

TELEPHONES To make a local call, simply dial the seven-digit number. You'll find specially marked AT& T USADirect phones at the airport, the cruise-ship dock in Hamilton, and King's Square and Ordnance Island in St. George's. You can also make international calls with a calling card from the main post office. You can make prepaid international calls from the Cable & Wireless Office, which also has international telex, cable, and fax services Monday through Saturday from 9 to 5.

Coming Ashore

Three Bermuda harbors serve cruise ships: Hamilton (the capital), St. George's, and King's Wharf at the Royal Naval Dockyard.

In Hamilton, cruise ships tie up right on the city's main street, Front Street. A Visitors Service Bureau is next to the ferry terminal, also on Front Street and nearby; maps and brochures are displayed in the cruise terminal itself.

St. George's actually has two piers that accommodate cruise ships. One is on Ordnance Island, which is in the heart of the city; another pier is nearby. Visitors Service Bureau offices are at each pier.

King's Wharf, in the Royal Naval Dockyard at the westernmost end of the island, is the most isolated of the three cruise-ship berthing areas, and it is where the largest vessels dock. But it is well-connected to the

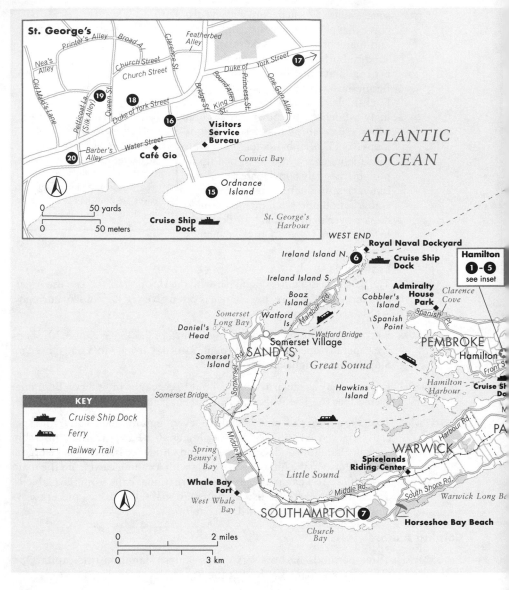

St. George's

Printer's Alley
Nea's Alley
Broad A...
Featherbed Alley
Church Street
Church Street
Clarence St.
Featherbed Alley
Duke of York Street
17
York Street
Old Maid's Lane
Petticoat La. (Silk Alley)
19
Queen St.
Duke of York Street
18
Bridge St.
Pound Alley
Princess St.
King St.
One Gun Alley
Barber's Alley
Water Street
20
16
Café Gio
Visitors Service Bureau
Convict Bay

0   50 yards
0   50 meters

Ordnance Island
15

Cruise Ship Dock

St. George's Harbour

ATLANTIC OCEAN

WEST END   **Royal Naval Dockyard**

Ireland Island N.   **6**   **Cruise Ship Dock**

Ireland Island S.

Boaz Island   Cobbler's Island   **Admiralty House Park**   Clarence Cove

Somerset Long Bay   Watford Is.   Spanish Point   Spanish Pt.

Daniel's Head   Watford Bridge   PEMBROKE

Somerset Village   Hamilton S...

Somerset Island   **SANDYS**   Great Sound   Hamilton Harbour   **Cruise Sh Do**

Somerset Bridge   Hawkins Island   Hamilton Harbour

KEY
🚢 *Cruise Ship Dock*
⛴ *Ferry*
├─┼─┤ *Railway Trail*

Spring Benny's Bay   Middle Rd.   Little Sound   **Spicelands Riding Center**   WARWICK   Harbour Rd.   PA

Whale Bay Fort   West Whale Bay   Middle Rd.   South Shore Rd.   Warwick Long B...

SOUTHAMPTON   **7**   **Horseshoe Bay Beach**

Church Bay

0   2 miles
0   3 km

Hamilton
1-**5**
see inset

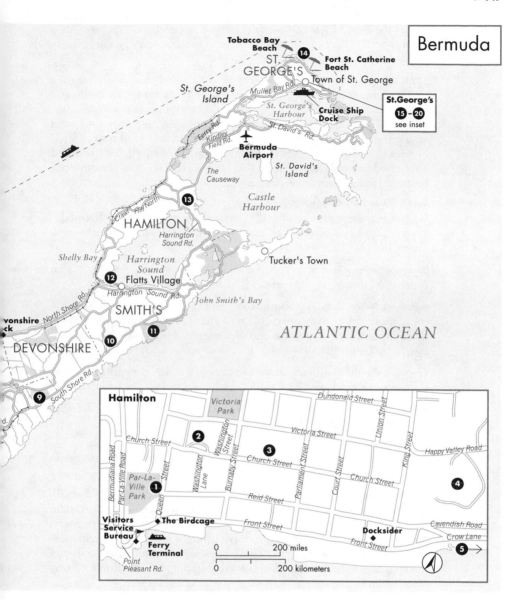

Bermuda

Tobacco Bay
Beach

ST.
GEORGE'S

Fort St. Catherine
Beach

St. George's
Island

Mullet Bay Rd.

Town of St. George

St. George's
Harbour

Cruise Ship
Dock

St.George's
⑮ – ⑳
see inset

Ferry Rd.

Kindley
Field Rd.

St. David's Rd.

Bermuda
Airport

St. David's
Island

The
Causeway

Castle
Harbour

Crawl Hill North

⑬

HAMILTON

Harrington
Sound Rd.

Shelly Bay

Harrington
Sound

Flatts Village

⑫

Harrington Sound Rd.

John Smith's Bay

North Shore Rd.

SMITH'S

vonshire
ck

DEVONSHIRE

⑩

⑪

Tucker's Town

ATLANTIC OCEAN

South Shore Rd.

⑨

d.

Hamilton

Victoria
Park

Dundonald Street

Union Street

❷

Church Street

Victoria Street

Washington Street

❸

Church Street

Parliament Street

Church Street

King Street

Happy Valley Road

Bermudiana Road

Par-La-Ville Road

Par-La-
Ville
Park

❶

Queen Street

Washington Lane

Burnaby Street

Reid Street

Court Street

❹

Visitors
Service
Bureau

◆ **The Birdcage**

Front Street

Docksider

Cavendish Road

Crow Lane

Front Street

Ferry
Terminal

Point
Pleasant Rd.

0   200 miles

0   200 kilometers

❺

rest of the island by taxi, bus, and ferry. The nearby Cooperage has a Visitors Service Bureau office, and bus stops and the ferry pier are clearly marked.

Taxis are the fastest and easiest way to get around the island, but they are also quite expensive. Four-seaters charge $5.35 for the first mile and $2 for each subsequent mile. You can hire taxis for around $30 per hour (3-hour minimum) if you want to do some exploring, and if you can round up a group of people, this is often cheaper than an island tour offered by your ship. Tip drivers 15%. Rental cars are prohibited, but the island has a good bus and ferry system. You can also rent scooters, but this can be dangerous and is not recommended.

Best Shore Excursions

We consider these to be among the better shore excursions for Bermuda. They may not be offered by all lines, and tour names may differ as well. Times and prices are approximate.

Dockyard Segway Tour. See the Royal Naval Dockyard by Segway. It's an expensive but unique experience. ⊙ *2 hrs* ▭ *$78.*

Horseback Riding. Between South Road and the Warwick beaches, sandy trails, most of which are open only to walkers or horseback riders, wind through strands of dune grass and oleander, and over coral bluffs to the beach. ⊙ *1½ hrs* ▭ *$65–$130.*

Kayaking. Paddle in protected coves or the open ocean, depending on your skill level, accompanied by a skilled guide and trainer. ⊙ *3 hrs* ▭ *$68.*

Railway Trail Tour. Tour the Bermuda Railway Trail by 21-speed bike with time for a swim. ⊙ *3½ hrs* ▭ *$72.*

Exploring Bermuda

Numbers in the margin correspond to points of interest on the Bermuda map.

Hamilton. Bermuda's capital since 1815, the City of Hamilton is a small, bustling harbor town. It's the economic and social center of Bermuda, with busy streets lined with shops and offices. International influences, from both business and tourism, have brought a degree of sophistication unusual in so small a city. There are several museums and galleries to explore, but the favorite pastimes are shopping in Hamilton's numerous boutiques and dining in its many upscale restaurants.

★ ❶ The **Museum of the Bermuda Historical Society/Bermuda Public Library** was once the home of Hamilton's first postmaster, William Bennet Perot, and his family. Mark Twain once lamented that the rubber tree in the front yard didn't bear fruit in the form of hot-water bottles and rubber overshoes. The library was founded in 1839, and its reference section has virtually every book ever written about Bermuda. The museum depicts Bermuda history with household goods and other artifacts, including an 18th-century sedan chair. ⊠ *13 Queen St.* ☎ *441/295–2905 library, 441/295–2487 museum* ▭ *Donations accepted* ⊙ *Library Mon.–Thurs. 8:30–7, Fri. 10–5, Sat. 9–5, Sun. 1–5; closed Sun. in July and Aug.; museum Mon.–Sat. 9:30–3:30* ☞ *Tours by appointment.*

★ ☾ **2** Set back from the street behind a fountain and lily pond, **City Hall & Arts Centre,** built in 1960, houses Hamilton's administrative offices as well as two art galleries and a performance hall. Rather than a clock, its tower has a wind vane—not surprising in a land where the weather is as important as the time. Massive cedar doors open into a large lobby with beautiful chandeliers and high ceilings. On the first landing, in the East Exhibition Room, is the Bermuda National Gallery, the home of Bermuda's national art collection. Farther up the stairs, in the West Wing, the Bermuda Society of Arts Gallery displays work by its members. ⊠ *17 Church St.* ☎ *441/292–1234* ☒ *Galleries free* ☉ *City Hall weekdays 9–5; National Gallery and Society of the Arts Mon.–Sat. 10–4.*

★ **3** Designed in early Greek-revival flourishes, the **Cathedral of the Most Holy Trinity** was constructed out of Bermuda limestone and materials imported from France, Nova Scotia, and Scotland. The cathedral was completed in 1911. It has a copper roof, unusual in Bermuda's sea of whitetopped buildings. After exploring the interior, you can purchase tickets to climb the 150-odd steps (143 feet) of the tower. ⊠ *Church St.* ☎ *441/292–4033* ⊕ *www.anglican.bm* ☒ *Cathedral free; Tower $3* ☉ *Church daily 7:30–5 and for Sun. services, tower weekdays 10–4.*

★ ☾ **4** The imposing **Fort Hamilton** has a moat, 18-ton guns, and underground passageways that were cut through solid rock by Royal Engineers in the 1860s. Built to defend the West End's Royal Naval Dockyard from an attack by land, it was outdated even before its completion, though it remains one of the finest surviving examples of a mid-Victorian polygonal fort in Bermuda. ⊠ *Happy Valley Rd.* ☎ *441/292–1234* ☒ *Free* ☉ *Daily 9:30–5.*

★ ☾ **5** The Bermuda Underwater Exploration Institute's harborside **Ocean Discovery Centre** has numerous multimedia and interactive displays designed to acquaint you with the deep sea and its inhabitants. Never heard of a bathysphere? See a replica of this deep-sea diving vehicle, which allowed oceanographer William Beebe and Otis Barton to venture 1/2 mi down into the deep in 1934. ⊠ *40 Crow La., off E. Broadway* ☎ *441/292–7219* ⊕ *www.buei.org* ☒ *$12.50* ☉ *Weekdays 9–5, weekends 10–5, last admission at 4.*

8 **Paget Marsh.** This small, easily walkable slice of unspoiled native Bermuda

Fodor's Choice is just minutes from bustling Hamilton. Listen for the cries of the native

★ and migratory birds who visit this natural wetland, jointly owned and preserved by the Bermuda National Trust and the Bermuda Audubon Society. ⊠ *Lover's La., Paget Parish* ☎ *441/236–6483* ⊕ *www.bnt.bm* ☒ *Free* ☉ *Daily dawn–dusk.*

★ ☾ **7** **Gibb's Hill Lighthouse.** The second cast-iron lighthouse ever built soars above Southampton Parish. Designed in London and opened in 1846, the tower stands 117 feet high and 362 feet above the sea. It's a long haul up the 185 spiral stairs, but you can stop to catch your breath at platforms along the way, where photographs and drawings of the lighthouse divert your attention. ⊠ *68 St. Anne's Rd., Southampton Parish* ☎ *441/238–8069* ⊕ *www.bermudalighthouse.com* ☒ *$2.50* ☉ *Daily 9–5; Closed Jan.*

7

⑥ Bermuda Maritime Museum and Dolphin Quest. Inside Bermuda's largest fort,
Fodor'sChoice built between 1837 and 1852, the Maritime Museum exhibits its collec-
★ tions in six old stone munitions warehouses, which surround the parade
grounds and the Keep Pond. On top of the hill is the Commissioner's
House, an unusual cast-iron building constructed from 1823 to 1828 in
England and shipped to Bermuda for the chief administrator of the
Dockyard. The Maritime Museum's most popular attraction is **Dolphin**
Quest, within the fortress's historic Keep. ⊠ *Maritime Museum, Dockyard* ☎ *441/234–1418 for Museum, 441/234–4464 for Dolphin Quest*
⊕ *www.bmm.bm* ⊠ *$10; Dolphin Quest programs $125–$275* ⊙ *Daily*
9:30–5, last admission 4.

⑨ Botanical Gardens. A fragrant haven for the island's exotic subtropical
plants, flowers, and trees, the 36-acre Botanical Gardens encompass a miniature forest, an aviary, a hibiscus garden with more than 150 species, and
other plant collections, such as orchids and cacti. The pretty white house
within the Gardens is **Camden,** the official residence of Bermuda's premier. Camden is open for tours Monday through Saturday noon to 2, except when official functions are scheduled. Behind Camden is the old
Arrowroot Factory, home to the Masterworks Arts Centre. ⊠ *169 South*
Rd., Paget Parish ☎ *441/236–5902 for Gardens, 441/236–5732 for*
Camden ⊠ *Free* ⊙ *Daily dawn–dusk; Camden tours Tues. & Fri. noon–2.*

★ ⊙ ⑩ **Verdmont.** Though it was used as a home until the mid-20th century, the
house has had virtually no structural changes since it was built in about
1710. Verdmont holds a notable collection of historic furnishings. Some
are imported fromEngland—such as the early-19th-century piano—but
most of the furniture is 18th-century cedar, crafted by Bermudian cabi-
netmakers. ⊠ *6 Verdmont La., off Collector's Hill, Smith's Parish*
☎ *441/236–7369* ⊕ *www.bnt.bm* ⊠ *$5; $10 combination ticket with*
Bermuda National Trust Museum in the Globe Hotel and Tucker House
⊙ *Tues.–Sat. 10–4.*

★ ⑪ **Spittal Pond Nature Reserve.** A showpiece of the Bermuda National Trust,
this nature park has 60 acres for carefree roaming, although you're
asked to keep to the walkways. On a high bluff overlooking the ocean,
Spanish Rock stands out as an oddity. It's now believed that a Portuguese ship was wrecked on the island in 1543 and that her sailors built
a new ship on which they departed. The carvings on Spanish Rock are
thought to be carved by the sailors, though the original has been removed.
⊠ *South Shore Rd., Smith's Parish* ☎ *441/236–6483* ⊕ *www.bnt.bm*
⊠ *Free* ⊙ *Daily dawn–dusk.*

⊙ ⑫ **Bermuda Aquarium, Museum & Zoo.** The aquarium has always been a pleas-
Fodor'sChoice ant diversion, but thanks to an ambitious expansion project it has be-
★ come truly great. The 145,000-gallon tank holding the North Rock
Exhibit, in the main gallery, gives you a diver's view of Bermuda's famed
living coral reefs and colorful marine life. ⊠ *40 North Shore Rd., Flatts*
Village, Hamilton Parish ☎ *441/293-2727* ⊕ *www.bamz.org* ⊠ *$10*
⊙ *Daily 9–5, last admission at 4; free interpretive tours 1:10 daily*
Apr.–Dec. (call for winter tour schedule).

🔄 ⑬ **Crystal Caves.** This fantastic cavern 120 feet underground, which was dis-
Fodor'sChoice covered in 1907, has spectacular stalactite formations. ⊠ *8 Crystal*
    ★ *Caves Rd., off Wilkinson Ave., Bailey's Bay, Hamilton Parish* ☎ *441/*
293–0640 ⊕ *www.bermudacaves.com* ☞ *One cave $15; combination*
ticket $21 ⊙ *Daily 9:30–4:30, last combination tour at 4.*

★ 🔄 ⑭ **Fort St. Catherine.** This restored fortress is one of the most impressive on
the island. The original fort was built around 1613, but it was remodeled and enlarged at least five times. As you travel through the tunnels,
you'll come across some startlingly lifelike figures tucked into niches. ⊠ *15*
Coot Pond Rd., St. George's Parish ☎ *441/297–1920* ☞ *$5* ⊙ *Daily 10–4.*

St. George's. The settlement of Bermuda began in what is now the Town
of St. George nearly 400 years ago, when the *Sea Venture* was shipwrecked
on Bermuda's treacherous reefs on its way to the colony of Jamestown,
Virginia. No trip to Bermuda is complete without a visit to this historic
town and UNESCO World Heritage Site.

★ ⑯ The **Bermuda National Trust Museum at the Globe Hotel** was built in
1700. During the American Civil War, Confederate Major Norman
Walker was stationed in the building, where he coordinated the flow of
guns, ammunition, and war supplies through Union blockades in American ports. The house saw service as the Globe Hotel during the mid-
19th century and became a National Trust property in 1951. ⊠ *32*
Duke of York St. ☎ *441/297–1423* ⊕ *www.bnt.bm* ☞ *$5; $10 combi-*
nation ticket includes admission to Tucker House and Verdmont
⊙ *Mon.–Sat. 10–4.*

★ ⑲ In early 2005, **Bermuda Perfumery & Gardens** moved from Bailey's Bay
(Smith's Parish) to Stewart Hall, one of the oldest buildings in St.
George's. The Lili Perfume Factory has been in existence since 1929, when
it began extracting natural fragrances from the island's flowers. Visitors
may browse the showroom and walk through the lovely garden behind
the building to the old cottage, where the perfumes are actually made.
⊠ *5 Queen St.* ☎ *441/293–0627* ⊕ *www.bermuda-perfumery.com*
☞ *Free* ⊙ *Mon.–Sat. 9–5.*

⑰ The history, trials, and accomplishments of black Bermudians are highlighted in **Bermudian Heritage Museum.** A model of the slave ship *En-*
terprise is part of a display that describes how the ship, with its load of
human "cargo," was blown off its course from Virginia to South Carolina in 1835; it landed in Bermuda, where slavery had already been abolished, so most of the slaves accepted freedom in Bermuda. ⊠ *Water and*
Duke of York Sts. ☎ *441/297–4126* ☞ *$3* ⊙ *Tues.–Sat. 10–3.*

★ 🔄 ⑮ A splendid bronze statue of Sir George Somers dominates **Ordnance Is-**
land. The dunking stool is a replica of the one used to dunk gossips, nagging wives, and suspected witches. Demonstrations are sometimes given,
although volunteers report that getting dunked is no picnic. Also on the
island is the *Deliverance II,* a replica of one of two ships—the other was
the *Patience*—built by the survivors of the 1609 wreck of the *Sea Ven-*
ture to carry them to Jamestown, Virginia, their original destination.
⊠ *Across from King's Sq.* ☎ *441/297–1459* ☞ *$3* ⊙ *Apr.–Oct., week-*
days 9:30–5.

★ ⑱   Because parts of **St. Peter's Church** date to its construction in 1620, it holds the distinction of being the oldest continuously operating Anglican church in the Western Hemisphere. It was not the first church to stand on this site, however. It replaced a 1612 structure of posts and palmetto leaves that was destroyed in a storm. The present church was extended in 1713, and the galleries on either side were added in 1833. ⊠ *33 Duke of York St.* ☎ *441/297–2459* ⊕ *www.anglican.bm* ✉ *Donations accepted* ⊗ *Daily 10–4:30; Sun. service at 11:15.*

★ ⑳   Constructed out of native limestone, **Tucker House** is typical of many early Bermudian houses. It was built in 1711 for a merchant who used the basement as storage space for his wares, and it was originally close to the shore—though landfill has since moved the water back. The house is at the corner of Barber's Alley, named for Joseph Haine Rainey, a freed slave from South Carolina who fled to Bermuda at the outbreak of the American Civil War and made his living here as a barber. After the war, Rainey returned home and, in 1870, became the first black man to be elected to the U.S. House of Representatives. ⊠ *5 Water St.* ☎ *441/297–0545* ⊕ *www.bnt. bm* ✉ *$5; $10 combination ticket includes admission to the National Trust Museum in the Globe Hotel and Verdmont* ⊗ *Mon.–Sat. 10–4.*

Shopping

Hamilton has the greatest concentration of shops in Bermuda, and Front Street is its pièce de résistance. Lined with small, pastel-color buildings, this most fashionable of Bermuda's streets houses sedate department stores and snazzy boutiques, with several small arcades and shopping alleys spinning away from it. A smart canopy shades the entrance to the 55 Front Street Group, which houses Crisson Jewellers. Modern Butterfield Place has galleries and boutiques selling, among other things, Louis Vuitton leather goods. The Emporium, a renovated building with an atrium, has a range of shops, from antiques to souvenirs.

In **St. George's,** Water Street, Duke of York Street, Hunters Wharf, Penno's Wharf, and Somers Wharf are the sites of numerous renovated buildings that house branches of Front Street stores, as well as artisans' studios. Historic King's Square offers little more than a couple of T-shirt and souvenir shops.

In the West End, **Somerset Village** has a few shops, but they hardly merit a special shopping trip. However, the **Clocktower Mall,** in a historic building at the Royal Naval Dockyard, has a few more shopping opportunities, including branches of Front Street shops and specialty boutiques. The **Dockyard** is also home to the Craft Market, the Bermuda Arts Centre, and Bermuda Clayworks.

Sports & Activities

BICYCLING   The best (and sometimes only) way to explore Bermuda's nooks and crannies—its little hidden coves and 18th Century tribe roads—is by bicycle or motor scooter. A popular option for biking in Bermuda is the **Railway Trail,** a dedicated cycle path blissfully free of cars. Running intermittently the length of the old Bermuda Railway (old "Rattle 'n' Shake"), this trail is scenic, paved, and restricted to pedestrian and bicycle traffic. You can ask the staff at any bike-rental shop for advice on where to access the trail. **Eve's Cycle Livery** (✉ Water St., St. George's ☎ 441/236–0839 ✉ Reid St., Hamilton ☎ 441/236–4491) has two locations convenient for cruise-ship passengers, Eve's rents standard-size mountain bikes, as well as motor scooters, including your mandatory helmet. The staff readily supplies advice on where to ride, and there is no charge for a repair waiver. **Wheels Cycles** (✉ Front St., near the docks, Hamilton ☎ 441/292–2245) has 13 branches all over the island, including one near the cruise-ship pier in Hamilton. You can rent mountain bikes for children and adults.

KAYAKING Good sea-kayaking areas can be found in protected coves and the open
★ ocean. Calm Mangrove Bay in Somerset is an especially popular spot. **SurfShack** (✉ 9 Beaches Resort, Daniel's Head, Somerset ☎ 441/239–2995 ⊕ www.surfshack.bm), based out of the 9 Beaches resort in Somerset, is the newest water-sports center in Bermuda and is fast becoming the place to go for all things aquatic. You can rent kayaks for $15 for an hour. Snorkel safaris, for groups up to 12 people, take you to some of the most secluded and beautiful locations around the island on one- or two-hour jet-ski tours.

GOLF Golf courses make up nearly 17 percent of the island's 21.6 square miles. The scenery on the courses is usually spectacular, with flowering trees and shrubs decked out in multicolored blossoms against a backdrop of brilliant blue sea and sky. The layouts are remarkably challenging, thanks to capriciousocean breezes, daunting natural terrain, and the clever work of world-class golf architects.

Fairmont Southampton Golf Club is known for its steep terrain. ✉ *Fairmont Southampton, South Rd., Southampton Parish* ☎ *441/239–6952* ⊕ *www. fairmont.com/Southampton* ✉ *Greens fees $70 with mandatory cart, $30 sunset walking. Pull-cart rental $7.50. Shoe rentals $10. Titleist-club rentals $25. Lessons $40 a half hour, $80 per hour.*

Mid Ocean Club, a classic 1921 Charles Blair Macdonald design revamped by Robert Trent Jones Sr. in 1953, is ranked as one of the top 50 courses outside the U.S. by *Golf Digest.* ✉ *Mid Ocean Dr., off South Shore Rd., Tucker's Town* ☎ *441/293–0330* 🖶 *441/293–8837* ⊕ *www. themidoceanclubbermuda.com* ✉ *Greens fees $210 ($70 when playing with a member). Nonmembers must be introduced by a club member (your hotelier can arrange this); nonmember starting times available Mon., Wed., and Fri. until noon, except holidays. After noon, every second tee time is available to nonmembers. Caddies $40 per bag, single, or $35 per bag, double (tip not included). Cart rental $25 per person.*

Port Royal Golf Course was once called one of the world's best public courses by Jack Nicklaus. ✉ *Off Middle Rd., Southampton Parish* ☎ *441/234–0974, 441/234–4653 for automated tee-time reservations up to 7 days in advance* 🖶 *441/234–3562* ⊕ *www.portroyalgolf.bm* ✉ *Greens fees: $139 including cart. Sunset rates are $85 with cart, $70 walking in summer; and $60 with cart, $50 walking in winter. Club rentals $37. Pull cart rentals $10. Shoe rentals $15. Lessons $50 for half hour.*

St. George's Golf Club, short but daunting, dominates a secluded headland at the island's northeastern end. In 2005 the course revamped its greens, which are small and were perpetually thin from constant buffeting by salty air. ✉ *1 Park Rd., St. George's Parish* ☎ *441/297–8353 pro shop, 441/234–4653 tee times* 🖶 *441/297–2273* ⊕ *www.stgeorgesgolf.bm* 🖃 *Greens fees $65. Cart rental $28 per person. Pull cart rental $10. Club rentals $35. Shoe rental $15. Lessons $50 half hour.*

Beaches

★ **Elbow Beach.** Swimming and body surfing are great at this beach, which is a pleasant setting for a late-evening stroll, with the lights from nearby hotels dancing on the water, but the romance dissipates in daylight, when the beach is noisy and crowded. Protective coral reefs make the waters the safest on the island, and a good choice for families. ✉ *Off South Rd., Paget Parish* Ⓜ *Bus 2 or 7 from Hamilton.*

FodorśChoice
★ **Horseshoe Bay Beach.** When locals say they're going to "the beach," they are generally referring to Horseshoe Bay Beach, the island's most popular. With clear water, a ⅓-mi crescent of pink sand, a vibrant social scene, and the uncluttered backdrop of South Shore Park, Horseshoe Bay has everything you could ask of a Bermudian beach. The undertow can be strong, especially on the main beach. ✉ *Off South Rd., Southampton Parish* ☎ *441/238–2651* Ⓜ *Bus 7 from Hamilton.*

Tobacco Bay Beach. The most popular beach near St. George's—about 15 minutes northwest of the town on foot—this small north-shore strand is huddled in a coral cove. It's a 10-minute hike from the bus stop in the town of St. George's, or you can flag down a St. George's Minibus Service van and ask for a lift here ($2 per person). ✉ *Coot Pond Rd., St. George's Parish* ☎ *441/297–8199* Ⓜ *Bus 1, 3, 10, or 11 from Hamilton.*

Where to Eat

¢–$ ✕ **Docksider.** Locals come to mingle at this sprawling Front Street sports bar. It's generally more popular as a drinking venue, but standard pub fare is available. Go for the English beef pie, fish-and-chips, or a fish sandwich and sip your dessert—a Dark 'n Stormy—out on the porch as you watch Bermuda stroll by. The pub has a good jukebox and there is often a DJ or a band on summer weekends, when it can become a lively night spot. ✉ *121 Front St., Hamilton* ☎ *441/296–3333* 🖃 *MC, V.*

$–$$ ✕ **Cafe Gió.** With a waterside terrace on the harbor, Cafe Gió offers tasty Italian cuisine in a pleasant, romantic setting. The fettuccine is good and the caesar salad is great. ✉ *36 Water St., St. George's* ☎ *441/297–1307* 🖃 *MC, V.*

BONAIRE (KRALENDIJK)

Vernon
O'Reilly
Ramesar

Starkly beautiful Bonaire is the consummate desert island. Surrounded by pristine waters, it is a haven for divers and snorkelers who flock here from around the world to take advantage of the excellent visibility, easily accessed reefs and bountiful marine life. Bonaire is the most rustic of the three ABC islands and despite its dependence on tourism it manages to maintain its identity and simple way of life. There are many very good restaurants most of which are located within walking distance of the port. Most of the island's 11,000 inhabitants live in and around the Kralendijk which must certainly qualify as one of the cutest and most compact capitals in the Caribbean. The best shopping is to be found along the very short stretch of road that constitutes "downtown". Bonaire's beaches tend to be small and rocky but there is a nice stretch of sandy beach at Lac Bay. It is entirely possible to see almost all of the sights and sounds of the island in one day by taking one of the island tours on offer.

CURRENCY The NAF guilder (NAF 1.78 to US$1); U.S. currency is accepted almost everywhere on the island, and the island has several ATMs, particularly in Kralendijk.

> **BONAIRE BEST BETS**
>
> ■ **Diving.** Bonaire is one of the world's top diving destinations. Certified divers shouldn't miss out.
>
> ■ **Snorkeling.** With reefs close to shore, snorkeling is good even from the beach in many spots.
>
> ■ **Washington-Slagbaai National Park.** Bonaire's best land-based sight is this well-preserved national park.

HOURS Banks are generally open weekdays from 8:30 to 3:30. Stores in the Kralendijk area are generally open Monday through Saturday from 8 to noon and 2 to 6 but may open earlier or stay open later depending on the season.

INTERNET **Bonaire Access** (⊠ Harbourside Mall, Kralendijk ☎ No phone). **Cyber City** (⊠ City Café, Kaya Grandi 7, Kralendijk ☎ 599/717–8286).

TELEPHONES You can make international calls from the Telbo central phone company office (next to the tourism office in Kralendijk), which is open 24 hours a day. The country code for Bonaire is 599; 717 is the exchange for every four-digit telephone number on the island. When making interisland calls, dial 717 plus the local four-digit number.

Coming Ashore

One of the great benefits of Bonaire to cruise passengers is that the port is right in downtown Kralendijk. Ships usually tender passengers ashore. A 4-minute walk gives access to most of the best shopping and restaurants on the island.

Bonaire lives for tourism, so upon the arrival of a cruise, the locals are ready. Taxis wait right at the port and operate on fixed government rates. All of the sights of Kralendikj are within easy walking distance, and a taxi ride to one of the larger resorts on the island will run between $5 and $8. A half-day island tour by taxi costs about $30 for up to 4 passengers.

Best Shore Excursions

We consider these to be among the better shore excursions for Bonaire. They may not be offered by all lines, and tour names may differ as well. Times and prices are approximate.

Best of Bonaire Island Tour Few roads, small size and absolutely no traffic means you can take in all of the island's major sights with ease. Explore Kralendijk, the salt pans and flamingoes, the slave huts and the rugged Northern coast in just a few hours with time left for shopping. ☉ *3 hrs* ▱ *$50.*

Mangrove Kayaking. A quick presentation on the fascinating world of mangroves is followed by a brief kayaking lesson and then a relaxing

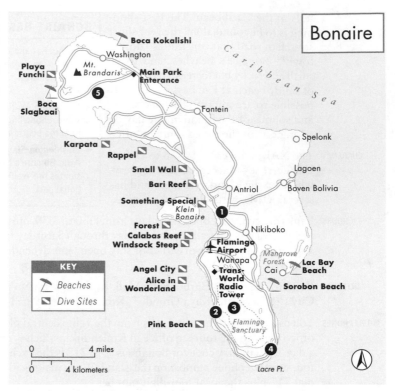

and scenic tour of the mangrove. These excursions also include refreshments. ☉ *3 hrs* 🚐 *$90.*

Shore Snorkel. It would almost be a sin to visit Bonaire without exploring the underwater wonders of the Bonaire Marine Park. Instructions, transportation and snorkeling equipment are included. ☉ *2–4 hrs* 🚐 *$50.*

Exploring Bonaire

Numbers in the margin correspond to points of interest on the Bonaire map.

❶ **Kralendijk.** Bonaire's small, tidy capital city (population 3,000) is five minutes from the airport. The main drag, J. A. Abraham Boulevard, turns into **Kaya Grandi** in the center of town. Along it are most of the island's major stores, boutiques, and restaurants. Across Kaya Grandi, opposite the Littman jewelry store, is Kaya L. D. Gerharts, with several small supermarkets, a handful of snack shops, and some of the better restaurants. Walk down the narrow waterfront avenue called Kaya C. E. B. Hellmund, which leads straight to the **North and South piers.** In the center of town, the Harborside Mall has chic boutiques. Along this route is **Fort Oranje,** with its cannons. From December through April, cruise ships dock in the harbor once or twice a week. The diminutive ochre-and-white structure that looks like a tiny Greek temple is the **fish market;** local anglers no longer bring their catches here (they sell out of their homes these days), but you can find plenty of fresh produce brought over from Colombia and Venezuela. Pick up the brochure *Walking and Shopping in Kralendijk* from the tourist office to get a map and full listing of all the monuments and sights in the town.

③ Salt Flats. You can't miss the salt flats—voluptuous white drifts that look something like mountains of snow. Harvested once a year, the "ponds" are owned by Cargill, Inc., which has reactivated the 19th-century salt industry with great success (one reason for that success is that the ocean on this part of the island is higher than the land—which makes irrigation a snap). Keep a lookout for the three 30-foot obelisks—white, blue, and red—that were used to guide the trade boats coming to pick up the salt. Look also in the distance across the pans to the abandoned solar saltworks that's now a designated **flamingo sanctuary.** With the naked eye you might be able to make out a pink-orange haze just on the horizon; with binoculars you will see a sea of bobbing pink bodies. The sanctuary is completely protected, and no entrance is allowed (flamingos are extremely sensitive to disturbances of any kind).

② Slave Huts. The salt industry's gritty history is revealed in Rode Pan, the site of two groups of tiny slave huts. The white grouping is on the right side of the road, opposite the salt flats; the second grouping, called the red slave huts (though they appear yellow), stretches across the road toward the island's southern tip. During the 19th century, slaves working the salt pans by day crawled into these huts to rest. Each Friday afternoon they walked seven hours to Rincon to weekend with their families, returning each Sunday. Only very small people will be able to enter, but walk around and poke your head in for a look.

④ Willemstoren Lighthouse. Bonaire's first lighthouse was built in 1837 and is now automated (but closed to visitors). Take some time to explore the beach and notice how the waves, driven by the trade winds, play a crashing symphony against the rocks. Locals stop here to collect pieces of driftwood in spectacular shapes and to build fanciful pyramids from objects that have washed ashore.

⑤ Washington–Slagbaai National Park. Once a plantation producing divi-divi trees (the pods were used for tanning animal skins), aloe (used for medicinal lotions), charcoal, and goats, the park is now a model of conservation. It's easy to tour the 13,500-acre tropical desert terrain on the dirt roads. As befits a wilderness sanctuary, the well-marked, rugged routes force you to drive slowly enough to appreciate the animal life and the terrain. If you're planning to hike, bring a picnic lunch, camera, sunscreen, and plenty of water. The short one (15 mi [24 km]) is marked by green arrows. Goats and donkeys may dart across the road, and if you keep your eyes peeled, you may catch sight of large iguanas camouflaged in the shrubbery. A useful guide to the park is available at the entrance for about $6. To get here, take the secondary road north from the town of Rincon. ☎ *599/717–8444* ⊕ *www.bonairenature.com/washingtonpark* ▤ *Free* ☉ *Daily 8–5; you must enter before 3.*

Shopping

Though it is a relatively small town Kralendijk offers a good range of high-end items like watches and jewelry at attractive prices. There are a number of souvenir shops offering T-shirts and trinkets lining the main stretch of Kaya Grandi.

Bon Tiki (⊠ Kaya C. E. B. Hellmund 3, Kralendijk ☎ 599/717–6877) sells unique works from Bonaire's finest artists. **JanArt Gallery** (⊠ Kaya Gloria 7, Kralendijk ☎ 599/717–5246), on the outskirts of town, sells unique watercolor paintings, prints, and art supplies; artist Janice Huckaby also hosts art classes. Whatever you do, make a point of visiting **Jenny's** ★ **Art** (⊠ Kaya Betico Croes 6, near post office, Kralendijk ☎ 599/717–5004). Lots of fun (and sometimes kitschy) souvenirs made out of driftwood, clay, and shells are all handmade by Jenny.

★ **Atlantis** (⊠ Kaya Grandi 32B, Kralendijk ☎ 599/717–7730) carries a large range of precious and semiprecious gems. The tanzanite collection is especially beautiful. Since gold jewelry is sold by weight here, it's an especially good buy. **Littman's** (⊠ Kaya Grandi 33, Kralendijk ☎ 599/717–8160 ⊠ Harborside Mall, Kaya Grandi 31, Kralendijk ☎ 599/717–2130) is an upscale jewelry and gift shop where many items are handpicked by owner Steven Littman on his regular trips to Europe.

Activities

DIVING & SNORKELING
Diving and snorkeling are almost a religion on Bonaire and are by far the most popular activities for even cruise visitors. Bonaire has some of the best reef diving this side of Australia's Great Barrier Reef. It takes only 5 to 25 minutes to reach many sites, the current is usually mild, and although some reefs have sudden, steep drops, most begin just offshore and slope gently downward at a 45-degree angle. General visibility runs 60 to 100 feet, except during surges in October and November. You can see several varieties of coral: knobby-brain, giant-brain, elkhorn, staghorn, mountainous star, gorgonian, and black. **Wanna Dive** (⊠ Hotel Rochaline, Kaya Grandi 7, next to City Café, Kralendijk ☎ 599/790–8880 ⊕ www. wannadivebonaire.com).

BICYCLING
Bonaire is generally flat, so bicycles are an easy way to get around. Because of the heat it's essential to carry water if you're planning to cycle for any distance and especially if your plans involve exploring the deserted interior. There are more than 180 mi (290 km) of unpaved routes (as well as the many paved roads) on the island. **Cycle Bonaire** (⊠ Kaya Gobernador N. Debrot 77A, Kralendijk ☎ 599/717–2229) rents mountain bikes and gear (trail maps, water bottles, helmets, locks, repair and first-aid kits) for $15 a day.

Beaches

Don't expect long stretches of glorious powdery sand. Bonaire's beaches are small, and though the water is blue (several shades of it, in fact), the sand isn't always white. In 2005, Bonaire's National Parks Foundation introduced a new "nature fee" that basically requires all nondivers to pay a $10 annual fee in order to enter the water anywhere around the island.

Lac Bay Beach. Known for its festive music on Sunday nights, this open bay area with pink-tinted sand is equally dazzling by day. It's a bumpy drive (10 to 15 minutes on a dirt road) to get here, but you'll be glad when you arrive. It's a good spot for diving, snorkeling, and kayaking (as long as you bring your own), and there are public restrooms and a restaurant for your convenience. ⊠ *Off Kaminda Sorobon, Cai.*

★ **Pink Beach.** As the name suggests, the sand here has a pinkish hue that takes on a magical shimmer in the late-afternoon sun. The water is suitable for swimming, snorkeling, and scuba diving. Take the Southern Scenic Route (E. E. G. Boulevard) on the island's western side; the beach is close to the slave huts. It's a favorite Bonairean hangout on the weekend, but it's almost deserted during the week. Because of the coral that is thrown up on the beach, sandals are recommended. ⊠ *Southern Scenic Hwy., south of airport.*

Windsock Beach. Near the airport (just off E. E. G. Boulevard), this pretty little spot, also known as Mangrove Beach, looks out toward the north side of the island and has about 200 yards of white sand along a rocky shoreline. It's a popular dive site, and swimming conditions are also good. ⊠ *Off E. E. G. Blvd., near airport.*

Where to Eat

$$-$$$ ✕ **City Café/City Restaurant.** This busy waterfront eatery is also one of the most reliable nightspots on the island, so it's always hopping day or night. Breakfast, lunch, and dinner are served daily for reasonable prices. Seafood is always featured, as are a variety of sandwiches and salads. The pita sandwich platters are a good lunchtime choice for the budget challenged. Weekends, there's always live entertainment and dancing. ⊠ *Hotel Rochaline, Kaya Grandi 7, Kralendijk* ☎ *599/717–8286* ⊟ *AE, MC, V.*

★ **$-$$** ✕ **Le Flamboyant.** This intimate restaurant offers good food at affordable prices. The cozy historic house—conveniently downtown—also has a small gourmet food shop, espresso bar, and lovely cocktail bar. The main attraction is the tree-covered courtyard at the back. Lunch offers a selection of ample sandwiches and salads; dinner is mostly seafood and pastas. Vegetarians will not have to pick and hunt for suitable items, as there's a comprehensive vegetarian menu. ⊠ *Kaya Grandi 12, Kralendijk* ☎ *599/717–3919* ⊟ *AE, MC, V* ☾ *Closed Sun.*

CALICA, MEXICO

Michele Joyce Just minutes away from Calica, Playa del Carmen has become one of Latin America's fastest-growing communities, with a pace almost as hectic as Cancún's. Hotels, restaurants, and shops multiply here faster than you can say "Kukulcán." Some are branches of Cancún establishments whose owners have taken up permanent residence in Playa—or who commute daily between the two places; others are owned by American and European expats who came here years ago, as early adopters. It makes for a varied, international community. Avenida 5, the first street in town parallel to the beach, is a long, colorfully tiled pedestrian walkway with shops, cafés, and street performers; small hotels and stores stretch north from this avenue. Avenida Juárez, running east–west from the highway to the beach, is the main commercial zone for the Riviera Maya corridor. Here, locals visit the food shops, pharmacies, auto-parts and hardware stores, and banks that line the curbs. People traveling the coast by car usually stop here to stock up on supplies—its banks, grocery stores, and gas stations are the last ones until Tulum.

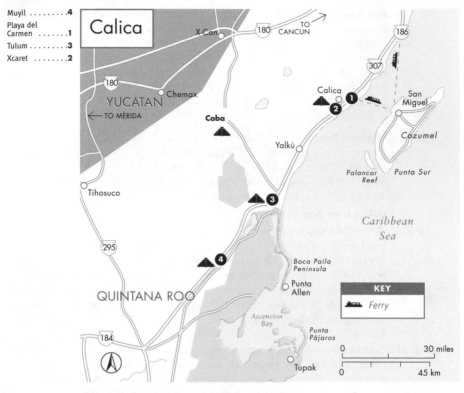

Essentials

CURRENCY   The Mexican peso (MX$11.13 to US$1). U.S. dollars and credit cards are widely accepted in the area, from the port to Playa del Carmen, but it's best to have pesos—and small bills—when you visit ruins where cashiers often run out of change. There is no advantage to paying in dollars, but there may be an advantage to paying in cash.

HOURS   Many Playa del Carmen restaurants are open for breakfast, lunch, and dinner, operating from around 10 in the morning until 10 at night. On weekends, especially around the busy Avenida 5 area, restaurants and bars stay open later, often until around midnight. Banks are generally open weekdays 9 to 5.

INTERNET   There are several Internet cafes on Avenida 5 in Playa del Carmen. **24 Com Center** (⊠ Av. 24, between Calle 1 and Calle 8, Playa del Carmen ☎ 984/803–5778).

TELEPHONES   Most pay phones accept prepaid Ladatel cards, sold in 30-, 50-, or 100-peso denominations. To use the card, insert it in the pay phone's slot, dial 001 (for calls to the U.S.) or 01 (for calls within Mexico), followed by the area code and number. Credit is deleted from the card as you use it, and the balance is displayed on the small screen on the phone.

Coming Ashore

The port at Calica, about 3 mi south of the town of Playa del Carmen (between Playa del Carmen and Xcarat), is small. Sometimes ships actually dock, and other times passengers are tendered to shore. There is a make-shift market at the port, where locals sell crafts. Beyond that, there is not much to do, and you'll need to head into Playa del Carmen proper to find restaurants and even tour operators. If you really want to shop, skip the vendors at the port and head to Playa del Carmen's Avenida 5, where you can easily spend an afternoon browsing shops and enjoying restaurants.

Taxis and tour buses are available at the port to take you to Playa del Carmen and other destinations, but lines often form as passengers wait for taxis, so hurry to the front of the line if you really want to pack a lot of activity into your day. Your taxi will have you in Playa del Carmen or in Xcaret in under 10 minutes, but you'll pay a whopping $10 for the short trip.

> ### CALICA BEST BETS
>
> **A Day at Xcaret.** Particularly for families, this ecological theme park is a great way to spend the day.
>
> **Beaches.** The beaches in the Riviera Maya are some of the best along the Yucatan's Caribbean coast.
>
> **Diving.** From Playa del Carmen, you're a short hop from some of the Yucatan's best dive sites.
>
> **Shopping.** Playa del Carmen's Avenida 5 can easily keep you occupied for your day in port if you are a shopaholic.

Shore Excursions

We consider these to be among the better shore excursions for Calica. They may not be offered by all lines, and tour names may differ as well. Times and prices are approximate.

ATV Tour. The tours in the Calica area usually include some driving both inland and on the beach. Lunch (or at least snacks) are usually provided. ☺ *6 hrs* ▨ *$84.*

Catamaran Snorkeling Cruise. Because of the exceptionally clear water, non-divers may wish to do this trip to see some of the wonderful sights below the sea and to visit undiscovered beaches. ☺ *6 hrs* ▨ *$84–$97.*

Diving. Certified divers who don't feel like making their own arrangements may wish to opt for ship-arranged diving trip to the excellent reefs around Cozumel. ☺ *3 hrs* ▨ *$90.*

Tulum. Because of the distance and crowds, it's sometimes better to take a ship-sponsored tour to Tulum rather than trying to go it alone. You'll go by bus. ☺ *6 ½ hrs* ▨ *$97.*

Exploring Calica

Numbers in the margin correspond to points of interest on the Playa del Carmen map.

❶ **Playa del Carmen.** Once upon a time, Playa del Carmen was a fishing village with a ravishing deserted beach. The villagers fished and raised coconut palms to produce copra (the roasted coconut that is pressed to render coconut oil), and the only foreigners who ventured here were beach bums. That was a long time ago, however. These days, although the beach is still delightful—alabaster-white sand, turquoise-blue waters—it's far from deserted. In fact, Playa has become one of Latin America's fastest-growing communities, with a population of more than 135,000 and a pace almost as hectic as Cancún's. The ferry pier, where the hourly boats arrive from and depart for Cozumel, is another busy part of town. The streets leading from the dock have shops, restaurants, cafés, a hotel, a basketball court, and food stands. If you take a stroll north from the pier along the beach, you'll find the serious sun worshippers. On the pier's south side is the edge of the sprawling Playacar complex. The development is a labyrinth of residences and all-inclusive resorts bordered by an 18-hole championship golf course. ⊠ *3 mi (5 km) north of Calica.*

The excellent 32-acre **Xaman Ha Aviary** (⊠ Paseo Xaman-Ha, Playacar ☎ 984/873–0235), in the middle of the Playacar development, is home to more than 30 species of native birds. It's open daily 9–5, and admission is $15.

Tres Rios Eco Park (⊠ Carretera Cancún–Tulum, Km 54 ☎ 998/850–4849 ⊕ www.tresrios.com), located just 7 mi north of Playa, is a great place to get a sense of this region's ecology and natural wonders. Three rivers converge in the expansive 800-acre property (a lush rarity in the dry Yucatán landscape), and you can explore them by kayaking, canoeing, or snorkeling along them. You can also take horseback rides along the beach or bike rides along jungle paths, keeping an eye out for birds and animals; if you're lucky, you might spot a white-fronted parrot, or even a coatimundi. Admission is $18, including lunch; $35 includes lunch and a choice of one activity. The park is open daily from 9 to 5.

② **Xcaret.** Once a sacred Maya city and port, Xcaret (pronounced *ish*-caret) is now a 250-acre ecological theme park on a gorgeous stretch of coastline. A Mexican version of Epcot Center, the park has done a good job to showcase, celebrate, and help preserve the natural environment of the Caribbean coast. ■ TIP➜ You can easily spend at least a full day here; there's tons to see and do. Among the most popular attractions are the Paradise River raft tour that takes you on a winding, watery journey through the jungle; the Butterfly Pavillion, where thousands of butterflies float dreamily through a botanical garden while New Age music plays in the background; and an ocean-fed aquarium where you can see local sea life drifting through coral heads and sea fans without getting wet. The list of Xcaret's attractions goes on and on. ⊠ *11 km (6½ mi) south of Playa del Carmen* ☎ *998/881–2451 in Cancún* ⊕ *www.xcaret.net* ⊠ *$53, including show* ☉ *Daily 8:30 AM–9 PM.*

③ **Tulum.** Tulum (pronounced tool-*lum*) is the Yucatán Peninsula's most-visited Maya ruin, attracting more than 2 million people annually. Though most of the architecture is of unremarkable Postclassic (1000–1521) style, the amount of attention that Tulum receives is not entirely undeserved. Its location by the blue-green Caribbean is breathtaking. Tulum is one of the few Maya cities known to have been inhabited when the conquistadores arrived in 1518. In the 16th century, it functioned as a safe harbor for trade goods from rival Maya factions; it was considered neutral territory where merchandise could be stored and traded in peace. The city reached its height when traders, made wealthy through the exchange of goods, for the first time outranked Maya priests in authority and power. When the Spaniards arrived, they forbade the Maya traders to sail the seas, and commerce among the Maya died. Tulum has long held special significance for the Maya. A key city in the League of Mayapán (AD

987–1194), it was never conquered by the Spaniards, although it was abandoned about 75 years after the conquest. For 300 years thereafter, it symbolized the defiance of an otherwise subjugated people; it was one of the last outposts of the Maya during their insurrection against Mexican rule in the War of the Castes, which began in 1846. Uprisings continued intermittently until 1935, when the Maya ceded Tulum to the government. ⊠ *2 km (1 mi) south of Tankah, 62 km (38 mi) south of Playa del Carmen* ⌨ *$9, use of video camera extra* ☉ *Daily 8–5.*

❹ **Muyil.** This photogenic archaeological site at the northern end of the Reserva de la Biosfera Sian Ka'an is underrated. Once known as Chunyaxché, it's now called by its ancient name, Muyil (pronounced mool-*hill*). It dates from the Late Preclassic era, when it was connected by road to the sea and served as a port between Cobá and the Maya centers in Belize and Guatemala. The most notable site at Muyil today is the remains of the 56-foot **Castillo**—one of the tallest on the Quintana Roo coast—at the center of a large acropolis. During excavations of the Castillo, jade figurines representing the moon and fertility goddess Ixchel were found. Recent excavations at Muyil have uncovered some smaller structures. The ruins stand near the edge of a deep-blue lagoon and are surrounded by almost impenetrable jungle—so be sure to bring bug repellent. You can drive down a dirt road on the side of the ruins to swim or fish in the lagoon. The bird-watching is also exceptional here. ⊠ *24 km (15 mi) south of Tulum, 86 km (53 mi) south of Playa del Carmen* ⌨ *$4, free Sun.* ☉ *Daily 8–5.*

Shopping

Playa del Carmen's Avenida 5 between Calles 4 and 10 is the best place to shop along the coast. Boutiques sell folk art and textiles from around Mexico, and clothing stores carry lots of sarongs and beachwear made from Indonesian batiks. A shopping area called Calle Corazon, between Calles 12 and 14, has a pedestrian street, art galleries, restaurants, and boutiques. **La Calaca** (⊠ Av. 5 between Calles 12 and 14 ☎ 984/873–0174) has an eclectic collection of wooden masks, whimsically carved angels and devils, and other crafts. **Maya Arts Gallery** (⊠ Av. 5 between Calles 6 and 8 ☎ 984/879–3389) has an extensive collection of hand-carved Maya masks and *huipiles* (the traditional, white, embroidered cotton dresses worn by Maya women) from Mexico and Guatemala.

Activities

DIVING The PADI-affiliated **Abyss** (⊠ Calle 12 ☎ 984/873–2164) offers training ($80 for an introductory course) in addition to dive trips ($50 for one tank, $70 for two tanks) and packages. The oldest shop in town, **Tank-Ha Dive Shop** (⊠ Av. 5 between Calles 8 and 10 ☎☎ 984/873–5037 ⊕ www.tankha.com), has PADI-certified teachers and runs diving and snorkeling trips to the reefs and caverns. A one-tank dive costs $35; for a two-tank trip it's $55; and for a cenote two-tank trip it's $90. Dive packages are also available.

GOLF Playa's golf course is an 18-hole, par-72 championship course designed by Robert Von Hagge. The greens fee is $180; there's also a special twilight fee of $120. Information is available from the **Casa Club de Golf** (☎ 984/873–0624 or 998/881–6088).

Where to Eat

¢–$ Babe's Noodles & Bar. Photos and paintings of old Hollywood pinup models decorate the walls and are even laminated onto the bar of this Swedish-owned, Asian restaurant, known for its fresh and interesting fare. Everything is cooked to order—no prefab dishes here. Try the spring rolls with peanut sauce, or the sesame noodles, made with chicken or pork, veggies, lime, green curry, and ginger. In the Buddha Garden, you can sip a *mojito,* or sit at the bar and watch the crowds on nearby 5th Avenue. ⊠ *Calle 10 between Avs. 5 and 10* ☎ *984/804–2592* ⊕ *www. babesnoodlesandbar.com* ⊟ *No credit cards* ⊠ *Av.5, between Calle 28 and 30* ☎ *984/803–0056.*

$–$$$$ La Parrilla. Reliably tasty Mexican fare is the draw at this boisterous, touristy restaurant. The smell of sizzling *parrilla mixta* (a grilled, marinated mixture of lobster, shrimp, chicken, and steak) can make it difficult to resist grabbing one of the few available tables. The margaritas here are strong, and there's often live music. ⊠ *Av. 5 and Calle 8* ☎ *984/873–0687* ⊟ *AE, D, MC, V.*

CARTAGENA, COLOMBIA

Jeff Van Fleet Ever wondered what the "Spanish Main" refers to? This is it. Colombia's Caribbean coast invokes ghosts of conquistadores, pirates, and missionaries journeying to the New World in search of wealth, whether material or spiritual. Anchoring this shore is Cartagena—poetically, officially *Cartagena de Indias* (Cartagena of the Indies)—founded in 1533 and one of Latin America's magnificent colonial cities. Gold and silver passed through here en route to Spain, making the city an obvious target for pirates, hence the construction of Cartagena's trademark walls and fortresses. Outside the *Ciudad Amurallada* (walled city) lie less historic (but no less interesting) beaches and water excursions. If Colombia conjures up images of drug lords and paramilitary guerillas, think again; security is quite visible (without being oppressive) here in the country's top tourist destination. Take the same precautions you'd follow visiting any city of 800,000 people, and you should have a grand time.

Essentials

CURRENCY The Colombian peso (COP 2,203 to US$1). In Colombia, peso prices are denoted with the "$" sign too. If they carry a lot of zeroes, they likely are not dollar prices, but always ask. ATMs are ubiquitous around town.

HOURS Many tourist sights close by 6 PM, meaning you should do your touring early in the day. (It's cooler before noon, as well.) Tourist-oriented shops keep hours from 9 to 9, although many close from 12:30 to 2, and little is open on Sunday. (Truly entrepreneurial store owners don't close when cruise ships are in port.)

INTERNET Upon arrival or before departure, you can check your e-mail at the bank of computers in the Terminal de Cruceros. In town, the computers at **Micronet** (⊠ Calle de la Estrella No. 4–47 are quite zippy and will set you back only 2,000 pesos per hour.)

PRECAUTIONS Security is tighter in Cartagena than elsewhere in Colombia, so you certainly can navigate the city on your own. (Knowing some Spanish helps.)

However, the scarcity of English speakers or English signage at the city's tourist attractions and the persistence of vendors, street touts and the periodic con artist—they *do* speak English—mean that many cruise passengers opt for the reassurance of an organized shore excursion. If you set out on your own, under no circumstances should you deal with anyone who approaches you on the street offering to change money; rip-offs are guaranteed.

TELEPHONES The Terminal de Cruceros has ample phones for your use. Local numbers in Cartagena have seven digits. For international calls, dial 009 followed by country and area codes and local number. The U.S. mobile carrier Cingular offers roaming options in this region of Colombia for calls back to the United States. **AT&T** (☎01-800/911–0010). **MCI** (☎01-800/916–0001). **Sprint** (☎ 01-800/913–0010).

Coming Ashore

Cruise ships dock at the modern Terminal de Cruceros (cruise terminal) on Isla de Manga, an island connected by a bridge to the historic city center, about 3 km (2 mi) northwest of the docks. You'll find telephones, Internet computers, and a duty-free shop in the terminal.

A small army of taxis waits in front of the terminal. Expect to pay 5,000 pesos for the 10-minute drive to the walled city; about 8,000 pesos will get you to the nearby beaches at Bocagrande. Drivers are all too happy to take you on your own do-it-yourself guided tour. Most charge around

10,000 to 15,000 pesos for an hour of waiting time. There's little need to rent a car here. Cartagena, at least that of tourist interest, is so compact, and walking its labyrinth of cobblestone streets in the old city is far more enjoyable than driving them.

Best Shore Excursions

We consider these to be among the better shore excursions for Cartagena. They may not be offered by all lines, and tour names may differ as well. Times and prices are approximate.

Cruise the Harbor. Approach Cartagena as did everyone in colonial times, from newly arriving residents, to pirates wishing to plunder the city. A boat trip around the city's inner bay allows to you appreciate the city's formidable walls and fortresses, without which, there would likely be no Cartagena today. Some cruise lines allow you to do it aboard a replica Spanish Galleon. ☺ *2 hrs* ⎙ *$42–$50.*

Mangrove & Swamp Eco-Tour. Better for birdwatchers than anyone else, these kayak tours take you into an extensive mangrove swamp to see the flora and fauna. ☺ *4 hrs* ⎙ *$56.*

Swim at Isla Barú. Cartagena is history, but nature beckons about 30 minutes away by boat. The beaches of nearby Isla Barú make a far more picturesque alternative to those closer to the city and offer ample swimming and snorkeling opportunities. ☺ *4 hrs* ⎙ *$60.*

Exploring Cartagena

Numbers in the margin correspond to points of interest on the Cartagena map.

Nothing says Cartagena quite like a ride in a horse-drawn carriage, or *coche,* as it known locally. Drivers are a wealth of information about Cartagena, and many do speak English. The downside for you is that the rides begin near dusk—it's a far cooler time of the day, after all—and your need to be back on ship may not coincide with that schedule. Do check. You can pick up carriages many places around, including the Plaza de los Coches, near the Puerta del Reloj in the walled city, or the Hotel Caribe in Bocagrande. Expect to pay around $170 to $200 for a 2-hour tour (this kind of excursion is best when the cost is split among a group of four).

❺ Castillo de San Felipe de Barajas. Designed by Antonio de Arévalo in 1639, the Fort of St. Philip's steep-angled brick and concrete battlements were arranged so that if part of the castle were conquered the rest could still be defended. A maze of tunnels, minimally lighted today to allow for spooky exploration, still connects vital points of the fort. Acoustics were perfect in the tunnels, allowing occupants of the fort to hear the footsteps of the

---

CARTAGENA BEST BETS

- **Ride a Coche.** If your ship stays in port until after dark, you can take the quintessential horse-and-buggy ride through the streets.

- **Walk La Murallas.** Walking the city's massive stone walls is a favorite tourist pastime, and for good reason; the distinctive walls made the city what it is today.

- **Visit Palacio de la Inquisición.** Cartagena's most-visited sight is this historic—and creepy—center for the Spanish Inquisition.

approaching enemy. You can walk here from the walled city in about 30 minutes; an 8,000-peso taxi ride is an easier option. ⊠ *Avenida Pedro de Heredia at Carrera 17* ☎ *666–4790* 🗐 *10,000 pesos* ⊙ *Daily 8–6.*

② **Catedral.** Any Latin American city centers on its cathedral and main square. Cartagena's Plaza de Bolívar is a shady place from which to admire Cartagena's 16th-century cathedral, with its colorful bell tower and 20th-century dome. Inside is a massive gilded altar. A stautue of South American liberator Simón Bolívar stands watch over his namesake plaza. ⊠ *Plaza de Bolívar.*

⑥ **Cerro de la Popa.** For spectacular views of Cartagena, ascend this hill, the FodorśChoice highest ground around. Because of its strategic location, the 17th-century hilltop convent did double duty as a fortress during the colonial era. ★ It now houses a museum and a chapel dedicated to the Virgin de la Candelaria, Cartagena's patron saint. No public transport exists to get up here; taxis change about 6,000 pesos. ✛ *3 km (2 mi) southeast of Ciudad Amurallada* ☎ *666-2331* 🗐 *5,000 pesos* ⊙ *Daily 9–5.*

❶ **Las Murallas.** Cartagena survived only because of its walls, and its *murallas* remain today the city's most distinctive feature. Repeated sacking by pirates and foreign invaders convinced the Spaniards of the need to enclose the region's most important port. Construction began about 1600 and was completed in 1796. Walking along the thick walls remains one of Cartagena's time-honored tourist pastimes. The **Puerta del Reloj** is the principal gate to the innermost sector of the Ciudad Amurallada. Its foursided clock tower was a relatively late addition (1888), and has become the best known symbol of the city. ⊠ *Area bounded by Bahía de las Ánimas, Caribbean Sea, and Laguna de San Lázaro* ⊙ *24 hours.*

❸ **Museo del Oro y Arqueología.** The Gold and Archaeological Museum, a project of Colombia's Central Bank, displays an assortment of artifacts culled from the Sinús, an indigenous group that lived in the region 2,000 years ago. ⊠ *Carrera 4 No. 33–26* ☎ *660–0778* 🗐 *Free* ⊙ *Tues.–Fri. 10–1 and 3–6, Sat. 10–1 and 2–5.*

❹ **Palacio de la Inquisición.** Arguably Cartagena's most visited tourist attraction documents the darkest period in the city's history. The 1770 Palace FodorśChoice of the Inquisition served as the second headquarters of the repressive arbiters of political and spiritual orthodoxy who once exercised jurisdiction ★ over northern South America. Although the museum also displays benign colonial and pre-Columbian artifacts, everyone heads to the ground floor to "Eeeewww" over the implements of torture—racks and thumbscrews, to name but two. ⊠ *Carrera 4 No. 33–26* ☎ *664–4113* 🗐 *3,000 pesos* ⊙ *Daily 9–5.*

Shopping

Think "Juan Valdez" if you're looking for something to take the folks back home. Small bags of fine Colombian coffee, the country's signature souvenir, are available in most tourist-oriented shops. Colombia also means emeralds, and you'll find plenty in the jewelry shops on or near Calle Pantaleón, beside the cathedral. Don't forget the duty-free shop in the Terminal de Cruceros for those last-minute purchases. On the high end of Cartagena's shopping spectrum lies **Galería Cano** ✉ *Plaza de Bolí-var* ☎ *664–7078.*, which has assembled an exquisite selection of indige-nous artisan work from around Colombia. The hats, hammocks, and jewelry here are admittedly pricey, but they do make a lovely souvenir of your day in Cartagena. The name of **Las Bóvedas** (✉ North of Plaza Fernández de Madrid ☎ No phone) translates as "the vaults," and the city's best crafts shops occupy this row of storerooms built in the 18th century to hold gunpowder and other military essentials. Your stockpile here will consist of hats, hammocks and leather goods.

Activities

DIVING Coral reefs line the coast south of Cartagena, although warm-water cur-rents have begun to erode them in recent years. There is still good div-ing to be had in the Islas del Rosario, an archipelago of 27 coral islands about 35 km (21 mi) southwest of the city. The **Caribe Dive Shop** (✉ Car-rera 1A, No. 2–87, Bocagrande ☎ 665–0155) at the Hotel Caribe or-ganizes snorkeling trips to the Islas del Rosario and scuba diving at underwater wrecks.

Beaches

Bocagrande. For most people, "beach" plus "Cartagena" equals "Boca-grande," the resort area on a 5 km- (3 mi-) long peninsula south of the walled city. High-rise hotels and condos front the gray-sand beach. It gets quite crowded and is very lively, but Bocagrande is probably not the Caribbean beach of which you've always dreamed. ✉ *2 km (1 mi) south of Cartagena Bocagrande.*

Playa Blanca. The area's quintessential postcard-perfect white-sand beach lies at Playa Blanca on Isla Barú southeast of Cartagena, a far nicer op-tion than Bocagrande if you have the time. Barú is an island in name only—a canal separates this long peninsula from the mainland—but boat is realistically the only way to get there from Cartagena. Many private boats leave from the Muelle de los Pegasos (the tourist dock) just south of the walled city on the way to Bocagrande, yet their speed frequently trans-lates into recklessness. An organized shore excursion through your ship offers the most reliable trip. ✉ *35 km (21 mi) southwest of Cartagena, Isla de Barú.*

Where to Eat

$–$$ ✗ **Café de la Plaza.** One of seven cafés spilling out onto the Plaza Santo Domingo, this popular eatery serves tasty food in generous portions and is one of those perfect places to watch the world go by. The menu is pre-dominantly Italian, with a good selection of pastas, salads, and sandwiches. It's also a good place to stop for breakfast. ✉ *Plaza Santo Domingo* ☎ *664–0920* ▭ *AE, DC, MC, V.*

$–$$ ✗ **Café San Pedro.** Although it serves primarily Colombian fare, this restaurant's eclectic menu includes dishes from Thailand, Italy, and Japan. You can also drop by to nurse a drink for as long as you like and to watch the activity on the plaza from one of the outdoor tables. ✉ *Plaza San Pedro* ☎ *664–5121* ▭ *AE, DC, MC, V.*

COLÓN, PANAMA

Linda Coffman   When you consider the decades it took to build the canal, not to mention the lives lost and government failures and triumphs involved during its construction, it comes as no surprise that the Panama Canal is often called the 8th Wonder of the Modern World. Best described as an aquatic bridge, the Panama Canal connects the Caribbean Sea with the Pacific Ocean by raising ships up and over Central America, through artificially created Gatún Lake, the highest point at 85 feet above sea level, and then lowering them back to sea level by using a series of locks, or water steps. A masterful engineering feat, three pairs of locks—Gatún, Pedro Miguel, and Miraflores—utilize gravity to fill and drain as ships pass through chambers 1,000 feet long by 110 feet wide that are "locked" by doors weighing 80 tons apiece, yet actually float into position. Most cruise ships pass through the canal seasonally, when repositioning from one coast to the other; however, partial transits have become an increasingly popular "destination" on regularly scheduled 10- and 11-night Caribbean itineraries. These loop cruises enter the canal from the Caribbean Sea and sail into Gatún Lake, where they remain for a few hours as passengers are tendered ashore for excursions. Ships then pass back through the locks, returning to the Caribbean and stopping at either Cristobal Pier or Colón 2000 Pier to retrieve passengers at the conclusion of their tours.

A day transiting the canal's Gatún Locks begins before dawn as your passenger ship passes through *Bahia Limon* and lines up with dozens of other vessels to await its turn to enter. Before your ship can proceed, two pilots and a narrator will board. The sight of a massive cruise ship being raised dozens of feet into the air by water is so mesmerizing that passengers eagerly crowd all forward decks at the first lock. If you don't find a good viewing spot, head for the rear decks, where there is usually more room and the view is just as intriguing. If you remain aboard, as many passengers do, you'll find plenty of room up front later in the day as your ship retraces its path down to the sea. Due to the tight scheduling of the day's activities—it takes at least 90 minutes for a ship to pass through Gatún Locks—passengers who wish to go ashore early in the day are advised to sign up for one of the many available shore excursions.

Essentials

CURRENCY   The balboa is permanently at par with the U.S. dollar. Panama does not print paper money, and U.S. dollars are used regularly. There is no need to acquire Panamanian money.

HOURS   It's all about the cruise ships here. If your ship is docked at the Colón 2000 Pier, the stores will be open.

INTERNET   There's an internet café at the Colón 2000 Pier.

TELEPHONES   You'll find telephones inside Colón's cruise terminals, where you can purchase phone cards, which are a handy and inexpensive way to make calls.

Coming Ashore

Colón, Panama's second-largest city, has little to offer of historic interest and is simply a jumping-off point to the rain forest and a wide variety of organized tours. Once in a while, a cruise's itinerary may include a day docked in Colón, rather than a partial canal transit. However, no matter how much time your ship spends in Colón, we strongly recommend that you leave the ship on an organized shore excursion, either arranged with the cruise line or through independent tour operators. Taxi drivers await ship arrivals, and some can be acceptable private guides; however, as in any foreign port, before setting out with any unofficial car and driver, you should set a firm price and agree upon an itinerary as well as look over the vehicle carefully.

Although entry time into the canal is always approximate, passenger ships have priority and most pass through Gatún Locks early in the morning. Passengers booked on shore excursions begin the tendering process soon after the ship sets anchor, which can be as early as 8:30 AM. Alternatives to excursions offered by your cruise ship are available from independent tour operators that can be arranged in advance through Web sites or, possibly, travel agents. You will likely be informed that Panamanian regulations restrict passengers going ashore in Gatún Lake to only those who have booked the cruise line's excursions; however, anyone who has a shore excursion reservation with a local company should be able to leave the vessel. Before making independent tour arrangements, confirm with your cruise line that you will be allowed to go ashore after presenting your private tour confirmation to the shore-excursion staff on board the ship.

Upon completion of either full or partial canal transits, cruise ships generally dock at either Cristobal Pier or Colón 2000 Pier late in the afternoon, where they may remain for several hours. Passengers who remained on board throughout the canal passage have the opportunity to go ashore and those who set out on land tours end at the terminals, where they rejoin the ship. All of Colón is considered a high crime area, and pickpockets have been known to strike even in the seemingly secure areas of the cruise-ship terminals. If you go ashore, you are well advised to leave jewelry and other valuables aboard your ship and carry only the cash you need.

SHORE EXCURSIONS If you wish to see a bit of Panama during your canal transit, you'll almost certainly need to book a shore excursion. This is one of the few cruise destinations where that is the case. The following shore excursions are offered by major cruise lines in Panama. They may not be offered by all lines, and tour names may differ as well. Times and prices are approximate.

Authentic Embera Indian Village. You travel by dugout canoe to an Embera village in the Chagres National Park. The village chief greets you with a traditional welcome, and his people perform native song, dance, and music and display their crafts. ⊗ *3½ hrs* ▱ *$99.*

Caribbean Rain Forest Nature & Wildlife Hike. Explore remote jungle trails on the western shore of the canal during your guided nature hike through Fort Sherman, site of the former United States Army elite jungle-training school. You may see toucans, sloths, anteaters, and howler monkeys in the intricate jungle ecosystem. ⊗ *4½–5 hrs* ▱ *$59.*

Gatún Lake Kayak & Eco Adventure. After a short bus ride, you arrive at the kayak staging area where you will set out on your ecological tour through the islands that surround Gatún Lake. Afterward, you will trade in your kayak for a bus and stop at the Gatún Locks Observation Area to watch ships traverse the locks. The observation platform has 80 steps; an alternate viewing site is available at ground level. Beverages and snacks are included. ⊗ *4 hrs* ▱ *$62.*

Panama Canal Railway Journey. Travel Panama's transcontinental railroad from Colón to Panama City, where you will then take a scenic drive and stop at Amador Causeway before returning to Colón by air-conditioned bus. Snacks and beverages are served on the train. The more expensive trip is in a dome car. ⊗ *5½ hrs* ▱ *$139–$199.*

Panama City Tour. Drive from the Atlantic to the Pacific through the rain forest from Colón to Panama City, where you will tour the city's highlights. Depending on when you leave, you'll get lunch or dinner. ⊗ *8 hrs* ▱ *$99.*

Panama's Rain Forest Aerial Tram. Transfer by bus from Colón to Gamboa Rain Forest Resort, where the aerial tram ride begins. After your narrated ascent through the forest canopy, you can walk to the observation platform before stopping for a picnic lunch on the way back to Colón. ⊗ *4½ hrs* ▱ *$99.*

SHOPPING While the Colón Free Zone is the world's second-largest tax-free zone—and is within walking distance of Colón 2000—it is situated amid uninviting squalor sure to intimidate even the boldest shopper; further, merchants here are supposed to do only wholesale sales. We can't recommend that you shop here, though some merchants will sell to tourists.

Better bets are within the large terminals adjacent to both Cristobal Pier and Colón 2000 Pier, where you will find Internet access, telephones, refreshments, and duty-free souvenir shopping in relatively secure environments. Stores in both locations feature local crafts such as baskets, wood carvings, and toys, as well as liquor, jewelry, and the ubiquitous souvenir T-shirts. In addition to shops and cafés, Cristobal Pier features an open-air arts and crafts market; Colón 2000 Pier has a well-stocked supermarket. The most unique locally made souvenirs are colorful appliquéd *molas,* the whimsical textile artwork created by native Kuna women, who come from the San Blas Islands; they are likely to be hand stitching new designs while they sell the ones they just completed. The Kuna ladies drive a hard bargain and, considering the intricate nature of their handiwork, prices are quite fair. This is not a particularly authentic experience, but prices can be good.

Watch for local folkloric dancers who often perform for tips in the terminal areas or pierside at sailaway.

COSTA MAYA, MEXICO

Michele Joyce   The newest cruise-ship destination on Mexico's Caribbean Coast, Puerto Costa Maya is an anomaly. Unlike other tourist attractions in the area (the island of Cozumel being the primary Yucatán cruise port), this port of call near Majahual has been created exclusively for cruise-ship passengers. The shops, restaurants, activities, and entertainment you'll find here aren't open to the general public. At first glance, the port complex itself may seem to be little more than an outdoor mall. The docking pier (which can accommodate three ships at once) leads to a 70,000 square-foot bazaar-type compound, where shops selling local crafts-jewelry, pottery, woven straw hats and bags, and embroidered dresses are interspersed with duty-free stores and souvenir shops. There are two alfresco restaurants, which serve seafood, American-friendly Mexican dishes like tacos and quesadillas, and cocktails at shaded tables. An outdoor amphitheater stages eight daily performances of traditional music and dance. The strip of beach edging the complex has been outfitted with colorful lounge chairs and *hamacas* (hammocks), and may tempt you to linger and sunbathe. If you want to have a truly authentic Mexican experience, though, you'll take advantage of the day tours offered to outlying areas. These give you a chance to see some of the really spectacular sights in this part of Mexico, many of which are rarely visited. This is one port where the shore excursion is the point, and there are no options except to purchase what your ship offers. You can preview what excursions may be offered on the Puerto Costa Maya's own Web site. Among the best tours are those that let you explore the gorgeous (and usually deserted) Mayan ruin sites of Kohunlich, Dzibanche, and Chacchoben. The ancient pyramids and temples at these sites, surrounded by jungle that's protected them for thousands of years, are still dazzling to behold. Since the sites are some distance from the port complex—and require some road travel in one of the port's air-conditioned vans—these tours are all-day affairs.

Essentials

CURRENCY   The Mexican peso (MX$11.13 to US$1). U.S. dollars and credit cards are accepted by everyone at the port. There is no advantage to paying in dollars, but there may be an advantage to paying in cash. Ten pesos are worth a little bit less than $1.

INFORMATION   **Puerto Costa Maya** (⊕ www.puertocostamaya.com).

TELEPHONES   Most pay phones accept prepaid Ladatel cards, which are sold in 30-, 50-, or 100-peso denominations. To use the card, insert it in the pay phone's slot, dial 001 (for calls to the U.S.) or 01 (for calls within Mexico), followed by the area code and number. Credit is deleted from the card as you use it, and the balance is displayed on a small screen on the phone.

SHORE
EXCURSIONS
We consider these to be among the better shore excursions for Costa Maya. They may not be offered by all lines, and tour names may differ as well. Times and prices are approximate. This is one place where your choice of a shore excursion can be crucial. You can reach some less-visited Maya sites that aren't easily reached from other parts of the country.

Catamaran and Snorkel. If you prefer your adventures on—or under—the water, an excellent tour choice is the catamaran and snorkeling trips to the nearby reef at Banco Chinchorro. ⊘ 3 hrs ⌨ $48.

Chacchoben. An air-conditioned bus transports you to a secluded jungle setting near the border with Belize. Your guide will explain the significance of the excavated portion of the 10-acre site, which includes detailed Maya temples and the remains of the Maya village. Afterwards, you have time for more exploration or to shop for crafts. Walking and climbing is over uneven surfaces. ⊘ 4 hrs ⌨ $72.

Jungle Beach Break. If you just want to relax, take a shuttle to nearby Uvero Beach. Included are an open bar and use of beach chairs, hammocks, and non-motorized water sports. Stay as long as you like. Freshwater showers, rest rooms, and changing rooms are available. There's a restaurant, but you must pay for the food here. ⊘ At your discretion ⌨ $40.

Kohunlich. An air-conditioned bus takes you to an isolated site near the Belize border where, spread over a wide area, the ruins include a variety of architectural styles, from the wide lawns of the ball courts and public plazas to the great temples with sculpted masks. Considerable walking and climbing is over uneven surfaces. A snack is included. Some tours (usually called "Mayan Explorer") also include Dzibanche and last eight hours. ⊘ 7–8 hrs ⌨ $82–$98.

Speed Boat Trip. If you enjoy the power of a speedboat, then this tour will appeal to you. These are among the fastest speed boats you'll find, and you'll be able to reach some less visited beaches for downtime before returning to the ship. ⊘ 3½ hrs ⌨ $96.

COZUMEL, MEXICO

Maribeth
Mellin
Cozumel, with its sun-drenched ivory beaches fringed with coral reefs, fulfills the tourist's vision of a tropical Caribbean island. It's a heady mix of the natural and the commercial. Despite a mini-construction boom in the island's sole city, San Miguel, there are still wild pockets scattered throughout the island where flora and fauna flourish. Smaller than Cancún, Cozumel surpasses its fancier neighbor in many ways. It has more history and ruins, superior diving and snorkeling, more authentic cuisine, and a greater diversity of handicrafts at better prices. The numerous coral reefs, particularly the world-renowned Palancar Reef, attract divers from around the world. On a busy cruise-ship day, the island can seem completely overrun, but it's still possible to get away, and some good Maya sights are within reach on long (and expensive) shore excursions.

Essentials

CURRENCY
The Mexican peso (MX$11.13 to US$1). U.S. dollars and credit cards are widely accepted in the area, from the port to Playa del Carmen, but

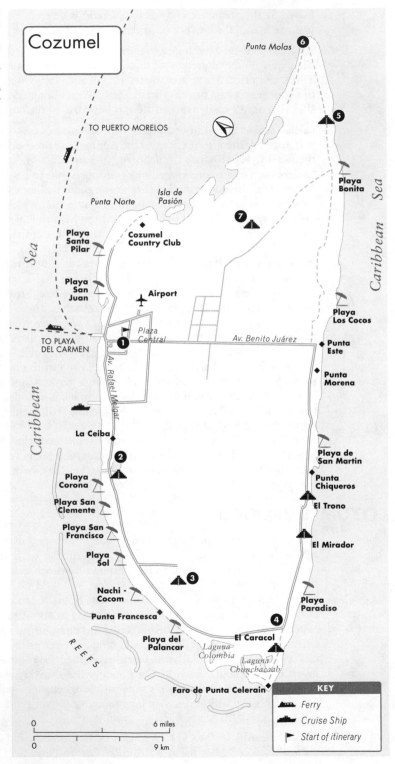

Cozumel

TO PUERTO MORELOS

Punta Molas

Sea

Caribbean Sea

Playa
Bonita

Punta Norte

Isla de
Pasión

Playa
Santa
Pilar

Cozumel
Country Club

Playa
San
Juan

Airport

Playa
Los Cocos

Plaza
Central

Av. Benito Juárez

Punta
Este

TO PLAYA
DEL CARMEN

Av. Rafael Melgar

Punta
Morena

La Ceiba

Playa
Corona

Playa de
San Martín

Punta
Chiqueros

Playa San
Clemente

El Trono

Playa San
Francisco

El Mirador

Playa
Sol

Nachi -
Cocom

Playa
Paradiso

Punta Francesca

El Caracol

Playa del
Palancar

Laguna
Colombia

Laguna
Chinchacaab

R E E F S

Faro de Punta Celerain

Caribbean

Sea

0   6 miles

0   9 km

it's best to have pesos—and small bills—when you visit ruins where cashiers often run out of change. There is no advantage to paying in dollars, but there may be an advantage to paying in cash.

HOURS Many Cozumel restaurants are open for breakfast, lunch, and dinner, operating from around 10 in the morning until 10 at night. Banks are generally open weekdays 9 to 5.

INTERNET **Calling Station** (✉ Av. Rafael E. Melgar 27, at Calle 3 Sur ☎ 987/872–1417). **The Crew Office** (✉ Av. 5, No. 201, between Calle 3 Sur and Av. Rosada Salas ☎ 987/ 869–1485). **CreWorld Internet** (✉ Av. Rafael E. Melgar and Calle 11 Sur ☎ 987/872–6509).

> ## COZUMEL BEST BETS
>
> ■ **Diving & Snorkeling.** Excellent reefs close to shore make either diving or snorkeling a must-do activity.
>
> ■ **Maya Ruins.** Some of the most famous and dazzling ruins are reachable from Cozumel, and if you have never seen a Maya pyramid, this is your chance.
>
> ■ **Shopping.** Because the dollar is still worth something in Mexico, you can get very good buys, and Cozumel is a major shopping destination.

TELEPHONES Most pay phones accept prepaid Ladatel cards, sold in 30-, 50-, or 100-peso denominations. To use the card, insert it in the pay phone's slot, dial 001 (for calls to the U.S.) or 01 (for calls within Mexico), followed by the area code and number. Credit is deleted from the card as you use it, and the balance is displayed on a small screen on the phone.

Coming Ashore

As many as six ships call at Cozumel on a busy day, tendering passengers to the downtown pier in the center of San Miguel or docking at the two international piers 4 mi (6 km) away. From the downtown pier you can walk into town or catch the ferry to Playa del Carmen. Taxi tours are also available. An island tour, including the ruins and other sights, costs about $50 to $70, but negotiate the price before you get in the cab. The international pier is close to many beaches, but you'll need a taxi to get into town. There's rarely a wait for a taxi, but prices are high, and drivers are often aggressive, asking double or triple the reasonable fare. Expect to pay $10 for the ride into San Miguel from the pier. Tipping is not necessary.

Passenger ferries to Playa del Carmen leave Cozumel's main pier approximately every other hour from 5 AM to 10 PM. They also leave Playa del Carmen's dock about every other hour on the hour, from 6 AM to 11 PM (but note that service sometimes varies according to demand). The trip takes 45 minutes. Verify the times: bad weather and changing schedules can prompt cancellations.

Shore Excursions

Cozumel offers more worthwhile shore excursions than most Caribbean ports. If you want to see Maya sites, then you should take a ship-sponsored tour because of the travel distances (often ships stop briefly off Playa del Carmen to discharge passengers going on these tours, a real time-saver). The following shore excursions are offered by major cruise lines in Cozumel. They may not be offered by all lines, and tour names may differ as well. Times and prices are approximate.

Atlantis Submarine Trip. Since the reefs here are so amazing, it's worth the money to take this submarine trip if you're not an accredited diver. You'll go 100 feet below the surface without getting wet. ⊘ 2¼ hrs ⊠ $98.

Diving. If you're an accredited diver, it can be worth taking a ship-sponsored excursion to maximize your time and minimize the arrangements you have to make. ⊘ 4½ hrs ⊠ $98.

Jungle ATV Tour. This off-road tour is good if you want to release some of your adrenaline. ⊘ 3½ hrs ⊠ $89.

Snorkel Tours. Popularized by Jacques Cousteau, Cozumel's coral reefs are considered to be some of the world's finest. Most ships offer snorkeling excursions, some with lessons and equipment provided. Locales and tour lengths vary by cruise line; the more expensive tours take you closer to the reefs; the cheaper tours include snorkeling from the beach only. ⊘ Approx. 4 hrs ⊠ $44.

Tequila Tasting Seminar. With the popularity of high-end tequilas has come this chance to learn more about the spirit and how to tell good from bad. This is a popular trip. ⊘ Approx. 3 hrs ⊠ $82.

Tulum Mayan Ruins. The only Maya settlement built on a cliff overlooking the sea was dedicated to the setting sun. After taking the public ferry to Playa del Carmen, you travel by bus to the site and tour the ruins. A stop at Xel-ha for snorkeling and swimming is usually an option; otherwise, you go back to Cozumel for shopping rather than to the ship. ⊘ 6½–8 hrs ⊠ $109.

Exploring Cozumel

Numbers in the margin correspond to points of interest on the Cozumel map.

San Miguel is tiny—you cannot get lost—and is best explored on foot. The main attractions are the small eateries and shops that line the streets, and the activity centers at the main square, where the locals congregate in the evenings.

⑤ Castillo Real. A Maya site on the coast near the island's northern end, the "royal castle" includes a lookout tower, the base of a pyramid, and a temple with two chambers capped by a false arch. The waters here harbor several shipwrecks, and it's a fine spot for snorkeling because there are few visitors to disturb the fish. Note, however, that you can't get here by rental car; plan to explore the area on a guided tour.

❸ El Cedral. Spanish explorers discovered this site, once the hub of Maya life on Cozumel, in 1518. Later, it became the island's first official city, founded in 1847. Today it's a farming community with small well-tended houses and gardens. Conquistadores tore down much of the Maya temple and, during World War II, the U.S. Army Corps of Engineers destroyed the rest to make way for the island's first airport. All that remains of the Maya ruins is one small structure with an arch. Nearby is a green-and-white cinder-block church, decorated inside with crosses shrouded in embroidered lace; legend has it that Mexico's first Mass was held here. Each May there's a fair here with dancing and bullfights. More small ruins are hidden in the surrounding jungle, but you need a guide to find them. Check with horseback riding companies for specialized tours. ⊠ *Turn at Km 17.5 off Carretera Sur or Av. Rafael E. Melgar, then drive 3 km (2 mi) inland to the site* 🕾 *No phone* 🎫 *Free* ⊙ *Daily dawn–dusk.*

★ 🐚 ➋ **Parque Chankanaab.** Chankanaab (which means "small sea") is a national park with a saltwater lagoon, an archaeological park, and a botanical garden. Scattered throughout are reproductions of a Maya village, and of Olmec, Toltec, Aztec, and Maya stone carvings. The gardens were severely damaged by Hurricane Wilma in 2005 and are slowly recovering. You can enjoy a cool walk through pathways leading to the sea, where parrot fish and sergeant majors swarm around snorkelers. You can swim, scuba dive, or snorkel at the beach. There's plenty to see: underwater caverns, a sunken ship, crusty old cannons and anchors, and a sculpture of la Virgen del Mar (Virgin of the Sea). To preserve the ecosystem, park rules forbid touching the reef or feeding the fish. Dive shops, restaurants, gift shops, a snack stand, and dressing rooms with lockers and showers are right on the sand. A small museum has exhibits on coral, shells, and the park's history, as well as some sculptures. ⊠ *Carretera Sur, Km 9* 🕾 *987/872–2940* 🎫 *$10* ⊙ *Daily 7–5.*

🐚 ➍ **Parque Punta Sur.** This 247-acre national preserve at Cozumel's southernmost tip is a protected habitat for numerous birds and animals, including crocodiles, flamingos, egrets, and herons. Cars aren't allowed, so you'll need to use park transportation (rented bicycles or public buses) to get around here. From observation towers you can spot crocodiles and birds in **Laguna Colombia** or **Laguna Chunchacaab.** Or visit the ancient Maya lighthouse, **El Caracol,** constructed to whistle when the wind blows in a certain direction. At the park's (and the island's) southernmost point is the **Faro de Celarain,** a lighthouse that is now a museum of navigation. Climb the 134 steps to the top; it's a steamy effort, but the views are incredible. Beaches here are wide and deserted, and there's great snorkeling offshore. Snorkeling equipment is available for rent, as are kayaks. The park also has an excellent restaurant (it's prohibited to bring food and drinks to the park), an information center, a small souvenir shop, and restrooms. Without a rental car, expect to pay about $40 for a round-trip taxi ride from San Miguel. ⊠ *Southernmost point in Punta Sur Park and the coastal rd.* 🕾 *987/872– 2940 or 987/872–8462* 🎫 *$10* ⊙ *Daily 9–5.*

➐ **San Gervasio.** Surrounded by a forest, these temples comprise Cozumel's largest remaining Maya and Toltec site. San Gervasio was once the island's capital and ceremonial center, dedicated to the fertility goddess Ixchel. The Classic- and Postclassic-style buildings were continuously occupied from AD 300 to 1500. Typical architectural features include limestone plazas and arches atop stepped platforms, as well as stelae and bas-reliefs. Be sure to see the "Las Manitas" temple with red handprints all over its altar. Plaques clearly describe each structure in Maya, Spanish, and English. ⊠ *From San Miguel, take the cross-island road (follow signs to the airport) east to San Gervasio access road; turn left and follow road for 4½ mi (7 km)* 🎫 *$5.50* ⊙ *Daily 7–4.*

7

★ ❶ **San Miguel.** Cozumel's only town feels more traditional the farther you walk away from the water; the waterfront has been taken over by large shops selling jewelry, imported rugs, leather boots, and souvenirs to cruise-ship passengers. Head inland to the pedestrian streets around the plaza, where family-owned restaurants and shops cater to locals and savvy travelers.

Shopping

San Miguel's biggest industry—even bigger than diving—is selling souvenirs to cruise-ship passengers. The primary items are ceramics, onyx, brass, wood carvings, colorful blankets and hammocks, reproductions of Maya artifacts, shells, silver, gold, sportswear, T-shirts, perfume, and liquor. Look for Mexican pewter; it's unusual, affordable, and attractive. Almost all stores take U.S. dollars. If your ship docks at International Pier, you can shop dockside for T-shirts, crafts, and more.

Before you spend any serious cash, though, keep in mind the following tips. Don't pay attention to written or verbal offers of "20% discount, today only" or "only for cruise-ship passengers"—they're nothing but bait to get you inside. Similarly, many of the larger stores advertise "duty-free" wares, but prices tend to be higher than retail prices in the United States. Avoid buying from street vendors, as the quality of their merchandise can be questionable, which may not be apparent until it's too late. Don't buy anything from the black coral "factories." The items are overpriced, and black coral is an endangered species.

The center of the shopping district is the main square off Avenida Melgar, across from the ferry terminal, where you'll find some upscale malls geared toward cruise-ship shoppers. The district extends north along Avenida Melgar and Calles 5 Sur and Norte. As a general rule, the newer, trendier shops line the waterfront, and the better crafts shops can be found around Avenida 5a. Other plazas include Plaza del Sol (on the east side of the main plaza), Villa Mar (on the north side of the main plaza), and the Plaza Confetti (on the south side of the main plaza).

Los Cinco Soles (⊠ Av. Rafael E. Melgar and Calle 8 Norte ☎ 987/872–0132) is the best one-stop shop for crafts from around Mexico. Several display rooms, covering almost an entire block, are filled with clothing, furnishings, home decor items, and jewelry. **Diamond Creations** (⊠ Av. Rafael E. Melgar Sur 131 ☎ 987/872–5330) lets you custom-design pieces of jewelry from a collection of loose diamonds, emeralds, rubies, sapphires, or tanzanite. The shop and its affiliates, Tanzanite International, Diamond Creations, and Silver International, have multiple locations along the waterfront and in the shopping malls—in fact, you can't avoid them. At Cozumel's best art gallery, **Galeria Azul** (⊠ Calle 10 Sur between Av. Salas and Calle 1 ☎ 987/869–0963), artist Greg Deitrich displays his engraved blown glass along with paintings, jewelry, and other works by local artists. **Mr. Buho** (⊠ Av. Rafael E. Melgar between Calles 6 and 8 ☎ 987/869–1601) specializes in white and black clothes and has well-made guayabera shirts and cotton dresses. **Viva Mexico** (⊠ Av. Rafael E. Melgar and Calle Adolfo Rosada Salas ☎ 987/872–0791) sells souvenirs and handicrafts from all over Mexico; it's a great place to find T-shirts, blankets, and trinkets.

Sports & Activities

DIVING & SNORKELING Cozumel is famous for its reefs. In addition to Chankanaab Nature Park, a great dive site is La Ceiba Reef, in the waters off La Ceiba and Sol Caribe hotels. Here lies the wreckage of a sunken airplane blown up for a Mexican disaster movie. Cozumel has plenty of dive shops to choose from. **Aqua Safari** (⊠ Av. Rafael E. Melgar 429, between Calles 5 and 7 Sur ☎ 987/872–0101) is one of the oldest and most professional shops and offers PADI certification. **Blue Angel** (⊠ Caribe Blu Hotel, Carretera Sur, Km 2.3 ☎ 987/872–1631) has an ideal location for both boat and shore dives. **Dive Cozumel-Yellow Rose** (⊠ Calle Adolfo Rosado Salas 85, between Avs. Rafael E. Melgar and 5 Sur ☎ 987/872–4567) specializes in cave diving for experienced divers.

Eagle Ray Divers (⊠ La Caleta Marina, near the Presidente Inter-Continental hotel ☎987/872–5735) offers snorkeling trips. The company also tracks the eagle rays that appear off Cozumel from December to February and runs trips for advanced divers to walls where the rays congregate.

FISHING Regulations forbid commercial fishing, sportfishing, spear fishing, and collecting any marine life in certain areas around Cozumel. It's illegal to kill some species within marine reserves, including billfish, so be prepared to return prize catches to the sea. You can charter high-speed fishing boats for about $420 per half-day or $600 per day (with a maximum of six people). **Albatross Deep Sea Fishing** (☎ 987/872–7904 or 888/333–4643) offers full-day rates that include boat and crew, tackle and bait, and lunch with beer and soda. **3 Hermanos** (☎ 987/872–6417 or 987/876–8931) specializes in deep-sea and fly-fishing trips. Their rates for a half-day deep-sea fishing trip start at $350.

Beaches

Cozumel's beaches vary from sandy treeless stretches to isolated coves to rocky shores. Most of the development is on the leeward (western) side. Beach clubs have sprung up on the southwest coast; admission, however, is usually free, as long as you buy food and drinks. Clubs offer typical tourist fare: souvenir shops, *palapa* (thatch-roofed) restaurants, kayaks, and cold beer. A cab ride from San Miguel to most clubs costs about $15 each way. Reaching beaches on the windward (eastern) side is more difficult, but the solitude is worth it. A small parking lot on the side of Carretera Sur just south of town marks the entrance to **Playa Caletita**. A few palapas are up for grabs, and the small restaurant has restrooms and beach chairs. South of the resorts lies the mostly ignored (and therefore serene) **Playa Palancar** (⊠ Carretera Sur ☎ 987/878–5238). Offshore is the famous Palancar Reef, easily accessed by the on-site dive shop. There's also a water-sports center, a bar-café, and a long beach with hammocks hanging under coconut palms. The aroma of grilled fish with garlic butter is tantalizing. Playa del Palancar keeps prices low and rarely feels crowded. If it weren't for the pretentious stone arch at the entrance, **Playa San Francisco** would look much like it did a decade ago. The inviting 3-mi (5-km) stretch of sandy beach, which extends along Carretera Sur, south of Parque Chankanaab at about Km 10, is among the longest and finest on Cozumel. Encompassing beaches known as Playa Maya and Santa Rosa, it's typically packed with cruise-ship passengers in high season. On Sunday, locals flock here to eat fresh fish and hear live music. Amenities include two outdoor restaurants, a bar, dressing rooms, gift shops, volleyball nets, beach chairs, and water-sports equipment rentals. Divers use this beach as a jumping-off point for the San Francisco reef and Santa Rosa wall. The abundance of turtle grass in the water, however, makes this a less-than-ideal spot for swimming. **Punta Chiqueros**, a half-moon-shaped cove sheltered by an offshore reef, is the first popular swimming area on the windward side as you drive north on the coastal road (it's about 8 mi [12 km] north of Parque Punta Sur). Part of a longer beach that some locals call Playa Bonita, it has fine sand, clear water, and moderate waves. This is a great place to swim, watch the sunset, and eat fresh fish at the restaurant, also called Playa Bonita.

Where to Eat

Some restaurants serving large groups may add a 10% to 15% service charge to the bill. Otherwise, a 15% to 20% tip is customary.

★ **$–$$$** ✕ **Guido's.** Chef Ivonne Villiger works wonders with fresh fish—if the wahoo with spinach is on the menu, don't miss it. But Guido's is best known for its pizzas baked in a wood-burning oven, which makes sections of the indoor dining room rather warm. Sit in the pleasantly overgrown courtyard instead, and order a pitcher of sangria to go with the puffy garlic bread. ✉ *Av. Rafael E. Melgar 23, between Calles 6 and 8 Norte* ☎ *987/872–0946* ▤ *AE, D, MC, V.*

¢–$ ✕ **El Foco.** Locals fuel up before and after partying at this traditional *taquería* (it's open until midnight, or until the last customer leaves). The soft tacos stuffed with pork, chorizo, cheese, or beef are cheap and filling. ✉ *Av. 5 Sur 13B, between Calles Adolfo Rosado Salas and 3 Sur* ☎ *987/872–5980* ▤ *No credit cards.*

CURAÇAO

Elise Rosen

Try to be on deck as your ship sails into Curaçao. The tiny Queen Emma Floating Bridge swings aside to allow ships to pass through the narrow channel. Pastel gingerbread buildings on shore look like dollhouses, especially from a large cruise ship. Although the gabled roofs and red tiles show a Dutch influence, the gleeful colors of the facades are peculiar to Curaçao. It's said that an early governor of the island suffered from migraines that were aggravated by the color white, so all the houses were painted in hues from magenta to mauve. Thirty-five mi (56 km) north of Venezuela and 42 mi (67 km) east of Aruba, Curaçao is, at 38 mi (61 km) long and 3 to 7½ mi (5 to 12 km) wide, the largest of the Netherlands Antilles. Although always sunny, it's never stiflingly hot here because of the constant trade winds. Water sports attract enthusiasts from all over the world, and the reef diving is excellent.

Essentials

CURRENCY   The NAf guilder (NAF1.78 to US$1); U.S. currency is accepted almost everywhere on the island, and ATMs are plentiful.

HOURS   Banks are open weekdays from 8 to 3:30. Post office hours are from 7:30 to 5 weekdays. Most shops are open Monday through Saturday from 8

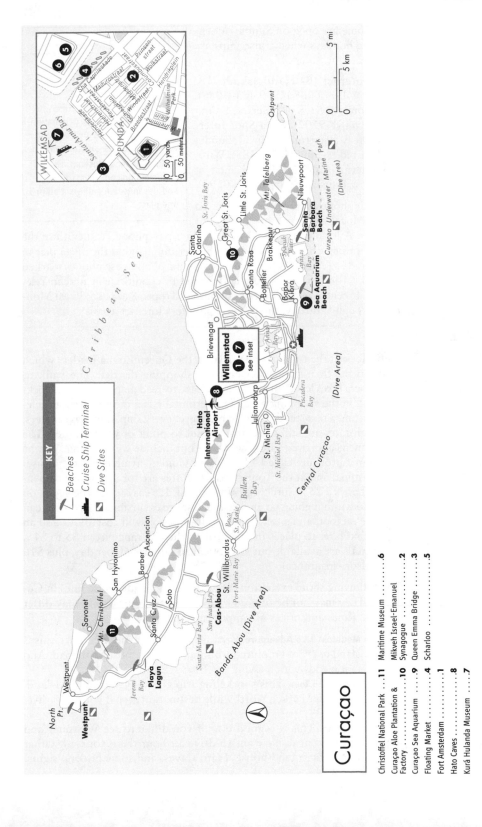

Curaçao

Christoffel National Park	. . . **11**	Maritime Museum **6**
Curaçao Aloe Plantation &		Mikveh Israel-Emanuel
Factory **10**		Synagogue **2**
Curaçao Sea Aquarium **9**		Queen Emma Bridge **3**
Floating Market **4**		Scharloo **5**
Fort Amsterdam **1**		
Hato Caves **8**		
Kurá Hulanda Museum **7**		

KEY

- ⚓ Cruise Ship Terminal
- Beaches
- Dive Sites

WILLEMSTAD

PUNDA

1 Fort Amsterdam
2 Mikveh Israel-Emanuel Synagogue
3 Queen Emma Bridge
4 Floating Market
5 Scharloo
6 Maritime Museum
7 Kurá Hulanda Museum

Santa Anna Bay
Sha Caprileskade
Handelskade
Madurostraat
Breedestraat
Winterstraat
Columbusstraat
Consciëntiesteeg
Heerenstraat
Prinsenstraat
Wolkstraat
Hendrikplein
Wilhelmina Park
Wilhelminaplein

Caribbean Sea

North Pt.
Westpunt
Westpunt
Jeremi Bay
Mt. Christoffel
Savonet
Santa Cruz
Solo
San Hyronimo
Barber
Ascencion
Santa Marta Bay
San Juan Bay
Port Marie Bay
St. Willibrordus
St. Michiel
Cas-Abou
Playa Lagun
Banda Abou (Dive Area)
Boca St. Matie
Bullen Bay
St. Michiel Bay
Hato International Airport
Julianadorp
Willemstad 1–7
see inset
Brievengat
St. Anna Bay
Piscadera Bay
Central Curaçao (Dive Area)
Santa Catarina
Santa Rosa
St. Joris Bay
Little St. Joris
Great St. Joris
Mt. Tafelberg
Ostpunt
Nieuwpoort
Curaçao Underwater Marine Park (Dive Area)
Santa Barbara Beach
Bapor Kibra
Sea Aquarium Beach
Bottelier
Brakkeput
Caracas Bay
Spanish Water

8 Hato Caves
9 Curaçao Sea Aquarium
10 Curaçao Aloe Plantation & Factory
11 Christoffel National Park

0 ___ 5 mi
0 ___ 5 km

0 ___ 50 yards
0 ___ 50 meters

to 6. Some are open on Sunday mornings and holidays when cruise ships are in port.

INTERNET **Café Internet** (⊠ Handelskade 3B, Punda, Willemstad ☎ 5999/465–5088). **Dot Com** (⊠ Saliña Galleries, Saliña ☎ 5999/461–9702). **Suya-Spot Internet C@fe** (⊠ Pietermaaiplein 13, Punda, Willemstad ☎ 5999/461–5388). **Wireless Internet Café** (⊠ Hanchi Snoa 4, Punda, Willemstad ☎ 5999/461–0590).

> ### CURAÇAO BEST BETS
>
> ■ **Diving.** After Bonaire, Curaçao has probably the best diving in the region.
>
> ■ **The Floating Market.** This unique market is a fun destination, even though it's mostly fruits and vegetables; go as early as you can.
>
> ■ **Kurá Hulanda Museum.** History is one of Curaçao's best offerings, and this museum gathers it all in one place.

TELEPHONES The telephone system is reliable. To place a local call, dial the seven-digit number. A local call costs NAf.50 from a pay phone. You can use the AT&T calling center at the cruise-ship terminal and at the mega pier in Otrobanda to call the U.S. From other public phones, use phones marked "Lenso." You can also call direct from the air-conditioned Curaçao Telecom (CT) center using a prepaid phone card (open 8 AM to 5:30 PM Monday through Saturday; the center also offers Internet access).

Coming Ashore

Ships dock at the terminal just beyond the Queen Emma Bridge, which leads to the floating market and the shopping district. The walk to downtown takes less than 10 minutes. Easy-to-read maps are posted dockside and in the shopping area. The terminal has a duty-free shop, telephones, and a taxi stand. Taxis, which meet every ship, now have meters, although rates are still fixed from point to point of your journey. The government-approved rates, which do not include waiting time, can be found in a brochure called "Taxi Tariff Guide," available at the cruise-ship terminal and at the Tourist Board. Rates are for up to four passengers. There's a 25% surcharge after 11 PM. It's easy to see the sights on Curaçao without going on an organized shore excursion. Downtown can be done on foot, and a taxi for up to four people will cost about $30 an hour. Taxi fares to places in and around the city range from $5 to $15. Car rentals are available but are not cheap (about $60 per day, plus $10 compulsory insurance).

SHORE EXCURSIONS The following shore excursions are offered by major cruise lines in Curaçao. They may not be offered by all lines, and tour names may differ as well. Times and prices are approximate.

Curaçao Mountain Bike Adventure. Because it's not too mountainous, this is a good island to try out mountain-biking, which is mostly off-road. And the excursion ends with a swim. ⏲ 3½ hrs 🎫 $58.

Curaçao Snorkeling Tour. This snorkeling trip goes to Caracas Bay Island, in the Underwater Park, a worthwhile destination even if you don't dive. ⏲ 2½ hrs 🎫 $34.

Discover Curaçao. This is a good tour if you'd like to see Westpunt and Mt. Christoffel but don't want to drive an hour there yourself. Other stops are made at a land house, Hato Caves, and some historic sights. ⏲ 3½ hrs 🎫 $40.

Scuba Dive with Equipment. Many of the best sites in Curaçao are under the sea. If you're a certified diver, this is a good place to do some underwater exploring. ☉ *4 hrs* ☒ *$95.*

Exploring Curaçao

Numbers in the margin correspond to points of interest on the Curaçao map.

Willemstad. Willemstad is small and navigable on foot. You needn't spend more than two or three hours wandering around here, although the narrow alleys and various architectural styles are enchanting. English, Spanish, and Dutch are widely spoken. Narrow Santa Anna Bay divides the city into two sides: Punda, where you'll find the main shopping district, and Otrabanda (literally, the "other side"), where the cruise ships dock. Punda is crammed with shops, restaurants, monuments, and markets. Otrabanda has narrow, winding streets full of colonial homes notable for their gables and Dutch-influenced designs.

You can cross from Otrabanda to Punda in one of three ways: walk over the Queen Emma Bridge; ride the free ferry, which runs when the bridge swings open to let seagoing vessels pass; or take a cab across the Juliana Bridge (about $7). On the Punda side of the city, Handelskade is where you'll find Willemstad's most famous sights—the colorful colonial buildings that line the waterfront. The original red roof tiles came from Europe on trade ships as ballast.

★ ❹ Each morning dozens of Venezuelan schooners laden with tropical fruits and vegetables arrive at the bustling **Floating Market** on the Punda side of the city. Mangoes, papayas, and exotic vegetables vie for space with freshly caught fish and herbs and spices. The buying is best at 6:30 AM—too early for most cruise-ship visitors—but there's plenty of action throughout the afternoon. Any produce bought here, however, should be thoroughly washed or peeled before being eaten. ☒ *Sha Caprileskade, Punda.*

❶ Step through the archway of **Fort Amsterdam** and enter another century. The entire structure dates from the 1700s, when it was the center of the city and the island's most important fort. Now it houses the governor's residence, the Fort Church, the Council of Ministers, and government offices. Outside the entrance, a series of majestic gnarled wayaka trees are fancifully carved with human forms—the work of local artist Mac Alberto. ☒ *Foot of Queen Emma Bridge, Punda* ☎ *5999/461–1139* ☒ *Free; $1.75 for church museum* ☉ *Weekdays 9–noon and 2–5, Sun. service at 10.*

❼ Opened in 1999, the **Kurá Hulanda Museum** features exhibits on African
Fodor'sChoice history and is the largest of its kind in the Caribbean. Displays include
★ a full-size reconstruction of a slave ship's hold and gut-wrenching first-hand accounts of the slave-trade era. ☒ *Klipstraat 9, Otrobanda* ☎ *5999/462–1400* ⊕ *www.kurahulanda.com* ☒ *$6* ☉ *Daily 10–5.*

❻ The 40-odd chronological exhibits at the **Maritime Museum** truly give you a sense of Curaçao's maritime history, using ship models, maps, nautical charts, navigational equipment, and audiovisual displays. The third floor hosts temporary exhibits, and the museum also offers a two-hour guided tour on its "water bus" through Curaçao's harbor—a route familiar to traders, smugglers, and pirates. When you're ready for a break, drop anchor at the Harbor Café or browse through the souvenir shop. ⊠ *Van der Brandhofstraat 7, Scharloo* ☎ *5999/465–2327* ⊕ *www. curacaomaritime.com* ☜ *Museum $6; museum and harbor tour $12* ⊘ *Tues.–Sat. 10–4.*

★ ❷ The **Mikveh Israel-Emanuel Synagogue** was founded in 1651 and is the oldest temple still in use in the Western Hemisphere. It draws 20,000 visitors a year. Enter through the gates around the corner on Hanchi Di Snoa. The Jewish Cultural Museum in the back displays antiques and fine Judaica. ⊠ *Hanchi Snoa 29, Punda* ☎ *5999/461–1067* ⊕ *www.snoa.com* ☜ *$5; donations also accepted* ⊘ *Weekdays 9–4:30.*

❸ The **Queen Emma Bridge** is affectionately called the Swinging Old Lady by the locals, and connects the two sides of Willemstad—Punda and Otrobanda—across the Santa Anna Bay. The bridge swings open at least 30 times a day to allow passage of ships to and from sea. The original bridge, built in 1888, was the brainchild of the American consul Leonard Burlington Smith, who made a mint off the tolls he charged for using it: 2¢ per person for those wearing shoes, free to those crossing barefoot. Today it's free to everyone.

❺ The **Wilhelmina Drawbridge** connects Punda with the once-flourishing district of **Scharloo,** where the early Jewish merchants built stately homes. The end of the district closest to Kleine Werf is now a run-down red-light district, but the rest of the area is well worth a visit. The architecture along Scharlooweg (much of it from the 17th century) is intriguing, and many of the structures that had become dilapidated have been meticulously renovated.

⓫ **Christoffel Park** is a good hour from Willemstad but worth a visit. This 4,450-acre garden and wildlife preserve with Mt. Christoffel at its center consists of three former plantations. As you drive through the park, watch for deer, goats, and smaller wildlife that might suddenly dart in front of your car. If you skip everything else on the island, it's possible to drive to the park and climb 1,239-foot Mt. Christoffel, which takes two to three strenuous hours. On a clear day you can then see the mountain ranges of Venezuela, Bonaire, and Aruba. ⊠ *Savonet* ☎ *5999/864–0363 for information and tour reservations, 5999/462–6262 for jeep tours, 5999/864–0535 for horseback tours* ☜ *$10* ⊘ *Mon.–Sat. 8–4, Sun. 6–3; last admission 1 hr before closing.*

❿ Drop in at the **Curaçao Aloe Plantation & Factory** for a fascinating tour that takes you through the various stages of production of the aloe vera plant, renowned for its healing powers. You'll get a look at everything from the aloe fields to the final products. At the gift shop, you can buy CurAloe products including homemade goodies like aloe wine, soap, pure aloe gel, and pure aloe juice, as well as sunscreen and other skin care products made off-site. The plantation is right on the way to the Ostrich Farm, which is run by the same owner. Tours begin every hour. ⊠ *Weg Naar Groot St. Joris z/n, Groot St. Joris* ☎ *5999/767–5577* ⊕ *www. aloecuracao.com* ☜ *$4* ⊘ *Mon.–Sat. 9–4; last tour at 3.*

9 At the **Curaçao Sea Aquarium** more than 400 varieties of exotic fish and vegetation are displayed. Outside is a 1,623-foot-long artificial beach of white sand, well suited to novice swimmers and children. There's also a platform overlooking the wreck of the steamship SS *Oranje Nassau* and an underwater observatory where you can watch divers and snorkelers swimming with stingrays and feeding sharks.

At the **Dolphin Academy** (☎ 5999/465–8900 ⊕ www.dolphin-academy. com), you can watch a fanciful dolphin show (included in the price of Sea Aquarium admission). For more up-close interaction, you may choose from several special programs (extra charges apply and reservations are essential) to encounter the dolphins in shallow water, or to swim, snorkel, or dive with them. ⊠ *Bapor Kibra z/n, Sea Aquarium Beach* ☎ *5999/ 461–6666* ⊕ *www.curacao-sea-aquarium.com* 🎫 *$15; animal encounters $54 for divers, $34 for snorkelers; sea lion programs $39–$149; Dolphin Academy $69–$300* ⊙ *Sea aquarium daily 8:30–5:30; Dolphin Academy daily 8:30–4:30.*

8 Hour-long guided tours of the **Hato Caves** wind down into various chambers to the water pools, a "voodoo" chamber, a wishing well, fruit bats' sleeping quarters, and Curaçao Falls, guarded by a limestone "dragon." Hidden lights illuminate the limestone formations and gravel walkways. This is one of the better Caribbean caves open to the public, but keep in mind that there are 49 steep steps to reach the entrance, and the cave itself is dank and hot (though they've put electric fans in some areas to provide relief). To reach the caves, head northwest toward the airport, take a right onto Gosieweg, follow the loop right onto Schottegatweg, take another right onto Jan Norduynweg, a final right onto Rooseveltweg, and follow signs. ⊠ *Rooseveltweg z/n, Hato* ☎ *5999/868–0379* 🎫 *$7* ⊙ *Daily 10–5.*

Shopping

Curaçao has some of the best shops in the Caribbean, but in many cases the prices are no lower than in U.S. discount stores. Hours are usually Monday through Saturday, from 8 to noon and 2 to 6. Most shops are within the six-block area of Willemstad described above. The main shopping streets are Heerenstraat, Breedestraat, and Madurostraat. **Bamali** (⊠ Breedestraat, Punda, Willemstad ☎ 5999/461–2258) sells funky, fabulous women's apparel, including Indonesian batik clothing; charming jewelry made of beads, shells, gemstones, and silver; handbags of leather and other fabrics; and lots of other unique accessories. Custom-made clothing is available here, too. **Boolchand's** (⊠ Heerenstraat 4B, Punda, Willemstad ☎ 5999/461–6233) sells electronics, jewelry, Swarovski crystal, Swiss watches, and cameras behind a facade of red-and-white checkered tiles. A sweet aroma permeates **Cigar Emporium** (⊠ Gomezplein, Punda, Willemstad ☎5999/465–3955), where you can find the largest selection of Cuban cigars on the island, including H. Upmann,

> ### SUNGLASSES
>
> When selecting sunglasses, the most important considerations are the amount of UV light that is blocked by the lenses and a proper fit. The lenses should shield your eyes from most angles. Darker lenses do not necessarily offer better UV protection. Look for sunglasses that block 99% of harmful UV rays.

Romeo & Julieta, and Montecristo. Visit the climate-controlled cedar cigar room. However, remember that Cuban cigars cannot be taken back to the United States legally. **Julius L. Penha & Sons** (⊠ Heerenstraat 1, Punda, Willemstad ☎ 5999/461–2266), near the Pontoon Bridge, sells French perfumes and cosmetics, clothing, and accessories, in a baroque-style building dating from 1708. **New Amsterdam** (⊠ Gomezplein 14, Punda, Willemstad ☎ 5999/461–2437 ⊠ Breedestraat 29, Punda, Willemstad ☎ 5999/461–3239) is the place to price hand-embroidered tablecloths, napkins, and pillowcases, as well as blue delft.

Sports & Activities

BIKING So you wanna bike Curaçao? **Wanna Bike Curaçao** (☎ 5999/527–3720 ⊕ www.wannabike.net) has the fix: kick into gear and head out for a guided mountain-bike tour through the Caracas Bay peninsula and the salt ponds at the Jan Thiel Lagoon. Although you should be fit to take on the challenge, mountain-bike experience is not required. A two-hour tour runs about $29 and covers the bike, helmet, water, refreshments, park entrance fee, and the guide, but don't forget to bring a camera.

DIVING & The **Curaçao Underwater Marine Park** is about 12½ mi (21 km) of untouched
SNORKELING coral reef that has national park status. Mooring buoys mark the most
★ ☽ interesting dive sites. **Ocean Encounters** (⊠ Lions Dive & Beach Resort, Bapor Kibra z/n, Sea Aquarium Beach ☎ 5999/461–8131 ⊕ www.oceanencounters.com) is the largest dive operator on the island and also
★ operates Toucan Diving at Kontiki Beach, which caters to walk-ins. **Sunset Divers** (⊠ Sunset Waters Beach Resort, Santa Marta Bay ☎ 5999/864–1708 ⊕ www.sunsetdiver.com), the closest full-service PADI operation to the famous Mushroom Forest, offers daily one- and two-tank dives, 24-hour shore diving, and custom dives. The friendly, expert staff takes you to dive sites along the west-side reef system, which has gently sloping walls with lots of coral growth, soft and hard. Lesser known but no less spectacular sites the company often visits include Harry's Hole and Boca Hulu.

Beaches

Curaçao doesn't have long, powdery stretches of sand. Instead you'll discover the joy of inlets: tiny bays marked by craggy cliffs, exotic trees, and scads of interesting pebbles, and coral that has washed up on the beaches. **Cas Abou** is a white-sand gem with the brightest blue water in Curaçao. Divers and snorkelers will appreciate the on-site dive shop, and sunbathers can make use of the small snack bar. The restrooms and showers are immaculate. Entry is $3. You'll pay a fee ($3 per person) to enter **Sea Aquarium Beach**, but the amenities (restrooms, showers, boutiques, watersports center, snack bar, restaurants with beach bars, thatched shelters and palm trees for shade, security patrols) on this 1,600-foot (490-m) man-made sandy beach and the calm waters protected by a carefully placed breakwater are well worth it. Two protected coves offer crystal-clear, turquoise water at **Playa Knip**, an expanse of alluring white sand, perfect for swimming and snorkeling. You can rent beach chairs and hang out under the palapas, or cool off with ice cream at the snack bar. There are rest rooms here, but no showers. Best of all, there's no fee, but that means it's popular with locals and particularly crowded on Sunday.

Where to Eat

Restaurants usually add a 10% to 15% service charge.

🕊 **$–$$** ✕ **Mambo Beach.** Spread over the sand, this open-air bar and grill serves hearty sandwiches and burgers for lunch. Steaks, fresh seafood, and pasta fill the dinner menu. There's an excellent fish buffet on Friday. ⊠ *Bapor Kibra z/n, Sea Aquarium Beach* ☎ *5999/461–8999* ▤ *MC, V.*

¢–$$ ✕ **Time Out Café.** In the shopping heartland of Punda, this outdoor spot serves up light bites like tuna sandwiches and grilled cheese, as well as heartier fare, including chicken shwarma. From Breedestraat facing Little Switzerland, take the alley to the left of the store (Kaya A. M. Prince) and walk about 20 yards, or look for the sign in Gomezplein Square and follow the arrow. ⊠ *Keukenplein 8, Punda, Willemstad* ☎ *5999/524–5071* ▤ *No credit cards* ⊘ *Closed Sun.*

DOMINICA (ROSEAU)

Roberta
Sotonoff

In the center of the Caribbean archipelago, wedged between the two French islands of Guadeloupe, to the north, and Martinique, to the south, Dominica is a wild place. So unyielding is the terrain that colonists surrendered efforts at colonization, and the last survivors of the Caribbean's original people, the Carib Indians, have made her rugged northeast their home. Dominica—just 29 mi (47 km) long and 16 mi (26 km) wide—is an English-speaking island, though family and place names are a mélange of French, English, and Carib. The capital is Roseau (pronounced rose-oh). If you've had enough of casinos, crowds, and swim-up bars and want to take leave of everyday life—to hike, bike, trek, spot birds and butterflies in the rain forest; explore waterfalls; discover a boiling lake; kayak, dive, snorkel, or sail in marine reserves; or go out in search of the many resident whale and dolphin species—this is the place to do it.

7

Essentials

CURRENCY Eastern Caribbean dollar (EC$2.70 to the US$1). U.S. currency is readily accepted, but you will get change in E.C. dollars. Most major credit cards are accepted, as are traveler's checks.

HOURS Banks are open Monday through Thursday from 8 to 2, until 5 on Friday. Most stores are open Monday from 8 to 5, until 4 Tuesday through Friday, and until 1 on Saturday. Some stores have longer hours, especially if a cruise ship is in port on a Saturday.

INTERNET You'll find two cyber cafés in Roseau. **Cornerhouse Café** (⊠ Old and King George V Sts., Roseau ☎ 767/449–9000) **Cyber Land Internet Café** (⊠ George St., Roseau ⊠ Woodstone Shopping Mall, Roseau).

DOMINICA BEST BETS
■ **Rain Forest Trips.** Dominica has some of the Caribbean's best undeveloped rain forest. Hiking is the best way, but try to get out and see the scenery, even if you only view it from the comfort of a car.
■ **Snorkeling in Champagne.** You can snorkel near a bubbling volcanic vent near the island's southern tip that puffs steam into the sea, which makes you feel as if you are swimming in warm champagne.
■ **Whale-Watching.** If you're there in season, the island has the best whale-watching in the Caribbean.

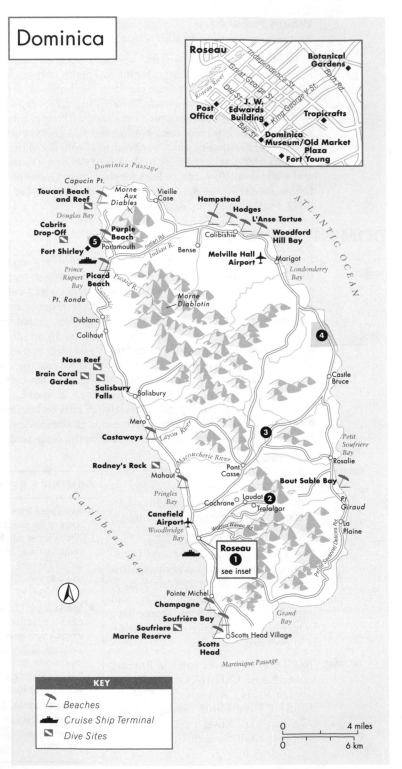

Dominica

Roseau

Botanical
Gardens

Post
Office

J. W.
Edwards
Building

Tropicrafts

Dominica
Museum/Old Market
Plaza

Fort Young

Dominica Passage

Capucin Pt.

Toucari Beach
and Reef

Morne
Aux
Diables

Vieille
Case

Hampstead

Hodges

L'Anse Tortue

Douglas Bay

Cabrits
Drop-Off

Purple
Beach

Portsmouth

Calibishie

Woodford
Hill Bay

Fort Shirley

Bense

Melville Hall
Airport

Marigot

Indian R.

Indian Rd.

ATLANTIC OCEAN

*Prince
Rupert
Bay*

Picard
Beach

Picard R.

*Londonderry
Bay*

Pt. Ronde

*Morne
Diablotin*

Dublanc

Colihaut

Castle
Bruce

Nose Reef

Brain Coral
Garden

Salisbury
Falls

Salisbury

Mero

Layou River

*Petit
Soufriere
Bay*

Rosalie

Castaways

Macoucherie River

Rodney's Rock

Mahaut

Pont
Casse

Bout Sable Bay

Pt.
Giraud

*Pringles
Bay*

Cochrane

Laudat

Trafalgar

La
Plaine

Caribbean Sea

Canefield
Airport

*Woodbridge
Bay*

Watton Waven Rd.

Roseau
see inset

Petite Savanne Delices Rd.

Pointe Michel

Champagne

Soufrière Bay

Soufriere
Marine Reserve

Scotts
Head

Scotts Head Village

*Grand
Bay*

Martinique Passage

KEY

Beaches

Cruise Ship Terminal

Dive Sites

0   4 miles
0   6 km

TELEPHONES   The island has direct-dial international service. All pay phones are equipped for local and overseas dialing, accepting either EC coins, credit cards, or phone cards, which you can buy at many island stores and at the airports. To call Dominica from the United States, dial the area code (767) and the local access code (44), followed by the five-digit local number. On the island, dial only the seven-digit number that follows the area code.

Coming Ashore

In Roseau, most ships dock along the Bayfront. Across the street from the pier, in the Old Post Office, is a visitor information center. Taxis, minibuses, and tour operators are available at the berths. If you do decide to tour with one of them, choose one who is certified, and be explicit when discussing where you will go and how much you will pay—don't be afraid to ask questions. The drivers usually quote a fixed fare, which is regulated by the Division of Tourism and the National Taxi Association. Drivers also offer their services for tours anywhere on the island beginning at $25 to $30 an hour for up to four people; a 4- to 5-hour island tour for up to four people will cost approximately $150. You can rent a car in Roseau for about $40, not including insurance and a mandatory EC30 driving permit, but it can be difficult to find things, so you might do better on a guided tour here.

Shore Excursions

We consider these to be among the better shore excursions for Dominica. They may not be offered by all lines, and tour names may differ as well. Times and prices are approximate.

Dominica Favorites. This excursion normally hits two very popular natural sites: Emerald Pool, in Morne Trois Pitons World Heritage Site, and Trafalgar Falls. The visit to Trafalgar Falls requires a 10-minute hike. ☉ *5 hrs* ▱ *$49.*

Kayak & Snorkel. Done at the southern tip of the island, the kayaking trip hits some hard-to-reach areas and allows time for snorkeling. ☉ *3½ hrs* ▱ *$59.*

Layou River Tubing. Travel down the Layou River by inner tube, passing unspoiled vegetation and the soaring cliffs above. Many tours also visit the Emerald Pool on the way back to the ship. ☉ *4 ½ hrs* ▱ *$69.*

Whale & Dolphin Watching. Dominica is one of the best whale-watching destinations in the Caribbean, so if you are there during the season and have the opportunity to do this excursion, take it. Most tours include a stop for snorkeling. ☉ *4 hrs* ▱ *$79.*

Exploring Dominica

Most of Dominica's roads are narrow and winding, so you'll need a few hours to take in the sights. Be adventurous, whether you prefer sightseeing or hiking—you'll be amply rewarded.

Numbers in the margin correspond to points of interest on the Dominica map.

♨ ➎ **Cabrits National Park.** The Cabrits National Park's Ft. Shirley ruins are among the most significant historic sites in the Caribbean. Just north of the town of Portsmouth, this 1,300-acre park includes a marine park and herbaceous swamps, which are an important environment for several species of rare birds and plants. At the heart of the park is the Ft. Shirley military complex. Built by the British between 1770 and 1815, it once comprised 50 major structures, including storehouses that were also quarters for 700 men. With the help of the Royal Navy (which sends sailors ashore to work on the site each time a ship is in port) and local volunteers, historian Dr. Lennox Honychurch restored the fort and its surroundings, incorporating a small museum that highlights the natural and historic aspects of the park and an open canteen-style restaurant. ⊠ *Portsmouth* 🕾 *No phone* 🎫 *$2* ⊘ *Museum daily 8–4.*

★ ℭ ❹ **Carib Indian Territory.** In 1903, after centuries of conflict, the Caribbean's first settlers, the Kalinago (more popularly known as the Caribs), were granted a portion of land (approximately 3,700 acres) on the island's northeast coast, on which to establish a reservation with their own chief. Today it's known as Carib Territory, clinging to the northeasterly corner of Dominica, where a group of just over 3,000 Caribs live and try to maintain their cultural heritage. **Kalinago Barana Autê** (⊠ Crayfish River 🕾 767/445–7979 🌐 www.kalinagobaranaaute.com) is Carib Territory's place to learn about Carib customs, history, and culture. A guided, 45-minute tour explores the village, stopping along the way to learn about plants, dugout canoes, basket weaving, and *kasava* bread making. The path offers wonderful viewpoints of the Atlantic and a chance to witness Isukati Falls. Admission is $8; the site is closed on Monday from October 15–April 15 and on Wednesday and Sunday the rest of the year.

ℭ ❸ **Emerald Pool.** Quite possibly the most-visited nature attraction on the island, this emerald-green pool fed by a 50-foot waterfall is an easy trip to make. To reach this spot in the vast Morne Trois Pitons National Park, you follow a trail that starts at the side of the road near the reception center (it's an easy 20-minute walk). Along the way you can pass lookout points with views of the windward (Atlantic) coast and the forested interior. If you don't want a crowd, check whether there are cruise ships in port before going out, as this spot is popular with cruise-ship tour groups.

❷ **Morne Trois Pitons National Park.** A UNESCO World Heritage Site, this 17,000-acre swath of lush, mountainous land in the south-central interior (covering 9% of Dominica) is the island's crown jewel. Named after one of the highest (4,600 feet) mountains on the island, it contains the island's famous "boiling lake," majestic waterfalls, and cool mountain lakes. Access to the park is possible from most points of the compass, though the easiest approaches are via the small mountaintop villages of Laudat (pronounced low-*dah*) and Cochrane.

About 5 mi (8 km) out of Roseau, the Wotton Waven Road branches off toward Sulphur Springs, where you can see the belching, sputtering, and gurgling releases of volcanic hot springs. At the base of Morne Micotrin you can find two crater lakes: the first, at 2,500 feet above sea level, is **Freshwater Lake.** According to a local legend, it's haunted by a vindictive mermaid and a monstrous serpent. Farther on is **Boeri Lake,** fringed with greenery and with purple hyacinths floating on its surface. The undisputed highlight of the park is **Boiling Lake.** Reputedly the world's largest such lake, it's a cauldron of gurgling gray-blue water, 70 yards wide

Fodor'sChoice
★

and of unknown depth, with water temperatures from 180°F to 197°F. The lake is actually a flooded fumarole, a crack through which gases escape from the molten lava below. As many visitors discovered in late 2004, the "lake" can sometimes dry up, though it fills again within a few months and, shortly after that, once more starts to boil. The two- to four-hour (one way) hike up to the lake is challenging (on a very rainy day, be prepared to slip and slide the whole way up and back). You'll need attire appropriate for a strenuous hike, and a guide is a must. Most guided trips start early (no later than 8:30 AM) for this all-day, 7-mi (11-km) round-trip trek, which passes through the Valley of Desolation and offers some opportunities for swimming in cold mountain streams along the way.

Just beyond the village of Trafalgar and up a short hill, there's the reception facility, where you can purchase passes to the national park and find guides to take you on a rain-forest trek to the twin **Trafalgar Falls;** the 125-foot high waterfall is called the Father, and the wider, 95-foot high one, the Mother. If you like a little challenge, let your guide take you up the riverbed to the cool pools at the base of the falls. Guides for this hike are available at the trailheads; still, it's best to arrange a tour before even setting out.

① **Roseau.** Although it's one of the smallest capitals in the Caribbean, Roseau has the highest concentration of inhabitants of any town in the Eastern Caribbean. Caribbean vernacular architecture and a bustling marketplace transport visitors back in time. Although you can walk the entire town in about an hour, you'll get a much better feel for the place on a leisurely stroll. **Lilac House,** on Kennedy Avenue, has three types of gingerbread fretwork, latticed veranda railings, and heavy hurricane shutters. The **J. W. Edwards Building,** at the corner of Old and King George V streets, has a stone base and a wooden second-floor gallery. **The old market plaza** is the center of Roseau's historic district, which was laid out by the French on a radial plan rather than a grid, so streets such as Hanover, King George V, and Old radiate from this area. South of the marketplace is the Fort Young Hotel, built as a British fort in the 18th century; the nearby state house, public library, and Anglican cathedral are also worth a visit.

The 40-acre **Botanical Gardens,** founded in 1891 as an annex of London's Kew Gardens, is a great place to relax, stroll, or watch a cricket match. In addition to the extensive collection of tropical plants and trees, there's also a parrot aviary. At the Forestry Division office, which is also on the garden grounds, you can find numerous publications on the island's flora, fauna, and national parks. The forestry officers are particularly knowledgeable on these subjects and can also recommend good hiking guides. ⊠ *Between Bath Rd. and Valley Rd.* ☎ *767/448–2401 Ext. 3417* ☞ *$2* ☉ *Mon. 8–1 and 2–5, Tues.–Fri. 8–1 and 2–4.*

The old post office now houses the **Dominica Museum.** This labor of love by local writer and historian Dr. Lennox Honychurch contains furnishings, documents, prints, and maps that date back hundreds of years; you can also find an entire Carib hut as well as Carib canoes, baskets, and other artifacts. ⊠ *Dame M. E. Charles Blvd., opposite cruise-ship berth* ☎ *767/448–8923* ☞ *$3* ☉ *Weekdays 9–4:30 and Sat. 9–1, closed Sun. except when a cruise ship is in port.*

Shopping

Dominicans produce distinctive handicrafts, with communities specializing in materials-at-hand: *vertivert* straw rugs, screwpine tableware, *larouma* basketware, and wood carvings are just some. Also notable are local herbs, spices, condiments, and herb teas.

One of the easiest places to pick up a souvenir is the Old Market Plaza. Slaves were once sold here, but today it's the scene of happier trading: key rings, magnets, dolls, baskets, handcrafted jewelry, T-shirts, spices, souvenirs, and batiks are available from a select group of entrepreneurs in open-air booths set up on the cobblestones. **Baroon International** (⊠ Kennedy Ave., Roseau ☎ 767/449–2888) sells unusual jewelry from Asia, the United States, and other Caribbean islands; there are also pieces that are assembled in the store, as well as personal accessories, souvenirs, and special gifts. **Dominica Pottery** (⊠ Bayfront St. and Kennedy Ave., Roseau ☎ No phone) carries products made from various local clays and glazes. **Tropicrafts** (⊠ Independence St. and Turkey La., Roseau ☎ 767/448–2747) has a back room where you can watch local ladies weave grass mats. You can also find arts and crafts from around the Caribbean, local wood carvings, rum, hot sauces, perfumes, and traditional Carib baskets, hats, and woven mats.

> **BIBS**
>
> With limited and expensive laundry facilities on ships, you may not want to spend your free time cleaning up after your child. It's convenient to bring along a pack of disposable bibs for mealtimes to keep baby's clothing cleaner and stain-free, avoiding messy garments after meals and a lot of laundry time on board the ship.

Activities

ADVENTURE PARKS
The **Rainforest Aerial Tram** (⊠ Laudat ☎ 767/448–8775, 767/440–3266, 866/759–8726 in U.S. ⊕ www.rfat.com) gives you a bird's-eye view of a pristine forest aboard an open, eight-person gondola. For 90 minutes to two hours, you slowly skim the tree-top canopy while a guide provides scientific information about the flora and fauna. At the top, there is an optional walking tour, which is worth the steps. The price is $65; with transportation and lunch, $85. It's popular with cruise-ship passengers, so try to reserve ahead.

Wacky Rollers (⊠ Front St., Roseau ⌂ Box 900, Roseau ☎ 767/440–4386 ⊕ www.wackyrollers.com) will make you feel as if you are training for the Marines as you swing on a Tarzan-style rope and grab onto a vertical rope ladder, rappel across zip lines and traverse suspended log bridges, a net bridge, and four monkey bridges (rope loops). It costs $60 and should take from 1½ to 3½ hours to conquer the 28 "games." There is also an abbreviated kids' course. Wacky Rollers also organizes adventure tours around the island. Although the office is in Roseau, the park itself is in Hillsborough Estate, about 20 to 25 minutes north of Roseau.

DIVING & SNORKELING
Dominica's dive sites are awesome. The best are those in the southwest—within and around **Soufrière/Scotts Head Marine Reserve**. This bay is the site of a submerged volcanic crater. Within a ½ mi (1 km) of the shore, there are vertical drops of 800 feet (240 m) to more than 1,500 feet (450 m), with visibility frequently extending to 100 feet (30 m). Shoals of boga fish, creole wrasse, and blue cromis are common, and you might even

see a spotted moray eel or a honeycomb cowfish. Crinoids (rare elsewhere) are also abundant here, as are giant barrel sponges. The going rate is about $65–$85 for a two-tank dive. All scuba-diving operators also offer snorkeling; equipment rents for $10 to $20 a day; trips with gear begin at about $15. The **Anchorage Dive & Whale Watch Center** (⊠ Anchorage Hotel, Castle Comfort ☎ 767/448–2638 ⊕ www.anchoragehotel.dm) has two dive boats that can take you out day or night. It also offers PADI instruction (all skill levels), snorkeling and whale-watching trips, and shore diving. One of the island's first dive operations, it offers many of the same trips as Dive Dominica. **Dive Dominica** (⊠ Castle Comfort Lodge, Castle Comfort ☎767/448—2188 or 888/414-7626 ⊕www.divedominica.com), one of the island's dive pioneers, conducts NAUI, PADI, and SSI courses as well as Nitrox certification. With four boats, it offers diving, snorkeling, and whale-watching trips and packages including accommodation at the Castle Comfort Lodge. Its trips are similar to Anchorage's.

HIKING The island is crisscrossed by ancient footpaths of the Arawak and Carib Indians and the Nègres Maroons, escaped slaves who established camps in the mountains. Existing trails range from easygoing to arduous. To make the most of your excursion, you'll need sturdy hiking boots, insect repellent, a change of clothes (kept dry), and a guide. Hikes and tours run $25 to $50 per person, depending on destinations and duration. Some of the natural attractions within the island's national parks require visitors to purchase a site pass. These are sold for varying numbers of visits. A single-entry site pass costs $2, a day pass $5, and a week pass $10. Local bird and forestry expert **Bertrand Jno Baptiste** (☎ 767/446–6358) leads hikes up Morne Diablotin and along the Syndicate Nature Trail; if he's not available, ask him to recommend another guide. Hiking guides can be arranged through the **National Development Corporation** (NDC or Dominica Tourist Office) (⊠ Valley Rd., Roseau ☎ 767/448–2045 ⊕ www.dominica.dm).

Beaches

★ On the west coast, just south of the village of Pointe Michel, **Champagne,** a stony beach, is one of the island's best spots for swimming, snorkeling, and diving. It gets its name from volcanic vents that constantly puff steam into the sea, which makes you feel as if you are swimming in warm

★ champagne. **Pointe Baptiste.** Extravagantly shaped, red-sandstone boulders surround this beautiful golden-sand beach. Access is a 15-minute walk, entering through private property, so the beach is quiet and unpopulated. Come here to relax, tan, take dips in the ocean, and climb these incredible rock formations. There are no facilities, but this is one of the nicest beaches on the island. It's near the Pointe Baptiste Guest House. ⊠ *Calibishie.*

Where to Eat

There is a 5% sales tax added to all bills. Some restaurants include a 10% service charge in the final tab; otherwise tip 10% for good service.

¢ ✕ **Cornerhouse Café.** Just off the Old Market Plaza in a historic, three-story stone-and-wood town house, this is Dominica's only true Internet café. An eclectic menu of meals and other treats is on offer to sustain you during your surfing: bagels with an assortment of toppings, delicious soups, fish, sandwiches, salads, cakes, and coffee. Computers are rented by the half hour; relax on soft chairs and flip through books and magazines while you wait. ⊠ *Old and King George V Sts., Roseau* ☎ *767/449–9000* ⊕ *www. avirtualdominica.com/cornerhouse* ▤ *No credit cards* ☉ *Closed Sun.*

$–$$$$ ✕ **Guiyave.** This popular restaurant in a quaint Caribbean town house also has a shop downstairs serving a scrumptious selection of sweet and savory pastries, tarts, and cakes. These can also be ordered upstairs, along with more elaborate fare such as garlic shrimp and spicy crab backs, when in season. Choose to dine either in the airy dining room or on the sunny, narrow balcony perched above Roseau's colorful streets—the perfect spot to indulge in one of the fresh-squeezed tropical juices. ⊠ *15 Cork St., Roseau* ☎ *767/448–2930* ▤ *AE, D, MC, V* ☉ *Closed Tues. and Wed.*

FREEPORT-LUCAYA, BAHAMAS

Chelle Koster Walton

Grand Bahama Island, the fourth-largest island in the Bahamas, lies only 52 mi (84 km) off Palm Beach, Florida. In 1492, when Columbus first set foot in the Bahamas, Grand Bahama was already populated. Skulls found in caves attest to the existence of the peaceable Lucayans, who were constantly fleeing the more bellicose Caribs. But it was not until the 1950s, when the harvesting of Caribbean yellow pine trees (now protected by Bahamian environmental law) was the island's major industry, that American financier Wallace Groves envisioned Grand Bahama's grandiose future as a tax-free port for the shipment of goods to the United States. It was in that era that the city of Freeport and later Lucaya evolved. They are separated by a 4-mi (6-km) stretch of East Sunrise Highway, although few can tell you where one community ends and the other begins. Most of Grand Bahama's commercial activity is concentrated in Freeport, the Bahamas's second-largest city. Lucaya, with its sprawling shopping complex and water-sports reputation, stepped up to the role of island tourism capital. Resorts, beaches, a casino, and golf courses make both cities popular with visitors.

Essentials

CURRENCY
The Bahamian dollar, which trades one-to-one with the U.S. dollar, which is universally accepted. There's no need to acquire any Bahamian currency.

HOURS
Banks are generally open Monday–Thursday 9:30 to 3 and Friday 9:30 to 4:30. Hours for attractions vary; most open by 9 or 10 and close by 5. Most shops are open from 10 to 6.

INTERNET
Port Lucaya Marina has free Wi-Fi service if you have your own laptop.

TELEPHONES
Calling locally or internationally is easy in the Bahamas. To place a local call, dial the seven-digit phone number. To call the United States, dial 1 plus the area code. Pay phones cost 25¢ per call; Bahamian and U.S. quarters are accepted, as are BATELCO phone cards. To place a call

---

FREEPORT-LUCAYA BEST BETS

- **Diving with UNEXSO.** Simply one of the world's most respected diving facilities.

- **Lucayan National Park.** The highest peak in the Virgin Islands has breathtaking views and is a great hiking destination.

- **Shopping.** Duty-free shopping in the Port Lucaya Marketplace is still good; be sure to haggle if you shop at the straw markets.

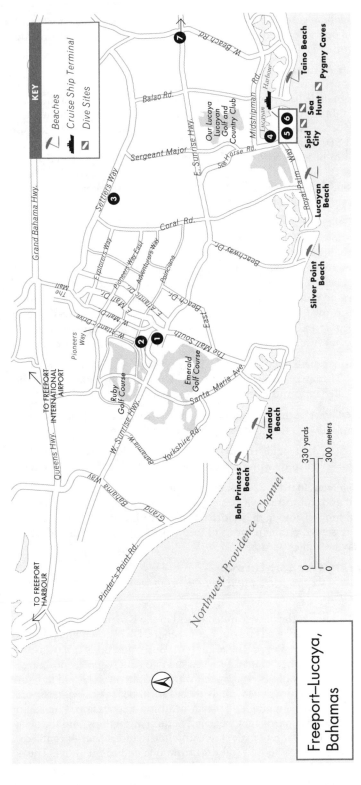

Freeport–Lucaya, Bahamas

KEY

⚓ Beaches

🚢 Cruise Ship Terminal

▨ Dive Sites

Bahamas National Trust
Rand Nature Centre **3**

The Dolphin Experience **6**

International Bazaar **1**

Lucayan National Park **7**

Perfume Factory **2**

Port Lucaya Marketplace **4**

Underwater Explorers
Society (UNEXSO) **5**

330 yards

300 meters

using a calling card, use your long-distance carrier's access code or dial 0 for the operator. Be aware that when placing a toll-free call from your hotel, you are charged as if for a regular long-distance call.

Coming Ashore

Cruise-ship passengers arrive at Lucayan Harbour, which has a clever Bahamian-style look, extensive cruise-passenger terminal facilities, and an entertainment-shopping village. The harbor lies about 10 minutes west of Freeport. Taxis and limos meet all cruise ships. Two passengers are charged $16 and $24 for trips to Freeport and Lucaya, respectively. Fare to Xanadu Beach is $17; it's $24 to Taino Beach. The price per person drops with larger groups. It's customary to tip taxi drivers 15%. A three-hour sightseeing tour of the Freeport-Lucaya area costs $25 to $35. Four-hour West End trips cost about $40.

Grand Bahama's flat terrain and straight, well-paved roads make for good scooter riding. Rentals run $35 a day (about $15 an hour). Helmets are required and provided. Look for small rental stands in parking lots and along the road in Freeport and Lucaya and at the larger resorts. It's usually cheaper to rent a car than to hire a taxi. Automobiles, jeeps, and vans can be rented at the Grand Bahama International Airport. Some agencies provide free pickup and delivery service to the cruise-ship port and Freeport and Lucaya, but prices are still not cheap; cars begin at $50 per day, but insurance of up to $17 per day is also required by law.

SHORE EXCURSIONS We consider these to be among the better shore excursions for Freeport-Lucaya. They may not be offered by all lines, and tour names may differ as well. Times and prices are approximate.

Jeep safari. Part of this trip goes off-road to explore the island's interior, but there's always time for a stop by the beach. ⊙ 5½ hrs 🎫 $89.

Kayaking Tour. A kayaking trip in Lucayan National Park is combined with a stop for lunch and swimming on a nice beach. ⊙ 6 hrs 🎫 $83–$89.

Snorkeling Tour. Board a 72-foot catamaran with a slide and rock-climbing wall and sail to Lucaya Beach, where you anchor near an offshore reef and snorkel among the colorful fish. Refreshments and (sometimes) lunch are served on the return sail to the dock; if lunch is included, the cost may be higher. ⊙ 3 hrs 🎫 $40.

Exploring Freeport-Lucaya

Numbers in the text correspond to numbers in the margin on the Freeport-Lucaya map.

Grand Bahama is the only planned island in the Bahamas. Its towns, villages, and sights are well laid out but far apart. Downtown Freeport and Lucaya are both best appreciated on foot. Buses and taxis can transport you the 4-mi (6-km) distance between the two. In Freeport, shopping is the main attraction. Bolstered by the Westin & Sheraton Grand Bahama Island resort complex, Lucaya has its beautiful beach and water-sports scene, plus more shopping and a big, beautiful new casino. Outside of town, isolated fishing villages, beaches, natural attractions, and the once-rowdy town of West End make it worthwhile to hire a tour or rent a car. The island stretches 96 mi (154 km) from one end to the other. The island is still recovering from hurricanes in 2004 and 2005.

EXPLORING FREEPORT
❸

PLASTIC BAGS

Use Ziploc bags for all toiletries and anything that might spill. Toss a few extras into your suitcase. You may need them later to pack dirty or damp clothes.

Bahamas National Trust Rand Nature Centre. On 100 acres just minutes from downtown Freeport, ½ mi (1 km) of self-guided botanical trails shows off 130 types of native plants, including many orchid species. The center is the island's birding hot spot, where you might spy a red-tailed hawk or a Cuban emerald hummingbird sipping hibiscus nectar. The center's flamingo flock was killed off by raccoons and is in the process of being replaced. The new visitors center hosts changing local art exhibits and some resident live animals such as the Bahama boa. Outside, you can visit a caged one-eyed Bahama parrot the center has adopted. The reserve is named for philanthropist James H. Rand, the former president of Remington Rand, who donated a hospital and library to the island. ⊠ *E. Settlers Way, Freeport* ☎ *242/352–5438* 🕿 *$5* ☉ *Weekdays 9–4.*

❶ **International Bazaar.** The effect of recent hurricanes on the now-closed Royal Oasis Resort & Casino results in a down-at-the-heels look for this once-vibrant shopping arena. Some restaurants and shops remain open, along with the straw market. At the entrance stands a 35-foot *torii* arch, a red-lacquered gate that is a traditional symbol of welcome in Japan. ⊠ *W. Sunrise Hwy. and Mall Dr.* ☎ *242/352–2828* 🕿 *Free* ☉ *Mon.–Sat. 10–6.*

★ ❷ **Perfume Factory.** The quiet and elegant Perfume Factory is in a replica 19th-century Bahamian mansion—the kind built by Loyalists who settled in the Bahamas after the American Revolution. The interior resembles a tasteful drawing room. This is the home of Fragrance of the Bahamas, a company that produces perfumes, colognes, and lotions using the scents of jasmine, cinnamon, gardenia, spice, and ginger. Take a free five-minute tour of the mixology laboratory. For $30 an ounce, you can blend your own perfume using any of the 35 scents ($15 for 1.5 ounces of blend-it-yourself body lotion). Sniff mixtures until they hit the right combination, then bottle, name, and take home the personalized potion. ⊠ *Behind International Bazaar, on access rd.* ☎ *242/352–9391* ⊕ *www.perfumefactory. com* 🕿 *Free* ☉ *Weekdays 9–5, Sat. 11–3.*

EXPLORING LUCAYA Lucaya, on Grand Bahama's southern coast and just east of Freeport, was developed as the island's resort center. These days, it's booming with the megaresort complex called the Westin & Sheraton Grand Bahama Island resort, a fine sandy beach, championship golf courses, a casino, a first-class dive operation, and Port Lucaya's shopping and marina facilities.

❻ **The Dolphin Experience.** Encounter Atlantic bottle-nosed dolphins in Sanctuary Bay at one of the world's first and largest dolphin facilities, about 2 mi (3 km) east of Port Lucaya. A ferry takes you from Port Lucaya to the bay to observe and photograph the animals. If you don't mind getting wet, you can sit on a partially submerged dock or stand waist deep in the water, and one of these friendly creatures will swim up and touch you. You can also engage in one of two swim-with-the-dolphins

FodorśChoice ★

programs (children must be 55-inches or taller). The Dolphin Experience began in 1987, when it trained five dolphins to interact with people. Later, the animals learned to head out to sea and swim with scuba divers on the open reef. A two-hour dive program is available. Buy tickets for The Dolphin Experience at the Underwater Explorers

> **HANGERS**
>
> Folding or inflatable travel hangers are useful if you need to dry out hand laundry or a bathing suit in your cabin. The ones in your cabin's closet may not be removable.

Society (UNEXSO) in Port Lucaya. Make reservations as early as possible. ⊠ *The Dolphin Experience, Port Lucaya* ☎ *242/373–1244 or 800/ 992–3483* 🖷 *242/373–8956* ⊕ *www.unexso.com* ✉ *2-hr interaction program $75, 2-hr swim program $169, dolphin dive $159, open-ocean experience $199* ⊘ *Daily 9–5.*

★ ❹ **Port Lucaya Marketplace.** Lucaya's capacious and lively shopping complex—a dozen low-rise, pastel-painted colonial buildings whose style was influenced by traditional island homes—is on the waterfront 4 mi (6 km) east of Freeport and across the street from a massive resort compound. The shopping center, whose walkways are lined with hibiscus, bougainvillea, and croton, has about 100 well-kept establishments, among them waterfront restaurants and bars, and shops that sell clothes, crystal and china, watches, jewelry, perfumes, and local arts and crafts. A straw market embraces the complex at both ends. ⊠ *Sea Horse Rd., Port Lucaya* ☎ *242/373–8446* ⊕ *www.portlucaya.com* ⊘ *Mon.–Sat. 10–6.*

❺ **Underwater Explorers Society (UNEXSO).** One of the world's most respected FodorśChoice diving facilities, UNEXSO welcomes more than 50,000 individuals each ★ year and trains hundreds of them in scuba diving. Their newest program, Mini-B Shallow Water Scuba Diving, uses a lightweight and compact scuba kit for three levels of short training and dive sessions. UNEXSO's facilities include an 18-foot-deep training pool with windows that look out on the harbor, changing rooms and showers, docks, equipment rental, and an air-tank filling station. ⊠ *On the wharf at Port Lucaya MarketPl.* ☎ *242/ 373–1244 or 800/992–3483* ⊕ *www.unexso.com* ✉ *Resort dives $85, dives from $35, dolphin dives $159, shark dives $89* ⊘ *Daily 8–5.*

BEYOND Grand Bahama Island narrows at picturesque West End, once Grand Ba-
FREEPORT- hama's capital and still home to descendants of the island's first settlers.
LUCAYA Seaside villages, with concrete block houses painted in bright blue and pastel yellow, fill in the landscape between Freeport and West End. The East End is Grand Bahama's "back-to-nature" side. The road east from Lucaya is long, flat, and mostly straight. It cuts through a vast pine forest to reach McLean's Town, the end of the road.

❼ **Lucayan National Park.** In this 40-acre seaside land preserve, trails and el-
FodorśChoice evated walkways wind through a natural forest of wild tamarind and
★ gumbo-limbo trees, past an observation platform, a mangrove swamp, sheltered pools containing rare marine species, and what is believed to be the largest explored underwater cave system in the world (7 mi long). You can enter the caves at two access points. One is closed during bat nursing season (June and July). Just 20 mi (32 km) east of Lucaya, the park contains examples of the island's five ecosystems: beach, sandy or

whiteland coppice (hardwood forest), mangroves, rocky coppice, and pine forest. Across the road, trails and boardwalks lead through pine forest and mangrove swamp to Gold Rock Beach, a beautiful, lightly populated strand of white sand, aquamarine sea, and coral reef. Signs along the trail detail the park's distinctive features. ⊠ *Grand Bahama Hwy.* ☎ *242/352–5438* ⊠ *$3 (tickets must be purchased in advance at Rand Nature Centre)* ⊙ *Daily 8:30–4:30.*

Shopping

In the stores, shops, and boutiques in Freeport's International Bazaar and at the Port Lucaya Marketplace, you can find duty-free goods costing up to 40% less than what you might pay back home. At the numerous perfume shops, fragrances are often sold at a sweet-smelling 25% below U.S. prices. Be sure to limit your haggling to the straw markets.

Sports & Activities

FISHING Fishing charters for up to four people cost $250 to $500 for a half-day and $350 and up for a full-day trip; many fishing outfitters charge by the person—often about $100. In deep waters, anglers pull up dolphin-fish, kingfish, or wahoo. Along the flats, the elusive bonefish is the catch of fishing aficionados. **Reef Tours Ltd.** (⊠ Port Lucaya Market Pl. ☎ 242/373–5880) offers sportfishing for four to six people on custom boats. Equipment and bait are provided free.

GOLF Because Grand Bahama is such a large island, it can afford long fairways puddled with lots of water and fraught with challenge. Two championship golf courses at the Westin & Sheraton and one 9-hole course keep duffers busy. **Fortune Hills Golf & Country Club** (⊠ E. Sunrise Hwy., Lucaya ☎ 242/373–2222) is a 3,453-yard, 9-hole, par-36 course designed by Dick Wilson and Joe Lee. **Lucayan Course** (⊠ The Westin & Sheraton Grand Bahama Island Resort, Lucaya ☎ 242/373–1066, 242/373–1333)—6,824-yards, par-72—is a dramatic 18-hole course. The course features tree-lined holes and fast, well-bunkered greens. The 18th hole has a double lake, and a new clubhouse is being built nearby. The property is home to the Jim McLean School of Golf, the school's first international location. The state-of-the-art instruction facilities include a practice putting green with bunker and chipping areas, covered teaching bays, and a teaching seminar area. **Reef Course** (⊠ Westin & Sheraton Grand Bahama Island Resort, Lucaya ☎ 242/373–2002), a 6,930-yard, par-72 course, was designed by Robert Trent Jones Jr. It has lots of water, wide fairways flanked by strategically placed bunkers, and a tricky dog-leg left on the 18th hole.

HORSEBACK **Pinetree Stables** (⊠ Beachway Dr., Freeport ☎ 242/373–3600) runs trail
RIDING and beach rides twice-daily for $75; it's closed on Monday. All two-hour trail rides are accompanied by an experienced guide. Rides for expert equestrians are also available. Reservations are essential.

Beaches

Some 60 miles of magnificent, pristine stretches of sand extend between Freeport-Lucaya and the island's eastern end. Most are used only by people who live in adjacent settlements. The beaches have no public facilities, so beachgoers often headquarter at one of the local beach bars, which often provide free transportation. **Lucayan Beach** is readily accessible from the town's main drag and is always lively and lovely. **Taíno Beach**, near

Freeport, is fun for families, water-sports enthusiasts, and partiers. Near Freeport, **Xanadu Beach** provides a mile of white sand.

Where to Eat

¢–$ ✕ **Becky's Restaurant & Lounge.** This popular eatery opens at 7 AM and may be the best place in town to fuel up before a full day of gambling or shopping. Its diner-style booths provide a comfortable backdrop for the inexpensive menu of traditional Bahamian and American food, from conch salad and curried mutton to seafood or a BLT. Pancakes, eggs, and special Bahamian breakfasts—"stew" fish, "boil" fish, or chicken souse (the latter two are both lime-seasoned soups), with johnnycake or grits—are served all day. ⊠ *E. Beach Dr. and E. Sunrise Hwy., Freeport* ☎ *242/ 352–5247* ▭ *D, MC, V.*

¢–$$ ✕ **Pub at Lucaya.** On the Port Lucaya waterfront, this amiable pub has a reputation for dependable English fare, such as bangers 'n' mash and shepherd's and steak-and-ale pies. You also can't go wrong with the frenched lamb chops, Bahamian lobster tail, or strip sirloin. Lunchtime brings burgers, pasta, and deli sandwiches. The nautical decor incorporates antiques, heavy rustic tables, and ersatz Tiffany lamps suspended from a wood-beam ceiling. Ask for a table on the outside terrace. ⊠ *Port Lucaya MarketPl.* ☎ *242/373–8450* ▭ *AE, DC, MC, V.*

GRAND CAYMAN, CAYMAN ISLANDS

Marvette Darien

The largest and most populous of the Cayman Islands, Grand Cayman is also one of the most popular cruise destinations in the Western Caribbean, largely because it doesn't suffer from the ailments afflicting many larger ports: panhandlers, hasslers, and crime. Instead, the Cayman economy is a study in stability and the environment is healthy and prosperous. Though the island is rather featureless, Grand Cayman is a diver's paradise, with pristine waters and a colorful variety of marine life. Compared with other Caribbean ports, there are few things to see on land here; instead, the island's most impressive sights are underwater. Snorkeling, diving, and glass-bottom boat and submarine rides top every ship's shore-excursion list and can also be arranged at major aquatic shops if you don't go on a ship-sponsored excursion. Grand Cayman is also famous for the 554 off-shore banks in George Town; not surprisingly, the standard of living is high, and nothing is cheap.

Essentials

CURRENCY The Cayman Island dollar (CI$1 to US$1.25). The U.S. dollar is accepted everywhere, and ATMs often dispense cash in both currencies, though you may receive change in Cayman dollars. Prices are often quoted in Cayman dollars, so make sure you know which currency you're dealing with so you don't end up paying 25% more than you expected.

GRAND CAYMAN BEST BETS

- **Diving.** If you're a diver, this is an excellent place to get underwater with several good sites close to shore.

- **Shopping.** Georgetown has a wide range of shops that are easy to get to from the cruise-ship pier.

- **Singray City.** Whether you go on a crowded ship-sponsored excursion or not, this is one of the most fun adventures the island has to offer.

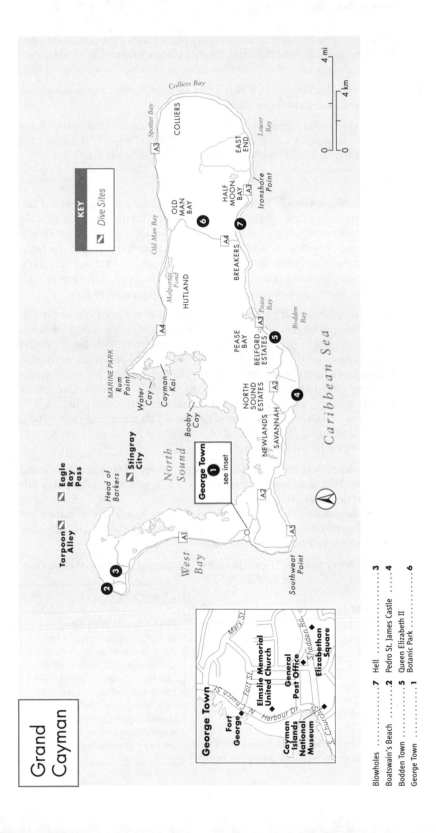

Grand Cayman

KEY

◪ Dive Sites

Colliers Bay

Spotter Bay

COLLIERS

A3

Lower Bay

EAST END

A3

Ironshore Point

HALF MOON BAY

OLD MAN BAY

6

7

Old Man Bay

A4

BREAKERS

Malportas Pond

HUTLAND

Pease Bay

A3

Bodden Bay

A4

MARINE PARK

Rum Point

Water Cay

Cayman Kai

PEASE BAY

BELFORD ESTATES

5

NORTH SOUND ESTATES

NEWLANDS

SAVANNAH

A2

4

Booby Cay

North Sound

George Town 1
see inset

A2

Caribbean Sea

Head of Barkers

◪ **Stingray City**

◪ **Eagle Ray Pass**

◪ **Tarpoon Alley**

2

3

West Bay

A1

Southwest Point

A5

4 mi

4 km

George Town

Mary St.

Fort George

Elmslie Memorial United Church

N. Church St.

Fort St.

Shedden Rd.

General Post Office

Cayman Islands National Museum

Harbour Dr.

Elizabethan Square

S. Church St.

Blowholes . . . . **7**   Hell **3**
Boatswain's Beach . . . . **2**   Pedro St. James Castle **4**
Bodden Town . . . . **5**   Queen Elizabeth II **5**
George Town . . . . **1**   Botanic Park **6**

HOURS Banks are open Monday through Friday from 9 to 4. Post offices are open weekdays from 8:30 to 3:30 and Saturday from 9:00 to 12:30. Shops are open weekdays from 9 to 5 and Saturday in George Town from 10 to 2.

INTERNET **Caybiz** (✉ The Village, 7 Dr. Roy's Dr., George Town) is an Internet café within walking distance of the cruise-ship pier.

TELEPHONES To dial the United States, dial 1 followed by the area code and telephone number. To place a credit-card call, dial 1–800/744–7777; credit-card and calling-card calls can be made from any public phone.

Coming Ashore

Ships anchor in George Town Harbour and tender passengers onto Harbour Drive, the center of the shopping district. If you just want to walk around town and shop or visit Seven Mile Beach, you're probably better off on your own, but the Stingray Sandbar snorkeling trip is a highlight of many Caribbean vacations and fills up quickly on cruise-ship days, so it's often better to order that excursion from your ship even though it will be more crowded than if you took an independent trip.

A tourist information booth is on the pier, as is the taxis queue for disembarking passengers. Taxi fares are determined by an elaborate structure set by the government, and although rates may seem high, cabbies rarely try to rip off tourists. Ask to see the chart if you want to check a quoted fare. Taxi drivers won't usually do hourly rates for small-group tours; you must arrange a sightseeing tour with a company. Car rentals are not terribly expensive, beginning at about $50 a day (plus a $7.50 driving permit), so they are a good option if you want to do some independent exploring. You can easily see the entire island and have time to stop at a beach in a single day.

SHORE EXCURSIONS We consider these to be among the better shore excursions for Grand Cayman. They may not be offered by all lines, and tour names may differ as well. Times and prices are approximate.

Atlantis Submarine. Your real submarine dives beneath the waters off Grand Cayman to reveal marine life and an underwater vista usually only visible to scuba divers. ⊙ *2 hrs* ▨ *$94.*

Reef and Wreck Snorkel. Trips will show you several good snorkeling sites, including the wreck of the *Cali.* ⊙ *2 hrs* ▨ *$44.*

Seaworld Explorer **Cruise.** A semi-submersible boat with seating five feet below the water's surface takes you on an air-conditioned, narrated voyage around George Town Harbour to view sunken ships, tropical fish, and coral reefs. Some ships offer a longer (and more expensive) tour that involves snorkeling. ⊙ *1 hr* ▨ *$37.*

Stingray City Snorkel Tour. A boat brings you offshore to a shallow sandbar inside

STROLLERS

Parents should bring along an umbrella stroller for walks around the ship as well as the ports of call; people often underestimate how big ships are. It also comes in handy at the airport. Wheel baby right to the departure gate–the stroller is gate checked and will be waiting for you when you arrive at your port of embarkation.

the North Sound reef where guides feed the waiting stingrays as you swim and play with the gentle creatures; you follow-up with a snorkeling stop. This is by far the most popular water excursion for non-divers, and while the area is overrun for most of these cruise-ship visits, it's still a thrilling experience. ☉ *3 hrs* ✉ *$45; an additional land tour increases price to $69.*

Exploring Grand Cayman

Numbers in the margin correspond to points of interest on the Grand Cayman map.

❼ Blowholes. When the trade winds blow hard, crashing waves force water into caverns and send geysers shooting up through the ironshore. The blowholes were partially filled during Hurricane Ivan in 2004, so the water has to be pretty rough before they are as dramatic as they once were. ✉ *Frank Sound Rd., near East End.*

❷ Boatswain's Beach. What was Cayman's premier attraction, the Turtle Farm, has been transformed into a marine theme park and rebranded as Boatswain's Beach. The expanded complex now has several shops for souvenirs, jewelry, and cigars as well as restaurants, a nature trail, butterfly garden, and small zoo. A snorkel lagoon provides the adventure of swimming with some of the marine life that are found just offshore the Cayman coastline. Unfortunately, the particularly steep new admission price may give you some serious second thoughts. ✉ *West Bay Rd., West Bay* ☎ *345/949–3893* ⊕ *www.boatswainsbeach.ky* ✉ *$60* ☉ *Daily 8–4:30.*

❺ Bodden Town. In the island's original south-shore capital you can find an old cemetery on the shore side of the road. Graves with A-frame structures are said to contain the remains of pirates. There are also the ruins of a fort and a wall erected by slaves in the 19th century. A curio shop serves as the entrance to what's called the Pirate's Caves, partially underground natural formations that are more hokey (decked out with fake treasure chests and mannequins in pirate garb) than spooky.

❶ George Town. Begin exploring the capital by strolling along the waterfront, Harbour Drive to **Elmslie Memorial United Church,** named after the first Presbyterian missionary to serve in the Caymans. Its vaulted ceiling, wooden arches, and sedate nave reflect the religious nature of island residents. In front of the court building, in the center of town, names of influential Caymanians are inscribed on the **Wall of History,** which commemorates the islands' quincentennial in 2003. Across the street is the Cayman Islands Legislative Assembly Building, next door to the 1919 Peace Memorial Building. In the middle of the financial district is the **General Post Office,** built in 1939. Let the kids pet the big blue iguana statues.

Built in 1833, the home of the **Cayman Islands National Museum** has had several different incarnations over the years, including that of courthouse, jail (now the gift shop), post office, and dance hall. It's small but fascinating, with excellent displays and videos that illustrate local geology, flora and fauna, and island history. At this writing, the museum was expected to reopen sometime in 2007. ✉ *Harbour Dr., George Town* ☎ *345/949–8368* ✉ *$5* ☉ *Weekdays 9–5, Sat. 10–2.*

❸ **Hell.** The touristy stopover in West Bay is little more than a patch of incredibly jagged black rock formations. The attractions are the small post office and a gift shop, where you can get cards and letters postmarked from Hell.

🐾 ❹ **Pedro St. James Castle.** Built in 1780, the great house is Cayman's oldest stone structure and the only remaining late-18th-century residence on the island. The buildings are surrounded by 8 acres of natural parks and woodlands. You can stroll through landscaping of native Caymanian flora and experience one of the most spectacular views on the island from atop the dramatic Great Pedro Bluff. Don't miss the impressive multimedia theater show complete with smoking pots, misting rains, and two film screens where the story of Pedro's Castle is presented. The show plays on the hour; see it before you tour the site. ⊠ *Savannah* ☎ *345/947–3329* 🖃 *$8* ☉ *Daily 8:30–5.*

❻ **Queen Elizabeth II Botanic Park.** This 65-acre wilderness preserve showcases a wide range of indigenous and nonindigenous tropical vegetation. Rare blue iguanas are bred and released in the gardens and seen regularly. If you're lucky, you'll see the brilliant green Cayman parrot—not just here but virtually anywhere in Cayman. ⊠ *Frank Sound Rd., Frank Sound* ☎ *345/947–9462, 345/947–3558 info line* 🖃 *$3* ☉ *Daily 9–6:30; last admission at 5:30.*

Shopping

The **Anchorage Centre** across from the cruise-ship North Terminal has 10 of the most affordable stores and boutiques selling duty-free goods from such great brand names as John Hardy, Movado, and Concord, as well as designer ammolite jewelry. Downtown is the **Kirk Freeport Plaza**, known for its boutiques selling fine watches, duty-free china, Gucci goods, perfumes, and cosmetics. Just keep walking—there's plenty of shopping in all directions. Stores in the **Landmark** sell perfumes, treasure coins, and upscale beachwear; Breezes by the Bay restaurant is upstairs.

★ The **Camera Store** (⊠ Waterfront Centre, N. Church St., George Town ☎ 345/949–4551) has friendly and knowledgeable service, lots of duty-free digital cameras, accessories, and fast photo printing from self-serv-
★ ice kiosks. **Cathy Church's Underwater Photo Centre & Gallery** (⊠ S. Church St., George Town ☎ 345/949–7415) has a collection of Cathy's spectacular color and limited-edition black-and-white underwater photos. Framed prints are shipped to the United States at no extra charge. Have her autograph her latest coffee-table book. One of many local artists,
★ Horacio Esteban, from Cayman Brac, sculpts Caymanite at **Esteban Gallery** (⊠ AALL Trust Bank Bldg., ground floor, Waterfront, George Town ☎ 345/946–2787). His work is beautiful, uniquely Cayman, and worth a look. The **Heritage Crafts Shop** (⊠ Harbour Dr., George Town ☎ 345/
★ 945–6041), near the harbor, sells local crafts and gifts. **Pure Art** (⊠ S. Church St., George Town ☎ 345/949–9133) sells watercolors, wood carvings, lacework, and much more by local artists. It is about 1½ mi (2½ km) south of George Town. This is a great place to browse even if you aren't planning a purchase.

Activities

DIVING &
SNORKELING

Pristine water (visibility often exceeding 100 feet [30 m]), breathtaking coral formations, and plentiful and exotic marine life mark the **Great Wall**— a world-renowned dive site just off the north side of Grand Cayman. A must-see for adventurous souls is **Stingray City** in the North Sound, noted as the best 12-foot (3½-m) dive in the world, where dozens of stingrays congregate, tame enough to suction squid from your outstretched palm. Nondivers gravitate to **Stingray Sandbar**, a shallower part of the North Sound, which has become a popular snorkeling spot; it is also a popular spot for the stingrays. **Don Foster's Dive Cayman Islands** (⊠ 218 S. Church St., George Town ☎ 345/949–5679 or 800/833–4837 ⊕ www.donfosters. com) has a pool with a shower and also snorkeling along the ironshore. The shore diving includes a few interesting swim-throughs, or you can book a boat dive. **Eden Rock Diving Center** (⊠ 124 S. Church St., George Town ☎ 345/949–7243 ⊕ www.edenrockdive.com), south of George Town, provides easy access to Eden Rock and Devil's Grotto. It has full equipment rental, lockers, and shower facilities. **Red Sail Sports** (☎ 345/ 949–8745 or 877/733–7245 ⊕ www.redsailcayman.com) offers daily trips from most of the major hotels. Dives are often run as guided tours, a perfect option for beginners. If you're experienced and if your air lasts a long time, discuss this with the boat captain to see if he requires that you come up with the group as determined by the first person who runs low on air. There is a full range of kids' dive options for ages 5 to 15. The company also operates dinner and sunset sails.

FISHING

Cayman waters are abundant with blue and white marlin, yellowfin tuna, sailfish, dolphinfish, bonefish, and wahoo. Two dozen boats are available for charter. **Sea Star Charters** (☎ 345/949–1016, 345/916–5234 after 8 AM) is run by Clinton Ebanks, a fine and very friendly Caymanian, who will do whatever it takes to make sure that you have a wonderful time on his small, 28-foot cabin cruiser, enjoying light-tackle, bone-, and bottom-fishing. He's a good choice for beginners and offers a nice cultural experience, as well as sailing charters. Only cash and traveler's checks are accepted.

HIKING

The National Trust's **Mastic Trail** (⊠ Frank Sound Rd., entrance by fire station at botanic park, Breakers ☎ 345/949–0121 for guide reservations) is a rugged 2-mi (3-km) slash through woodlands, mangrove swamps, and ancient rock formations. In the 1800s this woodland trail was used as a direct path to and from the North Side. A comfortable walk depends on weather, winter being better because it is drier. Call the National Trust to determine suitability and to book a guide for $45; tours are run daily from 9 to 5 by appointment only. Or walk on your own with a $5 guidebook. The trip takes about three hours.

Beaches

The west coast, the island's most developed area, is where you'll find the famous **Seven Mile Beach.** This white, powdery, 5½-mi-long (9-km-long) strand is Grand Cayman's busiest vacation center, and most of the island's resorts, restaurants, and shopping centers are along this strip. At the public beach toward the north end you can find chairs for rent ($10 for the day, including a beverage) and plenty of water toys, two beach bars, restrooms, and showers.

Where to Eat

Many restaurants add a 10% to 15% service charge. If a service charge is not added, tip 15% of the total bill.

$–$$$ ✕ **Breezes by the Bay.** This cheerful restaurant overlooks the busy George Town harbor from across Harbor Drive, so go to the second floor to avoid traffic noise. Prices are a bargain, especially for peel-and-eat shrimp. The desserts are huge. The bar mixes great specialty drinks. Inside is no-smoking. ⊠ *Harbor Dr., George Town* ☎ *345/943–8469* ▤ *AE, MC, V.*

★ **¢–$$** ✕ **Full of Beans Cafe.** If you want freshly squeezed juices, homegrown herbs, lots of vegetarian options, low prices, and three meals a day, seek out this strip-mall café. You can get takeout, delivery, and even catering if you're planning a party. A surprisingly large, eclectic menu includes everything from fresh banana bread and mango smoothies to cranberry-Brie salad, a Thai chicken wrap, and steak au poivre, not to mention choice salads. Plus you get to feast your eyes on the interesting collection of art, some from local artists, that adorns the walls. ⊠ *Pasadora Place, Smith Rd., George Town* ☎ *345/943–2326* ▤ *No credit cards* ☉ *Closed Sun.*

GRAND TURK, TURKS & CAICOS ISLANDS

Ramona Settle Just 7 mi (11 km) long and a little over 1 mi (2½ km) wide, Grand Turk, the political capital of the Turks & Caicos Islands, has been a longtime favorite destination for divers eager to explore the 7,000-foot-deep pristine coral walls that drop down only 300 yards out to sea. On shore, the tiny, quiet island is home to white-sand beaches, the National Museum, and a small population of wild horses and donkeys, which leisurely meander past the white-walled courtyards, pretty churches, and bougainvillea-covered colonial inns on their daily commute into town. The main settlement on the island is tranquil Cockburn Town, and that's where most of the small hotels, not to mention Pillory Beach, can be found. Although it has the second-largest number of inhabitants of all the Turks & Caicos Island, Grand Turk's permanent population has still not reached 4,000. Grand Turk is new to the cruise-ship scene, welcoming its first ships in 2006, but estimates place the number of likely cruise-ship visitors at 300,000 in relatively short order.

Essentials

CURRENCY The U.S. dollar. You'll find branches of Scotiabank and FirstCaribbean on Grand Turk, with ATMs; all of these are in tiny Cockburn Town.

HOURS Banks are open Monday through Thursday from 9 to 3, Friday 9 to 5. Post offices are open weekdays from 8 to 4. Shops are generally open weekdays from 8 or 8:30 to 5.

GRAND TURK BEST BETS

■ **Beaches.** Powdery soft sand is prevalent on the island's beaches, and you'll have a wide variety.

■ **Diving.** If you're certified, there are several world-class dive sights within reach.

■ **Gibb's Cay.** If you're not a diver, this might be the best offshore day-trip; tours include a picnic on the beach and swimming with stingrays, but you'll have to take a ship-sponsored trip.

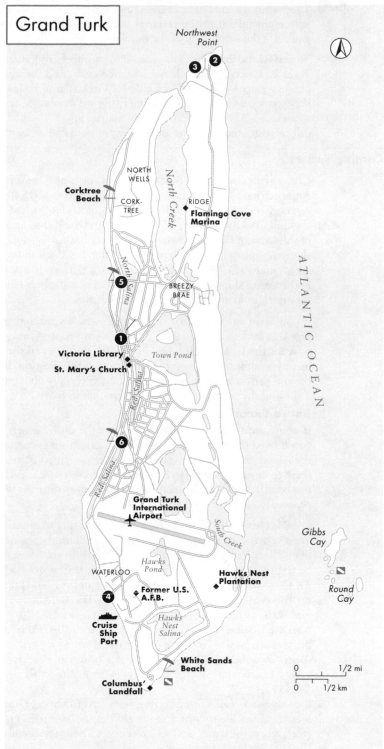

Grand Turk

Northwest Point

3 **2**

NORTH WELLS

North Creek

Corktree Beach

CORK-TREE

RIDGE

Flamingo Cove Marina

North Salina

5

BREEZY BRAE

1

Town Pond

Victoria Library

St. Mary's Church

Red Salina

6

Red Salina

Grand Turk International Airport

South Creek

Gibbs Cay

Hawks Pond

WATERLOO

Hawks Nest Plantation

Round Cay

4

Former U.S. A.F.B.

Hawks Nest Salina

Cruise Ship Port

White Sands Beach

Columbus' Landfall

ATLANTIC OCEAN

0   1/2 mi
0   1/2 km

INTERNET There's no Internet café at the cruise center, but if you have a laptop, you might take it to the restaurant at the Osprey Beach Hotel, where you can take advantage of the hotel's free Wi-Fi.

TELEPHONES To make local calls, dial the seven-digit number. To make calls from the Turks & Caicos, dial 0, then 1, the area code, and the number. All telephone service is provided by Cable & Wireless, and your U.S. cell phone may work on Grand Turk. Calling cards are available, or you can make a call using AT&T's USADirect by dialing 800/872–2881 to charge the call to your credit card or an AT&T pre-paid calling card.

Coming Ashore

Cruise ships dock at the southern end of the island, near the former U.S. Air Force base south of the airport. The purpose-built, $40-million cruise center, which opened in February 2006, is about 3 mi (5 km) from the tranquil Cockburn Town, Pillory beach, and the Ridge, and far from most of the western shore dive-sites. The center has many facilities, including shopping, a large, free-form pool, car-rental booths, and even a dock from which many sea-bound excursions depart. Governor's Beach is adjacent to the cruise-ship complex and one of the island's best beaches, but others are right in and around Cockburn Town.

If you want to come into Cockburn Town, it's reachable by taxi. You can also rent a car. However, all cruise-ship passengers can purchase a pass for the Guana "Hop On, Hop Off" Bus Tour of the island, which includes admission to several attractions, including the lighthouse and the old prison in Cockburn Town. This is usually cheaper than renting a car and drops you near the good beaches in town.

Shore Excursions

If you want to do more than just enjoy the cruise center or the beach, you'll need to sign up for one of the many shore excursions offered on the island, most geared exclusively for cruise-ship visitors. We consider these to be among the better shore excursions for Grand Turk. They may not be offered by all lines, and tour names may differ as well. Times and prices are approximate.

Certified Diving. Grand Turk lies in close proximity to amazing reefs; if you are a certified diver, that's the activity you should consider. Most cruise lines also offer programs for non-certified divers (these programs will be slightly more expensive and not as long). ☉ *4 hrs* ▱ *$109.*
4 X 4 Excursion. A multi-passenger 4x4 tour of the island takes you to some off-the-beaten-track places in the north. The tour includes a short stop and walk-around in Cockburn Town. ☉ *2 hrs* ▱ *$90.*
Dune Buggy Safari. This excursion is good for thrill-seekers, and these dune buggies are inspired by those used in the Peruvian desert. ☉ *2 hrs* ▱ *$99.*
Gibbs Cay with Stingrays. Gibbs Cay is a beautiful deserted island with a lovely beach and playful stingrays who are used to people. ☉ *2 hrs* ▱ *$59.*
Ultimate Snorkeling. With amazing reefs just offshore, Grand Turk has a wealth of sea life to visit and see close up. These trips go to Horseshoe Reef, where the water is 6 to 12 feet deep. There's a second stop at Round Cay. ☉ *2½ hrs* ▱ *$49.*

Exploring Grand Turk

Numbers in the margin correspond to points of interest on the Grand Turk map.

WATER
Tap water on your ship is perfectly safe to drink; purchasing bottled water is only necessary if you prefer the taste.

Pristine beaches with vistas of turquoise waters, small local settlements, historic ruins, and native flora and fauna are among the sights on Grand Turk. Fewer than 5,000 people live on this 7½-square-mi (19-square-km) island, and it's hard to get lost, as there aren't many roads.

1 **Cockburn Town.** The buildings in the colony's capital and seat of government reflect a 19th-century Bermudian style. Narrow streets are lined with low stone walls and old street lamps, which are now powered by electricity. The once-vital salinas have been restored, and covered benches along the sluices offer shady spots for observing wading birds, including flamingos that frequent the shallows. Be sure to pick up a copy of the Tourist Board's Heritage Walk guide to discover Grand Turk's rich architecture.

In one of the oldest stone buildings on the islands, the **Turks & Caicos National Museum** houses the Molasses Reef wreck, the earliest shipwreck—dating to the early 1500s—discovered in the Americas. The natural-history exhibits include artifacts left by Taíno, African, North American, Bermudian, French, and Latin American settlers. The museum has a 3-D coral reef exhibit, a walk-in Lucayan cave with wooden artifacts, and a gallery dedicated to Grand Turk's little-known involvement in the Space Race (Grand Turk was John Glenn's first earthside landfall after his moon walk). An interactive children's gallery keeps knee-high visitors even more "edutained." The museum also claims that Grand Turk was Columbus's first landfall in the New World. ⊠ *Duke St., Cockburn Town* ☎ *649/946–2160* ⊕ *www.tcmuseum.org* ☞ *$5* ☉ *Mon., Tues., Thurs., and Fri. 9–4, Wed. 9–5, Sat. 9–1.*

2 **Grand Turk Lighthouse.** More than 150 years old, the lighthouse, built in the United Kingdom and transported piece by piece to the island, used to protect ships in danger of wrecking on the northern reefs. Use this panoramic landmark as a starting point for a breezy clifftop walk following the donkey trails to the deserted eastern beach. ⊠ *Lighthouse Rd., North Ridge.*

Shopping

There's not much to buy in Grand Turk, and shopping isn't a major activity here. However, a duty-free mall is located right at the cruise-ship center, where you'll find the usual array of upscale shops, which were just beginning to open at this writing. There are also shops in Cockburn Town itself.

Sports & Activities

CYCLING   The island's mostly flat terrain isn't very taxing, and most roads have hard surfaces. Take water with you: there are few places to stop for refreshment. Most hotels have bicycles available, but you can also rent them for $10 to $15 a day from **Oasis Divers** (✉ Duke St., Cockburn Town ☎ 649/946–1128 ⊕ www.oasisdivers.com).

DIVING &
SNORKELING
★

In these waters you can find undersea cathedrals, coral gardens, and countless tunnels, but note that you must carry and present a valid certificate card before you'll be allowed to dive. As its name suggests, the **Black Forest** offers staggering black-coral formations as well as the occasional blacktip shark. In the **Library** you can study fish galore, including large numbers of yellowtail snapper. At the Columbus Passage separating South Caicos from Grand Turk, each side of a 22-mi-wide (35-km-wide) channel drops more than 7,000 feet. From January through March, thousands of Atlantic humpback whales swim through en route to their winter breeding grounds. **Gibb's Cay**, a small cay a couple of miles off of Grand Turk, makes a great excursion swimming with stingrays.

Dive outfitters can all be found in Cockburn Town. Two-tank boat dives generally cost $60 to $80. **Blue Water Divers** (✉ Duke St., Cockburn Town ☎ 649/946–2432 ⊕ www.grandturkscuba.com) has been in operation on Grand Turk since 1983 and is the only PADI Gold Palm five-star dive center on the island. Owner Mitch will doubtless put some of your underwater adventures to music in the evenings when he plays at the Osprey Beach Hotel or Salt Raker Inn. **Oasis Divers** (✉ Duke St., Cockburn Town ☎ 649/946–1128 ⊕ www.oasisdivers.com) specializes in complete gear handling and pampering treatment. It also supplies Nitrox and rebreathers. Besides daily dive trips to the Wall, **Sea Eye Diving** (✉ Duke St., Cockburn Town ☎ 649/946–1407 ⊕ www.seaeyediving.com) offers encounters with friendly stingrays on a popular snorkeling trip to nearby Gibbs Cay.

Beaches

Grand Turk is spoiled for choices when it comes to beach options: sunset strolls along miles of deserted beaches, picnics in secluded coves, beachcombing on the coralline sands, snorkeling around shallow coral heads close to shore, and always the impossibly turquoise-blue waters to admire. **Pillory Beach** is at the north end of Cockburn Town, **Osprey Beach** is at the south end. **Governor's Beach** is a crescent of powder-soft sand and shallow, calm turquoise waters that fronts the official British governor's residence, called Waterloo, is framed by tall casuarina trees that provide plenty of natural shade. It's close to the cruise-ship center and is fairly crowded when there is a ship in port. For more of a beach-combing experience, **Little Bluff Point Beach**, just west of the Grand Turk Lighthouse, is a low, limestone cliff-edged, shell-covered beach that looks out onto shallow waters, mangroves, and often flamingos, especially in spring and summer.

Where to Eat

There's a Margaritaville restaurant right at the cruise-ship center, so many people won't even want to leave to dine.

$–$$ ✕ **Sand Bar.** Run by two Canadian sisters, this popular beachside bar is a good value, though the menu is limited to fish-and-chips, quesadillas, and similarly basic bar fare. The tented wooden terrace jutting out on to the beach provides shade during the day, making it an ideal lunch spot.

The service is friendly, and the local crowd often spills into the street. ⊠ *Duke St., Cockburn Town* ⊟ *MC, V.*

¢–$ ✗ **Courtyard Café.** A great spot for people-watching, this spot offers omelets, wraps, and giant subs, as well as cakes for those with sweeter tastes. Daily specials range from lasagna and quiche to island-style beef patties. ⊠ *Duke St., Cockburn Town* ☎ *649/946–1453* ⊟ *AE, MC, V.*

GRENADA

Jane Zarem

Nutmeg, cinnamon, cloves, cocoa . . . those heady aromas fill the air in Grenada (pronounced gruh-*nay*-da). Only 21 mi (33½ km) long and 12 mi (19½ km) wide, the Isle of Spice is a tropical gem of lush rain forests, white-sand beaches, secluded coves, exotic flowers, and enough locally grown spices to fill anyone's kitchen cabinet. St. George's is one of the most picturesque capital cities in the Caribbean—and St. George's Harbour is one of the most picturesque harbors. Grenada's Grand Anse Beach is one of the region's finest beaches. The island has friendly, hospitable people and enough good shopping, restaurants, historic sites, and natural wonders to make it a popular port of call. About one-third of Grenada's visitors arrive by cruise ship, and that number continues to grow each year.

Essentials

CURRENCY Eastern Caribbean (E.C.) dollar (EC$2.70 to US$1). U.S. dollars are generally accepted, but change is given in E.C. dollars.

HOURS Banks are open Monday through Thursday from 8 to 2, Friday from 8 to 4. The main post office, at Burns Point by the port in St. George's, is open weekdays from 8 to 3:30. Stores are generally open weekdays from 8 to 4 or 4:30 and Saturday from 8 to 1; some close from noon to 1 during the week.

INTERNET **Java-Kool Internet Cafe** (⊠ The Carenage, St. George's ☎ 473/435–3506) is open Monday through Saturday from 9 AM to 9 PM.

TELEPHONES Prepaid phone cards, which can be used in special card phones throughout the Caribbean for local or international calls, are sold in various denominations at shops, attractions, transportation centers, and other convenient outlets. For international calls using a major credit card, dial 111; to place a collect call or use a calling card, dial 800/225–5872 from any telephone. Pay phones are available at the cruise-ship welcome center, or at the Cable & Wireless office on the Carenage in St. George's, shopping centers, and other convenient locations.

Coming Ashore

A new cruise-ship terminal opened in 2005 near Market Square on the north side of St. George's, allowing larger ships to dock rather than anchor outside the harbor. Passenger facilities are available at the terminal, and more are being added. You can easily tour the capital on foot, but be prepared to climb up and down steep hills. If you don't want to walk up and down through town, you can find a taxi ($3 or $4 each way) or a water taxi ($2 per person each way) right at the terminal to take you around The Carenage. To explore areas outside St. George's, hiring a taxi or arranging a guided tour is more sensible than renting a car. Taxis are plentiful, and fixed rates to popular island destinations are posted at the terminal's welcome center.

A taxi ride from the terminal to the beach will cost $13, but water taxis are a less expensive and more picturesque way to get there; the one-way fare is $6 to Grand Anse. Minibuses are the least expensive way to travel between St. George's and Grand Anse; pay EC$1.50 (55¢), but hold on to your hat. They're crowded with local people getting from here to there and often take turns at quite a clip! Still, it's an inexpensive, fun, and safe way to travel around the island. If you want to rent a car and explore on your own, be prepared to pay $12 for a temporary driving permit and about $55 to $75 for a day's car rental.

GRENADA BEST BETS

- **Fishing.** Deep-sea fishing is excellent in these waters, and if you can get a group together a half-day trip is not too expensive.
- **Grand Anse Beach.** Grenada has one of the Caribbean's most beautiful beaches, and the market here is also one of the island's best.
- **Spice Tours.** It's not known as the island of spice for nothing; touring one of the fragrant processing facilities is a highlight.

Shore Excursions

We consider these to be among the better shore excursions for Grenada. They may not be offered by all lines, and tour names may differ as well. Times and prices are approximate.

4 X 4 Adventure. After driving through St. George Parish, travel north, stopping at a sulphur spring and pond, then pass through Grenada's central mountain range to the rain forest, Crater Lake, and Grand Étang National Park. ◷ *4 hrs* 🖼 *$74.*

Island Tours. Tours of Grenada usually focus on either the island's natural beauty, which includes Concord Falls and Grand Étang, or the historical sights, which include Dougaldston Estate, the Gouyave Nutmeg Cooperative, and a rum distillery. Some include a bit of both. Day-long tours usually include lunch and cover a lot of ground. ◷ *4–8 hrs* 🖼 *$49–$95.*

Nature Walk & Swim. You travel to an undisturbed rain forest, which is an important island watershed. There, you'll climb to the summit of the hill (1,420 feet) and get a panoramic view from Port Salines in the south all the way to Grand Étang forest. Most tours end at Grande Anse Beach for a swim and refreshments. ◷ *4 hrs* 🖼 *$54.*

Rhum Runner Cruise. The cruise on this 60-foot catamaran is a favorite of island visitors. You normally stop at a deserted beach for a swim on half-day cruises. ◷ *3 hrs* 🖼 *$42.*

Exploring Grenada

Numbers in the margin correspond to points of interest on the Grenada map.

❸ **Concord Falls.** About 8 mi (13 km) north of St. George's, a turnoff from the West Coast Road leads to Concord Falls—actually three separate waterfalls. The first is at the end of the road; when the currents aren't too strong, you can take a dip under the cascade. Reaching the two other waterfalls requires an hour's hike into the forest reserve. The third and

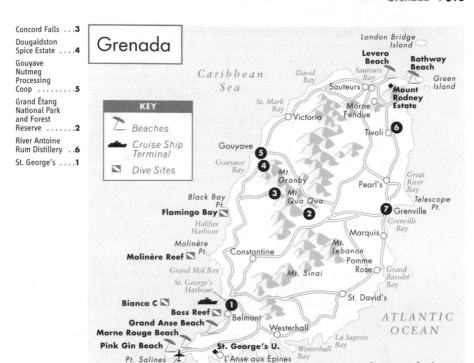

Grenada

KEY

🏖 *Beaches*

🚢 *Cruise Ship Terminal*

◥ *Dive Sites*

Caribbean Sea

London Bridge Island

Levera Beach **Bathway Beach**

David Bay *Sauteurs Bay* *Green Island*

Sauteurs ◗◗ ◆**Mount Rodney Estate**

St. Mark Bay Morne Fendue

◗Victoria

Tivoli ❻

Gouyave ❺

Gouyave Bay ❹

Mt. Granby Pearl's

Great River Bay

Black Bay Pt. ❸ *Mt. Qua Qua* *Telescope Pt.*

Flamingo Bay◥ ❷ ❼Grenville

Halifax Harbour *Grenville Bay*

Molinère Pt. Constantine Marquis◗

Molinère Reef◥ *Mt. Lebanon*

Grand Mal Bay Pomme Rose◗ *Grand Bacolet Bay*

St. George's Harbour *Mt. Sinai*

Bianca C◥ St. David's◗

Boss Reef◥ ❶ Belmont

Grand Anse Beach🏖 Westerhall *ATLANTIC OCEAN*

Morne Rouge Beach🏖

Pink Gin Beach🏖 **St. George's U.**◆ *La Sagesse Bay*

Pt. Salines ✈ L'Anse aux Epines *Westerhall Bay*

Pt. Salines International Airport **La Sagesse Beach**🏖

0 _____ 2 miles

0 _____ 2 kilometers

most spectacular waterfall, at Fountainbleu, thunders 65 feet over huge boulders and creates a small pool. It's smart to hire a guide. The path is clear, but slippery boulders toward the end can be treacherous without assistance. ⊠ *Main interior road, 15 mins northeast of St. George's, St. George* ☎ *473/440–2452* 🎟 *$1* ⊙ *Daily 9–5.*

🖐❹ **Dougaldston Spice Estate.** Just south of Gouyave, this historic plantation, now primarily a living museum, still grows and processes spices the old-fashioned way. You can see cocoa, nutmeg, mace, cloves, and other spices laid out on giant racks to dry in the sun. A worker will be glad to explain the process (and will appreciate a small donation). You can buy spices for about $2 a bag. ⊠ *Gouyave, St. John* ☎ *No phone* 🎟 *Free* ⊙ *Weekdays 9–4.*

🖐❺ **Gouyave Nutmeg Processing Cooperative.** Touring the nutmeg processing co-op, in the center of the west coast fishing village of Gouyave (pronounced *gwahve*), is a fragrant, fascinating way to spend half an hour. You can learn all about nutmeg and its uses, see the nutmegs laid out in bins, and watch the workers sort them by hand and pack them into burlap bags for shipping worldwide. The three-story plant turned out 3 million pounds of Grenada's most famous export each year prior to Hurricane Ivan's devastating effect on the crop in 2004. It will take a few more years for the nutmeg industry to get back to that level. ⊠ *Gouyave, St. John* ☎ *473/444–8337* 🎟 *$1* ⊙ *Weekdays 10–1 and 2–4.*

★ ♺ ❷ **Grand Étang National Park and Forest Reserve.** Deep in the mountainous interior of Grenada is a bird sanctuary and forest reserve with miles of hiking trails, lookouts, and fishing streams. **Grand Étang Lake** is a 36-acre expanse of cobalt-blue water that fills the crater of an extinct volcano 1,740 feet above sea level. Although legend has it the lake is bottomless, maximum soundings are recorded at 18 feet. The informative **Grand Étang Forest Center** has displays on the local wildlife and vegetation. A forest manager is on hand to answer questions. A small snack bar and souvenir stands are nearby. ⊠ *Main interior road, between Grenville and St. George's, St. Andrew* ☎ *473/440–6160* 🎟 *$1* ⊗ *Daily 8:30–4.*

> ## ID CASES
>
> You can keep track of your boarding pass, shipboard charge/key card, and picture ID when you go ashore by slipping them into a bi-fold business-card carrying case. Cases with a sueded finish are less likely to fall out of your pocket. With security as tight as it is these days, you don't want to lose your ID.

❻ **River Antoine Rum Distillery.** At this rustic operation, kept open primarily as a tourist attraction, a limited quantity of Rivers rum is produced by the same methods used since the distillery opened in 1785. The process begins with the crushing of sugarcane from adjacent fields in the River Antoine (pronounced an-*twine*) Estate. The result is a potent overproof rum, sold only in Grenada, that will knock your socks off. ⊠ *River Antoine Estate, St. Patrick* ☎ *473/442–7109* 🎟 *$2* ⊗ *Guided tours daily 9–4.*

❶ **St. George's.** Grenada's capital is a busy West Indian city, most of which remains unchanged from colonial days. Narrow streets lined with shops wind up, down, and across steep hills. Pastel-painted warehouses cling to the waterfront, while small rainbow-hue houses rise from the waterfront and disappear into steep green hills.

St. George's Harbour is the center of town. Schooners, ferries, and tour boats tie up along the seawall or at the small dinghy dock. On weekends a tall ship is likely to be anchored in the middle of the harbor, giving the scene a 19th-century flavor. **The Carenage** (pronounced car-a-*nahzh*), which surrounds horseshoe-shape St. George's Harbour, is the capital's main thoroughfare. Warehouses, shops, and restaurants line the waterfront. At the south end of the Carenage, the Grenada Board of Tourism has its offices. At the center of the Carenage, on the pedestrian plaza, sits the *Christ of the Deep* statue. It was presented to Grenada by Costa Cruise Line in remembrance of its ship *Bianca C*, which burned and sank in the harbor in 1961 and is now a favorite dive site.

♺ The **Grenada National Museum** (⊠ Young and Monckton Sts. ☎ 473/440–3725 🎟 $1 ⊗ Weekdays 9–4:30, Sat. 10–1), a block from the Carenage, is built on the foundation of a French army barracks and prison that was originally built in 1704. The small museum has exhibitions of news items, photos, and proclamations relating to the 1983 intervention, along with Empress Josephine's childhood bathtub and other memorabilia from earlier historical periods.

Ft. George (⊠ Church St.) is high on the hill at the entrance to St. George's Harbour. It's Grenada's oldest fort—built by the French in 1705 to protect the harbor. No shots were ever fired here until October 1983, when Prime Minister Maurice Bishop and some of his followers were assassinated in the courtyard. The fort now houses police headquarters, but is open to the public daily; admission is free. The 360-degree view of the capital city, St. George's Harbour, and the open sea is spectacular. An engineering feat for its time, the 340-foot-long **Sendall Tunnel** was built in 1895 and named for an early governor. It separates the harborside of St. George's from the Esplanade on the bay side of town, where you can find the markets (produce, meat, and fish), the cruise-ship terminal, and the public bus station.

Don't miss St. George's picturesque **Market Square** (⊠ Granby St.), a block from the cruise-ship terminal. It's open every weekday morning, but really comes alive on Saturday from 8 to noon. Vendors sell baskets, spices, brooms, clothing, knickknacks, coconut water, and heaps of fresh produce. Market Square is historically where parades and political rallies take place—and the beginning of the minibus routes to all areas of the island.

Built in 1825, the beautiful **St. George's Anglican Church** (⊠ Church St.) is filled with statues and plaques depicting Grenada in the 18th and 19th centuries. **St. George's Methodist Church** (⊠ Green St., near Herbert Blaize St.) was built in 1820 and is the oldest original church in the city. The Gothic tower of **St. George's Roman Catholic Church** (⊠ Church St.) dates from 1818, but the current structure was built in 1884; the tower is the city's most visible landmark. **York House** (⊠ Church St.), dating from 1801, is home to Grenada's Houses of Parliament and Supreme Court. It, the neighboring Registry Building (1780), and Government House (1802) are fine examples of early Georgian architecture.

Overlooking the city of St. George's and the inland side of the harbor, historic **Fort Frederick** (⊠ Richmond Hill) provides a panoramic view of two-thirds of Grenada. The fort was started by the French and completed in 1791 by the British; it was also the headquarters of the People's Revolutionary Government during the 1983 coup. Today you can get a bird's-eye view of much of Grenada from here.

Shopping

Grenada's best souvenirs or gifts for friends back home are spice baskets filled with cinnamon, nutmeg, mace, bay leaves, cloves, turmeric, and ginger. You can buy them for as little as $2 in practically every shop, at the open-air produce market at **Market Square** in St. George's, at the vendor stalls near the pier, and at the **Vendor's Craft & Spice Market** on Grand Anse Beach. Vendors also sell handmade fabric dolls, coral jewelry, seashells, and hats and baskets handwoven from green palm fronds. Bargaining is not appropriate in the shops, and it isn't customary with vendors—although most will offer you "a good price." **Art Fabrik** (⊠ 9 Young St., St. George's, St. George ☎ 473/440–0568) is a studio where you can watch artisans create batik before turning it into clothing or accessories. In the shop you can find fabric by the yard or fashioned into dresses, shirts, shorts, hats, and scarves. **Art Grenada** (⊠ Grand Anse Shopping Centre, Suite 7, Grand Anse, St. George ☎ 473/444–2317) displays and sells paintings, drawings, and watercolors exclusively by Grenadian artists, among them Canute Caliste, Lyndon Bedeau, and Susan

Mains. Exhibitions change monthly, and you can have your purchases shipped. **Tikal** (✉ Young St., St. George's, St. George ☎ 473/440–2310) is known for its exquisite baskets, artwork, jewelry, batik items, and fashions, both locally made and imported from Africa and Latin America.

Activities

DIVING You can see hundreds of varieties of fish and some 40 species of coral at more than a dozen sites off Grenada's southwest coast—only 15 to 20 minutes by boat. Depths vary from 20 to 120 feet, and visibility varies from 30 to 100 feet.

A spectacular dive is *Bianca C,* a 600-foot cruise ship that caught fire in 1961, sank to 100 feet, and is now encrusted with coral and a habitat for giant turtles, spotted eagle rays, barracuda, and jacks. **Boss Reef** extends 5 mi (8 km) from St. George's Harbour to Point Salines, with a depth ranging from 20 to 90 feet. **Flamingo Bay** has a wall that drops to 90 feet and is teeming with fish, sponges, sea horses, sea fans, and coral. **Molinère Reef** slopes from about 20 feet below the surface to a wall that drops to 65 feet. It's a good dive for beginners, and advanced divers can continue farther out to view the wreck of the *Buccaneer,* a 42-foot sloop.

Aquanauts Grenada (✉ Grand Anse Beach, Grand Anse ☎ 473/444–1126 ⊕ www.aquanautgrenada.com ✉ True Blue Bay Resort, True Blue ☎ 473/439–2500) has a multilingual staff, so instruction is available in English, German, Dutch, French, and Spanish. Two-tank dive trips, accommodating no more than eight divers, are offered each morning to both the Caribbean and Atlantic sides of Grenada. **Dive Grenada** (✉ Flamboyant Hotel, Morne Rouge, St. George ☎ 473/444–1092 ⊕ www.divegrenada.net) offers dive trips twice daily (at 10 AM and 2 PM), specializing in diving the *Bianca C.* **EcoDive** (✉ Grenada Grand Beach Resort, Grand Anse, St. George ☎ 473/444–7777 ⊕ www.ecodiveandtrek.com) offers two dive trips daily, both drift and wreck dives. The company also runs Grenada's marine conservation and education center, which conducts coral-reef monitoring and turtle projects.

FISHING Deep-sea fishing around Grenada is excellent, with marlin, sailfish, yellowfin tuna, and dolphinfish topping the list of good catches. You can arrange a half-day sportfishing trip for $375 or so, depending on the number of people. **True Blue Sportfishing** (☎ 473/444–2048) offers big-game charters on its "purpose-built" 31-foot Sport Fisherman, *Yes Aye.* It has an enclosed cabin, fighting chair, and professional tackle. British-born Capt. Gary Clifford, who has been fishing since the age of six, has operated True Blue Sportfishing since 1998. Refreshments and courtesy transport are included.

Beaches

Bathway Beach, a broad strip of sand with a natural reef that protects swimmers from the rough Atlantic surf on Grenada's far northern shore, has changing rooms at the Levera National Park headquarters.

Grand Anse Beach, in the southwest about 3 mi (5 km) south of St. George's, is Grenada's loveliest and most popular beach. It's a gleaming 2-mi (3-km) semicircle of white sand lapped by clear, gentle surf. Sea grape trees and coconut palms provide shady escapes from the sun. Brilliant rainbows frequently spill into the sea from the high green mountains that frame St. George's Harbour to the north. A public entrance is at Camerhogne Park, just a few steps from the main road. Beachfront hotels have water-sports centers where you can rent small sailboats, Windsurfers, and Sunfish (as well as beach chairs). The Grand Anse Craft & Spice Market is at the midpoint of the beach.

Where to Eat

Restaurants add an 8% government tax to your bill and usually add a 10% service charge; if not, tip 10% to 15% for a job well done.

★ **$–$$$** ✕ **Coconut Beach Restaurant.** Take local seafood, add butter, wine, and Grenadian spices, and you have excellent French creole cuisine. Throw in a beautiful location on Grand Anse Beach, and this West Indian cottage—rebuilt by owner Dennot "Scratch" McIntyre after Hurricane Ivan ripped it to shreds—becomes a perfect spot for an alfresco lunch or oceanfront dinner. Lobster is a specialty, perhaps wrapped in a crepe, dipped in garlic butter, or added to pasta. Or try the Caribbean chicken, seafood platter, lambi, or even grilled steak. Homemade coconut pie is a winner for dessert. On Wednesday and Sunday nights in season, dinner is a beach barbecue with live music. ⊠ *Grand Anse, St. George* ☎ *473/444-4644* ▭ *AE, D, MC, V* ⊗ *Closed Tues.*

¢–$ ✕ **The Nutmeg.** West Indian specialties, fresh seafood, great hamburgers, and a waterfront view make this a favorite with locals and visitors alike. It's upstairs on the Carenage (above Sea Change bookstore), with large, open windows from which you can watch the harbor activity as you eat. Try the callaloo soup, curried lambi, fresh seafood, or a steak—or just stop by for a rum punch and a roti, a fish sandwich and a Carib beer, or a hamburger and a Coke. ⊠ *The Carenage, St. George's, St. George* ☎ *473/440–2539* ▭ *AE, D, MC, V.*

GUADELOUPE (POINT-À-PITRE)

Eileen Robinson Smith

On a map, Guadeloupe looks like a giant butterfly resting on the sea between Antigua and Dominica. Its two wings—Basse-Terre and Grande-Terre—are the two largest islands in the 1,054-square-km (659-square-mi) Guadeloupe archipelago. The Rivière Salée, a 6-km (4-mi) channel between the Caribbean and the Atlantic, forms the "spine" of the butterfly. A drawbridge near Pointe-à-Pitre, the main city, connects the two islands. Guadeloupe is one of the most physically endowed islands in the Caribbean. If you're seeking a resort atmosphere, casinos, and white sandy beaches, your target is Grande-Terre. On the other hand, Basse-Terre's Parc National de la Guadeloupe, laced with mountain trails and washed by waterfalls and rivers, is a 74,100-acre haven for hikers, nature lovers, and anyone brave enough to peer into the steaming crater of an active volcano. The tropical beauty you will see equates to the mythical Garden of Eden.

> ## GUADELOUPE BEST BETS
>
> ■ **Diving.** Jacques Cousteau called the reef off Pigeon Island one of the world's top dive sites.
>
> ■ **Hiking.** The Parc National de la Guadeloupe is one of the Caribbean's most spectacular scenic destinations.
>
> ■ **Shopping.** Though Point-à-Pitre itself can be frenetic, it does have a good choice of European wares, though you may not be so excited about the prices.

7

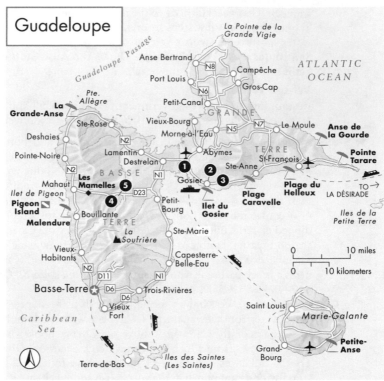

Essentials

CURRENCY   The euro (€1 to US$1.31). Some of the larger liquor and jewelry stores may accept dollars, but don't count on that. You cannot cash traveler's checks or dollars at the bank, only at a bureau de change, so ATMs are your best bet if you need euros; there is one right outside the tourist office.

HOURS   Banks are open weekdays from 8 to noon and 2 to 4. Most shops stay open all day, but some still close from noon to 2 or 2:30.

INTERNET   Pointe-à-Pitre has several Internet cafés; the tourist office can point you in their direction.

TELEPHONES   To call the United States from Guadeloupe, dial 001, the area code, and the local number. For calls within Guadeloupe, you now have to put 0590 before the six-digit number. You'll need to purchase a *télécarte* at the post office or at tobacco and grocery shops in order to use the phone booths.

Coming Ashore

Ships dock at the Maritime Terminal of Centre St-John Perse in downtown Pointe-à-Pitre, about a five-minute walk from the shopping district. Passengers are greeted by local musicians and hostesses, usually dressed in the traditional madras costumes—and often dispensing samplings of local rum and creole specialties. These multilingual staffers operate the information booth and can pair you up with an English-speaking taxi driver for a customized island tour. To get to the main tourist office, walk along the quay to the Place de la Victoire.

Taxi fares (more expensive here than on most other islands) are regulated by the government and posted at taxi stands. Renting a car is a good way to see Guadeloupe even though rentals can be expensive. Just be aware that traffic around Pointe-à-Pitre can be dreadful during rush-hour, so allow plenty of time to drop off your car rental and get back to the ship. There are several rental agencies at the airport near Pointe-à-Pitre.

Shore Excursions

We consider these to be among the better shore excursions for Guadeloupe. They may not be offered by all lines, and tour names may differ as well. Times and prices are approximate.

Botanical Garden & Distillery. This is a good tour if you want to see a little of Basse-Terre but aren't feeling too adventurous. It starts at the beautiful Deshaies Botanical Garden; after, you visit the Domaine de Séverin distillery for some rum-tasting. ⊙ *4 hrs* ✉ *$69.*

Cousteau Reserve. This trip to Pigeon Island, which was dubbed one of the world's best dive sites by Jacques Cousteau, won't give you time to do any diving, but there is a stop for snorkeling. ⊙ *4 hrs* ✉ *$86.*

Plantation Tour. You get a glimpse of the life of the plantocracy on this visit to Bel Air Plantation, which includes a stop at a rum distillery on the way back. ⊙ *4 hrs* ✉ *$69.*

Rainforest Excursion. If you want to see what makes Guadeloupe so amazing, take this tour to the rain forest on wild Basse-Terre, where you do a canopy walk and stop at the Cascade aux Ecrevisses, one of the island's grandest waterfalls. ⊙ *4 hrs* ✉ *$89.*

Exploring Guadeloupe

Numbers in the margin correspond to points of interest on the Guadeloupe map.

❶ Pointe-à-Pitre, a city of some 100,000 people, lies almost on the "backbone" of the butterfly, near the bridge that crosses the Salée River. This is not a postcard-pretty destination, but the Place de la Victoire, surrounded by wood buildings with balconies and shutters and lined with sidewalk cafés, has charm. The large, white Victorian building, with the wraparound veranda, is the tourist bureau. The square was named in honor of Victor Hugues's 1794 victory over the British. During the French Revolution a guillotine here lopped off the heads of many an aristocratic planter.

Anyone with an interest in French literature and culture won't want to miss the **Musée St-John Perse,** which is dedicated to Guadeloupe's most famous son and one of the giants of world literature, Alexis Léger, better known as St-John Perse, winner of the Nobel Prize for literature in 1960. Some of his finest poems are inspired by the history and landscape—particularly the sea—of his beloved Guadeloupe. The museum contains a collection of his poetry and some of his personal belongings. Before you go, look for his birthplace at 54 rue Achille René-Boisneuf. ⊠ *At rues Noizières and Achille René-Boisneuf* ☎ *0590/90–01–92* ✉ *€2* ⊙ *Thurs.–Tues. 8:30–12:30 and 2:30–5:30.*

Musée Schoelcher celebrates Victor Schoelcher, a high-minded abolitionist from Alsace who fought against slavery in the French West Indies in the 19th century. The museum contains many of his personal effects, and exhibits trace his life and work. Come for the architecture, the works of art, and the music history. ⊠ *24 rue Peynier* ☎ *0590/82–08–04* 📧 *€3* ⊙ *Weekdays 9–5.*

For fans of French ecclesiastical architecture, there's the imposing **Cathédrale de St-Pierre et St-Paul** (⊠ Rue Alexandre Isaac at rue de l'Eglise), built in 1807. Although battered by hurricanes, it has fine stained-glass windows and creole-style balconies and is reinforced with pillars and ribs that look like leftovers from the Eiffel Tower.

② **Aquarium de la Guadeloupe.** Unique in the Antilles, this aquarium in the marina near Pointe-à-Pitre is a good place to spend an hour. The well-planned facility has an assortment of tropical fish, crabs, lobsters, moray eels, puffy coffers, a shark or two, and some live coral. It's also a turtle rescue center. The retail shop has sea-related gifts, toys, and jewelry. ⊠ *Pl. Créole, off Rte. N4, Pointe-à-Pitre* ☎ *0590/90–92–38* 📧 *€7.50* ⊙ *Daily 9–7.*

③ **Fort Fleur d'Épée.** The main attraction in Bas-du-Fort is this 18th-century fortress, which hunkers down on a hillside behind a deep moat. It was the scene of hard-fought battles between the French and the English in 1794. You can explore its well-preserved dungeons and battlements and take in a sweeping view of Iles des Saintes and Marie-Galante. ⊠ *Bas-du-Fort* ☎ *0590/90–94–61* 📧 *€6* ⊙ *Mon. 10–5, Tues.–Sun. 9–5.*

★ **④** **Parc National de la Guadeloupe.** This 74,100-acre park has been recognized by UNESCO as a Biosphere Reserve. Before going, pick up a *Guide to the National Park* from the tourist office; it rates the hiking trails according to difficulty, and most are quite difficult indeed. Most mountain trails are in the southern half of the park. The park is bisected by the Route de la Traversée, a 16-mi (26-km) paved road lined with masses of tree ferns, shrubs, flowers, tall trees, and green plantains. It's the ideal point of entry to the park. Wear rubber-sole shoes and take along a swimsuit, a sweater, and perhaps food for a picnic. Try to get an early start to stay ahead of the hordes of cruise-ship passengers making a day of it. Check on the weather; if Basse-Terre has had a lot of rain, give it up. In the past, after intense rainfall, rockslides have closed the road for months. ⊠ *Administrative Headquarters, Rte. de la Traversée, St-Claude* ☎ *0590/80–86–00* ⊕ *www.guadeloupe-parcnational.com* 📧 *Free* ⊙ *Weekdays 8–5:30.*

⑤ **Cascade aux Ecrevisses.** Part of the Parc National de la Guadeloupe, Crayfish Falls is one of the island's loveliest (and most popular) spots. There's a marked trail (walk carefully—the rocks can be slippery) leading to this splendid waterfall, which dashes down into the Corossol River—a good place for a dip. Come early, though; otherwise you definitely won't have it to yourself.

Shopping

For serious shopping in Pointe-à-Pitre, browse the boutiques and stores along rue Schoelcher, rue Frébault, and rue Noizières. The multicolored market square and stalls of La Darse are filled mostly with vegetables, fruits, delicious homemade rum liqueurs, and housewares. The air is filled with the fragrance of spices and they have lovely gift baskets of spices and vanilla lined with madras fabric.

Au Bonheur des Dames (⊠ 49 rue Frébault, Pointe-à-Pitre, Grande-Terre ☏ 0590/82–00–30) sells several different lines of cosmetics and skin-care products in addition to its perfumes. **Délice Shop** (⊠ 45 rue Achille René-Boisneuf, Pointe-à-Pitre, Grande-Terre ☏ 0590/82–98–24) is the spot for island rum and edibles from France—from cheese to chocolate. **DODY** (⊠ 31 rue Frébault, Pointe-a-Pitre, Grande-Terre ☏ 0590/82–18–59) is the place if you have wanted to purchase white eyelet—blouses, skirts, dresses, or even bustiers—the shop has a high-quality designer line, but you will pay. There's lots of madras, too, which is especially cute in children's clothing. **Rosebleu** (⊠ 5 rue Frébault, Pointe-à-Pitre, Grande-Terre ☏ 0590/82–93–43) sells china, crystal, and silver by top manufacturers, including Christofle. **Vendôme** (⊠ 8–10 rue Frébault, Pointe-à-Pitre, Grande-Terre ☏ 0590/83–42–84) is Guadeloupe's exclusive purveyor of Stendhal and Germaine Monteil cosmetics.

Sports & Activities

DIVING The main diving area at the **Cousteau Underwater Park,** just off Basse-Terre near Pigeon Island, offers routine dives to 60 feet. But the numerous glass-bottom boats and day-trippers make the site feel like a crowded marine parking lot. The underwater wonders, however, are spectacular. Guides and instructors here are certified under the French CMAS (some also have PADI). Most operators offer two-hour dives for about €45–€50 per dive; three-dive packages are €120–€145. **Les Heures Saines** (⊠ Rocher de Malendure, Plage de Malendure, Bouillante, Basse-Terre ☏ 0590/98–86–63 or 0690/55–40–47 ⊕ www.plongee-guadeloupe.com) is the premier operator for dives in the Cousteau Reserve. Trips to Les Saintes offer one or two dives, for medium and advanced cardholders, with time for lunch and sightseeing. The instructors, many English-speaking, are excellent with children. The company also offers sea kayaking and winter whale- and dolphin-watching trips with marine biologists as guides, all aboard a 60-foot catamaran equipped with hydrophones.

HIKING With hundreds of trails and countless rivers and waterfalls, the Parc National de la Guadeloupe on Basse-Terre is the main draw for hikers. Some of the trails should be attempted only with an experienced guide. All tend to be muddy, so wear a good pair of boots. Know that even the young and fit can find these outings arduous; the unfit may find them painful. Start off slowly, with a shorter hike, then go for the gusto. **Vert Intense** (⊠ Basse-Terre ☏ 0590/99–34–73 or 0690/55–40–47 ⊕ www.ecotourisme-guadeloupe.net) organizes fascinating hikes in the Parc National de la Guadeloupe. You will move from steaming hot springs to an icy waterfall in the same hike. The French-speaking guides, who also know some English and Spanish, can also take you to other tropical forests and rivers, but hikes must be booked in advance.

Beaches

Plage Caravelle. Just southwest of Ste-Anne is one of Grande-Terre's longest and prettiest stretches of sand, the occasional dilapidated shack notwithstanding. Protected by reefs, it's also a fine snorkeling spot. Club Med occupies one end of this beach, where nude bathing is no longer permitted. Nonguests can enjoy its beach and water sports, as well as lunch and drinks by buying a day-pass (approximately €90). ⊠ *Rte. N4, southwest of Ste-Anne, Grande-Terre.*

Pointe des Châteaux. This is one of the island's most dramatic, wild seascapes; looming above are rugged cliffs topped by a huge crucifix. Pointe Tarare, a secluded, sandy strip just before the tip, is the island's only nude beach. If you don't feel comfortable with that, just keep walking and find your own white, sandy spot. Makeshift bars and snack stands crowd the parking area, but it's still best to bring some water and food. ⊠ *Rte. N4, southeast of St-François, Grande-Terre.*

La Grande-Anse. One of Guadeloupe's widest beaches, La Grande-Anse has soft, beige sand sheltered by palms. To the west is a round, verdant mountain. There's a large parking area and some food concessionaires, but no other facilities. The beach can be crowded, not to mention littered, on Sunday. Beyond the parking lot you can see signs for the creole restaurant Le Karacoli; if you have lunch there (it's not inexpensive), you can take a nap on the chaise lounges. ⊠ *Rte. N6, north of Deshaies, Basse-Terre.*

Where to Eat

Restaurants are required to include a 15% service charge in the menu price. Extra gratuities make Americans popular.

★ **$$-$$$$** ✗ **Le Rocher de Malendure.** Guests climb the yellow stairs for the panoramic sea views but return for the food. If you arrive before noon, when the divers pull in, you might snag one of the primo tables in a gazebo, which literally hang over the Caribbean. Begin with a perfectly executed mojito. With such fresh fish, don't hesitate to try the sushi *antilliaise*, a mixed-fish ceviche. The housemade, golden raisin rolls are perfect with the warm goat cheese salad with honey sauce perfumed by *herbes du Provence*. Grilled crayfish and lobster; octopus fricasse, shellfish bouillabaisse, and *dorade* (mahimahi) with a vanilla cream sauce have contemporary presentations and classic good flavor. Stone and steam cooking at the table are so guilt-free. UAC member. ⊠ *Bord de Mer, Malendure de Pigeon, Bouillante* ☎ *0590/98–70–84* ⊟ *AE, MC, V* ⊗ *Closed Wed. and Sept.*

¢–$ ✗ **Caraïbes Café.** This sidewalk café straight out of Paris is the *in* place for lunch and also a spot for a quick breakfast, a fresh juice cocktail (try *corossel/mangue*), a cappuccino, a sundae (*un coupe*), or a Pernod while you watch the people and listen to French crooners and "Desperado." The *formule* (fixed-price menu) is always the best deal. Then there are crepes, both main course and dessert crepes, sandwiches and grilled sirloin steak (*entrecote*) with perfect *pommes frites*. Service is fast, friendly and can even be in English. ⊠ *Place de la Victoire, Pointe-à-Pitre* ☎ *0590/82–92–23* ⊟ *MC, V* ⊗ *Closed Sun. No dinner.*

ISLA MARGARITA, VENEZUELA

Venezuelans are enormously fond of the island they call the "pearl in the Caribbean." Margarita's status as a duty-free port and its proximity to the mainland make it the top vacation spot for Venezuelans. Miles of white sandy beaches, glittering hotels and restaurants, and vibrant nightlife, as well as 16th-century forts and national parks, have transformed Isla Margarita into a newly popular destination for cruise-ship visitors as well. Isla Margarita is split into two sections linked by an 11-

mi (18-km) spit of sand. Most of the island's 350,000 residents occupy the more developed eastern half, especially the bustling city of Porlamar and the adjoining Pampatar. Others are found in the much smaller city of La Asunción, the capital of the region that also encompasses the neighboring islands of Coche and Cubagua. Roads on Isla Margarita are good, which means a car is the easiest way to venture out on your own. Taxis and vans serve as public transportation throughout the island.

Essentials

CURRENCY The Honduran bolívar (Bs2,147 to US$1). Italcambio, the largest of the *casas de cambio* (exchange houses), is permitted to exchange dollars and American Express traveler's checks denominated in dollars for bolívars, but not vice-versa. (Most banks will not exchange currency, and none will accept traveler's checks.) Given Venezuela's currency restrictions at this writing, there will be no shortage of black market dealers approaching you quietly about changing money in public places, but the so-called *mercado negro* is officially illegal and a dangerous risk for robbery.

HOURS Stores and attractions will be open if there is a cruise ship in port.

INTERNET **Tucupita Expeditions** (⊠ Boulevard Playa El Agua, Playa El Agua, in front of Playa El Agua Beach Hotel ☎ 0295/249–1864) is an Internet café and travel agency in the most popular beach area on the island.

TELEPHONES All telephone numbers have seven digits. Area codes begin with a "0" followed by a three-digit number, the first of which is a 2. International calls are extremely expensive; the average international rate per minute is $3.50 to the United States and $10 to Europe. You can reach an English-speaking long-distance operator by dialing 122. To use a calling card or credit card, or to place a collect call, use the various international access numbers from your home country.

Coming Ashore

Ships dock at El Guamache, which is in an isolated area about 45 minutes by taxi from the main city of Porlamar. Outside the dock, you'll find both indoor and outdoor shopping ranging from arts and crafts to high-end duty-free items. There is also a lively bar in the complex.

Margarita is a largely desert island, but it is easy enough to rent a car at the port and take a scenic drive around. Roads are well paved, and the driving conditions are quite good. If you plan to do any serious off-road exploring, then a 4x4 is essential. Taxis are clearly marked and are readily available at the port and in the major towns. Fares are posted on the taxi windows, but be sure to agree on a price to your destination beforehand, as some taxis will try to tack on a little extra to the fare. The fare to Porlamar from the port is about $50 for the round trip; fares in and around Porlamar usually do not exceed $5.

ISLA MARGARITA BEST BETS

- **Beaches.** This is a great place to simply relax on the beach. Try the busy strand at Playa El Agua.
- **Kayaking.** Good mangrove forests mean good kayaking, particularly in the Parque Nacional Laguna de la Restinga.
- **Snorkeling.** There's enough sea life in these waters to make a snorkeling trip a worthwhile endeavor.

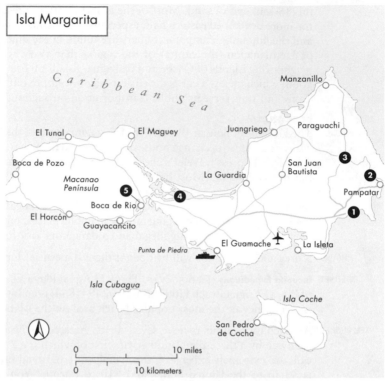

Isla Margarita

Caribbean Sea

Manzanillo

El Tunal   El Maguey   Juangriego   Paraguachi

Boca de Pozo   San Juan Bautista   **3**

Macanao Península   La Guardia   **2**

5   Pampatar

Boca de Rio   **4**   **1**

El Horcón

Guayacancito

El Guamache   La Isleta

Punta de Piedra

Isla Cubagua

Isla Coche

San Pedro de Cocha

0   10 miles

0   10 kilometers

SHORE   The following shore excursions are offered by major cruise lines in Isla
EXCURSIONS   Margarita. They may not be offered by all lines, and tour names may
differ as well. Times and prices are approximate.

Caribbean Kayaking Tour. After 90 minutes of kayaking, you have time to
relax on the beach. ⊙ *5 hrs* *$65.*
Land Cruiser Nature Adventure. You'll take off in a four-wheel drive vehicle
to explore some of the island's natural beauty. ⊙ *4 hrs* *$74.*
Margarita Splash. It's hard to resist the opportunity to drive your own speedboat around the island. ⊙ *4½ hrs* *$98.*
Round the Island Tour. This full-day tour takes in basically every sight on
the island and includes detailed explanations of points of interest. Cul-
ture-seekers will be pleased by the inclusion of the museum, and fun-seek-
ers will enjoy the beach stop in *Playa El Agua.* The tour also includes
refreshments and a chance to shop for local handicrafts. ⊙ *5 hrs* *$28.*

Exploring Margarita Island
*Numbers in the margin correspond to points of interest on the Margarita
map.*

③   La Asunción. From the mountains in the center of the island there are striking views as the road slowly descends to La Asunción, the small capital
of the region. The sleepy little town, ignored by the bargain-hunting
throngs, is the opposite of the bustling Porlamar. A handful of pretty colonial buildings are found around La Asunción's tree-covered Plaza Bolívar. ✉ *3 mi (5 km) north of El Valle.*

On Bolivar Square in the capital city of Asuncion the **Catedral de Nuestra Señora of La Asunción** built in 1617 is one of the oldest churches in Venezuela. Built of lime and local stone the small structure features beautiful statuary of various saints that date back many centuries.

❷ Diverland. A giant Ferris wheel leads you to the island's largest amusement park. There are 16 attractions, including a roller coaster and water slide. ⊠ *Av. Jóvito Villalba Pampatar* ☎ *0295/262–0813* 🎫 *$5* ☉ *Dec.–Apr. daily, 10 AM–11 PM; May–Nov., most weekends only (call for hours).*

❸ Museo Marino de Margarita. This museum's eight exhibit halls serve as a repository for Venezuela's astounding variety of marine life. As aquariums go, this is a small facility, but you can find everything from barracudas to flying fish. Many of the exhibits focus on the history of sea exploration in northern South America. ⊠ *Boulevar El Paseo, Boca del Rio, Macanao Peninsula* ☎ *0295/291-3231* 🎫 *Bs 6,000* ☉ *Daily 8–4:30.*

❹ Parque Nacional Laguna de la Restinga. The mangrove forests of this national reserve cover the 12-mi (20-km) thread of sand that makes up the tenuous link between the main part of the island and the Península de Macanao. Here you'll find a variety of colorful birds, such as the scarlet ibis. The park has an unspoiled beach and a sprinkling of fishermen's huts where you can buy the catch of the day.

❶ Porlamar. Porlamar, with about a third of Isla Margarita's population, is the island's center of commerce. Since it was granted free-port status in 1973, its boutique-lined avenues have been mobbed with tourists in search of tax-free bargains. Many of the goods found here are no cheaper than on the mainland, however. Porlamar is also the most cosmopolitan city on Isla Margarita, boasting countless restaurants, bars, clubs, and casinos.

Museo de Arte Contemporáneo Francisco Narvá is named after the native Margariteño sculptor whose works also can be viewed on the grounds of the Bella Vista Hotel. Here you'll find a permanent collection of Narváez's works, plus a rotating exhibit of national and international artworks. ⊠ *Calle Igualdad at Calle Diaz* ☎ *0295/261-8668* 🎫 *Bs 1,000* ☉ *Tues.–Fri. 9–5, Sat.–Sun. 10–4.*

Shopping

Although Isla Margarita is a major destination for Venezuelan day-trippers taking advantage of the duty-free prices, real bargains are hard to find. Your best bets are liquor and jewelry. Aside from the less expensive shops along Bulevar Guevara and Bulevar Gómez, shoppers are attracted to boutiques along Avenidas Santiago Mariño and 4 de Mayo, all in Porlamar. More and more shoppers are heading to the ubiquitous malls that are taking over the island. One

PACK AHEAD

When you put your summer wardrobe away for the winter, set aside the casual outfits, sandals, swimwear, and sleepwear you want to wear on your cruise and store them in the suitcase you plan to use. You will already be half-packed and will not be hunting down an outfit or a pair of shoes later.

of the most popular is the massive **Jumbo Mall** on 4 de Mayo. The stadium-size **Centro Sambil** has 137 stores and is the offspring of its mammoth parent shopping center in Caracas.

Sports & Activities

GOLF **Hesperia Playa El Agua** (⊠ Av. 31 de Julio, Pedro González ☎ 0295/249–0433), is a hotel that has the island's only 18-hole golf course. It is also handy that there is a lovely deserted beach located nearby for an after game cool down.

HORSEBACK **Walter's Tours** (⊠ C.C. La Redoma, Local #05, Los Robles ☎ 0295/174–
RIDING 1265 ⊕ www.margaritaislandguide.com) offers two-hour horseback riding tours in either the morning or afternoon. The route begins at the Cabatucan Ranch.

Beaches

Easily the most famous and crowded beach on the island, palm-lined **Playa El Agua** is a remarkable stretch of fine white sand that runs along the coast just north of Pampatar. For much of its 2-mi (3-km) length, restaurants and bars lure sunbathers with blaring salsa music and ice-cold beers. **Playa Guacuco** sits just outside Porlamar and is comparatively quiet compared to many other beaches on the island. The beach is lined with palm trees and there are gentle waves that allow for excellent body surfing. **Playa Parguito** is popular with surfers and offers excellent restaurants and shower facilities. It is located on the north of the island. It is also an excellent beach for people watching.

Where to Eat

There are many excellent restaurants on Isla Margarita and seafood is a favorite theme. On popular Playa El Agua, there are many casual beachside restaurants.

$$–$$$ ✕ **Bahi.** With large bay windows overlooking the beach, this place has a long-standing reputation for serving fine Spanish-style seafood dishes. Expect strolling musicians while you struggle to decide between the tasty paella and the succulent crab. Best of all, the prices are quite reasonable. ⊠ *Av. Raúl Leoni, Porlamar* ☎ *0295/261–4156* ▤ *AE, D, MC, V.*

$$–$$$ ✕ **Poseidón.** The god of the sea serves top-quality seafood artfully presented with a local touch, and is among the most exclusive—and best— in Isla Margarita. The restaurant has a tropical fish aquarium. ⊠ *Centro Comercial Jumbo, Av. 4 de Mayo, Porlamar* ▤ *AE, MC, V.*

KEY WEST, FLORIDA

Diane Bair
and Pamela
Wright

Along with the rest of Florida, Key West—the southernmost city in the continental United States—became part of American territory in 1821. In the late 19th century, it was Florida's wealthiest city per capita. The locals made their fortunes from "wrecking"—rescuing people and salvaging cargo from ships that foundered on nearby reefs. Cigar making, fishing, shrimping, and sponge gathering also became important industries. Capital of the self-proclaimed "Conch Republic," Key West today makes for a unique port of call. A genuinely American town, it nevertheless exudes the relaxed atmosphere and pace of a typical Caribbean island. Major attractions include the home of the Conch Republic's most famous residents, Ernest Hemingway and Harry Truman; the imposing Key West Museum of Art & History, a former U.S. Customs House and site of the military inquest of the USS *Maine*; and the island's renowned sunset celebrations.

Essentials

CURRENCY The U.S. dollar.

HOURS Many museums are closed on Mondays. Otherwise, regular 9–5 hours apply for most businesses.

INTERNET **Crossroads Internet Cafe** (✉ 500 Truman Ave. #7 ☎ 305/294–9118)

TELEPHONES Public phones are found at or near all three cruise docks: Mallory Square, Pier B at the Hilton, and Outer Mall (where the Conch Train drops passengers at Duval and Front streets). They're also along the major tourist thoroughfares.

Coming Ashore

Cruise ships dock at three different locations. Mallory Square and Pier B are within walking distance of Duval and Whitehead streets, the two main tourist thoroughfares. Passengers on ships that dock at Outer Mall are shuttled via Conch Train to Duval and Front streets. Because Key West is so easily explored on foot, there is rarely a need to hire a cab. If you plan to venture beyond the main tourist district, a fun way to get around is by bicycle or scooter. Key West is a cycling town. In fact, there are so many bikes around that cyclists must watch out for one another as much as for cars. You can get tourist information from the Greater Key West Chamber of Commerce, which is just off Mallory Square.

The Conch Tour Train can be boarded at Mallory Square or Flagler Station every half-hour; it costs $25 for the 90-minute tour. The Old Town Trolley operates trolley-style buses starting from Mallory Square every 30 minutes for the same price, but the smaller trolleys go places the train won't fit. Scooters can be easily rented. **Keys Moped & Scooter** (✉ 523 Truman Ave. ☎ 305/294–0399) rents beach cruisers with large baskets as well as scooters. Rates for scooters start at $30 for three hours. Look for the huge American flag on the roof. **Moped Hospital** (✉ 601 Truman Ave. ☎ 305/296–3344) supplies balloon-tire bikes ($18 a day) with yellow safety baskets, as well as mopeds ($40) and double-seater scooters ($65).

SHORE EXCURSIONS The following shore excursions are offered by major cruise lines in Key West. They may not be offered by all lines, and tour names may differ as well. Times and prices are approximate.

Fury Catamaran Reef Snorkeling. You sail out to the only living coral reef in the continental U.S., where the catamaran drops anchor and gives you the chance to snorkel. Refreshments are served on the way back. ⊙ *3 hrs* ▣ *$49.*

Harley Poker Run. This tour is scandalously expensive, but how often do you get a chance to ride on the overseas highway on a Harley? ⊙ *3½ hrs* ▣ *$375.*

Lloyd's Original Tropical Bike Tour. This leisurely tour takes you around Key West by bike. ⊙ *2½ hrs* ▣ *$45.*

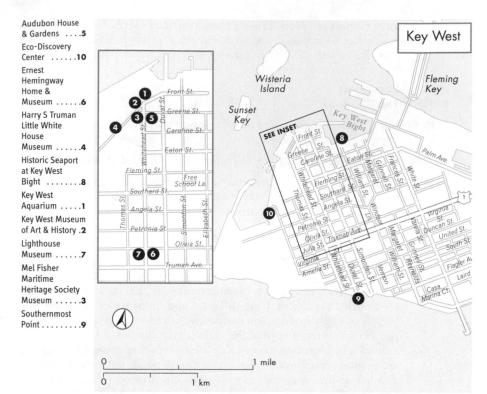

Exploring Key West

Numbers in the margin correspond to points of interest on the Key West map.

5 **Audubon House & Gardens.** If you've ever seen an engraving by ornithologist John James Audubon, you'll understand why his name is synonymous with birds. (OK, he shot a lot of them so they would lie still enough for his art, but we consider him to be part of our environmental conscience.) See his work in this three-story house, which was built in the 1840s for Captain John Geiger but now commemorates Audubon's 1832 stop in Key West. Several rooms of period antiques and a children's room are also of interest. Admission includes an audiotape (in English, French, German, or Spanish) for a self-guided tour of the house and tropical gardens, complemented by an informational booklet and signs that identify the rare indigenous plants and trees. ⊠ *205 Whitehead St.* ☎ *305/294–2116 or 877/294–2470* ⊕ *www.audubonhouse.com* ⊠ *$10* ⊙ *Daily 9:30–5; last tour starts at 4.*

★ **10** **Eco-Discovery Center.** Walk through a model of Key Largo's Aquarius, the world's only underwater ocean laboratory, to discover what lurks beneath the sea. Opened in January 2007, this 6,400 square-foot underwater attraction encourages visitors to venture through a variety of Florida Key habitats, from pinelands, beach dunes and mangroves to the deep sea. Touch-screen computer displays and live underwater cameras show-off North America's only contigiuous barrier coral reef. ⊠ *35 East Quay Rd., at* *end of Southard St. in Truman Annex* ☎ *305/809–4750* ⊕ *www. floridakeys.noaa.gov/eco.discovery.html* ✉ *$10* ⊘ *Tues.-Sat. 9–4.*

★ ❻ **Ernest Hemingway Home & Museum.** Guided tours of Ernest Hemingway's home are full of anecdotes about the author's life in the community and his household quarrels with wife Pauline. While living here between 1931 and 1942, Hemingway wrote about 70% of his life's work, including *For Whom the Bell Tolls.* Few of the family's belongings remain, but photographs help illustrate his life, and scores of descendants of Hemingway's cats have free reign of the property. Literary buffs should be aware that there are no curated exhibits from which to gain much insight into Hemingway's writing career. Tours begin every 10 minutes and take 25–30 minutes; then you're free to explore on your own. ✉ *907 Whitehead St.* ☎ *305/294– 1136* ⊕ *www.hemingwayhome.com* ✉ *$10* ⊘ *Daily 9–5.*

❹ **Harry S Truman Little White House Museum.** Personal glimpses are among the things that make many of the city's museums worth visiting, and this stop is no exception. For instance, in a letter to his wife during one of his visits, President Harry S Truman wrote, "Dear Bess, you should see the house. The place is all redecorated, new furniture and everything." If he visited today, he'd write something similar. There's a photographic review of visiting dignitaries and permanent audiovisual and artifact exhibits on the Florida Keys as a presidential retreat; Ulysses S. Grant, John F. Kennedy, and Jimmy Carter are among the chief executives who passed through here. Tours lasting 45 minutes begin every 15 minutes until 4:15. On the grounds of **Truman Annex,** a 103-acre former military parade grounds and barracks, the home served as a winter White House for presidents Truman, Eisenhower, and Kennedy. The two-bedroom Presidential Suite, with a veranda and sundeck, is available for a novelty overnight stay. ✉ *111 Front St.* ☎ *305/294–9911* ⊕ *www.trumanlittlewhitehouse. com* ✉ *$11* ⊘ *Daily 9–5, grounds 8–sunset; last tour at 4:30.*

❽ **Historic Seaport at Key West Bight.** What used to be a funky—in some places even seedy—part of town is now an 8½-acre historic restoration project of 100 businesses, including waterfront restaurants, open-air people- and dog-friendly bars, museums, clothing stores, bait shops, docks, a marina, a wedding chapel, the Waterfront Market, the Key West Rowing Club, and dive shops. It's all linked by the 2-mi (3 km) waterfront **Harborwalk,** which runs between Front and Grinnell streets, passing big ships, schooners, sunset cruises, fishing charters, and glass-bottom boats. Additional construction continues on outlying projects.

🖐 ❶ **Key West Aquarium.** Explore the fascinating underwater realm of the Keys without getting wet at this kid-friendly aquarium. Hundreds of tropical fish and sea creatures live here. A touch

---

KEY WEST BEST BETS

■ **Boat Cruise.** Whether you take a catamaran out to do some snorkeling or just do a sunset booze cruise, being out on the water is what Key West is all about.

■ **Kayaking.** Kayaking, either around Florida Bay or in the Great Heron National Wildlife Refuge, is a great way to spend a few hours.

■ **Sunset in Mallory Square.** The nightly street party is the quintessential Key West experience, and no one should miss it.

tank enables you to handle starfish, sea
cucumbers, horseshoe and hermit crabs,
even horse and queen conchs—living
totems of the Conch Republic. Built in
1934 by the Works Progress Administration as the world's first open-air
aquarium, most of the building has been
enclosed for all-weather viewing. Guided
tours include shark petting and feedings.
Tickets are good for the entire day. ⊠ *1 Whitehead St.* ☎ *305/296-2051*
⊕ *www.keywestaquarium.com* ✉ *$10* ⊙ *Daily 10–6; tours at 11, 1, 3,
and 4:30.*

> ## USED BOOKS
>
> Leave any paperback novels you
> have finished for the crew library.
> You will have more room in your
> suitcase, and crew members will
> have fresh reading material.

② **Key West Museum of Art & History.** If you didn't get enough Hemingway at
Fodor'sChoice his museum, you can meet him and his "mob," a.k.a., friends, here
★ through photographs and other visuals. But this is more about the city
than the noted author. When Key West was designated a U.S. port of entry
in the early 1820s, a customhouse was established. Salvaged cargoes from
ships wrecked on the reefs could enter here, thus setting the stage for
Key West to become the richest city in Florida. Following a $9-million
restoration, the imposing redbrick-and-terra-cotta Richardsonian Romanesque–style U.S. Custom House reopened as a museum. Its main gallery
displays major rotating exhibits. Smaller galleries have long-term and
changing exhibits about the history of Key West, such as *Remember the
Maine.* ⊠ *281 Front St.* ☎ *305/295-6616* ⊕ *www.kwahs.com* ✉ *$10*
⊙ *Daily 9–5.*

❼ **Lighthouse Museum.** For the best view in town and a history lesson at the
same time, climb the 88 steps to the top of this 92-foot lighthouse. It
was built in 1847. About 15 years later, a Fresnel lens was installed at
a cost of $1 million. The keeper lived in the adjacent 1887 clapboard
house, which now exhibits vintage photographs, ship models, nautical
charts, and lighthouse artifacts from all along the Key reefs. This site is
a nearby affiliate of the Key West Museum of Art and History. ⊠ *938
Whitehead St.* ☎ *305/294-0012* ✉ *$10* ⊙ *Daily 9:30–4:30; last admission at 4:15.*

❸ **Mel Fisher Maritime Heritage Society Museum.** The late Mel Fisher was a crusty
character who battled the state of Florida for more than a decade over
the remains of two riches-laden Spanish galleons that sank 40 miles off
the Keys in 1622 during a hurricane. In 1985, Mel Fisher recovered the
treasures from the lost ships, the *Nuestra Señora de Atocha* and the *Santa
Margarita.* In this museum, see, touch, and learn about some of the artifacts, including a gold bar weighing 6.3 troy pounds and a 77.76-carat
natural emerald crystal worth almost $250,000. Exhibits on the second
floor rotate and might cover slave ships, including the excavated 17th-
century *Henrietta Marie,* or the evolution of Florida maritime history.
⊠ *200 Greene St.* ☎ *305/294-2633* ⊕ *www.melfisher.org* ✉ *$11*
⊙ *Daily 9:30–5.*

❾ **Southernmost Point.** At the foot of Whitehead Street, a huge concrete marker
proclaims this spot to be the southernmost point in the continental

United States. Turn left on South Street. To your right are two dwellings that both claim to be the Southernmost House. Take a right onto Duval Street, which ends at the Atlantic Ocean, and you will be at the Southernmost Beach.

Shopping

Passengers looking for T-shirts, trinkets, and other souvenirs will find them along Duval Street and around the cruise-ship piers. **Fast Buck Freddie's** (✉ 500 Duval St. ☎ 305/294–2007) sells a classy, hip selection of crystal, furniture, tropical clothing, and every flamingo item imaginable. It also carries such imaginative items as a noise-activated rat in a trap and a raccoon tail in a bag. **Key West Aloe** (✉ 540 Greene St., at Simonton St. ☎ 305/294–5592 or 800/445–2563) was founded in a garage in 1971; today it produces some 300 perfume, sunscreen, and skin-care products for men and women. After years downtown on Front Street, it has moved back to a new showroom at the original factory location. The **Key West Island Bookstore** (✉ 513 Fleming St. ☎ 305/294–2904) is the literary bookstore of the large Key West writers' community. It carries new, used, and rare titles and specializes in Hemingway, Tennessee Williams, and South Florida mystery writers. **Lucky Street Gallery** (✉ 1130 Duvall St. ☎ 305/294–3973) sells high-end contemporary paintings, watercolors, and a few pieces of jewelry by internationally recognized Key West–based artists.

Sports & Activities

BOAT TOURS **M/V Discovery** (✉ Land's End Marina, 251 Margaret St., Key West 33040 ☎ 305/293–0099) glass-bottom boats have submerged viewing rooms for 360-degree marine watching and cost $35. **Adventure Charters & Tours** (✉ 6810 Front St., 33040 ☎ 305/296–0362 or 888/817–0841 ⊕ www.keywestadventures.com) takes kayaks to the Great Heron National Wildlife Refuge for full-day tours; they also offer half-day tours that paddle out from Key West.

DIVING & SNORKELING **Captain's Corner** (✉ Corner of Greene and Elizabeth ☎ 305/296–8865), a PADI five-star shop, has dive classes in several languages and twice-daily snorkel and dive trips to reefs and wrecks aboard the 60-foot dive boat *Sea Eagle* ($30 to $35). **Snuba of Key West** (✉ Garrison Bight Marina, Palm Ave. between Eaton St. and N. Roosevelt Blvd. ☎ 305/292–4616) takes you out to the reef on a catamaran, where you listen to a 20-minute orientation, then follow your guide underwater for a one-hour tour of the coral reefs. You wear a regulator with a breathing hose that is attached to a floating air tank on the surface of the water, so you do not need to be certified. You must know how to swim. The $95 cost includes beverages.

FISHING **Key West Bait and Tackle** (✉ 241 Margaret St. ☎ 305/292–1961) carries live bait, frozen rigged and unrigged bait, and fishing and rigging equipment. It also has the Live Bait Lounge; unwind and sip ice-cold beer while telling tall tales after fishing. **Key West Fishing Pro Guides** (☎ 866/259–4205) has several guides and trips ranging from flats fishing ($400 to $600) to offshore ($500 to $800) fishing.

Beaches

Key West doesn't have any great swimming beaches, but there are a few that might be worth a visit. **Fort Zachary Taylor State Historic Site** (⊠ End of Southard St., through Truman Annex) has an uncrowded beach, which is the best in Key West. There is an adjoining picnic area with barbecue grills and shade trees. **Smathers Beach** (⊠ S. Roosevelt Blvd.) has nearly 2 mi (3 km) of sand, restrooms, picnic areas, and volleyball courts, all of which make it popular with the spring-break crowd. Trucks along the road rent rafts, Windsurfers, and other beach "toys."

Where to Eat

$$–$$$ ✕ **Alice's Key West Restaurant.** A rather plain-Jane storefront gives way to

Fodor's Choice   a warm and cozy dining room, where chef-owner Alice Weingarten

★   works whimsical creations that are very far from plain. Color, zing, and spice are Weingarten's main ingredients. Take the tuna tartare tower: it's spiced with a garlic-chili paste, topped with tomato ginger jam, and served between crisp wonton wafers. The Brazilian churrasco pan-seared skirt steak is served with garlicky chimichurri sauce and green chili and manchego cheese mashed potatoes. Or, try the Asian spiced wild boar baby back ribs or Cuban-style mojo marinated ostrich. It's open for break-fast and lunch, too; end your Duval Crawl here for a breakfast of eggs, fries, and toast for as little as $4. ⊠ *1114 Duval St.* ☎ *305/292–5733* ⊟ *AE, D, MC, V* ☉ *No lunch.*

¢–$$ ✕ **Turtle Kraals.** In a city that prides itself on the battle of the bizarre, tur-tle races certainly are a contender for the title. They're held Monday and Friday evenings at 6 inside this restaurant and saloon named for the *kraals* (corrals) where turtles were kept from the mid 1800s until the 1970s. Today, much smaller box turtles provide the live entertainment while the menu offers an assortment of marine cuisine that includes seared jerk tuna, seafood enchiladas, and, our favorite, mango crab cakes with key lime mustard, yellow rice, black beans, and fried plantains. (If your ship leaves before race time, you can still meet the contenders during a mid-day visit.) ⊠ *231 Margaret St.* ☎ *305/294–2640* ⊟ *MC, V.*

Nightlife

Three spots stand out for first-timers among the saloons frequented by Key West denizens. All are within easy walking distance of the cruise-ship piers. In its earliest incarnation, back in 1851, **Capt. Tony's Saloon** (⊠428 Greene St. ☎ 305/294–1838) was a morgue and icehouse, then Key West's first telegraph station. It became the original Sloppy Joe's in the mid-1930s, when Hemingway was a regular. Later, a young Jimmy Buf-fett sang here. Bands play nightly. The **Schooner Wharf Bar** (⊠ 202 William St. ☎ 305/292–9520), an open-air waterfront bar and grill in the his-toric seaport district, retains its funky Key West charm. There's live is-land music all day, plus happy hour, and special events. There's more history and good times at **Sloppy Joe's** (⊠ 201 Duval St. ☎ 305/294–5717), the successor to a famous 1937 speakeasy named for its founder, Captain Joe Russell. Ernest Hemingway came here to gamble and tell stories. Dec-orated with Hemingway memorabilia and marine flags, the bar is pop-ular with travelers and is full and noisy all the time. Live entertainment plays daily 10 AM–2 AM.

LA ROMANA, DOMINICAN REPUBLIC

Eileen
Robinson
Smith

Dominicans will extend a gracious welcome, saying, "This is your home!" and, indeed, are happy to share what they have, which is a physically beautiful island bathed by the Atlantic Ocean to the north and the Caribbean Sea to the south. Among its most precious assets are 1,000 miles of gorgeous beaches studded with coconut palms and sands ranging from pearl white to golden brown to volcanic black. The Caribbean sun kisses this exotic land (temperatures average 82°F). It's a fertile country blessed with resources, particularly cocoa, coffee, rum, tobacco, and sugar cane.

The contrasts here can be dramatic. You will most definitely see signs of wealth, for the upper strata of society lives well indeed here. However, on the country roads you'll be amazed that four people with sacks of groceries and a stalk of bananas can fit on a smoky old *motoconcho* (motor bike/taxi). Similarly, Dominicans can be fair-skinned with light eyes, or black, but mostly they are shades of brown. Poverty still prevails, though the standard of life has really come up along with the growth of North American tourism. Islanders have an affinity for all things American, and many speak English. A great Dominican dream is to go to the States and become the next Sammy Sosa, then return to be a philanthropist in his own hometown.

> ## LA ROMANA BEST BETS
>
> - **Altos de Chavó.** Casa de Campo's own Tuscan hill town offers shopping and dining as well as great views. It's a worthwhile place to spend a couple of hours and perhaps have lunch.
> - **Golf.** The Teeth of the Dog is one of the Caribbean's best courses; if you are a golfer—and can get a tee time—you will never regret the expense.
> - **Kandela.** The Dominican folkloric show is a highlight if your ship stays late in port.

Essentials

CURRENCY The Dominican peso (RD$32.38 to US$1). At Casa de Campo, you can use U.S. dollars, but you may need to change some money if you explore further afield. You will get change in pesos.

HOURS Offices and shops are open weekdays from 8 to noon and 2 to 6, Saturday from 8 to noon. About half the stores stay open all day, no longer closing for a midday siesta. Attractions are generally seen between 9:00 a.m. and 5:00 to 6:00 p.m.

INTERNET Unfortunately, there is no Internet café where cruise-ship passengers can access their e-mail, either at the dock or at Casa de Campo.

TELEPHONES Telephones are available at the dock, as soon as passengers disembark, and telephone cards can be purchased there as well. Similarly, at the Marina Chavón, where a shuttle drops passengers off, you'll also find phones. Tele-cards can be bought at the supermarket. To call the U.S. or Canada from the D.R., just punch in 1 plus the area code and number. To make calls on the island, you must tap in the area code (809), plus the seven-digit number; if you are calling a Dominican cell phone, you must first punch in 1.

La Romana, Dominican Republic

Coming Ashore

Ships enter the Casa de Campo International Tourist Port (Muelle TurÍstico Internacional Casa de Campo.) A group of folkloric dancers and local musicians play merengue and greet passengers as they come down the gangway. An information booth with smiling, English-speaking staffers is there to assist cruise-ship passengers; the desk is open the entire time that the ship is in port. Most passengers explore the resort, take an excursion, and then have dinner on the ship or at the resort, and perhaps catch the bus to "Kandela" a Dominican-themed, Las Vegas–style revue performed under the stars in an amphitheater in Altos de Chavón.

It is a 15-minute walk into the town of La Romana, or you can jump into a waiting taxi. It's safe to stroll around town, but it's not particularly beautiful, quaint, nor even historic; however, it is a real slice of Dominican life. Most people just board the complimentary shuttle and head for La Marina Chavón and/or Altos de Chavón, both of which are at the Casa de Campo resort. Shuttles run all day long. Since many taxi drivers do not speak English, staff members from the information kiosk will help to make taxi arrangements. Most rates are fixed and spelled out on a board: $15 to Casa de Campo's Marina Chavón, $20 to Altos de Chavón. You may be able to negotiate a somewhat lower rate if a group books a taxi for a tour. You can also rent a car at Casa de Campo (Hertz and Avis have offices near the resort reception area); rates are expensive, usually more than $70 a day. Driving into Santo Domingo can be a hair-raising experience and isn't for the faint of heart.

Shore Excursions

The following shore excursions are offered by major cruise lines in La Romana. They may not be offered by all lines, and tour names may differ as well. Times and prices are approximate.

Horseback Riding. One popular activity at the Casa de Campo resort is horseback riding from the resort's excellent equestrian center. The 90-minute ride isn't exactly backcountry riding: you're going around the manicured grounds and golf courses, but it's fun. ⊙ *2 hrs* 🚌 *$60.*

Kandela. If your ship stays late at La Romana, you may have the opportunity to see "Kandela," a splashy, Las Vegas–style Dominican cultural show, at the amphitheater in Altos de Chavón. It's usually cheaper to book this show through your ship than on your own since transportation is included. ⊘ *2 hrs* ▧ *$31.*

Saona Adrenaline Experience. Casa de Campo's own beach is disappointing. This one isn't. After a speedboat ride down the river, you dock at Saona island for swimming at an excellent beach. Some tours stop for snorkeling in the bay on the way back. Other tours include a buffet lunch—and may cost more. ⊘ *4 hrs* ▧ *$70.*

Santo Domingo Tour. The largest and oldest city in the Caribbean, Santo Domingo can be overwhelming, but it's historic and only 90 minutes from La Romana. The trip includes a walk around the Zona Colonial, the oldest part of the city. ⊘ *6½ hrs* ▧ *$72.*

Exploring La Romana

Altos de Chavón is a replica of a 16th-century Mediterranean hill town with dramatic views of the Chavón River. You feel transported to centuries past as you stroll the cobblestoned streets, stopping into the quaint shops, exclusive boutiques, and art galleries located near the archaeological museum, design school, a medieval-style cathedral, and rows of restaurants, along with a French bakery and coffee bar.

Spanish civilization in the New World began in the 12-block Zona Colonial of **Santo Domingo**. Strolling its narrow streets, it's easy to imagine this old city as it was when the likes of Columbus, Cortés, and Ponce de León walked the cobblestones, pirates sailed in and out, and colonists were settling themselves. Tourist brochures tout that "history comes alive here"—a surprisingly truthful statement. A fun horse and carriage ride throughout the Zone costs $20 for an hour. The steeds are no thoroughbreds, but they clip right along, though any commentary will be in Spanish. The drivers usually hang out in front of the Sofitel Nicolas Ovando. History buffs will want to spend a day exploring the many "firsts" of our continent, which will be included in any cruise-ship excursion. Do wear comfortable shoes.

Shopping

Altos de Chavón also has many shops and art galleries, as well as restaurants. It also has the amphitheater where "Kandela" is performed most nights. Shops and galleries here are expensive, as are the restaurants. The **Casa de Campo Marina** is home to more than 60 upscale shops, galleries, and jewelers scattered among restaurants and an ice-cream parlor, a Euro-style bar, and a yacht club. It is a great place to spend a leisurely morning or afternoon of shopping and strolling, particularly if you enjoy staring at the extravagant yachts often moored here. The Jenny Polanco Boutique sells the work of a Dominican designer known for her white resort-wear for women; the shop now includes her line of contemporary jewelry and handbags. Although upscale is the operative word here, you can still buy a postcard, a pair of shorts, or a logo shirt. A supermarket sells sundries, postcards, and snacks.

> ### CABIN OUTLETS
>
> Most ships' cabins have only one or two electrical outlets located near the desk/vanity table (not counting the shaver-only outlet in the bathroom). A short extension cord allows you to use more than one electrical appliance at once and gives you a bit more flexibility to move around, particularly if you bring a laptop computer.

Activities

Most activities available at Casa de Campo are open to cruise-ship passengers. You'll need to make reservations on the ship, particularly for golf.

FISHING Marlin and wahoo are among the fish that folks angle for here (fishing is best between January and June). **La Marina Chavon** (⌷ Casa de Campo, Calle Barlovento 3, La Romana ☎ 809/523–8646 ⊕ www.marinacasadecampo.com) is the best charter option near La Romana. Costs to charter a boat—with a crew, refreshments, bait, and tackle—generally range from $592 to $1,616 for a half-day and from $790 to $3,191 for a full day.

GOLF *Golf* magazine has called "Teeth of the Dog" at **Casa de Campo** (⌷ La Romana ☎ 809/523–3333 ⊕ www.casadecampo.com.do) the finest golf resort in the Caribbean. In 2005 it was closed for some months for a complete renovation, but it is once again luxuriant, with new tees, greens, and contoured bunkers by Pete Dye himself. Greens fees are now $232 though it drops to $145 from May through October. A second course near Altos de Chavón, "Dye Fore" ($203) hugs a cliff overlooking the ocean, as well as Río Chávon and its palm groves. A third 18-hole course called "The Links" ($145) is inland. For all courses, non-guests must reserve tee times more than a day in advance, which makes booking on the ship essential.

Beaches

Las Minitas Beach at Casa de Campo is reserved exclusively for hotel guests and villa owners. Cruise passengers must take a beach excursion or make their own arrangements for transportation to nearby beaches. In truth, all of these are better than the beach at the resort.

Catalina Island is a diminutive, picture-postcard Caribbean island off the coast of the mainland. Some cruise ships actually anchor off Catalina Island and offer excursions by tenders to it as well as to Casa de Campo. To get to the island, you'll have to take an excursion. Catalina is about a half-hour away by catamaran, and most excursions offer the use of snorkeling equipment as well as a beach barbecue.

Playa Bayahibe is a beautiful stretch of beach. It is also pleasant to browse and shop in the village of Bayahibe. Shore excursions are organized by the cruise lines to the beach, which is about 30 minutes away from the cruise-port by bus. You can also book your own taxi here, and the trip may be cheaper than the cost of a shore excursion if you come with a group.

Saona Island was once a pristine, idyllic isle. Now, on a busy cruise-ship day, there may be as many as 1,000 bathers there. However, the beach is beautiful. To get here, you'll have to book an excursion with your ship, often a power boat from Altos de Chavón; otherwise, you are bused to Bayahibe and board a boat there. There is usually a stop at a natural, shallow pool with a white-sand bottom, populated with starfish. The day-trip usually includes a Dominican BBQ lunch.

Where to Eat

There are some casual places to eat at Marina de Chavón, but in truth the restaurants at Altos de Chavón are fairly expensive, and you'd be better off doing some shopping and then heading back to your ship for lunch. If you want to have something a little nicer at the marina, then Peperoni is the best choice.

$$–$$$ ✕**Peperoni.** Although the name sounds as Italian as *amore*, this classy restaurant's menu is much more eclectic than Italian. It has a classy, contemporary, white-dominated decor; waiters are also dressed in white with long aprons. The classic pasta dishes, osso buco, and risottos with rock shrimp or porcinis are authentic and delectable as are such specialties as polenta-encrusted sea bass with lentils. But you can also opt for stylishly simple charcoal-grilled steaks, burgers, pizzas, and sandwiches. ✉ *Plaza Portafolio 16, Marina Chavón* ☎ *809/523–2228* 🖃 *AE, MC, V.*

MARTINIQUE (FORT-DE-FRANCE)

Eileen
Robinson
Smith

The largest of the Windward Islands, Martinique is 4,261 mi (6,817 km) from Paris, but its spirit and language are decidedly French, with more than a soupçon of West Indian spice. Tangible, edible evidence of the fact is the island's cuisine, a superb blend of French and creole. Martinique is lushly landscaped with tropical flowers. Trees bend under the weight of fruits such as mangoes, papayas, lemons, limes, and bright-red West Indian cherries. Acres of banana plantations, pineapple fields, and waving sugarcane stretch to the horizon. The towering mountains and verdant rain forest in the north lure hikers, while underwater sights and sunken treasures attract snorkelers and scuba divers. Martinique is also wonderful if your idea of exercise is turning over every 10 minutes to get an even tan and your taste in adventure runs to duty-free shopping. A popular cruise-ship excursion goes to St-Pierre, which was buried by ash when Mont Pelée erupted in 1902.

Essentials

CURRENCY The euro (€1 to US$1.31). You will not be able to use dollars, so plan on getting some euros. You cannot cash traveler's checks or dollars at the bank, only at a bureau de change, so ATMs are your best bet if you need euros. Change Caraïbes—which has an office in Fort-de-France at 14 rue Victor Hugo and Le Bord de Mer—will still exchange both dollars and traveler's checks and usually offers fair rates.

HOURS Banks are open weekdays from 7:30 to noon and 2:30 to 4. Post offices are generally open weekdays from 7 to 6, Saturday from 8 until noon. Stores that cater to tourists are generally open weekdays from 8:30 to 6, Saturday 8:30 to 1. Many stores in Fort-de-France close from 12:30 to 2 for lunch.

INTERNET **Cyber Club Caraïbé** (✉ 16 rue Francois Arago, Fort-de-France ☎ 0596/70–31–62). **Internet Haut Depot** (✉ 61 rue Victor Hugo, Fort-de-France ☎ 0596/63–12–20).

TELEPHONES There are no coin-operated phone booths. Public phones now use a *télécarte,* which you can buy at post offices, café-tabacs, hotels, and at *bureaux de change.* To call the United States from Martinique, dial 00 + 1, the area code,

---

MARTINIQUE BEST BETS

- **Beaches.** If you want to simply relax, the most beautiful beach is Les Salines.

- **Shopping.** Shopping in Fort-de-France's many upscale boutiques is good, but never cheap.

- **St-Pierre.** Like Pompeii transported to the Caribbean, Martinique's former capital was buried by ash but has been reborn.

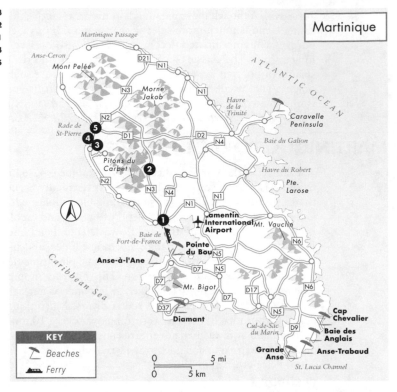

Martinique

and the local number. To call locally, you now have to dial 0596 before the six-digit number. You can make collect calls to Canada through the Bell operator; you can get the AT&T or MCI operators from blue, special-service phones at the cruise ports and in town (try Super Sumo snack bar, on rue de la Liberté, near the library).

Coming Ashore

Most cruise ships call at the Maritime Terminal east of Fort-de-France; however, some large ships that anchor in the Baie des Flamands may tender passengers directly to the Fort-de-France waterfront. To reach the tourist information booth, which is staffed by helpful, English-speaking personnel, turn right and walk along the waterfront. Uniformed dispatchers assist in finding English-speaking taxi drivers. Ask about guided walking tours that can be arranged at the nearby open-air market.

The only practical way to get into the city from the Maritime Terminal is to take a cab, approximately €15 round-trip. Taxis are metered, and there's no extra charge for extra passengers; however, rates are fairly expensive. A journey of any distance can cost €25 or more, and traffic in Fort-de-France can be nightmarish. If you want to go to the beach, a much cheaper option is to take a ferry from Fort-de-France. *Vedettes* (ferries) operate daily between Quai d'Ensnambuc in Fort-de-France and the marina in Pointe du Bout, Anse-Mitan, and Anse-à-l'Ane. Any of the three trips takes about 15 minutes, and the ferries operate about every 30 minutes on weekdays. Renting a car in Fort-de-France is possible, but the heavy traffic can be forbidding. Rates start at €60 per day for a car with manual transmission; those with automatic transmissions are substantially more expensive and rarely available.

Shore Excursions

We consider these to be among the better shore excursions for Martinique. They may not be offered by all lines, and tour names may differ as well. Times and prices are approximate.

Island Tour with St-Pierre. Ride along the coastal road to St-Pierre, which was once the capital of Martinique. The ruined city is a museum of devastated houses, monuments, and industries destroyed by the volcanic eruption of Mt. Pelée in 1902. Some tours include the Depaz Rum Distillery. ⊘ *4 hrs* ✉ *$76.*

Jardin de Balata. This botanical garden is one of the island's loveliest spots. A nearby church is an exact replica of Sacre Coeur. ⊘ *3 hrs* ✉ *$69.*

Martinique 4x4 You'll definitely hit the backroads on this trip, but you'll get to see some of the wildly beautiful landscape that you'll miss if you just stick to the main highways. This tour usually includes St-Pierre and the Depaz Distillery. ⊘ *4½ hrs* ✉ *$99.*

Exploring Martinique

Numbers in the margin correspond to points of interest on the Martinique map.

If you want to see the lush island interior and St-Pierre on your own, take the N3, which snakes through dense rain forests, north through the mountains to Le Morne Rouge, then take the coastal N2 back to Fort-de-France via St-Pierre. You can do the 40-mi (64-km) round-trip in half a day—that is if you don't get lost, can comprehend the road signs, avoid collisions in the roundabouts, drive as fast as the flow of frenetic traffic, and can ask directions in French (probably of someone on the street who only speaks a creole patois). But your best option is to hire an English-speaking driver.

③ Aqualand. This U.S.-style water park is a great place for families to have a wet, happy day. ✉ *Rte. des Pitons, Carbet* ☎ *0596/78–40–00* ⊕ *www.aqualand-martinique.fr* ✉ *€17.50* ⊘ *Daily 10–6.*

② Balata. Built in 1923 to commemorate those who died in World War I, **Balata Church** is an exact replica of Paris's Sacré-Coeur Basilica. The **Jardin de Balata** (Balata Gardens), has thousands of varieties of tropical flowers and plants. There are shaded benches from which to take in the mountain view. ✉ *Rte. de Balata, Balata* ☎ *0596/64–48–73* ✉ *€7* ⊘ *Daily 9–5.*

① Fort-de-France. With its historic fort and superb location beneath the towering Pitons du Carbet on the Baie des Flamands, Martinique's capital should be a grand place. It isn't. The most pleasant districts, such as Didier, Bellevue, and Schoelcher, are on the hillside; there are some good shops with Parisian wares and lively street markets. Near the harbor is a marketplace where local crafts and souvenirs are sold.

The heart of Fort-de-France is **La Savane**, a 12½-acre park filled with trees, fountains, and benches. It's a popular gathering place and the scene of promenades, parades, and impromptu soccer matches. Along the east side are numerous snack wagons. Alas, it's no longer a desirable oasis, what with a lot of litter and other negatives often found in urban parks. A statue of Pierre Belain d'Esnambuc, leader of the island's first settlers, is unintentionally upstaged by Vital Dubray's vandalized—now

> **PRE-PACK**
>
> Set aside a few moments every day to pack up your dirty clothes, then spend the last afternoon of your cruise doing fun things instead of packing.

headless—white Carrara marble statue of the empress Joséphine, Napoléon's first wife. Across from La Savane, you can catch the ferry *La Vedette* for the beaches at Anse-Mitan and Anse-à-l'Ane and for the 20-minute run across the bay to Pointe du Bout. It's relatively cheap as well as stress-free—much safer, more pleasant, and faster than by car.

The most imposing historic site in La Savane (and in Fort-de-France) is **Fort St-Louis,** which runs along the east side of La Savane. It's open Monday through Saturday from 9 to 3, and admission is €4.

The **Bibliothèque Schoelcher** is the wildly elaborate Romanesque public library. It was named after Victor Schoelcher, who led the fight to free the slaves in the French West Indies in the 19th century. The eye-popping structure was built for the 1889 Paris Exposition, after which it was dismantled, shipped to Martinique, and reassembled piece by ornate piece. ⊠ *At rue de la Liberté, runs along west side of La Savane, and rue Perrinon* ☎ *0596/70–26–67* ✉ *Free* ⊙ *Mon. 1–5:30, Tues.–Fri. 8:30–5:30, Sat. 8:30–noon.*

★ Le **Musée Régional d'Histoire et d'Ethnographie** is a learning experience that will help you better understand the history, background, and people of the island. Housed in an elaborate former residence (circa 1888) with balconies and fretwork, its displays are far-ranging. ⊠ *10 bd. Général de Gaulle* ☎ *0596/72–81–87* ✉ *€3* ⊙ *Mon. and Wed.–Fri. 8:30–5, Tues. 2–5, Sat. 8:30–noon.*

Rue Victor Schoelcher runs through the center of the capital's primary shopping district, a six-block area bounded by rue de la République, rue de la Liberté, rue de Victor Severe, and rue Victor Hugo. Stores sell Paris fashions and French perfume, china, crystal, and liqueurs, as well as local handicrafts. The Romanesque **Saint-Louis Cathedral** (⊠ Rue Victor Schoelcher) with its lovely stained-glass windows, was built in 1878, the sixth church on this site (the others were destroyed by fire, hurricane, and earthquake).

The **Parc Floral et Culturel,** in the northeastern corner of the city center, will acquaint you with the island's exotic flora. There's also an aquarium. The park contains the island's official cultural center, where there are sometimes free evening concerts. ⊠ *Pl. José-Marti, Sermac* ☎ *0596/71–66–25* ✉ *Grounds free; aquarium €5.60* ⊙ *Park daily dawn–10 PM; aquarium daily 9–7.*

❹ **Musée Gauguin.** Martinique was a brief station in Paul Gauguin's wanderings, but a decisive moment in the evolution of his art. Disappointingly, this modest museum has no originals, only reproductions. ⊠ *Anse-Turin, Carbet* ☎ *0596/78–22–66* ✉ *€6* ⊙ *Daily 9–5:30.*

⑤ St-Pierre. By the turn of the 20th century St-Pierre was a flourishing city, known as the Paris of the West Indies. But on May 8, 1902, as the nearby volcano erupted, Mont Pelée split in half, belching forth a cloud of burning ash, poisonous gas, and lava that raced down the mountain at 250 mph. At 3,600°F, it instantly vaporized everything in its path; 30,000 people in St-Pierre were killed in two minutes. Only one man, a prisoner in an underground cell in the town jail, survived. Today, the city has the feel of a European seaside hill town. Stroll the main streets and check the blackboards at the sidewalk cafés before deciding where to lunch. The **Cyparis Express,** a small tourist train, will take you around to the main sights with running narrative (in French) for €10.50; English-speaking guides are available. Like stage sets for a dramatic opera, there are the ruins of the island's first church (built in 1640), the imposing theater, and toppled statues.

★ ☙ For those interested in the eruption of 1902, the **Musée Vulcanologique Frank Perret** is a must. Established in 1932, it houses photographs of the old town, documents, and a number of relics—some gruesome—excavated from the ruins, including molten glass, melted iron, and contorted clocks stopped at 8 AM. ⊠ *Rue Victor Hugo* ☎ *0596/78–15–16* ⊡ *€5* ☙ *Daily 9–5.*

An excursion to **Depaz Distillery** is one of the island's nicest treats. There is a self-guided tour, and the tasting room sells their rums, including golden and aged rum (notably Rhum Dore) and distinctive liqueurs made from ginger and basil. ⊠ *Mont Pelée Plantation* ☎ *0596/78–13–14* ⊡ *Free* ☙ *Mon.–Sat. 9–5.*

Shopping
French products, such as perfume, wines, liquors, designer scarves, leather goods, and crystal, are good buys in Fort-de-France. Luxury goods are discounted 20% when paid for with traveler's checks or major credit cards. Look for creole gold jewelry; white, dark, flavored, and aged rums; and handcrafted straw goods, pottery, madras fabric, and tapestries. Shops that sell luxury items are abundant around the cathedral in Fort-de-France, particularly on rue Victor Hugo, rue Moreau de Jones, rue Antoine Siger, and rue Lamartine.

The work of **Antan Lontan** (⊠ 213 rte. de Balata, Fort-de-France ☎ 0596/ 64–52–72) has to be seen. Sculptures, busts, statuettes, and artistic lamps portray the creole women and the story of the Martiniquaise culture. **Cadet Daniel** (⊠ 72 rue Antoine Siger, Fort-de-France ☎ 0596/71–41–48) sells Lalique, Limoges, and Baccarat. **Roger Albert** (⊠ 7 rue Victor Hugo, Fort-de-France ☎ 0596/71–71–71) carries designer crystal.

Activities
FISHING Fish cruising these waters include tuna, barracuda, dolphinfish, kingfish, bonito, and the big game—white and blue marlins. The **Centre de Peche** (⊠ Port de Plaisance, bd. Allegre, Le Marin ☎ 0596/76–24–20 or 0696/ 28–80–58), a fully loaded Davis 47-foot fishing boat, is a sportfisherman's dream. It goes out with a minimum of four anglers for €195 per person for a half day, or €390 per person for a full day, including lunch. Nonanglers can come for the ride for €95 and €190, respectively. Captain Yves speaks English fluently and is a fun guy.

7

GOLF   The 18-hole **Golf Country Club de la Martinique** (⊠ Les Trois-Ilets ☎ 0596/ 68–32–81 ⊕ www.golfmartinique.com) has a par-71 Robert Trent Jones course with an English-speaking pro, pro shop, bar, and restaurant. The club offers special greens fees to cruise-ship passengers (€46 for green fees and another €46 for an electric cart). For those who don't mind walking while admiring the Caribbean view between the palm trees, club trolleys are €8. There are no caddies.

HIKING   Two-thirds of Martinique is designated as protected land. Trails, all 31 of them, are well marked and maintained. At the beginning of each, a notice is posted advising on the level of difficulty, the duration of a hike, and any interesting facts. The **Parc Naturel Régional de la Martinique** (⊠ 9 bd. Général de Gaulle, Fort-de-France ☎ 0596/73–19–30) organizes inexpensive guided excursions year-round. If there have been heavy rains, though, give it up. The tangle of ferns, bamboo trees, and llanai vines is dramatic, but during rainy season, the springs and waterfalls and wet, muddy trails will negate any enthusiasm.

HORSEBACK   At **Black Horse Ranch** (⊠ Les Trois-Ilets ☎ 0596/68–37–80), one-hour
RIDING   trail rides (€35) go into the countryside and across waving cane fields; two hours on the trail (€40) bring riders near a river. Only western saddles are used for adults; children can ride English. Semi-private lessons in French or English are €40 a person, less for kids if they can join a group. Some guides are English-speaking at **Ranch de Caps** (⊠ Cap Macré, Le Marin ☎ 0596/74–70–65 or 0696/23–18–18), where you can take a half-day ride (western) on the wild southern beaches and across the countryside for €45. Rides go out in the morning (8:30 to noon) and afternoon (1:30 to 5) every day but Monday. If you can manage a full day in the saddle, it costs €75. A real treat is the full-moon ride. Most of the mounts are Anglo-Arabs. Riders are encouraged to help cool and wash their horses at day's end. Reserve in advance. Riders of all levels are welcomed. **Ranch Jack** (⊠ Anse-d'Arlets ☎ 0596/68–37–69 or 0596/ 68–63–97) has trail rides (English style) across some beautiful country for €35 an hour; half-day excursions for €50 (€58 with transfers from nearby hotels) go through the fields and forests to the beach. The lessons for kids are recommendable.

Beaches

Topless bathing is prevalent at the large resort hotels. The clean, golden sand at **Anse-Mitan** (⊠ Les Trois-Ilets) is lined by inexpensive waterfront hotels; there is excellent snorkeling just offshore. Chaise lounges are available for rent from hotels for about €5. **Pointe du Bout** (⊠ Les Trois-Ilets) has small, man-made beaches that are lined with luxury resorts. Across from the main pedestrian entrance to the marina, if you take a left—between the taxi stand and the Kalenda Hotel, then go left again, you will reach the Sofitel beach, which has especially nice facilities and options for lunch. If not crowded with hotel guests, the beach boys might rent you a chaise. Otherwise, just plop your beach towel down in the sand and admire the great bay view. **Les Salines** (⊠ Ste-Anne), a cove of soft white sand lined with coconut palms, is about an hour from Fort-de-France. (This is doable if you cut the cost by taking a group taxi.) Les Salines is awash with families and children during holidays and on weekends, but quiet and uncrowded during the week. You can't rent chaise longues, so bring a beach towel or two (there are showers). Food vendors roam the sand.

Where to Eat

All restaurants include a 15% service charge in their prices. Leaving a little extra gives Americans a good name.

¢–$ ✕ **Linda's Café.** You will be satisfied at this classy café. You must order at the counter (it's OK to just point). Offerings are displayed in the glass case. Breakfast can be fresh-squeezed juice, gourmet coffee, and just-baked croissants. Lunch is the best possible sandwich situation. Choices abound, from fresh thyme bread with rare roast beef, to baby shrimp and avocado. Have creamy *fromage blanc* instead of mayo, and even turkey bacon. Dessert can be a perfect, dark-chocolate brownie. ⊠ *15 rue Victor Hugo, Fort-de-France* ☎ *0596/71–91–92* ⊟ *MC, V* ☺ *No dinner Sun.*

$–$$ ✕ **Chez Carole.** After spending eight years in Toulouse, Carole now cooks her island's creole specialties in the simple surroundings of the market. Tourists often pass by the loud hawkers to settle here, where they will be welcomed in English and impressed by the awards on display. Creole prix-fixe meals might include accras, fricassee of octopus and conch, chicken in coconut milk, or grilled whole fish. Accompaniments are usually lentils, red beans, yellow rice, and breadfruit. Homemade ice cream and coconut flan are among the dessert possibilities. Cruise-ship passengers love the fresh-squeezed juices (with rum, if you like) and coconut milk shakes. Dollars and traveler's checks work equally well here. ⊠ *Le Grand Marché, Rue Isambert, Fort-de-France* ☎ *0696/44–12–31* ⊟ *No credit cards* ☺ *Closed Sun. No dinner.*

MONTEGO BAY, JAMAICA

John Bigley &
Paris
Permenter

Today, many explorations of MoBay are conducted from a reclining chair—frothy drink in hand—on Doctor's Cave Beach. As home of Jamaica's busiest cruise pier and the north-shore airport, Montego Bay—or MoBay—is the first taste most visitors have of the island. Travelers from around the world come and go in this bustling community, which ranks as Jamaica's second-largest city. The name Montego is derived from *manteca* ("lard" in Spanish). The Spanish first named this Bahía de Manteca, or Lard Bay. Why? The Spanish once shipped hogs from this port city. Jamaican tourism began here in 1924, when the first resort opened at Doctor's Cave Beach so that health-seekers could "take the waters." If you can pull yourself away from the water's edge and brush the sand off your toes, you can find some very interesting colonial sights in the surrounding area.

Essentials

CURRENCY The Jamaican dollar (J$67 to US$1). Currency-exchange booths are set up on the docks at Montego Bay whenever a ship is in port; however, the U.S. dollar is accepted virtually everywhere, though change is made in Jamaican dollars.

HOURS Normal business hours for stores are weekdays from 8:30 to 4:30, Saturday 8 to 1 with extended hours for shops in tourist areas.

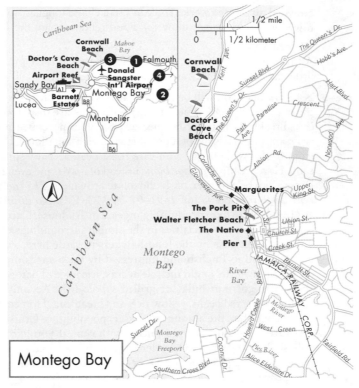

Montego Bay

INTERNET   A growing number of Internet cafés have sprung up in recent years in Montego Bay hotels and cafés. A popular option for many cruise passengers is the Internet café at **Doctor's Cave Beach** (✉ Montego Bay ☎ 876/971–1050).

TELEPHONES   Public telephones (and fax machines) are at the communications center at the Montego Bay Cruise Terminal. Travelers also find public phones in major Montego Bay malls such as the City Centre Shopping Mall. Some U.S. phone companies won't permit credit-card calls to be placed from Jamaica because they've been victims of fraud so collect calls are often the top option. GSM cell phones equipped with tri-band or world-roaming service will find coverage throughout the Montego Bay region.

Coming Ashore

Ships dock at the Montego Cruise Terminal, operated by the Port Authority of Jamaica. Located west of Montego Bay, the cruise terminal has five berths and accommodates both cruise and cargo shipping. The terminal has shops, a communications center, a Jamaica Tourist Board visitor information booth, and a taxi stand supervised by the Jamaica Tourist Board. The cruise port in Montego Bay is not within walking distance of the heart of town; however, there's one shopping center within walking distance of the docks. If you just want to visit a beach, then Doctor's Cave, a public beach, is a very good nearby alternative, and it's right in town.

From the Montego Cruise Terminal, both taxis and shuttle buses take passengers downtown. Taxi service is about US $10 each way to downtown. Expect to pay $2 per person each way by shuttle bus to the City Centre Shopping Mall or $3 each way to Doctor's Cave Beach. Jamaica is one place in the Caribbean where it's usually to your advantage to take an organized shore excursion offered by your ship unless you just want to do a bit of shopping in town. Taxis aren't particularly cheap, and a full-day tour for a small group will run $150 to $180 (because of road conditions and the distances in Jamaica, most tours take a full day).

If you take a private taxi, you should know that only some of Jamaica's taxis are metered; rates are per car, not per passenger. You can flag cabs on the street. All licensed and properly insured taxis display red Public Passenger (PP) license plates. Licensed minivans also bear the red PP plates. If you hire a taxi driver as a tour guide, be sure to agree on a price before the vehicle is put into gear. Because of the cost of insurance, which you must buy since most credit cards offering coverage exclude Jamaica, it's expensive to rent a car; you may also find it difficult to arrange a rental on-island. It's far easier to arrange a taxi.

> ### MONTEGO BAY BEST BETS
>
> - **Doctor's Cave Beach.** The public beach club right in the heart of Montego Bay is on an excellent stretch of white-sand beach and has many facilities to make a day at the beach a pleasure.
> - **Dunn's River Falls.** A visit to the falls is nothing but a touristy experience, and yet it's still exhilarating.
> - **Martha Brae Rafting.** A slow rafting trip down the river is a relaxing and enjoyable way to spend a few hours.
> - **Shopping.** If you just want some retail therapy, MoBay has several good shopping centers.

SHORE EXCURSIONS
We consider these to be among the better shore excursions for Montego Bay. They may not be offered by all lines, and tour names may differ as well. Times and prices are approximate.

Canopy Tour. The "tour" consists of flying from platform to platform through a forest on a zip line. It's a great experience. ☉ 4–4¼ hrs ▦ $99.

Dunn's River Falls with Lunch. Some kind of Dunn's River Falls trip is offered on all Montego Bay port calls, and it may be a combination of Dunn's River Falls with another attraction in Ocho Rios for more money. The basic (and usually cheapest) option includes a visit to the Falls and lunch at a local restaurant in Ocho Rios. ☉ 7½ hrs ▦ $79.

Montego Bay Highlights with Rose Hall. After a quick tour of town, the highlight of this trip is a visit to the supposedly haunted Rose Hall Great House. ☉ 3½ hrs ▦ $49.

Rafting on the Martha Brae River. Pass the verdant plant life as you glide down the river on a 30-foot, two seat bamboo raft. This is decidedly still-water rafting. ☉ 4¼ ▦ $69.

Exploring Montego Bay
Numbers in the margin correspond to points of interest on the Jamaica map.

❶ **Greenwood Great House.** Although this historic home has no spooky legend to titillate, it's much better than Rose Hall at evoking life on a sugar plantation. The Barrett family, from whom the English poet Elizabeth Barrett Browning descended, once owned all the land from Rose Hall to Falmouth; they built this and several other great houses on it. (The poet's father, Edward Moulton Barrett, "the Tyrant of Wimpole Street," was born at nearby Cinnamon Hill, the estate of the late country singer Johnny Cash.) Highlights of Greenwood include oil paintings of the Barretts, china made for the family by Wedgwood, a library filled with rare books from as early as 1697, fine antique furniture, and a collection of exotic musical instruments. There's a pub on-site as well. It's 15 mi (24 km) east of Montego Bay. ⊠ *Greenwood* ☎ *876/953–1077* ⊕ *www.greenwoodgreathouse.com* ✑ *$12* ⊙ *Daily 9–6.*

❷ **Martha Brae River.** A gentle waterway about 25 mi (40 km) southeast of Montego Bay, it takes its name from an Arawak Indian who killed herself because she refused to reveal the whereabouts of a local gold mine to the Spanish. According to legend, she agreed to take them there and, on reaching the river, used magic to change its course, drowning herself and the greedy Spaniards with her. Her *duppy* (ghost) is said to guard the mine's entrance. Rafting on this river is a very popular activity.

❸ **Rose Hall Great House.** In the 1700s, Rose Hall may have been the greatest of great houses in the West Indies. Today it's popular less for its architecture than for the legend surrounding its second mistress: Annie Palmer was credited with murdering three husbands and a *busha* (plantation overseer) who was her lover. The story is told in a novel that's sold everywhere in Jamaica: *The White Witch of Rose Hall.* There's a pub on-site. The house is across the highway from the Rose Hall Resort. ⊠ *North Coast Hwy.* ☎ *876/953–9982* ✑ *$15* ⊙ *Daily 9–6.*

❹ **Dunn's River Falls.** A top shore excursion from Montego Bay despite the two-hour drive to get here, the falls are an eye-catching sight: 600 feet of cold, clear mountain water splashing over a series of stone steps to the warm Caribbean. The best way to enjoy the falls is to climb the slippery steps: don a swimsuit, take the hand of the person ahead of you, and trust that the chain of hands and bodies leads to an experienced guide. The leaders of the climbs are personable fellows who reel off bits of local lore while telling you where to step; you can hire a guide's service for a tip of a few dollars. After the climb, you exit through a crowded market, another reminder that this is one of Jamaica's top tourist attractions. ⊠ *Off A1, between St. Ann's and Ocho Rios* ☎ *876/974–2857* ✑ *$15* ⊙ *Daily 8:30–5.*

FodorśChoice ★

Shopping

Jamaican artisans express themselves in silk-screening, wood carvings, resort wear, hand-loomed fabrics, and paintings. Jamaican rum makes a great gift, as do Tia Maria (the famous coffee liqueur) and Blue Mountain coffee. Wood carvings are one of the top purchases; the finest carvings are made from the Jamaican national tree, lignum vitae, or tree of life, a dense wood that requires a talented carver to transform the hard, blond wood into dolphins, heads, or fish. Bargaining is expected with crafts vendors.

Gallery of West Indian Art (⊠ 11 Fairfield Rd., Montego Bay ☎ 876/952–4547) is the place to find Jamaican and Haitian paintings. A corner of the gallery is devoted to hand-turned pottery (some painted) and beautifully carved and painted birds and animals.

Activities

DIVING & SNORKELING Jamaica isn't a major dive destination, but you can find a few rich underwater regions, especially off the north coast. MoBay, known for its wall dives, has **Airport Reef** at its southwestern edge. The site is known for its coral caves, tunnels, and canyons. The first marine park in Jamaica, the **Montego Bay Marine Park,** was established to protect the natural resources of the bay; a quick look at the area and it's easy to see the treasures that lie beneath the surface. The north coast is on the edge of the Cayman Trench, so it boasts a wide array of marine life.

Scuba Jamaica (⊠ Half Moon, N. Coast Hwy., Montego Bay ☎ 876/381–1113 ⊕ www.scuba-jamaica.com) offers serious scuba facilities for dedicated divers. This operator is a PADI and NAUI operation and also offers Nitrox diving and instruction as well as instruction in underwater photography, night diving, and open-water diving. There's a pickup service for the Montego Bay, Runaway Bay, Discovery Bay, and Ocho Rios areas.

DOLPHIN SWIM PROGRAMS Dolphin lovers find two well-run options in both Montego Bay and Ocho Rios. **Dolphin Cove** (⊠ N. Coast Hwy., adjacent to Dunn's River Falls, Ocho Rios ☎ 876/974–5335 ⊕ www.dolphincovejamaica.com) offers dolphin swims as well as lower-priced dolphin encounters for ages eight and up; dolphin touch programs for ages six and over; or simple admission to the grounds, which also includes a short nature walk. Programs cost between $39 and $179, depending on your depth of involvement with the dolphins. Advance reservations are required.

GOLF Golfers appreciate both the beauty and the challenges offered by Jamaica's courses and some of the best are found in the Montego Bay area. Caddies are almost always mandatory throughout the island, and rates are $15 to $45. Cart rentals are available; costs are $20 to $40. Some of the best courses in the country are found near MoBay.

★ **Half Moon Golf, Tennis & Beach Club** (⊠ Montego Bay ☎ 876/953–2560), a Robert Trent Jones–designed 18-hole course 7 mi (11 km) east of town, is the home of the Red Stripe Pro Am (greens fees are $150). In 2004 the course received an upgrade and once again draws international attention. **Ironshore** (⊠ Montego Bay ☎ 876/953–2800), 3 mi (5 km) east of the airport, is an 18-hole links-style course (the greens fees are $50). The **Rose Hall Resort & Country Club** (⊠ Montego Bay ☎ 876/953–2650) hosts several invitational tournaments (greens fees run $150 for nonguests). **Tryall Golf, Tennis & Beach Club** (⊠ North Coast Hwy., Sandy Bay ☎ 876/956–5681), 15 mi (24 km) west of Montego Bay, has an 18-hole championship course on the site of a 19th-century sugar plantation (greens fees are $125).

> **BINOCULARS**
>
> Binoculars are as useful indoors as they are outside. You might think they are only for bringing far-off wildlife and sights within view, but take them into museums, churches, and other buildings to examine the details of artwork, sculptures, and architectural elements.

RIVER RAFTING Jamaica's many rivers mean a multitude of freshwater experiences, from mild to wild. Relaxing rafting trips aboard bamboo rafts poled by local boatmen are almost a symbol of Jamaica; this was the island's first tourist activity outside the beaches. Jamaicans had long used bamboo rafts to transport bananas downriver; decades ago actor and Jamaica resident Errol Flynn saw the rafts and thought they'd make a good tourist attraction. Today the slow rides are a favorite with romantic travelers and anyone looking for a quiet few hours with a trip down the **Martha Brae River,** about 25 mi (40 km) from MoBay, **River Lethe,** about 12 mi (19 km) southwest, or the **Great River,** which travels through the rain forest.

Jamaica Tours Limited (⊠ Providence Dr., Montego Bay ☎ 876/953–3700 ⊕ www.jamaicatoursltd.com) conducts trips down the River Lethe, approximately 12 mi (19 km; a 50-minute trip) southwest of MoBay; the four-hour excursion costs about $54 per person, includes lunch, and takes you through unspoiled hill country. Bookings can also be made through hotel tour desks. **Martha Brae River Rafting** (⊠ Claude Clarke Ave., Montego Bay ☎ 876/952–0889 ⊕ www.jamaicarafting.com) leads trips down the Martha Brae River, about 25 mi (40 km) from most hotels in MoBay. The cost is $45 per person for the 1½-hour river run.

If you're looking for a more rugged adventure, then consider a white-water rafting trip with **Caliche Rainforest** (⊠ Montego Bay ☎ 876/940–1745 ⊕ www.whitewaterraftingmontegobay.com); you must be 14 years old for this trip. The company also offers a less strenuous rafting trip for all ages.

Beaches

Doctor's Cave Beach. Montego Bay's tourist scene has its roots right on the Hip Strip, the bustling entertainment district along Gloucester Avenue. The best beach in Jamaica outside one of the more developed resorts is also here, thanks to its plantation-style clubhouse with changing rooms, showers, gift shops, bar, grill, and even a cybercafé. Nearby, you'll find the always-popular Margaritaville. There's a fee for admission; beach chairs and umbrellas are also for rent. It's also a good spot for snorkeling, as it's within the Montego Bay Marine Park, with protected corals and marine life. More active travelers can opt for parasailing, glass-bottom boat rides, or jet skiing.

Walter Fletcher Beach. Though not as pretty as Doctor's Cave Beach—or as tidy—it's home to Aquasol Theme Park. Along with a large beach (which includes lifeguards and security), the park offers water trampolines, Jet Skis, banana boat rides, Wave Runners, glass-bottom boats, snorkeling, tennis, go-cart racing, a disco at night, a bar, and a grill. The beach is near the center of town, and there's protection from the surf on a windy day, so you can find unusually fine swimming here; the calm waters make it a good bet for children.

Where to Eat

Many restaurants add a 10% service charge to the bill. Otherwise, a tip of 10% to 20% is customary.

★ ¢–$$ ✕ **The Native.** Shaded by a large poinciana tree and overlooking Gloucester Avenue, this open-air stone terrace serves Jamaican and international dishes. To go native, start with smoked marlin, move on to the *boonoonoonoos* platter (a sampler of local dishes), and round out with coconut pie or *duckanoo* (a sweet dumpling of cornmeal, coconut, and banana wrapped in a banana leaf and steamed). Live entertainment and candlelighted tables make this a romantic choice for dinner on weekends. ⊠ *29 Gloucester Ave.* ☎ *876/979–2769* ≜ *Reservations essential* ▭ *AE, MC, V.*

¢–$ ✕ **The Pork Pit.** A favorite with many MoBay locals, this no-frills eatery serves Jamaican specialties, including some fiery jerk—note that it's spiced to local tastes, not watered down for tourist palates. Many get their food to go, but you can also find picnic tables just outside. ⊠ *27 Gloucester Ave.* ☎ *876/940–3008* ▭ *No credit cards.*

NASSAU, BAHAMAS

Cheryl Blackerby

Nassau, the capital of the Bahamas, has witnessed Spanish invasions and hosted pirates, who made it their headquarters for raids along the Spanish Main. The heritage of old Nassau blends the Southern charm of British loyalists from the Carolinas, the African tribal traditions of freed slaves, and a bawdy history of blockade-running during the Civil War and rum-running in the Roaring 1920s. The sheltered harbor bustles with cruise-ship hubbub, while a block away, broad, palm-lined Bay Street is alive with commercial activity. Over it all is a subtle layer of civility and sophistication, derived from three centuries of British rule. Nassau's charm, however, is often lost in its commercialism. There's excellent shopping, but if you look past the duty-free shops, you'll also find sights of historical significance that are worth seeing.

Essentials

CURRENCY The Bahamian dollar, which trades one-to-one with the U.S. dollar, which is universally accepted. There's no need to acquire any Bahamian currency.

HOURS Banks are generally open Monday–Thursday 9:30 to 3 and Friday 9:30 to 4:30. Hours for attractions vary; most open by 9 or 10 and close by 5. Most shops are open from 10 to 6.

INTERNET You'll find Internet kiosks at Prince George Wharf.

TELEPHONES Calling locally or internationally is easy in the Bahamas. To place a local call, dial the seven-digit phone number. To call the United States, dial 1 plus the area code. Pay phones cost 25¢ per call; Bahamian and U.S. quarters are accepted, as are BATELCO phone cards. To place a call using a calling card, use your long-distance carrier's access code or dial 0 for the operator. Be aware that when placing a toll-free call from your hotel, you are charged as if for a regular long-distance call.

Coming Ashore

Cruise ships dock at one of three piers on Prince George's Wharf. Taxi drivers who meet the ships may offer you a $2 "ride into town," but the historic government buildings and duty-free shops lie just steps from the dock area. As you leave the pier, look for a tall pink tower—diagonally across from here is the tourist information office. Stop in for maps of the island and downtown Nassau. On most days you can join a one-hour

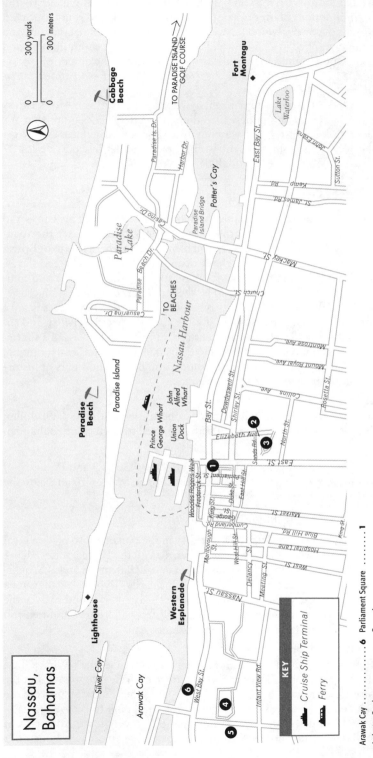

Nassau, Bahamas

Silver Cay

Arawak Cay

Lighthouse

Paradise Beach

Paradise Island

Cabbage Beach

300 yards
300 meters

TO PARADISE ISLAND
GOLF COURSE

Paradise Lake

Paradise Is. Dr.
Harbor Dr.
Casino Dr.
Paradise Beach Dr.
Casuarina Dr.

Potter's Cay

Paradise Island Bridge

Nassau Harbour

TO BEACHES

Prince George Wharf
John Alfred Wharf
Union Dock

Woodes Rogers Walk

Western Esplanade

Bay St.
Frederick St.
Parliament St.
Shirley St.
Dowdeswell St.
Elizabeth Ave.
Sands Rd.
North St.
East St.
East Bay St.
Mackey St.
Church St.
Montrose Ave.
Mount Royal Ave.
Collins Ave.
Rosetta St.
St. James Rd.
Kemp Rd.
John Evans
Sutton St.

Lake Waterloo

Fort Montagu

King St.
Duke St.
George St.
East Hill St.
Market St.
Cumberland Rd.
Blue Hill Rd.
Hospital Lane
West St.
Meeting St.
Delancy St.
West Hill St.
Marlborough St.
Nassau St.
West Bay St.
Infant View Rd.

KEY

🚢 Cruise Ship Terminal

⛴ Ferry

Arawak Cay 6
Ardastra Gardens
and Conservation Centre 5
Fort Charlotte 4
Fort Fincastle and the
Water Tower 3

Parliament Square 1
Queen's
Staircase 2

walking tour ($10 per person) conducted by a well-trained guide. Tours generally start every hour on the hour from 10 AM to 4 PM; confirm the day's schedule in the office. Just outside, an ATM dispenses U.S. dollars.

As you disembark from your ship, you will find a row of taxis and air-conditioned limousines. Fares are fixed by the government by zones. The fare is $6 for trips within downtown Nassau and around Paradise Island; $9 from downtown Nassau to Paradise Island (which includes the bridge toll); $8 from Paradise Island to downtown Nassau; and $18 from Cable Beach to Paradise Island, including toll ($17 for the return trip). Fares cover two passengers; each additional passenger is $3, regardless of destination. It is customary to tip taxi drivers 15%. You can also hire a car or small van for sightseeing for $45 to $60 per hour or about $13 per person.

Beautifully painted horse-drawn carriages will take as many as four people around Nassau at a rate of $10 per adult and $5 per child for a 30-minute ride; don't hesitate to bargain. Most drivers give a comprehensive tour of the Bay Street area, including an extensive history lesson. Look for the carriages on Woodes Rogers Walk, in the center of Rawson Square.

Two people can ride around the island on a motor scooter for about $40 for a half-day, $50 for a full day. Helmets and insurance for both driver and passenger are mandatory and are included in the rental price. Many hotels have scooters on the premises. You can also try Knowles, on West Bay Street, in the British Colonial Hilton parking lot, or check out the stands in Rawson Square. Remember to drive on the left.

The cheapest way to get to Paradise Island on your own is to take the ferry from the dock area ($3 each way).

Shore Excursions

We consider these to be among the better shore excursions for Nassau. They may not be offered by all lines, and tour names may differ as well. Times and prices are approximate.

Harbor Tour & Atlantis. After a half-hour harbor tour, your boat docks near the Atlantis Resort on Paradise Island, where you will be admitted to tour the world famous "Atlantis Dig" aquarium. Some lines also offer lunch, but these cost considerably more; most tours do not include use of the Atlantis beach or pools. ☉ *2½ hrs* 🚌 *$56.*

Nassau & Ardastra Gardens. Your tour takes in the major points of interest in Nassau, such as the Queen's Staircase and Fort Fincastle as well as Ardastra Gardens, a tropical zoo featuring pink flamingos, the national bird. ☉ *2½ hrs* 🚌 *$49.*

Sail & Snorkel. You sail, usually on a large catamaran, to a snorkeling spot, where

NASSAU BEST BETS

- **Ardastra Gardens.** Flocks of flamingos, the country's national bird, "march" in three daily shows (you can mingle with the flamboyant pink stars afterward).

- **Shopping.** To many, shopping is one of Nassau's great delights.

- **Western Esplanade Beach.** Head to this beach (also known as Long Wharf Beach) and sit in the shade of a coconut palm while admiring a glistening white-sand beach and the mega-cruise ships coming into the harbor. (It's only a 10-minute walk from the duty-free shops on Bay Street.)

the boat anchors while you swim among the fishies. Refreshments are provided. ⏱ 3½ hrs 🎫 $49.

Stingray Snorkel & Beach Break. You're taken to Blackbeard's Cay, where you'll get to snorkel among stingrays. Food and beverages are sold on-site. Snorkeling equipment is provided. ⏱ 3 hrs 🎫 $49.

Exploring Nassau

Numbers in the margins correspond to points of interest on the Nassau map.

Nassau's sheltered harbor bustles with cruise-ship hubbub, while a block away, broad, palm-lined Bay Street is alive with commercial activity. Shops angle for tourist dollars with fine imported goods at duty-free prices, yet you will find a handful of stores overflowing with authentic Bahamian crafts, foods, and other delights. Most of Nassau's historic sites are centered around downtown.

With its thoroughly revitalized downtown—the revamped British Colonial Hilton leads the way—Nassau is recapturing some of its glamour. Nevertheless, modern influence is apparent: fancy restaurants, suave clubs, and trendy coffeehouses have popped up everywhere. This trend comes partly in response to the burgeoning upper-crust crowds that now supplement the spring-breakers and cruise passengers who have traditionally flocked to Nassau.

Today the seedy air of the town's not-so-distant past is almost unrecognizable. Petty crime is no greater than in other towns of this size, and the streets not only look cleaner but feel safer. You can still find a wild club or a rowdy bar, but you can also sip cappuccino while viewing contemporary Bahamian art or dine by candlelight beneath prints of old Nassau, serenaded by soft, island-inspired calypso music.

⑥ Arawak Cay. For a literal taste of Bahamian culture throughout the island chain, take the slightly long walk west on Bay Street to this cluster of eateries and shops. You can buy crafts and food, especially squeaky-fresh conch salad, often made before your very eyes. An ice-cold Kalik beer makes the perfect foil. ⊠ *W. Bay St.* 🎫 *Free* ⏱ *Daily.*

⑤ Ardastra Gardens & Conservation Centre. Marching flamingos? These national birds of the Bahamas give a parading performance at Ardastra daily at 10:30, 2, and 4. The zoo, with more than 5 acres of tropical greenery and flowering shrubs, also has an aviary of rare tropical birds, native Bahamian creatures such as rock iguanas, and a global collection of small animals. ⊠ *Chippingham Rd., south of W. Bay St.* ☎ *242/323–5806* ⊕ *www.ardastra.com* 🎫 *$12* ⏱ *Daily 9–5.*

★ ④ Fort Charlotte. Built in the late 18th century, this imposing fort comes complete with a waterless moat, drawbridge, ramparts, and dungeons. Lord Dunmore, who built it, named the massive structure in honor of George III's wife. At the time, some called it Dunmore's Folly because of the staggering expense of its

CAUTION	
Mail overflowing your mailbox is a neon sign to thieves that you aren't home. Have someone pick it up, or, better, have the post office hold all your mail for you.	

construction. It cost eight times more than was originally planned. (Dunmore's superiors in London were less than ecstatic with the high costs, but he managed to survive unscathed.) Ironically, no shots were ever fired in battle from the fort. It is about 1 mi (1½ km) west of central Nassau. ⊠ *W. Bay St. at Chippingham Rd.* ☒ *Free* ⊗ *Local guides conduct tours daily 8–4.*

❸ **Fort Fincastle.** Shaped like a paddle-wheel steamer and perched near the top of the **Queen's Staircase,** Fort Fincastle—named for Royal Governor Lord Dunmore (Viscount Fincastle)—was completed in 1793 to serve as a lookout post for marauders trying to sneak into the harbor. It served as a lighthouse in the early 19th century. The fort's 126-foot-tall **water tower,** which is more than 200 feet above sea level, is the island's highest point but has been closed for some time for renovations. ⊠ *Top of Elizabeth Ave. hill, south of Shirley St., Nassau* ⊗ *Daily 8–5.*

❶ **Parliament Square.** Nassau is the seat of the national government. The Bahamian Parliament comprises two houses—a 16-member Senate (Upper House) and a 40-member House of Assembly (Lower House)—and a ministerial cabinet headed by a prime minister. Parliament Square's pink, colonnaded government buildings were constructed in the early 1800s by Loyalists who came to the Bahamas from North Carolina. The square is dominated by a statue of a slim young Queen Victoria that was erected on her birthday, May 24, in 1905. In the immediate area are a half dozen magistrates' courts (open to the public; obtain a pass at the door to view a session). Behind the House of Assembly is the **Supreme Court.** Its four-times-a-year opening ceremonies (held the first weeks of January, April, July, and October) recall the wigs and mace-bearing pageantry of the Houses of Parliament in London. The Royal Bahamas Police Force Band is usually on hand for the event. ⊠ *Bay St., Nassau* ☎ *242/322–7500 for information on Supreme Court ceremonies* ☒ *Free* ⊗ *Weekdays 10–4.*

❷ **Queen's Staircase.** These 65 steps are thought to have been carved out of a solid limestone cliff by slaves in the 1790s. The staircase was later named to honor Queen Victoria's 65-year reign. Recent innovations include a waterfall cascading from the top, and an ad hoc straw market along the narrow road that leads to the site. ⊠ *Top of Elizabeth Ave. hill, south of Shirley St.*

Shopping

Duty-free shopping is a major pastime in Nassau, and there are plenty of bargains to be found. Most of the stores selling duty-free items are clustered along an eight-block stretch of Bay Street in Old Nassau and on a few downtown side streets. Most stores are open Monday through Saturday from 9 to 5 and accept credit cards.

On Bay Street at Market Street, the **Straw Market** has convened for hundreds of years. After a disastrous fire in 2001, it relocated to a nearby concrete structure. Its counterpart on Paradise Island, **BahamaCraft Centre,** is set up in a collection of colorful kiosks. The straw markets carry inexpensive straw and carved items, plus T-shirts and other souvenir apparel and jewelry.

Doongalik Studios Gallery (⊠ 18 Village Rd., Paradise Island ☎ 242/394–1886) showcases Bahamian fine art, crafts, and culture in an old-Bahamian setting with a focus on the islands' annual Junkanoo festival.

Sports & Activities

FISHING   The waters here are generally smooth and alive with many species of game fish, which is one of the reasons why the Bahamas has more than 20 fishing tournaments open to visitors every year. A favorite spot just west of Nassau is the Tongue of the Ocean, so called because it looks like that part of the body when viewed from the air. The channel stretches for 100 mi. For boat rentals, parties of two to six will pay $300 or so for a half day, $600 for a full day.

Born Free Charters (☎ 242/393–4144 ⊕ www.bornfreefishing.com/) has three boats and guarantees a catch on full-day charters—if you don't get a fish, you don't pay. **Brown's Charters** (☎ 242/324–2061) specializes in 24-hour shark fishing trips, as well as reef and deep-sea fishing. **Chubasco Charters** (☎ 242/324–3474 ⊕ www.chubascocharters.com) has four boats for sportfishing and shark fishing charters.

GOLF   **Cable Beach Golf Club** (⊠ Cable Beach ☎ 800/214–4281 ⊕ www.radisson-cablebeach.com), at 7,040 yards and with a par of 72, is the oldest golf course in the Bahamas. The links are owned by the Radisson Cable Beach Casino & Golf Resort. **Ocean Club Golf Course** (⊠ Paradise Island Dr., Paradise Island ☎ 242/363–6682, 800/321–3000 in the U.S. ⊕ www.oneandonlyresorts.com) was designed by Tom Weiskopf. The par-72 championship course is surrounded by the ocean on three sides, which means that winds can get stiff. Tee times can be reserved 60 days in advance.

Beaches

New Providence is blessed with stretches of white sand studded with palm and sea grape trees. Some of the beaches are small and crescent-shaped; others stretch for miles. On the north side of the island lies Paradise Island's showpiece, **Cabbage Beach,** which is popular with locals and tourists and is the home of most of the island's resorts. The beach rims the north coast from the Atlantis lagoon to Snorkeler's Cove. At the north end you can rent Jet Skis and nonmotorized pedal boats and go parasailing. **Cable Beach** is on New Providence's north shore, about 3 mi (5 km) west of downtown Nassau. Resorts line much of this beautiful, broad swath of white sand, but there is public access. Jet-skiers and beach vendors abound, so don't expect quiet isolation. Just west of Cable Beach is a rambling pink house on the Rock Point promontory, where much of the 1965 James Bond movie *Thunderball* was filmed. Downtown, the **Western Esplanade** sweeps westward from the British Colonial Hotel on Bay Street (a 10-minute walk from the cruise-ship pier). It's just across the street from shops and restaurants, and it has restrooms, a snack bar, and changing facilities. **Paradise Beach** stretches for more than 1 mi (1½ km) on the western end of Paradise Island.

Where to Eat

$–$$ ✕ **Athena Café.** A mainstay since 1960, this Greek restaurant provides a break from the Nassau culinary routine. Sit on the second floor among Grecian statuary, or on the balcony overlooking the action below. Enjoy souvlaki, moussaka, and spanakopita, among other specialties, along with

Greek beer in a relaxed and friendly atmosphere. Gregarious owner Peter Mousis and his family serve tasty fare at moderate prices, including breakfast seven days a week. ⊠ *Bay St. at Charlotte St.* ☎ *242/322–8833* ⊟ *AE, D, MC, V* ☯ *No dinner Sun.*

$–$$ ✕ **Portofino.** Nassau's movers and shakers meet here for breakfast, lunch, and dinner. In the British Colonial Hilton Nassau, Portofino offers homemade Italian pasta dishes and pizza as well as Bahamian favorites such as pan-seared snapper with mango sauce, conch chowder, and guava duff. The lavish lunch buffet far surpasses the usual hotel fare. For breakfast, don't miss the Bahamian johnnycakes. Ask for a window seat so you can see the cruise ships come and go in the harbor. After dinner, you can walk to the hotel's private beach for a lovely view of the harbor and Paradise Island. ⊠ *No. 1 W. Bay St., Nassau* ☎ *242/322–3301* ⊟ *AE, MC, V.*

Nightlife

Some ships stay late into the night or until the next day so that passengers can enjoy Nassau's nightlife. You'll find nonstop entertainment nightly along Cable Beach and on Paradise Island. All the larger hotels offer lounges with island combos for listening or dancing and restaurants with soft guitar or piano music.

CASINOS At 50,000 square feet (100,000 if you include the dining and drinking areas), the **Atlantis Casino** (⊠ Atlantis Resort, Paradise Island ☎ 242/363–3000 ⊕ www.atlantis.com) is the Caribbean's largest gambling hall. Ringed with restaurants, it offers more than 1,000 slot machines, baccarat, blackjack, roulette, craps tables, and such local specialties as Caribbean stud poker. There's a high-limit table area, additional games available at most of the eateries within its walls, and a spectacularly open and airy design. Tables are open from 10 AM to 4 AM daily; slots, 24 hours daily. At the **Crystal Palace Casino** (⊠ Nassau Marriott Resort, Cable Beach ☎ 242/327–6200), slots, craps, baccarat, blackjack, roulette, Big Six, and face-up 21 are among the games in the 35,000-square-foot space. There's a Sports Book facility for sports betting, equipped with big-screen TVs, which air ongoing sporting events. Both VIPs and low-limit bettors have their own areas. Casino gaming lessons are available for beginners. Tables and slots are open 24 hours daily.

NIGHTCLUBS **Club Waterloo** (⊠ E. Bay St., Nassau ☎ 242/393–7324) claims to be Nassau's largest indoor-outdoor nightclub, with five bars and nonstop dancing Monday through Saturday until 4 AM (with bands on weekends). Try the spring-break-special Waterloo Hurricane, a mixture of rums and punches.

NEVIS (CHARLESTOWN)

Jordan Simon In 1493, when Columbus spied a cloud-crowned volcanic isle during his second voyage to the New World, he named it Nieves—the Spanish word for "snows"—because it reminded him of the peaks of the Pyrenees. Nevis rises from the water in an almost perfect cone, the tip of its 3,232-foot central mountain hidden by clouds. Even less developed than sister island St. Kitts—just 2 mi (3 km) away at their closest point, Nevis is known for its long beaches with white and black sand, its lush greenery, the charming if slightly dilapidated Georgian capital of Charlestown, and its restored sugar plantations that now house charming inns. Even on a day-trip Nevis feels relaxed and quietly upscale. You might run into celebrities at the Four Seasons or lunching at the beach bars on Pinney's, the showcase strand. Yet Nevisians (not to mention the significant expat American and British presence) never put on airs, offering warm hospitality to all visitors.

> ### NEVIS BEST BETS
>
> ■ **Hiking.** Even if you don't want to tackle Mount Nevis, getting out in the countryside on foot is one of the best ways to experience this small island.
>
> ■ **Horseback Riding.** For those who would rather someone (or something) else do the walking for them, the views from horseback are just as good as those from closer to the ground.

Essentials

CURRENCY The Eastern Caribbean dollar (EC$$2.70 to US$1). U.S. dollars, major credit cards, and traveler's checks are readily accepted, although large U.S. bills may be difficult to change in small shops—and you'll receive change in the local currency.

HOURS Most stores remain open Monday through Saturday from 9 to 4. Some attractions close early on Saturday.

INTERNET **Downtown Cybercafe** (✉ Main St., Charlestown ☎ 869/469–1999).

TELEPHONES Phone cards, which you can buy in denominations of $5, $10, and $20, are handy for making local phone calls, calling other islands, and accessing U.S. direct lines. To make a local call, dial the seven-digit number. To call Nevis from the United States, dial the area code 869, then access code 465, 466, 468, or 469 and the local four-digit number.

Coming Ashore

Cruise ships dock in Charlestown harbor; all but the smallest ships bring passengers in by tender to the central downtown ferry dock. The pier leads smack onto Main Street, with shops and restaurants steps away. Taxi drivers often greet tenders, and there's also a stand a block away. Fares are fairly expensive, but a three-hour driving tour of Nevis costs about $60 for up to four people. Several restored great-house plantation inns are known for their lunches; your driver can provide information and arrange drop-off and pickup. Before setting off in a taxi, be sure to clarify whether the rate quoted is in E.C. or U.S. dollars.

If your ship docks in St. Kitts, Nevis is a 30- to 45-minute ferry ride from Basseterre. You can tour Charlestown, the capital, in a half hour or so, but you'll need three to four hours to explore the entire island. Most cruise ships arrive in port at around 8 AM, and the ferry schedule (figure $18 round trip) can be irregular, so many passengers sign up for a cruise line–run shore excursion. If you travel independently, confirm departure times with the tourist office to be sure you'll make it back to your ship on time.

Shore Excursions

We consider these to be among the better shore excursions for Nevis. They may not be offered by all lines, and tour names may differ as well. Times and prices are approximate.

Beach & Trail Horseback Riding. The horseback ride takes you on trails through small villages as well as down to the beach. ☯ 2 ½ hrs ⌨ $109.

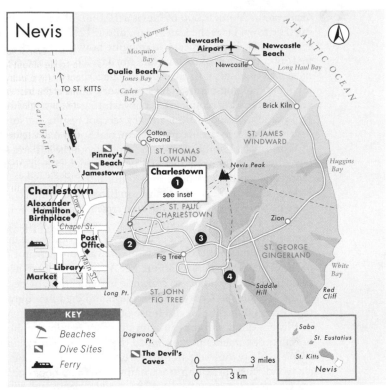

Hiking Herbert Heights. This hiking trip goes from Rawlins Plantation up to Herbert Heights. Some of the trips go by donkey. ⊙ *3 hrs* 💷 *$59.*

Exploring Nevis
Numbers in the margin correspond to points of interest on the Nevis map.

② **Bath Springs.** The Caribbean's first hotel, the Bath Hotel was so popular in the 19th century that visitors, including such dignitaries as Samuel Taylor Coleridge and Prince William Henry, traveled two months by ship to "take the waters" in the property's hot thermal springs. It suffered extensive hurricane and probably earthquake damage over the years and languished in disrepair until recently. Local volunteers have cleaned up the spring and built a stone pool and steps to enter the waters; now, residents and visitors enjoy the springs, which range from 104°F to 108°F, though signs still caution that you bathe at your own risk. Follow Main Street south from Charlestown. ⊠ *Charlestown outskirts.*

★ ④ **Botanical Gardens of Nevis.** In addition to terraced gardens and arbors, this remarkable 7.8-acre site in the glowering shadow of Mt. Nevis has natural lagoons, streams, and waterfalls, superlative bronze mermaids, egrets and herons, and extravagant fountains. You can find a proper rose garden, sections devoted to orchids and bromeliads, cacti, and flowering trees and shrubs—even a bamboo garden. A splendid re-creation of a plantation-style great house contains a tearoom with sweeping sea views and a souvenir shop. ⊠ *Montpelier Estate* ☎ *869/469–3509* 💷 *$9* ⊙ *Mon.–Sat. 9–4:30.*

★ ❶ **Charlestown.** About 1,200 of Nevis's 10,000 inhabitants live in the capital. The town faces the Caribbean, about 12½ mi (20 km) south of Basseterre on St. Kitts. It's easy to imagine how tiny Charlestown, founded in 1660, must have looked in its heyday. The weathered buildings still have their fanciful galleries, elaborate gingerbread fretwork, wooden shutters, and hanging plants. The stonework building with the clock tower (1825, but mostly rebuilt after a devastating 1873 fire) houses the courthouse and the second-floor **library** (a cool respite on sultry days). The little park next to the library is Memorial Square, dedicated to the fallen of World Wars I and II. Down the street from the square, archaeologists have discovered the remains of a Jewish cemetery and synagogue (Nevis reputedly had the Caribbean's second-oldest congregation), but there's little to see. The **Alexander Hamilton Birthplace,** which contains the Museum of Nevis History, is on the waterfront, covered in bougainvillea and hibiscus. This Georgian-style house is a reconstruction; the original had been built in 1680 and is thought to have been destroyed during an earthquake in the mid-19th century. Hamilton was born here in 1755 and moved to St. Croix when he was about 12. A few years later, at 17, he moved to the American colonies to continue his education; he became Secretary of the Treasury to George Washington and died in a duel with political rival Aaron Burr. The Nevis House of Assembly occupies the second floor of this building, and the museum downstairs contains Hamilton memorabilia, documents pertaining to the island's history, and displays on island geology, politics, architecture, culture, and cuisine. The gift shop is a wonderful source for historic maps, crafts, and books on Nevis. ⊠ *Low St., Charlestown* ☎ *869/469–5786* ⊕ *www.nevis-nhcs.org* ⊠ *$5 ($7 includes admission to Nelson Museum)* ⊗ *Weekdays 9–4, Sat. 9–noon.*

❸ **Nelson Museum.** This collection merits a visit for its memorabilia of Lord Horatio Nelson, including letters, documents, paintings, and even furniture from his flagship. Historical archives of the Nevis Historical and Conservation Society are housed here and are available for public viewing. Nelson was based in Antigua but on military patrol came to Nevis, where he met and eventually married Frances Nisbet, who lived on a 64-acre plantation here. Half the space is devoted to often provocative displays on island life, from leading families to vernacular architecture to the adaptation of traditional African customs, from cuisine to Carnival. ⊠ *Bath Rd., outside Charlestown* ☎ *869/469–0408* ⊕ *www.nevis-nhcs. org* ⊠ *$5 ($7 includes admission to Museum of Nevis History)* ⊗ *Weekdays 9–4, Sat. 9–noon.*

Shopping

Nevis is certainly not the place for a shopping spree, but there are some wonderful surprises, notably the island's stamps, fragrant honey, and batik and hand-embroidered clothing. Other than a few hotel boutiques and isolated galleries, virtually all shopping is concentrated on or just off Main Street in Charlestown. The lovely old stonework and wood floors of the waterfront Cotton Ginnery Complex make an appropriate setting for shops of local artisans.

★ Cheryl "Cherrianne" Liburd's **Bocane Ceramics** (⊠ Main St., Stoney Grove ☎ 869/469–5437) stocks beautifully designed and glazed local pottery, such as platters painted with marine life, pineapple tea sets, and coffee tables topped with mosaic depictions of chattel houses. **The CraftHouse** (⊠ Pinney's Rd., Charlestown ☎ 869/469–5505) is a marvelous source for local specialties from vetiver mats to leather moccasins; there's a smaller branch in the Cotton Ginnery. **Island Fever** (⊠ Main St., Charlestown ☎ 869/ 469–0867) has become the island's classiest boutique, with an excellent selection of everything from bathing suits and dresses to straw bags and jewelry. The **Nevis Handicraft Co-op Society** (⊠ Main St., Charlestown ☎ 869/469–1746), next to the tourist office, offers works by local artisans (clothing, ceramic ware, woven goods) and locally produced honey, hot sauces, and jellies (try the guava and soursop).

Activities

GOLF Duffers doff their hats to the beautiful, impeccably maintained Robert
Fodor'sChoice Trent Jones, Jr.–designed 18-hole, par-72, 6,766-yard championship **Four**
★ **Seasons Golf Course** (⊠ Four Seasons Resort Nevis, Pinney's Beach ☎ 869/ 469–1111): the virtual botanical gardens surrounding the fairways almost qualify as a hazard in themselves. The signature hole is the 15th, a 660-yard monster that encompasses a deep ravine; other holes include bridges, steep drops, rolling pitches, extremely tight and unforgiving fairways, sugarmill ruins, and fierce doglegs. Attentive attendants canvas the course with beverage buggies, handing out chilled, peppermint-scented towels. Greens fees are $120 per person for 9 holes, $195 for 18.

HIKING The center of the island is Nevis Peak—also known as Mount Nevis— which soars 3,232 feet and is flanked by Hurricane Hill on the north and Saddle Hill on the south. If you plan to scale Nevis Peak, a day-long affair, it's highly recommended that you go with a guide. Your hotel can arrange it (and a picnic lunch) for you. The **Upper Round Road Trail** is a 9-mi (14½-km) road constructed in the late 1600s and cleared and restored by the Nevis Historical and Conservation Society. It connects the Golden Rock Hotel, on the east side of the island, with Nisbet Plantation Beach Club, on the northern tip. The trail encompasses numerous vegetation zones, including pristine rain forest, and impressive plantation ruins. The original cobblestones, walls, and ruins are still evident in many places.

Herbert Heights Village Experience (☎ 869/469–2856 ⊕ www.herbertheights. com) is run by the Herbert family, who have fashioned their own unique activities. They lead four-hour nature hikes up to panoramic Herbert Heights, where you drink in fresh local juices and the views of Montserrat; the powerful telescope makes you feel as if you're staring right into that island's simmering volcano. The price is $15; for $35 you can ride one of their donkeys. **Sunrise Tours** (☎ 869/469–2758 ⊕ www. nevisnaturetours.com), run by Lynell and Earla Liburd, offers a range of hiking tours, but their most popular is Devil's Copper, a rock configuration full of ghostly legends. Local people gave it its name because at one time the water was hot—a volcanic thermal stream. The area features pristine waterfalls and splendid bird-watching. Hikes range from
★ $20 to $40 per person, and you receive a certificate of achievement. **Top to Bottom** (☎ 869/469–9080 ⊕ www.walknevis.com), run by Jim and Nikki Johnston, offers ecorambles (slow tours) and hikes that emphasize Nevis's volcanic and horticultural heritage (including pointing out folkloric herbal and "murderous" medicines). Three-hour rambles or hikes are

$20 per person (snacks and juice included); it's $35 for more strenuous climbs (two offered) up Mount Nevis.

HORSEBACK RIDING **Nevis Equestrian Centre** (✉ Cotton Ground, Pinney's Beach ☎ 869/469–8118) arranges leisurely beach rides, more demanding trail rides ($55–$80), and lessons from caring, careful owners Erika and John.

WINDSURFING ★ Waters are generally calm and northeasterly winds steady yet gentle, making Nevis an excellent spot for beginners and intermediates. **Windsurfing Nevis** (✉ Oualie Beach ☎ 869/469–9682 ⊕ www.windsurfingnevis.com) offers top-notch instructors (Winston Crooke is one of the best in the islands) and equipment for $25 per half hour. Groups are kept small (eight maximum), and the equipment is state-of-the-art from Mistral North and Tushingham.

Beaches

★ All beaches are free to the public (the plantation inns cordon off "private" areas on Pinney's Beach for guests), but there are no changing facilities, so wear a swimsuit under your clothes. **Oualie Beach,** south of Mosquito Bay and north of Cades and Jones bays, is a beige-sand beach where the folks at Oualie Beach Hotel can mix you a drink and fix you up with water-sports equipment. **Pinney's Beach,** the island's showpiece, has almost 4 mi (6½ km) of soft, golden sand on the calm Caribbean. The Four Seasons Resort is here, as are the private cabanas and pavilions of several mountain inns and casual beach bars.

Where to Eat

$–$$$ ✕ **Sunshine's.** Everything about this beach shack is larger than life, including the Rasta man Llewelyn "Sunshine" Caines himself. Flags and license plates from around the world complement the international patrons (including an occasional movie star), who wander over from the adjacent Four Seasons. Picnic tables are splashed with bright sunrise-to-sunset colors; even the palm trees are painted. Fishermen cruise up with their catch—you might savor lobster rolls or snapper creole. Don't miss the lethal house specialty, Killer Bee rum punch. As Sunshine boasts, "One and you're stung, two you're stunned, three it's a knockout." ✉ *Pinney's Beach* ☎ *869/469–1089* ▭ *No credit cards.*

$–$$$ ✕ **Unella's.** It's nothing fancy here—just tables on a second-floor porch overlooking Charlestown's waterfront. Stop for exceptional lobster (more expensive than the rest of the menu), curried lamb, island-style spare ribs, and steamed conch, all served with local vegetables, rice, and peas. Unella opens shop around 9 AM, when locals and boaters appear eager for their breakfast, and stays open all day as island ladies stop by in curlers, and cops and cabbies flirt shyly with the waitresses. ✉ *Waterfront, Charlestown* ☎ *869/469–5574* ▭ *No credit cards.*

OCHO RIOS, JAMAICA

John Bigley & Paris Permenter

About two hours east of Montego Bay lies Ocho Rios (often just "Ochi"), a lush destination that's favored by honeymooners for its tropical beauty. Often called the garden center of Jamaica, this community is perfumed by flowering hibiscus, bird of paradise, bougainvillea, and other tropical blooms year-round. Ocho Rios is a popular cruise port and the destination where you'll find one of the island's most recognizable attractions: the stair-step Dunn's River Falls, which invites travelers to climb in daisy-chain fashion, hand-in-hand behind a sure-footed guide This spectacular waterfall is actually a series of falls that cascades from the mountains to the sea. That combination of hills, rivers and sea also means many activities in the area from seaside horse-back rides to mountain biking and lazy river rafting.

> ## OCHO RIOS BEST BETS
>
> ■ **Chukka Cove.** Any of the great adventure tours here is sure to please, though you'll need to book them through your shp.
>
> ■ **Dunn's River Falls.** A visit to the falls is nothing but a touristy experience, and yet it's still exhilarating.
>
> ■ **Reggae Xplosion.** Reggae fans should check out this museum of the island sound that's right in Ocho Rios in one of the town's largest shopping centers.

Essentials

CURRENCY The Jamaican dollar (J$67 to US$1). Currency-exchange booths are set up on the docks at Ocho Rios whenever a ship is in port. The U.S. dollar is accepted virtually everywhere; at some places, change is made in Jamaican dollars. Prices given are in U.S. dollars unless otherwise indicated.

HOURS Normal business hours for stores are weekdays from 8:30 to 4:30, Saturday 8 to 1, with extended hours for shops in tourist areas.

INTERNET A growing number of facilities offer Internet service; expect to pay about US$2 for 20 minutes. At the Taj Mahal Centre, **Jerkin £ Taj Internet Bar and Grill** (✉ Ocho Rios ☎ 876/974–7438) offers numerous terminals for staying in touch by e-mail while traveling.

TELEPHONES Public telephones are located at the communications center at the Ocho Rios Cruise Pier. Travelers also find public phones in major Ocho Rios malls. Some U.S. phone companies won't permit credit-card calls to be placed from Jamaica because they've been victims of fraud so collect calls are often the top option. GSM cell phones equipped with tri-band or world-roaming service will find coverage throughout the Ocho Rios region.

Coming Ashore

Most cruise ships dock at this port on Jamaica's north coast, near Dunn's River Falls. Less than 1 mi (2 km) from the Ocho Rios pier are the Taj Mahal Duty-Free Shopping Center and the Ocean Village Shopping Center. Getting anywhere else in Ocho Rios will require a taxi; expect to pay $10 for a taxi ride downtown. The pier, which includes a cruise terminal with the basic services and transportation, is also within easy walking distance of Turtle Beach.

Licensed taxis are available at the pier; expect to pay about $35 per hour for a guided taxi tour. Jamaica is one place in the Caribbean where it's usually to your advantage to take an organized shore excursion offered by your ship unless you just want to go to the beach or do a bit of shopping in town. Car rental isn't recommended in Jamaica due to high prices, bad roads, and aggressive drivers.

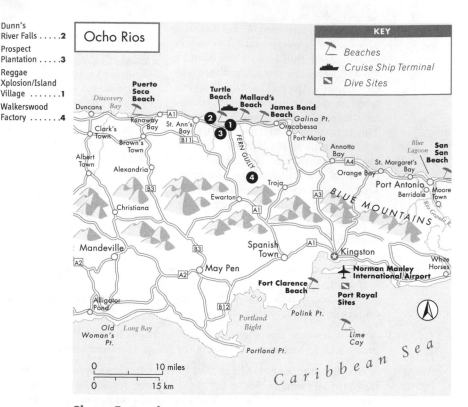

Ocho Rios

KEY

⤷ *Beaches*

⛴ *Cruise Ship Terminal*

◪ *Dive Sites*

Shore Excursions

We consider these to be among the better shore excursions for Ocho Rios. They may not be offered by all lines, and tour names may differ as well. Times and prices are approximate.

ATV Tour. You'll drive your own ATV around the hills outside Ocho Rios. ☾ *3½ hrs* ▦ *$89.*

Beach Horseback Riding. After riding your horse along a beach, you'll then ride it bareback into the surf for a swim. ☾ *4 hrs* ▦ *$89.*

Canopy Tour. The "tour" consists of flying from platform to platform through a forest on a zip line. It's a great experience. ☾ *4–4¼ hrs* ▦ *$99.*

Green Grotto Caves & Dunn's River Falls. Some kind of Dunn's River Falls trip is offered on all Ocho Rios port calls, and it may be a combination of Dunn's River Falls with another attraction for more money. The basic (and usually cheapest) option combines the Green Grotto Caves with nearby Dunn's River Falls. ☾ *4½ hrs* ▦ *$59.*

Rafting on the Martha Brae River. Pass the verdant plant life as you glide down the river on a 30-foot, two seat bamboo raft. This is decidedly still-water rafting. ☾ *6 hrs* ▦ *$58.*

Exploring Ocho Rios

Numbers in the margin correspond to points of interest on the Ocho Rios map.

② **Dunn's River Falls.** The falls are an eye-catching sight: 600 feet of cold, clear mountain water splashing over a series of stone steps to the warm Caribbean. The best way to enjoy the falls is to climb the slippery steps: don a swimsuit, take the hand of the person ahead of you, and trust that the chain of hands and bodies leads to an experienced guide. The leaders of the climbs are personable fellows who reel off bits of local lore while telling you where to step; you can hire a guide's service for a tip of a few dollars. After the climb, you exit through a crowded market, another reminder that this is one of Jamaica's top tourist attractions. ⊠ *Off A1, between St. Ann's and Ocho Rios* ☎ *876/974–2857* 🖅 *$10* ⊙ *Daily 8:30–5.*

> **BINOCULARS**
>
> Binoculars are as useful indoors as they are outside. You might think they are only for bringing far-off wildlife and sights within view, but take them into museums, churches, and other buildings to examine the details of artwork, sculptures, and architectural elements.

❸ Prospect Plantation. To learn about Jamaica's former agricultural economy, a trip to this working plantation, just west of town, is a must. But it's not just a place for history lovers or farming aficionados; everyone seems to enjoy the views over the White River Gorge and the tour by jitney (a canopied open-air cart pulled by a tractor). The grounds are full of exotic fruits and tropical trees, some planted over the years by such celebrities as Winston Churchill and Charlie Chaplin. You can also go horseback riding on the plantation's 900 acres or play miniature golf, grab a drink in the bar, or buy souvenirs in the gift shop. ⊠ *Hwy. A1, west of Ocho Rios* ☎ *876/994–1058* 🖅 *$29* ⊙ *Daily 8–5; tours Mon.–Sat. 10:30, 2, and 3:30.*

★ ❶ Reggae Xplosion. In the open-air Island Village shopping and entertainment center, which is owned by Island Records tycoon Chris Blackwell, this attraction traces the history of Jamaican music. Ska, mento, dancehall, reggae, and more are featured in a series of exhibits spanning two stories. Special sections highlight the careers of some of Jamaica's best-known talents, including Bob Marley, Peter Tosh, and Bunny Wailer. The museum also includes an extensive gift shop with recordings and collectibles. ⊠ *N. Coast Hwy., Island Village* ☎ *876/675–8895* ⊕ *www.islandjamaica. com* 🖅 *$10* ⊙ *Mon.–Sat. 9–5.*

★ ❹ Walkerswood Factory. To learn more about Jamaican cuisine (as well as the island's bountiful supply of herbs, fruits, and spices), visit the source of many sauces and seasonings. Walkerswood produces everything from jerk sauces to jams and pepper sauces. A one-hour guided tour provides a look at herb gardens, a visit to a re-created hut to learn more about historic countryside life, a jerk marinade demonstration, and samples of Walkswood products. The site includes a gift shop and snack bar featuring local dishes. ⊠ *About 6 mi (10 km) south of Ocho Rios on A3 in Walkerswood, St. Ann* ☎ *876/917–2318* ⊕ *www.walkerswood.com* 🖅 *$15* ⊙ *Mon.–Sat. 9–4.*

Shopping

Resort wear, jewelry, Jamaican rum, and Blue Mountain coffee are all popular offerings throughout Ocho Rios stores, while the crafts market is filled with wood carvings and paintings. The crafts market is located steps from the cruise ship dock but, before launching into a shopping expedition, consider your tolerance for pandemonium and price haggling. If you're looking to spend money, head for Pineapple Place, Ocean Village, the Taj Mahal, Coconut Grove, and Island Plaza. Some cruise lines run shore excursions that focus on shopping. A fun mall that also serves as an entertainment center is **Island Village.** Located near the cruise port, this mall is home to shops selling Jamaican handicrafts, duty-free goods and clothing, a Margaritaville restaurant, a Jamaican music museum, and a small beach area with a water trampoline.

Harmony Hall (✉ Hwy. A1, Ocho Rios ☎ 876/975–4222), an eight-minute drive east of the main part of town, is a restored great house, where Annabella Proudlock sells her unique wooden boxes (their covers are decorated with reproductions of Jamaican paintings). Also on sale—and magnificently displayed—are larger reproductions of paintings, lithographs, and signed prints of Jamaican scenes and hand-carved wooden combs. In addition, Harmony Hall is well-known for its shows by local artists.

Activities

DOLPHIN SWIM PROGRAMS

Dolphin Cove (✉ N. Coast Hwy., adjacent to Dunn's River Falls, Ocho Rios ☎ 876/974–5335 ⊕ www.dolphincovejamaica.com) offers dolphin swims as well as lower-priced dolphin encounters for ages eight and up; dolphin touch programs for ages six and over; or simple admission to the grounds, which also includes a short nature walk. Programs cost between $39 and $179, depending on your depth of involvement with the dolphins. Advance reservations are required.

GOLF

Although not as well known as a golf capital as Montego Bay, the Ocho Rios area is home to several excellent courses. Caddies are almost always mandatory throughout the island, and rates are $15 to $45. Cart rentals are available.

The Runaway Bay golf course is found at **Breezes Runaway Bay** (✉ N. Coast Hwy., Runaway Bay ☎ 876/973–7319). This 18-hole course has hosted many championship events (greens fees are $80 for nonguests; guests play for free) and is also home to an extensive golf academy. The golf course at **Sandals Golf & Country Club** (✉ Ocho Rios ☎ 876/975–0119) is 700 feet above sea level (greens fees for 18 holes are $100, or $70 for 9 holes for nonguests; complimentary greens fees for guests).

HORSEBACK RIDING

Ocho Rios has excellent horseback riding, but the best of the operations is **Chukka Cove Adventure Tours** (✉ Llandovery, St. Ann's Bay ☎ 876/972–2506 ⊕ www.chukkacaribbean.com), which is adjacent to the polo field, just west of town. The trainers here originally exercised the polo ponies by taking them for therapeutic rides in the sea; soon there were requests from visitors to ride the horses in the water. The company now offers a three-hour beach ride that ends with a bareback swim on the horses in the sea from a private beach. It's a highlight of many trips to Jamaica. Rather than be part of a guided group ride, you can opt to rent a horse by the hour at **Prospect Plantation** (✉ Ocho Rios ☎ 876/994–1058), which offers horseback riding for $48 per hour, but advance reservations are required.

MOUNTAIN BIKING

Ocho Rios's hilly terrain makes the region a fun challenge for mountain bikers. **Blue Mountain Bicycle Tours** (✉ 121 Main St., Ocho Rios ☎ 876/974–7075 ⊕ www.bmtoursja.com) takes travelers on guided rides in the spectacular Blue Mountains. The excursion, an all-day outing, starts high and glides downhill, so all levels of riders can enjoy the tour. The trip ends with a dip in a waterfall; the package price includes transportation from Ocho Rios, brunch, lunch, and all equipment. From its location outside of Montego Bay, **Chukka Caribbean Adventures** (⊠ Sandy Bay, Hanover ☎ 876/972–2506 ⊕ www.chukkacaribbean.com) offers both biking and ATV tours. There's a minimum age of 16 on the ATV tours. The noisy ATVs jostle and splash their way along trails on a 10-mi (16-km) ride through the hills before returning so visitors can take a dip in the sea. From its Ocho Rios location, **Chukka Caribbean Adventures** (⊠ Llandovery, St. Ann's Bay ☎ 876/972–2506 ⊕ www.chukkacaribbean.com) offers a 3½-hour bike tour through St. Ann and the village of Mount Zion with several stops and even snorkeling at the end. There is also an ATV tour. There's a minimum age of 6 for bikes, 16 for ATVs.

RIVER RAFTING Jamaica's many rivers mean a multitude of freshwater experiences, from mild to wild. Bamboo rafting is almost a symbol of Jamaica, and in the Ocho Rios area, relaxing floats are offered on the **White River.** For white-water buffs, **Chukka Caribbean Adventures** offers white-water tubing on the White River, a soft adventure that doesn't require any previous rafting experience. Rafters travel in a convoy along the river and through some gentle rapids. ⊠ *Ocho Rios* ☎ *876/972–2506* ⊕ *www.chukkacaribbean.com.*

Beaches
★ **Dunn's River Falls Beach,** at the foot of the falls, is usually crowded. Although tiny—especially considering the crowds—it's got a great view, as well as a beach bar and grill. Look up from the sands for a spectacular view of the cascading water, whose roar drowns out the sea as you approach. ⊠ *Rte. A1, between St. Ann's and Ocho Rios.*

East of Ocho Rios in the village of Oracabessa is **James Bond Beach,** which is popular because of the reggae performances that take place on its bandstand. There's a $5 admission fee. **Turtle Beach,** stretching behind the Sunset Jamaica Grande, is the busiest beach in Ocho Rios (where the islanders come to swim). Though much more convenient for cruise-ship passengers, it's not nearly as pretty as James Bond Beach. There's also a small beach at the foot.

Where to Eat
Many restaurants add a 10% service charge to the bill. Otherwise, a tip of 10% to 20% is customary.

$$–$$$ ✕ **Evita's Italian Restaurant.** Just about every celebrity who has visited Ocho
FodorsChoice Rios has dined at this hilltop restaurant, and Evita has the pictures to
★ prove it. Guests feel like stars themselves, with attentive waitstaff helping to guide them through a list of about 30 kinds of pasta, ranging from lasagna Rastafari (vegetarian) and fiery jerk spaghetti to *rotelle colombo* (crabmeat with white sauce and noodles). Kids under 12 eat for half price, and light eaters will appreciate half portions. The restaurant offers free transportation from area hotels. ⊠ *Mantalent Inn, Eden Bower Rd.* ☎ *876/ 974–2333* ▭ *AE, D, MC, V.*

¢–$ ✕ **Scotchie's Too.** The new Ocho Rios branch of the longtime Montego Bay
FodorsChoice favorite has already been lauded by international chefs for its excellent
★ jerk. The open-air eatery offers plates of jerk chicken, sausage, fish, pork, and ribs, all accompanied by festival, bammy, and some fire-

breathing hot sauce. Be sure to step over to the kitchen to watch the preparation of the jerk over the pits. ⊠ *North Coast Hwy., Drax Hall* ☎ *876/794–9457* ▱ *AE, D, MC, V.*

PROGRESO, MEXICO

Michele Joyce   The waterfront town closest to Mérida, Progreso is not particularly historic. It's also not terribly picturesque; still, it provokes a certain sentimental fondness for those who know it well. On weekdays during most of the year, the beaches are deserted, but when school is out (Easter week, July, and August) and on summer weekends it's bustling with families from Mérida. Progreso's charm—or lack of charm—seems to hinge on the weather. When the sun is shining, the water looks translucent green and feels bathtub-warm, and the fine sand makes for lovely long walks. When the wind blows during one of Yucatán's winter *nortes,* the water churns with whitecaps and looks gray and unappealing. Whether the weather is good or bad, however, everyone ends up eventually at one of the restaurants lining the main street, Calle 19. Across the street from the oceanfront malecón, these all serve up cold beer, seafood cocktails, and freshly grilled fish. Most cruise passengers head immediately for Mérida or one of the nearby archaeological sites.

Essentials

CURRENCY   The Mexican peso (MX$11.13 to US$1). U.S. dollars and credit cards are accepted by everyone at the port. There is no advantage to paying in dollars, but there may be an advantage to paying in cash. Ten pesos are worth a little bit less than $1 dollar.

HOURS   Many shops close between 1 and 4. Banks are generally open weekdays 9 to 5, and offices are usually open weekdays 9 to 2 and 4 to 7.

INTERNET   The cruise terminal isn't terribly close to Progreso's downtown area, but if you take a bus or taxi into town, you'll easily find an Internet café with pretty cheap service. If you take an excursion to Mérida, you'll find that Internet cafés there are ubiquitous, particularly the main square and Calles 61 and 63; most charge $1 to $3 per hour.

TELEPHONES   Most pay phones accept prepaid Ladatel cards, sold in 30-, 50-, or 100-peso denominations. To use the card, insert it in the pay phone's slot, dial 001 (for calls to the U.S.) or 01 (for calls within Mexico), followed by the area code and number. Credit is deleted from the card as you use it, and the balance is displayed on the small screen on the phone.

Coming Ashore

The pier in Progreso is long, and cruise ships dock at its end, so passengers are shuttled to the foot of the pier, where the Progreso Cruise Terminal offers visitors their first stop. The terminal houses small restaurants and shops selling locally produced crafts. These are some of the best shops in sleepy Progreso (a much wider selection is available in nearby Mérida). The beach lies just east of the pier and can easily be reached on foot. If you want to enjoy the sun and a peaceful afternoon, a drink at one of the small palapa-roof restaurants that line the beach is a good option.

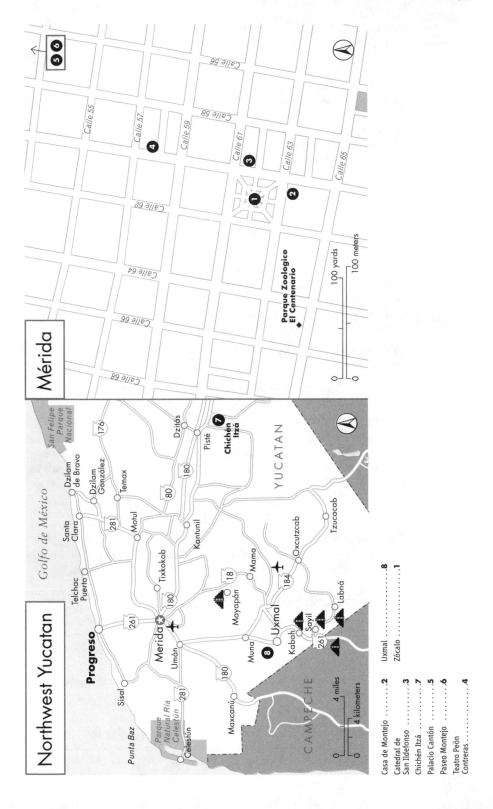

Northwest Yucatan

Golfo de México

San Felipe Parque Nacional

Punta Baz

Celestún
Parque Natural Ría Celestún

Sisal

Santa Clara

Telchac Puerto

Progreso

Dzilam de Bravo

Dzilam González

Temax

176

281

Motul

Tixkokob

Umán

261

Mérida

180

Maxcanú

Muna

Kantunil

Mama

18

Mayapán

80

180

Pisté

Dzidás

Chichén Itzá 7

YUCATAN

184

Uxmal 8

Kabah

Sayil

Labná

261

Oxcutzcab

Tzucacab

CAMPECHE

0 ———— 4 miles
0 ———— 4 kilometers

Mérida

Calle 55

Calle 57

Calle 59

Calle 61

Calle 63

Calle 65

Calle 62

Calle 64

Calle 66

Calle 68

Calle 56

Calle 58

5 6

4

3

1

2

Parque Zoologico El Centenario

0 ———— 100 yards
0 ———— 100 meters

If you are looking to explore, there are plenty of taxis around the pier. A trip around town should not cost more than $5, but ask the taxi driver to quote you a price. If you want to see more of Progresso, a cab can also take you to the local sightseeing tour bus, a bright blue, open-air, double-decker bus that travels through town and only costs $2. A taxi ride from Progreso to Mérida runs about $22, and most drivers charge around $12 per hour to show you around. If you plan on renting the cab for a good part of the day, talk about the number of hours and the cost with the driver before you take off. It's difficult to rent a car, so most people just band together in a taxi.

> ## PROGRESO BEST BETS
>
> **Chichén Itzá.** Difficult to reach from Cancún and most other Yucatan ports, the famous Maya city is an easy day-trip from Progreso.
>
> **Mérida.** This delightful, though busy, town is where you should head immediately upon landing if you aren't interested in the region's archaeological sites.
>
> **Uxmal.** One of the most beautiful Maya cities is reachable on a day-trip from Progreso. If you've seen Chichén Itzá, go here.

Shore Excursions

We consider these to be among the better shore excursions for Progreso. They may not be offered by all lines, and tour names may differ as well. Times and prices are approximate.

Caves & Cavern Snorkeling. This unique trip gives you the opportunity to snorkel in the clear waters of an underground river. ⊘ *7 hrs* ▣ *$84.*

Chichén Itzá. While you could probably do the trip on your own by rental car, it's easier to jump on a ship-sponsored bus for the 2-hour trip and tour that includes a box lunch. ⊘ *7 hrs* ▣ *$89.*

Progreso Beach Break. If ruins aren't your thing, a day-pass for a resort on a lovely white-sand beach may be. Since good beaches are in short supply here, it's better to bite the bullet and go to this resort for an all-inclusive beach day. ⊘ *4 hrs* ▣ *$79.*

Uxmal. Another major Maya archaeological site is easily reached by ship-sponsored excursion. ⊘ *7 hrs* ▣ *$89.*

Exploring Mérida

Numbers in the margin correspond to points of interest on the Mérida map.

Just south of Progreso (about 20 or 30 minutes by taxi), Mérida, the cultural and intellectual hub of the Yucatán, offers a great deal to explore. Mérida is rich in art, history, and tradition. Most streets are numbered, not named, and most run one-way. North-south streets have even numbers, which descend from west to east; east-west streets have odd numbers, which ascend from north to south. One of the best ways to see the city is to hire a *calesa*, a horse-drawn carriage. They congregate on the main square or at the Palacio Cantón, near the anthropology museum; expect to pay at least $13 per hour.

❷ **Casa de Montejo.** This stately palace sits on the south side of the plaza, on Calle 63. Francisco de Montejo—father and son—conquered the peninsula and founded Mérida in 1542; they built their "casa" 10 years later.

In the late 1970s, it was restored by banker Agustín Legorreta and converted to a branch of the Banamex bank. Built in the French style, it represents the city's finest—and oldest—example of colonial plateresque architecture, which typically has elaborate ornamentation. A bas-relief on the doorway—the facade is all that remains of the original house—depicts Francisco de Montejo the younger, his wife, and daughter as well as Spanish soldiers standing on the heads of the vanquished Maya. Even if you have no banking to do, step into the building weekdays between 9 and 5, Saturday 9 to 1, to glimpse the leafy inner patio.

❸ Catedral de San Ildefonso. Begun in 1561, St. Ildefonso is the oldest cathedral on the continent. It took several hundred Maya laborers, working with stones from the pyramids of the ravaged Maya city, 36 years to complete it. Designed in the somber Renaissance style by an architect who had worked on the Escorial in Madrid, its facade is stark and unadorned, with gunnery slits instead of windows, and faintly Moorish spires. Inside, the black Cristo de las Ampollas (Christ of the Blisters)—at 7 meters tall, perhaps the tallest Christ in Mexico—occupies a side chapel to the left of the main altar. The statue is a replica of the original, which was destroyed during the revolution; this is also when the gold that typically decorated Mexican cathedrals was carried off. According to one of many legends, the Christ figure burned all night yet appeared the next morning unscathed—except that it was covered with the blisters for which it is named. You can hear the pipe organ play at 11 AM Sunday Mass. ⊠ *Calles 60 and 61, Centro* ☎ *No phone* ☉ *Daily 7–11:30 and 4:30–8.*

❺ Palacio Cantón. The most compelling of the mansions on **Paseo Montejo,** the stately palacio was built as the residence for a general between 1909 and 1911. Designed by Enrique Deserti, who also did the blueprints for the Teatro Peón Contreras, the building has a grandiose air that seems more characteristic of a mausoleum than a home: there's marble everywhere, as well as Doric and Ionic columns and other Italianate Beaux Arts flourishes. The building also houses the air-conditioned **Museo de Antropología e Historia,** which gives a good introduction to ancient Maya culture. Temporary exhibits sometimes brighten the standard collection. ⊠ *Paseo Montejo 485, at Calle 43, Paseo Montejo* ☎ *999/923–0469* ⊡ *$3* ☉ *Tues.–Sat. 8–8, Sun. 8–2.*

❻ Paseo Montejo. North of downtown, this 10-block-long street was *the* place to reside in the late 19th century, when wealthy plantation owners sought to outdo each other with the opulence of their elegant mansions. Inside, the owners typically displayed imported Carrara marble and antiques, opting for the decorative styles popular in New Orleans, Cuba, and Paris rather than the style in Mexico City. (At the time there was more traffic by sea via the Gulf of Mexico and the Caribbean than there was overland across the lawless interior.) The broad boulevard, lined with tamarind and laurel trees, has lost much of its former panache; some of the once-stunning mansions have fallen into disrepair. Others, however, are being restored as part of a citywide, privately funded beautification program, and it's still a great place to wander, or to see by horse-drawn carriage.

❹ Teatro Peón Contreras. This 1908 Italianate theater was built along the same lines as grand turn-of-the-20th-century European theaters and opera houses. In the early 1980s the marble staircase, dome, and frescoes were restored. Today, in addition to performing arts, the theater also houses the **Centro de Información Turística** (Tourist Information Center), which provides maps, brochures, and details about attractions in the city and state. The theater's most popular attraction, however, is the café/bar spilling out into the street facing Parque de la Madre. It's crowded every night with people enjoying the balladeers singing romantic and politically inspired songs. ⊠ *Calle 60 between Calles 57 and 59, Centro* ☎ *999/924–9290 Tourist Information Center, 999/923—7344 and 999/924–9290 theater* ⊙ *Theater daily 7 AM–1 AM; Tourist Information Center daily 8 AM–8 PM.*

❶ **Zócalo.** Mérida's main square is in the oldest part of town—the Centro Histórico. It is a good spot from which to begin a tour of the city, to watch music or dance performances, or to chill in the shade of a laurel tree when the day gets too hot. Cafés along this route are perfect places from which to watch the parade of people as well as folk dancers and singers. Calle 60 between Parque Santa Lucía and the main square gets especially lively; restaurants here set out tables in the streets, which quickly fill with patrons enjoying the free hip-hop, tango, salsa, or jazz performances. ⊠ *Bordered by Calles 60, 62, 61, and 63.*

Further Afield

❼ **Chichén Itzá.** One of the most dramatically beautiful of the ancient Mayan cities, Chichén Itzá was discovered by Europeans in the mid-1800s, and much here remains a mystery. Experts have little information about who the Itzás might have been and the reason that they abandoned the city around 1224 is also unknown. ⊠ *Approximately 120 km (75 mi) east of Mérida on Carretera 180* ⊞ *Site, museum, and sound-and-light show $9.50; parking $2; use of video camera $3 (keep this receipt if visiting other archaeological sites on the same day)* ⊙ *Daily 8–5; sound-and-light show just after 5pm (at 8pm in Spanish with translations for $2.50)* ⊕ *www.inah.gob.mx.*

❽ **Uxmal.** If Chichén Itzá is the most expansive Mayan ruin in Yucatán, Uxmal is arguably the most elegant. The architecture here reflects the Late Classical renaissance of the 7th to the 9th century and is contemporary with that of Palenque and Tikal. ⊠ *78 km (48 mi) south of Mérida on Carretera 261* ⊞ *Site, museum, and sound-and-light show $9.50; parking $1; use of video camera $3 (keep this receipt if visiting other archaeological sites on the same day)* ⊙ *Daily 8–5; sound-and-light show just after dusk (at 7 or 8pm depending on the time of year)* ⊕ *www.inah. gob.mx.*

Shopping

In Progreso, there is also a small downtown area that is a better place to walk than to shop, between Calle 80 and Calle 31, with small restaurants that serve simple Mexican fare (like *tortas* and *tacos*), small shops with everyday goods for locals, banks, and supermarkets.

Just south of Progreso, Mérida offers more places to shop, including colorful Mexican markets selling local goods. The **Mercado Municipal** (⊠ Calles 56 and 67, Centro) has lots of things you won't need, but which are fascinating to look at: songbirds in cane cages, mountains of mysterious fruits and vegetables, dippers made of hollow gourds (the same way they've been made here for a thousand years). There are also lots of crafts for sale, including hammocks, sturdy leather *huaraches,* and piñatas in every imaginable shape and color. Sunday brings an array of wares into Mérida; starting at 9 AM, the Handicrafts Bazaar, or **Bazar de Artesanías** (⊠ At main square, Centro), sells lots of *huipiles* (traditional, white embroidered dresses) as well as hats and costume jewelry. As its name implies, popular art, or handicrafts, are sold at the **Bazar de Artes Populares** (⊠ Parque Santa Lucía, at Calles 60 and 55, Centro) beginning at 9 AM on Sunday. If you're interested in handicrafts, **Bazar García Rejón** (⊠ Calles 65 and 62, Centro) has rows of indoor stalls that sell items like leather goods, palm hats, and handmade guitars.

The **Mercado de Artesanís Garcí Rejón** (⊠ Calles 60 and 65) sells some quality items, and the shopping experience here can be less of a hassle than at the municipal market. You'll find reasonable prices on palm-fiber hats, hammocks, leather sandals, jewelry, and locally made liqueurs; persistent but polite bargaining may get you even better deals.

Activities

Progreso is not so much about lovely beaches, but you can easily walk to the town beach from the cruise-ship pier. Aside from archaeological sites, the main activity in the region is bird-watching, especially watching the many flamingos that nest in the region.

BIRD-WATCHING One of the most spectacular area sports and activities is bird watching, which you can enjoy at the **Parque Natural Ri` Lagartos**, about 2½ hours from Progreso by car. The real spectacle these days is the birds; more than 350 species nest and feed in the area, including flocks of flamingos, snowy and red egrets, white ibis, great white herons, cormorants, pelicans, and peregrine falcons. The easiest way to book a trip is through the Núñez family at the Isla Contoy restaurant, where you can also eat a delicious meal of fresh seafood. Call ahead to reserve an English- or Italian-speaking guide through their organization, Ría Lagartos Expeditions. This boat trip will take you through the mangrove forests to the flamingo feeding grounds (where, as an added bonus, you can paint your face or body with supposedly therapeutic green mud). A 2½-hour tour, which accommodates five or six people, costs $60; the 3½-hour tour costs $75 (both per boat, not per person). Other tour options are available. ⊠ *Calle 19 No. 134, at Calle 14* ☎ *986/862–0000* ⊕ *www.riolagartos.com* ▭ *No credit cards.*

Where to Eat

$ **Flamingos.** This restaurant facing Progreso's long cement promenade is a cut above its neighbors. Service is professional and attentive, and soon after arriving you'll get at least one free appetizer—maybe black beans with corn tortillas, or a plate of shredded shark meat stewed with tomatoes. The creamy cilantro soup is a little too cheesy (literally, not figuratively), but the large fish fillets are perfectly breaded and lightly fried. Breakfast is served after 7:00 AM. There's a full bar, and although there's no air-conditioning, large, glassless windows let in the ocean breeze. ⊠ *Calle 19 No. 144-D, at Calle 72, Progreso* ☎ *969/935–2122* ▭ *MC, V.*

$ ✕ **La Vía Olimpo.** Lingering over coffee is a great way to relax at this great Internet café. In the air-conditioned dining room, you can feast on poc chuc (slices of pork marinated in sour-orange juice and spices), turkey sandwiches, or burgers and fries. Crepes are also popular, and there are lots of salads and juices. ⊠ *Calle 62 No. 502, between Calles 63 and 61, Mérida* ☎ *999/923–4843* ▭ *MC, V.*

PUERTO LIMÓN, COSTA RICA

Jeff Van Fleet   Christopher Columbus became Costa Rica's first tourist when he landed on this stretch of coast in 1502 during his fourth and final voyage to the New World. Expecting to find vast mineral wealth, he named the region "Costa Rica" (rich coast). Imagine the Spaniards' surprise eventually to find there was none. Save for a brief skirmish some six decades ago, the country *did* prove itself rich in a long tradition of peace and democracy. No other country in Latin America can make that claim. Costa Rica is also abundantly rich in natural beauty, managing to pack beaches, volcanoes, rain forests and diverse animal life into an area the size of Vermont and New Hampshire combined. It has successfully parlayed those qualities into its role as one the world's great eco-tourism destinations. A day visit is short, but time enough for a quick sample.

Essentials

CURRENCY   The colón (₡529 to US$1). Most businesses in port gladly accept U.S. dollars.

HOURS   Stores and businesses open weekdays from 8 AM to 6 PM, with a two-hour break at midday. Places close at noon or 2 PM on Saturday, and little is open on Sunday. Most tourist-oriented businesses remain open when cruise ships are in port.

INTERNET   A bank of Internet computers is yours to use at the cruise terminal. In town, log on at **Internet Cinco Estrellas** (⊠ 50 m north of Terminal de Cruceros ☎ 758–5752).

TELEPHONES   Telephone numbers have seven digits. Merely dial the number. There are no area codes. You'll find ample phones for use in the cruise terminal. Public phones accept locally purchased calling cards.

Coming Ashore

Ships dock at Limón's spacious, spiffy Terminal de Cruceros (cruise terminal), one block south of the city's downtown. You'll find telephones, Internet computers, a crafts market, tourist information and tour operators' desks inside the terminal, as well as a small army of manicurists who do a brisk business. Step outside and walk straight ahead one block to reach Limón's downtown.

A fleet of red taxis waits on the street in front of the terminal. Drivers are happy to help you put together a do-it-yourself tour. Most charge $75 to $100 per carload for a day of touring. There is no place to rent a car here, but you're better off leaving the driving to someone else. Cruise lines offer dozens of shore excursions in Costa Rica, and if you want to go any farther afield than Limón or the coast south, we suggest you take

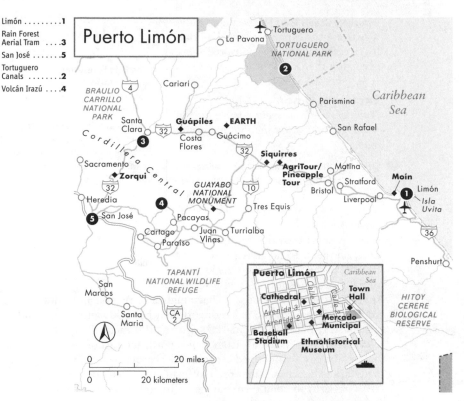

an organized tour. The country looks disarmingly small on a map—it is—but hills give rise to mountains the farther inland you go, and road conditions range from "okay" to "abysmal." Distances are short as the toucan flies, but travel times are longer than you'd expect.

Shore Excursions

We consider these to be among the better shore excursions for Puerto Limón. They may not be offered by all lines, and tour names may differ as well. Times and prices are approximate.

Flower Farm Tour. One of the world's largest ornamental plant farms operates a couple of hours inland from the coast. That diffenbachia sitting near your picture window back home might have come from here. Tours conclude with your chance to arrange a take-away tropical flower bouquet. ☉ *5 hrs* 🚘 *$59.*

Ride the Jungle Train. Passenger rail service once connected San José to Limón, but, alas, no longer. You can recapture some of that romantic era on a restored train that rumbles on tracks that still serve the region's banana plantations, and stop to see how the country's favorite yellow fruit is harvested, processed and packaged. ☉ *3¼ hrs* 🚘 *$69.*

Sloth Sanctuary. This quintessential animal-lover's shore excursion is arguably what Costa Rica is all about. Kind-hearted owners Luis and Judy Arroyo operate Aviarios del Caribe, a sloth rescue center an hour south of Limón. (Your entry fee supports their work.) Follow the tour with a hike and canoe ride through the estuary on the grounds. ☉ *5 hrs* 🚘 *$84.*

Tortuguero Canals Tour. The best (and only) way to see the canals is aboard a boat. It's easier to take a ship-sponsored shore excursion than to do it on your own. ⏱ *4 ½ hrs* 🎫 *$59.*

Exploring Limón

Numbers in the margin correspond to points of interest on the Puerto Limón map.

❶ Limón. "Sultry and sweltering" describes this port community of 90,000. The country's most ethnically diverse city mixes the Latino flavor of the rest of Costa Rica with Afro-Caribbean and Asian populations, descendants of laborers brought to do construction and farming in the 19th century. As in most of the rest of Costa Rica, you'll see no street signs here. Locals use a charmingly archaic system of designating addresses: The place you're looking for may be "100 meters south and 75 meters west of some landmark," where "100 meters" equals one city block, regardless of actual distance. Just north and east of the cruise terminal lies the city's palm-lined central park, **Parque Vargas**, with a promenade facing the ocean. Nine or so Hoffman's two-toed sloths live in its trees; ask a passerby to point them out, as spotting them requires a trained eye.

> ## PUERTO LIMÓN BEST BETS
>
> ■ **The Rain Forest Tram.** This attraction takes you up into the canopy of the rain forest to see it from a unique angle.
>
> ■ **Tortuguero Canals.** Whether you go on a ship-sponsored tour or arrange it on your own, you see a wild part of Costa Rica that isn't reachable by anything but boat.
>
> ■ **Zip-Line Tours.** If you have never done one of these thrilling tours, flying from tree to tree, Costa Rica is the original place to do it.

❸ Rain Forest Aerial Tram. This 4-square-km (2½-square-mi) preserve houses a privately owned and operated engineering marvel: a series of gondolas strung together in a modified ski-lift pulley system. (To lessen the impact on the jungle, the support pylons were lowered into place by helicopter.) The tram gives you a way of seeing the rain-forest canopy and its spectacular array of epiphyte plant life and birds from just above, a feat you could otherwise accomplish only by climbing the trees yourself. Though purists might complain that it treats the rain forest like an amusement park, it's an entertaining way to learn the value and beauty of rain-forest ecology. ⊠ *Braulio Carrillo National Park, 120 km (76 mi) west of Limón* ☎ *257–5961* ⊕ *www.rfat.com* 🎫 *$55* ⏱ *Mon. 9–4, Tues.–Sun. 6:30–4.*

❺ San José. Costa Rica's sprawling, congested capital sits in the middle of the country about three hours inland from the coast. Despite the distance, San José figures as a shore excursion—a long one to be sure—on most ships' itineraries. (The vertical distance is substantial too; the capital sits on a plateau just under a mile above sea level. You'll appreciate a jacket here after so many days at sea level.) Although the city dates from the mid-18th century, little from the colonial era remains. The **Teatro Nacional** (National Theater) is easily the most enchanting building in Costa Rica, and San José's must-see sight. Coffee barons constructed the Italianate sandstone building, modeling it on a composite of European opera houses, and inaugurating it in 1897. ⊠ *Plaza de la Cultura* ☎ *221–1329* ⊕ *www.teatronacional.go.cr* 🎫 *$5* ⏱ *Mon.–Sat. 9–4.*

The **Museo Nacional** is housed in a whitewashed fortress dating from 1870 that now serves as the country's National Museum. Notice the bullet holes: this former army headquarters saw fierce fighting during a brief 1948 civil war. But it was also here that the government abolished the country's military in 1949. ⊠ *C. 17, between Avdas. Central and 2* ☎*257–1433* ⊕*www.museocostarica.go.cr* ✉*$4* ☉*Tues.–Sat. 8:30–4:30, Sun. 9–4:30.*

The northeastern San José suburb of **Moravia** is chock full of souvenir stores lining a couple of blocks behind the city's church. ⊠ *160 km (100 mi) west of Limón.*

❷ **Tortuguero Canals.** The largely forested region north of Limón is one of those Costa Rican anomalies: roadless and remote, it's nevertheless one of the country's most-visited places. A system of inland canals runs parallel to the shoreline providing provide safer access to the region than a dangerous journey for smaller vessels up the sea coast. Some compare the densely layered greenery highlighted by brilliantly colored flowers, whose impact is doubled by the jungle's reflection in the mirror-smooth canal surfaces, to the Amazon. That might be stretching it, but there's still an Indiana Jones mystique to the journey up here, especially when you get off the main canals and into the narrower lagoons. Your guide will point out the abundant wildlife: sloths hang in the trees; howler monkeys let out their plaintive calls; egrets soar above the river surface; and crocodiles laze on the banks. ⊠ *North of Limón.*

❹ **Volcán Irazú.** Five active volcanoes loom over Costa Rica's territory (as well as many inactive ones). Irazú clocks in at the highest at about 3,700 meters (11,000 feet) and the farthest east and most accessible from Limón, though still a three-hour drive. The volcano last erupted in 1965, but gases and steam have billowed from fumaroles on its northwestern slope ever since. You can go right up to the top, although cloudy days—there are many—can obscure the view. ⊠ *140 km (84 mi) southwest of Limón* ✉ *$7* ☉ *Daily 8–3:30.*

Shopping

The cruise-ship terminal contains an orderly maze of souvenir stalls. Vendors are friendly, and there's no pressure to buy. Many shops populate the restored port building across the street. Here's the place to stock up on some of Costa Rica's signature products, most notably the country's pride and joy, its coffee. **Caribean Banana** (⊠ 50 m north Terminal de Cruceros, west side of Parque Vargas ☎ No phone) Spelling is not its forte, but this shop stands out from the others in the cruise-terminal area with a terrific selection of wood carvings.

Activities

WHITEWATER RAFTING You can experience some of the world's premier whitewater rafting in Costa Rica. The Río Reventazón in the eastern part of the country offers a few Class II–III sectors if you've never rafted before. **Ríos Tropicales** (⊠ Siquirres, 72 km (44 mi) west of Limón ☎ 233–6455 ⊕ www.riostropicales.com), one of Costa Rica's long-established outfitters, leads excursions on the Reventazón River from its operations center about an hour from Limón.

ZIP LINE TOURS   Costa Rica gave birth to the so-called canopy tour, a system of zip lines that transports you from platform to platform in the rainforest treetops courtesy of a very secure harness. Though billed as a way to get up close with nature, your Tarzan-like yells will probably scare any wildlife away. Think of it more as an outdoor amusement-park ride. **Original Canopy Tour** (⊠ Veragua de Liverpool, 15 km (9 mi) west of Limón ☎ 291–4465 ⊕ www.canopytour.com) opened only in 2006, but these folks are a branch of the oldest canopy-tour operator in the country.

Beaches

The dark-sand beaches on this sector of the coast are pleasant enough, but won't dazzle you if you've made previous stops at Caribbean islands with their white-sand strands. Nicer beaches than Limón's Playa Bonita lie farther south along the coast and can be reached by taxi or organized shore excursion. Strong undertows make for ideal surfing conditions on these shores, but risky swimming. Exercise caution.

Playa Bonita. The name of Limón's own strand translates at "pretty beach," but it's your typical urban beach, a bit on the cluttered side. ⊠ *2 km (1 mi) north of Limón.*

Playa Blanca. One of the coast's only white-sand beaches lies within the boundaries of Cahuita National Park right at the southern entrance of the pleasant little town of Cahuita. The park's rain forest extends right to the edge of the beach, and the waters here offer good snorkeling. ⊠ *44 km (26 mi) southeast of Limón Cahuita.*

Playa Cocles. The region's most popular strand of sand lies just outside Puerto Viejo de Talamanca, one of Costa Rica's archetypal beach towns, with its attendant cafés and bars and all-around good times to be had. ⊠ *63 km (38 mi) southeast of Limón, Puerto Viejo de Talamanca.*

Where to Eat

$–$$ ✕ **Brisas del Caribe.** You'll undoubtedly run across a few of your fellow passengers here at this old standby fronting the north side of the park. The food is good and filling. Seafood and surprisingly decent hamburgers, a real rarity in Costa Rica, are the fare here. ⊠ *North side of Parque Vargas* ☎ *758–0138* ⊟ *AE, DC, MC, V* ☺ *Breakfast served.*

$–$$ ✕ **Hotel Park.** Take refuge from the sweltering mid-day heat in the air-conditioned restaurant of Limón's pastel-and-pink, mid-range business-class hotel. Decent pastas, seafood and desserts are on the menu, and the pleasant ocean view is tossed in for free. ⊠ *Avda. 3, between Cs. 2 and 3* ☎ *798–0555* ⊟ *AE, DC, MC, V.*

ROATÁN, HONDURAS

Jeff Van Fleet   You'll swear you hear Jimmy Buffett singing as you step off the ship onto Roatán. The flavor is decidedly Margaritaville, but with all there is to do on this island off the north coast of Honduras, you'll never waste away here. Roatán is the largest and most important of the Bay Islands, though at a mere 65 km (40 mi) from tip to tip, and no more than five km (three mi) at its widest, "large" is relative here. As happened elsewhere on Central America's Caribbean coast, the British got here first—the Bay Islands didn't become part of Honduras until the mid-1800s—and left an indelible imprint in the form of place names such as Coxen Hole, French Harbour, and West End, and of course, their language, albeit a Caribbean-accented English. The eyes of underwater enthusiasts mist over at the mention of Roatán, one of the world's premier diving destinations, but plenty of topside activity will keep you busy too.

CURRENCY The Honduran leimpira (L18.9 to US$1). You'll find an ATM at Banco BAC in the town of Coxen Hole, where cruise ships arrive. Credit cards are widely accepted, although merchants frequently add a surcharge to offset the high processing fees they are charged by card companies.

> **ROATÁN BEST BETS**
>
> ■ **Diving.** Roatán is one of the world's great diving destinations. If you're certified, suit up. There's snorkeling too.
>
> ■ **Explore Garífuna Culture.** You'd never know it wandering West End, but the island has an original culture that predated the arrival of tourism, and which still dominates Roatán's eastern side.
>
> ■ **Copán.** It will have to be done on a very expensive, ship-sponsored tour, but Copán is one of the best Maya sites in the Caribbean.

HOURS Stores and businesses are open from 8 to 6. Many close for a couple of hours over lunch, as well as all day on Sunday, although those catering to the tourist trade make a point to stay open when cruise ships are in port.

INTERNET Check your e-mail at **Hondusoft Internet** (✉ Main St. Coxen Hole), just a couple of blocks from the cruise terminal.

TELEPHONES Phone numbers in Honduras have seven digits. There are no area codes, so just dial the number. You'll find public phones at the cruise terminal, as well as around populated areas on the island.

Coming Ashore

Ships dock at the Terminal de Cruceros (cruise terminal) in the village of Coxen Hole, the island's administrative center. You'll find telephones, Internet computers, and stands with tour information inside the terminal, as well as a flea market of crafts vendors just outside the gate. At this writing, a public concession has been granted to Royal Caribbean to construct and operate a new $16-million cruise terminal nearby. The current terminal dates only from 2001, but traffic here has outpaced its capacity. The new terminal, which will be open to all cruise lines, is expected to open in 2009.

A fleet of white taxis waits outside the gate, and here is your contact with one of the few negatives about Roatán. Drivers use a two-tier fare system, one for locals, and another, much higher "gringo" level. The $15 you'll be charged for the few miles to West End bears no resemblance to what a resident pays. Negotiate if you feel up to it. The local public-transport system consists of blue minivans that leave from Main Street in Coxen Hole to various points on the island until 6 PM. A journey to even the farthest reaches of the island does not exceed $1. Look for the cadre of tourist po-

Roatán Island

0   6 miles

0   6 kilometers

lice if you need help with anything. They wear yellow shirts and dark-green trousers and are evident on cruise days. You certainly can rent a car here, but the island's compact size makes it unnecessary. Taxis will happily take you anywhere; expect to pay $40 to $80 for a day's private tour.

Shore Excursions

We consider these to be among the better shore excursions for Roatan. They may not be offered by all lines, and tour names may differ as well. Times and prices are approximate.

Diving Excursion. For certified divers who don't want to make their own arrangements, a ship-sponsored diving excursion is the best route. This two-tank boat-dive excursion will explore some of the island's best reefs. ☺ 4 ½ hrs 🎫 $125.

Discover Roatán. A tour by boat and land will explore some of the island's interesting coves and includes a trip to visit the Garéfuna on the east end. ☺ 4 hrs 🎫 $54.

Eco-Hike with Beach. After climbing Carombola Mountain, you visit the botanical gardens there and then head down to Las Palmas for a beach break. ☺ 4 ½ hrs 🎫 $76.

Shipwreck Snorkel & Beach. For non-divers, a guided snorkeling trip will allow you to see something of the island's great reefs, as well as an interesting shipwreck. ☺ 4 ½ hrs 🎫 $52.

Exploring Roatán

Numbers in the margin correspond to points of interest on the Roatán map.

④ Carambola Botanical Gardens. One of the country's premier gardens contains an extensive orchid collection, and is home home to many different varieties of tropical plants. Take a self-guided tour. The trails and plants are well marked. The complex also serves as a breeding area for iguanas. ✉ *Across from Anthony's Key Resort, Sandy Bay* ☎ *445–3117* 💳 *$5* 🕐 *Daily 7–5.*

⑦ Copán. The magnificent Maya city of Copán easily wins the "Honduras' Most Famous Sight" title, and this mainland destination is included on a few ships' shore-excursion itineraries. A cadre of colorful parrots greets you at the gate to one of the most breathtaking archaeological sites in Central America. Down a tree-lined path you'll find a series of beautifully reconstructed temples. The intricate carvings on the stone structures, especially along the Hieroglyphic Stairway, are remarkably well preserved. Here you can marvel at the artistry of a city that many have called the "Paris of Central America."

The area open to the public covers only a small part of the city's ceremonial center. Copán once extended for nearly 2 km (1¼ mi) along the river, making it as large as many Maya archaeological sites in Guatemala. It's also just as old—more than 3,000 years ago there was an Olmec settlement on this site. Because new structures were usually built on top of existing ones, the great temples that are visible today were built during the reigns of the city's last few rulers. Nearby stands the pleasant little town of Copán Ruinas, chock full of pleasant little cafés and shops. ✉ *1½ km (1 mi) east of Copán Ruinas* ☎ *No phone* 💳 *$10* 🕐 *Daily 8–4.*

② Roatán Butterfly Garden. Hundreds of butterflies fluttering around you, all species native to Honduras. More than 20 colorful varieties are found here at any given time. Outside the screened-in butterfly house you will find a variety of tropical trees, including cashews, hogplums, and breadfruit. ✉ *West side, Sandy Bay* ☎ *445–1096* ⊕ *www.roatanbutterfly.com* 💳 *$5* 🕐 *Sun.–Fri. 9–5.*

③ Roatán Institute for Marine Sciences. Roatán's answer to Florida's Sea World is famous for its dolphin shows, always a crowd pleaser as the animals leap through hoops and balance balls on their noses, but don't ignore the informative bilingual exhibits about the geology and marine life of the Bay Islands. ✉ *Anthony Key Resort, Sandy Bay* ☎ *445–1327* 💳 *$5* 🕐 *Daily 8–5; dolphin shows Thurs.–Tues. 10 AM and 4 PM.*

⑤ Sherman Arch's Iguana Farm. Somebody has to love iguanas, and bless longtime resident Sherman Arch for doing so. He has opened his farm to some 2,700 of four species found on the island, and the animals roam freely here. (Feeding time is around noon.) Your visit is a chance to learn about iguanas, and your admission goes to the conservation of an animal that was slowly being lost to hunters on the island. ✉ *French Harbour turnoff, French Key* ☎ *445–1498* 💳 *$5* 🕐 *Daily 8–4.*

① West End. At the far western tip of the island lies one of the world's quintessential beach towns, and tourism central for Roatán. The town pulses but at half-pace—most of its streets are still unpaved—and is an enjoyable place to stroll and take in the shops and bars. ⊠ *West End.*

6 **Yubu.** The intermarriage of African slaves with European and indigenous peoples on Honduras' Caribbean coast gave rise to the region's distinctive Garífuna culture, which holds sway on the less-traveled east side of the island. Yubu is part museum, part theater, part store, and an opportunity to learn about a side of Roatán just 20 miles—but a world away—from the tourism hubbub of West End. ⊠ *Punta Gorda just before you enter town* 🕾 *No phone* 🖃 *$5* ⊙ *Tues.–Fri. 9–3.*

Shopping

Crafts vendors set up shop outside the cruise terminal gates, and a small selection of souvenir shops are scattered around the center of Coxen Hole, a short walk from the docks. Few of the souvenirs for sale here—or anywhere else on the island for that matter—were actually made in Roatán; most come from mainland Honduras. Standout shop **Yaba Ding Ding** (⊠ Main St.,, Coxen Hole 🕾 445–1683) takes its name from a Garífuna expression that loosely translates as "artifact." The shop, just a short stroll from the cruise terminal, deals in quality reproductions of indigenous artifacts, most of which were made in the mainland highlands near Copán. You'll also find a good selection of quality T-shirts here, far more distinctive than the standard, ubiquitous LIFE'S A BEACH ones.

Activities

DIVING & SNORKELING

Most of the activity on Roatán centers on scuba diving and snorkeling, as well as the newest sensation, snuba, a cross between the two, whereby your mask is connected to an air tube above. Warm water, great visibility, and thousands of colorful fish make the island a popular destination. Add to this a good chance of seeing a whale shark, and you'll realize why so many people head here each year. Dive sites cluster off the island's western and southern coasts. Competition among the dive shops is fierce in West End, so check out a few. When shopping around, ask about the condition of the diving equipment, and the safety equipment on the dive boat. **Native Sons** (⊠ Half Moon Bay, West End 🕾 445–1335 ⊕ www.nativesonsroatan.com) is one of the most popular dive shops in town. It's run by a native of Roatán who really knows the area. In business for more than a decade, **West End Divers** (⊠ Half Moon Bay, West End 🕾 445–1531 ⊕ www.westendivers.com) has a pair of dive boats. The company is committed to protecting the fragile marine ecology.

Beaches

You almost can't go wrong with any of Roatán's white-sand beaches. Even those adjacent to populated areas manage to stay clean and uncluttered, thanks to efforts of residents. Water is rougher for swimming on the less-protected north side of the island.

Half Moon Bay. Roatán's most popular beach is also one of its prettiest. Coconut palms and foliage come up to the crescent-shape shoreline. The beach lies just outside the tourist-friendly West End. Crystal-clear waters offer abundant visibility for snorkeling. ⊠ *North side, West End.*

Tabyana Beach. Locals refer to this lovely beach simply as "West Bay," but the travel brochures name it after its prominent Tabyana Beach Resort.

It's a de rigueur listing on every shore-excursions list, and the resort sets aside its facilities for its cruise passengers as a private beach. The complex also offers zip-line tours, which take you through the treetops courtesy of a series of cables and a very secure harness. ⊠ *West Bay.*

Where to Eat

$$ ✗ **¿Qué Tal? Café.** A good spot for a quick and simple meal, this friendly little café serves up salads, sandwiches, and other light fare. Located opposite the main road into Coxen Hole, it also offers Internet access. It's only open until 4 PM, however. ⊠ *Thicket Rd., Coxen Hole* ☏ *445–1007* ▤ *No credit cards* ⊘ *No dinner.*

$$–$$$ ✗ **Rudy's.** By far the best place in West End for breakfast, this little café opens at 6:30 AM. Divers crowd into the little garden to devour the excellent banana pancakes. For lunch try one of the fruit smoothies. ⊠ *West End* ☏ *No phone* ▤ *No credit cards* ⊘ *No dinner.*

SAMANÁ, DOMINICAN REPUBLIC

Eileen Robinson Smith

Samaná, the name of both a peninsula in the Dominican Republic as well as the largest town on Samaná Bay, is one of the least known regions of the country, but the new international airport that opened in late 2006 may change that perception quickly. Much development is planned, so a visit now will be to a place that is not yet geared to a great deal of mainstream, mass tourism. But with the use of the port by some mega-ships, that too is changing quickly. Samaná is one of the Dominican Republic's newest cruise-ship destination, with one of the island's greatest varieties of shore excursions. You can explore caves and see an amazing waterfall. And since many humpback whales come here each year to mate and give birth, it's a top whale-watching destination from January through March. While some cruise lines still use Cayo Levantado as a private-island type of experience, for other lines it is just one of several options.

Essentials

CURRENCY The Dominican peso (RD$32.50 to US$1). Get local currency if you are touring on your own, but most places accept U.S. dollars, though any change will be in pesos. Banks and *cambios* (currency exchange offices) are common.

HOURS Stores and attractions are typically open from 10 to 6. Many places close from noon to 2 for a lunch/siesta break, but when a ship is in port, you may find more businesses open.

INTERNET You'll find several convenient Internet cafés in town. The price of going on line ranges between RD$30 and RD$80 per hour, inexpensive to be sure. However, don't be surprised if you go and are told that the computers: *"No sirve, porque no hay electricidad."* Translation: this is still a developing destination, and often half the day is spent without electricity. Although most hotels and restaurants have generators, usually these shops do not. **Centro Llamada Edwards** (⊠ 4 Francisco Rosario Sanchez, Samaná ☏ 809/538-2476) has 5 computers and charges only RD$30 an hour to connect. **Deleon Communications** (⊠ 13 Maria Trinidad Sanchez, Samaná, across from the landmark Palacio Justicia ☏ 809/538-3538)

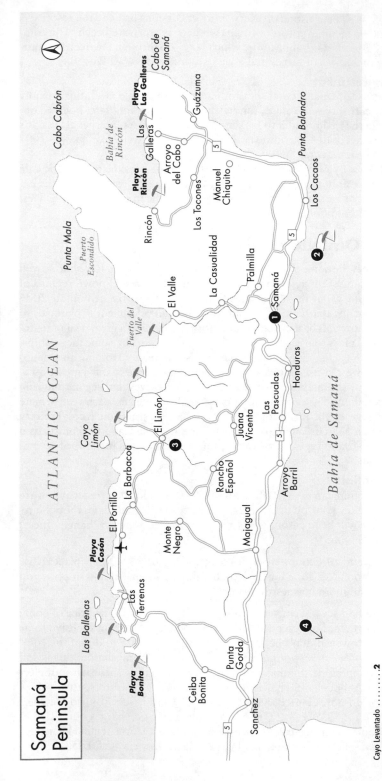

Samaná Peninsula

has six computers and four phone booths.

TELEPHONES You can call a U.S. or Canadian numbers easily; just dial 1 plus the area code and number. **Centro de Communicationes Verizon** (✉ 8 Francisco Rosario Sanchez, Samaná ☎ 809/538–2901 ✉ Maria Trinidad Sanchez, Samaná, next door to Pharmacia Gisella) is a good place to make phone calls. Only cash is taken, preferably pesos. At the first location, there are public computers for checking your e-mails; at the second, you won't be able to go online, but it is closer to the pier.

> **SAMANÁ BEST BETS**
>
> ■ **Cayo Levantado.** This resort island in the bay does put on an excellent show for day-trippers.
> ■ **Los Haitises National Park.** The caves filled with Taïno drawings and the pristine mangrove forests make this a top ecotourism destiantion in the region.
> ■ **Whale-watching.** In season, this is the top activity in the Samaná Peninsula.

Coming Ashore

Cruise ships anchor at a point that is equidistant between the town of Samaná and Cayo Levantado, an island at the mouth of Samaná Bay with a great beach and facilities to receive 1,500 cruise-ship passengers. Tenders will take you to one of three docks, located on the Malecón, referred to as the Samaná Bay Piers. The farthest is a five-minute walk from the town center. The Verizon office is just before the public market.

Renting a car, although possible, isn't a good option. Driving in the D. R. can be a hectic and even harrowing experience; if you are only in port one day, don't risk it. Yes, taxis are expensive, but the so are rental cars. You'll do better if you combine your resources with friends from the ship and share a taxi to do some independent exploring. Negotiate prices, and settle before getting in the taxi. To give you an idea of what to expect, a minivan that can take eight people will normally charges $90 for the round-trip to Las Terranas, including a two-hour wait while you explore or enjoy the beach. Similarly, you'll pay $80 to travel to Las Galleras or Playa Rincón. Many of the drivers speak some English. Within Samaná, rickshaws are far less costly and are also fun. Called *motoconchos de carretas,* they are not unlike larger versions of the Thai tuk-tuk, but can hold up to six people. The least you will pay is RD$10. They're fine to get around town, but don't even think about going the distance with them.

If you decide to rent a car, consider using **Javier Inversiones Rent-a-Car** (✉ 7 Francisco Rosario Sanchez, Samaná ☎ 809/249–5937), which can put you in a Jeep or even a Toyota Camry, although there is not a large inventory of automatics. You can expect to pay at least $50 a day—more for an automatic—but that does include insurance.

Shore Excursions

We consider these to be among the better shore excursions for Samaná. They may not be offered by all lines, and tour names may differ as well. Times and prices are approximate.

ATV Tours. ATVs go inland, halfway to the town of Sanchez, where there are incredible mountain views. The route follows a meandering jungle river. Normally, there is a stop at a coconut plantation to watch the processing, and to have a tasting. Then it's off to Playa El Valle, a golden beach, for a swim and even a siesta, after what is quite a bumpy ride. More expensive tours may include lunch. ⊙ *3½–6 hrs.* ☞ *$65–$109.*

Cave and Mangrove Exploration. Guided tours are the only way to explore the caves and mangrove forests of Los Haitises (pronounced Hi *tee* sis). The boat docks to allow passengers to walk quietly around a mangrove swamp and visit various cavern systems. Some trips also hike to the village of Crystal in the rain forest, where you can bathe in a crystal-clear, fresh water lagoon. ⊙ *3 hrs.* ☞ *$70–$79.*

Jeep Safaris. These four-wheel-drive vehicles follow the same course as the ATVs. Along the way you will stop at a typical Dominican country home, see beautiful beaches, rock formations, and rivers that emanate from caves. Some guides take you on a 15-minute walk to witness a stunning waterfall. ⊙ *4½ hrs.* ☞ *$64–$70.*

Salto El Limón Cascade. The best way to do this trip is on horseback, and that makes it a very worthwhile excursion. The waterfall itself is beautiful, and you will have the opportunity to swim in the clear pool. ⊙ *4½ hrs.* ☞ *$65.*

Exploring Samaná
Numbers in the margin correspond to points of interest on the Samaná map.

② **Cayo Levantado.** Residents of Samaná call Cayo Levantado their *pasa dia en la playa* (the place to pass the day on the beach). Today, the small island in Samaná Bay has been improved to receive up to 1,500 cruise-ship passengers per day, with dining facilities, bars, rest rooms, and lounge chairs on the beautiful beach. The company that runs cruise-ship services on the island has even applied for the coveted "Blue Flag" that designates a beach as clean and unpolluted. Independent restaurants and vendors also ply their wares. This isn't the most tranquil island, but you can quite happily spend the day here if you don't want to go into the town of Samaná. The new Grand Bahia Principe Cayo Levantado, an upscale, all-inclusive resort opened in December 2006 and claims the eastern two-thirds of the island for its private use. Day-use of the island will either be included in your cruise fare or will be treated as a regular shore excursion, for which the lines usually charge $40 to $60. ⊠ *Samaná Bay* ☎ *809/538-2579* ☞ *Donations appreciated* ⊙ *Daily dawn–dusk.*

④ **Los Haitises National Park.** A guided tour is the only way to explore Los Haitises' (pronounced Hi *tee* sis), which is across Samaná Bay from the peninsula. The park is famous for its Karst limestone formations, caves, and grottoes filled with pictographs and petroglyphs left by the indigenous Taíno before the discovery of the Americas. Mangrove forests shelter many coastal bird species, including Louisiana night herons and the magnificent American frigate birds, making this a birdwatchers' delight as well. Typical trips cruise the coastline dotted with small islands and spectacular cliff faces, finally docking to allow passengers to walk quietly around a mangrove swamp and visit the various caves. Some trips allow you to hike to the village of Crystal in the rain forest, where you can swim in a crystal-clear, freshwater lagoon.

3 **Salto el Limón Cascade** Provided that you are fit, an adventurous guided trip to this spectacular waterfall is a delight. The journey is usually done mostly on horseback but includes walking down rocky, sometimes muddy trails. The well-mannered horses take you across rivers and up mountains to El LimÛn, where you'll find the waterfall amidst luxuriant vegetation. Some snacks and drinks are usually included in the guided trip. ⊠ *El Limón.*

1 **Samaná.** The official name of the city is Santa Barbara de Samaná; alas, that saint's name is falling into disuse, and you'll more often hear simply "Samaná" these days. An authentic port town, not just a touristic zone, it has a typical *malecón* (seaside promenade) with gazebos and park benches, ideal for strolling and watching the boats in the harbor. The main road that borders this green zone, Avenida Malecón, is lined with restaurants, shops, and small businesses. A small but bustling town, Samaná is filled with friendly residents, skilled local craftsmen selling their wares, and many outdoor cafés.

The **Whale Museum & Nature Center** is dedicated to the mighty mammals of the sea, and you will learn everything you have ever wanted to know about whales here. Samaná has one of the largest marine mammal sanctuaries in the world and is a center for whale-watching in the migration season. The C.E.B.S.E (Center for Conservation and Ecodevelopment of Samaná Bay and its Environment) manages this facility. ⊠ *Tiro Blanco* ☎ *809/538–2042* ⊕ *samana.org.do* ⊠ *RD $50* ⊙ *Daily 8–12 and 2–5.*

The historic **Dominican Evangelical Church** is the oldest original building left in Samanę. It actually came across the ocean from England in 1881 in a hundred pieces and was reassembled here, serving the spiritual needs of African-American freedmen who emigrated here from Philadelphia, Pennsylvania in 1824. ⊠ *Calle Chaseurox, in front of the Catholic church* ☎ *809/ 538–2579* ⊠ *Donations appreciated* ⊙ *Daily dawn–dusk.*

Shopping
Rum, coffee, and cigars are popular local products. You may also find good coconut handicrafts, including coconut-shell candles. Whale-oriented gift items are particularly popular. Most of the souvenir shops are on Samań's Malecón or in the market plaza; you will find more on the major downtown streets in town, all within easy walking distance of the tender piers. A shopping mall called **Plublito Carabeño Plaza** (⊠ 20 Francisco Rosario Sanchez) is near the piers; it has a bevy of shops and food outlets (including American fast-food).

Activities
At this writing, only one excursion company, Bahia Cruise Services, is licensed to offer services to ships, so some of the tours in the region may be available only on ship-sponsored excursions. But there are some independent companies in the area.

DIVING & SNORKELING In 1979, three atolls disappeared following a seaquake off of Las Terrenas, providing an opportunity for truly memorable dives. **Aqua Center** (⊠ Viva Wyndham Samaná Resort, Las Terrenas ☎ 809/240—5050 ext. 2217 ⊕ www.aqua-center.com) offers one close dive at Las Ballenas (i.e., "the Whales"), a cluster of four little islands for $43 for certified divers only. You can also sign up for a resort dive for $85, but you will only be allowed to go down to 40 feet. Trips can be tailored around your cruise ship's schedule. Also, there are four dive masters here who offer PADI, PIRA, and SSI instruction that can count toward certification. In addition to transportation time, allow 2 hours to do a dive, with 45 minutes underwater. The center also offers snorkeling trips aboard a 35-foot catamaran to Playa Jackson, a tranquil virgin beach. This 3½-hour trip costs $25 per person. A longer trip includes lunch, but you must reserve in advance.

WHALE WATCHING   Humpback whales come to Samaná Bay to mate and give birth each year, from approximately January 15 through March 30. Samaná Bay is considered one of the top 10 destinations in the world to watch whales. **Victoria Marine/ Whale Samaná** (⊠ Across the street from the cement town dock, beside the park Samaná ☏ 809/538–2494) is owned by Kim Beddall, a Canadian who is incredibly knowledgeable about whales and Samaná at large, having lived here for 20-some years. Her operation is the region's best. Kim herself does almost all the English-speaking trips. The $50 price does not include the RD$100 Marine Mammal Sanctuary entrance fee. Kim welcomes cruise passengers but requires advance reservations. You must be able to arrive on shore by 9 AM for the morning trip and by 1:30 PM for the afternoon trip.

Beaches

There are no recommendable beaches in Samaná itself. You will have to travel to one of the beautiful ones elsewhere on the peninsula, another reason why the Cayo Levantado excursion is very popular on most ships.

Playa Bonito. Las Terrenas, about an hour away from Samaná, is a bohemian enclave favored by the French. It has become commercialized and can have a frenetic energy, but its beaches are legendary. On Playa Bonito you can bounce between the golden beach (BYO towel—no chaises) and one of the hotels directly across the rough road, where you can have lunch. Hotel Acaya is one of these hotels and has an open-air restaurant. Just yards away, at Hotel Bahia Las Bellenas, is Paco's, which specializes in fresh seafood. ⊠ *Las Terrenas.*

Playa Cosón. The closest good beach to Samaná is some 15 minutes away from the town of Las Terranas, and about an hour from Samaná. You can buy a day-pass for a reasonable price (about $35) at the resort Viva Wyndham Samaná, which is smack on Bahia Cosón. ⊠ *Bahia Cosón, Las Terrenas.*

Playa Las Galleras. The beach within this tiny coastal town, a 30-minute drive northeast from the port, is lovely, long, and uncluttered. The sand is white, and the Atlantic waters are generally calm. It has been designated a "Blue Flag" beach, which means that it is crystal clean with no pollution, though there are several hotels here. Generally, cruisers gravitate towards Casa Marina Bay Resort, and many cruise lines sell day passes for that all-inclusive resort. This is a good snorkeling spot, too. ⊠ *Las Galleras.*

Playa Rincón. This beautiful, white-sand beach is considered one of the top beaches in the Caribbean. It is relatively undeveloped, and at the far-right end is a sheltered area, where you can snorkel. At the other end, cliffs segue way into the turquoise water of Caño Frio, an ice-cold river that runs down from the mountains and forms a splash pool, ideal for rinsing off the salt water. There are no facilities per se, but local ladies will sell you the freshest lobster and fish in coconut sauce with rice, and other creole dishes as well as cold drinks. ⊠ *Turn right at the tiny town of El Rincón.*

Where to Eat

$–$$ ✕ **Le France.** From your first glance, you can tell that this corner restaurant has a charismatic appeal. With a red-tile roof and just one white wall, it has a massive mirror that reflects the tranquil bay view and the busy pedestrian traffic. It could be called a coconut palace, what with all the decorations. The food is not easy to categorize; expect a *comida international* that is French-accented, with seafood a major element. You can get off easy by ordering crêpes or pasta, or you can splurge on grilled shrimp. For starters, consider the original gazpacho with lambi (conch). This is one time you might want to chance beef tartare; loyal followers come all the way from Santo Domingo for it. ⊠ *6 Ave. de la Marina* ☏ *809/538–2257* ▤ *No credit cards* ⊙ *Closed Mon.*

$–$$$ ✕ **La Mata Rosada.** A popular pick of local expats and foodies, this spot will guarantee you a water view and some flavorful food, be it the sea and country salad (conch, potatoes, greens, and bacon) or the "gourmet" plate (a mix of grilled lobster and other shellfish). There is even a daily plat du jour for a song. Ceviche, a specialty of this port town, is made with dorado (mahimahi) here and is speckled with capers, tomatoes, and even mushrooms. Whether you go local or international, order the creole shrimp or a substantial salad, and you should leave satisfied. ⊠ *5 Avenida Malecon* ☏ *809/538–2388* ▤ *AE, V, MC* ⊙ *Closed Tues. June–Nov.*

ST. BARTHÉLEMY (GUSTAVIA)

Hilly St. Barthélemy, popularly known as St. Barth (or St. Barts) is just 8 square mi (21 square km), but the island has at least 20 good beaches. What draws visitors is its sophisticated but unstudied approach to relaxation: the finest food, excellent wine, high-end shopping, and lack of large-scale commercial development. A favorite among upscale cruise-ship passengers, who also appreciate the shopping opportunities and fine dining, St. Barths isn't really equipped for mega-ship visits, which is why most ships calling here are from smaller premium lines. This is one place where you don't need to take the ship's shore excursions to have a good time. Just hail a cab or rent a car and go to one of the many wonderful beaches, where you will find some of the best lunchtime restaurants, or wander around Gustavia, shopping and eating. It's the best way to relax on this most relaxing of islands.

Essentials

CURRENCY The euro (€1 to US$1.31); however, U.S. dollars are accepted in almost all shops and in many restaurants. Credit cards are widely accepted.

HOURS Stores are usually open from 8:30 to noon and 2 to 5 on weekdays (some say open until 7), and 8:30 to noon on Saturdays. Many stores are closed Wednesday afternoon.

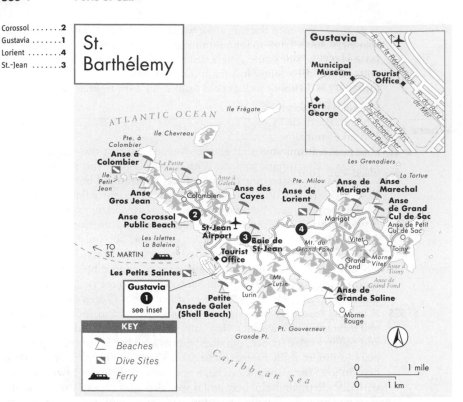

St.
Barthélemy

Gustavia

Municipal
Museum
Tourist
Office

Fort
George

ATLANTIC OCEAN

Ile Frégate

Les Grenadiers

Pte. à
Colombier

Ile Chevreau

La Tortue

Anse à
Colombier

La Petite
Anse

Anse à
Galets

Pte. Milou

Anse de
Marigot

Anse
Marechal

Ile.
Petit
Jean

Anse
Gros Jean

Colombier

Anse des
Cayes

Anse de
Lorient

Anse
de Grand
Cul de Sac

Anse Corossol
Public Beach

2

St-Jean
Airport

Marigot

Anse de Petit
Cul de Sac

Les Islettes
La Baleine

3

Baie de
St-Jean

4

Vitet

Toiny

← TO
ST. MARTIN

Tourist
Office

Mt. du
Grand Fond

Grand
Fond

Morne
Vitet

Anse à
Toiny

Les Petits Saintes

Mt.
Lurin

Anse de
Grand Fond

Gustavia
1
see inset

Petite
Ansede Galet
(Shell Beach)

Lurin

Anse de
Grande Saline

KEY

Morne
Rouge

Pt. Gouverneur

Beaches

Grande Pt.

Dive Sites

Caribbean Sea

Ferry

0   1 mile

0   1 km

INTERNET   Check your e-mail at the **Centre Alizes** (⊠ Rue de la République, Gustavia).

TELEPHONES   Public telephones accept *télécartes,* prepaid calling cards that you can
buy at the gas station next to the airport and at post offices in Lorient,
St-Jean, and Gustavia. Making an international call using a télécarte is
the best way to go.

Coming Ashore

Even medium-size ships must anchor in Gustavia Harbor and bring passengers ashore on tenders. The tiny harbor area is right in Gustavia, which
is easily explored on foot. Taxis, which meet all cruise ships, can be expensive. Technically, there's a flat rate for rides up to five minutes long.
Each additional three minutes is an additional amount. In reality, however, cabbies usually name a fixed rate—and will not budge. Fares are
50% higher on Sundays and holidays. St. Barths is one port where it's
really worth it to arrange a car rental for a full-day exploration of the
island, including the island's out-of-the-way beaches. But be aware that
during high season there is often a three-day minimum, so this may not
be possible except through your ship (and then you'll pay premium rates
indeed). Most car-rental firms operate at the airport; expect to pay about
€50 a day, which is cheaper than what you'll get if you go with one of
the ship's car rentals. The new St. Barth Shuttle service can be convenient and much less expensive than a taxi if you are just one or two people, but it still doesn't completely negate the need for a car.

Shore Excursions

Catamaran Snorkel Tour. Superb coral reefs are only a short sail from Gustavia Harbor, where you board your catamaran at the pier and head for your snorkel site. Equipment and instructions are provided and refreshments are served during the sail back to the pier. ⊙ *3 hrs* 🖭 *$149.*

Independent Exploration. One of the best—and most popular—ways to explore St. Barths is by rental car, so you can stop at your favorite beaches and take your time on the twisting roads. But you must be able to drive a manual transmission. ⊙ *5½ hrs* 🖭 *$129–$149.*

Island Tour. Your tour encompasses the highlights on a round-the-island trip by minibus. ⊙ *1¼ hrs* 🖭 *$49.*

Exploring St. Barths

With a little practice, negotiating St. Barths' narrow, steep roads soon becomes fun. Free maps are everywhere, roads are well marked, and painted signs will point you where you want to be. Take along a towel, sandals, and a bottle of water, and you will surely find a beach upon which to linger.

Numbers in the margin correspond to points of interest on the St. Barthélemy map.

❷ **Corossol.** The island's French-provincial origins are most evident in this two-street fishing village with a little rocky beach. Older local women weave lantana straw into handbags, baskets, hats, and delicate strings of birds. Ingenu Magras's **Inter Oceans Museum** has more than 9,000 seashells and an intriguing collection of sand samples from around the world. You can buy souvenir shells. ⊠ *Corossol* ☎ *0590/27–62–97* 🖭 *€3* ⊙ *Tues.–Sun. 9–12:30 and 2–5.*

❶ **Gustavia.** You can easily explore all of Gustavia during a two-hour stroll. Street signs in both French and Swedish illustrate the island's history. Most shops close from noon to 2, so plan lunch accordingly. A good spot to park your car is rue de la République, where catamarans, yachts, and sailboats are moored. The **tourist office** (☎ *0590/27–87–27*) on the pier can provide maps and a wealth of information. It's open Monday from 8:30 to 12:30, Tuesday through Friday from 8 to noon and 2 to 5, and Saturday from 9 to noon. On the far side of the harbor known as La Pointe is the charming **Municipal Museum,** where you can find watercolors, portraits, photographs, and historic documents detailing the island's history as well as displays of the island's flowers, plants, and marine life. ☎ *599/29–71–55* 🖭 *€2* ⊙ *Mon., Tues., Thurs., and Fri. 8:30–12:30 and 2:30–6, Sat. 9–12:30.*

❹ **Lorient.** Site of the first French settlement, Lorient is one of the island's two parishes; a restored church, a school, and a post office mark the spot. Note the

ST. BARTHS BEST BETS

- **Soaking up the Atmosphere.** It's the French Riviera transported to the Caribbean. Simply enjoy.

- **Beautiful Beaches.** Pick any of the lovely, uncrowded beaches and spread out for a day in the sun.

- **French Food.** St. Barths has some of the best restaurants in the Caribbean. This is the best place to splurge on a leisurely French lunch.

- **Shopping.** The Caribbean's best selection of high fashion is not cheap but it is unparalleled.

gaily decorated graves in the cemetery. One of St. Barths' secrets is **Le Manoir** (☎ 0590/27–79–27), a 1610 Norman manor, now a guesthouse, which was painstakingly shipped from France and reconstructed in Lorient in 1984. Look for the entrance by the Ligne St. Barths building.

❸ **St-Jean.** The half-mile-long crescent of sand at St-Jean is the island's most popular beach. Windsurfers skim along the water here, catching the strong trade winds. A popular activity is watching and photographing the hair-raising airplane landings. You'll also find some of the best shopping on the island here, as well as several restaurants.

Shopping

St. Barths is a duty-free port, and with its sophisticated crowd of visitors, shopping in the island's 200-plus boutiques is a definite delight. In Gustavia, boutiques line the three major shopping streets. The **Quai du République,** nick-named "Rue du Couturier," which is right on the harbor, rivals New York's Madison Avenue, or Paris's Avenue Montaigne for high-end "designer" retail. These shops often carry items that are not available in the U.S. Shops are also clustered in **La Savane Commercial Center** (across from the airport), **La Villa Créole** (in St-Jean), and **Espace Neptune** (on the road to Lorient). It's worth working your way from one end to the other at these shopping complexes—just to see or, perhaps, be seen. Boutiques in all three areas carry the latest in French and Italian sportswear and some haute couture. You probably are not going to find any bargains as long as the euro remains high, but you might be able to snag that *pochette* that is sold out stateside, and in any case, you'll have a lot of fun hunting around.

Look for Fabienne Miot's unusual gold jewelry at **L'Atelier de Fabienne** (⊠ Rue de la République, Gustavia ☎ 0590/27–63–31). Fans of Longchamp handbags and leather goods will find a good selection at about 20% off stateside prices at **Elysée Caraïbes** (⊠ Le Carré d'Or, Gustavia ☎ 0590/52–00–94). The **Hermès** (⊠ Rue de la République, Gustavia ☎ 0590/27–66–15) store in St. Barths is an independently owned franchise, and prices are slightly below those in the States. Don't miss **Lolita Jaca** (⊠ Le Carré d'Or, Gustavia ☎ 0590/27–59–98) for trendy, tailored sportswear. **Sindbad** (⊠ Carré d'Or, Gustavia ☎ 0590/27–52–29) is a tiny shop with funky, unique couture fashion jewelry by Gaz Bijou of St. Tropez, crystal collars for your pampered pooch, chunky ebony pendants on silk cord, Nomination bracelets, and other reasonably priced, up-to-the-minute styles. **Pati de Saint Barth** (⊠ Passage de la Crémaillière, Gustavia ☎ 0590/29–78–04) is the largest of the three shops that stock the chic, locally made T-shirts that have practically become the logo of St. Barths. The newest styles have hand-done graffiti-style lettering. **Stéphane & Bernard** (⊠ Rue de la République, Gustavia ☎ 0590/27–69–13) stocks a well-edited, large selection of superstar French fashion designers, including Rykiel, Tarlazzi, Kenzo, Feraud, and Mugler.

In Lorient, don't miss the superb skin-care products made on-site from local tropical plants by **Ligne de St. Barths** (⊠ Rte. de Saline, Lorient ☎ 0590/27–82–63).

Black Swan (⊠ Le Carré d'Or, Gustavia ☎ 0590/27–65–16 ⊠ La Villa Créole, St-Jean) has an unparalleled selection of bathing suits. The wide range of styles and sizes is appreciated. Local works of art, including paintings, are sold in the bright **Made in St-Barth La Boutique** (⊠ La Villa Créole, St-Jean ☏ 0590/27–56–57). **SUD SUD.ETC.Plage** (⊠ Galerie du Commerce, St-Jean ☏ 0590/27–98–75) stocks everything for the beach: inflatables, mats, bags, and beachy shell jewelry.

Activities

BEACHES   There are many *anses* (coves) and nearly 20 *plages* (beaches) scattered around the island, each with a distinctive personality and each open to the general public. Even in season you can find a nearly empty beach. Topless sunbathing is common, but nudism is technically forbidden—although both Saline and Gouverneur are de facto nude beaches. Because **Anse du Gouverneur** is so secluded, nude sunbathing is popular here; the beach is truly beautiful, with blissful swimming and views of St. Kitts, Saba, and St. Eustatius. Like a mini Côte d'Azur—beachside bistros, bungalow hotels, bronzed bodies, windsurfing, and lots of day-trippers—the reef-protected strip along **Baie de St-Jean** is divided by Eden Rock promontory, and there's good snorkeling west of the rock. The shallow, reef-protected beach at **Anse de Grand Cul de Sac** is especially nice for small children, fly fishermen, and windsurfers; it has excellent lunch spots and lots of pelicans. The big salt ponds of Grande Saline are no longer in use, and the place looks a little desolate. Don't be put off—by all means, climb the short hillock behind the ponds for a surprise. Secluded, with a sandy ocean bottom, **Anse de Grande Saline** is just about everyone's favorite beach and a great place for swimmers. In spite of the prohibition, young and old alike go nude. It can get windy here, so go on a calm day.

BOATING   St. Barths is a popular yachting and sailing center, thanks to its location midway between Antigua and St. Thomas. Gustavia's harbor, 13 to 16 feet deep, has mooring and docking facilities for 40 yachts. There are also good anchorages available at Public, Corossol, and Colombier. Day sails are popular activities and will take you to snorkeling spots that aren't reachable by land. **Marine Service** (⊠ Gustavia ☏ 0590/27–70–34 ⊕ www.st-barths.com/marine.service) offers full-day outings, either on a 42- or 46-foot catamaran, to the uninhabited Île Fourchue for swimming, snorkeling, cocktails, and lunch. The cost is $100 per person; an unskippered motor rental runs about $260 a day.

DIVING & SNORKELING   You can arrange scuba excursions to several local sites. Depending on the weather conditions, you may dive at Pain de Sucre, Coco Island, or even nearby Saba. There's also an underwater shipwreck to explore, plus sharks, rays, sea tortoises, coral, and the usual varieties of color fish. The waters on the island's leeward side are the calmest. If you're not a certified diver, there's an accessible shallow reef right off the beach at Anse de Cayes if you want to do snorkeling from the beach. **Plongée Caraïbe** (☏ 0590/27–55–94) is recommended for its up-to-the-minute equipment and dive boat. Marine Service operates the only five-star, PADI-certified diving center on the island, called **West Indies Dive** (☏ 0590/27–70–34 ⊕ www.westindiesdive.com). Scuba trips, packages, resort dives, night dives, and certifications start at $90, including gear.

WINDSURFING   Windsurfing fever has definitely caught on in St. Barths. Gentle, constant trade winds make conditions ideal on some beaches, such as Anse de Grand

Cul de Sac or Baie de St-Jean. You can rent boards for about €20 an hour at water-sports centers on the beaches. Lessons are offered for about $40 an hour at **Eden Rock Sea Sport Club** (⊠ Eden Rock Hotel, Baie de St-Jean ☎ 0590/27–74–77), which also rents boards. **Wind Wave Power** (⊠ St. Barth Beach Hotel, Grand Cul de Sac ☎ 0590/27–82–57) offers an extensive, six-hour training course. For €60, you can have a one-hour introductory lesson, along with the use of the Windsurfer for as long as you can stand up.

Where to Eat

Check restaurant bills carefully. A service charge is always added by law, but you should leave the server 5% to 10% extra in cash. It is generally advisable to charge restaurant meals on a credit card, as the issuer will offer a better exchange rate than the restaurant.

$$–$$$ ✕ **Le Repaire.** This friendly brasserie overlooks Gustavia's harbor and is a popular spot from its early-morning opening at 7 AM to its late-night closing at midnight. The menu ranges from cheeseburgers, which are served only at lunch along with the island's best fries, to simply grilled fish and meat. The composed salads always please. Wonderful ice-cream sundaes round out the menu. ⊠ *Quai de la République, Gustavia* ☎ *0590/ 27–72–48* ▤ *MC, V.*

★ ✕ **Le Tamarin.** A leisurely lunch here en route to Grand Saline beach is a **$$$–$$$$** St. Barths *must.* Delicious French and creole cuisine is served at this sophisticated open-air restaurant. Get to know the parrot, or relax in a hammock after the house-special carpaccios of salmon, tuna, and beef. The lemon tart deserves its excellent reputation. ⊠ *Salines* ☎ *0590/27–72–12* ▤ *AE, MC, V* ☼ *Open erratically May–Nov. Call to confirm.*

ST. JOHN, U.S. VIRGIN ISLANDS

Lynda Lohr

St. John's heart is Virgin Islands National Park, a treasure that takes up a full two-thirds of St. John's 20 square mi (53 square km). The park helps keep the island's interior in its pristine and undisturbed state, but if you go at midday, you'll probably have to share your stretch of beach with others, particularly at Trunk Bay. The island is booming, and while it can get a tad crowded at the ever-popular Trunk Bay Beach during the busy winter season, you won't find traffic jams or pollution. It's easy to escape from the fray, however: just head off on a hike. St. John doesn't have a grand agrarian past like her sister island, St. Croix, but if you're hiking in the dry season, you can probably stumble upon the stone ruins of old plantations. The less adventuresome can visit the repaired ruins at the park's Annaberg Plantation and Caneel Bay resort. Of the three U.S. Virgin Islands, St. John, which has 5,000 residents, has the strongest sense of community, which is primarily rooted in a desire to protect the island's natural beauty.

ST. JOHN BEST BETS

- **Hiking in the National Park.** Most of the island has been preserved, and the hiking trails that crisscross the terrain are easy enough for beginners and offer breathtaking scenery.

- **Snorkeling Cruises.** There are almost countless islands within easy reach, many with very good snorkeling possibilities.

- **Trunk Bay Beach.** St. John's national park beach is beautiful and has an underwater snorkeling trail.

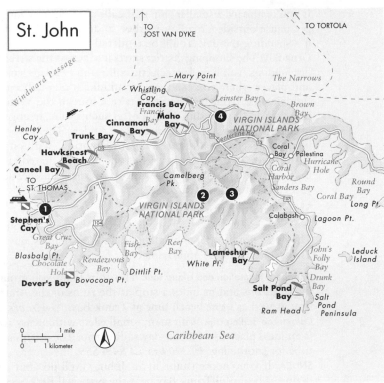

Annaberg
Plantation **4**

Bordeaux
Mountain **3**

Cruz Bay **1**

Reef Bay Trail . .**2**

St. John

TO
JOST VAN DYKE

TO TORTOLA

Windward Passage

Mary Point

The Narrows

Whistling
Cay

Francis Bay
Francis Bay

Leinster Bay

*Brown
Bay*

**Maho
Bay**

4

**VIRGIN ISLANDS
NATIONAL PARK**

**Cinnamon
Bay**

Bay

Henley
Cay

Trunk Bay

Centerline Rd.

**Hawksnest
Beach**

Coral
Bay

Palestina

*Hurricane
Hole*

Caneel Bay

*Coral
Harbor*

TO
ST. THOMAS

*Camelberg
Pk.*

Sanders Bay

*Round
Bay*

1

2

3

Coral Bay

Long Pt.

**Stephen's
Cay**

**VIRGIN ISLANDS
NATIONAL PARK**

Calabash

Lagoon Pt.

*Great Cruz
Bay*

*Fish
Bay*

*Reef
Bay*

*John's
Folly
Bay*

*Leduck
Island*

Blasbalg Pt.

*Rendezvous
Bay*

**Lameshur
Bay**

*Chocolate
Hole*

Dittlif Pt.

White Pt.

Dever's Bay

Bovocoap Pt.

*Drunk
Bay*

**Salt Pond
Bay**

*Salt
Pond
Peninsula*

Ram Head

0   1 mile
0   1 kilometer

Caribbean Sea

Essentials

CURRENCY The U.S. dollar is the official currency of the U.S. Virgin Islands; you'll find a few ATMs in Cruz Bay.

HOURS Bank hours are generally Monday through Thursday 9 to 3 and Friday 9 to 5; a handful open Saturday 9 to noon. On St. John, store hours run from 9 or 10 to 5 or 6. Wharfside Village and Mongoose Junction shops in Cruz Bay are often open into the evening.

INTERNET **Keep Me Posted** (⊠ Cocoloba shopping center, Rte. 107, Coral Bay, St. John ☎ 340/775–1727) **Surf da Web** (⊠ St. John Marketplace, 2nd floor, Cruz Bay, St. John ☎ 340/693–9152 ⊕ www.surfdaweb.com).

TELEPHONES Both GSM and Sprint phones work in most of St. John (take care that you're not roaming on the Tortola cell network on the island's north coast, though). It's as easy to call home from St. John as from any city in the United States. On St. John, public phones are in front of the post office, east of the tender landing, and at the ferry dock.

Coming Ashore

While smaller ships drop anchor at St. John, most people taking a cruise aboard a larger ship visit St. Thomas' sister island on a shore excursion or on an independent day trip from St. Thomas. If you prefer to not take a tour, ferries leave St. Thomas from the Charlotte Amalie waterfront and Red Hook. You'll have to take a taxi to reach the ferry dock.

If you're aboard a smaller ship that calls in St. John, your ship may simply pause outside Cruz Bay Harbor to drop you off or drop anchor if it's spending the day. You'll be tendered to shore at the main town of Cruz Bay. The shopping district starts just across the street from the tender landing. You'll find an eclectic collection of shops, cozy restaurants, and places where you can just sit and take it all in. The island has few sights to see. Your best bet is to take a tour of the Virgin Islands National Park. (If your ship doesn't offer such a tour, arrange one with one of the taxi drivers who will meet your tender.) The drive takes you past luscious beaches to a restored sugar plantation. With only a single day in port, you're better off just using the island's shared taxi vans rather than renting a car, but if you want to do some independent exploring, you can rent a car in Cruz Bay.

Shore Excursions

We consider these to be among the better shore excursions for St. John. They may not be offered by all lines, and tour names may differ as well. Times and prices are approximate.

Annaberg Plantation and Island Tour. This tour takes you around the island by safari bus and includes a stop at the ruins of the Annaberg Plantation as well as some beach time at Trunk Bay. ☉ 4 ½ hrs ⌑ $34–$49.

Catamaran Sailing Trip. With many small islets within easy reach, St. John is an ideal place to do a half-day sailing trip. These trips always include time for snorkeling. ☉ 3 ½ hrs ⌑ $49–$59.

SNUBA. If you choose snuba in St. John, you'll do your shallow-water diving at beautiful Trunk Bay near the National Park Service's snorkeling trail. ☉ 2 ½ hrs ⌑ $75–$84.

Exploring St. John

★ ❹ **Annaberg Plantation.** In the 18th century, sugar plantations dotted the steep hills of this island. Slaves and free Danes and Dutchmen toiled to harvest the cane that was used to create sugar, molasses, and rum for export. Built in the 1780s, the partially restored plantation at Leinster Bay was once an important sugar mill. Although there are no official visiting hours, the National Park Service has regular tours, and some well-informed taxi drivers will show you around. Occasionally you may see a living-history demonstration—someone making johnnycake or weaving baskets. For information on tours and cultural events, contact the St. John National Park Service Visitors Center. ⌂ *Leinster Bay Rd., Annaberg* ☎ *340/776–6201* ⊕ *www.nps.gov/viis* ⌑ *Free* ☉ *Daily sunrise–sunset.*

★ ❸ **Bordeaux Mountain.** St. John's highest peak rises to 1,277 feet. Route 10 passes near enough to the top to offer breathtaking views. Don't stray into the road here—cars whiz by at a good clip along this section. Instead, drive nearly to the end of the dirt road that heads off next to the restaurant and gift shop for spectacular views at Picture Point and the trailhead of the hike downhill to Lameshur. Get a trail map from the park service before you start. ⌂ *Rte. 10.*

❶ **Cruz Bay.** St. John's main town may be compact (it consists of only several blocks), but it's definitely a hub: the ferries from St. Thomas and the BVI pull in here, and it's where you can get a taxi or rent a car to travel around the island. There are plenty of shops in which to browse, a number of watering holes where you can stop for a breather, many restaurants, and a grassy square with benches where you can sit back and take everything in. Look for the current edition of the handy, amusing "St. John Map" featuring Max the Mongoose. To pick up a useful guide to St. John's hiking trails, see various large maps of the island, and find out about current park service programs, including guided walks and cultural demonstrations, stop by the **V. I. National Park Visitors Center** (⊠ Near the baseball field, Cruz Bay ☎ 340/776–6201 ⊕ www.nps.gov/ viis). It's open daily from 8 to 4:30.

★ ❷ **Reef Bay Trail.** Although this is one of the most interesting hikes on St. John, unless you're a rugged individualist who wants a physical challenge (and that describes a lot of people who stay on St. John), you can probably get the most out of the trip if you join a hike led by a park service ranger who can identify the trees and plants on the hike down, fill you in on the history of the Reef Bay Plantation, and tell you about the petroglyphs on the rocks at the bottom of the trail. A side trail takes you to the plantation's great house, a gutted but mostly intact structure that maintains vestiges of its former beauty. Take the safari bus from the park's visitor center. A boat takes you from the beach at Reef Bay back to the visitor center, saving you the uphill climb. ⊠ *Rte. 10, Reef Bay* ☎ *340/776–6201 Ext. 238 reservations* ⊕ *www.nps.gov/viis* ☒ *Free, safari bus $6, return boat trip to Cruz Bay $15* ☉ *Tours at 9:30 AM, days change seasonally.*

Shopping

In St. John, the small shopping district runs from Wharfside Village near the ferry landing to Mongoose Junction, just up the street from the cruise-ship dock and tender landing, with lots of shops tucked in between. The owner of **Bamboula** (⊠ Mongoose Junction, N. Shore Rd., Cruz Bay ☎ 340/693–8699), Jo Sterling, travels the Caribbean and beyond to find unusual housewares, art, rugs, bedspreads, accessories, shoes, and men's and women's clothes for this multicultural boutique. If you want to look like you stepped out of the pages of the resort-wear spread in an upscale travel magazine, try **Bougainvillea Boutique** (⊠ Mongoose Junction, N. Shore Rd., Cruz Bay ☎ 340/693–7190). Owner Susan Stair carries chic men's and women's clothes, straw hats, leather handbags, and fine gifts. Owner Radha Speer of **Caravan Gallery** (⊠ Mongoose Junction, N. Shore Rd., Cruz Bay ☎ 340/779–4566) travels the world to find much of the unusual jewelry she sells here. And the more you look, the more you see— folk art, tribal art, and masks cover the walls and tables, making this a great place to browse.

Pink Papaya (⊠ Lemon Tree Mall, King St., Cruz Bay ☎ 340/693–8535) is the home of longtime Virgin Islands resident M. L. Etre's well-known artwork, plus a huge collection of one-of-a-kind gifts, including bright tablecloths, unusual trays, dinnerware, and unique tropical jewelry. **St. John Editions** (⊠ N. Shore Rd., Cruz Bay ☎ 340/693–8444) has nifty cotton dresses that go from beach to dinner with a change of shoes and accessories. Owner Molly Soper also carries attractive straw hats and inexpensive jewelry.

7

Activities

DIVING & **Cruz Bay Watersports** (☎ 340/776–6234 ⊕ www.divestjohn.com) has two
SNORKELING locations: in Cruz Bay at the Lumberyard Shopping Complex and at the
Westin St. John Resort. Owners Marcus and Patty Johnston offer regular reef, wreck, and night dives and USVI and BVI snorkel tours. The
company holds both PADI five-star facility and NAUI Dream Resort status. **Low Key Watersports** (☎ 340/693–8999 or 800/835–7718 ⊕ www.
divelowkey.com), at Wharfside Village, offers one- and two-tank dives
and specialty courses. It's certified as a PADI five-star training facility.

FISHING Well-kept charter boats—approved by the U.S. Coast Guard—head out
to the north and south drops or troll along the inshore reefs, depending
on the season and what's biting. The captains usually provide bait,
drinks, and lunch, but you need to bring your own hat and sunscreen.
Fishing charters run between $550 and $750 per half day for the boat.
Gone Ketchin' (☎ 340/714–1175 ⊕ www.goneketchin.com), in St. John,
arranges trips with old salt Captain Grizz.

HIKING Although it's fun to go hiking with a Virgin Islands National Park guide,
don't be afraid to head out on your own. To find a hike that suits your
ability, stop by the park's visitor center in Cruz Bay and pick up the free
trail guide; it details points of interest, dangers, trail lengths, and estimated hiking times. Although the park staff recommends long pants to
protect against thorns and insects, most people hike in shorts because it
can get very hot. Wear sturdy shoes or hiking boots even if you're hiking to the beach. Don't forget to bring water and insect repellent. The
Fodor'sChoice **Virgin Islands National Park** (✉ 1300 Cruz Bay Creek, St. John ☎ 340/776–
★ 6201 ⊕ www.nps.gov/viis) maintains more than 20 trails on the north
and south shores and offers guided hikes along popular routes. A full-
day trip to Reef Bay is a must; it's an easy hike through lush and dry forest, past the ruins of an old plantation, and to a sugar factory adjacent
to the beach. It can be a bit arduous for young kids, however. Take the
$6 safari bus from the park's visitor center to the trailhead, where you
can meet a ranger who'll serve as your guide. The park provides a boat
ride back to Cruz Bay for $15 to save you the walk back up the moun-
tain. The schedule changes from season to season; call for times and reservations, which are essential.

Beaches

Long, sandy **Cinnamon Bay** (✉ North Shore Rd., Rte. 20, about 4 mi (6
km) east of Cruz Bay) faces beautiful cays and abuts the national park
campground. Facilities are open to the public and include cool showers,
toilets, a commissary, and a restaurant. You can rent water-sports equipment here. There's excellent snorkeling off the point to the right; look
for the big angelfish and large schools of purple triggerfish. Afternoons
on Cinnamon Bay can be windy, so arrive early to beat the gusts. **Hawksnest Beach** (✉ North Shore Rd., Rte. 20, about 2 mi (3 km) east of Cruz
Bay) is the closet beach to Cruz Bay, so it's often crowded. Sea grape trees
line this narrow beach, and there are rest rooms, cooking grills, and a
Fodor'sChoice covered shed for picnicking. **Trunk Bay** (✉ North Shore Rd., Rte. 20, about
★ 2½ mi (4 km) east of Cruz Bay), St. John's most-photographed beach,
is also the preferred spot for beginning snorkelers because of its underwater trail, but if you're looking for seclusion, don't come here because

it's the island's busiest. Crowded or not, this stunning beach is still beautiful. There are changing rooms, a snack bar, picnic tables, a gift shop, phones, lockers, and snorkeling-equipment rentals. You have to pay an entrance fee of $4 if you don't have a National Park Pass.

Where to Eat

☕ **$–$$** ✕ **Uncle Joe's Barbecue.** Juicy ribs and tasty chicken legs dripping with the house barbecue sauce make for one of St. John's best dining deals. An ear of corn, rice, and a generous scoop of macaroni salad or coleslaw round out the plate. This casual spot crowds the edge of a busy sidewalk in the heart of Cruz Bay. Even though there are a few open-air tables for dining "in," the ambience is more than a tad on the pedestrian side, so take-out is a better bet. ⊠ *North Shore Rd., across from post office* ☎ *340/ 693–8806* ▭ *No credit cards.*

$ ✕ **Sun Dog Cafe.** There's an unusual assortment of dishes at this charming alfresco restaurant, which you'll find tucked into a courtyard in the upper reaches of the Mongoose Junction shopping center. Kudos to the white pizza with artichoke hearts, roasted garlic, mozzarella cheese, and capers. The Jamaican jerk chicken sub and the black-bean quesadilla are also good choices. ⊠ *Mongoose Junction, North Shore Rd.* ☎ *340/ 693–8340* ▭ *AE, MC, V* ⊗ *No dinner.*

ST. KITTS (BASSETERRE)

Jordan Simon

Mountainous St. Kitts, the first English settlement in the Leeward Islands, crams some stunning scenery into its 65 square mi (168 square km). Vast, brilliant green fields of sugarcane (the former cash crop, now slowly being replanted) run to the shore. The fertile, lush island has some fascinating natural and historical attractions: a rain forest replete with waterfalls, thick vines, and secret trails; a central mountain range, dominated by the 3,792-foot Mt. Liamuiga, whose crater has long been dormant; and Brimstone Hill, known in the 17th century as the Gibraltar of the West Indies. St. Kitts and Nevis, along with Anguilla, achieved self-government as an Associated State of Great Britain in 1967. In 1983, St. Kitts & Nevis became an independent nation. English with a strong West Indian lilt is spoken here. People are friendly but shy; always ask before you take photographs. Also, be sure to wear wraps or shorts over beach attire when you're in public places.

CURRENCY Eastern Caribbean (E.C.) dollar (EC$2.70 to US$1). U.S. dollars are accepted practically everywhere, but you'll usually get change in E.C. currency.

HOURS Hours vary somewhat for banks but are typically Monday through Thursday from 8 to 2 and Friday from 8 to 4. There are numerous ATMs. Post offices are open Monday and Tuesday from 8 to 4, Wednesday through Friday from 8 to 3:30, and occasionally Saturday

ST. KITTS BEST BETS

- **Brimstone Hill Fortress.** This UN World Heritage Site has some of the best views on St. Kitts.

- **Nevis.** If your ship doesn't stop there, a trip to St. Kitts' beautiful sister island of Nevis is a worthwhile way to spend your day.

- **Romney Manor.** This partially restored manor house is a treat, and it's made better by the chance to view the wares of excellent Caribelle Batik.

7

from 8 to noon. Although shops used to close for lunch from noon to 1, more and more establishments are remaining open Monday through Saturday from 8 to 4.

INTERNET **Leyton's Sun Surf Internet Cafe** (✉ TDC Mall, Fort St., Basseterre, St. Kitts ☎ 869/465–5925).

TELEPHONES Phone cards, which you can buy in denominations of $5, $10, and $20, are handy for making local phone calls, calling other islands, and accessing U.S. direct lines. To make a local call, dial the seven-digit number. To call St. Kitts from the United States, dial the area code 869, then access code 465, 466, 468, or 469 and the local four-digit number.

Coming Ashore

Cruise ships calling at St. Kitts dock at Port Zante, which is a deep-water port directly in Basseterre, the capital of St. Kitts. The cruise-ship terminal is right in the downtown area, two minutes' walk from sights and shops. Taxi rates on St. Kitts are fixed and should be posted right at the dock. If you'd like to go to Nevis, several daily ferries (30 to 45 minutes, $8 one-way) can take you to Charlestown in Nevis; the byzantine schedule is subject to change, so double check times.

Taxi rates on St. Kitts are fairly expensive, and you may have to pay $32 for a ride to Brimstone Hill (for one to four passengers). A four-hour tour of St. Kitts is about $70. It's often cheaper to arrange an island tour with one of the local companies than to hire a taxi driver to take your group around. Several restored great-house plantations are known for their lunches; your driver can provide information and arrange drop-off and pickup. Before setting off in a cab, be sure to clarify whether the rate quoted is in E.C. or U.S. dollars.

SHORE EXCURSIONS
We consider these to be among the better shore excursions for St. Kitts. They may not be offered by all lines, and tour names may differ as well. Times and prices are approximate.

Brimstone Hill Fortress & Gardens. You will visit Brimstone Hill, a 300-year old fortress and World Heritage Site before going to Romney Gardens, where you can browse through the wares of Caribelle Batik Studio. Your tour ends after a drive through Basseterre. ☺ *3 hrs* ✉ *$54.*

Nevis Catamaran Getaway. Sail from St. Kitts to the island of Nevis for a day of snorkeling and a beach barbeque at Pinneys Beach. Some tours also include a bus trip to Alexander Hamilton Museum and the Botanical Garden, but these will cost more. ☺ *7 hrs* ✉ *$109.*

Sea Kayaking & Snorkeling. After kayaking in White House Bay, you have the opportunity to snorkel in Friars Bay. ☺ *3 hrs* ✉ *$89.*

St. Kitts Scenic Railway. After a bus trip to the rail station, you board a double-decker, narrow-gauge railway car for a trip partway around the island. Each passenger gets a comfortable downstairs air-conditioned seat fronting vaulted picture windows and an upstairs open-air observation spot. The conductor's running discourse embraces not only the history of sugar cultivation but the railway's construction, island folklore, island geography, even other agricultural mainstays from papayas and pineapples to pigs. Refreshments are provided. ☺ *3½ hrs* ✉ *$109.*

Exploring St. Kitts

Numbers in the margin correspond to points of interest on the St. Kitts map.

❶ Basseterre. On the south coast, St. Kitts's walkable capital is graced with tall palms, and although many of the buildings appear run-down, there are interesting shops, excellent art galleries, and some beautifully maintained houses. Duty-free shops and boutiques line the streets and courtyards radiating from the octagonal Circus, built in the style of London's famous Piccadilly Circus. There are lovely gardens on the site of a former slave market at **Independence Square** (⊠ Off Bank St.). The square is surrounded on three sides by 18th-century Georgian buildings. **St. George's Anglican Church** (⊠ Cayon St.) is a handsome stone building with a crenellated tower originally built by the French in 1670 and called Notre-Dame. The British burned it down in 1706 and rebuilt it four years later, naming it after the patron saint of England. Since then it has suffered a fire, an earthquake, and hurricanes, and was once again rebuilt in 1869. In the restored former Treasury Building, the **National Museum** (⊠ Bay Rd., Basseterre ☎ 869/465–5584) presents an eclectic collection reflecting the history and culture of the island—as a collaboration of the St. Christopher Heritage Society and the island government. Admission is $1, and it's open Tuesday through Friday from 9–1 and 2–5 (only from 9:30–2 Monday and Saturday).

★ ❹ Brimstone Hill. The well-restored 38-acre fortress, a UNESCO World Heritage Site, is well worth a trip, particularly if military history and/or spectacular views interest you. After routing the French in 1690, the English erected a battery here, and by 1736 the fortress held 49 guns, earning it the moniker "Gibraltar of the West Indies." A hurricane severely damaged the fortress in 1834, and in 1852 it was evacuated and dismantled. The citadel

CAUTION	⚠
Pack a small flashlight just in case there's an emergency. You don't want to be stumbling around in the dark.	

has been partially reconstructed and its guns remounted. A seven-minute orientation film recounts the fort's history and restoration. An on-site museum is mildly interesting, but it's the views that are astounding. Nature trails snake through the tangle of surrounding hardwood forest and savanna (a fine spot to catch the green vervet monkeys—inexplicably brought by the French and now outnumbering the residents—skittering about). ⊠ *Main Rd., Brimstone Hill* ☎ *869/465–2609* ⊕ *www.brimstonehillfortress.org* 🖾 *$8* ⊘ *Daily 9:30–5:30.*

★ ❸ **Romney Manor.** The ruins of this partially restored house and surrounding cottages that duplicate the old chattel-house style are set in 6 acres of gardens, with exotic flowers, an old bell tower, and an enormous, gnarled, 350-year-old *samaan* tree (sometimes called a rain tree). Inside, at **Caribelle Batik,** you can watch artisans hand-printing fabrics. Look for signs indicating a turnoff for Romney Manor near Old Road.

❷ **St. Kitts Scenic Railway.** The old narrow-gauge train that had transported sugarcane circles the island in just under four hours. Each passenger gets a comfortable, downstairs air-conditioned seat fronting vaulted picture windows and an upstairs open-air observation spot. The conductor's running discourse embraces not only the history of sugar cultivation but the railway's construction, local folklore, island geography, and even other agricultural mainstays from papayas to pigs. You can drink in complimentary tropical beverages (including luscious guava daiquiris) along with the sweeping rain-forest and ocean vistas. There's a break at the halfway point (La Vallee), where cruise-ship passengers on ship-sponsored tours disembark. By then, the trip may seem slow as molasses, but it's certainly uniquely Caribbean. ⊠ *Needsmust* ☎ *869/465–7263* ⊕ *www.StKittsScenicRailway.com* 🖾 *$89* ⊘ *June–Sept., departures Mon. at 1 PM and Wed. at 9:30 AM; Oct.–May, departures vary according to cruise-ship schedules.*

Shopping

St. Kitts has limited shopping, but there are a few duty-free shops with good deals on jewelry, perfume, china, and crystal. Don't forget to pick up some CSR, a "new cane spirit drink" that's distilled from fresh sugarcane right on St. Kitts or Brinley Gold's luscious flavored rums. Most shopping plazas are in downtown Basseterre—try the **Shoreline Plaza,** next to the Treasury Building; the **Pelican Mall,** across the street from Port Zante (which has a tourism office); and **Port Zante,** which has about 25 shops of its own.

Caribelle Batik (⊠ Romney Manor, Old Road ☎ 869/465–6253) sells batik wraps, kimonos, caftans, T-shirts, dresses, wall hangings, and the like. **Kate Design** (⊠ Bank St., Basseterre ☎ 869/465–5265) showcases the highly individual style of Kate Spencer, whose original paintings, serigraphs, note cards, and other pieces that she regularly introduces, are also available from her studio on the Rawlins Plantation grounds. **The Potter's House** (⊠ Camps Estate Great House, Camps Estate ☎ 869/465–5947) is the atelier-home of Carla Astaphan, whose beautifully glazed ceramics and masks celebrate the Afro-Caribbean heritage. **Spencer Cameron Art Gallery** (⊠ 10 N. Independence Sq., Basseterre ☎ 869/465–1617) has historical reproductions of Caribbean island charts and prints, in addition to owner Rosey Cameron's popular Carnevale clown prints and a wide selection of exceptional artwork by Caribbean artists. They will mail anywhere.

Activities

DIVING & SNORKELING
St. Kitts has more than a dozen excellent dive sites. The surrounding waters feature shoals, hot vents, shallows, canyons, steep walls, and caverns at depths from 40 to nearly 200 feet, with hundreds of wrecks. **Dive St. Kitts** (⊠ Frigate Bay, 2 mi [3 km] east of Basseterre ☎ 869/465–1189 ⊕ www.divestkitts.com), a PADI–NAUI facility, offers competitive prices; friendly, laid-back dive masters; and an international clientele. The Bird Rock location features superb beach diving: common sightings 20 feet to 30 feet out include octopi, nurse sharks, manta, spotted eagle rays, and sea horses. Shore dives are unlimited when you book packages. Kenneth Samuel of **Kenneth's Dive Center** (⊠ Bay Rd., Newtown ☎ 869/465–2670 ⊕ www.kennethsdivecenter.com) takes small groups of divers with C cards to nearby reefs. Rates average $40 for single-tank dives, $75 for double-tank dives; add $10 to $15 for equipment. After 25 years' experience, former fisherman Samuel is considered an old pro and strives to keep groups small and prices reasonable. Austin Macleod, a PADI-certified dive master–instructor and owner of **Pro-Divers** (⊠ Ocean Terrace Inn, Basseterre ☎ 869/466–3483 ⊕ www.prodiversstkitts.com), offers resort and certification courses. His prices for an open-water certification course and dive package prices are the lowest on the island. He also takes groups to snorkeling sites accessible only by boat.

GOLF
The **Royal St. Kitts Golf Club** (⊠ St. Kitts Marriott Resort, Frigate Bay ☎ 869/466–2700 ⊕ www.royalstkittsgolfclub.com) is an 18-hole, par-71 links-style championship course that underwent a complete redesign by Thomas McBroom to maximize Caribbean and Atlantic views and increase the challenge. Greens fees are $135 for Marriott guests in high season, $175 for nonguests. The development includes practice bunkers, putting green, and a short-game chipping area.

HIKING
Trails in the central mountains of St. Kitts vary from easy to don't-try-it-by-yourself. Monkey Hill and Verchild's Peak aren't difficult, although the Verchild's climb will take the better part of a day. Don't attempt Mt. Liamuiga without a guide. Tour rates range from $35 for a rain-forest walk to $65 for a volcano expedition. Earl of **Duke of Earl's Adventures** (☎ 869/465–1899) is as

---

STORAGE

Take along a hanging shoe organizer for the closet to extend storage space for small items and to keep shoes off the floor. An over-the-door, pocket-style shoe organizer can be hung on the bathroom door. Slip bathroom necessities in the pockets so they are handy and out of the way.

entertaining as his nickname suggests—and his prices are slightly cheaper. He genuinely loves his island and conveys that enthusiasm, encouraging hikers to swing on vines or sample unusual-looking fruits during his rain-forest trip. He also conducts a thorough volcano tour to the crater's rim. Greg Pereira of **Greg's Safaris** (☎ 869/465–4121 ⊕ www.gregssafaris. com), whose family has lived on St. Kitts since the early 19th century, takes groups on half-day trips into the rain forest and on full-day hikes up the volcano and through the grounds of a private 18th-century great house. The rain-forest trips include visits to sacred Carib sites, abandoned sugar mills, and an excursion down a 100-foot coastal canyon containing a wealth of Amerindian petroglyphs. The Off the Beaten Track Plantation Tour provides a thorough explanation of the role sugar and rum played in the Caribbean economy and colonial wars. He and his staff relate fascinating historical, folkloric, and botanical information. Oliver Spencer of **Off the Beaten Path** (☎ 869/465–6314) leads rain-forest treks to the ruins of an abandoned coffee plantation taken over by spreading banyan trees, explaining folklore and flora, including herbal remedies, along the way.

HORSEBACK RIDING Wild North Frigate Bay and desolate Conaree Beach are great for riding, as is the rain forest. Guides from **Trinity Stables** (☎ 869/465–3226) offer beach rides ($40) and trips into the rain forest ($50). The latter is intriguing as guides discuss plants' medicinal properties along the way (such as sugarcane to stanch bleeding) and pick oranges right off a tree to squeeze fresh juice. Otherwise, the staffers are cordial but shy, and this isn't a place for beginners' instruction.

Beaches

The powdery white-sand beaches of St. Kitts, free and open to the public (even those occupied by hotels), are in the Frigate Bay area or on the lower peninsula. **Banana Bay,** one of the island's loveliest beaches, stretches over 1 mi (1½ km) at the southeastern tip of the island, with majestic views of Nevis. **Cockleshell Bay,** Banana Bay's twin beach, is another eyebrow of glittering sand backed by lush vegetation and reachable on foot. Locals consider the Caribbean (southern) side of **Friar's Bay** the island's finest beach. Unfortunately, the upcoming Marine World development has co-opted nearly half the strand. Still, several hopping, happening bars, including Shipwreck and Sunset Grill serve terrific, inexpensive local food and cheap, frosty drinks. You can haggle with fishermen here to take you snorkeling off the eastern point. The waters on the Atlantic (northern) side are rougher, but the beach has a wild, desolate beauty. On the Caribbean side of **Frigate Bay** you'll find talcum powder–fine sand and several lively thatched beach boîtes, while the 4-mi-wide (6½-km-wide) Atlantic side—regrettably dominated by the leviathan Marriott—is a favorite with horseback riders.

Where to Eat

Restaurants occasionally add a 10% service charge to your bill; if this information isn't printed on the menu, ask about it. When there's no service charge, a tip of 15% is appropriate.

★ $$–$$$ ✗ **Turtle Beach Bar & Grill.** Treats at this popular daytime watering hole at the south end of S.E. Peninsula Road include honey-mustard ribs, coconut-shrimp salad, grilled lobster (a best-buy special Friday nights), decadent bread pudding with rum sauce, and an array of tempting tropical libations. Business cards and pennants from around the world plaster the bar; the room is decorated with a variety of nautical accoutrements. You can snorkel here, spot hawksbill turtles, feed the tame monkeys that boldly belly up to the bar (they adore green bananas and peaches), serve Wilbur the pig a beer, laze in a palm-shaded hammock, or rent a kayak or snorkel gear. Locals come Sunday afternoons for dancing to live bands and for fun but fiercely contested volleyball. ⊠ *S.E. Peninsula Rd., Turtle Beach* ☎ *869/469–9086* ⊟ *AE, D, MC, V* ☉ *No dinner Mon.–Thurs.*

$–$$$ ✕ **Ballahoo.** This second-floor terrace restaurant creates an appropriately tropical ambience with decor featuring whirring ceiling fans, potted palms, and colorful island prints, and lilting calypso and reggae on the sound system. Specialties include chili shrimp, conch simmered in garlic butter, Madras beef curry, and a toasted rum-and-banana sandwich topped with ice cream. Go at lunchtime, when you can watch the bustle of the Circus, and specials such as rotis bursting with curried chicken or vegetables slash prices nearly in half. Grab fresh local juices (tamarind, guava) if you can. Though the service is lackadaisical bordering on rude, the food is at least plentiful, the daiquiris killer, and the people-watching delightful. ⊠ *Fort St., Basseterre* ☎ *869/465–4197* ⊟ *AE, MC, V* ☉ *Closed Sun.*

ST. LUCIA (CASTRIES)

Jane Zarem

Magnificent St. Lucia—with towering mountains, dense rain forest, fertile green valleys, and acres of banana plantations—lies in the middle of the Windward Islands. Nicknamed "the Helen of the West Indies" because of its natural beauty, St. Lucia is distinguished from its neighbors by its unusual geological landmarks, the Pitons—the twin peaks on the southwest coast that soar nearly ½ mi (1 km) above the ocean floor and have become a symbol of this island. Nearby, outside the former French colonial capital of Soufrière, is a "drive-in" volcano, neighboring sulfur springs that have rejuvenated bathers for nearly three centuries, and one of the most beautiful botanical gardens in the Caribbean. A century and a half of battles between the French and English resulted in St. Lucia's changing hands 14 times before 1814, when England established possession. In 1979 the island became an independent state within the British Commonwealth of Nations. The official language is English, although most people also speak a French-creole patois.

Essentials

CURRENCY   Eastern Caribbean (E.C.) dollar (EC$2.70 to US$1). U.S. dollars are generally accepted, but change is given in E.C. dollars.

HOURS   Banks are open Monday through Thursday from 8 to 3, Friday 8 to 5; a few branches in Rodney Bay are also open Saturday from 9 to noon. Post offices are open weekdays from 8:30 to 4:30. Most stores are open weekdays from 8:30 to 12:30 and 1:30 to 4:30, Saturday from 8 to 12:30.

INTERNET   There are several Internet cafés in the Rodney Bay Marina. **Cyber Connections** (⊠ Rodney Bay Marina, Gros Islet ☎ 758/450–9309). **Destination St. Lucia (DSL) Ltd.** (⊠ Rodney Bay Marina, Gros Islet ☎ 758/452–8531).

TELEPHONES   You can make direct-dial overseas and interisland calls from St. Lucia, and the connections are excellent. You can charge an overseas call to a major credit card with no surcharge by dialing 811. Phone cards can be purchased at many retail outlets.

Coming Ashore

Most cruise ships dock at the capital city of Castries, on the island's north-west coast. Either of two docking areas is used: Pointe Seraphine, a port of entry and duty-free shopping complex, or Port Castries, a commercial wharf across the harbor. Ferry service connects the two piers. Smaller vessels occasionally call at Soufrière, on the island's southwest coast. Ships calling at Soufrière must usually anchor offshore and bring passengers ashore via tender. Tourist information booths are located at Pointe Seraphine in Castries and along the waterfront on Bay Street in Soufrière. Downtown Castries is within walking distance of the pier, and the produce market and adjacent crafts and vendors' markets are the main attractions. Soufrière is a sleepy West Indian town, but it's worth a short walk around the central square to view the French colonial architecture; most of the island's best sights are near Soufrière. Taxis are available at the docks in Castries. Although they are unmetered, the standard fares are posted at the entrance to Pointe Seraphine. Taxi drivers are well informed and can give you a full tour—often an excellent one—thanks to government-sponsored training programs. From the Castries area, full-day island tours cost about $140 for up to four people; sightseeing trips to Soufrière, around $120. If you plan your own day, expect to pay the driver at least $20 per hour plus a 10% tip. Whatever your destination, negotiate the price with the driver before you depart—and be sure that you both understand whether the rate is in E.C. or U.S. dollars.

Shore Excursions

We consider these to be among the better shore excursions for St. Lucia. They may not be offered by all lines, and tour names may differ as well. Times and prices are approximate.

Gros Piton Climb. While very strenuous, you get a unique view from the top of Gros Piton, making this trip quite worthwhile for the physically fit. ☉ 7 hrs ⌨ $129.

Pigeon Island Sea Kayaking. This is a good kayaking adventure for the novice. You paddle from Rodney Bay to Pigeon Island, tour the island itself, and spend some time at the beach. The return is by bus. ☉ 3 hrs ⌨ $62.

Rain-forest Hike. St. Lucia has a well-protected rain forest, and this hike will take you into the forest along the Canaries River. There's a refreshment stop on the way back to Castries. ☉ 5½ hrs ⌨ $52.

Soufrière Coastal Cruise The best tours travel down to Soufrière by catamaran

ST. LUCIA BEST BETS

- **The Pitons.** You have to see St. Lucia's famous twin peaks, and the most pleasant way to get down here from Castries is by boat.

- **The Rain Forest.** Whatever activity you might be interested in, do it. St. Lucia's lush rain forest is one of the best natural environments in the Caribbean.

- **Pigeon Island.** This national park is both historic and a great natural environment good for kayaking.

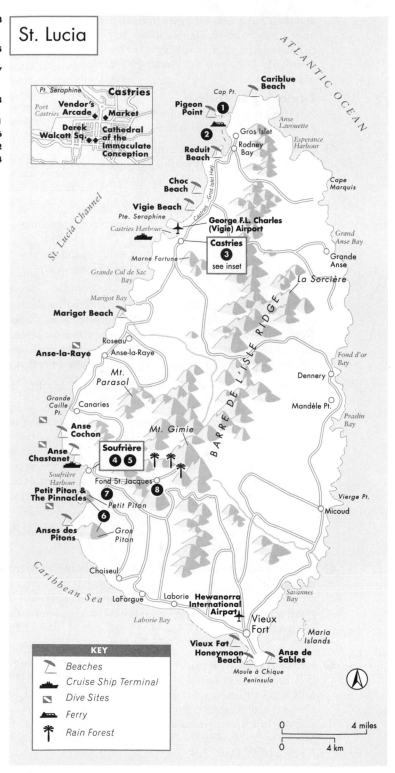

St. Lucia

ATLANTIC OCEAN

Castries

Pt. Seraphine

Port
Castries

**Vendor's
Arcade** ◆ **Market**

**Derek
Walcott Sq.** ◆ ◆ **Cathedral
of the
Immaculate
Conception**

**Cariblue
Beach**

Cap Pt.

**Pigeon
Point** ❶

❷

Gros Islet

Anse
Lavouette

Esperance
Harbour

**Reduit
Beach**

Rodney
Bay

Cape
Marquis

**Choc
Beach**

Vigie Beach

Pte. Seraphine

Castries Harbour

**George F.L. Charles
(Vigie) Airport**

Castries ❸
see inset

Grand
Anse Bay

Grande
Anse

La Sorcière

Morne Fortune

St. Lucia Channel

Castries – Gros Islet Hwy.

*Grande Cul de Sac
Bay*

Marigot Bay

Marigot Beach

Roseau

Anse-la-Raye

Anse-la-Raye

**Mt.
Parasol**

Grande
Caille
Pt.

Canaries

**Anse
Cochon**

**Anse
Chastanet**

*Soufrière
Harbour*

Fond St. Jacques

**Petit Piton &
The Pinnacles**

Petit Piton

**Anses des
Pitons**

*Gros
Piton*

Mt. Gimie

Soufrière
❹ ❺

❽

❼

❻

BARRE DE L'ISLE RIDGE

Fond d'or
Bay

Dennery

Mandéle Pt.

Praslin
Bay

Vierge Pt.

Micoud

Caribbean Sea

Choiseul

LaFargue

Laborie

**Hewanorra
International
Airport**

Laborie Bay

Savannes
Bay

**Vieux Fort
Honeymoon
Beach**

*Moule à Chique
Peninsula*

**Vieux
Fort**

**Anse de
Sables**

*Maria
Islands*

KEY	
⚓	*Beaches*
🚢	*Cruise Ship Terminal*
◻	*Dive Sites*
⛴	*Ferry*
🌴	*Rain Forest*

0 ___ 4 miles

0 ___ 4 km

and then put guests on buses that stop to visit the volcano, Diamond Botanical Gardens, and lunch at Morne Coubaril. Then you sail back. ☼ 7½ hrs ✉ $84.

Exploring St. Lucia
Numbers in the margin correspond to points of interest on the St. Lucia map.

❸ **Castries.** The capital, a busy commercial city of about 65,000 people, wraps around a sheltered bay. Morne Fortune rises sharply to the south of town, cre-

> **BAG IT**
>
> A mesh laundry bag or a "pop-up" mesh clothes hamper are two fairly light items that pack flat in your suitcase. The bag can hang from the closet, but either will keep your closet neat, allow damp clothing to dry out, and help you tote dirty clothes to the self-service laundry room so you can avoid high cleaning charges.

ating a dramatic green backdrop. The charm of Castries lies almost entirely in its liveliness, since most of the colonial buildings were destroyed by four fires that occurred between 1796 and 1948. Freighters (exporting bananas, coconut, cocoa, mace, nutmeg, and citrus fruits) and cruise ships come and go daily, making Castries Harbour one of the Caribbean's busiest ports.

Derek Walcott Square, a green oasis bordered by Brazil, Laborie, Micoud, and Bourbon streets, honors the hometown poet who won the 1992 Nobel prize for literature. Buildings from the 19th century can be seen on Brazil Street, the square's southern border. On the Laborie Street side, a huge, 400-year-old samaan tree shades a good portion of the square.

Directly across Laborie Street is the Roman Catholic **Cathedral of the Immaculate Conception,** which was built in 1897.

At the corner of Jeremie and Peynier streets, spreading beyond its brilliant orange roof, is the **Castries Market.** Full of excitement and bustle, the market is open every day except Sunday. It's liveliest on Saturday morning, when farmers bring their fresh produce and spices to town, as they have for more than a century. Next door to the produce market is the Craft Market, where you can buy pottery, wood carvings, and handwoven straw articles.

Across Peynier Street from the Craft Market, at the **Vendor's Arcade,** there are still more handicrafts and souvenirs.

🦢 ❺ **Diamond Botanical Gardens & Waterfall.** Water bubbling to the surface from underground sulfur springs streams downhill in rivulets to become Diamond Waterfall, deep within these splendid botanical gardens. For a small price, you can soak in one of the curative mineral baths. ⊠ *Soufrière Estate, Soufrière* ☎ *758/452–4759 or 758/454–7565* ✉ *$2.75, outside bath $2.50, private bath $3.75* ☼ *Mon.–Sat. 10–5, Sun. 10–3.*

❼ **Fond Doux Estate.** This plantation just outside Soufrière was one of the earliest French estates established by land grant (1745 and 1763); its 135 hilly acres still produce cocoa, citrus, bananas, coconut, and vegetables; the restored plantation house (built in 1864) is still in use. A tour can include lunch; souvenirs are sold at the boutique. ⊠ *Chateaubelair, Soufrière* ☎ *758/459–7545* ⊕ *www.fonddouxestate.com* ✉ *$6, buffet lunch $14* ☼ *Daily 9–4.*

❽ **La Soufrière Drive-In Volcano.** As you approach, your nose will pick up the strong scent of the sulfur springs. You actually drive up within a few hundred feet of the gurgling, steaming mass, then follow a guide around a fault in the substratum rock on foot. ⊠ *Bay St., Soufrière* ☎ *758/459– 5500* ⊠ *$1.25* ☉ *Daily 9–5.*

❶ **Pigeon Island.** This former hideout for pirate Jambe de Bois (Wooden Leg) is now a national landmark. You can swim or snorkel at two small beaches, look at ruins that date from 18th century French and English battles, or take in a multimedia display about the island's ecological and historical significance. ⊠ *Pigeon Island, St. Lucia National Trust, Rodney Bay* ☎ *758/452–5005* ⊕ *www.slunatrust.org* ⊠ *$4* ☉ *Daily 9–5.*

❻ **The Pitons.** These two unusual mountains, which rise precipitously from the cobalt blue Caribbean Sea just south of Soufrière, have become the symbol of St. Lucia. Covered with thick tropical vegetation, the massive outcroppings were formed by lava from a volcanic eruption 30 to 40 million years ago. They are not identical twins since—confusingly—2,619-foot Petit Piton is taller than 2,461-foot Gros Piton, though Gros Piton is, as the word translates, broader. You can also climb Gros Piton. ☎ *758/450–2231, 758/450–2078 for St. Lucia Forest & Lands Department, 758/459–9748 for Pitons Tour Guide Association* ⊠ *Guide services $45* ☉ *Daily by appointment only.*

❷ **Rodney Bay.** This man-made lagoon is home to the Rodney Bay Marina, where you can arrange yacht charters and sightseeing day trips. The Rodney Bay Ferry makes hourly crossings between the marina and the shopping complex, as well as daily excursions to Pigeon Island.

❹ **Soufrière.** The wharf is the center of activity in this sleepy town, the oldest in St. Lucia and the former French colonial capital. It's located 1 1/2 hours from Castries by car, 45-minutes by boat. The **Soufrière Tourist Information Centre** (⊠ Bay St., Soufrière ☎ 758/459–7200) provides information about area attractions. Note that outside some of the popular attractions in and around Soufrière, souvenir vendors can be persistent. Be polite but firm if you're not interested in their wares.

Shopping

The island's best-known products are artwork and wood carvings; clothing and household articles made from batik and silk-screen fabrics, designed and printed in island workshops; and clay pottery. You can also take home straw hats and baskets and locally grown cocoa, coffee, and spices. The only duty-free shopping is at **Pointe Seraphine** or **La Place Carenage,** on opposite sides of the harbor. You must show your passport and cabin key card to get duty-free prices. You'll want to experience the **Castries Market** and scour the adjacent **Vendor's Arcade** and **Craft Market** for handicrafts and souvenirs at bargain prices.

Artsibit Gallery (⊠ Brazil and Mongiraud Sts., Castries ☎ 758/452–7865) exhibits and sells moderately priced pieces by St. Lucian painters and sculptors. **Bagshaw Studios** (⊠ La Toc Rd., La Toc Bay, Castries ☎ 758/452–2139 or 758/451–9249) sells clothing and table linens in colorful tropical patterns using Stanley Bagshaw's original designs. The fabrics are silk-screened by hand in the adjacent workroom. At **Caribelle Batik** (⊠ La

Toc Rd., Morne Fortune, Castries ☎ 758/452–3785), craftspeople demonstrate the art of batik and silk-screen printing. Meanwhile, seamstresses create clothing and wall hangings, which you can purchase in the shop. **Eudovic Art Studio** (✉ Morne Fortune, Castries ☎ 758/452–2747) is a workshop and studio where you can buy trays, masks, and figures sculpted from local mahogany, red cedar, and eucalyptus wood. **Noah's Arkade** (✉ Jeremie St., Castries ☎ 758/452–2523 ✉ Pointe Seraphine, Castries ☎ 758/452–7488) has hammocks, wood carvings, straw mats, T-shirts, books, and other regional goods.

Activities

DIVING   The coral reefs at Anse Cochon and Anse Chastanet, on the southwest coast, are popular beach-entry dive sites. In the north, Pigeon Island is the most convenient site. **Buddies** (✉ Rodney Bay Marina, Rodney Bay ☎ 758/452–8406) offers wall, wreck, reef, and deep dives; open-water certification with advanced and specialty courses are taught by PADI-certified instructors. **Dive Fair Helen** (✉ Vigie Marina, Castries ☎ 758/451–7716 or 888/855–2206 in the U.S. and Canada ⊕ www.divefairhelen.com) is a PADI center that offers half- and full-day excursions to wreck, wall, and marine reserve areas, as well as night dives. **Scuba St. Lucia** (✉ Anse Chastanet, Soufrière ☎ 758/459–7755 ⊕ www.scubastlucia.com) is a PADI five-star training facility. Daily beach and boat dives and certification courses are offered; underwater photography and snorkeling equipment are available. Day-trips from the Castries port area include round-trip speedboat transportation.

FISHING   Among the deep-sea creatures you can find in St. Lucia's waters are dolphin (also called dorado or mahimahi), barracuda, mackerel, wahoo, kingfish, sailfish, and white or blue marlin. Sportfishing is generally done on a catch-and-release basis. Neither spearfishing nor collecting live fish in coastal waters is permitted. Half- or full-day deep-sea fishing excursions can be arranged at either Vigie Cove or Rodney Bay Marina. A half-day of fishing on a scheduled trip runs about $75 to $80 per person. Beginners are welcome. **Captain Mike's** (✉ Vigie Cove ☎ 758/452–1216 or 758/452–7044 ⊕ www.captmikes.com) has a fleet of Bertram power boats (31- to 38-feet) that accommodate as many as eight passengers; tackle and cold drinks are supplied. **Mako Watersports** (✉ Rodney Bay Marina, Rodney Bay ☎ 758/452–0412) takes fishing enthusiasts out on the well-equipped six-passenger *Annie Baby*.

GOLF   **St. Lucia Golf & Country Club** (✉ Cap Estate ☎ 758/452–8523 ⊕ www.stluciagolf.com), the island's only public course, is at the island's northern tip and offers panoramic views of both the Atlantic and Caribbean. It's an 18-hole championship course (6,829 yards, par 71). The clubhouse has a bar and a pro shop where you can rent clubs and shoes and arrange lessons. Greens fees are $70 for 9 holes or $95 for 18 holes; carts are required and included; club and shoe rentals are available. Reservations are essential. Complimentary transportation from your cruise ship is provided for parties of three or more people.

HORSEBACK RIDING   Creole horses, an indigenous breed, are fairly small, fast, sturdy, and even-tempered animals suitable for beginners. Established stables can accommodate all skill levels and offer countryside trail rides, beach rides with picnic lunches, plantation tours, carriage rides, and lengthy treks. Prices run about $40 for one hour, $50 for two hours, and $70 for a three-hour beach ride and barbecue. Transportation is usually provided between the stables and nearby hotels. People sometimes appear on beaches with their steeds and offer 30-minute rides for $10; ride at your own risk. **Country Saddles** (⊠ Marquis Estate, Babonneau ☎ 758/450–5467), 45 minutes east of Castries, guides beginners and advanced riders through banana plantations, forest trails, and along the Atlantic coast. **International Riding Stables** (⊠ Beauséjour Estate, Gros Islet ☎ 758/452–8139 or 758/450–8665) offers either English- or western-style riding. Their beach-picnic ride includes time for a swim—with or without your horse. **Trim's National Riding Stable** (⊠ Cas-en-Bas, Gros Islet ☎ 758/452–8273 or 758/450–9971), the island's oldest establishment, offers four riding sessions per day, plus beach tours, trail rides, and carriage tours to Pigeon Island.

Beaches

All of St. Lucia's beaches are open to the public, but Pigeon Point, Reduit, and Vigie beaches are particularly accessible to cruise-ship passengers. At **Pigeon Point**, a small beach within Pigeon Island National Historic Park, a restaurant serves snacks and drinks, but this is also a perfect spot for picnicking. It's about a 30-minute taxi ride ($20) from Pointe Seraphine. **Reduit Beach**, a long stretch of golden sand, is next to Rodney Bay. The Rex St. Lucian Hotel, which faces the beach, has a water-sports center. Many feel that Reduit (pronounced red-*wee*) is the island's finest beach. **Vigie Beach**, a 2-mi (3-km) strand in Castries, is not far from the port. It runs parallel to the George F. L. Charles Airport runway and continues on to become Malabar Beach, the beachfront for the Rendezvous resort.

Where to Eat

An 8% government tax is applicable to your bill, and most restaurants add a 10% service charge in lieu of tip.

★ **$$** ✕ **Jacques Waterside Dining.** Chef-owner Jacky Rioux creates magical dishes in his open-air garden restaurant (known for years as Froggie Jack's) overlooking Vigie Cove. The cooking style is decidedly French, as is Rioux, but fresh produce and local spices create a fusion cuisine that's memorable at lunch or dinner. You might start with a bowl of creamy tomato-basil or pumpkin soup, a grilled portobello mushroom, or octopus and conch in curried coconut sauce. Main courses include fresh seafood, such as oven-baked kingfish with a white wine and sweet pepper sauce, or breast of chicken stuffed with smoked salmon in a citrus butter sauce. The wine list is also impressive. ⊠ *Vigie Marina, Castries* ☎ *758/458–1900* ⚓ *Reservations essential* ▭ *AE, MC, V* ⊗ *Closed Sun.*

$–$$ ✕ **Lifeline Restaurant at the Hummingbird.** Cajou, the chef at this cheerful restaurant-bar in the Hummingbird Beach Resort, specializes in French creole cuisine, starting with fresh seafood or chicken seasoned with local herbs and accompanied by a medley of vegetables just picked from the Hummingbird's garden. Sandwiches and salads are also available. If you stop for lunch, be sure to visit the batik studio and art gallery of proprietor Joan Alexander and her son, adjacent to the dining room. ⊠ *Hum-*

mingbird Beach Resort, Anse Chastanet Rd., Soufrière ☎ *758/459–7232* ▭ *AE, D, MC, V.*

ST. MARTIN/ST. MAARTEN (PHILLIPSBURG)

Roberta
Sotonoff

St. Martin/St. Maarten: one tiny island, just 37 square mi (59 square km), with two different accents, and ruled by two sovereign nations. Here French and Dutch have lived side by side for hundreds of years, and when you cross from one country to the next there are no border patrols, no customs. In fact, the only indication that you have crossed a border at all is a small sign and a change in road surface. St. Martin/St. Maarten epitomizes tourist islands in the sun, where services are well developed but there's still some Caribbean flavor. The Dutch side is ideal for people who like plenty to do. The French side has a more genteel ambience, more fashionable shopping, and a Continental flair. The combination makes an almost ideal port. On the negative side, the island has been completely developed. It can be fun to shop, and you'll find an occasional bargain, but many goods are cheaper in the United States.

Essentials

CURRENCY Legal tender on the Dutch side is the Netherlands Antilles florin (guilder), written NAf; on the French side, the official currency is the euro (€1.31 to US$1). There's little need to exchange money. Prices are usually quoted in both NAf and U.S. dollars on the Dutch side and euros on the French side, but dollars are accepted all over the island.

HOURS Banks on the Dutch side are open Monday through Friday from 8:30 to 3:30. French banks are open weekdays from 8:30 to 12:30 and 2:30 to 4; they are usually closed on Wednesday afternoons and afternoons preceding holidays. Shops on the Dutch side are generally open Monday through Saturday from 9 to noon and 2 to 6; on the French side, Monday through Saturday from 9 to 1 and 3 to 7. Increasingly, shops on both sides remain open during lunch. Some of the larger shops are open on Sunday and holidays when cruise ships are in port.

INTERNET There is Wi-Fi service on the boardwalk behind Front Street if you have your own laptop. **Cyber Link** (✉ 53 Front St., Phillipsburg).

TELEPHONES To phone from the Dutch side to the French, you first must dial (00–590–590) for local numbers, or (00–590–690) for cell phones, then the six-digit local number. To call from the French side to the Dutch, dial "00–599" then the seven-digit local number. Remember that a call from one side to the other is an international call.

At the Landsradio in Philipsburg, there are facilities for overseas calls and a USADirect phone, where you're directly in touch with an operator who will ac-

---

ST. MAARTEN BEST BETS

- **The 12-metre Challenge.** This mock America's Cup race is considered by many to be the best shore excursion in the whole Caribbean.

- **Loterie Farm.** On the slopes of Pic du Paradis, this is an amazing eco-friendly preserve with fun activities and even food.

- **Shopping.** Phillipsburg's Front Street is chockablock with stores of every strip, but hit those in Marigot for more French fashions.

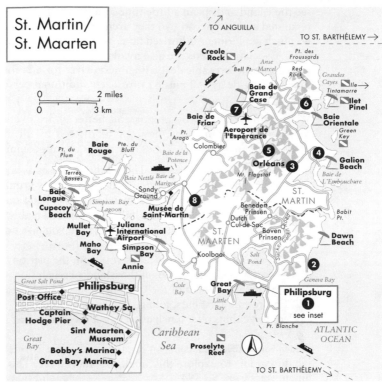

cept collect or credit-card calls. To call direct with an AT&T credit card or operator, dial 001–800/872–2881. On the French side, AT&T can be accessed by calling 080–099–00–11. If you need to use public phones, go to the special desk at Marigot's post office and buy a *télécarte*. There's a public phone at the tourist office in Marigot where you can make credit-card calls: the operator takes your card number (any major card) and assigns you a PIN (Personal Identification Number), which you then use to charge calls to your card.

Coming Ashore

Most cruise ships drop anchor off the Dutch capital of Philipsburg or dock in the marina at the southern tip of the Philipsburg harbor. If your ship anchors, tenders will ferry you to the town pier in the middle of town, where taxis await passengers. If your ship docks at the marina, downtown is a 15-minute taxi ride away. The walk is not recommended. The island is small, and most spots aren't more than a 30-minute drive from Marigot or Phillipsburg.

Doing your own thing will be much less expensive here than a ship-sponsored tour, and since rental cars are cheap (starting at $25 per day for a local car rental), you can easily strike out as soon as your ship docks. This is the best thing to do if you just want to

> ⚠ **CAUTION**
>
> Germicidal hand cleaner is a must-have for adventure excursions or where water might be at a premium. Bring a small bottle you can carry along with you.

see the island and spend a little time at a beach. Taxis are government-regulated and fairly costly, so they aren't really an option if you want to do much exploring. Authorized taxis display stickers of the St. Maarten Taxi Association. Taxis are also available at Marigot. You may be able to negotiate a favorable deal with a taxi driver for a 2- to 3-hour island tour for as little as $40 plus $15 for each additional person.

Shore Excursions

We consider these to be among the better shore excursions for St. Maarten/St. Martin. They may not be offered by all lines, and tour names may differ as well. Times and prices are approximate.

America's Cup 12-Metre Challenge. This yacht race uses actual sailing ships used in the America's Cup. Anyone can help the crew grind winches, trim sails, and punch the stop watch, or you can just sit back and watch everyone else work. The St. Maarten Challenge imitates an abbreviated America's Cup route. It's difficult to book this trip if you don't do it with your ship. ☉ *3 hrs* ⌷ *$99.*

Beach Sojourn. A short bus ride takes you from the pier on the Dutch side of St. Martin to Orient Beach on the island's French side. Often referred to as the French Riviera of the Caribbean, it's a lively beach where you will find restaurants, bars, lounge chairs, and umbrellas. Drinks are included; some ships offer lunch as well, but these trips cost more. ☉ *3 hrs* ⌷ *$44.*

Hidden Forest Adventure Tour. You're taken to Loterie Farm, on the hills of Pic du Paradis to explore this small private reserve. This tour includes lunch. ☉ *3½ hrs* ⌷ *$94.*

Marigot and the Butterfly Farm. Explore the upscale boutiques, duty-free shops and bistros of Marigot, stroll its waterfront, then visit the Butterfly Farm. At any given time in the terrarium-like sphere, as many as 600 butterflies (40 different species) flutter inside its garden. ☉ *3½ hrs* ⌷ *$39.*

Exploring St. Martin/St. Maarten

Numbers in the margin correspond to points of interest on the St. Martin/St. Maarten map.

❹ Butterfly Farm. Visitors enter a serene, tropical environment when they walk through the terrarium-like Butterfly Sphere. At any given time, as many as 600 butterflies, representing some 40 species, flutter inside the garden under a tented net. ⌷ *Rte. de Le Galion, Quartier d'Orléans* ☎ *590/87-31-21* ⊕ *www.thebutterflyfarm.com* ⌷ *$12* ☉ *Daily 9–3.*

❻ French Cul de Sac. North of Orient Bay Beach, the French colonial mansion of St-Martin's mayor is nestled in the hills. The area is peaceful and good for hiking. From the beach here, shuttle boats make the five-minute trip to Ilet Pinel, an uninhabited island that's fine for picnicking, sunning, and swimming.

❼ Grand Case. The island's culinary hotspot is in the heart of the French side on a beach at the foot of green hills and pastures. Though it has only a 1-mi-long (11/2-km-long) main street, it's known as the restaurant capital of the Caribbean. Grand Case Beach Club is at the end of this road.

② **Guana Bay Point.** On the rugged, windswept east coast about 10 minutes north of Philipsburg, Guana Bay Point offers isolated, untended beaches and a spectacular view of St. Barths.

❽ **Marigot.** This town's southern European flavor is most in evidence at its beautiful harborfront, with its shopping stalls, open-air cafés, and fresh-food vendors. From here, you can catch the ferry for Anguilla or St. Barths. Though not much remains of the structure itself, **Le Fort Louis,** completed by the French in 1789, commands a sweepingview of Marigot, its harbor, and the English island of Anguilla, which alone makes it worth the climb. ⊠ *Marigot.*

❸ **Orléans.** The island's oldest settlement, also known as the French Quarter, has classic, vibrantly painted West Indian style homes with elaborate gingerbread fretwork.

❶ **Philipsburg.** The capital of Dutch St. Maarten stretches about 1 mi (1½ km) along an isthmus between Great Bay and the Salt Pond and has five parallel streets. Most of the village's dozens of shops and restaurants are on Front Street, narrow and cobblestoned, closest to Great Bay. Because of its numerous duty-free shops and several casinos, it's generally congested when cruise ships are in port. Little lanes called *steegjes* connect Front Street with Back Street, which has fewer shops and considerably less congestion.

Wathey Square (pronounced watty), is in the heart of the village. Directly across from the square are the town hall and the courthouse, in the striking white building with the cupola. The structure was built in 1793 and has served as the commander's home, a fire station, a jail, and a post office. The streets surrounding the square are lined with hotels, duty-free shops, fine restaurants, and cafés. The **Captain Hodge Pier,** just off the square, is a good spot to view Great Bay and the beach that stretches alongside. The **Sint Maarten Museum** hosts rotating cultural exhibits and a permanent historical display called Forts of St. Maarten–St. Martin. The artifacts range from Arawak pottery shards to objects salvaged from the wreck of the HMS *Proselyte.* ⊠ *7 Front St., Philipsburg* ☎ *599/ 542–4917* ✆ *Free* ☉ *Weekdays 10–4, Sat. 10–2.*

❺ **Pic du Paradis.** From Friar's Bay Beach, a bumpy, tree-canopied road leads inland to this peak. At 1,492 feet, it's the island's highest point. There are two observation areas. From them, the tropical forest unfolds below and the vistas are breathtaking. The road is quite isolated, so it's best to travel in groups. It's also quite steep and not in particularly good shape, becoming a single lane as you near the summit; if you don't have a four-wheel-drive vehicle, you will not make it. Parking at the top is iffy, and it's best if you turn around before you park. It may not be so easy later. Near the bottom of Pic du Paradis is **Loterie Farm,** a peaceful 150-acre private nature preserve opened to the public in 1999 by American expat B. J. Welch. Designed to preserve island habitats, Loterie Farm offers a rare glimpse of Caribbean forest and mountain land. Welch has renovated an old farmhouse and welcomes visitors for horseback riding, hiking, mountain biking, ecotours, or less strenuous activities, such as meditation and yoga. Raves accompany lunch and dinner fare at the Hidden Forest Café since chef Julie Purkis took over the kitchen. The restaurant is open Tuesday through Sunday. The Loterie Farm's newest attraction, the **Fly Zone**, allows Tarzan wannabes to soar over the forest canopy via a series of ropes, cables, and suspended bridges. ⊠ *Rte. de Pic du Paradis* ☎ *590/87–86–16 or 590/57–28–55* ⊕ *www.loteriefarm. com* 🎫 *$5, 1½-hr tour $25, 4-hr tour $45* ⊙ *Daily sunrise–sunset.*

Shopping

It's true that the island sparkles with its myriad outdoor activities—diving, snorkeling, sailing, swimming, and sunning—but shopaholics are drawn to sparkle within the jewelry stores. The huge array of such stores is almost unrivaled in the Caribbean. In addition, duty-free shops offer substantial savings—about 15% to 30% below U.S. and Canadian prices—on cameras, watches, liquor, cigars, and designer clothing. It's no wonder that each year 500 cruise ships make Philipsburg a port of call. As is the case on many of the port stops, it is just common sense to keep a close watch on your valuables.

Philipsburg's **Front Street** has reinvented itself. Now it's mall-like, with red-brick walks and streets, palm trees lining the sleek boutiques, jewelry stores, souvenir shops, outdoor restaurants, and the old reliables—including McDonald's and Burger King. Here and there a school or a church appears to remind visitors there's more to the island than shopping. On Back Street is the **Philipsburg Market Place**, an open-air market where you can haggle for bargains on items such as handicrafts, souvenirs, and cover-ups. **Old Street**, near the end of Front Street, has stores, boutiques, and open-air cafés offering French crêpes, rich chocolates, and island mementos. You can find an outlet mall amid the more upscale shops at the **Maho** shopping plaza. The **Plaza del Lago** at the Simpson Bay Yacht Club complex has an excellent choice of restaurants as well as shops.

On the French side, wrought-iron balconies, colorful awnings, and gingerbread trim decorate Marigot's smart shops, tiny boutiques, and bistros in the **Marina Royale** complex and on the main streets, **rue de la Liberté** and **rue de la République**. Also in Marigot is the pricey **West Indies Mall** and the **Plaza Caraïbes**, which houses designer shops like Hermès and Ralph Lauren.

Activities

DIVING &
SNORKELING
Although St. Maarten is not known as a dive destination, the water temperature here is rarely below 70°F, and visibility is usually excellent, averaging about 100 feet (30 m). For snorkelers, the area around Orient Bay, Caye Verte (Green Key), Ilet Pinel, and Flat Island is especially lovely and is officially classified, and protected, as a regional underwater nature reserve. You can take a half-day snorkeling trip for around $25. On the Dutch side, **Dive Safaris** (⊠ Bobby's Marina, Yrausquin Blvd., Philipsburg ☎ 599/544–9001 ⊕ www.thescubashop.net) is a full-service outfit for divers. SSI- (Scuba Schools International) and PADI-certified dive centers include **Ocean Explorers Dive Shop** (⊠ 113 Welfare Rd., Simpson Bay ☎ 599/544–5252 ⊕ www.stmaartendiving.com).

On the French side, **Blue Ocean** (⊠ Sandy Ground Rd., Baie Nettlé ☎ 590/ 87–89–73) is a PADI-certified dive center that also offers regularly scheduled snorkeling trips. Arrange equipment rentals and snorkeling trips through **Kontiki Watersports** (✉ Northern beach entrance, Baie Orientale ☎ 590/87–46–89).

FISHING You can angle for yellowtail snapper, grouper, marlin, tuna, and wahoo on deep-sea excursions. Costs range from $150 per person for a half-day to $250 for a full day. Prices usually include bait and tackle, instruction for novices, and refreshments. Ask about licensing and insurance. **Big Sailfish Too** (✉ Anse Marcel ☎ 690/27–40–90) is your best bet on the French side of the island. **Lee's Deepsea Fishing** (✉ Welfare Rd. 82, Simpson Bay ☎ 599/544–4233 or 599/544–4234 ⊕ www.leesfish.com) organizes excursions, and when you return, Lee's Roadside Grill will cook your tuna, wahoo, or whatever else you catch and keep. **Rudy's Deep Sea Fishing** (✉ 14 Airport Rd., Simpson Bay ☎ 599/545–2177 or 599/522–7120 ⊕ www.rudysdeepseafishing.com) has been around for years and is one of the more experienced sport-angling outfits.

GOLF St. Maarten is not a golf destination. Although **Mullet Bay Golf Course** (✉ Airport Rd., north of the airport ☎ 599/545–2801), on the Dutch side, is an 18-hole course, it's the island's *only* one. Though lately it has been better tended, it's still not in the best of shape and many feel not worth the cost.

Beaches

The island's 10 mi (16 km) of beaches are all open to cruise-ship passengers. You can rent chairs and umbrellas at most of the beaches, primarily from beachside restaurants. The best beaches are on the French side. Topless bathing is common on the French side. If you take a cab to a remote beach, be sure to arrange a specific time for the driver to return for you. Don't leave valuables unattended on the beach or in a rental car, even in the trunk.

★ The nice, well-maintained beach at **Baie des Friars** is at the end of a poorly maintained dirt road. On a small, picturesque cove between Marigot and Grand Case, it attracts a casual crowd of locals and has a couple of good beachside restaurants. Getting to secluded **Baie Longue**, a 1-mi-long (1½-km-long) curve of white sand on the island's westernmost tip, requires a bumpy, 10-minute, we-must-be-lost drive off the main road, with just one small, unmarked entry down to the water. Though the beach is gravelly in places, this is a good place for snorkeling and swimming, but beware of a strong undertow when the waters are rough. If you want privacy, visit this isolated spot. There are no facilities or vendors.

FodorsChoice ★ By far the most beautiful beach on the island, 1-mi-long (1½-km-long) **Baie Orientale** has something for everyone, with its clean white sand, clear blue water, and an assortment of beach bars serving Mexican, Caribbean, American, and even kosher fare. There are plenty of places to rent equipment for water activities. The conservative north end is more family-oriented while the liberal south end is clothing-optional and eventually becomes a full-scale nude beach. A protected nature reserve, kid-friendly **Ilet Pinel** is a five-minute ferry ride from French Cul de Sac ($5 per person round-trip). The water is clear and shallow, and the shore is sheltered. If you like snorkeling, don your gear and swim along both sides of the coasts of this pencil-shape speck in the ocean. Food is available at the isle's two restaurants.

Where to Eat

Restaurants on the French side often figure a service charge into the menu prices. On the Dutch side, most restaurants add 10% to 15% to the bill. You can, if so moved by exceptional service, leave a tip.

$$–$$$ ✕ **Claude Mini-Club.** This brightly decorated upstairs restaurant, with a sweeping view of Marigot Harbor, has served traditional creole and French cuisine since 1969. The chairs and madras tablecloths are a mélange of sun yellow and orange. The whole place is built (tree-house-style) around the trunks of coconut trees. It's the place to be on Wednesday and Saturday nights, when the dinner buffet (40€) includes conch or onion soup, baked ham, blackened goose meat, lobster, roast beef, and all the trimmings. Fresh snapper is one of the specialties on the à la carte menu. There's live music nightly. ⊠ *Front de Mer, Marigot* ☎ *590/87–50–69* ▭ *AE, MC, V* ☾ *No lunch Sun.*

¢–$ ✕ **Kangaroo Court Café.** This little restaurant is renowned for its great coffee, but the gourmet burgers, pizza, salads, fruit frappés, and one of the island's largest selection of wines by the glass are not too shabby either. The funky patio area in the former childhood home of well-known islander Norman Wathey, is a pleasant place to enjoy your repast. Ruins from an old salt storage area, a small waterfall, and a huge ficus tree are the main decor. Almond trees shade it so well that nets are installed to keep nuts and leaves from hitting diners. ⊠ *6 Henrick St., Philipsburg* ☎ *599/542–7557 or 599/542–1644* ▭ *AE, D, MC, V* ☾ *No dinner.*

ST. THOMAS, U.S. VIRGIN ISLANDS

Carol
Bareuther

St. Thomas is the busiest cruise port of call in the world. Up to eight giant ships may visit in a single day. Don't expect an exotic island experience: one of the three U.S. Virgin Islands (with St. Croix and St. John), St. Thomas is as American as any place on the mainland, complete with McDonald's and HBO. The positive side of all this development is that there are more tours here than anywhere else in the Caribbean, and every year the excursions get better. Of course, shopping is the big draw in Charlotte Amalie, but experienced travelers remember the days of "real" bargains. Today, so many passengers fill the stores that it's a seller's market. On some days, there are so many cruise passengers on St. Thomas that you must book a ship-sponsored shore excursion if you want to do more than just take a taxi to the beach or stroll around Charlotte Amalie.

Essentials

CURRENCY   The U.S. dollar is the official currency of U.S. Virgin Islands, and ATMs are plentiful.

HOURS   Bank hours are generally Monday through Thursday 9 to 3 and Friday 9 to 5; a handful open Saturday 9 to noon. Stores on Main Street in Charlotte Amalie are open weekdays and Saturday 9 to 5. The hours of the shops in the Havensight Mall (next to the cruise-ships dock) are the same, though occasionally some stay open until 9 on Friday, depending on how many cruise ships are at the dock. You may also find some shops open on Sunday.

INTERNET   **Beans, Bytes & Websites** (⊠ Royal Dane Mall, behind Tavern on the Waterfront, Charlotte Amalie, St. Thomas ☎ 340/775–5262 ⊕ www.usvi.

net/cybercafe). **Cyber Zone** (⊠ Port of $ale, Charlotte Amalie, St. Thomas ☎ 340/714–7743).

TELEPHONES   Both GSM and Sprint phones work in St. Thomas. It's as easy to call home from St. Thomas and St. John as from any city in the United States. On St. Thomas, public phones are easily found, and AT&T has a telecommunications center across from the Havensight Mall and on the Waterfront in Charlotte Amalie across from Emancipation Gardens.

Coming Ashore

Depending on how many ships are in port, cruise ships drop anchor in the harbor at Charlotte Amalie and tender passengers directly to the waterfront duty-free shops, dock at the Havensight Mall at the eastern end of the crescent-shaped bay, or dock at Crown Bay Marina a few miles west of town.

The distance from Havensight to the duty-free shops is 1½ mi (3 km), which can be walked in less than half an hour; a taxi ride there costs $6 per person ($5 for each additional person). Tourist information offices are at the Havensight Mall (across from Building No. 1) for docking passengers and downtown near Fort Christian (at the eastern end of the waterfront shopping area) for those coming ashore by tender. Both offices distribute free maps. From Crown Bay, it's also a half-hour walk or a $5 per person cab ride ($4 for each additional person). Taxi drivers on St. Thomas do not typically do island tours, but there are myriad tour operators who will. You can rent a car in St. Thomas, but with all the tour options, it's often easier and cheaper to take an organized excursion or just hop in a cab.

SHORE   We consider these to be among the better shore excursions for St. Thomas.
EXCURSIONS   They may not be offered by all lines, and tour names may differ as well. Times and prices are approximate.

Helmet Dive. This is a unique diving opportunity for non-divers at Coral World Marine Park in St. Thomas, using helmets that provide oxygen as you walk along the bottom of the sea. Afterward, you can also visit the aquarium. ⏱ *3 hrs* 💳 *$89–$99.*

Kayaking & Snorkeling Tour. Paddle your kayak through a marine sanctuary as your guide narrates both the above- and underwater scenery. ⏱ *3½ hrs* 💳 *$72–$89.*

Turtle Cove Sail & Snorkel. Sail aboard a private yacht with a small group to Turtle Cove on St. Thomas's own Buck Island for snorkeling and swimming to view a sunken ship, tropical fish, and coral. ⏱ *3½ hrs* 💳 *$59.*

St. John Eco Hike. After a ferry ride to St. John, you hike approximately 1¼ mi (3 km) to Linde Point and then to Honeymoon Beach for a swim. Continue on to Caneel Bay to visit some ruins before

---

ST. THOMAS BEST BETS

■ **Coral World Marine Park.** This aquarium attraction is a great bet for families, and it's on one of the best snorkeling beaches.

■ **Magen's Bay Beach.** St. Thomas has one of the most picture-postcard perfect beaches you'll ever see. It's great for swimming.

■ **St. John.** It's easy to hop on the ferry to St. John for a day of hiking, then relax for an hour or two on the beach afterward.

■ **Shopping.** Charlotte Amalie is one of the best places in the Caribbean to shop.

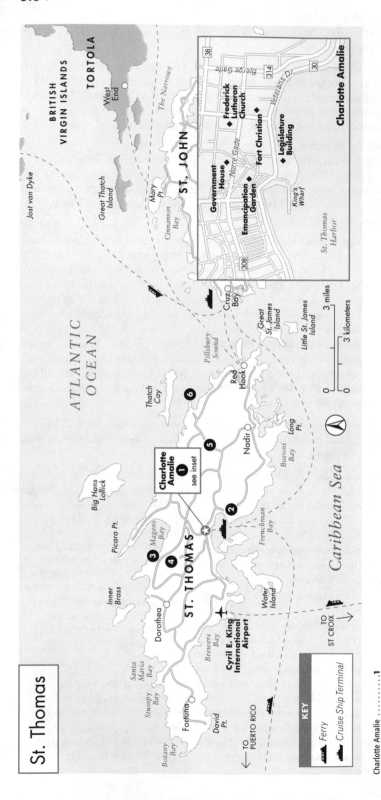

St. Thomas

KEY

🚢 Ferry

⛴ Cruise Ship Terminal

returning to the ferry landing by safari van. ☉ *4½ hrs* 🖅 *$54–$58.*

St. John Island Tour. Either your ship tenders you to St. John before docking in St. Thomas or you are transferred to the St. Thomas ferry dock in for the ride to St. John. On St. John, an open-air safari bus winds through the national park to a beach for snorkeling, swimming, and sunbathing. (If you have the option, you might avoid the often-crowded beach at Trunk Bay.) ☉ *4½ hrs* 🖅 *$46.*

Water Island Bike Trip. After riding a mountain bike around Water Island, which is just off the western end of St. Thomas, you stop for a refreshing swim at a beautiful sandy beach. ☉ *3½ hrs* 🖅 *$79.*

Exploring St. Thomas

Numbers in the margin correspond to points of interest on the St. Thomas map.

❶ Charlotte Amalie. St. Thomas's major burg is a hilly shopping town. There are also plenty of interesting historic sights—so take the time to see at least a few.

Emancipation Garden was built to honor the freeing of slaves in 1848; a bronze bust of a freed slave blowing a symbolic conch shell commemorates the 150th anniversary of this event. A bust of Denmark's King Christian and a scaled-down model of the U.S. Liberty Bell show the island's Danish-American ties. ✉ *Between Tolbod Gade and Fort Christian.*

Fort Christian, St. Thomas's oldest standing structure, was built between 1672 and 1680 and now has U.S. National Landmark status. The clock tower was added in the 19th century. This remarkable building has, over time, been used as a jail, governor's residence, town hall, courthouse, and church. Closed for major structural renovations since 2005, the building is scheduled to reopen in 2007. ✉ *Waterfront Hwy., east of shopping district* 🕾 *340/776–4566.*

Frederick Lutheran Church has a massive mahogany altar, and its pewsóeach with its own door were once rented to families of the congregation. ✉ *Norre Gade* 🕾 *340/776–1315* ☉ *Mon.–Sat. 9–4.*

Built in 1867, **Government House** houses the offices for the governor of the Virgin Islands. Inside, the staircases are of native mahogany, as are the plaques hand lettered in gold with the names of the governors appointed and, since 1970, elected. ✉ *Government Hill* 🕾 *340/774–0294* 🖅 *Free* ☉ *Weekdays 8–5.*

The pastoral-looking lime-green exterior of the **Legislature Building,** seat of U.S. Virgin Islands elected representatives, conceals the vociferous political wrangling of the Virgin Islands Senate going on inside. You're welcome to sit in on sessions in the upstairs chambers. ✉ *Waterfront Hwy., across from Fort Christian* 🕾 *340/774–0880* ☉ *Daily 8–5.*

❻ Coral World Ocean Park. Coral World has an offshore underwater observatory that houses the Predator Tank, one of the world's largest coral-reef tanks, and an aquarium with more than 20 portholes providing close-ups of Caribbean sea life. *Sea Trekkin'* lets you tour the reef outside the park at a depth of 15 feet, thanks to specialized high-tech headgear and a continuous air supply that's based on the surface. A guide leads the ½-hour tour and the narration is piped through a specialized microphone inside each trekker's helmet; the minimum age to participate is eight years. The park also has several outdoor pools where you can touch starfish, pet a baby shark, feed stingrays, and view endangered sea turtles. In addition there's a mangrove lagoon and a nature trail full of lush tropical flora. Daily feedings and talks take place at most every exhibit. ⊠ *Coki Point, north of Rte. 38, Estate Frydendal* ☎ *6450 Estate Smith Bay, St. Thomas 00802* ☎ *340/775–1555* ⊕ *www.coralworldvi. com* ☞ *$18, Sea Trek $68, Shark Encounter $43* ☉ *Daily 9–5.*

🐚 ❸ **Drake's Seat.** Sir Francis Drake was supposed to have kept watch over his fleet and looked for enemy ships from this particularly good vantage point. The panorama is especially breathtaking (and romantic) at dusk. ⊠ *Rte. 40, Estate Zufriedenheit.*

🐚 ❹ **Mountain Top.** Stop at Mountain Top for a banana daiquiri and spectacular views from the observation deck more than 1,500 feet above sea level. Kids will like talking to the parrots and hearing them answer back. ⊠ *Head north off Rte. 33, look for signs* ⊕ *www.greathouse-mountaintop. com.*

★ 🐚 ❷ **Paradise Point Tramway.** Fly skyward in a gondola to Paradise Point, an overlook with breathtaking views of Charlotte Amalie and the harbor. There are several shops, a bar, restaurant, and a wedding gazebo; kids enjoy the tropical bird show held daily at 10:30 AM, 1:30 PM, and 3:30 PM. A ¼-mi (½-km) hiking trail leads to spectacular views of St. Croix to the south. Wear sturdy shoes; the trail is steep and rocky. ⊠ *Rte. 30, across from Havensight Mall, Charlotte Amalie* ☎ *340/774–9809* ⊕ *www. paradisepointtramway.com* ☞ *$16* ☉ *Thurs.–Tues. 9–5, Wed. 9–9.*

❺ **Tillett Gardens.** East of Charlotte Amalie, Tillett Gardens is an oasis of artistic endeavor across from the Tutu Park Shopping Mall. You can watch artisans produce silk screen fabrics, pottery, candles, watercolors, jewelry, and other handicrafts. ⊠ *Rte. 38.*

Shopping

The prime shopping area in **Charlotte Amalie** is between Post Office and Market squares; it consists of three parallel streets that run east–west (Waterfront Highway, Main Street, and Back Street) and the alleyways that connect them. Particularly attractive are the historic **A. H. Riise Alley, Royal Dane Mall, Palm Passage,** and pastel-painted **International Plaza**—quaint alleys between Main Street and the Waterfront. **Vendors Plaza,** on the waterfront side of Emancipation Gardens in Charlotte Amalie, is a central location for vendors selling handmade earrings, necklaces, and bracelets; straw baskets and handbags; T-shirts; fabrics; African artifacts; and local fruits. Look for the many brightly colored umbrellas.

At the Crown Bay cruise-ship pier, the **Crown Bay Center,** off the Harwood Highway in Sub Base about ½ mi (¾ km) has quite a few shops.

Havensight Mall, next to the cruise-ship dock, may not be as charming as downtown Charlotte Amalie, but it does have more than 60 shops. It also has an excellent bookstore, a bank, a pharmacy, a gourmet grocery, and smaller branches of many downtown stores. The shops at **Port of Sale,** adjoining Havensight Mall (its buildings are pink instead of brown), sell discount goods. Next door to Port of $ale is the **Yacht Haven Grande** complex, with many upscale shops.

Shopping maps are available at the tourist offices and often from your ship's shore-excursion desk. Remember that you must pack any alcohol in your checked bags. **A. H. Riise Liquors** (⌧ 37 Main St., at Riise's Alley, Charlotte Amalie ☎ 340/776–2303 ✉ Havensight Mall, Bldg. I, Rte. 30, Charlotte Amalie ☎ 340/776–7713) offers a large selection of tobacco and liquor. The wine selection is large at warehouse-style **Al Cohen's Discount Liquor** (⌧ Rte. 30 across from Havensight Mall, Charlotte Amalie ☎ 340/774–3690).

Caribbean Marketplace (⌧ Havensight Mall, Rte. 30, Charlotte Amalie ☎ 340/776–5400) is a great place to buy handicrafts from the Caribbean and elsewhere. **Down Island Traders** (⌧ Waterfront Hwy. at Post Office Alley, Charlotte Amalie ☎ 340/776–4641) carries hand-painted calabash bowls; finely printed Caribbean note cards; jams, jellies, spices, hot sauces, and herbs; teas made of lemongrass, passion fruit, and mango; coffee from Jamaica; and handicrafts from throughout the Caribbean.

Little Switzerland (⌧ 5 Dronningens Gade, across from Emancipation Garden, Charlotte Amalie ☎ 340/776–2010 ✉ 3B Main St., Charlotte Amalie ☎ 340/776–2010 ✉ Havensight Mall, Bldg. II, Rte. 30, Charlotte Amalie ☎ 340/776–2198) is a good source for china, crystal, and jewelry. **Local Color** (⌧ Royal Dane Mall, at Waterfront, Charlotte Amalie ☎ 340/774–2280) carries casual and island clothing. More than 40 local artists—including schoolchildren, senior citizens, and people with disabilities—create the handcrafted items for sale at **Native Arts & Crafts Cooperative** (⌧ Tolbod Gade, across from Emancipation Garden and next to visitor center, Charlotte Amalie ☎ 340/777–1153).

Activities

DIVING & SNORKELING **Chris Sawyer Diving Center** (☎ 340/775–7320 or 877/929–3483 ⊕ www. sawyerdive.vi) is a PADI five-star outfit that specializes in dives to the 310-foot-long *Rhone,* in the British Virgin Islands. Hotel-dive packages are offered through the Wyndham Sugar Bay Beach Club & Resort. **Snuba of St. Thomas** (⌧ Rte. 388, at Coki Point, Estate Smith Bay ☎ 340/693–8063 ⊕ www.visnuba.com) offers something for nondivers, a cross between snorkeling and scuba diving: a 20-foot air hose connects you to the surface. The cost is $68. Children must be eight or older to participate.

FISHING Fishing here is synonymous with blue marlin angling. If you're not into marlin fishing, try hooking sailfish in the winter, dolphinfish come spring, and wahoo in the fall. To really find the trip that will best suit you, walk down the docks at either American Yacht Harbor or Sapphire Beach Marina in the late afternoon and chat with the captains and crews. The **Charter Boat Center** (⌧ 6300 Red Hook Plaza, Red Hook ☎ 340/775–7990 ⊕ www.charterboat.vi) is a major source for sportfishing charters, both marlin and inshore. For inshore trips, **Peanut Gallery Charters** (⌧ Crown Bay Marina, Rte. 304, Estate Contant ☎ 340/775–5274 ⊕ www. fishingstthomas.com) offers trips on its 18-foot *Dauntless* or 28-foot custom sportfishing catamaran.

GOLF The **Mahogany Run Golf Course** (⊠ Rte. 42, Estate Lovenlund ☎ 340/777–
★ 6006 or 800/253–7103 ⊕ www.mahoganyrungolf.com) attracts golfers
for its spectacular view of the British Virgin Islands and the challenging
3-hole Devil's Triangle. At this Tom and George Fazio–designed par-70,
18-hole course, there's a fully stocked pro shop, snack bar, and open-air
club house. Greens and half-cart fees for 18 holes are $150. The course
is open daily, and there are frequently informal weekend tournaments.
It's the only course on St. Thomas.

Beaches

All beaches in the USVI are public, but occasionally you'll need to stroll
Fodor's Choice through a resort to reach the sand. **Coki Beach** (⊠ Rte. 388, next to Coral
★ World Marine Park), next to Coral World (turn north off Route 38), is
the island's best snorkeling spot. Colorful beachside shops rent water-
sports equipment. Some also sell snack foods, cold drinks, and even fish
food (dry dog food).

Fodor's Choice On Route 35, **Magens Bay** (⊠ Rte. 35, at end of road on north side of is-
★ land) is usually lively because of its spectacular crescent of white sand,
more than ½ mi (¾ km) long, and its calm waters, which are protected
by two peninsulas. It's often listed among the world's most beautiful
beaches. (If you arrive between 8 AM and 5 PM, you have to pay an entrance fee of $3 per person, $1 per vehicle, and 25¢ per child under age
12.) The bottom is flat and sandy, so this is a place for sunning and swimming rather than snorkeling. There's also a bar, snack bar, and bathhouses
with toilets and saltwater showers. Close to Charlotte Amalie and
★ fronting the Marriott Frenchman's Reef Hotel, pretty **Morning Star Beach**
(⊠ Rte. 315, 2 mi (3 km) southeast of Charlotte Amalie, past Havensight Mall and cruise-ship dock) is where many young locals bodysurf
or play volleyball. Snorkeling is good near the rocks when the current
doesn't affect visibility. There's a fine view of St. John and other islands
★ from **Sapphire Beach** (⊠ Rte. 38, Sapphire Bay). The snorkeling is excellent at the reef to the right, or east, near Pettyklip Point. The constant
breeze makes this a great spot for windsurfing. The condo resort at **Secret Harbor** (⊠ Rte. 32, Red Hook) doesn't detract from the attractive-
ness of the cove-like beach. Not only is this East End spot pretty, but it
also has superb snorkeling—head out to the left, near the rocks.

Where to Eat

Some restaurants add a 10% to 15% service charge. If not, leave a
15% tip.

$$ ✗ **Cuzzin's Caribbean Restaurant & Bar.** The top picks in this restaurant in a
19th-century livery stage are Virgin Islands staples. For lunch, order ten-
der slivers of conch stewed in a rich onion butter sauce, savory braised
oxtail, or curried chicken. At dinner, the island-style mutton, served in
a thick gravy and seasoned with locally grown herbs, offers a tasty treat
that's deliciously different. Side dishes include peas and rice, boiled green
bananas, fried plantains, and potato stuffing. ⊠ 7 *Wimmelskafts Gade,
also called Back St.* ☎ *340/777–4711* ▭ *AE, MC, V.*

$–$$ ✗ **Gladys' Cafe.** Even if the local specialties—conch in butter sauce, salt
Fodor's Choice fish and dumplings, hearty red bean soup—didn't make this a recom-
★ mended café, it would be worth coming for Gladys's smile. While you're

here, pick up a $5 or $10 bottle of her special hot sauce. There are mustard-, oil and vinegar-, and tomato-based versions; the last is the hottest. ✉ *Waterfront, at Royal Dane Mall* ⌖ *28 Dronningens Gade, Charlotte Amelie St. Thomas 00802* ☎ *340/774–6604* ▤ *AE* ⊗ *No dinner.*

ST. VINCENT (KINGSTOWN)

Jane Zarem

You won't find glitzy resorts or flashy discos in St. Vincent. Rather, you'll be fascinated by picturesque villages, secluded beaches, and fine sailing waters. St. Vincent is the largest and northernmost island in the Grenadines archipelago; Kingstown, the capital city of St. Vincent & the Grenadines, is the government and business center and major port. Except for one barren area on the island's northeast coast—remnants of the 1979 eruption of La Soufrière, one of the last active volcanoes in the Caribbean—the countryside is mountainous, lush, and green. St. Vincent's mountains and forests thwarted European settlement for many years. As colonization advanced elsewhere in the Caribbean, in fact, the island became a refuge for Carib Indians—descendants of whom still live in northeastern St. Vincent. After years of fighting and back-and-forth territorial claims, British troops prevailed by overpowering the French and banishing Carib warriors to Central America. Independent since 1979, St. Vincent & the Grenadines remains a member of the British Commonwealth.

Essentials

CURRENCY Eastern Caribbean (E.C.) dollar (EC$2.70 to US$1). U.S. dollars are generally accepted, but change is given in E.C. dollars.

HOURS Banks are open Monday through Thursday from 8 to 1 or 3, Friday until 3 or 5. The General Post Office, on Halifax Street in Kingstown, is open weekdays from 8:30 to 3, Saturday from 8:30 to 11:30. Shops and businesses in Kingstown are open weekdays from 8 to 4; some close for lunch from noon to 1. Saturday hours are from 8 to noon.

INTERNET **E@gles Internet Cafe** (✉ Halifax St., opposite the General Post Office, Kingstown, St. Vincent) offers high-speed computers and broadband Internet access for as little as $2 per hour.

TELEPHONES Pay phones are readily available and best operated with the prepaid phone cards that are sold at many stores and can be used on many Caribbean islands. Telephone services are available at the cruise-ship terminal in Kingstown, St. Vincent. For an international operator, dial 115; to charge your call to a credit card, call 117.

Coming Ashore

The cruise-ship terminal at Kingstown, St. Vincent's capital city, accommodates two cruise ships; additional vessels anchor outside the harbor and bring passengers to the jetty by launch. The facility has about two dozen shops that sell duty-free items and handicrafts. There's a communications center, post office, tourist information desk, restaurant, and food court.

Buses and taxis are available at the wharf. Taxi drivers are well equipped to take you on an island tour; expect to pay $25 per hour for up to four passengers. The ferry to Bequia (one hour each way) is at the adjacent pier.

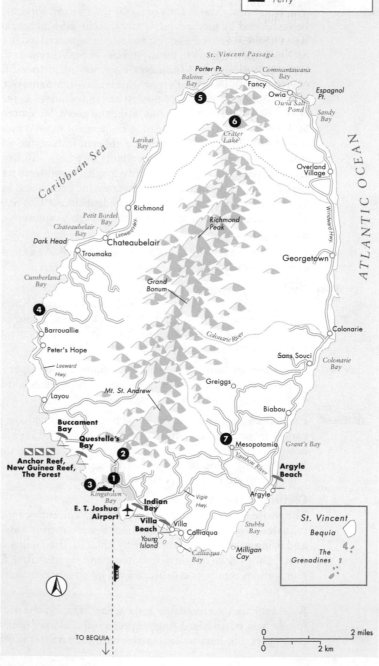

St. Vincent

Renting a car for just one day isn't advisable, since car rentals are expensive (at least $55 per day) and require a $20 temporary driving permit on top of that. It's almost always more financially favorable to take a tour, though you don't have to limit yourself to those offered by your ship.

SHORE EXCURSIONS We consider these to be among the better shore excursions for St. Lucia. They may not be offered by all lines, and tour names may differ as well. Times and prices are approximate. Ships that dock in St. Vincent often include some shore excursions to Bequia. In that case, they will include a one-hour ferry ride, each way, between St. Vincent and Bequia.

ST. VINCENT BEST BETS

■ **Ferry to Bequia.** You can easily get to laid-back Bequia on a one-hour ferry trip for better beaches than you'll find on St. Vincent.

■ **Hiking.** Whether you hike in the rain forest or do the more difficult climb of La Soufrière, it's worth exploring some of the island's rugged terrain.

■ **Tobago Cays.** These uninhabited islands are the top destination in the southern Grenadines for snorkeling, and it's reachable on a day-long excursion from St. Vincent.

Bequia by Catamaran. This day-long sailing trip takes you to Bequia and Petit Nevis with time to stroll, shop, and swim. The trip includes a beach picnic at Princess Margaret Beach. It's expensive but worthwhile. ⊙ *7 hrs* ✉ *$149.*

Scenic Island Tour. It's hard to appreciate how beautiful St. Vincent is unless you get out and do some exploring. This tour takes you to Fort Charlotte, the Botanical Garden, and the Mesopotamia Valley. ⊙ *3 hrs* ✉ *$52.*

Hiking the Vermont Nature Trail. This hike takes you about a mile through the rain forest and includes a refreshment stop. ⊙ *4 hrs* ✉ *$52.*

St. Vincent Garden Tour. This tour includes both the Montreal Estate and the St. Vincent Botanical Garden, which has breadfruit trees brought by Captain Bligh of the *Bounty*. ⊙ *4 hrs* ✉ *$56.*

Exploring St. Vincent

Numbers in the margin correspond to points of interest on the St. Vincent map.

★ ☾ ❷ **Botanical Garden.** A few minutes north of downtown by taxi is the oldest botanical garden in the Western Hemisphere, founded in 1765. Captain Bligh—of *Bounty* fame—brought the first breadfruit tree to this island for landowners to propagate. The prolific bounty of the breadfruit tree was used to feed the slaves. You can see a direct descendant of this original tree among the specimen mahogany, rubber, teak, and other tropical trees and shrubs in the 20 acres of gardens. Two dozen rare St. Vincent parrots live in the small aviary. Guides explain all the medicinal and ornamental trees and shrubs; they also appreciate a tip at the end of the tour. ⊠ *Off Leeward Hwy., Montrose* ☎ *784/457–1003* ✉ *$3* ⊙ *Daily 6–6.*

★ ❺ **Falls of Baleine.** The falls are impossible to reach by car, so book an escorted, all-day boat trip from Villa Beach or the Lagoon Marina. The boat ride along the coast offers scenic island views. When you arrive, you have to wade through shallow water to get to the beach. Then local guides help you make the easy five-minute trek to the 60-foot falls and the rock-enclosed freshwater pool the falls create—plan to take a dip.

★ ⏺ ❸ **Fort Charlotte.** Started by the French in 1786 and completed by the British in 1806, the fort was named for King George III's wife. It sits on Berkshire Hill, a dramatic promontory 636 feet above sea level, with a stunning view of Kingstown and the Grenadines. Interestingly, cannons face inward—the fear of attack by native peoples was far greater than any threat approaching from the sea, though, truth be told, the fort saw no action. Nowadays the fort serves as a signal station for ships; its ancient cells house paintings, by Lindsay Prescott, depicting early island history.

❶ **Kingstown.** The capital city of St. Vincent and the Grenadines is on the island's southwestern coast. The town of 13,500 residents wraps around Kingstown Bay; a ring of green hills and ridges, studded with homes, forms a backdrop for the city. This is very much a working city, with a busy harbor and few concessions to tourists. Kingstown Harbour is the only deepwater port on the island.

What few gift shops there are can be found on and around **Bay Street,** near the harbor. Upper Bay Street, which stretches along the bayfront, bustles with daytime activity—workers going about their business and housewives doing their shopping. Many of Kingstown's downtown buildings are built of stone or brick brought to the island in the holds of 18th-century ships as ballast (and replaced with sugar and spices for the return trip to Europe). The Georgian-style stone arches and second-floor overhangs on former warehouses create shelter from midday sun and the brief, cooling showers common to the tropics.

Grenadines Wharf, at the south end of Bay Street, is busy with schooners loading supplies and ferries loading people bound for the Grenadines. The **Cruise Ship Complex,** south of the commercial wharf, has a mall with a dozen or more shops, plus restaurants, a post office, communications facilities, and a taxi–minibus stand.

An almost infinite selection of produce fills the **Kingstown Produce Market,** a three-story building that takes up a whole city block on Upper Bay, Hillsboro, and Bedford streets in the center of town. It's noisy, colorful, and open Monday through Saturday—but the busiest times (and the best times to go) are Friday and Saturday mornings. In the courtyard, vendors sell local arts and crafts. On the upper floors, merchants sell clothing, household items, gifts, and other products.

Little Tokyo, so called because funding for the project was a gift from Japan, is a waterfront shopping area with a bustling indoor fish market and dozens of stalls where you can buy inexpensive homemade meals, drinks, ice cream, bread and cookies, clothing, and trinkets, and even get a haircut.

St. George's Cathedral, on Grenville Street, is a pristine, creamy-yellow Anglican church built in 1820. The dignified Georgian architecture includes simple wooden pews, an ornate chandelier, and beautiful stained-glass windows; one was a gift from Queen Victoria, who actually commissioned it for London's St. Paul's Cathedral in honor of her first grandson. When the artist created an angel with a red robe, she was horrified and sent it abroad. The markers in the cathedral's graveyard recount the history of the island. Across the street is **St. Mary's Cathedral**

of the Assumption (Roman Catholic), built in stages beginning in 1823. The strangely appealing design is a blend of Moorish, Georgian, and Romanesque styles applied to black brick. Nearby, freed slaves built the **Kingstown Methodist Church** in 1841. The exterior is brick, simply decorated with quoins (solid blocks that form the corners), and the roof is held together by metal straps, bolts, and wooden pins. **Scots Kirk** (1839–80) was built by and for Scottish settlers but became a Seventh-Day Adventist church in 1952.

❻ La Soufrière. The volcano, which last erupted in 1979, is 4,000 feet high and so huge in area that it covers virtually the entire northern third of the island. The eastern trail to the rim of the crater, a two-hour ascent, begins at Rabacca Dry River.

❼ Montreal Gardens. Welsh-born landscape designer Timothy Vaughn renovated 7½ acres of neglected commercial flower beds and a falling-down plantation house into a stunning, yet informal, garden spot. Anthuriums, ginger lilies, birds-of-paradise, and other tropical flowers are planted in raised beds; tree ferns create a canopy of shade along the walkways. The gardens are in the shadow of majestic Grand Bonhomme mountain, deep in the beautiful Mesopotamia Valley, about 12 mi (19 km) from Kingstown. ⊠ *Montreal St., Mesopotamia* ☎ *784/458–1198* ☑ *$3* ⊙ *Dec.–Aug., weekdays 9–4.*

❹ Wallilabou Bay. *The Pirates of the Caribbean* left their mark at Wallilabou (pronounced wally-la-*boo*), a location used for filming the recent movies. Many of the buildings and docks built as stage sets remain, giving the pretty bay an intriguingly historic appearance. You can sunbathe, swim, picnic, or buy your lunch at Wallilabou Anchorage. This is a favorite stop for day-trippers returning from the Falls of Baleine and boaters anchoring for the evening. Nearby there's a river with a small waterfall where you can take a freshwater plunge.

Shopping

The 12 blocks that hug the waterfront in **downtown Kingstown** comprise St. Vincent's main shopping district. Among the shops that sell goods to fulfill household needs are a few that sell local crafts, gifts, and souvenirs. Bargaining is neither expected nor appreciated. The **Cruise Ship Complex,** on the waterfront in Kingstown, has a collection of a dozen or so boutiques, shops, and restaurants that cater primarily to cruise-ship passengers but welcome all shoppers. St. Vincent is not a major duty-free shopping port, but you will find a few duty-free shops.

At **FranPaul's Selections** (⊠ 2nd fl., Bonadie's Plaza, Bay St., Kingstown ☎ 784/456–2662), Francelia St. John fashions dresses, pants, and shirts from colorful fabrics she selects in Trinidad. The emphasis is on African, Afro-Caribbean, and casual wear. **Nzimbu Browne** (⊠ McKie's Hill, Kingstown ☎784/457–1677) creates original art from dried banana leaves, carefully selecting and snipping bits and arranging them on pieces of wood to depict local scenes. He often sets up shop on Bay Street, near the Cobblestone Inn. **St. Vincent Craftsmen's Centre** (⊠ Frenches St., Kingstown ☎ 784/457–2516), three blocks from the wharf, sells locally made grass floor mats, place mats, and other straw articles, as well as batik cloth, handmade West Indian dolls, hand-painted calabashes, and framed artwork. The large grass mats can be rolled and folded for easy transport home. No credit cards are accepted.

Activities

DIVING &
SNORKELING
Novices and advanced divers alike will be impressed by the marine life in the waters surrounding St. Vincent and the Grenadines—brilliant sponges, huge deepwater coral trees, and shallow reefs teeming with colorful fish. The best dive spots on St. Vincent are in the small bays along the coast between Kingstown and Layou; many are within 20 yards of shore and only 20 feet to 30 feet down.

Anchor Reef has excellent visibility for viewing a deep-black coral garden, schools of squid, sea horses, and maybe a small octopus. **The Forest,** a shallow dive, is still dramatic, with soft corals in pastel colors and schools of small fish. **New Guinea Reef** slopes to 90 feet (28 m) and can't be matched for its quantity of corals and sponges. The pristine waters surrounding the **Tobago Cays,** in the Southern Grenadines, will give you a world-class diving experience.

Fantasea Tours (⊠ Villa Beach, St. Vincent ☎ 784/457–5555 ⊕ www. fantaseatours.com) will take you on a 38-foot power cruiser to the Falls of Baleine, Bequia, and Mustique, or on a snorkeling trip to the Tobago Cays. **Dive St. Vincent** (⊠ Young Island Dock, Villa Beach ☎ 784/457–4714 or 784/547–4928 ⊕ www.divestvincent.com) is where NAUI- and PADI-certified instructor Bill Tewes and his staff offer beginner and certification courses and dive trips to the St. Vincent coast and the southern Grenadines.

FISHING
From Villa Beach or Indian Bay on St. Vincent, you can go on a full-day fishing trip or boat ride around the Grenadines for about $120–$140 per person, including all equipment and lunch. **Crystal Blue Charters** (⊠ Indian Bay ☎ 784/457–4532 ⊜ 784/456–2232) offers sportfishing charters on a 34-foot pirogue for amateur and serious fishermen.

Beaches

St. Vincent's origin is volcanic, so its beaches range in color from golden-brown to black. Swimming is recommended only in the lagoons and bays along the leeward coast. By contrast, beaches on the Bequia and the rest of the Grenadines have pure white sand, palm trees, and crystal-clear aquamarine water; some are even within walking distance of the jetty. **Buccament Bay** is good for swimming. This tiny black-sand beach is 20 minutes north of Kingstown. South of Kingstown, **Indian Bay** has golden sand but is slightly rocky; it's a good place for snorkeling. **Questelle's Bay** (pronounced keet-*ells*), north of Kingstown and next to Campden Park, has a black-sand beach.

Where to Eat

A 7% government tax is applicable to your bill, and most restaurants add a 10% service charge in lieu of tip. If they do not, leave an appropriate tip; otherwise, anything additional is expected only for special service.

$$–$$$ ✕ **Lime Restaurant & Pub.** Named for the *pursuit* of liming (relaxing), this sprawling waterfront restaurant also has mostly green decor. An exten-

sive all-day menu caters to beachgoers and boaters who drop by for a roti and a bottle of Hairoun—or burgers, curries, sandwiches, gourmet pizzas, pastas, soups, and salads. Dinner choices include fresh seafood, volcano chicken (with a creole sauce that's as spicy as lava is hot), curried goat, and pepper steak. Casual and congenial by day, it's candlelit and romantic at night—enhanced by the twinkling lights of anchored boats and the soft sound of waves quietly breaking against the seawall. ⊠ *Young Island Channel, Villa Harbour* ☎ *784/458–4227* ▭ *AE, D, DC, MC, V.*

$–$$ ✕ **Basil's Bar & Restaurant.** It's not just the air-conditioning that makes this restaurant cool. Downstairs at the Cobblestone Inn is owned by Basil Charles, whose Basil's Beach Bar on Mustique is a hangout for the vacationing rich and famous. This is the Kingstown power-lunch venue. Local businesspeople gather for the daily buffet or a full menu of salads, sandwiches, barbecued chicken, or fresh seafood platters. Dinner entrées of pasta, local seafood, and chicken (try it poached in fresh ginger and coconut milk) are served at candlelit tables. There's a Chinese buffet on Friday, and takeout is available that night only. ⊠ *Cobblestone Inn, Upper Bay St., Kingstown* ☎ *784/457–2713* ▭ *AE, MC, V.*

SAN JUAN, PUERTO RICO

7

Mark Sullivan Although Puerto Rico is a commonwealth of the United States, few cities in the Caribbean are as steeped in Spanish tradition as San Juan. Within a seven-square-block area in Old San Juan are restored 16th-century buildings, museums, art galleries, bookstores, and 200-year-old houses with balustraded balconies overlooking narrow, cobblestone streets. In contrast, San Juan's sophisticated Condado and Isla Verde areas have glittering hotels, fancy boutiques, casinos, and discos. Out in the countryside is the 28,000-acre El Yunque rain forest, with more than 240 species of trees growing at least 100 feet high. You can stretch your sea legs on dramatic mountain ranges, numerous trails, vast caves, coffee plantations, old sugar mills, and hundreds of beaches. No wonder San Juan is one of the busiest ports of call in the Caribbean. Like any other big city, San Juan has its share of crime, so guard your wallet or purse, and avoid walking in the area between Old San Juan and the Condado.

CURRENCY The U.S. dollar is the official currency of Puerto Rico.

HOURS Street shops are open Monday through Saturday from 9 to 6. Banks are generally open weekdays from 8 to 4 or 9 to 5; a few branches are open Saturday from 9 to noon or 1.

INTERNET You can check your e-mail at **CyberNet Café** (⊠ 1128 Av. Ashford, Condado). **Diner's Restaurant** (⊠ 357 Calle San Francisco, Old San Juan) has Internet service.

TELEPHONES Calling the United States from Puerto Rico is the same as calling within the U.S. You can use the long-distance telephone service office in the cruise-ship terminal, or you can use your calling card by dialing the toll-free access number of your long-distance provider from any pay phone. You'll find a phone center by the Paseo de la Princesa.

Coming Ashore

Cruise ships dock within a couple of blocks of Old San Juan. The Paseo de la Princesa, a tree-lined promenade beneath the city wall, is a nice place for a stroll—you can admire the local crafts and stop at the refreshment kiosks. A tourist information booth is in the cruise-terminal area. Major sights in the Old San Juan area are mere blocks from the piers, but be aware that the streets are narrow and steeply inclined in places.

It's particularly easy to get to Cataño and the Bacardí Rum Plant on your own; take the ferry (50¢) that leaves from the cruise piers every half-hour and then a taxi from the other side. Taxis, which line up to meet ships, are the best option if you want to explore the city istelf. White taxis labeled TAXI TURISTICO charge set fares of $6 to $16. Metered cabs authorized by the Public Service Commission charge an initial $1; after that, it's about 10¢ for each additional ⅓ mi. If you take a metered taxi, insist that the meter be turned on, and pay only what is shown, plus a tip of 10% to 15%. You can negotiate with taxi drivers for specific trips, and you can hire a taxi for as little as $25 per hour for sightseeing tours.

SAN JUAN BEST BETS
■ **El Morro.** The labyrinthine fort is a National Historic Site as well as a UN World Heritage Site.
■ **Shopping.** Within a few blocks of the port, you can stroll and shop.
■ **El Yunque.** Just an hour away, this is a great day-trip destination if you don't want to stay in Old San Juan.
■ **Casa Bacardí.** Rum lovers can jump on the public ferry by the cruise-ship pier and then taxi over to the factory for a tour and tasting.

SHORE EXCURSIONS Don't waste your money on an expensive guided walking tour of Old San Juan; the area is easily accessible, though some streets are steep and covered with uneven cobblestones. Free tourist trolleys will take you to all the top sights in Old San Juan from a stop across from Pier 4. If you want to see more of the island but don't want to drive, then you may want to consider a shore excursion, though almost all trips can be booked with local tour operators. The following are good choices in San Juan. They may not be offered by all cruise lines. Times and prices are approximate.

ATV Tour of El Yunque. This ATV tour goes around the El Yunque foothills. It's a very popular tour. ⊙ 4 hrs ☞ $109.

Bio-lumniscent Bay Kayaking Trip. Laguna Grande in Fajardo has a good bioluminscent bay. Kayaking, which will bring you closer to the water, is the best way to do the trip. ⊙ 5 ½ hrs ☞ $69.

El Yunque Rain Forest Hike. A 45-minute bus ride delivers you to the Caribbean National Forest, where you will be taken on a guided 2-hour hike. ⊙ 5½ hrs ☞ $49.

Horseback Riding. It's also possible to ride Paso Fino horses in the El Yunque foothills. ⊙ 4 hrs ☞ $89.

Exploring San Juan

Numbers in the margin correspond to points of interest on the Old San Juan map.

Old San Juan

ATLANTIC OCEAN

0 ..... 1/4 mile
0 ..... 400 meters

El Campo Del Morro

Bahía de San Juan

KEY

Cruise Ship Terminal

❶ What to See

Ferry

🛈 Tourist Information

Old San Juan, the original city founded in 1521, contains authentic and carefully preserved examples of 16th- and 17th-century Spanish-colonial architecture. Graceful wrought-iron balconies decorated with lush hanging plants extend over narrow, cobblestone streets. Seventeenth-century walls still partially enclose the old city. Designated a U.S. National Historic Zone in 1950, it is packed with shops, open-air cafés, private homes, tree-shaded squares, monuments, plaques, pigeons, people, and traffic jams. It's faster to walk than to take a cab. If your feet fail you in Old San Juan, climb aboard the free open-air trolleys that rumble through the narrow streets. Take one from the docks or board anywhere along the route.

❽ **Alcaldía.** San Juan's city hall was built between 1604 and 1789. In 1841 extensive alterations were made so that it would resemble the city hall in Madrid. Renovations have refreshed the facade of the building and some interior rooms, but the architecture remains true to its colonial style. ✉ *153 Calle San Francisco, Plaza de Armas, Old San Juan* ☎ *787/724–7171* 🎫 *Free* ☉ *Weekdays 8–4.*

❹ **Casa Blanca.** The original structure on this site was a frame house built in 1521 as a home for Ponce de León. But he died in Cuba, never having lived in the home, which was virtually destroyed by a hurricane in 1523. Afterward, his son-in-law had the present masonry home built. His descendants occupied the house for 250 years. A museum devoted to archaeology is on the second floor. The surrounding garden, cooled by fountains, is a tranquil spot for a restorative pause. ✉ *1 Calle San*

Sebastián, Old San Juan ☎ *787/725–1454* ⊕ *www.icp.gobierno.pr* ⊠ *$2* ⊙ *Tues.–Sat. 8:30–4:20.*

⑤ Catedral de San Juan. The Catholic shrine of Puerto Rico had humble beginnings in the early 1520s as a thatch-top, wooden structure. Hurricane winds tore off the thatch and destroyed the church. It was reconstructed in 1540, when it was given a graceful circular staircase and vaulted Gothic ceilings. Most of the work on the present cathedral, however, was done in the 19th century. The remains of Ponce de León are in a marble tomb near the transept. ⊠ *151 Calle Cristo, Old San Juan* ☎ *787/722–0861* ⊕ *www.catedralsanjuan.com* ⊠ *$1 donation suggested* ⊙ *Mon.–Sat. 8–5, Sun. 8–2:30.*

❸ Convento de los Dominicos. Built by Dominican friars in 1523, this convent often served as a shelter during Carib Indian attacks and, more recently, as headquarters for the Antilles command of the U.S. Army. Now home to some offices of the Institute of Puerto Rican Culture, the beautifully restored building contains religious manuscripts, artifacts, and art. The institute also maintains a book and music shop on the premises. Classical concerts are held here occasionally. ⊠ *98 Calle Norzagaray, Old San Juan* ☎ *787/721–6866* ⊠ *Free* ⊙ *Mon.–Sat. 9–5.*

❻ La Fortaleza. Sitting on a hill overlooking the harbor, La Fortaleza was built as a fortress in 1533. Not a very good fortress, mind you. It was attacked numerous times and taken twice, by the British in 1598 and by the Dutch in 1625. When the city's other fortifications were finished, La Fortaleza was transformed into a palace. Guided tours of the extensive gardens and the circular dungeon are conducted on the hour in English, on the half hour in Spanish; both include a short video presentation. ⊠ *Calle Recinto Oeste, Old San Juan* ☎ *787/721–7000 Ext. 2211* ⊕ *www.fortaleza.gobierno.pr* ⊠ *Free* ⊙ *Weekdays 9–3:30.*

🖐 ❾ Fuerte San Cristóbal. This 18th-century fortress guarded the city from land attacks. Even larger than El Morro, San Cristóbal was known in its heyday as the Gibraltar of the West Indies. ⊠ *Calle Norzagaray, Old San Juan* ☎ *787/729–6960* ⊕ *www.nps.gov/saju* ⊠ *$3; $5 includes admission to El Morro* ⊙ *Daily 9–5.*

🖐 ❶ Fuerte San Felipe del Morro. On a rocky promontory at the Old City's northwestern tip is El Morro, which was built by the Spaniards between 1540 and 1783. Rising 140 feet above the sea, the fort boasts six massive levels. It's a labyrinth of dungeons, barracks, towers, and tunnels. Its museum traces the history of the fortress. Tours and a video show are available in English. ⊠ *Calle Norzagaray, Old San Juan* ☎ *787/729–6960* ⊕ *www.nps.gov/saju* ⊠ *$3; $5 includes admission to Fuerte San Cristóbal* ⊙ *Daily 9–5.*

❷ Museo de las Américas. On the second floor of the imposing former military barracks, Cuartel de Ballajá, the Museum's permanent exhibit, "Las Artes Populares en las Américas," focusing on the popular and folk art of Latin America, contains religious figures, musical instruments, basketwork, costumes, and farming and other implements. ⊠ *Calle Norzagaray and Calle del Morro, Old San Juan* ☎ *787/724–5052* ⊕ *www. museolasamericas.org* ⊠ *Free* ⊙ *Tues.–Sun. 10–4.*

❼ Plaza de Armas. This is the original main square of Old San Juan. The plaza, bordered by Calles San Francisco, Fortaleza, San José, and Cruz, has a lovely fountain with 19th-century statues representing the four seasons.

In **Puerta de Tierra,** ½ mi (1 km) east of the pier, is **El Capitolio,** Puerto Rico's white-marble capitol, dating from the 1920s. Another ½ mi(1 km) east, at the tip of Puerta de Tierra, tiny **Fort San Jerónimo** perches over the Atlantic like an afterthought. Added to San Juan's fortifications in the late 18th century, the structure barely survived the British attack of 1797.

Santurce, the district between Miramar on the west and the Laguna San José on the east, is a busy mixture of shops, markets, and offices. A Georgian-style structure, once a public school, is home of the **Museo Contemporáneo del Arte de Puerto Rico** (Museum of Contemporary Puerto Rican Art; ⊠ Av. Ponce de León at Av. R. H. Todd, Santurce ☎ 787/ 977–4030 ⊕ www.museocontemporaneopr.org). Closed Monday; free. The former San Juan Municipal Hospital is now the **Museo de Arte de Puerto Rico** (Museum of Puerto Rican Art; ⊠ 299 Av. José De Diego, Santurce ☎ 787/977–6277 ⊕ www.mapr.org), which displays a permanent collection of Puerto Rican art and changing exhibits. Closed Monday; $6 admission.

Casa Bacardí Visitor Center. Exiled from Cuba, the Bacardí family built a small distillery here in the 1950s. Today it's one of the world's largest, with the capacity to produce 100,000 gallons of spirits a day and 221 million cases a year. You can hop on a little tram to take a 45-minute tour of the bottling plant, distillery, and museum. Yes, you'll be offered a free sample. If you don't want to drive, you can reach the factory by taking the ferry from Pier 2 for 50¢ each way and then a public car from the ferry pier to the factory for about $2 or $3 per person. ⊠ *Rte. 888, Km 2.6, Cataño* ☎ *787/788–1500 or 787/788–8400* ⊕ *www.casabacardi.org* ☒ *Free* ⊘ *Mon.–Sat. 8:30–5:30, Sun. 10–5. Tours every 15–30 min.*

Shopping

San Juan is not a duty-free port, so you won't find bargains on electronics and perfumes. However, shopping for native crafts can be fun. Popular souvenirs and gifts include *santos* (small, hand-carved figures of saints or religious scenes), hand-rolled cigars, handmade lace, and carnival masks. Look for vendors selling crafts from kiosks at the **Artesanía Puertorriqueña** (⊠ Plaza Dársenas, Old San Juan, San Juan ☎ 787/722–1709) in the tourism company's La Casita near Pier 1. Several vendors also set up shop to sell articles such as belts, handbags, and toys along Calle San Justo in front of Plaza Dársenas. **Artefacto** (⊠ 99 Calle Cristo ☎ 787/386–6164) is the cleverest shop in San Juan. At first the items on display look like traditional crafts, but look again and you notice that everything is a little offbeat. A little wooden shrine, for example, might be sheltering an image of Marilyn Monroe. At the **Convento de los Dominicos** (⊠ 98 Calle Norzagaray, Old San Juan, San Juan ☎ 787/721–6866)—the Dominican Convent on the north side of the old city that houses the offices of the Instituto de Cultura Puertorriqueña—you can find baskets, masks, the famous *cuatro* guitars, santos, and reproductions of Taíno artifacts.

Sports & Activities

GOLF Though there are no courses in San Juan proper, it's possible to do a golf outing to one of Puerto Rico's stellar courses as a day trip. The Robert Trent Jones–designed courses at the **Hyatt Dorado Beach Resort & Country Club** (⊠ Rte. 693, Km 10.8, Dorado ☎ 787/796–1234 or 800/233–1234) got a facelift in 2005. Six new holes and six redesigned holes mean that the Pineapple and the Sugar Cane courses feel completely different. With El Yunque as a backdrop, the two 18-hole courses at the **Westin Río Mar Beach Golf Resort & Spa** (⊠ 6000 Río Mar Blvd., Río Grande ☎ 787/888–6000) are inspirational. The River Course was designed by Greg Norman, the Ocean course by George and Tom Fazio.

Beaches

By law, all of Puerto Rico's beaches are open to the public. The **Balneario de Carolina** is so close to the airport that the leaves rustle when planes take off. The long stretch of sand, which runs parallel to Avenida Los Gobernadores, is shaded by palms and almond trees. **Playa del Condado** is overshadowed by an unbroken string of hotels and apartment buildings. Beach bars, water-sports outfitters, and chair-rental places abound. The stretch of sand near Calle Vendig is especially popular with the gay community.

Where to Eat

Tips of 15% to 20% are expected, and appreciated, by restaurant waitstaff if a service charge is not included in the bill.

$$$–$$$$ ✕ **Aguaviva.** The name means "jellyfish," which explains why this ultra-cool, ultra-modern place has lighting fixtures shaped like that sea creature. Elegantly groomed oysters and clams float on cracked ice along the raw bar. The extensive menu is alive with inventive ceviches, some with tomato or roasted red peppers and olives, and fresh takes on classics like paella. For something more filling, try dorado served with a shrimp salsa, or tuna accompanied by seafood enchiladas. ⊠ *364 Calle La Fortaleza, Old San Juan* ☎ *787/722–0665* ⚐ *Reservations not accepted* ▤ *AE, D, MC, V.*

$–$$ ✕ **La Fonda del Jibarito.** Sanjuaneros have favored this casual, family-run restaurant for years. The conch ceviche and chicken fricassee are among the specialties on the menu of comida criollo dishes. The back porch is filled with plants, and the dining room is filled with fanciful depictions of life on the street outside. ⊠ *280 Calle Sol, Old San Juan* ☎ *787/725–8375* ⚐ *Reservations not accepted* ▤ *AE, MC, V.*

Nightlife

Almost every ship stays in San Juan late or even overnight to give passengers an opportunity to revel in the nightlife—the most sophisticated in the Caribbean.

CASINOS By law, all casinos are in hotels. The atmosphere is refined, and many patrons dress to the nines, but informal attire (no shorts or tank tops) is usually fine. Casinos set their own hours, which change seasonally, but generally operate from noon to 4 AM, although the casino in the Condado Plaza Hotel & Casino is open 24 hours. Other hotels with casinos include the Inter-Continental San Juan Resort & Casino, the Ritz-Carlton San Juan Hotel, Spa & Casino, and the Sheraton Old San Juan Hotel & Casino.

BARS &
DANCE CLUBS
A wildly popular hole-in-the-wall, **El Batey** (⊠ 101 Calle Cristo, Old San Juan ☎ 787/725–1787) won't win any prizes for its decor. Grab a marker to add your own message to the graffiti-covered walls, or add your business card to the hundreds that cover the lighting fixtures. The ceiling may leak, but the jukebox has the best selection of oldies in town. Join locals in a game of pool. **Candela** (⊠ 110 San Sebastián, Old San Juan ☎ 787/977–4305), a lounge–art gallery housed in a historic building, hosts some of the most innovative local DJs on the island and often invites star spinners from New York or London. This is the island's best showcase for experimental dance music. The festive, late-night haunt is open Tuesday through Saturday from 8 PM onward, and the conversation can be as stimulating as the dance floor. At **Liquid** (⊠ Water Club, 2 Calle Tartak, Isla Verde ☎ 787/725–4664 or 787/725–4675), the lobby lounge of San Juan's chicest boutique hotel, glass walls are filled with undulating water, and the fashionable patrons drink wild cocktails to pounding music. With a large dance and stage area and smokin' Afro-Cuban bands, **Rumba** (⊠ 152 Calle San Sebastián, Old San Juan, San Juan ☎ 787/725–4407) is one of the best parties in town. Popular with gay men and lesbians, **Starz** (⊠ 365 Av. de Diego, at Av. Ponce de León, Santurce ☎ 787/721–8645) is this cavernous club with dancing on Friday and Saturday nights, as well as a popular after-the-beach party on Sunday evening.

SANTO DOMINGO, DOMINICAN REPUBLIC

Eileen
Robinson
Smith
Spanish civilization in the New World began in Santo Domingo's 12-block Zona Colonial (Colonial Zone). As you stroll its narrow streets, it's easy to imagine this old city as it was when the likes of Columbus, Cortés, and Ponce de León walked the cobblestones, when pirates sailed in and out of the harbor, and when colonists first started building the New World's largest city. Tourist brochures tout that "history comes alive here"—a surprisingly truthful statement. However, many tourists bypass the large, sprawling, and noisy city; it's their loss. The Dominican Republic's seaside capital—despite such detractions as poverty and sprawl, not to mention a population of some 2 million people—has some of the country's best hotels, restaurants, and nightlife (not to mention great casinos). Many of these are right on or near the Malecón and within the historic Zona Colonial area, which is separated from the rest of the city by Parque Independencia. If your ship calls or even embarks here, you'll be treated to a vibrant cultural center unlike any other in the Caribbean.

Essentials

CURRENCY
The Dominican peso (RD$32.38 to US$1). Independent merchants willingly accept U.S. dollars, but you may need to change some money. Cambios (money exchange offices) are common, but you'll get the best rates at either a bank or a casino. Banco Popular has ATMS in the Zona Colonial, but you will be able to get only pesos.

HOURS
Offices and shops are open weekdays from 8 to noon and 2 to 6, Saturday from 8 to noon. About half the stores stay open all day, no longer closing for a midday siesta. Attractions are generally seen between 9:00 a.m. and 5:00 to 6:00 p.m.

INTERNET In the Colonial Zone, a convenient place to check your e-mail is **Verizon Comunicaciones** (✉ 256 Calle Conde, Zona Colonial ☎ 809/221–4249). You will have to pay cash—pesos or dollars. Look "up," and you will see many Internet cafés on The Conde, usually with second-floor locations.

TELEPHONES From the D.R., you need only dial 1 plus the area code and number to call the U.S. To make a local call, you must now dial 809 plus the seven-digit number. Phone cards, which are sold at gift shops and grocery stores, can give you considerable savings on your calls home. If you have a tri-band GSM phone, it should work on the island. Verizon calling centers, like **Verizon Comunicaciones** (✉ 256 Calle Conde, Zona Colonial ☎ 809/221–4249) have equally good rates to the States and Canada, now about 35¢ U.S. a minute. Know you need to pay in cash.

> ## SANTO DOMINGO BEST BETS
>
> - **Dining** Some of the D.R.'s best restaurants can be found in the capital. Take advantage of them if you have any extra time to spend here.
> - **Shopping.** The country's best shopping scene can be found in Santo Domingo, and Calle Conde is the main shopping street of Zona Colonial.
> - **Zona Colonial.** Santo Domingo's colonial zone is a World Heritage Site and a great place to shop and stroll.

Coming Ashore

Santo Domingo has two cruise ship terminals. The Port of Don Diego is on the Ozuma River, facing the Don Diego Highway, and across the street are steps that lead up to the main pedestrian shopping street of the Zona Colonia, Calle Conde. Diagonally across the river from Don Diego is the Sans Souci Dock, on avenida Francisco Alberto Caaman; from Sans Souci, you will need to jump into a waiting taxi ($5). Should you want to go to The Malecón or shop in the modern city, $20 an hour is the going rate. Don't rent a car; it's expensive, and traffic and parking are both difficult.

The new Don Diego terminal is a lovely yellow and white building, with faux gas lights and artistic mosaic work with an ocean theme on the facade; unfortunately, it has few passenger facilities except for three ATMs. When a ship is in, vendors set up colorful tables to sell their wares: cigars; larimar and amber jewelry, and handicrafts. The Ministry of Tourism has a table with an English-speaking staffer to answer questions and to assist passengers with taxi negotiations. No formal tours are offered here, although some passengers do partake of the tours offered on board their ship. The remodeling of the Sans Souci Dock is a work in progress, which is slated for completion on November 2007.

You can easily tour the Zona Colonial on your own; you can get a free walking-tour map and (usually) brochures in English at the Secretaria de Estado de Turismo office at Parque Colón, where you may be approached by freelance, English-speaking guides. They'll work enthusiastically for $20 an hour for four people. Do wear comfortable shoes.

AIRPORT TRANSFERS If you are embarking in Santo Domingo, you should fly into **Las Américas International Airport** (SDQ ✉ Santo Domingo ☎ 809/549–0450), about

7

Santo
Domingo

24 km (15 mi) east of downtown. Transportation into the city is strictly by taxi; figure on $35 for a taxi to or from hotels on the Malecón or in the Zona Colonial. You'll be greeted by a melee of hawking taxi drviers and their English-speaking solicitors (who expect to be tipped, as do the freelance porters who will undoubtedly scoop up your luggage). If you are spending the night in Santo Domingo before a cruise, you can probably arrange a driver through your hotel, so you'll be met with someone holding a sign with your name (it's worth the extra $10 or so to avoid the hassle). If you're going straight to your cruise ship, consider taking the cruise line's pre-arranged transfer. When you disembark from your ship, expect long lines at check-in, and be sure to give yourself a full two hours for check-in and security.

Best Shore Excursions

All-inclusive Beach Trip. If you don't want to see the historic parts of Santo Domingo, then this is probably your best alternative, though you'll find better and cheaper options on other islands. You'll get free food and drink and the option to lie about and do nothing. ☉ *5 hrs* ⛴ *$89.*

Santo Domingo Walking Tour. The best way to see the Zona Colonial is on foot, and if you don't feel comfortable doing it on your own, this is your best option. ☉ *3½ hrs* ⛴ *$45.*

Santo Domingo Sightseeing. If you want to do a bus tour of the city, the better option is one that includes a tour of the botanical gardens as well as the other main sights. ☉ *3¾ hrs* ⛴ *$39.*

Exploring Santo Domingo
Numbers in the margin correspond to points of interest on the Santo Domingo map.

History buffs will want to spend a day exploring the many "firsts" of our continent. A horse and carriage ride throughout the Colonial Zone costs $20 an hour. The steeds are no thoroughbreds, but they clip right along, though any commentary will be in Spanish. You can also negotiate to use them as a taxi, say down to the Malecón. The drivers hang out in front of the Sofitel Nicolas Ovando hotel.

❶ **Alcazar de Colón.** The 22 room castle of Don Diego Colón, built in 1517, has 40-inch-thick coral-limestone walls. The Renaissance-style structure, with its balustrade and double row of arches, is furnished in a style to which the viceroy of the island would have been accustomed. ⊠ *Plaza de España, off Calle Emiliano Tejera at foot of Calle Las Damas, Zona Colonial* ☎ *809/ 687–5361* ⊠ *RD$20* ⊗ *Mon. and Wed.–Fri. 9–5, Sat. 9–4, Sun. 9–1.*

❸ **Calle Las Damas.** The Street of the Ladies was named after the elegant ladies of the court who, in the Spanish tradition, promenaded in the evening. Here you can see a sundial dating from 1753 and the Casa de los Jesuitas, which houses a fine research library for colonial history as well as the Institute for Hispanic Culture; admission is free, and it's open weekdays from 8 to 4:30.

❹ **Catedral Santa María la Menor.** The coral-limestone facade of the first cathedral in the New World (1540) towers over the south side of the Parque Colón. Spanish workmen began building the cathedral in 1514, but left to search for gold in Mexico. The church, with its altar of hammered silver, is composed of architectural elements from the late Gothic. Style. ⊠ *Calle Arzobispo Meriño, Zona Colonial* ☎ *809/689–1920* ⊠ *Free* ⊗ *Mon.–Sat. 9–4; Sun. Masses begin at 6 AM.*

❺ **El Malecón.** Avenida George Washington, better known as the Malecón, runs along the Caribbean and has tall palms, cafés, hotels, and sea breezes.

❷ **Parque Colón.** The huge statue of Christopher Columbus in the park named after him dates from 1897 and is the work of French sculptor Gilbert. Like all the parks in The Zone, this one has been restored. ⊠ *El Conde at Arzobispo Meriño, Zona Colonial.*

Beaches
If you are just in port for a day, you'll have a better time if you skip the beach and spend some time in the Zona Colonial and on The Malecón. The closest good beach to Santo Domingo is **Boca Chica** (⊠ Autopista Las Americas, 21 mi (34 km) east of Santo Domingo Boca Chica), which is popular mainly with Dominicans and Europeans, but is one of the better places to go to the beach. Hang out at one of the popular restaurants, like El Pelicano.

Shopping
Exquisitely hand-wrapped cigars continue to be the hottest commodity coming out of the D.R. Only reputable cigar shops sell the real thing. Dominican rum and coffee are also good buys. *Mamajuana,* an herbal

liqueur, is said to be the Dominican answer to Viagra. Look also for the delicate, faceless ceramic figurines that symbolize Dominican culture. Though locally crafted products are often very affordable, expect to pay for designer jewelry made of amber and larimar, an indigenous semiprecious stone the color of the Caribbean. Amber, a fossilization of resin from a prehistoric pine tree, often encasing ancient animal and plant life, from leaves to spiders to tiny lizards, is mined extensively. (Beware of fakes, which are especially prevalent in street stalls.)

One of the main shopping streets in the Zone is **Calle El Conde,** a pedestrian thoroughfare. The dull and dusty stores with dated merchandise are giving way to some hip, new shops. However, many of the offerings, are still of a caliber and cost that the Dominicans can afford. The **Malecón Center,** is the newest complex and is adjacent to the nearly-new Hilton Santo Domingo. It will house 170 shops, boutiques, and services plus several movie theaters, when completely occupied. In the tower above are luxury apartments and Sammy Sosa, in one of the penthouses. **Plaza Central,** between Avenidas Winston Churchill and 27 de Febrero, is where you can find many top international boutiques and a Jenny Polanco shop (an upscale Dominican designer who has incredible white outfits, artistic jewelry, and purses).

Ambar Tres (⊠ La Atarazana 3, Zona Colonial ☎ 809/688–0474) carries a wide selection of amber jewelry. **Cigar King** (⊠ Calle Conde 208, Baguero Bldg., Zona Colonial ☎ 809/686–4987) keeps Dominican and Cuban cigars in a temperature-controlled cedar room.**L'Ile Au Tresor** (⊠ Arzobispo Merino #352, Esq. Calle Mercedes (across from Sofitel Frances), Zona Colonial ☎ 809/685–3983) may have a "pirates of the Caribbean" theme, but it is fun and has some of the most attractive and creative designer pieces in native larimar, amber, and even conch. **Plaza Toledo Bettye's Galeria** (⊠ Isabel la Católica 163, Zona Colonial ☎ 809/688–7649) sells a fascinating array of artwork, including Haitian vodoo banners, metal sculptures, even souvenirs, chandeliers, and estate jewelry.

Where to Eat

★ **$–$$$** ✕ **Café Bellini.** This café has always had a panache far and above its counterparts, for the Italian owners also have the adjacent furniture design center. The moderne, wicker-weave barrel chairs, and the contemporary art and light fixtures, are all achingly hip. Previously, the domineering Italian chef would send out what he wanted you to eat and the cost was celestial. The present chef is right on and the prices are democratic. The menu is the same at lunch and dinner and your first glance should be at the daily specials, where a main course, like the trio of raviolis made with spinach, beet, and pumpkin prices out at about $10. If local king crab is on the menu, order it. It's served in its crimson shell with a fresh tomato-basil sauce over spaghetti. Service is laudable and it's friendly and fun here; you can even choose the CDs, say a Tony Bennett. ⊠ *Arzobispo Merino, corner of Padre Bellini, Zona Colonial* ☎ *809/686–3387* ⚏ *Reservations essential* ▤ *AE, MC, V.*

★ **$–$$$** ✕ **La Residence.** This fine-dining enclave has always had the setting—Spanish colonial architecture, with pillars and archways overlooking a courtyard—and an esoteric lunch-dinner menu with high prices that did not always deliver. Now it has a seasoned French chef (and manager) serving classic yet innovative cuisine with many moderately priced choices. The daily Menu del Chef has a main course for less than $10. It could be brochettes of spit-roasted duck, chicken with poivre sauce, and vegetable risotto. You could start with a salad of panfried young squid for about $5 and go bonkers over the $3 dark- and white-chocolate terrine. Veer from the daily specials menu and it's certainly more pricey but fair; even the grilled fillet and braised oxtail with foie gras sauce and wild mushrooms is reasonable. ⊠ *In Sofitel Nicolas de Ovando, Calle Las Damas, Zona Colonial* ☎ *809/685–9955* ▭ *AE, MC, V.*

Where to Stay

Since Santo Domingo is the home port for at least one cruise ship, we've recommended some places to stay in case you choose to spend the night here before you sail. When looking for a good price at a Santo Domingo hotel, go on-line first when checking rates, as the Internet deals can be a fraction of the rack rates. Last-minute price breaks are another possibility.

★ **Sofitel Nicolas Ovando.** This luxury hotel, sculpted from the residence $$$–$$$$ of the first Governor of the Americas, is the best thing to happen in the Zone since Diego Columbus's palace was finished in 1517. Colonial rooms have canopied king-size beds, tall ceilings, original stone window benches, and shutters. Some prefer the sunny (smaller) rooms in the contemporary annex; with the river views, these are smart examples of French minimalist style. The pool is shaded by trees and tropical plantings, and swimmers leave the sun for a fitness break in the gym. The bar is a social scene, particularly when the music man plays at cocktail hour, which includes complimentary hors d'oeuvres. The breakfast spread is lavish. ⊠ *Calle Las Damas, Zona Colonial* ☎ *809/ 685–9955 or 800/763–4835* ⊟ *809/685–9302* ⊕ *www.sofitel.com* ⇨ *100 rooms, 4 suites* ♿ *In-room: safe, refrigerator. In-hotel: restaurant, room service, bars, pool, gym, concierge, laundry service, public Internet, public Wi-Fi, parking (no fee), some pets allowed* ▭ *AE, MC, V* ⼌ *BP.*

★ $–$$ **The Hilton Santo Domingo.** This has become *the* address on the Malecón for businesspeople, convention attendees, and leisure travelers. The five luxurious executive floors are wired for business, each with three phones, Internet ports, actual corner offices with imposing desks and ergonomic leather chairs, and DSL lines. Creature comforts are satisfied with the plush duvets, rain showers, and surround sound in the bathrooms, oversize flat-screen TVs, and sea views. Service might just be the best in the country, and rates are surprisingly moderate, particularly with online packages that include a lavish and healthy buffet breakfast. ⊠ *Av. George Washington 500, Zona Colonial* ☎ *809/685–0000* ⊟ *809/685–0202* ⊕ *www.hiltoncaribbean.com* ⇨ *228 rooms, 32 suites* ♿ *In-room: safe, refrigerator, Ethernet. In-hotel: 2 restaurants, bars, pool, gym, spa, concierge, executive floor, public Internet, public Wi-Fi* ▭ *AE, D, MC, V* ⼌ *EP.*

SANTO TOMÁS DE CASTILLA, GUATEMALA

Jeff Van Fleet Guatemala's short Caribbean shoreline doesn't generate the buzz of that of neighboring Belize and Mexico. The coast weighs in at a scant 123 km (74 mi), and this mostly highland country, which wears its indigenous culture on its sleeve, has historically looked inland rather than to the sea. You'll be drawn inland, too, with a variety of shore excursions. This is the land of the Maya, after all. But there's plenty to keep you occupied here in the lowlands. Tourist brochures tout the Caribbean coast as "The Other Guatemala." The predominantly indigenous and Spanish cultures of the highlands give way to an Afro-Caribbean tradition that listens more closely to the rhythms of far-off Jamaica rather than taking its cue from Guatemala City. Think of it as mixing a little reggae with your salsa.

Essentials

CURRENCY The Guatemalan quetzal, named for the brightly plumed bird that is the symbol of the country (Q7.67 to US$1). Take care of any banking matters in the cruise terminal in Santo Tomás de Castilla. You'll find ATMs in Puerto Barrios and Livingston but nowhere else in this region.

HOURS Businesses generally are open from 8 to 6, with many closing for a couple of hours over lunch.

INTERNET The Terminal de Cruceros in Santo Tomás de Castilla has Internet computers for your use, the easiest option if you're a day visitor.

TELEPHONES Guatemalan phone numbers have eight digits. There are no city or area codes. Simply dial the number for any in-country call. Most towns have offices of Telgua, the national telephone company, where you can place both national and international calls. Avoid the ubiquitous public phones with signs promising FREE CALLS TO THE USA. The number back home being called gets socked with a hefty bill.

Coming Ashore

Cruise ships dock at the modern, spacious Terminal de Cruceros, where you'll find a bank, post office, money exchange, telephones, Internet access, a lively crafts market, and an office of INGUAT, Guatemala's national tourist office. A marimba band serenades you with its clinking xylophone-like music; a Caribbean ensemble dances for you (and may even pull you in to take part.)

Taxis, both vehicular and water, take you to various destinations in the area. Plan on paying $2 to Santo Tomás de Castilla proper, and $5 to Puerto Barrios. Boats transport cruise visitors to Livingston, charging about $5 for the 20-minute trip. The Amantique Bay Resort provides

SANTO TOMÁS BEST BETS

- **Quiriguá.** If you want to see Maya ruins but don't want to spend an entire day on the bus, nearby Quiriguá can be impressive.

- **Copán.** In neighboring Honduras, this Maya site is a worthwhile day-trip from Santo Tomás.

- **Riding on the Río Dulce.** The ride on this river is one of Guatemala's most beautiful boat trips.

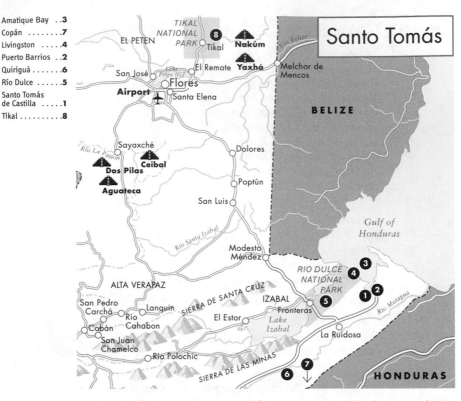

water taxis from port to resort of $8 per person. Vehicular taxis charge $15 per head to travel by land to the resort.

Shore Excursions

We consider these to be among the better shore excursions for Santo Tomás. They may not be offered by all lines, and tour names may differ as well. Times and prices are approximate.

Río Dulce Tour. Spanish explorers and pirates all made their way upriver on the Río Dulce—the construction of a 16th-century fort stopped the latter from getting too far—and your journey through the heavily forested canyon will be no less intriguing and exciting. Tours often include a stop in Livingston. ⊙ *4 hrs* ⊠ *$8.*

Quiriguá Archaeological Ruins. Other Maya ruins in the region are bigger and more spectacular, but those of the sixth-century AD city of Quiriguá offer you no less a fascinating experience, on a smaller and more manageable scale. The added bonus? Quiriguá lies close to the coast, making it a doable half-day excursion. ⊙ *4 ½ hrs* ⊠ *$89.*

Banana Plantation Tour. Neighboring Honduras was the original "banana republic," but the name once applied to Guatemala too. The Caribbean is still banana country, and Chiquita is still one of the region's main employers. A visit to its plantation at nearby Omagua lets you see the processing from cultivation to packing and shipping of the country's second most famous crop. (Coffee is the first.) ⊙ *4 hrs* ⊠ *$49.*

Exploring Santo Tomás de Castilla
Numbers in the margin correspond to points of interest on the Santo Tomás map.

③ Amatique Bay. "Bahía de Amatique" denotes the large bay that washes the Caribbean coast of Guatemala and southern Belize, but for most travelers the name is inexorably linked with the Amatique Bay Resort & Marina, part of the Clarion chain, and the region's only five-star hotel. The 61-room resort opens itself up for day visitors, and many cruise passengers stop by for a drink, a meal, or an entire day of swimming, watersliding, kayaking, horseback riding, or bicycling. ⊠ *10 km (6 mi) north of Santo Tomás* ☎ *7948–1800, 2421–3333 in Guatemala City* ⊕ *www. amatiquebay.net.*

⑦ Copán. The famous Maya ruins of Copán lie just across the border from this region in neighboring Honduras, but are accessible enough from Santo Tomás to be an excursion on many itineraries. Bring your passport since this entails an international border crossing. For a description of the ruins and what you will experience there, see ⇨ *Copán Ruinas in Roatán, Honduras* ⊠ *50 km (30 mi) south of Quiriguá* ☎ *No phone* ▤ *$10* ⊙ *Daily 8–4.*

④ Livingston. Visitors compare Livingston with Puerto Barrios across the bay, and the former wins hands down, for its sultry, seductive Caribbean flavor. Wood houses, some on stilts, some on stilts, congregate in this old fishing town, once an important railroad hub, but today inaccessible by land from the outside world. Livingston proudly trumpts its Garífuna heritage, a culture unique to Central America's eastern coast and descended from the intermarriage of African slaves with Caribbean indigenous peoples. Music and dance traditions and a Caribbean-accented English remain, even if old timers lament the creeping outside influences, namely Spanish, rap and reggae. ⊠ *25 km (15 mi) by water northwest of Santo Tomás.*

② Puerto Barrios. Puerto Barrios maintains the atmosphere of an old banana town, humid and a tad down at the heels, perhaps longing for better days. Santo Tomás has replaced it as the country's largest port, and you'll likely zip through the Caribbean coast's biggest city on your way to somewhere else, but the cathedral and municipal market are worth a look if you find yourself here. Water taxis depart the municipal docks for Livingston, across the bay, from where you start your trip up the Río Dulce. ⊠ *5 km (3 mi) north of Santo Tomás de Castilla.*

⑥ Quiriguá. Construction began on the Guatemalan lowlands' most important Maya ruins about AD 500. Its hieroglyhics tell its story: Quiriguá served at the time as a satellite state under the control of Copán, about 50 km (30 mi) away in present-day Honduras. By the height of its power in the seventh century, Quiriguá had overpowered Copán, but just as quickly, fell back into submissive status. Quiriguá's ruins still today live in the shadow of their more well-known neighbor across the border, and of the Tikal ruins in the northern part of Guatemala, but a visit here is rewarding for the carvings of *stelae*, the ornate sculptures depicting the city's rulers, and the largest such works in Central America. (Quiriguá's stelae stand 10 meters (33 feet) tall, dwarfing those of Copán.) Ease of access from the

Caribbean coast makes Quiriguá well worth a visit too. ✉ *90 km (54 mi) southwest of Santo Tomás* ☎ *No phone* 🎫 *$4* ⊙ *Daily 8–4.*

5 **Río Dulce.** The natural crown jewel of this region is the 13,000-hectare (32,000-acre) national park that protects the river leading inland from Livingston to Lago de Izabal, Guatemala's largest lake. Pelicans, herons, egrets, and terns nest and fly along the Río Dulce, which cuts through a heavily forested limestone canyon. Excursions often approach the park by land, but we recommend making the trip upriver from Livingston to immerse yourself in the entire Indiana Jones experience. ✉ *Southwest of Livingston.*

The **Castillo de San Felipe de Lara** (☎ No phone ⊙ Daily 8–5 🎫 $1) looms inland over the river's entrance to Lake Izabal near the town of Fronteras. Spanish colonists constructed the fortress in 1595 to guard the inland waterway from incursions by Dutch and English pirates. A 1999 earthquake in this region destroyed the river pier as well as damaging portions of the fort. If you wish to visit, rather than simply see the fort from the water, you need to approach the park overland rather than upriver.

A short launch from Fronteras takes you to **Hacienda Tijax** (☎ 7902–0859), an old rubber plantation, now reforestation project, which offers hiking and kayaking, and a chance to view the cultivation of orchids and spices.

1 **Santo Tomás de Castilla.** Belgian immigrants settled Santo Tomás in the 19th century, but little remains of their heritage today, save for the preponderance of French and Flemish names in the local cemetery. Most visitors move on. Santo Tomás has experienced a small renaissance as the country's most important port, receiving growing numbers of cruise and cargo ships, and serving as the headquarters of the Guatemalan navy.

8 **Tikal.** The high point of any trip to Guatemala is a visit to Tikal, Central America's most impressive indigenous ruins. There's nothing quite like the sight of the towering temples, ringed on all sides by miles of virgin forest, but you need a lot of *quetzales* to get here—tour operators charge about $500 for a day-trip from Santo Tomás. The cruise lines that do offer Tikal on their itineraries transport you via plane from the airstrip outside Santo Tomás to the small airport in Santa Elena near the ruins.

Although the region was home to Maya communities as early as 600 BC, Tikal itself wasn't established until sometime around 200 BC. By AD 500 it's estimated that the city had a population of close to 100,000. For almost 1,000 years Tikal remained engulfed by the jungle. The conquistadors who came here searching for gold and silver must have passed right by the overgrown ruins, mistaking them for rocky hills. Excavation began in earnest in the mid-1800s. Today, after more than 150 years of digging, researchers say that Tikal includes some 3,000 buildings. Countless more are still covered by the jungle. The ancient city's center is filled with awe-inspiring temples and acropolises. **Temple I,** known as the Temple of the Great Jaguar, is in the dramatic **Great Plaza.** It was built around AD 700 by Ah-Cacao. His tomb was discovered beneath the Temple of the Great Jaguar, and the theory is that his queen is buried beneath **Temple II,** called the Temple of the Masks. The **North Acropolis** is a mind-boggling conglomeration of temples built over layers of previous construction. Be sure to see the stone mask of the rain god at Temple 33.

If you climb to the top of one of the pyramids, you'll see the roofs of others rising above the rain forest's canopy. **Temple V** is now open to the public, and **Temple IV**, the tallest-known structure built by the Maya, offers and unforgettable view from the top. At the park headquarters, two good archaeological museums display Mayan artifacts. ⊠ *Parque Nacional Tikal* ☎ *No phone* ⊠ *$7* ☉ *Daily 6–6.*

Shopping

The rest of Guatemala overflows with indegnous crafts and art, but the famous market towns of the highlands are nowhere to be found in Caribbean region. Quite honestly, your best bet for shopping is the Terminal de Cruceros at Santo Tomás de Castilla, and you'll have plenty of opportunity to buy before you board your ship. What you'll find here comes from the Guatemala's highlands—the Caribbean has never developed a strong artisan tradition—with a good selection of fabrics, weavings, woodwork and basketry to choose from. Markets in Puerto Barrios and Livingston, the only real urban areas you'll encounter in this region, are more geared to the workaday needs of its residents rather than visitors.

Activities

BEACHES & WATER SPORTS — A beach culture has just never developed in this region of Guatamala the way it has in neighboring Belize and Mexico. The only real beach in the region is found within the confines of the **Amantique Bay Resort & Marina.**

(⊠ 5 km (3 mi) north of Puerto Barrios), which is the only place here that has a resort feel to it. Day visitors partake of swimming, waterslides, and kayaking. The resort's launch will bring you over from the cruise-ship terminal in Santo Tomás.

HIKING & KAYAKING — **Hacienda Tijax** (⊠ Las Fronteras ☎ 7902–0859), inland, near the point where the Río Dulce meets Lake Izabal provides kayaking and hiking for day visitors.

Where to Eat

$–$$$$ ✗ **Amatique Bay Resort & Marina.** Most cruise visitors pass through the Amatique Bay Resort to drink or dine, and you have three options to choose from at this complex: diners line up for the Caribbean-style buffet at Puerto Chico; Mango's provides a romantic place to take in the sunset—the resort sits on the eastern side of Amantique Bay, so, yes, the sunsets are fabulous; and El Berrinche offers a formal dining experience unmatched by any other place in the region (and by few other places in Guatemala). Seafood reigns at all the restaurants. ⊠ *5 km. (3 mi.) north of Puerto Barrios* ☎ *7948–1800* ⊟ *AE, DC, MC, V.*

TORTOLA, BRITISH VIRGIN ISLANDS

Lynda Lohr   Once a sleepy backwater, Tortola is definitely busy these days, particularly when several cruise ships tie up at the Road Town dock. Passengers crowd the streets and shops, and open-air jitneys filled with cruise-ship passengers create bottlenecks on the island's byways. That said, most folks visit Tortola to relax on its deserted sands or linger over lunch at one of its many delightful restaurants. Beaches are never more than a few miles away, and the steep green hills that form Tortola's spine are fanned by gentle trade winds. The neighboring islands glimmer like emeralds in a sea of sapphire. Tortola doesn't have many historic sights, but it does have abundant natural beauty. Beware of the roads, which are extraordinarily steep and twisting, making driving demanding. The best beaches are on the north shore.

Essentials

CURRENCY The U.S. dollar is the official currency. Some places accept cash only, but major credit cards are widely accepted. You'll find ATMs in Road Town.

HOURS Banking hours are usually Monday through Thursday from 9 to 2:30 and Friday from 9 to 2:30 and 4:30 to 6. Post offices are open weekdays from 9 to 5 and Saturday from 9 to noon. Stores are generally open Monday through Saturday from 9 to 5. Some may be open on Sunday.

INTERNET **Trellis Bay Cybercafé** (✉ Trellis Bay, Tortola ☎ 284/495–2447).

TELEPHONES To call anywhere in the BVI once you've arrived, dial all seven digits. A local call from a pay phone costs 25¢, but such phones are sometimes on the blink. An alternative is a Caribbean phone card, available in $5, $10, and $20 denominations. They're sold at most major hotels and many stores and can be used to call within the BVI, as well as all over the Caribbean, and to access USADirect from special phone-card phones. If you're coming ashore at the cruise-ship dock, you'll find pay phones right on the dock. If a tender drops you right in Road Town at the ferry dock, phones are located in the terminal.

Cingular has service in nearby St. John, USVI, so it's possible to get service from there in some spots in Road Town and along the waterfront highway that leads to the West End. You may not have to pay international roaming charges on some U.S. cell phone plans if you can connect with this network.

Coming Ashore

Large cruise ships usually anchor in Road Town Harbor and bring passengers ashore by tender. Small ships can sometimes tie up at Wickham's Cay dock. Either way, it's a short stroll to Road Town. If your ship isn't going to Virgin Gorda, you can make the 12-mi (19 km) trip by ferry from the dock in Road Town in about 30 minutes for about $27 round-trip, but you'll still have to take a taxi to get to The Baths for swimming and snorkeling, so it's not necessarily a bad deal to go on your ship's shore excursion.

There are taxi stands at Wickham's Cay and in Road Town. Taxis are unmetered, and there are minimums for travel throughout the island, so it's usually cheaper to travel in groups. Negotiate

---

TORTOLA BEST BETS

- **The *Rhone*.** For certified divers, this is one of the best wreck dives in the Caribbean.

- **Sage Mountain.** The highest peak in the Virgin Islands has breathtaking views and is a great hiking destination.

- **Sailing Trips.** Because of its proximity to small islets and good snorkeling sights, Tortola is the sailing capital of the Caribbean.

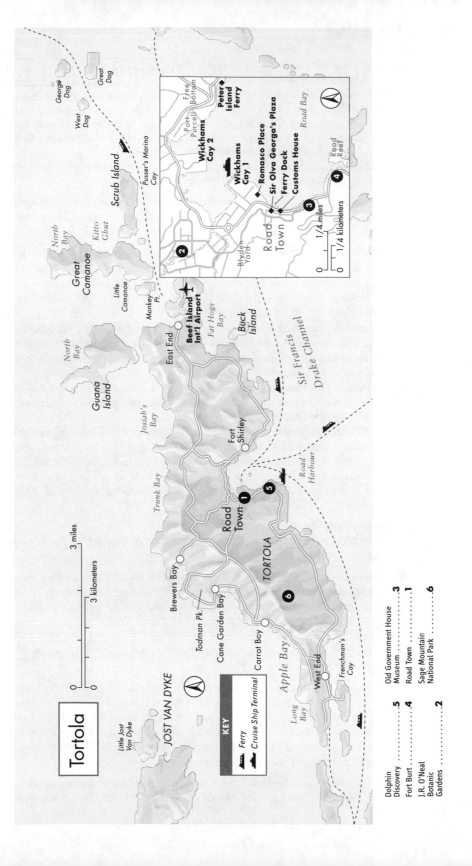

Tortola

0 3 miles
0 3 kilometers

JOST VAN DYKE

Little Jost
Van Dyke

KEY

Ferry
Cruise Ship Terminal

Dolphin
Discovery **5**
Fort Burt **4**
J.R. O'Neal
Botanic
Gardens **2**

Old Government House
Museum **3**
Road Town **1**
Sage Mountain
National Park **6**

West End
Frenchman's
Cay
Long
Bay
Apple Bay
Carrot Bay
Cane Garden Bay
Todman Pk.
Brewers Bay

TORTOLA

Road
Town
Fort
Shirley

Trunk Bay
Josiah's
Bay
North
Bay
Guana
Island

East End
Monkey
Pt.
Little
Camanoe
Great
Camanoe
North
Bay
Kitto
Ghut
Scrub Island
Pusser's Marina
Cay
George
Dog
West
Dog
Great
Dog

Beef Island
Int'l Airport
Fat Hogs
Bay
Buck
Island

**Sir Francis
Drake Channel**

Road
Harbour

Road Reef

**Road
Town**

Blyden
Yard
Port
Purcell
Free
Bottom

**Wickhams
Cay 2**
**Wickhams
Cay 1**
Romasco Place
Sir Olva Georga's Plaza
Ferry Dock
Customs House
**Peter
Island
Ferry**

Road Bay
Road
Reef

0 1/4 miles
0 1/4 kilometers

to get the best fares, as there is no set fee schedule. If you are in the islands for just a day, it's usually more cost-effective to share a taxi with a small group than to rent a car, since you'd have to pay an agency at Wickham's Cay or in Road Town $10 for a temporary license and car-rental charges of at least $50 a day. You must be at least age 25 to rent a car.

> **CAUTION**
>
> If you pick an outside cabin, check to make sure your view of the sea is not obstructed by a lifeboat. The ship's deck plan will help you figure it out.

SHORE EXCURSIONS We consider these to be among the better shore excursions for Tortola. They may not be offered by all lines, and tour names may differ as well. Times and prices are approximate.

Sage Mountain National Park Hike and Snorkel. The first stop on this excursion is the highest peak in the Virgin Islands, where you do a 1-mi (1½-km) hike through the rain forest to get to the best view. Then it's to a white-sand beach (usually Cane Garden Bay) for some swimming and snorkeling. ☉ 3½ hrs ☒ $35.

Sailing Excursion. Embark on a sailing yacht in Road Town harbor, Tortola, and sail past some of the smaller surrounding islands with stops to swim and snorkel. Full-day trips, which are usually considerably more expensive, include lunch. ☉ 4 hrs ☒ $54.

Scuba Diving the Wreck of the *Rhone*. If you are a certified diver, this trip explores one of the best wreck dives in the Caribbean region. No kids under 12. ☉ 5½ hrs ☒ $142.

Virgin Gorda Highlights & the Baths. From Tortola, you take a regularly scheduled ferry for the 40-minute cruise to Virgin Gorda, where you see the island sights and stop at the famous Baths and later for snorkeling at Savannah Bay, where most cruise lines provide snorkeling equipment. ☉ 5 ½ hrs ☒ $59 (sometimes less if your cruise ship anchors off Spanish Town).

Exploring Tortola
Numbers in the margin correspond to points of interest on the Tortola map.

⑤ Dolphin Discovery. Get up close and personal with dolphins as they swim in a spacious seaside pen. There are two different programs that provide a varying range of experiences. In the Royal Swim, dolphins tow participants around the pen. The less expensive Encounter allows you to touch the dolphins. ☒ *Prospect Reef Resort, Road Town* ☎ *284/494–7675* ⊕ *www.dolphindiscovery.com* ☒ *Royal Swim $139, Encounter $79* ☉ *Daily, by appointment only.*

④ Fort Burt. The most intact historic ruin on Tortola was built by the Dutch in the early 17th century to safeguard Road Harbour. It sits on a hill at the western edge of Road Town and is now the site of a small hotel and restaurant. The foundations and magazine remain, and the structure offers a commanding view of the harbor. ☒ *Waterfront Dr., Road Town* ☎ *No phone* ☒ *Free* ☉ *Daily dawn–dusk.*

② J. R. O'Neal Botanic Gardens. Take a walk through this 4-acre showcase of lush plant life. There are sections devoted to prickly cacti and succulents, hothouses for ferns and orchids, gardens of medicinal herbs, and plants and trees indigenous to the seashore. From the Tourist Board office in Road Town, cross Waterfront Drive and walk one block over to Main Street and turn right. Keep walking until you see the high school. The gardens are on your left. ⊠ *Botanic Station, Road Town* ☎ *284/494–3904* ✉ *$3* ⊙ *Mon.–Sat. 9–4:30.*

❸ Old Government House Museum. The seat of government until 1987, this gracious building now displays a nice collection of items from Tortola's past. The rooms are filled with period furniture, handpainted china, books signed by Queen Elizabeth II on her 1966 and 1977 visits, and numerous items reflecting Tortola's seafaring legacy. ⊠ *Waterfront Dr., Road Town* ☎ *284/494–3701* ✉ *Free* ⊙ *Weekdays 8:30–4:30.*

❶ Road Town. The laid-back capital of the BVI looks out over Road Town Harbour. It takes only an hour or so to stroll down Main Street and along the waterfront, checking out the traditional West Indian buildings, painted in pastel colors and sporting high-pitched, corrugated-tin roofs; bright shutters; and delicate fretwork trim. For hotel and sightseeing brochures and the latest information on everything from taxi rates to ferryboat schedules, visit the BVI Tourist Board office. Or just choose a seat on one of the benches in Sir Olva Georges Square, on Waterfront Drive, and watch the people come and go from the ferry dock and customs office across the street.

❻ Sage Mountain National Park. At 1,716 feet, Sage Mountain is the highest peak in the BVI. From the parking area, a trail leads you in a loop not only to the peak itself (and extraordinary views) but also to a small rain forest, sometimes shrouded in mist. Most of the forest was cut down over the centuries to clear land for sugarcane, cotton, and other crops; to create pastureland; or to simply utilize the stands of timber. In 1964 this park was established to preserve what remained. Up here you can see mahogany trees, white cedars, mountain guavas, elephant-ear vines, mamey trees, and giant bullet woods, to say nothing of such birds as mountain doves and thrushes. Take a taxi from Road Town or drive up Joe's Hill Road and make a left onto Ridge Road toward Chalwell and Doty villages. The road dead-ends at the park. ⊠ *Ridge Rd., Sage Mountain* ☎ *284/494–3904* ⊕ *www.bvinationalparkstrust.org* ✉ *$3* ⊙ *Daily dawn–dusk.*

Shopping

Many shops and boutiques are clustered along and just off Road Town's **Main Street.** You can shop in Road Town's **Wickham's Cay I** area adjacent to the marina, where cruise ships tender their passengers in. Don't be put off by an informal shop entrance; some of the best finds in the BVI lie behind shabby doors.

The **BVI Post Office** (⊠ Main St., Road Town ☎ 284/494–3701) is a philatelist's dream. It has a worldwide reputation for exquisite stamps in all sorts of designs. Although the stamps carry U.S. monetary designations, they can be used for postage only in the BVI. The **Gallery**

CAUTION	⚠
Check the balance of your shipboard account before the end of your cruise. You'll avoid a long line at the Purser's Desk that last morning after the final bill arrives.	

(⊠ 102 Main St., Road Town ☎ 284/494–6680) carries art by owner Lisa Gray and paintings by other Tortola artists. **Pusser's Company Store** (⊠ Main St. at Waterfront Rd., Road Town ☎ 284/494–2467 ⊠ Soper's Hole Marina, West End ☎ 284/495–4599) sells nautical memorabilia, ship models, and marine paintings. There's also an entire line of clothing for both men and women, handsome decorator bottles of Pusser's rum, and gift items bearing the Pusser's logo. **Samarkand** (⊠ Main St., Road Town ☎ 284/494–6415) crafts charming gold-and-silver pendants, earrings, bracelets, and pins, many with island themes like seashells, lizards, pelicans, and palm trees. There are also reproduction Spanish pieces of eight (old Spanish coins worth eight reals) that were found on sunken galleons. **Sunny Caribbee** (⊠ Main St., Road Town ☎ 284/494–2178), in a brightly painted West Indian house, packages its own herbs, teas, coffees, vinegars, hot sauces, soaps, skin and suntan lotions, and exotic concoctions—Arawak Love Potion and Island Hangover Cure, for example. There are also Caribbean books and art and hand-painted decorative accessories.

Activities

DIVING & SNORKELING

Clear waters and numerous reefs afford some wonderful opportunities for underwater exploration. In 1867 the RMS *Rhone,* a 310-foot-long royal mail steamer, split in two when it sank in a devastating hurricane. It's so well preserved that it was used in the movie *The Deep.* You can see the crow's nest and bowsprit, the cargo hold in the bow, and the engine and enormous propeller shaft in the stern. Every dive outfit in the BVI runs superlative scuba and snorkel tours here. Rates start at around $60 for a one-tank dive and $85 for a two-tank dive. **Blue Waters Divers** (⊠ Nanny Cay ☎ 284/494–2847 ⊠ Soper's Hole, West End ☎ 284/495–1200 ⊕ www.bluewaterdiversbvi.com) teaches resort, open-water, rescue, and advanced diving courses, and also makes daily dive trips. If you're chartering a sailboat, the company's boat will meet your boat at Peter, Salt, or Cooper Island for a rendezvous dive. Rates include all equipment as well as instruction. Make arrangements two days in advance. **Dive Tortola** (⊠ Prospect Reef ☎ 284/494–9200 ⊕ www.divetortola.com) offers beginner and advanced diving courses and daily dive trips. Trainers teach open-water, rescue, advanced diving, and resort courses. Dive Tortola also offers a rendezvous diving option for folks on charter sailboats.

FISHING

Most of the boats that take you deep-sea fishing for bluefish, wahoo, swordfish, and shark leave from nearby St. Thomas, but local anglers like to fish the shallower water for bonefish. A half-day of bone fishing runs about $480, a full day around $850. Call **Caribbean Fly Fishing** (⊠ Nanny Cay ☎ 284/494–4797 ⊕ www.caribflyfishing.com).

SAILING

The BVI are among the world's most popular sailing destinations. They're close together and surrounded by calm waters, so it's fairly easy to sail from one anchorage to the next. **Aristocat Charters** (⊠ West End ☎ 284/499–1249 ⊕ www.aristocatcharters.com) sets sail daily to the Indians and Peter Island aboard a 48-foot catamaran. **White Squall II** (⊠ Village Cay Marina, Road Town ☎ 284/494–2564 ⊕ www.whitesquall2.com) takes you on regularly scheduled day sails to the Baths at Virgin Gorda, Jost Van Dyke, or the Caves at Norman Island on an 80-foot schooner.

Beaches

Tortola's north side has several perfect palm-fringed white-sand beaches that curl around turquoise bays and coves. Nearly all are accessible by car (preferably one with four-wheel-drive), albeit down bumpy roads that corkscrew precipitously. Facilities run the gamut from absolutely none to a number of beachside bars and restaurants as well as places to rent water-sports equipment. The water at **Brewers Bay** is good for snorkeling, and you can find a campground with showers and bathrooms and beach bar tucked in the foliage right behind the beach. An old sugar mill and ruins of a rum distillery are just north of the beach along the road. The beach is easy to find, but the paved roads leading down the hill to it can be a bit daunting. You can get there from either Brewers Bay Road East or Brewers Bay Road West. Enticing **Cane Garden Bay** has exceptionally calm, crystalline waters and a silky stretch of sand except when storms at sea turn the water murky. Snorkeling is good along the edges. Casual guesthouses, restaurants, bars, and even shops are just steps off the beach in the growing village of the same name. It's a laid-back, even somewhat funky, place to put down your beach towel. Water-sports shops rent equipment. It's the closest beach to Road Town—one steep uphill and downhill drive—and one of the BVI's best-known anchorages; it's where cruise ships usually send their passengers. Have your camera ready for snapping the breathtaking approach to the 1-mi (2-km) stretch of white sand at **Long Bay West.** Although Long Bay Resort sprawls along part of it, the entire beach is open to the public. The water isn't as calm here as at Cane Garden or Brewers Bay, but it's still swimmable. Rent water-sports equipment and enjoy the beachfront restaurant at the resort. Turn left at Zion Hill Road, then travel about a ½ mi (1 km).

Where to Eat

$-$$ ✕ **Pusser's Road Town Pub.** Almost everyone who visits Tortola stops here at least once to have a bite to eat and to sample the famous Pusser's Rum Painkiller (fruit juices and rum). The nonthreatening menu includes cheesy pizza, shepherd's pie, fish-and-chips, and hamburgers. Dine inside in air-conditioned comfort or outside on the veranda, which looks out on the harbor. ✉ *Waterfront Dr.* ☎ *284/494–3897* 🖃 *AE, D, MC, V.*

★ **¢-$$** ✕ **Capriccio di Mare.** The owners of the well-known Brandywine Bay restaurant also run this authentic Italian outdoor café. Stop by for an espresso, fresh pastry, a bowl of perfectly cooked penne, or a crispy tomato and mozzarella pizza. Drink specialties include a mango Bellini, an adaptation of the famous cocktail served at Harry's Bar in Venice. ✉ *Waterfront Dr.* ☎ *284/494–5369* 🖄 *Reservations not accepted* 🖃 *MC, V* 🕓 *Closed Sun.*

TRINIDAD (PORT OF SPAIN)

Vernon
O'Reilly
Ramesar

Trinidad, the big sister in the twin island republic of Trinidad & Tobago, is the most southerly in the Caribbean and a melting pot of African, Indian, European, and South American cultures, which happily exist together. But it's not a typical Caribbean island since it is a major energy producer and relies very little on tourism for income. But Trinidadians do know how to party, and the island's population is always celebrating or preparing for some sort of festival, the biggest of which is, undoubtedly Carnival, which takes over much of Port-of-Spain every year for two days of bacchanalian excess. Those expecting pristine white beaches may find the island disappointing, but lovers of the rain forest and wildlife will find paradise.

Essentials

CURRENCY   The Trinidad & Tobago dollar (TT$6.20 to $1US). Most places catering to tourists will accept U.S. currency, but the exchange rate may vary wildly from place to place.

HOURS   Most shops are open weekdays from 8 to 4:30, Saturday from 8 to noon; malls stay open later during the week, often until at least 6 or 7 PM, and operate all day Saturday.

INTERNET   **Computer Planet Ltd.** (⊠ Corner of Ariapita Ave. and Luis St., Port of Spain, Trinidad ☎ 868/622–6888).

TELEPHONES   Pay phones are located in the cruise terminal. To make an international call from a pay phone, you must first purchase a pre-paid "companion" card, which is readily available from most convenience stores, then simply follow the instructions on the card. Cards are available in various denominations. Phones and calling cards are also available from the main phone company, TSTT, which has an office on Independence Square about 10 minute walk from the port.

Coming Ashore

Port of Spain is a bustling and sprawling metropolis with seemingly endless traffic jams. The capital of the twin-island republic is a work in progress, with government investing billions of dollars into upgrading the port area and many other areas of the city. The scale of this project means that the port will be a construction zone for some time to come, but the result is expected to be a mile-long facility designed to offer a range of facilities and services to visitors.

Because of the driving habits of Trinidadians and the often confusing road signs and narrow roads, it is not advisable to rent a car. Taxis flock to the port whenever a cruise ship arrives. Authorized taxis always have a license plate starting with the letter "H" (for "hire"). Though rates are technically fixed, it is never a bad idea to negotiate with the driver.

Shore Excursions

We consider these to be among the better shore excursions for Trinidad. They may not be offered by all lines, and tour names may differ as well. Times and prices are approximate.

Port of Spain Tour. Explore the vibrant capital city full of architectural surprises ranging from the huge red parliament building to a replica of a Scottish castle. Visit the botanical gardens, and then enjoy a cultural show. ⊗ 3½ hrs ⊠ $45.

Maracas Bay. The drive to this peach-

TRINIDAD BEST BETS

- **Caroni Bird Sanctuary.** This maze of swamps is one of the island's top birding spots.

- **Port of Spain.** Madly busy and hectic, this is still an interesting place if you can stand the crowds. For most people, a guided tour will be the better option.

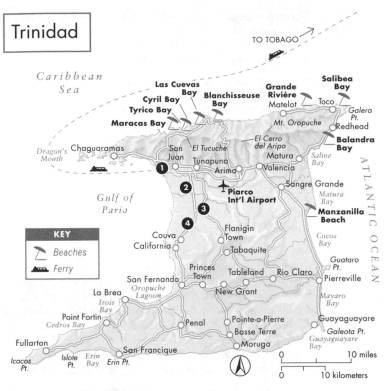

Trinidad

*Caribbean
Sea*

*Dragon's
Mouth*

TO TOBAGO

Chaguaramas

Las Cuevas
Bay Blanchisseuse
Bay

Cyril Bay
Tyrico Bay

Maracas Bay

Grande
Rivière
Matelot

Salibea
Bay

Toco

*Galera
Pt.*

Redhead

San
Juan   El Tucuche
Tunapuna

*El Cerro
del Aripo*

Mt. Oropuche

**Balandra
Bay**

Arima

Valencia

Matura   *Saline
Bay*

1

2

3

4

Piarco
Int'l Airport

Sangre Grande

*Matura
Bay*

**Manzanilla
Beach**

*Gulf of
Paria*

Couva
California

Flanigin
Town

Tabaquite

*Cocos
Bay*

KEY

🏖 Beaches

⛴ Ferry

San Fernando

La Brea
*Oropuche
Lagoon*

*Irois
Bay*

Point Fortin
Cedros Bay

Fullarton

*Icacos
Pt.*   *Islote
Pt.*   *Erin
Bay* Erin Pt.

San Francique

Princes
Town

Tableland   Rio Claro

New Grant

Penal

Pointe-a-Pierre

Basse Terre

Moruga

*Guataro
Pt.*

Pierreville

*Mayaro
Bay*

Guayaguayare

*Galeota Pt.
Guayaguayare
Bay*

ATLANTIC OCEAN

0   10 miles

0   10 kilometers

7

sand beach is as breathtaking as the beach itself, heading straight through the rain forest of Trinidad's Northern range of mountains with the ocean below on one side and lush greenery on the other. The descent allows for some magnificent aerial shots of the beach. Once at the beach there is ample time for sunning and swimming ⊙ *4 hrs* 🎫 *$40.*

Exploring Trinidad

Numbers in the margin correspond to points of interest on the Trinidad map.

👆 **2** **Caroni Bird Sanctuary.** This large swamp with mazelike waterways is bordered by mangrove trees, some plumed with huge termite nests. If you're lucky, you may see lazy caimans idling in the water and large snakes hanging from branches on the banks taking in the sun. In the middle of the sanctuary are several islets that are home to Trinidad's national bird, the scarlet ibis. ✚ *½ hr from Port of Spain; take Churchill Roosevelt Hwy. east to Uriah Butler south; turn right and in about 2 min, after passing Caroni River Bridge, follow sign for sanctuary* 🎫 *Free* ⊙ *Daily dawn–dusk.*

3 **Chaguaramas Military History & Aerospace Museum.** On the former U.S. military base, this is a must-see for history buffs. The exhibits are in a large hangarlike shed without air-conditioning, so dress appropriately. Exhibits cover everything from Amerindian history to the Cold War, but the emphasis is on the two World Wars. There's a decidedly charming and homemade feel to the place; in fact, most exhibits were made by the curator and founder, Commander Gaylord Kelshall of the T&T Coast Guard.

The museum is set a bit off the main road but is easily spotted by the turquoise BWIA L1011 jet parked out front (Trinidad and Tobago's former national airline). ⊠ *Western Main Rd., Chaguaramas* ☎ *868/634–4391* ☜ *TT$20* ☉ *Mon.–Sat. 9–5.*

🐣 ❹ **Dattatreya Yoga Centre.** This impressive temple site was constructed by artisans brought in from India. It is well worth a visit to admire the intricate architectural details of the main temple, learn about Trinidad Hinduism, and marvel at the towering 85-foot statue of the god Hanuman. This is a religious site, so appropriate clothing is required (no shorts), and shoes must be left outside the temple door. The temple is half an hour from Port of Spain; take Churchill Roosevelt Highway east to Uriah Butler south; turn right until the Chase Village flyover; follow the signs south to Waterloo; then follow signs to the temple. ⊠ *Datta Dr. at Orangefield Rd., Carapichaima* ☎ *868/673–5328* ☜ *Free* ☉ *Daily dawn–dusk, services daily.*

❶ **Port of Spain.** Most organized tours begin at the port. If you're planning to explore on foot, which will take two to four hours, start early in the day; by midday the port area can be as hot and packed as Calcutta. It's best to end your tour on a bench in the Queen's Park Savannah, sipping a cool coconut water bought from one of the vendors operating out of flatbed trucks. For about 50¢ he'll lop the top off a green coconut with a deft swing of the machete and, when you've finished drinking, lop again, making a bowl and spoon of coconut shell for you to eat the young pulp. As in most cities, take extra care at night; women should not walk alone.

The town's main dock, **King's Wharf,** entertains a steady parade of cruise and cargo ships, a reminder that the city started from this strategic harbor. When hurricanes threaten other islands, it's not unusual to see as many as five large cruise ships taking advantage of the safety of the harbor. It's on Wrightson Road, the main street along the water on the southwest side of town. The National Government has embarked on a massive development plan, which means that most of the wharf area is an active construction zone. The plan is to turn the area into a vibrant and attractive commercial and tourism zone, but it's likely to be a work in progress for several years.

Across Wrightson Road and a few minutes' walk from the south side of King's Wharf, the busy **Independence Square** has been the focus of the downtown area's major gentrification. On its south side the cruise-ship complex, full of duty-free shops, forms an enclave of international anonymity with the Crowne Plaza Trinidad. On the eastern end of the square is the Cathedral of the Immaculate Conception; it was by the sea when it was built in 1832, but subsequent landfill around the port gave it an inland location.

Frederick Street, Port of Spain's main shopping drag, starting north from the midpoint of Independence Square, is a market street of scents and sounds—perfumed oils sold by sidewalk vendors and music tapes being played from vending carts—and crowded shops. Although it may be tempting to purchase CDs from these street vendors, they are selling pirated material and doing so robs local artists of their livelihood.

At Prince and Frederick streets, **Woodford Square** has served as the site of political meetings, speeches, public protests, and occasional violence. It's dominated by the magnificent Red House, a Renaissance-style building that takes up an entire city block. Trinidad's House of Parliament takes its name from a paint job done in anticipation of Queen Victoria's Diamond Jubilee in 1897. The original Red House was burned to the ground in a 1903 riot, and the present structure was built four years later. The chambers are open to the public.

If the downtown port area is the pulse of Port of Spain, the great green expanse of **Queen's Park Savannah,** roughly bounded by Maraval Road, Queen's Park West, Charlotte Street, and Saddle Road, is the city's soul. You can walk straight north on Frederick Street and get there within 20 minutes. Its 2-mi (3-km) circumference is a popular jogger's track. The northern end of the Savannah is devoted to plants. A rock garden, known as the Hollows, and a fishpond add to the rusticity. In the middle of the Savannah you will find a small graveyard where members of the Peschier family—who originally owned the land—are buried. While the perimeter of the Savannah is busy and safe, you shouldn't walk across the park, as there have been occasional reports of muggings.

A series of astonishing buildings constructed in several 19th-century styles—known collectively as the **Magnificent Seven**—flanks the western side of the Savannah. Notable are Killarney, patterned (loosely) after Balmoral Castle in Scotland; Whitehall, constructed in the style of a Venetian palace; Roomor, a flamboyantly baroque colonial house with a preponderance of towers, pinnacles, and wrought-iron trim; and the Queen's Royal College, in German Renaissance style, with a prominent tower clock that chimes on the hour. Sadly, several of these fine buildings have fallen into advanced decay.

Head over to the southeast corner of the Savannah to see the **National Museum & Art Gallery,** especially its Carnival exhibitions, the Amerindian collection and historical re-creations, and the fine 19th-century paintings of Trinidadian artist Cazabon. ⊠ *117 Upper Frederick St., Port of Spain* ☎ *868/623–5941* ✎ *Free* ☉ *Tues.–Sat. 10–6.*

The cultivated expanse of parkland north of the Savannah is the site of the president's and prime minister's official residences and also the **Emperor Valley Zoo & Botanical Gardens.** A meticulous lattice of walkways and local flora, the parkland was first laid out in 1820 for Governor Ralph Woodford. In the midst of the serene wonderland is the 8-acre zoo, which exhibits mostly birds and animals of the region—from the brilliantly plumed scarlet ibis to slithering anacondas and pythons; you can also see (and hear) the wild parrots that breed in the surrounding foliage. The zoo draws a quarter of a million visitors a year. The admission prices are a steal, and tours are free. ⊠ *Botanical Gardens, Port of Spain* ☎ *868/622–3530 or 868/622–5343* ✎ *Zoo TT$4, gardens free* ☉ *Daily 9:30–5:30.*

Shopping

Trinidad offers the choice of shopping in the hectic downtown core of Port of Spain, where the prices are generally cheaper, or in any of a number of air-conditioned malls, where the atmosphere is calmer and the prices are higher. Local calypso and steelband music CDs are a popular choice as is rum produced on the island. For painted plates, ceramics, aromatic candles, wind chimes, and carved wood pieces and instruments, check out **Cockey** (✉ Long Circular Mall, Long Circular Rd., St. James, Port of Spain ☎ 868/628–6546). **Just CDs and Accessories** (✉ Long Circular Mall, Long Circular Rd., St. James, Port of Spain ☎ 868/622–7516) has a good selection of popular local musicians as well as other music genres. A fine designer shop, **Meiling** (✉ Kapok Hotel, Maraval, Port of Spain ☎ 868/627–6975), sells classically detailed Caribbean resort clothing. **Radical** (✉ The Falls at West Mall, Western Main Rd., Westmoorings ☎ 868/632–5800 ✉ Long Circular Mall, Long Circular Rd., St. James, Port of Spain ☎ 868/628–5693 ✉ Excellent City Centre, Independence Square, Port of Spain ☎ 868/627–6110), which carries T-shirts and original men's and women's clothing, is something like the Gap of the Caribbean. **Poui Boutique** (✉ Ellerslie Plaza, Long Circular Rd., Maraval, Port of Spain ☎ 868/622–5597) has stylish handmade batik articles, Ajoupa ware (an attractive, local terra-cotta pottery), and many other gift items. The miniature ceramic houses and local scenes are astoundingly realistic, and are all handcrafted by owners Rory and Bunty O'Connor. The design duo of Barbara Jardine and Rachel Ross creates the Alchemy jewelry line. Their handmade works of art with sterling silver, 18K gold, and precious and semiprecious stones are for sale at **Precious Little** (✉ 5 Pole Carew St., Woodbrook ☎ 868/622–7655).

Activities

Golf

The best course in Trinidad is the 18-hole course at **St. Andrew's Golf Club** (✉ Moka, Saddle Rd., Maraval, Port of Spain ☎ 868/629–2314), just outside Port of Spain. Greens fees are approximately $45 for 9 holes. The most convenient tee times are available on weekdays.

Beaches

★ **Maracas Bay** (✉ North Coast Rd.), a long stretch of sand with a cove and a fishing village at one end, is *the* local favorite, so it can get crowded on weekends. Lifeguards will guide you away from strong currents. Parking sites are ample, and there are snack bars and restrooms. Try a shark-and-bake ($2, to which you can add any of dozens of toppings, such as tamarind sauce and coleslaw) at one of the beach huts or in the nearby car park (Richard's is by far the most popular). Take the North Coast Road from Maraval (it intersects with Long Circular Road right next to KFC Maraval) over the Northern Range; the beach is about 7 mi (11 km) from Maraval.

Where to Eat

$–$$$ ✗ **The Verandah.** Owner and hostess Phyllis Vieira has been hosting din-
Fodor'sChoice   ers since the 1980s and prides herself on her "free-style Caribbean" menu,
★   which is one of the best-kept secrets on the island. But the reasonable prices and consistently excellent cuisine make this a secret we can no longer keep. The open veranda, interior, and courtyard of this beautiful ginger-bread-style colonial house provide a suitable setting for the menu, which

changes weekly and is brought to you on a blackboard by the attentive, white-garbed staff. ✉ *10 Rust St., St. Clair, Port of Spain* ☎ *868/622– 6287* ⌖ *Reservations essential* ▭ *No credit cards* ⊘ *Closed Sun. No dinner Mon.–Wed. and Fri.*

❂ **$–$$** ✕ **Veni Mangé.** The best lunches in town are served in this traditional West
Fodor's Choice Indian house. Credit Allyson Hennessy—a Cordon Bleu–trained chef and
★ local television celebrity—and her friendly, flamboyant sister and partner, Rosemary (Roses) Hezekiah. Despite Allyson's training, home cooking is the order of the day here. The creative creole menu changes regularly, but there's always an unusual and delicious vegetarian entrée. Veni's version of Trinidad's national dish, callaloo, is considered one of the best on the island. The *chip chip* (a small local clam) cocktail is deliciously piquant and is a restaurant rarity. ✉ *67A Ariapita Ave., Woodbrook, Port of Spain* ☎ *868/624–4597* ⌖ *Reservations essential* ▭ *AE, MC, V* ⊘ *Closed weekends. No dinner Mon., Tues., or Thurs.*

VIRGIN GORDA, BRITISH VIRGIN ISLANDS

Lynda Lohr Virgin Gorda, or "Fat Virgin," received its name from Christopher Columbus. The explorer envisioned the island as a pregnant woman in a languid recline with Gorda Peak being her big belly and the boulders of the Baths her toes. Different in topography from Tortola, with its arid landscape covered with scrub brush and cactus, Virgin Gorda has a slower pace of life, too. Goats and cattle own the right-of-way, and the unpretentious friendliness of the people is winning. The top sight (and beach for that matter) is The Baths, which draws scores of cruise-ship passengers and day-trippers to its giant boulders and grottoes that form a perfect snorkeling environment. While ships used to stop only in Tortola, saving Virgin Gorda for shore excursions, smaller ships are coming increasingly to Virgin Gorda directly.

Essentials

CURRENCY The U.S. dollar is the official currency here. Some places accept cash only, but major credit cards are widely accepted. First Caribbean International, which has an ATM, isn't far from the ferry dock in Spanish Town.

HOURS Banking hours are usually Monday through Thursday from 9 to 2:30 and Friday from 9 to 2:30 and 4:30 to 6. Post offices are open weekdays from 9 to 5 and Saturday from 9 to noon. Stores are generally open Monday through Saturday from 9 to 5. Some may be open on Sunday.

INTERNET At this writing, there are no Internet cafés on Virgin Gorda.

TELEPHONES To call anywhere in the BVI once you've arrived, dial all seven digits. A local call from a pay phone costs 25¢, but such phones are sometimes on the blink. An alternative is a Caribbean phone card,

> **VIRGIN GORDA BEST BETS**
>
> ■ **The *Rhone*.** For certified divers, this is one of the best wreck dives in the Caribbean.
>
> ■ **Sage Mountain.** The highest peak in the Virgin Islands has breathtaking views and is a great hiking destination.
>
> ■ **Sailing Trips.** Because of its proximity to small islets and good snorkeling sights, Tortola is the sailing capital of the Caribbean.

Virgin Gorda

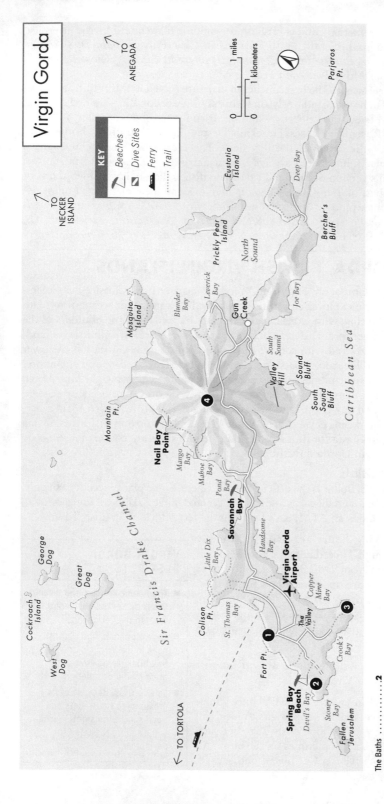

TO NECKER ISLAND

TO ANEGADA

KEY
- Beaches
- Dive Sites
- Ferry
- Trail

0 1 miles
0 1 kilometers

Parjaros Pt.

Eustatia Island

Deep Bay

Bercher's Bluff

Prickly Pear Island

North Sound

Leverick Bay

Blunder Bay

Mosquito Island

Gun Creek

South Sound

Joe Bay

Mountain Pt.

Valley Hill

Sound Bluff

South Sound Bluff

South Bluff

Caribbean Sea

4

Nail Bay Point

Mango Bay

Mahoe Bay

Pond Bay

Savannah Bay

Little Dix Bay

Handsome Bay

Colison Pt.

St. Thomas Bay

Virgin Gorda Airport

Copper Mine Bay

The Valley

Crook's Bay

Fort Pt.

1

3

Sir Francis Drake Channel

George Dog

Great Dog

Cockroach Island

West Dog

TO TORTOLA

Spring Bay Beach

Devil's Bay

2

Stoney Bay

Fallen Jerusalem

available in $5, $10, and $20 denominations. They're sold at most major hotels and many stores and can be used to call within the BVI, as well as all over the Caribbean, and to access USADirect from special phone-card phones. If you're coming ashore at the cruise-ship dock, you'll find pay phones right on the dock. If a tender drops you right in Road Town at the ferry dock, phones are located in the terminal.

You'll find pay phones in Spanish Town at the public dock, Virgin Gorda Yacht Harbor, and the Post Office, all located near spots where cruise-ship tenders land. If Leverick Bay is your destination, you'll find pay phones in the marina. Passengers coming ashore in North Sound will find pay phones at the Gun Creek public dock.

Coming Ashore

Ships often dock off Spanish Town, Leverick Bay, or in North Sound and tender passengers to the ferry dock. A few taxis will be available at Leverick Bay and at Gun Creek in North Sound—you can set up an island tour for about $45 for two people—but Leverick Bay and North Sound are far away from The Baths, the island's must-see beach, so a shore excursion is often the best choice. If you are tendered to Spanish Town, then it's possible to take a shuttle taxi to The Baths for as little as $4 per person each way. Of you are on Virgin Gorda for just a day, it's usually more cost-effective to share a taxi with a small group than to rent a car, since you'd have to pay an agency $10 for a temporary license and car-rental charges of at least $50 a day. You must be at least age 25 to rent a car.

SHORE EXCURSIONS We consider these to be among the better shore excursions for Virgin Gorda. They may not be offered by all lines, and tour names may differ as well. Times and prices are approximate.

Anegada. After a short flight, you'll get a tour of the only coral atoll in the British Virgin Islands ☉ *5 ½ hrs* 🖭 *$TK.*
Island Tour. You'll see all the island's sights on this tour, including Gorda Peak and The Baths. ☉ *2½ hrs* 🖭 *$TK.*
Snorkeling Trip. With many sights within easy reach, a snorkeling excursion is a worthwhile tour here. ☉ *2 hrs* 🖭 *$TK.*

Exploring Virgin Gorda

There are few roads on Virgin Gorda, and most byways don't follow the scalloped shoreline. The main route sticks resolutely to the center of the island, linking The Baths at the tip of the southern extremity with Gun Creek and Leverick Bay at North Sound and providing exhilarating views. The craggy coast, scissored with grottoes and fringed by palms and boulders, has a primitive beauty. If you drive, you can hit all the sights in one day. Stop to climb Gorda Peak, in the island's center.

Numbers in the margin correspond to points of interest on the British Virgin Islands map.

The Baths. At Virgin Gorda's most celebrated sight, giant boulders are scattered about the beach and in the water. Some are almost as large as houses and form remarkable grottoes. Climb between these rocks to swim in the many pools. If it's privacy you crave, follow the shore northward to quieter bays—Spring Bay, the Crawl, Little Trunk, and Valley Trunk—

Fodor'sChoice
★

or head south to Devil's Bay. ⊠ *Off Tower Rd., The Baths* ☎ *284/494–3904* ⊕ *www.bvinationalparkstrust.org* ☞ *$3* ☉ *Daily dawn–dusk.*

❸ **Copper Mine Point.** Here stand a tall, stone shaft silhouetted against the sky and a small stone structure that overlooks the sea. These are the ruins of a copper mine established 400 years ago and worked first by the Spanish, then by the English, until the early 20th century. In April 2003 this historic site became the 20th park under the BVI National Parks Trust jurisdiction. ⊠ *Copper Mine Rd.* ☎ *No phone* ⊕ *www.bvinationalparkstrust.org* ☞ *Free.*

> **CAUTION**
>
> If you pick an outside cabin, check to make sure your view of the sea is not obstructed by a lifeboat. The ship's deck plan will help you figure it out.

❶ **Spanish Town.** Virgin Gorda's peaceful main settlement, on the island's southern wing, is so tiny that it barely qualifies as a town at all. Also known as The Valley, Spanish Town has a marina, some shops, and a couple of car-rental agencies. Just north of town is the ferry slip. At the Virgin Gorda Yacht Harbour you can stroll along the dock and do a little shopping.

❹ **Virgin Gorda Peak National Park.** There are two trails at this 265-acre park, which contains the island's highest point, at 1,359 feet. Small signs on North Sound Road mark both entrances. It's about a 15-minute hike from either entrance up to a small clearing, where you can climb a ladder to the platform of a wooden observation tower and a spectacular 360-degree view. ⊠ *North Sound Rd., Gorda Peak* ☎ *No phone* ⊕ *www. bvinationalparkstrust.org* ☞ *Free.*

Shopping

Most boutiques are within hotel complexes—one of the best is at Little Dix Bay. There is a respectable and diverse scattering of shops in the bustling yacht harbor complex in Spanish Town.

Thee Artistic Gallery (⊠ Virgin Gorda Yacht Harbour, Spanish Town ☎ 284/ 495–5104) has Caribbean-made jewelry, 14-karat-gold nautical charms, maps, collectible coins, crystal, and Christmas tree ornaments with tropical themes. **Margo's Boutique** (⊠ Virgin Gorda Yacht Harbour, Spanish Town ☎ 284/495–5237) is the place to buy handmade silver, pearl, and shell jewelry. **Next Wave** (⊠ Virgin Gorda Yacht Harbour, Spanish Town ☎ 284/ 495–5623) sells T-shirts, canvas tote bags, and locally made jewelry.

Activities

DIVING & SNORKELING There are some terrific snorkel and dive sites off Virgin Gorda, including areas around The Baths, North Sound, and The Dogs. The **Bitter End Yacht Club** (⊠ North Sound ☎ 284/494–2746 ⊕ www.beyc.com) offers two snorkeling trips a day. **Dive BVI** (⊠ Virgin Gorda Yacht Harbour, Spanish Town ☎ 284/495–5513 or 800/848–7078 ⊠ Leverick Bay Resort and Marina, Leverick Bay ☎ 284/495–7328 ⊕ www.divebvi.com) offers expert instruction, certification, and day trips. **Sunchaser Scuba** (⊠ Bitter End Yacht Club, North Sound ☎ 284/495–9638 or 800/932–4286 ⊕ www.sunchaserscuba.com) offers resort, advanced, and rescue courses.

FISHING   The sportfishing here is so good that anglers come from all over the world. **Charter Virgin Gorda** (✉ Leverick Bay, North Sound ☎ 284/495–7421 ⊕ www.chartervirgingorda.com) offers a choice of trips aboard its 46-foot Hatteras, the *Mahoe Bay,* for full-day marlin hunting. Plan to spend $800 to $1,200.

SAILING   The BVI waters are calm, and terrific places to learn to sail. The **Bitter End Sailing & Windsurfing School** (✉ Bitter End Yacht Club, North Sound ☎ 284/494–2746 ⊕ www.beyc.com) offers classroom, dockside, and on-the-water lessons for sailors of all levels. Private lessons are $60 per hour. If you just want to sit back, relax, and let the captain take the helm, choose a sailing or power yacht from **Double "D" Charters** (✉ Virgin Gorda Yacht Harbour, Spanish Town ☎ 284/499–2479 ⊕ www.doubledbvi.com). Rates are $60 for a half-day trip and $95 for a full-day island-hopping excursion. Private full-day cruises or sails for up to eight people run $950. If you'd rather rent a Sunfish or Hobie Wave, check out **Leverick Bay Watersports** (✉ Leverick Bay, North Sound ☎ 284/495–7376 ⊕ www.watersportsbvi.com).

Beaches

The best beaches are easily reached by water, although they're also accessible on foot, usually after a moderately strenuous 10- to 15-minute hike. Anybody going to Virgin Gorda should experience swimming or snorkeling among its unique boulder formations, which can be visited at several beaches along Lee Road. The most popular of these spots is The Baths, but there are several others nearby that are easily reached. **The Baths** is usually crowded midday with day-trippers. Public bathrooms and a handful of bars and shops are close to the water and at the start of the path that leads to the beach. Beach lockers are available to keep belongings safe. Admission is $3. **Savannah Bay** is a wonderfully private beach close to Spanish Town. It may not always be completely deserted, but it's a long stretch of soft, white sand. There are no facilities. **Spring Bay Beach,** just off Tower Road, gets much less traffic than the nearby Baths and has the similarly large, imposing boulders that create interesting grottos for swimming. The snorkeling is excellent, and the grounds include swings and picnic tables.

Where to Eat

$$ ✕ **The Bath & Turtle.** You can sit back and relax at this informal tavern with a friendly staff—although the noise from the television can sometimes be a bit much. Well-stuffed sandwiches, homemade pizzas, pasta dishes, and daily specials like conch soup round out the casual menu. Live musicians perform Wednesday night. ✉ *Virgin Gorda Yacht Harbour, Spanish Town* ☎ 284/495–5239 ▭ *AE, MC, V.*

¢ ✕ **Mad Dog's.** Piña coladas are *the* thing at this breezy bar just outside the entrance to the Baths. The menu includes great triple-decker sandwiches and hot dogs. ✉ *The Valley* ☎ 284/495–5830 ▭ *No credit cards* ☉ *No dinner.*

INDEX

ABOUT OUR WRITER

Linda Coffman is a freelance travel writer and the originator of CruiseDiva.com, her Web site, which has been dishing out cruise-travel advice and information since 2000. Before that, she was the cruise guide for About.com. Her columns and articles have appeared in *Cruise Travel, Porthole, Consumers Digest,* and other regional and national magazines; the *Chicago Sun-Times*; and on numerous Web sites, including those for *USA Today* and the Travel Channel. She's an avid cruiser, who enjoys sailing on ships of every size to any port worldwide but spends most of her time cruising the Caribbean. Linda thinks cruising is in her Norwegian blood and credits her heritage for a love of all things nautical. When not at sea, she makes her home in Augusta, Georgia, with her husband, Mel, and two very finicky teenage cats.

ACKNOWLEDGMENTS

No writer could compile a guidebook such as this alone, and the task would not have been possible without the tireless assistance of public relations representatives of all the cruise lines profiled. A trio of special travel journalists also generously contributed their time and work: Anita Dunham Potter, creator of AnitaVacation.com; Alan Wilson, publisher of *Cruise News Daily* and Cruiseblogger.com; and Robert W. Bone, whose writing and photographs appear in Bob Bone's TravelPieces.com. In addition, Anita was first reader of the manuscript, and her sharp eye eliminated several missteps and bloopers. Susan Young, cruise editor of *Travel Agent Magazine,* provided valuable insight into the cruise industry. Numerous veteran cruise passengers, especially Sue, Bob, Amber, and Pete, added firsthand input about ships and their Caribbean travels—a timely "go, girl" went a long way with a deadline looming. Brad lifted my spirits with doses of encouragement and chocolate. As only a true friend can do, Diane Duke kept me going with her enthusiasm and offered peace of mind by cat-sitting during my weeks at sea. Special lifetime-achievement husband points are awarded to Mel for patiently enduring rushed meals, a messy house, and last-minute trips. Finally, to my editor Doug Stallings at Fodor's, I offer heartfelt thanks for making the past year my most creative and productive.

ica Line. 212–17 (all), *MSC Cruises.* 218–23 (all), *Norwegian Cruise Line.* 224–25, *Michel Verdure/Norwegian Cruise Line.* 226–27 (all), *Michel Verdure/Norwegian Cruise Line.* 228–31 (all), *Norwegian Cruise Line.* 232–37 (all), *Oceania Cruises.* 238–41 (all), *Princess Cruises.* 242 (top), *Andy Newman/Princess Cruises.* 242 (bottom), *Princess Cruises.* 243–49 (all), *Princess Cruises.* 250–59 (all), *Regent Seven Seas Cruises.* 260–62 (all), *Royal Caribbean International.* 264–65, *Hugh Stewart/Royal Caribbean International.* 265–75 (all), *Royal Caribbean International.* 278 (top), *Johansen Krause/Seabourn Yacht Club.* 278 (bottom), *Seabourn Yacht Club.* 279 (top), *Johansen Krause/Seabourn Yacht Club.* 279 (bottom), *Seabourn Yacht Club.* 280 (top), *Johansen Krause/Seabourn Yacht Club.* 280 (center and bottom), *Seabourn Yacht Club.* 282–83 (all), *Seabourn Yacht Club.* 284–89 (all), *SeaDream Yacht Club.* 290–95 (all), *Silversea Cruises.* 296–303 (all), *Star Clippers.* 304–11 (all), *Windjammer Barefoot Cruises.* 312–19 (all), *Windstar Cruises.* **Chapter 6: Ports of Embarkation:** 323, *Royal Caribbean International.* **Chapter 7: Ports of Call:** 403, *Celebrity Cruises.*

Color Section: Kayakers from the SeaDream II: *SeaDream Yacht Club*
Cocktails on Crystal Harmony: *Crystal Cruises*
The sun deck on Seven Seas Mariner: *Radisson Seven Seas Cruises*
Norwegian Cruise Line buffet: *Norwegian Cruise Line*
Jogging on the deck of MSC Lirica: *MSC Cruises*
Carnival Victory departing: *Andy Newman/Carnival Cruise Lines*
Entertainment on Costa: *Costa Cruises*
Service on Silversea Cruises: *Silversea Cruises*
Deck service on Holland America Line: *Holland America Line*
Star Clipper under sail: *Star Clippers*
Water slide on a Disney ship: © *Disney*
A luxury suite on Queen Mary 2: *Michel Verdure/Cunard Line*
MSC Opera pool deck: *MSC Cruises*
The planetarium on Queen Mary 2: *Cunard Line*
Dinner on Windstar Cruises: *Windstar Cruises*
Oceania Cruises' Regatta: *Oceania Cruises*
Casino on Seven Seas Voyager: *Radisson Seven Seas Cruises*
Compass Rose Bar on Windstar Cruises' Wind Surf: *Windstar Cruises*
Captain Max on Windjammer's Mandalay: *Windjammer Barefoot Cruises*
Yoga class on Celebrity Cruises: *Celebrity Cruises*
An aqua–bike excursion from a Princess ship: *Princess Cruises*
Sky Bar on Seabourn Legend: *Seabourn Yacht Club*
Putting practice on Royal Caribbean's Navigator of the Seas: *Royal Caribbean International*
Pampering at SeaDream spa: *SeaDream Yacht Club*